Innovations in Client-Centered Therapy
  by David A. Wexler and Laura North Rice
The Rorschach: A Comprehensive System, in two volumes
  by John E. Exner, Jr.
Theory and Practice in Behavior Therapy
  by Aubrey J. Yates
Principles of Psychotherapy
  by Irving B. Weiner
Psychoactive Drugs and Social Judgment: Theory and Research
  edited by Kenneth Hammond and C. R. B. Joyce
Clinical Methods in Psychology
  edited by Irving B. Weiner
Human Resources for Troubled Children
  by Werner I. Halpern and Stanley Kissel
Hyperactivity
  by Dorothea M. Ross and Sheila A. Ross
Heroin Addiction: Theory, Research and Treatment
  by Jerome J. Platt and Christina Labate
Children's Rights and the Mental Health Profession
  edited by Gerald P. Koocher
The Role of the Father in Child Development
  edited by Michael E. Lamb
Handbook of Behavioral Assessment
  edited by Anthony R. Ciminero, Karen S. Calhoun, and Henry E. Adams
Counseling and Psychotherapy: A Behavioral Approach
  by E. Lakin Phillips
Dimensions of Personality
  edited by Harvey London and John E. Exner, Jr.
The Mental Health Industry: A Cultural Phenomenon
  by Peter A. Magaro, Robert Gripp, David McDowell, and Ivan W. Miller III
Nonverbal Communication: The State of the Art
  by Robert G. Harper, Arthur N. Wiens, and Joseph D. Matarazzo
Alcoholism and Treatment
  by David J. Armor, J. Michael Polich, and Harriet B. Stambul
A Biodevelopmental Approach to Clinical Child Psychology: Cognitive Controls and Cognitive Control Theory
  by Sebastiano Santostefano
Handbook of Infant Development
  edited by Joy D. Osofsky
Understanding the Rape Victim: A Synthesis of Research Findings
  by Sedelle Katz and Mary Ann Mazur
Childhood Pathology and Later Adjustment: The Question of Prediction
  by Loretta K. Cass and Carolyn B. Thomas
Intelligent Testing with the WISC-R
  by Alan S. Kaufman
Adaptation in Schizophrenia: The Theory of Segmental Set
  by David Shakow
Psychotherapy: An Eclectic Approach
  by Sol L. Garfield
Handbook of Minimal Brain Dysfunctions
  edited by Herbert E. Rie and Ellen D. Rie
Handbook of Behavioral Interventions: A Clinical Guide
  edited by Alan Goldstein and Edna B. Foa
Art Psychotherapy
  by Harriet Wadeson

D0891652

Continued on back

HANDBOOK OF SOCIAL SKILLS
TRAINING AND RESEARCH

Handbook of Social Skills Training and Research

Edited by
Luciano L'Abate and Michael A. Milan
Georgia State University

A WILEY-INTERSCIENCE PUBLICATION
JOHN WILEY & SONS
New York · Chichester · Brisbane · Toronto · Singapore

Library of Congress Cataloging in Publication Data:

Main entry under title:
Handbook of social skills training and research.

  (Wiley series on personality processes, ISSN 0737-7920)
  Includes index.
  1. Social skills—Study and teaching—Therapeutic use—
Handbooks, manuals, etc.   2. Psychotherapy—Handbooks,
manuals, etc.   I. L'Abate, Luciano, 1928–
II. Milan, Michael A.   III. Series.
RC489.S63H35   1985   616.89'14   84-20889
ISBN 0-471-89832-5

Printed in the United States of America

10 9 8 7 6 5 4 3 2 1

Contributors

FRANK ANDRASIK, PH.D.
Associate Professor of Psychology
Department of Psychology
State University of New York
Albany, New York

STEVEN R. ASHER, PH.D.
Professor of Educational Psychology
 and Psychology
Director of Bureau of Educational
 Research
University of Illinois
Champaign, Illinois

DENNIS BAGAROZZI, PH.D.
Associate Professor
School of Social Work
East Carolina University
Greenville, North Carolina

GREGORY BROCK, PH.D.
Associate Professor of Family Studies
 and Marriage and Family Therapy
Department of Family Studies
University of Wisconsin at Stout
Menomonie, Wisconsin

DAVID K. BROOKS, M.A.
Ph.D. Candidate
Department of Counseling and Human
 Development Services
University of Georgia
Athens, Georgia

KAREN S. BUDD, PH.D.
Assistant Professor
C. Louis Meyer Children's
 Rehabilitation Institute
University of Nebraska Medical Center
Omaha, Nebraska

KAREN A. CHRISTOFF, PH.D.
Assistant Professor of Psychology
Department of Psychology
University of Mississippi
University, Mississippi

JEANETTE D. COUFAL, PH.D.
Assistant Professor
Department of Family Studies
University of Wisconsin at Stout
Menomonie, Wisconsin

JAMES P. CURRAN, PH.D.
Associate Professor of Psychiatry and
 Human Behavior
VA Medical Center
Brown University Medical School
Providence, Rhode Island

ANTHONY D'AUGELLI, PH.D.
Associate Professor of Human
 Development
College of Human Development
Pennsylvania State University
University Park, Pennsylvania

JUDITH FRANKEL D'AUGELLI, PH.D.
Private Practice
State College, Pennsylvania

WAYNE DOW, B.A.
Graduate Student
Department of Psychology
Georgia State University
Atlanta, Georgia

NORMAN EPSTEIN, PH.D.
Associate Professor
Department of Family and Community
 Development
University of Maryland
College Park, Maryland

ALBERT D. FARRELL, PH.D.
Associate Professor
Department of Psychology
Virginia Commonwealth University
Richmond, Virginia

ADRIAN FURNHAM, PH.D.
Lecturer
Department of Psychology
University College
London, England

MARYANNE GALVIN, ED.D.
Assistant Professor
Division of Child Psychiatry
Tufts New England Medical Center
Boston, Massachusetts

EILEEN GAMBRILL, PH.D.
Professor of Social Work
School of Social Welfare
University of California
Berkeley, California

GEORGE M. GAZDA, ED.D.
Regents Professor
School of Education
University of Georgia
Athens, Georgia

N. JANE GERSHAW, PH.D.
Clinical Assistant Professor of
   Psychiatry
Chief, VA Mental Health Clinic
Syracuse, New York

ARNOLD P. GOLDSTEIN, PH.D.
Professor
Department of Psychology
Syracuse University
Syracuse, New York

KATHERINE K. GORDON, M.A.
Consultant
Gainesville, Florida

RICHARD E. GORDON, M.D., PH.D.
Associate Professor
Department of Psychiatry
University of Florida Medical Center
Gainesville, Florida

BERNARD GUERNEY, JR., PH.D.
Professor of Human Development
Director, Individual and Family Studies
College of Human Development
The Pennsylvania State University
University Park, Pennsylvania

LOUISE GUERNEY, PH.D.
Associate Professor of Human
   Development
College of Human Development
The Pennsylvania State University
University Park, Pennsylvania

HARVEY JOANNING, PH.D.
Associate Professor
Texas Tech University
Lubbock, Texas

DAVID KEARNS, M.A.
Ph.D. Candidate
Department of Psychology
Georgia State University
Atlanta, Georgia

JEFFREY A. KELLY, PH.D.
Associate Professor of Psychiatry
Department of Psychiatry and Human
   Behavior
University of Mississippi Medical
   Center
Jackson, Mississippi

DAVID J. KOLKO, PH.D.
Assistant Professor
Division of Child and Adolescent
   Psychiatry
Staff Psychiatrist
Western Psychiatric Institute and Clinic
University of Pittsburgh Medical School
Pittsburgh, Pennsylvania

JUDITH L. KOMAKI, PH.D.
Associate Professor
Department of Psychological Sciences
Purdue University
West Lafayette, Indiana

LUCIANO L'ABATE, PH.D.
Professor of Psychology
Director of Family Studies Center
Department of Psychology
Georgia State University
Atlanta, Georgia

GARY W. LADD, PH.D.
Assistant Professor of Child
   Development and Psychology
Department of Child and Family Studies
Purdue University
West Lafayette, Indiana

JOHNNY L. MATSON, PH.D.
Department of Learning and
   Development
Northern Illinois University
DeKalb, Illinois

RICHARD M. MCFALL, PH.D.
Professor of Psychology
Department of Psychology
Indiana University
Bloomington, Indiana

MICHAEL A. MILAN, PH.D.
Associate Professor
Department of Psychology
Georgia State University
Atlanta, Georgia

E. LAKIN PHILLIPS, PH.D.
Professor of Psychology
Director of Counseling Center
George Washington University
Washington, D.C.

WILLIAM RICHARDSON, M.ED.
Ph.D. Candidate
Department of Counseling and
   Psychological Services
Georgia State University
Atlanta, Georgia

ESTHER D. ROTHBLUM, PH.D.
Assistant Professor
Department of Psychology
University of Vermont
Burlington, Vermont

DAVID G. SCHLUNDT, PH.D.
Assistant Professor
Department of Psychiatry and Human
   Behavior
University of Mississippi Medical
   Center
Jackson, Mississippi

LAURA SOLOMON, PH.D.
Assistant Professor
Department of Psychology
University of Vermont
Burlington, Vermont

ROBERT P. SPRAFKIN, PH.D.
Coordinator of Drug Treatment
   Program
VA Medical Center
Syracuse, New York

DANIEL B. WACKMAN, PH.D.
Professor
Interpersonal Communications
   Program, Inc.
School of Journalism and Mass
   Communications
Minneapolis, Minnesota

JAN L. WALLANDER, PH.D.
Assistant Professor
Department of Psychology
University of Southern California
Los Angeles, California

KAREN SMITH WAMPLER, PH.D.
Associate Professor
Department of Child and Family
   Development
College of Home Economics
The University of Georgia
Athens, Georgia

STACEY ZLOTNICK, B.S.
Ph.D. Candidate
Department of Organizational Behavior
Yale University
New Haven, Connecticut

Series Preface

This series of books is addressed to behavioral scientists interested in the nature of human personality. Its scope should prove pertinent to personality theorists and researchers as well as to clinicians concerned with applying an understanding of personality processes to the amelioration of emotional difficulties in living. To this end, the series provides a scholarly integration of theoretical formulations, empirical data, and practical recommendations.

Six major aspects of studying and learning about human personality can be designated: personality theory, personality structure and dynamics, personality development, personality assessment, personality change, and personality adjustment. In exploring these aspects of personality, the books in the series discuss a number of distinct but related subject areas: the nature and implications of various theories of personality; personality characteristics that account for consistencies and variations in human behavior; the emergence of personality processes in children and adolescents; the use of interviewing and testing procedures to evaluate individual differences in personality; efforts to modify personality styles through psychotherapy, counseling, behavior therapy, and other methods of influence; and patterns of abnormal personality functioning that impair individual competence.

IRVING B. WEINER

University of Denver
Denver, Colorado

Preface

Social skills training and research is among the most recent and most robust of the approaches to the remediation of psychological problems, the enhancement of interpersonal effectiveness, and the general improvement of the quality of life. From its early beginnings as "assertiveness training," the scope of this movement has expanded until now it must be considered one of the most widely deployed intervention strategies for the delivery of mental health services. As the range of topics included within this handbook demonstrates, virtually no population or problem has been neglected by the social skills training and research movement. In the process, assertiveness training has been incorporated within these applications and has lost its original, distinctive meaning. Indeed, most of the contributions to this handbook could be viewed as variations on the assertiveness training theme.

The growing popularity of social skills training is not without its attendant problems. In the rush to deploy skills training as an intervention modality in its own right or as an adjunct to other approaches, it is quite likely that some practitioners have not devoted the care to the development of skills training programs that is necessary to assure their effectiveness. This haste is in part understandable, for at first glance skills training appears deceptively simple. Indeed, one of its most desirable attributes is that the *training* aspect of the social skills

training can be conducted by competent paraprofessionals with a modicum of professional training and supervision. Unfortunately, determining the *content* of social skills training programs (i.e., the *skills* that are trained) is another matter. As several of the chapters within this handbook make clear, the identification of the skills to be taught is often a time-consuming and laborious process requiring extensive professional expertise. It is quite likely, therefore, that practitioners will be tempted to circumvent the empirical identification and validation of the skills to be taught and will instead rely upon their professional judgment when deciding what to teach. However, professional judgment is often a poor substitute for empirical development, and it is quite likely that programs based upon such a foundation will not be maximally effective if, indeed, they are effective at all.

The chapters contained within this handbook demonstrate the careful attention that must be paid to the development of skills training programs and to the evaluation of their effectiveness as they are employed in different settings, with various population groups, and for diverse problems. Lacking this continued assessment of skills training endeavors, it is quite possible that the good that can be accomplished by the movement may be undermined by the potential harm caused by well-intentioned but less rigorous individuals whose failures may taint us all. Social skills training is still struggling with problems of definition, identity, and usefulness. We shall attempt to identify some of these problems here. However, most of the chapters in this volume will come to grips with many of these issues and more. Among some of these issues we take particular note of the following:

1. Defining social skills training.
2. Education or therapy?
3. Direct versus delegated leadership.
4. Costs and efficiency.

Defining Social Skills Training.

Social skills training (SST) may be described as a form of psychological intervention based on prearranged topics or sequences of topics designed to improve the interpersonal functioning of the target population. This definition is posed to underscore certain themes that define the SST movement. In the first place, this definition recognizes the gradual, stepwise, linear progression of topics that may go from the simple issue of reinforcement identification or basic response definition to the more complex chaining of responses or systemic transactions. In the second place, this definition recognizes the prearranged nature of each program. The nature of the concept *program* implies in itself a specific topic, and, therefore, a formal diagnosis and prescriptive process is followed in which validated skills training programs are matched to the needs and characteristics of the clients. In the third place, this definition recognizes that most psychological skills deficits are *interpersonal,* and therefore these deficits will manifest themselves interpersonally. Hence, there is the need to *train* people (individuals, groups of individuals, couples, groups of couples, families, and groups of families) to learn new skills. It was hoped that the learning of new skills

would interfere with old inappropriate or inadequate skills and would generate the practice and even overpractice of new, more appropriate, and more adequate skills.

Education or Therapy?

In many ways, asking whether social skill training is education or therapy is to pose a misleading question. It implies an artificial dichotomy between what is education and what is therapy but one that is still propagated by those who view *education* as focusing "directly" upon troublesome emotions, thoughts, or behaviors while reserving the term *therapy* for "indirect" efforts whose goal is the resolution of the hypothesized intrapsychic conflicts and dynamics that are thought to "underly" them. Within this restricted and somewhat outdated framework, social skills training is certainly education. However, in the contemporary sense of therapy as an endeavor directed toward the remediation of problems-in-living, be they termed *neurosis, delinquency, psychosis, development delay,* and so forth, social skills training is certainly a powerful therapeutic endeavor.

Social skills training is depicted as a scientific (i.e., replicable) methodology whereas psychodynamic forms of therapy typically consist of nonreplicable techniques with little or no accountablilty. In this regard, social skills training differs from the various psychodynamic therapies by attending to two basic aspects of therapeutic intervention: (1) replication and (2) generalization. An approach, in order to be viable, must be replicable, that is, someone other than the originator needs to reproduce it and its effects. Social skills training involves, then, a *methodological* approach to the delivery of mental health services. As a method, rather than a technique, the intervention strategies are specified in a clear and unambiguous manner so that they are indeed reproducible by others. Techniques, on the other hand, are processional interventions that rely on a therapist's characteristic and style to achieve beneficial effects. These, of course, vary from therapist to therapist and prevent unambiguous evaluation of such therapeutic endeavors as a whole.

Generalization requires that therapeutic accomplishments in one setting show themselves in other appropriate settings as well (i.e., tranfer of training) and that these effects endure (i.e., maintenance). To ensure these aspects of generalization, skills trainers typically train to a predetermined, stringent criterion, include "homework" assignments in their curriculum, monitor *in vivo* efforts, and the like, rather than assume that the "individual has changed" and that the effects of these changes are transituational and permanent.

Direct versus Delegated Leadership

If a program is replicable, it is so specific as to allow others to learn it and to reproduce it. Consequently, trainers with less training and experience than the developer of the program can actually carry out most of the training under appropriate supervision. This is perhaps one of the major differentiations between the social skills training movement and the formal psychotherapies. Although the latter are still based on the notion of the *expert* therapist with unique (nonreplicable!) skills imparting directly his/her knowledge as no one else can, the social skills training movement has implicit in its operations the notion of a hierarchical organization in the delivery of services. In this organization, the one-therapist–one-patient (couple, family) notion is given up in favor of many trainers–many patients under the supervision of superordinate professionals. Thus, in the psychodynamic therapies, the

therapist takes complete responsibility for treatment, whereas in social skills training the *program* itself takes the major responsibility for producing change. Therapists usually cannot be monitored; programs, instead, can be debugged, corrected, and refined. In social skills training, as the chapters in the handbook will demonstrate, each program is continuously monitored, revised, and retested.

Costs and Efficiency

Much more than the formal psychotherapies, the social skills training movement is more concerned with issues of economics and effectiveness. Direct leadership is expensive because expert time is expensive. Delegated responsibilities recognize the inherent hierarchy of professional and technical skills and the importance of costs in mental health delivery. Therefore, this movement pays more attention to cost-effectiveness by using paraprofessional personnel as on-line service providers.

In many respects, then, as a method of intervention, the social skill training movement is much closer to what psychologists call the Boulder model, that is, the ideal blend of scientist–practitioner that clinical psychology for so many years has tried to reach but that in many ways it has failed to fulfill. In its empirical emphasis, the social skills training movement attempts to fulfill criteria of testability (verifiability and accountability). In its educational emphasis with clinical and nonclinical populations, the social skills training movement also attempts to fulfill professional criteria for generalizability and efficiency.

LUCIANO L'ABATE
MICHAEL A. MILAN

Atlanta, Georgia
March 1985

Contents

PART 1   HISTORICAL TRENDS AND METHODOLOGICAL ISSUES

1. Social Skills: History and Prospect, 3
    E. Lakin Phillips

2. New Directions in the Assessment of Social Competence and Social Skills, 22
    David G. Schlundt and Richard M. McFall

3. Conceptual and Methodological Issues in the Behavioral Assessment of
    Heterosocial Skills, 50
    David J. Kolko and Michael A. Milan

PART 2   PROGRAMS FOR SPECIAL PROBLEMS

4. Life Skills Training, 77
    George M. Gazda and David K. Brooks

5. Social Skills Training and Complementary Strategies in Anger Control and the
    Treatment of Aggressive Behavior, 101
    Michael A. Milan and David J. Kolko

6. Heterosocial Skills Training, 136
    James P. Curran, Jan L. Wallander, and Albert D. Farrell

7. The Enhancement of Sexual Skills and Competence: Promoting Lifelong
    Sexual Unfolding, 170
    Anthony D'Augelli and Judith Frankel D'Augelli

8. Social Skills Training for Divorced Individuals, 192
    Harvey Joanning

PART 3   PROGRAMS FOR SPECIAL POPULATIONS

9. Social Skill Training and Children's Peer Relations, 219
    Gary W. Ladd and Steven R. Asher

10. Parents as Mediators in the Social Skills Training of Children, 245
     Karen S. Budd

11. Parent Education as Skills Training, 263
     Gregory Brock and Jeanette D. Coufal

12. Structured Learning: Research and Practice in Psychological Skill Training, 284
     Arnold P. Goldstein, N. Jane Gershaw, and Robert P. Sprafkin

13. Social Skills Problems Experienced by Women, 303
     Laura Solomon and Esther D. Rothblum

14. Social Skills Training with the Elderly, 326
     Eileen Gambrill

PART 4   PROGRAMS FOR THE SEVERELY IMPAIRED

15. A Behavioral Approach to Social Skills Training with Psychiatric Patients, 361
     Karen A. Christoff and Jeffrey A. Kelly

16. A Program of Modular Psychoeducational Skills Training for Chronic Mental
     Patients, 388
     Richard E. Gordon and Katherine K. Gordon

17. Social Skills Training for the Mentally Retarded, 418
     Frank Andrasik and Johnny L. Matson

PART 5   PROGRAMS FOR COUPLES AND FAMILIES

18. The Couple Communication Program, 457
     Daniel B. Wackman and Karen Smith Wampler

19. Structured Approaches to Couples' Adjustment, 477
     Norman Epstein

20. The Relationship Enhancement Family of Family Therapies, 506
     Louise Guerney and Bernard Guerney, Jr.

PART 6   CURRENT STATUS AND FUTURE DIRECTIONS

21. Skills Training for Professional Helpers, 527
     Maryanne Galvin

22. Toward Effective Supervision in Business and Industry, 539
     Judith L. Komaki and Stacey Zlotnick

23. Social Skills Training: A European Perspective, 555
     Adrian Furnham

24. Enrichment, Structured Enrichment, Social Skills Training, and
    Psychotherapy: Comparisons and Contrasts, 581
       Luciano L'Abate, David Kearns, William Richardson, and Wayne Dow

25. Implications of Social Skills Training for Social and Interpersonal
    Competence, 604
       Dennis Bagarozzi

Author Index   *619*

Subject Index   *639*

HANDBOOK OF SOCIAL SKILLS
TRAINING AND RESEARCH

PART ONE

Historical Trends
and Methodological Issues

CHAPTER 1

Social Skills

History and Prospect

E. LAKIN PHILLIPS

The history of many seminal ideas in science reveals a checkered career. The same is true for the history of the present social skills movement. It took about 150 years for the notion of feedback, originally derived from Watt's steam engine, to find impetus and generality in the cybernetics movement of the mid-1940s and afterward., Darwin's ideas on evolution had precursors for years before his formulation developed the salience we now understand it to have. In psychology, social imitation learning may go back at least as far as Mary Cover Jones (1924), to be picked up and developed decades later by Bandura (1969).

Although some would say that the social skills movement came about in the recent past, there is evidence, if we view matters broadly, that social skills as a research idea and as an area of understanding human behavior is decades old. Bellack and Hersen (1977) state that social skills training techniques stem from two sources: the early work of Salter (1949), Wolpe (1958), and Lazarus (1971), mainly as psychotherapists and the work of Zigler and Phillips (1960, 1961) on "social competence." This latter fruitful research area showed that the greater the prior social competence of hospital-admitted patients, the less their length of stay in the hospital and the lower their recidivism rate. The level of social competence prior to hospitalization turned out to be a better predictor of posthospitalization adjustment than psychiatric diagnosis or the particular type of treatment received in the hospital (Bellack & Hersen, 1977, p. 143).

The historical background of social skills arising from psychotherapeutic intervention stressed the importance of *assertiveness*. Wolpe's contributions in this connection differentiated between positive approachful behaviors and those that were assertive but critical and/or disapproving. Patients and clients have been taught by psychotherapists for years to be candid, open, honest, self-revealing, and the like. These are presumably examples of assertiveness. Assertiveness training has held an important place in psychotherapy for at least two decades as well as having enjoyed a more specific role in changing behavior in nonclinical, "popular" settings for nearly as long. There is much advice today to the maladjusted who read the popular mental health literature to be "more assertive." Assertiveness has for some time in the United States (not so in England) been almost wholly equated with social skills training and with much of the social skills research literature. More recently, social skills have included more than assertiveness as the subtleties of interaction have been broken down into ever finer and more far-reaching details.

A recent trend has also emphasized

"positive" or "prosocial" behavior and its relationship to morality and to altruism (Staub, 1978, 1979). In relation to psychotherapy, social skills have also had an important place, especially in retrospect, in that the Frank study (1974) of short-term psychotherapy over a 25-year span at Johns Hopkins University showed social skills improvement to be one of the two major positive outcomes of brief therapy. It is extremely doubtful if the original motives for short-term or brief psychotherapy emanated from social skills training because at the beginning of the Johns Hopkins project, social skills (as we know it today) in relation to psychotherapy was not generally recognized. Rather, the motivation for the brief therapy project was more a matter of service-delivery economy and the observation that crisis intervention and timely support to patients or clients could often assist them in regaining their normal or usual status in their community and that long-term therapy has never been cost-effective, whereas brief therapy with its emphasis on social interaction, rather than intropsychic processes, has been relatively cost-effective. Thus, the *outcome* from brief psychotherapy emphasized social skills as the chief positive result from this kind of psychotherapeutic intervention.

DEFINITION

Once a movement takes some shape and is individuated from other areas of research and application, common sense definitions give way to more unified and articulate definitions. In Wolpe's (1958, pp. 72–74) use of the word *assertive,* he referred to the outward (i.e., interpersonal) expression of all feelings, both positive and negative, other than anxiety. In the Wolpe context, anxiety is the inhibitor of an appropriate response (appropriate to one's feelings and to the interpersonal exchange); hence Wolpe

emphasized that assertive behavior inhibits anxiety. In assertive behavior, positive or negative, the exchange between persons is reasonably clear; with anxiety, assertiveness is largely blocked, and the exchange between persons is vague, unresolved, and often generates more anxiety.

Libet and Lewinsohn (1973, p. 304) defined social skills as "the complex ability both to emit behaviors which are positively or negatively reinforced and not to emit behaviors that are punished or extinguished by others." Social competence or skill pivots on positively reinforced exchanges with others and few or no punished or ignored exchanges. Part of this definition, at least by implication, is that many social skills are situational; that is, people usually experience difficulty (or success) primarily in certain types of situations. Few, if any, are wholly lacking or wholly competent in social skills. Gambrill (1978, p. 535) relates this situational characteristic of much social skills to the degree of intimacy involved; whether the feeling generally is positive or negative; the assorted characteristics of persons involved such as status, age, and sex; how one regards oneself (role) in a given context; and number of people present. There may be other dimensions such as knowledge of, or interest in, topics under discussion, a person valuing listening over verbal assertiveness, anxiety over possibly stuttering or other speech inhibitions, and so on. Eisler, Miller, and Hersen (1973) indicated operationally that more socially skilled persons speak louder, respond more rapidly to others, give longer replies, evidence more affect, are less compliant, request more exchanges, and are more open minded in their expressiveness, compared to less socially skilled persons. Bellack and Hersen (1977, p. 145) refer to social skill as "an individual's ability to express both positive and negative feelings in the interpersonal context without suffering consequent loss of social reinforcement . . . in a large variety of interpersonal contexts . . . [involving] . . . the coordinated delivery of appropriate verbal and nonverbal responses.''

Moving to a somewhat different notion of social skills, Welford (1980) says the modern concept arose in England in the early 1960s. It was derived not so much from psychotherapy theory but rather largely from concepts of skill applied to human–machine interactions, where the analogy with human–machine systems involved perceptual, decisional, motoric, and other information-processing characteristics (Welford, 1966). There is not much referring to reinforcement, anxiety inhibition, or related concepts in Welford's definition. Welford says further that ''skill itself, of any kind, whether social or other, is conceived as the use of efficient strategies to relate the demands of tasks or situations to the performer's capacities'' (1980, p. 11) Although this definition may be a first approximation and encourage us to look into possibly useful analogies with other skill areas, the definition may lack the specificity needed for the complexity of social exchanges. ·

Welford's work (1966, 1980) requires further comments. Coming from human–machine systems research (ergonomics), Welford draws analogies between human–human social interactions and human–machine systems, wherein ''information processing'' requirements are applicable to understanding both areas of research and practical application. Human–machine systems require the use of human capacities to meet the demands of the situation (making machines work, producing via machine use, etc.), resulting in the use of *strategies* to combine the first two that result in a product. Extrapolating from the human–machine system complex to human–human social interaction, we call these strategies ''skills'' or, more specifically, social skills. Human–machine and human–human systems do show some differences, however, so the analogue is not complete; for example, person–person systems use feedback, but the feedback interaction is reciprocal to a greater degree than with human–machine interaction. Argyle (1981) calls this interaction *metaperception,* indicating that two participants in a social interaction not only judge each other in a primary sense but are concerned as well with each's judgment of the other. Each participant may be more interested in the other's notions of her/him than in the other person (''metaperception'' would presumably be more common in inerviews, in job evaluation, in psychotherapy, and in public performance situations where how-is-the-other-person-judging-me notions would be strong). Welford further points out (1980) that what we call ''skill'' results in the efficient and effective use of strategies. It may be, today, that the plethora of social skills written about are mainly the almost endless lists of strategies that complex human social interaction requires, and social skill is the ability to shift and pivot according to a variety of demands, thus making skill a matter of versatility rather than hard-and-fast contributions to a repertoire (it is that social skill is more a matter of managing a ''behavioral economy'' than drawing on a repertoire in the musical analogy sense). For example, many strategies (skills) are needed in the performance of a man asking a woman to dance: eye contact, bodily movements of anticipation, actual physical contact in a way that is inviting and reinforcing, and, of course, the complex movements of the dance itself, and (perhaps) the conversation accompanying it. Teaching-a-person-to-dance, then, is, in a sense, a social skill made up of a large number of strategies (elementary skills) that are seen throughout a series of junctures over time and that culminate in some final reinforcement of the whole chain or loop of events. As the current literature on social skills abundantly recognizes, analysis of the skills demands (strategies, combining capacity, and situational demands) is preeminent, and the taking-for-granted that we know what makes up social interaction in skilled ways is ill advised. To make the social skills situation even more complicated, think of the behaviors that go into ending or disengaging oneself from an interaction: all the way from hastening away from a person met casually on the street corner to ending a long-term relationship. We have not studied these "disengaging" kinds of interaction nearly as much as the engaging variety, but they are probably equally important and will come more into view as we gain expertise in analyzing social interactions of all types.

Welford makes another point that is important in understanding the history of social skills research and application. He observes that Crossman's work (1960) on information-processing approaches to human performance in England, being primarily a skill analysis of human–machine systems, led to teaming up with Argyle, the British social psychologist, in developing research sponsored by the British Department of Industrial and Scientific Research, to explore analogies between human–machine and human–human interactions. As we know, this research on social skills by Argyle and his group led to the first published book that specifically contained the term *social skills* in the title and that delineated many of the dimensions of social skills research and performance respected today as one of the best technical statements of then-current social skills knowledge (Trower, Bryant, & Argyle, 1978; Argyle, 1975). The technical background from which this research publication emanated was largely due, in England, to the work of Argyle and associates (Argyle, 1967, 1969; Argyle & Kendon, 1967). The work of Trower et al. seems, in retrospect, to have launched a formal set of research approaches into the study of social skills in that there were research models to follow, areas of clinical application suggested or exemplified, techniques proposed for identifying and approaching a myriad of specific social skills, and a general viewpoint that related social skills deficits to various more or less formidable clinical/personality areas such as depression. The Trower et al. volume also pointed up the importance of analyzing the social skills needs of individuals and assessing competence in actual life situations rather than relying on questionnaires and judges' ratings, although the latter are often needed and useful. Thus, social skills research had a different origin and a different emphasis in England than it did in America, although there have been many convergences in topic, method, and outcome in the two settings.

Social skill was defined somewhat more broadly by Phillips. He said that a person is socially skilled according to "the extent to which he or she can communicate with others in a manner that fulfills one's rights, requirements, satisfactions, or obligations to a reasonable degree without damaging the other person's similar rights, requirements, satisfactions, or obligations, and shares these rights, etc., with others in free and open exchange" (Phillips, 1978, p. 13). The emphasis on sharing, reciprocity, and responsibility are important here, they and largely preclude the "advantage-taker" salesperson (often regarded by others as "skilled") who can talk people into buying what they do not want or need. This emphasis disallows the teacher intimidating or threatening students in order to induce them to be productive, and it disallows skill to the parent or supervisor who freezes out the child or the employee from emotional expression in order to control unwanted or untoward behavior. Social skill is proactive, prosocial, and reciprocally productive of mutually shared reinforcement. By the same token, it addresses the importance of not being taken advantage of, saying no in order to prevent being intimidated, and holding firmly to one's rights to avoid being bilked. Advantage taking is not sharing, intimidation is not prosocial persuasion, and threatening is not likely to induce the best problem-solving behavior of others. In social skill exchange, reinforcement must be mutual, even if not wholly equal. That behaviors that are reinforcing only to the promulgator at the cost of the recipient are not prosocial skills behaviors: Their unfortunate examples can be found all the way from profound disregard of the other as in rape to the seemingly harmless and almost negligible purloining of store merchandise or other possessions by playful schoolchildren. These limitations on social skills are clear enough in dyadic relationships, but the clarity may become overcast in larger aggregates of persons: The politician who wins congressional moneys for some clearly needed agricultural project in his or her jurisdiction (a prosocial act) but buys up or allows his or her friend's prior knowledge enabling him or her to buy up properties or land that will profit from the governmental behest is not an example of prosocially skilled behavior. Or the drug company that promises cures of dreaded diseases on the basis of scant evidence thus incurring extreme costs and sacrifices on the part of the victims with few (doubtfully) profiting therefore among the patients but affording high profits to the drug company and stockholders is also the opposite to prosocial behavior. Whether social skills as a sharing of responsibility and reinforcement in any two-person or more exchange can be generalized to larger aggregates of persons in productive ways remains to be seen. It should be tried. A child in a preschool setting who becomes more prosocial by developing interpersonal, self-control, and play skills does not do so at the expense of the other children. Jonny's growth

does not take away from Susan or Bill. But in society, one man's fortune and profit may well be made at the expense of many others, even though the others may still profit somewhat in the fallout that results from some (economic) boon to a community. Is GM "skilled in persuading" the people of Detroit's Polish section and the government of Detroit to allow the building of a large industrial plant at the expense of making thousands of people homeless in order to bring some possible economic benefit to the area? Who is being reinforced? Is this an exchange that is socially skilled? Is it equitable, reciprocal, concerned with mutual rights and obligations of all parties? I doubt it. Applying some of the dyadic notions of reinforcement—parity, mutual reinforcement, equity, responsibility—to larger social aggregates may lead to the clarification of problems in the latter situation that go beyond the usual confines of legality in our society. Further, how social skill is envisioned and practiced in the aggregate may have a lot to say about social skill in the smaller orbits of our lives.

This small excursion into moral and ethical problems in relation to social skills has anticipated some recent interest in morality and social competence (Arbuthmet & Faust, 1981; Staub, 1978, 1979), and it will be returned to later.

EARLY HISTORY

Consulting recent publications in the social skills area might leave one with the notion that social skill—by that name or by the name of social competence—began a couple of decades ago among psychotherapists and with the work of Zigler and Phillips in the United States or with the work of Welford and Argyle and others in England. I believe the story is older than these accounts imply. A look at some earlier work of a social skills training nature among children may enlarge our understanding of developments.

Thompson (1952) wrote about developmental trends in social behavior. In analyzing social behavior among young children, although the emphasis was on developmental aspects, he observed the child's effect on others (his or her value as a social stimulus), the dynamics of social behavior sequences, how the child seeks satisfaction for his or her social interactional needs, and how well his or her efforts satisfy his or her social needs (reinforcement). Illustrating even earlier social developmental trends was Williams (1935) who performed a factoral analysis of social behavior patterns among young children. He identified items we would today subsume under *assertiveness:* seeking approbation, being affectionate, not depending upon the group wholly for direction, respecting other's rights, sympathizing, avoiding being unduly controlled, being responsible, showing ascendant behavior (he might have said "assertive"), being sociable (reinforcing others), and so on. We could today lift out a number of concepts, observational practices, and theorizing from these works, now four to five decades old, and be in considerable harmony with present-day social skills interests. Today we would talk about social reinforcement, imitation, modeling, the control of aversive consequences, and a few similar changes, but the substance would still be there. Reading these reports with some liberalism allows us to make connections with earlier child and social psychology.

Note, further, the discussion by Murphy, Murphy, and Newcomb (1937) wherein they write about "two distinct types of aggressiveness" among children —one that is socially assertive and one that is socially obnoxious. It is true they did not then lift out assertiveness and treat it as we do today, but the substance is still there, and the concept is available for uses we have only recently begun to

extend. What today we would call "assertiveness" is seen even more cogently in the study by Jack (1934) on ascendant behavior in preschool children. Her research had two aspects: (1) to study ascendant behavior and compare it with selected aspects of personality and— more related to our interest in social skills—(2) to experiment in building up the confidence of the least ascendant children in the group (increasing assertive behaviors). Eighteen 4-year-old children were paired with each of 10 other children and observed playing for 5 minutes in a sandbox containing three sets of toys. Behavioral observations were made on eight variables: the child's verbal attempt to secure play materials, defending (or snatching back) materials taken from child's possession, directing other child's behavior verbally, compliance with verbal direction of other child, acting critically toward companion (forbidding, criticizing), and initiating behavior that the child's companion imitated. The originally nonascendant children, observed on the playground, showed lacks of self-confidence four times as frequently as did ascendant children, including such behavior as fear of physical objects (slides, swings), loudness in manner and laughter, and reacting strongly to criticism. The experimental modification of weak ascendant behavior was carried out among the five lowest scoring children on seven occasions (10 to 15 minutes each) by teaching them to use three kinds of materials: making designs with mosaic blocks, assembling a picture puzzle, and learning a story in a picture book. (Note: These were *indirect* or broad-based approaches to the problem of changing nonascendant behavior.) Upon the completion of training in ascendant behavior, the originally unascendant children were paired again with ascendant children and observed as to their ascendant behavior relative to their former position vis-à-vis their paired companion and in terms of their own original scores. Both absolute and relative scores for four of the five experimental children showed marked increases in ascendance when the experiment was repeated in the play situation.

The author of the study (Jack, 1934) and the discussants of the social behavior of children (Murphy et al., 1937) pointed out that the study had many implications: It went against the grain of laissez faire educational policies then extant in preschool education; it showed that self-confidence could be trained and that it was related to specifiable items of self-assertiveness (ascendance) observable in the child's behavior; and that training in the handling of commonly used play and educational materials, both large and small, could facilitate the social adjustment and ascendance of preschool children. Further, the authors pointed out that before this study was performed, there was a great tendency to think of social behaviors (shyness, confidence, ascendance, etc.) as more or less fixed traits, commonly observed over a wide variety of social situations among peers or associates, whereas the study showed that social ascendance was more a matter of a three-cornered relationship between persons and between each person and environmental opportunities or demands (games, social skills) in which the persons were participating. The emphasis shifted, conceptually speaking, from a trait-bound notion, inherent in the individual and developmentally anchored, to a functional relationship between persons and situations. How modern that sounds today.

Page (1936) carried the Jack study further, using 107 preschool children, 73 of whom were from the University of Iowa Child Welfare Research Station (of high IQ and socioeconomic status [SES], and 34 from a cooperative research preschool at an orphan's home and were of lower IQ and SES. The children were observed in what we would today call a baseline set of measurements: From behind a one-way screen they were observed in play situations in sandboxes and with appropriate toys, each child being observed in five pairings, resulting in an "ascendance score" based on eight occasions, each sampling behavior in 5-minute pairings. The population was divided into ascendant, moderately ascendant, and nonascendant groups, and they were taught specific skills with a nontrained group serving as controls. The high-intelligence children ($n = 14$) almost doubled their pretraining scores (16.7 vs. 28.8, pre- and postscores, respectively). The effects of training seemed to be cumulative, and they also appeared to be stable over time among the experimental subjects whereas the controls stayed the same or lost ground. Increases in ascendance were noted in terms of "directing behavior," and a decrease in scores related to "defending or getting property," in contrast to controls.

The discussion of these studies included the point that previous studies of children of nursery school age looked upon aggression or ascendance in complex situations without trying to specify what were the apparent causal factors. Early studies looked for consistency, or lack of it, in social behaviors across situations, and systematic effort to change social behavior had been seldom encountered prior to the Jack and Page studies. These studies of what we would today call social skills pointed out further that preschool training in educational matters was then commonly thought to be related to school and teacher responsibilities, whereas the child could teach himself or herself, so to speak, play and social skills behaviors. We know today that this was a short-sighted view, but we have the advantage of almost 50 years of experience and a behavioral movement now two to three decades old to bolster our present observations. We learn from these studies, now nearly five decades old, that there was, indeed, a social skills movement in the form of actual behavior modification in an experimental context. The amazing thing is that such an impetus seemed to have been lost for about another 25 years—up to the point of the beginnings of the behavior modification movement of the late 1950s or early 1960s. Why was this so? Why the hiatus between these seminal studies and the beginning of the behavior modification movement? I think, but I do not know for sure, that the emphasis then was on *development* as an unfolding, in the Gesell sense. Important then was the notion that all behaviors correlated with and perhaps followed on general physical and intellectual development, and the situational and specific social context aspects escaped the researchers until conceptual tools were more readily available, better understood, and seen as salient to social behavior.

The earlier period emphasized traits and their measurement, in the sense of following the style of intelligence tests and measurements, and, in turn, related them to a variety of other variables, mostly demographic. Social behavior, especially ascendance, aggression, shyness, and the like were seen as byproducts of development, of trait theory, of more or less stable (even static?) conditions characterizing the child's age, sex, and SES. Little was thought of in the way of functional relationships between the environmental contingencies and the social skills, between the partners in social interaction, their skills, and the situational demands. Theories were "inside" theories, and we may have a return recently to this tendency to locate variables inside the person in a mentalistic sense (it is called "cognitive" today) and not to pursue as vigorously as we might the myriad functional relationships in the environment. The environment was then seen with some clarity, but it was a static, striated, demographic-type environment, not a specific, contingency-related, rein-

forcement-conditioned environment that allowed and encouraged exchange between participants in task-related activities. Researchers were looking then for the kind of social behavior stability that had been seemingly acquired in the study of intelligence with its vast emphasis on a particular kind of measurement, set in a context of demographic, class, racial, and sex variables. There was no better model than developmental studies of intelligence for the social behavior researcher to follow,* and an occasional study set in the manner we are more familiar with today did not make much headway.

These studies show, also, that the bare accumulation of facts may, at a given time, go begging for conceptual clarity and for relationship to the larger scientific picture. It is easy for us today to look back on this period in the study of social behavior among children and reconceptualize the investigations and place them in our present context, but that conceptual leap probably was impossible then and awaited the advent of the behavioral movement with its more salient and sharper variables. We often haul bricks to the constructions site, preparing to erect an edifice, but if no conceptual tools—no acrchitectural plans— are present or emerge, we have merely a collection of interesting parts without direction as to how to construct, integrate, and use them. Science is replete with as many conceptual breakthroughs as it is with empirical revelations. Even the empirical revelations are not thus fully noted unless they fit a conceptual context. Facts do not always speak for themselves; otherwise there would be

---

*Several examples of this manner of thinking are contained in the leading books on child psychology in the 1940s and 1950s: Anderson and Anderson (1954), Carmichael (1954), Morgan (1942), and Thompson (1952). All of these texts viewed child social behavior as an unfolding, developmenal process primarily, with circumstances or environmental contingencies falling into minor roles.

less lag between the accumulation of seminal facts and the development of a conceptual overview.

A final comment on the Jack and Page studies: They modified ascendant behavior by *general* skills training, using toys, and games and puzzles as the instructional media. They did not use specific ascendant skills themselves to modify ascendant behavior. We might do well today to contemplate this emphasis and empirically examine whether general social competence skills are not as instrumental in producing specific behavior change as are specific skill efforts with highly specified target behaviors in view. Perhaps social skills versatility, longer lasting social skills, and task generality would be enhanced by a broader based initial attack on social skills development. The Jack and Page studies went from the general (ascendance) to the specific (toys, games, etc.) to the general (ascendance behavior improved), whereas today we tend to go from the specific (target behavior) to the specific (skills training) to the general (more social competence as well as specific skills improvement). Whether these two models are really dissimilar is an empirical matter; we can hardly answer that question today.

Related to this observation of the choice of intervention variables in the Jack and Page studies versus today's methodology, one should note the critical comments of Trower (1982). Trower noted among other critical issues in social skills training that we teach component skills without sufficient regard to the person's own purposes, intentions, and skills status. Perhaps the Jack and Page studies addressed this notion without knowing they were doing so, and we have even today probably not differentiated the issue clearly enough. More broadly based social skills instruction might be an advantage for improving dating behavior, conversational skills, dealing with rejection, and so forth, and such

training might apply to varying extents across a wide spectrum of social skills, precisely because it addresses wider issues.

Trower's point and the present reply may focus, also, on Trower's notions that we lack precise social skill definitions because assessment and interference strategies are bound to suffer in the wake of such incomplete information. Knowing that we can probably improve upon any state of knowledge, we might consider that more broadly based social skills should be tried out, utilizing various different component skills. For example, in teaching social exchange and conversational skills, differing approaches such as learning about current events and relevant topics in the everyday world might be compared with teaching more specific component skills without attending to the content of conversational exchanges. Social skills in such a context may not be simple conversational adequacy but a vantage point of knowledge that one then learns to exchange with others, now on one basis, now on another.

THE ROLE OF THE ENVIRONMENT IN RECENT HISTORY

Returning to the importance of the Zigler and Phillips studies (1960, 1961; Phillips, 1968), it is apparent that although the connection between these studies and those of the recent social skills types is noticeable, less extrapolation from the past to the present has taken place than can now be judged desirable. For example, Phillips pointed out some very cogent results from his studies and those of others regarding the social basis of psychopathology. Studies in Stamford, Connecticut, and in St. Paul, Minnesota, (Buell, Bradley, & Associates, 1952; Phillips, 1968, p. 208) showed that poverty, ill health, family disorganization, mental illness, child abuse, and other signs of social disorganization go together, along with economic and chronic unemployment problems. The clustering of the ill effects for health and adjustment arising from poor social integration were anticipated 25 years ago in a study by Holmes et al. (1957), in which it was shown that the onset and course of tuberculosis appeared in "marginal people" and that social adjustment problems preceded the onset of or relapse into the disease, during which time broken marriages and changes in occupation and residence commonly preceded the illness. In these and other studies of social disorganization leading to a myriad of illnesses, economic problems, and personal maladjustment, there may be a common tread of social skills lacks. Dohrenwend and Dohrenwend (1969) said that what is commonly labeled as *psychiatric disorder* is no more than the transient and mostly to-be-expected reaction of otherwise normal individuals who face unusually severe stresses. Phillips (1978) made the same point in offering the study of social skills as an alternative to abnormal psychology and psychiatry. Are such "normal individuals" simply overcome with environmental stress owing to skills lacks on the one hand and to undue pressure and strain on the other hand, such that any of us would, under similar circumstances, succumb? Are those in more fortunate social circumstances—albeit they have their problems, too—simply more able to draw on and develop social skills to the point that they are not so much immune to breakdown but more adequately prepared for stress when it does (inevitably?) come?

The clustering of social/health/financial distress in thousands of families in the St. Paul and Stamford studies suggest that the density of problem areas is great and that if one bug does not get them, another one will. And once one is "down," all kinds of adversity may follow—when it rains, it pours. Social competence is a general state of affairs, one

mustering the skills to meet a variety of situations, no one of which is all-adequate or all-encompassing. The use of specific skills as strategies, reminiscent of the human–machine skill analogy, may be lacking in the "marginal" folk who have neither enough basic social skill nor enough experiences in selecting strategies to cope. Phillips said that "pathology eventuates when a deficiency in personal resources combines with stressful circumstances to create a situation in which the person lacks the adaptive skills for a successful resolution of his difficulties" (Phillips, 1968, p. 212). But people's coping skills fluctuate with environmental opportunities. The lessons of the recent past in the development and training of social skills tells us that the amount of variance in a person–environment deficit can perhaps be altered more readily by and through methods focused on the individual's social skills—in fairly well-structured social contexts—rather than waiting for larger scale environmental changes to allow the individual to solve his or her problems and flourish. However, larger scale changes may be needed in some cases to secure and support individual change and to prevent simply ad hoc adjustment at the individual level.*

---

*This point needs more elaboration than can be fully given here. Viewing social skills as basic to psychopathology does not imply that one goes straightforwardly from changing a given social skill (or set of skills) to an elimination of psychopathology (L'Abate, 1980, p. 217; Phillips, 1980, pp. 19–20; Singleton, 1980, pp. 1–9). Besides resting heavily on empirical support, the general notion of social skills in also a conceptual redirection concerning the causes and treatment of psychopathology. Social skills view-points are also programmatic in that changes are not only envisioned at the individual level but *programmatically* at small group (family groups, peer groups, etc.) and aggregate levels. In the latter case we observe that delinquent behaviors might not change much when intervention occurs only or primarily at the individual level but requires larger social setting changes. Individuals change within family groups but more profound and lasting changes occur through whole-

Obviously, there are many person–environment problems nested in these observations. What we lack in our present state of knowledge and what we have always lacked is what Phillips observed: "The concept of coping potential and its behavioral expression in social competence have been elaborated in considerable detail [in Phillips' book]. An equivalent amount of data are not available on the nature of the social environment nor on just what aspects of environment are of consequence in adaptation and failure" (Phillips, 1968, p. 213).

Following this line of reasoning, some of the social skills movement of the last decade or two may have gained its assertive and ascendant position on the backs of the relative personal, social, and environmental stability of the participants. One can list such things as training students in interpersonal skills, improving inpatient self-care, training physicians in better "doctor–patient" relationships, improving staff development via social skills, improving managerial skills in social interaction in businesses and industries, teaching and altering conversational skills, improving interviewing skills, and so on through a myriad of interesting, challenging, and sometimes very important settings and problems (Singleton, Spurgeon, & Stammers, 1980). But some of these are settings in which the participants have much at stake, where already there are overall social competencies and skill strategy repertoires, and where failure in training may have only minor or passing consequences, although personal functioning,

happiness, and well-being may be somewhat at issue. Social skills training in the manner proposed in the Singleton et al. volume has not been tried in settings like the Stamford and St. Paul community studies (Buell et al., 1952), the Hollingshead and Redlich (1958) setting, in the Srole et al. community studies (1962), nor in the more recently documented studies of depression and social skill lacks among lower class women in the London area (Brown & Harris, 1979).

We are at a stage in the development of social skills research and intervention as far as the social aggregate level is concerned where we were in the 1930s in regard to the individual child level, namely mainly describing extant social-structural conditions with relatively less intervention. Our present repertoire of social skills intervention is primarily at the individual level in essentially well-structured and well-maintained social contexts. These interventions are of considerable importance, and in time, they may well take us beyond the traditional clinic and the consulting room; social skills training may eventually supplement or further influence psychotherapy (Argyle, Bryant, & Trower, 1974; Coyne, 1976; Phillips, 1978, 1980; Trower et al., 1978). Also, social skills analysis and training may largely displace psychiatric diagnosis and move treatment away from traditional hospitalization and institutionalization into more specific social skills research and training areas (perhaps operating as centers), fashioned to meet the needs now so poorly met by hospitalization. But we will not have tackled the larger issues—the breeding grounds—if you will, of social and personal psychopathology until we have posited strong intervention programs in segments of society or in social aggregate settings now available to us in elementary and secondary schools, on university campuses, in corporations and businesses, in communities as well as in prisons and hospitals. As we make more excursions into the so-

family changes (L'Abate, 1977). In another parallel manner we speak of science as a way to solve human problems, not just in some crucial/technical situation (although this might come about) but in the larger *programmatic* sense. The social skills viewpoint is a vastly different way of looking at psychopathology than that offered in the traditional past; these differences must not be viewed superficially or masked (Kalish, 1981).

cial environment, we will not only better understand individual social behavior and social skills development, we will presumably enhance the value the individual has for the social group and vice versa by making the contribution to change and stability greater for each.

In regard to getting into the broader social matrix more thoroughly, it is important to realize that we do not have in our educational system and child-rearing practices what we might call a "social curriculum." We have curricula for most every other subject matter area but not for social behavior. We are in many ways still at the stage of thinking about social behavior that Murphy, Murphy, and Newcomb (1937) observed nearly a half century ago, namely that we "teach" intellectual skills, but we leave social skills largely to the individual's own initiative or to chance. Even the social skills movement of the past decade or so has been mainly centered on the remediation of social skills lacks (Phillips, 1980, p. 172) and not on the study of the social environment and/or on what aspects of the social environment are of importance in the social competence and adjustment of individuals (Phillips, 1968, p. 213). Argyle has recently stated that "I would . . . greatly welcome the inclusion of SST (Social Skills Training) as part of the school curriculum" (Argyle, 1981, p. 284). Some preliminary attempts are being made in England to train children in social competence (McPhail, 1972; McPhail, Middleton, & Ingram, 1978). The recent interest in the United States in moral behavior and prosocial development may generate more interest in a social curriculum in a manner that is teachable to any and all children. Arbuthmet & Faust, 1981; Hargie, Saunders, & Dickson, 1981; Staub, 1978, 1979). The far-reaching issues lie in the larger social fabric and in the teaching of social competence from the cradle onward. As already noted, the movement of social skills research and training might well be in the direction of studying larger social aggregates; our own dormitories in colleges and universities are good starting points, especially for preventive work, but few of us have tackled this environment. Prisons and mental hospitals are equally challenging areas for study and have been studied (as captive populations) more than the normal settings such as dormitories. In the former, however, the emphasis has been on the individual's social skills and has been, of course, remedial. Preventive work might better go on in dormitories, in apartment houses and developments, and in factories and offices. A social curriculum might be developed for each setting, fitting in nicely with the rules of conducting dorms, managing offices and factories, and constructively influencing how marriages and families function (de-Jong, 1980; Ellis & Whittington, 1981; Joanning, Brock, Avery, & Coufal, 1980, Scherer & Scherer, 1980;). Elementary and secondary schools are, of course, prime targets for social skills training. Some recent work of social psychologists (Harré, 1979) suggest support for the larger scale study of social skills and the curriculum route to better social skills training; for example, Harré suggests that social "meaning" is derived not from the personal, private history of the individual but from the place meaning—as social action—has in the network of public convention. The network-of-public-convention phrase suggests studying more thoroughly the social environment and preparing people for its demands and assessing its characteristics in a variety of settings. Harré further suggests that individuals' accounts of their behavior are not best understood as introspectively available data but as expressions of how people comprehend and report on their social world. We see the latter when clinical patients/clients attribute their concerns to "anxiety" when they are more angry and hostile than anything else; their introspective accounts simply mirror their interpretation of what is a social commonplace explanation (it is more acceptable to be anxious than angry), not what is true for them. The "individualistic culture" in the United States probably encourages one kind of social skills training—that placed at the individual "corrective" and assertive levels (which may be waning in importance [Galassi, Galassi, & Vedder, 1981]—but may inhibit equally forcefully social skills and social competence that have a larger social matrix as their starting point; whereas in England, as Argyle noted (1981, p. 262), people are less attuned to assertiveness and more interested in forming and maintaining friendships. The recent emphasis on "cognitive" psychology and "cognitive behavior" therapy may also act to inhibit proper attention to the larger social matrix in understanding the role of social skills (McArthur, 1981; Sampson, 1981).

The social skills concept has not only had an impact of improving the status of hospitalized persons; it has more recently invaded the psychotherapy office (Argyle, 1981; Argyle et al., 1974; Lewisohn 1975; Phillips, 1977, 1978, 1980; Trower et al., 1978). It is quite likely that if social skills training aids the plights of people hospitalized for psychological problems, those in outpatient settings engaging in psychotherapy may lack some of the same skills—perhaps to a lesser degree—and can be aided by proper training aimed at remediation and social enhancement. One reason for viewing outpatients and clients as suitable subjects for social skills enhancement is survey information indicating these populations have noticeable social concerns. Zimbardo (1977) reported on 2500 American college students, where 42% reported they were shy now, and of these, over 60% reported the problem had been serious. Bryant and Trower (1974), in a survey of a 10% sample of Oxford University students, found many

reporting social difficulties and a tendency to avoid some social situations, with 42% of freshmen students reporting moderate to great difficulty. Phillips (1978) found in a survey of 100 men and 100 women consecutive applicants for psychotherapy in a university mental health clinic that a higher proportion endorsed problem areas on the Mooney Problem Checklist in regard to social and recreational activities, social psychological activities, and personal psychological relations than any other, or all other, of 11 areas of personal experience. Similarly, 138 depressed inpatients and outpatients in a mental hospital setting showed profiles on the Minnesota Multiphasic Personality Inventory (MMPI) evidencing appreciable social introversion as a function of subtypes of depressive scale elevations (Phillips, 1978, pp. 54–100). These and other studies of the use of, or relevance of, social skills training in otherwise ostensible psychotherapy cases raises to an even higher consideration the applicability of social skills intervention as an adjunct to, or perhaps even in place of, psychotherapy (Phillips, 1978, 1980). In some research, social skills training had a more positive effect on clients than did either individual or group psychotherapy (Argyle et al., 1974; Maxwell, 1976; Marzillier, 1978; Twentyman & Zimering, 1979). Compared to most psychotherapy, the more specific nature of social skills training—identification of target behaviors, discussion and rehearsal, homework assignments, keeping logs, tryouts in natural settings, and the like—increases the on-task behaviors of the participants and may result in more concrete behavior change. These social skills programs also tend to encompass more areas—nonverbal behavior, for example—than does psychotherapy (Argyle, 1981; Hargie et al., 1981). The lasting power of various social skills training programs compared to psychotherapy and group therapy are yet to be amply investigated. It should be easier and less time consuming to update social skills training effects, if needed, than to have clients reenter psychotherapy if the need arises. There is probably no aspect of the general delivery of mental health services—from intake through individual and group psychotherapy, in both in- and outpatient setting—that would fail to profit from a social skills approach, although our confidence in the specifics of such training and its longer range effects are yet to be demonstrated. However these empirical issues may turn out, conceptually the application of social skills training methods to psychotherapy clients has given rise to the notion that people are "sick" because they lack social skills and general social competence, rather than viewing the lack of social skills as by-products of a "sick" mind (Hargie et al., 1981). With the shoe on the proper foot, from the standpoint of social skills research and application, researchers and clinicians can now proceed with some confidence in emphasizing the acquisition and polishing of social competencies rather than trying to fathom the causes and remediation of psychopathology strictly in individual, intropsychic terms. This change may have profound effects in time.

Social skills training in relation to children has had a resurgence in recent years (Cartledge & Milburn, 1980; Hargie et al., 1981; Staub, 1978, 1979;, Wine & Syme, 1981). Because the social skills movement with children covers not only common social skills but also moral and altruistic behaviors, it may have, or take on, larger meaning and cause us to reflect more on issues such as that suggested previously in the way of a social curriculum. Children are ideal for studying a social curriculum and already, by virtue of their development, are actually providing a kind of social curriculum for themselves. Adult provisions for childhood social development have never been analyzed in terms of a social curriculum; yet if we look at myths and rhymes

and the moral lessons found in poetry we observe an approximation to the social skills curriculum idea.

The natural or culturally given prescriptions for a social skills curriculum—assuming we call it that—tend to harbor negative lessons, fear, intimidation, and hostility. There is no better example of this set of social influences perpetrated on the child than the Mother Goose rhymes (deAngelis, 1954) that are so hoary in tradition over the years. Also, Bettelheim (1976) has institutionalized "enchantment" as a lesson given to children and emphasizes the use of myths and allegories as the basis for emotional catharsis that is presumably needed by the child as coping behavior in the face of developmental crises and intropsychic conflict.

The social skills movement, however, goes against the grain of the Bettelheim thesis and all other theses about child social development that place cathartic relief by vicarious means (poetry, myth, allegory) so prominent in child behavior. Social skills, in contrast, supports the notion of a positive, prosocial curriculum and puts little or no emphasis on cathartic relief, although recognizing that some such need may occasionally happen. Not only is there very little notice given to the possible cathartic role of myths in steering child social development, some would say that traditional mythology as taught to children may cause problems (Milburn, 1982). The depiction of children and child behavior in ancient and modern myths may do injustice to children and to understanding their social development; such mythology can adversely affect adult behavior and belief and child–adult interactions.

The social skills movement, then, is not simply an in-place set of techniques for resolving some child (or adolescent, or adult) social skills needs and conflicts. It is a movement that properly places much maturation for change and development in the social matrix and not in intropsychic development that allegedly unfolds despite the social circumstances. The variables are those relating to the person–environment exchange or interaction as with all behavior research and conceptualization.

CONCLUDING COMMENT

In summary, then, the social skills movement has had a number of historical features not commonly recognized. In the recent rush to empirical reports on a large variety of topics—many of which are highly instructive and useful—we have not looked back far enough to observe our roots. The earlier signs of social skills training from the 1930s has been largely ignored, and, more importantly, we have consequently failed to anchor ourselves in our intellectual past. We had a good beginning then but it got away, and for 20–25 years (after the 1930s) what we now term social skills had a limbo status.

The more recent work on social competence, growing out of the study of institutionalized adults, found that social competence prior to hospitalization was a good measure of how the patient would fare in the hospital and afterward. We did not build on this trend by further studying the environment, but let it, too, go somewhat into limbo.

About the same time, a third aspect of social skills training and research found its way into prominence from a somewhat different origin, namey human–machine systems and the emphasis on motor and perceptual skills training, with the eventual crossing-over from human–machine to human–human systems giving rise to a burgeoning work in social skills research and practice in the United Kingdom. A fourth trend, coming out of our own behavior modification movement and mostly stimulated by assertiveness training in the United States first equated social skills more or less completely with assertiveness, but has now broadened out to include a much larger set of considerations, moving the social skills area more into the larger social matrix with an emerging emphasis on prosocial behavior, moral behavior, the study of small social aggregates, and a slightly greater emphasis on preventive work. The real work of building a social curriculum remains to be done, but is at least being dimly recognized.

A fifth trend is seen in the development of corrective or remedial work where social skills training has begun to be applied to potential individual and group therapy clients. This trend has helped replace the traditional notions of abnormal psychology and psychiatry that people are lacking in social competence because the are "sick," rather than the other way around.

The sixth trend suggests, in part, the dropping of assertiveness as a unitary and unifying concept and putting more emphasis on response-specific and situation-specific behaviors. This trend may meld with greater concerns for the social aggregate and with the study of moral and prosocial issues. It also fits with, or may be synonymous with, the importance of assessment. This trend is unusually important, it appears, becuase it allows for assessment effort aimed at situation-specific variables without risking the traditional tendency to reify assessment outcome.

Child development and children's prosocial behaviors, in relation to social skills, is a newly burgeoning field, although, as we have seen, it has a hoary past. The new trend among child studies takes research more into moralistic and altruistic directions and asks more questions about the size of the social units (component behaviors) studied. Flexibility in choice of social variables and components may throw additional light on some knotty issues in the general study of social skills.

The final trend affecting social skills

research and training, now barely emerging, may be more in prospect than reality: that the social matrix more than individual cognitions will become the focus of inquiry, allowing us to understand better the shared social environment and the basic elements of social behavior. It may encourage progress in preventive work and treat the patient or clinical client not as an abnormality or psychiatric case but as an instance of social influence and skills training gone wrong, largely derived from an unhealthy and unwholesome social environment.

The recognition of these trends is beginning to be institutionalized by large-scale meetings of researchers in various social skills areas (L'Abate, 1982; Singleton et al., 1980; L'Abate & Milan, 1982, 1985). As the social skills movement takes further root, more such publications and societies might be anticipated, to the point where social skills becomes an integral part of clinical. therapeutic, and social psychology.

Looking backward at the social skills movement over the past several decades may allow some extrapolation toward the future. The movement, as such, appears to be a robust one, with numerous books, articles, and training and workshop programs being offered widely over the country and in foreign countries. Social skills research has permeated most fields of behavioral psychology as well as having at least a foot in the door among social psychologists, developmental psychologists, and philosophical and theoretical speculators in almost all settings in which psychological research and practice are carried out. The field is not only characterized by energetic empirical activities, but there is healthy ferment within the movement on the choice of variables, the location of the variables studied, and the importance of social skills formulations for adjacent or related areas of applied psychology. So early in the game, one could hardly ask for more

gainful activities. Add to this energy the formation of a professional association (Interpersonal Skills Training & Research Association [ISTARA]) (L'Abate & Milan, 1982 1983), and one sees more formal direction and purpose emerging from the now very broad social skills movement. Whether a formal association will stimulate the research and practice that are needed for scientific and humanitarian purposes remains to be seen, but without the bricks and mortar of associational strength any movement may meander about for years or decades and contribute less than it otherwise might. Now is the time for the association to lend purpose to the social skills movement without preempting research initiative or variety in application. In addition to research productivity and salience in application, we have to meet criteria related to accountability, conceptual clarity, and generalizability of outcome findings. If we can place all these dials and pointers in clear perspective, the social skills movement may turn out to be one of the most heuristic contributors to psychological and social knowledge to arrive on the scene in decades.

REFERENCES

Anderson, H. H., & Anderson, G. L. (1954). Social development. In L. Carmichael (Ed.), *Manual of child psychology*. New York: Wiley.

Arbuthmet, J. B., & Faust, D. (1981). *Teaching moral reasoning: Theory and practice*. New York: Harper & Row.

Argyle, M. (1967). *The psychology of interpersonal behavior*. London: Penguin.

Argyle, M. (1969). *Social interaction*. London: Methuen.

Argyle, M. (1975). *Bodily communication*. London: Methuen.

Argyle, M. (1981). The contribution of social interaction research to social skills training. In J. W. Wine & M. D. Syme (Eds.), *Social competence*. New York: Guilford Press.

Argyle, M., Bryant, B., & Trower, P. (1974). Social skills training and psychotherapy: A comparative study. *Psychological Medicine, 4,* 435–443.

Argyle, M., & Kendon, A. (1967). The experimental analysis of social performance. In L. Berkowitz (Ed.), *Advances in social psychology*. New York: Academic Press.

Bandura, A. (1969). *Principles of behavior change*. New York: Holt, Rinehart & Winston.

Bandura, A. (1971). *Social learning theory*. Morristown, NJ: Learing Press.

Bellack, A. S., & Hersen, M. (1977). *Behavior modification: An introductory textbook*. Baltimore: Williams & Wilkins.

Bellack, A. S., & Hersen, M. (Eds.) (1979). *Research and practice in social skills*. New York: Plenum.

Bettelhcim, B.(1976). *The uses of enchantment: The meaning and importance of fairy tales. New York: Vintage.*

Brown, G. W., & Harris, T. (1979). *Social origins of depression. A study of psychiatric disorders in women*. New York: Free Press.

Bryant, B., & Trower, P. (1974). Social difficulty in a student population. *British Journal of Educational Psychology, 44,* 13–21.

Buell, Bradley, & Associates (1952). Community planning for social services. New York: Columbia University Press.

Carmichael, L. (Ed.) (1954). *Manual of child psychology*. New York: Wiley.

Cartledge, G., & Milburn, J. F. (1980). Teaching social skills to children. New York: Pergamon.

Coyne, J. C. (1976). Toward an interactional description of depression. *Psychiatry, 39,* 14–27.

Crossman, E. R. F. W. (1960). Automation and skill. D.S.I.R. Problems of Progress in Industry, No. 9, HMSO, London.

deAngelis, M. (1954). *Book of nursery and Mother Goose rhymes*. New York: Doubleday.

deJong, J. R. (1980). Social skill aspects of industrial organizations. In W. T. Singleton, P. Spurgeon, & R. B. Stammers (Eds.), *The analysis of social skill*. London: Plenum.

Dohrenwend, B. R., & Dohrenwend, B.S. (1969). *Social status and psychological inquiry*. New York: Wiley.

Eisler, R. M., Miller, P. M., & Hersen, M. (1973). Components of assertive behavior. *Journal of Clinical Psychology, 29,* 295–299.

Ellis, R., & Whittington, D. (1981). *A guide to social skills training*. London: Crown Helm.

Frank, J. D. (1974). Therapeutic components of psychotherapy: A 25 year progress report of research. *Journal of Nervous & Mental Disease, 159,* 325–342.

Galassi, J. P., Galassi, M. D., & Vedder, M. J. (1981). Perspectives on assertion as a social skills model. In J. D. Wine & M. D. Syme (Eds.), *Social competence*. New York: Guilford Press.

Gambrill, E. D. (1978). *Behavior modification: Handbook of assessment, intervention, and evaluation*. San Francisco: Jossey-Bass.

Hargie, O., Saunders, C., & Dickson, D. (1981). *Social skills in interpersonal communication*. London: Crown Helm.

Harré, R. (1979). *Social being*. Totowa, NJ: Rowman & Littlefield.

Hollingshead, A. B., & Redlich, F. C. (1958). *Social class and mental illness*. New York: Wiley.

Holmes, T. H., Hawkins, N. G., Bowerman, E. C., Clark, E. R., Jr., & Joffee, J. R. (1957). Psychosocial and psychophysiological studies of tuberculosis. *Psychosomatic Medicine, 19,* 134–143.

Jack, L. M. (1934). An experimental study of ascendant behavior in preschool children. Iowa City: *University of Iowa Studies in Child Welfare*.

Joanning, H., Brock, G. W., Avery, A. W., & Coufal, J. D. (1980). The educational approach to social skills training in marriage and family intervention. In W. T. Singleton, P. Spurgeon, & R. B. Stammers (Eds.). *The analysis of social skills*. London: Plenum.

Jones, M. C. (1924). The elimination of children's fears. *Journal of Experimental Psychology, 7,* 383–390.

Kalish, H. I. (1981). *From behavior science to Behavior Modification.* New York: McGraw-Hill.

L'Abate, L. (1977). *Enrichment: Structured interventions with couples, families and groups.* Washington D.C.: University Press of America.

L'Abate, L. (1980). Toward a theory and technology for social skills training: Suggestions for curriculum development. *Academic Psychology Bulletin, 2,* 207–225.

L'Abate, L. (1982) Interpersonal Skills Training and Research Association, Box 564, G Georgia State University, Atlanta, Georgia.

L'Abate, L., & Milan, M. A. (1982). Conference Directors: National Conference on Social Skills Training and Research, Georgia State University, Atlanta, Georgia, March 5-6, 1982.

L'Abate, L., & Milan, M. A. (1985). *Handbook of social skills training and research.* New York: Wiley.

Lazarus, A. A. (1971). *Behavior therapy and beyond.* New York: McGraw-Hill.

Lewinsohn, P. M. (1975). The behavioral study and treatment of depression. In M. Hersen, R. M. Eisler, & P. M. Miller (Eds.), *Progress in behavior modification* (Vol. 1). New York: Academic Press.

Libet, J. M., & Lewinsohn, P.M. (1973). Concept of social skill with special reference to the behavior of depressed persons. *Journal of Consulting and Clinical Psychology, 40,* 304–312.

McArthur, G. N. (1981) An evaluation of social skills training. In E. T. Higgins, C. P. Herman, & M. P. Zanna (Eds.), *Social cognition.* Hillsdale, NJ: Erlbaum.

McPhail, P. (1972) *In other people's shoes.* London: Longman.

McPhail, P., Middleton, D., & Ingram, D. (1978). *Moral education in the middle years.* London: Longman.

Marzillier, J. (1978) Outcome studies in social skills training: A review. In P. Trower, B. Bryant, & M. Argyle (Eds.). *Social skills and mental health.* London: Methuen.

Maxwell, G. M. (1976). *An evaluation of social skills training.* Unpublished manuscript, University of Otago, Dunedin, New Zealand.

Milburn, D. (1982). *Felicido: The mythic reality of childhood.* Lanham, MD: University Press of America.

Morgan, J. J. B. (1942). *Child psychology.* New York: Farrar & Rinehart.

Murphy, G., Murphy, L. B., & Newcomb, T. M. (1937) *Experimental social psychology.* New York: Harper & Bros.

Page, L. M. (1936). The modification of ascendant behavior in preschool children. Iowa City: University of Iowa Studies in Child Welfare.

Phillips, E. L. (1977). *Counseling and psychotherapy: A behavioral approach.* New York: Wiley.

Phillips, E. L. (1978). *The social skills basis of psychopathology: Alternative to abnormal psychology and psychiatry.* New York: Grune & Stratton.

Phillips, E. L. (1980). Social skills instruction as adjunctive/alternative to psychotherapy. In W. T. Singleton, P. Spurgeon, & R. B. Stammers (Eds.), *The analysis of social skill.* London: Plenum.

Phillips, L. (1968). *Human Adaptation* New York: Academic Press.

Salter A. (1949) *Conditional reflex therapy.* New York: Farrer, Straus & Geroux, 1949.

Sampson, E. E. (1981). Cognitive psychology as ideology. *American Psychologist, 36,* 730–743.

Scherer, U., & Scherer, K. R. (1980) Psychological factors in bureaucratic encounters. In W. T. Singleton, P. Spurgeon, & R. B. Stammers (Eds.), *The analysis of social skill.* London: Plenum.

Singleton, W.T., Spurgeon, P., & Stammers, R. B. (Eds.) (1979). *The analysis of social skill.* London: Plenum.

Srole, L., Langner, T. S., Michael, S. T., Opler, M. K., & Rennie, T. A. C. (1962). *Mental health in the metropolis: Midtown Manhattan study (Vol. 1).* New York: McGraw-Hill.

Staub, E. (1978). *Positive social behavior and morality: Social and personal influences* (Vol. 1). New York: Academic Press.

Staub, E. (1979). *Positive social behavior and morality: Socialization and development* (Vol. 2). New York: Academic Press.

Thompson, G. G. (1952). *Child psychology.* Boston: Houghton-Mifflin.

Thorpe, L. P. (1946) *Child psychology and development.* New York: Ronald Press.

Trower, P. (1982). Toward a generative model of social skills: A critique and synthesis. In J. P. Curran & P. M. Monti (Eds.). *Social skills training.* New York: Guilford Press.

Trower, P., Bryant, B., & Argyle, M. (Eds.) (1978). *Social skills and mental health.* London: Methuen.

Twentyman, C. T., & Zimering, R. T. (1979). Behavioral training of social skills: A review. *Progress in Behavior Modification, 7,* 319–400.

Welford, A. T. (1966). The ergonomic approach to social behavior. *Ergonomics, 9,* 357–369.

Welford, A. T. (1980). The concept of skill and its application to social performance. In W. T. Singleton, P. Spurgeon, & R. B. Stammers (Eds.), *The analysis of social skill.* London: Plenum.

Williams, H. M. (1935). A factor analysis of Berne's social behavior in young children. *Journal of Experimental Education 4,* 142–146.

Wine, J. D., & Syme, M. D. (Eds.) (1981). *Social competence.* New York: Guilford Press.

Wolpe, J. (1958). *Psychotherapy by reciprocal inhibition.* Stanford: Stanford University Press.

Zigler, E., & Phillips, L. (1960). Social effectiveness and symptomatic behaviors. *Journal of Abnormal and Social Psychology, 61,* 231–238.

Zigler, E., & Phillips, L. (1961). Social competence and outcome in psychiatric disorder. *Journal of Abnormal and Social Psychology, 63,* 264–271.

Zimbardo, P. G. (1977). *Shyness: What it is, what to do about it.* Reading, MA: Addison-Wesley.

CHAPTER 2

New Directions in the Assessment of Social Competence and Social Skills

DAVID G. SCHLUNDT AND RICHARD M. McFALL

Writing a chapter on the assessment of social competence and social skills in 1983 is no easy task. The literature in this area has grown enormously in the 15 years or so since the first studies evaluating the effectiveness of social skills training were published (Eisler, Hersen, & Miller, 1973; Eisler, Miller & Hersen, 1973; McFall & Lillesand, 1971; McFall & Marston, 1970; Rehm & Marston, 1968). Therefore, this chapter will not attempt an exhaustive review of the literature on social skills, nor will it attempt to provide a cookbook on *how to* assess social skills because that would require much more space than is available. Instead, this chapter will develope an outline of a taxonomic system that might be useful for organizing the literature on the assessment of social competence and social skills and will relate this taxonomic system to some of the available methods that may prove useful for skills assessment.

Previous reviews of skills assessment have organized the literature around an implicit taxonomy. For example, Van Hasselt, Hersen, Whitehill, and Bellack (1979) organized their review of social skills assessment in children around two headings: direct observation of behavior and role playing. Foster and Richey (1979) opted for a similar taxonomy of skills assessment for children; they

discussed sociometrics and direct observation of behavior as the major approaches. Bellack (1979) organized his review of skills assessment literature around three major categories: self-report, naturalistic observations, and role playing. Eisler (1976), on the other hand, placed emphasis on the types of problem areas to be assessed (assertiveness, heterosocial skills, and depression) and then discussed four methods of gathering data (interviews, self-report questionnaires, role-playing assessments, and naturalistic observation of behavior).

There are several other ways that reviews of the social skills assessment literature could be organized. For example, skills assessment could be classified according to the populations for which they were intended (e.g., adults, children, adolescents, college students); according to the purposes for which they were to be used (e.g., clinical assessment, program evaluation, basic research); or according to the settings in which behaviors were sampled (e.g., naturalistic vs. laboratory).

DEFINITION OF SOCIAL COMPETENCE AND SOCIAL SKILLS

In a recent critical review of the social skills literature, McFall (1982) identified two major ways in which the concept of social skills has been used. It has been used in a traitlike manner to refer to stable characteristic of persons, and it has been used in a molecular manner to refer to specific component behaviors. McFall found that both of these uses were inadequate on conceptual and empirical grounds and proposed a reformulated conception involving a two-tiered model of social competence and social skills.

Social Competence

When a behavior is called *socially competent,* this involves a value-based judgment by an observer concerning the effectiveness of an individual's performance in a specific task. Three aspects of this definition need to be stressed: First, competence is a judgment about behavior and not a judgment about some enduring characteristic of the performer; second, the judgment is based on an episode of behavior within a context, not merely on a single, isolated molecular act; and third, the judge who evaluates the competence of a performance does so on the basis of certain implicit or explicit values. Competence judgments are inherently relativistic. They depend on the particular task in question, the particular context, and the values employed by the judge.

The assessment of social competence involves two components: (1) the study of the tasks that are relevant and important for the individual, and (2) the analysis of behaviors that relevant judges consider to be effective ways of handling each of these important tasks.

Social Skills

Social skills are the specific component processes that enable an individual to behave in a manner that will be judged as "competent." Skills are the abilities necessary for producing behavior that will accomplish the objective of a task. In

general, different tasks will require different skills because the specific shape of competent behavior will vary from one task to the next. Skills are also relativistic because they are tied to the value-based criterion used to judge competence. For example, one judge may consider conciliatory behavior to be the most competent way to handle interpersonal conflict, whereas another judge may believe that assertive behavior is the most competent way to respond. Thus, the particular skills required for competently handling interpersonal conflict will depend on which judge's conception of competence is being applied.

Implications

These definitions of social competence and social skills have important assessment implications. If a person is judged to perform incompetently at a particular task, then it is possible to infer that the person is deficient in one or more of the requisite skills for that task. Of course, a global judgment that a performance was incompetent does not help us identify the individual's particular skills deficits. A skills assessement requires independent methods for isolating and measuring each of the requisite skills underlying competent performance. We must be able to assess specific skills independently in order to avoid the problem of circularity. That is, explaining incompetent performance in terms of skills deficits is only valid if these deficits can be identified and measured independently of the performance that was used to make the competence judgment.

Distinguishing between competence and skill has other assessment implications. To the extent that a particular skill is required for competent performance in several different tasks, then an independent measure of that skill will contribute to our ability to predict a person's behavoir across several tasks. This prediction should hold true even if the tasks seem very dissimilar topographically, as long as they require the same component skill.

Suppose, for example, that an individual has a deficit in the skill of estimating the probability of negative consequences. Now consider two dissimilar tasks requiring this skill: (1) initiating sex on a date; and (2) investing money in the stock market. If we had an independent measure of a skill called "estimating negative outcome probabilities" and we could identify an individual who was deficient in this skill, then we could predict that the individual would be judged to behave incompetently in both tasks. In the first instance, the person might overestimate the probability that the partner would be unwilling to become involved in a sexual relationship. In the second intance, the person might overestimate the probability of losing a large sum of money.

The proposed model is potentially very powerful, especially when compared to other models of behavoiral assessment, which only predict that similar behaviors will be observed in similar situations (e.g., Goldfried & Linehan, 1977). Although it may be true that similar situations lead to similar levels of performance competence, the reason for this probably is that similar tasks require similar skills. The model proposed here is potentially more powerful because it is theoretically capable of predicting behavior across dissimilar as well as similar tasks.

Trait theories were attempts to predict behavior across tasks, but they failed to perform well, in part, because they made no attempt to match the relevance of different traits to different tasks. The behavioral assessment movement, which developed in reaction to the predictive failures of trait psychology (Goldfried & Kent, 1972), has led to the development of numerous behavioral measurement techniques and situational sampling strategies; however, it has also made relatively little progress toward the goal of successfully predicting cross-situational behavior. McFall's (1982; McFall & Dodge, 1982) two-tiered model of social competence and social skills conceptualizes the interface among behavior, abilities, and tasks in a way that points to the development of an assessment technology aimed at making cross-situational predictions.

TASKS AS UNITS OF ANALYSIS

Within the proposed two-tiered model, the concept of *task* plays a central role. Therefore, a number of questions concerning the task concept need to be addressed. For example, how do we identify the relevant assessment tasks for a particular individual? In what way does competent or incompetent performance on one task affect the competence of performance on other tasks? How can we conceptualize taks clearly enough to classify them reiably? What are the relevant concepts and terms to use in describing and identifying tasks? Only after such questions have been addressed can we begin to approach the issue of actually assessing competence and skill (see McFall & McDonel, 1984).

Identifying the Relevant Tasks for the Individual

How do we identify the most relevant tasks for a particular individual? It makes little sense to evaluate an individual's competence at handling a task that never occurs or is irrelevant in the individual's life. For example, an assessment of a person's competence in speaking a particular foreign language would be irrelevant if that person was never called upon to perform that language in "real life."

The judgment that someone is incompetent at a particular task is meaningful only if that task is part of that individual's life space. *Life space* is defined as the set of tasks that structure the individual's time and activity on a day-to-day basis. The concept of life space as used here, is similar, but not identical, to Lewin's (1935, 1936) original use of the term. Lewin used the concept to refer to the totality of stimuli and cognitions that impinge on an individual's awareness. Our use refers to the totality of tasks around which an individual's behavior is organized.

A thorough assessment of social competence and social skills must begin with an analysis of the individual's life space. To the extent that persons share certain characteristics, such as age, sex, race, socioeconomic status, or geographic location, they will also tend to have similar life spaces. Similarities in people's environments lead to similarities in relevant tasks, and this opens the way for the development of standardized assessments. For example, we know that all college students need to be competent in the task of studying for exams; therefore, a standardized competence assessment for college students would contain common items related to studying for exams (see Fisher-Beckfield & McFall, 1982).

In addition to these population-specific tasks, there probably are certain very basic tasks that nearly all people need to be able to handle. Virtually everyone's life space requires the ability to initiate and terminate conversations, to count money and make change, to navigate from one place to another, and to establish close relationships. The list of common human tasks is likely to be quite extensive.

To illustrate the task concept and its relevance to assessment, we will provide a concrete example of its use in two treatment programs. As part of the development of life skills training programs in a group home for male juvenile delinquents and in a halfway house for psychiatric patients, we generated the following typology of common tasks:

navigation, self-care, commerce, vocation/education, recreation, social/interpersonal, family, and community. We broke down each of these task domains further into a series of specific subtasks and ordered the subtasks hierarchically. Skills in the tasks early in the series needed to be mastered and combined in order to accomplish the more complex tasks later in the training sequence. Moreover, the individual needed to demonstrate competence in all of the tasks at one level before graduating to the next stage of the program. For example, in navigation, the individual had to demonstrate competence in map reading, giving directions, locating addresses in different parts of town, arranging and paying for transportation, and planning for future transportation needs. The final task in the navigation series was the "drop test" in which the client was dropped in an unfamiliar part of town with only 25 cents and was required to make it home in a reasonable time period.

These programs integrated assessment and training. We observed an individual's performance on each task and evaluated it in terms of its competence. If the performance was not deemed satisfactory, then training was begun, and the person was taught the necessary skills to perform the task competently. When the person's performance on one task reached criterion level, the next task in the assessment/training sequence was introduced.

By the end of this assessment and training sequence, the individual had demonstrated mastery across a series of increasingly complex tasks and, presumably, was prepared to handle most situations within that domain in "real life." Even after such assessment and training, it is inevitable that certain tasks would arise that the individual had not been prepared to handle. However, demonstration of mastery over a subset of common cultural tasks ensured that the individual had at least a foundation of

HUTCHINGS PSYCHIATRIC CENTER
Box 27
University Station
Syracuse, New York 13210

basic skills that would enable her/him to perform competently in a representative sample of real-world situations.

The development of these assessment/training sequences was based more on rational than empirical grounds. We relied heavily on our clinical experiences and our personal knowledge of the client's culture when choosing the components in this series of tasks. However, several empirical methods are available for conducting life-space analyses. First, one can interview members of the relevant population and ask them how they spend their time and what kinds of life problems they encounter. Second, self-monitoring records or diaries of critical incidents can be collected to identify the common tasks facing a given population. Third, systematic, careful observations of population members can be conducted to identify common tasks.

Barker (1963, 1968) has been a pioneer in developing methods for studying behavior in its natural context. Such methods could be used to enumerate the tasks an individual faces in her/his day-to-day life. For example, Barker (1963) had an observer follow a child around all day long and write an ongoing narrative description of the child's behaviors and the contexts in which they occurred. Detailed descriptive records such as these might be used to determine empirically the task profile of an individual's (or a population's) life space.

Another method of enumerating the relevant life-space tasks of individuals is the situational analysis of Goldfried and D'Zurilla's (1969) behavioral analytic approach to competence assessment. The approach has been used to construct a number of assessment inventories (see Fisher-Beckfield & McFall, 1982; Freedman, Rosenthal, Donahoe, Schlundt, & McFall, 1978; Goldsmith & McFall, 1975; MacDonald, 1978; Perri & Richards, 1979). What these inventories have in common is that they consist of lists of common tasks, or problem situations, that have been determined empirically to be important to members of the target population.

One major shortcoming of most competence inventories created by the behavioral-analytic method is that they consist of a list of isolated problem situations to which subjects are instructed to make brief, one-shot, role-played responses. Such inventories may sample subjects' responses to specific problems, but they do not assess the more basic processing skills required to perform competently in everyday life nor do they assess how these basic skills are interrelated over time. That is, they do not reveal how subjects perform on a sequence of subtasks that eventually make up a higher order task. This criticism is less true of Fisher-Beckfield and McFall's (1982) Problem Inventory for College Students (PICS) because approximately half of the items on this inventory were problem-solving situations in which the subject was required to enumerate a strategy, rather than simply role playing a single static response.

Systems of Interrelated Tasks

The tasks that comprise an individual's life space are not like the items on a list. Rather, they are the constituents of a complex, interrelated life system. Borrowing from Graham, Argyle, and Furnham's (1980) discussion of goal interrelationships, we can identify at least five ways in which the tasks comprising a life system interact with each other: (1) the accomplishment of one task can facilitate success in another task: (2) both tasks can be subtasks of a common superordinate task; (3) one task can be prerequisite to the accomplishment of another task; (4) the accomplishment of one task can interfere with success in another task; and (5) two tasks can be mutally exclusive.

In conceptualizing the task structure of an individual's life space, we suggest the following strategy: First, subdivide the life space into a set of task domains, such as navigation, self-care, commerce, education/vocation, recreation, social/interpersonal, family, and community. Within each domain, enumerate a list of subtasks. Next, organize these subtasks, where possible, into hierarchies. Then, examine the relationships between the different hierarchical components to see which facilitate, which interfere, and which are mutually exclusive.

To illustrate this process of analysis, consider the following three specific tasks: maintaining physical fitness, publishing at least three papers a year, and having a mutually satisfying marital relationship. Each of these larger tasks can be broken down into subtasks, and the specific relationships among them could be analyzed. Furthermore, we could examine the relationships among major task hierarchies. On the one hand, for example, success in maintaining physical fitness might facilitate performance of the publication and marriage tasks by increasing a person's strength and stamina and by preventing depression. On the other hand, work on the physical fitness task might interfere with performance of the other tasks to the extent that the time devoted to exercise-related activities interfered with the available time for publishing and marriage. Similarly, many of the subtasks involved in publishing three articles a year may interfere with, or even be mutually exclusive with, the subtasks required to have a good marriage.

We are not in a position to review the empirical literature on the task structure of people's lives or the interrelation of tasks and subtasks. To date, there is little empirical literature on these topics. Much of what has been written is found in the areas of ecological and environmental psychology (e.g., see Barker, 1968, 1978; Bell, Fisher, & Loomis, 1978; Moos, 1975; Proshansky, Ittelson, & Rivlin, 1976), and is primarily descriptive, with little attention to the problem of analyzing the structure of individual's life spaces. Much of this literature is devoted to basic research, with little relevance to assessment. Specific methods need to be developed for translating these basic, descriptive conceptualizations into useful assessment procedures. (See Willems, 1976, for a rare example of the applications of ecological psychology to assessment problems.)

The Structure of Tasks

In this chapter, we have suggested that the first step in the assessment of social competence and social skills is a systematic analysis of the task structure of an individual's environment or life space. The concept of a social situation, or a social task, is pivotal for the behavioral psychologist and the interactional personality theorist. Behavioral assessment involves analyzing behavior obtained in naturalistic or seminaturalistic situations. The interactionist conceptualizes behavior as a joint function of the person and the situation (Endler & Magnusson, 1976; Magnusson & Endler, 1977; Mischel, 1973; Peterson, 1979). With all of the theoretical importance attached to situations as determinants of behavior by behavioral assessors and interactional psychologists, it is surprising that better conceptual definitions and empirical methodologies for studying situations have not emerged. In most research studies, the problem of specifying what constitutes a situation has been finessed through the use of operational definitions. For example, the Survey of Heterosexual Interactions (SHI) is a self-report behavioral inventory that asks subjects to rate the likelihood of initiating an interaction with a member of the opposite sex (Twentyman, Boland, & McFall,

1981; Twentyman & McFall, 1975). Each item in the inventory is merely a short, intuitively derived description of a situation, such as the following:

You are walking to your mail box in the large apartment building where you live. When you get there, you notice that two women are putting their names on the mail box of the vacant apartment beneath yours. In this situation you would . . .

A number of assessment instruments have used items like this (Freedman et al., 1978; Gambrill & Richey, 1975; Hersen, Bellack, & Turner, 1978; Levenson & Gottman, 1978; Richardson & Tasto, 1976; Warren & Gilner, 1978). Because subjects seem to have very little difficulty responding to such items, no one in this research area has seemed to be bothered by the fact that such intuitively based descriptions do not constitute a clear definition of a situation.

Another method for operationalizing situations, particularly those involving interpersonal conversation, has been to instruct subjects to converse with trained or untrained confederates (e.g., Arkowitz, Lichtenstein, McGovern, & Hines, 1975; Barlow, Abel, Blanchard, Bristow, & Young, 1977; Clark & Arkowitz, 1975; Conger & Farrell, 1981; Greenwald, 1977; Heimberg, Madsen, Montgomery, & McNabb, 1980; Pilkonis, 1977; Royce & Arkowitz, 1978; Twentyman, Boland, & McFall; 1981). Again, this assessment approach readily generates responses, but fails to provide a clear definition of the particular situational context for such responses.

A related strategy for studying subjects' behavior in operationally defined social situations has been to create conditions in which behavior in a pseudonaturalistic contrived context is studied unobtrusively. The environment is arranged in such a way that the subject's behavior can be observed without the subject's being aware of it. A popular ex-

ample of this strategy is to place a subject in a waiting room with an experimental confederate whom the subject believes to be another subject. The real subject is given some ruse, such as that the experiment is running late and that there will be a short wait. Then, the ensuing interaction between the subject and the confederate is taken as a sample of that subject's behavior in a "social conversational" situation (e.g., Conger & Farrel, 1981; Curran, Little, & Gilbert, 1978; Greenwald, 1977; Pilkonis, 1977; Twentyman, Boland, & McFall, 1981). Similarly, in working with married couples, interpersonal situations have been simulated by giving couples hypothetical problems to solve and observing their subsequent behaviors. In some studies, couples have been instructed to identify and solve an actual problem (e.g., Gottman, 1979; Raush, Berry, Hertel, & Swain, 1974' Royce & Weiss, 1975).

In all the previously mentioned methods for simulating situations, the problem of defining a naturalistic situation is simply avoided. The situation is defined strictly in terms of the experimenter's or confederate's behavior. Such simulated assessments fail to provide clear situational definitions that allow us to link the assessment to those classes of situations that naturally occur in people's day-to-day environments. Clear-cut definitions are necessary if competence assessments are to have applicablilty outside the fixed stimulus properties of the psychological laboratory or clinic.

Toward a Definition of Situations

Forgas (1978a, 1978b) investigated social perceptions in the natural environment. He used an environmental unit of analysis called the *social episode*. According to Forgas (1978b), social episoder are

recurring, stereotypical sequences of social interactions withing a culturally defined environment with consensually defined boundaries and with a set of subculture-specific rules and norms relating to appropriate and inappropriate behavior. (p.435)

In one study, Forgas (1978b) analyzed informants' descriptions of social episodes that routinely occurred in an academic department. The episodes were characterized by a specific time, place, set of participants, and focus of activity. He had subjects rate each of 17 social episodes on a set of paired adjective scales and, by using multidimensional scaling, accounted for subjects' perceptions using four dimensions: (1) the extent to which the activity was anxiety provoking; (2) subjects' degree of behavioral involvement in the episode; (3) the pleasantness of the episode; and (4) whether the episode was socioemotional or task directed.

Argyle (1979) discussed situations and proposed a set of concepts for describing situations. *Social situations,* according to him, are discretely different entities that are composed of a system of highly interdependent parts. He suggested a number of situational components, including behavioral repertoires, goals, cognitive constructs, environmental props, and rules.

Graham, Argyle, and Furnham (1980) asked a group of subjects to write down all the possible goals a participant could have in each of several common situations. Over 100 goal descriptions were elicited, which were then collapsed by the authors into 18 goal categories. Subsequently, it was shown that another group of subjects could match the goal categories to the list of situations with a high degree of agreement.

A third line of research relevant to describing and defining social tasks is the work aimed at empirically developing situational taxonomies (see Ekehammar & Magnusson, 1973; Frederiksen, 1972; Price & Blashfield, 1975; Sells, 1963). Schlundt (1979) argued that because

of the situational specificity of social behaviors, a systematic method for grouping situations into functionally equivalent classes was needed. Schlundt used a method known as *numerical taxonomy* (Sneath & Sokal, 1973; Sokal & Sneath, 1963) to contruct a classification for the 52 descriptions of problem situations in Fisher-Beckfield and McFall's (1982) Problem Inventory for College Students (PICS). Numerical taxonomy consists of the following steps:

1. The selection of a set of objects to be classified.
2. The identification of a set of descriptive features that vary among the objects.
3. The measurement of the features that are present in each object.
4. The use of cluster analysis to form a classification of the objects based on the empirical similarities of their features.

Of most interest to the present discussion is the set of features that Schlundt used to describe the set of situations. Among these situational features were antecedents of the situation (such as the individual's previous behavior); the other people in the situation (e.g., friend vs. acquaintance); behavioral demands to change internal states (such as reduce anxiety or acquire information); behavioral demands to alter the environment (such as creating a product or influencing another's behavior); and possible consequences in the situation (e.g., rewards and punishments). Schlundt asked coders to judge the presence or absence of each feature in each of the 52 PICS situations. He then used cluster analysis to form a hierarchical taxonomy of situations. As a validation, he demonstated that situations that were similar according to the derived taxonomy also tended to elicit similar behavior patterns from subjects.

Summary

To a participant, a *social task* is an environmental state of affairs characterized by a distinctive pattern of perceptual features, including such things as the setting, its props, its participants, and the antecedent behaviors of the participants. The identification of a situation on the basis of its perceptual features implies a specific set of objectives, constructs, and rules that the participants use to select and guide their behavior. *Competence* refers to whether or not a particular person's behavior achieves the implicit or explicit objectives of the task. *Skills* are the processes involved in the perceptual identification of the task and its objectives and in the use of concepts and rules to translate the chosen objective into a sequence of behavior that achieves the situational objectives.

ASSESSING COMPETENCE

Brunswik's Lens Model

In this section, conceptual and methodological issues involved in the assessment of competence will be expored within the framework provided by Brunswik's (1952, 1955) lens model. As part of his exposition of probabilistic functionalism, Brunswik developed a conceptual model for understanding perception and behavior in complex natural contexts, which he named the *lens model*. There are three basic components to this lens model: the organism, the proximal cues in the environment, and the distal effects or end states in the environment. As a way of conceptualizing perception, organisms use proximal cues to draw inferences about distal states of the environment. As a way of conceptualizing achievement, the immediate behaviors of organisms are treated as proximal variables that are used to achieve certain distal end states or outcomes in the environment.

An important aspect of the lens model is the assumption that there is only a probabilistic relationship between proximal cues and distal end states. Likewise, the relationship between behaviors and eventual outcomes also is probabilistic. The presence of proximal cues gives the organism information about the relative probabilities of certain end states. In the lens model, as in life, nothing is absolutely certain, only more or less likely.

The lens model translates quite easily into a mathematical model based on multiple linear regression (see Hammond, 1955; Hammond, Hursch, & Todd, 1964). The task of the organism is to predict the *distal state* of the environment E_i from a set of *proximal cues* C_1, C_2, C_3, . . . C_n. The organism is presented with a series of sample cue distributions and makes a judgment about the probable outcome for each trial. The distal end state is also known after each trial.

The organism's *judgment* can be represented as O_j (the subscripts on the variables simply indicate that each may take on a number of values). The organism's success in predicting the distal end state is called the organism's *achievement* and is measured quite simply as the correlation between O_j and E_i. That is, r_{oe} is a measure of how well the organism is able to predict the distal end state from the proximal cues.

The multiple regression of the cues on the distal end state, R_{ec}, is referred to as the *ecological validity* of the cues. The ecological validity represents the extent to which the cues actually predict the distal end state. The fact that this multiple correlation can be less than 1 represents the probabilistic or uncertain nature of the natural environment. The ecological validity of the cues sets an upper limit on the organism's achievement.

That is, unless the organism is effectively using a nonlinear judgment stategy (see Einhorn, 1970), r_{oe} cannot exceed R_{ec}. The validity of a judgment cannot exceed the validity of the cues upon which the judgment is based.

In a similar manner, the cues can be regressed onto the subject's judgment, R_{oc}, resulting in a linear model referred to as the organism's *cue utilization*. This model describes how the organism takes information from the proximal environment and combines it to make a prediction about the distal environment.

A final term, $r_{\hat{o}e}$, represents the correlation between the prediction made by the cue utilization equation and the distal environment. This is the predictive success that would be achieved by replacing the judge by a *mathematical model of the judge* (see Hoffman, 1960).

The lens model has found its most extensive use in studies of clinical judgment (Dawes & Corrigan, 1974; Hammond, 1955; Hammond, Hursch, & Todd, 1964; Sawyer, 1966) and in studies of multiple cue probability learning (Castellan, 1972; Todd & Hammond, 1965). For example, Goldberg (1965) showed Minnesota Multiphasic Personality Inventory (MMPI) profiles (proximal cues) of 861 patients who had been diagnosed as psychotic or neurotic (distal state) to 29 clinical psychologists and graduate students (organisms). Each judge was instructed to rate the degree of psychosis for each of the 861 MMPI profiles on an 11-point scale. Goldberg compared each judge's achievement (i.e., the judge's accuracy in diagnosing psychosis from the MMPI profiles as measured by the correlation between the judgments and the criterion diagnoses) to the model of the judge derived from the cue utilization equation. In all cases, he found that the model of the judge was as good as or better than the judge's actual achievement. This is a robust finding that has been replicated in numerous studies. Sawyer

(1966), for example, reviewed 45 studies comparing clinical and statistical prediction and concluded that models of the judge were consistently superior to the judge (see also Dawes & Corrigan, 1974).

The Lens Model in Competence Assessment

In order to discuss the assessment of competence from this new perspective, we first need to link the three key components of the lens model (organism, proximal cues, and distal end states) to our model of social competence and social skills. The *organism,* in this version of the lens model, is the observer who makes a competence judgment. The *proximal cues* are the behaviors of some subject whose competence is being judged. The *distal end state* is the outcome of the subject's behaviors; that is, the subject's success in achieving the objectives of the task. Thus, the lens model fits quite nicely with our earlier definition of competence as a value-based judgment about the effectiveness of an individual's behavior in achieving the objectives of a particular task.

Figure 2.1 presents a pictorial representation of the lens model of compe-

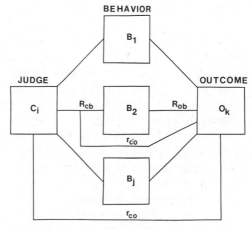

Figure 2.1. Brunswik's lens model applied to the assessment of social competence.

tence assessment. Note that the general shape of the figure is that of a convex lens, which is how the model got its name.

On the left of the figure is an observer who views a distribution of behavior and makes a rating of the competence of the observed performance. The distribution of behavior affects the environment to achieve certain end states or task outcomes. The task outcome is represented on the right of the figure.

The relationship between the observer's competence rating and the task outcome is a reflection of the observer's values. The correlation r_{co} will be referred to as the observer's *outcome evaluation*. Thus, for any particular end state that is measured, a high positive correlation indicates that achievement of the end state is weighted positively in forming a competence judgement. A high negative correlation indicates that the achievement of the end state is associated with a judgment of incompetence. A low or zero-order correlation indicates that the judge does not consider the end state to be relevant to a judgment of competence. Through this model, we can take a step toward operationalizing and measuring the value system of the competence judge and relating it to the assessment situation.

The relationship between the behavioral distribution and the observer's competence rating corresponds to the cue utilization equation of the lens model. This equation predicts which patterns of behavior will be considered competent and which incompetent. The weights given to the various behaviors in the cue utilization equation are indications of which behaviors the judge considers important components of competent performance.

The cue utilization equation can be used to develop an empirical model of the judge. Operationally, a model of the judge can be developed using a data set consisting of behavioral measures and competence ratings from a sample of subjects. Regression analysis is used to form a model of the judge. This model can then be used as an assessment tool. That is, the behaviors of a subject are sampled in an assessment task and a measure of the distribution of the subject's behaviors is taken. These behavioral measures are plugged into the model of the judge equation, and a predicted competence score is computed. Given the literature cited previously which shows that a model of the judge is a more valid predictor of criterion end states than the actual jduge, the computed competence score can be expected to be high-quality assessment data. Of course, research needs to be conducted to verify this hypothesis.

The relationship between the distribution of behaviors and the task outcome variable can also be modeled using a regression equation. This model will provide information about behavior-outcome contingencies. Thus, independent of any judge's value-based ratings, this component of the model will lead to the identification of if-then relationships between behavioral performances and task outcomes. These if-then relationships form the basis of a description of task performance as a rule-governed phenomenon (see Collett, 1977; Schlundt, 1982a).

Competence Ratings

The methodology involved in obtaining competence ratings is fairly simple. The judge views each sample of behavior and rates how effective the behavior was on a Likert-type scale. A 5- to 7-point scale typically is used, although there is some evidence that a 3-point scale may be adequate for many purposes (see Donahoe, 1978).

A number of dimensions have been used in past research to obtain global ratings of performance. Most notably, global ratings have been made of competence, skill, effectiveness, and anxiety. There has been much debate as to whether ratings should be made of skill or anxiety (see Bellack, 1979). Our recommendation is that judges be asked instead to indicate how effective they thought the subject's behavior was. As Bellack has pointed out, anxiety ratings are of interest, but they are not the best evidence upon which to base an assessment of competence.

The behavior samples can be live, on videotape, on audiotape, or presented as transcripts. Each method of presentation involves a loss of information about the behavior sample. For example, when using audiotapes, there is a loss of information about nonverbal body movements and facial expressions. Live ratings are preferred, from the standpoint of richness of information; however, videotapes are more practical because they preserve most of the information, can be rated at any time, can be rerated, and can be viewed in slow motion.

Selection of judges is another factor to be considered in obtaining competence ratings. The major decision is whether to use trained or untrained judges. For example, Curran, Monti, Corriveau, Hay, Hagerman, Zwick, and Farrel (1980) used trained judges to rate both the social skill and anxiety of subjects' videotaped performances in role-played social interactions. Based on a generalizability analysis, they concluded that the major source of variance in skill and anxiety ratings was differences among subjects and among subject's performances in different situations. Many studies have employed trained raters (e.g., Arkowitz, Lichtenstein, McGovern, & Hines, 1975; Clark & Arkowitz, 1975; Twentyman & McFall, 1975), and, in general, trained raters have been able to discriminate between subjects drawn from extreme

groups, such as high- and low-frequency daters (Borkovec, Stone, O'Brien, & Kaloupek, 1974). Training in most cases has involved coaching raters on what behaviors to look for, giving them practice in rating videotapes, providing feedback on the accuracy of practice ratings, and requiring raters to show agreement either with a standard protocol or with one another's ratings.

It is only sensible that persons being used to rate samples of behavior should be allowed to practice the rating procedure and become familiar with the task before rating the actual samples; however, teaching judges what behaviors to look for when making their judgments probably is inadvisable given the present definition of social competence. Because competence is a relativistic social judgment, it probably is best not to tell judges what to look for; instead, we should allow them to use their own value system to make the ratings.

If untrained raters are used, the selection of the raters becomes crucial. The key, if this approach is taken, is to insure that the persons selected as judges are representative of those individuals who would be in a position to define what is competent or incompetent behavior in the natural environment. Raters should be carefully selected from specific, well-defined populations. Persons who naturally deliver consequences in the task being studied make the ideal raters because their evaluations of performance competence make a real difference. For example, if an adolscent's competence in interacting with police is being evaluated, then the ideal populations to draw from would be police and adolescents. Similarly, if competence of heterosexual behavior is being evaluated, then the ideal population from which to select the judge would be peers of the opposite sex.

To summarize, we suggest that competence ratings be obtained from untrained judges drawn from the relevant population of naturalistic evaluators. The judges should rate either live or videotaped behavior samples, and the judgments should be ratings of effectiveness made on a 3-point to 7-point Likert scale.

Measuring Behavior

A number of very complex issues are involved in the measurement of behavior, but we can do little more than enumerate them here. One of the most relevant issues concerns the best methodology for the direct observation of behavior (see Colgan, 1978; Sackett, 1978).

The measurement of behavior can be conceptualized as involving three steps: (1) dividing the continuous stream of behavior into segments; (2) quantifying each segment; and (3) summarizing the component measures.

Segmenting Behavior

There are essentially two methods for dividing the stream of behavior into segments (see Barker, 1963; Fagen & Young, 1978; Sackett, 1978). In *time sampling,* the stream of behavior is divided into equal time intervals. For example, Conger and Farrell (1981) examined the behavioral components of social competence in heterosexual conversations by dividing conversations into 5-second intervals and then rating the presence or absence of each of a number of behaviors in each time interval.

The other method of segmenting behavior streams is called *event sampling.* In this method, units of behavior are based on changes in the behavior being observed. This results in a division of the behavior stream into natural units that represent complete behavioral acts. For example, Raush, Berry, Hertel, and Swain (1974), in a study of conflict resolution in marriage, used floor changes, defined as the end of one person's speech and the beginning of the next person's speech, as the way to segment behavior.

Bakeman and Dabbs (1976) argued that time sampling with very small units becomes equivalent to event sampling, as long as the time units are shorter than the duration of the most brief behavior. Schlundt (1982a), in a study of the expression of affective cues in heterosexual interactions, used a time sampling interval of 1 second and recorded the type of behavior that occurred during each interval. Behaviors lasting more than 1 second resulted in a series of repeated codes. When a change in behaviors occurred, there was a discontinuity between the entries for two successive time intervals. The data analyses he performed were based on event changes. The advantages of Schlundt's coding method were that it preserved information about event type, event timing, event duration, and event order along with facilitating the computation of reliability.

Functional behavior units for event-based and time-based sampling can be formed at a variety of levels of molarity. The stream of behavior can be broken down into many microscopic behaviors, such as muscle movements, head nods, glances, or speech dysfluencies. The behavior stream also can be segmented at more molar levels, in which case one is looking for units like behaviors episodes, response strategies, moods, topics of conversations, goals, or actions. The level of molarity and the behavior sampling strategy that an investigator chooses will depend on the subject population, subjects' problems, the purposes of the assessment, and the task in which the behavior is being assessed. Inevitably, choice always means that some information is lost, so the choices of the unit size and sampling strategy are critical.

Quantification of Behavior

Once the stream of behavior has been segmented, then some method must be used to assign a quantitative interpretation to each behavioral unit. There are several methods available for accomplishing this task: (1) Each unit can be rated or scaled on one or more continuous dimensions; (2) the presence or absence of each behavior can be recorded for each unit; and (3) each unit can be placed into one of a set of mutually exclusive and exhaustive behavior categories.

Dimensional ratings of behavior are most useful with a time sampling strategy. Note that the entire interaction can be considered a single unit. In this case, the ratings are not much different from the competence ratings discussed in the previous section. There is, however, one major difference. The raters who are measuring the behaviors should be trained to a much greater degree than the judges who are asked to make competence ratings. The personal values of the judges in competence ratings are important and should be allowed to vary. In behavioral measurement or coding, however, the effects of the judges' values should be minimized. This can be accomplished by making the rating scales as concrete as possible. For example, Kolotkin, Judd, and Weiser (1980) examined role-played responses to assertion situations. Each response was rated on 19 behavioral dimensions. The dimensions ranged from very specific, like giggling and duration of eye contact, to more global, such as body posture and overall aggression. Kolotkin et al. showed that many of the behavioral categories changed in a predictable way as a function of assertion training.

Coding each of a set of behaviors as either present or absent in each unit is also well suited to a time-based sampling strategy. In fact, this approach to quantification represents a degenerate form of rating in which the scale has only two points—present and absent. Binary rating scales, however, may be useful when judgments are complex or when there is little or no basis for estimating degree.

Presence-or-absence judgments can be quite reliable even when the behaviors being observed are quite subtle. Also, when samples from very short time intervals are being coded, presence–absence judgments can be used to measure the duration of behavior.

Romanczyk, Kent, Diament, and O'Leary (1973), in a study of how the conditions of assessment affect the reliability of behavioral measurement, identified nine disruptive behaviors that could occur in the classroom. They used 20-second sampling units and recorded the presence or absence of each behavior in each unit.

Categorical coding systems are the most widely used strategy for quantifying behavior (see Rosenblum, 1978; Sackett, 1978). In a categorical coding system, each behavior is placed into one of a set of mutually exclusive and exhaustive behavior categories. A coding system quantifies behavior at a nominal scale of measurement.

Categories can be based on either the form or the function of behavior. For example, Ekman (1979) developed a coding system for use in the analysis of facial expressions of emotion that was based on the contractions of different facial muscle groups. Among other things, he has used this coding system to distinguish between facial expression used as signals in conversations and facial expressions that are used to communicate emotion. Ekman's coding system is based on topographic descriptions of behavior and requires almost no inference. More often, however, the use of a coding system requires some inference concerning the function of a behavior (see Searle, 1976). Dodge (1981), for example, studied the social interaction of boys in unstructured play groups by coding each interactive behavior into one of 15 functional categories, such as cooperative play, aggressive play, insults, physical affection, and norm-setting statements. In addition to coding the target child's behavior, Dodge identified the peer with whom the interaction was occurring and measured the peer's response on a 3-point rating scale (positive, neutral, and negative). He used both frequencies and patterns of these behaviors to show that popular and rejected children behaved quite differently in this group context. Gottman (1979) also employed a functionally based behavior coding system in his studies of marital interactions.

In addition to the form-functional continuum, there are several other methodological issues to be considered in the use of categorical coding systems (see Altmann, 1965). One issue is how many categories should be used. Dodge (1981), for example, started with 30 coding categories but later collapsed these into 15 categories for analysis. There is a temptation when developing a coding system to form many categories that make fine distinctions among behaviors. A coding system with too few categories will miss important differences among behaviors, but a coding system with too many categories is too unwieldy and unreliable to be useful. In addition, most of the categories in a large and complex coding system typically occur with such a low base rate that they are virtually useless as predictors. Unless a tremendous number of behaviors is sampled (2000 +), the coding system probably should not have more than 20 categories.

Behaviors can be quantified in many ways, and various combinations of these quantification strategies may be used within the same study. For example, Hersen, Bellack, and Turner (1978) coded behaviors like smiles, physical gestures, compliance, requests, and praise. They also rated each response for appropriateness of intonation on a 5-point scale and noted the presence of speech and eye contact to the nearest second.

There are relatively few restrictions on how the various quantification strategies can be used. In fact, by combining different segmentation and quantification techniques, quite complex hybrid behavioral measurement schemes can be devised. All methods share the common feature of being a way to quantify behavior. The methods differ, however, in the way behavioral units are formed and in the scale of measurement used to quantify behavioral units.

Summarizing Behavior

Once a behavior sample has been segmented into units and the units have been quantified, the final step is to summarize the results of this process in some useful way. One of the major issues in this summarization is whether (and how) to include information about the sequential relationships among the coded behaviors.

Nonsequential Summaries

Most previous research in social skills assessment has used data summarization procedures that ignore the sequential character of the coded behaviors. The data within a category typically have been collapsed across time to yield a summary statistic. For example, in research by Eisler, Hersen, Miller, and Blanchard (1975), ratings of overall assertiveness, loudness, and affective appropriateness were made on 5-point scales for each role-played response. These ratings then were summed and averaged for each subject across all the test items within each situational type.

Similarly, when the data consist of presence–absence judgments across a series of time-sampling periods, nonsequential summary methods typically are used to compute either the *total* number or *percentage* of sampling units in which each type of behavior was judged to be present. Eisler et al. used this approach to summarize smiles, compliance, requests for new behavior, praise, and spontaneous positive behaviors. They also timed certain behaviors, such as the duration of response, to the nearest second. This type of duration measure is merely equivalent to noting the presence or absence of speech during each 1-second interval and summing the number of intervals in which it was present.

Minkin, Braukmann, Minkin, Timbers, Timbers Fixsen, Phillips, and Wolf (1976) scored the presence of questions and positive feedback in each 10-second interval during a 4-minute conversation, and then summarized their data by simply adding up the total number of coding intervals in which each behavior was judged present. They also measured the presence or absence of speech to the nearest second. They summarized behavior even further by adding together the number of questions, positive feedback, and total talk time divided by 10. Questions, positive feedback, total talk time, and the composite index were all positively correlated with judges' ratings of overall quality of the conversations. What these investigators ignored, of course, was the temporal and sequential nature of the coded behavior. Quite possibly, such informaion about subjects' performances would have been even more informative.

Often it is quite useful to convert the presence–absence data into a proportion by dividing the number of units during which the behavior was coded as present by the total number of units sampled. This type of summary statistic is particularly appropriate when the total nubmer of units sampled differs from on subject to another. Proportional summaries also facilitate comparisons across similar studies and provide more useful comparative data than absolute frequency data. Eisler et al. followed this summarization strategy, for example, when they divided the frequency of speech disturbances by the duration of speech.

When using categorical data, as opposed to presence–absence data, in a nonsequential fashion, one also has the choice of computing either frequencies or proportions. Frequency is computed by summing the absolute number of times behavioral units were placed in each of the coding categories over the entire observation period. Proportion (or probability) is simply the frequency of each category divided by the total number of units observed. Frequencies should be used when a difference in total number of units is important, and probabilities should be used to make the results from different sample sizes comparable.

Arkowitz, Lichtenstein, McGovern, and Hines (1975) divided subjects' verbal behaviors into utterances. Each utterance was coded as either substantive or responsive. Substantive reponses were coded as statements, questions, or responses to questions, whereas responsive utterances were coded as restatements, acknowledgments, agreements, or disagreements. These measurements were summarized by computing the frequencies of each type of behavior. When they treated each behavior category as a separate variable and compared the observed frequencies of high- and low-frequency daters using t tests, they found no significant differences between the two groups.

The method of data analysis used in a study should be consistent with the scale of measurement underlying the behavioral measurement. Arkowitz et al.'s use of t tests was inappropriate for nominal scale data. Application of a categorical coding system results in only one variable, which is behavior. In the Arkowitz et al. Study, this single variable was subdivided into seven categories of behavior. A nominal scale variable should be treated as a sample drawn from a multinomial distribution (see Hays, 1973) and should be analyzed with a technique suitable for nominal scale data, such as a chi-square test. In the study by Arkowitz et al., a chi-square test should have been used to compare two multinomial distributions, one drawn from a sample of 20 high-frequency daters and the other drawn from a sample of 15 low-frequency daters. It is quite possible that this test might have been statistically significant whereas the *t* tests were not.

In general, nonsequential data summary techniques involve computing means, frequencies, or proportions. Use of these statistics in data analysis should be consistent with the measurement scale used to quantify the data. Interval ratings and binary judgments can be analyzed using parametric statistics such as regression, *t* tests, and analysis of variance; however, categorical coding is more appropriately analyzed using statistical tests based on an underlying multinomial distribution (see Anderson, 1961; Colgan & Smith, 1978; Feinberg, 1977; Goodman, 1970; Gottman, 1978; Schlundt, 1982b).

Sequential Data Summary

Gottman (1979) pointed out that sequential data can always be converted to nonsequential data by summing over time, but that nonsequential data can never be used to reconstruct information about the ordering of events.

When events are measured on an interval or binary scale, sequential information can be captured using time-series analysis (see Glass, Wilson, & Gottman, 1975; Gottman & Glass, 1978; Hartmann, Gottman, Joes, Gardner, Kazdin, & Vaught, 1980; McCleary & Hay, 1980). Of particular interest is the use of bivariate time-series analysis to represent the sequential structure of social interaction (see McCleary & Hay, 1980).

Schlundt* used bivariate time-series analysis to study affective reciprocity during a heterosexual social interaction.

---

*Schlundt, D. G. (1983). *The use of bivariate time-series analysis to study dyadic social interaction: An n-of-one study.* Unpublished manuscript, University of Mississippi Medical Center, Jackson, Mississippi.

Each subject's emotional expression was coded during each second of a 2-minute interaction. Schlundt then used time-series analysis on these data to study four sources of causality in the interaction: (1) male autocorrelation—the effect of the male's past behavior on the male's present behavior; (2) female autocorrelation—the effect of the female's past behavior on the female's present behavior; (3) woman–man cross-correlation—the effect of the woman's past emotional behavior on the man's present emotional behavior; and (4) man –woman cross-correlation—the effect of the man's past behavior on the woman's present behavior. The results indicated that both autocorrelational components (1 and 2) operated on a lag 1 structure, whereas both cross-correlational components (3 and 4) operated on a lag 0 structure. Thus, and individual's affective tone could best be predicted from her/his own affective tone of 1-second prior and from the concurrent affective tone of the partner.

Revenstorf, Hahlweg, and Schindler (1978) used time-series analysis to model the sequential structure of marital interactions over a 70-day period and found a number of simultaneous and lag 1 cross-correlational relationships between the husband's and wife's behaviors. In addition, Revenstorf et al. noted that the absence of predicted cross-correlations, such as the absence of a lag 0 correlation between engaging in physical tenderness and feeling close, yielded diagnostic information about the dynamics of the couple's relationship. Binary data, where the presence or absence of each behavior is independently coded in each time interval, can also be analyzed using time-series analysis (see Gottman, 1979).

The sequential structure of behavior when the behavior is measured using a categorical coding system can be represented using Markov chain theory (see Chatfield & Lemon, 1970; Crane, 1978; Gottman & Notarius, 1978; Raush,

1972). A *Markov chain* is a table of conditional probabilites that describe the transition of a system from one state to the next over time. With a Markov chain analysis, one computes the probability that each behavior is followed by each other behavior. Van den Bercken and Cools (1980) reviewed several methodolgical approaches to the application of Markov chains to the summary and analysis of social behavior. They developed a model in which analogs of the concepts of autocorrelation and cross-correlation can be computed from Markov transition probability matrices. Although the application of Markov chain theory to the sequential summary of behavioral data is technically quite complex, the basic idea is that a Markov chain is a mathematical representation of a process that generates sequences of behaviors (see Binder & Wolin, 1964).

Methodologically, sequential analysis of categorical data based on Markov chains becomes a matter of analyzing multidimensional contingency tables, where one or more of the dimensions of the table is behaviors with different lag relationships (see Allison & Liker, 1982; Gottman & Notarius, 1978). For example, Schlundt (1982a) used log-linear contingency table analysis and multivariate information theory statistics to study the sequential aspects of turn taking in heterosexual conversations. He was able to identify particular conversational behaviors, such as questions and statements of opinion, that were followed by an increased probability of an exchange of speaking turns at the next time lag. Dodge, Schlundt, Schocken and Delugach (1983) used a similar multivariate information theory analysis of contingency tables to postulate a sequential model of how children initiate social interactions with peers.

Lag sequential analysis (Bakeman, 1978; Gottman & Notarius, 1978; Gottman, 1979) is an alternative procedure for summarizing the sequential structure of a behavior sample. In this procedure, some criterion behavior—for example, an aggressive act—is first identified. All instances of this type of behavior are located in the behavior sample. The probability of occurrence of each other type of behavior is then computed at different time lags before and after the criterion behavior. Statistical tests are used to identify sequences of behaviors that occur with greater-than-chance probability. Dodge (1981) used this model to identify the types of events that preceded acts of aggression dursing children's play activities. Gottman (1979) used a similar lag sequential analysis to study sequences of problem-solving behaviors in distressed and nondistressed married couples.

Measuring Outcomes

The final component of the lens model focuses on the outcome side of the equation. The measurement of two classes of outcomes—short-term and long-term—will be discussed.

A *short-term outcome* is an event that occurs as a direct result of behavior and in temporal contiguity with the behavior. Measures of the subject's success in achieving the specific objectives of a task fall into this category.

Short-term outcomes in social interactions can be measured in several ways. The most direct method is to have the participants in an interaction rate the effects of one another's task performance. For example, Jaremko, Meyers, Daner, Moore, and Allin (1982) had subjects make semantic differential ratings of their impressions of their partners after a brief interaction. These ratings presumably measured each subject's success in the task of "making a good impression."

Another method of measuring short-term outcomes is to develop an objective coding system that observers can use to categorize the effects of behaviors. For example, Dodge, Schlundt, Schocken, and Delugach (1983) used this approach to study the social initiation behavior of children. For each child's attempt at initiating a social interaction, observers coded the outcome as positive, neutral, or negative. The authors were able to identify specific behaviors and behavior sequences that were most likely to result in positive outcomes and used these findings to postulate a model of competent social initiation behavior.

Long-term outcomes refer to consequences of behavior that extend in time beyond the immediate situation. One of the simplest methods of obtaining a measure of long-term outcomes is to index subjects according to their memberships in relevant populations. This "known groups" method (see McFall, 1976) involves identifying homogeneous groups of subjects who share common characteristics that result from their typical pattern of behavior. Examples of common known groups outcome variables used in the social skills literature would be the classification of subjects on the basis of psychiatric diagnosis (e.g., Hersen, Bellack, & Turner, 1978) or dating frequency (e.g., Greenwald, 1977). Ordinarily, information about these variables is obtained from interviews, self-report questionnaires, or archival records. In dating frequency, for example, a questionnaire is used to identify which subjects date frequently and which subjects rarely or never date. Dating frequency is considered an index of long-term outcome because the number of dates one has over a period of time is likely to reflect the cumulative results of moment-to-moment heterosexual interactions. Likewise, psychiatric diagnosis is the long-term culmination of an individual's more immediate, day-to-day patterns of behavior.

Much of the research thus far in social skills assessment has used a known groups, or contrasting groups, methodology. It has been assumed that persons who share group membership on the basis of common long-term outcomes also will tend to display important similarities in the way they handle day-to-day situations that eventually lead to the long-term outcomes. Therefore, systematic comparisons between contrasting groups should help us identify the specific situations and behaviors that are the antecedents of the long-term outcomes. Although the known groups method has proven useful, it also has limitations. The most serious problem is that the method is based on a logical error—the "error of assumed essence." Simply because the subjects within a group are homogeneous with respect to one variable, it does not follow that they will be homogeneous on all other variables. It may be that they are extremely heterogeneous with respect to the key variables involved in the etiology of their problems. Stated another way, there may be several different ways of achieving the same long-term consequences. Thus, comparisons between known groups in the hope of finding common antecedents within the groups may be inappropriate and misleading.

Experimental Manipulations versus Stimulus Sampling

The lens model was developed by Brunswik as a complement to his ideas concerning the "representative design" of experiments (see Brunswik, 1955). In a truly *representative design,* the investigator might sample situations in much the same way that subjects are routinely sampled in most research designs. Brunswik's recommendations about stimulus sampling tend to have been overlooked. The typical experimental design employs a deliberate manipulation of experimental situations. This distinction between manipulation and sampling corresponds roughly to the distinction between fixed and random effects in analysis of variance.

Behaviors and outcomes alike have

usually been experimentally manipulated, rather than sampled, in research on competence assessment. For example, Dow, Glaser, and Biglan (1981) constructed several videotapes in which a female actor's behaviors were varied systematically so that she exhibited either high or low amounts of questions, compliments, and pauses in a $2 \times 2 \times 2$ factorial design. Each subject in the study viewed a single tape and then rated the female actor's social skills. Dow et al. found higher frequencies of questions and compliments led to more positive social skills ratings. Kupke, Hobbs, and Cheney (1979) also used experimental manipulation, rather than behavior sampling, in a study of the behavioral components of perceived social skills.

Instructional or experimental manipulations prior to the sampling of behaviors and competence ratings can be treated like an outcome variable in a lens model analysis. Although they did not analyze their data using the lens model, Kazdin, Matson, and Esveldt-Dawson (1981), in a study of skills assessment in children, manipulated outcomes using feedback and incentive. These manipulations affected both behavioral distributions and global ratings of skill.

A Lens Model Study

Although a number of studies contain the full components of the lens model, we will describe only one such study here in order to illustrate the way in which the lens model structures the assessment of social competence. Royce and Weiss (1975) conducted a study of the behavioral components of marital interactions. They showed judges videotapes of distressed and nondistressed couples engaged in dyadic interactions. The judges then rated the apparent degree of marital satisfaction for each couple and listed the behavioral cues that led to their judgments. Next, the videotapes were coded by the researchers for the presence or absence of each of the behavioral cues suggested by the judges. Judgments of marital satisfaction were correlated with the clinical status (distressed vs. nondistressed) of the couples. A regression analysis showed that judges relied heavily on the cues of compromise and positive attention in making their satisfaction judgments. A regression model of how the judges combined behavioral information was more accurate in predicting clinical status than were the judges' global ratings of marital satisfaction.

SOCIAL SKILLS ASSESSMENT

We have defined *social skills* as the component processes necessary for producing situational responses that will be considered competent. We also insisted that in order to avoid the problem of circularity, social skills must be assessed independently of the behavior sample used to assess competence. Elsewhere (McFall, 1982; McFall & Dodge, 1982; Schlundt, 1982a), we have proposed the tentative outline of a model of social skills. The model describes a general set of component skills that would be necessary for competent task performance in specific situations. The components skills correspond to a sequential information-processing model (see Massaro, 1975).

The model was logically derived from an input–output analysis of human information processing. Social skills must be studied as one would analyze the contents of an operating system that transforms the input of social stimuli into the output of social behavior. Thus, social skills can be thought of as the sequential transformation processes required to generate behavior that will be considered appropriate or competent for a given stimulus task.

The transformation process involved in responding differentially to stimuli can be broken into three major sequential stages: (1) stimulus decoding; (2) decision making, and (3) response encoding. The stages are interdependent; output of decoding is the input to decision making and the output of decision making is the input to encoding.

Just as the entire information-processing system can be divided into three stages, each major stage can be subdivided further into a series of substages. Decoding of stiuational input requires the reception of information by the sense organs, the perceptual identification of the important stimulus features of the situation, and the interpretation of those features within an existing knowledge framework.

In the decision-making stage, the individual must generate response alternatives, test the alternatives by matching them to the task, select a response alternative, search the repertoire to see if the selected response is available, and evaluate the utility of implementing the selected response, given all the available information. The decision-making stage takes as its input a situational interpretation and returns as its output a response proposition that the subject believes will be the most cost-effective way of dealing with the stimulus task. Presumably, the decision-making process involves the use of information transformation and contingency rules stored in long-term memory. By contingency rules, we mean rules that associate specific actions with circumstances (see Collett, 1977, for a discussion of rules governing interpretation and action).

The encoding stage of the information-processing sequence involves the translation of a propositional response program into a coordinated sequence of observable behaviors. The execution of a response program also requires an ongoing feedback process in which the form and impact of specific behaviors are compared to the expected form and impact, and subtle adjustments are made in

order to maximize the correspondence. Thus, execution (generating sequences of behaviors) and self-monitoring (adjusting based on feedback) are subcomponents of encoding skills. We assume that contingency rules stored in long-term memory are accessed in order to match specific behaviors with circumstances.

Schlundt (1982a) has suggested that it may be useful to distinguish between two possible types of skill deficits, structural and content. A *structural* deficit involves a defect in the information-processing system itself. An individual with a structural deficit would nearly always behave deficiently because that person's method of decoding, decision making, or encoding would be intrinsically faulty. This type of deficit would tend to result in transituationally incompetent behavior. An example of a structural deficit would be a failure in a sensory system, such as vision. An inability to process visual cues would produce ineffective performance in situations requiring use of visual information.

A *content deficit* would involve a defect in one or more of the information transformation or contingency rules that are stored in long-term memory and used in decoding, decision making, or encoding. Faulty rules and constructs would tend to cause situation-specific performance problems because the only behaviors to be affected would be those that occur when the faulty rule is applied. For example, an irrational fear of small furry animals probably involves a faulty rule stored in long-term memory—a rule that associates small furry animals with danger and that implies such actions as escape and avoidance. This faulty rule would lead to incompetent behavior (i.e., phobic behavior) in the presence of stimuli related to small furry animals. Structural deficits, which are more fundamental, may be more difficult to treat than content deficits, which should be amenable to learning-oriented interventions.

Assessment of Decoding Skills

Decoding skills can be assessed by presenting stimuli with known characteristics to subjects and observing the accuracy of their interpretations. For example, Rosenthal, Hall, Archer, Dimatteo, and Rogers (1979) have developed a set of test stimuli for assessing subjects' abilities to decode emotional messages. The Profile of Nonverbal Sensitivity (PONS) consists of 220 two-second film clips in which an actress portrays a variety of emotional expressions. The subject's task is to identify each of these expressions correctly. To complicate the task, the channel of information available to the subject is varied. Different combinations of face, body, face plus body, content-filtered speech, and random-spliced speech are used. In an extensive cross-cultural study, Rosenthal et al. (1979) investigated individual differences in decoding skills, as measured by the PONS, and found that although there was much variability in subjects' accuracy, all subject were able to perform at better than chance levels on the task. They showed that psychiatric patients scored lower than normal subjects and that people who scored high on the PONS reported more satisfaction from interpersonal relationships (see Rosenthal & DePaulo, 1979).

Although there are problems with the PONS test (see O'Sullivan, 1982), improved measures along similar lines might be developed to assess decoding skills. The assessment strategy would be simply to encode information into stimulus materials, to present the encoded information to subjects, and then to measure their decoding accuracy. McFall's (1982) model predicts that subjects who are poor decoders will be judged to behave les competently in relevant tasks.

Decision-Making Skills

Examples of available measures that tap decision-making skills would be interpersonal problem-solving measures such as those developed by Spivack and Shure (1974). These measures tap the subject's ability to generate alternative responses to a given set of problem situations. Generating response alternatives is clearly a component of the decision-making stage of information processing, as we have described it, although it does not capture all of that stage.

Additional measures of decision-making skills might be adapted from research paradigms in cognitive psychology. For example, studies in risk taking by Slovic (1964) might serve as models for the development of assessments of decision-making skills. Tversky and Kahnemen's (1974) discussion of a decision-making heuristic is another possible source of paradigms for developing skill assessments. Slovic, Fischoff, and Lichtenstein's (1977) review of behavioral decision making provides other prototypes for promising assessment paradigms.

Encoding Skills

The assessment of encoding skills requires that the decoding and decision-making stages be controlled, leaving the encoding stage as the only source of variability in the subject's task performance. In fact, much of the work done thus far in the behavioral assessment of social skills and social competence has focused on the assessment of encoding skill. Typically, subjects are asked to role play their responses to descriptions of problematic situations. Subjects are sometimes told how to interpret the situation and what their behavioral goals are. In role-played assertion situations, for example, subjects might be told that the situation involves an unreasonable request and that they should try to refuse it. Given the same interpretation and behavioral goals, differences in subjects' responses would be due to differences in encoding skills.

The fact that role-playing assessments typically tap only one of the three stages of information processing may explain why behavior in role-playing situations has been found to be so imperfectly related to behavior in the natural environment (see Bellack, Hersen, & Lamparski, 1979).

Trower's (1980) research might be used as a model for the development of possible measures of self-monitoring skills. In this research, subjects who were rated as skilled (e.e., competent) also showed more variability in their behavior as a function of changes in the situation. That is, the subjects whose behavior was considered more competent seemed to be more sensitive to situational variations and to adapt their repsonses accordingly. Measures of behavioral variability in structured tasks should be explored as potential ways of assessing the self-monitoring component of encoding skill.

CONCLUDING COMMENT

The assessment of social competence and social skills is becoming increasingly sophisticated. We hope that this chapter has provided a useful taxonomic framework for conceptualizing and organizing assessment approaches in social skills and social competence. We hope that the ideas presented also will stimulate further research and that the chapter has pointed out new directions for the development of more sophisticated and comprehensive assessment strategies.

One of the most serious unresolved issues in all of behavioral assessment concerns the definition and classification of situations. We have discussed this issue at some length and proposed the use of the "task" construct as a possible way of addressing this issue. We urge behaviorally oriented investigators to pay increased attention to the development of situational taxonomies as prerequisites to the further development of better methods of assessing social competence and social skills.

REFERENCES

Allison, P. D., & Liker, J. K. (1982). Analyzing sequential categorical data on dyadic interactions: A comment of Gottman. *Psychological Bulletin, 91*, 393–403.

Altmann, S. A. (1965). Sociobiology of rhesus monkeys II: Stochastics of social communication. *Journal of Theoretical Biology, 8*, 490–522.

Anderson, N. H. (1961). Scales and statistics: Parametric and nonparametric. *Psychological Bulletin, 53*, 305–316.

Arkowitz, H., Lichtenstein, E., McGovern, K., & Hines, P. (1975). The behavioral assessment of social competence in males. *Behavior Therapy, 6*, 3–13.

Bakeman, R. (1978). Untangling streams of behavior: Sequential analysis of observational data. In G. P. Sackett (Ed.), *Observing behavior: Data collection and analysis methods (Vol. 2).* Baltimore: Univeristy Park Press.

Bakeman, R., & Dabbs, J. M. Jr. (1976). Social interaction observed: Some approaches to the analysis of behavior streams. *Personality and Social Psychology Bulletin, 2*, 335–345.

Barker, R. G. (1963). The stream of behavior as an empirical problem. In R. G. Barker (Ed.), *The stream of behavior.* New York: Appleton-Century-Crofts.

Barker, R. G. (1968). *Ecological psychology: Concepts and methods for studying the environment of human behavior.* Stanford: Stanford University Press.

Barker, R. G. (Ed.). (1978). *Habitats, environments, and human behavior.* San Francisco: Jossey-Bass.

Barlow, D. H., Abel, G. C., Blanchard, E. B., Bristow, A. R., & Young, L. D. (1977). A heterosexual skills behavior checklist for males. *Behavior Therapy, 8,* 229–239.

Bell, P. A., Fisher, J. D., & Loomis, R. L. (1978). *Environmental psychology.* Philadelphia: Saunders.

Bellack, A. S. (1979). A critical appraisal of strategies for assessing social skill. *Behavioral Assessment, 1,* 157–176.

Bellack, A. S., Hersen, M, & Lamparski, D. (1979). Role-play test for assessing social skills: Are they valid? Are they useful? *Journal of Consulting and Clinical Psychology, 47,* 335–342.

Binder, A., & Wolin, B. R. (1964). Informational models and their uses. *Psychometrika, 29,* 25–54.

Borkovec, T. D., Stone, N. M., O'Brien, G. T., & Kaloupek, D. C. (1974). Evaluation of a clinically relevant target behavior for analog outcome research. *Behavior Therapy, 5,* 503–513.

Brunswik, E. (1952). *The conceptual framework of psychology.* Chicago: The University of Chicago Press.

Brunswik, E. (1955). Representative design and probabilistic theory. *Psychological Review, 62,* 193–217.

Castellan, N. J. Jr. (1972). The analysis of multiple criteria in multiple cue judgment tasks. *Organizational Behavior and Human Performance, 8,* 242–261.

Chatfield, C., & Lemon, R. E. (1970). Analyzing sequences of behavioural events. *Journal of Theoretical Biology, 29,* 427–445.

Clark, J., & Arkowitz, H. (1975). Social anxiety and self-evaluation of interpersonal performance. *Psychological Reports, 36,* 211–221.

Colgan, P. W. (Ed.). (1978). *Quantitative ethology.* New York: Wiley.

Colgan, P. W., & Smith, J. (1978). Multidimensional contingency table analysis. In P. W. Colgan (Ed.). *Quantitative ethology.* New York: Wiley.

Collett, P. (1977). The rules of social conduct. In P. Collett (Ed.), *Social rules and social behavior.* Totowa, NJ: Rowman & Littlefield.

Conger, J. C., & Farrell, A. D. (1981). Behavioral components of heterosocial skills. *Behavior Therapy, 12,* 41–55.

Crane, V. R. (1978). On fitting low-order Markov chains to behavior sequences. *Animal Behavior, 26,* 332–338.

Curran, J. P., Little, L. M., & Gilbert, F. S. (1978). Reactivity of males of differing heterosexual social anxiety to female approach and nonapproach cue conditions. *Behavior Therapy, 9,* 961–970.

Curran, J. P., Monti, P. M., Coriveau, D. P., Hay, L. R., Hagerman, S., Zwick, W. R., & Farrell, A. D. (1980). The generalizability of a procedure for assessing social skills and social anxiety in a psychiatric population. *Behavioral Assessment, 2,* 389–401.

Dawes, R.M., & Corrigan, B. (1974). Linear models in decision making. *Psychological Bulletin, 81,* 95–106.

Dodge, K. A. (1981). *Behavioral antecedants of peer social rejection and isolation.* Paper presented at the biennial meeting of the Society for Research in Child Development, Boston.

Dodge, K. A., Schlundt, D. G., Schocken, I., & Delugach, J. (in press). Social competence and children's sociometric status: The role of peer group entry strategies. *Merrill-Palmer Quarterly.*

Donahoe, C. P. Jr. (1978). *Definitions of competence and the assessment of social skills in adolescent boys.* Unpublished master's thesis, University of Wisconsin, Madison.

Dow, M. G., Glaser, S.R. & Biglan, A. (1981). The relevance of specific conversational behaviors to ratings of social skills: An experimental analysis. *Journal of Behavioral Assessment, 3,* 233–242.

Einhorn, H. J. (1970). The use of nonlinear, noncompensatory models in decision making. *Psychological Bulletin, 73,* 221–230.

Eisler, R. M. (1976). The behavioral assessment of social skills. In M. Hersen & A. S. Bellack (Eds.), *Behavioral assessment: A practical handbook.* New York: Pergamon.

Eisler, R.M., Hersen, M., & Miller, P. M. (1973). Effects of modeling on components of assertive behaviors. *Journal of Behavior Therapy and Experimental Psychiatry, 4*, 1–6.

Eisler, R. M., Hersen, M., Miller, P. M., & Blanchard, E. B. (1975). Situational determinants of assertive behavior. *Journal of Consulting and Clinical Psychology, 43*, 330–340.

Eilser, R. M., Miller, P. M., & Hersen, M. (1973). Components of assertive behavior. *Journal of Consulting and Clinical Psychology, 29*, 295–299.

Ekehammar, B., & Magnusson, D. (1973). A method to study stressful situations. *Journal of Personality and Social Psychology, 27*, 176–179.

Ekman, P. (1979). About brows: Emotional and conversational signals. In M. von Cranack, K, Foppa, W. Lepenies, & D. Ploog (Eds.), *Human ethology*. Cambridge: Cambridge University Press.

Endler, N. S., & Magnusson, D. (1976). Towards an interactional psychology of personality. *Psychological Bulletin, 85*, 956–974.

Fagen, R. M., & Young, D. Y. (1978). Temporal patterns of behavior: Durations, intervals, and latencies. In P. W. Colgan (Ed.), *Quantitative ethology*. New York: Wiley.

Feinberg, S. E. (1977). *The analysis of cross-classified categorical data*. Cambridge, MA.: M.I.T. Press.

Fisher-Beckfield, D. & McFall, R. M. (1982). Development of a competence inventory for college men and evaluation of relationships between competence and depression. *Journal of Consulting and Clinical Psychology, 50*, 697–705.

Forgas, J. P. (1978a). The effects of behavioral and cultural expectation cues on the perception of social episodes. *European Journal of Social Psychology, 8*, 203–213.

Forgas, J. P. (1978b). Social episodes and social structrure in an academic setting: The social environment of an intact group. *Journal of Experimental Social Psychology, 14*, 434–448.

Foster, S. L., & Richey, W. L. (1979). Issues in the assessment of social competence in children. *Journal of Applied Behavior Analysis, 12*, 625–638.

Frederiksen, N. (1972). Toward a taxonomy of situations. *American Psychologist, 27*, 114–123.

Freedman, B. J., Rosenthal, L., Donahoe, C. P. Jr., Schlundt, D. G., & McFall, R. M. (1978). A social-behavioral analysis of skill deficits in delinquent and nondelinquent adolescent boys. *Journal of Consulting and Clinical Psychology, 46*, 1448–1462.

Gambrill, E. D., & Richey, C. A. (1975). An assertion inventory for use in assessment and research. *Behavior Therapy, 6*, 550–561.

Glass, G. V., Wilson, V. L., & Gottman, J. M. (1975). *Design and analysis of time-series experiments*. Boulder: Colorado Associated University Press.

Goldberg, L. R. (1965). Diagnosticians vs. diagnostic signs: The diagnosis of psychosis vs. neurosis from the MMPI. *Psychological Monographs, 79* (9, Whole No. 602).

Goldfried, M. R., & Kent, R. N. (1972). Traditional versus behavioral assessment: A comparison of methodological and theoretical assumptions. *Psychological Bulletin, 77*, 409–420.

Goldfried, M. R., & D'Zurilla, T. J. (1969). A behavioral-analytic model for assessing competence. In C. D. Spielberger (Ed.), *Current topics in clinical and community psychology (Vol 1.)* New York: Academic Press.

Goldfried, M. R., & Linehan, M. H. (1977). Basic issues in behavioral assessment. In A. R. Ciminero, K. S. Calhoun, & H. E. Adams (Eds.), *Handbook of behavioral assessment*. New York: Wiley.

Goldsmith, J. B., & McFall, R. M. (1975). Development and evaluation of an interpersonal skill training program for psychiatric patients. *Journal of Abnormal Psychology, 84*, 51–58.

Goodman, L. A. (1970). The multivariate analysis of qualitative data: Interactions among multiple classifications. *Journal of the American Statistical Association, 65*, 226–256.

Gottman, J. M. (1978). Nonsequential data analysis techniques. In G. P. Sackett (Ed.), *Observing behavior: Data collection and data analysis methods. (Vol 2)*. Baltimore: University Park Press.

Gottman, J. M. (1979). *Martial interactions: Experimental investigations.* New York; Academic Press.

Gottman, J. M., & Glass, G. V. (1978). Analysis of interrupted time series experiments. In T. R. Kratochwill (Ed.), *Single subject research: Strategies for evaluating change.* New York: Academic Press.

Gottman, J. M., & Notarius, C. (1978). Sequential analysis of observational data using Markov chains. In T. R. Kratochwill (Ed.), *Single subject research: Strategies for evaluating change.* New York: Academic Press.

Graham, J. A., Argyle, M., & Furnham A. (1980). The goal structure of situations. *European Journal of Social Psychology, 10,* 345–366.

Greenwald, D. P. (1977). The behavioral assessment of differences in social skill and social anxiety in female college students. *Behavior Therapy, 8,* 925–937.

Hammond, K. (1955). Probabilistic functionalism and the clinical method. *Psychological Review, 62,* 255 262.

Hammond, K., Hursch, C., & Todd, F. (1964). Analyzing components of clinical inferences. *Psychological Review, 72,* 438–456.

Hartmann, D. P., Gottman, J. M., Jones, R. R., Gardner, W., Kazdin, A. E., & Vaught, R. S. (1980). Interrupted time-series analysis and its application to behavioral data. *Journal of Applied Behavior Analysis, 13,* 543–559.

Hays, W. L. (1973). *Statistics for the social sciences (2nd ed.).* New York: Holt, Rinehart & Winston.

Heimberg, G., Madsen, C. H., Montgomery, D., & McNabb, C. E. (1980). Behavioral treatments for heterosocial problems. *Behavior Modification, 4,* 147–172.

Hersen, M., Bellack, A. S., & Turner, S. M. (1978). Assessment of assertiveness in female psychiatric patients: Motor and autonomic measures. *Journal of Behavior Therapy and Experimental Psychiatry, 9,* 11–16.

Hoffman, P. (1960). The paramorphic representation of clinical judgment. *Psychological Bulletin, 57,* 116–131.

Jaremko, M. E., Myers, E. J., Daner, S., Moore, S., & Allin, J. (1982). Differences in daters: Effects of sex, dating frequency, and dating frequency of partner. *Behavioral Assessment, 4,* 307–316.

Kazdin, A. E., Matson, J. L., & Esveldt-Dawson, K. (1981). Social skill performance among normal and psychiatric inpatient children as a function of assessment conditions. *Behavior Research and Therapy, 19,* 145–152.

Kolotkin, R. A., Judd, B. B., & Weiser, S. A. (1980). *The behavioral assessment of assertion: Behavioral componets of perceived social skill.* Paper presented at the 14th annual convention of the Association for the Advancement of Behavior Therapy, New York.

Kupke, T. E., Hobbs, S. A., & Cheney, T. H. (1979). Selection of heterosocial skills: I. Criterion related validity. *Behavior Therapy, 10,* 327–335.

Levenson, R. W., & Gottman, J. M. (1978). Toward the assessment of social competence. *Journal of Consulting and Clinical Psychology, 46,* 453–562.

Lewin, K. (1936). *A dynamic theory of personality.* New York: McGraw-Hill.

Lewin, K. (1936). *Principles of topological psychology.* New York: McGraw-Hill.

MacDonald, M. L. (1978). Measuring assertion: A model and a method. *Behavior Therapy, 8,* 889–899.

Magnusson, D., & Endler, N. S. (Eds.). (1977). *Personality at the crossroads: Current issues in interactional psychology.* New York: Wiley.

Massaro, D. W.. (1975. *Experimental psychology and information processing.* Chicago: Rand McNally.

McCleary, R., & Hay, R. A. Jr. (1980). *Applied time-series analysis for the social sciences.* Beverly Hills: Sage.

McFall, R. M. (1976). *Behavioral training: A skill acquisition approach to clinical problems.* Morristown, NJ: General Learning Press.

McFall, R. M. (1982). A review and reformulation of the concept of social skills. *Behavioral Assessment, 4,* 1–33.

McFall, R. M., & Dodge, K. A. (1982). Self-management and interpersonal skills learning. In P. Karoly & F. Kanfer (Eds.), *Self-management and behavior change: From theory to practice.* New York: Pergamon.

McFall, R. M., & Lillesand, D. B. (1971). Behavioral rehearsal with modeling and coaching in assertion training. *Journal of Abnormal Psychology, 77,* 313–323.

McFall, R. M., & Marston, A. R. (1970). An experimental investigation of behavior rehearsal in assertive training. *Journal of Abnormal Psychology, 76,* 295–303.

McFall, R. M., & McDonel, E.C. (1984). The continuing search for units of analysis in psychology: Beyond persons, situations, and their interactions. In R. O. Nelson and S.C. Hayes (Eds.), *Conceptual foundations in behavior assessment.* New York: Guilford Press.

Minkin, N., Braukmann, C. J., Minkin, B. L., Timbers, G. D., Timbers, B. J., Fixsen, D. L., Phillips, E. L., & Wolf, M. M. (1976). The social validation and training of conversational skills. *Journal of Applied Behavior Analysis, 9,* 127–139.

Mischel, W. (1973). Towards a cognitive social learning reconceptualization of personality. *Psychological Review, 80,* 252–283.

Moos, R. H., (1975). *The human context: Environmental determinants of behavior.* New York: Wiley.

O'Sullivan, M. (1982). Measuring the ability to recognize facial expressions of emotion. In P. E. Ekman (Ed.), *Emotion in the human face (2nd ed.). Cambridge: Cambridge University Press.*

Perri, M., & Richards, C. S. (1979). Assessment of heterosocial skills in male college students: Empirical development of a behavioral role-playing test. *Behavior Modification, 3,* 337–354.

Peterson, D. (1979). Assessing relationships by means of interaction records. *Behavioral Assessment, 1,* 221–236.

Pilkonis, P. A. (1977). The behavioral consequences of shyness. *Journal of Personality, 45,* 596–611.

Price, R. H., & Blashfield, R. K. (1975). Explorations in the taxonomy of behavior settings: Analysis of dimensions and classification of settings. *American Journal of Community Psychology, 3,* 335–351.

Proshansky, H. H., Ittelson, W. H., & Rivlin, L. G. (1976). *Environmental psychology: Persons in their physical settings.* New York: Holt, Rinehart & Winston.

Raush, H. L. (1972). Process and change: A Markov model for interaction. *Family Process, 41,* 275–298.

Raush, H. L, Berry, W. A., Hertel, R. K., & Swain, M. A. (1974). *Communication conflict and marriage.* San Fransisco: Jossey-Bass.

Rehm, L. P., & Marston, A. R. (1968). Reduction of social anxiety through modification of self-reinforcement. *Journal of Consulting and Clinical Psychology, 32,* 565–574.

Revenstorf, D., hahlweg, K, & Schindler, L. (1978). Lead and lag in aspects of marital interaction. *Behavioural Analysis and Modification, 2,* 174–184.

Richardson, F. C., & Tasto, D. L. (1976). Development and factor analysis of a social anxiety inventory. *Behavior Therapy, 7,* 453–462.

Romanczyk, R. G., Kent, R. N., Diament, C., & O'Leary, K. D. (1973). Measuring the reliability of observational data: A reactive process. *Journal of Applied Behavior Analysis, 6,* 175–184.

Rosenblum, L. A. (1978). The creation of a behavioral taxonomy. In G. P. Sackett (Ed.), *Observing behavior: Data collection and analysis methods (Vol. 2).* Baltimore: University Park Press.

Rosenthal, R., & De Paulo, B. M. (1979). Sex differences in accomodation in nonverbal communication. In R. Rosenthal (Ed.), *Skill in nonverbal communication: Individual differences.* Cambridge, MA.: Oelgeschlager, Guinn & Hain.

Rosenthal, R. Hall, J. A., Archer, D., Dimatteo, M. R., & Rogers, P. L. (1979). Measuring sensitivity to nonverbal communication: The PONS test. In A. Wolfgang (Ed.), *Nonverbal behavior: Applications and cultural implications.* New York: Academic Press.

Royce, W. S., & Arkowitz, H. (1978). Multimodal evaluation of practice interaction as a treatment for social isolation. *Journal of Consulting and Clinical Psychology, 46,* 239–245.

Royce, W. S., & Weiss, R. L. (1975). Behavioral cues in the judgment of marital satisfaction: A linear regression analysis. *Journal of Consulting and Clinical Psychology, 43,* 816–824.

Sackett, G. P. (1978). Measurement in observational research. In G. P. Sackett (Ed.), *Observing behavior: Data collection and analysis methods (Vol. 2).* Baltimore: University Park Press.

Sawyer, J. (1966). Measurement and prediction, clinical and statistical. *Psychological Bulletin, 66,* 178–200.

Schlundt, D. G. (1979). *A comparison of three approaches to the construction of a psychologically relevant taxonomy of situations.* Unpublished master's thesis, University of Wisconsin, Madison.

Schlundt, D. G. (1982a). *An observational study of the behavioral components of social competence: The rules of topic management, speaking turn regulations, and the expression of affect in heterosexual dyadic conversations.* Unpublished doctoral dissertation, Indiana University, Bloomington.

Schlundt, D. G., (1982b). Two PASCAL programs for managing observational data bases and for performing multivariate information theory analysis and log-linear contingency table analysis of sequential and nonsequential data. *Behavior Research Methods and Instrumentation, 14,* 351–352.

Searle, J. A. (1976). A classification of illocutionary acts. *Language in Society, 5,* 1–23.

Sells, S. B. (1963). Dimensions of stimulus situations which account for behavior variance. In S. B. Sells (Ed.), *Stimulus determinants of behavior.* New York: Ronald Press.

Slovic, P. (1964). Assessment of risk-taking behavior. Psychological Bulletin, 61, 220–223.

Slovic, P., Fischoff, B., Lichtenstein, S. (1977). Behavioral decision theory. *Annual Review of Psychology, 28,* 1–39.

Sneath, P. H. A., & Sokal, R. R. (1973). *Numerical taxonomy.* San Fransisco: Jossey-Bass.

Sokal, R. R., & Sneath, P. H. A. (1963). *Principles of numerical taxonomy.* San Fransisco: Jossey-Bass.

Spivack, G., & Shure, M. B. (1974). *Social adjustment of young children: a cognitive approach to solving real-life problems.* San Fransisco: Jossey-Bass.

Todd, F. J., & Hammond, K. R. (1965). Differential feedback in two multiple cue learning tasks. *Behavioral Science, 10,* 429–435.

Trower, P. (1980). Situational analysis of the components and processes of behavior of socially skilled and unskilled patients. *Journal of Consulting and Clinical Psychology, 48,* 327–339.

Tversky, A., & Kahneman D. (1974). Judgment under uncertainty: Heuristics and biases. *Science, 185,* 1124–1131.

Twentyman, C. T., Boland, T., & McFall, R. M. (1981). Heterosexual avoidance in college males: Four studies. *Behavior Modification, 5,* 523–552.

Twentyman, C. T., & McFall, R. M. (1975). Behavior training of social skills in shy males. *Journal of Consulting and Clinical Psychology, 43,* 384–395.

Van den Bercken, J. H. L., & Cools, A. R. (1980). Information statistical analysis of social interaction and communication: An analysis of variance approach. *Animal Behavior, 28,* 172–188.

Van Hasselt, V. B., Hersen, M., Whitehill, M. B., & Bellack, A. S. (1979). Social skill assessment and training for children: An evaluative review. *Behavior Research and Therapy, 17,* 413–437.

Warren, N. J., & Gilner, F. H. (1978). Measurement of positive assertive behavior: The behavioral test of tenderness expression. *Behavior Therapy, 9,* 178–184.

Willems, E. P. (1976). Behavioral ecology, health status, and health care: Applications to the rehabilitation setting. In J. Dittman & J. F. Wohwill (Eds.), *Human behavior and environment: Advances in theory and research (Vol. 2).* New York: Plenum.

CHAPTER 3

Conceptual and Methodological Issues in the Behavioral Assessment of Heterosocial Skills

DAVID J. KOLKO AND MICHAEL A. MILAN

As several recent handbooks document (Bellack & Hersen, 1979; Curran & Monti, 1982; Eisler & Frederiksen, 1980; Kelly, 1981), behavioral research has highlighted the potential contribution of training procedures to the development and enhancement of a variety of social skills across a broad range of contexts and populations. One important area of study within this empirical literature has been concerned with the investigation of heterosocial interactive ability and competence in individuals characterized by minimal dating experience, heterosocial anxiety, and heterosocial skills deficits (Arkowitz, 1977; Curran, 1977). Although it has not yet been possible to construct a generally acceptable definition of *heterosocial competence,* the specific skills involved have been defined as those relevant to initiating, maintaining, and terminating a social and/or sexual relationship with a member of the opposite sex (Barlow, Abel, Blanchard, Bristow & Young, 1977).

The development and effective utilization of skills required for effective social relationships with members of the opposite sex constitute important developmental tasks that confront the college student (Havighurst, 1972). Little difficulty is experienced in the acquisition and expression of these skills in the ma-jority of college students. However, with certain individuals, these skills are either poorly developed or their expression is inhibited (Curran, 1977).

To help clarify the nature and extent of these adjustment problems, research bearing upon the prevalence and general significance of dating and heterosocial interaction problems will be reviewed and summarized in this chapter. This will be followed by a brief overview of the major conceptual models guiding heterosocial skills research and practice. The methodological issues bearing upon the identification of social skills will then be discussed, and an exposition of contemporary empirical approaches to the designation of effective social skills will be presented. Finally, several general assessment and treatment considerations will be offered.

PREVALENCE AND SIGNIFICANCE OF HETEROSOCIAL DIFFICULTIES

The prevalence of heterosocial difficulties has been estimated in several early studies. In a report of heterosocial problems in college students at a Midwestern university, Shmurak (1973) found that for males and females, 54% and 42% respectively, of the difficult social situa-

50

tions they reported dealt with dating. In a survey of men and women at Oxford University, Bryant and Trower (1974) noted that 25% of the situations designated as problematic concerned "seeking contact with strangers," especially of the opposite sex. Twenty-five percent of the males and 12% of the females in this survey claimed that they felt anxious when going out on a date. Other difficult situations involved public social contact and more intimate social contact. In another survey of male and female undergraduates, Borkevec, Stone, O'Brien, and Kaloupek (1974) found that 15.5% and 11.5%, respectively, reported at least some fear of being with the opposite sex. Thirty-two percent of the males and 38.5% of the females indicated a fear of meeting persons for the first time. The authors also note that heterosocial anxiety may be viewed as a clinically relevant and empirically quantifiable target behavior for therapy-outcome research.

These early findings detailing the incidence of heterosocial difficulties have been corroborated and extended in more recent investigations. Zimbardo, Pilkonis, and Norwood (1975) found that 42% of a sample of 817 high school and college students described themselves as "shy persons." Of those individuals who at one time had described themselves as shy, 85% disliked being shy, and 63% considered shyness a real "problem." In a follow-up study by Pilkonis (1977a), 41% of the sample of 263 undergraduates described themselves as shy. More men than women in this study reported themselves as shy. Further, their shyness was considered situationally specific. Shy persons were characterized as less sociable, less extroverted, less capable of monitoring their social behavior, more socially anxious, and more neurotic. Twenty-four percent of the shy respondents indicated an interest in counseling in order to remediate their social anxiety.

Martinez-Diaz and Edelstein (1980) found that 13% of their sample of 876 college men felt somewhat or very anxious and inhibited with women. A similar survey indicated that 64% of a college sample ranked dating concerns as their primary problem (McEwan, 1983). In one of the largest survey studies reported to date, 31% of 3800 randomly selected undergraduates described themselves as either somewhat or very anxious in dating situations (Arkowitz, Hinton, Perl, & Himadi, 1978). Half of the total sample expressed an interest in a program designed to facilitate their comfort and activity in these situations. A higher percentage of men versus women rated themselves as anxious about dating (31 vs. 25%) and interested in a program (56 vs. 43%). Arkowitz et al. proposed that these sex differences were associated with traditional sex-role stereotypes in which males were the expected initiator of heterosocial interactions.

The severity and prevalence of heterosocial difficulties appears to be amply documented. Their relationship to a host of concomitant psychosocial concerns has also been investigated. For example, Arkowitz et al. observed that problems such as depression, anxiety, academic failure, and avoidance of members of the opposite sex frequently accompanied dating anxiety. They proposed that dating anxiety represents a precursor to subsequent psychosocial adjustment difficulties in adult life. This is consistent with the results of social survey research conducted by Bryant, Trower, Yardley, Urbieta, and Letemendia (1976) and by Klaus, Hersen, and Bellack (1977).

Himadi, Arkowitz, Hinton, and Perl (1980) investigated low-dating men and women in same-sex and opposite-sex interactions. Low-dating men showed deficiencies in same-sex friendship interactions and greater psychological maladjustment than high-dating men. Specifically, low-dating men were less skilled and active during these interactions, and their scores on the Eysenck Personality Inventory (EPI) suggested greater neuroticism and less extraversion when compared with high-dating men. However, such findings were not obtained for low-dating women, in line with the results reported by Pilkonis (1977a).

Based on the evidence described thus far, it appears that certain minimal and problem daters often report heightened anxiety and discomfort in heterosocial situations and that some individuals, discriminated on the basis of dating frequency and discomfort measures, evidence different levels of interactional competences, skills, and psychopathology (Phillips, 1978). Although there is debate as to the relative significance attributed to dating experience (Arkowitz, 1977; McEwan, 1983), researchers have attempted to describe problematic dating and heterosocial tasks more accurately in college populations to develop the content and guidelines for intervention programs (Curran, 1977; Muehlenhard, 1983).

Two studies, both of which focus upon the specification of dating problems, highlight the task deficits that underlie many heterosocial difficulties. Thomander (1975) described several frequently reported dating problems that were reported by 26 minimal dating college students who experienced considerable anxiety while on a date. The social skills deficits most often reported included: (1) initiating and maintaining conversations; (2) behaving in a natural fashion; (3) expressing interest in another person; (4) and perceiving that one is liked by the other person. Contributing factors consisted of excessive choosiness and, for males, not asking or, for females, not being asked.

Klaus, Hersen, and Bellack (1977) conducted a survey of 90 male and 105 female college students to assess the degree of difficulty associated with nine tasks related to dating activities. For both groups, greatest difficulty was reported in the following tasks: (1) finding possible dates; (2) initiating sexual activity; (3) initiating contact with prospective dates; (4) avoiding or curtailing sex; and (5) ending a date. Although males indicated greater difficulty in initiating contact by phone with prospective dates, women indicated greater difficulty in finding dates, feeling comfortable on a date, making conversation, ending a date, and obtaining a date with the same partner. The sex differences in the levels of difficulty associated with a number of common dating activities are generally coincident with the findings of Arkowitz et al. (1978). Although these few studies shed light on some of the specific dating difficulties of college students in general, the majority of studies in the area have been designed to document more fully the specific behavioral differences between high- and low-effectiveness groups in various skill areas thought to be important in the development and expression of heterosocial competence. In large part, the areas explored have reflected the various conceptual models of heterosocial inhibition that have been postulated to underlie the difficulties experienced.

CONCEPTUAL MODELS

A variety of conceptual models representing diverse etiological factors and controlling variables have been proposed to account for heterosocial interaction difficulties (Arkowitz, 1981; Curran, 1977; Galassi & Galassi, 1979; Twentyman, Boland, & McFall, 1981). Four major models have been described: social skills deficits, conditioned anxiety, cognitive distortions, and physical attractiveness. Each model entails the measurement and modification of particular target behaviors. In order to highlight the evidence that supports each model, a brief description of the conceptual underpinnings, relevant research, and procedures that follow from each will be presented.

Social Skills Deficits

The assumption underlying this model is that unassertive individuals lack the requisite social and interpersonal skills for effective interaction (Eisler, 1976; McFall & Twentyman; 1973). The individual's failure to acquire these skills may result in inadequate social functioning and, thus, may serve as an antecedent of heterosocial anxiety, avoidance of social interactions, and maladaptive cognitive evaluations. Understandably, treatment from this perspective emphasizes a response-acquisition approach (McFall, 1976) in which effective interpersonal skills are trained according to established principles of learning.

Numerous investigations have been conducted to identify the behavioral referrents of heterosocial skills and their corresponding deficits in minimally dating individuals. Although some studies have failed to identify social skills differences between high- and low-frequency male daters (Arkowitz, Lichtenstein, McGovern, & Hines, 1975; Borkevec et al., 1974; Glasgow & Arkowitz, 1975; Martinez-Diaz & Edelstein, 1980), others have succeeded in differentiating the two groups. The general behavioral indexes of skills that have been identified include (1) initiations (Lipton & Nelson, 1980; Pilkonis, 1977b; Twentyman & McFall, 1975; Twentyman et al., 1981); (2) verbal responses to approach cues (Curran, Little, & Gilbert, 1978); (3) conversation content, voice quality, and affect indexes (Barlow et al., 1977; Pilkonis, 1977b); (4) verbal content quality (Perri & Richards, 1979); (5) personal attention (Kupke, Hobbs, & Cheney, 1979); (6) talk time (Arkowitz et al.,

1975; Conger & Farrell, 1981; Martinez-Diaz & Edelstein, 1980; Pilkonis, 1977b); and (7) response timing (Fischetti, Curran, & Wessberg, 1977). Females have not received the attention that males have. In four studies concerned with the behavioral assessment of social skills in females, only the following few indexes have been identified: eye contact (Greenwald, 1977; Kolko & Milan, in press); talk time (Glasgow & Arkowitz, 1975; Greenwald, 1977); response timing (Peterson, Fischetti, Curran, & Arland, 1981); interest and initiation (Kolko & Milan, in press; Williams & Ciminero, 1978), and both questions and compliments (Dow, Glaser, & Biglan, 1981; Kolko & Milan, in press). Overall, self-report measures and judges' global ratings of skill and anxiety have differentiated between social competency groups for both males and females better than direct behavioral measures of skill (Conger & Conger, 1982).

Interventive efforts to remediate social skills deficits have attempted to facilitate the acquisition of behavioral skills considered essential to the initiation and maintenance of heterosocial relationships (Eisler, 1976). A concise overview of this approach can be found in Curran (1977). Although few specific behavioral differences between groups have been consistently reported subsequent to treatment, studies have generally demonstrated the clinical utility of the skills training model on some self-report and role-playing or interactive measures relative to wait list, no-treatment, or baseline conditions (Bander, Steinke, Allen, & Mosher, 1975; Kelly, Urey, & Patterson, 1980; MacDonald, Lindquist, Kramer, McGrath, & Rhyne, 1975; McGovern, Arkowitz, & Gilmore, 1975; Melnick, 1973; Richey, 1979; Urey, Laughlin, & Kelly, 1979); assessment controls (Twentyman & McFall, 1975); sensitivity training (Curran, Gilbert, & Little, 1976); and systematic desensitization (Curran & Gilbert, 1975; Geary & Goldman, 1978).

Conditioned Anxiety

Wolpe (1969; Wolpe & Lazarus, 1966) has suggested that it is the anxiety initially conditioned to and later elicited by interpersonal situations that precludes the expression of socially competent behavior. In this model, the individual's unadaptive anxiety and resulting avoidance are the consequences of an aversive respondent conditioning experience. Thus, the competent expression of one's skills is inhibited and interfered with by conditioned anxiety. Treatment from this perspective has included systematic desensitization and practice-dating programs to produce anxiety reduction, both of which derive from a deconditioning or response-disinhibition approach (Bandura, 1969).

Few specific behavioral indexes of anxiety have been identified, although anxiety indexes are often difficult to distinguish from social skills indexes (Galassi & Galassi, 1979). Nevertheless, some studies have found differences in behavior between male heterosocial competency groups identified on the basis of global ratings of anxiety. Among the behavioral indexes identified in these studies were response latency (Arkowitz et al., 1978); gaze (Conger & Farrell, 1981); silences (Pilkonis, 1977b); heart rate (Borkevec et al., 1974); and avoidance (Twentyman & McFall, 1975). For females no particular behavioral indexes of anxiety have been obtained, although differences have been found in self-reported anxiety (Glasgow & Arkowitz, 1975; Greenwald, 1977; Williams & Ciminero, 1978).

Studies of the effectiveness of treatment have shown desensitization to be superior to wait list controls and placebo conditions (Curran, 1975; Curran & Gilbert, 1975). The comparative effectiveness of counterconditioning and skills

training approaches to treatment is unclear. Two studies have found desensitization to be comparable to skills training (Curran, 1975; Heimberg, Madsen, Montgomery, & McNabb, 1980), whereas three studies have found it to be less effective than skills training (Bander et al., 1975; Curran & Gilbert, 1975; Curran et al., 1976).

Several treatment programs have also investigated the efficacy of semistructured interactions in reducing dating anxiety. Martinson and Zerface (1970) initially demonstrated the superiority of prearranged interactions between male clients and college coeds over individual counseling. A series of subsequent investigations examined a related procedure—practice dating—in which the individual participates in weekly practice dates, each time with a novel partner (Christensen & Arkowitz, 1974). Practice dating has been shown to be superior to a control condition and comparable in efficacy to behavior rehearsal and practice dating with cognitive restructuring (Kramer, 1975).

Practice dating has also been successfully applied in reducing shyness in same-sex friendship interactions (Royce & Arkowitz, 1978). Perl, Hinton, Arkowitz, and Himadi (1977) reported negative results in that no differences were found in dating frequency between subjects in three practice-dating groups and those participating in a wait list control condition and group discussion. In explaining these results, Arkowitz (1977) argues that the mechanism underlying the anxiety reduction observed with practice-dating interactions is some form of desensitization. Future studies may begin to address the empirical adequacy of this conceptual position.

Cognitive Distortions

This model attributes the individual's heterosocial difficulties to maladaptive cognitive-evaluative appraisals and distortions (Linehan, 1980; Meichenbaum, Butler, & Gruson, 1981). Although capable of performing competently in heterosocial situations, the individual is said to think in ways that generate anxiety or compete with adaptive coping cognitions. These, in turn, lead to the performance deficit. Therefore, treatment from this perspective may best be described as involving the acquisition of cognitive responses in that the strategies focus on the replacement of maladaptive self-statements and evaluations with more adaptive ones (Meichenbaum, 1977).

Arkowitz et al. (1975) were among the first to suggest that a social-evaluative anxiety contributed to heterosocial incompetence. This proposal has been empirically supported through documentation of a variety of cognitive distortions that have differentiated between competency groups. Among them are excessively high performance standards (Clark & Arkowitz, 1975); overly negative self-evaluations (Clark & Arkowitz, 1975; Glasgow & Arkowitz, 1975); expectancies of negative evaluation (Fiedler & Beach, 1978; Smith & Sarason, 1975); irrational beliefs (Gormally, Sipps, Raphael, Edwin, & Varvil-Weld, 1981); selective attention to negative feedback (O'Banion & Arkowitz, 1977); deficient self-control (Perri & Richards, 1977); and insufficient knowledge of social norms (Twentyman et al., 1981). Additional studies have reported mixed results regarding the contribution of cognitive factors to overall social performance (Bellack, Hersen, & Turner, 1979; Eisler, Frederiksen, & Peterson, 1978). Moreover, contradictory evidence for the importance of cognitive processes has also been reported (Steffen & Reckman, 1978; Miller & Arkowitz, 1977).

Few studies have evaluated the effect of cognitively based treatment programs for heterosocial difficulties. In their classic study, Rehm and Marston (1968) found a self-reinforcement group consisting of structured homework (*in vivo* practice with females) and contingent self-reinforcement more effective than attention-control and no-treatment groups in reducing self-reporting anxiety and increasing dating frequency. Glass, Gottman, and Shmurak (1976) found that subjects receiving cognitive self-statement modification increased extra-therapy dating behavior and showed superior generalization to novel heterosocial situations relative to the performance of a response-acquisition group. However, the response-acquisition group and a combined treatment group performed better than cognitive self-statement modification alone in analog dating-behavior test situations. In a subsequent study comparing response-acquisition, cognitive-restructuring, and attention–placebo groups, the findings indicated the superiority of response acquisition in improving behavioral skills, whereas the cognitive-restructuring group evidenced greater reductions in self-reported and overt anxiety (Elder, Edelstein, & Fremouw, 1978). Finally, cognitive counseling has been found comparable to skills training or a combined group for socially anxious males, though all three treatment groups resulted in significant improvements on three of five dependent measures in comparison to a wait list control group (Gormally, Varvil-Weld, Raphael, & Sipps, 1981).

Physical Attractiveness

Although physical attractiveness has not been emphasized in conceptual and therapeutic formulations, it has been found to influence social anxiety powerfully (Glasgow & Arkowitz, 1975), dating frequency (Greenwald, 1977) as well as overall interpersonal attraction (Byrne, London, & Reeves, 1968; Dion, Berscheid, & Walster, 1972; Duck & Craig, 1975; Krebs & Adinolfi, 1975; Kupke, Calhoun, & Hobbs, 1979). The role of physical attractiveness has been highlighted in the discussion of dating behavior, especially its preliminary stages (Berscheid & Walster, 1973; Curran, 1973; Mathes & Kahn, 1975; Murstein, 1971). For example, Davis (1973) suggested that one of the first factors that may facilitate an initial encounter consists of an extraordinarily attractive appearance. He further indicates that "symbols of low status or ugliness" (p. 26) may disqualify the individual as an acceptable accoster or accostee.

Physical attractiveness has also been found to influence interpersonal judgments significantly about individuals, either male or female (Berscheid & Walster, 1973; Singer, 1964; Walster, Aronson, Abraham, & Rottman, 1966). Finally, children as well as adults have been found to be highly susceptible to the influence of physical attractiveness as a variable affecting the establishment of social relationships (Saxe, 1979). However, Goldman and Lewis (1977) found that even when their attractiveness was concealed, attractive persons were better able to get opposite-sex individuals to like them and view them as socially skilled relative to unattractive ones.

On the basis of these findings, it seems plausible that individuals reporting heterosocial problems may not be as physically attractive as those who do not experience such difficulties. Quite possibly, this situation may contribute to a reduction in approach behavior, thereby putting the comparably unattractive individual at a social disadvantage (Barocas & Karoly, 1972; Sigall & Landy, 1973). In light of the significant influence exerted by physical attractiveness, particularly in the initiation stage of a heterosocial relationship or "brief encounter," steps might be taken to enhance this factor in future training programs (Curran & Gilbert, 1975). At the very least, physical attractiveness should be assessed in studies investigating the behavioral referents of heterosocial competence (Arkowitz, 1981).

The preceding discussion of the effects of treatment based upon the various conceptual models of heterosocial skills development and expression makes clear that little can be said concerning their relative effectiveness. This should not be surprising, given the relatively primitive nature of most of these comparative studies. If it is indeed true that effective heterosocial performance depends upon several relatively independent factors (e.g., mastery of the skills involved, the control of anxiety that interferes with the performance of the skills, adaptive expectations, attractive appearance), then treatments directed at different factors in unselected populations in which all factors are present will continue to be seen as equally effective, for each is relevant to only particular subsets of those populations. What is called for, then, is not traditional comparative studies in which, for example, skills building is pitted against anxiety reduction, but, instead, diagnostic and prescriptive studies in which the specific nature of a "heterosocial deficit" is identified and specific procedures to remediate the relevant deficit or deficits are deployed in treatment. It might then be important to compare different approaches to the remediation of the same deficit. Such research awaits the development and validation of behavioral assessment instruments that allow the diagnosis of the specific deficit or deficits that are involved in an individual's heterosocial problem. Until that work is done and clinicians and researchers include a more precise diagnostic and prescriptive regimen in their work, the research that is conducted may well continue to provide answers to such primitive and inappropriate questions as whether skills training or anxiety reduction is more effective in overcoming personal appearance deficits.

METHODOLOGICAL ISSUES IN IDENTIFYING HETEROSOCIAL SKILLS

Despite the numerous research investigations that have discriminated competency groups, either in terms of the specific variables mentioned before or on the basis of global ratings, studies have had difficulty providing consistent evidence for specific behavioral differences that isolate important clusters of heterosocial skills (Arkowitz, 1981; Conger & Conger, 1982). Conger and Conger (1982) noted that the differences that have been found between competence groups have not been systematically replicated and, therefore, a profile of heterosocial competence at the performance level has not been elucidated. Nevertheless, as stated cogently by Curran and Mariotto (1980), "the search for empirically distinguishable subelements of the constructs involved in the social skills area is an important concern for behavioral assessors, because results of such studies dictate the elements to be included during assessments and the targets to be changed in treatment" (p. 9).

Several explanations implicating methodological limitations have been rendered for the failure to derive specific behavioral components of heterosocial skills. First, the selection of competent behaviors on the basis of face validity or "intuition" alone is a popular tactic, but an overall unsatisfactory means for generating the actual behaviors that influence personal judgments of an individual's competence (Conger, Wallander, Mariotto, & Ward, 1980; Hersen & Bellack, 1977; Spence, 1981). Early research in the area drew upon contrived assessment procedures and arbitrary target behaviors whose validity was not emprically established. Second, use of the contrasted or known groups approach, characteristic of the criterion-validity model so widely employed in this area,

may fail to elucidate the differences existing between groups that are unrelated to the criterion by which they were originally discriminated (McFall, 1976). As just one example, the use of dating frequency measures alone does not preclude differences between groups in terms of additional variables such as heterosocial avoidance and anxiety, currently regarded as comparably significant considerations in the subject selection process (Wallander, Conger, Mariotto, Curran, & Farrell, 1980; Twentyman et al., 1981). Thus, factors other than heterosocial skills may be responsible for the differences obtained between groups in several studies (Curran, 1977).

A third factor that accounts for the failure to derive a set of heterosocial skills empirically is that researchers have generally neglected to examine important differences between individuals in the more subtle process, rather than content, skills (Fischetti et al., 1977; Peterson et al., 1981; Trower, 1980). For example, Fischetti et al., and Peterson et al. found differences in response-timing skills (e.g., sequencing skills) between high and low heterosocially competent men and women, respectively. However, no group differences were found in the frequency of their responses. It must be noted that the aforementioned studies can also be contrasted on differences in observational recording procedures, the behaviors selected for assessment, subject populations, and selection criteria. The differences may further contribute to the failure to obtain a replicable behavioral composite of heterosocial competence (Conger & Farrell, 1981).

Of the more significant methodological considerations, several investigators have criticized the routine use of brief, single-response role plays in the assessment of social skills given their limited crtiterion validity and influence by instructional format (Arkowitz, 1981; Bellack, Hersen, & Turner, 1978a, 1978b; Bellack, Hersen, & Lamparski, 1979; Galassi & Galassi, 1976; Linehan, Goldfried, & Goldfried, 1979; McFall, 1976, 1977; Romano & Bellack, 1980). The behavioral measures obtained using such role-play situations have only minimally corresponded to those derived from more naturalistic situations and may yield artificial results that fail to capture the specific nature of an individual's skill deficiency adequately. Finally, selection instruments may be psychometrically unsound or inadequate, which may result in poorly discriminated samples prior to assessment (Curran, 1977; Bellack, 1979a). Researchers have only recently begun to evaluate the psychometric characteristics and validity of strategies for assessing heterrosocial skill (Farrell, Wallander, & Mariotto, 1978; Farrell, Mariotto, Conger, Curran, & Wallander, 1979; Heimberg, Harrison, Montgomery, Madsen, & Sherfey, 1980; Kolko & Milan, 1982; Lavin & Kupke, 1981; Wessberg, Mariotto, Conger, Farrell, & Conger, 1979).

EMPIRICAL APPROACHES TO THE DESIGNATION OF HETEROSOCIAL SKILLS

In light of these methodological issues, greater consideration should be given to the particular assessment approach adopted in order to designate a valid set of component behaviors empirically that discriminate skilled from unskilled individuals. To highlight these issues, several exemplary studies that draw upon empirical approaches to identifying heterosocial skills will be described.

One of the major approaches that has guided research efforts involves establishing the social validity or importance of the skills selected for measurement and modification by drawing upon the opinions of significant others (Kazdin, 1977; Wolf, 1978). In an attempt to de-

rive and train complex conversational skills in delinquent girls empirically, Minkin, Braukmann, Minkin, Timbers, Timbers, Fixsen, Phillips, and Wolf (1976) employed the following procedural components: (1) specification of significant component skills; (2) social validation of the importance of each skill; (3) behavioral training; and (4) social validation of the beneficial impact of training. Using this model, three component skills—questioning, providing feedback, and talk time—were identified and later found to enhance overall conversational ability as evaluated by various adult groups in the community.

Barlow et al. (1977) adopted a similar empirical strategy to identify the verbal and nonverbal components of social skills considered important when initiating heterosocial interaction with a female. Three groups consisting of socially adequate black and white males and socially adequate white male psychiatric patients participated in a videotaped role-play task with a female confederate that was later evaluated by six expert male and female judges. The resulting heterosocial checklist that consisted of three general categories—form of conversation, affect, and voice—significantly discriminated between adequate and inadequate competency groups.

Drawing upon the empirical strategy of Barlow et al., Conger et al. (1980) requested 134 college students to list the behavioral cues they employed in rating the performance of high and low heterosocially skilled males. This social validation approach was effective in generating a set of 12 individual behavioral cues that could be categorized on the basis of their association to rated social skills, anxiety, or both attributes. These cues suggest which behavioral referents should be evaluated during assessment. A similar approach to the determination of the behavioral referents of assertion in women was employed by Romano and Bellack (1980). Moreover, social validation has been employed to evaluate treatment outcome with adolescent patients following social skills training (Kolko, Dorsett, & Milan, 1981), and to assess the effects of duration of heterosocial role-play interactions on global ratings and the listing of behavioral cues (Dorsett, Milan, & Kolko, 1982). Muehlenhard and McFall (1981) employed a social validation approach to determining the most effective way for a woman to initiate a date with a man.

A second, complementary method for identifying heterosocial skills utilizes the criterion-validity model in which the relationships between specific behavioral measures and global ratings of skill and anxiety are evaluated. Kupke, Hobbs, & Cheney (1979) attempted to document empirically the significance of three measures of conversational behavior with global ratings of a female confederate's interpersonal attraction, a criterion that may reflect, in part, one's heterosocial competence. The confederate also rated the subject in physical attractiveness. Stepwise multiple regression analyses found that physical attractiveness significantly predicted overall interpersonal attraction. In terms of conversational behavior, the inclusion of personal attention, but not self-talk and minimal encourages, improved the prediction of attraction beyond physical attractiveness alone.

Conversational behaviors were also experimentally evaluated in a related study by Dow et al. (1981). Eight tapes of an identical heterosocial interaction were prepared in a $2 \times 2 \times 2$ experimental design in which the female's performance was either high or low on three behaviors: latency, questions, and compliments. Undergraduate students then rated the female on nine dimensions that taped global social skills and four dimensions that reflected halo effects (e.g., physical attractiveness, use of exercise, being a good cook). The results indicated that high compliments and questions were associated with higher social skill ratings as well as a physical attractiveness rating. In addition, there was no relationship between the skills and halo effect ratings, suggesting that subjects attended primarily to the female's social skills.

Conger and Farrell (1981) reported one of the most productive illustrations of this approach using males as subjects that included both social skills and anxiety ratings and a total of eight verbal and nonverbal behaviors. The behaviors were assessed during role play and waiting room situations with an interval recording procedure. The authors found that the behaviors were differentially correlated with skills (e.g., smiles, gestures, self-manipulations) or with both anxiety and skills (e.g., subject talk time, gaze, confederate talk time). Subject talk time and gaze were also strongly related to judges' global ratings of skills and anxiety in both assessment situations using multiple regression analyses. Similar empirical strategies have been employed in the specification of behavioral differences between skilled and unskilled adolescents (Spence, 1981); normals and psychopaths (Rime, Bouvey, Leborgne, & Rouillan, 1978); low- and high-anxiety individuals (Waxer, 1977); functional versus dysfunctional married couples (Royce & Weiss, 1975); and individuals classified as high and low in the ability to get others to talk and "open up" (Dabbs, Evans, Hopper, & Purvis, 1980; Purvis, Dabbs, & Hopper, 1981).

There is a third approach, infrequently employed, to selecting heterosocial skills. The ultimate criterion for determining which skills are important may rest upon a demonstration that improvements in skillful performance result in enhanced effectiveness and impact. Kupke, Calhoun, and Hobbs (1979) assessed the experimental validity of two conversational behaviors in males —personal attention and minimal encourages—in influencing a female confederate's rating of interpersonal attraction. Only personal attention was found to have a functional relationship to the female's global evaluation. A number of extraneous variables, such as physical attractiveness and frequency of verbalizations, were also analyzed but were found to contribute little to this relationship.

These studies demonstrate that the behavioral indexes of heterosocial skills can be derived if sufficient attention is given to assessment and methodological concerns, specifically, the use of empirically based strategies. An additional assessment approach that has implications for the determination and operationalization of criterion behaviors related to heterosocial skills is the behavior-analytic model (Goldfreid & D'Zurilla, 1969). The behavior-analytic approach to social competence involves the specification of problematic situations and potential responses as well as the empirical evaluation of the overall "competence" of the responses. From an assessment perspective, this strategy is advantageous in that the content validity of the assessment situations and their empirically determined criterion validity or significance are established, both of which have become important methodological concerns in the social skills literature (Curran & Mariotto, 1980; Linehan, 1979). Indeed, the behavior-analytic model has contributed to the construction and evbaluation of instruments for the behavioral assessment of assertiveness and general social skills (Freedman, Rosenthal, Donahoe, Schlundt, & McFall, 1978; Goldsmith & McFall, 1975).

Perri and Richards (1979) reported one of the first empirically derived assessment procedures for evaluating heterosocial competence. The test consisted of 22 situations that were previously validated as common and difficult by a sample of male undergraduates to which a male responded with a single statement. The content of the situations involved asking for a date, initiating, maintaining, and terminating conversations, describing one's feelings, and discussing contraception. An empirical criterion analysis of a broad range of responses to the items led to the construction of a five-level scoring system for assessing the effectiveness of each response. The test was found to discriminate known groups that differed in dating frequency and satisfaction as well as discomfort in heterosocial interactions. Perri and Richards also obtained evidence supporting the convergent validity of their assessment procedure.

In an empirical extension of this model, Fisher-Beckfield and McFall (1982) sought to develop a more comprehensive measure of general competence in male undergraduates. This measure consisted of 21 academic and 31 social interaction scenarios, some of which involved opposite-sex interactions. Fisher-Beckfield and McFall reported that scores of one's competency in both of these domains were significantly related to mild depression and grade point average. Although these few studies were successful in developing assessment procedures having relevance for heterosocial competence, they did not evaluate conversational skills from the verbal and nonverbal domains and, thus, provided little information about these potential clinical targets in need of remediation.

Kolko and Milan (in press) employed the behavior-analytic model to derive empirically a set of heterosocial skills that would discriminate skilled from unskilled college women. In the first step of this evaluation process, the role-play interactions of women classified as high and low heterosocially competent were shown to 30 male and 60 female peer judges who rendered global ratings and listed the behavioral referents on which their ratings were based. In the second step, 64 male and 104 female judges rated the quality of subjects' performances in the 10 most frequently listed cue categories from the first step and also listed the specific behavioral referents that influenced their ratings. The five most common referents were formulated into 3-point ordinal or nominal scales and then rated using a 30-second interval recording procedure. Of the original 34 behavioral definitions, 16 were found to discriminate the two competency groups and to possess adequate criterion validity. The skills represented a broad range of paralinguistic (e.g., loudness, tone, inflection); verbal (e.g., topic transition, reinforcing feedback, personal attention); and nonverbal behaviors (e.g., smiles, gaze, eye contact in listener role).

GENERAL ASSESSMENT AND TREATMENT CONSIDERATIONS

The preceding discussion has attempted to raise a number of methodological concerns that bear direct implications for the form and function of current approaches to assessing heterosocial skills. One general domain that may require some procedural modification involves the assessment stimuli or medium for eliciting heterosocial performances. Investigators are encouraged to select more critically the heterosocial situations used for assessment purposes through empirical analyses in order to ensure their relevance and content validity (cf. Freedman et al., 1978; Fisher-Beckfield & McFall, 1982). An attempt should also be made to state explicitly the purpose, setting, and associated interactant in each role play in order to equate each situation with a separate task or behavioral program (McFall, 1982). By attending to these assessment requirements, the rudiments of a taxonomy of empirically derived role-play situations will be established (Galassi, Galassi, & Vedder, 1981). The evaluation and categorization of relevant situations on the basis of different situational variables has been virtually neglected in this area (Kolotkin, 1980) and

deserves consideration, particularly in light of the situation-specific nature of the findings of other social skills investigations (Eisler, Hersen, Miller, & Blanchard, 1975; Phibbs & Arkowitz, in press; Himadi et al., 1980).

The content of a majority of the situations described in one study of the problems involved in heterosocial activities reflected difficulties in the initiation of a heterosocial encounter or the planning of a forthcoming one (Kolko & Milan, in press). The prominent role that was played by initiation or approach in heterosocial research has been suggested in several studies (Glasgow & Arkowitz, 1975; Lipton & Nelson, 1980). Bellack et al. (1979a) found that 35% of the variance associated with a self-report version of their empirically derived role-play items was accounted for by a factor involving "initiation of conversation with an unknown female" (p. 341). Twentyman et al. (1981), in a series of studies, found that daters and nondaters differed widely in terms of the likelihood of initiating conversations with a female, though few behavioral differences were observed once the two groups progressed from the initiation phase. Similar results have been obtained for women (Williams & Ciminero, 1978). If the findings for men bear significance for women, the necessity exists for training initiation—entry or "opener" skills in the modification of heterosocial interaction difficulties (McGovern et al., 1975).

Of comparable importance to the content of the role-play situations is the format taken by the role plays used in this area. The validity of these assessment stimuli and the generality of the findings based upon them have been called into question in several investigations. Consequently, role-play tasks should be of a duration sufficient enough to permit the development, assessment, and modification of several aspects of interpersonal interaction. This form of extended interaction has been reported in both assessment (Conger & Farrell, 1981; Kupke, Hobbs, & Cheney, 1979) and training (Heimberg et al., 1980) studies.

The role-play procedure and format also have considerable influence on the specific component behaviors enumerated for assessment purposes. Although many behaviors have relevance regardless of format (e.g., loudness, inflection, smiles, gaze), certain component behaviors will reflect the interactive and reciprocal nature of an extended role-play situation. For example, such behaviors as follow-up latency, follow-up answers to questions, topic transition, topic quality, topic development, and exchange ratio have been assessed (Kolko & Milan, in press). Single-response role plays would not be expected to capture these generally qualitative response patterns because they exclude any possibility for a continuous dyadic interaction. The work by Fischetti et al. (1977) and Peterson et al. (1981) on response synchronization with males and females, respectively, also highlights the importance of assessing high and low socially skilled subjects on skills that tap this process, rather than content, oriented interactive quality.

The importance of evaluating reciprocal measures is also seen in a related study documenting the effects of partner interaction on role-play performance by Jaremko, Myers, Daner, Moore, and Allin (1982). They found that the dating frequency of the partner with whom high- and low-frequency daters interacted either hindered or facilitated performance on a behavioral role-play task. For both males and females, interacting with a different dating-frequency partner (either high or low) hindered performance and was associated with lower global self-ratings relative to interacting with a same-frequency partner. It is plausible to assume that opposing partner-interaction effects may have obscured actual behavioral differences in heterosocial skills levels between con-

trasted groups, thereby yielding few significant behavioral discriminators. Furthermore, the fact that confederate variables have been found related to overall judgments of heterosocial competence (Conger & Farrell, 1981; Greenwald, 1977) warrants paying greater attention to behavioral changes in the responsivity of the confederate or partner. Skillful subjects may engage in more effective "elicitation" behaviors that draw the confederate out than unskilled subjects. The results of investigations by Dabbs et al. (1980), Moisan-Thomas and Conger (1980), and Purvis et al. (1981) support this supposition.

In addition to process skills, greater emphasis has been placed upon the complexity of the content of the skills that have been generally evaluated. These novel behavioral indexes have generally reflected complex conversational or verbal behavior patterns. Thus, such behaviors as interest, initiations, conversation structure, talk time, personal attention, and reinforcing feedback have been found to correlate with overall heterosocial skills (Barlow et al., 1977; Conger et al., 1980; Greenwald, 1977; Kolko & Milan, in press; Kupke, Hobbs, & Cheney, 1979; Pilkonis, 1977b). The fact that peer and expert judges pay greater attention to conversational variables (e.g., style, content) than researchers, in general, calls for further empirical examination of the relationships between various conversational behaviors and global competence judgments. Subsequent research should also be directed toward the systematic analysis of verbal behaviors involving the content, range, and integration of the topics that ensue in the initiation and maintenance phases of a heterosocial interaction. The incorporation of more sophisticated and effective conversational behaviors would potentially enhance the efficacy of extant skills training and confidence-boosting programs (Heimberg et al., 1980).

Although designation of the content of

heterosocial skills is of major empirical importance, further effort must also be directed toward an assessment of the consequences of these skills. Minimal attention has been paid to ascertaining those behaviors empirically that indeed contribute to a skillful heterosocial performance before a training program is initiated. Thus, increased effort should be devoted to assessing the response consequences or reactions elicited by the execution of each skill (Libet & Lewinsohn, 1973). An evaluation of the consequences that follow a given component behavior, irrespective of a particular content, might elucidate those behaviors that accrue maximum social reinforcement. Mullinix and Galassi (1981) proposed that studies concerned with specifying the content of social skills training programs consider the immediate behavior consequences that each skill generates. Such investigations must also take into account the characteristics of the judge or observer when the adequacy of a given behavior is evaluated. As found in different studies (Romano & Bellack, 1980; Trower, Bryant, & Argyle, 1978; Conger et al., 1980), male and female peer judges differ in their use of and sensitivity to skills-related cues.

As the relationship between role-play measures and naturalistic behavior has generally been less than adequate (Bellack et al., 1978a; 1979; Wessberg et al. 1979), the need exists for establishing the importance of behaviors selected for assessment to ongoing heterosocial interactions. The exploration of naturalistic heterosocial interactions has recently emerged in the behavioral assessment literature, particularly as a means for determining the external validity of selected component behaviors, that is, their association with "real-life" behaviors and consequences. Firth, Schneider, Conger, and Higbee (1981) attempted to cross-validate predictors obtained from a standard role-play procedure (Conger & Farrell, 1981) in naturalistic interactions

with two naive interactants. The results provided partial support for the relationship between two naturalistic behaviors—talk and gaze—and global judgments.

Some studies have also explored the ecological validity of novel role-play assessment formats. Kern (1982) compared the validity of brief and extended role plays with an unobtrusive naturalistic interaction (replication role play). The replication role play was generally superior to the two traditional role-play tests on various measures of heterosocial skill. In an extension of this study, Kern, Miller, and Eggers (1983) found that a specification role play in which respondents were instructed to simulate particular target behaviors evinced a more representative performance profile than either a replication or typically brief role play. The implications of these findings are that standard role plays assess general capability rather than typical or *in vivo* behavior and that those assessment procedures that minimize intructional demand, although maximizing situational and personal relevance, may enhance their external validity. Future studies are needed to refine and standardize current procedures used for assessment purposes.

In terms of conceptual developments, the major findings of several investigations have highlighted the need to examine sex differences further and not to generalize merely from males to females when evaluating heterosocial interactions and problem behaviors (Glasgow & Arkowitz, 1975; Hollandsworth & Wall, 1977; Klaus et al., 1977). For example, Glasgow and Arkowitz (1975) noted that minimal-dating males gave evidence of overly negative self-evaluations rather than social skill deficits, whereas minimal-dating females gave evidence of social skill deficits. Greater deficits in heterosocial skills in females have also been reported by Jaremko et al. (1982). Likewise, Klaus et al. (1977) found that low-frequency-dating women reported significantly more difficulty making contact with perspective dates than low-frequency-dating men. The men in the Klaus et al. (1977) study perceived themselves as more skillful and held more positive expectancies than women. The fact that sex differences have been obtained in these and additional investigations may limit the ability to generalize from males to females and speaks even more convincingly to the need for additional research with women (Galassi & Galassi, 1979; Himadi et al., 1980; Lipton & Nelson, 1980).

The studies briefly reviewed earlier suggest that heterosocial competence, like any other molar construct, is a function of numerous behavioral referents and etiological variables (Curran, 1979; Duck, 1978). The individual's skills, anxieties, cognitive expectancies, and physical attractiveness may differentially contribute to the performance that is observed during heterosocial interaction both in the laboratory and, more importantly, naturalistic settings. One variable, the likelihood of initiation or approach in a heterosocial encounter, has been investigated with both males (Twentyman & McFall, 1975; Twentyman et al., 1981) and females (Lipton & Nelson, 1980; Williams and Ciminero, 1978). It has also been incorporated in multidimensional self-report instruments (Kolko & Milan, 1982). Novel procedures for assessing the verbal and cognitive components of heterosocial difficulties have also emerged in the literature. The need exists for comprehensive assessment strategies that devote explicit attention to an understanding of the role of each of these causal factors (Bellack, 1979b; Glasgow & Arkowitz, 1975).

SUMMARY

The area of research and application of heterosocial skills is as important as is any of the other areas of adjustment of concern to the helping professions. The development and effective utilization of appropriate heterosocial skills is an important developmental accomplishment that can have profound direct or indirect impact upon social, educational, vocational, and interpersonal functioning as well as the psychological signs of stress and distress that accompany inadequacies and failures in these areas. It is important to continue research aimed at the behavioral elaboration of the complex of heterosocial skills that represent the developmental continuum from the earliest portions of the socialization process through the final phases of the span of life wherein major readjustments of heterosocial relationships are forced upon us. Such research provides the knowledge necessary to predict, effectively deal with, and prevent the serious psychological difficulties that can result from failures to cement these developmental tasks.

Heterosocial skills research has focused upon the developmental tasks of late adolescence and early adulthood. Additional research should be aimed at describing the tasks and skills involved in heterosocial readjustment following divorce or the dissolution of an enduring relationship with a lover, identifying the earliest stages of heterosocial skills development and the skills that characterize the successful beginnings of a lifelong period of fulfilling heterosocial relationships, and documenting the heterosocial skills necessary in old age to establish new relationships following the death of a spouse. As sparsely researched as these questions are, even less attention has been directed at the difficulties experienced by individuals seeking same-sex companions or partners at these various stages of the developmental continuum and in response to the predictable crises that many will encounter that parallel those encountered by peers with a heterosocial orientation. The skills necessary for satisfactory social adjustment and the resolution of additional developmental tasks as they arise in these all-but-neglected areas remain to be elaborated and validated (Curran, 1979).

Most behavioral skills research, whether in the area of heterosocial skills development or in other areas of concern, has focused upon fairly molecular responses, such as eye contact, posture, and speech intensity. Some research has been directed at the more complex domain of the content of verbal interactions, and the ingredients of such basic skills as the assertive response to unreasonable requests seem well established. However, the profession has not described the elaborated stream of give-and-take that characterizes meaningful human interactions. It appears that heterosocial skills training and research leaves the client all dressed up, making good eye contact, but with nothing to say. A new direction for innovative research in the area will involve more than methodological refinement after methodological refinement, each prompting another sifting of old soil that is already all but depleted. Richer soil abounds, and it is time that researchers turned away from the familiar and began to formulate the strategies and to develop the tools necessary to answer the challenging but critical questions that lie in these extensions of skills research.

We have alluded to the need for the development of assessment instruments that identify in specific terms the basic problems the person is experiencing. Little can be said at this point in the development of heterosocial assessment concerning the form these instruments should take. The behavioral tradition suggests that direct observation of actual performances would be the most productive direction to follow. However, the behavioral tradition also recognizes that difficulties are more often than not related to specific situations, tasks, settings, and social responses of other persons. Consequently, it is unlikely that valid and practical instruments will emerge that are directed at heterosocial competence per se and that researchers will be forced to view heterosocial competence as a convenient abstraction for a family of seemingly related concerns rather than a unitary construct.

In studying the more molecular and manageable components of heterosocial competence, it will be important to explore the relationship between self-reports and direct observations of performance. It may well develop that self-report instruments will prove more useful in the initial assessment of heterosocial difficulties than will direct observations of behavior. Self-report instruments will certainly allow for the more efficient sampling of a wide variety of potentially problematic circumstances than will direct observation. Moreover, direct observation typically implies the use of role plays and other obviously contrived strategies. The relationship between performance in these contrived situations and competence in real-life heterosocial interactions is far from isomorphic. Indeed, it may well be that self-report instruments that tap a client's skills, anxiety, response probability, expectancy of outcome, and other related domains for a variety of circumstances will prove more useful for general diagnostic and prescriptive purposes than will direct observations of limited samples of behavior in contrived situations. Direct observation of behavior samples might then prove useful for more precise specification of deficits to be remediated.

Finally, the specification of skills that are to be taught requires continued refinement and development. Many apparently important skills, such as the content of heterosocial interactions, are all but ignored in the literature. Moreover, even the development of knowledge concerning the form of heterosocial interactions is limited, focusing primarily as it does on white, middle-class college students. It is difficult to ascertain why behavioral scientists have not yet begun to address these issues and provide the information necessary to provide effective services so that groups could profit from such efforts. Perhaps the field has become hypertechnological and the evolving standards for methodologically adequate research has imposed unnecessary, unrealistic and unvalidated requirements that actually are working to impede progress rather than ensure quality.

A reading of the literature bearing upon the identification of social skills would suggest a course of action that would most probably dampen the enthusiasm of even the most dedicated researcher. Specifically, consider the time and effort required to accomplish the following tasks: (1) generate situations, (2) solicit the assistance of a large group of peers to identify empirically those situations that are most common and representative, (3) establish criteria for competence and identify individuals who range from skilled to unskilled along that continuum, (4) arrange for the individuals so identified to display their skills (usually via videotaped role plays), (5) solicit the assistance of a second, large group of peers to observe the displays to identify and list skill components, (6) combine and analyze the resulting data to deduce the distinguishing characteristics of competent performance, (7) train individuals to exhibit the skills and arrange for their display (again, usually via videotaped role plays), and (8) solicit the assistance of a third, large group of peers to observe the performances and rate competence before and after training in order to determine the social validity of the program. Such responsibilities would understandably discourage both researcher and clinician from embarking upon a social skills training and research program. Given these considerations, it is appropriate that alternative strategies for the identification of effective social skills be proposed and evaluated. It is perhaps the development and analysis of realistic and effective alternative strate-gies that is the most difficult challenge to the social skills movement. Much remains to be accomplished.

REFERENCES

Arkowitz, H. (1977). Measurement and modification of minimal dating behavior. In M. Hersen, R. M. Eisler, & P. M. Miller (Eds.), *Progress in behavior modification* (Vol. 5). New York: Academic Press.

Arkowitz, H. (1981). Assessment of social skills. In M. Hersen & A. S. Bellack (Eds.)., *Behavioral assessment: A practical handbook* (2nd ed.). New York: Pergamon.

Arkowitz, H., Lichtenstein, E., McGovern, K., & Hines, P. (1975). The behavioral assessment of social competence in males. *Behavior Therapy, 6,* 3–13.

Arkowitz, H., Hinton, R., Perl, J., & Himadi, W. (1978). Treatment strategies for dating anxiety in college men based on real-life practice. *The Counseling Psychologist, 7,* 41–46.

Bander, K. W., Steinke, G. U., Allen, G. J., & Mosher, D. L. (1975). Evaluation of three dating-specific treatment approaches for heterosexual dating anxiety. *Journal of Consulting and Clinical Psychology, 43,* 259–265.

Bandura, A. (1969). *Principles of behavior modification.* New York: Holt, Rinehart & Winston.

Barlow, D. H., Abel, G. G., Blanchard, E. B., Bristow, A. R., & Young, L. D. (1977). A heterosocial skills behavior checklist for males. *Behavior Therapy, 8,* 229–239.

Barocas, R., & Karoly, P. (1972). Effects of physical appearance on socialness. *Psychological Reports, 31,* 495–500.

Bellack, A. S. (1979a). A critical appraisal of strategies for assessing social skill. *Behavioral Assessment, 1,* 157–176.

Bellack, A. S. (1979b). Behavioral assessment of social skills. In A. S. Bellack & M. Hersen (Eds.), *Research and practice in social skills training.* New York: Plenum.

Bellack, A. S., & Hersen, M. (Eds.). (1979). *Research and practice in social skills training*. New York: Plenum.

Bellack, A. S., Hersen, M., & Lamparski, D. (1979). Role-play tests for assessing social skills: Are they valid? Are they useful? *Journal of Consulting and Clinical Psychology, 47,* 335–342.

Bellack, A. S., Hersen, J., & Turner, S. M. (1978a). Role-play tests for assessing social skills: Are they valid? *Behavior Therapy, 9,* 448–461.

Bellack, A. S., Hersen, M., & Turner, S. M. (1978b). Comments on the utility of suggestive versus definitive data: A reply to Curran. *Behavior Therapy, 9,* 469–470.

Bellack, A. S., Hersen, M., & Turner, S. M. (1979). Relationship of role playing and knowledge of appropriate behavior to assertion in the natural environment. *Journal of Consulting and Clinical Psychology, 47,* 670–678.

Berscheid, E., & Walster, E. (1973). Physical attractiveness. In L. Berkowitz (Ed.), *Advances in experimental social psychology* (Vol. 7). New York: Academic Press.

Borkevec, T. D., Stone, N. M., O'Brien, G. T., & Kaloupek, D. G. (1974). Evaluation of a clinically relevant target behavior for analogue outcome research. *Behavior Therapy, 5,* 503–513.

Bryant, B. M., & Trower, P. E. (1974). Social difficulty in a student sample. *British Journal of Educational Psychology, 44,* 13–21.

Bryant, B. M., Trower, P., Yardley, K., Urbieta, H., & Letemendia, F. (1976). A survey of social inadequacy among psychiatric outpatients. *Psychological Medicine, 6,* 101–112.

Byrne, D., London, O., & Reeves, K. (1968). The effects of physical attractiveness, sex, and attitude similarity on interpersonal attraction. *Journal of Personality, 36,* 259–271.

Christensen, A., & Arkowitz, H. (1974). Preliminary report on practice dating and feedback as treatment for college dating problems. *Journal of Counseling Psychology, 21,* 92–95.

Clark, J. V., & Arkowitz, H. (1975). Social anxiety and self-evaluation of interpersonal performance. *Psychological Reports, 36,* 211–221.

Conger, J. C., & Conger, A. J. (1982). Components of heterosocial competence. In J. P. Curran & P. M. Monti (Eds.), *Social skills training: A practical handbook for assessment and treatment.* New York: Guilford.

Conger, J. C., & Farrell, A. D. (1981). Behavioral components of heterosocial skills. *Behavior Therapy, 12,* 41–55.

Conger, A. J., Wallander, J. L., Mariotto, M. J., & Ward, D. (1980). Peer judgements of heterosexual-social anxiety and skill: What do they pay attention to anyhow? *Behavioral Assessment, 2,* 261–266.

Curran, J. P. (1973). Correlates of physical attractiveness and interpersonal attraction in the dating situation. *Social Behavior and Personality, 1,* 153–157.

Curran, J. P. (1975). Social skills training and systematic desensitization in reducing dating anxiety. *Behavior Research and Therapy, 13,* 65–68.

Curran, J. P. (1977). Skills training as an approach to the treatment of heterosexual-social anxiety: A review. *Psychological Bulletin, 84,* 140–157.

Curran, J. P. (1979). Social skills: Methodological issues and future directions. In A. S. Bellack & M. Hersen (Eds.), *Research and practice in social skills training.* New York: Plenum.

Curran, J. P., & Gilbert, F. S. (1975). A test of the relative effectiveness of a systematic desensitization program and an interpersonal skills training program with date anxious subjects. *Behavior Therapy, 6,* 510–521.

Curran, J. P., Gilbert, F. S. & Little, L. M. (1976). A comparison between behavioral replication training and sensitivity training approaches to heterosexual dating anxiety. *Journal of Counseling Psychology, 23,* 190—196.

Curran, J. P., Little, L. M., & Gilbert, F. S. (1978). Reactivity of males of differing heterosexual social anxiety to female approach and non-approach conditions. *Behavior Therapy, 9,* 961.

Curran, J. P., & Mariotto, M. J. (1980). A

conceptual structure for the assessment of social skills. In M. Hersen, R. M. Eisler, & P. M. Miller (Eds.), *Progress in Behavior Modification* (Vol. 10), New York: Academic Press.

Curran, J. P., & Monti, P. M. (Eds.). (1982). *Social skills training: A practical handbook for assessment and treatment.* New York: Guilford.

Dabbs, J. M., Evans, M. S., Hopper, C. H., & Purvis, J. A. (1980). Self-monitors in conversation: What do they monitor? *Journal of Personality and Social Psychology, 39,* 278–284.

Davis, M. (1973). *Intimate relations.* New York. The Free Press.

Dion, K., Berscheid, E., & Walster, E. (1972). What is beautiful is good. *Journal of Personality and Social Psychology, 24,* 285–290.

Dorsett, P. G., Milan, M. A., & Kolko, D. J. (1982). *The effects of duration of heterosocial role-play interactions on global ratings and cue-listing.* Paper presented at the annual meeting of the Southeastern Psychological Association, New Orleans.

Dow, M. G., Glaser, S. R., & Biglan, A. (1981). The relevance of specific conversational behaviors to ratings of social skill. *Journal of Behavioral Assessment, 3,* 233–242.

Duck, S. (1978). *The study of acquaintance.* Westmead, England: Saxon House.

Duck, S., & Craig, R. (1975). Effects of type of information upon interpersonal attraction. *Social Behavior and Personality, 3,* 157–164.

Eisler, R. M. (1976). The behavioral assessment of social skills. In M. Hersen & A. S. Bellack (Eds.), *Behavioral assessment: A practical handbook.* New York: Pergamon.

Eisler, R. M., & Frederiksen, L. W. (1980). *Perfecting social skills: A guide to interpersonal behavior development.* New York: Plenum.

Eisler, R. M., Frederiksen, L. W., & Peterson, G. L. (1978). The relationship of cognitive variables to the expression of assertiveness. *Behavior Therapy, 9,* 419–427.

Eisler, R. M., Hersen, M., Miller, P. M, & Blanchard, E. B. (1975). Situational determinants of assertive behaviors. *Journal of Consulting and Clinical Psychology, 43,* 330–340.

Elder, J. P., Edelstein, B. A., & Fremouw, W. J. (1978). *A comparison of response acquisition and cognitive restructuring in the enhancement of a social competence of college freshmen.* Paper presented at the annual meeting of the Association for the Advancement of Behavior Therapy, Chicago.

Farrell, A. D., Mariotto, M. J., Conger, A. M., Curran, J. P., & Wallander, J. L. (1979). Self-ratings and judges' ratings of heterosexual-social anxiety and skill: A generalizability study. *Journal of Consulting and Clinical Psychology, 47,* 164–175.

Farrell, A. D., Wallander, J. L., & Mariotto, M. J. (1978). *A preliminary evaluation of the survey of heterosexual interactions as a screening instrument for heterosocial research.* Paper presented at the annual convention of the Association for the Advancement of Behavior Therapy.

Fiedler, D., & Beach, L. R. (1978). On the decision to be assertive. *Journal of Consulting and Clinical Psychology, 46,* 537–546.

Firth, E. A., Schneider, P. A., Conger, J. C., & Higbee, G. H. (1981). *An exploration of naturalistic interactions for the assessment of heterosocial skills.* Paper presented at the annual meeting of the Association for the Advancement of Behavior Therapy, Toronto.

Fischetti, M., Curran, J. P., & Wessberg, H. W. (1977). Sense of timing: A skill deficit in heterosexual-socially anxious males. *Behavior Modification, 1,* 179–194.

Fisher-Beckfield, D., & McFall, R. M. (1982). Development of a competence inventory for college men and evaluation of relationships between competence and depression. *Journal of Consulting and Clinical Psychology, 50,* 697–705.

Freedman, B. J., Rosenthal, L., Donahoe, C. P., Schlundt, D. G., & McFall, R. M. (1978). A social-behavioral analysis of skill deficits in delinquent and nondelinquent adolescent boys. *Journal of Con-*

sulting and Clinical Psychology, 46, 1448–1462.

Galassi, M. D., & Galassi, J. P. (1976). The effects of role playing variations on the assessment of assertive behavior. *Behavior Therapy, 7,* 343–347.

Galassi, J., & Galassi, M. D. (1979). Modification of heterosocial skills deficits. In A. S. Bellack & M. Hersen (Eds.), *Research and practice in social skills training.* New York: Plenum.

Galassi, J. P., Galassi, M. D., & Vedder, M. J. (1981). Perspectives on assertion as a social skills model. In J. D. Wine & M. D. Smye (Eds.), *Social competence.* New York: Guilford.

Geary, J. M., & Goldman, M. S. (1978). Behavioral treatment of heterosexual social anxiety: A factorial investigation. *Behavior Therapy, 9,* 971–972.

Glasgow, R. E., & Arkowitz, H. (1975). The behavioral assessment of male and female social competence in dyadic heterosexual interactions. *Behavior Therapy, 6,* 488–498.

Glass, C. R., Gottman, J. M., & Shmurak, S. H. (1976). Response-acquisition and cognitive self-statement modification approaches to dating-skills training. *Journal of Counseling Psychology, 23,* 520–526.

Goldfried, M. R., & D'Zurilla, T. J. (1969). A behavioral-analytic model for assessing competence. In C. D. Spielberger (Ed.), *Current topics in clinical psychology* (Vol. 1). New York: Academic Press.

Goldman, W., & Lewis, P. (1977). Beautiful is good. Evidence that the physically attractive are more socially skilled. *Journal of Experimental Social Psychology, 6,* 352–356.

Goldsmith, J. B., & McFall, R. M. (1975). Development and evaluation of an interpersonal skill-training program for psychiatric inpatients. *Journal of Abnormal Psychology, 84,* 51–58.

Gormally, J., Sipps, G., Raphael, R., Edwin, D., Varvil-Weld, D. (1981). The relationship between maladaptive cognitions and social anxiety. *Journal of Consulting and Clinical Psychology, 49,* 300–301.

Gormally, J., Varvil-Weld, D., Raphael, R.,

& Sipps, G. (1981). Treatment of socially anxious college men using cognitive counseling and skills training. *Journal of Counseling Psychology, 28,* 147–157.

Greenwald, D. P. (1977). The behavioral assessment of social skill and social anxiety in female college students. *Behavior Therapy, 8,* 925–937.

Havighurst, R. M. (1972). *Developmental tasks and education* (3rd ed.). New York: David McKay.

Heimberg, R. G., Harrison, D. F., Montgomery, D., Madsen, C. H., & Sherfey, J. A. (1980). Psychometric and behavioral analysis of a social anxiety inventory: The situation questionnaire. *Behavioral Assessment, 2,* 403–416.

Heimberg, R. G., Madsen, C. H., Montgomery, D., & McNabb, C. E. (1980). Behavioral treatments for heterosocial problems: Effects on daily self-monitored and role-played interactions. *Behavior Modification, 4,* 147–172.

Hersen, M., & Bellack, A. S. (1977). Assessment of social skills. In A. R. Ciminero, K. S. Calhoun, & H. E. Adams (Eds.), *Handbook for behavioral assessment.* New York: Wiley.

Himadi, W. G., Arkowitz, H., Hinton, R., & Perl, J. (1980). Minimal dating and its relationship to other social problems and general adjustment. *Behavior Therapy, 11,* 345–352.

Hollandsworth, J. G., & Wall, K. E. (1977). Sex differences in assertive behavior: An empirical investigation. *Journal of Counseling Psychology, 24,* 217–222.

Jaremko, M. E., Myers, E. J., Daner, S., Moore, S., & Allin, J. (1982). Differences in daters: Effects of sex, dating frequency and dating frequency of partners. *Behavioral Assessment, 4,* 307–316.

Kazdin, A. E. (1977). Assessing the clinical or applied importance of behavior change through social validation. *Behavior Modification, 4,* 427–452.

Kelly, J. A. (1981). *Social-skills training.* New York: Springer.

Kelly, J. A., Urey, J. R., & Patterson, J. T. (1980). Improving heterosocial conversation skills of male psychiatric patients through a small group training procedure. *Behavior Therapy, 11,* 179–188.

Kern, J. M. (1982). The comparative external and concurrent validity of three role-plays for assessing heterosocial performance. *Behavior Therapy, 13,* 666–680.

Kern, J. M., Miller, C., & Eggers, J. (1983). Enhancing the validity of role-play tests: A comparison of three role-play methodologies. *Behavior Therapy, 14,* 482–492.

Klaus, D., Hersen, M., & Bellack, A. S. (1977). Survey of dating habits of male and female college students: A necessary precursor to measurement and modification. *Journal of Clinical Psychology, 33,* 369–375.

Kolko, D. J., & Milan, M. A. (1982). *Multimethod self-report assessment of heterosocial competence in males and females.* Paper presented at the annual meeting of the Association for Advancement of Behavior Therapy, Los Angeles.

Kolko, D. J., & Milan, M. A. (in press). Behavior-analytic development and validation of a women's heterosocial skill observational rating system. *Behavior Modification.*

Kolko, D. J., Dorsett, P. G., & Milan, M. A. (1981). A total-assessment approach to the evaluation of social skills training: The effectiveness of an anger control program for adolescent psychiatric patients. *Behavioral Assessment, 3,* 383–402.

Kolotkin, R. A. (1980). Situational specificity in the assessment of assertion: Considerations for the measurement of training and transfer. *Behavior Therapy, 11,* 651–661.

Kramer, S. R. (1975). *Effectiveness of behavior rehearsal and practice dating to increase heterosexual social interaction. Dissertation Abstracts International, 36,* 913B-914B. (University Microfilms, No. 75-16, 693)

Krebs, D., & Adinolfi, A. (1975). Physical attractiveness, social relations, and personality style. *Journal of Personality and Social Psychology, 31,* 245–253.

Kupke, T. E., Calhoun, K. S., & Hobbs, S. A. (1979). Selection of heterosocial skills. II. Experimental validity. *Behavioral Therapy, 10,* 336–346.

Kupke, T. E., Hobbs, S. A., & Cheney, T. H. (1979). Selection of heterosocial skills. I. Criterion-related validity. *Behavior Therapy, 10,* 327–335.

Lavin, P. F., & Kupke, T. E. (1981). Psychometric evaluation of the Situation Test of heterosocial skill. *Journal of Behavioral Assessment, 2,* 111–121.

Libet, J. M., & Lewinsohn, P. M. (1973). Concept of social skills with special reference to the behavior of depressed persons. *Journal of Consulting and Clinical Psychology, 40,* 304–312.

Linehan, M. M. (1979). Content validity: Its relevance to behavioral assessment. *Behavioral Assessment, 2,* 147–160.

Linehan, M. M. (1980). Structured cognitive-behavioral treatment of assertion problems. In P. C. Kendall & S. P. Hollon (Eds.), *Cognitive-behavioral interventions: Theory, research and procedures.* New York: Academic Press.

Linehan, M. M., Goldfried, M. R., & Goldfried, A. P. (1979). Assertion therapy: Skill training or cognitive restructuring. *Behavior Therapy, 10,* 372–388.

Lipton, D. N., & Nelson, R. O. (1980). The contribution of initiation behaviors to dating frequency. *Behavior Therapy, 11,* 59–67.

MacDonald, M. L., Lindquist, C. U., Kramer, J. A., McGrath, R. A., & Rhyne, L. D. (1975). Social skills training: Behavior rehearsal in groups and dating skills. *Journal of Counseling Psychology, 22,* 224–230.

McEwan, S. (1983). Isn't it time to leave minimal daters alone? *The Behavior Therapist, 6,* 101.

McFall, R. M. (1976). Behavioral training: A skill-acquisition approach to clinical problems. In J. T. Spence, R. C. Carson, & J. W. Thibaut (Eds.), *Behavioral approaches to therapy.* Morristown, NJ: General Learning.

McFall, R. M. (1977). Analogue methods in behavioral assessment: Issues and prospects. In J. D. Cone & R. P. Hawkins (Eds.), *Behavioral assessment: New directions in clinical psychology.* New York: Brunner/Mazel.

McFall, R. M. (1982). A review and reformulation of the concept of social skills. *Behavioral Assessment, 4,* 1–33.

McFall, R. M., & Twentyman, C. T. (1973). Four experiments on the relative contributors of rehearsal, modeling, and coaching on assertion training. *Journal of Abnormal Psychology, 81,* 199–218.

McGovern, K. B., Arkowitz, H., & Gilmore, S. K. (1975). Evaluation of social skills training programs for college dating inhibitions. *Journal of Counseling Psychology, 22,* 505–512.

Martinez-Diaz, J. A., & Edelstein, B. A. (1980). Heterosocial competence: Predictive and construct validity. *Behavior Modification, 4,* 115–129.

Martinson, W. D., & Zerface, J. P. (1970). Comparison of individual counseling and a social program with nondaters. *Journal of Counseling Psychology, 17,* 36–40.

Mathes, W. D., & Kahn, A. (1975). Physical attractiveness, happiness, neuroticism, and self-esteem. *Journal of Psychology, 90,* 27–30.

Meichenbaum, D. (1977). *Cognitive-behavior modification.* New York: Plenum.

Meichenbaum, D., Butler, L., & Gruson, L. (1981). Toward a conceptual model of social competence. In J. D. Wine & M. D. Smye (Eds.), *Social competence.* New York: Guilford.

Melnick, J. (1973). A comparison of replication techniques in the modification of minimal dating behavior. *Journal of Abnormal Psychology, 81,* 51–59.

Miller, W. R., & Arkowitz, H. (1977). Anxiety and perceived causation in the social success and failure experiences: Disconfirmation of an attribution hypothesis in two experiments. *Journal of Abnormal Psychology, 86,* 665–668.

Minkin, N., Braukmann, C., Minkin, B., Timbers, G., Timbers, B., Fixsen, D., Phillips, E. & Wolf, M. (1976). The social validation and training of conversational skills. *Journal of Applied Behavior Analysis, 9,* 127–139.

Moisan-Thomas, P. C., & Conger, J. C. (1980). *The effect of confederate responsivity on skill and anxiety.* Unpublished manuscript, Purdue University.

Muehlenhard, C. (1983). A response to McEwan. *The Behavior Therapist, 6,* 142.

Muehlenhard, C. L., & McFall, R. M. (1981). Dating initiation from a woman's perspective. *Behavior Therapy, 12,* 682–691.

Mullinix, S. B., & Galassi, J. P. (1981). Deriving the content of social skills training with a verbal response components approach. *Behavioral Assessment, 3,* 55–66.

Murstein, B. (1971). A theory of marital choice and its applicability to marriage adjustment. In B. Murstein (Eds.), *Theories of attraction and love.* New York: Springer.

O'Banion, K., & Arkowitz, H. (1977). Social anxiety and selective memory for affective information about the self. *Social Behavior and Personality, 5,* 321–328.

Perri, M. G., & Richards, C. A. (1977). An investigation of naturally occurring episodes of self-controlled behaviors. *Journal of Counseling Psychology, 3,* 178–183.

Perri, M. G., & Richards, C. S. (1979). Assessment of heterosocial skills in male college students: Empirical development of a behavioral role-playing test. *Behavior Modification, 3,* 337–354.

Perl, J., Hinton, R., Arkowitz, H., & Himadi, W. (1977). *Partner characteristics and the effectiveness of practice dating procedures in the treatment of minimal dating.* Paper presented at the annual meeting of the Association of the Advancement of Behavior Therapy, Atlanta.

Peterson, J., Fischetti, M., & Curran, J. P., & Arland, S. (1981). Sense of timing: A skill deficit in heterosocially-anxious women. *Behavior Therapy, 12,* 195–201.

Phibbs, J., & Arkowitz, H. (in press). Minimal dating, assertiveness, and depression. *Behavioral Counseling Quarterly.*

Phillips, E. L. (1978). *The social skills basis of psychopathology.* New York: Grune & Stratton.

Pilkonis, P. A. (1977a). Shyness, public and private, and its relationship to other measures of social behavior. *Journal of Personality, 45,* 585–595.

Pilkonis, P. A. (1977b). The behavioral consequences of shyness. *Journal of Personality, 45,* 596–611.

Purvis, J. A., Dabbs, J. M. & Hopper, C. H. (1981). *The "opener": Skilled user of facial expression.* Paper presented at the annual meeting of the American Psychological Association, Los Angeles.

Rehm, L. P., & Marston, A. R. (1968). Reduction of social anxiety through modification of self-reinforcement: An instigation therapy technique. *Journal of Consulting and Clinical Psychology, 32,* 565–574.

Rime, B., Bouvy, H., Leborgne, B., & Rouillan, F. (1978). Psychopathology and nonverbal behavior in an interpersonal situation. *Journal of Abnormal Psychology, 87,* 636–643.

Richey, C. A. (1979). *A program to increase social interaction skills among shy women.* Paper presented at the annual meeting of the American Psychological Association, New York.

Romano, J. M., & Bellack, A. S. (1980). Social validation of a component model of assertive behavior. *Journal of Consulting and Clinical Psychology, 48,* 478–490.

Royce, W. S., & Arkowitz, H. (1978). Multimodel evaluation of practice interactions as treatment for social isolation. *Journal of Consulting and Clinical Psychology, 46,* 239–245.

Royce, W. S., & Weiss, R. L. (1975). Behavioral cues in the judgement of marital satisfaction: A linear regression analysis. *Journal of Consulting and Clinical Psychology, 5,* 15–26.

Saxe, L. (1979). The ubiquity of physical appearance as a determinant of social relationships. In M. Cook & G. Wilson (Eds.), *Love and attraction.* New York: Pergamon.

Shmurak, S. H. (1973). *A comparison of types of problems encountered by college students and psychiatric inpatients in social situations.* Unpublished manuscript.

Sigall, H., & Landy, D. (1973). Radiating beauty: Effect of having a physically attractive partner on person perception. *Journal of Personality and Social Psychology, 28,* 218–224.

Singer, J. (1964). The use of manipulation strategies: Machiavellianism and attractiveness. *Sociometry, 27,* 138–150.

Smith, R. E., & Sarason, I. G. (1975). Social anxiety and the evaluation of negative interpersonal feedback. *Journal of Consulting and Clinical Psychology, 43,* 429.

Spence, S. H. (1981). Validation of social skills of adolescent males in an interview conversation with a previously unknown adult. *Journal of Applied Behavior Analysis, 14,* 159–168.

Steffen, J. J., & Reckman, R. F. (1978). Selective perception and interpretation of interpersonal cues in dyadic interactions. *The Journal of Psychology, 99,* 245–248.

Thomander, L. D. (1975). *The treatment of dating problems: Practice dating, dyadic interaction, and group discussion. Dissertation Abstracts International, 36,* 461B. (University Microfilms, No. 75-14, 850)

Trower, P. (1980). Situational analysis of the components and processes of behavior of socially skilled and unskilled patients. *Journal of Consulting and Clinical Psychology, 48,* 327–339.

Trower, P., Bryant, B. M., Argyle, M. (1978). *Social skills and mental health.* Pittsburgh: University of Pittsburgh Press.

Twentyman, C. T., & McFall, R. M. (1975). Behavioral training of social skills in shy males. *Journal of Consulting and Clinical Psychology, 43,* 384–395.

Twentyman, C. T., Boland, T., & McFall, R. M. (1981). Heterosocial avoidance in college males: Four studies. *Behavior Modification, 5,* 523–552.

Urey, J. R., Laughlin, C., & Kelly, J. A. (1979). Teaching heterosocial conversational skills to male psychiatric patients. *Journal of Behavior Therapy and Experimental Psychiatry, 10,* 323–328.

Wallander, J. L., Conger, A. J., Mariotto, M. J., Curran, J. P., & Farrell, A. D. (1980). *Behavior Therapy, 11,* 548–560.

Walster, E., Aronson, V., Abraham, D., & Rottman, L. (1966). Importance of physical attractiveness in dating behavior. *Journal of Personality and Social Psychology, 4,* 508–516.

Waxer, P. H. (1977). Nonverbal cues for anxiety: An examination of emotional leakage. *Journal of Abnormal Psychology, 86,* 306–314.

Wessberg, H. W., Mariotto, M. J., Conger, A. J., Farrell, A. D., & Conger, J. C. (1979). Ecological validity of role plays for assessing heterosocial anxiety and skill of male college students. *Journal of Consulting and Clinical Psychology, 47,* 525–535.

Williams, C. L., & Ciminero, A. R. (1978). Development and validation of a heterosocial skills inventory: The survey of heterosexual interactions for females.

Journal of Consulting and Clinical Psychology, 46, 1547–1548.

Wolf, M. M. (1978). Social validity: The case for subjective measurement or how applied behavior analysis is finding its heart. *Journal of Applied Behavior Analysis, 11,* 203–214.

Wolpe, J. (1969). *The practice of behavior therapy.* New York: Pergamon.

Wolfe, J., & Lazarus, A. A. (1966). *Behavior therapy techniques.* New York: Pergamon.

Zimbardo, P., Pilkonis, P. A., & Norwood, R. M. (1975). The social disease called shyness. *Psychology Today, 8,* 69–72.

PART TWO

Programs for Special Problems

CHAPTER 4

Life Skills Training

GEORGE M. GAZDA AND DAVID K. BROOKS

Life Skills Training (LST) is a comprehensive psychoeducational system with applications in psychotherapy, training, education, and rehabilitation. Firmly grounded in theories of human development, LST has been shown to be an effective modality for both prevention and remediation of psychological dysfunction. In its preventive applications, LST has been incorporated into school curricula at elementary and secondary levels. It has also been used with adult psychiatric inpatients, with outcomes often superior to more traditional treatment methods.

HISTORICAL BACKGROUND

Life Skills Training has evolved over the last 20 years as the result of Gazda's experiences with four movements or currents in contemporary psychological thought and practice. The first of these movements was group counseling and psychotherapy. The 1960s were probably the high-water mark of intense interest and experimentation in this area. Group approaches to therapy were advocated in texts (Gazda, 1968, 1969; Lifton, 1966; Slavson, 1964), explored in research reports and literature reviews (Lieberman, Yalom & Miles, 1973), and engaged in by practitioners and participants of every stripe. Gazda and his students conducted groups with schoolchildren of all ages, professional educators, psychiatric patients, recovering alcoholics, juvenile delinquents, convicted felons, and adults seeking personal growth, among others. Many of these activities were the subjects of doctoral dissertations and other research projects, whereas others were performed for the purpose of providing clinical training opportunities and community.

The second influential movement was the work of developmental theorists such as Erik Erikson (1950, 1963), Robert J. Havighurst (1953, 1972), and Donald E. Super, Crites, Hummel, Moser, Overstreet, & Warnath (1957) and Super (1963). These writers and others assumed that normal human development proceeded along a path from the simple to the complex; that development was more or less orderly, predictable, and age and/or stage related; and that progress from one developmental stage to the next depended upon mstery of appropriate developmental tasks. Their terminology and the finer points of their theories differed somewhat, but psychosocial development (Erikson, 1950, 1963; Havighurst, 1953, 1972) and vocational development (Super, 1963; Super et al., 1957) were viewed as organizing frameworks from which the coping skills appropriate to the tasks of normal development could be abstracted.

Group Counseling: A Developmental Approach

Gazda (1971) synthesized his experiences and research in group counseling with the growing conviction of the importance of developmental theories. The primary thesis was that the group counseling modality was applicable to a wide range of settings and client concerns and that it was most effective when the developmental needs of the particular age group being served were taken into account. It was hypothesized that preventive measures were likely to be more effective if deficits in coping skills could be regularly monitored. Remedial efforts therefore need not wait until clients were well beyond the optimum age for learning developmentally appropriate coping skills.

The second edition of *Group Counseling: A Developmental Approach* (Gazda, 1978) presented a broadened view of the developing person, adding to the existing psychosocial and vocational perspectives the dimensions of physical-sexual development, (Gesell, Ilg, Ames, 1946 and Bullis, 1956), cognitive development, a la Piaget (Flavell, 1963; Wadsworth, 1971), and moral development (Kohlberg, 1973; Kohlberg & Turiel, 1971). More recently the stages of ego development (Loevinger, 1976) and of affective development (Dupont, 1978) have been incorporated with the perspectives mentioned before into what is believed to be a conceptualization of the whole developing person (Gazda, 1984). From this model life skills can be abstracted, which are appropriate to all ages and stages of human development. These life skills are directly related to the successful accomplishment of developmental tasks appropriate to age and/or stage.

The third movement influential in the development of LST was Robert Carkhuff's work in human relations development during the late 1960s and early 1970s. Gazda was involved with several colleagues in the experimental application of interpersonal communication skills training to a variety of groups. Based on these experiences, Gazda et al.

developed training manuals for educators (1973, 1976, 1977, 1984), health care practitioners (1975, 1982), adolescents (1980), and criminal justice personnel (Sisson, Arthur, & Gazda, 1981). A decade's experience with the training approaches outlined in these materials has led to the conclusion that the *whole* person can be treated through *direct* training.

Concurrent with these developments was the experience of others using similar approaches. Based on the assumption that interpersonal skills are essential for progress in therapy, release from hospitalization, and reduced likelihood of readmission, Pierce and Drasgow (1969) implemented a systematic human relations training program for a group of chronic neuropsychiatric patients at a Veterans Administration (VA) hospital. This group received 20 hours of interpersonal communication skills training. Compared with four control groups receiving drug treatment, individual therapy, group therapy, and a combination of these, the experimental group was released from the hospital with greater frequency than control group members and had fewer readmissions.

The long-term effectiveness of such training has been demonstrated by another study, again involving VA patients, but in a different hospital. Powell and Clayton (1980) found that patients receiving interpersonal communication skills training experienced markedly lower rehospitalization rates two years after treatment than did a control group.

In a major literature review, Authier et al. (1975) made a persuasive case for training as the preferred mode of treatment. Psychotherapists should view themselves as teachers or trainers and their approaches to treatment as educational interventions. Training-as-treatment, then, is the fourth movement influential in the development of LST. Gazda's experience over the last decade as a consultant to the psychiatric division of a VA medical center has drawn these four elements—group counseling, developmental theories, human relations development, and training-as-treatment—together into a systematic, comprehensive approach that is the remedial dimension of LST. Interpersonal communication skills training was again found to be effective, but the conclusion was gradually reached that no *single* intervention could be expected to ameliorate *multiple* life skills deficits in patients who showed only modest gains after such training. It was hypothesized that multiple deficits should be addressed with multiple interventions.

After recruiting staff expertise from across health care disciplines, several LST modules were developed. In addition to interpersonal communication skills, training modules have been employed in career development, purpose in life, physical fitness/health maintenance, and problem solving, among others. May (1981) found that patients whose treatment program consisted of LST groups demonstrated significantly higher ratings of interpersonal communication and reported higher levels of meaningful purpose in life than those who received neither direct skills training nor a psychoeducational rationale for their treatment.

Preventive applications of LST were developed after the success of the system as a remedial modality had been demonstrated. A forerunner of this approach was the 1969 yearbook of the Association for Supervision and Curriculum Development—*Life Skills in School and Society* (Rubin, 1969). This collection of essays advocated the position that schools have the responsibility for preparing students for the business of living and that the scope of schooling ought to extend far beyond traditional academic skills development. A similar note was struck by Norman Sprinthall and Ralph Mosher (Mosher & Sprinthall, 1970, 1971; Sprinthall & Mosher, 1969)

in their work in "deliberate psychological education." Also influential were research reports such as that of the National Assessment of Educational Progress (1975), confirming how poorly our nation's schools were preparing students for the business of effective living. In speeches before professional audiences (Gazda, 1977), Gazda called for attention to "developmental education," an approach advocated concurrently by the Minnesota Department of Education (Miller, 1976). Others were pursuing parallel efforts during the 1970s. Adkins (1974) used the term *life-coping skills* as a rubric for his work with disadvantaged youth and adults. Life Skills Training (Gazda & Brooks, 1980) emerged as a synthesis of the previously mentioned influences and Gazda's experiences with psychiatric patients. The position was taken that, regardless of the setting, the primary objective of LST is the teaching/training of critical life skills related to the tasks and stages of various areas of human development.

During the late 1970s Gazda became involved as a consultant to an alternative education program at an elementary school in the Midwest. This program was the first attempt on the U.S. mainland to implement Corsini's (1977) "individual education" (IE) approach that was developed earlier in Hawaii. Initial work involved communication skills training for faculty and staff. Later, the LST group interventions originally developed at the VA medical center were adapted for use with pupils in the IE school. Setting, population, and intent were dramatically different, but feedback from pupils and staff indicated real promise for LST as a key element in the curriculum.

More recently, a series of LST modules have been developed for use with high school students. Research on the effectiveness of these efforts is sparse at present, but indications are strong that inclusion of LST in public school curricula can exert a powerful positive influence in a preventive sense on the future mental health of our citizens.

The position is taken (Gazda & Brooks, 1980) that Life Skills Training should be considered as an organizing framework for service delivery in university counseling centers, community mental health centers, and other multipurpose agencies. Because one of the benefits of an LST program is believed to be that it makes more effective use of staff time and talents, it is possible that cuts in human services budgets will hasten the time when LST or a similar approach will be implemented by these agencies.

THEORETICAL RATIONALE

The rationale for Life Skills Training rests on the following assumptions:

1.   Within the multiple dimensions of human development (i.e., psychosocial, vocational, physical-sexual, cognitive, moral, ego, and affective), there are *stages* through which all persons must progress if they are to lead effective lives. Some of these are age related; some are not.

2.   Satisfactory progression through the stages depends upon the successful accomplishment of *developmental tasks* (Havighurst, 1972) that are specific to the stages.

3.   Accomplishment of the developmental tasks is dependent upon mastery of *life skills* approrpiate to stage and task.

4.   Each individual encounters many agents (parents, siblings, teachers, peers, social institutions, etc.) through which life skills may be learned.

5.   There are certain age ranges in which certain life skills can be learned most easily.

6.   Individuals inherit their capacity for learning, but the degree to which they are able to achieve their maximum po-

tential is the result of the interaction between their genetic inheritance, their environment, and their life experiences.

7.   Individuals achieve optimal functioning when they attain operational mastery of fundamental life skills.

8.   Neuroses and functional psychoses frequently result from failure to develop one's life skills. Persons experiencing such dysfunctions are usually suffering from multiple life skills deficits. Within the context of an interview counseling group of in individual consultation with a therapist, such persons are able to identify their life skills deficits as well as the areas in which life skills mastery has been attained.

9.   Life skills can be taught most effectively through the medium of the small group, provided members are developmentally ready. Therefore, the most satisfactory means of ensuring positive mental health and of remediating psychological dysfunction when it occurs is through direct teaching/training in life skills, especially if two or more areas of life skills deficits are addressed concurrently (Gazda & Brooks, 1980).

Life skills are defined as any learned behaviors that are necessary for effective living, including requisite knowledge or conditions for the development or acquisition of such behaviors.* Such a broad definition obviously presents problems as well as benefits. Literally anything that human beings learn can be considered a life skill, so there is a need to be more specific as to what should be included in a program of Life Skills Training. On the other hand, such breadth allows for infinite flexibility in training with different populations in different settings.

Developmental tasks are defined by Havighurst (1972) as tasks that arise "at or about a certain period in the life of the

*Brooks, D. K. Jr. (1982). *Life-skills questionnaire*. Unpublished manuscript, University of Georgia.

individual, successful achievement of which leads to his happiness and to success with later tasks, while failure leads to unhappiness in the individual, disapproval by the society, and difficulty with later tasks'' (p. 2).

Can the major life skills be enumerated? Can they be classified under broad generic headings so that program development and/or treatment become more manageable? To answer these questions a 2-year Delphi survey was undertaken by Brooks (1984). The purpose of the study was to survey expert opinion to list major life skills for childhood, adolescence, and adulthood and then to classify these into generic categories across the life span. Based on the Delphi results and collapsing categories, Brooks (1984) was able to identify four generic life skill categories:

Fitness/health maintenance skills. These are skills necessary for motor development and coordination, nutritional maintenance, weight control, physical fitness, athletic participation, physiological aspects of sexuality, stress management, leisure activity selection, and the like.

Identity development/purpose in life skills. These are skills and awareness necessary for ongoing development of personal identity, including self-monitoring, maintenance of self-esteem, manipulating and accommodating to one's environment, clarifying values, sex-role development, making meaning, learning morals/values dimensions of sexuality, and so on.

Interpersonal communication/human relations skills. These are skills necessary for effective communication, both verbal and nonverbal, with others, including "core conditions" of empathy, warmth, and genuineness, clear expression of ideas and opinions, confrontation, giving and receiving feedback, and so forth.

Problem-solving/decision-making skills. These are skills necessary for information seeking, information assessment and analysis, problem identification, solution, implementation, and evaluation, goal setting, systematic planning and forecasting, time management, critical thinking, and the like.

THE TRAINING PROCESS

The training process of the LST system does not lend itself to elegant description at this point in its development. The theoretical assumptions upon which LST rests are the result of empirical eclecticism. The same process is operating in the development of the training model, but it is not quite so far along.

Even though LST has not reached the stage of a full-blown training paradigm, it is both possible and desirable to comment on the training process at its present state of development. Fundamental to the success of the system has been its reliance on the small group as the primary training vehicle. The small group medium is utilized in both the train-the-trainers and the training-as-treatment stages of the model. LST groups are similar in composition, structure, and dynamics to structured groups described frequently in recent literature (e.g., Drum & Knott, 1977), although the agenda for the LST group may be somewhat more flexible.

It is posited that learning and skills development in both stages take place as the result of the following sequence:

1. Brief instruction.
2. Leader Modeling.
3. Demonstration using simulations.
4. Trainee role playing and practice.
5. Feedback.
6. Homework.

The topical focus of LST groups necessitates a certain amount of didactic presentation of information, but such activity is kept to minimum except when the purpose of the groups is training trainers. It is important that trainers-in-training understand in more depth the developmental goals and processes inherent in training. Leader/facilitators model the target skills/behaviors throughout training. Simulated demonstrations, usually involving the facilitator and one or more trainees, are the next step, enabling trainees to understand the target behaviors more concretely. Practice via role playing follows, with frequent feedback from the leader and other trainees. At least half of each session is devoted to such practice, interspersed with appropriate feedback. Homework is regularly assigned, with the beginning of the following session devoted to individual reporting. There are, of course, elements of each LST group that are idiosyncratic to the leader and the trainees, but the sequential elements of brief didactic instruction, modeling, simulations, role playing, practice, feedback, and homework comprise the underlying training approach.

Essential Elements

The following items represent the essential elements incorporated in the LST model:

1.   Life skills are generated from the coping behaviors appropriate to the developmental tasks of a given age/stage (and sex, where applicable) across the seven dimensions of human development described previously.

2.   A Mastery learning model (cf. Bloom, 1976) is implemented whenever the life skills are hierarchical or progressive in nature.

3.   Activities are utilized throughout training to accommodate the three basic modes of learning: auditory, visual, and kinesthetic.

4.   Generic life skills are assumed to be a family of related skills that can be taught much like other subject-matter areas according to the developmental readiness of the client/trainee/student.

5.   The same training procedures are applied when teaching life skills for prevention as when teaching them for remediation. This is also true whether the goal is treatment or training trainers, although there is more didactic instruction with the latter goal.

6.   Extensive supervised practice is the core of training, utilizing role playing and simulation to ensure skills development.

7.   Homework is utilized to facilitate transfer of learned skills into everyday living for trainees/clients.

8.   Peer trainers are utilized whenever possible (especially when the goal is treatment) to increase transfer of learning and the credibility of the training process.

9.   Self-monitoring is emphasized and, where possible, scales for self-rating are employed.

10.   Trainees may repeat portions of training (or, if necessary, the entire training program) to increase and to solidify skills development.

11.   Training is based on an educational/instructional model rather than a treatment approach.

12.   A wide variety of training materials and methods are used, including extensive use of videotape recorders and playback equipment.

13.   Co-trainers are utilized in many instances to increase individualization of training.

14.   The training time, including length of sessions, spacing of sessions, and duration of training is flexible to accommodate the needs of trainees/clients at different levels of readiness.

15.   Training is conducted is small groups of 6 to 12 trainees/clients.

16.   Trainees are taught in a four-step pyramid sequence during which they

move from the role of trainee to that of trainer. Clients/patients may also, in special circumstances, progress through two or three steps of this sequence.

Pyramid of Training

All trainers are expected to achieve mastery of the generic life skill(s) that they are to teach. Mastery of the specific skills that make up the generic life skill(s) is essential in order to be able to model the skills effectively and to monitor skill development by trainees/clients. Trainers assume a range of roles including teacher, model, monitor/evaluator, motivator, encourager, facilitator, protector, and training media developer. The training activities most frequently used in each step of the training pyramid include the following:

Step 1.   Training in generic life skills.
1. Didactic presentation of the rationale for the model of the given life skill to be taught—"tell".
2. Modeling or demonstration of the behavior(s) or response(s) to be mastered—"show".
3. Role playing and practice by trainees/clients of the skills to be mastered—"do".
4. Self-monitoring/assessment (as well as monitoring/assessment by trainer and fellow trainees/clients) of skill level achieved—"feedback".
5. Trainees/clients assist each other in developing skills—"peer bonding".
6. Homework application of new skill(s) to daily living—"transfer."
Step 2.   Co-training with "master" trainer. This step always occurs, as do Steps 3 and 4, in the train-the-trainers stage of the model. It *may* also occur in the training-as-treatment stage in instances in which trainee/clients achieve mastery of one life skill, but are still working on others. In these cases, trainee/clients functioning as

peer helpers have proven beneficial in adding credibility to the training-as-treatment process.
Step 3.   Training under supervision of "master" trainer.
Step 4.   Training alone.

Steps 2, 3, and 4 contain within them the six elements of Step 1, but in each case the former trainee is gradually progressing through the status of co-trainer to becoming able to train without supervision.

The Life Skills Trainer

Because the LST system assumes that there are a number of generic life skills categories, it is important for trainers to decide which of the generic skills they will develop as specialties. Although it is possible to become an expert trainer in all of the skills areas, it is unlikely that most trainers will choose to specialize in more than two or three of them. Trainers generally develop expertise in skills areas that are somewhat closely related. For example, a trainer may wish to specialize in interpersonal communication/human relations skills and in the related area of problem-solving/decision-making skills. Regardless of the areas of intended specialization, all prospective trainers are first expected to become expert in interpersonal communication/human relations skills.

Once mastery of the generic life skills areas has been attained, attention is next focused on the group leadership skills a trainer must possess in order to be effective. Because LST typically involves didactic instruction, modeling, and practice, the group skills required of trainers include those of teacher as well as more typical group facilitation skills.

Teacher

As teacher, the trainer's first task is to determine the level of skills attainment as well as areas of skills deficits for potential group members. This task may be accomplished through interviews, staffings, psychological evaluations as well as less structured assessments and case history notes. A second task is to select training materials appropriate to the readiness level of the trainees/clients. The materials must then be organized according to a training schedule based on the length of time for training and the frequency of training sessions. Appropriate utilization of print and audiovisual media, especially videotape recorders, must be considered at this stage. Lesson plans for each session should be developed prior to the actual training. The nature of the skills to be developed will dictate the choice of instructional modes. Bloom's (1976) mastery learning model provides helpful structure and rationale for instruction.

Facilitator/Counselor

Carkhuff (1969a, 1969b) contended that effective facilitators must offer high levels of the "core conditions" of empathy, warmth, and respect as well as the more action-oriented dimensions of concreteness, genuineness, appropriate self-disclosure, confrontation, and immediacy. Life skills trainers are first trained systematically to offer effective levels of these dimensions of interpersonal communication/human relations skills. Until such skills are mastered, any attempt to teach other life skills will be unsuccessful.

Leader as Model

Bandura (1977) identified four processes in observational learning to explain the completed learning event: (1) attention; (2) retentin; (3) motor reproduction; and (4) motivation. Observer attention is influenced by the nature of the model. Characteristics such as interpersonal attractiveness, warmth, nurturance, perceived competence, perceived social power, age similarity, sex, and socioeconomic status influence the observer's attending behavior. Observer characteristics such as dependency, level of competence, sex, race, socioeconomic status, and previous social learning experiences are also related to learning.

The observed behavior must be symbolically coded to be retained. This coding can be either imaginal or verbal. Once coding has occurred, retention is enhanced by rehearsal strategies (Holland & Kobasigawan, 1980).

Motor reproduction of the images and thoughts acquired though observation depends upon the availability of the motor skills to the observer. When several components are to be mastered for motor reproduction, the missing or deficient skills must first be developed by observation and practice.

The motivational process is influenced by external reinforcement. Learned responses that are likely to result in direct external positive consequences are expressed overtly, whereas those that lead to neutral consequences or that may be negatively reinforced will probably not be translated into behavior. Modeled behavior is likely to be acquired and performed if the observed person is positively reinforced. If punishment is observed, the behavior will probably be suppressed (Holland & Kobasigawan, 1980). The observer may also manifest or inhibit an observed behavior based on evaluations of his/her own behavior compared to standards that have been assimilated through observation (Bandura & Kupers, 1964).

The effect of modeling in LST takes into account the characteristics outlined previously. Models are often presented on videotape after prior orientation (through didactic instruction) as to the rationale for the behavior to be modeled. Situations involving both positive and negative reinforcement are shown. In vivo modeling follows a similar program.

Fellow trainees are often used as models to accommodate sex and age similarity.

Leader Use of Role Playing

According to Shaw, Corsini, Blake, & Mouton (1980), no one has yet povided a completely satisfactory theory to explain the value of role playing for the purpose of changing human behavior. Nevertheless, role playing includes several features that appear to aid in behavioral change. Some of these features are an emphasis on personal concerns or problems, emphasis on personal behavior, active participation, feedback, and practice.

In order that training procedures are not too hypothetical or impersonal, role plays are based on relevant personal concerns of the trainee. Bradford (1945) stressed the importance of relevance and concreteness of the role play to the role player. Thus, when the role play is relevant to the client's own concerns or behaviors, he/she is motivated to experiment with more effective approaches as suggested through trainer critiques and feedback.

Bohart (1977), French (1945), and Moody (1953) note the importance of *active* involvement of the role player. They contend that role playing breaks through the verbal barriers and generates insights and skills where other methods fail. Research by Huyck (1975), O'Donnell (1954), and Planty (1948) supports their contention. Role playing, therefore, provides the trainee/client the opportunity to participate actively in the subject matter being studied through exploring, experimenting, and actually trying out new solutions (Shaw, et al., 1980).

Moody (1953) found that role playing can be used to expand social awareness, whereas Stahl (1953), Speroff (1953), and Cohen (1951) showed that it can be used to increase personal respect for the feelings of others. These characteristics are related to the *feedback* dimensions of

role playing. Feedback helps the client to identify his/her blind spots and to receive the kind of information that he/she ordinarily fails to see or hear. The trainee/client can check perceptions against those of others and can evaluate this behavior as well as that of others. Alternative ways of behaving that are explored under feedback conditions can be evaluated instantly. By testing various reactions the client can learn to be more comfortable when practicing new behavior (Shaw et al., 1980)

Finally, role playing allows trainees/clients to *practice* more effective methods of relating to others (Stahl, 1953). "The idea of skill practice is as appropriate in improving human relationships as it is in learning any new physical skill" (Shaw et al., 1980, p. 22). The position taken here is that a major deficit in current approaches to psychotherapy is the almost total lack of opportunity for clients to practice and perfect new responses or behaviors prior to using them in everyday life. Frequent use of role playing and behavioral rehearsal in Life Skills Training circumvents this problem.

Leader Facilitation of Transfer of Training

Several features of the LST model are aimed at ensuring the transfer of what is learned in training to the trainee/client's daily living. First, the training is typically done in small groups of 6 to 12. The use of the small group permits a degree of personal intimacy and cohesiveness that contributes to support and motivation. From a learning viewpoint, the small group represents a microcosm of society and helps to ensure stimulus variability. Skills learned in this context are more likely to transfer to a variety of situations that clients encounter on a daily basis.

Second, homework assignments between training sessions facilitate transfer. These assignments vary from workbook exercises that are intended to increase one's cognitive understanding of a given life skill to assignments that involve practice of the skill with significant others. The use of personal journals also facilitates self-monitoring of behavior that occurs between training sessions. In addition to the journal, self-rating devices are presented so that the trainee/client can monitor personal performance. For example, in interpersonal communication/human relations skills, a scale for rating one's global level of functioning is taught (see Global Scale in Gazda, Walters, & Childers 1975; Gazda, Asbury, Balzer, Childers, & Walters, 1977). In fitness/health maintenance skills, trainees are taught how to monitor their pulse rate during exercise activities.

Third, training is given to all members of a specific work, family, or educational unit so that external monitoring and mutual reinforcement can be built into the system. In other words, training is directed toward subsystems to enable them to play a constructive role in enhancing transfer of life skills.

Finally, trainee/clients are encouraged to attend intermittent "booster shot" training sessions to maintain their skill level. These sessions are analogous to in-service education for professionals such as teachers, physicians, and engineers. Learning life skills is considered to be a lifelong endeavor. Like any other skill, disuse can lead to deterioration.

Training Materials Required

The amount and kind of materials required vary with the generic life skill being taught. For example, when teaching fitness/health maintenance skills, one may use printed handouts dealing with basic food groups or effects of certain drugs on the body. Slides might be used to accompany minilectures on nutrition.

For exercise routines, exercise equipment may be employed along with monitoring devices for measuring physical stress, blood pressure, body weight, and changes in body conformity. The Health Hazard Appraisal (Milsum, 1980) may be given to assess and give computer feedback on a person's health assets and health hazards.

In teaching interpersonal communication/human relations skills, there is frequent use of books such as *Human Relations Development: A Manual for Health Sciences* (Gazda et al., 1975), *Realtalk: Exercises in Friendship and Helping Skills* (Gazda, Walters, & Childers, 1980), and *Human Relations Development: A Manual for Educators* (Gazda et al., 1977). Videotaped lectures are available, as are videotaped and slide-tape examples of appropriate and inappropriate responses. Trainee/clients can be videotaped as they practice to provide feedback opportunities. Rating scales can be used to enable trainee/clients to evaluate their performance and that of other training group members. The trainer is expected to accommodate the preferred learning styles of group members by providing a balanced use of materials appealing to auditory, visual, and kinesthetic learning modes.

Organizational Support/Resources Needed

Interdisciplinary cooperation is the key to success for LST in a treatment context. A motivating factor for such cooperation is the opportunity for professionals and paraprofessionals from various disciplines to choose a generic life skills area of special interest and to develop expertise in this area, usually working with a colleague from a different discipline but with similar interests. For example, in the VA medical center where the LST system has been under development, a clinical nurse specialist, a social worker, and a psychologist coordinate the LST program. A dietitian and a corrective therapist teach the fitness/health maintenance skills area. A nurse, a psychologist, and a social worker teach interpersonal communication/human relations skills. A chaplain teaches what is called the identity development/purpose-in-life skills area. Inservice training was provided for all trainers prior to initiating the LST model. A similar approach could be used in training community health and mental health personnel.

Interdisciplinary cooperation is a necessity for the success of LST when used for remediation or prevention. A secondary benefit is the increased communication and respect that dvelops between specialists from different disciplines, not to mention improvement in staff morale. Adequate physical space, availability of materials, and enlightened personnel are all necessary for a successful LST program. Also useful is the assistance of an audiovisual specialist who can provide access to videotape recording and playback equipment and who can train other staff members in its use.

Example of an LST Unit

What follows is an example of one unit or module outline from the LST program developed and implemented at the VA medical center:

I. *Name of group.* Decision-making/problem-solving training.
II. *Purpose.* Provide skill training to teach method of exploring and solving problems.
III. *Objectives.* At the completion of the training the learner will be able to:
    A. Identify primary values in his/her values hierarchy.
    B. Identify basic problem in problem areas.
    C. List and evaluate courses of action.
    D. Employ problem-solving technique to reach a decision.
    E. Identify step-by-step goals in implementing the decision.
IV. *Procedure.*
    A. *Selection of trainees/group members.* The following criteria will be used in selection of group members:
        1. Veterans who are actively psychotic are not candidates for this group.
        2. Veterans with organic brain syndrome with impaired reasoning abilities are not candidates.
        3. Veterans who acknowledge a need for problem-solving and decision-making skills will benefit from inclusion.
        4. Veterans who have had interpersonal communication/human relations skills training and/or assertiveness training are good candidates for this group.
        5. Veterans should be able to read and write to participate fully.
        6. Veterans must be willing to make commitment to continue the group the full 2 weeks.
    B. *Group size.* Eight (8) patients in a closed group.
    C. *Schedule.* Monday–Thursday 8:30–9:30 A.M. in Room 21, Building 94. The last 2 weeks of each month.
    D. *Description of Training.* Trainers will provide didactic instruction, demonstrations and return demonstrations,

paper-and-pencil exercises as follows:

1. Introduction to group members and purpose of training.
2. Values clarification exercises.
3. Introduction to *The Art of Problem Solving*, teaching the Carkhuff model in the following sequence:
   a. Exploration of problem areas.
   b. Identification of specific problem.
   c. Identification of realistic goal.
   d. Identification of all possible courses of action.
   e. Application of model.
   f. Demonstrations of use of the model, determining values hierarchy and weights of actions.
   g. Group participation on problem presented by each member using the model.
   h. Identification of "best" solution.
4. Evaluation of chosen solutions in terms of benefits and consequences.
5. Identification of small-step goals toward the implementation of the solution.
6. Teach purpose and value of commitments toward change.

V. *Evaluation.*
   A. Evaluation of training will be done by:
      1. Trainers' critiques.
      2. Questionnaire given to members at the conclusion of training.
   B. Evaluation of effects of training on participants will be done by:
      1. Self-report questionnaire.
      2. Instrument (to be developed for the LST evaluation form) administered pre- and post-training.

Name of Trainer: Kathy Brown, Staff Nurse.

CASE EXAMPLE *

If an observer were to "shadow" an individual patient during the course of treatment, something akin to the following actual case example might be noted. The patient's name has been changed, and minor details of the case have been altered in the interest of preserving confidentiality and the patient's privacy.

Presenting History

Mr. Green is a 30-year-old white male Vietnam War veteran. He had been admitted to the hospital by his mother because he was depressed over the loss of his job (carpenter's helper) and had threatened suicide. His mother reported that Mr. Green had had several serious episodes of drinking and that he had been fired from his last job because of drunkenness.

Mr. Green is a high school graduate with some vocational training. He entered a vocational-technical school following his military discharge, but he dropped out soon after getting married. He felt that he had made a mistake in quitting school.

Mr. Green described himself as shy. He had few friends (no close friends at all), and he frequently had to rely on his

*Provided by Mildred Powell, R.N., VA Medical Center, Augusta, GA.

wife for financial support when he was out of work. His wife is employed as a clerk. They have two children—a girl, 9, and a boy, 8.

Mr. Green also reported that he escaped from his troubles through drinking. He began drinking when he was in Vietnam. He had also used other drugs briefly while in service. Mr. Green's stated concern was the lack of progress in his work. He stated, "I'm not getting anywhere and I'm not progressing in job stability."

During his 3 meetings in the screening group prior to his referral for LST, Mr. Green voiced the same concerns cited before and requested assignment to the following groups: identity development/purpose in life, interpersonal communication/relationships, and vocational/career development. He was interviewed by the leader of the problem-drinking group and was also accepted into that group.

The following life skills deficits were identified by Mr. Green and his therapists:

Interpersonal communication/human relations. Had difficulty in conversations and sharing his problems; was shy, lonely, and nonassertive

Identity development/purpose-in-life. Felt he lost his purpose for living; threatened suicide because he felt he was a failure.

Vocational/career development. Had not followed through on his vocational school plans; work record was poor with frequent unemployment.

Fitness/health maintenance. Frequent episodes of drunkenness; poor fitness habits.

Leisure time. No hobbies or leisure activities outside of going to bars.

Problem-solving/decision-making. Used alcohol to avoid facing problems.

Family/marital relationships. Re-

sented his dependence on his wife and often felt inadequate as a father.

On the positive side, Mr. Green had above average intelligence, had a supportive wife, was physically able, was cooperative, and this was his first hospitalization.

Patient Progress

Mr. Green remained in the hospital for 5 weeks. During the first 2 weeks he participated in the following LST groups: identity development/purpose in life, interpersonal communication/human relations, and vocational/career development. Concurrently, he participated in the problem-drinking group, and remained in it for an additional 3 weeks.

Following completion of the three initial LST groups, Mr. Green volunteered for two more LST groups: problem-solving/decision-making, and fitness/health maintenance, thereby participating in all but one of the LST groups then available plus the auxiliary probem-drinking group. At the time of his discharge, he also agreed to follow-up counseling at a community mental health center.

The following progress report illustrates Mr. Green's behavioral changes

Interpersonal communication/human relations. Was able to self-disclose personal feelings and to be more specific in his communications; felt more comfortable in conversations on the ward; was more assertive in giving his opinions.

Identity development/purpose-in-life. Participated in group attempts to seek meaning from the things that happen in life, and had several talks with the chaplain.

Vocational/career development. Took interest and aptitude inventories; explored vocational options; was admitted to vocational school to resume his studies in carpentry.

Fitness/health maintenance. Attended every group session and developed a regimen of physical exercise including stretching and jogging; modified his diet to reduce alcoholic beverages.

Leisure time. Began a regular reading program in the hospital library, and worked regularly in the hospital green house.

Problem-solving/decision-making
Used a problem-solving model to decide to reenter vocational school.

Because Mr. Green's is a fairly recent case, there is no follow-up data to present that might indicate the posttreatment impact of LST in terms of successful adjustment or readmission to the hospital. The results of research studies indicate that patients participating in LST are readmitted less frequently and adjust to the demands of everyday life more satisfactorily than those receiving only traditional psychotherapy.

CLINICAL CONSIDERATIONS

Life Skills Training as a treatment modality is still in a state of evolutionary development. Expanding from a base of interpersonal communication skills training, other modules have been developed that are somewhat less established and systematic in their training procedures and less well supported by a substantial body of research studies. What is known is that LST *works* with patients. They become more involved in taking responsibility for the course of their treatment. Staff observations indicate that they are more motivated than patients receiving more traditional forms of treatment. Enthusiasm by staff members is a secondary gain not to be underestimated. A broad base of staff commitment tends to create an environment in which patient progress is *expected* rather than such progress being greeted with surprise. It is believed that such broad staff involve-

ment has led to a spirit of inventiveness in treatment approaches, to a willingness to challenge traditional but ineffective practices, and to a certain degree of risk taking while keeping patients' best interests uppermost in mind. This spirit of inventiveness and challenge has characterized such clinical aspects as diagnosis, assessment of progress, and criteria for release from hospitalization.

Diagnosis

Diagnosis of patients' specific disorders is not a matter of primary concern to life skills trainers. Patients are considered to be potential candidates for LST unless they are actively psychotic or their reasoning abilities are impaired by organic brain syndrome. Patients are referred for LST consideration by ward personnel in consultation with the primary therapist. Determination of LST eligibility is accomplished by several possible means. The most common determinant is patient staffing that serves a screening function. Patients have shown that in such a setting they are quite capable of identifying their life skills deficits and, with staff support, of consenting to requesting assignment to the LST groups most appropriate to their needs. Entry into LST may also be accomplished through consultation with a patient's individual therapist. Additionally, ward personnel monitor case histories to identify patients who might benefit from LST but who may be otherwise overlooked.

Participation in LST is strictly voluntary. Once involved in the program, patients are expected to complete their initial, jointly negotiated, training regimen unless it becomes obvious that their participation is counterproductive to their own progress or destructive to the training process. Such instances are rare, however.

Assessment of Progress

As illustrated by the preceding example of an LST unit, training objectives are specified in behavioral terms. When the unit is completed, those patients meeting the exit criteria are "graduated" to the next unit in the generic life skills sequence or enter training in a different life skills area. As dictated by the mastery learning concept, patients needing additional training and practice are permitted to do just that until mastery is achieved. Again, the voluntary principle operates. Patients are not forced into the next unit nor are they coerced to remain in their original unit. Negotiation and collaboration between patients and staff are ongoing procedures. Patients are not, however, permitted to participate in any LST group for which they have not mastered the prerequisite skills. Skills mastery is entered into patient records as are all pertinent treatment notes.

Criteria for Release

As is the case with diagnosis, release from treatment is not a matter of primary concern for life skills trainers. Such decisions are always based on a variety of factors, regardless of the treatment modality employed. It is noteworthy, however, that there is in almost all cases a direct relationship between success in training and other measures of patient progress, for example, decrease in medication, increased ward sociability, successful coping during weekend leaves, reported confidence at being able to "make it on the outside," and so forth. Participation in LST aids making recommendations and decisions about release because of the concrete, behavioral nature of entries in the records of patient/trainees. One can only complete a training unit by demonstrating the responsible prosocial behaviors that are also weighted heavily in release decisions.

At present, even though LST may be the only "treatment" a patient receives, decisions about reentry into the world outside the hospital are still based on some criteria from other treatment approaches. As LST increasingly becomes accepted as an effective treatment modality, it is expected that skills mastery will be the primary basis for decisions about release from treatment.

PREVENTIVE APPLICATIONS

Thus far, this chapter has focused almost exclusively on the train-the-trainer and training-as-treatment dimensions of LST. At least equally important is the developmental, training-as-prevention aspect. The theoretical assumptions and the framework of the training process are the same for prevention as for treatment. Trainers in preventive situations must possess the same skills as those involved in treatment. What is different is the characteristics of the target population, the content of the training units, and the aim of training as ensuring that life skills are mastered at the most developmentally appropriate ages and/or stages so that life skills deficits do not occur later in life. If one accepts the adage of an ounce of prevention being worth a pound of cure, then the preventive applications of LST are more important as a social agenda than are those of a remedial nature. (See the section on historical background for brief summaries of LST programs in elementary and secondary schools.) To date, training materials have been developed for four school systems. The following examples of training units will indicate their similarity in structure to units designed for psychiatric patients. The differences in content as well as their developmental, preventive intent should also be apparent.

Example of an LST Unit for Elementary Schools

I. Life skill: Interpersonal communication/human relations

II. Unit 2: Getting messages

III. Optional session, grades 4 and 5: Reflecting feeling and content

IV. Learner's objectives:
The student will reflect feelings and content of the speaker's messages.
Special Instructions: If students have mastered reflecting feelings, they are ready to move to reflecting feelings and content. Use as many of these activities as you have time for, selecting the ones that have the greatest appeal to your group.

V. Grades 4 and 5
Activity 1: Writing Responses: Feeling and content (10 minutes)
Say: "A person feels even more understood when the listener reflects feelings and content, or what the speaker is feeling and why he/she feels that way. An easy way to reflect feeling and content is to use the form, "You feel _____ when _____ _____." "Let's try writing responses." (Distribute worksheet). "Do the first and second writing examples; then we'll talk about them." (After discussion, have students complete exercise.)

Activity 2: Fishbowl (10 minutes)
The group is seated in a circle. Tell the students to think of something that happened to them the previous day that they felt strongly about. Ask someone to tell about that experience. As he/she talks, the leader is to model good listening behavior. Then, reflect the speaker's feeling and content using the form, "You feel _____ when _____." Next the listener becomes the speaker. Continue until each has been speaker and a listener.

Activity 3: Triad practice (10 minutes)
Divide the group into triads. The speaker is to talk about "the best things about this school" or "the worst things about this school" for 2 minutes. The listener is to reflect the feelings and content. The observer is to let the listener know how well he/she did. Rotate roles.

VI. Resources needed: For Activity 1, worksheets for each student.

VII. Learning styles: Auditory, visual, kinesthetic

VIII. Bloom's taxonomy:
A. Cognitive domain: Knowledge, comprehension, application.
B. Affective domain: Receiving, responding.

**Example of an LST Unit for
High Schools**

I. Generic life skill: Identity development/purpose in life

II. Unit 1; Title: Values

III. Session 2; Title: Values—Where do they come from?

IV. Learner's objectives:
A. The student will respect the right of others to hold different values.
B. The student will be aware of factors influencing the development of his/her values.
C. The student will be aware of his/her influence on others' values.
D. The student will learn that developing values is a life-long process.

Activity 1: Discussion of values written for homework (10 minutes)
Teacher instructions: This activity builds from the homework assignment. Begin with a 10-minute discussion of that exercise. Questions that may be helpful: (1) What was it like to think about and write your values in

the areas of money, friendship, love and sex, religion and morals, leisure, politics, and social organizations, work and school, family, maturity, and character traits? (You may want to list these areas on board.) (2) Which area was easiest? hardest? (3) What thoughts or questions came up as you wrote?

Peer facilitator instructions: Be ready to share your feelings and experiences in writing your values. You may be more in touch with difficulties other students had. Encourage group members to share these.

Activity 2: Where did I get these values? (25 minutes)

Teacher instructions: Divide students into dyads and distribute sheet "Where Did I Get These Values?" Go over instructions on sheet. Students are to complete sheet, then discuss with partner. Bring group back together and generate a list of sources of influence on values. Then consider the questions of which has the strongest influence now? Which did you do when you were ten? Which do you expect to influence you most when you're 21?

Activity 3: Whose values do I influence? How do I do that? (10 minutes)

Teacher instructions: Divide students into groups of four. Have them generate list of (1) Whose values do I influence? (2) How do I influence people? Regroup for discussion and homework.

In its training-as-prevention dimension, LST should be introduced into helping settings in schools, colleges, and community agencies. Support from administrators, staff members, and influential community persons is vital. In school settings LST can be taught every day at every grade level. Counselors and other pupil personnel staff can serve as the backbone of the program, but they cannot do all of the training and instruction. For example, the school nurse, lunchroom dietitian, and physical education director could team to teach fitness/health maintenance skills. The counselor, social worker, and social studies teachers could team to teach problem solving/decision making skills. Identity development/purpose in life skills can be taught by counselors with assistance from both vocational and academic teachers as well as community persons. It is desirable that the lead trainer in a school be in a nonteaching position because of the coordinating responsibilities that go with the task.

LST AND OTHER APPROACHES: SIMILARITIES AND DIFFERENCES

There are obviously a number of similarities between *elements* of LST and other training-oriented approaches. The effectiveness and advantages of interpersonal communication skills training as a treatment modality has been established for some time (Pierce & Drasgow, 1969) and has received consistent experimental and clinical support (e.g., Pierce, Schauble, & Wilson 1971; Vitalo, 1971). Both theoretical articles and literature reviews (e.g., Authier, Gustafson, Guerney, & Kasdorf, 1975; Guerney, Stollach, & Guerney, 1971) have urged that the focus be shifted from psychotherapeutic to psychoeducational modalities. Studies have also found positive relationships between physical fitness training and improved psychological functioning (Brown, 1978; Collingwood, 1976). D'Zurilla and Goldfried (1971) were among the first to argue for a problem-solving approach to therapy, using language that is descriptive of the LST view of etiology and that is applicable to other recent approaches as well (e.g., Brown, 1980):

Much of what we view clinically as "abnormal behavior" or "emotional disturbance" may be viewed as ineffective behavior and its consequences, in which the individual is unable to resolve certain situational problems in his life and his inadequate attempts to do so are having undesirable effects, such as anxiety, depression, and the creation of additional problems. (p. 107)

Just as the focus of these treatment approaches are similar to that of LST, there are at least two systems that are similar in structure. One is Arnold Lazarus's Multimodal Behavior Therapy (MBT). Lazarus (1975) defined MBT as "a systematic problem-solving process that examines and, if necessary, endeavors to remedy maladaptive responses across six separate but interrelated modalities—behavior, affect, sensation, imagery, cognition, and interpersonal relationships" (p. 150). The seventh dimension of diet and physical functioning permits the familiar acronym, BASIC ID. Lazarus further states that "the multi-modal behavior approach stresses the fact that the patients are usually troubled by a multitude of specific problems that should be dealt with by a similar multitude of specific treatments" (p. 165).

A basic difference between LST and MBT is the conceptualization of the human dimensions subject to deterioration and consequently in need of treatment. Another difference is in Lazarus's emphasis on locating deficits as opposed to the LST emphasis on locating areas of strength as well as those needing attention.

The other system that is structurally similar to LST is Arnold Goldstein's Structured Learning Therapy (Goldstein, Sprafkin, & Gershaw, 1976). Like LST, this system advocates direct training of specific behaviors and has both preventive and remedial dimensions. The primary differences are in the the-

oretical base and the derivation of the target skills. Whereas LST draws on human development theory, Goldstein and his colleagues used patient and staff surveys, clinical observations, and literature reviews to develop a list of 59 target skills involving social, personal, and interpersonal functioning.

The LST model presented in this chapter is unique in several respects. First, it is solidly grounded in human development theory. It thus lends itself equally well to prevention and remediation. Second, it emphasizes the small group as the medium of choice in all phases of training. Third, it places major responsibility on the trainee/client/patient for determining the course of training/ treatment. Fourth, it is firm in its insistence that training aimed at remediation take full account of existing areas of life skills mastery. Finally, it is an open system that permits endless permutations of training experiences in the course of individualized education/treatment.

RESEARCH SUPPORT

A research study of the effectiveness of LST with psychiatric inpatients (May, 1981) showed that the experimental group made significant gains over a group of patients receiving traditional treatment. The experimental LST group received 12 hours of training in interpersonal communication skills/human relations, 6 hours of what was then called purpose-in-life training (now known as identity development/purpose in life skills), and 10 hours of fitness/health maintenance skills training. The fitness training included instruction on diet and nutrition as well as practice in an exercise program.

A standard role play was used to assess progress in interpersonal communication/human relations skills. Responses were rated on the Global Scale (Gazda et al., 1975). The experimental group increased their communication skills significantly ($p<.001$) over the traditional treatment control group. Change on the purpose-in-life area was measured by the Purpose in Life test (Crumbaugh & Maholick, 1976). Again the LST group was significantly higher ($p<.025$) than the control group. Both experimental and control groups made significant pre-post physical fitness improvements on *forced vital capacity, blood pressure,* and *heart rate.* Both groups also showed a pre-post decrease in observed psychopathological behavior as measured by ward staff on the Nurse's Observation Scale for Inpatient Evaluation (NOSIE-30) (Honigfeld, Gillis, & Klett, 1966). The LST group also showed a trend ($p<.10$) toward satisfaction with treatment over the control group as measured by a semantic differential assessment.

Powell and Clayton (1980) studied the effects of interpersonal communication/human relations skills training on a group of psychiatric patients. They reported 50% fewer rehospitalizations and more gainful employment or productive volunteer work 2 years following treatment for patients receiving training compared to a Hawthorne treatment control group who received an equal amount of staff attention.

The LST system has also shown encouraging results in the training-as-prevention dimension even though the model was not fully implemented. Krebs (1981) compared students in three experimental classrooms, one each from the third, fourth, and fifth grades, with students in three control classrooms, one from each grade level. The students were posttested on the Barclay Classroom Climate Inventory (BCCI) (Barclay, 1978). Students in the experimental classes showed statistically significant gains ($p<.020$ to .001) over their peers on achievement motivation, control stability, energy activity, sociability/affiliation, and enterprising/dominance, and significant decreases on introversion/ex-

clusiveness ($p<.025$ to .046). Fifth- and sixth-grade classrooms also made educationally and statistically significant gains on all levels of the Iowa Test of Basic Skills: vocabulary, reading, language skills, work/study skills, mathematics, and composite scores. The experiment students at all grade levels also scored significantly higher ($p<.01$ to .04) on teacher ratings of responsibility, respect, resourcefulness, and responsiveness (Pratt & Mastroianni, 1981). Other studies (Bixler, 1972; Childers, 1973; Robinson, 1976) of the effects of interpersonal communication skills training with a variety of teacher groups showed significant positive gains for the teachers and/or their students.

The studies cited are admittedly few in number at this point, and all but one of them focus only on the outcomes of interpersonal communication/skills training rather than on the total impact of the LST system. Several new studies are under way or are in the planning stages. It is believed that in the next few years experimental and clinical applications of the LST model will increase in a variety of settings. The research studies accompanying these applications are expected to further confirm the efficacy of LST in both its preventive and remedial dimensions.

TENTATIVE CONCLUSIONS AND PREDICTIONS

Mahoney and Arnkoff (1978) reviewed the "cognitive and self-control" therapies for a recent clinical handbook (Garfield & Bergin, 1978). Their comments lend considerable support to LST and similar models. Their description of the problem-solving approaches appears consistent with the definition and rationale for LST presented here:

With the problem-solving approaches, clients are not only taught specific coping skills, but also the more general strategies of assessment, problem definition, and so on. In a sense, the therapist is sharing years of professional training by making the client an apprentice in therapy—a student of effective self-regulation. (p. 709)

Mahoney and Arnkoff (1978) summarized the criticisms of traditional psychotherapies as follows:

1. *Ineffectiveness,* particularly as defined by the client;
2. *Poor generalization* to problems and situations outside those specifically addressed by the therapist;
3. *Poor maintenance* (of therapeutic gains) over time;
4. *Poor cost-efficiency* as measured by both monetary and personal effort standards;
5. *Ethical dilemmas* in which the client's rights and responsibilities are not respected. (p. 709)

It is premature to compare clients' assessments of LST effectiveness with those of more traditional therapeutic approaches. Because of the strong emphasis on practice and homework in the teaching/training of generic life skills, however, one can predict satisfactory transfer or generalization of training. To the extent that such transfer is accomplished, the level of maintenance of therapeutic gains over time should also be satisfactory as measured by adjustment to the demands of everyday living and by a lower incidence of readmission to treatment. Because LST is based on effective models of life skills, trainees/clients/patients *understand* the process and rationale for the model they are using. This level of trainee investment in the learning process should be far more beneficial than would be the case if trainees were simply conditioned to give certain responses. Regarding cost-efficiency/effectiveness, LST is believed to be equally applicable to the prevention and remediation of life skills deficits. Preventive programs based on this approach

over the long term should reduce the need for remedial interventions, which are inherently more costly in all cases. An added cost benefit, of course, is the reliance on the small group as the primary modality. LST simply does not work as effectively as an individual treatment intervention. Finally, because LST is fundamentally an educational approach to treatment, ethical concerns should be minimized because participants are actively involved in their own learning and behavior change.

Life Skills Training is believed to be an appropriate model for both preventive and remedial mental health interventions. Although it was initially developed for use with an adult psychiatric population, it is proving to be quite effective as a curricular modality with schoolchildren. To date it has not been applied to mentally retarded or brain-damaged populations, but because it shares a number of characteristics with programs specifically designed for these persons, it should be applicable for adaptation in such settings.

Research and development efforts are underway to address the acknowledged "soft spots" of the model. The results of the Delphi survey helped to standardize the generic life skills. Existing training materials are being refined and new modules are under development. The goal of all these efforts is a comprehensive training paradigm that will be applicable to LST in all settings and with all populations. It is expected that the results of these activities will be shared with the professional community in the not-too-distant future.

We are aware of several obstacles that may hinder these efforts. One such obstacle is the attitude that the mission of education should be limited to the traditional "three R's" and that everything else is a frill that drains the taxpayer's pocket. It is expected that the incorporation of LST into school curricula will improve student motivation and achievement in academic areas. The resulting improvement in achievement test scores should overcome negative public attitudes. The real challenge for LST as a curricular intervention exists in teacher training institutions. The present state of siege under which many of these programs are laboring may provide the opportunity to make critical inroads on behalf of LST. It is hoped that the next generation of teachers, particularly at the secondary level, will be more receptive to psychoeducational approaches to learning than their predecessors have been.

The attitude of many in the mental health community regarding "treatment" is yet another obstacle. Professional status and credibility are, unfortunately, still determined by the level of diagnosable pathology of the patients one treats. Educational interventions are still not quite respectable. It is believed that the steady stream of research supporting the efficacy of such interventions and the oppressive financial burden of traditional treatment approaches will gradually cause these attitudes to change as well. Within the next 50 years positive mental health based on educational and training foundations will be as much a part of our society's commitments as is the goal of universal literacy at the present time.

REFERENCES

Adkins, W. R. (1974). Life-coping skills: A fifth curriculum. *Teachers College Record, 75*, 507–526.

Authier, J., Gustafson, K., Guerney, B., & Kasdorf, J. (1975). The psychological practitioner as a teacher: A theoretical-historical and practical review. *The Counseling Psychologist, 5*, 31–50.

Bandura, A. (1977). *Social learning theory*. Englewood Cliffs, NJ: Prentice-Hall.

Bandura, A., & Kupers, C. J. (1964). Transmission of patterns of self-reinforcement through modeling. *Journal of Abnormal and Social Psychology, 69*, 1–9.

Barclay, J. R. (1978). *Manual of the Barclay Classroom Climate Inventory*. Lexington, KY: Educational Skills Development.

Bixler, J. (1972). *Influence of trainer–trainee cognitive similarity on the outcome of systematic human relations training*. Unpublished doctoral dissertation, University of Georgia.

Bloom, B. S. (1976). *Human characteristics and school learning*. New York: McGraw-Hill.

Bohart, A. C. (1977). Role playing and interpersonal conflict reduction. *Journal of Counseling Psychology, 24*, 15–24.

Bradford, L. (1945). Supervisory training as a diagnostic instrument. *Personnel Administrator, 8*, 3–7.

Brooks, D. K. Jr. (1982). Life-skills questionnaire. Unpublished manuscript, University of Georgia.

Brooks, D. K. Jr., (1984). *A life-skills taxonomy. Defining elements of effective functioning through the use of the Delphi technique*. Unpublished doctoral dissertation, University of Georgia.

Brown, R. S. (1978). Jogging may be therapeutic for the psychiatric patient. *Clinical Psychiatry News, 6*, 1.

Brown, S. D. (1980). Coping skills training: An evaluation of a psychoeducational program in a community mental health setting. *Journal of Counseling Psychology, 27*, 340–345.

Carkhuff. R. R. (1969a). *Helping and human relations: A primer for lay and professional helpers* (Vol. 1): *Selection and training*. New York: Holt, Rinehart & Winston.

Carkhuff, R. R. (1969b). *Helping and human relations: A primer for lay and professional helpers* (Vol. 2): *Practice and research*. New York: Holt, Rinehart & Winston.

Childers, W. C. (1973). *An evaluation of the effectiveness of a human relations training model using in-class student teacher observation and interaction analysis*. Unpublished doctoral dissertation, University of Georgia.

Cohen, J. (1951). The technique of role-reversal: A preliminary note. *Occupational Psychology, 25,* 64–66.

Collingwood, T. R. (1976). Effective physical functioning: A pre-condition for the helping process. *Counselor Education and Supervision, 15,* 211–215.

Corsini, R. J. (1977). Individual education: A system based on individual psychology. *Journal of Individual Psychology, 33,* 295–349.

Crumbaugh, J. C., & Maholick, L. T. (1976). *PIL.* Munster, IN: Psychometric Affiliates.

Drum, D. J., & Knott, J. E. (1977). *Structured groups for facilitating development: Acquiring life skills, resolving life themes, and making life transitions.* New York: Human Sciences Press.

Dupont, H. (1978). *Affective development: A Piagetian model.* Paper presented at the UAP-USC 8th annual interdisciplinary conference "Piagetian Theory and the Helping Professions," Los Angeles, February 3–4.

D'Zurilla, T. J., & Goldfried, M. R. (1971). Problem solving and behavior modification. *Journal of Abnormal Psychology, 78,* 107–126.

Erikson, E. H. (1950). *Childhood and society.* New York: Norton.

Erikson, E. H. (1963). *Childhood and society* (2nd ed.). New York: Norton.

Flavell, J. H. (1963). *The developmental psychology of Jean Piaget.* New York: Van Nostrand.

French, J. R. P. (1945). Role playing as a method of training foremen. *Sociometry, 8,* 410–422.

Garfield, S. L., & Bergin, A. E. (Eds.). (1978). *Handbook of psychotherapy and behavior change: An empirical analysis* (2nd ed.). New York: Wiley.

Gazda, G. M. (Ed.). (1968). *Innovations to group psychotherapy.* Springfield, IL: Charles C Thomas.

Gazda, G. M. (Ed.). (1969). *Theories and methods of group counseling in the schools.* Springfield, IL: Charles C. Thomas.

Gazda, G. M. (1971). *Group counseling: A developmental approach.* Boston: Allyn and Bacon.

Gazda, G. M. (1977). Developmental education: A framework for a comprehensive counselling and guidance program. *Canadian Counsellor, 12,* 36–40.

Gazda, G. M. (1978). *Group counseling: A developmental approach* (2nd ed.). Boston: Allyn & Bacon.

Gazda, G. M. (1984). *Group counseling: A developmental approach* (3rd ed.). Boston: Allyn & Bacon.

Gazda, G. M., Asbury, F. R., Balzer, F. J., Childers, W. C., Deselle, E., & Walters, R. P. (1973). *Human relations development: A manual for educators.* Boston: Allyn & Bacon.

Gazda, G. M., Asbury, F. R., Balzer, F. J., Childers, W. C., & Walters, R. P. (1977). *Human relations development: A manual for educators* (2nd ed.). Boston: Allyn & Bacon.

Gazda, G. M., Asbury, F. R., Balzer, F. J., Childers, W. C., & Walters, R. P. (1984). *Human relations development: A manual for educators.* (3rd ed.). Boston: Allyn & Bacon.

Gazda, G. M., & Brooks, D. K. Jr. (1980). A comprehensive approach to developmental interventions. *Journal for Specialists in Group Work, 5,* 120–126.

Gazda, G. M., Childers, W. C., & Walters, R. P. (1982). *Interpersonal communication: A handbook for health professionals.* Rockville, MD: Aspen Systems.

Gazda, G. M., Duncan, J. A., Maples, M. F., & Brown, J. L. (1976). *The heart of teaching applications handbook: A training manual for enhancing the human relations skills of educators.* Bloomington, IN: Agency for Instructional Television.

Gazda, G. M., Walters, R. P., & Childers, W. C. (1975). *Human relations development: A manual for health sciences.* Boston: Allyn & Bacon.

Gazda, G. M., Walters, R. P., & Childers, W. C. (1980). *Realtalk: Exercises in friendship and helping skills.* Atlanta: Humanics.

Gesell, A., Ilg, F. L., Ames, L. B., & Bullis,

G. E. (1946). *The child from five to ten.* New York: Harper.

Gesell, A., Ilg, F. L., & Ames, L. B. (1956). *Youth: The years from ten to sixteen.* New York: Harper.

Goldstein, A. P., Sprafkin, R. P., & Gershaw, N. J. (1976). *Skill training for community living: Applying structured learning therapy.* New York: Pergamon.

Guerney, B., Stollak, G, & Guerney, L. (1971). The practicing psychologist as an educator: An alternative to the medical practitioner model. *Professional Psychology, 2,* 271–283.

Havighurst, R. J. (1953). *Human development and education.* New York: Longman, Green.

Havighurst, R. J. (1972). *Developmental tasks and education* (3rd ed.). New York: David McKay.

Holland, C. J., & Kobasigawan, A. (1980). In G. M. Gazda & R. J. Corsini (eds.), *Theories of learning.* Itasca, IL: F. E. Peacock.

Honigfeld, G., Gillis, R., & Klett, C. (1966). NOSIE-30: A treatment-sensitive ward behavior scale. *Psychological Reports, 19,* 180–182.

Huyck, E. T. (1975). Teaching for behavioral change. *Humanist Educator, 14,* 12–20.

Kohlberg, L. (1973). Continuities and discontinuities in childhood and adult moral development revisited. In P. L. Baltes & K. W. Schaie (Eds.), *Lifespan developmental psychology: Personality and socialization.* New York: Academic Press.

Kohlberg, L., & Turiel, E. (1971). Moral development and moral education. In G. Lesser (Ed.), *Psychology and educational practice.* New York: Scott Foresman.

Krebs, L. L. (1981). *The effects of the individual education system on grade school children on selected variables in the social and affective ares.* Unpublished master's thesis, DePaul University.

Lazarus, A. A. (1975). Multimodal behavior therapy in groups. In G. M. Gazda (Ed.), *Basic approaches to group psychotherapy and group counseling* (2nd ed.). Springfield, IL: Charles C Thomas.

Lieberman. M. A., Yalom, I. D., & Miles, M. B. (1973). *Encounter groups: First facts.* New York: Basic Books.

Lifton, W. M. (1966). *Working with groups* (2nd ed.). New York: Wiley.

Loevinger, J. (1976). *Ego development.* San Francisco: Jossey-Bass.

Mahoney, M. J., & Arnkoff, D. (1978). Cognitive and self-control therapies. In S. L. Garfield & A. E. Bergin (Eds.), *Handbook of psychotherapy and behavior change: An empirical analysis* (2nd ed.). New York: Wiley.

May, H. J. (1981). *The effects of life-skill training versus current psychiatric methods on therapeutic outcome in psychiatric patients.* Unpublished doctoral dissertation, University of Georgia.

Miller, G. D. (Ed.). (1976). *Developmental education and other emerging alternatives in secondary guidance programs.* St. Paul, MN: Minnesota Department of Education, Division of Instruction, Pupil Personnel Services.

Milsum, J. H. (1980). Lifestyle changes for the whole person: Stimulation through health hazard appraisal. In P. Davidson & S. Davidson (Eds.), *Behavioral medicine: Changing health lifestyles.* New York: Brunner/Mazel.

Moody, K. A. (1953). Role playing as a training technique. *Journal of Industrial Training, 7,* 3–5.

Mosher, R. L., & Sprinthall, N. A. (1970). Psychological education in secondary schools: A program to promote individual and human development. *American Psychologist, 25,* 911–924.

Mosher, R. L., & Sprinthall, N. A. (1971). Psychological education: A means to promote personal development during adolescence. *The Counseling Psychologist, 2*(4), 3–82.

National Assessment of Educational Progress. (1975). *Draft of basic skills objectives.* Denver: National Assessment of Educational Progress, a division of the Education Commission of the States.

O'Donnell, W. G. (1954). Role playing in training and management development. *Journal of the American Society of Training Directors, 8,* 76–78.

Pierce, R., & Drasgow, J. (1969). Teaching facilitative interpersonal functioning to psychiatric inpatients. *Journal of Counseling Psychology, 16,* 295–298.

Pierce, R., Schauble, P. B., & Wilson, R. R. (1971). Employing systematic human relations training for teaching constructive helper and helpee behavior in group therapy situations. *Journal of Research and Development in Education, 4,* 97–109.

Planty, E. G. (1948). Training employees and managers. In E. G. Planty, W. S. McCord, & C. A. Efferson (Eds.), *Training employees and managers for production and teamwork.* New York: Ronald Press.

Powell, M. F., & Clayton, M. S. (1980). Efficacy of human relations training on selected coping behaviors of veterans in a psychiatric hospital. *Journal for Specialists in Group Work, 5,* 170–176.

Pratt, A. B., & Mastroianni, M. (1981). Summary research on individual education. *Journal of Individual Psychology, 37,* 232–246.

Robinson, E. H. III. (1976). *Students' perceptions of teachers' abilities to provide certain facilitative conditions and their relationship to language arts achievement gains.* Unpublished doctoral dissertation, Duke University.

Rubin, L. J. (Ed.). (1969). *Life skills in school and society.* 1969 Yearbook. Washington: Association for Supervision and Curriculum Development.

Shaw, M. E., Corsini, R. J., Blake, R. R., & Mouton, J. S. (1980). *Role playing.* San Diego: University Associates.

Sisson, P. J., Arthur, G. L., & Gazda, G. M. (1981). *Human relations for criminal justice personnel.* Boston: Allyn & Bacon.

Slavson, S. R. (1964). *A textbook in analytic group psychotherapy.* New York: International Universities Press.

Speroff, B. J. (1953). The group's role in role playing. *Journal of Industrial Training, 7,* 17–20.

Sprinthall, N. A., & Mosher, R. L. (1969). *Studies of Adolescents in the secondary school.* Monograph No. 6. Cambridge, MA: Center for Research and Development, Harvard Graduate School of Education.

Stahl, G. R. (1953). Training directors evaluate role playing. *Journal of Industrial Training, 7,* 21–29.

Super, D. E. (1963). Vocational development in adolescence and early adulthood: Tasks and behaviors. In D. E. Super (Ed.), *Career development: Self-concept theory.* New York: College Entrance Examination Board.

Super, D. E., Crites, J. O., Hummel, R. C., Moser, H. P., Overstreet, P. L., & Warnath, C. F. (1957). *Vocational development: A framework for research.* Monograph No. 1. New York: Teachers College Press.

Vitalo, R. (1971). Teaching improved interpersonal functioning as a preferred mode of treatment. *Journal of Clinical Psychology, 27,* 166–171.

Wadsworth, B. J. (1971). *Piaget's theory of cognitive development.* New York: David McKay.

CHAPTER 5

Social Skills Training and Complementary Strategies in Anger Control and the Treatment of Aggressive Behavior

MICHAEL A. MILAN AND DAVID J. KOLKO

Aggression is a serious problem that has long been of concern to professionals and lay persons alike. It is not surprising, therefore, that a wide variety of theoretical formulations has been invoked to aid in our understanding and control of anger and aggression (Baron, 1977). Of these, the behavioral perspective is among the most extensively researched and documented (Patterson, Littman, & Bricker, 1967; Staub, 1971) and, primarily in the form of social learning theory (Bandura, 1973; Krasner & Ullmann, 1973), it will provide the basis of this review. Social learning theory identifies several variables that influence the expression of aggression; most notably the characteristics of a provocative situation, the manner in which the individual labels the situation, the interpersonal skills reportoire brought to bear upon the situation, and the consequences associated with aggressive behavior in response to the situation.

The relationship between anger and aggression has been highlighted in numerous descriptive formulations and has been elaborated upon in Megargee's (1973) distinction between *overcontrolled* and *undercontrolled* aggressive persons. Overcontrolled individuals are said to have failed to learn how to appropriately express their anger, whereas undercontrolled individuals are described as excessively prone to express their anger upon minimal provocation. The interpersonal difficulties of overcontrolled individuals and their experience of considerable anxiety when expressing anger as an emotion have been poignantly illustrated from the clinical perspective (Alberti & Emmons, 1978; Rothenberg, 1971; Rubin, 1970). As a result of their anger-expressiveness difficulties, both over- and undercontrolled individuals may resort to forms of aggressive behavior when confronted with a stressful situation (Rimm, 1977).

Typically, social learning theorists distinguish between aggressive behavior that is primarily under the control of its consequences (i.e., instrumental or operant aggression) and that that is elicited by its antecedents (i.e., emotional or respondent aggression). Social learning theory explanations of the learning of operant aggression have emphasized specific factors in individuals' early interpersonal experiences. Both the positive and negative reinforcement of aggressive behavior, experienced either directly by the individual (Patterson et al., 1967; Patterson, 1976) or vicariously through peer and parent modeling of aggression (Bandura, 1969; Oltmanns, Broderick, & O'Leary, 1977), have been identified as contributing to the development and maintenance of aggression. In addition, the learning of aggressive-disruptive behaviors in a coercive family system has been well documented in other studies (e.g., Johnson & Lobitz, 1974), and these formulations are consonant with the social psychological interpretation of aggression as the exercise of coercive power (Tedeschi, Smith, & Brown, 1974).

A review by Heatherington and Martin (1979) further confirms the contribution of early family experiences to aggression by documenting that aggressive response patterns are frequently acquired at an early age and, under certain social learning conditions, can become both frequent and habitual. Thus, it is not surprising that interpersonal difficulties involving anger and aggression are common in children, adolescents, and adults. Patterson (1956) and Jenkins (1968) reported that aggression was one of the most frequent behavior problems for which children are referred to outpatient clinics. Moreover, aggressive behavior in children and adults is associated with certain pathologies, such as antisocial and psychotic behavior patterns (Morris, 1956; Robins, 1966). Lefkowitz, Eron, Walder, and Huesman (1977) also reported that aggresive schoolchildren differed from their nonaggressive peers on several indexes of psychopathology.

Anger as an emotional respondent has been conceptualized by social learning theorists as a precursor of aggression. It has not been subjected to the same thorough examination as has aggressive behavior, however, if for no other reason than that it involves a subjective, internal state that confronts the scientist with methodological problems that are not easily solved. Novaco (1975) has come to grips with many of these problems and has advanced a comprehensive model of anger arousal and its treatment. He conceptualizes anger as the outcome of an initial provocation that can be conceived as an aversive event, mediating cognitive appraisals or interpretations of the provocative event, the individual's resulting somatic-affective condition, the label attached to it, and the behaviors that the individual emits to deal with the situation. The findings from several investigations (to be reviewed in a subsequent section of this chapter) have confirmed the model's conceptual framework and therapeutic recommendations.

Recognizing the prevalence and severity of anger and aggression problems, clinicians have devised an array of basic strategies to be used in their management (e.g., Berkowitz, 1973; Kolko, Dorsett, & Milan, 1981; Novaco, 1978; Patterson, Cobb, & Ray, 1972; Rimm, 1977). These programs have generally aimed at substituting prosocial for aggressive and coercive response patterns and have provided the basis for a differential diagnosis of the nature of the problem and the subsequent prescription of appropriate intervention strategies. The first question to be asked is whether the clients' difficulties represent a skills or a performance deficit (i.e., do clients have the skills in their repertories that are necessary to deal effectively with provocative situations in a prosocial manner?). If it appears that the problem reflects primarily a skills deficit, the course of action involves the teaching of the relevant social skills appropriate to the situations the client finds problematic (Hersen, 1979). The rationale for the teaching of social skills stems from social learning theory's emphasis on the acquisition of behavioral skills that serve as interpersonal alternatives to aggression. As noted by Eisler and Frederiksen (1980), the individual is explicitly trained in specific target behaviors that facilitate conflict resolution, thereby diminishing reliance upon inappropriate aggression.

If the appropriate social skills are present in the clients' repertoires, but emotional responses, such as anger or rage, and their overt counterparts, such as verbal or physical attack, interfere with the performance of the social skills, teaching of the self-control of anger in the form of coping strategies (Novaco, 1978) and the like has been shown to be beneficial. Here, the emphasis is upon the teaching of verbal and cognitive skills that the clients can employ to guide and control their responses to problematic interpersonal situations. Covert processes such as expectations and private speech have been most predominantly emphasized.

If the problem involves a performance deficit in that the client possesses the requisite social- and anger-control skills, either as entering competencies or as a result of a skills training program, but does not perform them, a contingency management program may be developed to encourage the client to practice them when in provocative situations. This is probably the most extensively explored approach to the treatment of aggression (Rimm & Masters, 1979), and it typically focuses upon existing contingencies of reinforcement and the rearrangement of antecedent and consequent events to encourage the control of anger and aggression. The purpose of this chapter is to review the various behavioral procedures and programs that have been applied in the treatment of anger difficulties and aggression in children, adolescents, and adults. Three approaches will be emphasized: (1) social skills training; (2) self-control training; and (3) contingency management.

An alternative approach to the control of anger involves the use of systematic desensitization (Wolpe, 1982) in which clients are exposed to progressively more anger-arousing provocations while maintaining an incompatible emotional state—typically relaxation. Although

this strategy will not be examined in detail in this chapter, its use alone or as a component of strategies that will be discussed holds considerable merit and is deserving of a brief review here. The justification for using desensitization in the modification of anger and aggressive outbursts comes from early experimental work with normal subjects (Ax, 1953; Funkenstein, King, & Drolette, 1957). Because desensitization had been widely used in the treatment of anxiety (Wolpe, 1976), it was not unreasonable to posit that it would show comparable utility in the case of individuals who experienced difficulty in controlling other forms of emotional responses.

Rimm, DeGrott, Boord, Herman, and Dillow (1971) reported one of the earliest applications of the desensitization of anger with 30 male subjects. After an anger–fear discrimination test, participants constructed hierarchies and learned relaxation skills before receiving formal desensitization treatment. The results indicated that following treatment a desensitization group showed lower self-ratings of anger and smaller Galvanic Skin Responses (GSR) than either a placebo or a control group. Working with a 19-year-old army officer, Herell (1971) found desensitization effective in reducing anger reactions and outbursts as well as the muscle tension with which they were associated. These improvements were also reported at an 8-week follow-up. Hearn and Evans (Evans & Hearn, 1973; Hearn & Evans, 1972) substantiated these findings with a group of 34 nurses. Desensitization clients showed a reduction in anger ratings on the stimulus scenes used during treatment relative to a no-treatment control group that remained unchanged. Furthermore, a 6-month follow-up indicated that these gains were maintained.

Relaxation is not the only counterconditioning response for use during desensitization. For example, Smith (1973) reported on an adult patient who failed to improve after seven standard desensitization sessions. Humorous content was then substituted for relaxation and embedded in the scenes used for imagination. Improvements in the client's GSR and cardiac responses along with positive changes in her Minnesota Multiphasic Personality Inventory (MMPI) profile and self-reported anger reflected the improvements made after humor was employed.

These results imply that desensitization therapy can be applied in treating individuals with anger difficulties. The data, however, consist mostly of physiological measures and self-ratings without direct observations in the natural environment to confirm the effectiveness of treatment. Furthermore, considerable variability exists in treatment duration. The range extends from 3 sessions (Rimm et al., 1971) to 18 sessions (Herell, 1971). Participants in the Rimm et al. (1971) study received all of 20 minutes of training to learn relaxation skills, whereas those in the Hearn and Evans (1972) study received 5 sessions of deep muscle relaxation. In sum, relaxation and formal desensitization therapy hold promise both as primary treatment modalities and as ingredients of multicomponent treatment packages to reduce inappropriate anger and aggression. More systematic research, including the use of direct measures of aggression, should be conducted to document their effectiveness as a primary treatment.

SOCIAL SKILLS TRAINING

The skills training effort itself typically involves 10 components. First, a general rationale for all skills components is provided including client-specific references that suggest the beneficial effects that will acrue to the client. Second, the therapist describes a representative provocative situation and then describes and models the to-be-mastered skills component. Third, the therapist and client role play the provocative situation with the client imitating the skills component the therapist has modeled. Fourth, the therapist critiques the client's performance with emphasis upon the correct aspects of the client's imitative behavior. Coaching, in the form of suggestions for more refined performance, is then provided. Fifth, the role play is repeated, critiqued, and additional coaching is provided until criterion-level performance is achieved. Sixth, a similar provocative situation is presented, and a somewhat abbreviated description and modeling of the component skills, modified somewhat to fit the situation, is provided. Seventh, the therapist and client again engage in the role play, critique, and coaching process until the client's performance again meets criterion. Eighth, a succession of similar situations and progressively less detailed descriptions and modelings of skills are presented, and performances are critiqued and coached until the client regularly produces criteron-meeting performances to novel situations when they are first presented. Once the client has mastered the skills in the therapy session, the ninth step involves strategies to encourage the performance of the newly acquired skills in the various real-life situations in which they are appropriate. Finally, arrangements are made for the client to record and report back to the therapist the characteristics of successful and unsuccessful performances so that progress may be reviewed in the subsequent session and refinements introduced as needed.

Several considerations enter into the construction and assessment of skills training programs. In general, the social skills training regimen requires that the skills to be taught are appropriate to the characteristics of the client, to the provocative encounters that set the occasion for anger and aggression, and to the social/cultural situations in which they occur. In addition, the role-play situations used in training and assessment should be determined to be representative of those with which the individual clients have difficulty in the natural environment. Extended role plays consisting of several interpersonal exchanges should be used in training to best simulate natural conditions. The molecular component skills that will be taught should be described in objective terms to facilitate instruction and should be quantified in a manner allowing objective assessment of the quality of performance before, during, and following training. The degree to which the training effort generalizes from the training setting and influences the client's behaviors in the natural environment should be determined. Finally, the degree to which the client's changed performance is seen by peers as improved or appropriate (the "social validity" of the training effort) should also be determined (Kolko et al., 1981).

The formal investigation of the role of social skills training in the treatment of aggressive behavior is relatively new with the early work of Wagner (1968) being among the first experimental investigations of the utility of the approach. In that study, Wagner demonstrated that "behavioral rehearsal" or role playing of appropriate forms of anger expression was effective in modifying modes of anger expression by adult psychiatric patients. Within the past decade there has been a dramatic and continuing increase in the number of publications describing and evaluating the skills training treatment of aggression. However, only recently has there been a turning away from the social-skills-training-works type of research that characterizes the beginnings of any movement and to an increased concern with the issues outlined previously that bear upon the construction and assessment of the training programs. Perhaps most importantly, we are now seeing the beginnings of attempts to specify and match the skills to be taught to the characteristics of the client and provoking situation.

The most recent research in the area is moving toward the behavior-analytic identification and validation of social skills (e.g., Kolko & Milan, Chapter 3). Unfortunately, this is an extremely time-consuming and laborious process, and it is therefore unlikely that skills trainers will be able to replicate this process for all the various circumstances they encounter in their therapeutic endeavors. Perhaps those who have the resources available to do so will employ the behavior-analytic method to identify and validate the skills appropriate to the situations and populations most commonly encountered in skills training programs. At the same time, additional research should be directed toward the development of more efficient strategies for the identification of social skills. Nonetheless, many skills trainers will be forced to continue to rely upon extrapolations from already-proven programs that approximate their requirements while individualizing their efforts as best they can to meet their needs. This, in turn, requires that particuar care be taken to evaluate the progress clients make in their programs and their effects on adjustments in problematic encounters.

One characteristic of the skills training model is the precise definition and quantification of the skills to be taught. Based on a review of reports of successful skills training programs, Kolko et al. (1981) developed and quantified a set of aggression-control skills for adolescent psychiatric patients to employ when responding to provocations. They are presented here as illustrative of the content of such programs:

Response latency
Score = 0: Provocation-to-response interval less than 3 seconds or greater than 6 seconds.
Score = 1: Provocation-to-response interval between 3 and 6 seconds.

Eye contact
Score = 0: Poor. Eyes oriented toward face of provocateur for less than 1/3 of client's total talk time.
Score = 1: Marginal. Eyes oriented toward face of provocateur between 1/3 and 2/3 of client's total talk time.
Score = 2: Good. Eyes oriented toward face of provocateur for more than 2/3 of client's total talk time.

Facial expression
Score = 0: Negative. Grimace, scowl, frown, raised eyebrows, or squinting eyes.
Score = 1: Positive. Smirk, smile, or grin.
Score = 2: Neutral. No salient changes of expression in the eyes or mouth and none of the behaviors indicated previously.

Voice loudness
Score = 0: Loud. Raises voice, shouts, or screams.
Score = 1: Soft. Mumbles to self, or no response at all.
Score = 2: Moderate. Normal, conversational loudness.

Verbal response
Score = 0: Antagonistic. Hostile, insulting statements, cursing, inappropriate requests, orders, and other remarks that set the occasion for further verbal attacks from provocation.
Score = 1: Irrelevant. Comment or question that fails to address the verbal content of the provacation, or no response at all.
Score = 2: Passive compliant. Overt behavior or verbal response that acquiesces to provocation, demands, or comments.

Score = 3: Expressive. One or more of the following responses, excluding any combination satisfying the criterion for a score of 4:
a. Acknowledgment: Any statement that acknowledges the provocateur's behavior or feelings.
b. Request: Any request, phrased as a question, for the provocateur to change behavior that does not imply harm.
c. Description: Any description of or statement about the client's behavior.
d. Explanation: Any statement that states the reason for the client's behavior.
Score = 4: Assertive (utilizing the four responses for "expressive" specified before). Either of the following two response combinations (in any order):
a. For the *first* response to provocation: a and/or b *plus* c and d.
b. For *subsequent* responses to continued provocations: a and/or b *plus* c and/or d.

An example of a 4 point assertive response to a first provocation might be "I know you're angry about being restricted (acknowledgement), but you shouldn't ask me to deliver a package for you (request). I'm not going to do things like that anymore (description) because my counselor says I'm doing good and I don't want to spoil my record (explanation)."

The manner in which Kolko et al. (1981) identified the skills they taught was certainly superior to reliance upon face validity and clinical judgment alone, for the skills were based upon the common ingredients of validated, clinically effective aggression treatment programs. In many cases, however, they, and other skills that were idiosyncratic of individual programs and for this reason *not* included, were originally based on face validity and clinical judgment. Consequently, the relative importance of all component skills is undetermined; the beneficial impact of idiosyncratic skills is untested; and the existence of additional skills is unknown. The following review of the literature on the skills training approach to the control of aggressive behavior focuses briefly upon general programs that sought to increase assertiveness and then reviews in some detail skills training programs designed specifically to decrease aggressive responses.

General Assertion Training

Assertion training has been used with considerable success with destructive and aggressive hospitalized patients. Wallace, Teigen, Liberman, and Baker (1973) combined assertion training and contingency contracting to reduce violent behavior in the treatment of a 22-year-old male patient. The patient was trained to respond appropriately to 25 individually tailored scenes across four different, personally relevant themes. The dependent measures included voice volume, eye contact, posture, and content of conversation. In addition, representative situations were constructed on the ward in order to assess progress. The results indicated that the patient responded assertively when later confronted with these situations without advance notice on the ward. In a follow-up study, Liberman, Wallace, Teigen, and Davis (1974) also found assertion training, consisting of modeling, rehearsal, and feedback, without contingency contracting, to be effective with an aggressive 20-year-old male resident.

Rimm (Rimm, 1977; Rimm, Hill, Brown, & Stuart, 1974) expanded upon this basic individual skills training format by designing and evaluating a group assertion training program. Individuals having difficulty controlling their tempers were exposed to common situations that often provoked them to anger. An assertion training group received a rationale for training, interpersonal exercises, behavioral rehearsal, feedback, and modeling. The members of a control group received the same rationale and then engaged in discussions of their feelings rather than receiving assertion training. The assertion training group showed improvements on behavioral measures of assertiveness and comfort, and decreases in self-ratings of anger and uptightness relative to the control group (Rimm et al., 1974). Rimm (1977) has made available an updated version of the format and content of group assertion training in the treatment of antisocial aggression based upon these procedures.

These early studies demonstrated the feasibility of assertion training in reducing aggressive behavior and angry outbursts. Both hospitalized and non-hospitalized patients were trained in both individual and group treatment programs to exhibit assertion skills that provided an alternative repertoire to their aggressive and coercive behavior. The importance of these studies lies not in their methodological characteristics that, like many early efforts in a new area, were sometimes problematic, but in their demonstration of the potential contribution of social skills training procedures to the control of anger and aggression. In furnishing optimistic results, they provided the clinical justification for pursuing additional investigations of the applicability of the skills training model to these problems.

Specific Skills Training

One of the earliest reports of a specific skills training program for the treatment of temper disorders was carried out with a 14-year-old adolescent by Kauffman and Wagner (1972). The authors developed a training program composed of modeling, role playing, cuing, prompting, coaching, cue fading, and social reinforcement. Skills were trained across several experimental phases that made use of reinforcement schedules, sitmulus generalization, multiple reinforcers, and a hierarchy of provocative training situations. Anecdotal results indicated that the boy's overall behavior improved and that he spent less time in isolation and time-out after treatment was initiated than before.

Foy, Eisler, & Pinkston (1975) reported a well-controlled investigation of the application of skills training in the case of an adult who was exhibiting explosive rage. Using a multiple baseline design across skills, Foy et al. investigated the role of modeling alone and when combined with social skills instruction. Whereas modeling alone produced initial decrements in undesirable behaviors, the addition of skills instruction facilitated not only the acquisition of appropriate skills but also their maintenance across time. At follow-up, the patient reported improved relationships at home and work. In a related study, Frederiksen, Jenkins, Foy, & Eisler (1976) replicated the results of Foy et al. (1975), using the basic skills training package of instructions, modeling, rehearsal, and feedback to teach appropriate responses to verbally abusive patients. The authors also assessed generalization to novel role-play participants and training scenes. Candid *in vivo* provocations were staged to test generalization to the patient's natural environment. Training produced dramatic changes in the patient's social skills that were also reflected in improved global ward ratings and increased skills use during assessment of generalization.

Several extensions of the skills training model with explosive psychiatric patients have been reported. Simon and Frederiksen (1977) employed the basic package of instructions, modeling, rehearsal, and feedback with an adult having a history of physical assault and rage attacks. Results indicated improvements in designated target behaviors as well as collateral measures of generalization on the ward. Matson and Stephens (1978) reported similar results with the same program plus social reinforcement in treating four combative female residents. Generalization of treatment gains to the ward environment was also reported. Working with adult male felons in a group format, Bornstein, Ulinegardner, Rychgtarck, Paul, Narfeh, Sweeney, and Justman (1979) demonstrated the efficacy of an interpersonal skills training program. Participants rehearsed each target skill until improvement was documented before advancing to the next skill. Differences were found between the training group and a new treatment control group on an interpersonal behavior role-play test after only six training sessions.

Matson and Zeiss (1978, 1979) have replicated these findings and have demonstrated that improvements in generalization can be achieved through the addition of *in vivo* rehearsal and feedback. In their first study, patients who were trained with *in vivo* rehearsal in addition to the basic skills training package improved more rapidly than those who received only the latter. In their second study, patients were provided a partner (or "buddy") who monitored their behavior and provided reinforcement, feedback, and suggestions in the hospital living environment when training was discontinued. Performance improvements were observed after training and were maintained at a 6-week follow-up.

The treatment of aggressive adolescents has also been conducted in a social skills training format. Goldstein, Sherman, Gershaw, Sprafkin, and Glick (1978) have documented the use of Structured Learning Therapy (SLT) in several studies aimed at improving the adolescent's prosocial repertoire. SLT, consisting of modeling, role playing, social reinforcement, and transfer (generalization) training, was found to produce significant gains in such skills as empathy, negotiation, self-control, and assertiveness when compared to control conditions or alternative treatment programs. Comparable procedures have been applied in the treatment of hospitalized and adjudicated adolescents. Elder, Edelstein, and Narick (1979) reported improvements in component skills following skills training and several indications of generalization in hospitalized patients, whereas Ollendick and Hersen (1979) obtained similarly impressive findings with adjudicated adolescents. In both programs, training entailed instructions, modeling, rehearsal, feedback, and social reinforcement. Ollendick and Hersen also included generalization instructions during the training program.

The study by Kolko et al. (1981) employed social skills training to promote anger control in hospitalized adolescent patients. Training consisted of modeling, instructions, discussion of therapists' modeled role plays, rehearsal, videotape and corrective feedback, and repeated coaching and rehearsal. The findings indicated that training facilitated the acquisition of five anger-control skills that generalized to novel role-play situations. Furthermore, the skills generalized to settings dissimilar to the treatment setting, as assessed during staged provocations, and were sufficiently large to be detected by staff members unassociated with the study. Professionals and members of the lay public provided social validation of the training effort.

With respect to the treatment of aggressive children, relatively few studies have been reported that have used social skills training procedures to modify aggressive behavior. Instead, contingency management appears to be the favored approach to date. In one of the studies

that did use social skills training, Matson, Esvelt-Dawson, Andrasik, Ollendick, Petti, and Hersen (1980) employed instructions, modeling, rehearsal, feedback, and social reinforcement with four aggressive, hospitalized children. Matson et al. reported that observation (modeling) alone produced few gains. However, substantial gains were made when the children were directly involved in the training program. Follow-up assessment indicated maintenance of these gains. Bornstein, Bellack, and Hersen (1980) found a similar training program, originally developed for unassertive children, to be effective with four highly aggressive children. Each client showed skills improvements once training was applied. However, generalization and follow-up probes indicated considerable variability among the four children on these measures. Bornstein et al. speculated that the children's reluctance to thoroughly adopt the skills that were taught may have influenced the overall efficacy of their intervention.

The literature reported thus far using social skills training procedures with aggressive adults, adolescents, and children is overwhelmingly positive. Several characteristics of this particular approach generate continued optimism regarding its continued implementation. Both single-case and group experimental design have been employed to assess the effects of the training program. Although the most widely used design has been the multiple baseline design (Hersen & Barlow, 1976) of single-case research methodology, this research area has also employed between-groups methods, thereby allowing relatively unambiguous conclusions acceptable to both methodological "camps" (Curran, 1979).

In addition, many of the studies have assessed both generalization to the clients' natural environments (Frederiksen et al., 1976; Kolko et al., 1981; Matson & Stephens, 1978; Spence & Marzillier, 1979) and maintenance across time (Elder et al., 1979; Matson & Stepehns, 1978; Matson et al., 1980). Follow-up assessments have documented the longer term maintenance of treatment following the completion of treatment. The work reported by Matson and Zeiss (1978, 1979) complements this trend by suggesting methods to program generalization and maintenance once training has been terminated.

Finally, skills training programs can be flexibly adapted to suit the needs of diverse client populations (Twentyman & Zimering, 1979). For example, training can be conducted both individually and/or in groups. In addition, skills training programs and materials have been made commercially available for use in psychiatric hospitals, schools, mental health centers, and residential institutions. This medium is particularly effective given the relatively brief duration of training that is required. In sum, social skills training provides a powerful alternative to traditional psychodynamic psychotherapy in the treatment of aggression and anger-control difficulties. Skills training programs have effectively developed prosocial response repertoires that facilitate the handling of interpersonal conflicts in children, adolescents, and adults who lack such skills. Its encouraging data base and use of empirically derived component procedures should encourage researchers to extend the skills training model in this and other areas that have proven refractory to traditional forms of psychodynamic intervention.

SELF-CONTROL TRAINING

It is possible that even some of the most motivated clients will acquire and perform in training sessions the general assertive and specific aggression control skills outlined previously, but when they encounter provocative situations in the natural environment they will continue to respond in their old angry and aggressive ways. This problem in generalization of training effects from the therapeutic setting to the real world is shared by all treatment modalities. When this situation is encountered in a social skills training program and fails to yield to the forms of generalization training discussed in the previous section, the use of self-control training to foster generalization and inhibit anger that blocks the performance of appropriate behavior appears to be a viable addition to the skills training regimen. Moreover, it serves as a treatment strategy in its own right when clients enter treatment with the skills but experience difficulty using them consistently.

The working definition of *self-control* that will be used here is modeled after that of Skinner (1953) and involves doing something at one point in time (the "controlling response") that influences what is done at a subsequent point in time (the "controlled response"). The controlled response may immediately follow the controlling response, or it may be delayed from relatively short to relatively long periods of time. Numerous examples of self-control so defined are available: refraining from purchasing junk food in the market so that one will not snack at home; engaging in relaxation exercises prior to an exam so that performance will be optimal; following logical problem-solving strategies so that correct solutions will emerge; and the like. This section will focus upon what has come to be termed "cognitive" forms of self-control as exemplified by the problem-solving exemplar of the preceding examples. In accord with Meichenbaum (1972), cognitions will be considered to consist primarily of thoughts or self-statements and will be viewed as a subset of covert (or private) behaviors that also include the emotions and other internal conditions as discussed by Skinner (1974).

Also, in accord with Meichenbaum

(1972), *cognitive modification* will be considered to consist of strategies that focus on thoughts or covert statements to produce therapeutic change. Although this may seem to be a somewhat narrow definition of the cognitive axis in modern psychology, its unification with behavior modification strategies to create a cognitive behavior therapy does encompass such strategies as self-instruction training, stress-innoculation training, problem-solving training, coping skills training, and the like. Strategies directed at the correction of false beliefs or, as Wolpe (1982) terms it, "the correction of misconceptions," would also be included (e.g., Kolko & Milan, 1980). However, this definition of cognitive modification appears to exclude strategies that are directed at the uncovering and correction of "unconscious" irrational beliefs (e.g., Ellis, 1970). Such strategies appear problematic for two reasons. First, the manner in which the unconscious wields its influence is difficult for cognitive therapy to specify. Second, when much time and effort is devoted to uncovering and making clear whether unconscious ideas exist and how they interfere with adjustment, it is often difficult to determine whether the irrational beliefs actually exist in the mind of the client or of the therapist.

The studies described in this section devote more systematic attention to the individual's cognitive or self-instructional skills than those discussed previously. Although they often include many of the strategies that have already been considered, their emphasis upon cognitive strategies merits a separate analysis. Indeed, a growing body of literature on cognitive behavior therapy has accumulated that, some argue, represents a bold new direction that behavior therapy has recently taken (Mahoney, 1974; Wilson, 1979). The accuracy of this characterization has been challenged by Wolpe (1982). As he points out, behavior therapists have, as a matter of course,

helped clients clarify the nature of their problem, reasoned with clients, corrected clients' misconceptions, discussed treatment strategies with clients, fostered the clients' confidence that change is possible, engaged in problem solving with the client, and the like.

Indeed, Wolpe (1982) notes that little was made of these "cognitive" practices in the writings of "noncognitive" behavior therapists "because to do so seemed as superfluous as to state that a syringe was used when recording that a patient received an injection" (p. 86). Nonetheless, the attention devoted to these practices by the cognitive behavior therapists has led to a more precise specification and evaluation of these components than otherwise would have occurred—an outcome all would agree can only serve to advance and refine the behavior therapy effort. The only risk increased attention to the cognitive components of behavior therapy would appear to pose is that therapists unduly emphasize the cognitive strategies and in the process deemphasize or discontinue the behavioral components of cognitive behavior therapy. Such a regression to cognitive therapy is certainly to be discouraged in light of what is known of the weak effects of pure forms of cognitive intervention (Wilson, 1979).

The programs that will be described have in common the use of self-control training to teach people to cope more effectively with provocative situations. Indeed, a distinction is sometimes made between what have been termed *coping* and *mastery* models in skills training. The coping model is depicted as teaching people general strategies that can be used under a variety of conditions, whereas the mastery model is characterized as teaching specific responses to specific provocations. The bulk of the work described in the preceding section is commonly attributed to the mastery model. Reflection upon the content of those skills training programs, however, indicates that considerable attention is routinely directed to teaching a variety of responses to an array of provocative situations in order to foster generalization. Consequently, it appears that the distinction between training for coping or mastery in terms of the goals of treatment is at best arbitrary and at worst artificial.

Although the strategies used to teach coping (or generality) may differ, the importance of such training has been amply documented. Goodwin and Mahoney (1975) demonstrated that the inclusions of coping responses in simple modeling resulted in improvement in the conduct of aggressive-impulsive boys. The children first viewed a model engaging in coping responses that were explicitly emphasized and illustrated. After viewing this film and practicing these coping responses, the children showed dramatic improvements in overall behavior that were maintained at follow-up. Similarly, Thelen, Fry, Dollinger, and Paul (1976) showed videotapes to delinquents residing in a group home in which a model had initial difficulty but was later successful in coping with various interpersonal situations. As indicated by staff behavior ratings, the boys showed better home adjustment after viewing and then enacting these situations.

The self-control training approach to teaching coping skills will be described in this section. Three major strategies will be reviewed: problem solving, self-instructions, and stress innoculation as well as packages combining these components. In fact, however, the distinctions between these strategies are often problematic, for they appear to embody common principles, as would be expected in light of their common cognitive base.

Problem Solving

D'Zurilla and Goldfried (1973) describe problem solving as the *process* of finding a solution and have developed and refined a five-component strategy that individuals may deploy in problematic situations in order to increase the likelihood that solutions will be hit upon that alter situations in a manner that reduces or eliminates their problematic nature. Their specification of the strategies that are taught could well serve as a standard against which other writers in the area could gauge their efforts. The first step in their problem-solving process is to assist the client in developing a problem-solving orientation that consists of a set or attitude to identify problematic situations when they occur and then to inhibit the tendency to either respond impulsively or withdraw. Second, problems are defined and objectives formulated. That is, the relevant aspects of problem situations are specified, and the changes to be made are identified for the various categories of problems that the client experiences. Third, the client is taught to generate as many alternative courses of action for the problematic situations as possible, which are independent of the probable outcomes of the solutions if implemented. Fourth, decision making, defined as selecting the best alternative for action, is taught. For each possible solution the client generates possible personal, social, short-term, and long-term consequences and on the basis of each solution's personal valence and probability identifies the one that maximizes positive outcomes while minimizing negative ones. The final step consists of the verification of the solution by actually acting upon it and observing the consequences. If the solution does not prove successful, the decision-making process is reactivated, and the resulting solution is verified. The process is repeated until a solution proves effective.

In one of the earliest investigations of the effects of problem-solving instructions on aggressive behavior, Chittenden (1942) conducted an experimental study in which appropriate responses to frustration were taught to aggressive and dominant school-aged children. In this classic study, the children were exposed to doll plays illustrating aggressive and then cooperative solutions to interpersonal problems, and the children discussed the advantages of cooperative responding with their teacher–trainer. The children showed a reduction in both domination and frustration-generated aggression during school following problem-solving training. Working within a group format, Gittelman (1965) applied this approach using role playing and rehearsal in the treatment of an aggressive 13-year-old boy. Participants in the group watched each other act out solutions to frustrating situations. Gittelman reported that the targeted child learned to inhibit his aggressive behavior and continued to show progress in conduct and academic performance at follow-up.

Also working in a group context, McNamara (1968) exposed an aggressive boy to children participating in a "re-learning group" in which verbal rehearsal and active problem-resolution strategies were taught. First, group members modeled prosocial responses to conflict-related situations. Then, the target child rehearsed these solutions before the group. After training, the intensity and frequency of aggressive behavior were reduced, and the child's social behavior improved significantly. As suggested by these findings, an active role in the formulation of problem solutions combined with prosocial modeling by other children can produce considerable behavior change as well as promote generalization. Such gains can be maximized when a variety of coping responses and solutions is included in the training program.

Self-Instructions

Self-instructional training (Meichenbaum, 1977) is typically described as teaching the covert statements or "thought processes" that competent individuals use to guide their activities. It usually involves five components. First, a model engages in competent behavior while speaking aloud the covert statements that guide behavior (i.e., by "thinking out loud"). This verbalizing of thought processes is also referred to as *cognitive modeling*. Second, the client performs the same behavior while the model verbally directs the client by asking the questions and prompting the instructions that were modeled in the first step. Third, the client performs the behavior while speaking aloud the questions and instructions modeled previously. Fourth, the client whispers the questions and instructions that are coming to guide activities while engaging in the behavior. Finally, the child engages in the behavior while guiding activities via subvocal speech (thinking to him- or herself the questions and instructions taught in the previous steps).

The instructions themselves usually consist of four basic performance-enhancing skills. First, the client identifies what the problem is. Second, instructions are given to focus attention on the task and guide behavior to produce a solution. Third, social reinforcement is provided as feedback to sustain appropriate behavior. Fourth, performance is evaluated, and steps are taken to correct errors while maintaining confidence that the client will succeed. With repeated practice, these instructions become abbreviated and automatic but emerge again when a difficult problem or situation is encountered. The relevance of self-instructional training is suggested in an unpublished report by Camp (1975, cited in Meichenbaum, 1977) who studied high- and low-aggressive boys and found that the aggressive boys differed from the nonaggressive boys in that they did not report the use of covert instructions and/or that when covert instructions were reported, they did not achieve functional control of the boys' activities.

By and large, the aggressive boys had the same self-instructional skills as the nonaggressive boys but failed to use them when thinking through and solving problems.

Blackwood (1970) demonstrated that disruptive and aggressive behaviors could be controlled through explicit instruction in the use of verbal self-control skills. Acting-out children copied, paraphrased, and recited oral essays concerning their misbehavior. The essays contained responses to four questions that the children were required to ask after each incident of misbehavior and that, it is presumed, the children came to use subsequently in the control of misbehavior. This form of verbal control was found more effective in decreasing misbehavior than one involving the use of unrelated essays as a form of punishment. Camp, Gasten, Hebert, and Doornick (1977) employed the same basic "think aloud" strategy with more aggressive children. The program consisted of the verbalization of guiding instructions to develop the requisite self-instructional skills for dealing with interpersonal difficulties. Participants were trained to respond with problem-solving instruction to questions concerning their behavior. Following intervention, improvements were reported in teacher ratings of prosocial behavior and the childrens' overall performance on cognitive tests.

Self-instruction training has also proven useful with adolescents showing a variety of behavioral problems, including aggression. Snyder and White (1979) described a self-instruction package that focused upon the verbalization of instructions and coping statements and the modifications of counterproductive statements. In conjunction with several techniques, the package was found more effective on three significant behavioral measures than a contingency awareness package. In a related study by Forman (1980), aggressive elementary-school children were assigned to either cognitive restructuring, response cost, or no-treatment control conditions. Children in the cognitive restructuring group focused upon the imagination of anger-provoking situations and appropriate self-statements consistent with the premise that each child was in control of the situation. Children in the response cost group lost 2 minutes recreation time for each incident of aggressive behavior. Both programs significantly reduced aggressive behavior relative to controls as measured by teacher ratings, records of aggressive behavior, and independent observations. However, the response cost program tended to produce greater decreases in aggression than the cognitive restructuring group.

Stress Inoculation

Perhaps the most comprehensive stress-inoculation package for dealing with angry outbursts and aggressive behavior is the anger-control program developed by Novaco (1975, 1978) who proposed both a conceptualization of anger arousal and an analysis of its various functions. His formulations rest upon the assumption that the experience and expression of anger can be regulated once a repertoire of skills has been developed. Novaco construes anger as being determined by external events (provocations), internal states (physiological arousal and the labeling of that subjective condition as "anger"), and overt behaviors that are enacted in response to those events. His stress-inoculation model of treatment of anger focuses on these components and involves three basic phases: (1) cognitive preparation; (2) skill acquisition; and (3) application practice.

The cognitive preparation phase is designed to educate clients about the functions of anger and their individual response style as well as to provide a common language system and a rationale for treatment. Emphasis is placed upon identifying provocative situations and persons, discriminating between anger as an affective state and agression as a voluntary behavior, distinguishing anger that is and is not justified, understanding the determinants of anger, identifying how interpersonal interaction patterns contribute to anger, and introducing the stress-inoculation procedures that will enable the clients to better manage provocative encounters and control their anger.

In the second phase of stress-inoculation training, skills acquisition, the clients are provided with cognitive and behavioral coping skills keyed to the results of the analysis of the determinants of their anger. After teaching the client to label provocative events differently and to deemphasize the importance often attributed to them, self-instructions are developed to control the anger itself. This involves four steps. First, the clients are taught to prepare for provocation by learning statements that will enable them to remain calm, maintain confidence, and anticipate the use of subsequent coping skills. In the second step—impact and confrontation—the clients are taught statements that will enable them to maintain control, continue the calm state, and look for a solution that will resolve the confrontation. The third step involves coping with the arousal that does occur. Emphasis is placed on the clients engaging in muscle relaxation and controlled breathing (Jacobsen, 1938) to inhibit anger reciprocally and then to initiate problem-solving activities. In the final step—subsequent reflection—the clients are taught social reinforcing statements for those situations in which the conflict or provocation has been successfully resolved and statements that minimize failure and maintain a relaxed and optimistic set about future provocations if the conflict has not been resolved successfully.

In the final phase of the stress-inoculation program, the clients practice the skills taught in role-play situations. Here, a hierarchy of provocative encounters is constructed, and the practice sessions begin with the least provocative and then move on to successively more provocative ones as skills are mastered and refined. Hence, the term *inoculation* is employed as a medical metaphor for this psychological procedure in which training proceeds by exposing the client to manageable "doses" of provocation that arouse anger but do not overwhelm the client as coping skills are practiced until the most arousing provocation is mastered. Results of Novaco's early research (1975) demonstrated the superiority of his stress-inoculation treatment program over cognitive self-control or relaxation procedures alone. The treatment program has also been successfully applied with adolescents (Schrader & Long, 1978) and law enforcement officers (Novaco, 1977a) as well as in a case of depression that was secondary to anger (Novaco, 1977b).

Self-Control Packages

There is, as is to be expected, much overlap among the three major strategies described previously. Nonetheless, writers and theorists have generally adhered to the distinctions between them. This section will review representative packages that have been described as combining ingredients from these (and other) strategies. To teach self-control to impulsive and aggressive children, Schneider (1974) developed a program called "The Turtle Technique." This package teaches children to control aggression by first closing their eyes, pulling their arms into the body, and putting their heads down; then they engage in relaxation exercises, and finally employ problem-solving strategies involving self-instructions that are rehearsed in imagination. Schneider and Robin (1976) reported that the package reduced aggressive and tantrum behavior in several emotionally disturbed children. In addition, various beneficial side effects of training were found that highlighted the participants' classroom adjustment. This particular self-control program is one of the few that aims specifically at the modification of children's disruptive behavior and aggressiveness using a diverse range of self-control procedures. Its basic techniques are similar to those used by Novaco (1975) in his highly successful anger-management package for adults, but without the stress-innoculation practice component.

McCullough, Huntsinger, and Nay (1977) designed a comparable package for an adolescent with violent temper tantrums. The boy was exposed to role playing followed by self-control training that included thought stopping, relaxation, and a contingency contract. After only one session of training, the boy's temper tantrums decreased and were maintained at low levels both at home and school. Packages such as this one have been applied in controlling outbursts in adults as well. Harvey, Karan, Bhargava, and Morehouse (1978) incorporated relaxation training, cue conditioning, and cognitively oriented procedures in the form of self-instructions, with time-out and positive reinforcement to reduce violent temper outbursts in a mentally retarded, adult female. The treatment program was designed to facilitate the client's self-control over her disruptive behavior. Its sequential application in two settings resulted in an immediate reduction in the frequency of temper tantrums. Furthermore, generalization and maintenance were facilitated by gradually thinning the schedule of token reinforcement so that naturally occurring reinforcers would come to maintain improvements in conduct.

Conceptually, cognitively oriented self-control strategies are presumed to differ from other strategies in terms of their emphasis on covert instructional control or active problem-solving strategies. As shown here, the combination of cognitive techniques and standard behavior therapy procedures has typically produced multiple behavioral improvements (Camp et al., 1977; Harvey et al., 1978; Novaco, 1978). In explaining such findings, it is said that these cognitive techniques provide one with an active, verbal repertoire that suppresses or competes with the overt expression of aggressive behavior. Private speech may summon up alternative strategies for handling interpersonal difficulties and, therefore, may function as verbal discriminative stimuli that are rehearsed in a response chain. Clearly, that the individual can employ covert instructions and other strategies to control unwanted aggressive behavior points to their obvious clinical utility. However, the manner in which instructions and covert coping strategies function to control overt behavior is still left for subsequent analysis.

The cognitively based programs and packages typically consist of several procedures, many of which are conventional behavioral strategies (e.g. rehearsal, modeling, feedback, relaxation). Unfortunately, only a few studies have attempted to investigate the role of specific cognitive strategies (Forman, 1980; Novaco, 1975; Snyder & White, 1979) apart from the contribution of these additional procedures. Components analyses are certainly needed in order to permit an evaluation of the incremental contribution of each specific procedure. Indeed, one aspect of training that most of these studies share is the active verbal participation and involvement of both client and therapist in the training process (Camp et al., 1977; Gittelman, 1965; McNamara, 1968). The individuals are directly involved in describing and reviewing the consequences of their behavior and in developing a variety of response alternatives through both overt and covert rehearsal. This training emphasis may enhance skills acquisition and promote generalization because of the intense level of involvement it engenders (Schrader & Long, 1978; Snyder & White, 1979). The fact that most studies reported brief treatment durations of less than 10 sessions as well as generalization of gains to naturalistic settings may offer some validity to this suggestion.

Thus, the programs reported here seem promising from a clinical standpoint. The lack of a clear methodology to investigate the contribution of cognitively oriented and behaviorally oriented procedures should encourage applied researchers to develop more sophisticated strategies to allow the necessary component analyses. Furthermore, cognitive-behavioral interventions require careful definition independent of the phenomena that they attempt to modify or eliminate so that circuitous, post hoc explanations of their efficacy are prevented (Rachlin, 1977). The research reported by Meichenbaum (1977) provides such a framework. In sum, the merger of cognitive and behavioral procedures has yielded encouraging clinical outcomes in the management of anger and aggression. These results will be more clearly evaluated when greater experimental sophistication is brought to bear upon these strategies and these often refractory clinical difficulties.

CONTINGENCY MANAGEMENT

An important component of both the social skills and self-control training programs described previously involves the practice of what is taught in real-life situations. The skills taught must be appropriate for the provocations that the client will encounter, and the client must use the skills in those provocations if anger is to be controlled and aggression is to be managed. Even the most motivated clients can experience difficulty doing so, and for this reason extended practice in training sessions and homework assignments of graduated difficulty are typically used to foster generalization from training to real-life situations. In some instances, little more can be done other than trust that preparation has been adequate and the naturally occurring contingencies have been correctly anticipated so that they will foster the real-life practice and strengthening of the new skills.

However, when the therapist does have the opportunity to influence the naturally occurring contingencies to better insure that they set the occasion for and reinforce the behaviors being taught, such strategies should be considered in order to maximize training effects. The contingency management procedures that are described in this section suggest how this may be done. As would be expected, most of these studies have been conducted in schools, inpatient mental health and mental retardation facilities, with parents, and the like, where the therapist can influence the manner in which others interact with the client. The contingency management studies generally do not explicitly include social skills and self-control components, whereas the social skills and self-control studies usually do not explicitly include contingency management components. The planned integration of these strategies can only facilitate training efforts.

Strategies will first be described that are designed to increase appropriate behavior through reinforcement: differential reinforcement, contingency contracting, and token reinforcement. Next to be described will be strategies to decrease undesirable behavior: time-out, response cost, and punishment through aversive stimulation. The utilization of these latter strategies is a matter of considerable controversy because of their past abuse and the degree of discomfort—both physical and psychological—that the more intrusive procedures can cause clients. Consequently, their use is not advocated, and anyone considering doing so would be well advised to review the precautions and client safeguards detailed by Martin (1975). At the very least, the therapist should subject the proposed program to a formal review process, document that the to-be-suppressed behavior is of danger to the client or to others, and insure that alternative, less intrusive strategies have been tried and have failed before the more intrusive of these strategies are considered. It must also be remembered that punishment procedures only suppress undesirable behavior and are therefore no substitute for social skills, self-control, and reinforcement programs that do teach and encourage appropriate alternative modes of expression. Consequently, no punishment program should be contemplated in the absence of concurrent positive programs to teach and strengthen desirable behavior.

An important component of any contingency management program is the rules that describe the behaviors that are expected. The relationship between rules and contingency management procedures in influencing behavior was made clear in a study by Madsen, Becker, and Thomas (1968). In this study, the aggressive and disruptive behaviors of two children in different classes were recorded using nine categories of inappropriate and one category of appropriate behavior. Results indicated that rules alone had little effect in changing classroom behavior, whereas conditions involving reinforcement and/or extinction with or without rules were more effective. Because teachers were worked with individually and given written instructions regarding the specification, posting, and rehearsal of their rules, it is unlikely that their relative ineffectiveness in controlling behavior with rules alone is an artifact of the manner in which the procedures were implemented. In this case, the use of rules in the absence of supporting contingency management procedures failed to control aggressive classroom behavior.

Graziano (1974) reported the use of physical restraint with repetition and reinforcement (lessening of restraint) of verbal rules with autistic children. He indicated that, although the statement of rules was initially ineffective in controlling tantrum and aggressive behavior, control was gradually established after sufficient repetition and reinforcement. Graziano speculated that the children gradually refrained from aggressive behavior as the rules took on the form of self-instructions when the clients' "overt verbal repetition of rules gradually diminished to a whisper, then to silent mouthings of phrases, and, finally dropped out altogether, while their control over behavior remained" (p. 160). The author also posited that the children's aggressive behavior came under internal verbal control after external control was imposed by the therapist. Alternatively, however, it is possible that punishment (i.e., restraint) of aggressive behavior may have been responsible for the reduced frequency of aggression.

Although little is known of how rules may be best used in contingency management programs, it seems useful to consistently precede the implementation of contingencies with rules that describe them. Although rules generally identify expected behavior, they can be expanded to also specify the potential consequences of engaging in the behavior that, in turn, may further influence whether the behavior will be emitted. Graziano's analysis further suggests that self-control may be facilitated with the presentation of verbal rules or admonitions. Still, however, the efficacy of rules in reducing aggressive behavior has yet to be determined clearly.

Differential Reinforcement

One of the most basic strategies to encourage appropriate behavior while discouraging inappropriate behavior involves the use of differential reinforcement, which involves positively reinforcing appropriate behavior while extinguishing (preventing the reinforcement of) inappropriate behavior. Early contingency management studies investigated the utility of reducing aggressive problem behaviors using this strategy. Working with a combative adult psychiatric patient, Ayllon and Michael (1959) instructed ward personnel to extinguish aggressive behavior and provide social reinforcement for the incompatible response of sitting on the floor. When the on-the-floor response was reinforced, the frequency of attacks decreased. Brown and Elliot (1965) gave similar instructions to teachers in order to reduce verbal and physical aggression in preschool children. The results of two classroom studies provide additional support for these findings. Allen, Turner, and Everett (1970) and Madsen et al. (1968) reported significant reductions in the frequency of children's aggressive behavior when similar differential reinforcement procedures were applied.

In the context of family therapy and parent training, differential reinforcement has played a major role in providing parents with a technique to alter their children's behavior at home. In an early study, Russo (1964) demonstrated the utility of this strategy in the case of an aggressive and destructive young girl. The mother was trained to reinforce cooperation and appropriate conduct with attention, and to extinguish loudness, outbursts, rudeness, and assaultiveness. After several months of treatment, the child became more cooperative, got along better with her mother, and was less disturbing and disruptive. Similarly, Bernal and her associates (Bernal, 1969, 1971; Bernal, Williams, Miller, & Reagor, 1972) have taught this technique to the parents of children whose behaviors have been collectively described as the "brat syndrome." Differential reinforcement was found to reduce these problem behaviors and facilitate compliance and parental control.

Overall, the previous studies indicate that differential reinforcement can be used to reduce the frequency of aggressive behaviors in a variety of settings and a wide range of clients. The success of this procedure is dependent upon a careful analysis of the reinforcing events that maintain aggressive behavior. For example, in designing a program for extinction, one must clearly assess the existing contingencies to ensure that the reinforcer to be withheld is, in fact, what sustains the behavior. This is perhaps most easily accomplished in controlled settings where the contingencies are defined and restricted. However, one must be mindful of differences in the duration of treatment in studies documenting the effectiveness of differential reinforcement. Russo (1964) reported a treatment duration of 9 months. The efforts of Allen et al. (1970) required 50 sessions, whereas those of Bernal et al. (1972) took 13 weeks. Clearly, wide discrepancies in treatment duration preclude any firm conclusions regarding the universal therapeutic potential of differential reinforcement.

Differential reinforcement has been useful in reducing aggression. However, it may require more time to produce response suppression than other techniques (Rimm & Masters, 1979). Thus, in cases of extreme and dangerous aggressive behavior, differential reinforcement may be contraindicated. Nevertheless, insofar as the procedure can be easily applied through the mere reversal of the extant contingencies and thereby requires little staff effort and time, it will continue to be applied under a wide range of circumstances.

Contingency Contracting

The contingency contract between the client and significant others is another method for establishing contingency control over behavior. It involves a negotiated and written specification of target behaviors and the reinforcers that are contingent upon them (Rimm & Masters, 1979). Contingency contracting has been clarified and implemented by Stuart (1971) who discussed the rationale, assumptions, and advantages of using contingency contracts.

The establishment of positive, non-coercive, and reciprocal control within a system is perhaps one of the most important advantages of the contract (Patterson, 1976). For example, a child's frequent aggressive behavior may be responses to a variety of coercive behaviors exhibited by the parents (Heatherington & Martin, 1979). Likewise, some parents may fail to apply reinforcing contingencies when their child's appropriate behavior warrants and attend instead to aggression. In rectifying these difficulties, the contract explicitly states agreed-upon desired behaviors and contingent consequences, while providing both parties with a format by which they can predict each other's behavior. Therefore, it becomes essential to include significant others in the treatment program in order to establish more adaptive reinforcement contingencies.

Thorne, Tharp, and Wetzel (1967) described the use of contingency contracts by a probation officer in modifying the assaultive behavior of a delinquent youth. A contract was developed between the youth and his parents in which he earned money for completing certain chores and showing obedience. Failures to comply with the terms of the contract resulted in restrictions from using the family car. Once the contract was in effect, the youth showed more responsible behavior, reentered school, and showed an improved relationship with his parents. In this case, the contract provided a more balanced schedule of reinforcement between family members.

Contractual arrangements have also proven useful in group therapy. Bardill (1972) established a contract between group members whereby appropriate conduct, active participation, and responsibility were reinforced with money and an off-campus trip. The program was successful in eliminating physical fights, destruction of property, and thefts. In one of the few studies with adults, Wallace, Teigen, Liberman, and Baker (1973) employed a contract with a hospitalized patient in which assault-free behavior for 7 days would earn the patient the opportunity to have a home visit. Over the first 11 days in which it was in effect, no assaultive incidents were observed. Unfortunately, no assessment of generalization to other settings was conducted in either study.

Finally, several programs have used contingency contracts in conjunction with additional procedures to produce rapid behavior change. Combining contracting and token reinforcement, Tobey and Thoreson (1976) reduced aggressive behavior in a child who earned home visits contingent upon appropriate behavior. Patterson and his associates (Patterson, 1976; Patterson et al., 1972; 1973; Patterson & Reid, 1973) have carefully constructed point systems in the homes of aggressive children specified in the form of a contract. The child actively negotiates with the parents to select reinforcers and the time period covered by the contract in order to work toward the receipt of substantial reinforcers. This contract system has proven effective in motivating appropriate behaviors in a short time period. Comparable effects were reported by Blackham and Silberman (1975) using a contract and response cost with a 9-year-old aggressive boy.

Contingency contracts are employed alone and in conjunction with other procedures. The studies reviewed indicate aggressive individuals often respond more appropriately with the implementation of a contract that specifies the behaviors to be engaged in and their contingent consequences, and that this procedure is of considerable value in modifying the coercive family system characteristic of many aggressive children and adolescents (Patterson, 1976).

Token Reinforcement

Perhaps the most popular single contingency management procedure is the token economy (Ayllon & Azrin, 1968). The following characteristics of tokens, all of which relate to their usefulness in behavior change programs, have been suggested by Krasner and Ullman (1973, pp. 281–283): Tokens are concrete and worthwhile indicators of social approval, which are backed up by exchanging them for goods; they can open up a limitless world of reinforcers, both primary and secondary; they provide a time bridge between the performance of an act and a later explicit reinforcement contingent upon the act; they can be given or withdrawn flexibly, frequently, and without interfering with ongoing behavior; and finally, they can be paired with social approval, eventually enabling material reinforcers to be replaced by social reinforcers, thus assisting the generalization to the outside world of the acquired or restored behavior.

A token reinforcement system may motivate prosocial behavior when extant contingencies have failed to reduce aggressive response patterns or have actually exacerbated them (Milan & McKee, 1974). Token systems have been established in outpatient treatment centers, psychiatric wards, classrooms, residential facilities, and homes. Their use in modifying aggression has provided an effective procedure for strengthening alternative, adaptive repertoires. Finally, the flexibility provided by the use of token systems permits the utilization of potent backup reinforcers in the construction of individualized treatment strategies (Ayllon, Milan, Roberts, & McKee, 1979).

Various forms of "tokens" have been used in aggression management programs. For example, Fineman (1968),

working with juveniles, established a merit–demerit token system in which plus or minus points were accumulated for appropriate or inappropriate behavior, respectively. Meichenbaum et al. (1968), also working with delinquents, utilized slips of paper showing the percentage of inappropriate behaviors and amount of money earned during class as tokens. Both of these studies reported significant reductions in aggressive behavior. Horton (1970) provided aggressive delinquent boys with tokens in the form of beans for exhibiting appropriate behaviors and observed similar reductions in aggression.

Although most token systems focus on the relationship of what clients do as individuals and what reinforcers they earn as a consequence of that behavior, some token economics have incorporated group contingencies wherein the reinforcers that individuals earn are a consequence of the behavior of the group to which they belong. For example, a group contingency within a token system was employed by Muller, Hasazi, Pierce, and Hasazi (1975) to reduce physical aggression in elementary-school children. Points were awarded to classes that did not engage in disruptive behavior that were then displayed in the hall and announced over the public address system. The levels of all of the inappropriate behaviors that were measured were dramatically reduced with these contingencies.

Finally, several noteworthy studies using a token system deserve mention. McConnahey, Thompson, and Zimmerman (1977) described a token economy for retarded women. After producing considerable behavior change, the authors began to fade out the contingencies by increasing the interval between token presentation and exchange and the physical distance between them. These procedures aided in promoting generalization and maintenance. A similar strategy was followed by Meichenbaum et al.

(1968). Bolstad and Johnson (1972) compared the efficacy of an externally regulated token system and an internally based one and found that both produced clinically significant effects and that children in the latter condition were slightly more successful in controlling their aggressive behavior than those in the former condition. It is clear that token reinforcement programs, alone and in combination with other strategies, can provide the incentive necessary to encourage patients to learn and use anger and aggression control skills.

Time-out

Time-out is probably the most widely employed strategy to suppress directly undesirable behavior, and it is therefore not surprising that it has been applied to aggressive-disruptive behaviors (Forehand & MacDonough, 1975). It is most often implemented in the form of a "period of time in which positive reinforcement is no longer available" (Leitenberg, 1965, p. 428) that is contingent upon an undesirable response. Following an instance of aggressive or disruptive behavior, the individual may be ignored or removed from all sources of reinforcement for a brief period of time. The time-out procedure has been employed in a diverse range of settings. In an early classroom study, time-out was found to reduce aggressive acting-out and fantasy play (Sloane, Johnson, & Bijou, 1967) in a male student. The child was placed in a separate room after each incident of assaultive and destructive behavior and remained there until he was quiet for 2 minutes. After treatment, the child's classroom behavior was significantly more manageable.

Hamilton, Stephens, and Allen (1967) described the use of time-out with severely retarded adolescents. Each incident of physical abuse resulted in immediate isolation for 1 hour in a restraining chair. Over a period of 13 months, the frequency of abuse decreased from 18 to 2 incidents per month. In another study, time-out took the form of wheeling a nonambulatory abusive patient to a nearby corner of the room and placing her on the floor for a minimum of 2 minutes (Bostow & Bailey, 1969). A second patient was placed in a booth whenever she bit, hit, and scratched others. Following the implementation of time-out, these problem behaviors were reduced to near-zero levels. Comparable results were found by Sand, Trieschman, Fordyce, and Fowler (1970) after isolating a 7-year-old boy who exhibited aggressive temper tantrums in a room for 15 minutes. A 5-minute time-out period was used by Cayner and Kiland (1974) with an adult patient who screamed aggressively. The frequency of screaming was reduced after 1 week of treatment and remained at low levels for several weeks until discharge. Allison and Allison (1971) controlled aggressive and oppositional behavior in a 26-month-old girl after instructing the mother to remove the child to her room. The child was released after a 5-minute period of silence had elapsed. Similar procedures were implemented by Sachs (1973) to reduce destructive-aggressive behavior in a 10-year-old boy. In both cases, the problem behaviors were reduced dramatically.

Studies using time-out have reported dramatic reductions in the frequency of aggressive, hostile, and violent behavior. Given the success demonstrated with this procedure, it becomes necesary to inquire into the parameters of time-out that produce the best results. For example, several studies have systematically investigated time-out duration. Burchard and Barrera (1972) found greater suppression with 30-minute than 5-minute time-out, whereas opposite results were found by Kendal, Nay, and Jeffers (1975). Freeman et al. (1976) investigated three durations of time-out seclusion: 1 hour, 3 minutes, and a requirement that the client be quiet for 15 minutes. Both the long and short durations were ineffective, whereas the latter produced dramatic suppression. To the contrary, a study of Hamilton, Stephens, and Allen (1967) found 1-hour seclusion to be effective, but the procedures cover an extended period of 11 months. White, Nielson, and Johnson (1972) reported no differences in suppression between 15- and 30-minute time-out.

These results, although often contradictory, do suggest that it is possible to reduce aggressive behavior through the use of relatively brief periods of time-out. In many cases, briefer periods of time-out have been shown to be as effective as longer durations of time-out and should be used when effective because the longer periods of time-out can deprive the individual of opportunities to participate in other treatment activities. Approximately half of the studies reviewed here have required a period of appropriate behavior prior to release from the time-out condition. The addition of this requirement precludes the inadvertent reinforcement of undesirable behaviors occurring at the time of release from time-out. Although the manner in which this contingency interacts with time-out duration is unclear from these studies, its inclusion within the time-out procedure may well produce greater suppression than time-out alone (Freeman, et al., Vukelich & Hake, 1971; 1976). Moreover, it does encourage appropriate behavior directly, and for these reasons it should be considered in time-out programs.

An extension of the practice of combining time-out with the requirement that persons engage in appopriate behavior before time-out is ended has been developed by Foxx and Azrin (1972). This strategy has been termed *overcorrection* and requires that the client practice the desirable alternative to the undesirable behavior throughout the time-out period. Foxx and Azrin reported the initial use of overcorrection in treating the aggressive-disruptive behaviors of a profoundly retarded patient. After time-out alone was applied to biting behavior with only minimal success, overcorrection in the form of oral hygiene training and medical assistance training was implemented. The patient's mouth was cleaned for 10 minutes with a toothbrush and, if tissue damage was found, her skin was cleaned and bandaged. In addition, she was required to listen to each line of the hospital incidence report. For grabbing and biting others, the patient received social insurance training in which she answered questions about imminent attacks and stroked the victim's back. These procedures immediately reduced the aggressive behavior, and these gains were maintained at near-zero levels for several months.

A further report by Matson and Stephens (1977) indicated similar results with a 62-year-old chronic patient who threw objects in other's faces. After each throwing incident, she was required to apologize for her misbehavior and receive 5 minutes of trash-pickup training. The trainers used manual guidance if she resisted in any way. Although differential reinforcement of incompatible behavior was found ineffective, overcorrection was successful in eliminating this behavior. These gains were also maintained at follow-up. Long-term maintenance of behavioral improvements following overcorrection have also been reported by Shapiro (1979). The author employed restitutional and positive practice overcorrection with a 5½-year-old girl exhibiting aggressive-disruptive behaviors. The procedure effected immediate and dramatic reductions in these problem behaviors that were maintained at 6-, 12-, and 18-month follow-up.

These preliminary investigations suggest that overcorrection offers an alternative to conventional contingency management procedures when the latter have failed to eliminate aggressive behaviors. When compared to punishment through aversive stimulation, overcorrection may be preferred by therapists and hospital staff. Moreover, the individual actually engages in "desirable" activities as part of the intervention. This noteworthy characteristic lends face validity to the use of overcorrection that, in the long run, may boost patient compliance with the technique.

Finally, the schedule of time-out administration has been investigated in only a few studies. Pendergrass (1971) reported that following each aggressive behavior with time-out was more effective than the intermittent application of time-out. Moreover, 5- and 20-minute durations were found equally effective in suppressing aggressive behavior. However, the findings of Clark, Rowbery, Baer, and Baer (1973) are not consistent with these data. The authors found that intermittent time-out was as effective as consistent time-out. Differential punishment of high-rate aggressive behavior was maximally effective and comparable in suppression to consistent time-out. Clearly, more research on schedule and duration effects is required before optimal parameters may be specified.

In summary, response-contingent time-out has been extensively applied to reduce aggressive behavior with excellent results. Attention should be paid to the various parameters governing the efficacy of time-out if maximal suppression is to be achieved. Only through the use of empirically sound methods can its parameters be explicated for clinical use. Insofar as aggressive behavior is frequently maintained by reinforcement from the social environment (e.g., Patterson et al., 1967; Patterson, Cobb, & Ray, 1973), time-out will continue to remain one of the more powerful techniques for its modification.

Response Cost

Response cost is closely related to time-out in that an undesirable behavior is fol-

lowed by the loss of positive reinforcers. However, whereas time-out is a period in which a person cannot acquire reinforcement, response cost requires that the client relinquish reinforcers that have already been earned. Consequently, the procedure requires the preexistence of a system in which the individual has earned or possesses a quantity of reinforcers from which portions may be subtracted or access may be limited. The response-cost procedure is often therefore associated with other procedures, such as basic reinforcement programs, contingency contracts, and token reinforcement systems.

Phillips (1968) investigated the effects of fines and warnings to reduce the aggressive statements of the residents of Achievement Place, a community-based group home program for predelinquent youths. The introduction of a 20-token fine produced an immediate decline in this behavior. Such statements gradually returned when fines were no longer levied and staff members merely warned that the fines would be used if aggressive behavior occurred. The response-cost procedure was compared to a time-out procedure in the control of four forms of aggression by institutionalized delinquents in a study by Burchard and Barrera (1972). The residents were exposed to either a 5- or 30-token fine, or a 5- or 30-minute isolation period. The higher values for both procedures were significantly more suppressive than the lower ones. In addition, the procedures implemented with higher values became more suppressive over time. No important differences in efficacy were identified between the two types of procedures.

Coe (1972) specified a response-cost procedure within a home-based contract to help manage the violent temper tantrums and aggressive behavior of a 12-year-old boy. The child was fined one token for every minute of tantrum behavior. In combination with positive reinforcement for appropriate behaviors, this procedure was effective in reducing both problem behaviors and restoring order to the home. In a similar but more complex program, Patterson (1976) reported positive findings with fines for aggressive and deviant behaviors in conduct problem children. Both privileges and points could be taken away for misbehavior, whereas they could be earned for prosocial behavior.

These findings indicate that fines can suppress aggressive behavior as well as other disruptive behaviors and provide additional evidence of their therapeutic benefits in these programs. However, because the studies reviewed have employed response cost procedures in conjunction with several other procedures, conclusions regarding the efficacy of response cost per se can be only tentative at best. One of the procedural difficulties associated with the implementation of response cost concerns its reliance upon the removal of an effective reinforcer. Where reinforcers cannot be easily withdrawn or removed, this paradigmatic requirement becomes a limiting pragmatic concern.

In conclusion, it appears that response cost can serve as a valuable component of comprehensive contingency management systems. If a sufficiently large magnitude of response cost is employed (Burchard & Barrera, 1972), maximal suppression may be produced. However, one of the limitations of this procedure derives from its dependence upon reinforcers that can be efficiently withdrawn. In cases where this is difficult to accomplish or where multiple reinforcers control aggressive behavior, alternative procedures may be preferred.

Punishment Through Aversive Stimulation

Although the contingent administration of aversive stimulation has been employed to reduce a wide range of problem behaviors (Johnston, 1972), only a relatively small number of studies have examined its effects upon aggression.

Risley (1968) reported one of the earliest laboratory investigations involving the contingent presentation of aversive stimulation in the form of electric shock to decrease aggressive behavior in a 6-year-old girl. Painful but harmless shock was initially employed to eliminate dangerous climbing behavior. The girl then began to aggress against her younger brother by striking him with objects or pushing him down the stairs. Contingent shock was applied to reduce her aggressive behavior and within 3 weeks its rate was reduced from 2.3 to 0 per day. In addition, the behavior was not reported to occur in the next 70 days of follow-up.

Browning (1971) and Browning and Stover (1971) discussed the use of several punishment techniques in reducing hitting responses in a 3-year-old girl admitted to residential treatment. A year's treatment consisting of time-out and verbal social punishment had proven inexpedient in decelerating her aggressive behavior. In fact, the data indicated that social censure had actually accelerated aggressive behavior. Therefore, contingent shock was introduced to decrease aggressive behavior and to condition verbal punishment concurrently. The results indicated that shock produced a dramatic deceleration. Unfortunately, subsequent reports indicated that the child's aggressive behavior at home was only moderately controlled. Assaultive behavior in a 20-year-old, schizophrenic female was treated by Liberman et al. (1974), using electric shock. The authors noted that assaultive behavior was reduced from an average of 0.9 incidents per day for a 10-day baseline to 2 incidents in the 30 days prior to discharge. However, her behavior deteriorated when she was transferred to another unit that did not implement the same contingencies as those that were found in her original ward.

Milder forms of aversive stimulation than shock have also been reported. Heriksen and Doughty (1967) paired facial (frown) and verbal disapproval

("That's a bad boy") with physical arm restraint contingent upon aggressive-disruptive behavior. These behaviors were reduced and remained at low levels, even following the withdrawal of restraint. Schwitzgebel (1967) consequated hostile statements with a mild aversive response or extinction in the form of a disagreement or inattention. Although the procedure resulted in some decrease in hostile statements, this reduction was not clinically significant. One study has reported the use of spanking in combination with other techniques to reduce the frequency of violent and aggressive temper tantrums in a 12-year-old boy (Coe, 1972). With the addition of spanking, the child's behavior was more controlled and less hostile. Finally, Geleerd (1945) instructed one mother to hold her tantrumming and aggressive daughter under a cold water faucet to "cool her down." The child rapidly learned to control her violent reactions.

In summary, the contingent administration of aversive stimulation following aggressive behavior has been mostly limited to use in institutions with highly refractory and dangerous behaviors. The overall effects of punishment alone do not appear sufficiently positive to warrant its use as a primary intervention modality except perhaps with self-injurious self-stimulation (Baer, 1970; Bucher & Lovaas, 1968). When contingent aversive stimulation is applied, it has typically been found advantageous to pair it with verbal stimuli in order to promote generalization and maintenance, and to combine it with reinforcement programs to teach alternative appropriate behavior. However, the use of punishment through aversive stimulation is of potential harm to clients, practitioners who advocate it, and the profession in whose name it is implemented. Consequently, it should be used only as a last resort and then with the full and careful attention to the legal and ethical safeguards required of such a hazardous undertaking.

CONCLUSIONS

The typical findings of the social skills training programs that have been used in the treatment of the behavior of explosive, aggressive, or hostile individuals have indicated relatively rapid and clinically significant improvements in specific problematic behaviors, classroom, ward, or unit functioning, and overall social adjustment. Such outcomes have commonly resulted from use of a basic skills package training combining instructions, modeling, rehearsal, feedback, coaching, and social reinforcement. Generalization and maintenance of treatment gains have largely been the rule, rather than the exception, when explicitly programmed for and tested. For example, both the addition of generalization instructions and the use of *in vivo* confederates have been shown to be advantageous in promoting skill use in the natural environment subsequent to the termination of treatment (Matson & Zeiss, 1979). Similarly, booster sessions at infrequent intervals to assess follow-up gains and provide retraining for skills showing deterioration have been shown to solidify treatment gains (Twentyman & Zimering, 1979).

The surge of interest in skills training procedures has prompted researchers to investigate the procedures and assessment strategies characteristic of this approach more fully. Several reviews have provided a critical perspective by which many skills programs can be evaluated (Bellack, 1979; Twentyman & Zimering, 1979), thereby advancing the methodological sophistication required of the skills training model. As noted by Curran (1979), consideration of previously neglected methodological details will further maximize the gains made subsequent to training.

The importance of improving assessment strategies to overcome the inadequacies of previous research receives continuing emphasis (Bellack, 1983). In sum, social skills training programs have been clinically useful with children, adolescents, and adults, and certainly warrant continued application. Perhaps in conjunction with a simple contingency management program, a skills training program could rapidly and effectively control hyperaggression while simultaneously developing an alternative prosocial repertoire. When such benefits are realized, the contingency management procedures can be withdrawn gradually.

Less is known about the cognitively oriented self-control techniques described here. Because cognitive strategies typically incorporate conventional behavioral procedures, few conclusions regarding their unique contribution to the training effort may be made. However, self-instruction and other covert self-control techniques are deserving of continued examination in the treatment of both aggressive behavior (Camp et al., 1977) and anger-expression difficulties (Novaco, 1978). The research to date bearing upon the clinical impact of cognitive behavioral strategies indicates that their use in treatment produces clinically significant therapeutic gains within short periods of time. Further research is required if necessary and sufficient components are to be identified and separated from those that do not contribute to these results. Studies combining external and "internal" strategies might, for example, examine the role of covert statements or guiding verbalizations by themselves and in combination with other cognitive and behavioral strategies (Forman, 1980; Snyder & White, 1979).

The contribution of contingency management procedures to controlling the frequency of aggressive outbursts and disruptive behavior in both children and adults is clear. Most of the studies reviewed have reported significant reductions in aggressive behavior, and they have been conducted in such a manner to conclude that the contingency management procedures, rather than other,

uncontrolled factors, have been responsible for the changes observed. As powerful as these procedures are, however, their implementation often poses considerable tactical and strategic problems. It is often difficult to program contingencies in a sufficient number of relevant settings to produce general effects (Combs & Slaby, 1977). In fact, the steps that are required to modify the contingencies in different settings may mitigate against doing so primarily because of time-and-cost limitations.

Another requirement of the contingency management approach is that the persons who carry these programs out (contingency managers) in the various settings in which the programs are implemented must receive the training and supervision required to insure that they do not deviate from effective procedure in their use of behavioral strategies. In order to maximize the gains produced by these methods, contingency managers routinely require this detailed training and continuing supervision. Finally, although contingency management can foster prosocial behaviors, it does not explicitly teach such skills to the clients. Consequently, supplementary social skill and self-control training in contingency management programs is often necessary.

Solutions to these difficulties appear to be limited only by the ingenuity of the therapists. For example, Rueveni's (1971) work with children demonstrates how peer therapists and peer-mediated contingencies can be incorporated in the treatment effort. In addition, children who have been trained to employ behavioral procedures during treatment have promoted behavioral improvements in other children's behavior (Johnson & Bailey, 1974). Alternatively, prosocial modeling may be facilitated if training includes a game, group therapy, or structured activity format. The studies also suggest that a successful treatment package might incorporate the use of brief time-out, moderate response cost, and explicit differential reinforcement of desirable behavior. If time-out is employed, release should be contingent upon some duration of appropriate behavior. The use of natural as well as token reinforcers would be suitable for response contingent presentation or withdrawal.

If the child is old enough, one might employ a contingency contract that requires prosocial behavior with continued progress required for the delivery of reinforcement (Stuart, 1971). Furthermore, as shown by Patterson's (1976) impressive work, parents can be trained to implement these and other techniques after receiving a structured course in behavior management principles and the implementation of behavior change projects. This comprehensive training program would not only facilitate rapid behavior change but would also enhance genealization and maintenance. Some of the same procedures appear to be appropriate for use with adults, particularly in controlled settings.

Thus, as documented in this review, a growing literature has accumulated on the application of behavioral procedures to socially disruptive aggressive behavior and anger-mediated excesses (Firestone, 1976; Foy et al., 1975; Frederiksen et al., 1976; Rimm et al., 1974). Conventional behavioral procedures such as contingency management and social skills training are a few of the methods that have been brought to bear upon these difficulties. For example, Eisler and Frederiksen (1980) and Rimm (1977) have discussed the use of social skills and assertion training, respectively, in the treatment of aggression. In both of these excellent accounts, the authors describe a conceptual framework for their treatment approach, assessment considerations, treatment guidelines, and illustrations of the model.

More recently, cognitive-behaviorists have reported the efficacy of treatment packages that draw upon both cognitive and behavioral procedures (Mahoney & Arnkoff, 1978). Novaco's (1975) anger-control program, for example, stands as the most comprehensive set of techniques that has been documented as useful in the management of excessive anger arousal. Its major emphasis lies in the formulation and training of cognitive self-control to regulate anger arousal and promote competency in dealing with provocation. The author's conceptual framework has received empirical support (Novaco, 1978).

The success of these behavioral and cognitive behavioral programs derives, in part, from their inclusion of a variety of different procedures designed to modify the individual's skill repertoire in an active and direct manner. When explicit training in fundamental skills is provided, competency in a particular situation and self-control are significantly encouraged. As demonstrated in a disappointingly small number of investigations (e.g., Harvey et al., 1978; McCullough et al., 1977), programs that explicitly alter both the environmental contingencies and the individual's prosocial repertoire are generally associated with both rapid and enduring improvements. Strategies designed to deal effectively with both of these important domains must be further investigated if maximum benefit is to be gained from their integration. Much effort has been devoted to the development and refinement of contingency management approaches to the control of aggression. We look forward to comparable advances in social skills and self-control training procedures to contribute to the design, implementation, and evaluation of potent programs for the treatment of anger difficulties and aggressive behavior. Their clinical impact will be maximized only through continued experimental examination.

REFERENCES

Alberti, R., & Emmons, M. (1978). *Your perfect right: A guide to assertive behavior.* San Luis Obispo, CA: Impact Publishers.

Allen, K., Turner, K., & Everett, D. (1970). A behavior modification classroom for Head Start children with problem behaviors. *Exceptional Children, 37,* 119–129.

Allison, T., & Allison, S. (1971). Time-out from reinforcement: Effect on sibling aggression. *The Psychological Record, 21,* 81–86.

Ax, A. (1953). The physiological differentiation of fear and anger. *Psychosomatic Medicine, 15,* 433–442.

Ayllon, T., & Azrin, N. (1968). *The token economy: A motivational system for therapy and rehabilitation.* New York: Appleton-Century-Crofts.

Ayllon, T., & Michael, J. (1959). The psychiatric nurse as a behavioral engineer. *Journal of the Experimental Analysis of Behavior, 2,* 323–337.

Ayllon, T., & Milan, M. A., with the assistance of Roberts, M. D., & McKee, J. M. (1979). *Correctional rehabilitation and management: A psychological approach.* New York: Wiley.

Baer, D. (1970). A case for the selective reinforcement of punishment. In C. Neuringer & J. L. Michael (Eds.), *Behavior modification in clinical psychology.* New York: Appleton-Century-Crofts.

Bandura, A. (1969). *Principles of behavior modification.* New York: Holt, Rinehart & Winston.

Bandura, A. (1973). *Aggression: A social learning analysis.* Englewood Cliffs, NJ: Prentice-Hall.

Bardill, D. (1972). Behavior contracting and group therapy with preadolescent males in a residential treatment setting. *International Journal of Group Psychotherapy, 22,* 333–337.

Baron, R. (1977). *Human aggression.* New York: Plenum.

Bellack, A. (1979). A critical appraisal of strategies for assessing social skill. *Behavioral Assessment, 1,* 157–176.

Bellack, A. S. (1983). Recurrent problems in the behavioral assessment of social skill. *Behavior Research and Therapy, 21,* 29–41.

Berkowitz, L. (1973). Control of aggression. In B. Caldwell & H. Ricciuti (Eds.), *Review of child development research* (Vol. 3). Chicago: The University of Chicago Press.

Bernal, M. (1969). Behavioral feedback in the modification of brat behaviors. *Journal of Nervous and Mental Disorder, 148,* 375–385.

Bernal, M. (1071). Training parents in child management. In R. Bradfield (Ed.), *Behavior modification of learning disabilities.* San Rafael, CA: Academic Therapy.

Bernal, M., Williams, D., Miller, W., & Reagor, P. (1972). The use of videotape feedback and operant learning principles in training parents in management of deviant children. In R. Rubin, H. Fensterheim, J. Henderson, & L. Ullmann (Eds.), *Advances in behavior therapy.* New York: Academic Press.

Blackham, G., & Silberman, A. (1975). *Modification of child and adolescent behavior* (2nd ed.). Belmont, CA: Wadsworth.

Blackwood, R. (1970). The operant conditioning of verbally mediated self-control in the classroom. *Journal of School Psychology, 8,* 251–258.

Bolstad, O., & Johnson, S. (1972). Self-regulation in the modification of disruptive classroom behavior. *Journal of Applied Behavior Analysis, 5,* 443–454.

Bornstein, P., Ulinegardner, J., Rychtarck, R., Paul, W., Narfeh, S., Sweeney, T., & Justman, A. (1979). Interpersonal skills training: Evaluation of a program with adult male offenders. *Criminal Justice and Behavior, 6,* 119–132.

Bornstein, M., Bellack, A., & Hersen, M. (1980). Social skills training for highly aggressive children: Treatment in an inpatient psychiatric setting. *Behavior Modification, 4,* 173–186.

Bostow, E., & Bailey, J. (1969). Modification of severe disruptive and aggressive behavior using brief time-out and reinforcement procedures. *Journal of Applied Behavior Analysis, 2,* 31–37.

Brown, P., & Elliot, R. (1965). Control of aggression in a nursery school class. *Journal of Exceptional Child Psychology, 2,* 103–107.

Browning, R. (1971). Treatment effects of a total behavior modification program with autistic children. *Behavior Research and Therapy, 9,* 317–327.

Browning, R., & Stover, D. (1971). *Behavior modification in child treatment: An experimental clinical approach.* Chicago: Aldine.

Bucher, B., & Lovaas, O. (1968). Use of aversive stimulation in behavior modification. In M. Jones (Ed.), *Miami symposium on the prediction of behavior 1967: Aversive stimulation.* Coral Gables: University of Miami Press.

Burchard, J., & Barrera, F. (1972). An analysis of time-out and response cost in a programmed environment. *Journal of Applied Behavior Analysis, 5,* 271–282.

Camp, B. (1975). *Verbal mediation in young aggressive boys.* Unpublished manuscript, University of Colorado School of Medicine. Cited in Meichenbaum, D. (1977).

Camp, B., Gaston, E., Hebert, F., & Doornick, W. (1977). ''Think-aloud'': A program for developing self-control in young, aggressive boys. *Journal of Abnormal Child Psychology, 5,* 157–169.

Cayner, J., & Kiland, J. (1974). Use of brief time-out with three schizophrenic patients. *Journal of Behavior Therapy and Experimental Psychiatry, 5,* 141–145.

Chittenden, G. (1942). An experimental study in measuring and modifying assertive behavior in young children. *Monographs of Society for Research in Child Development, 7* (Serial No. 31).

Clark. H., Rowbury, T., Baer, A., & Baer, D. (1973). Time-out as a punishing stimulus in continuous and intermittent schedules. *Journal of Applied Behavior Analysis, 6,* 443–455.

Coe, W. (1972). A behavioral approach to disrupted family interactions. *Psychotherapy: Theory, Research, and Practice, 9,* 80–85.

Combs, M., & Slaby, D. (1977). Social-skills training with children. In B. Lahey & A. Kazdin (Eds.), *Advances in clinical child psychology* (Vol. 1). New York: Plenum.

Curran, J. (1979). Social skills: Methodological issues and future directions. In A. Bellack & M. Hersen (Eds.), *Research and practice in social skills training.* New York: Plenum.

D'Zurilla, T. J., & Goldfried, M. R. (1973). Cognitive processes, problem solving, and effective behavior. In M. R. Goldfried & M. Merbaum, *Behavior change through self-control.* New York: Holt, Rinehart & Winston.

Eisler, R., & Frederiksen, L. (1980). *Perfecting social skills: A guide to interpersonal behavior development.* New York: Plenum.

Elder, J., Edelstein, B., & Narick, M. (1979). Adolescent psychiatric patients: Modifying aggressive behavior with social skills training. *Behavior Modification, 3,* 161–178.

Ellis, A. (1970). *The essence of rational psychotherapy: A comprehensive approach to treatment.* New York: Institute for Rational Living.

Evans, D., & Hearn, M. (1973). Anger and systematic desensitization: A follow-up. *Psychological Reports, 32,* 569–570.

Fineman, K. (1968). An operant conditioning program in a juvenile detention facility. *Psychological Reports, 22,* 1119–1120.

Firestone, P. (1976). The effects and side effects of time-out on an aggressive nursery school child. *Journal of Behavior Therapy and Experimental Psychiatry, 6,* 79–91.

Forehand, R., & MacDonough, S. (1975). Response contingent time out: An examination of outcome data. *European Journal of Behavioral Analysis and Modification, 1,* 109–115.

Forman, S. (1980). A comparison of cognitive training and response cost procedures in modifying aggressive behavior of elementary school children. *Behavior Therapy, 11,* 594–600.

Foxx, R., & Azrin, N. (1972). Restitution: A method of eliminating aggressive-disruptive behavior of retarded and brain damaged patients. *Behavior Research and Therapy, 10,* 15–27.

Foy, D., Eisler, R., & Pinkston, S. (1975). Modeled assertion in a case of explosive rages. *Journal of Behavior Therapy and Experimental Psychiatry, 6,* 135–137.

Frederiksen, L., Jenkins, J., Foy, D., & Eisler, E. (1976). Social skills training to modify abusive verbal outbursts in adults. *Journal of Applied Behavior Analysis, 9,* 117–125.

Freeman, B., Somerset, T., & Ritvo, E. (1976). Effect of duration of time-out in suppressing disruptive behavior of a severely autistic child. *Psychological Reports, 38,* 124–126.

Funkenstein, D., King, S., & Drolette, M. (1957). *Mastery of stress.* Cambridge, MA: Harvard University Press.

Geleerd, E. (1945). Observations on temper tantrums in children. *American Journal of Orthopsychiatry, 15,* 238–246.

Gittelman, M. (1965). Behavioral rehearsal as a technique in child treatment. *Journal of Child Psychology and Psychiatry, 6,* 251–255.

Goldstein, A., Sherman, M., Gershaw, N., Sprafkin, R., & Glick, B. (1978). Training aggressive adolescents in prosocial behavior. *Journal of Youth and Adolescents 7*(1), 73–92.

Goodwin, S., & Mahoney, M. (1975). Modification of aggression via modeling: An experimental probe. *Journal of Behavior Therapy and Experimental Psychiatry, 6,* 200–202.

Graziano, A. (1974). *Child without tomorrow.* New York: Pergamon.

Hamilton, J., Stephens, L., & Allen, P. (1967). Controlling aggressive and destructive behavior in severely retarded institutionalized residents. *American Journal of Mental Deficiency, 71,* 852–856.

Harvey, J., Karan, O., Bhargava, D., & Morehouse, N. (1978). Relaxation training and cognitive behavioral procedures to reduce violent temper outbursts in a moderately retarded woman. *Journal of Behavior Therapy and Experimental Psychiatry, 9,* 347–351.

Hearn, M., & Evans, D. (1972). Anger and reciprocal inhibition therapy. *Psychological Reports, 30,* 943–948.

Heatherington, E., & Martin, B. (1979). Family interaction and psychopathology in children. In H. Quay & J. Werry (Eds.), *Psychopathological disorders of children.* New York: Wiley.

Herell, J. (1971). Use of systematic desensitization to eliminate inappropriate anger. *Proceedings of the 79th Annual Convention of the American Psychological Association 6* (pp. 431–432). Washington, D. C.: American Psychological Association.

Heriksen, K., & Doughty, R. (1967). Decelerating undesirable behavior in a group of profoundly retarded boys. *American Journal of Mental Deficiency, 72,* 40–44.

Hersen, M. (1979). Modification of skills deficits in psychiatric patients. In A. Bellack & M. Hersen (Eds.), *Research and practice in social skills training.* New York: Plenum.

Hersen, M. & Barlow, D. (1976). *Single case experimental designs: Strategies for studying behavior change.* New York: Pergamon.

Horton, L. (1970). Generalization of aggressive behavior in adolescent delinquent boys. *Journal of Applied Behavior Analysis, 3,* 205–211.

Jacobsen, E. (1938). *Progressive relaxation.* Chicago: The University of Chicago Press.

Jenkins, R. (1968). The varieties of children's behavioral problems and family dynamics. *American Journal of Psychiatry, 124,* 134–139.

Johnson, S., & Lobitz, G. (1974). Parental manipulation of child behavior in home observations. *Journal of Applied Behavior Analysis, 7,* 23–31.

Johnson, M., & Bailey, J. (1974). Cross-age tutoring: Fifth graders as arithmetic tutors for kindergarten children. *Journal of Applied Behavior Analysis, 7,* 223–232.

Johnston, J. (1972). Punishment of human behavior. *American Psychologist, 27,* 1033–1054.

Kauffman, L., & Wagner, B. (1972). Barb: A systematic treatment technique for temper control disorders. *Behavior Therapy, 3*, 84–90.

Kendal, P., Nay, W., & Jeffers, J. (1975). Time-out duration and contrast effects: A systematic evaluation of a successive treatments design. *Behavior Therapy, 6*, 609–615.

Kolko, D., Dorsett, P., & Milan, M. (1981). A total-assessment approach in the evaluation of social skills training: The effectiveness of an anger control program for adolescent psychiatric patients. *Behavior Assessment, 3*, 383–402.

Kolko, D. J., & Milan, M. A. (1980). Misconception correction through reading in the treatment of a self-injection phobia. *Journal of Behavior Therapy and Experimental Psychiatry, 11*, 273–276.

Krasner, L., & Ullman, L. P. (1973). *Behavior influence and personality: The social matrix of human action.* New York: Holt, Rinehart & Winston.

Lefkowitz, M., Eron, L., Walder, L., & Huesman, R. (1977). *Growing up to be violent: A longitudinal study of the development of aggression.* New York: Pergamon.

Leitenberg, H. (1965). Is time-out from positive reinforcement an aversive event? A review of the experimental evidence. *Psychological Bulletin, 64*, 428–441.

Liberman, R., Wallace, C., Teigen, J., & Davis, J. (1974). Interventions with psychotic behaviors. In K. Calhoun, H. Adams, & K. Mitchell (Eds.), *Innovative treatment methods in psychopathology.* New York: Wiley.

Madsen, C., Becker, W., & Thomas, D. (1968). Rules, praise, and ignoring: Elements of elementary classroom control. *Journal of Applied Behavior Analysis, 1*, 139–150.

Mahoney, M. J. (1974). *Cognition and behavior modification.* Cambridge, MA: Ballinger.

Mahoney, M., & Arnkoff, D. (1978). Cognitive and self-control therapies. In S. Garfield & A. Bergin (Eds.), *Handbook of psychotherapy and behavior change* (2nd ed.). New York: Wiley.

Martin, R. (1975). *Legal challenges to behavior modification.* Champaign, IL: Research Press.

Matson, J., & Stephens, R. (1977). Overcorrection of aggressive behavior in a chronic psychiatric patient. *Behavior Modification, 1*, 559–564.

Matson, J., & Stephens, R. (1978). Increasing appropriate behavior of explosive chronic psychiatric patients with a social skills training package. *Behavior Modification, 2*, 61–76.

Matson, J., & Zeiss, R. (1978). Group training of social skills in chronically explosive severely disturbed psychiatric patients. *Behavioral Engineering, 5*, 41–50.

Matson, J., & Zeiss, R. (1979). The buddy system: A method for generalized reduction of appropriate interpersonal behavior of retarded psychiatric patients. *British Journal of Social and Clinical Psychology, 18*, 201.

Matson, J., Esveldt-Dawson, K., Andrasik, F., Ollendick, T., Petti, T., & Hersen, M. (1980). Direct, observational, and generalization effects of social skills training with emotionally disturbed children. *Behavior Therapy, 11*, 522–531.

McConahey, D., Thompson, T., & Zimmerman, R. (1977). A token system for retarded women: Behavior therapy, drug administration and their combination. In T. Thompson & J. Grabowski (Eds.), *Behavior modification of the mentally retarded.* New York: Oxford University Press.

McCullough, J., Huntsinger, G., & Nay, W. (1977). Self-control treatment of aggression in a sixteen-year-old male: A case study. *Journal of Consulting and Clinical Psychology, 45*, 322–331.

McNamara, J. (1968). The broad-based application of social learning theory to treating aggression in a preschool child. *Journal of Clinical Psychology, 26*, 245–247.

Megargee, E. (1973). Recent research on overcontrolled and undercontrolled personality patterns among violent offenders. *Sociological Symposium, 9*, 37–50.

Meichenbaum, D. (1972). Cognitive modification of test anxious college students. *Journal of Consulting and Clinical Psychology, 39*, 370–380.

Meichenbaum, D. (1977). *Cognitive behavior*

modification: An integrative approach. New York: Plenum.

Meichenbaum, D., Bowers, K., & Ross, R. (1968). Modification of classroom behavior of institutionalized female adolescent offenders. *Behavior Research and Therapy, 6,* 343–353.

Milan, M. A., & McKee, J. M. (1974). Behavior modification: Principles and applications in corrections. In D. Glaser (Ed.), *Handbook of criminology.* Chicago: Rand McNally.

Morris, H. (1956). Aggressive behavior disorders in children: A follow-up study. *American Journal of Psychiatry, 112,* 991–997.

Muller, A., Hasazi, S., Pierce, M., & Hasazi, J. (1975). Modification of disruptive behavior in a large group of elementary school students. In E. Ramp & G. Semb (Eds.), *Behavior analysis: Areas of research and application.* Englewood Cliffs, NJ: Prentice-Hall.

Novaco, R. (1975). *Anger control: The development and evaluation of an experimental treatment.* Lexington, MA: Heath.

Novaco, R. W. (1977a). A stress-innoculation approach to anger management in the training of law enforcement officers. *American Journal of Community Psychology, 5,* 327–346.

Novaco, R. (1977b). Stress innoculation: A cognitive therapy for anger and its application to a case of depression. *American Journal of Community Psychology, 5,* 327–346.

Novaco, R. (1978). Anger and coping with stress: Cognitive behavioral interventions. In J. Foreyt & D. Rathjen (Eds.), *Cognitive behavior therapy: Research and application.* New York: Plenum.

Ollendick, T., & Hersen, M. (1979). Social skills training for juvenile delinquents. *Behavior Research and Therapy, 17,* 1–8.

Oltmanns, T., Broderick, J., & O'Leary, K. (1977). Marital adjustment and the efficacy of behavior therapy with children. *Journal of Consulting and Clinical Psychology, 45,* 724–729.

Patterson, G. (1956). *A tentative approach to the classification of children's behavior*

problems. Unpublished doctoral dissertations. University of Minnesota.

Patterson, G. (1976). The aggressive child: Victim and architect of a coercive system. In E. Mash, L. Hamerlynch, & L. Handy. *Behavior modification with families.* New York: Brunner/Mazel.

Patterson, G., Cobb, J., & Ray, R. (1972). Direct interventions in the classroom: A set of procedures for the aggressive child. In F. Clark, D. Evans, & L. Hamerlynck (Eds.), *Implementing behavioral programs for schools and clinics.* Champaign, IL: Research Press.

Patterson, G., Cobb, J., & Ray, R. (1973). A social engineering technique for retraining the families of aggressive boys. In H. Adams & I. Unikel (Ed.), *Issues and trends in behavior therapy.* Springfield, IL: Charles C Thomas.

Patterson, G., & Gullion, M. (1976). *Living with children: New methods for parents and teachers.* Champaign, IL: Research Press.

Patterson, G., Littman, R., & Bricker, W. (1967). Assertive behavior in children: A step toward a theory of aggression. *Monographs of the Society for Research in Child Development, 32* (Serial No. 113).

Patterson, G., & Reid, J. (1973). Intervention for families of aggressive boys: A replication study. *Behavior Research and Therapy, 11,* 383–394.

Pendergrass, V. (1971). Effects of length of time out from positive reinforcement and schedule of application in suppression of aggressive behavior. *Psychological Record, 21,* 75–80.

Phillips, E. (1968). Achievement Place: Token reinforcement procedures in a home style rehabilitation setting for pre-delinquent boys. *Journal of Applied Behavior Analysis, 1,* 213–233.

Rachlin, H. (1977). Review of M. J. Mahoney's *Cognition and behavior modification. Journal of Applied Behavior Analysis, 10,* 369–374.

Rimm, D. (1977). Treatment of antisocial aggression. In G. Harris (Ed.), *The group treatment of human problems.* New York: Grune & Stratton.

Rimm, D., DeGroot, J., Boord, P., Herman, J., & Dillow, P. (1971). Systematic desensitization of an anger response. *Behavior Research and Therapy, 9,* 273–280.

Rimm, D., Hill, G., Brown, N., & Stuart, J. (1974). Group assertion training in the treatment of inappropriate anger. *Psychological Reports, 34,* 791–798.

Rimm, D., & Masters, D. (1979). *Behavior therapy: Techniques and empirical findings.* New York: Academic Press.

Risley, T. (1968). The effects and side effects of punishing the autistic behaviors of a deviant child. *Journal of Applied Behavior Analysis, 1,* 21–34.

Robins, L. (1966). *Deviant children grow up.* Baltimore: Williams & Wilkins.

Rothenberg, A. (1971). On anger. *American Journal of Psychiatry, 128,* 454–460.

Rubin, T. (1970). *The angry book.* New York: Collier Macmillan.

Rueveni, U. (1971). Using sensitivity training with junior high school students. *Children, 18,* 69–72.

Russo, S. (1964). Adaptations in behavioral therapy with children. *Behavior Research and Therapy, 2,* 43–47.

Sachs, D. (1973). The efficacy of time out procedures in a variety of behavior problems. *Journal of Behavior Therapy and Experimental Psychiatry, 4,* 237–242.

Sand, P., Trieschman, R., Fordyce, W., & Fowler, R. (1970). Behavior modification in the medical rehabilitation setting: Rationale and some applications. *Rehabilitation Research and Practice Review, 1,* 11.

Schneider, M. (1974). Turtle technique in the classroom. *Teaching exceptional children, 7,* 22–24.

Schneider, M., & Robin, A. (1976). The turtle technique: A method for the self-control of impulsive behavior. In D. Krumboltz & C. Thoresen (Eds.), *Behavioral counseling.*

Schrader, C., & Long, J. (1978). *An anger control package for adolescent drug abusers.* Paper presented at the annual convention of the Association for Behavior Analysis, Milwaukee, WI.

Schwitzgebel, R. (1967). Short-term operant conditioning of adolescent offenders on socially relevant variables. *Journal of Abnormal Psychology, 72,* 134–142.

Shapiro, E. (1979). Restitution and positive practice overcorrection in reducing aggressive-disruptive behavior: A long-term follow-up. *Journal of Behavior Therapy and Experimental Psychiatry, 10,* 131–134.

Simon, S., & Frederiksen, L. (1977). *Social skills training in the treatment of a physically abusive "explosive personality."* Paper presented at the annual convention of the Southeastern Psychological Association, New Orleans, LA.

Skinner, B. F. (1953). *Science and human behavior.* New York: The Free Press.

Skinner, B. F. (1974). *About behaviorism.* New York: Alfred A. Knopf.

Sloane, H., Johnson, M., & Bijou, S. (1967). Successive modification of aggressive behavior and aggressive fantasy play by management of contingencies. *Journal of Child Psychology and Psychiatry, 8,* 217–226.

Smith, R. (1973). The use of humor in the counterconditioning of anger responses: A case study. *Behavior Therapy, 4,* 576–580.

Snyder, J., & White, M. (1979). The use of cognitive self-instruction in the treatment of behaviorally disturbed adolescents. *Behavior Therapy, 10,* 227–235.

Spence, S., & Marzillier, J. (1979). Social skills training with adolescent male offenders: I. Short-term effects. *Behavior Research and Therapy, 17,* 7–16.

Staub, E. (1971). The learning and unlearning of aggression. In J. Singer (Ed.), *The control of aggression and violence.* New York: Acadmic Press.

Stuart, R. (1971). Behavioral contracting with the families of delinquents. *Journal of Behavior Therapy and Experimental Psychiatry, 2,* 1–11.

Tedeschi, J. T., Smith, R. B., & Brown, R. C. (1974). A reinterpretation of research on aggression. *Psychological Bulletin, 81,* 540–562.

Thelen, M., Fry, R., Dollinger, S., & Paul, S. (1976). Use of videotaped models to improve the interpersonal adjustment of delinquents. *Journal of Consulting and Clinical Psychology, 44,* 492.

Thorne, G., Tharp, R., & Wetzel, R. (1967). Behavior modification techniques: New tools for probation officers. *Federal Probation,* June 1967, 21–27.

Tobey, T., & Thoresen, C. (1976). Helping Billy reduce aggressive behaviors: A nine-year-old makes good. In J. Krumboltz & C. Thoresen (Eds.), *Counseling methods.* New York: Holt, Rinehart & Winston.

Twentyman, C., & Zimering, R. (1979). Behavioral training of social skills: A critical review. In M. Hersen, R. Eisler, & P. Miller (Eds.), *Progress in behavior modification,* Vol. 7. New York: Academic Press.

Vukelich, R., & Hake, D. (1971). Reduction of dangerously aggressive behavior in a severely retarded resident through a combination of positive reinforcement procedures. *Journal of Applied Behavior Analysis, 4,* 215–225.

Wagner, M. (1968). Comparative effectiveness of behavioral rehearsal and verbal reinforcement for effecting anger expressiveness. *Psychological Reports, 22,* 1079–1080.

Wallace, C., Teigen, J., Liberman, R., & Baker, V. (1973). Destructive behavior treated by contingency contracts and assertion training: A case study. *Journal of Behavior Therapy and Experimental Psychiatry, 4,* 273–274.

White, G., Nielsen, G., & Johnson, S. (1972). Time out duration and the suppression of deviant behavior in children. *Journal of Applied Behavior Analysis, 5,* 111–120.

Wilson, G. (1979). Cognitive behavior therapy: Paradigm shift or passing phase. In J. Foreyt & D. Rathjen (Eds.), *Cognitive behavior therapy: Research and application.* New York: Plenum.

Wolpe, J. (1976). *Theme and variations: A behavior therapy casebook.* New York: Pergamon.

Wolpe, J. (1982). *The practice of behavior therapy.* New York: Pergamon.

CHAPTER 6

Heterosocial Skills Training

JAMES P. CURRAN, JAN L. WALLANDER, AND ALBERT D. FARRELL

In this chapter we will first review a number of converging sources that appear to us to have contributed to the development of heterosocial skills training. We will then explain the rationale for heterosocial skills training as a treatment procedure for dating difficulties, and we will examine the evidence for the effectiveness of the various training components used in heterosocial skills programs. The content of various training programs will be discussed and procedures for identifying content components will be outlined. The effectiveness of heterosocial skills program will be reviewed. This treatment outcome review will be limited to those studies employing minimal standard control groups and those studies comparing the relative effectiveness of heterosocial skills training to other treatment alternatives. The last section of the chapter will summarize the present sate of the art with respect to heterosocial skills training and suggestions for future research practice will be made.

ORIGIN OF HETEROSOCIAL SKILLS TRAINING

Interest in heterosocial skills training as a treatment strategy can be traced to a number of sources. Four sources that we find particularly illuminating and that we will discuss in some detail are (1) the focus on interpersonal competence found in numerous theories of personality; (2) empiricial findings linking interpersonal competence to psychological functioning; (3) the development of response acquisition approaches to the treatment of distressed emotional states and disordered behaviors; and (4) the search by empirically oriented clinicians for an adequate therapy analog. The first three of these sources are common to a generic social skills training approach, but the fourth is more or less responsible for the interest in heterosocial skills training.

The Role of Interpersonal Competence in Personality Theories

Neo-Freudians and ego theorists such as Adler (1930), Horney (1939), Sullivan (1953), Erikson (1950), Hartmann (1958), and White (1960), objected to Freud's emphasis on instinct and drive as the basis of personality development and shifted the emphasis away from instincts to interpersonal relations, especially the parent–child relationship. These theories attempted to replace or supplement Freud's libido model for an interpersonal model. For example, Hartmann (1958) wrote that instincts alone could never account for adaptive behavior in humans nor the reality principle. He felt that there had to be an innate ego apparatus that developed autonomously from the id in a conflict-free sphere. Erikson (1950) outlined eight stages in the development of the ego. He introduced the notion of competence in each stage and specified the motor and cognitive capacities that determine the character of the crisis in each stage.

Of all the ego theorists, Robert White's (1960) writings emphasized the prominence of interpersonal competency most of all. In fact, White urged adoption of a competence model of human development to go along with Freud's instinctual model and the other ego theorists' interpersonal model. White felt that an individual's emotional development could not be adequately conceptualized by either an exclusively libido model or an exclusively interpersonal model. Feeling that a drive reduction theory of learning was inadequate, White instead saw individuals as active manipulators and explorers of their environments. An effectance motive was postulated whose most characteristic feature was seen in the production of effects on the environment. Its adaptive significance lay in the promotion of spare-time behavior that led to an extensive growth of competence, well beyond what could be learned in connection with drive reduction. White's effectance motivation has its immediate satisfaction in a feeling of efficacy and its adaptive significance in the growth of competence. White stated (1960, p. 185): "Effectance refers to the active tendency to put forth effort to influence the environment, while feelings of efficacy refers to the satisfaction that comes with producing effects." A child's actual competence and a sense of competence are built up from his or her history of dealing efficaciously with the environment. A sense of competence is held to be a crucial element in the psychology of the ego. White's notion of competence and efficacy are in some ways similar to Bandura's (1977a) notion of self-efficacy that we will address later in this section.

Early radical behaviorism with its concentration on S–R psychology to the exclusion of the organism, rejected notions such as competence and self-efficacy. Interest in competency and self-efficacy, however, was maintained by social psychology. Argyle and Kendon (1967), for example, proposed a model in which man was conceptualized as pursuing social and other goals, acting according to rules, and monitoring his or her performance in the light of continuous feedback from the environment. Harré and Secord (1972) emphasized man as an agent directing his or her own behavior. In their model, the agent is active rather than passive. Man seeks out and processes information and generates, monitors and controls his or her actions in order to achieve a goal.

Social learning theorists such as Mischel (1973) and Bandura (1977b) have also developed models that stress man as a more active organism than the more mechanistic S–R models. Mischel feels that through direct and observational learning an individual acquires information about the world. Man has the potential to generate vast repertoires of organized behavior including, among many other things, the social rules and conventions that guide conduct. The observer selectively constructs his or her renditions of reality by means of cognitive and behavioral construction competencies. Another set of Mischel's constructs deals with an individual's expectancies about the consequences of different behavioral possibilities including expectancies of reinforcing contingencies and how certain events predict certain other events. Mischel's conceptual model includes a self-regulatory system and plans wherein persons set performance goals for themselves and react with self-criticism or self-satisfaction depending on how well their behavior matches their expectations and criteria.

Bandura (1977a) developed the construct of *self-efficacy* as an attempt to explain the puzzle that most of our conceptual systems regarding the development of behavior are cognitive in origin; yet most of our effective treatment procedures tend to involve performance-base accomplishments. For Bandura, like White, an individual's self-efficacy is based upon a history of performance accomplishment mediated by cognitive events. Whether an individual attempts a task, persists to its goals, and overcomes obstacles to the goal, is mainly a function of his or her self-efficacy.

Phillips (1978) postulates *social incompetence* as the major psychological deficit and as the major cause of psychopathology. A lack of social skills leads to faulty problem solving and emotional distress that leads to psychopathology. For Phillips, psychopathology results from an organism's inability to solve problems, resolve conflicts, and reach goals. The organism's lack of requisite skills results in less adaptive, and in some cases, maladaptive strategies. Negative emotional states and maladaptive cognitions occur in lieu of social solutions to problems. Phillips perceives social skills training not just as another treatment approach but as an alternative model to the traditional medical model of psychopathology. Although we are not in agreement with Phillips regarding his notion that social skills are the major deficits leading to all psychopathology, we do feel it is an important parameter that, up to this point in time, has not received the emphasis it deserves. From the brief review, we can see that the notion of interpersonal competence has played a central role in numerous theories of psychological functioning. In these theories, socially competent individuals are perceived (everything else being equal) as better equipped to handle psychological crises. Consequently, it can be argued that one way to improve psychological functioning would to be increase interpersonal competency. The rationale for social skills training is precisely this notion that increasing interpersonal compe-

tency will lead to better resolutions of problematic interpersonal situations and improve psychological functioning.

The competence conceptualizations of all the theorists reviewed in this section have emphasized man as an active organism and the paramount role of cognitive processes in interpersonal competency. Trower (1982) has justifiably criticized social skills training approaches that emphasize the teaching of isolated behavioral components to the neglect of cognitive processes.

Empirical Findings Linking Social Competence and Psychopathology

Zigler and Phillips (1960, 1962) found that hospitalized psychiatric patients evidenced greater inpoverishment in social achievement than nonhospitalized individuals from the same socioeconomic strata of society. A number of studies (Phillips & Zigler, 1961; Zigler & Levine, 1973; Zigler & Phillips, 1960) demonstrated that level of premorbid social competence in a hospitalized psychiatric patient is a good predictor of posthospital adjustment. This relationship seems to hold, irrespective of the patient's diagnostic label and regardless of the treatment regime carried out during the course of hospitalization. Strauss and Carpenter (1972) indicated that premorbid levels of instrumental role behavior and instrumental skills are important predictors of competence in subsequent social adjustment, clinical outcome, and quality of interpersonal life for schizophrenic patients. Curran, Miller, Zwick, Monti, and Stout (1980) demonstrated that patients labeled as having social skills deficits have significantly longer admission stays to a psychiatric hospital and show less adequate psychiatric functioning after discharge. Hersen (1979) noted that many studies have demonstrated that the better the patient's social skills and adjustment are prior to being hospitalized for psychosis, the better the posthospital adjustment will be. Strauss, Klorman, and Kokes (1977) have also presented evidence supporting an association between premorbid functioning (especially in the area of social relationships) and poor outcome.

Paul (1969) noted that the biggest single deficit found in chronic psychiatric patients appears to be a lack of instrumental role functioning. He suggested the possible efficacy of developing treatment approaches that would attempt to teach chronic psychiatric patients instrumental skills systematically. In Paul's (Paul & Lentz, 1977) monumental study examining a psychosocial approach to the treatment of chronic schizophrenics, he found that one of the best predictors of whether a patient would be discharged from the hospital and whether he or she would have to be readmitted to the hospital was his or her social skills level.

Increasingly more researchers (Argyle & Kendon, 1967; Gladwin, 1977; Libet & Lewinsohn, 1973; Sylph, Ross, & Kedward, 1978) have stressed social skill deficits as a factor in the major forms of psychopathology. It also appears that social skills deficits are not only associated with major forms of psychopathology but with numerous other dysfunctional behaviors such as sexual problems (Barlow, 1973); alcohol abuse (Kraft, 1971; Miller, Hersen, Eisler, & Hilsman, 1974); drug addiction (Callner & Ross, 1976); marital dysfunctioning Eisler, Miller, Hersen, & Alford, 1974); and, of course, dating anxiety and deficits (Curran, 1977).

Response Acquisition Approaches to Treatment

A major influence in the development of social skills training was the theoretical work of Wolpe and Lazarus (1969). These theorists were concerned with distressed emotional states, especially anxiety. They developed assertion training as a means of assisting individuals over-

come anxiety reactions that they felt were inhibiting their performance in social encounters. The focus of the training was on teaching individuals how to release feelings of anger and frustration appropriately when they allow themselves to be coerced by others in interpersonal interactions. The theoretical rationale for the training was that by teaching an individual how to express his or her feelings appropriately, the inhibitive effects of anxiety would be gradually overcome via a process called *reciprocal inhibition*. Lazarus (1971) included the expression of positive emotions, such as warmth, compassion, and love, as also being assertive behaviors.

The assumption in these earlier works is that individuals have these skills in their repertoire but that these skills merely need to be drawn out of them. Assertion training was directed at reducing a hypothesized anxiety state, and it was assumed that once the anxiety was removed the natural adaptive responses in the patient's repertoire would be emitted. The presence of the requisite skills is implicit in this view.

Kanfer and Phillips (1970) saw that assertion training might have utility beyond an anxiety-reduction technique. They stressed the importance of instrumental role learning in behavior therapy and labeled such an approach *replication therapy*. They saw replication therapy as successful because new behaviors are developed, practiced, and acquired in settings designed to facilitate learning, and at the same time anxiety in problem situations is reduced. McFall and Twentyman proposed another label for this type of treatment and called it the *response acquisition* approach to treatment. They stated (1973, p. 199) the major premise of response acquisition training as

Maladaptive behaviors are construed in terms of the absence of specific response skills. The therapeutic objective is to provide patients with direct training in precisely those skills lacking in their repertoires. Very little attention is given to eliminating existing maladaptive behavior; instead, it is assumed that as skillful, adaptive responses are acquired, rehearsed and reinforced, the previous maladaptive responses will be displaced and disappear.

A movement began for a direct and systematic attempt to teach those skills deemed important in problematic situations in therapy. It was assured that if an individual could handle these situations more skillfully, there would be better psychological functioning.

Dating Anxiety as a Therapy Analog

Specific interest in heterosocial skills training was largely due to the search by psychologists in academic settings for a better analog for anxiety—related problems than the "small animal phobias," which had been popular in the late 1960s. When these psychologists, particularly behaviorally oriented clinicians, became interested in evaluating the effectiveness of various therapeutic techniques, they needed a sufficient number of subjects, exhibiting the same distressing behavior, in order to complete the cells of their tightly controlled factorial studies. Because homogeneous psychiatric populations of sufficient size were not readily available to academic researchers, college students with "small animal phobias" were chosen because they appeared to be an adequate substitute. During the 1960s a proliferation of "small animal phobias" studies appeared; however, the clinical relevance and the methodological soundness of these studies has been seriously questioned (Cooper, Furst, & Bridger, 1969).

Dating anxiety appears to be a good choice as a target behavior for analog research. Heterosexual social anxiety is a pervasive, complex, and debilitating type of anxiety reaction (Fishman & Nawas, 1973). Because social anxiety is so disruptive of daily functioning and because a complete avoidance of social stumuli is nearly impossible, recruitment of fairly large numbers of well-motivated subjects should be possible. Indeed, dating anxiety appears to be a major concern for college students. Martinson and Zerface (1970) noted that the most frequent complaint voiced by undergraduates, using a college counseling center, was with difficulties in dating relationships. Borkovec, Stone, O'Brien, and Kaloupek (1974), in a survey of college students at a Midwestern university, found that approximately 15% of the males and 11% of the females reported some fear of being with members of the opposite sex, with over 30% of each sex saying this was especially distressing when meeting someone for the first time. Pilkonis (1977) reported that approximately 40% of the undergraduates surveyed stated that they were shy, especially in dating situations. Glass, Gottam, and Shmurak (1976) discovered that approximately 54% of the males and 42% of the females surveyed rated dating situations as being difficult.

Borkovec et al. examined the "goodness" of heterosexual social anxiety as a target behavior for therapy research. They concluded (1974):

Heterosexual-social anxiety, then appears to be an ideal target behavior for analogue research. A large number of potential subjects exists; the behavior is clinically relevant; unobtrusive, non-deceptive measurement procedures validly discriminate low and high-anxious subjects; demand effects beyond repeated testing are negligible; and strong physiological arousal is elicited and does note readily habituate. p. 573

For these reasons, increasing attention was focused on heterosocial anxiety as a therapy analog.

Although the search for a therapy analog accounted for much of the initial interest in heterosocial anxiety, researchers in this area began to view it as worthy of study in its own right (Galassi & Galassi, 1979). Dating concerns are not limited to undergraduate populations, and dating problems would also appear to have implications for later social functioning (Galassi & Galassi, 1979). Landy and Gaupp (1971) found that interpersonal situations appeared to be a major stimulus for peoples' fears and anxieties. Bryant, Trower, Yardley, Urbieta, and Letemendia (1976) reported that socially incompetent psychiatric patients were likely to have a history of poor mixing with others and be regarded as failures in dating. They were reported as having considerable difficulty in meeting strangers, starting up friendships, going to parties, and so on.

Studies examining various therapeutic approaches to dating anxiety, including heterosexual social skills training, were conducted on this new target behavior. However, the exhuberance of the discovery of this new target behavior was soon tempered by the many methodological shortcomings of these treatment-outcome studies.

HETEROSOCIAL SKILLS TRAINING AS A TREATMENT FOR DATING ANXIETY

Heterosocial skills training was seen as one of several treatment approaches for the alleviation of dating anxiety. In fact, many of the studies examining the effect of heterosocial skills training were studies comparing its effectiveness to other procedures.

The assumption behind heterosocial skills training as a treatment method for dating anxiety is that the anxiety is reactive in nature (Paul & Bernstein, 1973). That is, deficiencies in skills lead to failure in heterosocial encounters, which produces anxiety. The rationale for skills training as a treatment modality is that increases in skills would lead to more successful heterosexual encounters that, in turn, would decrease anxiety. In order

to test this logic, it must be shown that the subjects are both anxious and deficient in heterosexual skills. In most studies it is not clear whether either of these assumptions has been met. Determining if an individual is, indeed, deficient in heterosocial skills is especially problematic. All we can observe is performance, and performance is only partially a function of skills. Even when a person possesses the requisite skills, they may not perform competently because of numerous other factors such as fear of undesirable consequences, poor discriminative cue-reading ability, and negative self-evaluations that inhibit the response, and so forth.

More puzzling than the failure to demonstrate heterosocial skills deficiencies is the lack of real evidence, in many studies, that the subjects were dating anxious. Although the original impetus for heterosocial skills training was in its potential utility in the treatment of dating anxiety, subjects in these studies were often selected based on criteria other than anxiety (Curran, 1977). Subjects were selected for these studies who were only slightly anxious or perhaps not anxious at all but who merely wished to improve their dating frequency. Consequently, the generalizability of the results of these studies to other types of anxiety reactions is questionable. This lack of attention to subject-selection criteria was unfortunate because it clouded the issue of the "goodness" of dating anxiety as a target behavior for analogue research. It appears to us that dating anxiety as a therapy analog got sidetracked, and we believe a refocus on dating anxiety as a therapy analog for anxiety reactions should be initiated.

We are not, however, suggesting that we abandon our interest in heterosocial skills in and of themselves. Heterosocial skills and heterosocial skills training are worthy of study, in and of themselves because dating concerns are a real and relevant clinical problem (Martinson &

Zerface, 1970). Maladaptive solutions to concerns of dating encounters may lead to other types of psychopathology (Barlow, Abel, Blanchard, Bristow, & Young, 1977). Lastly, knowledge generated in our attempts to understand those skills regarded as competent in dating encounters will help us understand the nature of competent interpersonal performance.

The skills taught in heterosocial skills training programs were most often intuitively rather than empirically determined. That is, investigators based the content of their skills programs on what they thought would be successful behaviors to exhibit in heterosocial encounters and not on empirical data. Investigators assumed that the behaviors being taught would make the subject more effective. There was little attempt to assess what the subjects did well, what they were doing wrong, and what they needed to learn. We need to identify the specific skills required for successful heterosocial encounters and be able to ascertain whether these skills are or are not in the subject's repertoire.

There are several procedures available for the identification of these skills. One procedure is identification of and surveying "critical others." Here, persons considered important because of their expertise or because they are similar to individuals in the criterion situation or control their reinforcers are surveyed to determine their opinions regarding skillful behaviors. Another method that could be used is a contrasted group procedure wherein competent and incompetent groups are observed to isolated differences in their behaviors. Examples of attempts to identify skills for a specific task or situation can be found in the literature, for example, Schwartz and Gottman's (1976) analysis of assertive behavior; McDonald's (1978) presentation of a model and a method for measuring assertive behav-

iors; Conger and Farrell's (1981) study of heterosocial behavioral components; Kupke, Hobbs, and Cheney's (1979) selection of heterosocial skills; Freedman, Rosenthal, Donahue, Schlundt, and McFall's (1978) analysis of skill deficits in delinquents; and Trower's (1980) situational analysis of the components and processes of skilled and unskilled psychiatric patients.

Our search for the skills that will serve as the content of our training packages is extremely important because it dictates what we teach, what we assess, and what serves as the social validation of our programs. If we do not know what the appropriate skills are, then our training programs might not make much sense. That is, we may be teaching subjects new responses, but these new responses will not increase their interpersonal effectiveness in dating situations. For example, in a series of studies described by Conger and Conger (1982), it was found that unskilled males were not particularly deficient in behaviors or knowledge about how to make dates or where to take them; rather they were deficient in conversational skills or in matters related to sexual activities. Consequently, a program employing the teaching of conversational skills would appear to have better chance of success than one teaching how to make dates. (We will describe in greater detail, in another section of the chapter, the methods we have been employing in trying to identify heterosocial skills that increase the probability of success in heterosexual encounters.)

TRAINING PROCEDURES

The construction of social skills training programs for heterosocial problems is based on the hypothesis that people display these problems because they lack requisite skills for successful opposite-sex interactions. Competing explanations for heterosocial problems include conditioned anxiety, cognitive misappraisal, or physical attractiveness as the central feature (see Arkowitz, 1977, and Curran, 1977, for details). These alternative hypotheses have led to the development of other treatment approaches for heterosocial problems. (In keeping with the title of this book, the focus of this section will be limited to the social skills training approach. In a later section these other approaches will be discussed briefly when the data on comparative outcome between social skills training and other approaches are discussed.)

Whether referred to as "behavior replication techniques" (Kanfer & Phillips, 1970), "behavior rehearsal" (Lazarus, 1971), or "behavioral training" (McFall & Twentyman, 1973), comprehensive social skills training for heterosocial problem behaviors typically consist of several elements: Information about appropriate response patterns is first provided to the subjects, who rehearse these new behavior patterns and receive feedback about their performance; this is often followed by an attempt to generalize these behaviors beyond the treatment situation. Few studies in the heterosocial skills training literature, however, have examined individual treatment components in order to isolate those that are necessary and sufficient for treatment progress. Instead, more typically, conglomerate training programs have been constructed, usually on intuitive bases and from information gleaned from research on other problem behaviors. These programs, then, have been applied to heterosocial problem behaviors, with the major interest being in clinical outcome and, at times, differential effectiveness, compared to other treatment approaches. Consequently, in order to obtain information about the effectiveness of the various skills training components for heterosocial problem behaviors, the research on general social skills training will have to be relied upon.

Providing Information

Intuitively, it seems that a prerequisite to the consistent display of appropriate heterosocial skills is the knowledge of what constitutes these skills and how they can best be displayed. Undoubtedly, most treatment programs have attempted to achieve this, even if only informally. About two-thirds of the programs described in the heterosocial skills literature have attempted to provide this information to the participants in a structured and documented fashion prior to any response practice. Exceptions are the programs specifically employing only response practice (Christensen & Arkowitz, 1974; Christensen, Arkowitz, & Anderson, 1975; Martinson & Zerface, 1970) and a program emphasizing self-administration techniques, including self-reinforcement (Rehm & Marston, 1968).

Typically, two methods are used to provide information, and they often are used in combination: (1) verbal instruction, where the information is presented verbally; and (2) modeling, where the information is provided visually when a model displays the behavior in question. Verbal instruction is a deductive procedure, in contrast to modeling, and it can take many forms. It has been used, in a formal manner, in about half of the studies in this area. Generally it is presented by the therapists, and it is usually supplemented by written material, which is followed by discussion. Verbal instruction can include, in addition to the specific information as to how to display a certain behavior, the rationale why this is an important skill, when it can be used, and even examples of inappropriate uses of the skill. Although most people would agree that information should be provided, there is no agreement as to what the content of this should be. That is, what are the necessary and sufficient skills for effective heterosocial interactions? (This major issue will be discussed in a later section). Therapists, instead, must rely on their or others' personal experience in determining the verbal instruction material. Verbal instruction has not been evaluated separately as a component of heterosocial skills training, but it has been included with other components in producing successful outcomes (e.g., Curran & Gilbert, 1975; Kramer, 1975; McGovern, Arkowitz, & Gilmore, 1975). In more general research on the unique effect of coaching, the results are equivocal and dependent upon the target population, specific skill, and how it is combined with other treatment components (cf. Twentyman & Zimering, 1979, for a review).

Modeling has been included in heterosocial skills training because the literature supports its use in numerous other training contexts (e.g., Rosenthal & Bandura, 1978). This literature points out several ways in which the effect of modeling can be enhanced, such as by increasing the similarity between the role model and the subject (Bandura, Ross & Ross, 1963); using multiple models (Kazdin, 1976); and allowing the model to experience positive consequences (Bandura, 1965). Because the typical target population for heterosocial skills training is male college students, these findings suggest using several male student role models, rather than graduate student therapists, and allowing the modeling situations to end with positive consequences for the target model (e.g., a phone call resulting in a date). These suggestions are based on research with other populations, however, and it is not yet known what parameters of modeling are important specifically for heterosocial skills training. Another question that could be asked is whether live or video modeling is most effective.

Modeling, both live and video, is a common treatment component in successful heterosocial skills training programs (e.g., Heimberg, Madsen, Montgomery, & McNabb, 1980; Morgan, 1975; Royce & Arkowitz, 1976). However, consistent positive results have not been found, even in the general social skills training literature, supporting the use of modeling procedures by themselves (cf. Twentyman & Zimering, 1979, for a review). This suggests modeling is best included in programs in combination with other treatment components, as is the case in most heterosocial skills training programs. In all, about one-half of these programs employed modeling in some form or another.

Rehearsal

Germane to skills training is the use of some type of rehearsal technique, where the clients overtly practice the new responses in order to add to their limited behavioral repertoires or, when the response is already present, to increase the probability of its occurrence. Without this treatment component, the treatment procedure being reviewed in this book probably would not be referred to as social skills *training*. Furthermore, every heterosocial skills training program reviewed in this chapter included it as a treatment component. Although rehearsal takes many different forms, the basic procedure involves the overt repetition of the desired response pattern during training sessions in the clinic. This basic procedure is then expanded or altered. Subjects can also rehearse the responses of the significant others in the situation (role reversal) as well as possible incompetent responses. Presumably, the latter is done to aid in the differentiation between competence and incompetence. These variations of rehearsal have been included in some successful heterosocial skills training programs (e.g., Clark, 1974; Curran & Gilbert, 1975), but thus far the effect of each technique has not been distinguished from that of others.

A distinctly different and relatively popular type of rehearsal procedure has taken the form of practice dating, where the subjects more informally rehearse the target behaviors in the natural situations for which treatment is intended. The therapist arranges dates for them, either with other clients or with confederates. It has been used in about one-fourth of the programs serving as the basis for this review. Research has shown that when used by itself, practice dating is significantly more effective in improving dating behavior when compared to a no-treatment control (e.g., Christensen & Arkowitz, 1974; Christensen et al., 1975). Because it appears cost-effective, such findings support its use as a treatment, at least for some clients. It seems that practice dating has the potential for increasing generalization. It also should increase the amount of time available for rehearsal because it does not rely on only scheduled training sessions. However, practice dating, without appropriate preparation through instruction and modeling, may be problematic for severely skills-deficient clients. The natural feedback they receive could be overly negative because the therapist has much less control over it, in contrast to when rehearsal occurs in the clinic. When practice dating has been compared directly to rehearsal in session as part of a comprehensive heterosocial skills training program, including all treatment elements, treatment outcome has been comparable (McGovern et al., 1975). That is, no differences have been found between programs including the two different rehearsal procedures. This again may argue for the use of rehearsal in sessions for severely deficient clients, whereas clients possessing a minimum amount of skills may benefit more from practice dating.

Although not yet incorporated in the treatment of heterosocial problem behaviors, several investigators have argued for the use of covert rehearsal or imaginal practice in social skills training (Kazdin, 1974; Nietzel, Martorano, & Melnick, 1977; Thorpe, 1973). This has been advocated, in part, to increase generalization by attempting to internalize the response. Thus far, however, unequivocal outcomes have not been demonstrated for covert rehearsal versus overt rehearsal; specific outcome, instead, is dependent on numerous variables (cf. Twentyman & Zimering, 1979, for a review).

Given the generally positive outcome of programs including rehearsal as a treatment component in heterosocial skills training, together with the positive outcome for practice dating by itself, some form of rehearsal appears to be the most important component for successful heterosocial skills treatment. This remains a hypothesis, pending more research.

Performance Feedback

After the subject has obtained information about a heterosocial skill through verbal instruction and/or modeling and has rehearsed the desired behavior, the skill usually is shaped through feedback and reinforcement. In this context, feedback provides specific information to the client to enable skill modification or improvement, whereas reinforcement is a motivational component intended to shape behavior or increase response rate. A feedback component could be identified as a specific treatment component in about one-half of the heterosocial skills training programs reviewed for this chapter. Feedback commonly is given by the therapist, but frequently an attempt is made also to obtain peer feedback by involving the other group members in the process (e.g., Curran, Gilbert, & Little, 1976).

Playback of videorecordings of rehearsal responses is a very powerful adjunct to feedback because both non-verbal and verbal behaviors can easily and clearly be evaluated and related to the response of the rehearsal partner. It is, however, also a potentially very anxiety-producing and at times embarassing procedure for subjects. Videotape playback should therefore be sensitively introduced into the training, possibly through familiarization prior to treatment. Furthermore, research on more general social skills training suggests that, in order to avoid possible deleterious effects, several rehearsal attempts should be allowed prior to feedback (McFall & Gailbraith, 1977; Sarason & Ganzer, 1973). The direct effect of feedback has been assessed in only one study of heterosocial skills training. Melnick (1973) found that groups receiving both rehearsal and videotape feedback were superior to those who received modeling only or rehearsal only. Nonetheless, research on general social skills training has found little or no additive effect for feedback (Gormally, Hill, Otis, & Rainey, 1975; Melnick & Stocker, 1977), making the status of feedback equivocal. The majority of the studies using feedback in combination with other training components have, however, reported positive results (cf. Twentyman & Zimering, 1979, for a review).

The usefulness of reinforcement has been documented in numerous and varied studies (e.g., Kazdin, 1978). Although it may not have been specified in some cases, reinforcement has undoubtedly been applied in some form in every study of heterosocial skills training. Although the therapist most often provides reinforcement in these training programs, some investigators have attempted to structure the reinforcement so that it is given by other group members as well (e.g., Curran et al., 1976). In one study reinforcement was self-administered by the subjects (Rehm & Marston, 1968). The subjects were first trained to set individual goals for a hierarchy of troublesome heterosocial situa-tions and then to evaluate their own performance using these goals as criteria as they performed *in vivo* in these situations. The results obtained suggest an enhanced effect from this program, which was maintained at 7- and 9-month follow-up.

Although not yet incorporated in a heterosocial skills training program, several social skills programs have formalized peer reinforcement by employing a "buddy system" (Azrin, Flores, & Kaplan, 1975; Rose, 1975; Shoemaker & Paulson, 1976). Subjects are paired up and instructed to monitor and reinforce each other's performance in the natural environment. Both the use of self-administered reinforcement and reinforcing heterosocial skills acquisition or display in the natural environment are consistent with recommendations for programming treatment maintenance and generalization. In general, systematic attempts to include "environmental reinforcers" should enhance the effectiveness of heterosocial skills training programs.

Generalization Strategies

Generalization of the skills acquired in treatment sessions to the natural environment is of course the goal of any heterosocial training program. Thus far in the heterosocial skills training area, generalization has been promoted primarily through assigning homework to the subjects. Subjects are requested to perform tasks between sessions outside of the clinic. Usually they are encouraged to rehearse (e.g., Curran, 1975; Twentyman & McFall, 1975) or self-monitor (e.g., Curran et al, 1976; Twentyman & McFall, 1975) skills targeted in the sessions. About one-third of the studies in this area have incorporated these features, with only one study thus far providing information about the additive effect of homework. MacDonald, Lindquist, Kramer, McGrath, and Rhyne (1975) did not find that homework assignments between treatment sessions improved upon the positive outcome observed for a standard heterosocial skills training package that included verbal instruction, rehearsal, and feedback, but no homework. Instead, a highly similar outcome was noted when homework was added to this package. Thus, whereas it appears a conceptually promising technique in light of poor generalization for many social skills training programs, more research is needed investigating the unique effects of homework. The intuitively positive aspects of assigning behavioral homework, however, include that the therapist is able to reinforce appropriate behavior outside of the laboratory and that the subject is likely to begin to engage in the very situations to which training is directed.

Summary

Because the work on heterosocial skills has been so strongly treatment-outcome oriented, little is known about which treatment components are necessary and sufficient. Inferences can only be made from work targeting other problem behaviors. Consequently, positive outcome must be attributed at this point to a combination of techniques aimed at providing information about the target skills, practicing these and receiving feedback on them, and generalizing their acquisitions to the natural environment. More research is needed to partial out the effect of each component. The primarily intuitive hypothesis that rehearsal and feedback are the most powerful techniques for acquisition might initially guide this research. In addition, special attention must be focused on what treatment components contribute to the generalization of skills to the natural environment and the maintenance of these gains.

TRAINING CONTENTS

Social skills training programs, as mentioned previously, are based on the assumption that individuals lack the necessary skills for successful interactions. The goal of social skills training is to correct these deficiencies through instruction in appropriate skills. Social skills training programs for heterosocial problems are distinguished from social skills training programs applied to other areas primarily by their content, rather than by the procedures employed.

Individual versus Actuarial Approaches

In designing a social skills training program for heterosocial problems, one must first determine the domain of skills that should be trained. This domin is actually a complex interaction of specific behaviors and situations. In a discussion of social skills training, McFall describes skills as "the specific abilities required to perform competently at a task" (McFall, 1982, pp. 12–13). In order to describe the domain of social skills adquately, it is thus necessary to specify both the domin of the tasks, or problematic situations, and the specific behaviors or abilities required to perform these tasks competently.

In developing social skills training programs, investigators may follow one of two approaches to defining this domain—an individual approach or an actuarial approach. In the individual or ideographic approach, the first step involves sampling an individual client's behavior across a variety of heterosocial situations to identify situations that are the most problematic for that individual. The next step is to determine the specific behavioral deficits in each of those situations. Finally, a treatment program would be designed to correct that specific deficit. This approach would thus insure a treatment program of maximum relevance for a given individual. The task of assessing an individual's behavior across the domain of potentially problematic situations is, however, extremely time consuming. The more expedient method of asking an individual client to identify heterosocial situations he or she perceives as problematic would involve much less time; however, this approach presents difficulties due to the inaccuracy of clients' self-reports (cf. Curran, Wallander, & Fischetti, 1977). Designing a new treatment program for each new client would also be extremely time consuming. In addition, determining the adequacy of social skills training and designing a sound treatment package would be difficult when treatment varied across subjects. A possible compromise to this approach might involve the development of treatment components or modules that could be combined to individualize treatment programs (cf. McFall, 1982).

In contrast to the individual approach, group social skills training programs for heterosocial problems have followed what might best be described as an actuarial approach to assessment and treatment. In this approach, individuals who experience heterosocial probems are observed or surveyed to identify specific difficulties experienced by a plurality of such clients. A good example of such an approach to problem identification is the behavioral-analytic model described by Goldfried and D'Zurilla (1969). Once problematic situations have been identified, criteria are developed for determining skilled and unskilled responses. These situations then serve as the basis for both assessment and the development of treatment programs. Although the contents of such a group program may not perfectly fit the needs of an individual client, it is assumed that the content of such a training program has a high probability of being relevant for the majority of clients. This may be referred to as an actuarial approach in the sense that it follows a model based on base rates, rather than individual assessment. An underlying assumption of this model is that social skills deficits are not randomly distributed across situations for different individuals, but rather that par-

ticular situations might be relevant to many individuals. This approach could be refined to identify subgroups of clients who experience problems in similar situations. Screening criteria and treatment programs may then be tailored to these subgroups of individuals. This is analogous to actuarial prediction where predictions are based, in part, on an individual's background.

Heterosocial Skills Training Programs

Given some of the difficulties associated with the individual approach, it is not surprising that many social skills investigations have employed the group actuarial approach to designing treatment programs. These "canned" treatment programs provide a ready basis for evaluative research due to their standardization and resulting replicability. The more individual approach has primarily been incorporated in single case studies. In the following discussion, an attempt will be made to describe the specific contents of a number of published social skills training programs and to describe the source of these contents. Determining the contents of social skills training programs for heterosocial problems from the published literature is a difficult task. Although studies are generally quite explicit in presenting the procedures employed (e.g., modeling, behavioral rehearsal, feedback), they are frequently vague about the specific content presented by these procedures. Details concerning the source of the training material are also rarely specified.

One of the more detailed training manuals for heterosocial skills was presented by Lindquist, Framer, McGrawth, MacDonald, and Rhyne (1975). This manual described a fairly comprehensive list of problematic heterosocial situations and specific suggestions for appropriate behaviors in these situations. Problematic situations included initiating a conversation; responding to an approach; how to leave a situation gracefully; cues for receptivity; initiating a second conversation; extending a conversation; giving compliments; making interesting conversation; silences; planning dates; evaluating a date; extending a relationship (second dates); meeting women at parties; telephoning; intimate conversation; and physical involvement. Although the preceding topics served as the basis for group meetings, individual differences in problems were handled by involving group members in specifying details of these situations during role playing. Although the contents of this treatment program appear intuitively very comprehensive, the empirical basis for selecting these specific situations was not presented. This manual served as the basis for the treatment program studied by MacDonald et al. (1975) and was also employed in a modified form by Heimberg et al. (1980).

Another detailed training manual was presented by Curran and Gilbert (1975). This manual also presented problematic heterosocial situations and suggestions for appropriate behaviors. Topics covered in this manual included giving and receiving compliments; feeling talk; listening skills; assertion; nonverbal methods of communication; handling periods of silence; planning and asking for dates; physical attractiveness; and physical intimacy. Selection of these particular topics was based on a literature search. This manual was employed in several studies comparing the effectiveness of social skills training to several other treatment approaches (Curran, 1975; Curran & Gilbert, 1975; Curran, Gilbert, & Little, 1976).

Glass et al. (1976) described a response acquisition program for heterosocial problems that included the use of a videotape training tape that presented 11 problem situations. These situations were chosen from a set obtained through interviews with 100 undergraduate psychology students who were asked to give a "play-by-play" of problematic social situations. In addition, several situations were adapted from Goldsmith & McFall (1975) who employed a behavioral-analytic model to determine problematic social situations for psychiatric inpatients. The nature of those situations and the criteria used for their final selection were not described. A similar treatment program that employed a videotape of male and female students in "progressively more psychologically intimate situations" was described by Melnick (1973).

McGovern et al. (1975) described a social interaction training manual developed to serve as a source of information about dating for college men. Major areas of training included initiating and maintaining an effective conversation; appearance and dress; telephoning and planning the date; and social "turn-ons" and "turn-offs." The contents of this manual were based on meetings between one of the authors and a group of undergraduate women with high dating frequencies. These women were asked to provide information about effective dating behaviors in men. The final revision of this manual was completed after receiving additional feedback from a second group of women with high dating frequency. The use of recipients of male dating behavior as judges of effective behavior is a very desirable feature of this training program. The use of high-frequency daters has the advantage of providing judges who have considerable experience with dating. The results obtained from this source should, however, be interpreted cautiously in light of the sampling bias introduced. It is unclear whether males completing social skills training programs will more frequently date the most popular women available. Attempts should also be made to determine the behaviors in heterosocial situations that are viewed as effective by females who are moderate or low-frequency daters. Although women, as recipients of male dating behavior, may serve a useful function as judges of effective behavior, males with heterosocial problems remain a valuable source to identify problematic heterosocial situations.

Twentyman & McFall (1975, p. 385) described a treatment program based on "an empirically derived set of discriminating problem situations in which nondaters manifested performance deficits." These problematic situations were obtained from an unpublished pilot study that identified competent responses to problematic situations based on interviews with college women. Although an informal approach to problem identification is preferable to clinical intuition, more formalized empirical study is needed. The results of these studies could then be compared across investigators to determine if the same problematic situations and behaviors are being targeted. In the words of the authors themselves:

The heterosexual behaviors that the shy subjects in the present study were taught were those for which coeds had indicated a preference in an informal pilot study. It would have been far better, however, if the training program's content had been based on a more systematic, empirical analysis of the topography and structure of competent heterosexual performance. (Twentyman & McFall, 1975, p. 394)

Elder, Edelstein, Frewmouw, Lively, Walker, and Womeldorf (1978) also have described a heterosocial skills training program. The contents of this program included nonverbal behaviors; becoming acquainted with strangers; giving and receiving compliments; self-disclosures; requesting information from others; negative assertion; and how to "generally appear socially competent." In this program an attempt was made to involve the subjects in identifying problematic situations: The role-played scenes involved social situations personally problematic to the various group members and situations determined on an a priori basis to be especially relevant to young college students. As is the case with other studies in this area, the empirical approach taken to problems identification is not clearly specified.

Bander, Steinke, Allen, and Mosher (1975) described a social skills training program that included five sessions on analysis of verbal and nonverbal communication methods and arranging dates; a session on sexual norms and girls' dating preferences obtained from surveys ($n = 70$) and interviews ($n = 48$) of undergraduate females; and two sessions that focused on individually identified problems. This survey and interview data appear to be very promising sources of information for subjects, particularly when the sources are presented. More detailed results of these surveys and interviews would have been useful to other investigators and clinicians.

Finally, West, Goethe, & Kallman (1980) discussed a combined behavioral/cognitive treatment program. The primary emphasis of this training program was on verbal and nonverbal conversational skills, how and where to meet people, and rejection of requests. One innovative feature of this program was its use of a stage model in which predetermined goals were set for each stage of the group. According to this approach, each client had to satisfy behavioral criteria for each stage before moving on to subsequent stages. Although the procedures for this program were spelled out in considerable detail, the empirical basis for its content and stage criteria were not discussed.

Researchers have developed a number of fairly comprehensive social skills training programs for heterosocial problems. Most of these programs covered initiating contact with women; conversational skills; appearance and dress; and planning dates. Although these topics were followed in the training sessions, the majority of training programs allowed for individual differences by involving the subjects in specifying the details during procedures such as role playing. The problematic situations presented in these treatment programs have been based on either very informal survey procedures or clinical intuition. A more systematic approach to identifying problematic heterosocial situations, such as the procedures used by Goldfried and D'Zurilla (1969) in their survey of college freshman, could provide a better basis for designing these programs. Replications of this approach across investigators and cross-investigator comparisons would reveal critical information about the frequency with which various heterosocial situations are viewed as problematic. As a minimum, such studies might validate our clinical intuitions and pilot studies.

In addition to identifying problematic situations, developers of skills training programs must also specify appropriate behaviors to employ in these situations. These have, at best, been based on rather informal pilot data. In order to assess the progress of subjects toward these standards, skills training programs have relied on the judgments of therapists (Melnick, 1973); women who served as role-play partners (Bander et al., 1975; McGovern et al., 1975); the subjects themselves (Twentyman & McFall, 1975); other group members and videotaped feedback (Curran & Gilbert, 1975); and therapists and other group members (Elder et al., 1978; Heimberg et al., 1980; Lindquist et al., 1975). Although peers are an important source of data, one must question the extent to which some of these individuals can provide socially valid criteria. Are subjects who require social skills training the best sources of information about appropriate social behavior? Although female confederates may provide more socially valid criteria, for males and vice versa, this source may also be biased, if not adequately sampled. A more systematic

sampling of undergraduate men and women and detailed specification of criteria would provide a more comprehensive and socially valid (Kazdin, 1977) source of material for training. As Twentyman and McFall pointed out: "Ideally the construction of training programs should be guided by an empirical analysis of subjects' training needs and a thorough understanding of the inherent structure of the training material" (1975, p.394).

Attempts at Identifying Content Components of Social Skills

Treatment programs for heterosocial skills training have relied on fairly informal evaluations of an individual's performance in problematic situations. Subjects role playing these situations are given feedback about their overall performance and specific behavioral changes are suggested (e.g., increase eye contact, use more relaxed posture, use partner's name more). What has been missing from these programs is an empirical basis for these behavioral components. In this section we will discuss several studies which attempted to identify specific behavioral components of social skills.

Initial attempts to identify specific behavioral components of heterosocial skills met with fairly discouraging and inconclusive results. "Unfortunately, these skills represent somewhat a will-o-the-wisp. Globally defined, effective skills can often be distinguished from ineffective ones. However, relatively little success has been enjoyed in identifying the specific behaviors that comprise them" (Galassi & Galassi, 1979, p. 131). The majority of early studies reported that, whereas global ratings of skill by judges differentiated between various groups of subjects (e.g., high-vs. low-frequency daters), specific behavioral measures such as frequency counts did not (e.g., Arkowitz, Lichtenstein,

McGovern, & Hines, 1975; Glasgow & Arkowitz, 1975; Twentyman & McFall, 1975). These studies led many researchers in this area to abandon specific behavioral measures in favor of more global ratings. Other investigators found this abandonment somewhat premature.

Being careful not to overemphasize skill deficits, we should not abandon the search for these deficits without first conducting studies that use the structural approach to investigating dyadic interactions. If judges can routinely detect global skill differences between crudely defined groups of competent and incompetent performers, it seems likely that they are responding to observable differences that current methodology has been unable to detect" (Galassi & Galassi, 1979, p. 177).

Conger and Farrell (1981) raised methodological criticisms of these earlier studies. Specifically, they pointed out inconsistencies in these studies due to (1) differences in the medium of observation (live, audio, or video recordings); (2) differences in the behaviors selected and their definitions; (3) differences in subject selection criteria; and (4) reliance on self-report measures for the criterion (Conger & Farrell, 1981). These investigators conducted a study that employed behavioral recordings of videotape interactions of male college students with female confederates. These interactions included two role plays—a pizza parlor interaction and student union interaction—both of which required the subject to maintain a conversation with a minimally responsive confederate for 4 minutes. In addition, videotaped interactions of subjects in two 3-minute waiting periods, ostensibly due to scheduling problems, were coded. This study employed multiple criterion measures including self-report and global ratings of anxiety and social skill. Specific behaviors included in this study were gestures, self-manipulations, smiles, head nods, leg moves, subject talk, and confederate talk and gaze. Selection of these be-

haviors was based on behaviors studied previously in the social skills area and behaviors identified as relevant to the judgment of skills and anxiety by observational research on verbal and nonverbal behavior in related areas. In contrast to earlier studies, results of this study indicated strong relationships between simple duration measures of subject talk, gaze, and confederate talk with judgments of anxiety and social skill. Multiple regression analyses employing behavioral measures of discrete behaviors as predictors and judges' ratings a criterion resulted in multiple correlations of .66 for predicting anxiety and .90 or higher for social skills for both the role-play and waiting-period interactions.

Positive results were also reported by Kupke Hobbs, & Cheney. (1979). These investigators obtained measures of verbal behaviors from audiotapes of male subjects participating in 15-minute interactions with female undergraduates. This study employed somewhat more complex conversational behaviors than were previously studied in the heterosocial skills research. Conversational behaviors were selected that were felt to possess social reinforcement value. Specific behaviors were personal attention, minimal encourages, and self-talk. The criterion was a composite measure of interpersonal attraction obtained from the women who interacted with the subjects in the role plays. Results indicated a strong relationship between one of the verbal measures, personal attention, and interpersonal attraction. Measures of the remaining two conversational behaviors were not related to interpersonal attraction.

The correlational methodology employed by Conger and Farrell (1981) and Kupke et al. (1979) provided some useful cues regarding the basis of judges' ratings of dimensions such as social skills and interpersonal attractiveness. Unfortunately, these studies do not provide a sufficient basis for determining the degree to which judges are actually influenced by these specific behaviors. This latter question was, however, addressed in a follow-up study by Kupke et al. (1979) that provided experimental validity for personal attention as a conversational skill for males. In this study, subjects were trained to increase their frequency of either personal attention, the behavior that had been shown to relate to interpersonal attractiveness, or minimal encourages, a behavior that had not been shown to relate to interpersonal attractiveness. In addition, a third group of subjects served as an experimental control, participating only in the pre- and postassessments. Results of this study indicated that subjects who increased their frequency of personal attention received higher ratings of interpersonal attraction by females than subjects in either of the other groups. This study was well designed, and checks were made to control for physical attractiveness and to validate the specific effect of the interventions on subject behavior in the role plays. As a result of these studies, it was demonstrated that personal attention is related to interpersonal attractiveness in conversations, and that increasing a subject's rate of personal attention will directly influence his or her interpersonal attractiveness in conversations. These studies thus serve as very useful models for identifying and experimentally validating component behaviors of social skill. A final step in this process would be to validate the relevance of this component for a clinial population.

Research described in the preceding studies attempted to determine empirically the relevance of various behavioral components for judgments of social skills. One weakness of these studies is that the investigators must still rely on their intuitions or empirical results in related areas to determine which behaviors to include. This approach could result in the exclusion of important behavioral components of social skills. An alternative approach to identifying the behavioral components individuals attend when judging social skills is to ask them. This simple approach served as a starting point for a series of investigations.

The Congers and their colleagues conducted a series of studies (see Conger & Conger, 1982, for a detailed review) aimed at identifying behavioral components of social skills. Based on pilot work identifying problematic heterosocial situations for college males (described in Conger & Conger, 1982), these investigators decided to focus their attention on conversational skills. The starting point in their program was a study in which male and female undergraduates served as peer judges (Conger, Wallander, Mariotto, & Ward, 1980). These subjects observed seven videotape segments of males interacting with female confederates and were asked to make ratings on 7-point scales for anxiety, social skill, and physical attractiveness. Subjects were then asked to generate the cues they used to judge the performance of the male in the last video segment they observed and to specify the dimensions these cues were related to (i.e., anxiety or social skill). These peers generated over 900 cues that were then put into a hierarchial structure by the investigators. Results of this study indicated that peers provided cues coincident with the primary components studied by investigators in the social skills area, though peers placed greater emphasis on conversational style than content. Although most of the cues were related to either anxiety or social skills, some cues were considered related to both dimensions. Finally, sex differences were found that suggested that females showed better discrimination in relating cues to skill and were able to specify more positive instances of social skill.

One criticism of the preceding study concerns the extent to which judges may have based their generated cues on popular notions of social skills rather than behaviors they actually observed on the videotapes. In order to address this question, Conger & Conger (1982) conducted a follow-up study to determine if subjects provided different cues depending upon which tape they were shown. In other words, if subjects generated these cues based on the videotapes they observed, subjects who observed different videotapes should have generated different cues. Results of this study indicated fairly specific relationships between the frequency with which subjects generated certain cues and the particular stimulus tape they observed. Given these results, it appeared unlikely that subjects were simply responding with popular definetions of social skills and anxiety. These results also tended to support the more individual or ideographic approach to assessment of social skills discussed earlier. That is, the finding that subjects generated different cues depending upon the particular subject they observed indicates the multitude of possible behaviors that may be judged inappropriate. Conger, Wallander, Mariotto, and Ward (1980) suggested that this may partially account for the different results found across studies attempting to identify behavioral components. The specific components generated in such studies may be largely due to the deficits shown by the particular subjects studied. Based on these findings, it was suggested that higher order behavioral categories that subsumed some of these specific behaviors may be a useful compromise between the global ratings and more specific, but perhaps ideosyncratic, behavioral deficits.

The potential utility of intermediate ratings led to the development of a set of behaviorally referenced ratings scales described by Wallander, Conger, & Conger, 1982). Based on the hierarchial structure described in the preceding studies, Wallander et al. (1982) developed a rating system in which the specific cues serve as behavioral referents for ratings on eleven 7-point intermediate-level scales (e.g., use of facial expression, personal conversational style, partner-directed behavior). The advantage of this approach is that ratings can be made on dimensions that target specific deficiences, yet are sufficiently general to be used across subjects. The more idiosyncratic behaviors provided a basis for identifying the specific deficiencies of a subject and arriving at an overall rating for that dimension. Wallander et al. (1982) then investigated the reliability and validity of this measure. Results of this study indicated good reliability across both raters and intervals, interdependency among component behaviors, and concurrent validity with global anxiety and social skills ratings, molecular-level behavioral codings, and a self-report measure.

In adapting this scale for use with psychiatric patients, Farrell, Rabinowitz, Wallander, and Curran (1982) introduced a modification that could further improve the utility of this scale for treatment planning. Instead of using the specific behaviors as referents for intermediate-level ratings, these behaviors were presented to raters individually in checklist format. The presence or absence of each behavior was coded by the rater. Each behavior in the checklist is associated with one of the intermediate-level dimensions used by Wallander et al. (1982), and each has been given a predetermined scale value reflecting its appropriateness. The advantage of this approach is that each subject is assigned a score on each intermediate level scale, and the individual behaviors that led to this score are also identified.

Summary

In the preceding section we reviewed the contents of social skills training programs for heterosocial problems. Based on the review it appears that although researchers in this area have developed a number of fairly comprehensive treatment programs, the empirical basis for these treatment programs rests on either clinical intuition or fairly informal pilot research. Problematic situations are most often described generally with specific details provided by subjects participating in these groups. Behavioral components identified in coaching are generally based on the clinical judgment of the therapist, other group members, role-play partners, and/or the subjects themselves. In order to design more relevant and replicable treatment programs, additional research aimed at identifying problematic situations and criterion for competent performance in these situations is needed. The behavioral-analytic approach described by Goldfried and D'Zurilla (1969) was recommended for identifying problematic heterosocial situations. Several lines of research attempting to identify behavioral components of conversational skills were presented as promising models for identifying behavioral components. Although this review has applied these criticisms to social skills training programs, they are equally valid criticisms of social skills assessment procedures (cf. Bellack, 1979; Curran & Mariotto, 1980; Curran & Wessberg, 1981).

In spite of these criticisms, these treatment programs have resulted in significant improvement for subjects displaying heterosocial problems. As such, they have provided a good starting point for developing more refined programs.

TREATMENT EFFECTIVENESS

Numerous studies have been published evaluating the efficacy of skills training as a treatment for heterosocial problem behaviors. Limiting our review to those studies utilizing group experimental designs, which had included a treatment condition that was based on an underlying skills-deficit hypothesis and that included one or more of the treatment components discussed before, 17 such reports were found. These studies have varied greatly in the degree to which alternative explanations for observed changes were controlled for in the experimental design. Several of these studies have investigated the comparative effectiveness of heterosocial skills training in comparison to alternative treatment approaches. In this section, the treatment-outcome literature relevant to heterosocial skills will be reviewed in two parts: first, those studies examining the effectiveness of heterosocial skills; these will be followed by a review of studies evaluating the effects of heterosocial skills training in comparison to alternative approaches.

Treatment Outcome with Experimental Control

Following Paul's (1969a) recommendations, we will discuss only studies that have controlled specifically for (1) the passage of time (through inclusion of a mminimal contact or assessment-only condition) and (2) nonspecific or placebo treatment effects (through inclusion of a condition where a credible treatment with an equivalent amount of therapist contact was administered). Only 7 of the 17 studies in this area meet these criteria all of which will be reviewed now in chronological order.

In the earliest evaluation of a social skills training program, Rehm and Marston (1968) randomly assigned 24 college male volunteers, who stated they felt uncomfortable in dating situations, to one of three conditions: (1) skills training with self-administered *in vivo* rehearsal, feedback, and reinforcement; (2) nondirective counseling (nonspecific control); and (3) minimal contact control where subjects were encouraged to think about their problems, but where no suggestions were given. Treatment consisted of 30 minutes of individual sessions per week for 5 weeks. Multiple therapists, who were crossed over conditions, were used. Assessment, consisting of self-report and behavioral measures, was conducted at pre- and posttreatment and at a 7- to 9- month follow-up. The results favoring the self-administered skills training groups were based primarily on self-report measures; none of the behavioral measures showed any significant differences between groups. Further, there were no significant differences between groups at follow-up on a generalization measure of dating frequency.

Martinson and Zerface (1970) employed a similar design in which they randomly assigned 24 college male volunteers, who had had less than one date in the previous month, to one of the following three treatment conditions: (1) skills training through practice dating where they were paired up with a different female volunteer each week; (2) individual, nonbehavioral professional counseling (nonspecific control); and (3) delayed treatment control (assessment only). Treatment lasted 5 weeks, and its effect was assessed with pre- and posttreatment self-report measures only. The skills training group was reported significantly more effective than both of the other groups in reducing specific dating fear and more effective than the delayed treatment group, but not the counseling group, in increasing dating frequency during 8- week posttreatment follow-up.

In an ambitious study, Melnick (1973) examined the incremental effectiveness of various skills training components including an adequate experimental control. He randomly assigned 59 males introductory psychology students, who reported feeling uncomfortable on dates and who dated less than twice a week, to one of six conditions: (1) video and overt modeling, rehearsal, video feedback, and reinforcement; (a) video and overt modeling, rehearsal, and video feed-

back; (3) verbal instruction, video and overt modeling, and rehearsal; (4) video modeling; (5) insight-oriented therapy (nonspecific control); and (6) waiting list control (assessment only). Treatment lasted four weekly sessions and was conducted individually by the same therapist in all conditions. Pre- and posttreatment assessment included both self-report and behavioral measures. Because of the small number of subjects in each condition, the two conditions with video feedback, the two without video feedback, and the two control conditions were combined within each pair for purpose of the analysis. In general, the behavioral measures showed that the combined video feedback skills training conditions were superior to the combined skills training conditions without video feedback, which in turn were superior to the combined control conditions. There were no differences, however, on self-report measures, including one based on dating frequency during treatment.

Bander et al. (1975) evaluated heterosocial skills training by randomly assigning 100 college males, who reported social anxiety and low dating frequency (although no specific criteria were stated), to one of five conditions: (1) skills training with verbal instructions, rehearsal, and homework; (2) skills training as in (1) plus systematic desensitization; (3) a half-day sensitivity group session; (4) nonspecific therapy including group exercises focusing on awareness but deemphasizing dating concerns; and (5) minimal contract control. Treatment, which lasted eight weekly sessions, was conducted in groups by therapists who were crossed over conditions. Assessment included self-report before and after the treatment and at follow-up to the treatment and a behavioral measure at posttreatment only. The skills training, both with and without systematic desensitization, was generally superior to the other groups at posttreatment and at follow-up. Systematic desensitization provided no measurable benefit over and beyond skills training in this study.

Curran (1975) included appropriate experimental control for passage of time and placebo effects in the first of a series of three studies evaluating heterosocial skills training. Twenty-two college students (including 3 females), who scored in the extreme one-third of the distribution on a social anxiety questionnaire and who reported minimal dating histories (although no specific figures were stated), were randomly assigned to one of four conditions: (1) skills training with verbal instructions, video modeling, rehearsal, video and group feedback, and homework; (2) systematic desensitization around dating situation; (3) relaxation training only (nonspecific control); and (4) waiting list control (assessment only). Therapists were crossed over conditions and treatment lasted six sessions over 2 weeks. Pre- and postassessment consisted of both self-report and behavioral measures. No follow-up assessment was conducted. Results indicated that the skills training and systematic desensitization conditions demonstrated significant changes over time on the behavioral measures, whereas the control conditions did not. These results led to a further study (Curran & Gilbert, 1975) that relates to comparative effectiveness (see the next section).

Using more stringent selection criteria than previous studies, MacDonald et al. (1975) randomly assigned 48 college males, who had had less than four dates the previous year, to one of four conditions: (1) skills training, including verbal instructions, rehearsal, and feedback; (2) skills training as in (1) plus homework; (3) attention placebo; and (4) waiting list control. Treatment was conducted in groups by therapists crossed over conditions and lasted for six weekly sessions. Pre- and postassessment included self-report and behavioral measures, while a

6-month follow-up was conducted on dating behavior. Results indicated a significant improvement over the control groups for both skills training conditions on some self-report and numerous behavioral measures from pre- to posttreatment. Dating frequency at follow-up, on the other hand, increased significantly for both the skills training with homework and the attention placebo condition.

Finally, McGovern et al. (1975) also controlled for passage of time and nonspecific effects in an evaluation of two forms of skills training. They randomly assigned 34 college males, all with less than three dates in the past month who stated they were anxious in social situations, to one of four treatment conditions: (1) skills training with verbal instruction, in session rehearsal, and feedback; (2) skills training with verbal instructions, practice dating, and feedback; (3) discussion groups centered around dating problems (nonspecific control); and (4) waiting list control (assessment only). The principal investigator was the sole therapist for all conditions. Treatments lasted six weekly sessions and were evaluated pre- and posttreatment with self-report measures only. The results indicated that the two skills training conditions were superior to the other conditions on most of these measures, but they did not differ from each other.

Summary

In combination, these studies indicate that heterosocial skills training of different forms typically results in significantly more improvement over the course of treatment than groups controlling for passage of time and therapist contact. However, these findings are not as conclusive as they first appear. First of all, the data are primarily of a self-report nature. Although four studies that did include behavioral measures (Curran,

1975; MacDonald et al., 1975; Melnick, 1973: Rehm & Marston, 1968) were supportive of the positive outcome of skills training, the self-report measures in two of these (Curran 1975; Melnick, 1973) were not consistent with the behavioral measures. Furthermore, only two studies (Bander et al., 1975; Rehm & Marston, 1968) assessed the maintenance of treatment gains at follow-up. Whereas they both confirm the positive outcome for social skills training, only self-report measures were used at follow-up. Finally, only four studies (MacDonald et al., 1975; Martinson & Zerface, 1970; Melnick, 1973; Rehm & Marston, 1968) employed measures of generalization, typically in the form of self-reported dating frequency. None of them demonstrated a superiority for skills training over control groups for *both* passage of time and placebo effects. (Martinson and Zerface reported superiority over the waiting list group but not over the attention placebo group.) An additional concern about these studies is, as noted by several previous reviewers (e.g., Arkowitz, 1977; Curran, 1977), the use of subjects whose status as skills deficient can be questioned. That is, the selection criteria commonly have been very lenient.

Comparative Outcome

Heterosocial problem behaviors have also been explained by theories other than social skills deficits (Curran, 1977). Most prominent of these alternative explanations have been *conditioned anxiety* and *faulty cognition*. With respect to the conditioned anxiety hypothesis, heterosocial problem behaviors are viewed as the result of classically conditioned episodes where previously neutral cues of heterosocial situations are associated with aversive stimuli, either through *in vivo* or vicarious experiences. This conceptualization naturally leads to the consideration of systematic desensitization as a treatment for heterosocial difficul-

ties. Several different types of faulty cognitions have been mentioned by Curran (1977) that may be responsible for heterosocial problem behaviors. These include unrealistic criteria, misperception of social cues, overly negative evaluation of performance, negative self-statements, and insufficient self-reinforcement. This conceptualization has given rise to the use of cognitive restructuring methods as a treatment for heterosocial difficulties. We will review the few studies that have evaluated one or both of these alternative treatment approaches in comparison to social skills training.

Curran directed two studies where systematic desensitization was compared to skills training. The first (Curran, 1975) has already been reviewed, and the results indicated that both conditions yielded significant positive effects on behavioral measures of social skills and anxiety at posttreatment in comparison to control groups. The two treatment conditions did not, however, differ significantly from each other. The subsequent study (Curran & Gilbert, 1975) also included a 6-month follow-up assessment and an indirect measure of generalization, self-reported dating frequency. The 35 subjects (14 of whom were females) selected for this study were in the extreme one-third of the distribution on two relevant questionnaires and appeared to be minimal daters (over 50% had not dated in the 7 to 8 weeks prior to treatment). They were randomly assigned to either (1) social skills training with verbal instructions, modeling, rehearsal, individual and group feedback, and homework assignments; (2) systematic desensitization around dating situations; or (3) a waiting list control (assessment only). Two pairs of therapists, who were crossed over conditions, were employed. Self-report and behavioral measures obtained at three intervals, indicated significant decreases for both treatment groups, but not for the control group, in anxiety at posttest and follow-up. Skills training and desensitization groups, however, did not differ in decreasing anxiety. Both treatment groups also demonstrated significant increases in dating frequency both during and after treatment, suggesting equal generalization effects. Ratings of social skills. in contrast, were higher for the skills training group than the control group at posttest, and significantly different from both the control and desensitization groups at follow-up. These results suggest a more general treatment for skills training.

The differential effectiveness of social skills training and cognitive restructuring was evaluated by Glass, Gottman, and Shmurak (1976). No selection criteria were used in recruiting 61 college males to volunteer for their study. These subjects were randomly assigned to one of five conditions: (1) social skills training with verbal instructions, audio modeling, and rehearsal for four sessions; (2) cognitive restructuring for four sessions; (3) combined social skills and cognitive restructuring training, as in (1) and (2), for five sessions; (4) social skills training as in (1), but for five sessions; (5) cognitive restructuring as in (2), but for five sessions; and (6) waiting list control (assessment only). Conditions (4) and (5) were included to control for the additional time involved in the combined treatment. The cognitive restructuring treatment was based on Meichenbaum's (1972) training model, where coping models demonstrate how to verbalize negative self-talk, recognize negative self-talk as such, and produce positive adaptive self-talk. This is then followed by verbal instruction, rehearsal, and feedback of these cognitive restructuring skills. Multiple therapists were used and crossed over treatment conditions. Dating history and behavioral data were collected at pre- and posttreatment and at 6-month follow-up to treatment. Behavioral data were obtained by observing

and rating the performance of the subjects in situations actually included in the treatment as practice situations and in situations unfamiliar to the subjects to assess generalization of treatment. Follow-up assessment also included a phone call measure of generalization. The results at posttreatment and follow-up indicated that all treatment groups performed significantly better than the waiting list control on the dating test situations on which they had training. However on the untrained generalization situations only the cognitive modification group showed significant improvement at posttreatment and follow-up. Length of treatment did not matter. Thus, it appears from these findings that, although social skills training can effectively teach individuals appropriate responses for specific situations, their training does not generalize to new situations without some direct cognitive restructuring. It should be noted, however, that cognitive modification is often informally included as part of many social skills training programs.

Heimberg et al. (1980) evaluated three treatment approaches. They included in their sample 69 college males who score at least one standard deviation above the mean on a relevant questionnaire and randomly assigned these to one of four conditions: (1) social skills training with verbal instructions, covert and overt rehearsal, and feedback; (2) group systematic desensitization around dating items; (3) practice dating with cognitive restructuring following Rehm and Marsten's (1968) procedures; and (4) assessment-only control. Treatment lasted eight weekly sessions and was conducted by graduate students who were apparently not crossed over conditions. Assessments, consisting of self-report and behavioral measures in the laboratory and self-monitoring of daily interactions (a generalization measure), were conducted at pre- and posttreatment and at a 9-week follow-up to treatment. The results indicated a significant general improvement from pre- to postassessment for *all* conditions, including the control. Some, but not all, effects were maintained at follow-up. The authors attributed the lack of differential as well as treatment-specific effects to large individual differences in pretest data across measures.

Summary

Given the few studies evaluating comparative effectiveness of social skills training, little can be stated at this point. Nonetheless, several tentative hypotheses can be generated: Social skills training for heterosocial problem behaviors may produce a more general positive behavioral effect than systematic desensitization (Curran & Gilbert, 1975), but in order for this to generalize beyond targeted situations, cognitive restructuring may be needed (Glass et al., 1976). These hypotheses, of course, need to be confirmed by further reseach. Moreover, the importance of person variables and person-with-treatment interactions is also strongly implicated by this research (Heimberg et al., 1980) and needs to be investigated further in further efforts.

CURRENT STATE OF THE ART AND FURTHER DIRECTIONS

Training Procedures of Heterosocial Programs

The literature regarding the relative effectiveness of various procedures of heterosocial skills programs is miniscule. Consequently, we were forced to review the literature regarding the procedure off skills programs for other types of targeted behaviors. Even then, it was extremely difficult to evaluate this literature because these studies differed on so many parameters, such as types of subjects, length of the programs, skills taught, the relative isolation or contamination of the procedures, and so on. From a review of the literature it appears that rehearsal and feedback techniques are perhaps the most powerful techniques with respect to the acquisition of a skill. However, the literature is so confusing that perhaps the only tentative conclusion that can be reached is that the effectiveness of the program is probably due to a combination of techniques. In future research special attention should be focused on those training procedures necessary for the generalization of these skills into the natural environment. More studies need to be conducted evaluating the use of homework assignments, *in vivo* practice, practice dating, and "buddy" systems in promoting generalization of these skills to the natural environment.

More systematic studies need to be conducted to evaluate the training components. These studies should attempt to control as many parameters as they possibly can and just attempt to manipuate the components. In all likelihood, the importance of each component is probably mediated by other parameters such as the subject population studied, the targeted behaviors, and the assessment procedures used to measure its effectiveness.

Content of Heterosocial Skills Programs

We find a hierarchical model useful in conceptualizing skills-content components in order to avoid the molecular versus molar controversy. We feel that both levels as well as intermediate levels will be crucial to our understanding of heterosocial skills.

More sophisticated training programs will require that the domain of problematic social situations and effective behaviors in these situations be better specified. A survey of a subject's competence across these situations will provide the basis for training. Within this approach, assessment will interface with treatment to identify problem areas and indicate progress, perhaps in a stage model (cf. West et al., 1980). The discussion of alternative models for social skills presented by McFall (1982) and Trower (1982) offers much promise in this regard. In order to provide a basis for these training programs, it will be necessary to go beyond the informal and intuitive approaches to determining the contents of treatment programs previously discussed and turn to more systematic empirical methods.

Specific components are only part of the puzzle, however; future research needs to uncover process or interactive patterns (for example, parameters of timing and sequencing). We need to understand both components and process variables and how they are integrated in competent individuals. That is, it is not only knowledge of what to say but when to say it that is critical. Most of the research that has been done with respect to the components has been correlational in nature. In future research we need to establish more functional relationships. For example, studies such as Rose and Tryon (1979) and Kupke et al. (1979) need to be conducted where components are varied in such a fashion as to determine how they alter judgments regarding successful performance.

Subject Selection

The vast majority of studies conducted on heterosocial skills were done on college students. One question that needs to be addressed is how representative is this population to other dating populations, such as high school students, non-college same-age peers, and older adults. It is conceivable that different types of skills might be needed for successful encounters by each of these populations.

The composition of groups of subjects undergoing heterosocial skills training has never been adequately assessed by any study in the literature. That is, it is not clear from reading the literature whether individuals selected for these heterosocial skills training programs were indeed deficient in heterosocial skills. This is probably due to the problem of assessing skills deficits in addition to less than rigorous research methodologies. The problem of assessing skills deficits is quite obvious; we can measure performance but not potential. Performance is influenced by numerous factors, in addition to existing behavioral repertories. Numerous motivational, emotional, or cognitive factors can interfere with successful performance. However, with the more refined methodologies we can attempt to eliminate these other factors. We can develop assessment protocols in such a fashion that we can be more confident whether a skills deficit exists or not. For example, we can construct structured interviews to obtain performance histories; we can attempt to motivate our subjects to perform up to their potential; we can assess social knowledge; and we can vary degree of difficulty of the task, and so on.

We need to assess our subjects more thoroughly because there is a good likelihood that an interaction effect exists between the source of the dating problem and the type of treatment implemented. For example, systematic desensitization may be ineffective for a truly skills-deficient individual, but highly effective for someone who is mildly anxious but possesses good interpersonal skills. We may also find that characteristics of the subjects might interact with the generalization of these skills to the natural environment. In the Glass et al. (1975) study, it appeared that subjects who were only minimally deficient in skill needed only a cognitive treatment, whereas subjects who were severely deficient in skills needed a skills acquisition and cognitive approach. We also may discover that certain programs might be effective for individuals who are experiencing problems complicated by multiple sources (cognitive, emotional, and skill deficits). For example, in a study by Trower, Yardley, Bryant, and Shaw (1978), individuals who were primarily or secondarily social phobics, benefited from a skills training program, whereas individuals who were secondarily social phobics did not benefit from a desensitization program that was successful with primarily social phobics. It may be, as Curran (1977) pointed out, that components within heterosocial skills training programs can also be viewed as decreasing anxiety and clearing up cognitive misconceptions.

Adequacy of Assessment Protocol

One of the most critical questions in all heterosocial skills research relates to the validity of the assessment measures used. As stated by Conger and Conger (1982, p. 322):

Research on heterosexual social problem behaviors based on different measurement instruments is not a homogeneous enterprise. The research indicated a lack of convergence of the measurement instruments on the unitary problem behavior or behavior construct and this lack most likely stems from the strategies used to develop the measures and the absence of consensually agreed upon criteria. We concluded there was a major need to specify more completely an empirically determined set of behavioral indicators related to heterosocial skill and anxiety and more specific guidelines for combining these indicators into heuristic composite measures of skill and anxiety.

We need to know whether the results of our treatment studies actually have social validation. That is, do they represent real and significant changes? Do these changes generalize from laboratory to the subject's natural environment? In developing our assessment procedures, we need to complete both a skills analysis

and a task analysis. As McFall (1982, p. 16) notes:

One must understand these important features of that task: its purpose, its contraints, its setting, the rules governing task performance, the criteria for distinguishing between successful and unsuccessful performance, and how the task relates to other aspects of the person's life system.

McFall (1982) sees the basic requirements for the assessment task as being (1) to identify the most relevant and critical life task for the person or group; (2) to conduct task analysis for each task; (3) to obtain a representative sample of each individual's performance on each task; (4) to establish task-specific criteria for evaluating competent performance; (5) to evaluate the performance samples; and (6) to summarize, integrate, and interpret the evaluation results.

We need to assess transfer of training better. Before we do this, a careful specification of what constitutes transfer must be obtained. That is, if situational variables are powerful determinants of behavior, we need to examine our training situations to look for commonalities. Less than perfect generalization may be due to situational determinants being different in the training situation rather than in the natural environment. So many different types of situations can occur on a date, and yet what we train for and assess in a training program usually involves only a limited number of situations like small talk, conversations, initiating dates, and the like. MacDonald and Cohen (1981) pointed out the diversity of interpersonal situations and how they might call for different types of skills. From reading descriptions of heterosexual programs, there appear to be numerous skills and situations neglected. For example, using McDonald and Cohen's (1981) list, we do very little training for situations requiring confiding, helping, pleading, competing, and respecting.

Development of a Comprehensive Model

When one reads the literature on social skills training, one gets the impression that most of the emphasis in training is on teaching specific component behaviors (i.e., teaching appropriate levels of eye contact, delivering an assertive response, and so on). The fact is that much more than component behaviors is taught in most training programs. However, not only have we not specified to any great extent these other goals of our training programs, we have not systematically studied and examined these goals. In our training programs we discuss with our subjects rules for social conduct, teach them to monitor their own behavior and the behavior of others, generate probability levels between actions and reinforcements, and so on. In most cases, these other goals of the training program are seldom discussed in the literature. This lack of attention probably reflects the unsystematic manner in which most skills programs attempt to impart these important parameters.

Trower (1982) makes the distinction between what he calls social skills and social skill. *Social skills* for Trower are the actual normative component behaviors or identifiable sequences of elements or acts or scripts that people use in social interaction, and that are governed by rules. *Social skill,* on the other hand, refers to the process of generating skilled behavior directed to a goal. He feels that in most training programs there is an overemphasis on teaching component skills rather than social skill per se (i.e., generative capability). Trower cites four important variables involved in the actual generative process: (1) monitoring capabilities (of both external and internal events); (2) a performance capability

(monitored); (3) goals or standards; and (4) cognitive representations and logical functions.

In addition to attempting to measure our subjects' response capabilities, Trower feels that we should be assessing an individual's possession of social knowledge, ability to produce appropriate plans, their outcome expectancies, and the beliefs that generate them. We need to assess the subject's own purpose, perception, inferences, and evaluations. We also need to know more about norms and rules for social behavior and the structure and function of social discourse. As for training, Trower (1982, p. 424) stated that it "should also include the monitoring, logical disputing, an empirical disproving of invalid inferences and negative evaluations, which commonly function to block both the acquisition and generation of social skill."

It should be kept in mind that possession of the requisite skill does not guarantee competent performance. Performance is a function of numerous variables, only one of which is possession of the requisite skill. In addition to response capability, the organism must be able to adequately receive, perceive, and interpret incoming stimuli. The organism must possess problem-solving skills, have task-relevant knowledge and experience, possess an adequate self-efficacy that he or she can perform competently, have favorable expectations about the likely consequences of competent performance, and so on.

It is our belief that social skills training programs will have to be more comprehensive if they are to have a significant long-lasting impact as a treatment procedure. Variables and processes that have been approached unsystematically must be studied more systematically in both evaluation and training. Social skills training in many ways is still in its infancy and must be nurtured properly in order to reach adulthood.

SUMMARY

Interest in heterosocial skills training as a treatment strategy can be traced to a number of sources. Four sources discussed were (1) the emphasis on interpersonal competence in personality theories; (2) the linkage between interpersonal competence and psychological functioning; (3) the development of response acquisition approaches to the treatment of deviant behavior; and (4) the search for appropriate targets for therapy analog research. Heterosocial anxiety appears to be an ideal target behavior for analog research because a large number of potential subjects exist, the behavior is clinically relevant, measurement procedures validly discriminate between low- and high-anxious subjects, strong physiological reactions are elicited that do not readily habituate, and the effects of repeated testing and experimental demand are negligible.

The assumption behind heterosocial skills training as a treatment method is that the anxiety is reactive in nature, that is, deficiencies in skills lead to failure in heterosocial encounter that produce anxiety. Theoretically, increases in skills would lead to more successful heterosexual encounters that in turn would decrease anxiety. Heterosocial skills training programs typically consist of the following elements: (1) information about appropriate response patterns is provided to the subjects by verbal instruction and modeling; (2) subjects are asked to rehearse in role plays these new behavior patterns; (3) subjects receive feedback regarding their performance from therapists, other subjects, and videotape playback; and (4) subjects are provided homework assignments in an attempt to promote generalization of these skills beyond the treatment situation.

The content of heterosocial skills training programs (i.e., the skills taught) should ideally be based on empirical data. The construction of training programs should be guided by empirical analysis of subjects training needs and an understanding of the problematic situations. A review of the literature indicates that most treatment programs rest on either clinical intuition or fairly informal pilot research. The behavior-analytic approach was recommended for identifying problematic heterosocial situations. Likewise, empirical strategies such as peer nomination procedures, contrasted groups procedures, and so on are encouraged in order to identify specific behavioral components of heterosocial skills.

A review of the literature indicates a tentative conclusion that heterosocial skills training is an effective treatment procedure. Studies indicate that heterosocial skills training of different forms typically results in significantly more improvement over the course of treatment than groups controlling for passage of time and therapist contact. However, little data exist regarding generalization of treatment effects to the natural environment. Because there are so few studies evaluating comparative effectiveness of social skills training, little can be stated on these matters at this point. The importance of person variables and person-with-treatment interactions are implicated by research.

Five areas of future research were addressed: (1) training procedures of heterosocial programs; (2) content of heterosocial programs; (3) problems in identifying subjects appropriate for heterosocial programs; (4) problems in assessing heterosocial competence, especially the issue regarding the social validation of our treatment outcome studies; and (5) the need for a generative model of social skills with inclusion of cognitive variables.

REFERENCES

Adler, A. (1930). Individual psychotherapy. In C. Murcheson (Ed.), *Psychologies of 1930.* Worcester, MA: Clark University Press.

Argyle, M., & Kendon, A. (1967). The experimental analysis of human performance. *Advances in Experimental Social Psychology, 3,* 55–98.

Arkowitz, H. (1977). The measurement and modification of minimal dating behavior. In M. Hersen, R. Eisler, & P. Miller (Eds.), *Progress in behavior modification.* New York: Academic Press.

Arkowitz, H., Lichtenstein, E., McGovern, K., & Hines, P. (1975) The behavioral assessment of social competence in males. *Behavior Therapy, 6,* 3–13.

Arzin, N.H., Flores, T., & Kaplan, S. J. (1975). Job-finding club: A group-assisted program for obtaining employment. *Behavior Research and Therapy, 13* 17–27.

Bander, K. W., Steinke, G. V., Allen, G. J. & Mosher, D. L., (1975). Evaluation of three dating-specific treatment approaches for heterosexual dating anxiety. *Journal of Consulting and Clinical Psychology, 43,* 259–265.

Bandura, A. (1965). Influence of model's reinforcement contingencies on the acquisition of imatative responses. *Journal of Personality and Social Psychology, 1,* 689–595.

Bandura, A. (1977a). Self-efficacy: Toward a unifying theory of behavioral change. *Psychological Review, 84,* 191–215.

Bandura, A. (1977b). *Social learning theory.* Englewood Cliffs, NJ: Prentice-Hall.

Bandura, A., Ross, D., & Ross, S. A. (1963). Vicarious reinforcement and imitative learning. *Journal of Abnormal and Social Psychology, 67,* 601–607.

Barlow, D. H., Abel, G. G., Blanchard, E. B., Bristow, A. R., & Young, L. D. (1977). A heterosocial skills behavior checklist for males. *Behavior Therapy, 8,* 229–239.

Bellack, A. S. (1979). A critical appraisal of strategies for assessing social skill. *Behavioral Assessment, 1,* 157–176.

Borkovec, T. T., Stone, N. M., O'Brien, G. T., & Kaloupek, D. G., (1974). Evaluation of a clinically relevant target behavior for analog outcome research. *Behavior Therapy, 5,* 503–513.

Bryant, B., Trower, R., Yardley, K., Urbieta, K., & Letemendia, F. J. (1976). A survey of social inadequacy among psychiatric patients. *Psychological Medicine, 6,* 102–112.

Callner, D. A. & Ross, S. M. (1976). The reliability and validity of three measures of assertion in a drug addict population. *Behavior Therapy, 7,* 659–667.

Christensen, A., & Arkowitz, H. (1974). Preliminary report on practice dating and feedback as a treatment for college dating problems. *Journal of Consulting and Clinical Psychology, 21,* 92–95.

Christensen, A., Arkowitz, H., & Anderson, J. (1975). Practice dating as treatment for college dating inhibitions. *Behavior Research and Therapy, 113,* 321–331.

Clark, K. W. *Evaluation of a group social skills training program with psychiatric inpatients: Training Viet Nam era veterans in assertion, heterosexual, and job interview skills.* (1974). Unpublished doctoral dissertation, University of Wisconsin.

Conger, J. C., & Conger, A. J., (1982). Components of heterosocial competence. In J. P. Curran & P. M. Monti (Eds.), *Social skills training: A practical handbook for assessment and treatment.* New York: Guilford.

Conger, J. C., & Farrell, A. D. (1981). Behavioral components of heterosocial skills. *Behavior Therapy, 12,* 41–55.

Conger, A. J., Wallander, J. L. & Conger, J. C., (1980). *Peer judgements of heterosexual-social anxiety and skill: They do pay attention!* Paper presented at the meeting of the Association for the Advancement of Behavior Therapy, New York.

Conger, A. J., Wallander, J. L., Mariotto, M. J., & Ward, D. (1980). Peer judgements of heterosexual-social anxiety and skill: What do they pay attention to anyhow? *Behavioral Assessment, 2,* 243–259.

Cooper, A., Furst, J. B., & Bridger, W. H. (1969). A brief commentary on the usefulness of studying fears of snakes. *Journal of Abnormal Psychology, 74,* 413–414.

Curran, J. P. (1975). An evaluation of a skills training program and a systematic desensitization program in reducing dating anxiety. *Behavior Research and Therapy, 13,* 65–68.

Curran, J. P. (1977). Skills training as an approach to the treatment of heterosexual-social anxiety: A review. *Psychological Bulletin, 84,* 140–157.

Curran, J. P., & Gilbert, F. S. (1975). A testing of the relative effectiveness of a systematic desensitization program and an interpersonal skills training program with date anxious subjects. *Behavior Therapy, 6,* 510–521.

Curran, J. P., Gilbert, F. S., & Little, L. M. (1976). A comparison between behavioral replication training and sensitivity training approaches to heterosexual dating anxiety. *Journal of Counseling Psychology, 23,* 190–196.

Curran, J. P., & Mariotto, M. J. (1980). A conceptual structure for the assessment of social skills. In M. Hersen, R. M. Eisler, & P. M. Miller (Eds.), *Progress in behavior modification* (Vol. 9). New York: Academic Press.

Curran, J. P. Miller, I. W., Zwick, W. R., Monti, P. M., & Stout, R. L. (1980). The socially inadequate patient: Incidence rate, demographic and clinical features, hospital and post-hospital functioning. *Journal of Consulting and Clinical Psychology, 48,* 375–382.

Curran, J. P., Wallander, J. L., & Fischetti, M. (1977). The importance of behavioral and cognitive factors in heterosexual-social anxiety and skill. *Journal of Personality, 48,* 285–292.

Curran, J. P., & Wessberg, H. W. (1981). The assessment of social inadequacy. In D. H. Barlow (Ed.), *Behavioral assessment of adult disorders.* New York: Guilford.

Eisler, R. M., Miller, P. M., Hersen, M., & Alford, H. (1974). Effects of assertive training on marital interaction. *Archives of General Psychiatry, 30,* 643–649.

Elder, J. P., Edelstein, B., Frewmouw, Lively, L., Walker, J., & Womeldorf, J. A. (1978). *A comparison of response acquisition and cognitive restructuring in the enhancement of social competence of college freshmen.* Paper presented at AABT.

Erikson, E. H. (1950). *Childhood and society.* New York: Norton.

Farrell, A. D., Rabinowitz, J. A., Wallander, J. L., & Curran, J. P. (1982). *Development and evaluation of a behavioral checklist for social skills assessment.* Unpublished manuscript.

Fishman, S., & Nawas, M. (1973). Treatment of polysomatic or global problems by systematic desensitization. In R. Rubin (Ed.), *Advances in behavior therapy,* New York: Academic Press.

Freedman, B. J., Rosenthal, L., Donahue, C. P. Jr., Schlundt, D. G., & McFall, R. M. (1978). A social-behavioral analysis of skill deficits in delinquent and nondelinquent adolescent boys. *Journal of Consulting and Clinical Psychology, 46,* 1448–1462.

Galassi, J. D. & Galassi, M. D., (1979). Modification of heterosocial skills deficits. In A. S. Bellack & M. Hersen (Eds.), *Research and practice in social skills training.* New York: Plenum.

Gladwin, T. (1977). Social competence and clinical practice, *Psychiatry, 30*–38.

Glasgow, R. E., & Arkowitz, H. (1975) The behavioral assessment of male and female social competence in dyadic heterosexual interactions. *Behavior Therapy,* 488–498.

Glass, C. R., Gottman, J. M., & Shmurak, S. H. (1976). Response-acquisition and cognitive self-statement modification approaches to dating-skills training. *Journal of Consulting and Clinical Psychology, 23,* 520–526.

Goldfried, M. R., & D'Zurilla, T. J. (1969). A behavioral analytic model for assessing competence. In C. D. Spielberger (Ed.), *Current topics in clinical and community psychology* (Vol. 1). New York: Academic Press.

Goldsmith, J. B., & McFall, R. M. (1975). Development and evaluation of an interpersonal skill-training program for psychiatry inpatients. *Journal of Abnormal Psychology, 84,* 51–58.

Gormally, J., Hill, C. E., Otis, M., & Rainey, L. A., (1975). A microtraining approach to assertion training. *Journal of Counseling Psychology, 22,* 299–303.

Hartmann, H. (1958). *Ego psychology and the problem of adaption.* (D. Rapaport, Trans.) New York: International University Press.

Heimberg, R. A. Madsen, C. H., Montgomery, D. & McNabb, C. E. (1980). Behavioral treatments for heterosocial problems: Effects on daily self-monitored and role-played interactions. *Behavioral Modification, 4,* 147–172.

Hersen, M. (1979). Modification of skill deficits in psychiatric patients. In A. S. Bellack & M. Hersen (Eds.), *Research and practice in social skills training.* New York: Plenum.

Horney, K. (1939). *New ways in psychoanalysis.* New York: Norton.

Harré, R., & Secord, P. F., (1979). *The explanation of social behavior.* Oxford: Blackwell.

Kanfer, R. H., & Phillips, J. S. (1970). *Learning foundations of behavior therapy.* New York: Wiley.

Kazdin, A. E. (1974). Effects of covert modeling and model reinforcement on assertive behavior. *Journal of Abnormal Psychology, 83,* 240–252.

Kazdin, A. E. (1976). Effects of covert modeling, multiple models, and model reinforcement on assertive behavior. *Behavior Therapy, 7,* 211–222.

Kazdin, A. E. (1977). Assessing the clinical and applied importance of behavior change through social validation. *Behavior Modification, 1,* 427–452.

Kazdin, A. E. (1978). The application of operant techniques in treatment, rehabilitation, and education. In S. L. Gargield & A. E. Bergin (Eds.), *Handbook of psychotherapy and behavior change: An empirical analysis* (2nd ed.). New York: Wiley.

Kraft, T. (1971). Social anxiety model of alcoholism. *Perceptual and Motor Skills, 33,* 797–798.

Kramer, S. R. (1975). *Effectiveness of behavior rehearsal and practice dating to increase heterosexual social interaction.* Unpublished doctoral dissertation, University of Texas at Austin.

Kupke, T. E., Calhoun, K. S., & Hobbs, S. A. (1979). Selection of heterosocial skills II: Experimental validity. *Behavior Therapy, 10,* 336–346.

Kupke, T. E., Hobbs, S. A. & Cheney, T. H. (1979). Selection of heterosocial skills I: Criterion-related validity. *Behavior Therapy, 10,* 327–335.

Landy, F. J. & Gaupp, L. A. (1971). A factor analysis of the Fear Survey Schedule-III. *Behavior Research and Therapy, 9,* 89–94.

Lazarus, A. A. (1971). *Behavior therapy and beyond.* New York: McGraw-Hill.

Libet, J. M. & Lewinsohn, P. M. (1973). Concept of social skills with special reference to the behavior of depressed persons. *Journal of Consulting and Clinical Psychology, 40,* 304–312.

Lindquist, C. W., Framer, J. A., McGrath, R. A., MacDonald, M. L. & Rhyne, L. D. (1975). Social skills training: Dating skills treatment manual. *JSAS Catalog of Selected Documents in Psychology, 5,* 279.

MacDonald, M. L. (1978). Measuring assertion: A model and method. *Behavior Therapy, 9,* 889–899.

MacDonald, M. L., & Cohen, J. (1981). Trees in the forest: Some components of social skills. *Journal of Clinical Psychology, 37,* 342–347.

MacDonald, M. L., Lindquist, C. U., Kramer, J. A., McGrath, R. A. & Rhyne, L. D. (1975). Social skills training: Behavior rehearsal in groups and dating skills. *Journal of Counseling Psychology, 22,* 224–230.

Martinson, W. D., & Zerface, J. P. (1970). Comparison of individual counseling and a social program with nondaters. *Journal of Counseling Psychology, 17,* 36–40.

McFall, R. M., & Galbraith, J. R. (1977). *Two studies examining feedback in assertion training*. Unpublished manuscript, University of Wisconsin.

McFall, R. M. (1982). A review and reformulation of the concept of social skills. *Behavioral Assessment, 4*, 1–33.

McFall, R. M., & Twentyman, C. T. (1973). Four experiments on the relative contributions of rehearsal, modeling and coaching to assertion training. *Journal of Abnormal Psychology, 81*, 199–218.

McGovern, K. B., Arkowitz, H., & Gilmore, S. K. (1975). Evaluation of social skills training programs for college dating inhibitions. *Journal of Counseling Psychology, 22*, 505–512.

Meichenbaum, D. (1972). Ways of modifying what clients say to themselves. *Rational Living, 7*, 22–27.

Melnick, J. A. (1973). Comparison of replication techniques in the modification of minimal dating behavior. *Journal of Abnormal Psychology, 81*, 51–59.

Melnick, J. A., & Stocker, R. B. (1977). An experimental analysis of the behavioral rehearsal with feedback technique in assertiveness training. *Behavior Therapy, 8*, 222–228.

Miller, P. M., Hersen, M., Eisler, R. M., & Hilsman, G. (1974). Effects of social stress on operant drinking of alcoholics and social drinkers. *Behavior Research and Therapy, 12*, 67–72.

Mischel, W. (1973). Toward a cognitive social learning reconceptualization of personality. *Psychological Review, 80* 252–283.

Morgan, J. M. (1975). *The effects of model exposure and behavioral rehearsal on the initiation of dating experiences by seldom dating college men*. Unpublished doctoral dissertation. Southern Illinois University.

Nietzel, M. T., Martorano, R. D. & Melnick, J. (1977). The effects of covert modeling with and without reply training on the development and generalization of assertive responses. *Behavior Therapy, 8*, 183–192.

Paul, G. L. (1969a). Behavior modification research: Design and tactics. In C. M. Franks (Ed.), *Behavior therapy: Appraisal and status*. New York: McGraw-Hill.

Paul, G. L. (1969b). Chronic mental patient: Current status—future directions. *Psychological Bulletin, 71*, 81–94.

Paul, G. L., & Lentz, R. J. (1977). Psychosocial treatment of chronic mental patients: Mileau vs. social learning program. Cambridge: Harvard Unviversity Press.

Paul, G. L., & Bernstein, D. A. (1973). *Anxiety and clinical problems: Systematic desensitization and related techniques*. Morristown, NJ: General Learning.

Phillips, E. L. (1978). *The social skills basis of psychopathology: Alternative to abnormal psychology and psychiatry*. New York: Grune & Stratton.

Phillips, L., & Zigler, E., (1961). Social competence: The action–thought parameter and vicariousness in normal and pathological behaviors. *Journal of Abnormal and Social Psychology, 63*, 137–146.

Pilkonis, P. A. (1977). Shyness, public and private, and its relationship to other measures of social behavior. *Journal of Personality, 45*, 585–595.

Rehm, L. P., & Marston, A. R., (1968). Reduction of social anxiety through modification of self-reinforcement: An instigation therapy technique. *Journal of Consulting and Clinical Psychology, 32*, 565–574.

Rose, Y. J., & Tryon, W. W. (1979). Judgements of assertive behavior as a function of speech loudness, latency, content, questions, inflection, and sex. *Behavior Modification, 3*, 112–123.

Rose, S. D. (1975). In pursuit of social competence. *Social Work, 20*, 33–39.

Rosenthal, T., & Bandura, A. (1978). Psychological modeling: Theory and practice. In S. L. Garfield & A. E. Bergin (Eds.), *Handbook of psychotherapy and behavior change: An empirical analysis* (2nd ed). New York: Wiley.

Royce, W. S., & Arkowitz, H. (1976). Multimodel evaluation of *in vivo* practice as treatment for social isolation. *Paper presented at the 10th Annual Convention of Association for Advancement of Behavior Therapy*.

Sarason, I. G., & Ganzer, V. J. (1973). Modeling and group discussion in the rehabilitation of juvenile delinquents. *Journal of Counseling Psychology, 20*, 442–449.

Schwartz, R. M., & Gottman, J. M. (1976). Toward a task analysis of assertive behavior. *Journal of Consulting and Clinical Psychology, 44*, 910–920.

Shoemaker, M. E., & Paulson, T. L. (1976). Group assertive training for mothers: A family intervention strategy. In E. J. Mash, L. C. Handy, & L. A. Hamerlynck (Eds.), *Behavior modification approaches to parenting.* New York: Brunner/Mazel.

Strauss, J. S., & Carpenter, W. T., (1972). The prediction of outcome in schizophrenia: I. Characteristics of outcome. *Archives of General Psychiatry, 21*, 739–746.

Strauss, J. S., Klorman, R., & Kokes, R. F., (1977) Premorbid adjustment in schizophrenia: The implications of finding for understanding, research and application. *Schizophrenia Bulletin, 3*, 240–244.

Sullivan, H. S. (1953). *The interpersonal theory of psychiatry.* New York: Norton.

Sylph, J. A., Ross, H. E., & Kedward, H. B. (1978). Social disability in chronic psychiatric patients. *American Journal of Psychiatry, 134*, 1391–1394.

Thorpe, G. L. (1973). *Short-term effectiveness of systematic desensitization, modeling, and behavior rehearsal, and self-instructional training in facilitating assertive-refusal behavior.* Unpublished doctoral dissertation. Rutgers University.

Trower, P. (1980). Situational analysis of the components and processes of behavior of socially skilled and unskilled patients. *Journal of Consulting and Clinical Psychology, 48*, 327–339.

Trower, P. (1982). Toward a generative model of social skills: A critique and synthesis. In J. P. Curran & P. M. Monti (Eds.), *Social skills training: A practical handbook for assessment and treatment.* New York: Guilford.

Trower, P., Yardley, K., Bryant, B. M., & Shaw, P. (1978). The treatment of social failure: A comparison of anxiety reduction and skill-acquisition procedures on two social problems. *Behavior Modification, 2*, 41–60.

Twentyman, C. T., & McFall, R. M. (1975). Behavioral training of social skills in shy males. *Journal of Consulting and Clinical Psychology, 43*, 384–395.

Twentyman, C. T. & Zimering, R. T. (1979). Behavioral training of social skills: A critical review. In M. Hersen, R. Eisler, & P. Miller (Eds.), *Progress in behavior modification.* New York: Academic Press.

Wallander, J. L. Conger, A. J., & Conger, J. C. (1982). *Development and evaluation of a behaviorally referenced, multicomponent rating system for heterosocial skills.* Manuscript submitted for publication.

West, B. L., Goethe, K. E., & Kallman, W. M. (1980). Heterosocial skills training: A behavioral-cognitive approach. In D. Upper & S. M. Ross (Eds.), *Behavioral group therapy, 1980: An annual review.* Champaign, IL: Research Press.

White, R. (1960). Competence and the psychosexual stages of development. In M. R. Jones (Ed.), *Nebraska symposium on motivation.* Lincoln: University of Nebraska Press.

Wolpe, J., & Lazarus, A. A. (1969). *Behavior therapy techniques.* New York: Pergamon.

Zigler, E., & Levine, J. (1973). Premorbid adjustment and paranoid–non-paranoid status in schizophrenia: A further investigation. *Journal of Abnormal Psychology, 82*, 189–199.

Zigler, E., & Phillips, L. (1960). Social effectiveness and symptomatic behaviors. *Journal of Abnormal and Social Psychology, 61*, 231–238.

Zigler, E., & Phillips, L. (1962). Social competence and the process-reactive distinction in psychopathology. *Journal of Abnormal and Social Psychology, 65*, 215–222.

CHAPTER 7

The Enhancement of Sexual Skills and Competence

Promoting Lifelong Sexual Unfolding

ANTHONY D'AUGELLI AND JUDITH FRANKEL D'AUGELLI

Chance was bewildered: there was clearly no place to which he could run away. He searched his memory and recalled situations on TV in which a woman advanced toward a man on a couch or a bed or inside a car. Usually, after a while, they come very close to each other, and, often they would be partly undressed. They would then kiss and embrace. But on TV what happened next was always obscured: a brand-new image would appear on the screen: the embrace of man and woman was utterly forgotten. And yet, Chance knew, there could be other gestures and other kinds of closeness following such intimacies.

JERZY KOSINSKI, *Being There* (1970)

Chance Gardiner's sexual predicament is only more extreme than most; the limits of his sexual socialization are more obvious. It takes little introspection to determine the boundaries of one's sexual expression, although more speculation is needed to reconstruct a psychosexual autobiography. No doubt our basic sexual preferences are formed early in life (for example, the recent Kinsey data on homosexuality [Bell, Weinberg, & Hammersmith, 1981] are described as consistent with a biological determinism of sexual preference), and later sexual development could be viewed as providing social training in meeting one's sexual needs in a particular cultural context. Physical development notwithstanding, sexual development is closely intertwined with social development. With the obvious exceptions of masturbation and fantasy, sexual behavior is social and interpersonal. Sexual behavior is ini-

tiated in the world of social norms and meanings: An intense gaze in a certain social context has distinct sexual meaning. Sexual exchanges occur in an interpersonal context, usually between two people. Sexual development involves a transition from comfortable transactions in social situations to satisfying contacts in physically and often psychologically intimate circumstances. Much variability exists in individual skillfulness in both the public and private realms of sexual behavior. Chance Gardiner is not alone in his awkwardness.

Very little attention has been paid by social scientists to the competencies or skills involved in actual sexual behavior. The assumption made is that most men and women meet their sexual needs adequately, if not with flair and creativity. We know little of sexual frustrations or dysfunctions unless people seek sex therapy and even less of unfulfilled sexual interests and fantasies. There is no doubt, however, that much variability exists in what is considered "adequate" sexuality. This variability in how people handle their sexuality is partially explained by the inability to observe, in a systematic way, effective models of diverse, comfortable, satisfying sexual behaviors. It is indeed the case that beyond a certain point one may not know how to behave—one's preparation has distinct limits, limits that simultaneously enhance mystery and excitement and cause anxiety and discomfort.

Consider these situations:

1. An adolescent female wishes to engage in sexual behavior with her somewhat shy friend but is unable to ask.

2. A married man wishes his wife to stimulate him orally but is too embarrassed to request it.

3. A recently divorced person seeks companionship but is confused about the social rules involved in meeting others in bars.

4. A gay male is uncomfortable telling his lover that he dislikes anal sex.

5. A middle-aged woman notices her husband's erections have become less strong but hesitates to mention it because she fears he will misunderstand.

6. A 20-year-old refuses to go on dates because she is increasingly aroused by physical closeness with men.

7. A 35-year-old woman hesitates to tell her younger lover that she prefers manual stimulation to intercourse.

8. A parent is uncomfortable telling his son about masturbation, avoiding direct answers to his questions.

9. A man fantasizes about having sex with two women but does not share this with his wife.

10. A gay woman finds a male friend staring at her intensely. Though she likes him, he does not know about her sexual preference.

These represent a small representative sample of sexual situations in which some response other than a purely physical one is necessary. Such a set of responses might be termed *sexual skills,* the nonverbal and verbal responses that occurred before, during, and after a sexual encounter. More specifically, *sexual skills* can be defined as interpersonal behaviors that are effective in meeting a person's goals for a sexual interaction, whether the goal is for a limited sexual experience, for the development of a new relationship, or for the maintenance or modification of an ongoing relationship. Effective sexual skills evolve as the person changes and develops, in response to changing social and cultural circumstances relating to sexuality. A clear example of this can be seen in changes in "effective" male sexual skills brought about by the women's movement: For young men at least, the hypermasculine, controlling macho approach may become increasingly problematic. Similarly, the increased prevalence of divorce and remarriage is evidence of the de facto need for behavioral flexibility in sexual matters. More people than ever before must meet the challenge of negotiating new sexual relationships in circumstances that in many ways are quite different from their earlier experience.

Specific skills involved in actual sexual situations are but one component of a broader set of capabilities related to effective sexual functioning over the life span. In a comprehensive definition, the World Health Organization (1975) described "sexual health" as

the integration of the somatic, emotional, intellectual, and social aspects of sexual being, in ways that are positively enriching and that enhance personality, communication, and love. Fundamental to this concept are the right to sexual information and the right to consider sexuality for pleasure as well as for procreation.

Maddock (1977) defines sexual health as:

1. The conviction that one's personal and social behaviors are congruent with one's gender identity, and a sense of comfort with one's sex-role behaviors
2. The ability to carry on effective interpersonal relationships with members of both sexes, including the capacity for love and long-term commitment
3. The capacity to respond to erotic stimulation in such a way as to make sexual activity a positive and pleasurable aspect of one's experience.
4. The judgment necessary to make rewarding decisions about one's sexual behavior which are consistent with one's over-all value system and belief about life. (p. 355)

Because health and the medical and physiological aspects of sexuality are but one component of human sexuality, a more comprehensive term is offered here, *sexual competence. Sexual competence is defined as the ability to meet one's own and others' goals for sexual activity*. Sexual competence includes knowledge of sexual functioning of men and women; an understanding of both one's own personal attitudes, values, and expectations regarding sexuality and the origins of this sexual ideology; the ability to make personally congruent decisions about sexual matters; the ability to assert one's sexual interests and their meanings to others; the ability to act in sexually satisfying ways to meet one's own and one's partner's needs; and the ability to discuss with others one's sexuality and its development over time.

This chapter will review current thinking about competent sexual behavior and will describe systematic methods that have been developed to enhance sexual functioning. The current status of interventions in the area of sexuality is that the predominant activity is sex ther-

apy and sex counseling, efforts that are designed to remediate clearly delineated dysfunctions and dissatisfactions. Because the focus of this chapter is on sexual enhancement, only a brief review of the clinical literature on sex therapy will be provided; the reader is referred to other sources, especially LoPiccolo and LoPiccolo (1978). Sex therapy is of note, however, because it provided the first historical context for direct, active training of sexual behavior. In addition, many of the approaches used by enhancement programs are taken directly from sex therapy procedures. Nor will traditional sex education programs, generally intended to dispense information and disseminate nonjudgmental views about the range and diversity of human sexual response, be reviewed. The impact of informational programs on sexuality has been reviewed by Kilmann, Wanlass, Sabalis, and Sullivan (1981). Their general conclusion is that sex education appears to result in gains in sexual knowledge and shifts toward more liberal sexual attitudes. The relationship between such changes and skillful sexual behavior and sexual satisfaction remains to be examined.

Both sex education with its focus on information distribution and sex therapy with its focus on ameliorating discrete problems have clear implications for enhancement. Yet both are inadequate for the task: Sex education, because of its limited domain (information), ignores the critical need for behavioral learning, and sex therapy, because its clinical raison d'être, reduces its impact to those willing to admit serious dissatisfaction. Neither provide systematic and comprehensive training in the many components of sexuality in a way to promote competence in the general population. This is left to the vicissitudes of routine socialization. As Roberts (1980c) notes:

In the past decade, three national commissions have stressed the importance of sexuality in one's life. At the same time, the research studies prepared for these commissions revealed that mythology and misunderstanding about sexuality pervade our society, underlie our social institutions, and contribute to uninformed and misinformed sexual decision making—particularly among the young. (p. 261)

It is easier for a curious individual to learn to become adept at gourmet cooking or basketball than to partake of carefully designed and supervised lessons in acquiring sexual competence. This review will provide direction for the development of such programs. The authors are sympathetic with Szasz's (1980) vituperative attack on sexology and its unstated ideology yet disagree with his conclusion: We believe that sex is learned and *can* be taught in a constructive, nonmanipulative way.

COMPONENTS OF SEXUAL FUNCTIONING

A description of the complexities of human sexual response makes very clear the breadth of possibilities for enhancement efforts. Human sexuality is a composite of inherited and acquired characteristics; an expression of changing individual, social, and interpersonal needs; a manifestation of physiological, cognitive, affective, psychological, and moral predispositions; a negotiation of interpersonal situations with direct and symbolic meanings; and, an expression of one's selfhood at different stages of life. Sexual functioning at any one point in life is but a transient episode in one's sexual development from birth (if not from intrauterine life) to death; there are continuities and discontinuities in one's sexual behavior across the life span. Sexual behavior is also social behavior and thus involves varying degrees of interaction with others and interdependence on and engagement with others.

Human sexuality is inexorably involved in interpersonal events. In addition, sexual expression is uniquely susceptible to changing cultural conditions. Social norms, values, and rules dictate sexual behavior. As Reiss (1981) notes, our sexual mores remain heavily colored by ideological rigidities and irrationalities. In sum, there are three broad sets of components that influence sexual development: *intraindividual developmental, social and interpersonal,* and *cultural and contextual.* These will be discussed briefly.

Individual Components

This set of components has received by far the most attention, reflecting an individualistic and personological bias. The process by which a person responds to a sexual stimulus is described by Walen (1980) as involving this sequence: perception of a sexual stimulus ▶ evaluation of the sexual stimulus ▶ physiological arousal ▶ perception of arousal (and sometimes, denial of arousal) ▶ evaluation of arousal ▶ overt sexual behavior ▶ perception of sexual behavior ▶ evaluation of sexual behavior. Tollison and Adams (1979) provide a comprehensive list of individual components:

1. Sexual arousal.
2. Gender role identification and sexual identification.
3. Heterosocial behavior (social behaviors needed to initiate, engage in, and maintain heterosocial relationships).
4. Heterosexual behavior (seduction behaviors, foreplay, and sexual techniques).

Graber (1981) lists four areas of sexual functioning—the physical, the intrapsychic, the interpersonal, and the learned. Unfortunately, these views, in addition to focusing exclusively on the individual, assume a static view of sexual behavior.

In actuality, arousal, evaluative, and behavioral components are constantly interacting. For instance, intense arousal can influence evaluation and vice versa. Indeed, the problems associated with excessive self-monitoring ("the spectator role") described by Masters and Johnson (1970) demonstrate the power of cognitive appraisal to override physiological processes and behavioral performance. Pleasurable behaviors can similarly influence evaluative processes, as seen in the repeated use of a new sexual behavior that had earlier been negatively evaluated.

Enhancement can be directed to an individual's arousal, evaluative processes, or behavioral repertoire. Arousal can be enhanced by a variety of means—by either reducing inhibitions or by shaping increased sensitivity to erotic stimuli. Evaluation processes can be enhanced by identification and modification of thoughts and feelings that interfere with sexual behavior. Performance itself can be directly improved by skills training— information, modeling, and graduated practice. Individual sexual competence can be recast in these terms and defined as the ability to be aroused by a range of sexual and erotic stimuli, the ability to evaluate the meanings of this arousal in terms that promote sexual satisfaction, and the ability to engage in varied and satisfying sexual acts.

Of critical importance in such enhancement is that the nature of individual sexual competence changes over the life span as the person's sexual identity emerges over time, crystallizes during adolescence and early adulthood, changes with other changes of the adult years, and is modified by the aging process. The complexities of sexual development over the life span have not been directly addressed, with isolated researchers dealing with different age groups. In contrast, a life span view stresses the diversity of factors resulting in behavior and the description and ex-planation of continuities and discontinuities over time. Baltes, Reese, and Lipsett (1980) provide four assumptions of the life span view that we have extrapolated to the sexual sphere: (1) sexual development is a lifetime process in which behavior change can occur at any point; (2) sexual development is influenced by its historical time, and generational effects must be considered; (3) sexual development is multidetermined and complex so that the person shows considerable heterogeneity over time and across situations; and (4) sexual development is best viewed as a flexible process in which multiple determinants induce continual change. Spanier (1977) labels the process of sexual development *sexual socialization,* which includes five components, any of which could be appropriately targeted for enhancement: the development of sex-object preference; the development of gender roles; the development of gender identity; the acquisition of sexual skills, knowledge, and values; and the development of sexual attitudes. The life span view points to the need for lifelong sexual enhancement: from rewriting the "unwritten sexual curriculum" of early socialization (Roberts, 1980a), to enhancing the "sexual unfolding" of adolescents (Sarrell & Sarrell, 1979), to realizing that adult sexual behaviors change, and to an affirmation of the sexual needs and interests of the elderly (LaTorre & Kear, 1977). Sarrel and Sarrel's (1979) concept of *sexual unfolding,* although they see it as describing adolescence, seems eminently suitable to a life span view of individual sexual competence. They detail the components of sexual unfolding as:

1. An evolving sense of the body, with a body image that is gender specific and fairly free of distortion.
2. The ability to overcome or moderate guilt, shame, and inhibitions associated with sexual thoughts and behavior.

3. The recognition of what is erotically pleasing and displeasing.
4. The absence of conflict and confusion about sexual orientation.
5. An increasingly satisfying and rich sexual life, free of dysfunction or compulsion, including satisfying autoeroticism.
6. A growing awareness of being a sexual person and the place of sex in one's life.
7. The ability to respond for oneself, one's partner, and society (use of contraception and avoidance of using sex for exploitation).
8. The ability to experience eroticism as *one* aspect of intimacy with another person.

Enhancement might focus on different aspects of this unfolding at points across the life span. Juhasz and Sonnenshein-Schneider (1980) argue that adolescents critically need to learn specific skills to evaluate influences on their behavior and decisions. Wagner's (1980) data on adolescent women—including, for example, the finding that many are unaware that the clitoris is the organ responsive to sexual stimulation—points to the need for specific sexual-arousal information. Johnson and Masters (1976) note that in adulthood the work ethic can have a deleterious impact on sexuality, turning sex into a task performed with discipline but little joy. Disruptions and disturbances in most adults' sexual histories have been reported in several studies (Edwards & Booth, 1976; Frank, Anderson, & Rubenstein, 1978). Hessellund (1976), in his sample of 38 couples, found that 63% of the women and 40% of the men do not now masturbate, suggesting a possible area for intervention for disinhibition. Martin (1981) reports that despite good health, 36% of his elderly sample reported no more than six sexual events (of any kind) within the last year. It is unfortunately the case that few interventions have been developed to promote sexual competence in any group except the adult male and female. Carrera (1976) quotes Margaret Mead as remarking that "there are probably very few young people in America who haven't been lied to magnificently about sex," but her comment seems generally true across the life span. Roberts (1980b) states that there is a critical need for programs for people of different ages to understand their sexuality and to improve conditions under which sexual learning occurs. She writes:

There are volumes of sexual literature and mountains of data available to us, but no one to discuss them with, no one to help us appraise and evaluate them. Most people are forced to make sense of their sexuality, and the frequently conflicting messages they receive, alone. Children, adolescents, and adults are required to find their way to responsible sexual satisfaction without ever talking about responsibility or sexuality or satisfaction. If these are the conditions of learning about sexuality, then the evidence that many persons find their own sexuality a source of difficulty should come to us as no surprise. (pp. 248–249)

Interpersonal Components

The inability of one distressed male to recognize the relationship of sexual behavior to interpersonal events is well illustrated by this wry report of Tollison and Adams (1979):

One patient reported being frustrated and perplexed over his inability to seduce a female plant worker in the back of the factory warehouse. It turned out that the patient had never entertained the female worker socially. His only contact with her and the resulting seduction attempts occurred each day in the warehouse after the couple had shared lunch, which the female worker had prepared. It is true that the back of the warehouse did represent a somewhat physically private location, but successful seduction is not easy amidst boxes of freight with the noises of engines and trucks in the background. (pp. 17–18)

Verhulst and Heiman (1979) correctly note that too often sex is seen as an individual matter with little recognition of the interpersonal dynamics always involved. Indeed, as Wiseman (1976) points out, this is the very essence of sex—the simultaneous focus on one's own sexual pleasure in relationship to another's and the ability to make this process seem spontaneous. Sex is an interpersonal engagement, as has been well described by Mosher (1980) in his definition of a "sexual contact episode" as:

the social-sexual interaction between partners which is bounded by the initiatory social or sexual acts leading to the phase of excitement and concluded by the social and/ sexual acts that acknowledge resolution or completion of the engagement. (p. 5)

This means that sexual competence involves both *social skills* (skills to meet one's sexual needs in social situations) and *relationship-development skills* (skills to allow for the development of a relationship, both to increase intimacy and commitment and, if desired, to disengage). The situation is complicated by the fact that the two interactants may be at different developmental levels in their individual sexual functioning and may differ in their current interpersonal style. A germane example might be a middle-aged person who, despite physical attraction to a younger partner, seeks commitment from a sexual partner, whereas the younger partner seeks companionship and excitement. This discrepancy in individual expectations would be likely to have an impact on the course of their sexual relationship.

That sexual competence involves skilled social behavior is readily shown. Trower (1979) describes the basic processes in social skills as perception, cog-

nition, and performance, the latter being subdivided into verbal and nonverbal components. He also notes the need to understand the rules and conversations of diverse social environments, something anyone who has visited a singles' bar will readily understand. Argyle (1981) provides components of socially skilled performance; we have added examples relating to sexual competence:

1. Accurate perception of others (ability to understand that someone else's interest is sexual).
2. Taking the role of the other (ability to avoid the use of sexual slang that a partner might find embarrassing).
3. Nonverbal communication of interpersonal attitudes and emotion (ability to convey sexual interest or sexual disinterest).
4. Nonverbal accompaniments of speech (ability to modulate vocal tone during a seduction attempt).
5. Completing and elaborating on verbal utterances (ability to negotiate a sexual-contact episode with a stranger).
6. Sending feedback signals (ability to provide information to a partner about his or her sexual technique).
7. Managing synchronization (ability to coordinate sexual behaviors).
8. Managing self-presentation (ability to request a certain kind of sexual experience assertively).
9. Managing different situations (ability to respond comfortably in a variety of sexual situations).

Tollison and Adams (1979) describe the specific skills needed to initiate sexual relationships as open-ended questions, extended conversational skills, self-disclosure, eye contact, and appropriate physical appearance; they view skills preceding sexual behavior as increased self-disclosure, ingratiation, and the ability to reward the other person. Verhulst and Heiman (1979) argue that the reciprocal nature of sexuality (one's arousal is conditional on the other's) demands that one be socially sensitive to one's partner's pattern of expressivity. Every sexual interaction has a broader meaning:

Every moment of interaction exchange always contains implicit information about gender identity and sexual behavior, about the degree of attachment between the partners and finally about the desire to get to know the other and to accept in turn some kind of exploratory behavior. (Verhulst & Heiman, 1979, p. 31)

This view suggests that other skills—those involved in developing relationships—are also necessary. Although many sexual episodes may consist of single interactions with others, the more common pattern is repeated sexual transactions with partners in which close relationships emerge. A comprehensive view of sexual competence must go beyond a person's ability to engage in a series of disconnected sexual acts, although this is a vital element of sexual skillfulness. Rather, such a view must be complemented by relationship-development skills so that such sexual encounters *can* be developed into the kinds of satisfying interpersonal relationships most individuals seek. Various stage models of relationship development exist, most notably Levinger's (Huston & Levinger, 1978; Levinger & Snoek, 1972) and Scanzoni's (1979). Different sexual skills are included in the three levels of involvement proposed by both models. Levinger's three levels—unilateral awareness, surface contact, and mutuality—and their implications for sexual behavior appear next:

Level	Definition	Behaviors
1. Unilateral awareness	One knows of the other, but no interaction has occurred.	Self-centered fantasies; attempts to enhance self-image to attract attention and interest; focus on physical attractiveness and its salience.
2. Surface contact	Formal and superficial contact; role performances.	Behaviors designed to maximize personal sexual fulfillment; behavior based on stereotypic expectations.
3. Mutuality	Relationship is personal, intense, and intimate.	Sexual expression tailored to needs and interests of other in idiosyncratic way. Partners assume responsibility for both their own and each other's pleasure.

Each of these levels encompasses many different kinds of relationships, but the implication is that enhancement programs can profitably operate at each, covering levels of individual functioning throughout the life span. The ability to move from one level to a more advanced level in meeting one's changing sexual needs is an important target for enhancement. Zilbergeld and Ellison (1979) give an excellent example of this in their social skills training for sex therapy clients. Their graduated model starts with initiating contact with a new person (going beyond unilateral awareness) to a limited first encounter (surface contact) with the ultimate goal of enabling clients to negotiate mutuality relationships. It is unfortunate that sex therapists have provided so little systematic training for different kinds of relationship goals; all too often, the focus has been on the mutuality relationships of committed couples (at least couples committed enough to enter a therapeutic situation).

In sum, enhancement of sexual competence must include careful attention to social and relationship-development skills. Depth of sexual involvement, Mosher (1980) argues, is dependent upon behaviors that help partners abandon their ordinary reality focus so that they can construct a sexual orientation of arousal, excitement, and fulfillment. Without effective social skills—nonverbal and verbal—in transitory encounters, little satisfaction can occur. Without the ability to communicate and meet the needs of someone in a mutually close relationship, the relationship may begin to deteriorate. As Jacobs (1978) writes, sex can be used to ward off intimacy. Sex in apparently close relationships that does not reinforce and extend intimacy can be reasonably seen as a form of masturbation—a "narcissistic preoccupation with sensation to exclude feelings of love and tenderness" (Jacobs, 1978, p. 43).

Contextual Components

It is hardly insightful to note the strong influence of culture on the development of sexuality. Szasz's (1980) treatise provides the interested reader with an entertaining review of religious prescriptions concerning sexuality, in particular the near-phobic attitudes toward masturbation. As Szasz notes, sex education and the cultural control of sexual expression are as old as civilization; the unique contribution of our age, as he sees it, is the medicalization of sexuality with its attendant "sex therapy" and "sex therapists." Masters and Johnson (Johnson & Masters, 1976; Masters & Johnson, 1970) note the destructive impact of the prevalent work ethic on sexual functioning, with its emphasis on performance and products. It is commonly presumed among sexologists that our culture provides a consistently ambivalent message to people abut sexuality—the remarkable candor presented in films, books, and the media is countered by an equally noteworthy reluctance to approach sexuality directly and honestly without moralization or romanticization. It is beyond the scope of this chapter to review contemporary sexual attitudes—the reader could consult, for instance, Hite's reports (1976, 1981)—but the cultural backdrop of sexual competence needs some detail. A succinct way to present this is to offer Albert Ellis's list of irrational ideas about sexuality that are perpetuated by the culture:

that [people] must have conventional coitus to have successful and enjoyable sex; that all normal men and women desire sex incessantly and can easily get aroused and satisfied; that spontaneous arousal by both partners must occur if they have good sex; that loving partners automatically and often feel aroused by their mates; that varietism proves unimportant in sex relations; that adulterous desires exist illegitimately and immorally; that foreplay, to seem proper, must wind up in penile-vaginal copulation; that any knowledgeable individual can easily turn on and give many orgasms to his or her partner. (Ellis, 1975, pp. 14–15)

Reiss (1981) also provides an excellent summary of contemporary sexual ideologies. He notes prevalent negative attitudes toward "body-centered sexuality" in contrast to "person-centered sexuality" and what he terms an "allegiance to heterosexual coitus." He suggests that widely held outlooks will evolve toward a new ideology, which he terms *modern/naturalistic*. This ideology is characterized by (1) gender roles that are equalitarian; (2) a positive valuing of both body- and person-centered sex; (3) the view that one's sexual emotions are both strong and manageable; (4) an affirmation of the major goals of sexuality as physical pleasure and psychological intimacy; and (5) an acceptance without guilt of a wide range of sexual behaviors that do not involve force or fraud. Such an ideology would provide a more constructive alternative for the development of individual sexual competence.

INTERVENTION FOR SEXUAL ENHANCEMENT

Life Development as a Framework

The three sets of components of sexual competence—individual developmental, social interpersonal, and contextual cultural—provide direction for a variety of programs designed to enrich human sexuality. Although it is probably true that the latter set of components would have the most pervasive impact, this area is influenced more by sweeping historical and social trends than by the planned interventions of social scientists. This is not to suggest that change at the societal level does not occur in a directed way. Bayer's (1981) review of the concerted efforts of gay activists and sympathetic psychiatrists to delete homosexuality from the psychiatric nomenclature is an excellent example of a contextual change that was vigorously engineered. Yet, by far the most common focus for programmatic intervention has been at the individual and social-interpersonal level. A framework that has utility for an analysis of such interventions is a life-development model (Danish & D'Augelli, 1980, 1983).

The life-development intervention model has been proposed as an alternative to prototypical models for the development of human services, especially in the mental health field. In contrast to views that focus on mental health problems and their treatment or prevention, life-development intervention focuses on the encouragement of competent behaviors across the life span. It thus avoids the stigmatization and iatrogenic conse-

quences of a treatment approach and the conceptual and operational ambiguities of prevention. A critical focus is on life events, which include predicted as well as unexpected occurrences that are experienced by most people, and on systematic efforts to provide opportunities that allow the successful mastery of such events. Basic to this viewpoint is the recognition that routine life occurrences are often stressful, that ineffective coping has lingering and deleterious consequences, that effective coping can be taught, and that successful acquisition of competence can generalize to new life events.

Certainly, the development of one's sexual competence fits into the life-development framework. It is clear that the events related to sexual development are stressful for most people thanks to ambiguous societal norms and erratic socialization processes; that many, if not most, people do not cope with the development of their sexuality in ways that are continuously satisfying and rewarding; that ineffective coping can lead to a wide range of behavioral disorders and general unhappiness; and, that there is no dearth of directions for the development of programs to promote more effective coping over the life span. The life-development framework is particularly useful in this area in its delineation of major areas for the developent of personal competence. Competence to cope effectively with a life event consists of four components:

1. *The acquisition of information.* This is detailed knowledge about a life event that allows the person to know what to expect, to develop rational rather than irrational attitudes, and to construct a value position based on informed judgments.
2. *The acquisition of skills.* This is skillful behavior related to a life event that leads the person to meet his or her needs successfully and at the

same time develop a sense of mastery and accomplishment.

3. *The ability to take risks.* Because any new circumstance demands novel behaviors, the person must be willing to manifest his or her skilled behavior in new circumstances. Overcoming the fears associated with change leads to a sense of control over one's life.

4. *The development of social support.* This is the ability to reach out to others and develop a predictable group of caring others that provides a buffer against life stresses and a vehicle for discussing and evaluating how one has approached a life event.

A comprehensive model for enhancing sexual competence should include components to deal with all four areas. *Basic information* about human sexuality is essential to sexual competence. One needs to know the physiology of the human sexual response cycle, information on current sexual attitudes and sexual behaviors, and information on the diversity of human sexual expression. It is also essential to know sexual-stimulation techniques both for oneself and for one's partner, the nature of personal reactions to sexual expression, and common uncertainties about sexuality. Information about sexually transmitted diseases and birth control are required as well. This information, however, must be provided from a life span perspective—the continuities and discontinuities of the life span can no longer be overlooked. Changes in sexual responsivity with aging should be understood lest normative occurrences become the source of intense personal worry. Information can challenge many myths about sexuality, as sex education proponents acknowledge. There is simply no substitute for direct and detailed information to help people begin the process of sexual-competence enhancement—whether the need is to determine the location of a

gay support group, a list of effective personal vibrators, the contraindications of diverse birth-control methods, or the typical refractory periods for men and women.

Specific skills training must be included in a comprehensive program. It is not reasonable to assume that people *know how to behave* in sexual situations, although one need not assume the presence of behavioral deficits to provide specific training in sexual behavior. Training in sexual behavior is in no way inconsistent with the development of spontaneous feelings, affection, and intimacy. As Szasz (1980) suggests, neither is practicing tennis serves inconsistent with becoming a highly accomplished tennis player. Effective sexual behavior is a highly skilled act that does not occur naturally; the best evidence of this is the large number of women who report not experiencing orgasm during intercourse. Indeed, unless a person develops skills for stimulation in addition to those needed for intercourse, it could be argued that his or her sexual potential is severely limited. The nearly exclusive focus on intercourse, which to many appears a "natural" sexual event, is a societal bias. This bias has led to a widespread misconception that sexual expression is not highly skilled (Reiss, 1981). Men could benefit from being taught a variety of stimulation techniques to enable their partners to experience orgasms; women could benefit from skills in noncoital pleasuring for men. But these behaviors are *skills*—they cannot simply be read about, despite the usefulness of the *Joy of Sex* and other explicit manuals of sexual skills. Skilled performance must be described in detail, must be discussed, must be observed, must be gradually practiced, and must be shaped by direct feedback and reinforcement. A woman who wishes to enhance her partner's sexual pleasure by the "squeeze" technique, for instance, can read about it, but she will only become skillful if she engages in a learning sequence. As Graber (1981) writes:

Sexual functioning is a psychomotor skill that may be compared to other psychomotor acts such as riding a bicycle. Both require attention and awareness to bodily functioning and a feedback mechanism for utilizing information as the body perceives it in order to perform the motor act. As with riding a bicycle, once the psychomotor skill is learned it becomes essentially automatic, and the learned nature of it fades from the consciousness. Most of us do not remember how we learned to control our ejaculation. If for some reason we did not learn how to ride a bicycle as a child, we can learn to do it as an adult. Having not learned the psychomotor function at the critical period when it was easiest to do, this is often a more difficult but not impossible task. (p. 485)

Experiences in *risk taking* are also essential in promoting sexual competence. Careful consideration of the advantages and disadvantages of behaving in a specific way can be accomplished to help the person make a decision (Danish & D'Augelli, 1982). Many sexual behaviors involve risk. Szasz (1980) writes that sex is "safe to watch but more fun to play. Although sex is a risky game, one is supposed to pretend it's not" (p. 3). All too often the risk is either ignored or imagined beyond proportion. Rejection, a lowered self-concept, fear of failure, and simple disappointment are all risks in any sexual situation, as is the possibility of disease in the case of sex with new partners. Individuals must not be encouraged to ignore these risks; rather, they need a method to weigh the presumed risks against the presumed gains. Providing a generic framework for such sexual risk assessment can have a durable effect and can promote the exploration of new forms of sexual expression.

Finally, the development of sexual competence involves the ability to extend oneself to others (nonpartners) to gain *social support*. Little research has been done on how people routinely deal with problems in their sexual lives that are not actual dysfunctions, but it is likely that many solve sexual dilemmas in a manner similar to how they solve other mental health problems—they turn to others for comfort, reassurance, and advice (Veroff, Kulka, & Douvan, 1981). It is likely that fewer turn to others for help with sexual problems, given the assumption that one should be intrinsically competent in the sexual domain, but the power of such informal help remains. It is worth considering why sex therapists have perpetuated the privatism attached to sexuality by not encouraging clients to share their sexual worries with close friends. A life span approach to sexual competence demands the development of support for sexual change and growth; a reliance on oneself and professional sexologists is extremely limited. Szasz (1980) notes how sexologists have transformed the human problems of sexuality into professional ones. His point is nowhere better made than in the support area. One needs to learn about sex from others because sexual behavior is so heavily influenced by cultural norms and conventions; expert opinion is but one set of judgments about sexuality. Much could be gained by encouraging individuals to consider creating their own personal support system, whether through informal contacts with close friends and relatives or through formal means such as self-help and other groups, to help them confront the issues in sexuality that do not directly involve knowledge, skills, or risk taking. These, indeed, are the larger issues—those of the meaning of sexuality in one's life, the relationship of sexual expression to other aspects of one's personality, the value attached to changes in sexual behavior over time, and so on. The more profound meanings of sexual behavior are best addressed by one's peers, friends, co-workers, and family in the context of one's existence. As Mosher (1980) writes,

The contact with the partner [in a profound sexual experience] has transcended personal identity into a homonoymous union that celebrates the spirit of life itself. The phases of human sexual response will have profound meaning. There are orgasms and there are profound sexual contact episodes. One physical description of orgasm is that it consists of rhythmical, .8 second contractions of the pubococcygeal muscles. Humans make meanings from these contractions and their total experience. Profound meanings embody the sexual experience with metavalues and numinous symbolism. (p. 25)

These meanings are not the domain of experts in sex information and behavior; yet they must be part of a total approach to enhancing lifelong sexual unfolding.

In sum, a complete approach to the enrichment of sexual competence over the life span should include elements of these four components—accurate and neutral information about all aspects of sexuality and its ramifications, explicit training in the diverse skills (social and personal) needed in engaging in sexual behavior in different kinds of relationships, assistance in careful consideration of the risks involved in the diverse forms of sexual expression and in the lack of such expression, and, finally, methods to help people develop social support so that they can consider the meaning of sex for their own development. Efforts that have been developed to date to enhance sexuality will not be reviewed with this perspective in mind. Two broad types of interventions will be considered—*sex therapy,* structured intervention to resolve specific sexual problems, and *sexual enrichment,* structured intervention to enhance sexuality in individuals with no current sexual problems. Finally, a brief section will review both therapeutic and enhancement-oriented efforts designed for gay men and women.

Sex Therapy

Despite important contributions to the remediation of sexual problems by such behaviorally oriented therapists as Albert Ellis (see Ellis, 1975) and Joseph Wolpe (1958), there is little doubt that Masters and Johnson's work has been the foundation of sex therapy. Sex therapy, as it is currently practiced, is a direct result of their intensive laboratory studies of the physiology of the human sexual response cycle (Masters & Johnson, 1966) and their lengthy experience with sexual dysfunctions (Masters & Johnson, 1970). Although other explanations for their impact, including the massive amount of publicity generated by their laboratory work, can be given, it is important to recognize that Masters and Johnson's work in sex therapy evolved directly from their physiological studies and observations. It is unlikely that any other investigations have ever had as extensive and intensive source of data about human sexuality upon which to base an intervention effort. Indeed, sex therapy may be the only psychologically oriented therapy for which extensive normative data about the domain of note are available. This is not to say that the St. Louis investigators are free from criticism; such has been offered, ranging from the thoughtful (Zilbergeld & Evans, 1980) to the hyperbolic (Szasz, 1980). In addition, substantive advances in sex therapy have been made by others. Kaplan (1974, 1980) has added a needed focus on psychodynamic issues in certain sexual problems, extending Masters and Johnson's essentially behavioral perspective. Annon (1976) has correctly conceptualized sexual interventions on a continuum of intensity, from the therapist's providing "permission" to engage in certain desired acts through in-depth therapy for more complex sexual concerns.

In any event, Masters and Johnson provided the critical insight—that improvement of a sexual problem must be seen as a *learning or relearning experience* and that *direct, active training* in sexual functioning is the "treatment" of choice for most sexual disorders. As they write:

The Foundation's therapeutic approach is based firmly upon a program of education for each member of the dysfunctional marital unit. Multiple treatment sessions are devoted to explanations of sexual functioning with concentration of both psychological and physiological ramifications of sexual responsivity. The educational process is more effectively absorbed if the dual-sex therapy teams function as translators to make certain that no misunderstandings develop due to emotional or sexual language barriers. (Masters & Johnson, 1970, pp. 4–5)

Kaplan also emphasizes the role of relearning experiences:

When individuals undergo psychoanalysis, marital therapy or even most forms of behavior therapy, the therapeutic process is conducted almost entirely in the office. . . . In contrast, sex therapy relies heavily for its therapeutic impact on erotic tasks which the couple conducts at home. *It is the integrated use of systematically structured sexual experiences with conjoint therapeutic sessions which is the main innovation and distinctive feature of sex therapy.* (Kaplan, 1974, p. xii; emphasis is in original)

Ellis (1975) notes that more than any other psychological problem, sexual difficulties require use of direct teaching, homework assignments, and training. LoPiccolo (1978) describes the basic principles of sex therapy as follows:

1. Partners share responsibility for the disorder.
2. Information and education are critical; they may not be sufficient, but they are necessary.
3. Attitude change must occur, from negative attitudes about sex to more positive ones.
4. Performance anxiety must be eliminated and replaced by a less demanding, yet skilled sense of sexual competence.
5. There must be increased communication and greater effectiveness in sexual technique; inhibitions about sex must be changed and openness to a wider range of sexual expressiveness must be encouraged.
6. Destructive life-style and sex roles need to be modified, especially lifestyles that relegate sex to an unimportant position and rigid sex-role behaviors.
7. Changes in behaviors must be prescribed; gradual steps must be taken to acquire skillful sexual behavior.

Schover (1982) notes that common sexual dissatisfactions revolve around five areas—difficulties with sexual communication, lack of skill in initiating sexual activity, disagreements about foreplay and nonsexual physical affection, disagreements about the variety of sexual activities, and disagreements about the frequency of sexual activities. Sex therapy deals with each of these problem areas in a direct way—by modeling and encouraging direct discussion of sex, by encouraging and prescribing certain sexual behaviors and disinhibiting partners from requesting such behaviors, by explicit discussion of stimulation and affection techniques, by careful training in a variety of sexual activities, and by helping couples negotiate contracts and agreements about their sexual preferences. Although considerable therapeutic power resides in the supportive, permission-giving nature of the sex therapists, sex therapy generally succeeds because of its explicit and implicit use of skills training—explanation, modeling, practice, feedback, and reinforcement of sexually satisfying behaviors. This can best be seen in the treatment of problems in men's ejaculatory control, which is accomplished by direct training in delaying orgasm, and in the treatment of low frequency of orgasm in women, which is accomplished by self-stimulation procedures. It is not surprising that these are the two sets of procedures that are the most clearly effective in the sex therapy armamentarium (Graber, 1981).

The sex therapy literature cannot

be reviewed in depth here: the reader should consult Kaplan (1974), LoPiccolo and LoPiccolo (1978), and Masters and Johnson (1970). The research on sex therapy has been accumulating for some time and has been reviewed in several places (Hogan, 1978; Wright & Mathieu, 1977). The research can be summarized by saying that it is very uneven; as Hogan (1978) concludes, no definite conclusions can be drawn because of inadequate research design. The specific techniques of sex therapy have not been carefully evaluated, although the "squeeze technique" is apparently consistent in its impact. Zilbergeld and Evans's (1980) critique of Masters and Johnson's (1970) research is relevant to the entire field of sex therapy. They note problems in delineating samples, describing procedures, specifying criteria for success and failure, detailing evaluative measures, and describing follow-up. Zilbergeld and Evans conclude that the high success rates of Masters and Johnson are "misleading," and until careful factorial designs are used, this conclusion is appropriate for other claims of success in this field. Most studies lack the rudimentary requirements of psychotherapy research, particularly relevant control groups. For example, two recent evaluation studies—Chesney, Blakeney, Chan, and Cole (1981) and Tullman, Gilner, Kolodny, Dornbush, and Tullman (1981)—did not compare the treatment groups with controls. No study has directly assessed the differential impact of expectancy versus specific training techniques by the inclusion of an attention–placebo group despite the repeated finding of the impact of expectancy in behavior change efforts. One wonders what the current status of many sex therapy techniques would be were they subjected to the kind of rigorous evaluation that helped to qualify the overly zealous proclamations originally given to systematic desensitization by behavior therapists.

Sexual Enhancement Programs

Much less professional time has been devoted to the design of enhancement programs for persons wishing to acquire increased sexual competence. One could speculate that this is so because there is no requirement for competent sexual behavior in our culture. If there were clear disincentives to poor or marginal sexual competence, enhancement efforts might evolve. Consider, as an example, the report of Heyl (1977) on the training of novice prostitutes by madams. That prostitutes receive more thoughtful training in sexual competence than most adults cannot be purely explained by the profit motive; it can be as easily understood as a direct, honest appreciation of the importance of *learning* about sex. Most of what Heyl's madams report teaching—physical and psychological pleasuring techniques, interpersonal skills, consideration of values—would be entirely appropriate in a sexual enhancement program!

Two enhancement programs that have been described in considerable detail have been developed by LoPiccolo (LoPiccolo & Miller, 1975) and by Maddock (1977). LoPiccolo's is a program for three couples and involves a series of structured exercises and homework assignments. In three sessions, couples engage in a verbal disinhibition game in which sexual terms are discussed, an exercise to initiate or refuse a sexual request, learning of various genital-pleasuring techniques, the development of lists of sexual "turn-ons" and "turn-offs," learning techniques of sensate forms of caressing, and writing an underground newspaper ad offering their spouse as a sexual partner. The goals are to disinhibit the participants as well as to teach them new sexual techniques. LoPiccolo reports the results of a research study comparing four treatment groups with an untreated control. Assessment was accomplished using the Sexual

Interaction Inventory and the Fundamental Interpersonal Relationship–Orientation–Behavior Scale (FIRO-B). Results indicated significant changes in the enhancement groups' scores and improvement over the controls on the Sexual Interaction Inventory. No changes were found on the FIRO-B. Gains were maintained at a 3-month follow-up. This research, however, is not reported in detail and must be considered suggestive. Despite the author's note that future research on the program would be attempted, no subsequent reports have appeared.

Maddock's (1977) enrichment efforts are part of a larger set of "sexual health services" based on several principles— the need to be responsible for oneself, the permission to be sexual, the need for sexual reeducation, the need for increased awareness, and the need for structured behavior change for sexual enhancement. He offers a series of "guided education and enrichment" experiences, which are conducted by sexual health "consultants." They include these components:

1. *Sexual attitude reassessment seminars (SAR).* These include large group presentations and discussions, multimedia presentations, and small group discussions of sexuality of various kinds. Films, slides, and audiotapes of masturbation, heterosexual and homosexual relationships, changing sex roles, sexual fantasy, and other topics are presented in an intensive way.

2. *Sexual communication group.* This is a small group workshop for couples in which they learn to communicate effectively about sex, verbally and nonverbally. Sexual feelings and fantasies are shared.

3. *Body awareness sessions.* These are meetings between a couple and a team in which the couple react to

their bodies, discussing positive and negative reactions. An internal body fantasy (imagining oneself on a trip inside one's body) and a sexological exam are included.

4. *Behavioral home assignments.* These are assignments to facilitate particular changes in sexual behaviors at home. Educational information and films are used. One assignment deals with general relaxation and the enhancement of sexual and sensual experiencing.

Maddock reports the results of evaluation efforts of these services. All couples were given a variety of measures, including the Minnesota Sexual Attitude Scale, a Sexual Problem Identification Form, the Sexual Interaction Inventory, and the Locke-Wallace Marital Adjustment Test. Participants' self-reports of their reactions to these experiences are highly positive; for instance, 96% found the SAR seminar beneficial, and 61% reported some change in sexual behavior (although its nature is unclear). Significant changes in attitudes as a consequence of SAR involvement were reported as well. Couples involved in these experiences also described more constructive attitudes and changes in marital satisfaction. Responses on the Sexual Interaction Inventory were all in the direction of increased sexual satisfaction, with most of the scales of the measure showing significant improvement. Scores on the Locke-Wallace measure also increased, showing greater marital satisfaction. Despite Maddock's positive results, considerable caution is called for in interpreting these findings because the research suffers from many methodological flaws, the most obvious being the lack of a simple control group. Despite the number of couples involved in these experiences, no definite statements can be made about outcome except to say that participants found their experience valuable.

Reports from others provide less information about their procedures. Several "enhancement groups" are essentially therapeutic experiences for people with sexual difficulties. Morton and Dion (1976) describe a group in a community mental health setting for women with a variety of sexual complaints. The seven sessions are based on Annon's (1976) tenets of permission giving, limited information (about self-stimulation and orgasm), and specific suggestions (to enhance intimacy and positive feelings toward partners). The 13 women in the group set their own personal goals for sexual enhancement. The results were called "highly positive" by the authors; all reached their personal goals, and 12 of the 13 indicated an increased enjoyment of sex and an increased ability to express sexual desire. No control group nor psychometric instruments were employed in this research. Sotile, Kilmann, and Follingstad (1977) describe a program that included women with sexual anxieties and involved their partners in a workshop including structured experiences. A weekend workshop for couples with problems is detailed by Leiblum and Rosen (1979). An evaluation showed increases in overall marital satisfaction and small but positive changes in sexual behavior. No control group was used in this study. Leiblum and Ersner-Hershfield (1977) conducted enhancement groups for dysfunctional women, comparing two groups with participation of partners with one group without such participation. Of the 16 participants, 14 became "reliably orgasmic." Partner participation did not enhance behavioral outcome but did enhance marital and sexual satisfaction. No control group was involved.

One program for women, described by Wilcox and Hager (1980), is oriented to enhancement of normal sexual functioning. Its goal is to teach women to have more realistic expectations for orgasm, and especially to disinhibit women of the notion that they should feel obli-

gated to reach orgasm predominantly via intercourse. They stressed four points —that there are normal differences in needs for sexual stimulation, that intercourse may be insufficient for orgasm, that the need for direct clitoral stimulation is normal, and that orgasm results from clitoral stimulation though it may be experienced vaginally. Compared to a control group, those receiving information on these points had more realistic views and were more positive about self-stimulation. There were no differences in actual use of direct clitoral stimulation, though the authors reported a "trend" toward higher rates in the program participants.

Several existing programs include a focus on the social behavior that is directly related to sexual enhancement. Zilbergeld and Ellison (1979) included a social skills training component to sex therapy groups and found it to be essential. No formal evaluation was conducted. A more specific form of social skills—assertiveness—has been the focus of two reports of sexual enhancement efforts for women (Carlson & Johnson, 1975; Liss-Levinson, Coleman, & Brown, 1975). Both are concerned with women's ability to stand up for their sexual rights, to openly express their sexual needs and preferences, and to become more comfortable with a wider range of sexual expressions. Carlson and Johnson's (1975) program for women includes role-playing responses to unreasonable requests, exploring "10 wants" related to sexuality, looking at themselves in a mirror to explore body images, and giving each other massages. Specific training in assertion was also included. Liss-Levinson et al.'s (1975) program's content is remarkably similar, but it also includes a section on assertion with gynecologists—a neglected part of female sexual coping. Both assertiveness programs affirm the importance of female sexuality, clearly attempting to disabuse women of the traditional dependence on men for their sexual competence. It is interesting to report that no such efforts have been attempted for men, despite the difficulties many men have in sexual assertion. Neither program was subjected to empirical research.

Much is yet to be done in this area. Significant portions of the life span are ignored in the published reports of sexual enhancement efforts. Only one report was found on enhancing sexuality in the elderly (Rowland & Haynes, 1978). This study, involving 10 couples, showed significant changes in sexual satisfaction, increased frequency of certain sexual behaviors, and more positive attitudes about one's marriage and one's life after participation in the program. Unfortunately, no control group was used. No report was found for adolescents or for young adults, not even for college students. Perhaps even more pessimistically, the current status of these programs is unclear. Most were apparently done on a time-limited basis, probably stimulated by one of the authors' personal interests. There is no evidence that any program, except Maddock's (1977), has been maintained, nor have any been subjected to rigorous evaluation. Indeed, the evaluative research in the area of sexual enhancement is even weaker than in sex therapy, which is not surprising given the fewer number of studies conducted. A major problem is a consistent lack of control or comparison groups, which is an elementary requirement for evaluation. Based on the weak current reports, it must be stated that the effectiveness of sexual enhancement has yet to be demonstrated, despite the generally positive conclusions of all these efforts. These efforts hold much promise to enhance sexual competence, but rigorous research is sorely needed.

Interventions for Gay Populations

Despite the long-standing recognition that a substantial minority of the population expresses their sexual interests and needs in same-sex relationships, remarkably little has been done to enhance the sexual competence of gay persons. The need is undocumented, but no doubt intense, as Meston (1975) writes:

The anxiety and confusion around sexuality is exacerbated in homosexuals. Not only is there ignorance and secretiveness of human sexuality in general, but there is overt societal disapproval and condemnation of both the person who seeks same-sex relationships and the sexual activities carried on within these relationships. Because of this, the homosexual has even fewer resources available for the supportive exploration of his or her sexuality. (p. 18)

Routinely, less information is available, fewer opportunities are provided to acquire skills, risk taking is exacerbated by societal stigmatization, and social support may be hard to find, especially outsde of the concentrated "gay ghettos" of metropolitan areas.

Two reports in this area have appeared in the literature, one detailing sex therapy for gay people and the other describing an enhancement program. McWhirter and Mattison (1978) report on the therapy of 22 gay men. They view the experience as similar to therapy with heterosexual couples except that their group exhibited less rigid sexual attitudes, did not assume traditional sex roles, used sex as a weapon to a lesser extent, and had greater empathy with their partners' dysfunction. Meston's (1975) enhancement group was similar to a Sexual Attitude Restructuring seminar in that it involved bombardment with explicit sexual material. The goal of the program was to provide a supportive environment to explore participants' sex histories, values, attitudes, and experiences and to discuss masturbation and forms of sexual relating. Of the group of 13 (11 men, 2 women), most were professionals. No formal evaluation was conducted, although Meston reports that participants' reactions were very positive.

The enhancement of sexual competence for sexual minority members is an area that needs future attention. This is likely to become increasingly important as homophobic attitudes decrease and the modern/naturalistic sexual ideology Reiss (1981) describes becomes widespread.

SUMMARY AND CONCLUSIONS

Several conclusions can be drawn from this review of sexual competence, its development over the life span, and the systematic efforts at remediation and enhancement.

1. Sexual competence consists of individual, social and interpersonal, and contextual components that change over the life span.
2. Sexual competence consists of the acquisition of factual information, skills in social and sexual behavior, experience in taking risks, and opportunities to create social support for one's sexuality.
3. Sexual learning must be integrated into one's total development and personality.
4. Presently, there are few norms for sexuality. Diversity of sexual expression and behavior is the rule rather than the exception, necessitating flexibility in sexual behavior and expression.
5. A sexually competent individual must be able to be responsive to others' sexual needs and interests.
6. Sexual competence involves considerable decision making.
7. The direct teaching methods developed by skills training can be used to increase an individual's sexual competence.
8. Enhancement efforts need to be expanded to provide increased access for more people. Particular focus must be given to a comprehensive, life span model of sexual enhancement as well as to the special needs of sexual minorities.

It is clear that more attention needs to be devoted to the development and dissemination of efforts to promote sexual competence. Social change is likely to provide the challenge. Francoeur (1980) paints a vivid portrait of the future as one in which there will be sexual equality, the absence of sexual stereotypes, the postponement of marriage, the dominance of premarital sex, common divorce, readily available and effective contraception, common extramarital sex, and more positive attitudes toward sex in which reproduction is generally incidental. Most of these changes will have clear implications for sexuality. We cannot be left in the position of Chance Gardiner:

EE stood up and rearranged her clothes. She looked at him; there was no enmity in her look. "I might just as well tell you this, Chauncey," she said. "I am in love with you. I love you, and I want you. And I know that you know it, and I am grateful that you have decided to wait until . . . until . . ." She searched, but could not find the words. She left the room. Chance got up and patted down his hair. He sat by his desk and turned on the TV. The image appeared instantly. (Kosinski, 1970, p. 66)

REFERENCES

Annon, J. S. (1976). *Behavioral treatment of sexual problems*. New York: Harper & Row.

Argyle, M. (1981). The contribution of social interaction to social skills training. In J. D. Wine & M. D. Smye (Eds.), *Social competence*. New York: Guilford.

Baltes, P. B., Reese, H. W., & Lipsett, L. P. (1980). Life-span developmental psychology. In M. R. Rosenzweig & L. W. Porter (Eds.), *Annual review of psychology, 31*, 65–110.

Bayer, R. (1981). *Homosexuality and Amer-*

ican psychiatry: The politics of diagnosis. New York: Basic Books.

Bell, A. P., Weinberg, M. S., & Hammersmith, S. K. (1981). Sexual preference: Its development in men and women. Bloomington: Indiana University Press.

Carlson, N. R., & Johnson, D. A. (1975). Sexuality assertiveness training: A workshop for women. The Counseling Psychologist, 5, 4, 53–59.

Carrera, M. A. (1976). Peer group sex information and education. Journal of Research and Development in Education, 10, 50–55.

Chesney, A. P., Blakeney, P. E., Chan, F. A., & Cole, C. M. (1981). The impact of sex therapy on sexual behaviors and marital communication. Journal of Sex and Marital Therapy, 7, 70–79.

Danish, S. J., & D'Augelli, A. R. (1980). Promoting competence and enhancing development through life development intervention. In L. A. Bond & J. C. Rosen (Eds.), Primary prevention of psychopathology (Vol. 4). Hanover, NH: University Press of New England.

Danish, S. J., & D'Augelli, A. R. (1983). Helping skills II: Life development intervention. New York: Human Sciences Press.

Edwards, J. N., & Booth, A. (1976). The cessation of marital intercourse. American Journal of Psychiatry, 133, 1333–1336.

Ellis, A. (1975). The rational-emotive approach to sex therapy. The Counseling Psychologist, 5, 14–21.

Francoeur, R. T. (1980). The sexual revolution: Will hard times turn back the clock? The Futurist, 14, 3–12.

Frank, E., Anderson, C., & Rubenstein, D. (1978). Frequency of sexual dysfunction in "normal" couples. New England Journal of Medicine, 299, 111–115.

Graber, B. (1981). Demystifying "sex therapy." American Journal of Psychotherapy, 35, 481–488.

Hessellund, H. (1976). Masturbation and sexual fantasies in married couples. Archives of Sexual Behavior, 5, 133–147.

Heyl, B. S. (1977). The madam as teacher: The training of house prostitutes. Social Problems, 25, 545–555.

Hite, S. (1976). The Hite report: A nation-wide study of female sexuality. New York: Macmillan.

Hite, S. (1981). The Hite report on male sexuality. New York: Knopf.

Hogan, D. R. (1978). The effectiveness of sex therapy: A review of the literature. In J. LoPiccolo & L. LoPiccolo (Eds.), Handbook of sex therapy. New York: Plenum.

Huston, T., & Levinger, G. (1978). Interpersonal attraction and relationships. In M. R. Rosenszweig & L. Porter (Eds.), Annual review of psychology (Vol. 29). Palo Alto: Annual Reviews.

Jacobs, L. I. (1978, July). Use of sex to ward off intimacy. Medical Aspects of Human Sexuality, 32–43.

Johnson, V. E., & Masters, W. H. (1976). Contemporary influences on sexual response: The work ethic. Journal of School Health, 46, 211–215.

Juhasz, A. M., & Sonnenshein–Schneider, M. (1980). Adolescent sexual decision-making: Components and skills. Adolescence, 15, 743–750.

Kaplan, H. S. (1974). The new sex therapy: Active treatment of sexual dysfunctions. New York: Brunner/Mazel.

Kaplan, H. S. (1980). Disorders of sexual desire. New York: Simon & Schuster.

Kilmann, P. R., Wanlass, R. L., Sabalis, R. F., & Sullivan, B. (1981). Sex education: A review of its effects. Archives of Sexual Behavior, 10, 177–205.

Kosinski, J. (1970) Being there. New York: Bantam Books.

LaTorre, R. A., & Kear, K. (1977). Attitudes toward sex in the aged. Archives of Sexual Behaviors, 6, 203–213.

Leiblum, S. R., & Ersner-Hershfield, R. (1977). Sexual enhancement groups for dysfunctional women: An evaluation. Journal of Sex and Marital Therapy, 3, 139–152.

Leiblum, S. R., & Rosen, R. C. (1979). The weekend workshop for dysfunctional couples: Assets and limitations. Journal of Sex and Marital Therapy, 5, 57–69.

Levinger, G., & Snoek, J. D. (1972). Attraction in relationship: A new look at interpersonal attraction. Morristown, NJ: General Learning Press.

Liss-Levinson, N., Coleman, E., & Brown, L. (1975). A program of sexual assertiveness training for women. *The Counseling Psychologist, 5,* 74–78.

LoPiccolo, J. (1978). Direct treatment of sexual dysfunction. In J. LoPiccolo & L. LoPiccolo (Eds.), *Handbook of sex therapy.* NY: Plenum.

LoPiccolo, J., & LoPiccolo, L. (Eds.). (1978). *Handbook of sex therapy.* New York: Plenum.

LoPiccolo, J., & Miller, V. H. (1975). A program for enhancing the sexual relationship of normal couples. *The Counseling Psychologist, 5,* 41–45.

Maddock, J. W. (1977). Sexual health: An enrichment and treatment program. In D. H. Olson (Ed.), *Treating relationships.* Lake Mills, IO: Graphic.

Martin, C. E. (1981). Factors affecting sexual functioning in 60–79-year-old married males. *Archives of Sexual Behavior, 10,* 399–420.

Masters, W. H., & Johnson, V. E. (1966). *Human sexual response.* Boston: Little, Brown.

Masters, W. H., & Johnson, V. E. (1970). *Human sexual inadequacy.* Boston: Little, Brown.

McWhirter, D. P., & Mattison, A. M. (1978). The treatment of sexual dysfunction in gay male couples. *Journal of Sex and Marital Therapy, 4,* 213–218.

Meston, J. T. (1975). The use of a sexual enrichment program to enhance self-concept and interpersonal relationships of homosexuals. *Journal of Sex Education and Therapy, 1,* 17–19.

Morton, T. L., & Dion, G. (1976). A sexual enhancement group for women. *Journal of Sex Education and Therapy, 2,* 35–38.

Mosher, D. L. (1980). Three dimensions of depth of involvement in human sexual response. *Journal of Sex Research, 16,* 1–42.

Reiss, I. L. (1981). Some observations on ideology and sexuality in America. *Journal of Marriage and the Family, 43,* 271–283.

Roberts, E. J. (1980a). Dimensions of sexual learning in childhood. In E. J. Roberts (Ed.), *Childhood sexual learning: The unwritten curriculum.* Cambridge, MA: Ballinger.

Roberts, E. J. (1980b). Sex education versus sexual learning. In M. Kirkpatrick (Ed.), *Women's sexual development: Explanation of inner space.* New York: Plenum.

Roberts, E. J. (1980c). Sexuality and social policy: The unwritten curriculum. In E. J. Roberts (Ed.), *Childhood sexual learning: The unwritten curriculum.* Cambridge, MA: Ballinger.

Rowland, K. F., & Haynes, S. N. (1978). A sexual enhancement program for elderly couples. *Journal of Sex and Marital Therapy, 4,* 91–113.

Sarrel, L. J., & Sarrel, P. M. (1979). *Sexual unfolding: Sexual development and sex therapies in late adolescence.* Boston: Little, Brown.

Scanzoni, J. (1979). Social exchange and behavioral interdependence. In R. L. Burgess & T. L. Huston (Eds.), *Social exchange in developing relationships.* New York: Academic Press.

Schover, L. R. (1982). Enhancing sexual intimacy. In P. Keller & L. Ritt (Eds.), *Innovations in clinical practice.* Sarasota, FL: Professional Resource Exchange.

Sotile, W. M., Kilmann, P., & Follingstad, D. R. (1977). A sexual enhancement workshop: Beyond group systematic desensitization for women's sexual anxiety. *Journal of Sex and Marital Therapy, 3,* 249–255.

Spanier, G. B. (1977). Sexual socialization: A conceptual review. *International Journal of Sociology of the Family, 7,* 87–106.

Szasz, T. (1980). *Sex by prescription.* Garden City, NY: Anchor Press.

Tollison, C. D., & Adams, H. E. (1979). *Sexual disorders.* New York: Gardner Press.

Tullman, G. M., Gilner, F. H., & Kolodny, R. C., Dornbush, R. L., & Tullman, G. D. (1981). The pre- and post-therapy measurement of communications skills of couples undergoing sex therapy at the Masters and Johnson Institute. *Archives of Sexual Behavior, 10,* 95–109.

Trower, P. (1979). Fundamentals of interpersonal behavior: A social psychological perspective. In A. S. Bellack & M. Hersen (Eds.), *Research and practice in social skills training.* New York: Plenum.

Verhulst, J., & Heiman, J. R. (1979). An interactional approach to sexual dysfunctions. *American Journal of Family Therapy, 7,* 19–36.

Veroff, J., Kulka, R. A., & Douvan, E. (1981). *Mental health in America: Patterns of help-seeking from 1957 to 1976.* New York: Basic Books.

Wagner, C. A. (1980). Sexuality of American adolescents. *Adolescence, 15,* 567–580.

Walen, S. R. (1980). Cognitive factors in sexual behavior. *Journal of Sex and Marital Therapy, 6,* 87–101.

World Health Organization. (1975). Technical report 572: Education and therapy in human sexuality. Geneva: World Health Organization.

Wilcox, D., & Hager, R. (1980). Toward realistic expectations for orgasmic response in women. *Journal of Sex Research, 16,* 162–179.

Wiseman, J. P. (1976). *The social psychology of sex.* New York: Harper & Row.

Wolpe, J. L. (1958). *Psychotherapy by reciprocal inhibition.* Stanford: Stanford University Press.

Wright, J. R., & Mathieu, M. (1977). The treatment of sexual dysfunction: A review. *Archives of General Psychiatry, 34,* 881–890.

Zilbergeld, B., & Ellison, C. R. (1979). Social skills training as an adjunct to sex therapy. *Journal of Sex and Marital Therapy, 5,* 340–350.

Zilbergeld, B., & Evans, M. (1980, August). The inadequacy of Masters and Johnson. *Psychology Today,* 29–43.

CHAPTER 8

Social Skills Training for Divorced Individuals

HARVEY JOANNING

Ten years ago this chapter would have begun with a number of alarming comments about the rising rate of divorce, its negative effect on individuals involved, and the need to do something about the problem before it became worse. Many facts and figures would have been cited to convince the reader of the enormity of the social problem involved in divorce and the need to eradicate this attack on the institution of marriage as quickly as possible. Today, the tone seems to be changing; divorce as a social problem has not been removed; in fact, attempts have been made to redefine divorce as a creative or growth-oriented life transition (Gettleman & Markowitz, 1974; Krantzler, 1975). Whether one chooses to perceive divorce as a social problem or as an opportunity for individuals to seek a better personal life, the phenomena of divorce is apparently here to stay. Furthermore, few would argue that divorce is a traumatic experience, an experience that often devastates the personal life of individuals experiencing the process. Consequently, much work has been done by researchers and practitioners to understand better the process of divorce and to design therapies of interventions to assist individuals attempting to adjust to divorce.

The general effects of divorce on individuals are readily apparent to friends and acquaintances of individuals who have separated from their spouse. The time following the termination of a marital relationship is often characterized by confusion, depression, and period of doubt and self-depreciation. The most pronounced emotional and behavioral changes associated with divorce begin at the time of physical separation (Raschke, 1975). This is the time when the divorcing individual and the individual's acquaintances become most acutely aware of the negative impact of the divorce process as well as the need to assist people attempting to survive the emotional upheavals caused by divorce.

A number of consequences of divorce have been identified by researchers First, a sense of loss, inadequacy, and decreasd self-esteem accompany the divorced person's realization that a discrepancy exists between what was expected of marriage and the reality of divorce. Few enter marriage expecting it to end in divorce (Konopka, 1976). Society reinforces the notion that once a couple marries, they will remain together (Brown, Feldberg, Fox, & Kohen, 1976). Failure to meet societal expectations of marriage leads the divorced individual to feel a sense of failure, rejection, and personal inadequacy. Consequently, self-esteem decreases and often becomes an obstacle to healthy postdivorce adjustment (Hart, 1976).

The fact that a relationship has ended and two spouses are no longer living together leads to the second consequence of divorce—changes in the divorced person's social support system. Weiss (1976) describes that tendencies of friends and relatives to rally around the divorced individual initially and provide support. This support gives way to reactions idiosyncratic to the individual friend or relative. Often, the divorced individual finds that he or she has lost not only the marital partner but most former friends and relatives as well. The effects of finding oneself alone as well as separated from a former spouse are easy to imagine.

A third consequence of divorce is the social stigma attached to divorce by friends, relatives, and society in general. Society tends to view each divorce as a failure—an index of social disorder (Mead, 1970). Having to face this social stigma in addition to being alone and having lost much of one's sense of self-worth leaves many divorced people ill equipped to adjust readily to the reality of divorce.

Fortunately, helping professionals have not ignored these hardships faced by divorcing and divorced individuals. Kaslow (1981) has reviewed therapeutic efforts designed to assist individuals experiencing the divorce adjustment process. Her focus was on therapies tailored to individuals or small groups of individuals seeking help dealing with the emotional trauma of divorce.

This chapter will review in detail intervention approaches that are generally more structured and systematic than the therapies reviewed by Kaslow. The purpose of this chapter is to review social skills training programs designed to assist individuals engaged in the process of divorce adjustment. Describing existing programs in some detail, highlighting similarities and unique features of the programs described, and suggesting directions for future program development and research are goals of this review.

Programs that approach or meet the following criteria will be reviewed in this chapter: (1) topics for each session of the program are defined prior to the beginning of training; (2) the number of sessions is set prior to the beginning of the program; and (3) a clear sequence of lessons or topics to be covered in th program is detailed prior to the beginning of training. These criteria will serve as an operational definition of social skills training programs for the purposes of this chapter. When possible, this review will include a description of the social skills taught in each program as well as how, if at all, the program assessed change in participants.

Following the detailed description of the programs developed to date and a review of the research of their effectiveness, a summary of the common elements of existing programs will be described followed by specific suggestions of components of an idealized social skills training program for divorced individuals.

Although few such programs exist at present, the intervention programs that have been developed are significant in terms of the range and depth of treatment intervention they entail. I hope that this review will assist the reader in developing future intervention programs and research designs.

PROGRAM DESCRIPTIONS AND RESEARCH

This section of the chapter will reveiw in detail six representative programs currently used in the country. Each program will be examined in terms of its structure and format, topics covered, and special characteristics of the particular program. A review of outcomes will be considered if research has been done on the program.

Transition Groups

The first program to be considered was developed by Morris and Prescott (1975). Their program, called Transition

Groups, was named in recognition of changes involved in returning to single life while adjusting to divorce. The groups focus on the adjustment stages individuals go through while adjusting to separation and divorce.

The transition groups discussed by Morris and Prescott were conducted on a university campus and involved 38 participants enrolled in the groups over a period of 18 months. Most of the students in the groups were between 18 and 22 years, but the average age of group members was 29 years, representing a skewed distribution over an age range of 18 to 50 years. The groups were made up equally of men and women at the University of Idaho. Most of the participants were experiencing their first divorce with five individuals having gone through a prior relationship termination.

A male–female co-facilitator model was used to lead the transition groups. The group leaders were role models for group members participating in the project. The leadership style used by the facilitators was to follow the conversation and feeling tone of the group, occasionally intervening to clarify a point or deal with an issue. The leaders tended to be reactive; that is, to allow the group participants to initiate topics. The co-facilitators intervened when appropriate to assure that concerns or issues were adequately processed before the group moved on to another topic.

Transition group members entered the program through referral from the university counseling center or in response to advertisements circulated across the campus. Individuals interested in the groups were screened by the co-facilitators prior to entering the group. The transition groups were designed for eight or nine weekly meetings of 2 hours each during a given semester. The group was disbanded at the close of each semester; however, five of six participants recontracted to join another group in subsequent semesters.

Participant needs early in the program included (1) support; (2) sharing of feelings and concerns with those who could empathize with their situation; and (3) gaining a better perspective on emotional reactions to relationship termination. Early stages of the group were characterized by mourning, feelings of grief, guilt, anxiety, and ventilation of strong emotion. Throughout the course of the program participants were given the opportunity to give and receive feedback about behavior observed in the group. Group cohesiveness developed rapidly as participants shared concerns regarding loneliness and the need to overcome feelings of isolation or alienation. Over the course of the program, participants made a transition from the examination of their past to a concern with the here and now. The most pressing need of participants during the intermediate stages of the program was developing a satisfying role in a life-style as a divorced individual. Late in the program, the emphasis switched to a focus on the future and planning for the future.

As a result of their experiences in conducting transition groups for divorced individuals, Morris and Prescott have made the following recommendations: (1) postpartnership adjustment groups should have male and female facilitators; (2) an individual intake interview should be conducted with each potential group member prior to entry into the group; and (3) both individuals from a marriage that has terminated should not be seen in the same group because of the disruptive potential of renewing old battles or the inhibiting effects of having a former spouse present in the group.

The transition group program has not been researched to date. However, the authors of the program have used the following questions in terms of future research questions regarding their program or similar programs: (1) Do transition group participants evidence better adjustment to partnership failure than individuals who do not experience the group treatment? (2) Is postpartnership adjustment accelerated in groups in which the leaders initiate activities or topics for consideration, or is a nondirective membership-centered approach better? (3) Can adjustment to separation or divorce be facilitated by a marathon session or a weekend workshop, or do weekly session ranging over a number of weeks produce better results? (4) Because transition groups appear to progress through a series of stages, would it inhibit the group process to bring in new members after an established group has been meeting for a few sessions?

In conclusion, the Transition Group developed by Morris and Prescott represents the earliest published report of a social skills training program designed specifically for divorced individuals. The program, as it was designed and reported, anticipated many of the programs to be developed over subsequent years. Although the program lacked the structure, depth of content, and research characteristics of later programs, the program laid the foundation for more broadly based and sophisticated programs that followed. In terms of the criteria specified earlier for social skills training programs, the transition groups reviewed here fit loosely within the criteria defined. The groups did focus on an agreed upon topic, that is, adjustment to separation and divorce. However, the topics for each session of the training program were not defined prior to the beginning of the program. Topics were allowed to emerge from the group, and the facilitators encouraged discussion of the topics rather than setting the agenda for each group session. Consequently, the first criterion for a social skills training program was met partially. The number of sessions for the program was apparently not set prior to beginning the sessions but was dictated by the length of the semester. The fact that the groups were eight or nine sessions long tended

to be an artifact of the service agency's schedule rather than a preordained decision on the part of the program organizers. The third criterion for social skills training programs was not met because a clear sequence of sessions or topics to be covered week by week was not detailed prior to the beginning of the program. Finally, although the program did not systematically teach social skills, involvement in the group encouraged people to self-disclose and gave participants an opportunity to plan for a future life-style. In effect, the program randomly exposed participants to skills taught formally in later programs. Even though the Transition Group program did not meet the criteria for a social skills training program, I have reviewed it here for its historic value. Clearly, the Transition Group program described by Morris and Prescott bridged the gap from individual therapeutic intervention with divorced individuals, treatment that tended to be nonstructured and tailored to the particular individual being served, to later programs that are highly structured and designed for the benefit of groups of individuals.

The Fisher Divorce and Personal Growth Seminar

The second divorce program was developed by Fisher (1981a, 1981b). The program has not been published in professional journals but has gained national attention because of the various materials Fisher has developed for individuals going through the process of divorce. These materials include the book *Rebuilding: When Your Relationship Ends* (Fisher, 1981a) and the Fisher Divorce Adjustment Scale (Fisher, 1976). These materials have been used widely in divorce adjustment groups and by researchers examining the effectiveness of such groups.

Fisher has developed a social skills training program called The Fisher Divorce and Personal Growth Seminar. The seminar is loosely described in his dissertation (Fisher, 1976). Fisher has since published a teacher's guide (1981b) for the seminar that gives a detailed description of the program session by session. The divorce adjustment seminar has the following behavioral objectives:

1. To help people gain an intellectual and emotional understanding of how to adjust to a crisis such as the ending of a love relationship.
2. To help people adjust socially and emotionally.
3. To help people learn to build a social support system.
4. To use the pain of the crisis as a motivation to learn new and productive patterns of living and interacting with family, friends, and lovers.

The seminar is held 3 hours per week for 10 weeks with an emphasis on informal group discussion. Participants are required to (1) attend and participate in all group sessions; (2) read the textbook; (3) read two books from the bibliography distributed during the first group session; (4) keep a weekly journal of thoughts, feelings, and reactions to class discussions and personal growth experiences during the week; (5) become involved in the "whatever" project—something you have wanted to do but have not had time for; (6) read weekly handouts to prepare for the following week's discussion; and (7) write an evaluation of the seminar during the 10th group session as a review of personal growth experiences.

The seminars have male and female co-facilitators. These leaders are used to assist individuals in working through the polarization of feelings about the opposite sex that often occur for divorcing individuals.

The typical class format is a minilecture followed by class discussion. The structure is flexible and allows for group

members to work through personal difficulties. Fisher describes the seminar as at times resembling a graduate college graduate seminar and at times a trust support group. The topics covered in the 10 weekly sessions include:

Session 1. Divorce process rebuilding blocks: A model of the divorce adjustment process.

Session 2. Transactional analysis for lovers: Transactional analysis as it applies to love relationships.

Session 3. Divorce grief: Grief as it relates to divorce.

Session 4. Angerism: A discussion of anger experienced during divorce.

Session 5. Self-concept: A discussion of how to improve feelings of self-worth.

Session 6. Fisher's theory of show, rebel, and love stages: A developmental model of growth resulting in improved personal identity.

Session 7. Masks: A discussion of emotional distance and loss of intimacy.

Session 8. Love: A discussion of love and self-love.

Session 9. Relationships: Relationships during the divorce process.

Session 10. Sexuality: Developing a meaningful sexuality.

Like Morris and Prescott's program, Fisher's format allowed participants an opportunity for self-disclosure and informal practice of interpersonal skills. Formal skills teaching was limited to cognitive reframing regarding the divorce process and adjustment to divorce.

Research regarding the effectiveness of Fisher's seminar has been limited to his dissertation (Fisher, 1976). The dissertation was a pretest, posttest control group design. Thirty experimental (19 female, 11 male) and 30 control (21 female,

& 9 male) subjects were used in the study. Subjects ranged in age from 20 to 59 years; however, subjects were not randomnly assigned to control and treatment conditions. In addition, experimental subjects were treated in two separate groups in different communities. Control subjects had been separated for a longer period of time than experimental subjects and were less motivated to be involved in the seminars. Obviously, these weaknesses limited generalizability of study findings.

Outcome measures of the study included the Personality Orientation Inventory, the Tennessee Self-Concept Scale, and the Fisher Divorce Adjustment Scale. Because the Personality Orientation Inventory and the Tennessee Self-Concept Scale are well documented in the literature, they will not be reviewed here. The Fisher Divorce Adjustment Scale was developed for the study. The purpose of the adjustment scale is to measure a perons's adjustment to the ending of his or her love relationship. The scale generates a total score and five subtest scores: (1) feelings of self-worth; (2) disentaglement of love relationship; (3) feelings of angerism; (4) symptoms of grief; and (5) rebuilding self-trust. The alpha internal reliability of the total score is .98 with the reliability of the subtests ranging from .87 to .95. More information on the scale is available from Fisher (1977).

Study findings indicated that experimental subjects experienced significantly greater growth through the divorce process in terms of self-acceptance of divorce, disentanglement of the love relationship, rebuilding social relationships, and overall adjustment to divorce. A 3-month follow-up indicated that these gains were maintained. Correlational analyses among the three out-come measures in the study indicated that divorce adjustment was easier for people with a good self-concept and a greater degree of self-actualization. In addition, the Fisher Divorce Adjustment Scale indicated a significant variation in the pace that individuals progressed through the divorce adjustment process. Overall, these findings indicate that the divorce and personal growth seminar holds potential for assisting individuals in the divorce adjustment process. Further research is needed to assess the effectiveness of the updated version of the seminar now being offered nationally as well as to overcome the design flaws apparent in the original dissertation.

Fisher's work in the area of divorce adjustment has contributed a well-developed program for the treatment of divorce adjustment, pertinent reading material for individuals experiencing divorce, an instrument for assessing the degree of divorce adjustment, and preliminary data to indicate that structured social skills training experiences for divorcing individuals can be helpful in facilitating the divorce adjustment process.

Divore Adjustment Groups

The third pioneer in the development of social skills training for divorced individuals is Kessler. Her works are described in two articles, the first of which details her original program (Kessler, 1976) and the second article, which reports an outcome study designed to measure the effectiveness of an expanded version of the program (Kessler, 1978). The original program also served as the basis of the expanded form tested by Kessler in her research reviewed later in this chapter.

In her first article, Kessler sees divorce adjustment groups as filling the need to help individuals (1) move through the divorce adjustment process more quickly; (2) develop a greater sense of autonomy and self-esteem; (3) let go of the past; (4) share and contrast experiences with other divorcing individuals; and (5) recognize that divorce demands adjustments. In addition, Kessler sees her groups helping divorcing individuals adjust to the divorce process without fear of being judged for having made the decision to divorce.

The goals of Kessler's program include (1) to help individuals regain emotional autonomy; (2) to mitigate the debilitating aspects of divorce; (3) to provide a pace to discharge safely some of the emotionality of divorce; (4) to help people develop a broader concept of divorce; (5) to assist people in meeting new friends in a meaningful way; and (6) to enable people to learn coping mechanisms that they can use in dealing with other losses.

Kessler stresses the importance of counselors being aware of dimensions unique to the divorcing population. She suggests counselors be aware that (1) everyone in a group will be at a different stage of divorce adjustment; (2) some group members may be looking for "instant intimacy"; (3) some individuals may exhibit guardedness; and (4) individuals entering groups may perceive themselves as having few options in coping with the divorce adjustment.

In working with groups of divorced individuals, Kessler gives some guidelines for selection of group members, duration of the group, and format of the group. In selecting group members, Kessler sees as appropriate any individual who has decided that the marriage is irrevocably over. In addition, she suggests two criteria for group membership; first, that the individual has definitely decided on divorce or has been cut off by a partner who has made that decision, and second, that the person is physically separated from the spouse. Finally, she suggests that 10–12 members is ideal for a group.

Kessler (1976) initially recommended that groups run for 5 weeks with a 2-hour session once a week; however, her second paper (1978), discussed later, used a longer format. In regard to treatment format, Kessler divided the groups into two main segments; lecturettes and unstruc-

tured group process. Each group begins with a 15–20-minute lecturette followed by a discussion. The lecturettes are designed to (1) provide structure for the emotional divorce experience by plotting stages and expectations of the experience; (2) give people a vocabulary to work with and material to relate to if they are having a difficult time expressing what is happening to them; (3) provide a structured experience at the beginning of each group so that each person can prepare for the group discussion in a safe and passive way; and (4) teach the specific therapeutic tools for changing thoughts, emotions, and behaviors in order to make divorce a constructive rather than destructive experience.

Lecturettes during the groups focus on (1) common stages of divorce; (2) transactional analysis as it relates to the divorce process; (3) techniques for making divorce a more palatable process; (4) divorce reform in the United States; and (5) legal aspects of divorce.

Kessler discusses issues and dynamics that occur during the course of divorce adjustment groups. Issues include "the emotional yo-yos," mood swings and heightened sensitivities that occur during the divorce process. These mood swings include an exaggerated time perspective and emotionally intense discussion of the divorce process. Kessler advises divorcing individuals to save their overcharged emotional experiences for the group so they do not engage in outbursts that may harm friendships, job, or family. She further encourages people that the emotional mood swings they are experiencing are a stage that will pass as the divorce process continues.

A second dynamic that people attending divorce adjustment groups may experience is what Kessler refers to as "sand in the gears," a tendency by divorcing individuals to find themselves behaviorally plugged up. Divorcing individuals may simply stop doing the thing necessary to continue coping with life on a day-to-day basis.

A third issue that may occur for group participants is "passivity that devours," a general passivity about life that blocks individuals from fully adjusting to divorce. This passivity is an emotional experience that seems to parallel the behavioral tendency by some divorcing individuals to get "sand in the gears."

A final issue that Kessler sees members of her divorce adjustment groups struggling with is the "burying-the-hatchet" phenomena. Divorcing individuals struggle with the decision to seek or not seek revenge during the divorce process. The groups tend to dampen an individual's desire to start divorce warfare with the ex-spouse. Kessler's groups help individuals deal with the desire to get revenge by having them focus on themselves and take responsibility for themselves rather than blaming their spouse for their predicament.

In her second article, Kessler (1978) built on the basic goals and concepts just discussed but added greater structure to her format and increased the number of sessions in order to conduct an outcome study to test the effectiveness of her divorce adjustment groups. Her study was designed to determine whether a structured or unstructured approach would be more effective in dealing with divorce adjustment groups.

Subjects for the group were 11 men and 19 women who volunteered for a group called "Beyond Divorce: Coping Skills for Adults." Nine students and 21 nonstudents ranging from 21 to 61 years of age were randomnly assigned to a structured treatment group, an unstructured treatment group, and a control group.

Outcome measures for the study included the Total, Identity, and Self-satisfaction subscales of the Tennessee Self-Concept Scale and the Initiative, Self-assurance, and Maturity subscales of the Self-Decription Inventory. In ad-

dition, Kessler administered the Self-Report Questionnaire that solicited information about the last 3 months of the subjects' lives, requesting information such as number of days absent from work, traffic tickets, and recent doctor visits. The questionnaire also asked participants to rate the quality of the group for them and their adjustment as compared to 2 months earlier.

Procedure for the study was as follows. The two treatment groups met for one Saturday 8-hour exerience followed by eight weekly meetings of 2 hours per week. In the unstructured group, the leader responded to the needs of the individual participants of the group as they arose. Spontaneous discussion and self-disclosure of feelings were encouraged. Members of the group expressed fears about being single, resentments about the injustices in marriage, concern for children, anger toward people who judge them, feelings of self-judgment. The leader encouraged people to discuss feelings rather than superficial topics. The structured group also began by discussing the same emotional concerns as individuals in the unstructured group had done. About half of the structured group time was spent in spontaneous discussion. The second half of each structured group session began with a film vignette designed to stimulate discussion and to introduce a skill-building exercise. The skill-building exercises focused on actual intra- or interpersonal situations that group members were experiencing. Role playing was used to assist group members in developing alternate ways of handling the specific situations stimulated by the film vignettes. The film used in the structured groups is entitled *Divorce: Part I* (Kessler & Whiteley, Producers). The film vignettes focused on topics such as parent–child interactions, assertive behavior, values clarification, and dealing with one's ex-spouse. Following the eight weeks of training, experimental and control subjects were administered the three outcome measures. A posttest only, control group design was chosen to eliminate pretest reactivity.

Kessler found significant differences between the treatment groups and the control group on all three subscales of the Tennessee Self-Concept Scale and the three subscales of the Self-Descriptive Inventory. The structured group scored significantly higher on each of the scales than the unstructured group, and both treatment groups scored significantly higher than the control group. No differences among groups were found for number of recent doctor visits, traffic tickets, days of depression, or days of sick leaves as reported on the Self-Report Questionnaire. Subjects attending the structured group were more satisfied with the group than individuals attending the unstructured group. Results of the analysis of the Tennessee Self-Concept Scale indicated that persons attending the structured group achieved the highest overall level of self-esteem and achieved a more positive self-identity and greater self-acceptance.

Kessler recommends structured group experiences for individuals in the divorce adjustment process. However, Kessler does mention that individuals in the structured group initially had difficulty moving from the unstructured to the structured part of the experience. By the end of 8 weeks, individuals in the structured group had learned to accept and appreciate the structured experience. Members of the unstructured group reported positive feelings about their group and a sense of cohesiveness at the end of the group. Kessler suggests that the unstructured group experience may not give group members the confidence to cope with day-to-day demands of the divorce experience. She postulates that ambiguity may not be constructive during a time that is already heavily laden with ambiguity. She further speculates that the structured experience may provide skill building that

makes floundering slightly more manageable. Finally, she feels the structured focus of the group may subtly encourage a more active stance in setting and obtaining goals in life.

Kessler's divorce adjustment group represents a further refinement of social skills training experiences for divorcing individuals. Her outcome study suggests that the addition of structure to group experiences for divorcing individuals strengthens the ability of such groups to assist in adjustment to divorce. Kessler's work is a clear departure from the first two programs reviewed.

The films employed in her program modeled specific interpersonal skills, whereas role playing further promoted behavior shaping. The combination of cognitive reframing and behavior change closely identifies Kessler's work as focusing on specific social skills. Although her group is partially spontaneous, she has clearly moved in the direction of structure and replicable format. Her work suggests that greater structure is associated with a more powerful training experience for divorced individuals.

The Treatment Seminar for Post-Divorce Adjustment

The fourth training program was developed by Granvold and Welch. They have described their program in two articles (Granvold & Welch, 1977; Welch & Granvold, 1977), the second of which focuses on training completed with 96 people who had participated in three separate seminars. Their second paper will be the focus of this discussion because apparently the program had been further refined by the time it was published. The reader is encouraged to read both articles for a full description of the program developed by these practitioners.

The Treatment Seminar for Post-Divorce Adjustment is a cognitive behavioral approach. In developing the model, the authors utilized empirical findings from sociological investigations of post-divorce adjustment, learning theory, and small group therapy. The philosophy underlying the treatment seminar is that postdivorce adjustment inherently involves emotive accomodation, cognitive restructuring, and behavior change. The overall strategy of the seminar is to move from generalized imparting of knowledge to specific problem solving. The seminars are structured around specific content areas. Groups begin with instructions regarding typical problems, practical logistics, and psychosocial implications of the process of separation and divorce and move to discussions of and problem solving around individual adjustment delimmas.

Ninety-six people at various stages in the divorce process participated in the three seminars reported in the second article. Participants ranged from 19–57 years of age and women outnumbered men by a 4:1 ratio. Participants responded to multimedia announcements of the seminar or were referred by area practitioners.

Seminars were conducted weekly for 7 weeks 3 hours per night with each successive session devoted to a new topic. All seminars were jointly conducted by the authors. Each session began with a 15- to 30-minute didactic introduction to the topic being considered that evening. Participants then divided into two small groups to facilitate group discussion. One to 1½ hours were devoted to group discussion, problem solving, modeling, and role rehearsal. A brief outline of the didactic portion of each session follows:

Weeks 1 and 2.   Emotional impact of separation/divorce.
Weeks 2 and 3.   The continuing relationship with the ex-spouse.
Weeks 3 and 4.   The impact of separation of family and friends.
Weeks 4 and 5.   Impact of separation on relationship with children.

Weeks 5 and 6.   Work and dating.
Weeks 6 and 7.   Sexual adjustment as a single adult.

Granvold and Welch report a number of group process observations as a result of having conducted a number of divorce seminars: (1) individual participants began to share problems of adjustment and creative approaches to problem resolution as they sensed the universality of experiences among group members; (2) the groups allowed for vicarious learning by their members; and (3) the groups served as sources of social reinforcement of their members.

The treatment seminars made use of cognitive restructuring on the assumption that behavior change can be brought about by modifying individual assumptions and expectations about the world and internal verbalizations. The goals of cognitive restructuring included the alteration of negative cognitive sets, irrational assumptions, and internal verbalizations. Four steps toward cognitive restructuring were taught participants: (1) presenting a rationale; (2) representing a method for identifying irrational assumptions; (3) self-intervention; and (4) creative problem solving. In addition, the authors used Rational-Emotive Therapy to attack irrational beliefs. Homework involved having participants apply rational viewpoints to current adjustment problems by writing short essays in which irrational cognitions were actively refuted. A final method of cognitive restructuring taught in the seminar was the development of creative solutions to problems. Participants were taught four sequential steps to creative problem solving: (1) the statement of a problem situation in clear, unambiguous language; (2) the suggestions of possible options for solution of the problem; (3) an analysis of possible consequences for each solution; and (4) the stimulation of the skills required to put the solution into action.

In addition to cognitive restructuring,

modeling and behavioral rehearsal were used to facilitate the participants' incorporation of desired behavioral actions and responses. Behaviors were modeled by the authors and rehearsed by participants. Therefore, social skills taught in the program were both cognitive and behavioral in nature.

Specific homework assignments were made to promote behavior transfer and generalization beyond the group setting. Homework assignments were (1) highly specific; (2) realistic and supportive of reasonable change; (3) verbally committed to by participants while in the group; and (4) reported to the group after an attempt had been made to carry out the assignment.

Like programs reviewed earlier, the Treatment Seminar for Postdivorce Adjustment incorporates weekly didactic instructions and discussions around topical issues; however, the program seems even more structured than other programs reviewed thus far in terms of the specificity of the agenda followed. In addition, the program emphasizes cognitive restructuring, modeling, and behavioral rehearsal as well as specific homework assignment.

Although the other programs utilized these methods to some extent, Granvold and Welch's approach seems more specific and well developed. Particularly interesting are the authors' attempts to blend a variety of therapeutic techniques in the development of a program for divorce adjustment. The program clearly draws on behavioral and cognitive approaches to psychotherapy. The fact that the seminar is conducted in a group setting also allows for emotional interaction among group members. In summary, this program tends to deemphasize the role of emotive treatment of divorce adjustment and emphasizes behavioral and cognitive treatment of individuals experiencing the adjustment stresses of divorce.

Unfortunately, Granvold and Welch have not researched the effectiveness of their program. Considering the degree to which the format of the program has been specified by the authors, development of an outcome research design to evaluate the effectiveness of the program appears straightforward. The results of such a study would be particularly interesting considering the positive outcome of Kessler's research regarding her structured approach to divorce adjustment. Granvold and Welch's program appears even more structured than Kessler's. Whether furthur increasing the structure of divorce adjustment programs would in turn increase the effectiveness of such programs is an interesting question for future research. Futhermore, process research regarding the interactive effects of cognitive, behavioral, and effective approaches to the treatment of divorce adjustment bears further exploration. Such research would shed light on the optimal mix of treatment components used to assist individuals experiencing the stresses of divorce.

Thus far, this chapter has focused on the work of individual researchers and practitioners throughout the country. This focus will now shift to hybrid programs that have been developed, building upon the research and programming of training approaches cited thus far. By the late 1970s, enough work in the area of social skills training for divorced individuals had been accomplished to allow researchers to develop hybrid models, drawing from the advantages of and avoiding the limitations of earlier studies and programs. Building on these earlier foundations are the interrelated research studies of the Texas Tech University group. Three studies growing out of these works are detailed next.

Communication Skills Training for Divorced Individuals

Thiessen, Avery, and Joanning (1981) developed and researched a communications skills training approach to facilitate the postdivorce adjustment of women. A review of earlier studies indicated a number of variables central to the divorce adjustment process. Included among these variables were the divorced person's age, income, sex, previous marital relationship, relationship to the initiation of the divorce, self-esteem, and social support system. Factors such as age, sex, income, previous marital relationship, and relationship to the initiation of divorce are beyond the influence of social skills training programs; therefore, the focus of this research was on self-esteem and social support systems. Prior research had indicated that the higher an individual's self-esteem and the greater a person's social support system, the more likely the person would adjust quickly and satisfactorily to divorce. The program developed for this study was designed to focus on these two important variables—self-esteem and social support—both of which are amenable to intervention. The study postulated that to build self-esteem and to strengthen social support systems, a divorcing individual must possess the necessary communication skills to develop in both areas. Because prior research had indicated that many recently divorced individuals lacked necessary communication skills or were unable to use existing skills, the intervention program developed for the study was designed to teach communication skills or to enhance existing communication skills and increase the possibility that such skills would be used to build and maintain a social support system and self-esteem. In addition, a communication focus was taken because earlier research had indicated that inadequate social skills were closely related to low self-esteem and that training in social skills provided the individual with greater self-confidence and self-esteem. Finally, other researchers have noted that communication skills were needed to improve both self-esteem and social support. Specific skills targeted in the study were self-disclosure skills (ex-

pression and ownership of feelings) and empathy skills (communication of understanding and acceptance). In summary, then, the purpose of this study was to teach recently divorced women the communication skills necessary to enhance their self-esteem, strengthen their social support system, and ultimately ease the distress of postdivorce adjustment.

Dependent measures for the study were (1) general postdivorce adjustment as measured by the total score of the Fisher Divorce Adjustment Scale (Fisher, 1977); (2) self-esteem as assessed by Rosenberg Self-Esteem Scale (Wylie, 1974) and the self-esteem subscale of the Fisher Divorce Adjustment Scale; (3) perceived quality of social support as assessed by the perceived Social Support Scale developed by Thiessen; (4) self-disclosure skill as assessed by the Self-Feeling Awareness Scale (Guerney, 1977); and (5) empathy skill as assessed by the Acceptance of Other Scale (Guerney, 1977).

Subjects in the experimental group met 3 hours per week for 5 weeks. Male and female facilitators represented and clarified information regarding materials presented in the groups, modeled empathy and self-disclosure skills, supervised skill practice, and provided feedback and reinforcement to the subjects. The training program was developed from the divorce adjustment seminars described earlier, existing communication skills training programs, and the authors' experience in divorce adjustment counseling. The training format followed a structured educational approach to dealing with problems faced by recently divorced persons. Each session began with a short talk on a topic of concern to the group. The topics included (1) the emotional imact of separation and divorce; (2) the continued relationship with the former spouse; (3) the impact of divorce on friends and family; (4) the problems of dating and sexual expression; (5) the effect of divorce on self-esteem; and (6) the effects of future relationship terminations. Following the introductory talk, at least 2 hours of each 3 hour session were spent presenting and practicing a specific skill that related to the topic presented in the first part of the session. Throughout the sessions, priority was given to practice and supervision of the skills presented.

Results of the study indicated that the experimental group, relative to the control group, increased its level of general postdivorce adjustment as measured by the Fisher Divorce Adjustment Scale. Likewise the Self-Esteem subscale of the Fisher Divorce Adjustment Scale indicated that members of the experimental group increased their level of self-esteem relative to controls. The Acceptance of Other Scale findings indicated that the experimental group's level of empathy increased significantly as compared to the control group. No significant differences between the experimental group and control group were found for self-esteem as measured by the Rosenberg Self-Esteem Scale, perceived level of social support, or self-disclosure skills.

Thiessen, Avery, and Joanning (1981) note that these findings imply that (1) divorced people can benefit from a short-term, structured, communication skills training program; (2) individual and group psychotherapy may not be the only means of diminishing postdivorce stress; and (3) structured intervention strategies designed to aid recently divorced and separated individuals provide a new and potentially fruitful area of research.

The mixed results in terms of increased self-esteem as measured by the Fisher Divorce Adjustment Scale but not the Rosenberg Self-Esteem Scale were explained by Thiessen et al. (1981) as possibly due to the degree of sensitivity of the Rosenberg Self-Esteem Scale, which may not be sensitive to short-term change in self-esteem and by the fact that the Self-Esteem Subscale of the Fisher Divorce Adjustment Scale consists of 25

items and has a larger range of content than the Rosenberg Self-Esteem Scale. Thiessen et al. suggest that further research utilizing a more extensive training procedure as well as self-esteem measures that include items covering a broad range of content areas is needed to clarify the effects of divorce adjustment training on self-esteem.

The fact that the program had a positive effect on general postdivorce adjustment but not on subjects' perceived level of social support was explained by Thiessen et al. (1981) as due to the following possible factors: (1) The program may not have contributed to the social support of the experimental group and consequently no increases were observed; (2) the perceived social support scale may not possess the sensitivity to monitor change over short periods of time; (3) the length of the intervention program may not have allowed sufficient time for participants to develop new social support systems or to enhance existing systems; and (4) the structured nature of the program may have worked against the participants developing a strong social support system among themselves. Thiessen et al. (1981) go on to suggest that their highly structured communication skills training format may have inhibited spontaneous interaction among group participants and thereby diminished the possibility of social support systems developing within the group. This observation is consistent with the findings of earlier researchers and practitioners previously discussed and suggests that some time during training should be set aside for group activities that allow for spontaneous participant interaction.

The results of this study indicated no difference between experimental and control groups in regard to self-disclosure skills following training. Thiessen et al. (1981) point to two factors that may contribute to these findings. The subjects chosen for the study may have had a particularly difficult time acquiring and demonstrating self-disclosure skills, or the lack of males in the group may have contributed to the lack of increase in self-disclosure skills. Thiessen et al. explain that the crisis-state nature of recently divorced and separated individuals may inhibit them from self-disclosure and that recently divorced women may find it easier to express their feelings to member of the opposite sex.

In contrast to the lack of acquisition of self-disclosure skills, the experimental group relative to the control group significantly increased in empathy skills. By the termination of training, the experimental group was able to acknowledge the content of the speaker's statement and to demonstrate acceptance of the speaker during training exercises. The study demonstrates that individuals experiencing emotional turmoil are able to learn a new mode of communication and that interpersonal communication skills training programs can be applied to individuals who are in a negative emotional state.

Thiessen et al. (1981) discuss the following sample characteristics that limit generalizability of the study finding: (1) All participants were women; therefore they were not representative of all divorced and separated individuals; (2) participants were limited to individuals divorced and separated less than 9 months; therefore the sample may not be representative of individuals who have been divorced or separated for longer periods of time; (3) the study included only a short-term assessment of the variables involved (this limitation was overcome and will be discussed shortly); (4) the small sample size may have been too small to be representative of the population of divorced individuals; and (5) the relative contributions of communication skills training and/or the group experience to the gains made by the experimental subjects is unclear.

This study makes several contribu-

tions to the field of social skills training for divorced individuals: (1) Earlier programming efforts as well as research on the process of divorce and treatment of divorce were incorporated in developing the program tested in the study; (2) the program clearly falls within the definitional framework of social skills training defined in this volume in that the number of sessions and topics for the program were preordained as were the sequence of sessions; (3) skills trained in the program were clearly defined and assessments were made of how well the skills were learned; (4) appropriate research methodology and statistical analyses were incorporated to assess the effectiveness of the program; and (5) directions for future program development and research were clearly indicated.

This study gives practitioners in the field important information for use in future program development and raises some interesting questions. In regard to suggestions for future programming, the study points out the importance of short-term, structured, communication skills training for divorced individuals. This study furthers the suggestion made by Kessler that training programs for divorced individuals can be structured and short term. Also, the study demonstrates that even people in a state of emotional turmoil such as recently divorced individuals can learn interpersonal skills. Additionally, the program suggests that divorced individuals can indeed help themselves through the crisis of divorce. This finding is, of course, consistent with earlier programs and studies described and is an obvious prerequisite if work in this area is to continue. The fact that this program did not increase the experimental group's social support systems is both interesting and disappointing. Such support systems are not only highly desirable but necessary for the successful adjustment of divorced individuals. Future research focusing on whether this lack of social support system building during training was due to the structured nature of the program would be very interesting. Perhaps this program goes too far in structuring the divorce adjustment group experience for participants. Again, the optimal balance beween structure and spontaneousness in the divorce adjustment group training experience is called into question.

One of the shortcomings of the Thiessen, Avery, and Joanning (1981) study was later overcome. A follow-up study was conducted 3 months following the completion of training by experimental subjects. This work was conducted as part of a dissertation effort by Goethal (1979). At follow-up, 12 of the 13 original experimental subjects and 13 of the 15 original control subjects were reevaluated. The same dependent variables and assessment measures were incorporated in the follow-up study. In addition, Goethal gave the experimental subject a questionnaire designed to assess the subject's perceived improvement in their divorce adjustment as a result of participating in the training program.

The results of the follow-up study indicated that (1) experimental subjects, relative to controls, continued to show an increase in general postdivorce adjustment; (2) the experimental subjects no longer showed an increase in self-esteem as measured by either the Fisher Postdivorce Adjustment Scale or the Rosenberg Self-Esteem Scale; and (3) the experimental group continued to exhibit a higher level of empathy skills relative to controls.

Except for the decrease in self-esteem at follow-up, the experimental subjects in the study continued to show benefits of the divorce adjustment training experience developed by Thiessen, Avery, and Joanning. To date, this study is the only indication available that social skills training programs for divorced individuals can have more than an immediate or short-term impact on the divorce adjustment of individuals.

Avery and Thiessen (1982) report an additional study designed to test a different format of the communication skills training program for divorced persons just described. The purpose of this study was to teach recent divorcees communication skills to assist them in developing new social support systems or to strengthen existing ones. The format tested in this study was an intensive weekend exerience as opposed to the weekly format described earlier.

Criteria for subject selection were physical separation from spouse for no more than 16 months and no prior divorce counseling or interpersonal skills training experience. Twenty-seven subjects met the criteria and were assigned to experimental or control conditions on the basis of available weekends. Five males and 8 females, ranging in age from 24–50, constituted the experimental group. Five males and 9 females, ranging in age from 25–50, constituted the control group. The experimental subjects had been separated an average of 8 months, whereas control subjects had been separated for 10 months. No differences were found between experimental and control subjects on any relevant demographic variables.

The dependent variables were perceived social support as measured by the Perceived Social Support Scale and the communications skills of self-disclosure and empathy as measured by the Self-Feeling Awareness Scale and the Acceptance of Others Scale.

During the week immediately preceding the weekend program and again during the week following the program, subjects in each treatment condition completed the measures. The experimental group met Friday evening and all day Saturday for a total of 13 contact hours. A male/female co-facilitator team conducted a condensed version of the training material used in Thiessen, Avery, and Joanning's earlier study. Results of the study indicated that the experimental group, relative to the control group, increased their perceived level of social support. In addition, the experimental group improved on measures of self-disclosure skills with females increasing more than males. Finally, experimental subjects also increased on measures of empathy skills, with females again demonstrating a greater increase in empathic abilities.

Avery and Thiessen speculated that being understood and accepted while recalling various aspects of divorce and separation during the group experience might have encouraged participants to further self-disclose and in turn to listen to and accept others. Such a situation would help to explain increased empathy and self-disclosure skills demonstrated by experimental group subjects in the study. Avery and Thiessen suggest that future research explore (1) the relationship between social support and self-disclosure and empathy skills; (2) the relationship among components of their program and increases in self-disclosure, empathy, and perceived social support; (3) the effectiveness of longer term programs; and (4) the degree to which gains are maintained a month or more following training.

Taken together, the two studies just reviewed give insight into the effectiveness of two different formats of the same training program; they test the effectiveness of a highly structured program and give some suggestion of the maintenance of skills taught in such a program. In addition, the studies set a precedent for continued development and refinement of a program through a series of research studies. Such efforts accelerate the rate at which an area of investigation is developed by saving the steps and time necessary in developing a new research program. I hope that other program developers and researchers will also continue their efforts beyond an initial effort to develop or research social skills training programs for divorced individuals.

Adjustment and Identity After Divorce

One final divorce adjustment program will be reviewed briefly. This program developed by Read (1980) and Waldren has also grown out of the work and research at Texas Tech University. The Adjustment and Identity after Divorce Seminar (AID) is similar in general design to the programs developed by Morris and Prescott and Fisher, which were both described earlier, in that the program is primarily affective and cognitive in its content.

The program is an intensive 2-day experience typically conducted on a Friday evening and all day Saturday. The program begins on Friday evening with introductory exercises followed by a discussion of processes and stages of divorce drawn from authors such as Kessler (1976) who have described the stages of divorce adjustment in some detail. The Friday-evening session closes with a long exploration of the emotional processes of separation and divorce experienced by group participants. The Saturday session begins with discussions and exercises focusing on self-concept and identity, self- and other perceptions as influenced by the divorce process. The workshop moves to discussion and work on identity obtained from roles, especially sex roles, to a discussion of myths about divorce, and emphasizes the importance of developing a single identity following divorce. The afternoon of the Saturday workshop deals with the divorced persons' future socially, personally, and vocationally. The Saturday-evening session closes out the workshop with a focus on clarification of issues and values as well as personal goal setting.

The AID workshop is more structured than other emotionally and cognitively oriented programs discussed previously in this chapter. The format is well detailed, and resource materials are available to guide didactic portions of the experience and group exercises. The program has been conducted on a regular basis over a 3-year period and has been developed to a point that the program format and material are well designed and readily usable. In addition, the authors have developed and conducted training workshops for practitioners interested in leading AID workshops. Although Read and Waldren do not specify social skills taught in their program, like Morris and Prescott as well as Fisher, they implicitly teach a number of cognitive and interpersonal skills.

Like several of the programs described earlier, the AID workshop has not been researched in terms of its effectiveness in facilitating the divorce adjustment process. Because of the structured nature of the program and the leader's guide and other resourse material available for the AID workshop, the program presents future researchers with an opportunity to compare an affective/cognitive program with a more behaviorally oriented program such as the one developed by Thiessen, Avery, and Joanning.

PRIMARY PROGRAM FEATURES

The six social skills training programs just described represent a variety of program characteristics and primary treatment components. A number of common theses emerge as program features are compared and contrasted. In addition, each program contributes some unique approach to intervening with individuals experiencing the divorce adjustment process (See Table 8.1).

All of the programs explored in this chapter used a group setting as a framework for intevention. Numbers of individuals in groups ranged from approximately 10 to 35 members, although not all of the authors specified the number of members treated. Five of the six programs met on a weekly basis, one time per week for 5 to 10 weeks; however,

Kessler (1976, 1978), Thiessen et al. (1981), and Read (1980) incorporated weekend meetings. Kessler began her program with an intensive weekend experience followed by weekly sessions, making her program the most intensive in terms of total hours. Thiessen, Avery, and Joanning used a weekly or weekend format in their program, with each approach involving participants in approximately the same total number of hours. Read tended to prefer a weekend format although she had experimented with weekly session to some degree. All the programs except Morris and Prescott planned a set number of session prior to the beginning of treatment. Morris and Prescott's program was timed to concide with the length of an academic semester.

Preplanned topics and predetermined sequencing of topices was established for five of the six programs. Again, Morris and Prescott were the exception in that their approach was designed to allow topics to emerge spontaneously from group discussions rather than have group leaders introduce specific topics in a specific order.

Fisher (1977), Kessler (1976, 1978), and Thiessen et al. (1981) all attempted to measure change in participants' behavior, attitude, or affective state as a result of completing their programs. Kessler (1978) along with Thiessen et al. (1981) demonstrated that their programs maintain their effect beyond the termination of treatment.

Morris and Prescott (1975) were the only authors who did not make use of instructional materials during the course of training, The other program developers had instructional materials that ranged from suggested bibliographies, filmed vignettes, and handout materials to published materials that were designed specifically for the program.

Program authors were also generally consistent in defining goals for their program; Morris and Prescott were the exception. Goal definition seemed to be a

TABLE 8.1 Program Characteristics

Authors	Interval Session No. Predetermined No.	Pre-planned Topics	Pre-determined Sequencing	Measurement of Change	Goals Defined	Instructional Materials	Leaders & Style	Format	Focus	Degree of Structure
Morris & Prescott	Weekly 8–9 No	No	No	No	No	No	Male–*female* Reactive	Discussion	Affective	Low
Fisher	Weekly 10 Yes	Yes	Yes	Yes	Yes	Yes	Male–*female* Directive	Lecture Discussion	Affective Cognitive	Moderate
Kessler	Weekend + Weekly 8 Yes	Yes	Yes	Yes	Yes	Yes	*Single* Directive	Lecture Discussion Skill Training	Affective Cognitive Behavioral	Moderate
Granvold & Welch	Weekly 7 Yes	Yes	Yes	No	Some-what	Yes	Male–male	Lecture Discussion Skill Training	Cognitive Behavioral	Moderate to High
Thiessen, Avery, & Joanning	Weekly 5 or Weekend Yes	Yes	Yes	Yes	Yes	Yes	Male–female	Lecture Skill Training	Cognitive Behavioral	High
Read	Weekend Yes	Yes	Yes	No	Yes	Yes	Male–female or Single	Lecture Discussion	Affective Cognitive	Moderate to High

necessary component of these social skills training programs because they aided in establishing the structure necessary to move from individually tailored therapy to programmed interventions appropriate for groups of individuals with similar needs.

Male–female co-leader teams were used in four of the six programs reviewed. Granvold and Welch (1977) were unique in their use of male–male teams; this arrangement was due to the fact that the authors were the leaders for all of the groups reviewed in their paper. Kessler and Read made use of single leaders, although Read also used male–female teams. Leadership style in all of the programs except Morris and Prescott's was moderately to highly directive; that is, the leaders actively took charge of the program, introduced topics for discussion or training, and generally directed the activities of each session. This directive leadership style was necessitated by the programmed nature of the interventions described. These social skills training programs for divorced individuals seemed to be much more leader controlled than the therapeutic interventions for individuals reviewed by Kaslow (1981). Morris and Prescott's work represented a bridge from individual to group intervention with divorced individuals in terms of therapist or leader style.

General program formats included discussion, lecture, and/or skill training. Morris and Prescott relied exclusively on group discussion to achieve a program focus that was decidedly affective or emotionally oriented. Fisher and Read were similar in that both authors incorporated lecture and discussion to achieve program focuses that were both affective and cognitively oriented. Kessler, Granvold, and Welch and Thiessen et al. all combined lecture, discussion, and skill training in their treatment format. Although Kessler tended to balance affective, cognitive, and behavioral in-

terventions as the focus of her treatment, Granvold and Welch along with Thiessen et al. tended to emphasize cognitive and behavioral interventions.

Not surprisingly, Morris and Prescott's program, with its emphasis on discussion and reactive leadership style, exhibited the lowest degree of program structure. Fisher and Kessler seemed to prefer a moderate degree of structure, allowing group process to dictate the structure to some degree. The remaining three programs tended toward a higher degree of structure as dictated by the specificity of their program formats. Thiessen et al. (1981) with their focus on communication skills training, were the most structured in their attempt to use a relatively small number of contact hours to achieve very specific interventions.

Table 8.2 illustrates program treatment components incorporated to one degree or another by each of the authors. The first program developed, by Morris and Prescott, used discussion groups exclusively to encourage group support,

TABLE 8.2.   Program Treatment Components

Morris & Prescott	Emotionally oriented discussion groups focusing on support, self-disclosure, and development of a single life-style.
Fisher	Topical lectures and emotionally oriented discussion groups.
Kessler	Topical lectures, emotionally oriented discussion groups, and some skill training in the structured format of the program.
Granvold & Welch	Topical lectures, cognitive restructuring, modeling, and behavioral rehearsal.
Thiessen, Avery, & Joanning	Topical lectures, modeling, supervised empathy, and self-disclosure skill training
Read	Topical lecture and structured emotive and cognitive group exercises.

individual self-disclosure, and development of a single life-style. Later programs, with their specified program goals and greater breadth of purpose, used a wider range of treatment or training components. Kessler's approach seemed the most broad, given the range of program focus and format. Thiessen, Avery, and Joanning were quite focused in their interest in cognitive and behavioral change and served as a counterpoint to Morris and Prescott's earlier, affectively oriented work.

In summary, Morris and Precott represented a first attempt to move divorce adjustment interventions out of the individual therapy office and into a group format available to large numbers of divorcing individuals with similar needs. Fisher, Kessler, and Read helped to evolve structured program formats with specified goals and a broad range of training/treatment components. Granvold and Welch and especially Thiesson, Avery, and Joanning empasized structure as well as a cognitive/behavioral focus in an attempt to achieve highly specified program goals.

FUTURE DIRECTIONS FOR RESEARCH AND PROGRAM DEVELOPOMENT

The future of social skills training for divorced individuals is certainly clearer now than it was when Morris and Prescott began their work in the early 1970s. The review just completed suggests a number of possible directions for further research and development in this area.

Clearly specified training/treatment goals appear to be at least a helpful if not necessary step in developing social skills training programs for divorced individuals. Without such goals, intervention tends to become reactive; that is, the therapist or leader follows the lead of the client or clients in the manner of traditional individual psychotherapy. Because social skills training programs are designed to help or assist larger numbers of individuals than can be treated in traditional psychotherapy, program developers must be clear as to the purpose of their intervention, method of intervention, and presentation of their program to the public. Having clearly defined training/treatment goals seems to facilitate this process.

The programs reviewed tend to focus, to one degree or another, on behavioral, affective, or cognitive interventions in order to obtain treatment goals. A real divergence exists among the programs, however, as practitioners attempt to discover the best mix of treatment focus. Several of the authors cited have suggested that future research explore which possible treatment foci are most influential in facilitating the divorce adjustment process. Research assessing the effects of different treatment focus on outcome is clearly indicated. In addition, different treatment packages for divorced individuals who differ on variables related to divorce adjustment (e.g., sex, age, length of time since divorce) may be shown to be more helpful than omnibus programs.

A related research question has to do with how much structure is appropriate in divorce adjustment programs. The range represented in this chapter is from low to high degrees of structure. The researchers have alluded to their struggle to determine what degree of structure is optimal. The research cited in this chapter has involved moderately to highly structured programs. A real question remains as to the long-term effectiveness of other less structured programs. Kessler's research is a step toward answering the question of how much structure is best.

The role of instructional material and leader style is another area of program development not clearly understood. The trend seems to be toward increasing use of structured materials such as textbooks, films, and bibliographies. Likewise, leader style is moving toward more directiveness as programs became more structured. This directiveness is necessary to hold group process to the specified agenda characteristic of the later programs described. The use of published resource material, specified agenda, and structured leader style certainly facilitates the efforts of researchers to explore process and outcome effects of programs. In fact, the emerging structure of materials and leader style may be at least in part an artifact of the increasing tendency to research social skills training programs for divorced individuals.

The length of treatment in terms of total contact hours varies considerably across the programs reviewed. Thiessen, Avery, and Joanning (1981) have been able to demonstrate clear behavioral change in trained participants over a rather short period of time. Kessler (1976, 1978) has also been able to show change over time but with a considerably more extensive program in terms of contact hours. The length of time necessary for a program to be effective probably hinges on the breadth of change desired; that is, the degree to which program authors attempt to produce change in affective, cognitive, and behavioral areas. Programs that attempt to change one or two of these areas may require less time than programs that are more pervasive in nature. The particularly interesting focus of intervention in terms of length of time needed to produce change seems to be the affective or emotionally oriented area. Several authors mentioned that producing emotional change, moving subjects from a negative to a positive emotional state, seems to take a longer period of time than introducing new information (cognitive change) or new skill (behavioral change).

An issue related to treatment length is mass versus interval practice. Most of the programs mentioned met weekly for 2 to 3 hours but two of the programs used a weekend format as part or all of their training paradigm. A weekend-only format has an advantage in that participants' schedules are only interrupted for 1 or 2 days, and emotional intensity can be raised more effectively than in a weekly format. Weekly meetings on the other hand, provide opportunity for more long-term support and generalization of learning from the group to home environments. Kessler's use of both weekend and weekly meetings combines the best of two worlds; however, scheduling and participant commitment could become an issue, given the length of the program. Research exploring the advantages and disadvantages of weekend versus weekly meetings certainly merits attention.

Program developers face another choice in deciding how many group leaders to employ, the sex of the leaders, and whether to use same-sex or mixed-sex leader teams. One of the authors mentioned the advantage of having opposite-sex group leaders to facilitate participant resolution of opposite-sex resentments that may exist because of the divorce. Another author mentioned the advantage of male/female teams in terms of providing same-sex and opposite-sex points of view relevant to divorce as well as modeling good heterosexual relationship. Leader teams, be they same sex or opposite sex, have a built-in disadvantage in that providing co-facilitators for a group is more costly than providing one leader. In addition, co-facilitators must feel comfortable working together and be coordinated in their leadership style so as to prevent participant confusion and group process dysfunction. Leader teams have one clear advantage over single-leader formats; that is, while one facilitator is speaking or conducting group process, the other leader can be making process observations or preparing for his or her turn to speak or direct. This arrangement can be a particular advantage in a large group or groups in which the facilitator teams are not experienced to the point of reacting more or less automatically to group process. Having time to think about and plan one's interventions can make group leadership less harrowing and probably more effective.

Another future direction for research has to do with the effects of divorce adjustment outlined in the beginning of this chapter. Do social skills training programs assist divorced individuals in coping with problems such as loss of self-esteem, decreased social support, and the shame of social stigma? If divorce adjustment intervention experiences do not impact positively on these issues, the value of such intervention is certainly called into question. Fortunately, some of the research already done on existing programs indicates that an impact on these issues is possible. The programs described do seem to have a positive effect upon self-esteem, social support system building, and the relief of guilt or shame associated with being a divorced person.

CONCLUDING COMMENTS

To conclude this chapter and to serve as a form of summary of the major points covered, some suggestions as to an idealized divorce adjustment program are in order. Using the information available from programs and research described here, a best guess of program components to be incorporated in an ideal program would include the following features:

1. It would include an initial session of a half day or more devoted to defusion of the negative emotions present for many recently divorced individuals, promotion of self-disclosure, a sense of universality of problems, and development of group cohesion. This initial session would be designed to prepare participants for cognitive and behavioral interventions as well as continued group support.

2. Groups would continue to meet on a weekly basis for a period of 4 to 8 weeks, depending on the scope of issues to be covered in the program. These weekly sessions would move from a primarily emotional focus to cognitive and behavioral interventions. Such interventions would be designed to change attitudes blocking adjustment to divorce as well as disseminating appropriate and accurate information regarding the divorce process. Behavioral interventions would be designed to overcome deficiencies in areas such as communication skills or general interpersonal skills. Such a program with its emphasis on emotional, cognitive, and behavioral change would provide a scope broad enough to assist a wide variety of clientele with different needs.

3. Male–female leader teams would be used to distribute the demands of group facilitation across two people, to provide role models for group participants, to provide a model male–female relationship, and to facilitate efficient group process.

4. Relevant instructional material such as bibliographies, printed material, and films would be used during sessions to stimulate group discussion, to set the theme for attitudinal and behavioral change, and to relieve the burden of structuring all of the group time from the leader. The use of such materials would also facilitate standardization of effective group interventions as well as research on the outcomes of such interventions.

5. Program goals and clear descriptions of the general intervention format would be made available to potential group participants. Such information

would allow interested parties to decide whether or not to become involved in the intervention program as well as to enhance motivation of participants prior to entering the program.

Other more specific suggestions for future programming and research could certainly be gleaned from the review just completed. Such specific suggestions would move beyond the purpose of this chapter; that is, to provide a general summary of work in the field done to date and a general direction for future efforts. I hope the materials in this chapter will serve as a stimulus and guide for those helping professionals interested in facilitating the adjustment of individuals who have recently experienced the realities of divorce.

REFERENCES

Avery, A., & Thiessen, J. (1982). Communication skill training for divorcees. *Journal of Counseling Psychology*.

Brown, C. A., Feldberg, R., Fox, E. M., & Kohen, J. (1976). Divorce: Chance of a new lifetime. *Journal of Social Issues, 32*, 110–133.

Fisher, B. (1976). *Identifying and meeting needs of formerly-married people through a divorce adjustment seminar.* Unpublished doctoral dissertation, University of Northern Colorado.

Fisher, B. (1977). *Fisher Divorce Adjustment Scale.* The Family Relations Learning Center, 450 Ord Drive, Boulder, Colorado 80303.

Fisher, B., (1981a) *Rebuilding: When your relationship ends.* San Luis Obispo, CA: Impact Press.

Fisher, B. (1981b). *Teacher's guide: Fisher's divorce and personal growth seminar.* The Family Relations Learning Center, 450 Ord Drive, Boulder, Colorado 80303.

Gettleman, S., & Markowitz, J. (1974). *The courage to divorce.* New York: Simon & Schuster.

Goethal, K. (1979). *A follow-up study of a skills training approach to post-divorce adjustment.* Unpublished doctoral dissertation, Texas Tech University.

Granvold, D., & Welch, G. (1977). Intervention for post divorce adjustment problems: The treatment seminar. *Journal of Divorce, 1*, 81–92.

Guerney, B. G. Jr. (1977). *Relationship enhancement.* San Francisco: Jossey-Bass.

Hart, N. (1976). *When marriage ends: A study in status passage.* London: Tavistock.

Kaslow, F. (1981). Divorce and divorce therapy. In A. S. Gurman & D. P. Kniskern (Eds.), *Handbook of family therapy* (pp. 662–696). New York: Brunner/Mazel.

Kessler, S. (1976). Divorce adjustment groups. *Personnel and Guidance Journal, 54*, 251–255.

Kessler, S. (1978). Building skills in divorce adjustment groups. *Journal of Divorce, 2*, 209–216.

Kessler, S., & Whiteley, J. (Producers). *Divorce: Part I.* (Film, available from the American Personnel and Guidance Association, 1607 New Hampshire Ave. N.W., Washington, DC 20009.)

Konopka, G. (1976). Adolescent girls: A two-year study. In E. Elridge & N. Meredity (Eds.), *Environmental issues: Family impact.* Minneapolis: Bargess.

Krantzler, M. (1975). *Creative divorce.* New York: M. Evans.

Mead, M. (1975). Anomalies in American postdivorce relationships. In P. Bohannon (Ed.), *Divorce and after.* Garden City, NY: Doubleday.

Morris, J. D., & Prescott, M. R. (1975). Transition groups: An approach to dealing with post-partnership anguish. *The Family Coordinator, 24*, 325–330.

Raschke, H. J. (1975). Social and psychological factors in voluntary post-marital dissolution adjustment. *Dissertation Abstracts International, 35*, 5549A–5550A. (University Microfilms No. 75-2143)

Read, J. (1980). *Single adjustment and identity after divorce: A manual.* Unpublished manuscript, Texas Tech University.

Thiessen, J., Avery, A., & Joanning, H. (1981). Facilitating postdivorce adjustment among women: A communication skills training approach. *Journal of Divorce, 4,* 35–44.

Weiss, R. S. (1976). *Marital separating.* New York: Basic Books.

Welch, G., & Granvold, D. (1977). Seminars for separated/divorced: An educational approach to post-divorce adjustment. *Journal of Sex and Marital Therapy, 3,* 31–39.

Wylie, R. C. (1974). *The self-concept.* Lincoln: University of Nebraska Press.

PART THREE

Programs for Special Populations

CHAPTER 9

Social Skill Training and Children's Peer Relations

GARY W. LADD AND STEVEN R. ASHER

With the exception of a few early studies in the 1930s and 1940s (see Renshaw, 1981), most research on social skill* training with children has been conducted during the past 15 years. During this relatively short period of time, more than 45 skill training studies have been published in over 15 different professional journals by authors working primarily in educational, clinical, developmental, and pediatric settings (for reviews of this literature see Asher & Renshaw, 1981; Conger & Keane, 1981; Ladd & Mize, 1983; Wanlass & Prinz, 1982). Of the studies comprising this literature, no less than 30 have been published in the last 7 years alone. Few topics in child development have received as much attention in so short a time from researchers representing such a wide range of disciplines.

Perhaps due to the youth and the rapid growth of this field, the promise of social skill training as a solution to such childhood maladies as peer rejection, so-cial isolation, and friendlessness is accompanied by an array of issues and problems that require solution in order for further progress to occur. This chapter will focus on interventions that have been aimed at improving children's peer relationships and status, and it will address several of the most critical current issues facing this field. Included among the topics and issues to be reviewed and discussed are (1) the impetus for social skill training with children; (2) the potential candidates for social skill training; (3) the link between sociometric status and social skills; (4) the methodology employed in social skill training, that is, the procedures to be followed in teaching skills; and (5) the types of research strategies used to assess the outcomes of training and the processes that contribute to gains in status. Finally, consideration will also be given to certain pragmatic and ethical issues facing those wishing to use social skill training interventions in educational settings or incorporate these procedures into clinical practice.

IMPETUS FOR SOCIAL SKILL TRAINING WITH CHILDREN

Although behavioral scientists, clinicians, and educators have long been concerned with methods for changing

---

*Note the use of the singular (social skill) in this chapter. Even though it is not consistent with the handbook's title and other chapters, we strongly favor the singular form for the following reasons: Skills (plural) implies multiple *behaviors,* whereas skill (singular) implies a more global competence *construct* that may consist of many components. Social *skill* training, then, implies change in the child's skillfulness and does not imply that the concept is limited to a set of behaviors.

children's behavior and guiding their development, systematic research on methods for influencing the course of children's peer interactions and relationships is a relatively recent undertaking. Contemporary interest in social skill training with unpopular children has grown out of recent trends and discoveries in research on peer socialization and preventative mental health. In this section, we provide a brief account of how these two research areas have contributed to concerns about socially disadvantaged children and to efforts to aid these children.

Research on the Consequences of Poor Peer Relations

Interest in social skill training with children is in part a response to research on the relationship between early peer experience and later social adjustment. Evidence concerning this relationship comes from both experimental research with primates and correlational studies with humans, and it has often been interpreted as support for the hypothesis that early peer isolation or rejection places children at risk for later social difficulties.

Research with Primates

Some of the evidence concerning the adaptive significance of early peer relations comes from research with nonhuman species such as the rhesus monkey. Beginning with the work of Harlow in the 1960s, questions concerning the relative importance of early maternal and peer experience have been addressed by contrasting the developmental progress of monkeys reared under conditions where the extent and timing of early maternal and/or peer contact has been varied. The results of early studies (see Harlow, 1969) indicated that, although developmental aberrations were most apparent for monkeys reared in total isolation, later social difficulties (i.e., extreme wariness and/or hyperaggressiveness toward age-mates) were also common among the animals deprived of peer but not maternal contact. Later studies, in which the onset of peer contact was varied (e.g., Suomi & Harlow, 1975) revealed that longer periods of peer isolation, especially during the early months of life, tended to produce more severe and debilitating social difficulties later in development. Researchers have also addressed the question of whether the long-term benefits of early peer contact are comparable to that provided by the parent or are perhaps mediated by maternal contact. Apparently, peer contact is at best a poor substitute for maternal stimulation. Studies by Goy and Goldfoot (1973) and Suomi and Harlow (1975) indicate that the combination of "peer rearing" and maternal deprivation lead to many of the same consequences observed for monkeys reared by their mothers in the absence of peers.

Research with Humans

Due to obvious ethical constraints, research with humans has been limited to correlational studies focusing on the relationship between children's early behavior patterns or status with peers and their later life adjustment. In most of these studies, investigators have employed one of three basic research designs (termed follow-back, follow-up, and follow-through strategies by Kohn, 1977), and they have selected their samples from institutions such as child guidance centers, mental hospitals, and public schools. Information about subjects' peer relations has typically been obtained from close associates (i.e., parents or teachers), retrospective self-reports, school or clinic records, or sociometric assessment of ongoing peer interactions and relationships.

Difficulty in relating to peers is one of several types of adjustment problems that may interfere with children's progress in school. Although actual incidence of peer-related adjustment problems has not been determined, research by Gronlund (1959) and Hymel and Asher (1977) indicates that somewhere between 6 and 11% of the children in third- through sixth-grades have no friends in their classrooms. Furthermore, there is some evidence to suggest that children's early patterns of peer interaction and their acceptance in the peer group remain relatively stable over time (see Asher & Hymel, 1981; Coie & Dodge, 1983; Van Alstnyne & Hattwick, 1939; Waldrop & Halverson, 1975).

In at least four published studies, investigators have reported a relationship between children's early peer relations and their later adaptation to the school environment. In an early study, Koch (1933) found that preschoolers' scores on a paired-comparison sociometric instrument were predictive of school adjustment, and concluded that children who were popular with classmates were better able to tolerate school routines and demands than were unpopular children. Based on measures of preschoolers' behaviors toward peers, Van Alstyne and Hattwick (1939) found that early difficulties with peers predicted children's later adjustment in elementary school. In a later study with ninth-grade students, Ullmann (1957) found that sociometric ratings from peers and teacher adjustment ratings, as compared to several personality measures, best discriminated between those pupils who later dropped out of school or became high school honor graduates. Further evidence concerning the relationship between children's social functioning with classmates and their achievement in school can be found in studies by Buswell (1953) and Kohn (1977). Buswell followed kindergarten and fifth-grade children who were most and least liked by peers into subsequent grades and found that the popular children at both age levels were most likely to become high achievers. Similar findings were reported by Kohn in a lon-

gitudinal study of children progressing from day-care programs in New York City into the early years of grade school. Specifically, teacher ratings of children's shyness–passivity and isolation from peers were obtained for a sample of 1232 children during preschool and found to predict children's underachievement as early as first grade.

Several investigators have also reported a relationship between early peer difficulties and subsequent mental health problems. In a retrospective study, Kohn and Clausen (1955) found that disturbed adults, as compared to a group of matched-normal controls, were more likely to describe themselves as socially isolated or friendless at age 13 or 14. Working with a large sample and a battery of measures first administered in the third grade (e.g., achievement, aptitude, personality indexes), Cowen, Pederson, Babigian, Izzo, and Trost (1973) found that classroom peer rejection was the best single predictor of subjects' tendencies to seek psychiatric assistance as adults 11 years later. Problematic peer relations may also be associated with mental health disorders during childhood. Reports of research and clinical services (e.g., Michael, Morris, & Soroker, 1957; Morris, Soroker, & Burruss, 1954; Rinn & Markle, 1979) suggest that a significant proportion of the children seen in mental health clinics and child guidance centers are diagnosed as having difficulties in peer relations. In addition, data from other sources suggest that problems such as suicide (Stengle, 1971) and alcoholism (Robins, 1966) may be related to peer rejection and isolation during childhood and adolescence.

There is also evidence to suggest that children who have trouble relating to peers are more likely to experience behavior or character disorders in adolescence and adulthood. Roff and colleagues (Roff & Sells, 1968; Roff, Sells, & Golden, 1972) found that, among middle-class boys, those who were rejected rather than accepted by peers in the third through sixth grades were more likely to be identified as juvenile offenders during the early years of high school. In contrast, the incidence of delinquency among lower-class boys with histories of peer acceptance or rejection did not differ significantly. Roff (1961) also studied the relationship between boys's peer acceptance and rejection and their later adjustment to the military service. Males who had been rejected by peers during childhood, as indicated in reports obtained from child-guidance clinics, were more likely than their accepted counterparts to have military records indicating severe behavior problems or conduct-related discharges. Finally, Janes and Hesselbrock (1978) used individual interviews to assess the interpersonal adjustment of adults who had been seen 9–15 years earlier in child guidance clinics and found that children who were described as withdrawn or antisocial toward peers in the clinic records had the poorest adjustment ratings as adults. Sex differences in the data suggested that later maladaptation was associated with early patterns of antisocial behavior for males and social withdrawal for females.

The hypothesis that restricted or disordered peer relations during childhood leads to short- and long-term adjustment problems gains the most support from the experimental research with primates and is strengthened by the correlational studies with humans. However, at present, the limited scope and numerous shortcomings associated with this research make any interpretation little more than a working hypothesis. For example, along with the interpretational difficulties raised by correlational designs, much of the research with humans has been conducted with nonrepresentative samples (e.g., clinic populations) and based on measures with questionable reliability and validity (e.g., antecdotal records).

Nonetheless, the notion that children

with a history of poor peer relations are more vunerable to later interpersonal disorders is one of the most frequently cited justifications for social skill training research. Furthermore, it appears that research on the consequences of poor peer relations has encouraged investigators to think in somewhat different terms about *who* is "at risk" during childhood and *what* might be considered the most appropriate intervention objectives. When designing social skill training interventions, some investigators appear to have focused on the research pertaining to peer deprivation and, thus, have tended to view children with very low levels of peer interaction as vulnerable or "at risk" (e.g., Furman, Rahe, & Hartup, 1979). Typically, these investigators have attempted to increase the quantity of children's peer interactions. In contrast, other investigators have placed greater weight on findings that link later maladjustment with children's early antisocial behavior patterns and peer rejection. When social skill training interventions have been designed from this perspective, investigators have typically sought to change the quality of children's social interactions and relationships (e.g., Ladd, 1981; Oden & Asher, 1977). This chapter emphasizes research within the latter tradition because of the greater evidence of the concurrent and predictive validity of measures associated with this approach (see Asher, Markell, & Hymel, 1981, and later sections of this chapter).

RESEARCH ON THE CONTRIBUTION OF PEER RELATIONS TO CHILDREN'S SOCIAL COMPETENCE

Even if the hypothesis that inadequate peer relations place children at risk for interpersonal disorders is accepted, there remains the question of the ways in which successful children benefit from relationships with age-mates. For this reason, many investigators interested in social skill training have recognized the relevance of research on the contributions of peers to the development of children's social competence.

Relationships with peers appear to serve a variety of functions, many of which may facilitate children's social learning and development. For example, social interactions provide children with opportunities to learn from peer's reactions. Studies of peer reinforcement indicate that children are more likely to inhibit their use of aggressive strategies with peers who resist such attacks (Patterson, Littman, & Bricker, 1967). Moreover, as has been suggested in recent reviews of the literature (Asher, 1978; Hartup, 1970, 1978), the acquisition and maintenance of many other forms of social behavior, personality dispositions, and attitudes during childhood (e.g., language patterns, altruistic gestures, peer popularity, moral beliefs) may depend, in part, on the reactions children receive from peers.

Numerous studies also suggest that children learn simply by watching their peers' behavior. Children's prosocial and aggressive behaviors are elicited by watching peers exhibit these responses (see Bandura, 1973; Rushton, 1976), and there is also evidence to suggest that children learn sex-typed behaviors (Kobasigawa, 1968), standards for self-reinforcement (Bandura & Kupers, 1964), and fearlessness (Bandura & Menlove, 1968) in the same manner.

In addition to acting as teachers, peers may also serve as a source of emotional support that, in turn, may provide a "secure base" for further social learning and discovery. Freud and Dann's (1951) classic study of six World War II orphans suggested that, in the absence of adult caretakers, children develop patterns of peer attachment and interdependency that closely resemble those found in most parent–child relationships. Sim-

ilarly, the results of laboratory-based investigations by Schwarz (1972) and Ispa (1977) indicate that when children are faced with unfamiliar or possibly threatening situations, a peer (a best friend) can serve many of the same comforting and distress-inhibiting functions as parents.

Other studies indicate that participation in peer activities provides children with unique opportunities to engage in various forms of play and role-related behaviors. Research on social interaction in children's affiliative relationships indicates that same-age friends often engage in complex forms of imaginary play (Gottman & Parkhurst, 1980), and frequently display affectively oriented and reciprocal patterns of behavior during joint activities (Newcomb, Brady, & Hartup, 1979). Apparently, age-mates also offer something unique to children in terms of opportunities to share interactive roles (e.g., teacher–learner) during play. Brody, Stoneman, and MacKinnon (1982) found that the time spent in these and other roles was more balanced when children played with same-age friends as opposed to younger siblings.

For persons interested in social skill training, the studies reviewed in this section are of primary importance as a source of information about peer socialization processes and their contribution to the development of interpersonal competence. Unlike the studies reviewed in the preceding section, these investigations tend to shed light on the conditions that prevent rather than cause later maladjustment. Furthermore, understanding the ecology of the peer culture is essential because, in most cases, the objective of this type of intervention is to help children adapt to the peer group or learn appropriate ways to establish and maintain peer relationships. Social skill training investigators also use information about the means by which children naturalistically learn from peers. For example, a number of studies, based on the assumption that children learn from peer models, have involved showing preschoolers films of age-mates demonstrating specific social responses (see O'Connor, 1969, 1972; Keller & Carlson, 1974). Moreover, as will be seen, investigators have often based their training curriculum on behaviors that are frequently employed by popular children or found to produce positive consequences in the peer group.

THE CANDIDATES FOR SOCIAL SKILL TRAINING

Social skill training should be best suited to children whose difficulties relating to peers are the result of deficits in specific interpersonal competencies. However, it is likely that the types of problems children experience with peers differ both in severity and the extent to which they are caused or maintained by skill deficits. Thus, the selection of candidates for social skill training would seem to be predicated on at least two criteria, including (1) the seriousness of the presenting problem (i.e., the degree of discomfort or developmental risk posed by the problem); and (2) the etiology of the problem (i.e., the extent to which specific skill deficits as opposed to other possible causes are responsible for the problem).

Past social skill training research has been designed to address several types of peer-related problems that may or may not satisfy these two selection criteria. The diagnostic terminology and assessment criteria found in these studies seem to delineate at least two major types of social difficulties, peer isolation/withdrawal and lack of popularity, including peer neglect and rejection. Consequently, it is useful to consider, based on available evidence, which of these groups of children may be regarded as most in need and likely to benefit from social skill training.

Several social skill training studies have been aimed at children who are considered to be socially withdrawn or isolated from peers. Although there is considerable debate about the exact meaning of this concept (see Wanlass & Prinz, 1982), it would appear that this category of social difficulty generally refers to children who actively avoid or often fail to interact with peers. Low rates of peer interaction are often taken as evidence of this type of problem (cf. Allen, Hart, Buell, Harris, & Wolfe 1964; O'Connor, 1969, 1972), and many investigators have intervened with children who are selected based on this criterion (see Hops, 1982, for a review). The seriousness of this problem, when viewed in terms of the possible developmental risks posed by low rates of interaction, remains unclear. Present evidence suggests that children's overall rate of peer interaction, without consideration of its quality, bears little relationship to measures of current or long-term social adjustment (Asher, Markell, & Hymel, 1981). However, recent research with preschool children by Rubin (1982) indicates that some forms of nonsocial behaviors (e.g., functional or sensori–motor forms of play) are more predictive of social maladjustment than others (e.g., more constructive forms of solitary play), and that certain types of infrequently interacting children may be at risk.

A second group of children targeted for social skill training are those with low levels of peer acceptance or popularity, as reflected by various sociometric measures. Until recently, most of this work was focused on "unpopular" children, that is, individuals who were least often nominated or most lowly rated by peers for specific social roles such as playmate or workmate (e.g., Oden & Asher, 1977; Ladd, 1981). Based on findings from studies linking low peer status with later adjustment problems, these children were considered to be at risk and, therefore, suitable candidates for social skill training. However, due to recent efforts to classify children further into various sociometric types, there has been increasing speculation about the long-term prognosis of rejected (i.e., actively disliked) as opposed to neglected (i.e., moderately liked but ignored or friendless) children. Relying on past studies and epidemiological reports (see Michael et al., 1957; Morris et al., 1954) and research on the stability of children's status classifications (e.g., Coie & Dodge, 1983), several researchers (see Coie & Kupersmidt, in press; Conger & Keane, 1981) have argued that neglected children are less likely to experience adjustment problems in later life than their rejected counterparts, and are, therefore, less in need of clinical attention during childhood. Although this is provocative, it would appear that the available evidence on this issue does not yet warrent firm conclusions.

A third potential group of children that might be identified for social skill training are those who may be generally accepted but have no close friends. Friendlessness per se has seldom been viewed as a justification for social skill training. Hymel and Asher (1977) found that there are some children who are generally well accepted yet have no best friends in their class. It seems plausible that many of these children have best friends elsewhere. Still, there may be a group of generally well-liked children who have no best friends, that is, who do not form close relationships with peers. Data on the short- or long-term developmental outcomes of chronic friendlessness during childhood does not exist. However, as Putallaz and Gottman (1982) have noted, there is evidence to suggest that adults who remain friendless are at greater risk for psychiatric difficulties and, therefore, there is reason to be concerned about children who fail to form at least one intimate or close relationship with peers during childhood.

Clearly, in view of the limitations and scope of past research, it would be difficult to conclude that any of these childhood social disorders are insignificant. Most of what *is* known about the long-term consequences of these problems, however, points to a relationship between early peer rejection, in particular, and later maladjustment. Although this may be a valid justification for early detection and treatment of rejected children, it does not preclude the need to intervene on behalf of isolated/withdrawn or friendless children. Rather, it appears that the latter problems have been understudied and, thus, deserve more attention in future research.

In addition to problem severity, the issue of whether or not these childhood maladies are best treated with social skill training procedures also depends on the extent to which each may be considered a function of (i.e., caused or maintained by) "deficits" in children's social skills. However, determining the contribution of skill deficits to children's peer-related problems promises to be a difficult task. As Wanlass and Prinz (1982) have suggested, behavioral data on social withdrawal/isolation can be attributed not only to skill deficits but also to a variety of other factors, including fearfulness or anxiety, or orientation or preference for being with adults rather than peers (see Evers-Pasquale & Sherman, 1975). Similarly, research on the concomitants of sociometric status suggest multiple etiologies for problems such as peer neglect and rejection. The antecedants of friendlessness, although largely unstudied, are undoubtedly no less complex. Moreover, even in the instances where skill deficits may be responsible for a child's peer difficulties, the appropriateness of social skill training as a treatment method may also depend on the type of deficit involved (see later discussion of the antecedents of status).

In sum, research is needed to explore further the consequences of peer isolation/withdrawal, rejection, and friendlessness during childhood, and to test the assumption that these problems can, at times, result from deficiencies in children's social skills. As will be seen in the next section, some of the most convincing evidence concerning the relationship between skill deficiencies and children's problems in peer relations comes from research on the antecedents and correlates of sociometric status.

THE LINK BETWEEN SOCIOMETRIC STATUS AND SOCIAL SKILLS

Of the considerable number of studies that have explored the classroom as a social system (see Dunkin & Biddle, 1974), perhaps none have been as instrumental in drawing attention to the plight of children with poor peer relations as those based on sociometric methodology. Sociometric research has a long and rich history. Moreno (1934) is usually credited with creating the sociometric measure. However, his early use of this technique to study interpersonal attraction and group membership in institutional settings (i.e., correctional facilities, reform schools) was paralleled by several sociometric studies of children's popularity and peer status in public school classrooms (see Bott, 1934; Koch, 1933). Over the years, there has been continuing interest in the use of sociometric data to distinguish patterns of interpersonal attraction and group membership in the peer culture.

The Identification of Sociometric "Types"

From the early stages of sociometry, researchers have used the technique not only to identify patterns of liking or attraction among class members (Bott, 1934) but to classify individuals according to their position in the classroom-liking hierarchy (Koch, 1933; Northway, 1946). In the late 1950s Gronlund (1959),

elaborating upon terminology first used by Moreno, identified four different sociometric classifications or membership groups: stars, isolates, neglectees, and rejectees. In contrast to Moreno, however, who employed these terms to characterize an individual's social position or role within a group, Gronlund used these categories to describe specific types of children, as defined by their social standing or status among classmates. Stars and rejectees were defined as the children receiving large numbers of positive or negative nominations, respectively, from peers on a sociometric test. Children who received few nominations were termed "neglectees," and those lacking any nominations were called "isolates."

Recently, several investigators have begun to reexamine the distinctions drawn between high- and low-status children (Coie, Dodge, & Coppotelli, 1982; Gottman, 1977; Peery, 1979). The combined use of positive and negative nominations makes it possible to distinguish between neglected children (few positive nominations or negative nominations) and rejected children (few positive nominations but many negative nominations), and between popular children (many positive nominations and few negative nominations) and controversial children (many positive and negative nominations). Distinguishing between these four groups is proving to be extremely important. Rejected status appears to be particularly stable over time (Coie & Dodge, 1983); rejected children are most likely to report being lonely (Asher & Wheeler, 1983) and, as will be seen, the four groups exhibit distinct behavioral styles in both existing (e.g., Dodge, Coie, & Brakke, 1982) and newly formed groups (e.g., Dodge, 1983).

Searching for the Behavior Antecedents of Sociometric Status

There is a long history of research focusing on the behavioral correlates of sociometric status. This research, spanning five decades (e.g., Goldman, Corsini, & DeUrioste, 1980; Gottman, Gonso, & Rasmussen, 1975; Hartup, Glazer, & Charlesworth, 1967; Koch, 1933; Lippitt, 1941; Marshall & McCandless, 1957) has usually involved the observation of children in existing groups with the classroom being the predominant setting for observation. More recently, investigators have begun to study children's behavior in newly formed groups (Coie & Kupersmidt, 1983; Dodge, 1983; Putallaz, 1983), and to make use of specially arranged or analog settings to study behaviors and events of special interest (Coie & Kupersmidt, 1983; Dodge, 1983; Putallaz, 1983; Putallaz & Gottman, 1981). These studies have made it possible to study the emergence of status, the influence of important behaviors (e.g., aggression) that may occur infrequently in natural settings, and, most importantly, to draw more confident inferences about the causal relationship of behavior and status. Earlier studies of children's behavior in existing groups made it impossible to determine whether behavior was the cause or consequence of low status.

An examination of research in both existing and newly formed groups suggests several generalizations about the social behavior of high- and low-status children. A consistent pattern emerging across several studies is the relationship between prosocial behavior and sociometric status. For example, among preschool children, popularity has been found to be associated with friendly approaches to peers (Marshall & McCandless, 1957), nurturance giving (Moore & Updegraff, 1964), and giving social reinforcement. These same types of behaviors have been reported as predictors of peer popularity in samples of grade-school children (e.g., Bonney, 1943; Campbell & Yarrow, 1961; Coie & Kupersmidt, 1983; Dodge, 1983).

A second theme in the behavioral observation research concerns the styles of play exhibited by popular versus unpopular children. Research by Rubin and his colleagues (Rubin, 1982; Rubin & Daniels-Beirness, 1983; Rubin, Daniels-Beirness, & Hayvren, in press) indicates that popular preschoolers are more likely to receive social overtures from others, participate in group dramatic play and games with rules, and generally have higher levels of social interaction with peers. Behaviors that appear to be negatively correlated with peer acceptance include negatively toned peer interactions, immature or high-activity types of solitary play activity (termed solitary functional and dramatic play), and participation in rough-and-tumble play (Rubin, 1982; Rubin & Daniels-Beirness, 1983). More constructive forms of noninteractive but parallel play (i.e., engaging in similar activities in the proximity of peers) were found to be positively related to peer popularity at this age (Rubin, 1982). Furthermore, Rubin and Daniels-Beirness (1983) found that a similar pattern of relationships emerged when many of these same behaviors, observed during kindergarten, were used to predict sociometric status in first grade.

A third theme emerging from recent research by Putallaz and Gottman (Putallaz, 1983; Putallaz & Gottman, 1981) is the greater tendency of popular children to behave in ways that are relevant to their peers' ongoing actions. Thus, Putallaz and Gottman find that when children are attempting to enter a dyad that is engaged in a game, popular children are more likely to adopt the frame of reference of the group and say things that "fit in" rather than distract. That unpopular children may, in general, be poorer communicators is also suggested by several studies of children's referential communication ability (e.g., Gottman et al., 1975; Rubin, 1972).

A fourth feature of the behavioral interaction style of popular children is that they are more responsive when sought out by other children (Benson & Gottman, as cited in Putallaz & Gottman, 1981; Dodge, 1983; Gottman et al.,

1975). Indeed, studies sometimes find larger effects of sociometric status on "receiver" behavior than "initiator" behavior, suggesting that a main contributor to the maintenance of status is being responsive to overtures from others. In a related vein, Dodge (1983) has found that popular children have longer interactions than unpopular children. Even 6-to-9-month-old infants appear to exhibit large individual differences in their responsiveness to the overture of a peer (Lee, 1973).

It is also clear that unpopular children engage in various aggressive and disruptive behaviors that may lead to their problems with peers. This generalization holds true in the preschool (Dunnington, 1957; Hartup, Glazer, & Charlesworth, 1967; McGuire, 1973), elementary school (e.g., Dodge, 1983; Gottman et al., 1975; Ladd, 1983), and high school years (e.g., Lesser, 1959). Recent efforts at distinguishing between unpopular children who are neglected versus rejected have been particularly productive (Coie, Dodge, & Coppotelli, 1982; Coie & Kupersmidt, 1983; Dodge, 1983). In his study of group formation, Dodge found that boys who engaged in relatively high frequencies of antisocial behavior were seen by peers as aggressive and eventually became rejected by their fellow playgroup members. In contrast, boys classified as neglectees were viewed by peers as shy and were far less antisocial, exhibiting no more antisocial behavior than their more popular peers. However, neglected children did not start out in the groups by engaging in a reclusive or withdrawn style. Indeed, in the early sessions, their interaction rates were high, but they were more likely to engage in certain kinds of inappropriate behaviors (e.g., standing on tables). By the end of the eight play sessions their interaction rate became quite low. Dodge's findings not only demonstrate behavioral differences between rejected and neglected children, but highlight the dis-

tinction between the emergence versus maintenance of status. A study by Coie and Kupersmidt (1983) reached similar conclusions about the behavior of rejected versus neglected children and also yielded the remarkable finding that children's status in school correlates significantly with status in a new group of previously unfamiliar peers after only three 1-hour play sessions.

Research on Underlying Processes

Historically, research on the antecedents of status has focused on the overt behavioral style of children in their interactions with peers. Recent efforts, however, have been aimed at several process variables that might underlie children's ability to behave competently in social groups. These include children's knowledge of interaction strategies, children's goals in social situations, and children's confidence in their ability to achieve interpersonal goals.

Gottman et al. (1975) assessed the social knowledge of high- and low-status children by providing children with a role-play task in which they had to pretend that the experimenter was a new child and their goal was to make a new friend. The results indicated that low-status children were less knowledgeable about how to make a friend than were more popular peers. Ladd and Oden (1979), in a follow-up study, provided third-graders with several situations involving a classmate in need of help. Unpopular children's ideas were more unique (less normative) and often situationally inappropriate. Pursuing this line of research, Asher and Renshaw (1981) provided children with nine situations involving initiation or entry, maintenance of ongoing interaction, or resolutions of a conflict. Children's ideas were rated by "blind" judges in terms of the assertiveness and friendliness of each strategy as well as the likelihood that the ideas would be effective at solving each problem. Unpopular children's ideas were found to be less friendly and effective. No differences in assertiveness were obtained. Content analysis of strategies suggested that unpopular children's ideas were more aggressive than popular children's in conflict situations and vaguer and less detailed or sophisticated in initiation and maintenance situations.

The Gottman et al. (1975), Ladd and Oden (1979), and Asher and Renshaw (1981) studies are important because they suggest that unpopular children actually lack knowledge about how to behave in various social situations. Because these role-play and interview studies are conducted in relatively "safe" or nonthreatening situations, they tend to rule out the interpretation that low-status children know what to do but simply cannot execute appropriate behavior in real-life, more anxiety-provoking, situations.

A second, recently examined process variable is children's construal of goals in social situations. Renshaw and Asher (1983) have hypothesized that children might behave inappropriately or suggest inappropriate strategies on social knowledge interviews because of the nature of the goals that they pursue. For example, in a game situation, children must reconcile or coordinate the goal of winning with the goal of making sure that the relationship with the game partner continues to go smoothly. A child who focuses exclusively on the goal of winning at the expense of the relationship aspects of the situation may be one who is more likely to cheat, disrupt the game when losing, gloat when ahead, and the like. A child who exhibits these sorts of dysfunctional behaviors may have knowledge of how to behave more prosocially but fail to do so due to inappropriate goal-construal processes. Renshaw and Asher (1983) asked third- through sixth-grade children not only what they would do in several social situations but why. Using a typology based on the dimensions of asser-

tiveness and friendliness, Renshaw and Asher found both age and sociometric status differences in children's goals.

A focus on children's goals may be particularly helpful in interpreting the social relationship problems of unpopular educable mentally retarded (EMR) children in mainstreamed settings. In a review of literature on the social competence of the retarded, Taylor (1982) proposed that EMR children's goals are essentially avoidant in nature. Due to a history of failure in social situations, EMR children often behave as though their goals were to maintain a low profile and not suffer further "hurts."

The behavior of aggressive children may also be open to a goal interpretation. Dodge and his colleagues (Dodge, 1980; Dodge & Frame, 1982; Dodge & Newman, 1981) have found that aggressive children are more likely to perceive another's actions as hostile when there is ambiguity concerning intention. This tendency to attribute aggressive motives to others may serve as the basis for the aggressive child's actions toward peers. In situations where the intentions behind a peer's actions are unclear, aggressive children not only construe the peer's intentions as hostile but also act upon this interpretation by employing aggressive or retaliatory behaviors. It appears as if biases in the processing of social information are leading to aggressive and self-protective goals rather than to goals that would focus on maintaining harmonious social relationships.

A third process variable that has been considered is children's confidence in social situations. Goetz and Dweck (1980) conducted research from a "learned-helplessness" perspective on the attributions children make about their own failure in social situations. Children who attributed social rejection to personal incompetence showed greater deterioration in their strategies for beginning a relationship than children who attributed rejection to factors such as incompatibility or traits of the rejector. Furthermore, children who were low in sociometric status were more likely than popular children to attribute rejection to their own personal incompetence.

Wheeler and Ladd (1982) also examined the relationship of children's confidence to their status in the peer group. They developed the Children's Self-Efficacy for Peer Interaction Scale to assess children's perceptions of their ability to be persuasive in conflict and nonconflict situations. Significant correlations were found between feelings of self-efficacy and sociometric status in two samples of third- through fifth-grade children. In addition, children reported feeling less efficacious in the conflict than nonconflict situations.

In sum, the search for behavioral antecedents of status is now being accompanied by a search for social/cognitive and motivational processes that might underlie and give rise to individual differences in social behavior and sociometric status. Efforts in this direction have been fruitful thus far and hopefully will continue.

Social Skill Training and Unpopular Children

Further evidence concerning a link between children's social skills and their status or acceptance from peers comes from research on social skill training with unpopular children. Generally, these studies are based on the hypothesis that a lack of social skills is responsible for children's low peer status, and that efforts to remediate these "skill deficits" will result in increased popularity or acceptance (Asher & Renshaw, 1981; Ladd, in press). Evidence bearing upon this hypothesis comes from seven published studies in which investigators have created a training curriculum based on skills that were known to be correlates of peer acceptance, and have evaluated the success of the intervention in terms of children's gains in peer status.

The first study to explore social skill training as a means of increasing children's peer status was conducted by Gottman, Gonso, and Schuler (1976). In this small n study, the investigators used a variety of instructional techniques, including videotaped instructions, role playing, and training on referential communication tasks, to teach two unpopular third-grade girls how to give and receive positive interaction, make friends, and take the listener's role. Compared to two unpopular girls in an attention-control condition, the trained children evidenced significant gains on a sociometric play-rating measure, and these gains lasted 9 weeks after the intervention when a follow-up evaluation was made.

In a subsequent study, Oden and Asher (1977) individually trained low-accepted third- and fourth-graders in four broad classes of interpersonal skills (i.e., communication, cooperation, participation, and validation support). This training or "coaching" procedure consisted of five sessions, each of which was designed to teach children the four skill concepts, provide an opportunity to rehearse the skills in a play session with a peer, and provide a review session for evaluating the concepts once the child had tried them in the play session. Both behavior observations and sociometric measures were used to assess the progress of the trained children and children who participated in a peer-pairing condition (i.e., children who were paired with a peer for a play session but did not receive the skill training). Although both groups increased in the amount of time spent playing with their partner in the play sessions, only the trained children showed improvement in the play ratings from classmates, and these gains were apparent both at the end of the intervention and in a follow-up assessment conducted 1 year later. An additional control group of children who received neither coaching nor peer pairing remained quite low in status 1 year later.

Hymel and Asher (1977) investigated the effects of training unpopular third- through fifth-graders with one of three procedures: the Oden and Asher coaching procedure, a more individualized coaching procedure that emphasized specific concepts that particular children seemed to need, and a procedure that paired children with a peer for play but provided no instruction. The results of this study were unexpected in that children in all three groups made substantial gains in sociometric status at posttest and in a follow-up assessment conducted 6 months later. Because children in all three groups were selected on the basis of extreme scores and a no-treatment control group was omitted in the experimental design, Hymel and Asher were unable to ascertain whether the gains evidenced in sociometric status were the result of a regression artifact or possibly due to comparable treatment effects within the three groups.

Gresham and Nagel (1980) compared the effectiveness of a coaching procedure similar to that used by Oden and Asher (1977) to two other types of interventions: a method that entailed presenting each of the trained social skills in a narrated film (modeling) and a combined modeling and coaching procedure. Unlike Oden and Asher, Gresham and Nagel coached children in dyads and triads, rather than individually. There was a total of six sessions and, within each session, children participated in a sequence of instructions, rehearsal, and performance reviews for each of 11 different social skills. Gresham and Nagel also assessed changes in children's social status and friendships with a battery of peer-rating and nomination measures and observed children's behaviors in their classrooms. Children in all three treatment conditions improved in sociometric standing and displayed higher levels of positive interactions with classmates. Children in the coaching condition, however, as compared to peers in the other experimental groups, showed the great-

est decreases in negative interactions following the training.

In a skill training procedure developed by La Greca and Santogrossi (1980), low-accepted grade-school children first watched narrated videotapes of peers demonstrating various social skills and then verbally reviewed and discussed each one as a strategy for use with classmates. Children then engaged in guided rehearsals by role playing the trained skills, and these attempts to enact the skills were videotaped and later used to provide suggestions about how to improve their performance. Finally, children were encouraged to employ the trained skills in external settings, such as the classroom, and were asked to review and discuss the outcomes of these "homework assignments" in subsequent sessions. The results of this study indicated that, compared to peers assigned to a control group, the trained children made greater gains in social knowledge and skill performance and also had higher levels of interactions with peers in school situations. No differences were obtained, however, on a measure of peer acceptance.

In an effort to investigate further and extend the Oden and Asher (1977) procedure, Ladd (1981) trained three specific skills (i.e., asking questions, leading peers, offering supportive statements) with third-graders who were selected on the basis of low sociometric ratings and infrequent use of social skills in the classroom. Within the first six of the eight training sessions, the Oden and Asher procedure was used to promote an understanding of the skills followed by an opportunity for children to rehearse the skills in the company of their training partner with the instructor's supervision. The final two sessions were used to foster skill maintenance and generalization by encouraging children to initiate the skills independently in a seminaturalistic situation with both familiar and unfamiliar peers, and by reviewing instances in which the children had attempted the skills in interactions with peers. The training procedure produced significant gains on two of the three trained skills, and these changes were still apparent in a follow-up assessment conducted 4 weeks later. Furthermore, the trained children evidenced significant gains in sociometric status at the conclusion of the intervention and at follow-up. Similar changes were not found for subjects assigned to either an attention-control or a nontreatment-control condition.

The training method and assessment procedures implemented in a recent study by Bierman & Furman (1984) were similar to those employed by Oden and Asher (1977) and Ladd (1981). Unlike their predecessors, however, Bierman and Furman worked with somewhat older children (sixth-graders). Although significant behavioral changes resulted from this intervention program, Bierman and Furman discovered that with older children, it was also necessary to increase peers' involvement and participation with the trained children before lasting sociometric gains could be achieved.

Thus, four of the seven studies reviewed before provide clear support for the notion that children's social skillfulness and their social status in the peer group are closely intertwined. Further, the results of the Hymel and Asher (1977) and Bierman and Furman (1984) studies do not necessarily rule out this interpretation but may instead point to methodological artifacts or possible changes in the effectiveness of these interventions as children grow older. Only La Greca and Santogrossi (1980) failed to find changes in sociometric status along with the observed gains in social skills. This finding may be due to the fact that, like the Bierman and Furman study, a substantial proportion of the children in this study were older (fifth-graders) and perhaps were faced with peer groups that were less willing to allow them to change their long-standing negative reputations.

Another point about these studies concerns the type of assessment tools employed in them. The observed gains in sociometric status were obtained on rating-scale measures in which children rated (typically on a 1–5 scale) how much they liked to play with the other members of the class. Thus, the unpopular children who participated in the training gained in the average rating they received from classmates. In contrast, children did not gain, even when the training resulted in higher average ratings, on a nomination measure soliciting children's best friendship choices (e.g., Gresham & Nagle, 1980; Oden & Asher, 1977). There is a useful distinction to be made, then, between acceptance (average degree of liking by peers) and friendship (number of best friendship nominations received), and it appears that skill training studies are more successful when judged by the former rather than the latter criterion. This conclusion is strengthened by the results of a study by Siperstein and Gale (1983). In this investigation, learning-disabled children participated in either a social skill training condition or an adult-attention control group and were evaluated on both sociometric rating-scale (play- and work-with ratings) and friendship-nomination measures. Previous studies limited children to nominating their three best friends in class. Thus, it could be that children receiving training could not gain on this measure because their classmates were constrained by the limited-nomination method. Siperstein and Gale modified this procedure to allow children to nominate an unlimited number of "best friends" and then an unlimited number of "other friends." Results indicated that children who received social skill training gained on rating-scale measures of acceptance but did not gain on the best friends measure. They did, however, gain on the "other friends" measure. These results, along with prior evidence, suggest that participation in available social skill programs is promoting children's ability to establish meaningful acquaintanceships or "colleague" relationships. Whether different program content will be required to promote closer friendship relations is an issue for further research (see Asher & Hymel, 1981, for a further discussion of the acceptance vs. friendship distinction).

The research findings reviewed in this section and those that precede it provide a foundation and impetus for social skills training with children having peer-relationship problems. In the sections that follow, we shall consider issues that pertain to the further development and implementation of this methodology.

SOCIAL SKILL TRAINING METHODOLOGY

Decisions concerning the purposes or objectives of social skill training that, in turn, help to define the candidates and curricula must eventually be translated into effective intervention methodology. More specifically, this issue concerns the mechanics of social skills training, or the ways in which a training curriculum can be implemented to accomplish the training objectives. Although most investigators have typically viewed social skill training as a means of transmitting or strengthening various social abilities, past efforts to develop and define training methodology have been based largely on implicit theories of skill learning and instruction or post hoc explanations of behavior change.

Until recently, investigators, have relied on broad instructional concepts or learning principles (e.g., modeling, shaping, coaching) to distinguish between various intervention methods and account for training outcomes (see Asher, Oden, & Gottman, 1977; Conger & Keane, 1981; Wanlass & Prinz, 1982). For example, methods in which children are encouraged to observe adults or peers demonstrate specific social behaviors have been termed "modeling strategies," and are perhaps best exemplified by a line of research that was begun by O'Connor (1969, 1972) and extended by other researchers (e.g., Evers & Schwarz, 1973; Keller & Carlson, 1974; Jakibchuck & Smeriglio, 1976).

The operant-based concept—shaping—has been used to describe training methods in which researchers engineer the social environment so that children are likely to experience favorable social or material rewards for engaging in specific social behaviors with peers. Examples of training strategies that have often been referred to as "shaping" can be found in studies by Allen et al. (1964) and O'Connor (1972).

The third category, termed "coaching," has been used to represent a variety of training methods that have been designed to interface concept-instruction and behavioral rehearsal procedures. Among the various training methods to be found in the literature, those reported in studies by Gresham and Nagle (1980), Oden & Asher (1977), and Ladd (1981) probably best exemplify strategies referred to as "coaching."

Although this tripartite taxonomy appears to provide a useful way to categorize social skill training methodologies, a closer look at the actual manipulations that constitute the various procedures reveals considerable redundancy across methods (see Ladd & Mize, 1983). Furthermore, this framework is of little utility for such purposes as identifying the manipulations that comprise a given training method, determining the arrangement of these variables in the training sequence, and explicating the functions of these manipulations in children's skill learning and behavior change. Consequently, there is a need to develop explicit models of skill learning and behavior change from which effective skill training methodology can be derived and tested.

Toward this end, Ladd and Mize (1983) have proposed a model of social skill training/learning based on a cognitive/social learning explanation of behavior change. This model is based on the assumption that effective social functioning among peers depends on the child's (1) knowledge of specific interpersonal behaviors and their likely functions within interpersonal situations; (2) ability to convert social knowledge into skillful social behavior in interactive contexts; and (3) ability to accurately evaluate skill performance and performance-related outcomes and maintain or adjust behavior accordingly. Deficits, such as a lack of mastery or coordination of these areas, are thought to place the child "at risk" for interpersonal difficulties and would, therefore, be targeted for remediation. Thus, the principal objectives of skill training, according to this model, include (1) enhancing children's skill knowledge or concepts: (2) helping children translate these concepts into skillful behaviors; and (3) fostering skill maintenance and generalization in the social environment.

Especially germane to the topic at hand is the skill training methodology that Ladd and Mize propose for achieving each of these objectives. First, a social concept-instruction procedure, similar to that developed by Klausmeier and colleagues (see Klausmeier, 1976; Klausmeier & Goodwin, 1975), is proposed as a means of helping children represent and store skill-related information. This procedure consists of five basic steps: First, the social skill instructor attempts to establish a learning set or perspective that can be used to organize skill information and motivate children to learn skill concepts. This may include steps such as providing children with an advanced organizer (e.g., "Let's talk about some ways to have fun with other kids when you play games"); translating the concept into specific skills (e.g., "One

way to make a game fun for everyone is to take turns"); and pointing out the functional relevance of the skills (e.g., "When you take turns in a game other kids will have fun too and want to play with you"). Second, the social skill instructor tries to help children define the concept by aiding them to identify its attributes (e.g., "During a game, taking turns means giving everyone chance to play"). This step is intended to correct deficiencies and misconceptions in skill knowledge and eliminates the need for children to infer a concept's meaning from its exemplars. Third, the instructor provides or encourages children to identify a series of examples and counterexamples of the concept to illustrate various aspects of the skill and prevent over- and undergeneralization (e.g., "Yes, waiting until others have finished before you begin would be taking turns, but always trying to be first or stopping others from having a try would not be taking turns"). Fourth, to facilitate retention and allow the instructor to monitor children's understanding of the presented skill information, the learner is encouraged to verbally rehearse and recall the information they have abstracted from concept instruction. Finally, the social skill instructor provides feedback about the ways in which the learner's rehearsed conceptualization does and does not correspond to the concept attributes and exemplars presented during instruction. In addition to corrective feedback, the instructor may encourage the learner to consider the concept's relationship to other social concepts or its applications in alternative social contexts or settings.

The second training objective, helping children translate the instructed skill concepts into skillful social behaviors, is accomplished by having the learner initially practice the skills in a context where instructor supervision (i.e., response guidance and feedback) is maximized where potential interpersonal risks (e.g., peer ridicule or rejection) are minimized. During this guided rehearsal phase, the learner is provided with explicit performance standards and corrective feedback as a means of promoting skill refinement and elaboration.

Fostering skill generalization and maintenance—the third training objective—is intended to increase the learner's independence and control over both performance and evaluation. Skill generalization is facilitated by having the learner practice the trained skill(s) in a graduated series of rehearsal contexts that approximate naturalistic social situations. To promote skill maintenance, the instructor's supervision, which is at a maximum during guided rehearsal, is withdrawn as the learner becomes more proficient and able to perform the skills in peer situations. At the same time, children are taught to conduct realistic self-evaluations of both their own skill performance and performance-related outcomes (e.g., peer's reactions), and to adjust their behaviors in light of this information so as to increase the likelihood of obtaining desired social outcomes or goals.

Unlike previous efforts to define and organize social skill training methodology, this model has the advantage of a theoretical rationale for guiding the inclusion and arrangement of specific manipulations as well as the interpretation of the obtained effects. Furthermore, this approach makes it possible to dismantle the training method into component manipulations and, therefore, makes possible an evaluation of the functions that these manipulations may serve in children's skill learning and behavior change. Considerable empirical work is needed to validate the functions of specific training manipulations (e.g., determine whether various types of concept-teaching procedures actually enhance children's skill concepts) and to determine which types and combinations of training objectives (and corresponding manipulations) are needed to ensure skill learning or behavior change.

EVALUATING PROCESSES AND OUTCOMES IN SOCIAL SKILL TRAINING

To date, investigators have emphasized outcome evaluation in social skill training studies, especially behavioral and sociometric outcomes. As noted before, evidence is accumulating concerning the beneficial effects of direct instruction in social skills on children's social behavior and peer acceptance. What remains to be understood, however, is *why* these changes occur. In three papers, Asher and Renshaw (1981), Asher and Taylor (1983), and Ladd and Mize (1983) have speculated about several reasons why interventions based on skills training may be effective with socially rejected children. Among the hypotheses advanced are that (1) children are learning new concepts or principles of interactions (e.g., participation, cooperation); (2) children are learning specific behaviors that enable them to translate general concepts into action (e.g., a specific cooperative action in a specific game); (3) children are learning about the necessity to monitor or pay attention to their social interactions; (4) children are acquiring increased confidence about their ability to interact successfully with peers; and (5) children are acquiring new goals for social situations and peer activities (e.g., the goal of game partners having a good time together).

Research has begun on several of these processes, and there now are methods for assessing processes such as children's social knowledge, confidence, and goals. With further research it should become possible to determine whether children who change in behavior and status also change in terms of these presumably underlying processes. Indeed, as suggested elsewhere (Asher & Taylor, 1983; Gottman & Markman, 1978; Ladd, in press; Ladd & Mize, 1983), the key issue in evaluating therapeutic or educational programs is not simply whether children change, but why. Indeed, an important contribution in this area would be to relate changes in process dimensions to changes in outcome measures.

FROM RESEARCH TO PRACTICE: PRAGMATIC AND ETHICAL ISSUES

Until recently, social skill training with children has remained an experimental undertaking and has been implemented largely by researchers. However, as is reflected by the growing volume of literature on this topic aimed at educators and child and family practitioners (see Asher, 1982; Asher, Renshaw, & Hymel, 1982; Oden, 1980; Stocking, Arezzo, & Leavitt, 1980; Stephans, 1978), social skill training may become a widely used method for treating school-aged children's social difficulties.

As might be expected with any new intervention method, social skill training involves practical and ethical problems that must be carefully weighed and hopefully resolved before the approach becomes fully integrated into educational and clinical practice. Widespread use and acceptance of social skill training methods may depend on both the availability of certain interpersonal and environmental resources and the answers to some rather complex and controversial ethical questions.

Parents, Teachers, or Educators as Social Skill Teachers?

Social skill training programs will influence limited numbers of children unless they are adopted by persons who are routinely in a position to guide children's

social development or respond to their interpersonal difficulties. For reasons to be discussed later, parents, educators, and clinicians seem to be in the best position to act as teachers of social skills, even though their potentially unique roles and responsibilities may help or hinder their effectiveness in this capacity.

Over the course of development, parents are likely to be the most consistent caretakers in children's lives and no doubt have considerable impact on their social development (see Chapter 10 in this volume). A growing body of evidence from research on early attachment and child rearing indicates that, along with peers, parents play an important role in the socialization of children's social competencies (Hartup, 1979; Lieberman, 1977). In fact, Asher et al. (1982) have suggested that over the normal course of child socialization, parents may play many of the roles prescribed for instructors in social skill training programs. Parents, for example, may operate as designers–planners of children's early social experiences and may model or perhaps "coach" their children in specific social skills. Yet parents and the types of contributions that parents make to children's social development have not been well studied or utilized by those concerned with aiding children with peer-related difficulties.

By virtue of their potential as providers of long-term individualized instruction, parents have a distinct advantage over other socialization agents. Because parents are also seen in our culture as particularly responsible for children's social and personality development, they may also experience fewer role conflicts when performing this function than some other socialization agents. However, the advantages that parents may possess as social skill teachers may also be offset by several disadvantages. Many of the social skill training methods that have appeared in the literature (e.g., filmed demonstrations, adult rewards for peer interaction) may not be compatible with parent teaching styles and values, or the routines and contexts of family life. Furthermore, many of the existing social skill training methods call for information and procedures that may exceed parents' immediate resources and expertise. For example, some methods would require parents to have considerable information about their child's typical behaviors in peer settings (e.g., school) and to arrange extended rehearsal sessions with carefully selected groups of agemates. Finally, it is possible that children would be less receptive to direct instruction from their parents, especially if there is a history of negative interaction cycles. In such circumstances, children are likely to perceive instruction as punitive in tone even when the parent attempts to communicate in a supportive or neutral manner.

Classroom teachers are also likely to exert considerable influence over children's social development and, in fact, are more often recommended and utilized by researchers to implement social skill training (see Allen et al., 1964; Cartledge & Milburn, 1978; Evers & Schwarz, 1973). Classroom teachers serve many of the same teaching functions (e.g., designers–planners, models, coaches) as parents in fostering children's social learning and development, except that their contributions take place in an environment that is geared toward group instruction and academic outcomes.

Unlike parents, teachers are often at a disadvantge as social skill instructors because their involvement with children is often "diluted" over the many individuals that comprise a classroom and is often limited to time intervals of a year or less. Compared to parents, time spent teaching children social skills may also produce greater role conflict for teachers because many school systems and communities tend to define the educator's role strictly in terms of academic activities. Preschool and primary teachers are usually an exception to this rule because most early childhood programs emphasize or place equal weight on social objectives. However, there are also advantages to having teachers act as administrators of social skill training programs. Teachers have considerable background and expertise at implementing educational programs with children and are likely to be familiar with many of the basic principles of learning and instruction used in social skill training procedures. In addition, teachers work in an environment that provides both regular opportunities to observe children's behavior across a wide sample of peer activities and many of the resources needed to implement social skill training procedures (see Mize, Ladd, & Price, in press). For example, arranging for children to practice new skills with both familiar and unfamiliar peers (see Ladd, 1981) would probably be less of a problem for teachers than parents.

Finally, social skill training can be carried out by child and family specialists and mental health professionals based in schools, clinics, and community agencies. Professionals of this type tend to be problem or prevention focused and can be viewed as providing socialization support to children through either direct services (e.g., conducting social skill training with children) or consultation (e.g., helping parents and teachers develop and implement social skill training programs). Compared to classroom teachers, it seems likely that mental health professionals could operate in both of these capacities with little or no role conflict and, yet, possess an equivalent level of familiarity and expertise with the principles and mechanics of social skill training. Unlike teachers, they also have the time for prolonged 1:1 interaction with individual children. For clinicians, the disadvantage of providing social skill training as a direct service to children is that "therapy" of this sort is typically expensive (both in terms of time and money) and, therefore, often unavailable or short lived. Furthermore, when social skill training is implemented in a clinic setting, limitations are often placed on the instructor's treatment and evaluation procedures (e.g., availability of nonclinic peers for rehearsal sessions, opportunity to assess improvement in the "problem" context). Professionals working in school or community settings (e.g., school social workers, school psychologists, Y counselors, etc.) would seem to have the option of providing social skill training either as a direct service or through consultation as well as the interpersonal and environmental resources to do so effectively.

Ethical Issues in Social Skill Training with Children

On the surface, the primary ethical question to be addressed by proponents of social skill training is whether adults should attempt to influence children's social orientations, behaviors, and peer relationships. Yet, when framed in the context of child socialization, this becomes a moot question. To argue that adults should not influence children's social behaviors and relationships is tantamount to rejecting their role as socializers in this area of development. In fact, it is easier to argue that adults cannot avoid influencing children's social development and relationships. Rather, it would seem more appropriate to consider social skill training as one of many ways adults may choose to influence children's social development, each of which is likely to raise certain ethical questions, depending on the extent to which its purposes, methods, and likely outcomes are judged to be in keeping with humanistic social values.

A more substantial ethical issue concerns children's rights to understand the purposes of social skill training, and, on this basis, accept or reject the opportunity to participate in the intervention. This issue raises several thorny questions including whether children should be informed about the purposes of social skill training and whether they should be encouraged to take part in this type of intervention against their wishes, even if their parents and teachers approve. With regard to the first question, informing children of the purpose of social skill training has the advantage of maintaining honest communication between the instructor and the child and, in cases where children are aware of and/or troubled by their social difficulties, it may also provide an added incentive for skill learning and behavior change. One disadvantage of this approach, however, is that such information may also heighten children's awareness of their own social difficulties and possible foster lowered self-expectations or a self-fulfilling prophecy. Some instructors may consider this risk to be a sufficient justification for concealing the actual purposes of an intervention. For example, Oden and Asher (1977) told third- and fourth-grade children that they were, in effect, consultants and that the adult (coach) was interested in finding out what kinds of things made games fun to play. This provided a framework for discussing social interaction concepts and suggesting ideas for the child to evaluate in the light of his or her interactions with peers. All children accepted this rationale, and their special status as "consultant" may have even been part of the treatment.

The second question, that is, whether children should be allowed to contest their parent's wishes by refusing treatment, pits the rights of children against those of their parents, and is complicated by differences in their respective legal responsibilities and maturity levels. From a parent's perspective, it is clear that children do not always choose what is best for themselves and, thus, require the benefit of an adult's wisdom and guidance. However, there may also be occasions in which parent's decisions do not reflect the best interests of their children.

Our discussion thus far presumes that consent is required either on the part of the child or parent. Yet, it is quite possible that certain children will have serious behavior problems and be at risk in terms of later adjustment, but they or their parents would prefer that they not participate in special programs designed to enhance children's functioning with peers. An analogy with reading instruction may highlight the dilemma and the difference between the ways in which we think about academic versus social skills. Educators would not allow children to "opt out" of programs designed to promote reading skills; yet choice is allowed with respect to certain social objectives. The difference in attitude may be due to the clearer rationale for reading as a critical academic and life-adjustment skill. Also, there are well-accepted, "standard" educational practices for teaching reading. In the area of social adjustment, evidence is only beginning to accumulate about the role of social skills and peer relations in the long-term academic and social adjustment of children. Furthermore, these findings have not been widely disseminated to the general public or even the average educator. As for the issue of "standard practice," it has been noted that educators have no established body of practice in the socialization areas and that this poses problems in terms of teacher training and the meaning of professional behavior (Katz, 1982). Nonetheless, as successful studies have accumulated over the past decade, it becomes possible to see certain successful skill training methods as emerging. In the future, educators may have "standard practices" for providing assistance to children with or without the child or the parents' consent.

Finally, professionals involved in social skill training must develop guidelines for determining when the information they obtain from various assessment and training procedures is of a confidential nature, and how this information is to be handled. Presumably, much of the information that is revealed during the course of training about children's friends, peer reputations, and social problems is privileged, and there is a responsibility to safeguard this information. Children's involvement in social skill training may also be regarded as confidential information and, therefore, depending on the setting in which the intervention is implemented, may be disguised or withheld from classmates and nonparticipating school personnel.

Determining whether confidential information about children can be shared with their parents has become a difficult issue for many child and family therapists (see Margolin, 1982), and it may also pose difficulties for those who teach social skills to children. Although probably less of a problem with younger children, many preadolescents may be hesitant or embarrassed to have their parents learn about their social activities or difficulties in the peer group. In such instances, the social skill instructor's failure to insure confidentiality may engender a lack of trust on the part of the child and thereby impede the effectiveness of the intervention.

SUMMARY AND CONCLUSIONS

Social skill training is a relatively new area of research that promises to yield ways of assisting children with peer-relationship problems. The premise underlying social skill training research is that many children experience social difficulties with peers because of deficiencies in basic interpersonal skills, and they can profit from interventions that are designed to transmit and/or facilitate these abilities. The purpose of this chapter has been to review the background and impetus for contemporary research on social skill training with children and examine certain key remaining issues and problems. Hopefully, as social skill training is applied in diverse settings and with various child populations, there will be a continuing dialogue between researchers and practitioners concerning the feasibility, effectiveness, and ethics of this approach to aiding children who might otherwise be seriously at risk.

REFERENCES

Allen, K. E., Hart, B., Buell, J. S., Harris, F. R., & Wolfe, M. A. (1964). Effects of social reinforcement on isolate behavior of a nursery school child. *Child Development, 35,* 511–518.

Asher, S. R. Children's peer relations (1978). In M. E. Lamb (Ed.), *Social and personality development.* New York: Holt, Rinehart & Winston.

Asher, S. R. (1982). Some kids are nobody's best friend. *Today's Education, 71,* 22–29.

Asher, S. R., & Hymel, S. (1981). Children's social competence in peer relations: Sociometric and behavioral assessment. In J. D. Wine & M. D. Smye (Eds.), *Social competence.* New York: Guilford.

Asher, S. R., Oden, S. L., & Gottman, J. M. (1977). Children's friendships in school settings. In L. G. Katz (Ed.), *Current topics in early childhood education* (Vol. 1). Norwood, NJ: Ablex.

Asher, S. R., Markell, R. A., & Hymel, ·S. (1981). Identifying children at risk in peer relations: A critique of the rate-of-interaction approach to assessment. *Child Development, 52,* 1239–1245.

Asher, S. R., & Renshaw, P. D. (1981). Children without friends: Social knowledge and social skill training. In S. R. Asher & J. M. Gottman (Eds.), *The development of children's friendships.* New York: Cambridge University Press.

Asher, S. R., Renshaw, P. D., & Hymel, S. (1982). Peer relations and the development of social skills. In S. G. Moore & C. R. Cooper (Eds.), *The young child:*

Reviews of research (Vol. 3). Washington, DC: National Association for the Education of Young Children.

Asher, S. R., & Taylor, A. R. (1983). Social skill training with children: Evaluating processes and outcomes. *Studies in Educational Evaluation, 8,* 237–245.

Asher, S. R., & Wheeler, V. A. (1983). *Children's loneliness: A comparison of rejected and neglected peer status.* Unpublished manuscript, University of Illinois, Urbana–Champaign.

Bandura, A. (1973). *Aggression: A social learning analysis.* Englewood Cliffs, NJ: Prentice-Hall.

Bandura, A., & Kupers, C. J. (1964). Transmission of patterns of self-reinforcement through modeling. *Journal of Abnormal and Social Psychology, 69,* 1–9.

Bandura, A., & Menlove, F. L. (1968). Factors determining vicarious extinction of avoidance behavior through symbolic modeling. *Journal of Personality and Social Psychology, 8,* 99–108.

Bierman, K. L., & Furman, W. (1984). The effects of social skill training and peer involvement on the social adjustment of pre-adolescents. *Child Development, 55,* 151–162.

Bonney, M. (1943). Personality traits of socially successful and socially unsuccessful children. *Journal of Educational Psychology, 34,* 449–472.

Bott, H. (1934). Personality development in young children. *University of Toronto Studies: Child Development Series I,* No. 2.

Brody, G. H., Stoneman, Z., & MacKinnon, C. E. (1982). Role asymmetries in interactions among school-aged children, their younger siblings, and their friends. *Child Development, 53,* 1364–1370.

Buswell, N. M. (1953). The relationship between the social structure of the classroom and the academic success of the pupils. *Journal of Experimental Education, 22,* 37–52.

Campbell, J. D., & Yarrow, M. R. (1961). Perceptual and behavioral correlates of social effectiveness. *Sociometry, 24,* 1–20.

Cartledge, G., & Milburn, J. F. (1978). The case for teaching social skills in the classroom: A review. *Review of Educational Research, 48,* 133–156.

Coie, J. D., & Dodge, K. A. (1983). Continuities and changes in children's social status: A five-year longitudinal study. *Merrill-Palmer Quarterly, 29,* 261–282.

Coie, J. D., Dodge, K. A., & Coppotelli, H. (1982). Dimensions and types of social status: A cross-age perspective. *Developmental Psychology, 18,* 557–570.

Coie, J. D., & Kupersmidt, J. (1983). A behavioral analysis of emerging social status in boys' groups. *Child Development, 54,* 1400–1416.

Conger, J. C., & Keane, A. P. (1981). Social skills intervention in the treatment of isolated or withdrawn children. *Psychological Bulletin, 90,* 478–495.

Cowen, E. L., Pederson, A., Babigian, H., Izzo, L. D., & Trost, M. A. (1973). Long-term follow-up of early detected vulnerable children. *Journal of Consulting and Clinical Psychology, 41,* 438–446.

Dodge, K. A. (1980). Social cognition and children's aggressive behavior. *Child Development, 51,* 162–170.

Dodge, K. A. (1983). Behavioral antecedents of peer social rejection and isolation. *Child Development, 54,* 1386–1399.

Dodge, K. A., Coie, J. D., & Brakke, N. P. (1982). Behavior patterns of socially rejected and neglected pre-adolescents: The roles of social approach and aggression, *Journal of Abnormal Child Psychology, 10,* 389–410.

Dodge, K. A., & Frame, C. L. (1982). Social cognitive biases and deficits in aggressive boys. *Child Development, 53,* 620–635.

Dodge, K. A., & Newman, J. P. (1981). Biased decision-making processes in aggressive boys. *Journal of Abnormal Psychology, 90,* 375–379.

Dunkin, M. J., & Biddle, B. J. (1974). *The study of teaching.* New York: Holt, Rinehart & Winston.

Dunnington, M. J. (1957). Behavioral differences of sociometric status groups in a nursery school. *Child Development, 28,* 103–111.

Evers, W., & Schwarz, S. A. (1973). Modifying social withdrawal in preschoolers:

The effects of filmed modeling and teacher praise. *Journal of Abnormal Child Psychology, 1,* 248–256.

Evers-Pasquale, W., & Sherman, M. (1975). The reward value of peers: A variable influencing the efficacy of filmed modeling in modifying social isolation in preschoolers. *Journal of Abnormal Child Psychology, 3,* 179–189.

Freud, A., & Dann, S. (1951). An experiment in group upbringing. In R. Eissler, A Freud, H. Hartmann, and E. Kris (Eds.), *The psychoanalytic study of the child* (Vol. 6). New York: International Universities Press.

Furman, W., Rahe, D. F., & Hartup, W. W. (1979). Rehabilitation of socially withdrawn preschool children through mixed-age socialization. *Child Development, 50,* 915–922.

Goetz, T. E., & Dweck, C. S. (1980). Learned helplessness in social situations. *Journal of Personality and Social Psychology, 39,* 246–255.

Goldman, J. A., Corsini, D. A., & DeUrioste, R. (1980). Implications of positive and negative sociometric status for assessing the social competence of young children. *Journal of Applied Developmental Psychology, 1,* 209–220.

Gottman, J. M. (1977). The effects of a modeling film on social isolation in preschool children: A methodological investigation. *Journal of Abnormal Child Psychology, 5,* 69–78.

Gottman, J. M., Gonso, J., & Rasmussen, B. (1975). Social interaction, social competence, and friendship in children. *Child Development, 46,* 709–718.

Gottman, J. M., Gonso, J., & Schuler, P. (1976). Teaching social skills to isolated children. *Journal of Abnormal Child Psychology, 4,* 179–197.

Gottman, J. M., & Markman, H. J. (1978). Experimental designs in psychotherapy research. In S. L. Garfield & A. E. Bergin (Eds.), *Handbook of psychotherapy and behavior Change: An empirical analysis.* New York: Wiley.

Gottman, J.M., & Parkhurst, J. T. (1980). The development of friendship and acquaintanceship processes. In A. Collins (Ed.), *Minnesota symposia on child psy-*

chology (Vol. 13). Hillsdale, NJ: Erlbaum.

Goy, R. W., & Goldfoot, D. A. (1973). Experimental and hormonal factors influencing the development of sexual behavior in the male rhesus monkey. In *The neurosciences, third study program*. Cambridge: I. T. Press.

Gresham, F. M., & Nagle, R. J. (1980). Social skills training with children: Responsiveness to modeling and coaching as a function of peer orientation. *Journal of Consulting and Clinical Psychology, 18*, 718–729.

Gronlund, N. E. (1959). *Sociometry in the classroom*. New York: Harper & Brothers.

Harlow, H. F. (1969). Age-mate or peer affectional system. In D. S. Lehrman, R. A. Hinde, & E. Shaw (Eds.), *Advances in the study of behavior* (Vol. 2). New York: Academic Press.

Hartup, W. W. (1970). Peer interaction and social organization. In P. Mussen (Ed.), *Carmichael's manual of child psychology* (Vol. 2). New York: Wiley.

Hartup, W. W. (1978). Children and their friends. In H. McGurk (Ed.), *Issues in childhood social development*. Cambridge: Methuen.

Hartup, W. W. (1979). The social worlds of childhood. *American Psychologist, 34*, 944–950.

Hartup, W. W. Glazer, J. A., & Charlesworth, R. (1967). Peer reinforcement and sociometric status. *Child Development, 38*, 1017–1024.

Hops, H. (1982). Social-skills training for socially withdrawn/isolate children. In P. Karoly & J. Steffen (Eds.), *Improving children's competence: Advances in child behavior analysis and therapy*. Lexington, MA: Lexington Books.

Hymel, S., & Asher, S. R. (1977). *Assessment and training of isolated children's social skills*. Paper presented at the biennial meeting of the Society for Research in Child Development, New Orleans (ERIC Documentation Reproduction Service, No. ED 136–930).

Ispa, J. (1977). *Familiar and unfamiliar peers as havens of security for Soviet nursery children*. Paper presented at the biennial

meeting of the Society for Research in Child Development, New Orleans.

Jakibchuk, Z., & Smeriglio, V. L. (1976). The influence of symbolic modeling on the social behavior of preschool children with low levels of social responsiveness. *Child Development, 47*, 838–841.

Janes, C. L., & Hesselbrock, V. M. (1978). Problem children's adult adjustment predicted from teacher ratings. *American Journal of Orthopsychiatry, 48*, 300–309.

Katz, L. G. (1982). Personal communication.

Keller, M. F., & Carlson, P. M. (1974). The use of symbolic modeling to promote social skills in preschool children with low levels of social responsiveness. *Child Development, 45*, 912–919.

Klausmeier, H. J. (1976). Instructional design and the teaching of concepts. In J. R. Levin & V. L. Allen (Eds.), *Cognitive learning in children: Theories and strategies*. New York: Academic Press.

Klausmeier, H. J., & Goodwin, W. (1975). *Learning and human abilities: Educational psychology*. New York: Harper & Row.

Kobasigawa, A. (1968). Inhibitory and disinhibitory effects of models on sex-inappropriate behavior in children. *Psychologia, 11*, 86–96.

Koch, H. L. (1933). Popularity among preschool children: Some related factors and a technique for its measurement. *Child Development, 4*, 164–175.

Kohn, M. (1977). *Social competence, symptoms, and underachievement in childhood: A longitudinal perspective*. Washington, DC: V.H. Winston & Sons.

Kohn, M., & Clausen, J. (1955) Social isolation and schizophrenia. *American Sociological Review, 20*, 265–273.

Ladd, G. W. (in press). Documenting the effects of social skill training with children: Process and outcome assessment. In B. Schneider, K. Rubin, and J. Ledingham (Eds.), *Peer relationships and social skills in childhood: Issues in assessment and training*. New York: Springer-Verlag.

Ladd, G. (1983). Social networks of popular, average, and rejected children in school settings. *Merrill-Palmer Quarterly, 29*, 283–308.

Ladd, G. W. (1981). Effectiveness of a social

learning method for enhancing children's social interaction and peer acceptance. *Child Development, 52,* 171–178.

Ladd, G. W., & Mize, J. (1983). A cognitive-social learning model of social skill training. *Psychological Review, 90,* 127–157.

Ladd, G. W., & Oden, S. (1979). The relationship between peer acceptance and children's ideas about helpfulness. *Child Development, 50,* 402–408.

LaGreca, A. M., & Santogrossi, D. A. (1980). Social skills training with elementary school students: A behavioral group approach. *Journal of Consulting and Clinical Psychology, 48,* 220–227.

Lee, L. C. (1973). *Social encounters of infants: The beginnings of popularity.* Paper presented at the annual meeting of the International Society for the Study of Behavioral Development, Ann Arbor.

Lesser, G. S. (1959). The relationships between various forms of aggression and popularity among lower-class children. *Journal of Educational Psychology, 50,* 20–25.

Lieberman, A. F. (1977). Preschoolers competence with a peer: Relations with attachment and peer experience. *Child Development, 48,* 1277–1287.

Lippitt, R. (1941). Popularity among preschool children. *Child Development, 12,* 305–332.

Margolin, G. (1982). Ethical and legal considerations in marital and family therapy. *American Psychologist, 37,* 788–801.

Marshall, H. R., & McCandless, B. R. (1957). A study in prediction of social behavior of preschool children. *Child Development, 28,* 149–159.

McGuire, J. M. (1973). Aggression and sociometric status with preschool children. *Sociometry, 36,* 542–549.

Michael, C. M., Morris, D. P., & Soroker, E. (1957). Follow-up studies of shy, withdrawn children II: Relative incidence of schizophrenia. *American Journal of Orthopsychiatry, 27,* 331–337.

Mize, J., Ladd, G. W., & Price, J. (in press). Promoting peer relations with young children: Rationales and strategies. *Child Care Quarterly.*

Moore, S. G., & Updegraff, R. (1964). Sociometric status of preschool children as related to age, sex, nurturance-giving, and dependence. *Child Development, 35,* 519–524.

Moreno, J. L. (1934). *Who shall survive?: A new approach to the problem of human interrelations.* Washington, DC: Nervous and Mental Disease Publishing Co.

Morris, D. P., Soroker, E., & Burruss, G. (1954). Follow-up studies of shy, withdrawn children I: Evaluation of later adjustment. *American Journal of Orthopsychiatry, 24,* 743–754.

Newcomb, A. F., Brady, J. E., & Hartup, W. W. (1979). Friendship and incentive condition as determinants of children's task-oriented behavior. *Child Development, 50,* 878–881.

Northway, M. L. (1946). Personality and sociometric status: A review of the Toronto studies. *Sociometry, 9,* 233–246.

O'Connor, R. D. (1969). Modification of social withdrawal through symbolic modeling. *Journal of Applied Behavior Analysis, 2,* 15–22.

O'Connor, R. D. (1972). Relative efficacy of modeling, shaping, and the combined procedures for modification of social withdrawal. *Journal of Abnormal Psychology, 79,* 327–334.

Oden, S. L. (1980). A child's social isolation: Origins, prevention, intervention. In G. Cartledge and J. F. Milburn (Eds.), *Teaching social skills to children.* New York: Pergamon.

Oden, S. L., & Asher, S. R. (1977). Coaching children in social skills for friendship making. *Child Development, 48,* 495–506.

Patterson, G. R., Littman, R. A., & Bricker, W. (1967). Assertive behavior in children: A step toward a theory of aggression. *Monographs of the Society for Research in Child Development, 32,* 5.

Peery, J. C. (1979). Popular, amiable, isolated, rejected: A reconceptualization of sociometric status in preschool children. *Child Development, 50,* 1231–1234.

Putallaz, M. (in press). Predicting children's sociometric status from their behavior. *Child Development. 54,* 1417–1426.

Putallaz, M., & Gottman, J. M. (1982). An interactional model of children's entry into peer groups. *Child Development, 52,* 986–994.

Putallaz, M., & Gottman, J. M. (1982). Conceptualizing social competence in children. In P. Karoly and J. J. Steffen (Eds.), *Improving children's competence: Advances in child behavior analysis and theory*. Lexington, Mass.: Lexington Books.

Renshaw, P. D. (1981). The roots of current peer interaction research: A historical analysis of the 1930s. In S. R. Asher & J. M. Gottman (Eds.) *The development of children's friendships*. Cambridge: Cambridge University Press.

Renshaw, P. D., & Asher, S. R. (1983). Children's goals and strategies for social interaction. *Merrill-Palmer Quarterly. 29*, 353–374.

Rinn, R. C., & Markle, A. (1979). Modification of social skill deficits in children. In A. S. Bellack & M. Hersen (Eds.), *Research and practice in social skills training*. New York: Plenum.

Robins, L. N. (1966). *Deviant children grow up: A sociological and psychiatric study of sociopathic personality*. Baltimore: Williams & Wilkins.

Roff, M. (1961). Childhood social interactions and young adult bad conduct. *Journal of Abnormal and Social Psychology, 63*, 333–337.

Roff, M., & Sells, S. B. (1968). Juvenile delinquency in relation to peer acceptance-rejection and socioeconomic status. *Psychology in the Schools, 5*, 3–18.

Roff, M., Sells, S. B., & Golden, M. M. (1972). *Social adjustment and personality development in children*. Minneapolis: The University of Minnesota Press.

Rubin, K. (1972). Relationship between egocentric communication and popularity among peers. *Developmental Psychology, 7*, 364.

Rubin, K. H. (1982). Non-social play in preschoolers: Necessarily evil? *Child Development, 53*, 651–657.

Rubin, K. H., & Daniels-Beirness, T. (1983). Concurrent and predictive correlates of sociometric status in kindergarten and grade one children. *Merrill-Palmer Quarterly. 29*, 337–352.

Rubin, K. H., Daniels-Beirness, T., & Hayvren, M. (in press). Social and social-cognitive correlates of sociometric status in preschool and kindergarten children, *Canadian Journal of Behavioral Science*.

Rushton, J. P. (1976). Socialization and the altruistic behavior of children. *Psychological Bulletin, 83*, 898–913.

Schwarz, J. C. (1972). Effects of peer familiarity on the behavior of preschoolers in a novel situation. *Journal of Personality and Social Psychology, 24*, 276–284.

Siperstein, G. N., & Gale, M. E. (April 1983). *Improving peer relationship of rejected children*. Paper presented at the biennial meeting of the Society for Research in Child Development, Detroit.

Stengel, E. (1971). *Suicide and attempted suicide*. Middlesex: Penguin.

Stephans, T. M. (1978). *Social skills in the classroom*. Columbus, OH: Cedars Press.

Stocking, H. S., Arezzo, D., & Leavitt, S. (1980). *Helping kids make friends*. Allen, TX: Argus Communications.

Suomi, S. J., & Harlow, H. F. (1975). The role and reason of peer relationships in rhesus monkeys. In M. Lewis & L. A. Roseblum (Eds.), *Friendship and peer relations*. New York: Wiley.

Taylor, A. R. (1982). Social competence and interpersonal relations between retarded and nonretarded children. In N. R. Ellis (Ed.), *International review of research in mental retardation* (Vol. II). New York: Academic Press.

Ullmann, C. A. (1957). Teachers, peers, and tests as predictors of adjustment. *Journal of Educational Psychology, 48*, 257–267.

Van Alstnyne, D., & Hattwick, L. A. (1939). A followup study of the behavior of nursery school children. *Child Development, 10*, 43–69.

Waldrop, M. F., & Halverson, C. F. (1975). Intensive and extensive peer behavior: Longitudinal and cross-sectional analyses. *Child Development, 46*, 19–26.

Wanlass, R. L., & Prinz, R. J. (1982) Methodological issues in conceptualizing and treating childhood social isolation. *Psychological Bulletin, 92*, 39–55.

Wheeler, V. A., & Ladd, G. W. (1982). Assessment of children's self-efficacy for social interactions with peers. *Developmental Psychology, 18*, 795–805.

CHAPTER 10

Parents as Mediators in the Social Skills Training of Children

KAREN S. BUDD

Most theorists and researchers of child development agree that parents play a formative role in the socialization of children (Cairns, 1979; Martin, 1975). From early infancy, parents engage their children's attention and respond enthusiastically to the smiles, frowns, coos, and tugs through which communication begins. As mobility and language enable children to explore their environment actively, parents begin imparting countless lessons of how the social world works and the behaviors expected of children. These lessons are directed at helping children learn to become socially competent—that is, interpersonally perceptive, cooperative, self-assertive, friendly with peers, and not intrusive with adults (Lamb & Baumrind, 1978). This chapter examines the role of parents in the social skills training of their children. First let us briefly consider other issues, however, that bear on children's socialization.

Although parents influence their children's acquisition of social knowledge through the child-rearing process, peer interactions provide another medium for social development. Hartup (1978) contended that peer relations provide children with unique experiences not available within the family. Because of children's egalitarian relationship with one another, peer interactions introduce children to the give-and-take that is essential to socialization of aggression. He observed that some events, such as play, rarely occur in adult–child interactions, and when they do they are different in form than in child–child interactions. Besides teaching children how to survive among equals, peer relationships provide children with a context for meaningful comparison of themselves with others and with the opportunity for group belonging (Rubin, 1980).

During the past decade, there has been a reawakening of scientific interest in the social development of children (Asher, 1978). Investigations of socialization have confirmed that children vary widely in their interaction styles but that some patterns are noticeably more effective than others in gaining peer acceptance. Combs and Slaby (1977), in their review of the social skills literature, reported that high peer acceptance has been consistently found to be associated directly with measures of friendliness, participation, nurturance, generosity, and responsiveness in peer interactions.

The importance of social relationships in childhood is underscored by longitudinal studies showing that poor peer relationships in childhood are correlated with emotional and academic problems in later adjustment (Cowen, Pederson, Babigian, Izzo, & Trost, 1973; Robins,

1972; Roff, Sells, & Golden, 1972). Although these studies do not prove a causal link between early social difficulties and adult problems, they do suggest that children with poor social relations are at risk for continuing troubles. Both socially anxious (shy and withdrawn) children and antisocial (aggressive and disruptive) children have been identified as at risk; however, the latter group has a poorer long-term prognosis (Conger & Keane, 1981).

The area of social skills training emerged in response to a recognition of the enduring nature of social problems for children and adults. Based on the assumption that interpersonal problems result from deficits in a person's behavioral repertoire, behavioral interventions focus on teaching specific responses presumed to characterize social competence (Bellack, 1979; Hops, 1983). More cognitively oriented interventions focus on teaching an understanding of social rules and concepts thought to underlie socially competent behavior (Urbain & Kendall, 1980). Because of the current emphasis on peer relations as indicative of children's social competence, social skills interventions typically have occurred in settings such as schools or playgrounds where same-age children naturally congregate. Training usually is provided by teachers, counselors, professional therapists, or occasionally through instruction of target children's own peers.

Noticeably absent from the social skills literature is consideration of the role of parents in interventions for their children. Perhaps this omission results from a view of parents as peripheral to children's peer relationships, as lacking in social skills themselves, or as less adequate teachers than the typical providers of social skills training. There is some evidence to suggest that the difficulties unpopular children experience in making and sustaining friendships is part of a more complex set of interpersonal problems existing within the family (Allen,

1981). A longitudinal study of children's social adjustment found the home atmosphere in families of low-peer-status children to be characterized by greater conflict, disharmony, and irritation among family members, as well as more authoritarian child-rearing practices than in families of medium- or high-peer-status children (Magnusson, Duner, & Zetterblom, 1975). Another longitudinal investigation found that children's peer acceptance was positively associated with a number of family factors, including loving, accepting, and consistent child-rearing practices, and peer rejection was correlated with family dissent and conflicting child-rearing patterns (Roff et al., 1972).

Although the nature and direction of parent–child influence is unclear, children's difficulties in peer relationships may well be tied to socialization problems at home. Considering the integral role of the family in children's social development, there is reason to consider parents as participants in the social skills training of children. Not only would parents provide an additional manpower resource, but their involvement could be crucial to producing enduring changes in children's social behavior. Including parents in children's social skills interventions might facilitate healthier family social interactions as well.

The purpose of this chapter is to examine the potential of parents as mediators in programs to improve children's social effectiveness. The term *mediators* is used here to imply any form of planned interceding role by parents in social skills interventions. Of particular interest is the feasibility of behavioral parent training as an approach to teaching parents to fulfill the mediational role. The field of behavioral parent training has developed over the past 20 years of clinical investigations, in which parents have been employed as treatment agents for their own children's behavior problems (see reviews by Gordon & Davidson,

1981; Graziano, 1977; O'Dell, in press). Through the application of social learning principles, parents have been taught to influence a host of child behavior patterns. These are the same principles being used by teachers, therapists, and peers in social skills interventions. Can behavioral parent training equip parents to serve as social skills teachers for their children?

In order to answer this question, the present chapter explores the interaction between the fields of behavioral parent training and social skills training. Ensuing sections delineate the dimensions of social skills, survey existing behavioral literature in which parents have participated in training children to be socially competent, examine the advantages and disadvantages of involving parents in social skills training, outline mediational roles for parents, and propose issues for future research.

DIMENSIONS OF SOCIAL SKILLS

Before delving into the literature on parents' involvement in social skills training, it is important to examine more carefully what is meant by the term *social skills*. Dyadic interactions between the parent and child often are the focus of behavioral parenting interventions, with the aim of increasing children's compliance or decreasing tantrums, fighting, or complaints. Conceivably, all these interventions could be viewed within the guise of social skills because their goal is to increase harmonious relationships between the child and other family members. However, Foster and Ritchey (1979) have pointed out that a global, overly inclusive conception of social skills has limited practical utility, because it conveys little or no information about the particular child responses that are effective in interpersonal interactions. Rather, they argued that labeling a behavior as *skillful* requires that the be-

havior is somehow better than the myriad incompatible responses available to the child.

Deciding on a definition of social skills is not only problematic with respect to the parent–child literature. Virtually all reviews of social skills training with children (e.g., Combs & Slaby, 1977; Conger & Keane, 1981; Foster, 1983; Hops, 1983; Van Hasselt, Hersen, Whitehill, & Bellack, 1979) have been prefaced by a discussion of the inexplicitness of the term and lack of a generally accepted definition. Despite these problems, there are some recurrent features across reviewers' definitions of social skills. These features include (1) a focus on discrete, learned behaviors (with or without attention to underlying cognitive processes) assumed to relate directly to a person's global social competence; (2) a presumption that there are qualitative and situation-specific differences in social behaviors that mark them as skillful within a particular context; and (3) an emphasis on interpersonal effectiveness in gaining positive outcomes without infringing on the rights of others. As a working base, this chapter employs the definition advanced by Rinn and Markle (1979), who described social skills as follows:

[They are] a repertoire of verbal and nonverbal behaviors by which children affect the responses of other individuals (e.g., peers, parents, siblings, and teachers) in the interpersonal context. This repertoire acts as a mechanism through which children influence their environment by obtaining, removing, or avoiding desirable and undesirable outcomes in the social sphere. Further, the extent to which they are successful in obtaining desirable outcomes and avoiding or escaping undesirable ones *without inflicting pain on others* is the extent to which they are considered "socially skilled" (p. 108).

The specific behavioral components ascribed to the area of social skills vary according to researchers' interests, children's ages, and environmental contexts; few components have been validated empirically for their ability to differentiate socially competent children from less competent peers (Conger & Keane, 1981; Van Hasselt et al., 1979). With these cautions in mind, there appear to be three general categories of social skills targeted across investigations with children: (1) assertiveness (e.g., Bornstein, Bellack, & Hersen, 1977; Rinn & Markle, 1979); (2) interpersonal problem solving (e.g., Spivak & Shure, 1974; Urbain & Kendall, 1980); and (3) play and friendship building (e.g., Gottman, Gonso, & Rasmussen, 1975; Oden & Asher, 1977; Walker, Greenwood, Hops, & Todd, 1979). Examples of target behaviors in each category are provided in Table 10.1. For purposes of this chapter, studies focusing on more general response classes (e.g., compliance or appropriate behavior) were not considered, because these classes contain both social and nonsocial responses. Other studies excluded from the current review were those directed at decreasing specific antisocial behaviors (e.g., aggression, talking back, criticism) without targeting alternative positive behaviors as well, because social skills are defined by the presence of prosocial behaviors rather than by the absence of antisocial acts.

RESEARCH REVIEW OF PARENT INVOLVEMENT IN SOCIAL SKILLS TRAINING

The basic theme underlying behavioral parent training has been to enhance parents' skills at influencing children's behavior by teaching parents effective use of social learning principles (e.g., reinforcement, punishment, modeling, discrimination). Application of these principles to ongoing parent–child interactions has led to substantial changes in children's adaptive and maladaptive response patterns. Parents have been taught to treat their children's somatic complaints, fears, developmental and language disorders, oppositional behavior, and everyday behavior problems (Graziano, 1977).

Although parents have been infrequent participants in social skills interventions for children, there are reports in the behavioral research literature where parents were trained to modify reponses similar to those targeted in social skills interventions. Mediating roles played by parents in these studies include providing differential consequences to ongoing prosocial behaviors in family interactions, implementing instructional training programs for children in social behaviors, participating in family problem-solving interventions, and serving as adjuncts to social skills interventions in school or clinic settings.

Some of the early demonstrations of behavioral parent training (O'Leary, O'Leary, & Becker, 1967; Wahler, Winkel, Peterson, & Morrison, 1965; Zeilberger, Sampen, & Sloane, 1968) focused on increasing children's cooperative play or independent play while decreasing commanding, dependent responses, and/or sibling aggression. In these studies, parents were trained to implement differential attention procedures, often in combination with timeout for serious transgressions. Lavigueur (1976) later demonstrated that nontarget siblings could be included along with their parents as treatment agents in the home. He taught family members to use differential attention procedures to increase effectively target children's positive verbalizations, helpfulness, and positive affect and decrease negative verbalizations, aggression, and negative affect. The preceding studies involved parents as reinforcement agents for prosocial interactions, whereas another study focused on facilitating a different area of social skills—assertiveness. Patterson (1972) involved a parent in

TABLE 10.1.   Dimensions of Social Skills Training with Children

Category	Description	Sample Target Behaviors
Assertiveness	Forthright expression of one's feelings and opinions	Eye contact Voice volume Speech duration Request new behavior Deny unreasonable request State opinion Agree or disagree with other's opinion
Problem solving	Verbal strategies for analyzing and resolving conflicts	State problem Label own feelings Label other's feelings Identify other's perception Identify alternatives Describe consequences Plan actions to attain goal
Play and friendship building	Affiliative and conversational responses to enhance acceptance	Greet others Invite to join activity Ask for information Show approval Provide help Take turns Share materials

teaching a child to defend himself when attacked by his younger brother. In this case report, Patterson provided the child with brief instruction in assertion through a wrestling game and then requested the mother to reinforce assertive acts at home. No formal data were collected, but the mother reported treatment to be effective.

The previous studies suggest that parents can apply appropriate consequences to social behaviors identified as desirable or undesirable by an experimenter. In a few later studies, parents themselves were trained to implement instructional training programs for their children in social behaviors. Arnold, Sturgis, and Forehand (1977) trained the mother of a retarded adolescent girl to implement a program for improving her daughter's conversational skills. Through a sequence of shaping procedures involving instructions, prompts, modeling, and positive feedback, the mother taught the girl to encourage others to talk (by indicating interest, enthusiasm, and attention) and to ask on-topic questions in social conversation. Audiotapes of mother–daughter conversations during training sessions confirmed the child's acquisition of target skills.

In another parent-implemented training study, Matson (1981) employed mothers of three retarded girls as treatment agents for the girls' excessive fear of adult strangers. He taught the mothers to implement a participant modeling procedure so the girls would approach and speak to strangers upon the mothers' requests. Training was conducted under the artificial conditions of a clinic setting, but experimental probes of the girls' behavior in the home with parents of the girls' friends demonstrated generalized effects of treatment up to 6 months later.

A more naturalistic demonstration of parent-implemented training of social skills has been provided by Powell, Salzberg, Rule, Levy, and Itzkowitz (1983). Their study was directed at increasing the play skills (e.g., sharing, play organizing, assisting, and affection) of four handicapped children with their nonhandicapped siblings. As an exploratory condition following baseline, parents in the four families were instructed to do their best to get the children to play with each other. This condition had no effect on the children's play, despite all the parents having previously completed behavioral training in child management. Parents were then provided 3 hours of formal instruction in recognizing, prompting, and reinforcing play behaviors, structuring the environment to enhance play, and managing child problems during play. Training led to marked increases in play for all children during structured training sessions and, in three of four families, to generalized increases in play periods where parents were not present.

The investigations by Arnold et al. (1977), Matson (1981), and Powell et al. (1983) demonstrate that parents can do more than carry out appropriate contingencies for socially skillful responses. Parents can also train the responses through a variety of procedures, such as instructions, modeling, role playing, and descriptive feedback. Arnold et al. documented the mother's appropriate use of positive attention in training sessions, and Powell and his colleagues provided evidence of parents' increased prompts and praise during training. None of the studies examined parents' behavior outside the training setting, so the generalized impact of intervention on the parents is unknown. Together, the findings suggest that, at least within the confines of a structured training setting, parents are capable of teaching specific social skills to their children.

In addition to training parents to apply consequences and/or implement teaching programs with children, parents have participated in interventions designed to enhance problem-solving skills of family members (see Urbain & Kendell, 1980, for a review). Several of these studies in-

volved families of adolescents referred for delinquency or severe negative interactions (e.g., Alexander & Parsons, 1973; Blechman, Olson, Schornagel, Halsdorf, & Turner, 1976; Kifer, Lewis, Green, & Phillips, 1974; Robin, 1981; Robin, Kent, O'Leary, Foster, & Prinz, 1977). Target behaviors and treatment methods varied somewhat across studies, but a central goal in each case was to increase verbal communication strategies for resolving conflicts (e.g., specifying problems, listing options, stating consequences, offering compromises, and adopting agreements). Family members entered into contingency contracts to implement agreed-upon solutions.

The positive outcomes of these studies suggest that family oriented problem-solving therapy is effective in teaching family members to use alternative communication patterns; in some cases, long-term improvements in adolescent adjustment also have been demonstrated (e.g., Alexander & Parsons, 1973). Because parents in these studies were introduced to therapeutic procedures along with their adolescent children, it is not clear whether the parents could serve initially as trainers of these skills in the family. Considering the reported history and severity of parent–child conflicts and the possible contributing function of adult maladaptive response patterns, initial training by a professional therapist may be necessary.

Problem-solving skills also have been the focus of intervention for preschool children in a series of research investigations by Shure and Spivak (Shure & Spivak, 1978; Spivak, Platt, & Shure, 1976; Spivak & Shure, 1974). These studies do not fit neatly within the behavioral intervention context, in that they focused on cognitive processes rather than on discrete behaviors and did not consider the contingencies operating in the teaching process. However, they are included here because one study illustrates parent involvement in teaching a sequence of verbal problem-solving steps. Shure and Spivak's program focused on teaching children covert thinking processes involved in solving conflicts by prompting children to describe problems, label their emotions, decide on what else they could do to deal with the problem, identify the consequences of their actions, and plan actions to attain the goal. Although initial experiments used classroom teachers as trainers (Spivak & Shure, 1974), the curriculum subsequently was taught by the children's mothers at home (Shure & Spivak, 1978). Across a 3-month period, mothers taught their children to verbalize the problem-solving steps in diverse situations. Measures of children's responses to hypothetical analog situations and teachers' blind ratings of the children in preschool suggest that children can acquire functional skills when training occurs in the classroom or at home.

Another example of involving parents in problem-solving intervention was provided by Kelley, Embry, and Baer (1979). In their study, both parents of a 5-year-old boy had been taught to deliver appropriate instructions, differential attention, and time-out to increase compliant behavior, but the parents reported still being dissatisfied with overall family interactions. An additional "support training" package was devised, in which the parents were taught to negotiate conflicts regarding child management rules, support and enforce one another's instructions to the child, attend positively to each other in front of the child, and arrange enjoyable activities in which all family members could participate. At the same time, the experimenter held several sessions with the child to train him in giving appreciative comments and showing affection to his parents. Treatment resulted in increased positive comments between spouses and from the child to his parents. Reportedly, this intervention satisfied the parents' concerns regarding family relationships, although the function of the training package was not experimentally analyzed.

In the preceding studies of problem-solving interventions, parents had different roles, either as therapy recipients along with their children (e.g., Alexander & Parsons, 1973; Blechman et al., 1976; Kifer et al, 1974; Robin, 1981; Robin et al, 1977), as trainers (Shure & Spivak, 1978), or in a combination of these roles (Kelley et al., 1979). The studies suggest that parents may need training in their own social skills repertoire as part of the overall intervention.

There have been two reports in the research literature of involving parents as adjuncts to social skills intervention conducted outside the home. Walker, Hops, and Greenwood (1981) developed the RECESS (Reprogramming Environmental Contingencies for Effective Social Skills) program as a comprehensive intervention package for use with socially negative and aggressive children in kindergarten through third grades. School treatment included systematic training in cooperative behaviors, a response–cost point system, adult praise, and group-activity rewards for the target child and classroom peers based on the target child's performance. In addition, the child's parents provided praise and individual rewards at home when target goals were met at school, based on a reward menu developed jointly by the parents and school personnel. To date, the independent function of the home-based reinforcement component has not been evaluated within RECESS, but other applications of home-based contingencies have demonstrated the effectiveness of this strategy for increasing adherence to classroom rules and completion of academic assignments (e.g., Budd, Leibowitz, Riner, Mindell, & Goldfarb, 1981; Shumaker, Hovell, & Sherman, 1977).

Parents also have served as adjuncts

to social skills training in an outpatient clinic setting. Rinn and Markle (1979) reported training parents in general behavior management skills concurrent with training the children in four categories of social behaviors: self-expressive skills, other-enhancing skills, assertive skills, and conversational skills. Parents received specific consultation on the social skills responses being taught so they could reinforce these responses at home. Rinn and Markle provided no data on the parent aspect of training or the children's use of the skills outside the clinic, but the overall program was reported to be successful.

In private practice, Rinn* has continued to train children and their parents in the manner described previously. During behavior-management training, parents and children jointly contract to follow common rules of etiquette in conflicts at home. After children are trained in social skills, parents are instructed to arrange opportunities for the children to practice the responses at home. For example, parents deliberately break an agreed-upon rule (e.g., yell at the child or use derogatory labels) and, if the children are appropriately assertive in confronting the parents about the incident, they earn a reward. By structuring occasions for children to practice the social skills at home, the generality of training presumably would be enhanced; however, these effects have yet to be demonstrated empirically.

In summary, existing research provides preliminary evidence that parents can participate successfully in children's social skills training, at least in circumscribed cases. However, most of the interventions were directed at social interchanges between the parent and child or between siblings rather than at children's competence in peer relationships. Most also were quite restricted in the tar-

*Rinn, R. C. Personal communication, February 1983.

gert behaviors and situations to which training was applied. Parents' roles varied from serving as therapy recipients along with their children, to applying differential contingencies for prosocial and antisocial behaviors, and to actively teaching socially skillful responses under the supervision of a professional. Given the limited information available to date, many questions remain about when, how, and to what extent parents can successfully participate in social skills interventions.

ADVANTAGES AND DISADVANTAGES OF INVOLVING PARENTS

Using the research literature as a guide, several arguments can be made for and against parents' involvement in formal training programs for children's social skills. On the positive side, much research attests to the ability of parents to modify many important child responses through behavioral intervention. Treatment programs have called for parents to alter ongoing social contingencies to child behavior as well as to teach specific skills. The teaching function of parents in behavioral interventions is most evident in programs for developmentally delayed children where parents have trained academic, self-help, and rudimentary interaction skills using, in some cases, quite sophisticated curricula (Altman & Mira, 1983). Because parents have demonstrated their capabilities in teaching other aspects of child behavior, one might presume that many parents would be similarly competent in training children's social skills.

A second reason for involving parents in social skills interventions is a pragmatic one—to increase the effectiveness of treatment. Research in social skills training (Berler, Gross, & Drabman, 1982; Strain & Fox, 1981) and other areas of behavioral intervention (Stokes

& Baer, 1977) consistently has found that treatment effects are short lived in the absence of specific programming for generalization and maintenance. Strain and Fox (1981) noted that existing friendship networks in classroom settings and a history of negative contacts between target children and classroom peers inhibit transfer of training into everyday peer social interactions. Parents have considerable potential as generalization–facilitation agents, both because they are a powerful source of reinforcement and because they interact with children across many environments. Even when social skills training occurs outside the home, parents could be involved by providing reinforcement at home, based on children's performance of criterion skills in the training setting (cf. Walker, Hops, & Greenwood, 1981). Parents also could participate as adjunct trainers to social skills programs initiated in school or clinic settings. In these roles, parents could provide children with instruction, practice, and encouragement in using social skills in parent–child, sibling, and neighborhood interactions. At the very least, parents should be informed of the goals and rationale for social skills interventions, so they do not unwittingly punish new behavior patterns at home.

A third argument in favor of involving parents relates to the possibility that parent–child interactions contribute to the origin and/or maintenance of children's social difficulties in other spheres. Urbain and Kendall (1980) noted that family conflicts present numerous significant and possibly prototypic interpersonal problems for children. Longitudinal studies of children with poor social adjustment often have reported early difficulties in family interactions and childrearing practices as well (Magnusson et al., 1975; Roff et al., 1972). If children's skill deficits arise out of maladaptive social interchanges or inadequate training in the home, including parents in the treatment process could be critical to

producing enduring changes in children's behavior. Parent involvement would not only extend children's practice of positive social responses to the home but would also educate parents about socially skillful behavior.

Balanced against these aruguments for parent involvement are a number of potentially significant problems. One concern is. that the area of social skills training may simply be too complex for most parents to participate in it in an integral way. Researchers in the field themselves have emphasized the elusiveness of the concept and have yet to reach agreement on the behaviors comprising social skills (Foster & Ritchey, 1979; Van Hasselt et al., 1979). In addition, they have repeatedly stressed the importance of situational context in assessing skillful responding (Foster, 1983). If the area of social skills is, in fact, characterized by subtle and multifaceted discriminations that challenge professionals' capabilities, it may be unreasonable to expect parents to acquire and train the skills in short-term intervention programs. The findings of Powell and his colleagues (1983) that even parents who had completed behavior management training were unable to increase their children's positive play interactions without specific instruction underscore this concern. If only a minority of parents are competent to serve as social skills trainers for their children, there is little chance that these parents will be found in the families where children are most in need of help.

Another possible barrier to involving parents in social skills interventions concerns their motivation. In programs that focus on increasing children's compliance or decreasing disruptive behaviors, parents are primary consumers of the intervention. By contrast, in social skills training, children are the most direct consumers. Parents may be less aware or concerned about children's difficulties in maintaining friendships, asserting themselves, or resolving peer conflicts as long as the children are basically manageable at home. Some parents may even oppose fostering their children's independence and self-expression within family interchanges, either out of fear that these efforts would lessen their control or, conversely, that such training would intrude on the children's freedom of development.

A third potential limitation to involving parents in children's social skills interventions relates to their availability in the situations where training is needed. All adults, by their presence, naturally exert some controlling influence on children's conversations and activities. Thus, perhaps the most salient test of a child's social skillfulness occurs in unsupervised interactions with other children. For parents to participate in social skills training, they must become informed about the relevant target skills, arrange opportunities for the child to practice the skills in their presence, and then monitor the child's application of the skills in naturalistic situations. To the extent that children's social deficits occur in environments accessible to parents, participation by parents in training should be feasible. However, for problems that arise mainly in school situations or in unsupervised interactions, parent involvement necessarily becomes more indirect. Also, as Rubin (1980) noted, when parents do take on a training role, care should be exercised that their efforts to prompt and reinforce skillful behavior do not interfere with ongoing peer interactions. This same precaution has been voiced in reference to teacher-mediated programs, based on evidence that immediate teacher reinforcement of social responses actually suppreseed peer interchanges (Walker, Greenwood, Hops, & Todd, 1979).

The preceding discussion has proposed several rationales for involving parents in social skills training along with some mitigating concerns. The pre-vious history of successful parent-mediated interventions in child treatment, the obvious need for generalization programming, and possible parental contributions to children's social maladjustment support the value of a parent-mediated approach. Yet parents' effectiveness as mediators depends in part on their competence, motivation, and availability as social skills agents—aspects that have yet to be evaluated. Further research is called for to explore the feasibility of parent involvement and its contribution to social skills interventions.

MEDIATIONAL ROLES FOR PARENTS

Given the preliminary state of knowledge about parents' involvement in social skills training, the future possibilities are vast. Perhaps a useful starting point would be to describe some of the mediational roles parents could take and to identify some of the research questions to be addressed in evaluating their efforts. Based on the existing literature and common-sense extrapolation, there appear to be at least six potential variations of parent involvement in social skills interventions:

1. *Informed parent.* In this minimum-involvement role, parents receive information about a training program in which their child participates, but parents have no formal part in the training themselves. The types of information provided might include any of the following: a summary of the child's incoming strengths and weaknesses regarding social skills; the target social responses being trained; the rationale for teaching these behaviors; a description of the training curriculum and techniques; periodic updates of the child's skill acquisition; suggestions for how the skills could be practiced at home; and suggestions

for parent support and reinforcement of newly learned skills. Some information to parents probably is standard procedure for social skills programs in school and clinic settings, but the specific types of information provided and the effects of this knowledge on parents' interactions with their children have not been reported.

2. *Home-based reinforcement agent.* In this role, parents provide their child access to specific privileges at home, based on achieving citerion goals in a social skills program conducted elsewhere. This procedure entails having the teacher or therapist jointly plan a menu of home rewards with the parents and send home frequent (e.g., daily or weekly) reports of the child's performance so parents can provide or withhold reinforcement accordingly. Presumably, parents would also be informed of the training goals, rationale, and techniques, and they might receive informal suggestions on ways to extend treatment effects to the home. The RECESS program developed by Walker, Hops, and Greenwood (1981) included home-based contingencies as one of several components in a school-based treatment program for socially negative and aggressive children. Although the overall program was successful, the contribution of home-based reinforcement to outcome was not assessed. In addition to evaluating the impact of this treatment component on the child's social behavior in the training setting, it would be interesting to examine whether having parents implement home-based contingencies produces any generalized changes in parent–child interactions.

3. *Adjunct trainer.* Concurrent with social skills training in a school or clinic setting, parents could participate in training and/or maintaining target skills in the home. This model of parent involvement is a formalization of the "informed parent" role, with specific parent responsibilities spelled out as part of the overall treatment program. For example, parents could review procedures with the child that are taught in another setting and demonstrate how they can be adapted to family situations, arrange for regular practice sessions at home, and/or provide reinforcement for children's displays of target skills at home. Rinn* reported informally that he has paired clinic treatment for children with parent-initiated practice opportunities at home to prompt carry-over and support of children's social skills outside the clinic setting. As adjunct trainers, parents could be given only as much responsibility as is judged appropriate for the individual case, while still insuring some systematic parent participation. Thus, this role appears to offer the benefits of parent involvement in social skills training without the risks inherent in programs implemented solely by parents.

The idea of using parents as adjunct trainers is not new; they often have served as tutors of children's academic skills. However, application of the model to other dimensions of child behavior is less common. Recently, my colleagues and I developed and evaluated a joint therapist–parent intervention program for treatment of children's stuttering (Budd, Itzkowitz, Madison, George, & Price, 1984). In this program, parents accompanied their children and speech therapists to an intensive 1-week clinic to learn a method of stutter-free speech. While speech pathologists worked individually with the children to train fluent speech patterns, parents learned how to implement a home-based therapy program consisting of a daily conversational activity with the child, contingency contracts to encourage the child's practice throughout the day, and frequent social reinforcement. The positive findings of this program to date suggest that the joint

*Rinn, R. C. Personal communication, February 1983.

therapist–parent approach might be successfully adapted to training other child behaviors. In fact, a variation of this approach was implemented by my staff colleagues (Von Seggern, Itzkowitz, & Fabry*) to train children's social skills. Small groups of children attended weekly clinic sessions to practice specific social skills, whereas their parents attended concurrent sessions to learn reinforcement and generalization techniques. Although no formal analysis was conducted, the parents' enthusiasm for their involvement and their initial naiveté regarding social skills suggest that including a parent component in the intervention was worthwhile.

4. *Therapy participant.* If the primary focus of intervention is parent–child interactions, parents can be involved as recipients of training along with their children. This model is exemplified by several family-oriented problem-solving interventions reviewed earlier (e.g., Alexander & Parsons, 1973; Blechman et al., 1976; Kifer et al., 1974; Robin, 1981; Robin et al., 1977) in which all family members were taught positive communication strategies for resolving conflicts. In this variant of parent involvement, the parents are presumed to have some social patterns that require modification in order for intervention to succeed with the target child or adolescent. After initially participating as therapy recipients, parents may become qualified to take on other roles to further the child's social skills development. This model appears most appropriate in cases where there is concern that the family contributes integrally to maintenance of the child's social problems.

5. *Trainer–trainee.* In this role, parents receive supervised instruction in social skills via workshops, curricula, or training sessions, and they, in turn, implement the primary intervention with

*Von Seggern, B., Itzkowitz, J., Fabry, P. Personal communication, February 1983.

their children. This model was used by Arnold et al. (1977) to train communication skills, by Matson (1981) to train assertiveness with strangers, and by Powell and his colleagues (1983) to increase play interactions between handicapped children and their siblings. It presumes that, following their own training, parents are competent to teach the target skills and that training by the parents is sufficient to develop the social responses of concern.

The teaching-family model developed initially by Achievement Place researchers (Phillips, Fixsen, Phillips, & Wolf, 1979; Phillips, Phillips, Fixsen, & Wolf, 1974) provides a valuable technology for training adults to serve in a teaching role. As part of the teaching-family program, professional house parents carry out intensive teaching interactions with delinquent and predelinquent youths on a wide range of skills, including many social skills. The teaching interaction consists of the following steps: initial praise, description of appropriate behavior, description of inappropriate behavior, demonstration of alternative behavior, rationale for alternative behavior, request for acknowledgment, practice, feedback, and encouragement. This teaching sequence also has been included as a component in training programs for parents (Leavitt, 1982), but little research has examined parents' ability to carry out teaching interactions with their children. Given the complexity of many social skills, this model appears to offer a useful framework for training parents to teach desired social patterns to their children explicitly, and thus it deserves further experimental investigation.

A key question related to this model of parent involvement (and, to a certain extent, to all the models proposed) is whether parents need prior or concurrent training in behavior management techniques in order to serve effectively as social skills trainers. Considering that parents are responsible for maintaining the child's attentiveness and cooperation during training, they must be able to exert control when needed. If child compliance is problematic, parents probably would need training in child management techniques, although this assumption has yet to be empirically validated.

6. *Independent trainer.* Perhaps the most common, yet least studied, role parents play in their children's social skills development is as independent trainers. In this role, parents ascertain areas where their children appear to be experiencing difficulty and take it upon themselves to provide instruction in new skills. Training may transpire in informal conversations or through structured activities; its occurrence may be spontaneous or planned; and its effects could be productive or insignificant.

Parents who wish to acquire information on how to promote their children's social skills can avail themselves of some recent publications directed toward a lay audience, such as Stocking, Arezzo, and Leavitt's *Helping Kids Make Friends* (1979), Rubin's *Children's Friendships* (1980), and Zimbardo and Radl's *The Shy Child: A Parent's Guide to Overcoming and Preventing Shyness from Infancy to Adulthood* (1982). These books all offer highly readable condensations of research on children's social development along with practical suggestions for fostering greater social competence. However, whether parents can translate the verbal knowledge acquired from such books into successful training experiences for their children is another matter. So far, the research on bibliotherapy with parents has shown wide variations in parents' acquisition and application of child management information, with the necessity for additional training in many cases (McMahon & Forehand, 1979).

Another potential mechanism by which parents could train social skills independently is through children's literature. Story time is a favorite activity of many families and offers broad possibilities for teaching and discussing information within a play context. Sapon-Shevin (1980) provided teaching suggestions and several references of books and games appropriate for teaching cooperation to preschool children in school settings; these same materials would be relevant for parents. Additional print and media resource materials for training social skills were compiled by Cartledge and Milburn (1980). It remains to be seen whether parents can effectively train social skills by using storybooks as the medium. Parents probably would need to provide prompts, feedback, and reinforcement directly in social interactions to promote children's carry-over of concepts from stories into practice. Parents themselves may need assistance in how to structure and conduct the training for it to have a substantial impact.

FUTURE DIRECTIONS

A recurrent theme emerging from the preceding discussion of mediational roles for parents is the need for research to address the many questions existent in the area. The most basic question is whether a parent-mediated approach is effective in teaching children social skills. The earlier review of research documents that parent involvement can succeed, at least in circumscribed cases, but the parameters of successful outcome are not at all clear. Useful information for analyzing effectiveness would include measures comparable to those employed in school- or clinic-based social skills interventions (e.g., structured role plays, naturalistic interactions with peers, and sociometric ratings). Most parent-implemented treatment studies provided data only on parent–child interactions; however, Powell et al. (1983) assessed sibling interactions using a coding system adapted from classroom-based social skills research. Ideally, parent-mediated investigations should provide information on children's social skills both with parents and with other children.

If parent-mediated treatment is found to be effective, a host of follow-up questions become important. For example, which variants of parent involvemnt are successful? What are the necessary ingredients of training for the parents? What effect does training have on the parents, children, and parent–child interactions beyond those aspects specifically targeted in training? What prerequisite skills, attitudes, or resources must parents possess for them to fulfill a mediational role? What characteristics of the child (e.g., age, intelligence, general compliance to parent instructions) influence the feasibiltiy of parent treatment? How does the nature, severity, and location of social responses to be trained affect the choice of involving parents in intervention? How does parent-mediated treatment compare with other forms of social skills intervention in terms of effectiveness, convenience, and cost? Each of the preceding questions merits serious investigation if we are to explore fully the potential of involving parents in children's social skills interventions.

Another issue that bears consideration is the adequacy of parenting procedures typically trained within a behavioral approach for fostering children's social competence. Using social learning principles as a base, parents typically are taught to provide generous amounts of positive reinforcement, ignore mild misbehaviors, exert consistent consequences, and use instructions, modeling, and prompts to shape new behaviors. However, behavioral therapists are less likely to emphasize communication strategies and mutual problem solving between parents and children as ingredients of training. When social skills are at issue, behavioral parenting training might be enriched by adopting some of the techniques advocated by affectively oriented therapies (Ginott, 1965; Gordon, 1970), such as encouraging parents and children to listen to one another and to express their feelings. Likewise, some procedures of cognitively oriented parent training curricula (Dinkmeyer & McKay, 1976; Dreikurs & Grey, 1968), such as providing rationales, allowing children to experience natural consequences, and promoting children's participation in coflict resolution, could be valuable additions to contingency-management training. (See Greenspan* for a discussion of the contributions of various theoretical orientations to child rearing.) Some behavioral training programs do reflect a blending of techniques from different orientations (e.g., Alexander & Parsons, 1973; Robin, 1981); however, as a field, behavioral parent training has not stressed the communication and problem-solving dimensions. It would be useful to evaluate the benefits of incorporating these components into parent-mediated interventions for children's social skills.

SUMMARY

Because the family plays an integral role in children's social development, there is reason to consider parents as participants in the social skills training of children. The successful involvement of parents in other behavioral treatment programs for children, the clear need for generalization programming, and the potential parental contributions to children's social maladjustment support the value of a parent-mediated approach. However, parents' effectiveness as mediators depends on their competence,

*Greenspan, S. *An integrative model of caregiver discipline.* Unpublished manuscript submitted for publication, April 1984. (Available from S. Greenspan, Boys Town Center for the Study of Youth Development, Boys Town, NE 68010.)

motivation, and availability as social skills agents, and these aspects have as yet undergone little experimental evaluation.

Several research directions have been suggested for further examining the intersection of behavioral parent training and social skills training. Given the rapid parallel growth of the two areas in recent years and their promising contributions to children's healthy development, an integration of the two approaches is well worth investigating. To the extent that this effort succeeds, both parents and children stand to gain handsomely. However, regardless of the outcome of future research, parents inevitably will continue to influence children's social development by whatever means they know. Thus, there is reason to search for constructive and mutually rewarding ways parents can contribute to the process.

ACKNOWLEDGMENTS

I would like to express my appreciation to several friends and colleagues who generously shared their ideas and suggestions during my writing of this chapter. The thoughtful comments of Pam Fabry, Beth Von Seggern, Judy Itzkowitz, Steve Greenspan, Sharon Foster, and Stan O'Dell were especially helpful to me. I also am grateful to Steven Asher for his editorial suggestions on the manuscript. This chapter was supported in part by Project 405 from Maternal and Child Health Services to the Meyer Children's Rehabilitation Institute of the University of Nebraska Medical Center.

REFERENCES

Alexander, J. F., & Parsons, B. V. (1973). Short-term behavioral intervention with delinquent families: Impact on family process and recidivism. *Journal of Abnormal Psychology, 81*, 219–225.

Allen, V. L. (1981). Self, social group, and social structure: Surmises about the study of children's friendships. In S. R. Asher & J. M. Gottman (Eds.), *The development of children's friendships.* Cambridge: Cambridge University Press.

Altman, K., & Mira, M. (1983). Training parents of developmentally disabled children. In J. L. Matson & F. Andrasik (Eds.), *Treatment issues and innovations in mental retardation.* New York: Plenum.

Arnold, S., Sturgis, E., & Forehand, R. (1977). Training a parent to teach communication skills. *Behavior Modification, 1*, 259–276.

Asher, S. R. (1978). Children's peer relations. In M. E. Lamb (Eds.), *Social and personality development.* New York: Holt, Rinehart & Winston.

Bellack, A. S. (1979). Behavioral assessment of social skills. In A. S. Bellack & M. Hersen (Eds.), *Research and practice in social skills training.* New York: Plenum.

Berler, E. S., Gross, A. M., & Drabman, R. S. (1982). Social skills training with children: Proceed with caution. *Journal of Applied Behavior Analysis, 15*, 41–53.

Blechman, E. A., Olson, D. H. L., Schornagel, C. Y., Halsdorf, M., & Turner, A. J. (1976). The family contract game: Technique and case study. *Journal of Consulting and Clinical Psychology, 44*, 449–455.

Bornstein, M. R., Bellack, A. S., & Hersen, M. (1977). Social-skills training for unassertive children: A multiple-baseline analysis. *Journal of Applied Behavior Analysis, 10*, 183–195.

Budd, K. S., Itzkowitz, J. S., Madison, L. S., George, C. H., & Price, H. A. (1984, November). *Therapists and parents as allies in behavioral treatment of children's stuttering.* Paper presented at the meeting of the Association for the Advancement of Behavior Therapy, Philadelphia.

Budd, K. S., Leibowitz, J. M., Riner, L. S., Mindell, C., & Goldfarb, A. L. (1981). Home-based treatment of severe disruptive behaviors: A reinforcement package for preschool and kindergarten children. *Behavior Modification, 5,* 273–298.

Cairns, R. B. (1979). *Social development: The origins and plasticity of interchanges.* San Francisco: W. H. Freeman.

Cartledge, G., & Milburn, J. F. (1980). Appendix: Resource materials for teaching social skills. In G. Cartledge & J. F. Milburn (Eds.), *Teaching social skills to children.* New York: Pergamon.

Combs, M. L. , & Slaby, D. A. (1977). Social-skills training with children. In B. B. Lahey & A. E. Kazdin (Eds.), *Advances in clinical child psychology* (Vol. 1). New York: Plenum.

Conger, J. C., & Keane, S. P. (1981). Social skills intervention in the treatment of isolated or withdrawn children. *Psychological Bulletin, 90,* 478–495.

Cowen, E. L., Pederson, A., Babigian, H., Izzo, L. D., & Trost, M. A. (1973). Long-term follow-up of early detected vulnerable children. *Journal of Consulting and Clinical Psychology, 41,* 438–446.

Dinkmeyer, D., & McKay, G. D. (1976). *Systematic training for effective parenting.* Circle Pines, MN: American Guidance Service.

Dreikurs, R., & Grey, L. (1968). *A new approach to discipline: Logical consequences.* New York: Hawthorn.

Foster, S. L. (1983). Critical elements in the development of children's social skills. In R. Ellis & D. Whittington (Eds.), *New directions in social skills training.* Beckenham, England: Croom Helm.

Foster, S. L., & Ritchey, W. L. (1979). Issues in the assessment of social competence in children. *Journal of Applied Behavior Analysis, 12,* 625–638.

Ginott, H G. (1965). *Between parent and child: New solutions to old problems.* New York: Macmillan.

Gordon, S. B., & Davidson, N. (1981). Behavioral parent training. In A. S. Gurman & D. P. Kniskern (Eds.), *Handbook of family therapy.* New York: Brunner/Mazel.

Gordon, T. (1979). *P.E.T: Parent effectiveness training.* New York: Wyden.

Gottman, J., Gonso, J., & Rasmussen, B. (1975). Social interaction, social competence, and friendship in children. *Child Development, 46,* 709–718.

Graziano, A. M. (1977). Parents as behavior therapists. In M. Hersen, R. M. Eisler, & P. M. Miller (Eds.), *Progress in behavior modification* (Vol. 4). New York: Academic Press.

Hartup, W. W. (1978). Peer interactions and the processes of socialization. In M. J. Guralnick (Ed.), *Early intervention and the integration of handicapped and nonhandicapped children.* Baltimore: University Park Press.

Hops, H. (1983). Children's social competance and skill: Current research practices and future directions. *Behavior Therapy, 14,* 3–18.

Kelley, M. L., Embry, L. H., & Baer, D. M. (1979). Skills for child management and family support: Training parents for maintenance. *Behavior Modification, 3,* 373–396.

Kifer, R. E., Lewis, M. A., Green, D. R., & Phillips, E. L. (1974). Training predelinquent youths and their parents to negotiate conflict situations. *Journal of Applied Behavior Analysis, 7,* 357–364.

Lamb, M. E., & Baumrind, D. (1978). Socialization and personality development in the preschool years. In M. E. Lamb (Ed.), *Social and personality development.* New York: Holt, Rinehart & Winston.

Lavigueur, H. (1976). The use of siblings as an adjunct to the behavior treatment of children in the home with parents as therapists. *Behavior Therapy, 7,* 602–613.

Leavitt, S. E. (1982). *Active parenting: A trainer's manual.* Boys Town, NE: The Boys Town Center.

Magnusson, D., Duner, A., & Zetterblom, G. (1975). *Adjustment: A longitudinal study.* New York: Wiley.

Martin, B. (1975). Parent–child relations. In F. D. Horowitz (Ed.), *Review of child development research* (Vol. 4). Chicago: The University of Chicago Press.

Matson, J. L. (1981). Assessment and treatment of clinical fears in mentally retarded children. *Journal of Applied Behavior Analysis, 14,* 287–294.

McMahon, R. J., & Forehand, R. (1979). Self-help behavior therapies in parent training. In B. B. Lahey & A. E. Kazdin (Eds.), *Advances in clinical child psychology* (Vol. 3). New York: Plenum.

O'Dell, S. L. (in press). Progress in parent training. In M. Hersen, R. M. Eisler, & P. M. Miller (Eds.), *Progress in behavior modification* (Vol. 19). New York: Academic Press.

Oden, S., & Asher, S. R. (1977). Coaching children in social skills for friendship making. *Child Development, 48,* 495–506.

O'Leary, K. D., O'Leary, S., & Becker, W. C. (1967). Modification of a deviant sibling interaction pattern in the home. *Behaviour Research and Therapy, 5,* 113–120.

Patterson, R. L. (1972). Time-out and assertive training for a dependent child. *Behavior Therapy, 3,* 466–468.

Phillips, E. L., Fixsen, D. L., Phillips, E. A., & Wolf, M. M. (1979). The teaching-family model: A comprehensive approach to residential treatment of youth. In D. Cullinan & M. P. Epstein (Eds.), *Special education for adolescents: Issues and perspectives*. New York: Charles E. Merrill.

Phillips, E. L., Phillips, E. A., Fixsen, D. L., & Wolf, M. M. (1974). *The teaching-family handbook* (rev. ed.). Lawrence, KS: Bureau of Child Research.

Powell, T. H., Salzberg, C. L., Rule, S., Levy, S., & Itzkowitz, J. S. (1983). Teaching mentally retarded children to play with their siblings using parents as trainers. *Education and Treatment of Children, 6,* 343-362.

Rinn, R. C., & Markle, A. (1979). Modification of social skills deficits in children. In A. S. Bellack & M. Hersen (Eds.), *Research and practice in social skills training*. New York: Plenum.

Robin, A. L. (1981). A controlled evaluation of problem-solving communication training with parent–adolescent conflict. *Behavior Therapy, 12,* 593–609.

Robin, A. L., Kent, R., O'Leary, K. D., Foster, S., & Prinz, R. (1977). An approach to teaching parents and adolescents problem-solving communication skills: A preliminary report. *Behavior Therapy, 8,* 639–643.

Robins, L. N. (1972). Follow-up studies of behavior disorders in children. In H. C. Quay & J. J. Werry (Eds.), *Psychopathological disorders of childhood*. New York: Wiley.

Roff, M., Sells, S. B., & Golden, M. M. (1972). *Social adjustment and personality development in children*. Minneapolis: University of Minnesota Press.

Rubin, Z. (1980). *Children's friendships*. Cambridge: Harvard University Press.

Sapon-Shevin, M. (1980). Teaching cooperation in early childhood settings. In G. Cartledge & J. F. Milburn (Eds.), *Teaching social skills to children*. New York: Pergamon.

Shumaker, J. B., Hovell, M. F., & Sherman, J. A. (1977). An analysis of daily report cards and parent-managed privileges in the improvement of adolescents' classroom performance. *Journal of Applied Behavior Analysis, 10,* 449–464.

Shure, M. B., & Spivak, G. (1978). *Problem-solving techniques in childrearing*. San Francisco: Jossey-Bass.

Spivak, G., Platt, J. J., & Shure, M. B. (1976). *The problem-solving approach to adjustment: A guide to research and intervention*. San Francisco: Jossey-Bass.

Spivak, G., & Shure, M. B. (1974). *Social adjustment of young children: A cognitive approach to solving real-life problems*. San Francisco: Jossey-Bass.

Stocking, S. H., Arezzo, D., & Leavitt, S. (1979). *Helping kids make friends*. Allen, TX: Argus Communications.

Stokes, T. F., & Baer, D. M. (1977). An implicit technology of generalization. *Journal of Applied Behavior Analysis, 10,* 349–367.

Strain, P. S., & Fox, J. J. (1981). Peer social initiations and the modification of social withdrawal: A review and future perspective. *Journal of Pediatric Psychology, 6,* 417–433.

Urbain, E. S., & Kendall, P. C. (1980). Review of social-cognitive problem-solving interventions with children. *Psychological Bulletin, 88,* 109–143.

Van Hasselt, V. B., Hersen, M., Whitehill, M. B., & Bellack, A. S. (1979). Social skill assessment and training for children: An evaluative review. *Behaviour Research and Therapy, 17,* 413–437.

Wahler, R. G., Winkel, G. H., Peterson, R. G., & Morrison, D. C. (1965). Mothers as behavior therapists for their own children. *Behaviour Research and Therapy, 3,* 113–124.

Walker, H. M., Greenwood, C. R., Hops, H., & Todd, N. M. (1979). Differential effects of reinforcing topographic components of social interaction: Analysis and direct replication. *Behavior Modification, 3,* 291–321.

Walker, H. M., Hops, H., & Greenwood, C. R. (1981). RECESS: Research and development of a behavior management package for remediating social aggression in the school setting. In P. S. Strain (Ed.), *The utilization of classroom peers as behavior change agents.* New York: Plenum.

Zeilberger, J., Sampen, S. E., & Sloane, H. N. (1968). Modification of a child's problem behaviors in the home with the mother as therapist. *Journal of Applied Behavior Analysis, 1,* 47–53.

Zimbardo, P. G., & Radl, S. L. (1982). *The shy child: A parant's guide to overcoming and preventing shyness from infancy to adulthood.* Garden City, NY: Doubleday.

CHAPTER 11

Parent Education as Skills Training

GREGORY BROCK AND JEANETTE D. COUFAL

For millennia, child-raising techniques and methods have been transferred from one generation to the next through folk wisdom and modeling. In recent decades, the popular press and audiovisual media have become important sources of parenting information (Clarke-Stewart, 1978), and within the past 15 years a new and promising source of parenting education has taken form. Today, in addition to traditional methods, parenting education is being provided to small classes of interested parents who acquire more knowledge about their roles, gain new attitudes, and learn skills to change and enhance interaction with their children. As a result of the demand for parenting training, there has been a proliferation of programs and materials designed to help parents view the enchancement of their parenting skills as an attractive way to strengthen family life.

The purpose of this chapter is to provide an overview of parenting programs that meet the following criteria: social skills training methodologies are used; a group format is employed; the programs are currently available to the public; and they have been evaluated. Although the programs reviewed here have different emphases, there are common themes. These generic content areas will be identified. In keeping with the emphasis of

the book, the behavioral and social skills training components of these programs will be discussed as well as the competencies required of group leaders. Finally, the future of parent training will be summarized.

OVERVIEW OF EXISTING GROUP PROGRAMS

Although many parenting group programs have been designed, only a few use social skills training methods, and only a few have been experienced by many parents. Parent Effectiveness Training (Gordon, 1970) and Systematic Training for Effective Parenting (Dinkmeyer & McKay, 1976) are the best-known programs.

Making up a second tier of existing programs that are less well known and are more the product of active research enterprises are the Parent–Child Relationship Enhancement program (Coufal & Brock, 1983), the parent–adolescent form of the Relationship Enhancement family of programs (Guerney, 1977), and the behavior modification group of programs (Hall, 1983; Patterson, 1975). In addition, two programs that are eclectic in content and parenting philosophy will be reviewed, the Parenting Skills Training program (L. Guerney, 1978) and Parenting Skills (Abidin, 1981).

Parent Effectiveness Training

The Parent Effectiveness Training program (PET) is probably the best-known parenting program in the United States. Developed by T. Gordon, the program has been popularized by his books and by the establishment of a commercial enterprise that has provided training to over 400,000 parents (Gordon, 1976).

PET groups are taught by instructors who have attended a training seminar sponsored by Gordon's Effectiveness Training Inc. The parenting groups themselves are usually made up of no more than 25 parents. A variety of procedures, including lectures, modeling, videotapes, parent exercises, role plays, group discussion, and home practice are used to train parents in several skills over 8 weeks with 3 hours of instruction provided each week.

One aspect of the PET program that deserves discussion is the conceptual framework on which the program is based. Few other parenting programs are as fully developed in terms of a parenting philosophy as is PET. There are two pervasive concepts in the PET philosophy, and several skills are taught to actualize these concepts in everyday parent–child interaction. The concepts are *acceptance* and *democracy*. Parents are to communicate acceptance to their children through active listening and the avoidance of 12 roadblocks to communication. When a parent objects to a specific child behavior, another skill, I messages, is used to convey the parent's feelings in a nonevaluative and nonthreatening manner. If I messages do not result in acceptable child behavior, a conflict-resolution skill is used to reach a mutually satisfactory resolution to the issue between parent and child. Through the use of these skills, a healthier, self-esteem-enhancing type of parent–child relationship is produced.

Research evaluating PET has yielded overall mixed and positive results (Rinn & Markle, 1977). Many studies are flawed with research design problems, and only a few have been published. Among the studies that employ a control group, attitude outcome measures have been used almost exclusively. A majority of the controlled studies have used the Parent Attitude Survey Scale (PASS) (Hereford, 1963) to assess changes in parents' confidence, acceptance, trust, and understanding of their children as well as parents' sense of influence over their children. For the most part, PET outcome studies have shown changes on the understanding and acceptance subscales of the PASS (Hanley, 1974; Larson, 1972; Lillibridge, 1971; Schmitz, 1975; Schofield, 1979). Three other published studies reported significant gains for PET groups as compared with control groups on empathic communication skills (Hetrick, 1979; Therrien, 1979) and on egalitarian attitudes for parents and moral reasoning for their adolescents (Stanley, 1978). When compared with alternate treatments, PET has not demonstrated clear-cut superiority (Anchor & Thomason, 1977; Larson, 1972; Miles, 1974; Stearn, 1971).

Systematic Training for Effective Parenting

Rudolf Dreikurs, one of Alfred Adler's students, wrote *Children: The Challenge* (1964) with Vicki Soltz in which Adler's theoretical principles were extended and translated into practical guidelines for parents. This book has served as the foundation for several generations of parenting programs that have evolved into the currently popular Systematic Training for Effective Parenting program (STEP).

STEP is a neatly packaged program

designed by Dinkmeyer and McKay (1976). STEP groups meet for 8 to 10 weeks, 2 hours each week, and the sessions are made up of lectures, audiovisual materials, exercises, discussion, and homework. The objective of the program is to change parent attitudes and behaviors that result in parent–child power struggles. The democratic or open family system (Constantine, 1977) is promoted. An important principle is that a misbehaving child is a discouraged child, and discouraged children resort to goals of attention, power, revenge, and inadequacy. Parents are taught to use encouragement, effective communication, logical/natural consequences, and family meetings with their children.

As with PET, the research evaluating STEP has been limited and the results mixed. McKay (1976) reported significant and positive changes in parents' perceptions of child behavior, but no change in parent behavior was found. This lack of behavior change was also reported by Goula (1976). In an earlier study, however, Freeman (1975) compared an Adlerian mother study group (AMS) with a Traditional mother study group (TMS)—a group with no particular approach and a no-treatment group. AMS mothers were found to use fewer coercive strategies with their children than those in the other group. Also, the AMS mothers viewed their children's behaviors as less bothersome than control mothers. In other group comparisons, the results were unclear as to which treatment (AMS or TMS) was superior.

Parent–Child Relationship Enhancement

Whereas PET and STEP involve only the parents, the Parent–Child Relationship Enhancement program (PCRE) is organized around participation by parents, together with their children, ages 2 through 10. PCRE emphasizes relationship-building skills (empathic responding and nonverbal attention) combined with parent assertion skills (limit setting and I messages). As with other programs, the training is carried out over 10, 2-hour sessions. Group facilitators follow an instructor's guide (Coufal & Brock, 1983) that outlines the format and goals for each session and the training methods of discussion, modeling, role plays, exercises, and home practice. Unlike other programs, the skills are learned through play sessions that parents conduct with their own children, first during group sessions when the leader and other group members observe and give feedback, and later at home.

The play sessions are valuable for two reasons. First, play sessions may improve parent–child relationships by providing the often cited but rarely operationalized "quality time". The child is given the parent's full attention, and she or he is encouraged to be expressive and self-directed in play. The adult is empathic and warm but sets clear limits on unacceptable behavior. Second, play sessions provide a time and place for parents to practice the skills and to receive supervision in the use of them. Through learning to perform the skills at a high level, a parent is more likely to use them after the PCRE group has ended and in situations outside the play sessions, and thus generalization may be enhanced.

The philosophy and design of PCRE is derived from Filial Therapy, which was developed by the Guerneys to train parents to serve as play therapists for their own children who have serious adjustment problems (Guerney, 1964: L. Guerney, 1976). PCRE differs from Filial Therapy because PCRE is a time-limited parent education program, more structured than Filial Therapy, and it may appeal to a different group of parents who are more interested in prevention than remediation.

In an evaluation study, Coufal (1982) randomly assigned 94 parents to three groups: PCRE, an alternate skills training experience in which parents participated without their children (ST), and a no-treatment control group. The results of the behavioral measures showed that PCRE parents scored higher than ST and control parents on personal involvement with the child, acceptance and nonverbal affection displayed toward the child, and allowing the child self-direction. When parents were asked to write out their verbal responses to hypothetical parent–child situations, PCRE parents were more accepting than the ST and control parents, and both PCRE and ST parents were superior to control parents on I messages and nonaccepting responses. The findings suggested that including children in parent education may result in more effective skills training.

Parent Adolescent Relationship Development

The Parent Adolescent Relationship Development program (PARD) is one of the Relationship Enhancment programs developed by B. Guerney (1977) to improve family communication and problem solving and thereby enhance family and personal development. PARD is designed for parents and their children who are old enough (ages 10 and up) to express their own needs directly and to assume equal responsiblity for family interactions. Both parents and adolescents are systematically trained in expressive skills and empathic listening skills. In addition, participants learn to facilitate other group members' use of the communication skills and to carry out problem-solving strategies. Groups of six to eight members (three to four parent–adolescent pairs) meet for 10–15 weeks in 2-hour sessions. The training methods include modeling, cuing, reinforcement, feedback, and home assignments. With some PARD groups, follow-up booster sessions are conducted every 6 weeks for up to 6 months after the initial training has been completed.

Ginsberg (1977) evaluated PARD with 58 fathers and their teenage sons randomly assigned to a PARD or a waiting list control group. The PARD group showed greater improvement than controls on behavioral measures of communication (expressive and empathic skills), and self-report measures of general communication, quality of relationship, and self-concept. In a large study, Guerney, Coufal and Vogelsong (1981) evaluated PARD with a population of 108 middle- and low-income mothers and adolescent daughters randomly assigned to PARD, a traditional discussion group, and a no-treatment control group. The findings showed the PARD group to be superior to the discussion and control group on indexes of specific communication skills, general communication patterns, and relationship quality. In a 6-month follow-up to this study, Guerney, Vogelsong, and Coufal (1983) found PARD participants maintained and increased their gains on the preceding three variables over the follow-up period, whereas the traditional discussion and control groups did not. These results at posttest and follow-up were attributed to the skills training administered to the PARD group.

Behavioral programs

The programs that fit into the category of behavioral programs are quite different from those described previously. Behavioral programs tend to be designed to train parents in the methodology of behavior modification, and the outcome tends to be change in some specific troublesome behavior exibited by a child. PET, STEP, PCRE, and PARD, on the other hand, are more general in that there is an attempt to impart a child-rearing philosophy to the parent who participates in the program. Behavioral programs could be said to be more value free than those previously reviewed; the training provides the methods, and the parent determines what behaviors they wish to reinforce, model, or change.

Applying behavior change methods based on social learning theory to parental concerns was popularized by G. Patterson beginning in the 1960s. In 1965, the Oregon Social Learning Project was organized to develop an empirically based, low-cost treatment for use with families of aggressive and predelinquent children. Each family was supplied with individual services that consisted of providing a programmed text for parents to read on the principles and applications of social learning theory, training in observation and data collection, role playing of family interaction situations, and then parents implementing the procedures at home. The effectiveness of the training was evaluated and found successful in decreasing deviant child behavior and in maintaining treatment gains (Patterson, Ray, & Shaw, 1968). These positive results led to the refinement of the training procedures, expansion of program content, and the development of a group approach to training.

The group approach developed by Patterson and his associates is carried out over a 10-week period with one training session each week. In the first session, parents are taught to observe and record problem child behaviors, and parents use these skills over the first 6 weeks of the treatment. Social and tangible-reward methods are trained in session 2 through the use of videotapes. Time-out as a method of behavior control is presented via videotape in session 3, and in session 4 parents are taught data-tracking procedures for use in evaluating their behavior change efforts. In session 5, parents present their behavior change program to their group for critique and discussion. The remainder of the sessions consists of training in be-

havior change strategies: attending and ignoring, shaping, problem solving, contingency contracting, and fading. For all these topics, role play, videotaped modeling, and discussion make up the training.

Evaluation of Patterson's time-limited, group training approach has shown it to be quite effective as a treatment for socially aggressive child behavior. The latest research work completed at the Oregon Social Learning Center (Patterson, Chamberlain, & Reid, 1982) was a study designed to control for variables other then those directly related to the treatment (e.g., regression, testing, expectancy of improvement, and maturation). The results of this study and that of two others (Walter & Gilmore, 1973; Wiltz & Patterson, 1974) showed that, as a result of treatment, actual changes in child behavior occurred; the changes were reliable across treatment groups and therapists; and the social learning approach was more effective than traditional family therapy.

One behavioral group program that has reached a large number of parents is the Responsive Parenting (RP) program (Hall 1983). A unique aspect of RP is that parents learn behavioral principles by undertaking a home project that involves establishing a baseline for one of their child's problematic behaviors, responding to that behavior in a specific way, and then stopping the parent response so the parent can understand his/her impact on the child's behavior. Another innovative feature is that parents who have previously participated in RP are selected and trained as group leaders. Over 3000 parents in the Shawnee Mission Kansas School District have received RP training, and it is now widely disseminated in other states.

In a 5 year study partially supported by the National Institutes of Mental Health, Hall (1983) found that the parents' individual behavior change projects consistently indicated positive changes in child target behaviors. On two pre-post mea-sures—the Walker Problem Identifica-tion Checklist and the Parent Evaluation Survey—the RP group showed signifi-cant changes as compared to those found in a control group.

Eclectic Programs

Some parenting skills programs embrace several theories and types of skills taught to parents. Two examples of these pro-grams are L. Guerney's Parenting Skills Training program (1978) and R. Abidin's Parenting Skills program (1981).

L. Guerney's Parenting Skills Train-ing program is an adaptation of the Fos-ter Parent Training program (1975) that she developed for the Pennsylvania Bu-reau of Children and Youth. The pro-gram is conducted over a 9-week period, 2 hours each session, and training is pro-vided in the areas of understanding child development, communication skills, changing the environment, setting limits, consequences, reinforcement, and skills in-tegration. The session devoted to under-standing child development is unique to parenting training programs because most parenting skills programs neglect develop-mental theory.

The program has been evaluated with foster parents of children aged 5 to 12 (L. Guerney, 1977). Using a pre-post, control group design, the skills training group displayed more accepting attitudes toward children, and they used more de-sirable parenting responses than the con-trols. An adaptation of the Parenting Skills Training program for use as a drug abuse prevention program (D'Augelli & Weener, 1976, 1978) was evaluated using a treatment ($n = 37$ parents) and control group ($n = 21$ parents) design. Parents in the treatment group increased their use of effective responses to drug-dilemma situations, whereas the control group demonstrated no change.

Abidin's Parenting Skills (1981) pro-gram represents a blend of concepts and skills from three theoretical orientations: humanistic, behavior change, and ra-tional emotive psychology. The basic course consists of 19 units that cover self-esteem, evaluating one's parent–child relationship, communication, be-havior change methods, and parent cog-nitive change methods. Abidin suggests several combinations of the 19 units to create shorter, less comprehensive pro-grams. Each 2-hour session consists of three parts: review of the past week's home practice, the teaching of the new lesson, and discussion of how the new ideas relate to each parent's situation. Cantor (1976) offered a 10-week version of Abidin's program containing behav-ioral and relationship-building skills to parents of high-risk first-graders. When compared with the control group, par-ents' perceptions of their children's gains in school adjustment approached significance. The parents' satisfaction with the program, attendance, and homework completion was high and comparable to results obtained with PET.

It is clear from the preceding program descriptions that different programs have different emphases of content and philosophy. A commonality of content among programs does exist, however, and in the next section the generic areas of program content will be discussed.

GENERIC PROGRAM CONTENTS

When the actual training content of the presently available programs is exam-ined, five areas of training emerge: com-munication skills, skills in environmental planning, parent change skills, skills in changing the child, and skills in family change or problem solving. All of the areas would be covered in a comprehen-sive or eclectic program. A noneclectic or theory-bound program would empha-size one or several of the preceding areas over others. For example, PET emphasizes communications skills, whereas the Responsive Parenting program focuses on changing parent and child behaviors. The content area(s) emphasized in a program indicate the value system or parenting assumptions made by a program designer.

Communication Skills

Nearly every parenting program addresses the topic of communication in some way. The programs choosing this emphasis usually operationalize communication as the effective performance of two skills—speaking and listening. The listening skill has been labeled variously as "empathy" (Briggs, 1970), "reflective listening" (L. Guerney, 1978), "mirroring" (Ginott, 1965), and "empathic responding" (Guerney, 1977). No matter what it is called, listening is defined by the acts of conveying attention, processing speaker messages, and then communicating understanding of those messages. The speaking skill has been labeled "I messages" (Gordon, 1970) and "parent messages" (L. Guerney, 1978), both of which refer to honest disclosure by the parent of his/her feelings and needs regarding a child's behavior. Both skills are products of the ongoing operationalization of effective interpersonal relations that has comprised much of the social-psychological and family studies research over the past three decades.

Skills in Planning The Environment

An area often overlooked as a way to enhance parent–child relations is planning the environment. Many conflicts can be avoided by enriching a child's surroundings to prevent mischief and boredom, reducing stimulation before quiet times, child proofing for safety, substituting one activity for another, and planning ahead for events and changes. Such child guidance methods that make up part of PET and the Parenting Skills Training pro-

gram are potentially powerful ways to influence child behavior and prevent problems, but they are perhaps not emphasized enough in parenting programs. With many programs, for example, planning the environment is discussed by a group of parents to increase their awareness, but this discussion is not accompanied with behavioral rehearsal of such skills as redirecting a child's attention. Unfortunately, the limited time and sessions that parents will allot to parenting training often force program designers to take shortcuts by covering material through discussion methods rather than by the modeling, training, and practice sequence that is specified later in this chapter.

Parent Self-Change

Upon being asked what they want from a program, parents often request training in how to change their child. This is certainly an important knowledge and skills area for parents, but several programs also include methods that parents can use to change themselves. The goal of this segment of a program is to broaden parents' perspective on problem solving to include the possibility of self-change, in addition to changing their child.

One approach to training parent self-change consists of helping parents understand the stages of child development (Dodson, 1974; Gesell & Ilg, 1943) and relating these stages to parents' expectations. Briggs (1970) warns parents that unrealistic expectations may damage children's self-esteem. Encouraging parents to make their implicit expectations explicit is a first step. Also, helping parents to compare notes with other parents can lead them to develop more realistic attitudes about what their child is able and unable to do.

Abidin (1981) described a second approach to parent change that is an interesting application of rational emotive therapy. He urges parents to change their "self-talk" from nonsense to sensible statements because our reactions and feelings are caused primarily by what we tell ourselves about a situation. As an example, consider the mother who is having a party for adults at her home. Suddenly, her 5 year-old son who has been playing by himself says to his mother in front of her guests, "I hate you! These people are just a bunch of old stink bugs!" The mother can react with nonsense self-talk such as, "He doesn't love me. The others will think I am a bad mother," or she can think in a more sensible fashion: "Poor kid, he's feeling ignored. Nevertheless, I'm going to have to show him a better way to get my attention." Her feelings and reactions differ according to her self-talk.

A third self-change approach is for parents to apply the behavior management process discussed in the next section to themselves. Watson and Tharp (1977) provide guidance in such self-modification methods.

Changing the Child

Many of the behavior management skills fit into this component of a parenting program. These skills include the following:

1. Clearly defining the inappropriate child behavior (the problem).
2. Clearly defining the desired behavior (the goal).
3. Observing and recording the child's present behavior.
4. Methods of maintaining and developing desirable behavior (reinforcement, shaping, and modeling).
5. Methods of stopping inappropriate behavior (extinction, time-out, and withdrawing reinforcers).

Becker (1971), Krumboltz and Krumboltz (1972), Patterson (1975), and Patterson and Gullion (1976) are excellent references of these skills.

Limit setting (Dobson, 1970; L. Guerney, 1978) and using natural and logical consequences for broken limits (Dreikurs & Stoltz, 1964) also are effective child change procedures that sometimes are more attractive to parents than the behavior management skills listed previously. Dreikurs recommends that parents attempt to understand their child's goals before deciding how to change the child's behavior. He believes that misbehavior from a child results from the mistaken goals of attention, power, revenge, or inadequacy that the child turns to after she/he discovers that self-importance and belonging cannot be earned through postive behavior.

Changing the Family

The four skill areas discussed before are often taught as segmented units. In a section of a parenting program that is designed to help change whole families, all of the four skills areas are integrated under the domain of problem solving. By the time this skill component is presented, parents need to be familiar with communication skills, environmental planning, and behavior change skills for themselves as well as for their children, and they need to have the child development information necessary to govern their expectations. Systematic ways to combine the skills units are offered in several leader manuals (D'Augelli & Weener, 1976; L. Guerney, 1978).

Problem solving is a systematic process of thinking through an issue before implementing a change strategy. Gordon's "No-loss" method or Dreikurs's "family council" are good guides to democratic family problem solving. The process of solving family problems consists of a series of steps beginning with a careful and specific description of the problem, after which alternative solutions are generated (brainstorming). One best solution is then selected, implemented, and evaluated. If the problem is not solved, either it must be redefined or another solution tried.

The key concept for parents to learn in this section of a program is that problems experienced by one or several members of their families are to be recognized as family difficulties. The resolution of problems, then, requires participation from everyone in the family and not a simple change on the part of one member. It is important to direct parents away from identifying one family member as the troublemaker or as the identified patient.

Implied in the preceding discussion of generic program contents is the idea that a general method of skills training exists—a method that can be used to teach any social skill effectively. Such a method is described in the next section.

THE SKILLS TRAINING PROCESS

Many of the parent training programs in the past were designed with the assumption that the right input of information or change in attitude would change parents' behavior automatically. Research has shown, however, that attitudes often are resistant to change and that even when attitudes are changed, new behavior does not necessarily follow (Sherif & Sherif, 1969; Tavormina, 1974). This is especially true of behaviors that parents have never observed or performed before. Program designers can potentially avoid this problem by taking the opposite approach of changing attitudes by first changing behaviors.

A strength of the skills training approach is that child-rearing concepts such as limit setting and empathy are behaviorally defined. General guidelines for parents such as, "Set appropriate limits" and "Do not be overprotective" may be helpful. But, to bring about the parent actions suggested by these guidelines, parents need more help than a mere discussion of such teachings. The skills training approach is based on learning principles that suggest:

1. Parents need guidelines for child rearing demonstrated.
2. Parents need structured practice to break old habits and to learn new ways of interacting with their children.
3. Parents need cuing and feedback along with their practice to give them reinforcement for what they are doing well.
4. Parents need support and encouragement when trying out new behaviors at home.

These principles suggest the components of a parent training methodology. The components are arranged in a stepwise order that is effective in parenting skills training (see the next sections.) Similar steps are followed in teaching athletic and technical skills to people (Whiting, 1969).

Step 1: Specify a Goal

Goals are signposts pointing out the direction of the training for parents. Nonspecific concepts such as empathy are broken down into a number of skills, and each subskill is given a clear and simple goal statement. Unless goals are made explicit, parent education has an undefined, general focus. Examples of goals for parents in a skills session on listening might be:

Too General   To listen to our children.
              To understand our
              children.
Specific   To enlarge our feeling
              vocabulary.
              To understand the
              roadblocks to
              communication.
              To listen for our
              children's feelings and
              respond with an
              empathic response.

Step 2: Present a Rationale

Before parents will invest themselves in learning something new, they must understand how a skill will be of value to them. For example, the rationale for responding to a child's feelings with empathy is to convey acceptance. When children sense they are accepted, they feel higher self-esteem, and they are usually easier to get along with and manage.

Step 3: Describe the Skill Clearly

Parents are interested in precise, how-to directions when they are first learning a skill. With the limit-setting skill for example, specifics such as these are helpful:

1. Set only the rules you are able and willing to enforce consistently.
2. State a rule to your child in positive terms—"Come home immediately after school," instead of "Don't dawdle after school is out."
3. Make the rule specific and behavioral—"Turn down the TV and talk in a calm tone of voice," instead of "Be considerate of your family."

Step 4: Group Discussion

Usually, it is hopeful at this stage in the training process to encourage parents to express their opinions about the skill to be learned. This discussion allows the group leader to clear up possible misunderstandings about the rationale and the skill. For example, with listening skills, parents often wonder if accepting all their children's feelings is being too permissive. The leader can explain that all feelings are acceptable, but that not all behavior is allowed.

Step 5: Presentation of Low Skill Level

Parents quickly learn a high skill level if they are first shown what not to do. This step should be modeled, with the leader exhibiting the low skill level. By exaggerating examples, the leader can make the demonstration entertaining and get the point across. Again, with listening skills as an example, parents can take turns briefly decribing a problem they are experiencing. The leader responds to them with poor, but fairly typical comments that adults also use with children. When the parents' reaction to the comments are discussed, they can gain more appreciation for how it feels to be nagged, criticized, interrogated, given advice, or consoled.

Step 6: Presentation of High Skill Level

In this step, the leader demonstrates the skill level with which the parents are to leave the session. The leader must be careful not to overwhelm or make the modeled skill too advanced. It is important that the skill that is presented is also learnable within the time limits of the session. Sometimes, and with some complex skills, two modeling segments can be presented at this point in the training: first, the skill level the leader wants the parents to achieve in that session, and second, the skill level that can be attained with extended practice.

Step 7: Practice of the Skill

The principle of successive approximations, or shaping, is used to practice a skill. The skill is divided into subskills, starting with an easy segment to complete successfully. Gradually, more difficult components of the skill are added and practiced. For example, asking parents to reflect their children's feelings is no easy task, and so, empathic response training begins with the parents reading children's statements and identifying the feelings they think are implied in them. This procedure sensitizes parents to feelings and broadens their vocabulary of feeling words.

Next, parents are given a sentence structure for responding with empathy and acceptance, and they are asked to write out responses to written child statements using this form. Parents then practice verbally responding to child statements that are role played by other parent-group members. Finally, before they try their skill at home with their children, they practice empathic responding with another group member who talks at length about a personal concern.

Parents need to experience success with each subskill before attempting the next. It is important that the leader monitor the practice to be sure parents have learned each subskill correctly before proceeding to the next.

Step 8: Extended Practice

After parents have practiced the skill in the classroom, the next step is for them to become more comfortable using the skill at home. Home practice follows the same successive approximation principle used in class. With PCRE, for example, parents initially are asked to be aware of times in which their children are experiencing feelings and to label those feelings silently to themselves. The next week, after more in-session practice, parents are asked to give spontaneous empathic responses when their children express problems and to record several of these instances on a home worksheet. In the following week, they carry out an extended dialogue (15 minutes) with their child at a time when she or he has a problem, and the parent responds to the child's feeling with empathic responses.

Step 9: Evaluate the Skill Level

In this final stage of the training process, the leader observes parents while they perform the skill. Both reinforcing and corrective feedback are given, and addi-

tional modeling and practice is provided if necessary. Parents are encouraged to share their successes and problems in using the skill at home.

Training Tips for Leaders

1. To teach any of the parenting skills, the leader must know and be able to perform the skills well.

2. One of the best ways to teach parents to use the skills with their children is for the group leader to model the skills while interacting with the parents. Many of the parenting skills are not only appropriate in the parent–child relationship but in adult relationships as well. For example, if a parent expresses reservations about the democratic problem-solving skill, the leader might first respond, "You're worried that this isn't going to work in your family." Such a response does show acceptance of the parent's feelings and she or he may continue to express other doubts. A skills training leader needs to disclose her/his feelings, listen well, respond to parent's feelings with empathy, and set limits to model the same skills that parents are encouraged to use with their families.

3. Try to present the skills as something that may be helpful to parents. Often, absolutes such as "Don't spank your children" encourage parents to find reasons not to get involved in a learning experience. Try not to get defensive about a skill being presented. Instead, present it as a potentially helpful alternative. Point out that the more alternatives parents have in their repertoires, the better prepared they will be to deal with each individual child in many different situations.

4. As a leader, it is important to refrain from lecturing and behaving in other "expert" ways. The group leader's role is that of a facilitator. Direct parents' questions back to the group for answers and use open-ended questions that begin with "What," "How," and

"Why" to encourage parents to discuss issues.

5. Some aspect of training involves entertainment. The first session is especially important in developing a relaxed, informal atmosphere, and including get-acquainted exercises at the beginning of a group is time well spent. The training process can be made enjoyable and stimulating by using humor, laughing at oneself, and maintaining a fairly rapid pace.

6. To keep track of parents' reactions, cue into their nonverbal messages and the atmosphere in the group. Notice puzzled looks and apprehensive expressions as well as nods and smiles. Set a norm for open expression of reservations and questions. Parents are much better off if their doubts are dealt with in the group instead of at home where misunderstanding can be compounded. A good facilitator has an agenda in mind for the best use of group time, but the situation may dictate that the agenda be discarded to attend to important issues that may later impede parent progress if ignored.

7. It is easy to get involved in an extended discussion about the value of a skill. Try to move into the training as soon as possible. Ask parents to try out the skill and reject it only after they have experienced it as ineffective. Remember, adopting new behaviors can lead to new attitudes.

8. Perhaps the most important aspect of the leader role is to reinforce parent success rather than punish failure. This does not mean letting errors go by without helping parents perfect their skills, but, at the same time, a leader should look for what parents are doing well and emphasize that success. For example, if a parent says, "I just couldn't bring myself to respond with empathy when Johnny was angry with his little brother," a good facilitator will say, "Good, that's the first step! You recognized that moment as the time when Johnny had feelings and as a chance for you to be empathic. That awareness is excellent."

9. Keep in mind the stages of skill learning. Typically, people go through five stages in acquiring a new skill, be it parenting, athletic, mechanical, or other skills:

(a) *Unawareness*. The individual is not aware of the existence of the skill and its potential usefulness. For example, parents often are unaware of the feelings underlying children's words, and they are unfamiliar with responding with empathy as a way to help a child who has a problem.

(b) *Awareness*. The individual understands a skill but has not yet translated it into behavior. Parents know what empathic responses are and why they are valuable in parent–child interaction. They are beginning to identify situations in which such responses might be helpful, but they are not yet actually performing the skill.

(c) *Awkward, unskilled*. The individual can perfom the skill, but it feels clumsy. Continuing with the example given before, the parent can respond with empathy, but he or she feels unnatural and self-conscious in doing so.

(d) *Skilled, comfortable*. The skill can be performed well. Past successes and practice with the skill have developed self-confidence. Parents who are at the skilled stage believe in the value of accepting and understanding their children's feelings, and they have practiced the empathy response enough to be comfortable with this new behavior.

(e) *Automatic*. The skill is used to such an extent that it is performed smoothly and effortlessly. Parents at this stage respond spontaneously to their children's feelings and the skill feels very natural. This stage comes only after considerable time and practice.

These stages of skill learning can be presented to parents early in their learning of the first skill as a way of explaining their feelings of unnaturalness and discomfort. Using an analogy like learning to ski, drive, or type will remind parents of the stages they went through when learning those skills and that practice over time was what made those skills natural and automatic. It is important to stress that feeling uncomfortable and unnatural is typical when just beginning to learn a new skill.

10.   The leader should aim to match the amount of time available to teach a skill with the capacity of the parents to learn. Present too little material rather than too much. Parents are eager to learn many skills, but one result of hurried training may be that parents never get beyond the awareness or awkward stage of learning any skill. Teaching parents a few skills that are learned well is better than attempting to teach many skills that are learned superficially.

The steps in skills training and the training tips just described make up a methodology that has been found to be successful and that typifies a social skills training approach to parent education. Along with understanding social skills training methods, several other areas of expertise are needed by parenting program leaders.

PARENT-EDUCATOR COMPETENCIES

If parenting programs are to be well planned, if they are to be led with expertise, and if the effects of programs are to be known, parent educators need competence in four areas: program planning, marketing, implementation, and evaluation.

Program Planning

The first competency area—program planning—involves the development of a parent program. It includes identifying target parents, assessing the needs of that population, developing training goals based on their needs, and coordinating content, teaching methods, and materials to accomplish these goals.

Planning how to deliver the parent program is an important consideration. Parent educators should understand the difference between the educational model of service delivery and the remedial, medical model (Authier, Gustafson, Guerney, & Kasdorf, 1975; Guerney, 1981). Under the educational model, parents are considered students instead of clients or patients. The educator's role is that of facilitator, leader, or teacher, rather than one of therapist or counselor. Parents attend parenting sessions for education, training, and enhancement, not to cure abnormality or illness. Parent programs can be called "parenting courses" to convey this educational focus. These labels may seem unimportant, but when working with parents who have been court referred or who are trying to improve their parenting skills at the suggestion of a therapist, the label used to describe the training is important. In addition, there is still a phobia in our society toward mental health services, and helping people call themselves "students" is more likely to attract group participants.

Program planning also concerns making decisions about the format of parent groups. The authors recommend that parent skills training be conducted in small groups of 8 to 16 parents. Larger groups can be conducted, but the individual attention the leader can give to each parent is reduced, and less thorough training may result.

In two-parent homes, spouses should be encouraged to participate in the program as couples because of the value of partners working together on family goals. Husbands and wives need support from one another if a family is to carry out the tasks of parenting successfully. For example, imagine this scene resulting from one spouse's receiving parenting training whereas the other does not:

Child comes home crying about being unfairly made to stay after school by a teacher. One parent states, "Just let me call that teacher, I'll find out what really happened!" The other parent wants to respond, "Sounds like this has been a tough day for you," to encourage the child to talk about the problem without the parent making it her/his own.

Husbands and wives need support from one another if a family is to carry out the tasks of parenting successfully. For example, both members of the parent team need to be able to share perceptions regarding the needs of their children and to share a skills repertoire that enables them to behave similarly in parent–child interactions.

Single parents can profit from parent education when the training is designed to meet their needs. Such parents can be placed together in groups so that they can support one another and deal with their special concerns. Putting parents with similar-aged children in the same group is also important. Parents who have preschool children have different concerns than parents of junior high school students. Combining parents with different-aged children may take some of the relevance out of a parenting group because the discussions and training must be of a more general nature to accomodate the different needs of parents with children at different levels of development.

The number of sessions for parent programs can range from one-shot presentations to 10–12 weekly meetings of 2 to 3 hours each. To train parent skills with some depth and sufficient practice, the 10–12-session format allotted by the broadly based programs such as PET is a guide. Some parents are reticent to commit themselves for that length of time, however. One alternative is to offer one-time sessions to parents whose schedules better fit a single-session format. Another approach to this difficulty is to break a broadly based program into modules that require instruction over only a few sessions. Parents could enroll in the modules as their schedules permit. Another approach to scheduling is to take programs to the parents, for example, offering classes over lunch hours at the work site.

Whether parents enroll for one module or decide to get involved in a complete program, it is important that whatever is offered be done so in depth. Learning new skills requires practice and supervision. Unless parents can be trained through the awkward stage of learning, they probably will not find the new skills effective at home. And if they find the skills ineffective, they may "turn off" to other parent education experiences and give parent education a negative recommendation to their friends.

Good program development results from a thorough understanding of the various theoretical approaches to child rearing and parent–child relationships. The program planner also needs to keep up to date with both the professional and the popular literature in these areas; in addition, he or she must be familiar with resources such as leader manuals, teaching materials, and media aids.

Callahan (1973) calls for authors of parenting books to explicitly state the theories and underlying assumptions on which their views are based. Parent educators, likewise, often fail to make clear their theoretical biases when they promote and present programs to parents. parent educators and program designers should be knowledgeable of child-rearing theory in general (e.g., Mead, 1976) and provide training in the parenting philosophy with which they feel most comfortable.

Marketing Parent Education

The population most interested in parent education is comprised of "normal" families. The parent educator cannot, therefore, count on the same motivators used to generate consumers as have the remedial services that are designed to help troubled families. Motivation and interest in parent education must arise from family values that place a high priority on high-quality family life and child rearing. Such values can be enhanced through public awareness; increased awareness, in turn, can come about through the marketing and promotion of parent programs. Too few parent educators, however, have expertise in selling their wares.

Two potential methods to market or stimulate interest in parenting programs will be discussed here. The first method relies on the media—a well-known book, educational television series, or regular column in the local newspaper. Gordon (1970, 1976) used this method, and he is a good example of a family relations professional who is also effective at program promotion, distribution, and sales. Some may find fault with his being an entrepreneur and developing his parenting program into a successful franchise business, but keep in mind how he has benefited the parent-education movement. His books have heightened public awareness of the need for parent education to an extent that no other family relations professional can claim.

Most parent educators will not write bestsellers as a first step in bringing attention to their programs. Instead, they are likely to use a second method—marketing their program through existing institutions and agencies. This method involves locating the community resources that are potential and willing outlets for parent education.

One suggestion is to take advantage of the surge of interest in adult education. A parenting class can be offered for college credit, continuing education, or professional in-service training. Another approach is to team up with professionals in the community by convincing ministers, family physicians, pediatricians, social workers, and school personnel of the value of adding parent education to

the services they provide. If the parent educator is also one of these service providers, a shift in emphasis from a remedial to a preventive orientation can reap many rewards. For example, elementary school guidance counselors can offer parent education in addition to their more traditional counseling services with the goal of preventing problems before they arise. Church organizations with a strong family service orientation can be stimulated to offer parent classes as part of their family and youth programming. Also, organizations such as the United Way, Junior League, YWCA–YMCA, and local service clubs can be asked to sponsor parenting groups.

Education for parenthood can be offered as part of the curricula at public schools and universities. In this context, parent education usually is provided to potential parents. In an interesting article, de Lissovoy (1977) reasons that parenting skills should be taught to this group only in the context of their day-to-day activities. For example, instead of teaching communication skills for a future time when young adults and teenagers become parents, the skills might be more effectively taught as interpersonal communication for use with peers, or child care skills could be taught in the context of baby-sitting. Setting up a certified child care course and awarding a certificate of expertise that is both an honor and a recommendation for employment could be another means of marketing parent education.

Regarding growth areas for parent education, many companies now have employee-assistance programs that are designed to enhance the family life of their personnel. Part of these services often includes parent education that is provided to employees at the work site. Most often, the companies contract for these services with outside professionals or refer employees to existing services. A marketwise parent educator would want to be on the company referral list, and she/he would also want to be known as a resource to the human resources officer or the employee assistance officer.

Program Implementation

Implementing the parent program is the third area of competence. Interpersonal relations skills, group leadership, and parenting knowledge along with expertise in the skills training methodology discussed previously are necessary to deliver a program effectively. The need for interpersonal skills is obvious; the success or failure of a parenting group very much depends on interacting with parents in ways that develop rapport, elicit their participation, and increase their self-confidence. This supportive role must be blended with leadership that encourages parents to examine their child-rearing philosophies and to consider alternative parenting skills and attitudes. In addition, group discussion and group management skills such as structuring, questioning, role playing, and feedback are necessary.

The parent-educator role closely resembles the parent role. The skills that parents learn to enhance their relationship with their children, such as listening with empathy, setting limits, and reinforcing desired behavior, are the same skills used by parent educators in conducting effective groups. The leader must be a model for parents and must convey parenting expertise via role playing, demonstrations, interacting with the parents' children, and responding to the parents themselves. Implied here is the need for leaders to be experienced with children. Although a leader may be competent as a parent educator without also being a parent, she/he must be knowledgeable about children of various ages and the problems parents typically want to address in parenting groups.

Program Evaluation

The role of parent educator is not merely one of parent group leader and expert in progam development. A fourth area of competencey is needed—progam evaluation. When a parent enrolls in a program, the implication is that she/he wants to do a better job as a parent. Likewise, an evaluation of a parent program indicates that the educator wants to improve her/his performance and program. The evaluation itself can be as informal as asking parents to give their verbal or written feedback at progressive stages of the program or at its end. A more systematic evaluation might involve assessing parents' knowledge, attitudes, and/or skills prior to and immediately following a training experience. A complete evaluation might include a follow-up assessment of the long-term effects of the program.

As a result of there being four competency areas, it is obvious that the role of parent educator is complex and that it is made up of several subroles: effective group leader, marketing expert, program planner, and evaluator. This is not to say that all parent educators need equal competence in the four areas. Both professionals and paraprofessionals can play important roles in the evolution of skills-based parent education. Professionals, for example, can assume the competencies of program development and evaluation as well as the training and supervision of group leaders. The groups themselves can be led by paraprofessionals who also market their services to the public. Research has shown the cost-effectiveness and service quality of the paraprofessional approach to providing mental health services (Danish & Brock, 1974).

This discussion of parent-educator competencies, the presentation of a generic skills training model, and the overview of existing programs communicates a positive picture of parent education. The field is not without need for new direction, however, and in the next section the future of parent education will be summarized.

THE FUTURE OF PARENT EDUCATION

Over time, parent education has evolved from the maternal associations of the 1820s in which mothers discussed their child-rearing concerns to the systematic training programs that have been explored in this chapter. What lies in the future for parent education?

There are a number of existing issues that may be used to define a future for parent education. These issues do not pertain so much to the skills training methodology that is commonly used to teach parents new skills but rather to program content, program structure, and research evaluation.

One issue of primary concern is whether the consumers of parent training are to remain largely mothers. Men do participate in parenting groups, but the majority of members are women. In addition, children are almost never full participants in the training process that takes place during parenting group sessions. Fathers and children are by and large relegated to the roles of either merely hearing about or being confused by what is going on in the parenting group, in the case of fathers (Doherty & Ryder, 1980), or the recipient of training aftereffects, in the case of children. If we assume that parent training is essentially a family intervention (Fine, 1980), then parent-education groups need to change content, structure, or both so that all members of a family can become involved in an active way.

The structure of the PCRE program is an example of one approach to including children in the training. That focus, however, is a minimal one because children do not play a substantive role in PCRE groups; they are present only to facilitate parent learning of empathic responding and limit-setting skills. To involve children fully, training content in which children are also taught skills such as parent reinforcement and parent management need to be developed. Improving the

participation of fathers may involve changing the content of parent education to include training mothers to train their absent spouses.

A change in program structure to one that requires less parental time investment may yield greater participation from fathers. Hampson, Schulte and Ricks (1983) found that an alternate service delivery system, consisting of training in the home, increased the participation of foster fathers in a foster parenting program. It is more likely, however, that the lack of male participation is due to cultural norms prescribing parenting education as part of the female role than to a lack of time on the part of fathers. Perhaps the equal involvement of fathers and mothers in parenting skills training will need to wait for social change in the definition of sex roles. An alternative to waiting for these changes to occur is redefining the goals of parent education toward more of a family-education emphasis that is designed to imrove the functioning of all family members. Such a change in the focus of parent education may also yield new program structures, content, and goals that are designed to meet the specific needs of alternate family forms.

Efforts to resolve these program structure and content issues can be aided by research, although there are also a number of critical empirical questions that remain unaddressed. The research and empirical issues of parent education summarized by Tavormina (1980) include the practical significance of the changes produced by parent training; the lack of attention that has been directed to the ripple effects of parent training on family process; the absence of failure reports in the literature; the apparent lack of interface between developmental theory and training program content, especially for parents of older children; and the need for more evaluation of the maintenance and generalization of skills learned by parents. These issues are not those one would expect of an area of intervention in its infancy. The preceding list of issues says that parent education as a field has gone beyond evaluating its general effectiveness. The future of parent education lies in better understanding why and with whom parent training is effective and in identifying the niche it is to occupy within the full range of mental health services.

The fit or place of parent education within the mental health system is perhaps the most important issue that deserves attention from researchers and practioners over the next decade. This issue manifests itself in the common decision to exclude some groups from the parent-education experience (e.g., psychotic parents [Wiltz, 1969], those with poor marriages [Bernal, 1973], severely dysfunctional adult–child relationships, or families in crisis). This decision is based on the assumption that education or training is not an appropriate treatment for less than functional segments of the society and that therapy is the treatment of choice for these clients. There is no evidence to support the assumption that clinical populations cannot benefit from training, be it parent training, marital communication training, or other social skills training. In fact, there is ample research to show that parent education, as one type of educational model intervention, is a very effective treatment for dysfunctional relationship systems. For example, in their review of behavioral parent-education programs, Gordon and Davidson (1981) pointed out that the majority of behavioral parent training research has been conducted in clinical settings. The positive results of these studies is good evidence that parent education and training is appropriate for use with a broad spectrum of clients. Equating social skills training and education with only the enrichment treatment modality and population, therefore, is inaccurate. Researchers, authors, and practitioners, however, persist in relegating educational model treatments

such as parent education to a status below that of therapy. The future of parent education and social skills training in general will depend greatly on whether the mental health field can adapt to the changes brought about by educational model interventions and whether the field is willing to challenge the bias of practitioners and researchers toward traditional mental health services.

SUMMARY

The purpose of this chapter was to provide an overview of the existing parenting education programs and the social skills training methods that are used in those programs to help parents learn new ways of interacting with their children. In addition to reviewing specific programs, the generic contents of social-skills-training-based parenting programs was discussed as was a general training model that has met with success in parent education. Lastly, the competencies of the parenting skills group leader and the issues related to marketing parent education were described.

Parent education has changed greatly since it was initiated at the turn of this century. The impetus for those changes has been our increased knowledge about the parenting role and the development of social skills training methods. Future developments in the parenting education expression of social skills training depend on these same sources.

REFERENCES

Abidin, R. (1981). *Parenting skills: Trainer's manual* (2nd ed.). New York: Human Sciences Press.

Anchor, K., & Thomason, T. (1977). A comparison of two parent training models with educated parents. *Journal of Community Psychology, 5,* 134–141.

Authier, J., Gustafson, K., Guerney, Jr., B.,

& Kasdorf, J. (1975). The psychological practitioner as a teacher: A theoretical-historical and practical review. *The Counseling Psychologist, 5,* 31–50.

Becker, W. (1971). *Parents are teachers.* Champaign, IL: Research Press.

Bernal, M. (1973, May). *Preliminary report of a preventive intervention project.* Paper presented at the Rocky Mountain Psychological Association, Las Vegas.

Briggs, D. (1970). *Your Child's self-esteem: The key to his life.* New York: Doubleday.

Callahan, S. (1973). *Parenting: Principles and politics of parenthood.* Baltimore: Penguin Books.

Cantor, D. (1976). *Evaluation of a parenting skills training program with the parents of first grade children at risk.* Unpublished doctoral dissertation, Rutgers University.

Clarke-Stewart, K. (1978). Popular primers for parents. *American Psychologist, 33,* 359–363.

Constantine, L. (1977). Open family: A lifestyle for kids and other people. *The Family Coordinator, 26,* 113–121.

Coufal, J. (1982). *An experimental evaluation of two approaches to parent skills training: Parent–child participation versus parents only.* Paper presented at the meeting of the National Council of Family Relations, Washington, DC.

Coufal, J., & Brock, G. (1983). *Parent–child relationship enhancement: A ten week education program.* Menomonie University of Wisconsin–Stout.

Danish, S., & Brock, G. (1974). The current status of paraprofessional training. *Personnel and Guidance Journal, 53,* 299–303.

D'Augelli, J., & Weener, J. (1976). *Communication and parenting skills: Leader's guide.* University Park: The Pennsylvania State University.

D'Augelli, J., & Weener, J. (1978). Training parents as metal health agents. *Community Mental Health Journal, 14,* 87–96.

de Lissovoy, V. (1977). *Parent education: White elephant in the classroom.* Paper presented at the meeting of the National Council on Family Relations, San Diego.

Dinkmeyer, D. & McKay, G. (1976). *Systematic training for effective parenting: Parent's handbook.* Circle Pines, MN: American Guidance Service.

Dobson, J. (1970). *Dare to discipline.* Wheaton, IL: Tyndale House.

Dodson, F. (1970). *How to parent.* New York: New American Library.

Dodson, F. (1974). *How to father.* New York: New American Library.

Doherty, W., & Ryder, R. (1980). Parent effectiveness training (PET): Criticisms and caveats. *Journal of Marital and Family Therapy, 6,* 409–420.

Dreikurs, R., & Soltz, V. (1964). *Children: The challenge.* New York: Hawthorn Books.

Fine, M. (1980). *Handbook on parent education.* New York: Academic Press.

Freeman, C. (1975). Adlerian mother study groups: Effects on attitudes and behavior. *Journal of Individual Psychology, 31,* 37–50.

Gesell, A., & Ilg, F. (1943). *Infant and child in the culture of today.* New York: Harper.

Ginott, H. (1965). *Between parent and child.* New York: Macmillan.

Ginsberg, B., (1977) Parent–adolescent relationship development. In B. Guerney (Ed.). *Relationship enhancement.* San Francisco: Jossey-Bass.

Gordon, S., & Davidson, N. (1981). Behavioral parent training. In A. Gurman & D. Kiniskern (Eds.), *Handbook of family therapy.* New York: Brunner/Mazel.

Gordon, T. (1970). *Parent effectiveness training.* New York: Wyden Books.

Gordon, T. (1976). *P.E.T. in action.* New York: Bantam Books.

Goula, J. (1976). The effect of Adlerian parent study groups with and without communication training on the behavior of parents and children. *Dissertation Abstracts International,* 1976, *37,* 1985A–1986A. (University Microfilms No. 76-22, 473).

Guerney, B. (1964). Filial Therapy: Description and rationale. *Journal of Consulting Psychology, 28,* 304–319.

Guerney, B. (1977). *Relationship Enhancement.* San Francisco: Jossey-Bass.

Guerney, B. (1981). The delivery of mental health services: Spiritual vs. medical vs. educational models. In T. Vallance & R. Sabre (Eds.), *Society's stepchildren: Mental health services in transition*. New York: Human Sciences Press.

Guerney, B., Coufal. J., & Vogelsong, E. (1981). Relationship enhancement versus a traditional approach to therapeutic/preventive/enrichment parent–adolescent programs. *Journal of Consulting and Clinical Psychology, 49*, 927–939.

Guerney, B., Vogelsong, E., & Coufal, J. (1983). Relationship enhancement versus a traditional treatment: Follow-up and booster effects. In D. Olson & B. Miller (Eds.), *Family Studies Review Yearbook*. Beverly Hills, CA: Sage Publications.

Guerney, L. (1975). *Foster parent training: A manual for parents*. University Park: The Pennsylvania State University.

Guerney, L. (1976). Filial Therapy program. In D. Olson (Ed.), *Treating relationships*. Lake Mills, IA: Graphic Publishing.

Guerney, L. (1977). A description and evaluation of a skills training program for foster parents. *American Journal of Community Psychology, 5*, 361–371.

Guerney, L. (1978). *Parenting: A skills training manual*. State College, PA: Institute for the Development of Emotional and Life Skills.

Hall, M. (1983). Responsive parenting: A large scale training program for school districts, hospitals and mental health centers. In R. Polster & R. Dangle (Eds.), *Parent training: Foundations of research and practice*. New York: Guilford.

Hampson, R., Schulte, M., & Ricks, C. (1983). Individual vs. group training for foster parents: Efficiency/effectiveness evaluations. *Family Relations, 32*, 191–202.

Hanley, D. (1974). Changes in parent attitudes related to a parent effectiveness training and enrichment program. (Doctoral dissertation, United States International University). *Dissertation Abstract International*, 1974, *34*, 7044A.

Hereford, C. (1963). *Changing parental attitudes through group discussion*. Austin: University of Texas Press.

Hetrick, E. (1979). Training parents of learning disabled children in facilitative communication skills. *Journal of Learning Disabilities, 12*, 275–277.

Krumboltz, J., & Krumboltz, H. (1972). *Changing children's behavior*. Englewood Cliffs, NJ.: Prentice-Hall.

Larson, R. (1972). Can parent classes affect family communications? *School Counselor, 19*, 261–270.

Lillibridge, E. (1971). The relationship of a Parent Effectiveness Training program to change in parent's self-assessed attitudes and children's perceptions of parents. (Doctoral dissertation, United States University). *Dissertation Abstracts International*, 1972, *32*, 5613A.

McKay, G. (1976). Systematic training for effective parenting: Effects on behavior change of parents and children. *Dissertation Abstracts International*, 1976, *37*, 3423A–3424A. (University Microfilms No. 76-28, 215).

Mead, D. (1976). *Six approaches to child rearing*. Provo, UT: Brigham Young University Press.

Miles, J. (1974). A comparative analysis of the effectiveness of verbal reinforcement group counseling and Parent Effectiveness Training on certain behavioral aspects of potential dropouts. (Doctoral dissertation, Auburn University). *Dissertation Abstracts International*, 1975, *35*, 7655A.

Patterson, G. (1975). *Families; Applications of social learning to family life*. Champaign, IL: Research Press.

Patterson, G., Chamberlain, P., & Reid, J. (1982). A comparative evaluation of a parent-training program. *Behavior Therapy, 13*, 638–650.

Patterson, G., & Gullion, M. (1976). *Living with children*. Champaign, IL: Research Press.

Patterson, G., Ray, R., & Shaw, D. (1968). Direct intervention in families of deviant children. *Oregon Research Institute Bulletin, 8*.

Rinn, R., & Markle. A. (1977). P.E.T.: A review. *Psychological Reports, 41*, 95–109.

Schmitz, K. (1975). A study of the relationship of Parent Effectiveness Training to changes in parents' self-assessed attitudes and behavior in a rural population. (Doctoral dissertation, University of South Dakota). *Dissertation Abstracts International*, 1975, *36*, 3526A.

Schofield, R. (1979). Parent group education and student self-esteem. *Social Work in Education, 1*, 26–33.

Sherif, M., & Sherif, C. (1969). *Social psychology*. New York: Harper & Row.

Stanley, S. (1978). Family education to enhance the moral atmosphere of the family and the moral development of adolescents. *Journal of Counseling Psychology, 25*, 110–118.

Stearn, M. (1971). The relationship of Parent Effectiveness Training to parent attitudes, parent behavior and child self-esteem. (Doctoral dissertation, United States International University). *Dissertation Abstracts International*, 1971, *32*, 1885B.

Tavorimina, J. (1974). Basic models of parent counseling. *Psychological bulletin, 81*, 827–835.

Tavormina J. (1980). Evaluation and comparative studies of parent education. In R. Abidin (Ed.), *Parent education and intervention handbook*. Springfield, IL: Charles C Thomas.

Therrien, M. (1979). Evaluating empathy skill training for parents. *Social Work, 24*, 417–419.

Walter, H., & Gilmore, S., (1973) Placebo versus social learning effects in parent training procedures designed to alter the behavior of aggressive boys. *Behavior Therapy, 4*, 361–377.

Watson, D, & Tharp R., (1977). *Self-directed behavior*. Monterey, CA.: Brooks-Cole.

Whiting, H. (1969). *Acquiring ball skills*. Philadelphia: Lea & Febager.

Wiltz, N. (1969). Modification of behavior through parent participation in a group technique. (Doctoral dissertation. University of Oregon). *Dissertation Abstracts International*, 1970, *30*, 4786-A.

Wiltz, N., & Patterson, G. (1974). An evaluation of parent training procedures designed to alter inappropriate aggressive behavior of boys. *Behavior Therapy. 5*, 215–221.

CHAPTER 12

Structured Learning

Research and Practice
in Psychological Skill Training

ARNOLD P. GOLDSTEIN, N. JANE GERSHAW, AND ROBERT P. SPRAFKIN

Until the early 1970s, there existed three major psychological approaches designed to alter the behavior of unhappy, ineffective, or disturbed individuals —psychodynamic/psychoanalytic, humanistic/nondirective, and behavior modification. Although each differed from the others in several major respects, one of their significant commonalities was the shared assumption that the patient had somewhere within himself or herself, as yet unexpressed, the effective, satisfying, or healthy behaviors whose expression was among the goals of the therapy. Such latent potentials, in all three approaches, would be realized by the patient if the therapist was sufficiently skilled in reducing or removing obstacles to such realization. The psychoanalyst sought to do so by calling forth and interpreting unconscious, material-blocking, progress-relevant awareness. The nondirectivist, who believes that the potential for change resides within the patient, sought to free this potential by providing a warm, empathic, maximally accepting therapeutic environment. And the behavior modifier,

by means of one or more contingency management procedures, attempted to see to it that when the latent desirable behaviors or approximations thereto did occur, the patient received contingent reinforcement, thus increasing the probability that these behaviors would recur. Therefore, whether sought by means of therapeutic climate or by dint of offering contingent rewards, all three approaches assumed that somewhere within the individual's repertoire resided the desired, effective, sought-after goal behaviors.

In the early 1970s, an important new intervention approach began to emerge —psychological skill training, an approach resting upon rather different assumptions. Viewing the helpee more in educational, pedagogic terms rather than as a patient in need of therapy, the psychological skills trainer assumed that he or she was dealing with an individual who was deficient, or at best weak, in the skills necessary for effective and satisfying daily living. The task of the skills trainer became, therefore, not interpretation, reflection or reinforcement, but the active and deliberate teaching of desirable behaviors. Rather than an intervention called psychotherapy, between a patient and a psychotherapist, what emerged was training, between a trainee and a psychological skills trainer.

The roots of the psychological skills

Sections of this chapter have been excerpted from Goldstein, A. P. *Psychological Skill Training.*. New York: Pergamon Press, 1981. Permission from Pergamon to reprint is gratefully acknowledged.

training movement lie within both education and psychology. The notion of literally seeking to teach desirable behaviors has often, if sporadically, been a significant goal of the American educational establishment. The Character Education movement of the 1920s and more contemporary Moral Education and Values Clarification programs are but a few of several possible examples. Add to this the institutionalized educational interest in skills training, the hundreds of interpersonal and planning skills courses taught in America's more than 2000 community colleges, and the hundreds of self-help books oriented toward similar skill-enhancement goals that are available to the American poublic, and it becomes clear that the formal and informal educational establishment in America provided fertile soil and explicit stimulation within which the psychological skills training movement could grow.

Much the same can be said for Amer ican psychology, as it, too, laid the groundwork by its prevailing philosophy and concerete interests in the development of this new movement. The learning process has above all else been the central theoretical and investigative concern of American psychology since the late 19th century. This focal interest also assumed major therapeutic form in the 1950s, as psychotherapy practitioners and researchers alike came to view psychotherapeutic treatment more and more in learning terms. The very healthy and still-expanding field of behavior modification grew from this joint learning–clinic focus and may be appropriately viewed as the immediately preceding context in which psychological skills training came to be developed. In companion with the growth of behavior modification, psychological thinking increasingly shifted from a strict emphasis on remediation to one that was equally concerned with prevention, and the bases for this shift included movement away from a medical model conceptual-

ization toward what may most aptly be called a "psychoeducational" theoretical stance. Both of these thrusts—heightened concern with prevention and a psychoeducational perspective—gave strong added impetus to the viability of the psychological skill training movement.

Perhaps psychology's most direct contribution to psychological skills training came from social learning theory, in particular, the work conducted and stimulated by Albert Bandura. Based upon the same broad array of modeling, behavioral rehearsal, and social reinforcement investigations, which helped stimulate and direct the development of the Structured Learning skill training approach, Bandura (1973) commented as follows:

The method that has yielded the most impressive results with diverse problems contains three major components. First, alternative modes of response are repeatedly modeled, preferably by several people who demonstrate how the new style of behavior can be used in dealing with a variety of . . . situations. Second, learners are provided with necessary guidance and ample opportunities to practice the modeled behavior under favorable conditions until they perform it skillfully and spontaneously. The latter procedures are ideally suited for developing new social skills, but they are unlikely to be adopted unless they produce rewarding consequences. Arrangement of success experiences, particularly for initial efforts at behaving differently, constitute the third component in this powerful composite method. . . . Given adequate demonstration, guided practice, and success experiences, this method is almost certain to produce favorable results. (p. 253)

Other events of the 1970s provided still further fertile ground for the growth of the skill training movement. The inadequacy of prompting, shaping, and related operant procedures for adding *new* behaviors to individuals' behavioral repertoires was increasingly apparent. The widespread reliance upon deinstitution-alization, which lay at the heart of the community mental health movement, re-sulted in the discharge from America's public mental hospitals of approximately 400,000 persons, the majority of whom were substantially deficient in important daily functioning skills. And, especially to these investigators, it has grown par-ticularly clear that what the American mental health movement had available to offer lower social class clients was grossly inadequate to meet their psy-chotherapeutic needs. These factors, relevant supportive research, the incom-pleteness of operant approaches, large populations of grossly skill-deficient in-dividuals, and the paucity of useful inter-ventions for a large segment of American society—all in the context of historically supportive roots in both education and psychology—came together in the think-ing of these writers and others as de-manding a new intervention, something prescriptively responsive to these sev-eral needs. Psychological skills training was the answer, and a movement was launched.

Our involvement in this movement, a psychological skill training approach that we have termed Structured Learn-ing (SL) began in the early 1970s. At that time and for several years thereafter, our studies were conducted in public mental hospitals with long-term, highly skill-de-ficient chronic patients. It was while conducting research with these trainees that three investigative themes emerged, themes we have continued to pursue as our research shifted over the years to other settings and other types of trainee populations. These central study con-cerns may be expressed by indicating that the overall goal of SL is to effec-tively lead trainees to high levels of (1) skill acquisition and (2) skill transfer, and to do so in a (3) prescriptive manner. Investigative concern with acquisition, transfer, and prescriptiveness will be re-visited in some depth later in this chap-ter.

THE LOW-INCOME PATIENT

Of the several forces noted as having precipitated our entry into skill training research and practice, perhaps most po-tent was our concern with the poverty of existing effective treatment approaches designed to serve the mental health needs of low-income patient popula-tions. It has by now been well estab-lished that the implications of a patient's social class for his or her psychothera-peutic treatment destiny are numerous, pervasive, and enduring. If the patient is lower social class, such implications are decidedly and uniformly negative. It has been consistently demonstrated that, in comparison with patients at higher social class levels, the lower-class patient–candidate seeking psychotherapeutic assistance in an outpatient setting is sig-nificantly more likely to:

1. Be found unacceptable for treat-ment.
2. Receive a socially less desirable for-mal diagnosis.
3. Drop out (or be dropped out) after in-itial screening.
4. Spend considerable time on the clin-ic's waiting list.
5. Be assigned to the least experienced staff members.
6. Hold expectations incongruent with those held by his or her therapist.
7. Form a poor relationship with his or her psychotherapist.
8. Terminate or be terminated earlier.
9. Improve significantly less from either his or her own or his or her thera-pist's perspective.

Analogous dimensions relevant to men-tal hospital settings yield an even grim-mer pattern for the lower-class inpatient. As but one example, in the United States, Canada, and other nations in-volved in the deinstitutionalization movement, this has been a decade during which the rate of mental hospital discharges has increased significantly. But the proportion of lower-class inpatients still hospitalized has *increased*. In a 10-year follow-up of Hollingshead and Redlich's (1958) research, Meyers, Bean, and Pepper (1965) discovered that significantly more middle- and upper-class patients had left the hospitals, as compared with those of lower social class standing. Furthermore, the likelihood of rehospitalization was significantly greater for those lower-class patients who had been discharged.

At the broadest level of generalization, we would assert that the lower social class patient has fared so poorly in psychotherapy because the type of psychotherapy we are most prone to offer—traditional, verbal, insight-oriented psychotherapy—is almost singularly a middle-class enterprise. It is middle class in its underlying philosophies of people, in its theoretical rationales, and in its specific therapeutic techniques. Schofield (1964) has taken an analogous position by suggesting that most psychotherapists prefer to work with what he described as the YAVIS patient—young, attractive, verbal, intelligent, and successful, and most typically, middle or upper social class. YAVISES seek psychotherapy voluntarily; they do not wish drug or physical therapy, but, as their therapist prefers, they expect to explore their inner worlds and actively participate in seeking insight. They tend to form a favorable therapeutic relationship, remain in treatment for an extended period, and, in about two-thirds of such therapist–patient pairings, YAVISES indeed derive psychotherapuetic benefit.

Our own clinical and research interest lies more with a contrasting type of patient, whom we might term non-YAVISES. They are typically lower or working class, are often middle aged, physically ordinary or unattractive, verbally reticent, intellectually unexceptional or dull, and vocationally unsuccessful or marginal. In our own studies, non-YAVISES have been formally diagnosed schizophrenic, psychoneurotic, inadequate personality, drug addict, retarded, or alcoholic, though it is their social-class levels and its associated lifestyles we consider of greater consequence than their diagnoses per se. How else might we describe the non-YAVIS patient? They seek psychotherapy often not with full volition. They anticipate not introspective behavior on their own part but advice and active guidance from their psychotherapist. Because the non-YAVISES often view their problems as physical in nature, physical or drug therapies are also consistent with their expectations and even preferences. As noted earlier, they tend to remain in treatment very briefly, form a poor therapeutic relationship, and derive minimal benefit from psychotherapy. In the United States, 50% of the psychotherapies involving non-YAVIS patients at community mental health centers last but one or two sessions—clearly less successful an effort than is therapy with middle-class clients.

ALTERNATIVE SOLUTIONS

Admonitions to Be Concrete

How are we to help the lower-class patient more effectively? Four approaches can be identified. The first consists of simple admonitions in the psychiatric, social work, and psychological literatures urging therapists to "be more directive, concrete, specific, advice-giving," and the like. Although this is indeed good prescriptive advice, it, like most advice, is rarely followed. Perhaps this is in part because the training analyst, psychology professor, or psychiatrist writing these articles rarely sees such patients in his or her own private therapy practices. Instead, while they write of the non-YAVISES and urge us on in their direction, they themselves treat the YAVISES! They ask us to do as they say, not as they do. Young therapists respond to their model's behavior, not the model's words. Thus, this approach, consisting of admonitions and beseeching in the literature, has essentially failed. The gap between the typically middle-class therapist and the lower-class patient—a gap in values, language, beliefs about psychopathology, and its remediation—is simply too great to close in this manner.

Paraprofessional Therapists

If this is the case, many have held that a second and viable solution to the psychotherapeutic needs of low-income patients is to employ therapists who share values, language, and therapy beliefs with the low-income non-Yavis patient, that is, the lower social class or working-class psychotherapist. If such therapists could be found, this position held, congruent therapist–patient expectancies, a positive relationship, and a favorable outcome all might well ensue. It was this set of assumptions and hopes that, in the United States, led to the so-called "paraprofessional therapist" movement. This was a period in the late 1960s and early 1970s during which individuals of lower- and working-class status were identified and (briefly) trained to function as what were termed "paraprofessional," "nonprofessional," "indigenous," "neighborhood," or "community therapists." And, in fact, many, indeed, proved to be therapeutic. Unfortunately, a series of subsequent economic and political events (the Viet Nam war, recession) have combined to keep this an underfunded movement, one that has yet to reach its full therapeutic potential.

Conformity Prescriptions

If admonitions are not enough and paraprofessionals are too scarce, what solutions remain? There are two, and both are what we have termed "prescriptive." The first seeks to "make the patient fit the therapy": It is a conformity prescription that seeks to alter the patient, his or her expectancies, relatability, or similar therapy-readiness characteristics so that the patient more adequately fits the patient role appropriate to whatever (unchanged) psychotherapy we are offering.

Goldstein's (1971) own earlier research program is one example of such a conformity prescription for the lower-class patient. The broad goal was to implement and evaluate procedures designed to enhance the favorablensess of the psychotherapeutic relationship. Social psychologists have focused much research attention upon procedures predicted to increase what they term "interpersonal attraction," that is, the degree to which one member of a dyad likes or is attracted to the other. Working in laboratory settings, usually with college student subjects, researchers have developed serveral different procedures for reliably enhancing interpersonal attraction. These procedures we extrapolated from laboratory to clinic as a means of seeking to increase the attraction of patients to their psychotherapists. Concretely, the procedures included the following:

1. Direct structuring, in which the patient is directly led to believe that he or she will like the therapist.
2. Trait structuring, in which the patient is provided with information about the therapist, such as therapist "warmth" or "experience".
3. Status, in which both verbal and physical information are used to lead the patient to believe that the therapist is of high status.
4. Effort, in which the therapeutic interaction itself is deliberately made more effortful for the patient.
5. Modeling, in which the patient is provided with the opportunity to view a

model who is hightly attracted to the psychotherapist.

6. Matching, in which therapist and patient are paired on the basis of test results concerning their interpersonal needs or therapy-relevant attitudes.

7. Conformity pressure, in which both an attracted model and cohorts rating him or her as attractive are utilized.

In a series of investigations, we examined each of these procedures with separate middle-and lower-class patient samples. Almost every one of our procedures worked successfully with the middle-class patient samples. Almost every procedure failed with our lower-class samples. This failure is not an uncommon outcome. Most efforts to teach low-income patients "good patient" skills, to socialize them into traditional, verbal, insight-oriented therapy, to have them play the therapeutic game as it is usually structured, have not been successful.

Reformity Prescriptions

In response to both these findings and the literature summarized earlier, an alternative approach to the lower-class patient seemed appropriate. Rather than make the patient fit the therapy, rather than a conformity prescription, we opted to try to develop a therapy to fit the lower-class patient, to try to alter or reformulate our psychotherapeutic offering to correspond to or be consistent with "where the patient was at." Stated otherwise, we sought what might be termed a "reformity prescription." To determine the nature of such an approach, we turned this time primarily to developmental psychology research on child rearing and sociological writing on social class and life-styles. These bodies of literatures consistently reveal that middle-class child rearing and life-style —with their emphasis upon intentions,

motivation, inner states, self-regulation, and the like—are excellent "basic training" for participation in traditional, verbal psychotherapies should such persons become emotionally disturbed in later life. Lower-class child rearing and life-styles—with their emphasis upon action, motor behavior, consequences rather than intentions, reliance upon external example, authority, and a restricted verbal code—ill prepare such persons for traditional psychotherapy but might, we speculated, prepare them very well for a treatment that was responsive to such life-style characteristics, that is, a treatment that was brief, concrete, behavioral, actional, authoritatively administered, and that required imitation of specific overt examples, taught role-taking skills, and provided early, continuing, and frequent reinforcement for enactment of seldom-used but adaptive skill behaviors. Borrowing liberally from and building upon the works of Bandura (1969), Lazarus (1966), and others, we have constructed and tested such a therapy, a class-linked therapy that we have shown over the course of several dozen investigations to be optimally appropriate for the lower-class patient. We call this approach Structured Learning Therapy (SLT) (Goldstein, 1973). Its major components are modeling, role playing, performance feedback, and transfer of training. That is, the patient is provided with specific, detailed, frequent, and vivid displays of adaptive behavior or of specific skills in which he or she is deficient (i.e., modeling); is given considerable opportunity and encouragement to behaviorally rehearse or practice such modeled behavior (i.e., role playing); is provided with positive feedback, approval, or reward for successful enactments (i.e., performance feedback); and is required to engage in a number of behaviors (to be described later) that enhance the likelihood that the behaviors taught in the therapy room will be used reliably in the community and other application settings (i.e., transfer of training).

At the very time that we were formulating this reformity prescription, Structured Learning Therapy, a major movement was developing in the United States—the deinstitutionalization movement. This is the movement from public mental hospital to community of chronic adult mental patients—85% of whom are socioeconomically lower or working class. In the United States, in the past 20 years, the mental hospital patient census has decreased from approximately 550,000 to 150,000 souls. In terms of the movement of people out of institutions, the deinstitutionalization movement seems to be a marked success.

For many of the persons thus moved, however, major problems have occurred. Years and years of colonization —increasing hospitalization; of an unskilled, chronic ward existence; of an existence far removed in its demands from the demands of adequate community function—left thousands of these ex-patients ill prepared for what was to confront them. As they moved from hospital to group home, welfare hotel, or halfway house, many proved too deficient in daily living skills to remain out of the hospital. They, too, often had moved from "back ward" to "back alley" and could not make it. It was to this challenge that we sought to respond by the full development, investigation, and dissemination of SLT.

STRUCTURED LEARNING THERAPY

SLT requires, first, that patients—called trainees in this approach—be exposed to expert examples of the behaviors we wish them to learn. The 6–12 trainees constituting the SL group are selected because of their shared skill deficiencies, essentially independent of their formal diagnoses. Each potentially problematic behavior is referred to as a skill. Each of the 59 tapes in the series of displays depicts a different daily living skill (see Table 12.1). Each skill is broken down into 4–6 different behavioral steps. The steps constitute the operational definition of the given skill. One tape consists of one skill. Each tape consists of 10 vignettes in each of which actors expertly portray the steps of that skill in a variety of community, hospital, and transitional settings. Trainers describe the first skill to be taught and hand out to all trainees cards (skill cards) on which the name of the skill and the behavioral steps are printed. The first modeling tape is then played (or the trainers present live modeling of the given skill). Trainees are told to listen closely to the way the actors in each vignette follow the behavioral steps for that skill.

Role Playing

A brief, spontaneous discussion almost invariably follows the presentation of a modeling display. Trainees comment on the steps, the actors, and, very often, on how the situation or skill problem portrayed occurs in their own lives. Because our primary goal in role playing is to encourage realistic behavioral rehearsal, a trainee's statements about his or her individual difficulties using the skill being taught can often develop into material for the first role play. To enhance the realism of the portrayal, the main actor is asked to choose a second trainee (co-actor) to play the role of the significant-other person in his or her life who is relevant to the skill problem. One trainer is responsible for keeping a record of those who have role played, which role, and for which skill—to be sure that all participate about equally. It is of crucial importance that the main actor seek to enact the steps that he or she has just heard modeled.

The main actor is asked to describe briefly the real skill problem situation and the real person(s) involved in it, with

TABLE 12.1   Structured Learning Skills for Adults

Basic Skills

Series   I.   Conversations: Beginning skills
Skill   1.   Starting a conversation
Skill   2.   Carrying on a conversation
Skill   3.   Ending a conversation
Skill   4.   Listening

Series II.   Conversations: Expressing oneself
Skill   5.   Expressing a compliment
Skill   6.   Expressing appreciation
Skill   7.   Expressing encouragement
Skill   8.   Asking for help
Skill   9.   Giving instructions
Skill 10.   Expressing affection
Skill 11.   Expressing a complaint
Skill 12.   Persuading others
Skill 13.   Expressing anger

Series III.   Conversations: Responding to others
Skill 14.   Responding to praise
Skill 15.   Responding to the feelings of others (empathy)
Skill 16.   Apologizing
Skill 17.   Following instructions
Skill 18.   Responding to persuasion
Skill 19.   Responding to failure
Skill 20.   Responding to contradictory messages
Skill 21.   Responding to a complaint
Skill 22.   Responding to anger

Series IV.   Planning skills
Skill 23.   Setting a goal
Skill 24.   Gathering information
Skill 25.   Concentrating on a task
Skill 26.   Evaluating your abilities
Skill 27.   Preparing for a stressful conversation
Skill 28.   Setting problem priorities
Skill 29.   Decision making

Series   V.   Alternatives to aggression
Skill 30.   Identifying and labeling your emotions
Skill 31.   Determining responsibility
Skill 32.   Making requests
Skill 33.   Relaxation
Skill 34.   Self-control
Skill 35.   Negotiation
Skill 36.   Helping others
Skill 37.   Assertiveness

Application Skills [a]

Skill 38.   Finding a place to live (through formal channels)
Skill 39.   Moving in (typical)
Skill 40.   Moving in (difficult)
Skill 41.   Managing money
Skill 42.   Neighboring (apartment house)
Skill 43.   Job seeking (typical)
Skill 44.   Job seeking (difficult)
Skill 45.   Job keeping (average day's work)
Skill 46.   Job keeping (strict boss)
Skill 47.   Receiving telephone calls (difficult)

TABLE 12.1   (*Continued*)

Skill 48.	Restaurant eating (typical)
Skill 49.	Organizing time (typical)
Skill 50.	Using leisure time (learning something new)
Skill 51.	Using leisure time (interpersonal activity)
Skill 52.	Social (party)
Skill 53.	Social (church supper)
Skill 54.	Marital (positive interaction)
Skill 55.	Martial (negative interaction)
Skill 56.	Using community resources (seeking money)
Skill 57.	Using community resources (avoiding red tape)
Skill 58.	Dealing with crises (inpatient to nonpatient transition)
Skill 59.	Dealing with crises (loss)

[a] Each application tape portrays a model enacting three to eight basic skills, in a sequence and combination chosen to deal completely with a real-life problem.

whom he or she could try these behavioral steps in real life. The co-actor is called by the name of the main actor's significant other during the role play. The trainer then instructs the role players to begin. It is the trainers' main responsibility at this point to be sure that the main actor keeps role playing and that he or she attempts to follow the behavioral steps while doing so. If he or she "breaks role" and begins making comments, explaining background events, and the like, a trainer firmly instructs him or her to resume the role. One trainer is positioned near the chalkboard and points to each step in turn as the role play unfolds, being sure that none is either missed or enacted out of order. If the trainers or the actors feel that the role play is not progressing well and wish to start over, this is appropriate. Trainers make an effort to have the actors complete the skill enactment before stepping down. Observers (the other trainees) are instructed to hold their comments until the role play has been completed.

The role playing continues until all trainees have had an opportunity to participate—even if all the steps must be carried over to a second or a third session. It should be noted that although the framework (behavioral steps) of each role play in the series remains the same, the actual content can and should change from role play to role play. It is the problem as it actually occurs, or could occur, in each trainee's real-life environment that should be the content of the given role play. When the role play has been completed, each trainee should be better armed to act appropriately in the given reality situation.

Feedback

Upon completion of each role play, a brief feedback period ensues. The goals of this activity are to let the main actor know how well he or she followed the steps for the skill or in what ways he or she departed from them, to explore the psychological impact of his or her enactment on the co-actor, and to provide him or her encouragement to try out the role-play behaviors in real life. In these critiques, it is crucial that the behavioral focus of SL be maintained. Comments must point to the presence or absence of specific, concrete behaviors and should not take the form of general evaluative comments or broad generalities.

Transfer of Training

Several aspects of the SL sessions described had, as their primary purpose, augmentation of the likelihood that learning in the therapy setting would transfer to the trainee's actual real-life environment.

Provisions of General Principles

Transfer of training has been demonstrated to be facilitated by providing trainees with general mediating principles governing successful or competent performance on the training and criterion tasks. This procedure has typically been operationalized in laboratory contexts by providing subjects with the organizing concepts, principles, strategies, or rationales that explain or account for the stimulus–response relationships operative in both the training and the application settings. The provision of general principles to SLT trainees is being operationalized in our training by the presentation in verbal, pictorial, and written form of appropriate information governing skill instigation, selection and implementation principles.

Overlearning

Overlearning is a procedure by which learning is extended to more trials than are necessary merely to produce initial changes in the subject's behavior. The overlearning, or repetition, or successful skill enactuments, in the typical SLT session is quite substantial, with the given skill taught and its behavioral steps (1) modeled several times; (2) role played one or more times by the trainee; (3) observed live by the trainee as every other group member role plays it; (4) read by the trainee from a blackborad and the skill card; (5) written by the trainee in his or her trainee's notebook; (6) practiced *in vivo* one or more times by the trainee as part of the formal homework assignment; (7) practiced *in vivo* one or more times by the trainee in response to adult and/or peer-leader coaching; and (8) practiced *in vivo* one or more times by the trainee in response to skill-oriented, intrinsically interesting stimuli introduced into his or her real-life environment.

Identical Elements

In perhaps the earliest experimental concern with transfer enhancement, Thorndike and Woodworth (1901) concluded that when there was a facilitative effect of one habit on another, it was to the extent that, and because, they shared identical elements. Ellis (1965) and Osgood (1953) have more recently emphasized the importance of transfer of similarity between stimulus and response aspects of the training and application tasks. The greater the similarity of physical and interpersonal stimuli in the SLT setting and the home or other setting in which the skill is to be applied, the greater the likely transfer.

The "real lifeness" of SLT is operationalized in a number of ways. These operational expressions of identical elements include (1) the representative, relevant, and realistic content and portrayal of the models, protagonists, and situations on the modeling tapes, all designed to be highly similar to what trainees are likely to face in their daily lives; (2) the physical props used in and the arrangement of, the role-playing setting to be similar to real-life settings; (3) the choice, coaching, and enactment of the co-actors or protagonists to be similar to real-life figures; (4) the manner in which the role plays themselves are conducted to be as responsive as possible to the real-life interpersonal simuli to which the trainee will actually respond with the given skill, and to provide behavioral rehearsal of that skill as the trainee actually plans to employ it; (5) the *in vivo* homework—coached, practiced, and intrinsically interesting skill-relevant stimuli described earlier; (6) the training of living units (all the members of a given ward) as a unit.

Stimulus Variability

Callantine and Warren (1955), Duncan (1958, 1959), and Shore and Sechrest (1961) have demonstrated that positive transfer is greater when a variety of relevant training stimuli are employed. Stimulus variability is implemented in our SLT studies by use of (1) rotation of group leaders across groups; (2) rotation of trainees across groups; (3) having trainees re-role-play a given skill with several co-actors; (4) having trainees re-role-play a given skill across several relevant settings; and (5) use of multiple homework assignments for each given skill.

Real-Life Reinforcement

Given successful implementation of both appropriate SLT procedures and the transfer enhancement procedures examined already, positive transfer may still fail to occur. As Agras (1967), Gruber (1971), Patterson and Gullion (1972), Tharp and Wetzel (1969), and literally dozens of other investigators have shown, stable and enduring performance in application settings of newly learned skills is very much at the mercy of real-life reinforcement contingencies.

We have found it useful to implement several supplemental programs outside the SLT setting, programs that can help to provide the rewards or reinforcements trainees need so that their new behaviors will be maintained. These programs include provision for both external social reward (provided by persons in the trainees' real-life environment) and self-reward (provided by the trainee himself or herself).

In several hospitals and agencies, we have actively sought to identify and develop environmental or external support by holding orientation meetings for hospital staff and for relatives and friends of trainees, that is, the real-life reward and punishment-givers. The purpose of these meetings was to acquaint significant others in the trainees' lives with SLT theory and procedures. Most important in these sessions is the presentation of procedures whereby staff, relatives, and friends can encourage and reward trainees as they practice their new skills. We

consider these orientation sessions for such persons a major value for transfer of training.

Frequently, environmental support is insufficient to maintain newly learned skills. It is also the case that many real-life environments in which trainees work and live will actively resist a trainee's efforts at behavior change. For this reason, we have found it useful to include in our transfer efforts a program of self-reinforcement. Trainees can be instructed in the nature of self-reinforcement and encouraged to "say something and do something nice for yourself" if they practice their new skills well.

The five transfer-enhancement procedures that we have briefly described do not exhaust the actual range of techniques employed for such purposes that we have examined in our research program. A complete listing of these procedures, with citation of our program's investigations, demonstrating their transfer-enhancing efficacy, appears in Table 12.2.

All of these demonstrated transfer-enhancing techniques as well as a substantial number of potentially fruitful techniques have been examined at length in two recent texts devoted to this all-important concern with generalization and endurance of treatment effects

TABLE 12.2.   Successful Transfer-Enhancing Procedures

1. Overlearning (Lopez, 1977a)
2. Helper role structuring (Litwack, 1970; Solomon, 1978)
3. Identical elements (Guzzetta, 1974; Wood, 1977)
4. Coping modeling (Fleming, 1976)
5. Stimulus variability (Hummel, 1977)
6. General principles (Lack, 1975; Lopez, 1977a)
7. Programmed reinforcement (Greenleaf, 1978; Gutride, Goldstein & Hunter, 1973)
8. *In vivo* feedback (Goldstein & Goedhart, 1973)
9. Teaching skills in tandem—reciprocal benefits (Hummel, 1977)
10. Mastery induction (Solomon, 1978)

(Goldstein & Kanfer, 1979; Koroly & Steffen, 1980).

A thorough review of psychotherapy outcome and follow-up research conducted by Goldstein and Stein (1976) revealed that "though the number of studies reporting positive therapeutic outcomes is high (85%), only 14% of the studies conducted report maintenance or transfer of therapeutic gains" (Goldstein & Kanfer, 1979, p. 2). This exceedingly low level of persistence of effect has also been documented by many others (e.g., Kazdin, 1975; Keeley, Shemberg, & Carbonell, 1976; Margolin, Siegel, & Phillips, 1976). It is to be noted and underscored in this context, however, that in our research on SL, we have been able to attain a skills transfer effect in approximately 45–50% of the trainees involved. This skills transfer effect appears to occur in direct proportion to the number of specific transfer-enhancing procedures (see Table 12.1) that are explicitly incorporated into the SL format.

Other Trainee Populations

We have described the history of SLT, its rationale, its procedures, and its application to chronic adult trainees who are seeking to function in community settings. It is the natural development of most therapies, however, that although developed for one population, they are applied in a testing-the-limits way to a number of other populations. This has been the case with SLT. Our research and clinical work have extended its demonstrated applicability to geriatric trainees, child-abusing parents, aggressive adolescents, disturbed preadolescents, and such other trainees as industrial managers, police officers, teachers, and hospital personnel.

Because the components of SL are commonly used didactic techniques, our skill training success with such diverse trainees is no surprise. Of special importance to our skill-acquisition and skill-

transfer success, however, has been our continued and energetic concern with prescriptiveness. Consistent with our reformity prescription belief, with our effort to make the therapy fit the patient, we have consistently adapted all aspects of SL to fit salient trainee characteristics. For example, our special interest during the past few years has been to use SL to teach prosocial skills to antisocial and aggressive adolescents (see Table 12.3 for a listing of the SL skills for adolescents). Our own interations with such youngsters and consultations about them reveal a number of training-relevant characteristics to which our efforts had to be responsive.

For such adolescents, raised on TV and perhaps low in imaginal patience, audio-only modeling display, hardly seemed appropriate. Thus, with such trainees, skills are modeled live by the trainers or on a filmstrip or videotape. When one observes such youngsters and, in a Premackian sense, sees what they choose to do when given freedom of choice, they will often listen to rock music, play board games, and read comic books. To capture such interests, to use their preferred channels of influence prescriptively, our filmstrip and videotape displays have rock music themes that reflect the behavioral steps of the given skill. We have a SL board game ("Making It"), and SL comic books are being developed. Our strategy may be summarized as "Study your trainees, learn how they learn, and prescriptively reflect these insights in your behavior change efforts."

EVALUATION

Starting in 1970, our research group has conducted a systematic research program oriented toward evaluating and improving the effectiveness of SL. Approximately 50 investigations have been conducted, involving a wide variety

TABLE 12.3   Structured Learning Skills for Adolescents

Series I.	Beginning social skills	
	Skill 1.	Listening
	Skill 2.	Starting a conversation
	Skill 3.	Having a conversation
	Skill 4.	Asking a question
	Skill 5.	Saying thank you
	Skill 6.	Introducing yourself
	Skill 7.	Introducing other people
	Skill 8.	Giving a compliment
Series II.	Advanced social skills	
	Skill 9.	Asking for help
	Skill 10.	Joining in
	Skill 11.	Giving instructions
	Skill 12.	Following instructions
	Skill 13.	Apologizing
	Skill 14.	Convincing others
Series III.	Skills for dealing with feelings	
	Skill 15.	Knowing your feelings
	Skill 16.	Expressing your feelings
	Skill 17.	Understanding the feelings of others
	Skill 18.	Dealing with someone else's anger
	Skill 19.	Expressing affection
	Skill 20.	Dealing with fear
	Skill 21.	Rewarding yourself
Series IV.	Skill alternatives to aggression	
	Skill 22.	Asking permission
	Skill 23.	Sharing something
	Skill 24.	Helping others
	Skill 25.	Negotiating
	Skill 26.	Using self-control
	Skill 27.	Standing up for your rights
	Skill 28.	Responding to teasing
	Skill 29.	Avoiding trouble with others
	Skill 30.	Keeping out of fights
Series V.	Skills for dealing with stress	
	Skill 31.	Making a complaint
	Skill 32.	Answering a complaint
	Skill 33.	Sportsmanship after the game
	Skill 34.	Dealing with embarrassment
	Skill 35.	Dealing with being left out
	Skill 36.	Standing up for a friend
	Skill 37.	Responding to persuasion
	Skill 38.	Responding to failure
	Skill 39.	Dealing with confusing messages
	Skill 40.	Dealing with an accusation
	Skill 41.	Getting ready for a difficult conversation
	Skill 42.	Dealing with group pressure
Series VI.	Planning skills	
	Skill 43.	Deciding on something to do
	Skill 44.	Deciding what caused a problem
	Skill 45.	Setting a goal
	Skill 46.	Deciding on your abilities
	Skill 47.	Gathering information
	Skill 48.	Arranging problems by importance
	Skill 49.	Making a decision
	Skill 50.	Concentrating on a task

of trainee populations. These include chronic adult schizophrenics (Goldstein, 1973; Goldstein, Sprafkin, & Gershaw, 1976, 1979; Liberman, 1970; Orenstein, 1969; Sutton-Simon, 1974); aggressive and other behavior-disordered adolescents (Goldstein, Sprafkin, Gershaw, & Klein, 1979, 1980; Greenleaf, 1977; Litwack, 1976; Trief, 1976; Wood, 1977); geriatric inpatients (Lopez, 1977a; Lopez, Hoyer, Goldstein, Gershaw, & Sprafkin, in press), child-abusing parents (Solomon, 1977; Sturm, 1980); young children (Hummel, 1977; Swanstrom, 1974); and such change-agent trainees as mental hospital staff (Berlin, 1974; Goldstein & Goedhart, 1973; Lack, 1975; Robinson, 1973; Schneiman, 1972) and persons employed in industry (Goldstein & Sorcher, 1973a, 1973b; Sorcher & Goldstein, 1972). The major findings of this lengthy series of studies, reported in the cited sources as well as in comprehensive form in *Psychological Skill Training* (Goldstein, 1981), may be summarized as follows:

1. *Skill Acquisition.* Across diverse trainee populations and target skills, skill acqustion is a reliable training outcome—occurring in well over 90% of SL trainees. Although pleased with this outcome, we are acutely aware of the manner in which therapeutic gains demonstrable *in the training context* are rather easily accomplished—given the potency, support, encouragement, and low threat value of trainers and therapists in that context—but that the more consequential outcome question by far pertains to trainee skill performance *in real-world contexts,* that is, skill transfer.

2. *Skill transfer.* As noted earlier, across diverse trainee populations, target skills, and applied (real-world) settings, skill transfer occurs with approximately 50% of SLT. Goldstein and Kanfer (1979) and Karoly and Steffens (1980) have indicated that across several dozen types of psychotherapy involving many different types of psychopathology, the average transfer rate of followup is between 15% and 20% of patients who are seen. The 50% rate consequent to SL is a significant improvement upon this collective base rate, though it must immediately be underscored that this cumulative average transfer finding also means that the gains shown by half of our trainees were limited to in-session acquisition. Of special consequence, however, is the consistently clear manner in which skill transfer in our studies was a function of the explicit implementation of laboratory-derived, transfer enhancing techniques (such as those described earlier).

3. *Prescriptiveness.* A prescriptive research strategy is, at heart, an effort to conceptualize, operationalize, and evaluate potentially optimal trainer × trainee × training method matches. Prior to constituting such combinations, trainer, trainee, and training characteristics that may be active contributors to such matches must be examined singly and in combination. In other words, active and inert ingredients must be identified. A small and continuing series of multiple regression investigations conducted by us have begun to point to state, trait, cognitive, demographic, and sociometric predictors of high levels of skill acquisition and transfer (Anderson, 1981; Hoyer, Lopez, & Goldstein, in press). More such prescriptive ingredients research seems worthy of pursuit.

Experimental Designs

With relatively few (mostly multiple regression) exceptions, our research program has relied upon factorial experimental designs as its investigative means, a reliance we chose mainly because of the potential utility of such designs in prescriptively oriented research. Although we believe this to be a sound decision on which we plan to continue to act, we do not wish to devalue the potential of other design orientations for the understanding and improvement of psychological skill training efforts. Studies employing single-case designs, for example, have been shown by Bellack and Hersen (1979) to be able to shed considerable light on the skill training process and thus are to be encouraged. Even at the rudimentary case study level, we have found that experiences with single groups of special types of trainees—depressed college students (O'Brien, 1981), convicted felons (Weiss, 1979), blind individuals (Meyer, 1978)—tell us much of value about the trainees themselves, about SL, and about the psychological skill training process in general.

Analog studies have long been a preferred companion research strategy of ours (Goldstein & Dean, 1966). We have conducted a subseries of SL analog investigations and found their outcomes to be sufficiently productive that we believe further use, in companion with nonanalog research, would be quite valuable. In this manner, we have examined the usefulness of SL in teaching change agents how to recognize trainee fearfulness (Berlin, 1974), anger (Healy, 1975), and certain paralinguistic affective cues (Lopez, 1977b); and we have examined which types of trainees are optimally matched in a SLT-like context with trainers who are high in hostility solidus guilt (Edelman, 1977), high in need to control (Robertson, 1977), high in aggression tolerance (Sturm, 1979), or high on certain compatibility indexes (O'Brien, 1977). At early parameter-identifying stages of a research program, in particular, analog research seems especially useful and might well be considered one of the tactics of choice as SL research ventrures into new terrain at the hands of other investigators.

Structured Learning Trainers

Although we have had relatively little to say about SL trainers throughout this chapter, we wish to point out that trainer characteristics and behavior are equal to trainee and method dimensions in their importance in the trainee × trainer × training method match. As Kiesler (1966) observed several years ago, we must operate no longer under the beliefs of a therapist uniformity myth. Trainers differ from one another and are probably different in ways that substantially influence training outcome (e.g., see the analog studies cited earlier). Systematic identification and investigation of such trainer characteristics seem to be an especially valuable research goal. Consistent with such an aspiration, we might note that the array of types of change agents who have seemingly functioned as effective SL trainers is quite broad—psychologists; social workers; teachers; nurses; occupational and recreational therapists; graduate, undergraduate, and high school students; home, parent, and teacher aides; and people who, by dint of their own (since overcome) skill-deficient history, might be called "been theres." Profession or level of credentials has not, it is our impression, been terribly important in determining who is or is not an effective SL trainer. Although we have provided our impressions of requisite general and specific trainer skills necessary for skilled leadership (see Goldstein, 1981), which characteristics do in fact lead to effective SL group leadership, to functionally skill-enhancing leadership, remains largely a domain for future investigation.

Future Research

Where is SL heading? In several directions, we hope. Some are already underway; some are yet to be pursued. We hope in particular that our own efforts as well as those of others will be successful in preventive directions. As we have commented elsewhere:

We hope investigators go beyond the remedial strategy implicit in certain of our studies

—in which we focused upon persons already displaying long-term skills deficiencies— and respond more to a preventive strategy by seeking to identify persons at risk and training them in a preparatory manner to confront future skill-demanding situations as they arise. Concretely, we refer here to . . . young children, adults in need of pre-marital training, adults profitably taught parenting, pre-retirement or other developmental-stage relevant skills, and so forth. (Goldstein, 1981, p. 128)

SUMMARY

Most contemporary approaches to social skill training can trace their immediate roots to social learning research of the 1960s and 1970s examining the efficacy of observational learning, behavioral rehearsal, and related techniques for the development of social competence. Although we, too, have been importantly influenced by this substantial body of literature, the antecedents of SLT were as much or more a matter of societal need. The failure of the mental health establishment to even approach meeting the remedial needs of the vast number of low-income clients and potential clients served historically as our motivation to develop a reformity prescription; that is, a treatment approach tailored to the accessibility channels of the typical low-income client. In the present chapter, we have described this developmental history, the procedures that constitute SLT, and its application and evaluation with diverse—but, especially, low-income—trainee populations. The social skill training movement has developed rapidly in the past decade or so, and in its several manifestations is contributing significantly to the interpersonal effectiveness and personal satisfactions of its recipients. We are indeed pleased that SLT has been and will continue to be a part of this effort.

REFERENCES

Agras, W. R. (1967.) Transfer during systematic desensitization therapy. *Behavior Research and Therapy, 5,* 193–199.

Anderson, L. (1981). Role playing ability and young children: The prescriptive question. Unpublished masters thesis, Syracuse University

Bandura, A. (1969.) *Principles of behavior modification.* New York: Holt, Rinehart & Winston

Bandura, A. (1973.) *Aggression: A social Learning analysis.* Englewood Cliffs, NJ: Prentice-Hall.

Bellack, A. S., & Hersen, M. (1979.) *Research and practice in social skills training.* New York: Plenum.

Berlin, R. J. (1974.) *Training of hospital staff in accurate affective perception fear-anxiety from vocal cues in the context of varying facial cues.* Unpublished master's thesis, Syracuse University.

Callantine, M. F., & Warren, J. M. (1955.) Learning sets in human concept formation. *Psychological Reports, 1,* 363–367.

Duncan, C. P. (1959.) Recent research on human problem solving. *Psychological Bulletin, 56,* 397–429.

Edelman, E. (1977.) *Behavior of high versus low hostility–guilt Structured Learning trainers under standardized client conditions of expressed hostility.* Unpublished master's thesis, Syracuse University.

Ellis, H. (1965.) *The transfer of learning.* New York: Macmillan.

Fleming, L. (1976.) *Training passive and aggressive educable mentally retarded children for assertive behaviors using three types of Structured Learning training.* Unpublished doctoral dissertation, Syracuse University.

Goldstein, A. P. (1971.) *Psychotherapeutic attraction.* New York: Pergamon Press.

Goldstein, A. P. (1973) *Structured Learning Therapy: Toward a psychotherapy for the poor.* New York: Academic Press.

Goldstein, A. P. (1981.) *Psychological skill training.* New York: Pergamon Press.

Goldstein, A. P., & Dean, S. (1966.) *The investigation of psychotherapy.* New York: Wiley.

Goldsein, A. P., Gershaw, N. J., & Sprafkin, R. P. (1975.) Structured learning Therapy: Skill training for schizophrenics. *Schizophrenia Bulletin, 14*, 83–88.

Goldstein, A. P., & Goedhart, A. (1973.) The use of Structured Learning for empathy-enhancement in paraprofessional psychotherapist training. *Journal of Community Psychology, 1*, 168–173.

Goldstein, A. P., & Kanfer, F. (Eds.). (1979). *Maximizing treatment gains*. New York: Academic Press.

Goldstein, A. P., & Sorcher, M. (1973a.) Changing managerial behavior by applied learning techniques. *Training & Development Journal*, March, pp. 36–39.

Goldstein, A. P., & Sorcher, M. (1973b.) *Changing supervisor behavior*. New York: Pergamon.

Goldstein, A. P., Sprafkin, R. P., & Gershaw, N. J. (1976.) *Skill training for community living: Applying Structured Learning Therapy*. New York: Pergamon.

Goldstein, A. P., Sprafkin, R. P., & Gershaw, N.J. (1979.) Structured Learning Therapy: Training for community living. *Psychotherapy: Theory, Research & Practice, 16*, 199–203.

Goldstein, A. P., Sprafkin, R. P., Gershaw, N. J., & Klein, P. (1979.) *Skillstreaming the adolescent*. Urbana, IL: Research Press.

Goldstein, A. P., Sprafkin, R. P., Gershaw, N. J., & Klein, P. (1980.) Structured Learning and the skill-deficient adolescent. In G. Cartledge & J. Milburn (Eds.), *Teaching social skills to children*. New York: Pergamon.

Goldstein, A. P., & Stein, N. (1976.) *Prescriptive Psychotherapies*. New York: Pergamon.

Greenleaf, D. (1978.) Peer reinforcement as transfer enhancement in Structured Learning Therapy. Unpublished master's thesis, Syracuse University.

Gruber, R. P. (1971.) Behavior therapy: Problems in Generalization. *Behavior Therapy, 2*,261–368.

Gutride, M. E., Goldstein, A. P., & Hunter, G. F. (1973.) The use of modeling and role playing to increase social interaction among schizophrenic patients. *Journal of Consulting and Clinical Psychology, 40*, 408–415.

Guzzetta, R. A. (1974.) *Acquisition and transfer of empathy by the parents of early adolescents through Structured Learning training*. Unpublished doctoral dissertation, Syracuse University.

Healy, J. A. (1975.) *Training of hospital staff in accurate, effective perception of anger from vocal cues in the context of varying facial cues*. Unpublished master's thesis, Syracuse University.

Hollingshead, A. B., & Redlich, F. C. (1958.) *Social class and mental illness*. New York: Wiley.

Hoyer, W. J., Lopez, M. A., & Goldstein, A. P. (1981). Correlates of social skill acquisition and transfer by elderly patients. Unpublished manuscript, Syracuse University.

Hummel, J. W. (1977.) *An examination of Structured Learning Therapy, self-control, negotiations training and variations in stimulus conditions*. Unpublished doctoral dissertation, Syracuse University.

Karoly, P., & Steffens, J. J. (Eds.). (1980.) *Improving the long-term effects of psychotherapy*. New York: Gardner Press.

Keeley, S. M., Shemberg, K. M., & Carbonell, J. (1976). Operant clinical intervention: Behavior management or beyond? *Behavior Therapy, 7*, 292–305.

Kazdin, A. E. (1975).*Behavior modification in applied settings*. Homewood, Ill.: Dorsey Press.

Kiesler, D. J. (1966.) Some myths of psychotherapy research and the search for a paradigm. *Psychological Bulletin, 65*, 110–136.

Lack, D. Z. (1975.) *Problem-solving training, Structured Learning training, and didactic instruction in the preparation of paraprofessional mental health personnel for the utilization of contingency management techniques*. Unpublished doctoral dissertation, Syracuse University.

Lazarus, A. A. (1966.) Behavioral rehearsal vs. nondirective therapy vs. advice in effecting behavior change. *Behavior Research and Therapy, 4*, 209–212.

Liberman, B. (1970.) *The effect of modeling procedures on attraction and disclosure in a psychotherapy analogue.* Unpublished doctoral dissertation, Syracuse University.

Litwack, S. E. (1970.) *The use of the helper theory principle to increase therapeutic effectiveness and reduce therapeutic resistance: Structured Learning Therapy with resistant adolescents.* Unpublished doctoral dissertation, Syracuse University.

Lopez, M. (1977a.) *The effects of overlearning and prestructuring in Structured Learning Therapy with geriatric patients.* Unpublished doctoral dissertation, Syracuse University.

Lopez, M. (1977b.) *The influence of vocal and facial cue training on the identification of affect communicated via paralinguistic cues.* Unpublished master's thesis, Syracuse University.

Lopez, M. A., Hoyer, W.J., Goldstein, A. P., Gershaw, N. J., & Sprafkin, R. P. (in press.) Effects of overlearning and incentive on the acquisition and transfer of interpersonal skills with institutionalized elderly. *Journal of Gerontology.*

Marholin, D., & Touchette, P. E. (1979). The role of stimulus control and response consequences. In A. P. Goldstein and F. H. Kanfer (Eds.), *Maximizing treatment gains: Transfer enhancement in psychotherapy.* New York: Academic Press.

Meyer, R. (1978.) *Structured Learning manual for blind trainees.* Unpublished (braille) manuscript, Syracuse, NY

Meyers, J. K., Bean, L. L., & Pepper, M. P. (1965.) Social class and psychiatric disorders. A ten-year follow-up. *Journal of Health and Human Behavior, 6,* 74–79.

O'Brien, D. (1977.) *Control and affection in Structured Learning Therapy trainers.* Unpublished master's thesis, Syracuse University.

O'Brien, D. (1981.) *Effects of cognitive therapy, using a Structured Learning Therapy format, and a mastery manipulation on depression.* Unpublished doctoral dissertation, Syracuse University.

Orenstein, R. (1969.) *The influence of self-esteem on modeling behavior in a psychotherapy analogue.* Unpublished master's thesis, Syracuse University.

Osgood, C. E. (1953.) *Method and theory in experimental psychology.* New York: Oxford University Press.

Patterson, G. R., & Gullion, M. E. (1972.) *Living with children.* Champaign, IL: Research Press.

Robertson, B. (1977.) *The effects of Structured Learning trainers' need to control on their group leadership behavior with aggressive and withdrawn trainees.* Unpublished master's thesis, Syracuse University.

Robinson, R. (1973.) *Evaluation of a Structured Learning empathy training program for lower socioeconomic status home-aide trainees.* Unpublished master's thesis, Syracuse University.

Schneiman, R. (1972.) *An evaluation of Structured Learning and didactic learning as methods of training behavior modification skills to lower and middle socioeconomic level teacher-aides.* Unpublished doctoral dissertation, Syracuse University.

Schofield, W. (1964.) *Psychotherapy, the purchase of friendship.* Englewood Cliffs, NJ: Prentice-Hall.

Shore, E., & Sechrest, L. (1961.) Concept attainment as a function of number of positive instances presented. *Journal of Educational Psychology, 52,* 303–307.

Solomon, E. (1978.) *Structured Learning Therapy with abusive parents: Training in self-control.* Unpublished doctoral dissertation, Syracuse University.

Sorcher, M., & Goldstein, A. P. (1972). A behavior modeling approach to manager and supervisor training. *Personnel Administration, 35,* 35–41.

Sturm, D. (1980.) *Therapist aggression tolerance and dependency tolerance under standardized client conditions of hostility and dependency.* Unpublished master's thesis, Syracuse University.

Sutton-Simon, K. (1974.) *The effects of two types of modeling and rehearsal procedures upon schizophrenics' social skill behavior.* Unpublished doctoral dissertation, Syracuse University.

Swanstrom, C. (1974.) *Training self-control in behavior problem children.* Unpublished doctoral dissertation, Syracuse University.

Tharp, R. G., & Wetzel, R. (1969.) *Behavior*

modification in the natural environment. New York: Acdemic Press.

Thorndike, E. L., & Woodworth, R. S. (1901.) The influence of improvement in one mental function upon the efficiency of other functions. *Psychological Review, 8,* 247–261.

Trief, P. (1971.) *The reduction of egocentrism in acting-out adolescents by Structured Learning Therapy.* Unpublished doctoral dissertation, Syracuse University.

Weiss, D. M. (1979.) *Effects of Structured Learning Therapy on social skill functioning of behavior-disordered convicted felons.* Unpublished master's thesis, Syracuse University.

Wood, M. (1977.) *Adolescent acquisition and transfer of assertiveness through the use of Structured Learning Therapy.* Unpublished doctoral dissertaion, Syracuse University.

CHAPTER 13

Social Skills Problems Experienced by Women

LAURA J. SOLOMON AND ESTHER D. ROTHBLUM

Few variables that distinguish individuals are as noticeable as gender. Writers throughout history have commented on the behavior of men versus women, much of it focused on the interpersonal realm. Personality theorists (e.g., McClelland, 1961) have contrasted men's need for achievement with women's need for affiliation. Developmental psychologists have noted the depth of knowledge that even very young children have about sex differences and social behavior.

Beliefs about the behavior of females and males are known as sex role stereotypes. The traditional masculine sex role stereotype highlights characteristics such as competence, logic, and assertiveness; the traditional feminine sex role stereotype stresses warmth and expressiveness (Deaux, 1976). Sex role stereotypes commonly refer to personality traits, such as active, adventurous, self-confident, and ambitious (for men), and dependent, passive, tactful, and gentle (for women). However, sex role stereotypes can be held about any behavior more commonly ascribed to one sex, such as "women go to college to find a husband" or "big boys don't cry." Thus, it is evident that sex role stereotypes govern a wide range of interpersonal functioning.

When mental health professionals were asked to indicate characteristics of either a normal man, a normal woman, or a normal person, the adjectives used to describe a healthy man and a healthy adult were highly similar and differed significantly from those used to describe a healthy woman (Broverman, Broverman, Clarkson, Rosenkrantz, & Vogel, 1970). Healthy men (but not women) were described as aggressive, independent, unemotional, dominant, direct, adventurous, not at all excitable in a minor crisis, blunt, loud, and rough. Healthy women (but not men) were ascribed such characteristics as talkative, tactful, quiet, expressive of tender feelings, submissive, dependent, easily tearful, emotional, home oriented, and not at all skilled in business. Healthy adults were characterized in a manner similar to healthy men. The results of this study indicate that it is difficult to be both a healthy adult and a healthy female in our society.

This chapter will focus on social skills problems that stem from the traditional feminine sex role stereotype. Because women have been socialized to be passive, submissive, tearful, and dependent, what difficulties arise when women attempt to stand up for their rights, turn down an unreasonable request, or provide positive or negative feedback to others?

The first section of this chapter will review briefly the assertion literature as it applies to women. Historically, women have been the participants in many assertion training groups as a result of their perceived deficits in this area. Assertion training has also been one of the major foci of behavioral research in the area of social skills. For these reasons, we will initially discuss the assertion literature as it relates to women.

Relatively little research has focused on the consequences of teaching women to become more assertive. The second section will discuss perceptions of assertive women and the special problems that such perceptions pose for women.

The traditional emphasis on the development of nurturing behavior in females prepared women for roles as wives, mothers, and homemakers. Partly as a result of the feminist movement and partly out of economic necessity, increasing numbers of women have entered the paid work force. The third section focuses on perceptions of women in the work setting as they relate to difficulties in interpersonal functioning. Specifically, the conflict between the traditional nurturant and expressive roles of women and the behavior of competent employees will be described.

Sex role stereotypes about women's use of language will be discussed in the fourth section of this chapter. Because a large component of interpersonal functioning is verbal, are there sex differences in linguistic styles that result in interpersonal problems for women?

The fifth section describes problems women face in personal relationships. Still socialized to marry and gain status vicariously from a husband's work, how are women coping with the realities of separation, divorce, widowhood, and single parenthood?

The final section will focus on intervention and prevention strategies for the previously mentioned social skills prob-

lems. The authors recognize the power and influence of societal socialization in the creation of social skills problems for women. Thus, the focus on strategies for overcoming these problems will generally be societal, rather than individual, implementations.

This chapter will not discuss social skills assets of women. Thus, areas in which women are considered highly competent, such as skills in expressing positive emotion, skills in self-disclosing, and the ability to listen effectively, to name just a few, are not the content of a chapter on social skills deficits. Rather, they might constitute the focus of a chapter on social skills problems that are specific to men.

LACK OF ASSERTION

Assertion training has enjoyed more publicity in the popular media than any other behavioral technique (Fodor, in press). Over 20 books on assertion reside on local bookstore shelves, some of them written specifically for women. It is not surprising that women are the targeted audience for many of these publications; women, as a group, report greater difficulty in handling both personal and professional situations assertively.

In general, women tend to report engaging in less assertive behavior than do men. Hollandsworth and Wall (1977) reviewed the research literature on self-report assessment scales of assertion. Of the 14 studies that analyzed sex differences cited by these researchers, all found women to report less assertion than did men. This difference reached statistical significance in four of these studies. This concern among women about lack of assertion has led large numbers of women to enroll in assertion training programs.

Jakubowski-Spector (1973) identified three historical trends to account for the popularity of assertion training for women. These include (1) the self-growth movement, which encouraged women to view self-fulfillment as their right and which prompted women to increase their potential in traditional and nontraditional areas; (2) the growing realization of the inflexibility of traditional sex roles, as women have taken on new jobs and experimented with new roles in personal relationships; and (3) the women's movement, which has encouraged women to increase their power and effectiveness.

Assertive behavior is defined in several fairly consistent ways. Jakubowski-Spector (1973) suggested that *assertive behavior* is evidenced by a person who stands up for legitimate rights in a way that does not violate the rights of others. She contrasted this with *aggressive behavior* in which the rights of others are violated. Winship and Kelley (1976) described assertive behavior as an honest expression of desires without infringing upon the rights of others. Eisler, Miller, and Hersen (1973) argued that *assertiveness* is a complex construct having both verbal and nonverbal component behaviors, and Lazarus (1973) elaborated on four components of the *assertive response*. He stated that nonassertive individuals have deficiencies in one or more of the following areas: (1) the ability to say "no"; (2) the ability to make requests; (3) the ability to express positive and negative feelings; or (4) the ability to begin, continue, and end conversations.

Specifically, women seem to experience greater difficulty than men expressing negative feelings, making requests, and setting limits. Hollandsworth and Wall (1977) found women to be less assertive than men on such items of the College Self-Expression Scale as refusing a boss's unreasonable request, asking a boss for favors, expressing anger to the boss, stating an opinion to the boss, standing up to the boss, asking a friend to repay a small loan, and stating

opinions during a discussion or debate. Women reported more assertion than men only on the item that concerned expressing their anger to their parents.

Data from other sources corroborate these findings. Haas (1979) found that women make fewer requests of their spouses than do men. Executives who supervise businesswomen report that the women are less assertive than desirable in such areas as delegating work, speaking up at meetings, making requests of others, dealing with criticism, and persuading others (Leonard, in Muehlenhard, 1983).

However, women report more skill than do men on positive areas of assertion. On the College Self-Expression Scale, women indicated greater assertion than did men on items related to expressing love, affection, and approval of others and complimenting others (Hollandsworth & Wall, 1977).

Women's greater skill in expressing positive rather than negative feelings is not surprising, given the research on sex role stereotypes (Broverman et al., 1970). The traditional feminine sex role stereotype is replete with adjectives consistent with positive assertive behavior, yet is virtually devoid of adjectives indicative of negative assertion. Muehlenhard (1983) compared a feminine stereotype to types of assertion. Women are characterized as sensitive to the feelings of others, open about emotions, and expressive of tender feelings, all of which correspond with positive assertion. However, women are also considered submissive, easily influenced, and sneaky, characteristics that appear incompatible with the expression of negative feelings.

The sex difference in areas of assertion suggests that assertive behavior is situation specific. Research on assertion (e.g., Eisler, Hersen, Miller, & Blanchard, 1975) indicates that an individual's assertive behavior is functionally related to the social context of the interpersonal interaction. Brumage (1976) investigated sex differences in assertive behavior in home- versus work-related situations. Females were perceived to behave more appropriately when displaying assertion at home; males were considered to behave more appropriately when displaying assertion at work.

In general, women who wish to become more assertive and who seek help from a professional therapist or assertion training program receive treatment that consists of several components (Fodor, in press). The first component, an assessment phase, usually includes self-report assertion scales and behavioral role-play situations to identify the extent of assertion deficits. The second phase of assertion training is largely educational. The therapist informs the client of the distinctions among assertive, aggressive, and passive responding; outlines the rationale for assertion training; discusses goals; and explains the training procedure. The third component involves assertion skills training. This typically incorporates direct instruction and practice of assertive behaviors in role-play situations that the client identifies as realistic and problematic. The skills training frequently includes modeling, where the client observes a demonstration of assertive behavior by the trainer, other participants, or a model on video or audiotape; behavioral rehearsal, where the client practices the assertive behaviors with the trainer or with other participants; feedback from the trainer and other participants regarding the specific verbal and nonverbal components of the response; coaching in improved strategies; and reinforcement in the form of social praise for appropriate assertive behaviors.

Many assertion training programs include components to counteract the inhibitory effects of excessive anxiety and/or negative, maladaptive cognitions (Fodor, in press). Anxiety reduction is usually accomplished by means of relax-

ation training, systematic desensitization, or exposure to the feared situation. Cognitive restructuring may be included to aid the client in changing her attitudes and values about the consequences of assertion. Finally, assertion training programs may include follow-up sessions to problem solve difficulties, to reinforce the use of new skills, and to assess and promote generalization of assertive behaviors to other people, circumstances, and situations.

Research on the overall efficacy of assertion training and the relative contributions of the various components has been extensive, although usually limited to either college student or inpatient psychiatric populations. To date, virtually no research has focused systematically on assertion training specifically targeted for women. That is, despite the fact that women, more often than men, report and demonstrate deficits in assertive behavior (particularly in the areas of expressing negative feelings, making requests, and setting limits), the assertion training intervention tends to be the same for both males and females. It is possible that this failure to tailor the assertion training procedure to the unique needs of women may contribute to some of the problems in generalization and transfer of training that are evident with this intervention.

Fodor (in press) suggests some considerations in assertion training that may be particularly salient to women. These factors, although based largely on clinical observation, serve as guides for further research on assertion training with women. They also serve as issues for the therapist to consider when planning assertion training for female clients.

Clinical observation reveals that women and men experience problems behaving assertively in different types of situations (Fodor, in press). Women, whether clerks or executives, frequently report difficulties standing up to men in the work setting. Some women experience difficulty displaying authority or wielding power, and some seem to view this behavior as too aggressive. In personal relationships with men, women report difficulty establishing an equal relationship, initiating contact, initiating sex, setting limits on sexual behavior, increasing power in the relationship, and voicing dissatisfaction (Fodor, in press). Fodor suggests that women in therapy often report difficulty asserting themselves with their mothers and daughters. In contrast, men in therapy often express difficulties controlling excessive aggression and coping with feelings of anger.

Despite the sex differences in areas of assertion, assertion training programs have presented both women and men with a standard treatment package. Societal issues confronting women (e.g., sexual harassment at work, family's expectations of dependency) are addressed on an individual case-by-case basis rather than as important themes affecting the lives and behavior of most women. Assertion trainers frequently encourage clients to focus on the specifics of problematic situations without also pointing out similarities across situations that may reflect societal expectations about appropriate behavior for women. Training may proceed with no attention to the facts that the majority of the group is female and that the areas in which the women experience difficulty asserting themselves are similar. The absence of these observations may perpetuate a notion that the women are individually responsible for their behavioral deficits. Instead, the prevalence of the problem among women suggests that societal expectations conspire to induce behavior incompatible with assertion in a number of situations. The value of this interpretation in changing behavior needs to be explored.

The ultimate goal of assertion training is the generalization of assertive behavior to a variety of situations. It is assumed that group exercises will result in clients engaging in similar assertive behaviors in their homes and work settings. An additional assumption holds that the clients' assertive behaviors will be well received by others in the environment. In fact, if a woman were to begin behaving assertively with her boss, husband, co-workers, mechanic, mother, and professor as the result of in-group role-playing exercises, it is unlikely that the results would be uniformly positive. Fodor and Epstein (in press) discussed the importance of significant others in determining success or failure. A woman may be encouraged to seek assertion training by her boss or husband, but their reactions to the newly assertive woman may be punitive. In contrast, a formerly unassertive man returning to the work or home environment is more likely to behave in accord with his expected role as the result of assertion training. Assertion training groups generally have not focused on the consequences of assertion for women. Women may be frightened or discouraged by initial unfavorable responses of significant others to their assertion. These negative responses may lead to quick extinction of the behavior. Fodor and Epstein (in press) conclude that research studies fail to focus on the relationship between assertive behavior, risk taking, and subsequent consequences for women.

Finally, there has been virtually no research exploring situations in which it may be inappropriate for women to use assertion. Battered women may wish to receive training in standing up for themselves. However, will assertion directed toward an abusing spouse result in additional battering? Will training women to "fight back" verbally to a physically stronger man have dangerous consequences for a woman's safety? The research on rape indicates that anger (Malamuth, 1982; Pithers, Marques, Gibat, & Marlatt, in press) increases the chances of a man's raping a woman. Because it is not known what the impact of assertive responding in these situations might be, therapists are advised against the wholesale promotion of assertion training with women. Careful research should precede widespread application, particularly in areas where the consequence might be further abuse.

In conclusion, there is ample evidence that assertion training programs are utilized by women and that such programs effectively increase assertion in the short run. However, the failure of training programs to focus on (1) the similarities among women and (2) possible initial negative responses from others in the environment may limit the generalization of assertion skills. Generalization and transfer of training problems plague the assertion training literature (see Chapter 15 on assertion training); thus, research on possible ways to enhance generalization is vitally needed. Finally, the consequences of assertion for women facing physical abuse require further investigation. Therapists are urged to weigh the risks carefully when considering assertion training with these special populations of women.

PERCEPTIONS OF ASSERTION

Although much research has focused on increasing assertion, there has been comparatively little investigation of people's perceptions of assertive women. Sex role stereotypes about women include such characteristics as passive, dependent, sneaky, easily influenced, and emotional (Broverman et al., 1970). Assertive women are thus interacting in a sex-inconsistent manner. How does society react to such out-of-role behavior on the part of women?

In general, although females have much to gain by engaging in effective interpersonal behavior, they also pay a price for behaving assertively. Assertive females tend to be viewed more negatively on certain characteristics compared to assertive males (Cowan & Koziej, 1979; Lao, Upchurch, Corwin & Grossnickle, 1975; Kelly, Kern, Kirkley, Patterson, & Keane, 1980). Lao et al. (1975) asked male and female undergraduates to view a videotape of male or female actors playing the role of either high-, medium-, or low-assertive faculty members. College students of both sexes rated actors on two 9-point scales as to their likeability and intelligence. High-assertive female actors were rated significantly less intelligent and less likeable than were high-assertive male actors.

Using a more elaborate methodological design, Kelly et al. (1980) had college subjects observe a videotape of a male or female college student behaving either assertively or nonassertively, and then rate these actors on interpersonal attraction. Unassertive male and female actors were rated similarly on items related to likeability. However, ratings of assertive actors differed by sex. Female assertive actors were rated significantly lower than male assertive actors on the items friendly, pleasant, considerate, open minded, good natured, kind, likeable, thoughtful, and warm, all comprising the likeability factor of the scale. Female assertive actors were also judged to be significantly less attractive, less desirable school committee members, and less likely to be spoken to at a party compared to male assertive actors. On ability and achievement items, assertive males were rated more positively than any other group. Thus, assertive women were viewed significantly more negatively on both likeability and achievement than were assertive males.

Cowan and Koziej (1979) asked college students to listen to audiotapes of a male and female interacting in either an in-role or out-of-role manner on the dimension of dominance/submission. The out-of-role (dominant) female was rated as more masculine, whereas the out-of-role (submissive) male was not viewed as more feminine. Thus, the findings of these perceptions of assertion studies suggest that assertive females are perceived more negatively than are assertive males in terms of likeability and achievement and that dominant females are perceived as more masculine or sex inappropriate.

Other researchers have examined a broader range of responses. Hull and Schroeder (1979) asked male and female undergraduates to interact with a female confederate who responded either nonassertively, assertively, or aggressively. Both males and females rated the female confederate positively when she behaved nonassertively, negatively when she behaved aggressively, and fair and nonrevengeful yet unsympathetic, aggressive, and dominant when she acted assertively. Unfortunately, Hull and Schroeder (1979) did not include a male confederate in their study. Thus, these "mixed" ratings of the assertive female cannot be interpreted more fully.

Assertive women tend to be evaluated more negatively by females than by males. Hess, Bridgewater, Bornstein, and Sweeney (1980) found that females rated assertive responses delivered by both male and female actors as more masculine and aggressive than did male raters. Denmark (1980) asked subjects to rate a written message by a male or female faculty member that was either "outspoken" or "conciliatory." Male subjects rated the outspoken woman more positively than did female subjects. Thus, men and women may have different standards regarding appropriate interpersonal behavior. More specifically, women appear to have more support for asserting themselves among men than among other women. This suggests that assertive behavior directed toward men may be more favorably received than that same behavior directed toward women. Further investigation is required, however, before this conclusion can be fully endorsed.

Because of negative evaluations of assertive women, researchers have attempted to identify modifying factors that temper the harshness of assertive responding while retaining its effectiveness. Woolfolk and Dever (1979) found that subjects perceived assertive behavior as more polite, less hostile, and more satisfying than aggressive behavior, but as less satisfying than nonassertive behavior. They included a fourth communication style, that of "assertion plus extra consideration" in which the speaker behaved in a manner that was assertive, but also friendly, tactful, and indicative of awareness of the needs of others. This empathic style received the highest ratings; it was considered both appropriate and kind. Woolfolk and Dever (1979) did not find an effect for sex of the actor.

In an investigation of corporate managers' perceptions of assertive males and females, Solomon, Brehony, Rothblum, and Kelly (1983) presented managers with audiotapes of individuals handling business-related conflicts in an assertive manner. The verbal content of the assertive response was modified to be either directly assertive, assertive but prefaced by empathic comments, or assertive but prefaced by self-effacing comments. Subjects were middle- and top-level managers of a large corporation. The results revealed that self-effacing models were evaluated significantly less favorably than directly assertive or empathic-assertive models. Managers rated empathic-assertive models significantly more favorably on several criteria, including fairness, intelligence, and an increased desire to be supervised by the model. On almost all measures, assertive females were rated as positively as assertive males. Female managers rated all models significantly more positively than did male managers on such dimensions as tact, education, attractiveness, desirability as a colleague, and desirability for promotion. There were no sex of subject by sex of model by type of assertion effects.

Several conclusions can be drawn from the preceding studies. First, there is a tendency for assertive women to be viewed more negatively than assertive men, although this is not a consistent finding. These negative evaluations of assertive women fall within the social domain (e.g., likeability, attractiveness) and the achievement domain (e.g., intelligence, competence). Secondly, some studies indicate that females relative to males have different standards for evaluating appropriate female interpersonal behaviors. Females, more than males, tend to view assertive behavior in females as aggressive and masculine. Finally, regardless of sex, tempering an assertive response with an empathic or positive preliminary statement appears to result in more positive social evaluations and in more favorable ratings of intellectual attributes. The impact of empathic assertive responding appears to be an avenue worthy of further systematic research.

PERCEPTIONS OF WOMEN'S SOCIAL SKILLS IN THE WORK SETTING

The woman in a managerial, supervisory, or leadership role at work faces out-of-role conflicts similar to the assertive woman. Both strive to be direct, effective, and able to say "no" where appropriate (Shaw & Rutledge, 1976). The media have begun to focus on the particular dilemmas of women in the work place (cf. such titles as "Masculine Traits Equal Business Success," *New York Times,* August 30, 1977; "Sex-Related Problems Aren't the Biggest Job Woes of Most Woman Managers," *Wall Street Journal,* May 29, 1979). However, there has been relatively little research on the social skills of women at work. The present review will focus on studies investigating interpersonal behavior of women in the work setting rather than on employee attitudes toward sex roles in general.

Research conducted in the work place generally reveals that the male sex role stereotype corresponds to the managerial role, whereas the female sex role stereotype does not. Schein (1973) asked middle managers to evaluate women in general, men in general, and successful middle managers on 92 descriptive adjectives that had previously been found to differentiate men and women. Her results indicated that the evaluations of men and of managers overlapped considerably, whereas there was a near-zero correlation between evaluations of women and of managers. Specifically, 60 of the 86 items on which managers were rated were more similar to ratings of men than of women, compared with 8 of the 86 items that were more similar to ratings of women than of men. Similar results depicting the lack of congruity between the roles of women and of managers have been obtained by Powell and Butterfield (1979) and by Massengill and Di-Marco (1979). These studies confirm the notion of "role conflict," that women in managerial roles are expected to behave both aggressively, competitively, and independently as well as emotionally and dependently. O'Leary (1974) has described this double bind as follows (p. 815):

The woman who seeks employment in a traditionally masculine position is faced with a dilemma. Society views the ideal woman as an expressive individual lacking in the masculine attributes of logic and drive. If she feels that because she is not a man she is not endowed with the competency characteristics ascribed to men, she may suffer from lack of confidence concerning her ability to do the job well. If, on the other hand, she feels that she has the potential to manifest masculine traits, she may feel that allowing such characteristics to surface might be detrimental to her femininity, rendering her less of a woman.

When supervisees are asked to evaluate the effectiveness of supervisory style, ratings are influenced by the supervisor's sex. Rosen and Jerdee (1973) asked undergraduates and bank supervisors to select effective styles of supervision from among four alternative supervisory styles. These included a threat style (supervisor told subordinates that they would be discharged if there was no improvement in performance), a reward style (supervisor told subordinates that salary increases would result from improved performance), a friendly-dependent style (supervisor approached subordinates in a friendly manner and asked for help from subordinates in the form of improved performance), and a helping style (supervisor offered to help subordinates with any problem that interfered with their performance). Both males and females rated the reward style as most appropriate for male supervisors. There were no sex differences in the appropriateness of either the threat or helping style, and the latter was regarded as effective for both sexes. Supervisors who adopted a friendly-dependent style were rated appropriate when using that style with subordinates of the opposite sex. Males were considered appropriate in their use of three of the four supervisory styles, whereas women were constricted from using the reward and threat styles. Thus, there appears to be less flexibility in the manner with which female supervisors can effectively perform their roles.

Similarly, Bartol and Butterfield (1976) asked students of business management to evaluate managers according to four dimensions of leadership that are stressed in the leadership literature: initiating structure (e.g., reorganizing the department), consideration (e.g., paying attention to the comfort of employees), production emphasis (e.g., putting in extra hours at work), and tolerance for freedom (e.g., promoting a relaxed and informal work atmosphere). Evaluations consisted of ratings of productivity, employee satisfaction, supervisor's satisfaction, and general effectiveness. Female leaders were evaluated more positively than were males on consideration, whereas males were evaluated more positively than were females on initiating structure. There were no sex differences on production emphasis (which was generally evaluated negatively) nor on tolerance for freedom. However, individuals who behaved in leadership styles of the opposite sex (e.g., considerate males, structuring females) were evaluated more negatively. Thus, what is considered an acceptable leadership style for women is not the same as that of men and vice versa.

Williams (1980) provides evidence for sex differences among raters in perceptions of work-related effectiveness. Students of business viewed a videotape of either an assertive or unassertive female manager. The assertive woman manager was rated significantly more favorably in terms of her managerial effectiveness than was the unassertive woman manager. Additionally, the assertive woman manager was viewed as more competent and dynamic, but less trustworthy than her unassertive counterpart. Female raters reported significantly more favorable attitudes toward women as managers than did male raters. Further, raters who scored high in assertiveness themselves were significantly more favorable toward women as managers compared to raters who scored low in assertiveness. Presumably, women managers will experience more positive evaluations if their subordinates are also assertive women.

In order to examine reactions to women engaged in traditional or nontraditional sex role pursuits, Spence and Helmreich (1972) presented undergraduates with a videotape of a female model who behaved either competently or incompetently and reportedly had either masculine interests (i.e., physics major, enjoyed tennis) or feminine interests (i.e., fine arts major, enjoyed cooking). Female subjects gave highest ratings of likability to the model who was either masculine in her interests or competent. Male subjects preferred the model who was both masculine in her interests and competent, and liked the masculine—incompetent model least. These results are contrary to the commonly held assumption that women pursuing masculine interests will experience negative social consequences (i.e., will not be liked). However, at least for women working in nontraditional roles primarily with men, the findings suggest they had best be competent in their pursuit of masculine activities.

The study by Spence and Helmreich (1972) did not compare female and male models. Other studies suggest that when males and females perform identical assertive, managerial behaviors, the women are viewed less positively than are the men.

Wiley and Eskilson (1982) asked middle managers to rate different ways of influencing people. A male or female actor attempted to influence either a male or female target person. Styles of influence consisted of either using reward power (e.g., "Doing it my way will get you credit; otherwise, I may not ensure you get credit") or expert power (e.g., "I've done this successfully before"). Managers were asked to rate the probable positions of the actor and the target person in the corporation and their degree of power, and to rate them on adjectives corresponding with sex role stereotypes. These researchers found that differences in perceived, but not actual, position in the corporate hierarchy accounted for much of women's devaluation in management. That is, women are assumed to have a lower position and less power. Wiley and Eskilson (1982, p. 8) suggest that "strong legitimazation of women in authority roles would appear to eliminate misperceptions of their power and obviate the need for different interaction

styles." Yet, these authors also found that women perceived as having equivalent positions to male managers were viewed as significantly colder than their male counterparts when engaging in identical assertive management behavior. Further, the way in which a manager attempts to influence a co-worker is differentially effective, depending on the manager's sex. Male managers were judged to be more effective when using expert-based influence attempts. In contrast, female managers were judged to be more effective when using reward-based influence attempts. This suggests, once again, that the management style that may be effective for men may not be effective when used by women. The reward-based influence attempts found to be effective for women in this study were not viewed as appropriate for women in the previously cited Rosen and Jerdee (1973) research. Methodological differences in the investigation may account for this inconsistency. However, it may be the case that there are fewer standards for appropriate female managerial behavior, and therefore, one might expect less consistency regarding what is appropriate behavior for women in managerial roles.

It does seem apparent, however, that merely training women to adhere to a "masculine" interpersonal style in management situations will not necessarily result in favorable evaluations. As Wiley and Eskilson suggest, legitimazation of women in positions of power is required. This involves the installation of more female role models into higher levels of the corporate hierarchy. It is really after women are given the opportunities to perform in managerial capacities that appropriate standards for behavior can be determined.

Women are not strangers to the role of subordinates, and when raters are asked to evaluate the effectiveness of subordinates rather than managers, sex differences are also apparent. Rosen and

Jerdee (1975) gave bank employers sample grievances by employees. Complaintants were either male or female and appealed in either a polite, pleading manner or in an aggressive, threatening manner. A passive, pleading appeal on the part of a female employee received the lowest evaluations, although such an appeal when presented by a male employee was rated positively. Aggressive, threatening demands by either males or females received moderately positive evaluations. This suggests that in order for women employees to have a grievance heard, they must use a more forceful, out-of-role approach. Male employees, on the other hand, have greater flexibility in voicing a grievance. In contrast, Mai-Dalton, Feldman-Summers, and Mitchell (1979) asked banking executives to evaluate how either a male or female manager requested that his/her superior approve a large business loan. The request was made in either a calm, unemotional manner or in an angry, emotional manner. In general, calm, unemotional behavior was evaluated more positively. However, angry, emotional females were rated more positively than males behaving in a similar manner. These authors considered the emotional behavior to be more consistent with women's roles and thus suggested that it was more appropriate behavior for women than for men. However, individuals behaving in the calm, unemotional manner were rated as possessing a greater chance for promotion.

In conclusion, there are mixed results regarding the degree to which in-role versus out-of-role behavior results in perceptions of greater effectiveness on the part of women in the work setting. On the one hand, the role of manager is highly dissimilar to the feminine sex role stereotype, and women who behave in "masculine" styles are evaluated negatively. On the other hand, there is evidence that women who behave nontraditionally and are effective are evaluated

positively. It would appear, then, that the woman who is able to surmount her history of socialization *both* to occupy the role of manager and to assert herself in that role may function most effectively. Unfortunately, the prevalence of managerial women is probably too low to permit a basis for standards of comparison among managerial styles.

SOCIAL SKILLS PROBLEMS RESULTING FROM SEX DIFFERENCES IN LINGUISTIC STYLE

Behavior therapy for social skills deficits, whether in the form of assertion training, interviewing skills training, or dating skills training, has recognized the importance of language use. In particular for women, sex role stereotypes hold that women's use of language renders them powerless, unassertive, and hesitant. A plethora of literature has focused on sex differences in language use (e.g., such books as *Man Made Language* and *Words and Women*). Beliefs about women's linguistic styles will be reviewed with corresponding confirming or disputing behavioral research evidence.

To "talk like a lady" connotes a tentative and powerless form of speech. The following pair of sentences differ only in choice of initial expletive:

Oh dear, it's raining again.
Shit, it's raining again.

Most people would assume that the former was spoken by a woman, the latter by a man (Lakoff, 1973). Research on the style of women's language does indeed confirm that women use hesitant features of speech as modifiers ("sort of," "I think"), "empty" adjectives ("divine," "fabulous"), tag questions (". . . Don't you agree?"), statement endings that turn into questions ("Dinner is ready?"), intensifiers ("I'm *so* happy"), and overly polite speech ("Would you be so kind . . .") (Crosby, Jose, & Wong-McCarthy, 1981).

The sex role stereotype holds that women are more talkative than men. The research indicates otherwise. Women tend to engage in listening and head nodding more readily, whereas men do more talking in all combinations of social interactions: in single-sex and mixed-sex dyads and in groups (Henley & Thorne, 1977). In mixed-sex interactions, men have been found to be more talkative in work-related situations such as faculty meetings (Kirsh, 1983) and state legislative meetings (Spender, 1980) as well as in conversations in the home environment (Fishman, 1978). Women perform the "interactional shit-work" (Fishman, 1978) by asking questions and by supporting the men's statements and opinions. Kirsh (1983) concluded that this only serves to perpetuate the image of the competent male leader and the passive, dependent female follower.

As a consequence of these speech patterns, women are frequently ignored and interrupted. In mixed-sex conversations, men tend to interrupt women, "talk over" women's speech, change the topic, and deny women access to topic control by often not responding to initiation (Fishman, 1978). This led Kirsh (1983) to suggest that men's power in conversations, as a result of ignoring and interrupting women and changing female-initiated topics, perpetuates the societal power hierarchy in which men have higher status than women and women have more menial, supportive roles.

Sex differences in linguistic styles are apparent in very young children. By age 4, boys use more language associated with males, such as giving out information, and girls are more compliant and deferential (Kirsh, 1983). Boys speak up more in mixed-sex groups, are spoken to more by boys and girls, and they receive more requests for permission and statements about needs (Kirsh, 1983). This early sex difference in language use revealing greater competence among boys is especially disconcerting in light of girls' earlier use of speech and greater verbal aptitude.

The powerlessness of women's speech is recognized clearly in adulthood. Research indicates that both men and women lapse into "women's language" when talking to the police (Crosby & Nyquist, 1977). Jury members are less likely to believe an individual using women's linguistic styles (O'Barr, 1982). Even voice pitch can be a stigma. Lower pitch voices carry more authority, and female newscasters are more likely to be hired if their voice has a lower pitch than a higher one. As a result, one can conclude that adult women face conflicts in appearing both competent and feminine in their language use.

It is presumptuous to assume that specific language-use intervention strategies directed to individual women will dramatically alter interpersonal functioning on a large scale. Given women's early and comprehensive training to be verbally hesitant, supportive, and deferential, and their continuing punishment for attempts to speak up, larger scale cultural changes are required in order to prevent and reverse a lifetime of stigma for the silent sex.

SOCIAL SKILLS PROBLEMS FOLLOWING MARITAL DISRUPTION

Traditionally, women have been socialized to fulfill the roles of wife and mother. Only 5 to 6% of women in high school and in the early years of college have no intentions of marrying (Donelson, 1977). Probably no other event in a woman's life is given as much attention by our society, and few other events are so expected in a woman's life.

The average age at marriage for women in this country is 20 years (Williams, 1983). Unmarried women who are older may begin to experience the pressure to "find a man" in order to avoid the connotations associated with the labels of "spinster" or "old maid." Donelson has pointed out that our culture is not so much "promarriage" as "antisingleness." She states (p. 233):

The pressures toward marriage and away from singleness are so pervasive and intense in contemporary society that many people have not in fact freely chosen the marriage they have or intend. There has been an idolatry of marriage as the only way to find peace and fulfillment. . . . Supporting the assumption of the necessity of marriage are strong assumptions about the disadvantages of not being married—although most single women are not particularly antimarriage, most other people are antisingleness. . . . Many women felt that marriage is the only way for them to be happy, and that singleness means only a loneliness and despair they think they can avoid by marriage.

In contrast to the interpersonal deficits that singleness connotes for women, unmarried men are considered to lead interpersonally fulfilling and sexually exciting lives.

Despite this socialization, a woman's chances of remaining married are statistically slim. A 1979 U.S. Bureau of the Census survey indicated that there were five divorces in this country for every 10 marriages (Worell & Garret-Fulks, 1983). There is less available information about marital separation rates, although a 1971 U.S. Bureau of the Census survey indicated that women are separated for longer periods of time than are men before reentering relationships (Bloom, Asher, & White, 1978). The number of divorces involving children is increasing dramatically, and over 90% of children are placed in the custody of the mother (Worell & Garett-Fulks, 1983). This has resulted in dramatic increases in the proportion of single-parent households headed by women. Finally, women are four times more likely than men to be widowed, given their longer life span and the tendency for them to marry men who are older (Worell & Garret-Fulks, 1983). Thus, the majority of women who marry cannot realistically expect to live "happily ever after" with their spouse.

Hetherington, Cox, and Cox (1979) investigated the immediate consequences of divorce for women and men in a 2-year longitudinal study of parent and child functioning after divorce. Divorced mothers felt physically unattractive, helpless, and complained of having lost the identity and status of the marital role. Divorced fathers, on the other hand, felt rootless and unstructured without the presence of children and a familiar setting.

Social activity for divorced fathers was marked in the Hetherington et al. (1979) sample. One year after the divorce, these men were engaged in a frenzy of social encounters at bars, parties, clubs, and gatherings. Divorced women were less likely to engage in such social activity. Furthermore, a subgroup of divorced women rapidly deteriorated in appearance and grooming.

Hetherington et al. also found that their divorced subjects demonstrated a rapid decline in contact with former friends who were married. This effect was more marked for women than for men. Males were more often included in social activities. Women reported less energy for social activities because of increased time demands, such as the time needed to seek employment and perform child care and housework. They reported feeling trapped or locked into a child's world. Although the social life of the divorced woman increased over the 2-year period, it did not approach that of married women. Both divorced men and women expressed dissatisfaction with causal sexual encounters and lack of intimacy. Women, however, were more likely to express dissatisfaction, high-lighting feelings of depression, desper-ation, and low self-esteem following casual sexual encounters (Hetherington et al., 1979).

Given the preceding results, it is not surprising that the divorced women in the Hetherington et al. study continued to feel attachment to their former hus-bands. They were more likely than the divorced men to feel that the divorce had been a mistake, and they experi-enced feelings of depression, anger, and panic when their ex-husbands remarried. Women were less prepared for the social and financial responsibilities facing the divorced person than were men. The pressures of taking the iniative in these areas, while simultaneously maintaining the domestic and child-rearing duties, may have led the newly divorced woman to view her ex-husband and marriage with undeserving affection.

The stigma associated with the role of divorced women has been discussed by Brandwein, Brown, and Fox (1974) and Borenzweig (1976). The family having a single mother at its head is termed "bro-ken," "disorganized," or "nonintact." The divorced woman is considered to have been unable to "keep her man" (Brandwein et al., 1974). On the other hand, she is viewed also as likely to se-duce other women's husbands. Divorced mothers are shown little respect and so-cietal attitudes toward them are gener-ally negative. In fact, they are often blamed for a variety of social problems, including the need for federal govern-ment expenditures in the form of welfare (Brandwein et al., 1974). As a result of the stigma, divorced women are fre-quently socially isolated. Borenzweig believes that divorced mothers are pun-ished as a result of having threatened so-cietal beliefs in monogamy, sex roles, and the nuclear family.

Marital disruption places the woman in a "deviant" gender role—that of head of the household. Socialized to depend on her husband for social activity and identity and to subordinate herself in the marital relationship, the divorced woman experiences difficulty managing her finances, her children, her former spouse, and her social life (Worell & Garret-Fulks, 1983). Rawlings and Car-ter (1979, p. 28) state:

Males and females both will experience fail-ure following divorce, but women have a heightened sense of personal failure over not succeeding at their most important societal role. The divorced woman's perception of failure is similar to that of a man's following the loss of employment and results in similar psychological consequences: lowered self-es-teem, depression, and guilt.

The social situation may be less am-biguous for widowed women than for di-vorced women, as there are clearer guidelines for the role of widow (Brand-wein et al., 1974; Worell & Garret-Fulks, 1973). Yet widows, too, are regarded as a "fifth wheel" in social situations (Wor-ell & Garret-Fulks, 1983) and have dif-ficulties coping with their new roles. Younger widows often do not have the support of women their age who are in similar circumstances. Widows of all ages are sometimes less prepared to as-sume their new roles than are divorced women due to the possible sudden na-ture of the husband's death.

Given the social stigma, it is not sur-prising that "single-again" women are considered to occupy a temporary role "between men" and are expected to re-marry. Yet the probability that women will remarry is less than that for men. About 13% of eligible men remarry each year compared with 4% of eligible women. The peak age of remarriage for women is 20–24 years; for men it is 25–29 years (Bloom, Asher, & White, 1978). For women, rates of remarriage are high-est for younger women without children (Hetherington et al., 1979). Similarly, widowed men are more likely to remarry than widowed women (Bloom et al., 1978). Remarriages also tend to show greater age discrepancies between partners. Bloom et al. indicate that whereas brides are 10 or more years younger than grooms in less than 2% of first marriages, in remarriages, 27% of brides are 10 or more years younger than their grooms. Thus, the woman over 30, especially if she has children, has a greatly decreased chance of ever remarrying. In contrast to pressures on women to remarry, there is some evidence that remaining single has interpersonal advantages for women. Women who left their spouses and who did not become reinvolved reported better social adjustment than those who did resume relationships with men (Rounsaville, Prusoff, & Weissman, 1980).

If we have succeeded in disbanding the myth of the "gay divorcee," it is not our intention to advocate that women necessarily remain married. Marriage may be considered society's ideal state for women; however, there is evidence to suggest that marriage is psychologically healthier for men than for women (Bloom et al., 1978; Gove, 1973; Radloff, 1975). The social benefits of marriage for men include acquiring a partner to meet domestic, social, and sexual needs; the social hazards of marriage for women involve fulfilling those same roles. Whereas divorce affects women more adversely than men, never-married women are as psychologically healthy as married men. Ironically, it is this very group of never-married women who would be considered socially deficient by their friends, family, and co-workers by virtue of their single status.

In summary, women are not prepared for "single-again" status. Not only does society look down on a woman in such a position, but also society expects these women to be able to handle social initiatives that are counter to the social behaviors women have been taught to display. The feminine sex role stereotype encourages passivity and dependency, behaviors that are least likely to result in successful coping with the single-again responsibilities or successful development of new supportive networks.

IMPLICATIONS FOR INTERVENTION AND PREVENTION

It is evident from the preceding sections that there is considerable overlap in the types of social skills problems experienced by women. The social skills deficits exposed in the work setting are consistent with the deficits found in women in the assertion literature and in the marital disruption literature. Similarly, the conflicts that women face are apparent across the various social skills areas. That is, women are criticized for not having managerial/leadership skills; yet they are appraised more negatively than are men when displaying these behaviors. Women are considered to be too deferent and emotional; yet they are judged less likable and intelligent than are males when making assertive responses. The common theme underlying these social skills problems is the socialization process that teaches females to be passive, dependent, and family oriented when the harsh realities of the world require a much broader behavioral repertoire.

Yet the broader behavioral repertoire, the inclusion of "male" behaviors within the female's social skills capabilities, does not solve her problems. Ours is a world of rapid social transition. The behaviors that may facilitate adaptation to swiftly changing roles are likely to be rewarded and punished intermittently. Women in new roles are unlikely to behave in ways that are pleasing to everyone. The general absence of female role models in positions of authority and power makes it difficult to determine what interpersonal behavior patterns are both effective and satisfying in such circumstances. Thus, the literature on social skills problems of women is fraught with unanswered questions.

In light of these issues, what are the implications for social skills training with women? Three general suggestions are offered to therapists for consideration when teaching women new ways to handle interpersonal situations. These suggestions are presented as components that may be incorporated into a standard skills training program that already includes instruction, behavioral rehearsal, feedback, and reinforcement, in order to better tailor the program to the unique needs of women. The authors acknowledge the absence of empirical support for their recommendations and encourage the systematic investigation of these suggestions: (1) Anticipate and discuss with the client the likelihood of intermittent success when she begins engaging in new assertive, nonstereotypic interpersonal behaviors; (2) address self-defeating cognitions that may inhibit risk taking in the interpersonal domain; and (3) decrease perceptions of isolation and increase exposure to relevant role models. Each of these suggestions will be discussed in turn.

There are sometimes harsh contingencies in the natural environment for women behaving in nontraditional ways (e.g., setting limits, making requests, supervising in the work setting). Because women may be punished for attempting assertive responses initially, therapists are wise to anticipate problems with generalization. The experience of failure is likely to be frustrating for both the client and the therapist. Thus, strategies that either prepare the woman for the difficulties she may face or attempt to make the environment more receptive to her new behavior could help enhance generalization. Specifically, therapists might familiarize themselves with the findings from the perception of assertion and women in the work setting literatures. These findings could be discussed realistically in terms of the types of responses women

may expect from others. Therapy sessions could include practicing how to handle the negative reactions of others to an assertive woman. With adequate preparation, the female client may be inoculated against early termination of new behaviors because of a few negative consequences.

The perception of assertion literature suggests that the inclusion of modifying factors in assertive responding results in positive evaluations of assertive women. That is, women who temper an assertive response with an empathic preliminary statement are judged to be both intelligent and likeable (Solomon et al., 1983; Woolfolk & Dever, 1979). Training in the use of such modifiers may encourage women to stand up for themselves while retaining their sensitivity to the concerns of others. It may allow others in the environment to better accept women's requests, criticisms, and general authority, as the behavior maintains an element of female role-consistent responding (i.e., the showing of interpersonal sensitivity).

Finally, when feasible, significant others from the client's natural environment could be brought into therapy to enhance the likelihood that the woman's new behavior will be favorably received. Involvement of a friend, spouse, or lover could permit more realistic appraisal of the behavior of both individuals and possibly could result in problem solving new solutions to the social skills dilemmas facing women.

As a result of socialization, women may possess self-defeating cognitions about the chances of effective interpersonal change. Kelly (1982) has pointed out that clients with a history of social skills deficits continue to attend selectively to the possibility of negative outcomes. For example, women may consider being liked by others more important than being assertive. Women may fear rejection disproportionally to the likelihood of its occurrence. Research by Eisler, Frederiksen, and Peterson (1978) has indicated that highly assertive subjects expected more positive evaluations from other people in social situations than did low-assertive subjects. In particular, high- and low-assertive subjects did not differ on expectations of negative evaluations (such as fear or anger expressed toward them, or fear of being taken advantage of). Rather, high-assertive subjects were significantly more likely than low-assertive subjects to expect positive consequences, such as admiration, respect, or understanding. Although this study did not investigate sex differences, the results imply that low-assertive subjects expect less favorable responses to be demonstrated toward them and thus may be less likely to exhibit assertive behavior. Thus, for example, a woman might repeatedly initiate a social contact without being turned down, yet still believe that such behavior is not approved of. Rather than enjoy the feelings of mastery that accompany behavior change, women may devalue their own performance or view others as not responding favorably.

Ellis and Harper (1976) have described irrational cognitions that interfere with effective functioning, such as fears of failure, self-blame, need for approval, and catastrophizing. Cognitive-oriented strategies (e.g., Ellis's Rational Emotive Therapy, Beck's Cognitive Behavior Therapy, Meichenbaum's Self-Instructional Training) to counteract such self-defeating beliefs seem particularly indicated for female clients. Therapists might investigate the nature of women's negative self-statements and provide alternative, competency-enhancing cognitions. A study by Linehan, Goldfried, and Goldfried (1979) combined behavioral social skills training with cognitive restructuring. The cognitive component included both identifying self-defeating thoughts and generating positive alternatives. Their results indicated that the combined behavioral and cognitive approach was more effective than either approach used alone. More research is necessary to investigate the nature of women's cognitions and to intervene effectively.

Finally, the effects that consciousness-raising groups have had on improving women's feelings of personal adequacy should be mentioned. Lange and Jakubowski (1978) suggest combining assertion training with consciousness-raising discussion. In this way, female clients are provided with both skills training and cognitive restructuring. Issues such as changes in self-concept, awareness of the role of socialization, discussion of achieving personal competency, and standards for appropriate behavior might be addressed.

Women in individual therapy may have the impression that they are unique and alone in their struggles to adapt to new roles or to stand up for what they believe. Although it is important to create in clients a sense of personal mastery and competence, it is also important to avoid blaming the victim—holding clients responsible for the problems they experience. By helping clients understand that the behaviors and beliefs that women are taught throughout their lives contribute to current difficulties, clients can recognize that they are not alone in their efforts. This "not-alone" status can empower individuals to change their circumstances. That is, the recognition that their problems fit into a larger context may encourage a level of activism inspired by group support. Thus, therapists may consider providing support groups for women experiencing similar circumstances (e.g., widows, single parents, women in management). Such groups enable women to problem solve with the benefit of group feedback and to practice new behaviors in the presence of peers who may understand and experience similar issues. Support groups also indicate to group members that they are not isolated but rather are part of a larger group of women with similar concerns. Therapists are advised to become aware of community groups (e.g., widow-to-widow programs, Parents without Partners, local women's business associations) that could help meet clients' needs.

The strategies discussed thus far have focused on therapy or tertiary intervention with female clients. Although it is important to consider ways to improve therapeutic efficacy, the magnitude of the problem warrants equal consideration of prevention strategies. Perpetuation of the traditional feminine sex role stereotype can only serve to place limits on appropriate female behavior, reduce the acceptance of women in nontraditional roles, and maintain punitive consequences for women who behave in ways contrary to the stereotype. If one agrees that societal expectations for females shape their social behaviors and help create their social skills problems, then an appropriate role for professionals intending to reduce behavior problems in women would include maximizing flexibility in both the behaviors and the expectations of females. Although this may appear to be an ominous task, there are realistic ways to promote healthy, flexible social functioning in females within the constraints of one's professional activities.

First, therapists working with female clients are encouraged to promote independent functioning and role flexibility whether or not the presenting problem is of a social skills nature. Just as a physician is encouraged to advise a patient to stop smoking even when the presenting complaint is unrelated to the smoking habit, the therapist may reduce the likelihood of future difficulties by suggesting and supporting independent, self-sufficient, and flexible behavior in women. For example, a couple in therapy might be encouraged to engage periodically in activities independent of the spouse, to rotate responsibility for household fi-

nances or maintain separate accounts, to swap specific household roles occasionally in order to gain exposure to tasks that may ultimately require their attention. Thus, within the context of therapy, the therapist can promote flexibility and independent functioning before a social skills problem arises.

Second, psychologists are in an excellent position to influence the manner in which children are taught sex role behavior. By consulting to teachers in the classroom and/or groups of parents of young children, psychologists can encourage positive responding to nonstereotypic behaviors in young girls. Mental health professionals can discuss the limitations of sex role stereotyping with these adults who ultimately shape female behavior and expectations. The psychologist can demonstrate ways to reinforce both male and female social behaviors regardless of the child's sex, suggest ways to handle children's questions and comments regarding the flexibility of behaviors and roles, offer advice on the adequacy of school textbooks in their portrayal of men's and women's roles, and encourage other adults to model nontraditional behaviors for young children to see.

Finally, mental health professionals can discuss the sex role conceptualization of women's social skills problems with their colleagues, thereby enhancing the likelihood of a trickle-down effect. As more professionals perceive the deficits in female's social functioning as inadequacies in our process of socialization, more emphasis may be placed on applied research designed to examine ways to prevent and/or intervene in this area.

Gisela Konopka, a noted social worker dedicated to social action as a means of preventing mental health problems, has stated (1981, p. 119):

Perhaps the most important quality of the professional who genuinely wants to be of help to mankind [sic] is an inquiring, flexible mind combined with an almost searing honesty and courage to stand up against comfortable dogmas within and fashionable ones without.

The prevention of the types of social skills problems experienced by women that were discussed in this chapter requires that we venture beyond the therapeutic hour and into the realm of social change. Efforts that ignore these societal issues are likely to have only limited impact.

CONCLUSIONS

This chapter focused on specific social skills problems experienced by women. The authors proposed that the traditional feminine sex role socialization process might contribute to the skills problems. The literature review revealed that many questions remain regarding (1) the nature of appropriate clinical interventions for social skills problems in women, and (2) the impact of changing sex role options available to women. These questions lend direction to future research.

In the area of assertion, available evidence suggests that women participate in assertion training programs and that many of these programs may effectively increase assertive responding in the short term. However, many programs have failed to address the similarities in assertion deficits experienced by women and the effects that assertive behavior might have on women's environments. Consequently, the newly assertive woman risks possible negative consequences of her behavior. This issue requires further investigation in light of the transfer of training problems that plague this clinical area.

Results from the perceptions of assertion literature suggest that women who behave in an assertive manner tend to be viewed more negatively than are assertive men, although this is by no means a consistent finding across all studies. The negative evaluations include lower expectations of assertive women in both social and achievement areas. Women appear to view assertive females as more aggressive or masculine than do men. However, prefacing an assertive response with an empathic or positive statement seems to temper the negative appraisals of women. Further research on the impact of empathic assertive responding is needed.

Research on women's social skills in the work setting revealed that the traditional feminine sex role stereotype bears little resemblance to the characteristics required of supervisors or executives. However, women who competently perform nontraditional roles seem to be evaluated positively. Unfortunately, women in the work setting have few female role models from which to emulate managerial functioning. The lack of female role models, no doubt, adds to the difficulty women face when attempting to incorporate nontraditional roles effectively. Training in managerial skills, organizational behaviors, and office politics may aid the individual woman aspiring for the executive office; however, we feel it is unlikely that individual skills training will be as effective as exposure to competent female models from an early age.

Women's use of language may contribute to social skills problems. Linguistic styles typically practiced by women include hesitant, tentative, overly polite, and powerless features of speech. Women talk less than men, get interrupted more, and engage in topics of conversation that are more readily ignored than are those initiated by men. These sex differences in language patterns are acquired at an early age suggesting that early intervention is required.

Finally, despite women's socialization for the role of wife, proportionately few women will remain married. Women who are single again as a result of divorce, separation, or widowhood are often stigmatized for having failed in their marriages. Newly single women may feel unprepared to handle the role of head-of-household and may lack supportive social networks to help ease the transition from married to single again. Never-married women, who tend to be psychologically healthier than their married counterparts, ironically are considered socially deficient by society because of their failure to marry. Societal norms must change in order to better accept the alternatives available to women in terms of marital-singleness status. Further, the value of supportive networks for single-again women requires investigation.

It is apparent that there is overlap in the social skills problems experienced by women in a variety of situations. Societal roles for women are changing rapidly, often without clear guidelines for effective functioning in these new roles. This chapter presented three recommendations for therapists who provide social skills training for women. First, therapists are encouraged to anticipate, discuss, and rehearse with women the difficulties they may encounter when engaging in sex-inconsistent behavior. Secondly, therapists are urged to focus on increasing women's cognitions of mastery and decreasing self-devaluating, self-defeating cognitions that often persist despite behavior change. Finally, therapists are encouraged to expose women to relevant role models and to decrease women's perceptions of isolation.

Whereas much can be done to improve therapeutic efficacy with female clients, the large-scale nature of the problems also warrants discussion of prevention strategies. Therapists can promote independent functioning in female clients even when social skills problems are not the presenting problem. Psychologists can influence the way in which children learn interpersonal behaviors, by consulting to schools and by training teachers and parents to model and encourage both traditional and non-traditional sex role behaviors. Finally, mental health professionals can discuss the sex role formulation of women's social skills problems with their colleagues in order to facilitate research on intervention and prevention strategies in this area and to promote the process of social change.

REFERENCES

Bartol, K. M., & Butterfield, D. A. (1976). Sex effects in evaluating leaders. *Journal of Applied Psychology, 61,* 446–454.

Bloom, B. L., Asher, S. J., & White, S. W. (1978). Marital disruption as a stressor: A review and analysis. *Psychological Bulletin, 85,* 867–894.

Borenzweig, H. (1976). The punishment of divorced mothers. *Journal of Sociology and Social Welfare, 3,* 291–311.

Brandwein, R. A., Brown, C. A., & Fox, E. M. (1974). Women and children last: The social situation of divorced mothers and their families. *Journal of Marriage and the Family, 36,* 498–514.

Broverman, I. H., Broverman, D. M., Clarkson, F. E., Rosenkrantz, P. S., & Vogel, S. R. (1970). Sex role stereotypes and clinical judgments of mental health. *Journal of Consulting and Clinical Psychology, 34,* 1–7.

Brumage, M. E. (1976). The influence of sex-role expectations on observers' perceptions and evaluations of persons behaving assertively. *Dissertation Abstracts International, 36,* 5338 B.

Cowan, G., & Koziej, J. (1979). The perception of sex-inconsistant behavior. *Sex Roles, 5,* 1–10.

Crosby, F., Jose, P., & Wong-McCarthy, W. (1981). Gender, androgyny, and conversational assertiveness. In C. Mayo & N. M. Henley (Eds.), *Gender and nonverbal behavior.* New York: Springer-Verlag.

Crosby, F., & Nyquist, L. (1977). The female register: An empirical study of Lakoff's hypotheses. *Language in Society, 6,* 313–322.

Deaux, K. (1976). *The behavior of women and men*. Monterey: Brooks/Cole.

Denmark, F. L. (1980). From rocking the cradle to rocking the boat. *American Psychologist, 35,* 1057–1065.

Donelson, E. (1977). Becoming a single woman. In E. Donelson & J. E. Gullahorn (Eds.), *Women: A psychological perspective* (pp. 228–246). New York: Wiley.

Eisler, R. M., Frederiksen, L. E., & Peterson, G. L. (1978). The relationship of cognitive variables to the expression of assertiveness. *Behavior Therapy, 9,* 419–427.

Eisler, R. M. Hersen, M., Miller, P. M., & Blanchard, E. B. (1975). Situational determinants of assertive behaviors. *Journal of Consulting and Clinical Psychology, 43,* 330–340.

Eisler, R. M., Miller, P. M., & Hersen, M. (1973). Components of assertive behavior. *Journal of Clinical Psychology, 29,* 295–299.

Ellis, A., & Harper, R. A. (1976). *A new guide to rational living*. North Hollywood: Wilshire.

Fishman, P. (1978). Interaction: The work women do. *Social Problems, 25,* 397–406.

Fodor, I. G. (in press). The treatment of communication problems with assertiveness training. In A. Goldstein and E. Foa (Eds.), *Handbook of behavioral interventions*. New York: Wiley.

Fodor, I. G., & Epstein, R. C. (in press). Assertiveness training for women: Where are we failing? In P. Emmelkamp & E. Foa (Eds.), *Failures in behavior therapy*. New York: Wiley.

Gove, W. R. (1973). Sex, marital status, and mortality. *American Journal of Sociology, 79,* 45–67.

Haas, A. (1979). Male and female spoken language differences: Stereotypes and evidence. *Psychological Bulletin, 86,* 616–626.

Henley, N., & Thorne, B. (1977). Womanspeak and manspeak: Sex differences and sexism in communication, verbal and nonverbal. In A. Sargent (Ed.), *Beyond sex roles*. New York: West Publishing.

Hess, E. P., Bridgewater, C. A., Bornstein, P. H., & Sweeney, T. M. (1980). Situational determinants in the perception of assertiveness: Gender-related influences. *Behavior Therapy, 11,* 49–58.

Hetherington, E. M. Cox, M., & Cox, R. (1979). Stress and coping in divorce: A focus on women. In J. E. Gullahorn (Ed.), *Psychology and women: In transition*. New York: Wiley.

Hollandsworth, J. G., & Wall, K. E. (1977). Sex differences in assertive behavior: An empirical investigation. *Journal of Counseling Psychology, 24,* 217–222.

Hull, D. B., & Schroeder, H. E. (1979). Some interpersonal effects of assertion, nonassertion, and aggression. *Behavior Therapy, 10,* 20–28.

Jakubowski-Spector, P. (1973). Facilitating the growth of women through assertive training. *The Counseling Psychologist, 4,* 75–86.

Kelly, J. A. (1982). *Social-skills training: A practical guide for interventions*. New York: Springer.

Kelly, J. A., Kern, J. M., Kirkley, B. G., Patterson, J. N., & Keane, T. M. (1980). Reactions to assertive versus nonassertive behavior: Differential effects for males and females and implications for assertive training. *Behavior Therapy, 11,* 670–682.

Kirsh, B. (1983). Sex roles and language use: Implications for mental health. In V. Franks & E. D. Rothblum (Eds.), *The stereotyping of women: Its effects on mental health*. New York: Springer.

Konopka, G. (1981). Social change, social action as prevention: The role of the professional. In J. M. Joffe & G. W. Albee (Eds.), *Prevention through political action and social change*. Hanover, NH: University Press of New England.

Lakoff, R. (1973). Language and woman's place. *Language in society, 2,* 45–79.

Lange, A. J., & Jakubowski, P. (1978). *Responsible assertive behavior*. Champaign, IL: Research Press.

Lao, R. C., Upchurch, W. H., Corwin, B. J., & Grossnickle, W. F. (1975). Biased attitudes toward females as indicated by ratings of intelligence and likeability. *Psychological Reports, 37,* 1315–1320.

Lazarus, A. A. (1973). On assertive behavior: A brief note. *Behavior Therapy, 4,* 697–699.

Linehan, M., Goldfried, M., & Goldfried, A. (1979). Assertion therapy: Skill training or cognitive restructuring. *Behavior Therapy, 10,* 372–388.

McClelland, D. C. (1961). *The achieving society.* Princeton: Van Nostrand.

Mai-Dalton, R. R., Feldman-Summers, S., & Mitchell, T. R. (1979). Effects of employee gender and behavioral style on the evaluation of male and female banking executives. *Journal of Applied Psychology, 64,* 221–226.

Malamuth, N. M. (1982). Rapists and normal men. *Treatment for Sexual Aggressiveness News, 5.*

Massengill, D., & DiMarco, N. (1979). Sex-role stereotypes and requisite management characteristics: A current replication. *Sex Roles, 5,* 561–570.

Muehlenhard, C. L. (1983). Women's assertion and the feminine sex-role stereotype. In V. Franks & E. D. Rothblum (Eds.), *The stereotyping of women: Its effects on mental health.* New York: Springer.

O'Barr, W. (1982). *Linguist evidence: Language, power and strategy in the courtroom.* New York: Academic Press.

O'Leary, V. E. (1974). Some attitudinal barriers to occupational aspirations in women. *Psychological Bulletin, 81,* 809–826.

Pithers, W. D., Marques, J. K., Gibat, C. C., & Marlatt, G. A. (in press). Relapse prevention: A self-control model of treatment and maintenance of change for sexual aggressives. In J. Greer & I. R. Stuart (Eds.), *Sexual aggression: Current perspectives on treatment.* New York: Van Nostrand Reinhold.

Powell, G. N., & Butterfield, D. A. (1979). The "good manager": Masculine or androgynous? *Management Journal, 22,* 395–403.

Radloff, L. (1975). Sex differences in depression: The effects of occupation and marital status. *Sex Roles, 1,* 249–265.

Rawlings, E. I., & Carter, D. K. (1979). Divorced women. *The Counseling Psychologist, 8,* 27–28.

Rosen, B., & Jerdee, T. H. (1973). The influence of sex-role stereotypes on evaluations of male and female supervisory behavior. *Journal of Applied Psychology, 57,* 44–48.

Rosen, B., & Jerdee, T. H. (1975). Effects of employee's sex and threatening versus pleading appeals on managerial evaluations of grievances. *Journal of Applied Psychology, 60,* 442–445.

Rounsaville, B. J., Prusoff, B. A., & Weissman, M. M. (1980). The course of marital disputes in depressed women: A 48-month follow-up study. *Comprehensive Psychiatry, 21,* 111–118.

Schein, V. E. (1973). The relationship between sex role stereotypes and requisite management characteristics. *Journal of Applied Psychology, 57,* 95–100.

Shaw, M. E., & Rutledge. P. (1976). Assertiveness training for managers. *Training and Development Journal,* September 8–14.

Solomon, L. J., Brehony, K. A., Rothblum, E. D., & Kelly, J. A. (1983). The relationship of verbal content in assertive responses to perceptions of the businessperson. *Journal of Organizational Behavior Management, 4,* 49–63.

Spence, J. T., & Helmreich, R. (1972). Who likes competent women? Competence, sex-role congruence of interests, and subjects' attitudes toward women as determinants of interpersonal attraction. *Journal of Applied Social Psychology, 2,* 197–213.

Spender, D. (1980). *Man made language.* Boston: Routledge & Kegan Paul.

Wiley, M. G., & Eskilson, A. (1982). Coping in the corporation: Sex role constraints. *Journal of Applied Social Psychology, 12, 1–11.*

Williams, C. A. (1980). An experimental study of the effects of assertiveness in the interpersonal communication style of a woman manager on perceptions of managerial effectiveness, credibility ratings, and attitudes toward women as managers. *Dissertation Abstracts International, 40,* 4804-A.

Williams, J. H. (1983). *Psychology of Women* (2nd ed.). New York: W. W. Norton.

Winship, B. J., & Kelley, J. D. (1976). A verbal response model of assertiveness. *Journal of Counseling Psychology, 23,* 215–220.

Woolfolk, R. L., & Dever, S. (1979). Perceptions of assertion: An empirical analysis. *Behavior Therapy, 10,* 404–411.

Worell, J., & Garret-Fulks, N. (1983). The resocialization of single-again women. In V. Franks & E. D. Rothblum (Eds.), *The stereotyping of women: Its effects on mental health.* New York: Springer.

CHAPTER 14

Social Skills Training with the Elderly

EILEEN GAMBRILL

Relatively little attention has been devoted to social skills training with the elderly in the behavioral literature (Patterson & Jackson, 1980; Rotheram & Corby, 1980). A number of reports involve older psychiatric patients; however, rarely is age singled out as a distinguishing feature (Hersen, 1979). The importance of effective social skills for the elderly has been highlighted by many authors. Social isolation is associated with health risks such as cardio-vas-cular disease (e.g., Lynch, 1977; Berkman & Syme, 1979). Social performance influences capacities to get along despite physical limitations (Kane & Kane, 1979). Kuypers and Bengston (1973) have emphasized that competent social behavior will help older people by decreasing susceptibility to loss and increasing self-confidence, by reducing dependency and increasing self-reliance, by encouraging older adults to view themselves as able, and by maintaining effective coping skills. These consequences are of special relevance for older adults, given the loss of significant others, the loss of important roles upon retirement, the increased dependence of many older adults, and the decreased status that advancing years often brings. Effective behavior is likely to yield the additional benefit of positive reactions from bystanders that may help to decrease negative stereotypes of the elderly. For example, older people who

acted assertively in a situation involving the return of merchandise were perceived more positively by younger people compared to older people who did not respond assertively (Baffra & Zarit, 1977).

Theoretical and methodological issues are first discussed in this chapter as well as empirical data from social gerontology that has been neglected. This is followed by a description and critique of social skills training programs with the elderly. Suggestions for enhancing the effectiveness of programs are offered.

Research to date supports a theoretical view of social behavior that attends to cognitions and emotions as well as overt behavior (e.g., Trower, 1982; Argyle, Furnham, & Green, 1981; Glass & Merluzzi, 1981). It is helpful to distinguish between *social skills* and *social skill*. The former term refers to the "normative component behaviors or actions —single elements (looks, nods, lexical items, etc.) or identifiable sequences of elements, or acts or scripts (greetings, etc.)—that ordinary people use in social interaction and that are governed by rules" (Trower, 1982, p. 418). These are acquired by experience, retained in memory, altered by emotional reactions, and retrieved as necessary. The particular meaning of any one component would depend on its meaning in the context of a larger episode. *Social skill* is defined as "the process of generating skilled behavior, directed toward a goal" (p. 418). *Social competence* is defined as the "capability to generate skilled behavior i.e., the possession of skill and skills)," and *social performance* is "the actual production of skilled behavior in specific situations" (p. 419) that requires appropriate expectancies and subjective values.

Trower argues correctly that much of the work in social skill training in the United States had emphasized social skills rather than this process model of social skill with its heavier emphasis on the cognitive components of socially effective behavior. This is certainly the case with social skills training with the elderly. A process model of effective behavior includes attention to goals and plans, perception and translation of social signals, feedback, self-presentation, ability to take the role of others, knowledge about the rules for appropriate behavior in specific situations as well as verbal and nonverbal skills (Argyle, 1980; Argyle et al., 1981; Trower, Bryant, & Argyle, 1978).

The same basic questions related to other populations are also of import with the elderly, for example: (1) What criteria should be used to define effective performance? (2) What specific situations are of most concern? (3) What specific goals can most effectively be pursued in what situations? (4) What verbal and nonverbal behaviors are important in achieving goals? (5) What factors impede or facilitate effective performance? (6) What are ingredients of effective training programs? (7) What progress indicators should be used? (8) How can generalization and maintenance of progress be encouraged?

MYTHS AND STEREOTYPES ABOUT THE ELDERLY

Every culture has myths about and stereotypes of particular groups of people including the elderly. Different cohorts (a cohort is a set of people born at the same time) have different views of age and aging (Riley, 1978). These myths and stereotypes influence how each individual reacts to older people as well as to themselves in terms of aging. They also influence the development of programs offered to the elderly. "Cohort definitions, even when false, can become institutionalized as new norms and new role expectations, crystallized as new customs or laws" (Riley, 1978, p. 46). Authors interested in the sociology of aging offer important insights as to where these stereotypes and myths originate. For example, Riley (1978) points to the "life course fallacy" that incorrectly interprets cross-sectional data as if they referred to the aging process (p. 42). Cohort differences in patterns of life course are overlooked. A second source is the "fallacy of age reification" in which chronological age itself is considered a causal factor. There is increasing evidence that this is not the case; that situational factors may play an overriding influence in relation to characteristics attributed to inevitable maturational factors. A third source is the "fallacy of cohort centrism," which involves overgeneralization from the experience of one cohort. For example, inaccurate predictions could be made about the cohort of people born in the United States in the 1950s based on data gathered from people born in the early 1920s. Some myths about aging that are especially likely to interfere with the design of effective programs to enhance social competencies are described next.

Peplau and her colleagues have recently explored the sollogism: old = alone = lonely (Peplau, Bikson, Rook, & Goodchilds, 1982). Being old *is* often associated with being alone. Thirty-three percent of women in their late 60s and early 70s and 41% of women in their late 70s or older live alone. The percentage of men living alone is much lower (Marquis, 1979). The percentage of older people living alone is increasing. But, does living alone entail being lonely? Here the syllogism breaks down. Most old people who live alone are not lonely (see for example, Tunstall, 1967). Older adults who live alone are usually not socially isolated (Cantor, 1975; Cohen & Sokolovsky, 1980; Kohen, 1983). Of course, as Peplau et al. (1982) note, the quantitative characteristics of interaction, such as frequency of contact, is only modestly associated with subjective well-being (Larson, 1978). A number of studies show that contacts with friends and neighbors influence well-being more than contact with grown children. Single older people who live with relatives report greater loneliness than those who live alone or with friends (Perlman, Gerson, & Spinner, 1978). One of the most frequent complaints of older people who live with their children is feeling isolated within the family group (Kutner, Fanshel, Togo, & Languer, 1956). Factors related to social satisfaction include availability of a confidant, a sense of personal control, kinds of social comparison that are made, factors such as health, housing, transportation, income, and gender (Peplau et al., 1982). These findings have implications for the types of programs that are developed to enhance social interactions of the elderly.

Yet another myth is that a high percentage of the elderly are housed in institutions. Only about 5% of people over the age of 65 live in institutions (Marquis, 1979). However, a much higher percentage may, at sometime, reside in a nursing home. Many people believe that physical and psychological problems severely limit the elderly. It is true that the elderly have more chronic ailments including arthritis, hypertension, hearing loss, and heart disease as compared to younger individuals. However, less than 14% of people over the age of 65 report that their health problems prevent them from carrying out major activities. The elderly have fewer acute conditions compared to younger people (Rooke & Wingrove, 1980, p. 29). Eighty-one percent of people 65 and over lead independent lives in the community and manage their own affairs (*Working with Older People*, 1970). Only a small proportion of people 65 and older suffer from severe cognitive impairment. Age per se accounts for a small amount of variance in intellectual functioning up to the early 70s. Up to ages 60–70, differences between cohorts equal or exceed the importance of chronological age differences (Shaie & Parham, 1977). Interindividual differences in intellectual aging are large. The belief that the majority of the elderly are idle and bored is also a myth. "The majority of elderly persons are active and involved with family, community, paid and volunteer work, and as caretakers of their own affairs" (Rooke & Wingrove, 1980, p. 83). There is increasing recognition that many negative characteristics ascribed to personal factors are directly related to environmental characteristics.

Yet another myth is that the elderly do not know what they want. Reviews of social policy and programs in relation to the elderly emphasize the extent to which selection of outcomes are often imposed on the elderly. For example, agencies often stress life-enhancement services, such as socialization activities, whereas older people report that their first priority is more support services in case of illness. Estes (1980) found that although staff members in community planning agencies for the elderly view problems of the elderly as having a social structural origin, professionals who worked in these settings often practice accommodative, adjustment-oriented approaches in which elderly people are discouraged from becoming independent and in which it is assumed that clients cannot accurately perceive their own problems; it is assumed that "the professional and planner are the appropriate experts to diagnose the client's problem'' (p. 127). The need for involving elderly people in making planning decisions was minimized.

Negative attitudes toward the elderly, an increasing elderly population, limited material resources of many elderly people, and diversity of the elderly population are not myths. Negative attitudes toward the elderly are found among professionals who work with the elderly as well as among laypeople. For example, Miller, Lowenstein, and Winston (1976) found that physicians who work with elderly ill people have very negative attitudes about these individuals. Inaccurate assignment of problems to the elderly may increase negative stereotypes of the elderly as idle, lonely, and bored (Rooke & Wingrove, 1980). Rodin and Langer (1980) found that both young and middle-age people view old people as mainly involved in nonsocial behaviors and passive activities, and as having negative psychological characteristics to a much greater degree than positive ones. Younger populations were more likely to perceive older people as sickly. When age-stereotyped behaviors are involved, the views of elderly people are more negative than those of younger people. These authors offer evidence that elderly people accept negative stereotypes of themselves. Acceptance of such stereotypes will decrease self-esteem, which in turn will decrease coping efforts and result in a decreased sense of personal control over environmental events. This in turn will further reduce self-esteem. Negative stereotypes (Rodin & Langer, 1980, p. 24) encourage people to make ''damaging self, rather than situational attributions for events, and so efforts to correct situations that are indeed changeable may not be made''.

The population of people 65 and over has increased from 4% in 1900 to over 11% today and is projected to continue to increase. By the year 2035, it is expected that 18% of the total population will be 65 years or over and that half of that age group will be 75 or over. Women will continue to outnumber men by significant proportions. By the year 2000, it is projected that there will be 154 older women for every 100 older men (*Facts about Older Americans,* 1975). Although the majority of people over 65 are not destitute, a minority have very low incomes. For example, 8% of the elderly in 1978 had incomes below $1,500 per year. Two and a half million had incomes between $1500 and $3000 a year (Siegel, et al., 1976). Exclusion from the labor force has increased among the elderly (*Population Bulletin,* 1975).

SOCIAL SITUATIONS OF CONCERN TO THE ELDERLY AND EFFECTIVE RESPONSE OPTIONS

Elderly people interact with family members, friends, and acquaintances, professionals such as physicians as well as with service personnel, such as waiters. In addition, many interact with fellow workers either in the course of paid employment or volunteer work. Some social skills may be of value in a range of situations, whereas others may have more specialized uses. Transitions to institutional settings, for example, may require special skills. Adaptations required will depend upon the match between personal and environmental characteristics. Turner, Tobin, and Liberman (1972) found that ''aggression'' and ''activity'' were related to adaptation and intact functioning 1 year after admission to an institution. Later years often require adaptations to loss of living companions and decrease of physical and sensory capabilities. Interpersonal problem-solving and emotion-coping skills will be required, such as arranging time-outs from negative thoughts, collecting needed information, gaining support from others, and gaining specific kinds of help from both formal and informal resource systems. Many service programs are founded on the assumption that more elders could continue living with family members for a longer period of time if required skills and environmental conditions were available. These include effective communication skills to negotiate conflicts that arise. Lindsley (1964) pointed out the importance of maintaining appropriate grooming behaviors. Examples of skill clusters important in a family context include decision-making and negotiation skills, rewardingness, and requesting behavior changes.

Ideally, a typology of social situations would be available that clearly described relevant situations, how frequently each is likely to occur, the goals that could be effectively pursued within each as well as the skills required to attain these goals for different subpopulations of the elderly. Efforts to generate such a typology in relation to the elderly are in their infancy. Although many studies are available within social gerontology that is concerned with identifying interpersonal situations of concern to the elderly, data offered are usually general rather than specific. For example, Sheidt and Shaie (1978) are engaged in research designed "to identify specific behavioral-situational interactions which might serve as criteria for a more ecologically-valid and sensitive assessment of adult competence" (p. 849), using a population of older adults in West Los Angeles. Situations were generated through self-report from, and interviews with, 100 subjects drawn from senior centers, church groups, volunteers, and the streets and parks of West Los Angeles. (The number from each is not given.) "Participants were asked to report events, episodes or situations occurring in their lives within the past year." Sixteen classes of situations were identified. These were divided into social and nonsocial activities and then further divided into high activity/low activity, and within these into various combinations of common (occurring frequently), un-

common, and supportive/depriving. An example of a social/common/depriving/low activity is offering money to a son or daughter who needs it. An example of a social/common/supportive/high activity is "arguing with a person about an important point" (p. 851). Dimensions were selected based on the literature. It is not clear that these are useful in terms of planning training programs.

Many reports concern specific contexts such as nursing homes. Examples included on the Perceived Environmental Control Scale (Wolk & Telleen, 1976) under "Satisfaction with nursing home" include (1) be close to family; (2) have activities that interest you; (3) have frequent contact with a doctor; (4) make new friends in the home; (5) have staff care about you; (6) be close to friends; and (7) have a good roommate. Data from such sources provide a rich source of exploratory information concerning relevant interpersonal situations. However, these must be defined with greater precision. For example, what does a good roommate do (and not do) and in what specific situations? What kinds of attention from staff are most valued by which residents? On what schedule should different kinds of attention be offered for maximal satisfaction? Little information is available concerning the most effective way to pursue specific social goals. Data gained from other populations should be of value in relation to people 65 and older. However, in some instances, unique characteristics of the elderly, such as looking old rather than young, may require special skills in specific situations. Quayhagen and Chiriboga (1976) selected 12 stressful situations that represent loss or threat in the areas of health, finances, competency, self-concept, and interpersonal relations relevant to the elderly residing in group-living situations. Respondents note for each story what they would have done, how they would have felt, and which emotion (from a list of 24) most closely resembles their feelings. Respondents are also asked to indicate on a 4-point scale how often they use each of 11 strategies to handle each situation. Examples included trying to find out more about the situation, talking with others about the problem, drawing upon past experience, and trying to see the humorous aspects of the situation. Examples of situations include a woman who is watching a favorite TV show and her roommate changes the station, and a man whose family wish to take over his financial affairs. In another instrument developed by Kahana and Kahana (1975), only one story is presented. This concerns a 70-year-old man who must move because his home will be torn down. Respondents first indicate how they would handle this situation and are then presented with a list of 23 possible strategies and are asked how likely it would be that they would use each, using a 4-point scale. Situations used were not empirically derived by interviewing elderly people and their significant others and by systematic observation in the natural environment. Nor were coping options empirically derived. Asking respondents to select options from a predesigned list of strategies neglects capacities to generate options (Mischel, 1981).

There is an extensive literature in the area of social gerontology concerned with the measurement of social functioning. Feasible, valid, and sensitive measures of social performance would be helpful in a number of clinical situations such as making decisions about the timing and type of long-term care for elderly people. Kane and Kane (1979) provide an informative description of measures of social functioning that will be of interest to those conducting social skills training with the elderly. They divide measures into three categories: (1) social interactions and resources; (2) personal coping and subjective well-being; and (3) environmental fit. They offer an incisive description of measurement problems, including the absence of age norms, the absence of longitudinal studies that offer information concerning scores on scales and later outcomes, vaguely defined concepts, lack of societal role expectations for the elderly, the variety of satisfying patterns of social functioning, and socioeconomic and cultural influences. Practical problems include limitations of self-report, choice of time frame to use, and cognitive impairments of some older people.

PROGRAM DEVELOPMENT IN SOCIAL SKILLS TRAINING PROGRAMS

Important ingredients of assessment can be seen in Figure 14.1. Successful program development will require selection of valid, reliable sources of information. A hallmark of a behavioral approach to social skills training is an individualized assessment in which empirically based answers are sought to questions such as what situations are of most concern, what are the most effective response

_____ 1. Clear description of socially validated goals including specific situations in which these can be pursued.

_____ 2. Clear description of verbal and nonverbal behaviors comprising competent behavior.

_____ 3. Collection of data concerning initial performance levels on component skills.

_____ 4. Identification of intermediate steps for each person.

_____ 5. Identification of unique factors that impede performance for each person.

_____ 6. Identification of personal and environmental resources that can be helpful in achieving outcomes for each individual.

Figure 14.1   Checklist for evaluating the quality of assessment.

options in each, and what factors interfere with and facilitate effective performance. This hallmark has not been faithfully followed. Gender differences are totally ignored. A few studies have included some components of a behavior-analytic approach to identifying situations of concern and effective response options (Goldfried & D'Zurilla, 1969). Situations should be identified by elderly respondents and significant others, and these should be cross-validated on other samples. Ideally, effective responses in each situation should be identified by observation in the natural environment. In some studies, the number of people involved in different stages of program development is not reported, nor is the duration of observation, nor the exact contexts in which observation occurred (e.g., Edinberg, Karoly, & Gleser, 1977). Edinberg et al. (1977) identified 106 situations based on interviews with senior center staff, observation, written responses, and role playing. No information is offered describing the content of these 106 situations. These were reduced to a final list of 20 situations using the following guidelines (Edinberg et al., 1977, p. 870):

(1) The final list would reflect the overall content of the 106-situation sample; (2) situations generally would be applicable to older adults; (3) a range of social roles for the elderly would be included; (4) situations would require a variety of assertive responses (e.g., initiating a discussion, making a request on one's behalf); and (5) some situations would be based on potentially serious outcomes, such as responding to a confidence man.

Examples of situations are offered next.

You sit down for a meal at the center, and you notice there is a salad at every place except yours. You want one. A serving person comes by your place, putting out salt and pepper. She says, "Excuse me, I have to put

this down here." Which of these would you say?

A staff worker at the center is talking to you. She explains how to get bus service so you can come for meals. *You do not hear her too well.* When she is through speaking, she says, "Do you understand?" Which of these would you say or do?

You are having a discussion with your children or family. They feel you should move into a nursing home. You do not feel that you need to. One of them says, "You are too old to take care of yourself." Which of these would you say or do?

Four or five response options were created for each situation. Some of these were drawn from the original list of 106 situations, and others were added to include a passive, assertive, and aggressive option for each situation. Additional criteria used were clear wording, behavioral descriptiveness, and perceived likelihood that older adults could respond in the manner described. Six people who worked with the elderly or had special training in gerontology rated each response for aggression and assertion on 7-point scales. (Judges were not asked to indicate the basis on which they made their judgments.) These data were used to categorize responses into assertive, aggressive, or passive categories. In addition, 18 elderly judges rated each response on a 10-point scale of appropriateness. The purpose of obtaining these ratings "was to determine which situations elicited appropriate assertive responses" (Edinberg et al., p. 870). Assertive responses appeared to be viewed as desirable behavior by the elderly. Sixty-four older adults were asked to respond to a paper-and-pencil assessment instrument based on the data collected during initial phases of program development. These subjects usually endorsed the "appropriate answers" regardless of their rated assertion. (How this was rated was not described.) The authors noted that response bias probably influenced results obtained; that is, respondents selected what they considered to be appropriate responses rather than indicate what they would actually do or say in a situation.

Eight situations were then selected for use in behavioral assessment, and scripts were developed for each. Criteria used to make this selection were not described. Examples, including response options, are given next:

You have just received a medical checkup. As you are getting dressed, the doctor comes in. He says, "Well, you might have a little high blood pressure." Which of these would you do or say?

1. You say nothing but nod your head in agreement.
2. You say, "You would too if you had my problems."
3. You say, "High blood pressure? What should I do about it?"
4. You say, "You can be honest. What's really wrong?"

You are in a grocery store. You have just paid for your groceries. The sales clerk gives you your change. You look at it and it is a dollar short. Which of these would you do or say?

1. You say, "You should be ashamed trying to cheat people."
2. You say nothing and leave.
3. You say, "I think I have another dollar coming to me."
4. You count your change and say, "This isn't right, is it?

Thirty-three elderly men and women drawn from two senior centers responded to four of the eight situations (two on audiotape and two in an extended role play). These included the two just described as well as one involving an offer of help from a family member, and one involving saying no to a "con man." Average age of the subjects was 70. Tape-recorded responses were rated in terms of assertion and content by two undergraduate psychology majors. A 5-point scale was used to assess assertion. Methods and criteria used for content ratings were the same as those used in making assertion ratings. It is not surprising, then, that a high correlation was found between assertion and content ratings (.93). Rater reliability was .89 and .91 for the two scales. Situations differed in the degree of assertion displayed, regardless of the person involved. Differences in assertion were also found among individuals.

This study demonstrates some of the problems with program development related to social skill training programs with the elderly: (1) failure to select situations of most concern to the population under consideration; (2) failure to determine specific goals respondents would like to achieve in each situation; (3) a priori selection of response options rather than determination of which options are most effective in real life; (4) failure to determine criteria on which judges base their evaluations of response options; (5) failure to compare evaluations of judges with the effectiveness of response options in real-life situations; (6) use of a small number of situations to obtain behavioral measures; (7) global ratings of skill; and (8) ignoring personal outcomes such as discomfort and satisfaction with responses offered.

Community residents were also employed in a study by Toseland and Rose (1978) (see also Toseland, 1977). Interviews were held with 20 older persons that yielded seven items. Following further assessment, four items were deleted, and a new set of eight items was constructed based on interviews with 40 people aged 55 and over. Degree of relevance to the elderly and degree of difficulty were considered in selection of items. Five response options to each situation were "developed on the basis of the situation's relevance and difficulty" (p. 29). These were then rank ordered from 1 (best option) to 5 (worst option) by eight gerontologists using criteria for effective responses derived from Eisler, Miller, and Hersen (1973). These include latency of reply, duration of reply, degree of compliance, request for behavior changes, voice loudness, and profoundness of affect. (Whether these criteria are of maximal relevance to the situation/person contexts used by Toseland is not known.) Examples of two situations together with ranked response options are given next (Toseland, 1977).

A neighbor or friend asks to borrow a punch bowl and serving plate that you own. The punch bowl and serving plate are valuable to you. This neighbor or friend is asking to borrow the punch bowl and serving plate and you do not want to lend them.

Rank	Responses
1	You would explain to your neighbor or friend the value of the items to you and refuse to loan it. Criteria:_____
2	You would simply refuse to loan the items. Criteria:_____
3	You would be hesitant about refusing because you don't want to offend this neighbor. Criteria:_____
5	You would loan the items. Criteria:_____
4	You would tell your friend that you will think about it, hoping that the friend will not ask a second time. Criteria:_____

You've brought your spring coat to the cleaner and stated clearly that you wanted a particular stain removed. The worker says, "I'll take care of it." When you pick up the coat the stain is still there. He says that the stain has been there for ages—it won't come out. He hands you your coat and the bill.

Rank	Responses
4	You would take the coat and never go back to that store. Criteria:_____
5	You would accept the coat figuring that they tried to do what they could. Criteria:_____
1	You would remind the worker of your previous statement and his response, and then ask that he try to remove the spot a second time. Criteria:_____
2	You would remind the worker of your previous statement and his response, and then tell him that you will not pay since he didn't render the service he said that he would. Criteria:_____

Elderly community residents were also the population of concern in a report by Gambrill and Barth (1982). Interviews were held with the staff members of senior and nutrition centers as well as with 83 persons attending these centers (34 men and 49 women). Three-quarters of the sample lived alone. The majority of the sample were either widows (41%) or widowers (15%). Twelve percent had never been married; 14% were currently married; 15% were divorced; and 4% were separated. Sixty-three percent had a high school education or less. Although most respondents reported that they were very satisfied (29%) or satisfied (37%) with their social contacts, 43% reported that they would like more social contacts. Only 4% of the sample was employed part- or full-time. Respondents were requested to identify specific social situations that they would like to handle differently. Interviewers (three graduate social work students) used a standard introduction to explain the purpose of the interview. Standard prompts were used to encourage respondents to identify situations of concern such as, "Can you think of any situations in which you wanted something but weren't sure what to say?'' After a situation was mentioned, prompts were employed to gain more specific information, such as who was involved, how often the situation arose, what the person wanted to achieve, what was said, where this occurred, and what resulted. Elderly respondents were also asked to complete a self-report inventory, listing 22 different situations. Situations included were drawn from the literature concerning social skills training, from a perusal of relevant literature in gerontology, and from initial pilot interviews with center staff and participants. Respondents indicated one of the following for each item: 1 = do it, it is easy; 2 = do it, but it is difficult; 3 = don't do it, even though I would like to; 4 = don't do it and don't want to; and 5 = the situation does not arise. Relevant situations were also noted during observation in the centers. Over 200 situations were generated. Most of these fell into 1 of the 22 situations included in the self-report inventory. Categories 2 (do it but it is difficult) and three (don't do it even though I would like to) were combined in determining items of most concern to respondents (see Table 14.1). Twelve professionals who work with the elderly (staff members of senior centers, second year master's degree social work students specializing in aging, and faculty members in this area) were asked to write down what they believed was most appropriate to do or say in each of the situations indicated as of most concern. Components of effective reactions were selected, based on their responses as well as on criteria shown to be important in the literature related to social skills.

Other studies employed elderly inpatients. Berger and Rose (1977) asked nursing home residents ($n = 22$) to recall recent interpersonal situations in which "the patient felt he could have responded more successfully or felt better than he actually did.'' (p. 348). Respondets were asked: ''(1) what lead up to the situation? (2) what was the purpose of the interaction?; (3) what were the characteristics of the other person(s)?; (4) what was the physical setting?; and, (5) what was the flow of interaction? i.e., who said what to whom?'' (p. 348). Thirty-four situations were offered. These included making a reasonable request, refusing an inappropriate request or responding to an unfair action or statement, and initiating and maintaining a conversation. Most situations included other residents, although some involved staff or relatives. These 34 situations were tape-recorded and presented to 11 of the residents who participated in the interview. Residents rated their comfort and competence and indicated whether situations "would ever come up.'' Sixteen situations met the following criteria: "fewer than half of the subjects rated their response as a 1—comfortable and able to handle it, and fewer than a third said that it "would never come up.'' Tape-recorded responses to each of the 16 situations were gathered from eight staff members. These responses were rated by an additional five "significant others'' on a scale from 1 = very effective, to 5 = very ineffective. Raters were asked to indicate "what it was that made him decide a response was effective or ineffective in that situation'' (Berger & Rose, 1977, p. 348). Criteria mentioned by more than one rater were retained. Two examples of situations together with responses are given next (Berger, 1976). Reactions judged to be effective are noted by an asterisk.

Let's suppose the regular doctor at the Home is in your room examining you. In the past you have not asked the doctor many questions because he has always been in a hurry and answered you in a very abrupt way. This time however, you have just asked the doctor about some tests and medication.

When the doctor finishes answering, you describe to him some new pains you began having recently. He says, "Don't you know

TABLE 14.1.   Percentage of Respondents Rating Items as of Concern

Percentage of Subjects Indicating that Item Is of Concern	Situation
36	1. Ask a favor of someone you are close to.
12	2. Resists sales pressure
24	3. Request expected service when this is not provided (e.g., in a restaurant).
26	4. Start conversations with other people.
33	5. Express an opinion that differs from that of the person you are talking to.
42	6. Turn down requests from other people.
6	7. Compliment another person.
47	8. Tell someone you are close to when he/she says or does something that bothers you.
18	9. Tell a person that you don't know something he or she expects you to know.
54	10. Turn off a talkative friend.
15	11. Request a meeting with a friend or acquaintence.
19	12. Ask a doctor for information about what is wrong or why you have to take a particular medication.
17	13. Ask a person to clarify or repeat information you don't understand.
14	14. Tell someone you like them.
39	15. Discuss openly with a person his or her criticism of something you've said or done.
41	16. Tell another person when you feel he or she has done or is doing something that is unfair.
41	17. Ask a person who is annoying you in a public situation to stop . . .
28	18. Request the return of borrowed items.
29	19. Continue to talk to someone who disagrees with you.
30	20. Ask for help from a stranger or acquaintence when you need it.
7	21. Ask for information when you need it.
19	22. Share your personal thoughts and feeling with a friend or acquaintence.

Source. Gambrill & Barth (1982).

you're getting old? You should expect to have some pains!"

Responses:

*a.   But even if I am getting old, it still hurts. Can you do anything to help?

b.   I know I am getting old. But I never had these pains before and I feel that they are not caused by my failing health.

c.   Yes, I know I'm getting old. But I would like to have a comfortable old age.

d.   (No response. Remain silent.)

e.   But some of these pains are not from what I feel is being old. Old age has nothing to do with the way I feel.

*f.   I know I'm getting old, but there are different kinds of pains. Now some stay and some go. For those that stay, I feel that's a little different.

g.   Well, it would help if you would be a little sympathetic on occasion.

h.   I know that I'm growing old. But good grief! Do I have to be this sick all the time?

Let's suppose that your children often visit you at the Home. Your son lives a short drive from the Home. You would like to visit with your son at *his* home.

Your son is in your room at the Home talking with you. He says, "How have things been going with you?"

a.   Fine, but I'd like to come visit you.

b.   Fair to good. Things could be better. Would it be convenient to come to your house some Sunday for a visit?

*c.   Fine, but I would like to have a visit at your house sometime.

d.   Well, it's home away from home. But there's no place like your own home.

*e.   I am lonesome and would like to come to visit you at your home.

f.   O.K., but could you take me out to see my home place.

*g.   I really can't complain, the food is good, they have many activities, the service is good. But I must say I do miss visiting with you and the family in your home.

*h.   I'm satisfied here, but my biggest desire would be to go to your home to visit some time. To sit in some homey surroundings and visit, only for a short time.

Lopez, Hoyer, Goldstein, Gershaw, and Sprafkin (1980) selected "starting a conversation" on the basis of its "concreteness and simplicity and its relevance for this conversational-skill deficient population" (p. 405) of long-term institutionalized elderly patients. Component steps, also determined on an a priori basis, included (1) greet the person; (2) make small talk; (3) decide if the person wants to talk to you; and (4) begin the topic. Six vignettes were designed that depicted situations that would be applicable to this population. Unlike the reports reviewed before, neither residents nor staff were asked to list relevant situations. Lopez (1980) selected the skill "expressing appreciation" on the basis of its concreteness, simplicity, and usefullness to employ in a social skills program for elderly psychiatric inpatients.

Patterson et al. (1982) designed a behavioral program to decrease the number of geriatric patients in state hospitals. The first phase of this program included program development and planning. One hundred and forty-one elderly people entered residential care during phase 2 of the project that included treatment, planning, and evaluation. Average length of stay in the program during phase 2 was 16.6 weeks. Elderly clients also participated in day treatment ($n = 134$) during phase 2. Two of the modules in the program involved interpersonal skills. The goal of the conversational module "was to increase the frequency with which cli-

ents engaged in informal social conversations with one another" (p. 212). The communication module included situations related to the expression of pleasure and displeasure. Clients "were taught to effectively say that they liked specific favors done by other people, that they were grateful for the favors, and then to deliver a personal message to the other person (e.g., "You're a nice person to do that for me"). They were also "taught to say that they did not like unfavorable actions by another and to ask them to stop the behavior or correct the problem. Behaviors required in these types of situations were selected because they are more basic to effective social interaction than mere casual conversations and because they are incompatible with apathy, passivity, or hostility." (p. 77). Situations included in the training were "not specifically related to any situation of any particular individual because the emphasis of the training was on the behavior itself and not on the situation" (pp. 77–78). Thus, situations were selected on an a priori basis. Component behaviors were also selected on this basis. These included three verbal behaviors (content, loudness, and voice-feeling quality) and three nonverbal behaviors (facial expression [including eye contact], body position and movement, and hand gestures) (p. 78). In addition, complete performance was evaluated.

This brief review indicates that information available is sparse in terms of identifying *specific* interpersonal situations of concern to different subpopulations of elderly people. In addition, the components of effective reactions in specific situations have, in most instances, not been identified empirically. Although efforts have been made in some studies to gain the input of elderly people themselves as well as significant others, often specific skills are selected on an a priori basis—they seem important. Significant others are neglected. The goals that people would like to achieve in specific situations, including both personal and, social ones, are not identified.

PROGRAM EVALUATION

Many components of social skills training complement those that facilitate learning in the elderly, including use of concrete tasks, a supportive atmosphere, encouragement of risk taking, structure, and presenting information via both visual and auditory modalities. Important ingredients of training programs can be seen in Figure 14.2. The studies described next include only some of these. Material developed during the program development stage of assessment was used in the program evaluation stage described next.

Programs Involving Community Residents

Edinberg (1975) compared a discussion group to a social skills training and a no-treatment control group. Eight 45-minute training sessions were held. The general procedure followed in each session is outlined next.

I.   Introduction and review by leader.
II.   Group exercise with demonstration by leader.
    A.   Statement about exercise.
    B.   Demonstration by leader and performance by group members.
    C.   Processing (feedback).
III. Practice of assertion situations (in sessions 2–5, these were predetermined; in sessions 6–8, members used their own examples).
    A.   Statement about the situation.
    B.   Individuals perform in presence of whole group (preferably in center of group).

_____ 1.   Intervention programs are based on individualized assessment.
_____ 2.   Goals pursued are validated for each person.
_____ 3.   Clear criteria are identified for increasing performance requirements.
_____ 4.   Models of effective behavior are provided.
_____ 5.   Multiple practice opportunities are arranged.
_____ 6.   Feedback is offered following each role play.
_____ 7.   Advancement to higher performance requirements are dependent on mastery of initial skill levels.
_____ 8.   Training settings are selected that will facilitate maintenance.
_____ 9.   Relevant, sensitive, and valid progress indicators are selected.
_____ 10. Significant others are included in the training program.
_____ 11. Homework assignments are selected that will facilitate use of skills in the natural environment.
_____ 12. Effective arrangements are made to encourage generalization and maintenance.

Figure 14.2   Checklist for evaluating the quality of social skills training programs.

1.   Covert rehearsal (thinking of what to do).
2.   Modeling (leader models response).
3.   Verbal rehearsal (person discusses what leader did).
4.   Performance.
5.   Feedback from leader, group.
6.   Repeat 3–5 if necessary.
IV.   Homework assignment.

The group exercises were designed to facilitate participation as well as learning effective responses. Topics included introducing oneself, learning what may prevent effective reactions, self-evaluation training, and giving and receiving positive feedback. Results indicated that the discussion group was just as effective as the social skills training group.

Toseland (1977) explored the effectiveness of a problem-solving group for older persons. Six volunteers aged 55 and over were recruited from a senior citizen's center. The group met for six 1-1/2 hour meetings. In addition, pre- and postassessment sessions were held. Interpersonal situations discussed included initiating interactions and conversations, confronting others and giving negative feedback, handling service situations, making requests, turning down requests, and responding to criticism. The problem-solving method employed consisted of the following six steps: "(1) defining the facts of the situation; (2) evaluating thoughts and feelings about the situation; (3) stating the preferred emotion, behavior, and consequences of the situation; (4) deciding on the best solution; and (5) practicing how to implement the decision" (p. 325). Measures used to evaluate progress included a self-report measure (the Assertion Inventory, Gambrill & Richey, 1975) and a behavioral role-play test. The latter measure consisted of seven tape-recorded situations. These were identified by asking older persons at the senior center for "common, difficult situations confronted by older persons that require much interpersonal skills for effective response" (p. 326). Eight experts in the field of aging rated five response options developed for each situation on a 5-point scale ranging from 1 (excellent) to 5 (very poor response) (origin of the response options is not described). The mean score was derived for all eight judges, and a coding manual developed based on this. A psychiatric nurse with more than 5 years' experience in research and treatment of psychiatric patients rated the tapes. Examination of gain scores indicated that participants improved both on the behavioral role-play test and on the Anxiety Scale of the Assertion Inventory. All participants stated that the group was helpful. Absence of a control group and an assessment-only condition make it

difficult to interpret results found. It is not clear why a person with extensive experience with psychiatric patients was selected to assess the behavior of senior center participants. Criteria on which judges based their ratings were not identified. No follow-up data are offered.

Toseland and Rose (1978) compared three groups (behavioral role play, problem solving, and social group work) to increase social skills of older adults who attended senior centers and who lived by themselves in the community. Fifty-three persons were divided into 15 groups, and groups were randomly assigned to methods. The mean age of subjects was 69 (range 55 to 84). Three-quarters of the participants were women. Mean education was 12 years. Groups of three to five subjects met for six 90-minute sessions. Twelve leaders worked with two groups each. Trainers included professional staff of agencies, outreach workers, and master of social work students. Each leader participated in 15 hours of training. Behavioral role play included modeling, rehearsal, feedback, coaching, and discussion. Four of the eight situations selected during assessment were practiced in the group sessions. Cognitive skills were emphasized in problem-solving groups. These included clear definition of situations and identifying alternatives and criteria to use in making decisions. The social group work method included description of situations, evaluation of preferred responses, and discussion of solutions. Both self-report [the Assertion Inventory (Gambrill & Richey, 1975)] and behavioral measures were used to evaluate progress. Two judges rated responses made to eight audiotaped situations using a 5-point scale of overall social skill. Interrater reliability for role plays averaged .76. Behavioral role play and problem solving were significantly more effective at posttraining compared to the social group work on the role-play test on trained as well as untrained test items. No between-group difference was found on the self-report measure. All three groups showed an increased ability to handle difficult interpersonal situations at a 3-month follow-up.

Some paraprofessional counseling programs involved older persons. These programs were often modeled on the microcounseling procedures developed by Ivy (1971) and Carkhuff (1971) and focused on skills such as attending, use of open questions, paraphrasing, reflection of feeling, and summarizations. Walters, Fink, and White (1976) reported that peer-group counseling programs had positive results in terms of enhancing functioning of older adults outside of the counseling group. Some programs were quite extensive. For example, a peer counseling program in St. Louis involving elderly people selected from nutrition sites involved 80 hours of training conducted in weekly 1-day sessions over 12 weeks. Objectives included preparation in the concepts of counseling/facilitative skills (based on Carkhuff), training in the basic concepts of gerontology, and becoming familiar with the aging network in the St. Louis area. Following training, counselors were expected to become more involved in helping peers at nutrition sites through attentive listening, reaching out, and sharing their knowledge of services (Bolton & Dignum-Scott, 1979). Support groups for the elderly sometimes include training in how to handle interpersonal situations (e.g., Petty, Moeller, & Campbell, 1976). Often, peer counseling programs and support groups are not clearly described nor carefully evaluated.

Social skills training was used together with other behavioral methods to decrease depression in elderly clients aged 55–78 (Steuer and Hammen, 1983). Groups met twice a week for 10 weeks and then weekly for 26 weeks in 1-1/2 hour sessions. Four case examples are reported highlighting modifications in cognitive-behavioral methods that may

be required when working with older people.

To date, there is little evidence that social skills training involving elderly people who live in the community is effective. Failure to find differences either right after intervention or at follow-up is not surprising given the deficiencies of the programs. These included their short-term nature, failure to select goals of most concern to participants and to include both personal and social outcomes, failure to attend to the variety of individual factors that may mediate effective performance of verbal and nonverbal skills that do exist (e.g., inappropriate goals or plans for achieving these, faulty perception of social signals, inaccurate use of feedback, inappropriate expectations and performance standards, and interfering emotional reactions such as anger and anxiety), and failure to plan for generalization and maintenance of skills. These program deficiencies are also present in social skills training programs with elderly people who live in residential settings.

Reports with Elderly Living in Residential Settings

Berger and Rose (1977) compared interpersonal skill training with discussion and assessment-only conditions using 25 nursing home residents. Mean age of respondents was 77 years. Eleven men and 14 women participated. Length of time in the nursing home ranged from .3 to 17 years. Training was carried out in three individual 45-minute sessions by graduate students. Eight situations were randomly selected from the 16 situations derived in the program development phase. One measure used to assess change was the Behavioral Role Play Test (BRT). Tape-recorded responses of participants to 16 situations identified during program development were used. Four raters independently scored each resident's BRT based on five criteria identified during program development. One point was assigned for each criteria satisfied. The final score for each person represented the mean proportion of criteria satisfied across situations. Correlations between all pairs of raters ranged from .80 to .84. Residents rated their satisfaction with their responses, and the experimentors recorded pulse rate right before and after the BRT. A real-life test was given to residents at the second posttreatment session. Each subject was asked to take the part of a resident and respond to the experimentor who played the part of a social worker requesting an interview. The task of the resident included asking the social worker to come back the next day. The experimenter recorded the number of tasks completed successfully, overall effectiveness of the role play (criteria for rating not stated), and the duration of the interaction. Residents rated their own ability and comfort. In addition, residents completed the Interpersonal Situation Inventory, consisting of 34 situations (see discussion under Program Development). The interpersonal skill training group was superior on the BRT to the discussion control and the combined control conditions on both posttest and at a 2-month follow-up on the subset of eight situations for which residents were trained. No significant differences were found on any other measures.

One interesting feature of this study was the measurement of pulse rate. Physiological reactions of clients are typically ignored in the evaluation of social skills training programs, whether with elderly or with younger people. The authors also asked respondents to indicate the degree of satisfaction with their responses. Ideally, ratings of comfort would also be obtained. One criterion for assessing the effectiveness of social behavior should be the degree of comfort. No measure was made of the extent to which skills generalized to real-life situations. Residents were not asked to iden-

tify personal and social goals related to the eight situations. Most of these limitations are also found in other social skills training programs with elderly residents.

Lopez (1980) explored the effectiveness of Structured Learning Therapy (SLT) (Goldstein, Sprafkin, & Gershaw, 1976) with residents of a state psychiatric hospital for elderly persons. Special attention was devoted to transfer training through use of overlearning in which practice was given over more trials than necessary to produce desired changes. One hundred and twenty residents were chosen by the psychology staff for possible participation in the study "on the basis of relatively high levels of functioning, cooperation, and general lack of social skills" (p. 287). Seventy residents from this group who scored highest on a measure of cognitive functioning were selected. Mean age of participants was 65, and mean duration of institutionalization was 20.7 years. Forty-five women and 25 men participated. Six experimental conditions included three groups receiving precounseling training and either high, medium, or low overlearning and three groups receiving high, medium, or low overlearning without precounseling. Ten residents were randomly assigned to each of the experimental conditions and to the control condition. Each experimental group consisted of two trainers and five residents. Training focused on "expressing appreciation," which was assumed to consist of three steps: "(a) Clearly describe to other people what they did for you that deserves appreciation, (b) tell other people why you appreciate what they did, (c) ask other people if there is anything you can do for them" (p. 288).

Dependent measures included tape-recorded responses to six related situations selected for their relevance to institutionalized elderly persons. Subjects were asked to say out loud what they would say in the situation. Three other measures were employed: (1) minimal transfer test in which residents responded to similar vignettes (given only as a posttest); (2) a role-play test in which residents interacted with a psychiatric aid in a prestructured role play, and; (3) an observation measure collected by staff consisting of a 5-day record of "expressing appreciation" on the unit. Responses to the first three measures were rated by independent raters on a 4-point scale of skill. Two pairs of raters were used. Interrater reliabilities were .86 and .90. Half of the subjects received a precounseling session prior to training. This consisted of offering information about trainer and trainee roles, discussion of how skills would be helpful, and a description of the training procedure. Control subjects received attention and brief instructions. High-, medium-, and low-overlearning groups met for eight, six, and four 40-minute sessions each (not including the precounseling session). Training included distribution of skill cards noting three learning points, model presentation, discussion of learning points and outcome of the vignettes presented, role playing, social reinforcement, positive feedback, and prompting. Each resident correctly role played the skill at least one time. In the high-overlearning condition, each participant role played the skill correctly three times, and in the medium-overlearning group, residents correctly role played the skill twice. Subjects in the attention/brief instruction group met for nine 40-minute sessions. Neutral topics were discussed, such as the weather and the food at the institution. All subjects in the training group acquired the skill. Precounseling structuring had no effect either on acquisition or transfer. Medium overlearning enhanced transfer; however, high overlearning decreased both skill acquisition and transfer.

Lopez et al. (1980) explored the effectiveness of the addition of a monetary incentive on skills acquisition and transfer of training in relation to the skills of

"starting a conversation." Fifty-six residents of a state psychiatric institution (31 women and 25 men) participated. Mean age was 65.7, mean length of institutionalization was 20 years, and mean years of education was 9. Ten subjects were randomly assigned to high-, medium-, or low-overlearning conditions (eight, six, and four sessions, respectively). Groups were further divided into SLT amd SLT plus incentive conditions. Sessions lasted 40 minutes. The incentive consisted of 5 cents for each correctly performed behavioral step or 25 cents if all four learning points were displayed (greeting, making small talk, deciding if the person wants to talk to you, beginning a topic). All subjects acquired the skills. Trainers included a doctoral student in clinical psychology and eight hospital staff members. Measures included audiotaped responses to six taped vignettes, a minimal transfer test, a face-to-face posttest in which an actor interacted with the resident to evaluate conversational skills, and an observational posttest in which residents were unobtrusively observed during an unstructured group session. There were no significant overall multivariate effects of either overlearning or incentive.

Here, too, residents were not asked what specific situations were of most concern to them and what goals they valued in these situations. Certainly, some elderly people may not be able to respond to such questions, even if posed in very simple language. However, it is likely that many could. Why not ask them? There is an underlying assumption that elderly residents are unable to say what they would like, which, although this may accurately describe some, certainly does not apply to all. Also, there are other ways to find out what social goals people value—for example, by reinforcer sampling. Lopez and her colleagues refer to one or two rehearsals as "overlearning." *Overlearning* refers to continued practice after mastery of a skill has been demonstrated. Do one or two rehearsals fulfill the requirements of overlearning? The negative effect found for high overlearning was probably a spurious finding. No plans were included to enhance generalization and maintenance. Selection of the incentive used in the second study was not based on client preference; individual differences in the value of different consequences was not considered.

Corby (1975) reported the use of assertion training focused on relationship initiation techniques. Participants consisted of a group of men and women residing in a retirement home. Their mean age was 86 years. Four 1-hour sessions were held. Differences between open and closed questions were discussed, and group members "practiced attending to and identifying the kinds of questions others asked and the responses they received, practiced asking different kinds of questions themselves, gave feedback to each other, picked up on free information offered, gave it themselves, and discussed the appropriateness of different communications in different settings" (p. 71). Homework assignments entailed observing nonverbal behaviors of others to which the participants would respond positively. Corby reports that interpersonal disclosure increased an average of 67%, participants made fewer negative judgments of the nonverbal behavior of others, and they talked more about engaging in "growth" activities.

Social skills training is included as one of many program components in some settings. For example Gordon, Patterson, Eberly, and Penner (1980) included three "training modules" under personal and social skills. Communication training "teaches basic oral communication, how to convey facts and feelings," and "how to express pleasure and displeasure." (p. 134). In conversation training, patients "practice skills of communication: learning to listen, to initiate conversations, to maintain two-way communication by positive response and eye contact." Interpersonal communication training includes "skills necessary for effectively dealing with others and resolving interpersonal conflicts." In another training module (leisure skills), residents "learn to participate, to initiate, and to teach others how to use table games, simple crafts and music." (p. 134). Individualized assessment is conducted by assessing current functioning within each skill area. Evaluation of results indicated that a higher percentage of patients participating in the modular training program were discharged compared to a group remaining in traditional care (74 vs. 53%). Recidivism was reduced to 4%. Because there were many components of this program, the unique contribution of social skills training is unknown.

Patterson, Smith, Goodale, & Miller (1978) randomly assigned psychogeriatric residents to either a social skills (SS) training group or a conversation maintenance (CM) training group (see also Patterson et al., 1982). Residents in the latter group were instructed to sit in the conversational area of the dayroom for about 1 hour each day and to talk to someone. They received tokens from raters if they were observed talking. Training in the communication module was carried out in a group setting. Groups met for 45-minute sessions three times a week for 22 sessions. A "scoreboard" was posted on one wall during group meetings on which ratings of behavior were placed. Signs were also posted that described how tokens could be earned. Modeling, role playing, feedback, and reinforcement were used to increase skills. Tokens were given for improvements in role playing and for offering accurate feedback to others. Training focused on expression of pleasure and displeasure, starting with the expression of pleasure. A behavior rating scale based on six behaviors (see discussion under Program Development) was used to offer feedback and assess behavior. Behavior was assessed before training and 4 weeks later. Ratings were made by "blind" observers based on videotapes presented in random order. Clients in the communication group showed more improvement compared to subjects in the conversation training group, as the authors anticipated. After training was completed, each participant was asked to select someone on the ward to whom they could honestly express pleasure and someone to whom they could honestly express displeasure and to do so. These episodes were observed. Residents in the social skills training group were rated significantly higher. No follow-up data are presented.

Communication of pleasure and displeasure was assessed at baseline, during the first progress evaluation and at discharge for 116 clients (Patterson et al., 1982). Scores for clients in both the day treatment and the residential programs increased for both pleasure and displeasure from the initial to the first progress assessment and from the first progress assessment to discharge evaluation. The authors noted that 33% of the clients failed to reach criterion for success in this module even after 12 or more weeks of training. (See Patterson et al., 1982, for further details concerning evaluation of this program.) Conclusions that can be drawn about the effectiveness of this program are limited by lack of follow-up measures of change in real-life settings, among other problems.

Social skills training programs developed for psychiatric populations include many older patients. Generally, age is not extracted as a separate factor in assessing the effectiveness of these programs. (See, for example, Anthony, Pierce, Cohen, & Cannon, 1980; Goldstein, Sprafkin, & Gershaw, 1976; Goldstein, 1981; Trower et al. 1978; Wallace, 1982). Some single-case studies describe the use of social skills training with older people. For example, one case study de-

scribes the use of assertion training with a 56-year-old carpenter who was hospitalized after an explosive argument with his foreman at work (Foy, Eisler, & Pinkston, 1975). Target behaviors included hostile remarks, compliance, irrelevant comments, and requests. A baseline was gathered over three sessions on all four behaviors, and then modeling and modeling plus instructions were introduced within a multiple baseline design. The addition of instructions enhanced the effects of modeling. A 6-month follow-up employing role plays indicated that gains were maintained. Improvements in real-life settings were also reported.

CRITIQUE OF PROGRAMS

This review clearly indicates the exploratory nature of efforts to date concerning social skills training with the elderly. Studies are flawed either in the program development phase (deciding on the focus of training) and/or in the intervention phase. Available studies typically emphasize component skills and ignore personal and social goals as well as cognitive and emotional factors that may interfere with effective social behaviors (see the first section of this chapter for further discussion). Problems in program development include failure to select situations of most concern to people who participate in training programs and failure to validate response components empirically. Response options are not selected based on what works best in real-life settings. Failure to gather relevant observational data is especially striking within residential settings that provide many opportunities for observation of staff–resident interaction. Individual baseline information is not reported in studies involving comparison of groups. Information concerning the environment in which behaviors are to be performed is lacking. Only if the social context in which a person lives is understood can the possible consequences of pursuing a particular goal be clearly evaluated. For example, one participant in a social skills training program offered to elderly innercity residents living in single-room dwellings said that if she complained to her landlady about others using her toilet and leaving it filthy, these people might hurt her (Gambrill, 1982).

Skills training agendas are typically not individually tailored to initial performance levels on component skills with advancement to higher skill levels contingent on demonstrated mastery of more elementary skills. Periods of intervention are often very short, for example, three 1-hour periods. Training is usually conducted in an artificial setting such as a group, and methods to encourage generalization to real-life settings such as homework assignments are typically not used. Procedures that would encourage maintenance are not taken advantage of, such as involvement of significant others. Between-group differences have not been found at short-term follow-up in some reports. Should we expect any more from training programs that are so brief?

Surprisingly little is reported concerning special steps taken to overcome possible sensory and cognitive deficits such as using large printing and sound-amplification devices. Observational data concerning changes in real-life settings were not collected in most studies. Thus, we do not know whether skills generalized to real-life settings. Should we expect generalization of skills that are not of most concern to participants in programs in which opportunities to maximize generalization are not used? Follow-up periods are very brief. Differences in individual responsiveness to programs may be obscured by use of group data alone. Ideally, data describing the progress of individuals should be gathered as well as data describing gains made by groups experiencing different programs.

A careful individual assessment would reveal which individuals would profit most from social skills training and which people would benefit from alternative procedures. Little systematic use has been made of the unique characteristics of a group setting. For example, systematic use of feedback can be encouraged by requesting group members to complete a rating sheet following each role play (Liberman, King, DeRisi, & McCann, 1975). Few studies take advantage of visible indicators of feedback such as tokens or points. These could also be used by staff in residential settings to support social behaviors during the day. Group settings provide opportunities to establish "buddy systems" in which pairs could assume responsibility for prompting and reinforcing relevant behaviors between sessions in real-life settings.

RECOMMENDATIONS FOR THE FUTURE

A search for new formats and greater attention to a process model of social competence should enhance the effectiveness of future programs. Possibilities for creating new social goals and contexts for pursuing these should be explored. Other procedures for enhancing social competence and participation that may be more effective than social skills training should not be overlooked.

Explore New Training Formats

The decreasing sensory capabilities of the elderly may require presentation of information and gathering of information via new formats. Research related to problem solving of elderly people points to learning aids that can help people to organize information and to use mediational techniques (Botwinick, 1978). Sensory mode of presentation (e.g., visual or auditory) should be carefully matched with individual differences. Tools such as magnifying glasses should be available and/or print made larger for participants as needed. Colors could be used to highlight differences. Lighting should be good. Participants should be encouraged to speak loudly so that all can hear. Audiotaped cassettes depicting effective behavior related to specific social goals may be used to develop and review required behaviors. Ideally, a bank of audiotape and videotape cassettes, each depicting behaviors related to a specific social goal, should be available. Selection could be individually tailored for each person. These tapes could be reviewed on an as-needed basis at home as a memory aid. Task cards with important points noted related to use of a skill could also be used as a memory aid.

It takes two to create a rewarding encounter between two people. Programs to date using a group format for social skills training have included only elderly people. Significant others such as family members or residential staff have not been included. Future research should explore the effectiveness of programs in which significant others are included (see for example Brahce, Silverman, Zielinski, Leon, Resch, & Haas, 1981).

Use a Process Model of Social Competence

A process model of social skill devotes attention to perception, expectations, causal attributions, standards of performance, goals, and adequacy of plans made to attain these (e.g., Argyle et al., 1981; Trower et al., 1978). Future efforts should devote more attention to such factors. How accurately can an elderly person identify feelings and attitudes of others, for example? Programs for enhancing such skills are available and should be drawn upon as relevant (e.g., Trower et al., 1978). Causal attributions are related to whether or not a person tries to attain desired social goals and, if he or she does, what the nature of these efforts will be. (See for example, Peplau, Russell, & Heim, 1979). Characterological self-blame in which attributions for negative experiences are made to relatively unchangeable aspects of the self is more likely to be associated with depression and a belief that one's fate is deserved than is behavioral self-blame in which negative outcomes are attributed to changeable aspects of behavior or self-presentation such as manner of dressing (Janoff-Bulman, 1979). Dysfunctional attributions for physical decline can be altered by programs that develop helpful explanations for the source of problems. A reattribution program for people entering nursing homes resulted in an increase in participation, sociability, and health and a decrease in stress (Rodin & Langer, 1980). The way in which a task is framed influences performance, that is, as a test or a "new activity" (Langer, Rodin, Beck, Weinman, & Spitzer, 1979).

A process model of social competence requires identification of personal and social outcomes of importance to elderly people in different situations. These may differ from person to person dependent upon individual values (Wrubel, Benner, & Lazarus, 1981). Social skills training programs for the elderly should be designed to achieve goals of importance to the participants of such programs for ethical as well as practical reasons. An important practical reason for such involvement is that participation is influenced by the degree of choice people have over their environments. For example, when residents of nursing homes were given an opportunity to make decisions and to assume increased responsibility, they became more involved and active as well as happier, and they showed significant health benefits (e.g., Langer & Rodin, 1976; Mercer & Kane, 1979). The influence of self-esteem and self-efficacy on subsequent coping efforts should sensitize social skills trainers to routinely include such measures when evaluating outcomes.

Research concerning problem-solving skills of the elderly suggest a number of helpful cognitive strategies (Botwinick, 1978; Meichenbaum, 1974). Hussian and Lawrence (1981) compared problem-solving training and social reinforcement of activity with depressed institutionalized residents. Problem-solving training consisted of five 30-minute sessions. No description was offered concerning special steps taken to include learning aids found to be of value to the elderly. No differences were found between training groups and a wait list control group on a measure of hospital adjustment. Gains on the Beck Depression Inventory found for subjects receiving problem-solving training were no longer present at a 3-month follow-up. Keller, Croake, and Brooking (1975) reported that rational-emotive training increased rational thinking and decreased anxiety among older people. (See also Labouvie-Viet & Gonda, 1976; Zarit, 1979).

Research clearly shows that lack of motivation is often responsible for lack of performance, not irreversible deficiencies resulting from aging. For example, Langer et al. (1979) found that expectations of elderly nursing home residents for higher performance and arrangement of contingent consequences resulted in significant improvement on standard short-term memory tests and improvement on nurses' ratings of alertness, mental activity, and social adjustment. Leech and Witte (1971) found that performance of older subjects improved when all responses were rewarded, but correct responses were followed by greater rewards than wrong ones. Lindsley (1964) stressed the importance of discovering optimal reinforcers and reinforcement schedules for older persons. Sociological studies of older people will offer an important source of information concerning factors that influence social performance (e.g., Gubrium, 1975; Lopata, 1979; Matthews, 1979).

Create New Social Goals and Contexts for Achieving These

Our vision should not be limited by what is, including the view of old age many people hold. Rather than viewing retirement as limiting options, this change of status can be viewed as offering new freedoms. Transitions, such as from full time work to retirement, could be prolonged rather than abrupt, allowing time to create new interests and goals. For examples of different perspectives on aging see *Harvest in May* (1965).

Assertively "standing up for one's rights" may be viewed as rude by many elderly people. Perceptions of given social behaviors and goals change over the course of life. For example, some elderly people who were interviewed in a recent study said that they no longer bothered to talk to people who disagreed with them (Gambrill & Barth, 1982). What new contexts can be created that would help older people to achieve a greater percentage of their social goals and to discover new ones they value? We should examine not only the cultures that exist in our own country but those that exist in other countries as well to discover contexts that might be created and the goals that may be succesfully pursued in these contexts. Little is known about the social goals pursued by people, seniors or otherwise, in specific situations. British researchers have stressed the importance of such information and have been pioneers in starting to gather data in this area (e.g., Argyle et al., 1981). Attention should be paid to both long-term and short-term personal (effects on one's self) and social (effects on others) goals as well as the likelihood that given consequences will occur and the person's capability to act effectively if the situation arises (Nezu & D'Zurilla, 1979). Many writers note the absence of general norms for behavior and roles of the elderly that provide an opportunity to create new goals. In addition to spontaneous helping that arises among elderly who live in proximity to each other, voluntary groups, including interest groups, such as the Gray Panthers, offer contexts for pursuit of a variety of goals as well as a source of effective models (Hess, 1976).

Taking Advantage of Other Options for Enhancing and Maintaining Opportunities

Social skills training addresses personal characteristics associated with attaining social goals. It does not directly address situational variables such as behavior of significant others or physical characteristics of the environment that may be as relevant or more important. Researchers in the area of loneliness have emphasized the importance of examining situational constraints related to pursuit of social outcomes (e.g., Peplau et al., 1982). Attention to hallmarks of a behavioral approach to assessment in which there is a careful analysis of both personal and situational factors related to desired outcomes will be important to determine the most effective, efficient procedures. Individual assessment is especially important with older people in view of the fact that physiological factors such as certain kinds of physical illness and prescribed medication can complicate assessment (Butler and Lewis, 1977; Hudson, 1982). Individually tailored assessment may indicate that social skills training will not be the most effective way to achieve desired outcomes. Some alternative routes that have been explored are briefly described next.

Prosthetic Devices

Lindsley (1964) suggested many ways in which behavioral technology could be utilized, including the introduction of prosthetic environments to restore or maintain competent performance (see also Baltes & Barton, 1977). Response-contingent access could prevent boredom and disinterest due to missing significant parts of a communication. Other modifications that could be made include increasing the intensity of environmental cues, response-force amplifiers, response devices that permit a variety of typographies, and feedback systems that permit error location and correction before its occurrence. Frail health and reduced capability to use transportation decrease mobility and thus decrease the potential for the reciprocity of social contacts that seems to be so important (Peplau et al., 1982). Communication opportunities for the frail elderly who are housebound could be increased by use of senior companion programs (Bowles, 1976), CB radios, and the exchange of audiotaped cassette messages. Physical illness may require the development of new repertoires to enable communication (Wisocki and Mosher, 1980). Prosthetic aids will be of value not only in institutions, but in other environments such as private homes, hotels, recreational settings, and social skills training groups.

Create New Social Environments by Rearranging Physical and Social Characteristics

Dependence and lack of participation often stem from deficient social and physical environments (Barton, Baltes, & Orzech, 1980). Social interaction can be altered by rearrangement of these environments. Relatively minor changes that do not entail great cost have resulted in striking changes in social participation. For example, serving coffee and orange juice for 1 hour in the morning in a solarium increased social interaction in a home for the aged (Blackman, Howe, & Pinkston, 1976; see also Quattrochi-Tubin & Jason, 1980). Serving food family style rather than on individual trays increased social interaction (Risley, Gottula, & Edwards, 1978). Other alterations of the physical environment that enhanced social interaction included setting up a store in the lobby of a nursing home (McClannahan & Risley, 1973), rearranging furniture (Melin & Götestam, 1981), and integrating sex-segregated wards (Silverstone & Wynter, 1975). Architectural design influences social interaction (Cluff & Campbell, 1975). Social participation and activity can also be changed by rearranging social prompts and consequences (see for example, MacDonald, 1978; McClannahan & Risley, 1975; Linsk, Howe & Pinkston, 1975; Mueller & Atlas, 1972). Abrams, Hines, Pollock, Ross, Stubbs, and Polyot (1974) found that giving transferable tokens to residents that could only be spent by someone else increased interaction. Development of programs in residential settings that enhance opportunities of the elderly for greater influence over their environments will require knowledge of organizational sources of power and formal and informal channels of communication. Gaining such information and using this for the benefit of elderly residents will require effective interpersonal skills on the part of program developers.

Residential staff interact with family members as well as residents. Blackman (1981) explored the effectiveness of interpersonal skills training in helping nurses aides and orderlies in a home for the aged to interact more effectively with residents' families. Forty staff members participated in the study. The five staff-identified problems with families included in the training program were (1) complaints about apparent nonperformance of specific services; (2) giving information about the resident's condition or treatment plan; (3) complaints about missing personal property; (4) requests for immediate attention or service; and (5) initiating and maintaining positive interactions. Half of the staff received

training in interpersonal skills. General communication principles used in the program included active listening, explanations of the source of the problem, related policies and procedures of the home, explanation of possible solutions, remaining "pleasant and attentive," and use of social reinforcement. Other staff members participated in a discussion group program. (Duration of training program was not reported.) Measures used to evaluate progress included a role-play test of conflictual staff–family interactions and a paper-and-pencil test concerning knowledge of policies and procedures of the home. Role-play analogs to assess generalization were also employed. Measures were gathered at pretraining, posttraining and at a 6-week follow-up. The group receiving training received significantly higher scores on four of the five problem situations presented during training and on three of the five situations not used during training. However, no between-group differences were found at follow-up.

Training materials for nursing home staff consisting of detailed checklists for providing high-quality service in specific areas such as offering feeding assistance have been developed by Risley and his colleagues (e.g., Risley and Edwards, 1978). Ongoing use of high-quality effective procedures will require administrative support. Effective reinforcers, both for staff and residents, will have to be identified. Staff may not always accurately identify events of most value to elderly residents (Wisocki, 1979).

Use of Natural Reinforcing Communities

Settings may exist such as foster home environments for the elderly or senior companion programs in which adaptive social repertoires would be maintained (Baer & Wolf, 1970). These should be taken advantage of because the only requirement is locating appropriate contexts and arranging entry. Foster Grandparents programs, for example, can be a success not only in relation to outcomes for children, but in positive outcomes for the elderly as well (Fabry & Reid, 1978). Helping others and being useful is a naturally occurring reinforcer for many elderly people as is illustrated by the popularity of the retired senior volunteer program (Bowles, 1976). Abrahams, Wallach, and Divens (1979) explored the use of group meetings between high school students and institutionalized geriatric patients. Students and residents met twice a week for 1-hour meetings over 15 weeks. Daytime napping decreased, and social participation increased. Information concerning social networks and social support systems will be required to identify promising opportunities and useful alterations that could be made (see, e.g., Goldstein and Baer, 1976; Gottlieb, 1981; Lally, Black, Thornock, & Hawkins, 1979; Lopata, 1979; Palmore, 1981). Reinforcer sampling offers one method of discovering reinforcers (Wisocki, 1977).

Offer Preventative Programs

Information concerning factors that impede the development of effective interpersonal skills and those that interfere with available skills is important in identifying promising opportunities for preventative efforts. Ideally, relevant training programs would be offered at an early age (Baltes & Willis, 1979). Information concerning sources of stress, coping skills available, and preferred and actual social networks will be helpful in predicting when additional skills will be required or rearrangements of the physical or social environment will be needed. This knowledge can be used to identify individuals who could benefit from services at an early point. Knowledge about a person's social support system can be used to predict who is most likely to be dependent if this changes. An elderly person living in a single-room innercity hotel who has but one friend who

helps him or her is more likely to require aid if his or her friend leaves or dies compared to a person who receives help from many individuals (Cohen & Sokolvsky, 1980).

Bereavement counseling (Ramsay, 1979) may be required to address unresolved grief that may get in the way of forming new social relationships following the death of a significant-other. Preventative opportunities are also provided by offering family members help with behaviors they complain of on the part of elderly relatives and offering respite from care-giving tasks (e.g., Haley, 1983).

Attend to Ethical Concerns

Ethical issues that are important in working with other populations are also important here. We must not promise more than we can deliver or offer less than is possible. Just as effective social skills training may decrease social or material deprivation in the midst of plenty, it will not decrease social deprivation in the midst of impoverished, unchangeable environments. The more imbalanced the power between individuals, such as between staff and residents in a nursing home, the greater vigilance should be exercised, for example, in terms of who selects social goals to pursue. Power is also imbalanced with many older people who live with relatives. The more imbalanced the power differential between people, the more likely those in power will select goals to pursue that do not really do anything to balance such differences. Social skills training programs should offer elderly participants cognitive, emotional, and behavioral competencies that increase "opportunities for real control, not simply strategies that increase perceived control while options for actual control remain unavailable" (Rodin & Langer, 1980, p. 27).

Only a portion of all those elders who would like to enhance their social skills will seek out training programs or volunteer to participate in those that are announced. What initiatives should be taken to encourage hesitant potential participants to sample what they may gain from training programs? What type of outreach programs should be developed? How aggressive should these be? Where does the boundary lie between invasion of privacy and deprivation of opportunities? What percentage of the elderly are isolated by choice, and how many are isolated against their will? How can we protect the privacy and choices of the former while offering desired services to the latter group? How can iatrogenic effects be prevented? (See, for example, Blenker, Bloom, & Nielson, 1971). Individual and cultural differences will require careful consideration of preferences of elderly participants concerning social goals to pursue as well as procedures selected to attain these.

SHOULD AGE BE SINGLED OUT AS A UNIQUE FACTOR?

Advantages of singling age out as a unique characteristic include the reminder to take advantage of the rich literatue that is available in gerontology, much of which has relevance to the development of social skills training programs with the elderly. This can point to useful prosthetic devices, effective environmental rearrangements, remind us of the plasticity of behavior that has been clearly shown in the literature, inform researchers of innovative service delivery systems, and sensitize them to concerns such as elderly people who accept a negative stereotype of themselves. One disadvantage is that researchers may not use this singling out as a cue to become informed about relevant empirical information but instead use this as an opportunity to impose inaccurate cohort-myopic views of the elderly. Failure to

ask participants what they would like suggests a view of the elderly as too feeble to participate actively in the selection of goals to pursue. A second possible disadvantage of singling out the aged as a separate group is that researchers may fail to appreciate the diversity of subgroups within the elderly population. Only as increased attention is devoted to a large group of individuals do unique subpopulations with special concerns emerge (see for example, Berger, 1982). One component of social skill identified by Argyle and his colleagues is special skills related to certain situations. It is likely that such special skills will be important with special populations. A third disadvantage is the possibility that we will fail to build training programs on what is already known about effective methods based on other populations.

SUMMARY AND CONCLUSIONS

Efforts to explore the utility of social skills training with the elderly are exploratory. Although many programs have attempted to apply an empirical approach to the selection of situations of concern and effective response options, this has typically been carried out in a fragmentary fashion without careful attention to individual and situational differences. Information concerning desired social goals and the behavioral and cognitive skills required to achieve these and identification of initial performance levels of each skill as well as environmental factors that may facilitate or constrain effective performance are typically lacking. Possible changes in self-esteem and self-efficacy are usually not explored. Social networks and support systems of involved subjects and opportunities for rearrangement are not described. Because these may be integrally related to selection of goals and intervention procedures, this is a major oversight. Intervention programs are often very brief with sparse efforts made to encourage generalization and maintenance, and little, if any, attention is devoted to enhancing helpful attributions. Follow-up studies indicate that between-group differences are often transitory. Reports are often difficult to evaluate because of missing information.

A careful assessment will be required to determine whether social skills training is the best option, and if it is, what factors may facilitate or impede progress, such as physical limitations. This should reveal whether personal deficiencies exist that should be altered, or whether social outcomes can be pursued more effectively by other means, such as rearrangement of physical and social characteristics of relevant environments. Future efforts to explore the effectiveness of social skills training with the elderly will benefit from being more attentive to individualized assessment and intervention. Only an individualized assessment will indicate, for each person, what goals are desired (and whether these are attainable), and the specific factors that should be increased, decreased, varied, or stabilized to attain these goals. This will require baseline information for each person in group studies as well as single-case studies and design of intervention programs tailored for each person's particular assessment picture. Information is needed concerning situations of concern to specific subgroups of the elderly. As increased attention is devoted to interpersonal concerns of the elderly, groups will emerge in which unique situations arise, which may require special skills, such as with gay/lesbian older people and members of ethnic minorities. Acceptance of a process model of social competence calls for greater attention to cognitions such as attributions and self-esteem that influence performance. Performance is also influenced by motivational variables; this calls for greater focus on identification of personally relevant goals and arrange-

ment of optimal schedules of reinforcement to maintain related behaviors. Greater attention should be paid to social validity, not only of goals selected, but also of procedures used and changes made. Significant others should comprise an important source of feedback concerning progress as should observation in real-life settings. The literature within social gerontology offers a rich source of information that should be drawn upon. Social networks and social support systems of the elderly has long been of interest in this area as have types of learning aids that may enhance performance.

Social skills training for the elderly will not irradicate negative stereotypes and impoverished environments. It will not equalize the skewed power arrangements of nursing homes. Nor will it prevent inevitable physical declines. It should, however, offer elderly people a greater range of options in dealing with everyday interpersonal situations, including negative stereotypes, and increase opportunities for reinforcement. Available social skills can be potentiated by prosthetic devices, rearrangement of physical and social characteristics of environments, and the creation of new social goals and contexts.

REFERENCES

Abrahams, J. P., Wallach, H. F., & Divens, S. (1979). Behavioral improvements in long-term geriatric patients during age-integrated psychosocial rehabilitation. *Journal of the American Geriatric Society, 27,* 218–221.

Abrams, L., Hines, D., Pollock, D., Ross, M., Stubbs, D. A., & Polyot, C. J. (1974). Transferable tokens: Increasing social interaction in token economies. *Psychological Reports, 35,* 447–452.

Anthony, W. A., Pierce, R. M., Cohen, M. R., & Cannon, J. R. (1980). The skills of rehabilitation programming. *Psychiat-*

ric rehabilitation practice series: Book 2. Baltimore: University Park Press.

Argyle, M. (1980). Interaction skills and social competence. In P. Feldman & J. Orford (Eds.), *Psychological problems: The social context*. New York: Wiley.

Argyle, M., Furnham, A., & Graham, J. A. (1981). *Social situations*. Cambridge: Cambridge University Press.

Baer, D. and Wolfe, M. (1970). The entry into natural communities of reinforcement. In R. Ulrich, T. Stachnick and J. Mabry (Eds.). *Control of Human Behavior, 2,* 319–324.

Baffra, G. A., & Zarit, S. H. (1977). *Age differences in the perception of assertive behavior*. Paper presented at the 30th annual meeting of the Gerontological Society, San Francisco.

Baltes, M. M., & Barton, W. M. (1977). New approaches toward aging: A case for the operant model. *Educational Gerontology: An Interpersonal Quarterly, 2,* 383–405.

Baltes, P. B., & Willis, S. L. (1979). Life span developmental psychology, cognitive functioning and social policy. In M. W. Riley (Ed.), *Aging from birth to death*. Washington: American Association for the Advancement of Science.

Barton, E. M., Baltes, M. M., & Orzech, M. J. (1980). Etiology of dependence in older nursing home residents during morning care: The role of staff behavior. *Journal of Personality and Social Psychology, 38,* 423–431.

Berger, R. M. (1976). *Interpersonal skill training with institutionalized elderly patients*. Doctoral dissertation, University of Wisconsin, Madison.

Berger, R. M. (1982). *Gay and gray: The older male homosexual man*. Urbana–Champaign: University of Illinois Press.

Berger, R. M., & Rose, S. D. (1977). Interpersonal skill training with institutionalized elderly patients. *Journal of Gerontology, 32,* 346–353.

Berkman, L. F., & Syme, S. L. (1979). Social networks, host resistance, and mortality: A nine-year follow-up study of Alameda County residents. *American Journal of Epidemiology, 109,* 186–204.

Blackman, D. K. (1981). *Interpersonal skills training for non-professional staff in a home for the aged*. Paper presented at the 15th Annual Convention of the Association for the Advancement of Behavior Therapy, Toronto.

Blackman, D. K., Howe, M., & Pinkston, E. M. (1976). Increasing participation in social interaction of the institutionalized elderly. *The Gerontologist, 16,* 69–76.

Blenker, M., Bloom, M., & Nielson, M. (1971). A research and demonstration project of protective service. *Social Casework, 52,* 483–499.

Bolton, C. R., & Dignum-Scott, J. E. (1979). Peer-group advocacy counseling for the elderly: A conceptual model. *Journal of Gerontological Social Work, 1,* 321–331.

Botwinick, J. (1978). *Aging and behavior: A comprehensive integration of research findings* (2nd ed). New York: Springer.

Bowles, E. (1976). Older persons as providers of services: Three federal programs. *Social Policy, 7,* 81-88.

Bralice, C. I., Silverman, A. G., Zielinski, C., Leon, J., Resch, J., & Haas, S. (1981). *As parents grow older: A manual for program replication*. Ann Arbor: Institute of Gerontology, University of Michigan.

Butler, R. & Lewis, M. (1977). *Aging and mental health*. St. Louis: Mosby.

Cantor, M. (1975). Lifespace and the social support system of the inner city elderly of New York. *Gerontologist, 15,* 23–27.

Carkhuff, R. P. (1971). Training as a necessary pre-condition of education: The development and generalization of a systematic training model. *Journal of Research and Development in Education, 4,* 3–15.

Cluff, P. J., & Campbell, W. H. (1975). The social corridor: An environmental and behavioral evaluation. *Gerontologist, 15,* 506–523.

Cohen, C. I., & Soklovsky, J. (1980). Social engagement versus isolation: The care of the aged in SRO hotels. *The Gerontologist, 20,* 36–44.

Corby, N. (1975). Assertion training with aged populations. *The Counseling Psychologist, 5,* 69–74.

Edinberg, M. A. (1975). *Behavioral assessment and assertion training of the elderly*. Unpublished doctoral dissertation, University of Cincinnati.

Edinberg, M. A., Karoly, P., & Gleser, G. C. (1977). Assessing assertion in the elderly: An application of the behavior-analytic model of competence. *Journal of Clinical Psychology, 33*, 869–874.

Eisler, R. M., Miller, P. M., & Hersen, M. (1973). Components of assertive behavior. *Journal of Clinical Psychology, 29*, 295–299.

Estes, C. L. (1980). Constructions of reality. *Journal of Social Issues, 36*, 117–132.

Fabry, P. L., & Reid, D. H. (1975). Teaching foster grandparents to train severely handicapped persons. *Journal of Applied Behavior Analysis, 11*, 111–123.

Facts About Older Americans. (1975). Washington: DHEW Publications, No. (OHD) 75-20006.

Foy, D. W., Eisler, R. M., & Pinkston, S. (1975). Modeled assertion in a case of explosive rages. *Journal of Behavior Therapy and Experimental Psychiatry, 6*, 135–137.

Gambrill, E. D. (1982). *Social skills training for the elderly: An exploratory study*. Unpublished manuscript, University of California, Berkeley.

Gambrill, E. D., & Barth, R. (1982). *Social situations of concern to elderly community residents*. Unpublished Manuscript, University of California, Berkeley.

Gambrill, E. D., & Richey, C. A. (1975). An assertion inventory for use in assessment and research. *Behavior Therapy, 6*, 547–549.

Glass, C. R., & Merluzzi, T. V. (1981). Cognitive assessment of social-evaluative anxiety. In T. V. Merluzzi, C. R. Glass, & M. Genest (Eds.), *Cognitive assessment*. New York: Guilford.

Goldfried, M. R., & D'Zurilla, T. J. (1969). A behavior-analytic model for assessing competence. In C. D. Spielberger (Ed.), *Current topics in clinical and community psychology* (Vol. I). New York: Academic Press.

Goldstein, A. P. (1981). *Psychological skill training: The structured learning technique*. New York: Pergamon.

Goldstein, A. P., Sprafkin, R. P., & Gershaw, N. J. (1976). *Skill training for community living: Applying structured learning therapy*. New York: Pergamon.

Goldstein, R. S., & Baer, D. M. (1976). A procedure to increase the personal mail and number of correspondents for nursing home residents. *Behavior Therapy, 7*, 348–354.

Gordon, R. E., Patterson, R. L., Eberly, D. A., & Penner, L. (1980). Modular treatment of psychiatric patients. In J. H. Masserman (Ed.), *Current psychiatric therapies*. New York: Grune & Stratton.

Gottlieb, B. H. (1981). Preventive interventions involving social networks and social support. In B. H. Gottlieb (Ed.), *Social networks and social support*. Beverly Hills: Sage.

Gubrium, J. F. (1975). *Living and dying at Murray Manor*. New York: St. Martin's Press.

Haley, W. E. (1983). A family-behavioral approach to the treatment of the cognitively impaired elderly. *The Gerontologist, 23*, 18–20.

Harvest in May: The promises of old age. (1965). *American Education, 1*, 20–21.

Hersen, M. (1979). Modification of skill deficits in psychiatric patients. In A. S. Bellack & M. Hersen (Eds.), *Research and practice in social skills training*. New York: Plenum.

Hess, B. B. (1976). Self-help among the aged. *Social Policy, 7*, 55–62.

Hudson, B. L. (1982). *Social Work with Psychiatric Patients*. London: Macmillan.

Hussian, R. A., & Lawrence, P. S. (1981). Social reinforcement of activity and problem-solving training in the treatment of depressed institutionalized elderly patients. *Cognitive Therapy and Research, 5*, 57–69.

Ivy, A. E. (1971). *Microcounseling: Innovations in interviewing training*. Springfield, IL: Charles C. Thomas.

Janoff-Bulman, R. (1979). Characterological versus behavioral self-blame: Depression and rape. *Journal of Personality and Social Psychology, 37*, 1798–1809.

Kahana, E., & Kahana, B. (1975). Strategies

of coping in institutional environments. Summary progress report, NIH. See E. Kahana, T. Fairchild, & B. Kahana. Adaptation. In D. J Mangen & W. A. Peterson (Eds.), *Research instruments in social gerontology* (Vol. I). Minneapolis: University of Minnesota Press.

Kane, R. A., & Kane, R. L. (1979). *Assessing the elderly*. Lexington, MA: Lexington Books.

Keller, J. F., Croake, J. W., & Brooking, J. Y. (1975). Effects of a program in rational thinking on anxieties in older persons. *Journal of Counseling Psychology, 22*, 54–57.

Kohen, J. A. (1983). Old but not alone: Informal social supports among the elderly by marital status and sex. *The Gerontologist, 23*, 57–63.

Kutner, B., Fanshel, D., Togo, A., & Languer, T. (1956). *Five hundred over sixty*. New York: Russell Sage.

Kuypers, J. A., & Bengston, V. L. (1973). Social breakdown and competence. *Human Development, 16*, 181–201.

Labouvie-Viet, G., & Gonda, J. N. (1976). Cognitive strategy training and intellectual performance in the elderly. *Journal of Gerontology, 31*, 327–332.

Lally, M., Black, E., Thornock, M., & Hawkins, J. D. (1979). Older women in single room occupant (SRO) hotels: A Seattle profile. *The Gerontologist, 19*, 67–73.

Langer, E., & Rodin, J. (1976). Effects of choice and enhanced personal responsibility for the aged. *Journal of Personality and Social Psychology, 34*, 191–198.

Langer, E., Rodin, J., Beck, P., Weinman, C., & Spitzer, L. (1979). Environmental determinants of memory improvement in late adulthood. *Journal of Personality and Social Psychology, 37*, 2003–2013.

Larson, R. (1978). Thirty years of research on the subjective well-being of older Americans. *Journal of Gerontology, 33*, 109–125.

Leech, S., & Witte, K. L. (1971). Paired associate learning in elderly adults as related to pacing and incentive conditions. *Developmental Psychology, 5*, 180.

Liberman, R. P., King, L. W., DeRisi, W. J., & McCann, M. (1975). *Personal effectiveness: Guiding people to assert themselves and improve their social skills*. Campaign, IL: Research Press.

Lindsley, O. R. (1964). Geriatric prosthetics. In R. Kastenbaum (Ed.), *New thoughts on old age*. New York: Springer-Verlag.

Linsk, N., Howe, M. W., & Pinkston, E. M. (1975). Behavioral group work in a home for the aged. *Social Work, 20*, 454–463.

Lopata, H. Z. (1979). *Women as widows*. New York: Elsevier-North Holland.

Lopez, M. A. (1980). Social-skills training with institutionalized elderly: Effects of precounseling structuring and overlearning on skill acquisition and transfer. *Journal of Counseling Psychology, 27*, 286–293.

Lopez, M. A., Hoyer, W. T., Goldstein, A. P., Gershaw, N. J., & Sprafkin, R. P. (1980). Effects of overlearning and incentive on the acquisition and transfer of interpersonal skills with institutionalized elderly. *Journal of Gerontology, 35*, 403–408.

Lynch, J. J. (1977). *The broken heart: The medical consequences of loneliness in America*. New York: Basic Books.

MacDonald, M. L. (1978). Environmental programming for the socially isolated aging. *The Gerontoloist, 18*, 350–354.

Marquis, Academic Media (1979). *Sourcebook on aging* (2nd ed.). Chicago: Marquis Who's Who.

Matthews, S. H. (1979). *The social world of old women*. Beverly Hills: Sage.

McClannahan, L. E., & Risley, T. R. (1973). A store for nursing home residents. *Nursing Homes, 7*, 26–31.

McClannahan, L. E., & Risley, T. R. (1975). Design of living environments for nursing-home residents: Increasing participation in recreational activities. *Journal of Applied Behavior Analysis, 8*, 261–268.

Meichenbaum, D. (1974). Self-instructional strategy training: A cognitive prosthesis for the aged. *Human Development, 17*, 273–280.

Melin, L., & Götestam, K. G. (1981). The effects of rearranging ward routines on communication and eating behaviors of psychogeriatric patients. *Journal of Applied Behavior Analysis, 14*, 47–51.

Mercer, S., & Kane, R. A. (1979). Helplessness and hopelessness among the institutionalized aged: An experiment. *Health and Social Work, 4,* 90–116.

Miller, D. B., Lowenstein, R., & Winston, R. (1976). Physicians' attitudes' toward the ill aged and nursing homes. *Journal of the American Geriatrics Society, 24,* 498–505.

Mischel, W. (1981). A cognitive-social learning approach to assessment. In T. V. Merluzzi, C. R. Glass, & M. Genest (Eds.), *Cognitive assessment.* New York: Guilford.

Mueller, D. J., & Atlas, L. (1972). Resocialization of regressed elderly residents: A behavioral management approach. *Journal of Gerontology, 27,* 390–392.

Nezu, A., & D'Zurilla, T. J. (1979). An experimental evaluation of the decision-making process in social problem solving. *Cognitive Therapy and Research, 3,* 269–277.

Palmore, E. (1981). *Social patterns in normal aging: Findings from the Duke longitudinal study.* Durham, NC: Duke University Press.

Patterson, R. L., & Jackson, G. M. (1980). Behavior modification with the elderly. In M. Hersen, R. M. Eisler, & P. M. Miller, (Eds.), *Progress in behavior modification* (Vol. 9). New York: Academic Press.

Patterson, R. L., Dupree, L. W., Eberly, D. A., Jackson, G. M., O'Sullivan, M. J., Penner, L. A. & Kelly, C. D. (1982). *Overcoming deficits of aging.* New York: Plenum.

Patterson, R. L., Smith, G., Godale, M., & Miller, C. (1978). *Improving communication skills of psycho-geriatric clients.* Paper presented at the 24th meeting of the Southwestern Psychological Association, Atlanta.

Peplau, L. A., Bikson, T. K., Rook, K. S., & Goodchilds, J. D. (1982). Being old and living alone. In L. A. Peplau & D. Perlman (Eds.), *Loneliness: A sourcebook of current theory, research and therapy.* New York: Wiley.

Peplau, L. A., Russell, D., & Heim, M. (1979). The experience of loneliness. In I. H. Frieze, D. Bar-Tal, & J. S. Carroll (Eds.). *New approaches to social problems.* San Francisco: Jossey-Bass.

Perlman, D., Gerson, A. C., & Spinner, B. (1978). Loneliness among senior citizens: An empirical report. *Essence, 2,* 239–248.

Petty, B. J., Moeller, T. P., & Campbell, R. Z. (1976). Support groups for elderly persons in the community. *The Gerontologist, 15,* 522–528.

Population Bulletin. (1975). The aged in America. Washington: Population Reference Bureau.

Quattrochi-Tubin, S., & Jason, L. A. (1980). Enhancing social interactions and activity among the elderly through stimulus control. *Journal of Applied Behavior Analysis, 13,* 159–163.

Quayhagen, M. P., & Chiriboga, D. (1976). *Geriatric coping schedules.* Paper presented at the annual meeting of the Gerontological Society, New York. See also E. Kahana, T. Fairchild, & B. Kahana. Adaptation. In D. J. Mangen & W. A. Peterson (Eds.), *Research instruments in social gerontology* (Vol. I). Minneapolis: University of Minneosta Press.

Ramsay, R. W. (1979). Bereavement: A behavioral treatment of pathological grief. In P. O. Sjöden, S. Bates, & W. S. Dockens (Eds.), *Trends in behavior therapy.* New York: Academic Press.

Riley, M. W. (1978). Aging, social change and the power of ideas. *Daedalus, 107,* 39–52.

Risley, T., & Edwards, A. (1978). *Behavioral technology for nursing home care: Toward a system of nursing home organization and management.* Paper presented at the conference on Applied Behavior Analysis, University of Auckland. *Australian Behavior Therapist, 6,* 1979, 35–53.

Risley, T. R., Gottula, P., & Edwards, K. (1978). *Social interaction during family and institutional style meal service in a nursing home dining room.* Paper presented at the Nova Behavioral Conference on Aging, Port St. Lucie, FL.

Rodin, J., & Langer, E. (1980). Aging labels: The decline of control and the fall of self-esteem. *Journal of Social Issues, 36,* 12–29.

Rooke, M. L., & Wingrove, C. R. (1980). *Benefaction or bondage? Social policy and the aged.* Washington: University Press of America.

Rotheram, M. J., & Corby, N. (1980). Social power and the elderly. In D. P. Rathjen and J. B. Foreyt (Eds.), *Social competence: Interventions for children and adults.* New York: Pergamon.

Schaie, K. W., & Parham, I. A. (1977). Cohort-sequential analyses of adult intellectual development. *Developmental Psychology, 13,* 649–653.

Scheidt, R. J., & Shaie, K. W. (1978). A taxonomy of situations for an elderly population: Generating situational criteria. *Journal of Gerontology, 33,* 848–857.

Siegel, J. S. (1976). Demographic aspects of aging and the older population in the United States. *Current Population Reports:* Special Studies, Series P-23, No. 59, May 26–27. U.S. Bureau of the Census, Washington, D. C. U.S. Government Printing Office (revised Jan. 1978).

Silverstone, B., & Wynter, L. (1975). The effects of introducing a heterosexual living space. *The Gerontologist, 15,* 83–87.

Steuer, J. L. & Hammen, C. L. (1983) Cognitive-behavioral group therapy for the depressed elderly: Issues and applications. *Cognitive Therapy and Research, 7,* 285–296.

Toseland, R. (1977). *A comparison of three group methods to train social skills in older persons.* Doctoral dissertation, University of Wisconsin, Madison.

Toseland, R., & Rose, S. D. (1978). Evaluating social skills training for older adults in groups. *Social Work Research and Abstracts, 44,* 25-33.

Trower, P. (1982). Toward a generative model of social skills: A critique and synthesis. In J. P. Curran & P. M. Monti (Eds.), *Social Skill Training.* New York: Guilford.

Trower, P., Bryant, B., & Argyle, M. (1978). *Social skills and mental health.* London: Methuen.

Tunstall, J. (1967). *Old and alone.* London: Routledge & Kegan Paul.

Turner, B. F., Tobin, S. S., & Leiberman, M. A. (1972). Personality traits as predictors of institutional adaptation among the aged. *Journal of Gerontology, 27,* 61–68.

Wallace, C. J. (1982). The social skills training project of the mental health clinical research center for the study of schizophrenia. In J. P. Curran & P. M. Monti (Eds.), *Social skills training: A practical handbook for assessment and treatment.* New York: Guilford.

Walters, E., Fink, S., & White, B. (1976). Peer group counseling for older people. *Educational Gerontology, 1,* 157–170.

Wisocki, P. A. (1977). *Sampling procedures: Tools for stimulating the activity and interest of institutionalized elderly.* Paper presented at the American Psychological Association, San Francisco.

Wisocki, P. A. (1979). *Actual and predicted responses of institutionalized elderly to the reinforcement survey schedule.* Paper presented at the Association for Advancement of Behavior Therapy meeting, San Francisco.

Wisocki, P. A., & Mosher, P. M. (1980). Peer facilitated sign language training for a geriatric stroke victim with chronic brain syndrome. *Journal of Geriatric Psychiatry, 13,* 89–102.

Wolk, S., & Telleen, S. (1976). Psychological and social correlates of life satisfaction as a function of residential constraint. *Journal of Gerontology, 31,* 89–98.

Working with Older People (Vol. III). (1970). The aging person: Needs and Services. U. S. Department of Health, Education and Welfare. Rockville, MD: Public Health Service.

Wrubel, J., Benner, P., & Lazarus, P. S. (1981). Social competence from the perspective of stress and coping. In J. D. Wine & M. D. Smye (Eds.). *Social competence.* New York: Guilford.

Zarit, S. H. (1979). Helping an aging patient to cope with memory problems. *Geriatrics, 34,* 82–90.

PART FOUR

Programs for the Severely Impaired

CHAPTER 15

A Behavioral Approach to Social Skills Training with Psychiatric Patients

KAREN A. CHRISTOFF AND JEFFREY A. KELLY

Chronic psychiatric patients, considered here to mean individuals with a history of institutionalization for the treatment of severe and usually schizophrenic disorders, represent a population often characterized by striking and pervasive interpersonal skills deficits. Bellack and Hersen (1978) have pointed out that although there are many different and often discrepant theories of why individuals develop psychotic disorders such as schizophrenia, there seems to be remarkable convergence when clinicians are asked to describe the appearance of a "chronic schizophrenic." In almost any clinician's description of how a chronic schizophrenic acts, one finds frequent reference to *interpersonal* deficits and idiosyncracies: social withdrawal, lack of spontaneity, inappropriateness, dull or blunted emotion, and peculiar style of communication with others. In the eyes of many professionals and quite certainly to most people in the community at large, it is the social "differentness" of chronic psychiatric patients that most immediately sets them apart from others.

During the past 15 years, there has been renewed interest in developing effective new treatment programs for chronic psychiatric patients. Much of the impetus for this interest was a movement toward noninstitutional forms of inter-

vention. In the early 1970s, policies of deinstitutionalization were adopted in most states; by the late 1970s, treatment of patients in the "least restrictive setting" possible became a widely accepted, and often legally mandated, mental health policy. With this emphasis on community-based treatment, patients who had been institutionalized for long periods were discharged back into the community; those who entered institutions for the first time often remained there for much shorter periods than in the past.

One consequence of the shift toward noninstitutional treatment of psychiatric patients was the need to develop applied research interventions for teaching skills that are needed to live effectively in the community. The focus of many skills training projects with institutionalized clients has been such basic but important community-living competencies as cooking, budgeting, housekeeping, and vocational preparedness (cf. Bauman & Iwata, 1977; Cuvo, Jacobi, & Supko, 1981; Johnson & Cuvo, 1981). However, there has also been a slowly growing recognition that many of the daily-living tasks faced by chronic psychiatric patients are social in nature and therefore require effective social skills. If one expects psychiatric patients to establish adequate interpersonal relationships with others, an apparent requisite to successful living outside institutions (Zigler & Phillips, 1962), they must first have the social conversational skills to develop those relationships. If one expects psychiatric patients to resist exploitation by others, they must be able to assert themselves when confronted by unreasonable demands and requests. To achieve financial self-sufficiency, skills in job finding (including the critically important social task of handling interviews effectively) are needed. To develop relationships with opposite-sex persons, successful and appropriate hetersocial or date-initiation skills are needed. In short, successful everyday living requires a variety of different interpersonal competencies, and many psychiatric patients seem to exhibit social skills deficits that limit their abilities to achieve successful relationships with others (Libet & Lewinsohn, 1973; Trower, Bryant, & Argyle, 1978; Wolpe, 1969; Zigler & Phillips, 1962).

The recognition that psychiatric patients encounter difficulty with interpersonal relationships is certainly not new. Traditional theories of personality and psychopathology, especially those of Adler, Sullivan, Horney, and George Kelly, have long stressed the relationship-interpersonal aspects of disordered functioning, often in eloquent detail. However, for most traditional theorists, the interpersonal deficits of psychiatric patients were viewed as "symptomatic" of their disorders, and social behavior deficits were rarely the target for direct intervention.

Efforts to specifically improve the social behavior of psychiatric patients received much more attention with the development of behavioral contingency management programs in the 1960s. Usually implemented in residential or institutional ward settings, operant programs (such as token economies) made use of explicit reinforcement contingencies to increase a wide variety of self-care and social interaction behaviors (see reviews by Ayllon & Azrin, 1968; Carlson, Hersen, & Eisler, 1972; Kazdin & Bootzin, 1972). Often focused on the most chronic back-ward patients, operant programs proved successful for increasing behavior related to social appearance (including hygiene, cleanliness, and dress) as well as appropriate, if somewhat rudimentary, aspects of social skill (spending less time alone in one's room, engaging in social activities on the ward, and communicating verbally and appropriately with others).

Although operant, token-based approaches represent one of the earliest successful attempts to improve the social skills of chronic psychiatric patients specifically, contingency management procedures used alone are limited in a number of ways. First, as Hersen and Bellack (1976a) point out, if an individual does not have appropriate skills in his or her behavioral repertoire, a contingency management system would be ineffective; if a patient is unable to emit some targeted skills response (such as assertiveness or maintaining a conversation), she or he will not have the opportunity to be reinforced. This, in turn, leads to a second limitation. Unlike relatively simple, discrete behaviors such as tooth brushing, hair combing, or even being physically present for ward activities, the skills needed to initiate and maintain social interactions successfully are extremely complex. Effective conversational skills, for example, require an individual to master a whole range of verbal behaviors (including asking appropriate questions, conveying interest in the other conversant, talking about topics of interest that are appropriate to the interaction); nonverbal behaviors (such as eye contact, suitable affect, voice tone, voice loudness, posture, and physical appearance); and stylistic skills (integrating all of the aforementioned components together smoothly, handling silences, appropriately maintaining or changing topics during the course of the conversation, and so on). Given the complexity of even routine interactions like short conversations, individuals who are seriously skills deficient require a very active, intensive teaching intervention beyond the practical scope of contingency management systems when used alone.

A final consideration is that social skills training with psychiatric patients usually entails treatment in one setting (within a hospital, a mental health center, aftercare program, or some other facility) that is primarily intended to alter the quality of an individual's behavior in different *in vivo* community settings (when talking to one's next-door neighbor, interviewing for a job, handling a problem with the landlord, asking someone for a date, and so on). For this reason, training approaches that explicitly foster skill generalization to critical *in vivo* environments are probably more useful than those limited to contingency management of patient behavior within a single setting, such as a hospital ward or a day treatment program.

As a result of these factors, research on social skills training with psychiatric patients expanded beyond purely operant institutional programs in the 1970s. Utilizing a number of behavioral principles including modeling, coaching, reinforcement/shaping, behavior rehearsal, and feedback, investigators developed intensive training programs intended to teach patients to handle specific types of social interaction more effectively. One of the first kinds of social skills to receive attention was assertiveness. Following from earlier success in assertion training for college students and other high-functioning individuals (cf. McFall & Lillesand, 1971; McFall & Marston, 1970), a number of investigators extended assertion training techniques to populations of psychiatric inpatients and outpatients (Bellack, Hersen & Turner, 1976; Edel-

stein & Eisler, 1976; Eisler, Hersen, Miller, & Blanchard, 1975; Fredericksen, Jenkins, Foy, & Eisler, 1976; Hersen & Bellack, 1976b; Kelly, Fredericksen, Fitts, & Phillips, 1978). All of these studies shared similar rationales: Because psychiatric patients are often passive during their interactions with others, specific training to assist them in expressing both negative feelings when confronted by the unreasonable actions of others ("refusal assertion") and positive feelings when others behave warmly ("commendatory assertion") may enhance the quality of their interpersonal relationships.

In addition to shared clinical rationales, most of the early assertion training interventions followed very similar training formats. Patients role played a series of short, usually standardized, vignettes in which someone else (the role-play partner) directed either unreasonable or positive comments to them. Ratings of role-play performance were made to identify skills components deficient in the subjects' responses. Training would then be introduced to shape skills components such as eye contact, speech quality, and the verbal content of the subjects' responses to his/her partner in each role-played scene. Although there was some variability in specific techniques, most assertive training projects with psychiatric patients made use of instruction, modeling, role-play rehearsal, and reinforcement/feedback over multiple treatment sessions to increase components of assertive responses.

The early assertive training research with psychiatric patients was impressive in several respects. For probably the first time, comprehensive "packages" of behavioral techniques were specifically used to improve the quality of social skills in a clearly "clinical" population. Although it was evident that social skills training was not in itself a sufficient treatment for chronic schizophrenics (the population most often studied in this literature), these studies demonstrated that basic skills training principles can be applied to remediate the obvious social deficits of this population, deficits that often remain even following treatment with psychotropic medications. Finally, by attempting to define socially skilled assertive behavior in terms of objective components, these interventions contributed to the development of new and more operationally precise conceptualizations of social skills.

The literature on assertive training with psychiatric patients, although innovative in many respects, can best be viewed as the early beginning of this treatment approach, rather than its current "state of the art" or its ideal application. Although a number of investigations demonstrated that one can improve patients' assertiveness during structured role plays in the clinic setting (Bellack et al., 1976; Edelstein & Eisler, 1976; Eisler et al., 1975; Fredericksen et al., 1976; Kelly et al., 1978), the critical question of whether skill use would generalize to interactions in the natural environment was largely unevaluated. One might also argue that much attention has been given to teaching skills that may be needed on only an occasional basis. Although being able to resist the unreasonable behavior of an antagonist (refusal assertion) is an adaptive skill, situations requiring refusal assertion probably occur with relatively low frequency for most people, including psychiatric patients. Other types of social interactions—initiating and maintaining conversations, for example—take place far more frequently and may be of greater adjustmental relevance for most psychiatric patients living in the community.

It is possible to broaden or stretch the term *assertiveness* to designate effective, appropriate, and skilled performance in any situation (e.g., assertively handling conversations, job interviews, or date initiations), and some investigators appear to use the terms *assertion*

training and *social skills training* interchangeably (Kelly, 1982). However, it may be more useful to think of social skills training as a generic, categorical description that subsumes various types of specific interventions. Some applications of social skills training that are relevant to psychiatric patients include interventions to improve physical appearance, conversational skills, job-seeking skills, hetersocial (date-initiation skills) and social problem-solving skills, in addition to assertiveness. As we will see when we review some of these applications, the most exemplary social skills interventions with psychiatric populations specifically focus their training attention on situations that the individual is currently unable to handle skillfully and that are necessary for the individual's community adjustment. Training procedures explicitly intended to foster generalization (skills use in the natural environment) are also receiving more attention.

SETTINGS, GOALS, AND TREATMENT FORMATS OF SOCIAL SKILLS TRAINING WITH PSYCHIATRIC PATIENTS

Social skills training can be conducted in most settings where psychiatric patients receive treatment. For patients who are in institutional or inpatient facilities, training can be structured to improve the quality of social interactions within the facility as well as to prepare patients to handle interpersonal situations they will face when returning to the community. Individuals with a long history of institutionalization and the severe social impairment that often accompanies chronic schizophrenia may exhibit skills deficits that are quite pervasive (Bellack & Hersen, 1978; Trower et al., 1978). Assuming that an overall aim is for these patients to adjust successfully to community living, intensive social skills training in a number of specific areas may be needed (appearance enhancement, conversational skills, job-interview training, and so on). One can, in fact, argue that it is highly irresponsible to discharge patients into the community when it is evident that they still lack the social skills needed to get along effectively with others.

The implementation of specific "modules" is an effective way to incorporate social skills training in the overall treatment program of an institution (Kelly, Patterson, & Snowden, 1979c). Using this approach, a facility could offer a variety of different training modules or classes (such as in appearance, conversational skills, date-initiation skills, job-finding skills, etc.), with patients scheduled to attend those groups that most met their future needs and current skills deficits. In this way, the patient who is single and date anxious could receive heterosocial skills training; the individual who will be seeking employment following discharge might receive job-seeking skills training; and so on (Kelly et al., 1979c). Presumably, decisions about which types of skills training a given individual needs could be made collaboratively by the facility staff and the patient.

Another important setting for social skills training is the facility that provides aftercare services when a patient has been discharged from institutional treatment. Mental health centers, partial hospitalization programs, and transitional living residences all deal with patients readapting to community living and, as a result of the deinstitutionalization policies of the past decade, aftercare has become a major activity of many mental health facilities. Although an advantage of social skills training conducted in institutional settings is that it can potentially assist patients in learning skills *before* the individual returns to the community, an advantage of incorporating skills training in aftercare programs is

that patients can practice the skills daily *while* actually living in the community. Once again, it is possible to provide various kinds of skills training interventions to aftercare patients, with a given individual offered the type(s) of training that most meet his or her needs (Kelly et al., 1979c; Liberman, DeRisi, King, Eckman, & Wood, 1970).

Assessment Issues Preceding Intervention

As we alluded to earlier and as Franks (1982) has cogently pointed out, decisions about whether social skills training is an appropriate intervention for a given patient (and, if so, what type of skills training that individual needs) must always be based on careful and detailed clinical assessment. To a certain degree, we feel that some forms of social skills intervention, such as assertiveness training, have become so well known, popular, and faddish that they are applied almost indiscriminatively across client populations and individuals. To evaluate the appropriateness of any social skills treatment for a patient properly, three related questions must be considered. First, *does the individual presently exhibit skills deficits in certain types of social interactions* (conversations, heterosocial interactions, job interviews, when confronted with the unreasonable behavior of others, etc.)? Second, *do the observed deficits appear to be present because the individual lacks the skills needed to handle such interactions effectively?* And, third, *is acquisition of improved social skills clinically relevant and important for this individual's functioning and adjustment?*

Assessment of Skills Deficits

A detailed discussion of procedures for social skills assessment is beyond the scope of this chapter. However, clinicians are usually first "alerted" to the possibility that social skills may be needed for a given patient in several ways. *Staff observation* of a patient's interpersonal functioning (such as on a hospital ward or a mental health center aftercare program) may reveal deficits in social skills. Isolation, deficient conversational behavior, inappropriately handled conversations, or extreme passivity with others are all potential indicators of social skills inadequacy. *Patient reports* of their own interpersonal difficulties may also alert the clinician that social functioning merits further attention. Patients' descriptions of loneliness, paucity of relationships, social anxiety, or difficulties getting along with others can all be signs that skills deficits are present. Finally, *new social interactions that will soon be faced* by the patient should lead the clinician to consider whether the individual has the skills needed to handle those new situations. For example, psychiatric patients successful in sheltered vocational rehabilitation programs may be encouraged to seek competitive employment on their own. If this is done, the clinician should attempt to anticipate what new social skills demands will be faced by the patient (e.g., telephoning potential employers to inquire about openings, interviewing for jobs, interacting with co-workers on the job) and, if indicated, assess and train these skills.

These initial and general factors can be followed by more specific skill assessment. Within the literature, behavior analytic methods for assessing social skills performance have received the greatest amount of attention. Using this approach, the therapist closely observes the behavior of the patient during social interactions that approximate the *in vivo* situations believed to be troublesome. For example, Urey, Laughlin, and Kelly (1979) assessed the hetersocial skills of formerly hospitalized male psychiatric patients by having them interact for 5 minutes with female confederates; this was intended to approximate the type of situation they would actually encounter when initiating dates or other hetersocial

interactions. Similarly, role-played employment interviews have been used to assess the interview skills of patients who would soon be job seeking (Furman, Geller, Simon, & Kelly, 1979; Kelly, Laughlin, Claiborne, & Patterson, 1979b; Kelly, Urey, & Kelly, 1979; Kelly, Laughlin, Claiborne, & Patterson, 1979b; Kelly, Urey, & Patterson, 1981), and role plays of situations requiring assertiveness are often used to assess this skill (Bellack et al., 1976; Eisler et al., 1975; Hersen & Bellack, 1976b). The clinician usually follows her/his initial impression that a patient is skills deficient with some more formalized, behavioral assessment of performance in a situation that approximates the troublesome interaction.

Are Social Deficits Due to Skills Inadequacies that Require Training or to Other Factors?

When psychiatric patients are observed to exhibit social behavior inadequacies, skills training may be an appropriate intervention. The rationale, of course, for most formalized social skills training is that because a patient lacks those behavioral competencies needed to handle interactions effectively, a systematic "teaching" program is needed. However, deficiencies in social skills performance can occur for other reasons, and alternative forms of intervention may be warranted. For example, the social environment of certain patients (especially those patients on institution "back" wards or those living in socially impoverished settings within the community) provides little opportunity to use, practice, and be reinforced for socially skilled behavior. Consequently, an absence of effective social skills in some patients may be attributed, not to patient skills deficits, but to environmental contingencies that provide very little reinforcement for interpersonal behavior that is deemed appropriate for the general population.

The deleterious influence of simply having few opportunities to practice socially skillful behavior has received little attention with psychiatric patient populations. However, some studies with college students suggest that hetersocial anxiety can be diminished and performance improved by providing repeated opportunities to practice skilled behavior, even without formal social skills training per se (Christensen & Arkowtiz, 1974; Christensen, Arkowitz, & Anderson, 1975). Although psychiatric patients typically exhibit more severe and pervasive skills deficits than the average socially anxious college student, clinicians should attempt to analyze whether a patient has sufficient opportunities to engage in (and be reinforced for) any skill behavior that is not currently observed. If not, intervention could be appropriately focused to this problem.

A final and certainly more difficult clinical problem is that some patients may exhibit social skills deficits because interpersonal interactions simply lack reinforcement value to them (Kelly, 1982). Most of us assume that interactions such as conversations are (or, at least, can be) positive and rewarding events. Therefore, the skills one uses to establish conversations and, ultimately, friendships can be seen as behavioral pathways to reach those rewarding goals. However, if the goals of being with others and having friends are *not* rewarding, one would have little reason to develop and exhibit the skills needed to attain them. Unfortunately, at least some psychiatric patients do not appear to find relationships with others as highly reinforcing goals and may exhibit skills deficits for this reason.

To summarize, the observation that a patient exhibits social inadequacies can indicate the need for social skills training. Alternatively and concurrently, skills deficits can be accounted for if the individual lacks opportunities to practice skilled behavior, if insufficient naturalistic reinforcement accompanies the exhi-

bition of appropriate skills, and/or if the goals attainable through socially skilled actions are not presently reinforcing to the individual. To the extent that any of these factors are present, they too will require intervention.

Is Skills Training Clinically Relevant for the Patient?

An additional practical matter is ensuring that skills training in a particular area is clinically relevant for the patient who will receive it. For example, most studies indicate that it is possible to teach refusal assertiveness to a wide variety of psychiatric patients. However, the fact that one is *able* to teach patients to behave assertively does not mean that they actually required assertion training. Presumably, refusal assertion training is an appropriate intervention only if there is evidence that a particular patient has been, or is likely to be, taken advantage of by others. In that case, refusal training is clinically relevant for the individual. Similarly, job interview training may be needed by patients who will soon be seeking employment but would not be relevant for individuals who are not yet vocationally competent.

Within the social skills literature, closely tailoring interventions to a patient's specific needs has not always received the attention it merits. For example, assertive training projects with psychiatric patients often rely on a set of standardized role-play scenes as both assessment and behavior practice vehicles (cf. The Behavioral Assertiveness Test; Eisler et al., 1975). Using this training method, subjects are taught to exhibit components of refusal assertion in scenes that involve, among other topics, returning overcooked steaks in a restaurant or asking someone to vacate your reserved seat at a sporting event. Although the use of standardized or "stock" scenes may be useful in assertiveness research, most available data indicate that social skills are quite situation specific (Eisler et al., 1975; Kelly et al., 1978). If a patient does not receive training in how to handle situations that very closely conform to the interactions that are actually problematic for him or her, little behavior-change benefit will be derived. Therefore, careful interviews and observations to pinpoint an individual's specific social skills problem interactions closely (followed by assessment and later practice in these areas) is undoubtedly more useful than simply presenting a standard set of published assessment/practice scenes that may be quite unrelated to the *in vivo* interactions causing the person difficulty (Kelly, 1982). This close tailoring of training may be especially important for lower functioning psychiatric patients who have limited ability to generalize skills to situations dissimilar from those used in training.

Treatment Formats and Components

As we will see shortly, most social skills interventions with psychiatric populations use an intensive package of behavioral procedures in training. Following a behavior assessment "sample" in which the subject's performance is observed and evaluated (and this might be an assertiveness or job interview role play, or an unstructured conversation), training is provided to improve and shape specific aspects of the subject's skills. *Instruction* or *coaching* from the therapist is used to convey information to the patient about some desired skill behavior (e.g., "I want you to practice looking directly at the other person's face when you are talking to him"). *Modeling,* either with the therapist demonstrating the skill "live" or by showing a videotaped model, is ordinarily used to expose the patient further to the desired behavior. *Opportunity for the patient to rehearse or practice* a simulated interaction provides a performance experience and allows the therapist to offer *feedback, reinforcement, and further shaping* of

the skill. These in-session procedures are relatively standard in social skills training for all client populations, and are widely used in interventions with psychiatric patients as well.

Several other procedural points are particularly salient when conducting training with severely skills-deficient individuals. The first involves the pace and intensity of treatment. Although brief interventions, consisting of several treatment sessions, have been reported for high-functioning clients with relativly circumscribed interaction problems (Christensen et al., 1975; Forrest & Baumgarten, 1975; Glass, Gottman, & Shmurak, 1976; Hollandsworth, Dressel, & Stevens, 1977), psychiatric patients with long-standing and severe social skills deficits often require much more intensive training. For example, the Urey et al. (1979) heterosocial-conversational training intervention required 16 individual training sessions, whereas Hersen and Bellack (1976b) reported that one patient required daily sessions, lasting 30 to 90 minutes each, for 5 weeks in order to fully shape his assertion skills. Intensive social skills training is undoubtedly necessary for individuals with extremely poor skills or slow response to treatment.

Another matter that we have observed involves the importance of ensuring that patients acquire social skills concepts or strategies, rather than memorized or "parroted" responses to highly specific social stimuli. Although some high-functioning clients are able to quickly grasp skills concepts or rules, many psychiatric patients (especially those who can be called "lower functioning") seem to have much more difficulty generalizing skills use to stimuli or settings different than those of training. As one example, patients who repeatedly role play the same situations calling for assertiveness or conversational initiation may learn adequate responses to those specific stimuli but encounter difficulty handling different situations that, in fact, call for the same social response (Eisler et al., 1975). This, of course, is a problem of generalization. Although it has not been extensively described in the literature, the problem of inadequate response discrimination also appears to occur with some lower functioning persons (Christoff & Kelly, in press). Here, a patient exhibits a social response indiscriminately, in situations where it is inappropriate as well as appropriate. For example, a schizophrenic patient might approach strangers and begin talking to them about some personal problem, even though this topic of conversation would only be appropriate with someone already well known to the individual. Similarly, a common (if unsubstantiated) fear is that people who first learn refusal assertive skills will overuse the responses in situations where they are not warranted, and come across to others as "pushy" or belligerent.

Although most research with psychiatric populations focused primarily on the *training* of social skills, interventions are clinically useful only to the extent that patients actually *use* their newly trained skills in the natural environment and thereby achieve more satisfactory relationships. As we turn now to a review of some representative interventions, we will consider both how skills training was accomplished and what efforts were made to ensure that patients could correctly use their newly acquired skills outside the immediate training setting.

POTENTIAL TARGET AREAS FOR SOCIAL SKILLS TRAINING WITH PSYCHIATRIC PATIENTS

The term *social skills* covers a wide variety of specific behavioral competencies that are functionally effective in different interpersonal situations. Skillful behavior requires the coordination of a complex pattern of discrete verbal and nonverbal response components that are appropriate to the situation and that will facilitate satisfaction of one's goals, needs, or objectives. Because different skills are needed in different kinds of situations, the next section of the chapter will be devoted to discussions of several classes of social skills that are relevant to psychiatric patients. Specifically, we will discuss (1) self-care skills, including grooming and dressing; (2) conversational skills; (3) assertiveness skills; (4) date initiation/hetersocial skills; and (5) employment-related social skills.

Self-Care Skills

Historically, social skills training has focused on verbal and cognitive skills. Although there is no question as to the relevance and importance of these, patients from institutionalized populations may also require attention to more basic elements of self-presentation such as grooming, dress, and self-care skills prior to training more complex verbal and interactive skills. Appearance is clearly important to social acceptance because impressions made on first sight may well bias the opinions of others. Much has been written with regard to appearance aspects of social skills in the form of advice to job interviewees, but the importance for day-to-day interactions has been largely neglected. The relevance of clothing and appearance in impression management has been well documented (Molloy, 1976, 1977), and the demonstrated impact of appearance warrants its inclusion in any training program designed to enhance the functional effectiveness of the client within her/his environment. If appearance is deficient in some way or if the therapist or ward staff members form negative impressions based on appearance, it is probably reasonable to assume that others with whom the client interacts will form these same impressions. Because grooming and dressing are very basic aspects of social skills, and because very negative responses are often elicited by deficits in these areas (such as body odor, poorly applied makeup, dirty unkempt hair and clothing, and so on), the practical impact of higher level training (such as assertiveness or conversational skills) may well be limited by problems in this more basic area.

Surprisingly, there are few controlled investigations of the impact of personal appearance training with psychiatric patients. Several studies have demonstrated that mentally retarded individuals can be trained to bathe, dress, and groom themselves appropriately (Martin, Kehoe, Bird, Jensen, & Darbyshire, 1971; Matson, DiLorenzo, & Esveldt-Dawson, 1981; Treffrey, Martin, Samels, & Watson, 1970). However, even these investigations have not specifically demonstrated that such training leads to increased acceptance of the trainees within the community. From a subjective point of view, we have noted that ward staff members often base judgments about when psychiatric inpatients are "getting better" on observations that the patients are "looking better" (i.e., bathing more frequently and with fewer prompts, combing their hair, brushing their teeth, washing and ironing their clothing, and so on).

In spite of the paucity of attention to the physical appearance of psychiatric patients, we believe this is an important area of social skills training, and propose that it should be addressed within the context of a complete social skills training program. Assessment must include evaluations of what skills in this area the patient is exhibiting in her/his day-to-day life as well as what skills she or he is capable of performing but simply does not use. As Kazdin, Matson, and Esveldt-Dawson (1981) have noted, one should not assume that a patient cannot perform required behaviors simply because she or he does not emit them spontaneously.

A behavior may not occur simply because it has gone unreinforced in the past or because other incompatible behaviors have been reinforced. Thus, a psychiatric patient may not bathe, groom, or dress properly simply because others have always assisted, prompted, or done it for her or him; not because she or he is incapable. Assessment must be directed at determining what appearance skills are deficient, and whether they need to be trained or the reinforcers for incompatible behaviors (i.e., helplessness) withdrawn, or both. Results of this assessment will then determine the content and process of training. If required, training can incorporate the discrete steps in bathing and dressing as described in Martin et al. (1971), Matson et al. (1981), and Treffrey et al. (1970). If the patient does not require this basic training, teaching simple rules such as "use deodorant every day," "don't wear plaid shirts with striped slacks," "don't wear blue jeans on a job interview," and so on may suffice. Attention must be directed toward determining exactly what aspects of dressing and grooming are deficient, and effective remediation will consist of specific training in the deficient areas.

Conversational Skills

Conversational skills refer to the abilities to begin and maintain informal conversations with others (Kelly, 1982). Trower (1980) has suggested that deficient conversational skills are prominent determinants of inferences of social incompetence. Presumably, basic conversational skills are prerequisites to competence in a wide variety of interpersonal situations. Obtaining employment, establishing and maintaining friendships and heterosexual relationships, and soliciting assistance from others all require a basic ability to communicate with others in conversation. Psychiatric patients, particularly those who have been institutionalized for long periods of time and who lack basic conversation skills, are often perceived by others as dull, peculiar, and even threatening (Bellack & Hersen, 1978; Kelly, 1982; Kelly, Urey, & Patterson, 1980b; Urey et al., 1979). In addition, several psychiatric diagnostic categories, most notably schizophrenia and depression, are characterized by withdrawal and social isolation. Presumably, training programs where patients are given opportunities to practice and receive reinforcement for appropriate conversational behavior will facilitate increased and improved social and conversational interactions for these patients. Thus, conversational skills training can be seen as critical to the rehabilitation of many psychiatric patients.

In assessing and training conversational skills, one must take into account not only the environment within which the individual presently functions but also other environments to which she or he might reasonably aspire. Psychiatric inpatients may converse quite appropriately and adequately within the institution. However, conversational behaviors that are acceptable within the institution may well not be acceptable to the community at large and may limit the individual's movement from the inpatient setting. In general, we believe that conversational behavior should be evaluated with respect to how closely it approximates that of same-aged ''normal'' (i.e., nonhospitalized) persons. Training should likewise be directed at teaching psychiatric patients to approximate the normal behavior of same-aged members of the community at large. Strange and stilted speech patterns, topic content, and mannerisms while speaking are often tolerated and even expected of patients within some institutions. However, outside of the institution they may prove problematic for the patient because they cause him or her to be targeted as ''different'' or ''strange.''

Assessment of conversational behav-

ior ordinarily focuses on specific components of the individual's conversational repertoire. The most commonly described components of conversational skills include conversational questions, self-disclosing statements, positive-opinion statements, reinforcing or acknowledging comments, appropriate conversational content, speech duration and latency, vocal fluency, voice intonation, affect or emotionality, appropriate smiling, eye contact, posture, and gestures (Bradlyn, Himadi, Crimmins, Christoff, Graves, & Kelly, 1983; Kelly, 1982; Kelly, Furman, Phillips, Hathorn, & Wilson, 1979a; Kelly, Wildman, Urey, & Thurman, 1979d; Minkin, Braukmann, Minkin, Timbers, Timbers, Fixen, Phillips, & Wolf, 1976; Stalonas & Johnson; 1979; Urey et al., 1979). All of these components can be operationally defined in a relatively objective manner; a sample of clients' conversational behavior can be rated for their presence, absence, or appropriateness; and any (or all) components can be targeted for treatment if they appear to be either excessive, absent, or inappropriately used.

Detailed operational definitions of components of conversational skills have been presented elsewhere (cf. Bellack & Hersen, 1978; Cotler & Guerra, 1976; Kelly, 1982) and will not be described in detail here. It is suggested that readers interested in assessing and training conversational skills consult these sources prior to initiating their treatment programs.

Behavioral assessments of these skills have typically consisted of having the client engage in a structured or semi-structured interaction with a confederate or therapist that can be audio- or video-taped and later rated for behaviors such as those previously mentioned. These interactions can consist of a series of structured scenes such as those contained in Eisler et al.'s (1975) Behavioral Assertiveness Test-Revised, or Goldsmith and McFall's (1975) Interpersonal Behavior

Role Playing Test, or of less structured extended conversations where the client is simply asked to converse with another person and "get to know him (her) better." We prefer the latter assessment procedure because its unstructured format seems to provide a better index of clients' general conversational skills (Bradlyn et al, in press, Kelly, 1982; Kelly et al., 1980b; Urey et al., 1979). Initial skills assessment requires that the therapist observe the adequacy of all aspects or components of the client's conversational skills. Then, skills aspects that are problematic (e.g., excessive, deficient, or inappropriately used) can be trained and evaluated during the course of treatment.

Many investigations have demonstrated that, after training, clients exhibit improved use of skills components such as those described earlier. Regardless of whether deficient conversational performance appears to result from never having learned appropriate social behaviors, from disuse and therefore lack of reinforcement for these behaviors, or from inhibition due to anxiety, behavior therapists seem to agree that training or retraining and repeated practice is likely to result in improved skills performance (Hersen & Bellack, 1976a; Kelly, 1982; Marzillier, Lambert, & Kellett, 1976; Wallace, Nelson, Liberman, Aitchison, Lukoff, Elder, & Ferris, 1980).

In addition, there seems to be general agreement that coaching and instructions, coupled with modeling and performance feedback are the most effective combination of treatment procedures (Edelstein & Eisler, 1976; Hersen & Bellack, 1976a; Kelly, 1982). Based on these findings, effective treatment programs usually consist of pretraining conversational assessment to determine specific problem areas, instructions in how to perform the targeted skills and presented rationale for their importance, modeling of the desired skills by the therapist, and repeated client practice of the skills that is followed by feedback from the therapist.

There are very few reported treatment interventions that specifically target the training of conversational skills in nonretarded psychiatric patients, other than those that directed attention to training the conversational aspects of assertion. Falloon, Lindley, McDonald, and Marks (1977) and Goldsmith and McFall (1975) did train some aspects of conversational skills (e.g. initiating and terminating conversations, self-disclosing, and making eye contact) within the context of more broadly based social skills training programs. In both of these programs, a combination of the previously described treatment methods were used. Urey et al. (1979) trained heterosocial conversational skills with two male psychiatric patients on an individual basis, and Kelly et al. (1980b) provided training for three male patients in a small group format. This latter investigation will be described in some detail to illustrate possible procedures for training.

The three subjects in this study were unmarried males, all diagnosed as schizophrenic, the residual type, and were participants in a mental health center's aftercare program. They were selected for training because staff members had found them to be deficient in conversational skills. Conversations with unfamiliar females were targeted for treatment because all subjects reported that these caused them the greatest difficulty. Skills levels were assessed by recording 8-minute conversations between each subject and a female confederate who was unfamiliar to him. These conversations were recorded prior to training (baseline), immediately following each treatment session, and at follow-up, and they were rated for the frequency of three specific conversational behaviors that were targeted sequentially for treatment. These skills, in order of training, were asking conversational questions, self-disclosing positive information, and complimenting the partner. Training sessions were held weekly for 9 weeks, and each lasted 40 minutes. Each group session began with a description of the skill targeted for the day and presentation of an 8-minute modeling videotape of a male and female demonstrating the target skill in a conversation. Following this, the group was led in a discussion that focused on the general class of the targeted skill, and how each subject might adapt it for his own use. Group members then practiced using the skill in conversations with each other.

Ratings of subjects' videotaped conversations indicated that for all subjects, frequency of the target behaviors increased following training. In addition, female judges who were uninvolved with the project and not familiar with the patients rated their posttraining tapes higher than their pretraining tapes on interest shown in partner, conversational skills and appropriateness, and genuineness of emotions. They also expressed more interest in actually meeting the subjects following listening to posttraining tapes.

In order for treatment programs to be maximally effective, attention must also be paid to the impact of training on naturally occurring, *in vivo* conversational behavior as well as to behavior exhibited in the more structured training-practice setting. To assess *in vivo* skills use, patients can be asked to monitor the frequency of their day-to-day conversations, including whether (and how well) they believe they performed the various components. Inpatients can also be observed when they converse with others on the ward, in the cafeteria, or in any other setting where they normally interact with others. Reports of skills performances can also be solicited from staff members or significant others who normally interact with the patient but are uninvolved with the training itself. Obviously, this type of assessment requires informed consent of the patient and/or

his or her legal representative, and therapists need to attend to their clients' right to confidentiality. However, without such procedures, there is little way to assess accurately whether treatment programs lead to improvements in the patients actual *in vivo* behavior.

Assertiveness Skills

Over the past two decades, much research has promoted the importance of assertiveness as a skill required for effective interpersonal functioning. There have been many definitions of the term *assertiveness* (cf. Alberti & Emmons, 1970; Kelly, 1982; Lazarus, 1971; Lange & Jakubowski, 1976; Wolpe, 1969), but almost all authors imply that assertion reflects the ability to express thoughts, feelings, ideas, opinions, or beliefs to others in an effective and comfortable manner. Although the terms *assertiveness* and *social skills* have occasionally been used synonymously, we do not believe these terms to be synonymous. Instead, we conceptualize assertiveness as a specialized subset of behavioral social skills that function to maximize the probability of attaining specific objectives. Although there are many possible taxonomies of assertive behavior, we will address three general categories: *refusal, commendatory,* and *request* assertiveness.

Refusal Assertiveness

In the context of a disagreement, or when one person is trying to block or interfere with the ongoing, goal-directed behavior of another, it may be appropriate (and socially skillful) to refuse to accept or allow the interference. Refusal assertions have generally received the bulk of attention in the social skills training literature (Eisler, 1976; Kelly, 1982), and are probably most representative of popular conceptions of assertiveness (i.e., standing up for one's rights and refusing to allow others to take advantage of one). This form of assertiveness may be particularly important for psychiatric patients, especially those who have been institutionalized for lengthy periods of time. Passivity and subservience to the rules and wishes of institutional staff may be functional within the institution, but the same passivity may place these patients at high risk for exploitation and perhaps ridicule by members of the external community. Because refusal assertiveness functions to prevent the loss of reinforcement in situations where one might otherwise be taken advantage of, assessment and training of those skills seems particularly important with this population. Deficits in refusal assertiveness can be inferred from patients' self-reports of exploitation or passivity, from staff or significant others' reports of non-assertive behavior, or from any other indications that a patient has a history of being exploited in some manner by others. In addition, it is important that one *not* assume that because the patient can verbally describe what she or he should do in an exploitative situation, she or he *will*, in fact, behave in the described manner. A growing body of evidence suggests that there is little correspondence between knowing what one should do and actually doing it when confronted with a situation requiring assertiveness (cf. Bellack, Hersen, & Turner, 1979; Zisfein & Rosen, 1974).

Assessment of skills in this area can take the form of role-play situations where the patient is asked to respond to unreasonable requests and her/his responses are rated for assertive content (i.e., does she or he refuse to comply) as well as stylistic elements (e.g., eye contact, appropriate affect, loudness and fluency of speech, and latency and duration of response). Deficits (or excesses) that are exhibited during role-play assessment scenes suggest the need for assertiveness training. However, the converse is not necessarily true (e.g., that skillful role-play assessment scenes

suggest the need for assertiveness training. However, the converse is not necessarily true (e.g., that skillful role-play performance indicates no need for training). Observations of how the patient handles conflict situations in her/his natural environment (whether on the ward, in a sheltered workshop, or during social activities) are also needed. If deficits are noted in these more naturalistic situations, effort should be direct toward identifying the specific situations where the client is unassertive as well as the verbal, nonverbal, and stylistic behaviors that are deficient so that they may be targeted for treatment.

In addition, therapists need to attend to the question of whether or not the patient can discriminate situations where refusal is appropriate (such as when asked to sign a blank document or to give away possessions or money) and situations where refusal is inappropriate (such as when asked to perform a job-related task by one's employer). Presenting patients with a variety of role-play situations, some in which refusal assertiveness is appropriate and some in which it is not, should facilitate the assessment of a patient's ability to make such discriminations and provide clinical information on whether discrimination training is needed in this area. Again, we prefer not to rely solely on information obtained from structured role plays in determining skills levels, but try to obtain, whenever possible, more naturalistic data, including reports from persons who observe the patient's daily interactions.

Commendatory Assertiveness

Expressions of positive feelings such as praise, appreciation, and liking can be seen as facilitative of positive interpersonal relationships (Kelly, 1982). The ability to commend others in a warm, sincere, and friendly manner can be an extremely powerful interpersonal skill and functions to make the individual a potent reinforcer and desirable interaction partner. For psychiatric patients who are withdrawn, isolated, and generally lacking in positive interpersonal relationships, appropriate use of this skill can be invaluable. Although warm, commendatory assertion has received relatively less attention in the literature than refusal assertiveness, training in its use seems warranted for patients who exhibit deficits in interpersonal relationships that can be attributed to a failure to communicate positive feeling or for those individuals who experience difficulty in responding to the positive behavior of others.

Skillful commendatory assertions are comprised of many of the same components as refusals (e.g., eye contact, affect, and speech loudness and fluency). The content differs, however, in its specific inclusion of praise or approval statements (Kelly et al., 1978), expression of positive feelings that have resulted from the other person's positive behavior (Schinke, Gilchrist, Smith, & Wong, 1979), and perhaps an offer to reciprocate a positive act to the person in the future (Kelly et al., 1978; Skillings, Hersen, Bellack, & Becker, 1978). Deficits in these skills components may indicate a need for training in how to exhibit commendatory skills, how to discriminate situations in which they are appropriate, or both.

Request Assertiveness

A third form of assertiveness occurs when one makes requests of others in order to facilitate meeting one's needs or attaining one's goals. These assertions can occur in conjunction with refusals in situations where the asserter turns down an unreasonable act and also requests a change in the requester's behavior ("No, I will not give you any money; *please don't ask me again"*). The request functions to increase the probability that the present conflict situation will not recur in the future. A request can also exist

by itself as a means to a specific goal, as in asking others for directions, ("How do I get to the bank?") or seeking assistance ("My social security check did not come. Can you look into your files to find out why?"). Like commendatory assertions, assessing and teaching appropriate request behavior has received relatively little attention. However, these skills are important for independent living within many community settings, especially because institutionalized persons have been frequently described as helpless, withdrawn, and passive (Bellack & Hersen, 1978; Goldsmith & McFall, 1975; Kelly et al., 1980b; Trower, 1980; Zisfein & Rosen, 1974). Role-played situations can be developed to assess whether, and how effectively, clients can exhibit request behavior in situations they may confront. However, as we have previously noted, one should be cautious in assuming that skillful behavior in a limited number of role-play situations is representative of generally skillful behavior in the natural environment. Further, assessment and intervention in this area should tap a range of everyday problem situations likely to be faced by the patient in the community, perhaps including asking a landlord to make needed apartment repairs, requesting that a store clerk refund money on a defective purchase, or asking another person to accompany her/him to a social event.

Deficits in assertiveness skills are often described as situation specific (Eisler et al., 1975). However, psychiatric patients frequently seem to exhibit deficient behaviors across a wide range of situations. Assessment for treatment planning should also take this into account and expose the patient to as many specific situations as possible. Treatment priorities can then be established by determining the particular situations that she or he finds most problematic.

Assertiveness training interventions, like those for training conversational skills, typically include instructions, modeling, behavior rehearsal, and feedback. Once assessment has identified the specific situations that are problematic for the patient and the particular response components that her/his performance reveals as deficient, training can focus on these problem areas. For example, in a typical assertion training project, instructions in how and why a skill behavior should be performed are given to the patient and she or he is then asked to role play an interaction in which she or he uses the particular skill. Ordinarily, interventions focus on one skill behavior (eye contact, voice quality, verbal content, etc.) at a time in order to avoid "overwhelming" the patient with information. Following a practice role play, the patient is given feedback to shape and refine her/his use of the skill. This feedback should be specific and worded as positively as possible in order to provide the patient with successful experiences and maintain her/his interest. Social reinforcement from the therapist is often critical to facilitating skill acquisition. Therapists can model the desired skill for the patient, such as by demonstrating an effective assertive response for the patient to observe and imitate. The sequence of instructions, modeling, role play, and feedback is then repeated until the targeted skill is mastered, perhaps over several sessions for difficult skills or low-functioning patients. In order to increase the likelihood that the trained skills will transfer to the natural environment, "homework" assignments are essential. These often take the form of specific instructions to practice the skills, monitor their use, and provide reports on how difficult situations were handled to the therapist at the next session. Assignments should be as specific as possible (e.g., "Ask someone for the time and practice looking at her/him when you do so") in order to maximize the probability that they will be carried out, and they should always be within the range of the patient's current level of skills acquisition so that she or he is likely to be able to complete them successfully. One would not, for example, ask clients to handle very difficult, complex assertion situations until they have become proficient at handling comparable situations during training.

The vast majority of the reported social skills interventions with psychiatric patients have been specifically directed at training assertive responses, rather than other kinds of social skills. These interventions have been conducted with individual patients (cf. Bellack et al., 1976; Edelstein & Eisler, 1976; Foy, Massey, Duer, Ross, & Wooten, 1979; Goldsmith & McFall, 1975; Hersen & Bellack, 1976b; Kelly et al., 1978), and in group formats (cf. Eisler, Blanchard, Fitts, & Williams, 1978; Field & Test, 1975; Lomont, Gilner, Spector, & Skinner, 1969).

Because Trower et al. (1978) have termed Goldsmith and McFall's (1975) project as "one of the best comparative studies" on social skills training with psychiatric inpatients, we will describe their procedures in some detail as a sample intervention. The subjects in this study were 36 psychiatric inpatients at a Veterans Administration hospital (18 schizophrenics and 18 neurotics or character disorders). Each was randomly assigned to one of three groups: interpersonal skills training, psychotherapy control, or assessment-only control (12 each). Assessment of skills levels before and after training consisted of subjects self-ratings of how well they interacted with others; how well they expected to be able to interact outside the hospital; their feelings of self-worth; their self-ratings of comfort and competence in 55 different interpersonal situations; and their role-play behaviors in 25 of these 55 situations. The interpersonal skills training group received three 1-hour individual training sessions within a 5-day period. These training sessions began with coverage of 11 of the 25 problem situations presented in the assessments. A problem situation was first described to the patient, and he was coached regarding how the situation could be handled effectively. He then heard an audiotaped model responding competently in the situation. This was followed by a review and description of probable consequences of his various response options. The situation was then represented, and the subject responded. The response was recorded and played back so that the subject and therapist could evaluate it and provide corrective feedback. Rehearsal continued until the therapist and subject agreed that the subject had responded in a competent manner for two consecutive times. Training then progressed to a new situation. The subjects in this group showed significantly greater improvement in their ability to handle interpersonal problem situations than did those in the assessment-only group or those in the psychotherapy control group who had discussed the same problem situations but received no training in how to deal with them effectively.

Although this intervention led to improved performance and utilized the same basic sequence of training methods (coaching, modeling, behavior rehearsal, corrective feedback) of virtually every assertion skills training program, it is certainly not the only possible approach. Component behaviors (such as eye contact, voice quality, response content) can be targeted sequentially, and/or different situations can be targeted hierarchically with those easiest for the patient trained first. It has also been our experience that 3 hours of training is seldom enough to lead to maintenance of improved performance or to generalization to settings other than that in which the training occurred. Lengthier interventions are generally needed, particularly with low-functioning patients.

Again, it should be noted that assertiveness is not the only skill required for effective interpersonal functioning. At-tention must also be directed to other skills areas in a comprehensive training program.

Date Initiation/Heterosocial Skills

Date initiation and heterosocial skills are a specialized example of conversation skills directed at teaching the specific goal of establishing an intimate sexual and/or social relationship with another person. Although most research to date on heterosocial and date-initiation skills training has been conducted with college student populations (Arkowitz, 1977; Curran, 1977), it may also be very relevant for certain psychiatric patients. Patients who are single can certainly have the same goal of establishing relationships with opposite-sex persons as do other single people in the community. Thus, if an overall aim when working with psychiatric patients is enhancing skills needed for community living, it is important to assess the degree to which a patient is able to establish intimate heterosocial relationships, provided that that goal is important to the individual. If skills deficits are present in this area (including heterosocial anxiety, socially inappropriate ways of interacting with opposite-sex persons, or poor general conversational skills that include deficient social behavior during heterosocial interactions), specific training may be needed.

Because interacting with opposite-sex persons and initiating dates each require skills that are quite similar to engaging in conversations, many of the elements comprising effective heterosocial behaviors are the same as those that comprise effective conversational skills. Asking and answering conversational questions, discussing topics of interest that are appropriate to the situation, maintaining eye contact, displaying warm affect, and conveying interest in the other person's behavior are components of social skills in both general conversations and heterosocial interactions. However, depending on the intimacy and intent of the interaction (e.g., simply talking with an opposite-sex person, asking for a date, or being on a date with someone already well known), other specific behaviors may be appropriate. These might include such components as verbal expressions of affection or liking, specifically requesting a date, touching, or holding hands (Bander, Steinke, Allen, & Mosher, 1975; Curran, 1975; Farrell, Mariotto, Conger, Curran, & Wallender, 1979; Heimberg, Madsen, Montgomery, & McNabb, 1980; Kelly, 1982; Kupke, Hobbs, & Cheney, 1979; Wessberg, Mariotto, Conger, Farrell, & Conger, 1979).

As we noted, the area of heterosocial competence in psychiatric patients has been almost entirely neglected, with most reported interventions in this area limited to adolescent populations (Arkowitz, 1977; Curran, 1977). Falloon et al. (1977) reported that they provided training in developing intimate friendships and sexual relationships for psychiatric outpatients, within the context of a broader based skills training program, but they did not describe specific procedures for this training. Kelly et al. (1980b) and Urey et al. (1979) trained conversational skills in formerly hospitalized psychiatric patients using opposite-sex practice partners. However, the focus of the training in these last two studies was not on increasing dating frequency per se. In spite of this paucity of research attention, many psychiatric patients, particularly those with lengthy histories of institutional living, seem to exhibit deficiencies in this area. Institutional living settings too often limit the opportunities of their residents to observe and engage in age-appropriate heterosocial and dating skills, and past expectations that these residents would remain institutionalized indefinitely seem to have led to an implicit denial that these skills are necessary for psychiatric patients. With the increasing

emphasis on deinstitutionalization, community-based treatment, and community work and living placements, many formerly hospitalized persons are functioning in settings where these skills are more relevant. We believe that psychiatric patients should be provided with training to facilitate the appropriate fulfillment of their heterosocial and heterosexual needs and desires and that these issues should be dealt with at whatever point the individual expresses an interest or when it becomes apparent to someone in the environment that these issues are relevant for the individual. In addition to the conversational skills components listed earlier, other functional/pragmatic aspects of dating behavior (such as knowledge of where to go to meet prospective dates and of appropriate dating activities, arranging a meeting time and place, dressing appropriately for the planned activity, arranging to pay for activities while on the date, and planning transportation to and from the activity) should be assessed and targeted for training if deficiencies are observed.

The same training techniques used for assertion and conversational skills training are useful for training heterosocial skills. Instructions, modeling, role playing, feedback, and *in vivo* practice are all likely to be components of an effective treatment program in this area. Again, skills training should always be accompanied by efforts to assist the client in using heterosocial or date-initiation skills appropriately in the natural environment.

Job-Interviewing Skills

Although vocational training has long been an important component of rehabilitation programs for psychiatric patients, it is only recently that attention has been directed toward the training of social skills necessary for locating potential jobs, convincing employers of vocational competence in employment interviews, and effectively interacting with co-workers and supervisors. Even patients who are successful in vocational skills training programs will be unlikely to obtain work outside the sheltered setting if they cannot locate potential employment and *convince* employers of their vocational competence.

Locating and using information about potential jobs, making telephone and personal contacts with potential employers, dressing and grooming appropriately for interviews, completing job application forms, and presenting oneself positively in the interview situation are all important steps in the job-finding process (Azrin, Flores, & Kaplan, 1975; Clark, Boyd, & Macrae, 1975; Jones & Azrin, 1973; Perrin, 1977). However, research has consistently shown that hiring decisions are based primarily on performance during job interviews (Cohen & Etheridge, 1975; Drake, Kaplan, & Stone, 1972; Springbett, 1958, Tschirgi, 1973).

Patients who are known to be vocationally competent based on successful completion of a vocational training program, effective workshop performance, or successful employment history, but who presently are unable to obtain non-sheltered or standard employment may be deficient in either job-finding or job-interviewing skills. If the patient is not obtaining interviews, assessment of how she or he is attempting to locate potential employers (e.g., job-finding skills) can be used to determine whether specific skills in this area need training. Potential problem areas might include an inability to use the telephone book or want ads skillfully, poorly handled telephone inquiries to employers, inadequately completed application forms, or so on. Because Jones & Azrin (1973) found that two-thirds of job leads come from friends and relatives, individuals who are not locating job leads should be assessed for social skills in asking about job leads or openings, asking others if they would be willing to serve as references as well as their ability to target appropriate people to ask.

If the patient is obtaining interviews but not experiencing success at them, a job-interview skills deficit may be present, and the client's performance in a role-played interview should be observed to assess for the presence, frequency, and/or appropriateness of effective interview self-presentation skills behaviors. Components of job-interviewing skills that have been noted in the literature include eye contact; appropriate affect; speech loudness; clarity and fluency; concise, direct answers to interviewers' questions; job-relevant questions asked of the interviewer; positive self-statements regarding past education, training, work experience, interests, hobbies, or activities; and expressions of enthusiasm and interest in the position applied for (Barbee & Keil, 1973; Furman et al., 1979; Hollandsworth et al., 1977; Hollandsworth, Glazeski, & Dressel, 1978; Kelly et al., 1979b; Kelly et al., 1980b; Kelly, Wildman, & Berler, 1980c; Pinto, 1979).

If a patient has a demonstrated ability to obtain employment but has a history of problematic relations with supervisors or co-workers, or has been fired, assessment and training of her/his skills in getting along with others may be required. Commendatory assertiveness toward co-workers and supervisors, refusals of unreasonable requests, requests for assistance or time off, ability to handle criticism, and general abilities to carry on appropriate conversations with others in the job setting are all reasonable targets for assessment and training where deficiencies are apparent.

Target skills for job-related social skills training programs will be determined by the assessment procedures. The techniques for training will, again, include instructions, modeling, role playing, feedback, and *in vivo* practice.

As an example of one such intervention, Kelly et al. (1979b) provided job-interview training for six formerly hospitalized psychiatric patients who were enrolled in a mental health center aftercare program. All six had been diagnosed as residual-type schizophrenics. Although all of these patients had either completed vocational rehabilitation or were judged to be employable based on their employment histories, none had been successful in obtaining a job for at least 1 year prior to training. Assessment of skills levels was accomplished by tape-recording each subject's responses to a series of 10 standard employment interview questions that were presented in a simulated interview format by a staff member. These assessment interviews were conducted three times prior to the onset of training and following each training session. They were later rated for the frequency with which the subject used the trained skills (asking the interviewer job-relevant questions, providing favorable information about her/his own past work or training history or qualifications, and verbally expressing interest and enthusiasm in the position applied for), and for the frequency of negative information statements. Subjects also participated in interviews with an experienced personnel interviewer before and after training. Interviewers were asked to conduct the interview as they would if the subject was actually applying for a job with their organization. These interviews were also tape-recorded and rated for the behaviors described previously. They were also presented to a different personnel manager who rated the subjects on ambitiousness, enthusiasm, qualifications, appropriate content, speech fluency, and likelihood of being hired based on the interview.

Training consisted of ten 45-minute sessions over a 3-week period. The three targeted skills components were trained during successive weeks. Each session began with a description of the particular skill component to be trained that day and a 10-minute modeling videotape of an effective job interview. Attention of the group members was direction to the model's demonstration of the specific targeted skill. The experimenter then instructed the group in the importance of the skill and provided examples. Group members then practiced using the skill in responding to interview questions posed by the experimenters. Corrective feedback and praise for skillful responses were then provided by the experimenters and other group members.

All subjects demonstrated increased use of the targeted skills following training in their use, and their inappropriate verbal content decreased as appropriate verbal skills were learned. The effects also generalized to interviews with actual personnel interviewers, and the interviewer–judges evaluated the subjects much more favorably following training. In addition, after this training intervention, five of the six subjects were able to obtain paid positions following real-life interviews.

This study provides strong support for the use of job-interview training as part of a comprehensive social skills training program for patients judged to be employable because all of the subjects had had at least four unsuccessful job interviews prior to training and five of the six interviewed successfully following training.

ISSUES FOR FUTURE RESEARCH AND APPLICATION

The use of social skills training procedures with psychiatric patient populations, although a fairly recent development, has already yielded promising results. In particular, behavioral treatment packages (including instructions, modeling, practice, feedback, and reinforcement), whether used in individual treatment or in groups, have been effective in teaching skills-deficient patients a variety of different social skills. However, there are also a number of issues in the skills training literature with chronic psychiatric populations that have received inadequate attention to date. These issues are of importance both to practitioners and to applied researchers, and we will conclude this section with a brief discussion of some of the area's current limitations that, we hope, will be addressed in future projects.

Clinically Relevant Tailoring of Skills Training to Specific Patient Needs

Social skills training is a broad, generic description of a type of treatment. As we noted earlier, many different types of specific interpersonal skills are subsumed under this categorical "umbrella," and training interventions must be tailored to specific types of social skills, such as assertiveness, conversational skills, dating/heterosocial skills, job-interview skills, or so on (Kelly, 1982). Presumably, for example, what one teaches clients in an assertion training program will be quite different than what one covers in a job-interview or date-initiation skills program. Further, the exact kind of social skills training needed by one client may be different than the type required by another. This, in turn, suggests that decisions about the appropriate form of social skills treatment for a given client be determined by analyzing specific situations the individual now handles poorly or might be expected to handle poorly in the future, the types of social skills training that are needed, and whether improved skills of those types will actually enhance the individual's adjustment or functioning level.

Within much of the social skills training literature to date, there has been relatively little attention to matching specific types of training closely to the specific

assessed needs of a given client. Franks (1982) has pointed out that patients often seem to be "put into" social skills training without closely assessing their exact social skills deficits and without ensuring that treatment focuses on the specific situations known to be problematic for them. In both clinical interventions and research projects, there is a need to tailor specific kinds of skills training more closely to the known skills deficits of patients and to demonstrate not only that skills responses can be taught but that they also improve the adjustment of the individual.

Generalization of Skills Training Effects to *in vivo* Interactions

It is well established that one can teach patients the skills to handle role-play antagonists assertively, to perform well in simulated conversations, or to present themselves favorably in role-played job interviews. All of the studies reviewed in this chapter demonstrate that socially skilled behavior in simulated or role-played interactions can be shaped and improved. However, there have been very few demonstrations that patients use their newly acquired skills during natural, *in vivo* social interactions occurring outside the treatment setting itself.

We would argue that most social skills training programs, at least those reported in the applied research literature, have focused attention primarily on teaching psychiatric patients new skills and have dealt very minimally with the equally important matter of helping patients to then actually apply and use those newly acquired skills in day-to-day living. One possible reason for this is that techniques for training persons to *exhibit* skills behaviors in practice situations are relatively well established, whereas optimal techniques for fostering skills *generalization* have received much less attention. For clinical interventions, the use of homework assignments to practice skills behaviors outside the treatment setting, teaching clients to adopt general social strategies rather than memorized responses, increasing the access of a person to social settings where skills behaviors can be used, the arrangement of contingencies in the natural environment that reinforce socially skilled behavior, teaching clients to discriminate when, where, and how to use new skills in their living environment, and decreasing cognitive inhibitions concerning performance in social interactions have all been described (Kelly, 1982) as key elements that may help to foster skills generalization. Clinical research to evaluate the utility of such techniques is clearly needed.

Refinement in the Definition, Assessment, and Teaching of Social Skills

Within the entire social skills area, including interventions with psychiatric patients, we are still at a very early point in our efforts to define and describe socially skilled behavior adequately. In general, a "component analysis" approach has been used to assess and teach most social skills. As we saw, refusal assertiveness has usually been defined in terms of components such as eye contact, firm affect, noncompliance, appropriate voice characteristics, and so on (Bellack et al., 1976; Eisler, Miller, & Hersen, 1973; Kelly et al., 1978; Schinke et al., 1979). Conversational skills have been assessed in terms of various verbal and nonverbal behaviors, such as asking or answering questions, talking about oneself, looking at the other person, making speech acknowledgers when the other person is speaking, and so on (Kelly et al., 1979a; Minkin et al., 1976; Stalonas & Johnson, 1979; Urey et al., 1979). Within most interventions, social skills are judged based on whether, or how frequently, the individual exhibits such components.

This component-based model of definition is useful because it permits us to assess and teach skills behaviors in a relatively specific manner. However, it ignores certain other aspects of effective social interactions. For example, it is possible for individuals to exhibit all of the correct behavioral components of a social skill but to do so in a poorly styled, awkward, and unskilled manner. In a conversation, the style and pacing of how one behaves is very critical to overall effectiveness and may involve such subtle stylistic qualities as when one asks questions, how the content of comments or questions are related to the content of the conversation that preceded them, when one smiles or does not smile, how silences are handled or terminated, and so on. These stylistic aspects of skills are certainly more difficult to define behaviorally than frequency counts or presence–absence ratings of discrete behaviors, but they may be extremely relevant determinants of overall skill. Within the social skills literature as a whole, it will be important to develop new definitional and assessment methodologies that take into account subtle stylistic aspects of effective interpersonal skills. For clinicians working with psychiatric patient populations, it will then be challenging to develop techniques for teaching these more subtle aspects of social skills style, often to clients who are extremely skills deficient.

The Need for Normative Data on Social Effectiveness in Various Situations

One final issue should be briefly noted: We still have very little empirical normative data on how skilled people behave in various types of interpersonal situations. For the most part, social skills interventions (including, but certainly not limited to, those with psychiatric patients) target specific behaviors that the therapist *thinks* contribute to social skills. Thus, what is taught in training interventions for almost all types of social skills—assertion, conversational skills, effective job interviewing, and so on—has been derived largely on intuitive judgment by therapists and researchers. Although efforts to validate socially or globally the behaviors taught in skills training interventions are now beginning to appear (Christoff & Edelstein, 1981; Kelly, Kern, Kirkley, Patterson, & Keane, 1980a; Romano & Bellack, 1980; Solomon, Brehony, Rothblum, & Kelly, in press), much more research in this area is still needed. It would be useful, for example, to locate individuals "everyone" considers to be good, skilled conversationalists and closely assess exactly what they do during conversations with others. The same type of normative-validation procedure could be used to gain empirical information on the determinants of skilled behavior in other types of social interactions as well. Such efforts will assist us in better understanding the behavioral makeup of social skills and, in turn, provide information that will ensure that skills training programs target relevant aspects of social effectiveness.

CONCLUDING COMMENT

In summary, psychiatric patients represent a population for whom social skills training is often useful and appropriate. Building from the clinical studies already conducted, it should be possible for projects to become even more effective and capable of enhancing the interpersonal adjustment of these clients. The future appears promising for clinical interventions, for applied research, and for the improved functioning of patients who receive this training.

REFERENCES

Alberti, R. E., & Emmons, M. L. (1970). *Your perfect right: A guide to assertive behavior.* San Luis Obispo, CA: Impact.

Ayllon, T., & Azrin, N. H. (1968). *The token economy: A motivational system for therapy and rehabilitation.* New York: Appleton-Century-Crofts.

Arkowitz, H. (1977). Measurement and modification of minimal dating behavior. In M. Hersen, R. Eisler, & P. Miller (Eds.), *Progress in behavior modification* (Vol. 5). New York: Academic Press.

Azrin, N. H., Flores, T., & Kaplan, S. J. (1975). Job-finding club: A group assisted program for obtaining employment. *Behaviour Reseach and Therapy, 13,* 17–27.

Bander, K. W., Steinke, G. V., Allen, G. J., & Mosher, D. L. (1975). Evaluation of three dating-specific treatment approaches for heterosexual dating anxiety. *Journal of Consulting and Clinical Psychology, 43,* 259–265.

Bauman, E. E., & Iwata, B. A. (1977). Maintenance of independent housekeeping skill using scheduling plus self-recording procedures. *Behavior Therapy, 8,* 554–560.

Barbee, J. R., & Keil, E. C. (973). Experimental techniques of job interview training for the disadvantaged: Videotape feedback, behavior modification, and microcounseling. *Journal of Applied Psychology, 58,* 209–213.

Bellack, A. S., & Hersen, M. (1978). Chronic psychiatric patients: Social skills training. In M. Hersen & A. S. Bellack (Eds.), *Behavior therapy in the psychiatric setting.* Baltimore: Williams & Wilkins.

Bellack, A. S., Hersen, M., & Turner, S. M. (1976). Generalization effects of social skills training in chronic schizophrenics: An experimental analysis. *Behaviour Research and Therapy, 14,* 391–398.

Bellack, A. S., Hersen, M., & Turner, S. M. (1979). The relationship of role-playing and knowledge of appropriate behavior to assertion in the natural environment. *Journal of Consulting and Clinical Psychology, 47,* 670–678.

Bradlyn, A. S., Himadi, W. G., Crimmins, D. B., Christoff, K. A., Graves, K. G., & Kelly, J. A. (1983). Conversational skills training for retarded adolescents. *Behavior Therapy, 14,* 314–325.

Carlson, C. G., Hersen, M., & Eisler, R. M. (1972). Token economy programs in the treatment of hospitalized adult psychiatric patients. *Journal of Nervous and Mental Disease, 155,* 192–204.

Christensen, A., & Arkowitz, H. (1974). Preliminary report on practice dating and feedback as treatment for college dating problems. *Journal of Counseling Psychology, 21,* 92–95.

Christensen, A., Arkowitz, H., Anderson, J. (1975). Practice dating as treatment for college dating inhibitions. *Behaviour Research and Therapy, 13,* 321–331.

Christoff, K. A., & Edelstein, B. A. (1981). *Functional aspects of assertive and aggressive behavior: Laboratory and in vivo observations.* Paper presented at the meeting of the Association for Advancement of Behavior Therapy, Toronto.

Christoff, K. A., & Kelly, J. A. (in press). Social skills. In J. L. Matson & S. E. Breuning (Eds.), *Assessing the mentally retarded.* New York: Grune & Stratton.

Clark, H. B., Boyd, S. B., & Macrae, J. W. (1975). A classroom program teaching disadvantaged youths to write bigraphic information. *Journal of Applied Behavior Analysis, 8,* 67–75.

Cohen, B. M., & Etheridge, J. M. (1975). Recruiting's main ingredient. *Journal of College Placement, 35,* 75–77.

Cotler, S. B., & Guerra, J. J. (1976). *Assertion training: A humanistic-behavioral guide to self-dignity.* Champaign, IL: Research Press.

Curran, J. P. (1975). An evaluation of a skills training program and a systematic desensitization program in reducing dating anxiety. *Behaviour Research and Therapy, 13,* 65–68.

Curran, J. P. (1977). Skills training as an approach to the treatment of heterosexual-social anxiety. *Psychological Bulletin, 84,* 140–157.

Cuvo, A. J., Jacobi, L., & Supko, R. (1981). Teaching laundry skills to mentally retarded students. *Education and Training of the Mentally Retarded, 16,* 54–64.

Drake, L. R., Kaplan, H. R., & Stone, B. A. (1972). How do employers value the interview? *Journal of College Placement, 32,* 47–51.

Edelstein, B. A., & Eisler, R. M. (1976). Effects of modeling with instructions and feedback on the behavioral components of social skills. *Behavior Therapy, 7,* 382–389.

Eisler, R. M. (1976). Assessment of social skills. In M. Hersen & A. S. Bellack (Eds.), *Behavioral assessment: A practical handbook.* Oxford: Pergamon.

Eisler, R. M., Blanchard, E. B., Fitts, H., & Williams, J. G. (1978). Social skill training with and without modeling for schizophrenic and non-hospitalized psychiatric patients. *Behavior Modification, 2,* 147–172.

Eisler, R. M., Hersen, M., Miller, P. M., & Blanchard, E. B. (1975). Situational determinants of assertive behaviors. *Journal of Consulting and Clinical Psychology, 43,* 330–340.

Eisler, R. M., Miller, P. M., & Hersen, M. (1973). Components of assertive behavior. *Journal of Clinical Psychology, 29,* 295–299.

Falloon, I. R. H., Lindley, P., McDonald, R., & Marks, I. M. (1977). Social skills training of out-patient groups. *British Journal of Psychiatry, 131,* 599–609.

Farrell, A. D., Mariotto, M. J., Conger, A. J., Curran, J. P., & Wallender, J. L. (1979). Self-ratings and judges' ratings of heterosexual social anxiety and skill: A generalizability study. *Journal of Consulting and Clinical Psychology, 47,* 164–175.

Field, G. D., & Test, M. A. (1975). Group assertive training for severely disturbed patients. *Journal of Behavior Therapy and Experimental Psychiatry, 6,* 129–134.

Forrest, D. V., & Baumgarten, L. (1975). An hour for job interviewing skills. *Journal of College Placement,* 77–78.

Foy, D., Massey, F., Duer, J., Ross, J., & Wooten, L. (1979). Social skills training to improve alcoholics' vocational interpersonal competency. *Journal of Counseling Psychology, 26,* 128–132.

Franks, C. M. (1982). Forward. In. J. A. Kelly, *Social-skills training: A practical guide for interventions.* New York: Springer.

Frederiksen, L. W., Jenkins, J. O., Foy, D. W., & Eisler, R. M. (1976). Social skills training in the modification of abusive verbal outbursts in adults. *Journal of Applied Behavior Analysis, 9,* 117–125.

Furman, W., Geller, M., Simon, S. J. & Kelly, J. A. (1979). The use of a behavior rehearsal procedure for teaching job-interviewing skills to psychiatric patients. *Behavior Therapy, 10,* 157–167.

Glass, C. R., Gottman, J. M., & Shmurak, S. H. (1976). Response–acquisition and cognitive self-statement modification approaches to dating-skills training. *Journal of Counseling Psychology, 23,* 520–526.

Goldsmith, J. B., & McFall, R. M. (1975). Development and evaluation of an interpersonal skill-training program for psychiatric inpatients. *Journal of Abnormal Psychology, 84,* 51–58.

Heimberg, R. G., Madsen, C. H., Montgomery, D., & McNabb, C. E. (1980). Behavioral treatments for heterosocial problems: Effects on daily self-monitored and role played interactions. *Behavior Modification, 4,* 147–172.

Hersen, M., & Bellack, A. S. (1976a). Social skills training for chronic psychiatric patients: Rationale, research findings, and future directions. *Comprehensive Psychiatry, 17,* 559–580.

Hersen, M., & Bellack, A. S. (1976b). A multiple baseline analysis of social skills training in chronic schizophrenics. *Journal of Applied Behavior Analysis, 9,* 239–245.

Hollandsworth, J. G., Jr., Dressel, M. E., & Stevens, J. (1977). Use of behavioral versus traditional procedures for increasing job interview skills. *Journal of Counseling Psychology, 24,* 503–510.

Hollandsworth, J. G., Jr., Glazeski, R. C., & Dressel, M. E. (1978). Use of social-skills training in the treatment of extreme anxiety and deficient verbal skills in the job-interview setting. *Journal of Applied Behavior Analysis, 11,* 259–269.

Johnson, B. F., & Cuvo, A. J. (1981). Teaching mentally retarded adults to cook. *Behavior Modification, 5,* 187–202.

Jones, R. J., & Azrin, N. H. (1973). An experimental application of a social reinforcement approach to the problem of job-finding. *Journal of Applied Behavior Analysis, 6,* 345–353.

Kazdin, A. E., & Bootzin, R. R. (1972). The token economy: An evaluative review. *Journal of Applied Behavior Analysis, 5,* 343–372.

Kazdin, A. E., Matson, J. L., & Esveldt-Dawson, K. (1981). Social skill performance among normal and psychiatric inpatient children as a function of assessment conditions. *Behaviour Research and Therapy, 19,* 145–152.

Kelly, J. A. (1982). *Social skills training: A practical guide for interventions.* New York: Springer.

Kelly, J. A., Frederiksen, L. W., Fitts, H., & Phillips, J. (1978). Training and generalization of commendatory assertiveness: A controlled single subject experiment. *Journal of Behavior Therapy and Experimental Psychiatry, 9,* 17–21.

Kelly, J. A., Furman, W., Phillips, J., Hathorn, S., & Wilson, T. (1979a). Teaching conversational skills to retarded adolescents. *Child Behavior Therapy, 1,* 85–97.

Kelly, J. A., Kern, J. M., Kirkley, B. G., Patterson, J., & Keane, T. M. (1980a). Reactions to assertive versus unassertive behavior: Differential effects for males and females and implications for assertiveness training. *Behavior Therapy, 11,* 670–682.

Kelly, J. A., Laughlin, C., Claiborne, M., & Patterson, J. (1979b). A group procedure for teaching job interviewing skills to formerly hospitalized psychiatric patients. *Behavior Therapy, 10,* 299–310.

Kelly, J. A., Patterson, J., & Snowden, E. E. (1979c) A pragmatic approach to mental health aftercare and partial hospitalization. *Social Work in Health Care, 4,* 431–443.

Kelly, J. A., Urey, J. R., & Patterson, J. (1980b). Improving heterosocial conversational skills of male psychiatric patients through a small group training procedure. *Behavior Therapy, 11,* 179–188.

Kelly, J. A., Urey, J. R., & Patterson, J. (1981). Small group job interview skills training in the mental health center setting. *Behavioral Counseling Quarterly, 1,* 202–212.

Kelly, J. A., Wildman, B. G., & Berler, E. S.

(1980c) Small group behavioral training to improve the job interview skills repertoire of mildly retarded adolescents. *Journal of Applied Behavior Analysis, 13*, 461–471.

Kelly, J. A., Wildman, B. G., Urey, J. R., & Thurman, C. (1979d). Group skills training to increase the conversational repertoire of retarded adolescents. *Child Behavior Therapy, 1*, 323–336.

Kupke, T. E., Hobbs, S. A., & Cheney, T. H. (1979). Selection of heterosocial skills, I. Criterion-related validity. *Behavior Therapy, 10*, 327–335.

Lazarus, A. (1971). *Behavior therapy and beyond*. New York: McGraw-Hill.

Lange, A. J., & Jakubowski, P. (1976). *Responsible assertive behavior: Cognitive/behavioral procedures for trainers*. Champaign, IL: Research Press.

Liberman, R. P., DeRisi, W. J., King, L. W., Eckman, T. H., & Wood, D. (1970). Behavioral measurement in a community mental health center. In P. O. Davidson, F. W. Clark, & L. A. Hamerlynck (Eds.), *Evaluation of behavioral programs in community, residential, and social settings*. New York: Brunner/Mazel.

Libet, J., & Lewinsohn, P. M. (1973). Concept of social skill with special reference to the behavior of depressed persons. *Journal of Consulting and Clinical Psychology, 40*, 304–312.

Lomont, J. F., Gilner, F. H., Spector, N. J., & Skinner, K. K. (1969). Group assertive training and group insight therapies. *Psychological Reports, 25*, 463–470.

Martin, G. L., Kehoe, B., Bird, E., Jensen, V., & Darbyshire, M. (1971). Operant conditioning in dressing behavior of severely retarded girls. *Mental Retardation, 9(3)*, 27–31.

Marzillier, J. S., Lambert, C., & Kellett, J. (1976). A controlled evaluation of systematic desensitization and social skills training for socially inadequate psychiatric patients. *Behaviour Research and Therapy, 14*, 225–238.

Matson, J. L., DiLorenzo, T. M., & Esveldt-Dawson, K. (1981). Independence training as a method of enhancing self-help

skills acquisition of the mentally retarded. *Behaviour Research and Therapy, 19*, 399–405.

McFall, R. M., & Lillesand, D. B. (1971). Behavior rehearsal with modeling and coaching in assertion training. *Journal of Abnormal Psychology, 37*, 313–323.

McFall, R. M., & Marston, A. R. (1970). An experimental investigation of behavior rehearsal in assertive training. *Journal of Abnormal Psychology, 76*, 295–303.

Minkin, N., Braukmann, C. J., Minkin, B. L., Timbers, G. D., Timbers, B. J., Fixsen, D. L., Phillips, E. L., & Wolf, M. M. (1976). The social validation and training of conversational skills. *Journal of Applied Behavior Analysis, 9*, 127–139.

Molloy, J. T. (1976). *Dress for success*. New York: Warner Books.

Molloy, J. T. (1977). *The woman's dress for success book*. Chicago: Follett.

Perrin, T. O. (1977). Job seeking training for adult retarded clients. *Journal of Applied Rehabilitation Counseling, 8*, 181–188.

Pinto, R. P. (1979). An evaluation of job-interview training in the rehabilitation setting. *Journal of Rehabilitation, 45*, 71–76.

Romano, J. M., & Bellack, A. S. (1980). Social validation of a component model of assertive behavior. *Journal of Consulting and Clinical Psychology, 48*, 478–490.

Schinke, S. P., Gilchrist, L. D., Smith, T. E., & Wong, S. E. (1979). Group interpersonal skills training in a natural setting: An experimental study. *Behaviour Research and Therapy, 17*, 149–154.

Skillings, R. E., Hersen, M., Bellack, A. S., & Becker, M. P. (1978). Relationship of specific and global measures of assertion in college females. *Journal of Clinical Psychology, 34*, 346–353.

Solomon, L. J., Brehony, K. A., Rothblum, E. D., & Kelly, J. A. (in press). Corporate managers' reactions to assertive social skills exhibited by males and females. *Journal of Organizational Behavior Management*.

Springbett, B. M. (1958). Factors affecting the final decision in the employment interview. *Canadian Journal of Psychology, 12,* 13–22.

Stalonas, P. M., & Johnson, W. G. (1979). Conversation skills training for obsessive speech using an aversive-cueing procedure. *Journal of Behavior Therapy and Experimental Psychiatry, 10,* 61–63.

Treffrey, D., Martin, G., Samels, J., & Watson, C. (1970). Operant conditioning of grooming behavior of severely retarded girls. *Mental Retardation, 8(4),* 29–33.

Trower, P. (1980). Situational analysis of the components and processes of behavior of socially skilled and unskilled patients. *Journal of Consulting and Clinical Psychology, 48,* 327–339.

Trower, P., Bryant, B., & Argyle, M. (1978). *Social skills and mental health.* Pittsburgh: University of Pittsburgh Press.

Tschirgi, H. D. (1973). What do recruiters really look for in candidates? *Journal of College Placement, 33,* 75–79.

Urey, J. R., Laughlin, C. S., & Kelly, J. A. (1979). Teaching heterosocial conversational skills to male psychiatric patients.

Journal of Behavior Therapy and Experimental Psychiatry, 10, 323–328.

Wallace, C. J., Nelson, C. J., Liberman, R. P., Aitchison, R. A., Lukoff, D., Elder, J. P., & Ferris, C. (1980). Social skills training with schizophrenic patients. *Schizophrenia Bulletin, 6,* 42–64.

Wessberg, H. W., Mariotto, M. J., Conger, A. J., Farrell, A. D., & Conger, J. C. (1979). Ecological validity of role plays for assessing heterosocial anxiety and skill of male college students. *Journal of Consulting and Clinical Psychology, 47,* 525–535.

Wolpe, J. (1969). *The practice of behavior therapy.* Oxford: Pergamon.

Zigler, E., & Phillips, L. (1962). Social competence and the process-reactive distinction in psychopathology. *Journal of Abnormal and Social Psychology, 65,* 215–222.

Zisfein, L., & Rosen, M. (1974). Effects of a personal adjustment training group counseling program. *Mental Retardation, 12(3),* 50–53.

CHAPTER 16

A Program of Modular Psychoeducational Skills Training for Chronic Mental Patients

RICHARD E. GORDON AND KATHERINE K. GORDON

This chapter describes how psychiatric patients are taught a variety of skills in order to improve their functional levels. It presents research findings from studies of chronic mental patients and describes aspects of the integrated psychoeducational training and treatment programs developed by the authors and their colleagues at the University of South Florida and the Florida Mental Health Institute (FMHI) (Gordon & Gordon, 1981).

Training will be discussed in terms of the Functional Level (FL) equation, which is adapted from Albee (1982) and Gartner and Riessman (1982). This equation provides a useful model with which to examine the different biopsychosocial components of skills-building treatments used with psychiatric patients. It brings together in one simple formula the major variables that affect patient adjustment and that the treatment process addresses (Gordon and Gordon, 1983):

$$FL = \frac{C + D + E}{A + B}$$

where FL = functional level
    A = aggravating stress
    B = biomedical impairment
    C = coping skill
    D = directive power
    E = environmental supports.

This report first will discuss the FL-equation and its use as a model for integrating skills training in psychiatric treatment. The present chapter will consider some of the categories of skills taught, along with a description of the training process. Brief discussions of behavior management and dynamic psychotherapy and their relationships to skills training of psychiatric patients will follow. Sections on assessment and treatment planning will come next. The chapter will conclude by discussing disincentives to the establishment of psychoeducational skills-building programs and methods of overcoming obstacles.

CHRONIC MENTAL PATIENTS AND THEIR SKILLS DEFICITS

Unlike typical mental and surgical patients with uncomplicated pneumonia or appendicitis, many chronic mental patients do not return to a previous high level of functioning when they recover from the acute phase of their mental illness. Many never attained it previously. People learn the skills needed for effective functioning in life from their family in the home, from teachers and fellow students in the school, from employers and fellow employees on the job, and from friends in organizations, and social and leisure groups. Many parents of psychiatric patients were unable to provide good role models and skills training. Chronic mental patients often quit school and failed to obtain either the formal knowledge that gives direction to their lives or the training in skills such as setting goals and persevering in their attainment. Both of these—lack of knowledge and lack of skills—are related to poor mental health and to poor response to traditional psychiatric treatment. In addition, chronic mental patients often fail to keep jobs, do not generally join clubs and organizations, and make few friends. Most of the last are not especially skillful. Their personal support systems are often deficient (Tolsdorf, 1976).

Because of chronic mental patients' inadequacies in social skills, competence, and support networks, they are especially vulnerable to stress and are poorly equipped to cope with it. Although psychiatric patients differ one from another, and each requires special treatment for personal idiosyncracies, most patients share many similar needs and problems—deficiencies in asserting themselves effectively, in enjoying leisure and social life, in parenting, and/or in solving personal problems and conflicts. More seriously ill patients often do not know why or how to take their medication, nor how to use buses and laundromats, nor how to handle checks and budget money, nor how to get and keep jobs. They usually have difficulty in planning and in setting long- and short-term goals. Most of these handicaps can be overcome through psychoeducation and training.

Chronic patients (and staff), however, must first change the attitude that seriously disabled mental patients are biologically helpless and incapable of learning, that they are hopelessly impaired by the illnesses, and that they are doomed to a life of failure and dependency. They need to realize that, like many stroke patients who have been left paralyzed or speechless by an injury to part of their brain, many chronic mental patients can be trained to use their unimpaired brain functions to overcome their defects. They can learn to be proficient in the psychosocial skills needed for solving their problems, coping with stress, maintaining their emotional equilibrium, and leading fruitful lives at better functional levels (FL). This and other variables in the FL-equation will now be defined and discussed.

IMPROVING FUNCTIONAL LEVEL

Functional Level (FL)

Functional level considers quality of life in social relations, functioning at work and school, use of leisure time, and performance of activities of daily living. Note that FL is a ratio; the denominator can be a very large number, and people can bear a large burden of stress (A) in the FL equation and chronic biomedical impairment (B) without becoming dysfunctional if they have developed compensating coping skills (C), direction over resources (D), and environmental supports (E), so that the numerator is also large. In treatment, patients can be helped to function at a higher level by training them to improve their coping skills, directive power, and environmental supports, to decrease their stresses and biomedical impairments, or to learn combinations of these. Functional level (FL) is measured on scales such as the one described in the *Diagnostic and Statistical Manual of Mental Disorders.* (DSM-III) (1980).

Aggravating Stress (A)

Stressors (A) may be related to ongoing realistic problems, or they may be largely associated with conditioned stimuli from the past. Many standardized instruments, such as the well-known Holmes and Rahe Scale (1967), have been developed to measure the severity of stressors. Patients learn in psychiatric treatment how to manage stress and solve personal problems as part of their psychoeducational training in personal/social skills. Table 16.1 outlines a group of skills categorized by age and population served that are being taught to patients in psychoeducational modules (Gordon & Gordon, 1981).

Biomedical Impairments (B)

Biomedical impairments include not only medical diagnoses and disorders but also other factors related to aging, obesity, malnutrition, substance abuse, lack of exercise, and apathy. Medical and surgical treatments affect the biomedical variables, especially with patients with acute disorders—pneumonia, appendicitis, and overt, active psychoses. They clear up bacterial infections, remove tumors, and reduce behavioral and psychophysiological symptoms.

Merely recovering from an operation or acute infection that temporarily confined a patient to bed may restore a person with mainly biomedical impairments to a high level of functioning (FL). But many patients with chronic impairments, including chronically ill mental patients,

TABLE 16.1.   Skills Taught in Modular Classes to Patients of Different Ages and Their Families

Categories of Skills	Components	Elderly	Young Adults	Chronic Adults	Adolescents	Children	Families
Survival skills	Medication training	X	X	X			X
	Personal information	X				X	
	Compliant behavior	X	X	X	X	X	X
Daily living skills	Personal hygiene/eating/toilet	X		X	X	X	X
	Home care	X	X	X	X	X	X
	Independent living	X	X	X	X		
Personal/social skills	Managing stress		X	X			
	Communicating	X	X	X	X	X	X
	Personal health	X	X	X	X		
	Problem solving	X	X	X	X		X
	Asserting	X	X	X	X		X
	Negotiating		X		X		X
	Relaxing	X	X				X
	Sex role		X		X		
	Peer support		X	X	X		X
	Leadership		X				
Academic/vocational skills		X	X	X	X	X	
Leisure skills		X	X	X	X	X	X
Self-integrative skills	Building self-esteem	X					
	Clarifying values		X		X		X
	Goal setting		X	X			
	Measuring personal achievement				X		
Cognitive skills	Managing anxiety and depression	X	X	X			X

Source. Gordon & Gordon (1981).

in particular, cannot readily return to good functioning after recovering from a bout of acute illness.

Many psychiatric patients require considerable training to take their medications regularly, to go for their periodic prescription refills and their laboratory tests, to exercise, to keep their diets as well as to learn the other skills shown in Table 16.1

Coping Skills (C)

Personal and social coping skills are learned throughout life. Many of them— communicating effectively, providing feedback, asserting, problem solving, making friends, parenting, using leisure, performing activities of daily living, and so forth—can be taught in short-term psychoeducational courses in several hours of class. Yet, many psychiatric patients have never learned effective ones before entering treatment. Table 16.1 includes a sampling of coping as well as other skills taught to patients. Numerous scales gauge patients' proficiencies in a variety of personal skills (Gordon & Gordon, 1983). Figure 16.1 presents a graph

that illustrates the improvement of a patient's coping skills during treatment (Gordon & Gordon, 1981).

Directive Power (D)

Directive power (D) is related to education, intelligence, vocation, and social position. It is the power to personally control one's own life and the reinforcers in it, and is measured on scales like that of Hollingshead and Redlich (1958). Rotter's (1966) Internal-External Locus of Control measure assesses patients' perception of their competence in controlling their lives and thoughts. A person of higher directive power, such as a YAVIS (young, attractive, verbal, intelligent, and successful), generally does much better in traditional psychiatric treatment than does a poorly educated lower-class, uncommunicative, and unintelligent person.

People benefit when they are reinforced for becoming more influential in a variety of diverse areas—vocational, educational, avocational, basic living, and leisure activities. When they must face

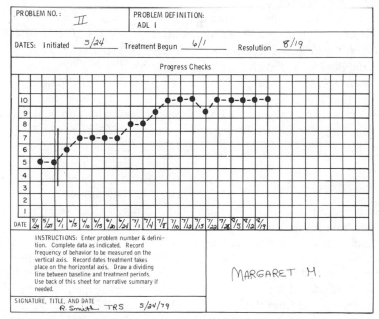

Figure 16.1.   Graph presenting a patient's progress in basic living skills (ADL 1) From Gordon and Gordon (1981).

a chronic frustration in some sector of activity, such as in their studies, marriages, or jobs, they can shunt their thoughts to other interests and pursue other goals where fewer obstacles impede their performance. Developing a diversity of competencies provides patients with a valuable technique for coping with stress: They obtain positive reinforcement with minimal effort, expense, or waste for their efforts in successful areas, and counteract, overcome, or avoid the depression, anger, or apathy that accompanies constant failure in stifled areas (Gordon, Gordon, & Gunther, 1961).

Different activities also bring patients into contact with groups of potential friends who share their interests. They then can benefit from creating a healthier personal social network through increasing the number and quality of support groups to which they belong. Diversity as a therapeutic technique is especially useful with elderly persons who cannot work, disabled veterans and others who lose the security of their monthly pension checks if they obtain gainful employment, and others who are unemployed because of economic recession or other job cutbacks. Psychiatric patients improve their control over resources by attending school, continuing education, and by learning new jobs. Psychoeducational treatment programs offer them skills training in such activities as paying attention in class, getting and holding jobs, and learning administrative and leadership skills.

Environmental Supports (E)

Environmental supports (E) include those provided not only by the family but also by friends and acquaintances of the patient. People's natural social networks of family and friends protect them against a wide range of physical and emotional problems and help them cope with stress (Tolsdorf, 1976). Environmental supports are assessed by in-

struments such as the Environmental Deprivation Scale (Rehabilitation Research Foundation Publications, 1977).

Improvements in patients' support systems do not just happen; they often must be carefully planned and implemented by professionals. In order to remedy deficiencies, therapists have attempted to strengthen or modify the personal support network of the individual patient, a procedure that is often effective with persons treated in outpatient settings. However, this approach has limited application to low-income, chronically ill patients who orbit in and out of mental institutions. Their personal network is frequently too impoverished and too pathological to justify the time and effort to attempt to repair it. For them a Community Network Development program (CND) has been established in which hospitalized patients are taught in modular psychoeducational skills-building classes to provide mutual support for each other. After discharge into the CND, they receive only backup assistance from trained paraprofessionals who are supervised by professionals (Gordon & Gordon, 1981).

MODULAR PSYCHOEDUCATIONAL SKILLS TRAINING

Young psychiatric patients and old, the acutely and chronically ill, low-income public patients, and those receiving private care, inpatients and outpatients, all benefit from modular psychoeducational skills training. Psychoeducational modules provides them with the information needed to acquire specified knowledge and skills, and measure their progress in attaining proficiency. Each module contains the following elements: (1) a clearly defined psychoeducational goal; (2) a statement of behavioral objectives; (3) a list of materials; (4) an instructional design; (5) a pretest; (6) the procedures —lesson plans and exercises—by which patients/students achieve each behavioral objective; (7) assessments that gauge proficiency before, during, and after treatment; (8) a posttest; and (9) a final section that provides feedback from the patients to the instructor (Gordon & Gordon, 1981; Gordon, Patterson, Eberly, & Penner, 1980).

Each manual's detailed written plan, stated objectives, built-in assessments, and precisely defined step-by-step procedures for achieving the objectives and for measuring progress in reaching them assures that a standard quality of service is being rendered that can be replicated exactly by other trained paraprofessional staff members in different settings with different patients (Bedell & Weathers, 1979).

Paraprofessional mental health workers serve as educators and trainers, teaching both the knowledge and the performance of the skills to be learned. Patients assume the role of students who participate actively in learning to enhance their skills. Patients in groups and classes also learn from fellow patients. They aid each other by providing information and feedback, by commenting on each other's performance, by themselves modeling appropriate personal and social behaviors, by expressing satisfaction with what they are learning, and by applying peer pressure on each other and positive reinforcement for step-by-step achievement. In the hospital setting, the example and high motivation of classroom peers help reduce the violence and destructiveness that typify some patients and help overcome the apathy and withdrawal that characterize others.

Categories of Skill-Enhancement Modules

Different levels of skills can be identified within the seven categories shown in Table 16.1:

1. *Survival skills* comprise behaviors essential to safety and life. Without

them, the patient cannot survive alone outside an institution. Self-injurious behavior, conduct that may harm others, and the confused wandering of a disoriented elderly patient require treatment at the level of survival skills. Personal information training improves many elderly patients' competence. Self-medication is often a survival skill for chronic patients who cannot function outside an institution without taking their prescribed drugs on a regular schedule and keeping their biomedical impairments controlled.

2. *Basic living skills* include elementary self-care activities such as dressing, grooming, and eating; at a higher level, self-help daily-living skills include doing laundry and handling finances. Successful training of these skills also improves competence.

3. *Personal and social skills* include asserting, planning, communicating, negotiating, cooperating, and behaving appropriately in social situations; managing stress and problem solving; providing peer support and leadership; and following good personal health habits.

Patients who learn to express their wants and feelings clearly but inoffensively are more likely to get their needs met, and not experience frustration. When they learn the skillful use of problem-solving techniques, they become more efficient in eliminating stresses that otherwise accompany unresolved life conflicts.

Skillful self-assertion reduces the stress that passive individuals habitually endure when they are easily exploited by others. It also decreases the punishment that overaggressive persons receive when they annoy others and provoke them to retaliate. Many reports provide evidence of how training in asserting, communicating, and problem solving improves functioning (Alberti, 1977; Bedell, Archer, & Marlowe, 1980; Davis, 1973; D'Zurilla & Goldfried, 1971; Eisler et al, 1974a; Eisler, Herson, & Miller, 1974b; Goldstein, Spraffin, & Gershaw,

1976; Liberman, King, De Risi, & Mc-Cann, 1975; Mahoney, 1974; Manis, 1974; Paul & Lentz, Phillips 1977; Phillips, & Fixen, 1973; Wallace et al., 1973).

The importance of negotiation has received less attention. Many patients lack skill in negotiation. They do not know how to ask questions and gain the information needed to make a good bargain because they have had little example in their early home life. As a result, those who have not learned to negotiate skillfully face frustration as they proceed through life because they come out on the short end of many deals. They rightfully feel that people are getting the better of them. They may wrongfully conclude, however, that people are out to get them; they do not realize that they simply are not well-trained negotiators. Patients' paranoia decreases after they have completed negotiation training, as measured on the Minnesota Multiphasic Personality Inventory (MMPI) (Archer, Bedell, & Amuso, 1980a; Gordon, Edmunson, & Archer, 1981).

4. *Academic and vocational skills* are achievement-oriented skills such as those required for competence in school or on the job. These include learning effective study habits and classroom decorum as well as seeking and maintaining gainful employment.

The previous groups of skills involve patients' interacting with the environment and other persons in efforts to reduce the stress affecting them. The subsequent three categories of skills—integrative, cognitive, and leisure—often involve the development of inner resources that reduce the impact of stress on the individual: They help him or her consciously to relax rather than be stirred up; to work off tensions in exercise; to develop new attitudes or thoughts about what is happening, so that he or she no longer feels stressed; to become inured to stress and tolerant of discomfort; and finally to learn perseverance, patience, and persistence.

5. *Leisure skills* involve a diversity of pleasurable, relaxing, exercising, and/or constructive avocational pursuits (Gordon et al, 1961; Gordon, Lyons, & Muniz, 1973; Gordon & Webb, 1973).

6. *Cognitive skills* are those dealing with forming and restructuring internal thought processes or belief systems. Training in the management of anxiety and/or depression teaches patients to control these emotions and to shunt aside their unwanted components (Vagg, Archer, Bedell, & Leggett, 1981).

7. *Integrative skills* are involved in such areas as clarifying and reassessing values, building self-esteem, setting goals, and measuring personal achievements. Patients learn to set priorities, to discriminate between high-risk and low-risk goals, and to postpone secondary objectives that require prior steps or additional support. They are taught to achieve short-term goals and to plan carefully to reach long-term ones by step-by-step efforts. All these integrative skills-building processes help improve patients' competence.

Modules are standardized, evaluated regularly, and revised periodically. Standardization allows procedures to be developed that can be readily understood, implemented, and assessed by minimally trained individuals. Evaluation submits the processes to objective scrutiny to determine if they work or not, under which conditions they do work, and how effective they are. Practices are not rigid; modules are revised and reevaluated in the light of feedback, new techniques, experience, theory, and specific treatment needs with different populations.

The package of modules provides a bank of highly specific standard techniques demonstrated to be effective with patients in groups; with minor modifications, they are suitable for adaptation to a wide variety of treatment settings. In psychiatric hospitals, classes, for the most part, are conducted (usually by activities or psychology department personnel) right on the wards where the patients reside, enabling every patient to participate in classes for 5, 6, or even 8 hours each day, not just a lucky few who can leave the building.

Paraprofessional staff in the authors' programs conducted both psychoeducational training and behavior management of patients. These staff worked in job classifications that at that time (1975–1979) paid $6765 to $10,127 per year. Educationally, staff were mostly at the junior college level; many were studying part-time toward AA degrees. As part of the orientation training for their jobs, each attended a 30-hour course in behavioral techniques that qualified for 4 hours of undergraduate credit toward their degrees. In addition to general training in behavior management, the paraprofessionals learned the modular skills-building components of the specific program area where they were employed. Their teachers were the professional members of the adult, children's, and gerontology treatment unit. Each program's course followed the same modular format and taught the same basic principles, as applied to the three different patient populations. Because their own training contained the same structure that they would use in training patients, the paraprofessionals became familiar from their earliest job experience not only with the content but with the method of the modular psychoeducational approach (Gordon & Gordon, 1981; Patterson, 1982).

Medication Training

For many patients who have developed psychiatric disorders, medication training is a key component of a psychoeducational treatment regimen. Medications modify constitutional reactions (variable B) and help control the body's excessive reactions to stress: They suppress hallucinations, delusions, and thinking disturbances, counteract anxiety and depression, lower blood pressure and gastrointestinal acidity, relax bronchial muscles, and reduce agitated behavior. Without the tranquilizing and suppressing effects of antipsychotic medication, many acutely psychotic mental patients usually are not fully able to benefit from behavioral and other psychoeducational interventions because their symptoms interfere too much with their learning.

Discontinuation of medication is a major cause of recidivism among chronic mental patients, and more than 40% of patients admitted to state hospitals each year are recidivists. Furthermore, illness and even death can befall persons who combine psychotropic medication with other substances, such as alcohol. Simply telling a departing patient to take medications as prescribed and to avoid combining them with certain other drugs often is ineffective. For patients to gain genuine understanding so that they become responsible self-medicators, they need training and practice in the use of medications. They receive these in psychoeducational classes that include playing two educational games developed by staff—Meds Bingo and Name That Pill (Weathers, Bedell, Marlowe, Gordon, Adams, & Reed, 1978).

Meds Bingo teaches drug classification, therapeutic effects, side effects, drug interactions, and precautions. In Name that Pill, patients learn visual identification of different medications and practice reciting the information they learned in Meds Bingo. These are part of a group of therapeutic board games developed to build the skills of patients. Typically, each game has four basic components: a scorekeeping device such as a marker to move around a playing board; a process for assigning tasks to patient players such as drawing cards, playing roles, or following rules; a peer-grading procedure to score each patient's response; and stimulus items such as cards that elicit practice. Figure 16.2 compares the steps in leader-led and game procedures for enhancing skills; it shows that the operations proceed in identical manner in both methods of training. However, staff participation is minimal in gaming therapy. Therapeutic games play a prominent part in the treatment programs of adult and adolescent patients. The gaming format is used to deliver training in communicating, asserting, problem solving, sexuality awareness, utilizing leisure time, family living as well as self-medicating (Gordon & Gordon, 1981)

In addition to medication training, the patients also receive training to go for periodic refills of their prescriptions and for monitoring of their blood levels of lithium and other psychoactive medications that are potentially toxic or might cause harmful side effects. They need

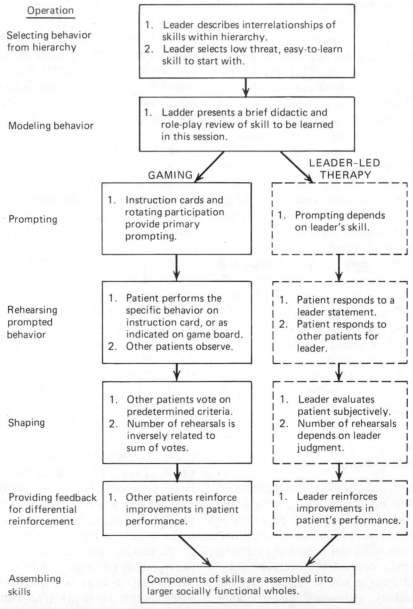

Figure 16.2.   A comparison of contemporary leader-led and game procedures for skills enhancements.

to learn to keep appointments for regular checkups on the amounts of MHPG (3-methoxy, 4-hydroxyphenylglycol), DHPG (3, 4-dihydroxyphenylglycol), and other biochemical markers in their body fluids. These tests are becoming increasingly useful and important in differential diagnosis, in selection of appropriate medications, and in monitoring patient response to therapy, especially with affective disorders in their acute stages.

It is much easier to teach self-medication to patients who are taking only one or two tablets or capsules at bedtime than those receiving five or six different medications at varying intervals throughout the day. Once patients have been stabilized to as large an extent as possible on bedtime medications, they are taught how to manage their medications independently in preparation for leaving the hospital (Cohen, Gordon, & Adams, 1979). In the peer-managed Community Network Development (CND) program (to be described), the patients themselves learn to prompt and reinforce each others' medicating and blood-monitoring activities (Gordon & Gordon, 1981).

However, patients cannot obtain social skills nor supportive friends from a bottle. No one has found a way to put tact in a pill nor courage in a powder. In fact, abuse of drugs and alcohol decreases patients' competence, brings them into contact with troublesome associates, and increases psychiatric and criminal recidivism.

Patients' Special Needs: Studying, Working, Playing, and Obtaining Environmental Supports

Different combinations of skills-building modules are required to improve coping abilities of patients of various ages, degrees of chronicity, or severity of illness. Patients are grouped together into three major program areas: those for children and adolescents aged 18 and below, for adults aged 19 to 54, and for persons aged 55 and older.

Children and adolescents return to their parents' or foster parents' homes and primarily need preparation for developing educational competencies in the school environment. Younger and middle-aged adults may live independently and require preparation for the working world. Physically handicapped and elderly patients with varying degrees of organic brain disease may need to live in sheltered settings and to develop skills that are not achievement oriented. Before establishing psychoeducational programs, therefore, facilities should conduct several needs assessments. They should identify both their patients' individual problems and also their community's special attitudes and needs.

In resort states, many public patients are new retirees or rootless drifters who wander in from out of state; the latter often run afoul of the law (Gordon et al., 1973). Their treatment needs differ from those of middle-class housewives who make up a large part of the typical suburban private psychiatric practice population (Pankratz & Lipkin, 1978).

Deinstitutionalization programs must ask where will the patients go after discharge from treatment. Many chronic patients remain in the hospital far longer than required for treatment because they have no place to go; they have no home; all the adult congregate living facilities in the area are filled, and the community's attitudes toward patients are negative.

Resources for community aftercare for psychiatric patients must be appraised and their availability determined before groups of patients can be discharged with confidence in the effectiveness of their remaining in the community and leading decent lives there. Slater, Gordon, Patterson, & Bowman (1978) conducted a survey in Florida of agency workers' perceptions of the best and worst deinstitutionalization programs for elderly patients imaginable in their communities. They arrived at the conclusions shown in Table 16.2. In planning the programs described here, care was therefore taken to make certain that (1) community workers knew about the survey and its results; (2) the patients' treatments provided the most frequently mentioned services desired and avoided those decried in the survey; and (3) agency personnel in the community were kept informed as to the treatments the patients were receiving and the response of each patient.

Staff must address the issue of what particular skills their patient groups require for effective functioning outside the hospital in their community. Patients gain little long-term benefits when hospitals that serve rural low-income residents teach them pottery making and using the kiln or jewelry making and crafting precious metals unless there are resources in their home communities for the patients to exercise their new skills and receive praise and recognition for their efforts.

Psychoeducational programs for adult mental patients teach them to be self-sufficient, to help each other, and to reduce their dependence on mental health agencies. Adult patients need to learn job-getting and job-keeping skills as well as to receive vocational rehabilitation. Without jobs, many eventually require rehospitalization. Work that earns praise and money helps maintain the patients' self-respect. Not working provokes criticism and rejection. These negative reinforcements may elicit abnormal behavior and contribute to mental disorders. Boredom and lack of stimulation of institutional life increases patients' mental deterioration. When abnormal symptoms and behavior result in transfer payments, attention, and sympathy, the patients' symptoms often worsen, a problem that is especially prevalent with VA psychiatric patients (Gordon & Webb, 1973). On the other hand, demands and satisfaction of work capture patients' attention and thus reduce inner preoccupation with hallucinations and delusions. Finally, working and learning to work provide an environment that improves patients' social contacts. Fellow employees on a job become major sources of community support for patients as with ordinary people.

Patients' workloads must be geared to their limitations and capabilities. Many are unable to work more than 10 to 20 hours per week. Staff therefore must also train employers, personnel departments, vocational rehabilitation, and other human service workers, to assess, place, and monitor the performance at work of previously hospitalized mental patients. Guidelines have been established by which a supervisor can rate the performance of working patients as a percentage of full effort, enabling them to earn pay that is appropriate to their performance (Cogan, 1972).

So that they can live outside an institution, elderly mental patients need to improve their competence—learn basic living skills and personal information and to reduce their biomedical impairments —learn how to use their medications; few, if any, of this population will enter the competitive job market; therefore, they are also taught diverse leisure and avocational skills. Pensioners whose disorders are reinforced by disability payments require similar training. They too must learn activities that help them occupy their leisure, increase the numbers of their friendship groups, and build self-esteem.

Treatment must plan not only for inpatient management, but also for aftercare. At the Florida Mental Health Institute (FMHI), a modular skills-building approach prepared elderly institutionalized chronic mental patients for living in the community. Program evaluation showed that it was successful in discharging 85% of the patients, as compared to results with traditional state

TABLE 16.2. Community Agency Workers' Perceptions of Deinstitutionalization Program Needs

The Best Deinstitutionalization Program Imaginable	N	The Worst Deinstitutionalization Program Imaginable	N
1. Support systems for development of recreation, nutrition, health, peer support, etc.	37	1. Lack of patient prerelease training, preparation, or planning	23
2. Adequate residential placements with graduated levels of supervision and care	29	2. Lack of sufficient follow-up or aftercare	20
3. Comprehensive integration of services	29	3. Inadequate community outreach resources and support services	18
4. Appropriate placements	25	4. Lack of coordination and communication	15
5. Day-treatment programs	23	5. No program at all or fragmented health and social services	13
6. Good preplacement preparation and planning	22	6. "Dumping" clients anyplace that will take them	11
7. Adequate foster and boarding home care	22	7. Little or no employee training and not enough qualified employees	10
8. Good follow-up and aftercare	21	8. Lack of consideration for patients' needs as individuals	9
9. Community awareness and involvement	17	9. Merely placing patients in foster or boarding homes	8
10. Qualified staff	17	10. Ignoring the elderly or isolating them	6
11. Prevention programs	16	11. Lack of case management and supervision	6
12. Proper funding	16	12. Not enough local programs and alternatives	5
13. Education and other activities built into residences	15	13. Lack of program and community residence assessment, evaluation, and supervision	4
14. Regular group therapy and skill building	15	14. Irresponsible or indiscriminate placement	4
15. Suitable, locally available residences	11		
16. Effective referral system	11		
17. Disability determinations before release	11		
18. Regular service visits by case management	7		
19. Home care	6		
20. Transportation services	6		
21. Nursing home care	5		
22. Easy mobility to and from each level of care	3		

Note. One hundred and ten persons participated in the survey.

Source. Slater et al. (1978).

hospital treatment where 37% of patients returned to the community (Patterson, 1982). However, further evaluation showed that over the course of the first year after discharge the percentages of discharged patients who needed to return to a psychiatric hospital tripled—increasing from 8.9% to 26.7% (Patterson, 1982).

Most likely, some of the elderly patients who needed to return to a hospital required even more environmental support in the community after discharge than they were receiving, in order to maintain the skills they were taught. A parallel project with younger FMHI chronic mental patients provides them with both training in skills for community living and also training in interacting positively with fellow patients in a peer-managed Community Network Development program (CND), a mutual support group that they enter after leaving the institution. This CND cut recidivism among a group of experimental patients to half that of a matched control group who only received community-living skills training. The CND patients required less than one-third as many days of rehospitalization (7.0 versus 24.6) and less than one-fifth as many hours of outpatient care (201 vs. 1158) (Gordon & Gordon, 1981).

These findings of the benefits of environmental supports in maintaining and even increasing psychiatric patient gains during a transition period—entering the community after leaving the institution—confirm previous researches with maternity patients and college students (Gordon & Gordon, 1960, 1963). In response to classroom orientation for the role changes they would encounter, experimental groups of antenatal-class pregnant women and of college freshmen made significantly greater numbers of changes in their lives than did matched control groups. These changes, which included improving environmental supports (E) and reducing stress (A), were associated with significantly better adjustments to the transition period by the experimentals in both cases. Follow-up studies with the women showed that the differences between the experimentals and the controls continued 4 to 6 years later. (Gordon, 1961; Gordon & Gordon, 1960; Gordon, Kapostins, & Gordon, 1967).

The experimental groups had maintained healthy emotional functioning better than did the controls ($p<.01$); had subsequently given birth to greater numbers of healthy children ($p<.05$); and had suffered fewer physical illnesses, marital conflicts, sex problems, and divorces.

These findings take on special significance in the light of a study by Neumann (1976). Traditional childbirth education classes were supplemented by reading and discussing a booklet about psychological aspects of childbearing, and by role playing postpartum stress situations. These training sessions produced no effect on postpartum anxiety or depression. "Evidently understanding and realistically anticipating postpartum adjustment problems is less helpful in reducing difficulties than is developing a network of supportive friends and family members" (Cogan, 1980, p. 5). However, many chronic mental patients do not have a helpful network of supportive friends and family members (Tolsdorf, 1976). A study by Edmunson points to relationships between a number of features of psychiatric patients' support networks and their social psychological characteristics (Gordon & Edmunson, 1981).

Poor network supports and less "reciprocity" (mutual providing and receiving assistance between patients and their network members) were related to long psychiatric hospitalizations (r ranged from $-.25$ to $-.33$; $p <.05$).

Patients with destructive networks (they contained aggravating persons who made them feel worse or who frustrated them) were more likely to be arrested for criminal behavior (r ranged from .39; p <.001 to .45; p <.0001).

Arrests were less likely to occur when patients felt warmly toward their network members (a positive "relationship valence") ($r = -.26$; p <.04).

Aggravators were associated with serious suicidal attempts (r ranged between .29; p <.02 and .40; p <.001).

Positive feelings toward network members tended to deter suicide ($r = .36$; p <.004).

Among personality variables, the following were found.

Percentages of aggravators in the network correlated positively with trait anxiety and with depression, psychopathy, paranoia, psychasthenia, mania, and schizophrenia scores on the MMPI (r ranged from .23; p <.04 to .30; p <.0003).

Patients felt a greater sense of personal control over their lives when their networks provided support ($r - .22$; p <.05).

Patients felt less personal control when there were more aggravators ($r = .22$; p <.05).

Because chronic mental patients' personal support networks are frequently inadequate, the previously mentioned Community Network Development program (CND) was established. In it, patients are trained while still in the hospital to support each other mutually in the community after they join the network (Edmunson, Kinder, & Marlowe, 1979; Edmunson, Bedell, Archer, & Gordon, 1982; Edmunson, Bedell, & Gordon, 1984; Gordon & Gordon, 1981).

TRAINING PATIENTS' MUTUAL SUPPORT SKILLS: THE COMMUNITY NETWORK DEVELOPMENT PROGRAM (CND)

While the patient remains inside the hospital, staff there control the environment; they selectively reinforce effective patient behaviors and extinguish unacceptable ones. But in the larger environment of the community outside the hospital, persons in the patient's support system may lack both knowledge and skill in effective reinforcement; indeed, they may unwittingly reestablish the patient's undesirable behaviors. Many programs for mental patients, alcoholics, and drug dependents, which initially were successful in returning the patient to the community, have floundered in the long run because the patients returned to a social network that eventually promoted and reinforced their pathological behaviors.

The Community Network Development program (CND) seeks to increase the amount of peer support available to patient members by arranging a variety of programs and activities where members can meet, socialize, and work together in a positively reinforcing atmosphere. Because emphasis is on peer support rather than on professional support, CND employs members of the network as activities organizers and managers.

Preparing for Discharge

CND staff begin preparing patients for the transition from residential treatment to community life during the last weeks of inpatient residence. Staff train patients in preemployment skills, peer counseling, group leadership, and community-living skills as well as review patient plans regarding housing, employment, finances, and medical follow-up. They use the modular psychoeducational skills training approach described earlier in this chapter.

PREEMPLOYMENT SKILLS TRAINING. Patients learn how and where to look for a job; how to express themselves well nonverbally in an interview; how to make an employer aware of their assets; and how to deal with such sensitive questions as, "Have you ever been hospitalized?" or "Have you ever been arrested?"

PEER-COUNSELING TRAINING. Patients learn to counsel each other. They learn to listen, to give and receive feedback, and to use positive reinforcement. CND staff observe patients as they are being trained and learn which patients are most effective as peer counselors.

GROUP LEADERSHIP SKILLS TRAINING. Patients learn group work and leadership, skills that increase their ability to interact effectively with people on the job, in their families, and among their friends. Training includes didactic lessons on leadership, discussions of experiences group members have had in which they made use of leadership qualities, and videotaped role plays of leadership situations. Each group member plans an agenda for a meeting, defines the roles that other group members will represent, presents the agenda to the group, and finally runs a meeting.

COMMUNITY-LIVING SKILLS TRAINING. Because patients often lack the basic living skills necessary to manage their lives effectively, the CND has developed a series of programmed instruction modules designed to teach these new skills. When people join CND, they receive copies of these modules with an orientation manual. The modules cover the following topics:

1. How to find a place to live.
2. How to obtain assistance from agencies.
3. How to manage money.
4. How to develop leisure skills.
5. How to ride a bus.

Each booklet is designed so that it can be used by CND members to obtain general information or as a resource when a specific need arises.

SELECTING COMMUNITY AREA MANAGERS (CAMs) AND NETWORK DIRECTORS. Patients apply for these positions, and staff make selections from applicants on the basis of personal qualities—overall emotional adjustment and motivation—and practical matters—possession of a current driver's license, a car, and a telephone. The CAMs and director receive special training as managers and, after discharge from the residential unit, are hired at the minimum wage for 20–30 hours of work per week. The network director coordinates the activities of three or four community area groups of 20–25 patients, each managed by a CAM. The CAMs and network director receive a peer-counseling manual, which describes 10 of the most common problems that patients may encounter in the community. These problems include (1) employment; (2) housing; (3) financial assistance; (4) noninvolvement in the group; (5) suicidal tendencies; (6) training and education; (7) transportation; (8) recreation; (9) patient crisis and instability; and (10) medical problems. The manual details step-by-step solutions to each problem and provides a referral resource file with addresses and telephone numbers of local helping agencies.

The CAMs work with members is supervised regularly by a staff member who also provides clinical back-up should the CAMs encounter problems beyond their skill level.

CND is more fully described in the references, so it is unnecessary to go into further detail here on its activities and the duties of the CAMs and network directors. Evaluations of the program showed that it was highly effective in maintaining patients' successful community functioning, as compared to results with matched controls. Further, those patients who held leadership positions in the network rated their jobs as rewarding and minimally stressful; their emotional outcomes were as good as, or better than, those of patients who did not take on leadership responsibilities. Rehospitalization rates of patients who took leadership roles in the CND were lower than those of their nonleader peers. As a result of this finding, all patients who can accept leadership and other responsibilities are now given these within the limits of their interests and capabilities (Edmunson et al., 1979, 1982, 1984; Gordon et al., 1981; Gordon & Gordon, 1981).

Other persons besides patients—people in the community who presently or potentially may provide support to the patients—parents and foster parents of child patients, spouses, siblings, and other friends and relatives, managers, owners, and operators of foster homes and boarding houses where patients reside in the community, employers, agency personnel, teachers, and others —also need training; like the patients, they too are taught in modular psychoeducational settings to manage behavior and provide support.

MANAGING UNACCEPTABLE HABITS, ABNORMAL THOUGHTS, AND HARMFUL BEHAVIORS

Patients may display a wide range of problem behaviors that evolved as responses to past and present stresses as well as those that resulted from poor training and modeling. Problems like a whining, irritable, or a whispering voice; withdrawal; pacing and restless behavior; eating too much or too fast; phobias, obsessions, and compulsions; overdependence on drugs or alcohol; poor grooming; or type A coronary artery disease-prone behavior, for example; the head banging of the autistic child; peculiar mannerisms and antisocial habits; incontinence; the uncontrollable rages of the paranoid adult—all these can benefit from behavioral management techniques in combination with medical,

psychodynamic, and psychoeducational treatments. A patient-managed token economy (TEP), where patients themselves learn to reinforce each other's appropriate performance and to extinguish unacceptable behaviors, is a very effective behavioral tool in treating these abnormalities (Gordon & Gordon, 1981; Kazdin, 1973, 1975, 1977; Kazdin & Bootzin, 1972).

In their individual and group behavioral therapy sessions, patients apply in their personal lives the general principles of communicating, asserting, problem solving, negotiating, and the like (see Table 16.1) that they learned in their psychoeducational classes. They learn both verbal and nonverbal methods of expressing their thoughts and feelings accurately—speaking clearly and distinctly, making eye contact with someone who is speaking to them or to whom they are speaking, listening and giving feedback, making small talk, initiating a conversation, disagreeing tactfully, changing a subject in an appropriate manner, or speaking before a group or to a stranger of either sex.

Their token economy provides them with a structure within which they reinforce each other's skills-building competence, practice being responsible, and learn behaviors needed for community living. They earn tokens for performing therapeutic tasks related to their personal problem—"initiate a conversation with a stranger," or for completing tasks that aid the transition to community life —"find the bus route from your home to the nearest supermarket" or "organize and participate in a car wash."

Because of this differential reinforcement of their skillful, productive, acceptable behaviors, most patients gradually cease to entertain delusional thoughts and ideas of reference or alien control, to hallucinate, or to behave in violent or aggressive manners that endanger themselves or others. In fact, in many public mental facilities, the most hard-to-manage, aggressive, and destructive patients are usually sent to receive treatment in the behavioral/psychoeducational unit. There they stop acting in an unacceptable fashion because they gain better control over their lives and destinies. Evaluation data confirm these clinical observations. Patients' personality characteristics underwent major changes from before to after combined psychoeducational and behavioral treatment. Their scores after treatment showed that they expected to exercise significantly greater personal internal control over their lives. Further, they reduced their disposition to perceive life situations as threatening. Their problem-solving skills were enhanced. They were better able to manage depression.

The peer-managed token economy was as effective as a traditional staff-managed program in maintaining patients' performance of target behaviors and produced significant increases in their social adequacy and community adjustment potential. Patients' trait anxieties were reduced, and their MMPI profiles revealed significantly less psychopathology after treatment. Objective tests confirmed findings from patient-scored measures (Archer, Bedell, & Amuso, 1980a) Archer, Bedell, &; Amuso, 1980b; Bedell & Archer, 1980; Bedell et al., 1980; Bedell & Weathers, 1979; Gordon & Gordon, 1981; Rotter, 1966; Spielberger, Gorsuch, & Lushene, 1979; Vagg et al., 1982).

Those patients who continue to behave in a manner that is harmful to themselves or to others may require treatment on the continuum between time-out from positive reinforcement (extinction), through overcorrection and facial screening, to more restrictive (aversive) procedures like seclusion and restraint. Where combined psychoeducational/behavioral procedures are fully utilized, facilities find that they rarely need to use the last, most heroic measures.

DYNAMIC, INSIGHT-GIVING THERAPY

Fear, anxiety, depression, and anger can inhibit rational thought, planning, and learning. Dynamic therapy can help reduce these blocking emotions in many patients. Insight into relationships between past and present difficulties and their influence upon patients' symptoms can result in extinction and unlearning of pathological emotional responses when the problems are largely in the past, and realistic present-day dangers can be controlled. However, psychodynamic therapy per se provides no intrinsic skills-building training, nor guidance in developing support networks (Gordon, 1959).

Many unskilled, chronic mental patients suffer not only from chaotically disorganized functioning of their inner mental processes, but also from many present-day life problems and personal deficits—financial insecurity, aggravating friends, inability to enjoy leisure, low self-esteem, and so forth. Insight therapy for them, before they have attained successes in using their new skills and support networks, may do more harm than good. These patients may be able to contribute to a variable extent to developing their treatment plan, but the main responsibility rests with the therapists. On the other hand, patients who are able to examine their needs, motives, and conflicts objectively can use these insights for helping set their own goals and plan their own rehabilitation. Self-understanding leads to greater competence in obtaining reinforcement.

Once patients have developed sufficient numbers of tools for effectively coping with their personal problems—personal skills and helpful, supportive friends—they can benefit from gaining insight into their problems. Fairly intact neurotics and patients with character disorders, who are mainly treated as outpatients in clinic and office practice, usually benefit from psychodynamic therapy early in treatment. Chronically ill mental patients with few effective psychosocial skills and those with acute psychoses whose flagrant symptoms distract them from concentrating on their problems need first to get their symptoms under control with the help of medications and to develop the necessary skills and supports, either in individual behavioral programs or in group psychoeducational classes. Later, they can begin to look into their personal conflicts and frustrations.

Insight can give direction to patients' self-help efforts. It also can motivate their learning to improve their psychosocial skills and community supports as they learn to use their new skills in resolving personal conflicts and improving their competence (variable D) (Gordon & Gordon, 1981). The extent to which each patient can benefit from insight therapy varies, but many become candidates, after they have undergone psychoeducation, have developed peer supports and have learned to integrate these new resources into their inner mental processes.

ASSESSING PATIENTS AND EVALUATING PROGRAMS

With many physical diseases, such as hypertension or diabetes, numerical physiological or biochemical measures such as those describing blood pressure and blood sugar levels are routinely used clinically to assess the degree of physical impairment and the progress in treatment of patients. Likewise, some chemical and physiological measures are useful for psychiatric assessment: The dexamethasone suppression test provides a chemical indicator of endogenous depression; blood levels of cholesterol are correlated with burdensome social stresses; those of uric acid are correlated with performance of pleasant tasks and responsibilities assumed as an expression of personal drive and effort to achieve (Gordon, Lindeman, & Gordon, 1967).

In clinical practice, assessment of level of functioning generally has required psychometric judgments by trained observers, by patients themselves, or by persons who know the patients—friends or relatives. In present-day psychiatric practice, these are often made in a subjective manner. Unsystematic measures of patients, made at different times, by different persons within a treatment facility, between different programs of treatment, or between various facilities, cannot be accurately combined and compared with each other for evaluating treatments, programs, and facilities.

Standardized psychiatric assessments can be made by such means as rating scales. These provide objective, accurate, reliable (reproducible), valid, numerical data about patients that can be compared. Many standardized rating scales have been developed since the 1950s to evaluate the efficacy of new psychotropic drug therapies. Many of these can be useful as general clinical instruments because (1) they offer a practical means of assessing patients that is sensitive to change and progress in therapy; and (2) they do not take long to administer.

However, we have observed in surveying psychiatric facilities throughout the country that most centers do not routinely use standardized rating scales for clinical assessment. Instead, most members of the professional staff spend 12 to 20 hours each week in meetings, discussing the condition and progress of one, two, three, or possibly four patients each hour. The staff tends to describe patient problems in subjective, general terms—"is violent and disturbed" or "is delusional and hallucinating"—rather than in objective, specific ones—"strikes at other patients and staff three to four times each week" or "sits in his room talking to voices unless kept occupied." This lack of systematic assessment in psychiatric practice contributes to the questioning by insurers and public officials as to the efficacy of psychiatric treatment.

In the psychoeducational programs described here, previously standardized general psychiatric rating scales such as the Nurses Observational Scale for Inpatient Evaluation (NOSIE-30) (Honigfeld, Gillis, & Klett, 1966), the Community Adjustment Potential Scale (CAP) (Hogarty & Ulrich, 1972), and the Social Adjustment Behavioral Rating Scale (SABRS) (Aumack, 1962) are regularly used to measure the effects of psychiatric treatment upon the observable behavior of adult and elderly patients (variable FL) (see Figure 16.3) (Gordon & Gordon, 1981). Other scales currently in use include an instrument under investigation by Edmunson (Gordon & Edmunson, 1981) and the Environmental Deprivation Scale (Rehabilitation Research Foundation, 1977) that measure patients' supports. The State-Trait Anxiety Measure (Spielberger et al., 1979) and the Minnesota Multiphasic Personality Inventory (MMPI) measure variable B. We currently are investigating the usefulness of five scales for measuring each of the independent (A through E) variables in the FL-equation (Gordon & Gordon, 1983).

Staff-developed scales also gauge patients' proficiency in specific skills. Assessments on these last scales, which are incorporated in the training manuals, help determine which skills-building classes a patient needs to attend. Reassessments objectively measure patients'

progress or lack of progress in treatment for each skill as well as in overall adjustment and, ultimately, their readiness for discharge (see Figure 16.3).

Nurses and the professionals they supervise remain with the patients on the treatment units throughout the entire day. Nurses learn to conduct assessments as part of their education, to measure blood pressure, pulse rate, and temperature of patients who require these tests. In turn, they train their subordinates to perform these measurements under their supervision. They and their staff are also taught to administer standardized rating scales such as the NOSIE-30.

Activities therapy, recreational therapy, vocational therapy, and other specialized treatment staff are with the patients only periodically, when they conduct their psychoeducational classes or other services. They learn to administer proficiency gauges that assess programs in the specific skills that they are teaching.

Numerical indicators make it possible for patient progress in developing proficiency in a skill as well as competence to be represented graphically in the patient's chart as shown in Figure 16.1. Psychotherapists can tell with a glance at the chart whether the patient is responding to psychiatric treatment, just as they can see by scanning the temperature or blood pressure graphs whether the patient is benefitting from treatment of high blood pressure or of an elevation of temperature. The importance of using standardized scales not only for research but for routine clinical care cannot be overemphasized (Gordon & Gordon, 1981).

Many psychiatric facilities fail to use numerical measures and to graph them; staff must often read several pages of progress notes and decipher hundreds of handwritten words to determine whether the patient's psychiatric condition is improving or not. Thus, in those facilities, staff spend much time behind closed doors in team meetings and also at office desks "treating the charts"—writing and reading notes in the patients' records. These activities seldom precisely measure progress in treatment. Standardized instruments can eliminate this imprecision, waste of time and effort, and inefficiency in psychiatry just as they do in medicine and surgery.

Facilities frequently encounter problems in describing specific programmatic goals and in evaluating the achievement of objectives. They often state objectives in immeasurable terms such as "to provide the highest possible level of patient care." Little effort is generally made to assess the special characteristics and needs of the specific population served (some of these were addressed in a prior section on patients' special needs); also, few facilities utilize psychoeducational modules to train the patients. Facilities that offer combined programs usually can express their plan for professional services in measurable terms. Further, the latter find that facility and program evaluations also can be done more easily.

When assessment scales are standardized, numerical data can be analyzed, displayed, and compared, and scores from a number of similar patients in the program may be pooled and used for statistical evaluation of the entire program. With data from valid and reliable tests, evaluators may readily examine the effectiveness of the program as well as the efficiency of resource utilization. For example, data on the NOSIE-30 showed that the gerontology program fulfilled its objectives: Patients became more active and showed greater interest in social participation; significant changes occurred within 4 weeks after admission; and patients continued to improve and maintained their earlier gains for the remainder of their treatment. Further, their scores on the Community Adjustment Potential (CAP) scale of the Discharge Readiness Inventory and on the SABRS indicated that they improved significantly from admission to discharge and that they were prepared for discharge into the community upon completing an average treatment period of 17.3 weeks (Patterson, 1982). Figures 16.3 and 16.4 present graphs that illustrate how pooled data can be used to evaluate the effectiveness of a treatment module (Figure 16.3) or an entire program (Figure 16.4) (Gordon & Gordon, 1981; Patterson, 1982).

TREATMENT PLANNING

In many psychiatric programs, patients' goals in treatment are poorly defined, criteria for achievement are inadequately developed, objectives are rarely specified and measured in an accurate and standardized manner, and times for achieving the goals are vague. Without these components of the treatment plan clearly spelled out, reviews and updates are inadequate, and feedback to staff and administration is minimal.

In psychoeducational programs, on the other hand, the patients receive standardized assessments upon entering each program. These measure their strengths, deficits, and symptoms (anxiety, depression, low self-esteem, etc.) in all the areas where there are psychoeducational modules (see Table 16.1).

The psychotherapist uses the results of patients' assessments to develop individualized treatment plans that include a variety of skills-building classes. Physicians can prescribe a specific regimen of treatment modules, along with their orders for psychoactive drugs, and enjoy as much (or possibly greater) confidence in the precise content, quality, and effects of the modular treatment as they can assume about the effects of the psychotropic medications ordered for the patient.

The different stages in treatment of chronically ill schizophrenic patients are

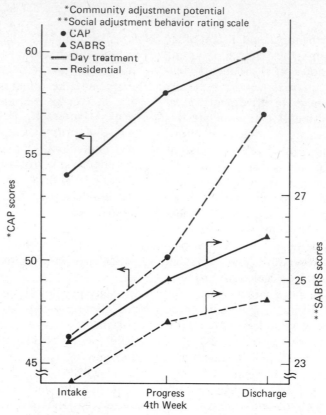

Figure 16.3. Asessment of readiness for community living. This figure presents pooled data collected from 133 elderly patients on the SABRS and CAPS scales. This figure was adapted from materials developed by Eberly, Penner, and the FMHI Gerontology staff. From Gordon and Gordon (1981).

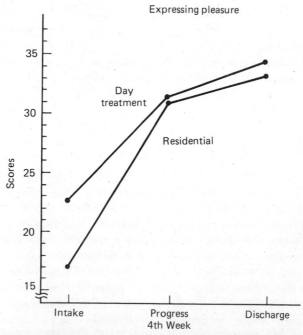

Figure 16.4. Assessment of communication skills acquisition. This figure presents pooled data collected from 116 elderly patients who were trained to communicate pleasure. This graph was adapted from materials developed by Eberly and the FMHI Gerontology staff. From Gordon and Gordon (1981).

illustrated in Figure 16.5. Treatment facilities, in describing their goals and objectives, need to identify which period(s) in their patients' care they primarily address with their treatment programs. Short-term crisis units in community mental health centers, for example, and acute care programs for psychiatric patients in general hospitals concentrate largely on the first phase. In it, medical treatments predominate along with behavioral control procedures. They are the major factors in bringing the symptoms of the acute phase of the patient's disorder under control. Within 1 to 6 weeks, as a rule, these procedures prepare patients for the main inpatient treatment in the care of the chronic mental patient—full-time programs of skills-building classes and peer support training. These, like other educational

curricula, are time limited and of moderate duration. Periods of no more than 9 to 12 weeks have generally been adequate for patients to complete the inpatient phase of their skills and support-building educational treatment (Gordon & Gordon, 1981).

The psychiatric staff charts the patients' scores on their periodic assessments on graphs in their record and follows their progress through the various stages of treatment primarily by reviewing these graphs. Individual and group therapies address individual conflicts that remain after the patients' most common problems have been treated in the classroom and they and their patient peers have learned to handle many of their difficulties themselves.

Ward staff learn to teach the skills-building classes, to administer the

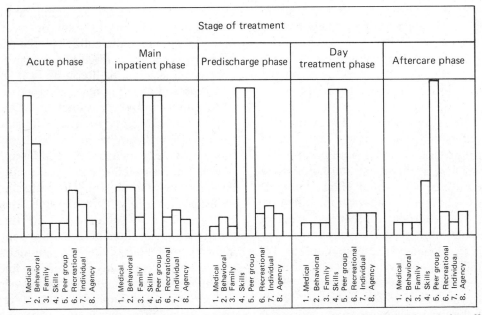

Figure 16.5.   Schematic representation of combined treatment. This schema illustrates the relative effort required in different phases of the treatment process with the chronically ill adult mental patient. Treatments include (1) diagnosis, assessment, and medical care, including the use of psychotropic medications; (2) behavior management, including token economies; (3) family assessment and therapy; (4) psychoeducational training in psychosocial skills; (5) peer management and support training; (6) recreational and other activities; (7) individual psychotherapy; and (8) involvement of community agencies, schools, and employers. Patients may not need to participate in every phase shown. Children usually need more behavior management and family therapy. Elderly patients require less use of peer management and support programs. However, this schema serves to clarify the relationships of the various components in combined therapy.

standard assessment tests, and to use behavioral methods for curbing patients' antisocial conduct. Staff who are college students or graduates usually require 60 to 80 hours of training in assessing and managing behavior and in teaching a specific skill, in order to assess and treat mental patients in a specific psychoeducational class.

Because patient progress is assessed with standardized scales, members of the psychiatric staff spend much less time writing lengthy progress notes and attending time-consuming team meetings. They treat two to three times as many patients, both because they have more time and because treatment programs that include psychoeducation are considerably more effective with patients than traditional ones. Professionals concentrate on problem patients and supervision rather than on "treating the chart." Ward staff are much happier with their new work. Once they learn to provide psychoeducation, they can be promoted to higher level paraprofessional job classifications where they receive better pay. Their new training and skills prepare them both for hospital and for community work. Repeated feedback from measured progress, both with individual patients and after evaluation of entire programs, keeps both paraprofessional and professional staff motivated and enthusiastic about their work. It helps counteract frustration, anxiety, and staff "burnout." Most important of all, patients benefit from programs that include psychoeducational courses for building psychosocial skills and training in peer management and support. Many more improve; they cooperate better with the treatment team; they progress at a faster pace; and they require much less rehospitalization and other psychiatric treatment after being discharged from inpatient care (Gordon & Gordon, 1981).

Returning to Figure 16.5, treatment facilities and individual therapists address different phases of the combined treatment continuum. Short-term programs, which many insurance policies cover, devote most of their effort to the acute phase. Therefore, they cannot offer much psychoeducational training to their patients. This component of treatment can be provided in a combined day-treatment aftercare program, paid for by partial hospitalization insurance. The patient is discharged from inpatient care and sent back to his or her referring professional for office treatment. He or she is also enrolled in a posthospitalization skills-building phase of care at the day-treatment center.

DISINCENTIVES TO UTILIZING PSYCHOEDUCATIONAL TREATMENT

Considerable interest has developed in the use of psychoeducational methods for coping with stress in combination with other traditional psychiatric treatment techniques. Publications on the use of the programs described here began to appear in the scientific literature in 1978, as did presentations at national meetings of scientific and professional organizations. Statewide and nationwide demand for the manuals prepared for adult patients provides a measure of need for and interest in the psychoeducational modular approach to treatment. The pattern of requests from July 1978 through May 1979 is shown in Table 16.3. Note that the most popular manuals are those dealing with problem solving, communicating, asserting, sexuality awareness, and managing anxiety and depression—in that order. Approximately 38% of requests came from within the state and 62% from the rest of the nation.

Despite evidence of the effectiveness of psychoeducational treatment and interest in this method of therapy, its use in psychiatry has grown slowly. A stumbling block to implementation is that most psychiatrists, nurses, activities therapists, social workers, psychiatric aides, and others, including many clinical psychologists, are not trained to use behavioral techniques. They have not learned in their previous schooling to conceptualize a mental health problem as a deficit in skills that can be treated by training and education—by skills building. Further, many have not learned in their personal lives to shape behavior by modeling and positive reinforcement. Some tend to overuse coercion and punishment, procedures that are often comparatively ineffective with seriously ill mental patients.

TABLE 16.3.   Approximate Numbers and Percentages of Training Manuals Requested by Persons Interested in the Modular Psychoeducational Approach to Psychiatric Treatment

	Manual	
Subject	Number Requested	Percentage of Total
Problem solving	3150	18
Communication	2450	14
Assertion	2050	12
Sexuality awareness	1870	10.5
Anxiety and depression management	1750	10
Relaxation	1400	8
Family	1280	7.5
Leisure skills	1205	7
Job hunting	1050	6
Assertion games	650	4
Nonverbal therapy	525	3
Totals	17,380	100%

Note. These data were collected by Neil Willemse during the period July 1978 through May 1979.

Although the benefits of behavioral and skills training classes and of developing a network of supportive friends among patient peers are well documented, insurance companies, Medicare and Medicaid, and other third-party payers generally do not provide payments to patients for improving their support networks and attaining psychoeducational services. Thus, hospitals that treat psychiatric patients may concentrate primarily on treating the acute phase of mental illness—phase A in Figure 16.6—in reducing symptoms and abnormal behavior. They provide little or no psychoeducational treatment for improving patients' functioning after they leave the hospital because there is little incentive to train patients to cope with nonhospital life.

Professional and paraprofessional staff in hospitals and in outpatient settings usually do not learn behavioral and psychoeducational treatment techniques because neither they nor the facilities where they work are reimbursed for teaching patients new, effective skills. There are also powerful disincentives to teaching patients to help themselves and each other. Hospitals need to keep their beds as filled as possible to justify their budgets; thus, they benefit primarily from hospitalizing and rehospitalizing sick people. The careers of staff at all levels—professionals, paraprofessionals, administrators, and even maintenance crew—depend upon people being mentally sick. Their life work and personal security motivate them to study about the biology, chemistry, and pharmacology of mental illness. Pharmaceutical companies also tend to emphasize the biomedical aspects of psychiatry in the courses they offer. They support research and training in physiology and psychopharmacology of mental disease rather than in psychoeducation. Patients and their families have much to benefit from the latter approach. In a free society, they might be expected to lobby for skills-building treatment. But, because of the very nature of their problem, they provide a weak constituency.

A facility's treatment philosophy may require that nurses, doctors, and other staff adopt an indiscriminately warm, tolerant, accepting approach to their patients, regardless of patient behavior. However, "tender, loving care" may not only encourage patients' talking about fears and worries, it may also inadvertantly reinforce the problem behaviors that treatment is intended to alleviate.

Psychiatric personnel working in many public and private treatment facilities for chronic mental patients often fail to specifically praise or support the positive activities of their patients. On the other hand, they show concern about deviant behaviors—disturbed shouting, for example. Passive behavior and withdrawal of patients, which causes no trouble on the ward, is encouraged; deviant behavior, that which psychiatric treatment is seeking to eliminate, receives extra attention; and these reinforcements increase the likelihood of both continuing.

Professionals who are not trained in behavioral and psychoeducational techniques and who are not aware of the effectiveness of these approaches when combined with traditional medical and psychodynamic ones, advocate a widespread community construction effort that includes building a wide spectrum of halfway houses, family and group homes, and therapeutic residential centers, and staffing them with a large complement of social workers and other mental health personnel. To implement such a program will foster the disability of those patients who are capable of learning to take care of themselves in their own homes and apartments. Possibly, a building campaign may be needed for some patients, but there is no concrete evidence that this is so for most. In any event, a large-scale program should not be instituted until patients first receive inexpensive skills-building and mutual support training. Patients who are more capable of functioning independently will learn to do so. Only those who continue to be dysfunctional will remain comparatively dependent; perhaps most of them will do just as well in present-day facilities for the mentally ill, and tax dollars can be put into better patient programs rather than new building construction.

Overcoming the Obstacles to Providing Combined Treatments

The benefits of peer support and psychoeducational services for coping with life stresses will reach increasing numbers of psychiatric patients as mental health planners take the following steps: (1) establish community partial hospitalization facilities that provide aftercare programs of psychoeducational classes and peer-support training for recently discharged former inpatients, for other patients who present a high risk for hospitalization, and for still other outpatients; (2) arrange for training for treatment staffs in behavioral, psychoeducational, and standardized assessment techniques; (3) employ behaviorally trained nurses, psychologists, and educators to participate as key members of the stress management teams; (4) utilize standardized assessment instruments and their test results to demonstrate to insurance companies and other third-party payers the benefits of their treatments; (5) obtain a library of psychoeducational modules with which to conduct treatment; and (6) expand partial hospitalization services to include additional stress and pain management programs for other nonpsychiatric medical patients.

Residential programs of psychoeducational classes and peer-support preparation are now being conducted in some psychiatric facilities around the nation, but partial hospitalization psychoeducational services and especially classes for outpatients are still a novelty. Partial hospitalization is at least as effective as residential care for many psychiatric patients and, as data with children, adolescents, and adult patients show, day treatment may be more appropriate for some (Gordon & Gordon, 1981).

The results of evaluations of psycho-

educational programs and their benefits to patients have been disseminated
widely—in workshops, conferences, on-
site visits, and the literature, to both private practitioners and public mental
health providers in state hospitals and
community mental health providers in
state hospitals and community mental
health centers. As a result, following cutbacks in federal support of CMHCs and
elimination of categorical funding for
mental health care in the states, public mental health providers have joined
forces with private practitioners in Florida. Together, they have persuaded the
legislature to include payments for partial hospitalization in the state's insurance statutes. Psychiatric hospitals
and other treatment facilities as well as
groups of psychotherapists practicing in
a community should expand their activities to include these services. Private
practitioners will need to pool resources
—both staff and patients—because
few individual therapists alone have sufficient numbers of either to warrant
setting up a solo psychoeducational,
peer-support, stress management program in a brief period of time. Third-
party payers are now willing to pay for
partial hospitalization, and psychoeducational classes should be included as a
major component of a total treatment
package provided under psychiatric
direction and management (Guilette,
Crowley, & Savitz, 1978). These programs can and should obtain accreditation from national agencies such as the
Joint Commission on Accreditation of
Hospitals.

Training in behavior management can
be arranged through many college and
university departments of psychology as
well as through attendance at national
meetings. Psychiatrists need not become
expert behavior managers and psychoeducators. Their task is primarily to learn
to supervise the paraprofessional staff
and to understand the psychoeducational

principles, practices, and procedures the
staff are carrying out. Once payments
are being obtained for providing 3 to
6 hours of psychoeducational sessions
each day of partial hospitalization, funds
for upgrading staff positions will be
available to motivate their learning these
treatment techniques.

Behaviorally trained professionals are
essential to a good combined treatment
program. When psychiatrists are not
trained and experienced psychoeducators, they may wish to collaborate with
allied health professionals who have
received this training. Competent, experienced health and psychoeducators
should be placed in responsible leadership positions in the treatment program
where they exert authority over the psychoeducational part of the program,
while psychiatric professionals supervise
and direct the medical and medicolegal
aspects. It is important to recognize that
many psychologists and others who attended graduate school prior to the 1970s
or received their graduate education in
schools that do not have a strong behavioral emphasis may not be able to
contribute much to a psychoeducational
program. Training in projective testing
and insight-giving therapy is not what is
needed.

It is hard to ignore the evidence of
objective standardized tests and assessments. When patients' MMPI and
internal versus external control scores
(Rotter, 1966; Gordon, Edmunson, &
Archer, 1981) show that their personality
profiles have become significantly less
pathological, insurance companies will
find it hard to deny payment for treatment. Patients should be tested on both
their individual skills and on their overall
personality and behavioral characteristics, using standardized instruments.

Psychoeducational modules are being
developed at hospitals throughout the
country. Many of the manuals, like the
set produced at FMHI, were written

with the help of public funds and are in the public domain. Many of these works are of variable quality from a literary standpoint and need editing, but there is no need for psychiatry to reinvent the wheel. The manuals can be purchased at cost; they provide a starting place for launching a psychoeducational program.

Many patients with nonpsychiatric medical conditions respond favorably to health and psychoeducational stress management training. Patients with chronic pain such as headache and backache benefit. Even patients with pain due to metastatic cancer respond because their attitudes and worries about their conditions affect their awareness of pain (Flinn, 1981). Health and psychoeducational programs help patients to manage their diets—whether for weight control or for diabetes; they help them control dependencies on alcohol, drugs, and smoking; they aid those with hypertension, angina pectoris, and other chronic tension disorders related to personality and life-style. Psychoeducational training helps patients to adapt to the stresses of executive responsibility, of combining career and child care, and of other complications of the two-career marriage. Psychiatric facilities and office practitioners can expand the range of stress management services they offer by supplementing residential and office practice with day treatments that include psychoeducation and peer support as new elements in their treatment armamentaria.

SUMMARY AND CONCLUSIONS

This chapter has described modular skills-building psychoeducational treatment programs for psychiatric patients that combine traditional psychodynamic, psychopharmacologic, and behavioral treatments with innovative peer support and psychiatric assessment techniques. Data have been presented that point to the effectiveness of this combined approach in helping patients cope with their personal problems, learn to continue taking their psychotropic medications after leaving the hospital, become proficient in a variety of personal psychosocial skills, make friends and build mutual aid networks, benefit from behavioral and psychodynamic therapies, rid themselves of abnormal thoughts and harmful behaviors, and improve their functional level.

The relationships between the different program components have been presented in the context of the Functional Level equation that relates six variables to each other—(A) aggravating stress; (B) biomedical impairment; (C) coping skill; (D) directive bower; (E) environmental support, and (FL) functional level. Because every variable in this equation can be assessed numerically, it serves as a useful model for planning and monitoring psychiatric treatment. Further, because the letters in the formula are easily memorized, the FL equation serves as a helpful mnemonic aid to use when developing biopsychosocial treatment programs.

The report has discussed treatment planning to incorporate the various components of the combined therapy program. It has commented on disincentives to establishing psychoeducational and peer support treatment, and it has suggested methods of overcoming these obstacles.

Psychotherapists have been shown how to implement a psychoeducational program as part of their own treatment regimen. They are encouraged to utilize standardized, objective tests to assess patients and measure the results of treatment. Standardized assessments help convince insurance companies, other third-party payers, and skeptics of the value of psychiatric programs as well as eliminate the inefficiency of time-consuming meetings and conferences devoted largely to assessing patients subjectively and planning their treatments. Psychotherapists are encouraged to expand the scope of their practices to include psychoeducational and peer-support techniques in outpatient, partial hospitalization, and residential care not only of psychiatric patients but also of other patients with stress and pain-related illnesses—diabetics, cardiacs, hypertensives, and others whose personalities and life-styles affect their illnesses.

REFERENCES

Albee, G. W. (1982). Preventing psychopathology and promoting human potential. *American of Psychologist, 37,* 1043–1050.

Alberti, R. E. (1977). *Assertiveness: Innovations, applications, issues.* San Luis Obispo, CA.: Impact.

Archer, R. P., Bedell, J. R., & Amuso, K. F. (1980a). Personality, demographic and intellectual variables related to discharge readiness. *Journal Psychology, 104,* 67–74.

Archer, R. P., Bedell, J. R., & Amuso, K. (1980b). Interrelationships and changes of locus of control and trait anxiety among residential psychiatric inpatients. *Social Behavior and Personality, 8,* 161–165.

Aumack, L (1962). Social adjustment behavior rating scale. *Journal of Clinical Psychology, 13,* 436–441.

Beck, A. T., Ward, C. H., Mendelson, M. et al. (1961). An inventory for measuring depression. *Archives of General Psychiatry, 4,* 561–571.

Bedell, J. R. & Archer, R. P. (1980). Peer managed token economies: Evaluation and description. *Journal of Clinical Psychology, 36,* 716–722.

Bedell, J. R., Archer, R. P., & Marlowe, H. A. (1980). A description and evaluation of a problem solving skills training program. In D. Upper & S.M. Ross (Eds.), *Annual review of behavior group therapy* (Vol. 2). Champaign, IL: Research Press.

Bedell, J. P., & Weathers, L. R. (1979). A psycho-educational model for skill training: Therapist-facilitated and game-facilitated applications. In D. Upper & S. M. Ross (Eds.); *Behavioral group therapy, 1979: An annual review.* Champaign, IL: Research Press.

Cogan, R. (1980). Postpartum depression. *ICEA Review, 4,* 5.

Cogan, M. E. (1972). *Step system of rehabilitation.* New York: Roerig.

Cohen, M., Gordon, R., & Adams, J. (1979). Single bedtime dose self-medication system. *Hospital and Community Psychiatry 30,* 30–33.

Davis, G. A. (1973). Strategies for stimulating solutions: Attribute listing, morphological synthesis, and idea checklists. In *Psychology of problem solving theory and practice.* New York: Basic Books.

Diagnostic and Statistical Manual of Mental Disorders. (DSM III). (3rd ed.) (1980). Washington: American Psychiatric Association.

D'Zurilla, T. J., & Goldfried, M. R. (1971). Problem solving and behavior modification. *Journal of Abnormal Psychology 73,* 107–126.

Edmunson, E., Bedell, J., Archer, R., & Gordon, R. E. (1982). The community network development project: Skill building and peer support. In A. Jeger & R. S. Slotnick, (Eds), *Community mental health and behavioral ecology.* New York: Plenum Press.

Edmunson, E. D., Bedell, J. R., & Gordon, R. E. (1984). Bridging the gap between self-help and professional aftercare. In A. Gartner & F. Riessman, (Eds.), *Peer support systems.* New York: Human Science Press.

Edmunson, E., Kinder, C., & Marlowe, A. (Eds.) (1979). Peer support systems: Concepts, prototypes, and developmental techniques, Tampa, FL: *Florida Mental Health Institute.*

Eisler, R. M., Miller, P. M., Hersen, M., Alford, H. (1974a). Effects of assertive training on marital interaction *Archives of General Psychiatry, 30,* 643–649.

Eisler, R. M., Herson, M., & Miller, P. M. (1974b). Shaping components of assertiveness with instructions and feedback. *American Journal of Psychiatry, 131,* 1344–1347.

Flinn, D. E. (1981). *Results of psychiatric inpatient treatment program for chronic pain.* Paper presented at the annual meeting of the Southern Psychiatric Association, Nashville.

Gartner, A. J., & Riessman, F. (1982). Self-help and mental health. *Hospital and Community Psychiatry, 33,* 631–635.

Goldstein, A. P., Spraffin, R. P., & Gershaw, N. J. (1976). Structured learning therapy: Training for community living. *Psychotherapy: Theory, Research, and Practice, 13,* 374–377.

Gordon, R. E. (1959). Sociodynamics and psychotherapy. *AMA Archives of Neurology and Psychiatry,* 1981, 486–503.

Gordon, R. E. (1961). *Prevention of postpartum emotional difficulties.* Ann Arbor, MI: University Microfilms.

Gordon, R. E., Edmunson, E. & Archer, R. (1981). *The use of networks and social support in therapy.* Paper presented at the 133rd Annual Meeting, American Psychiatric Association, San Francisco.

Gordon, R. E., & Gordon, K. K. (1959). Prediction and treatment of emotional disorders of pregnancy. *American Journal of Obstetrics and Gynecology, 77,* 1074–1133.

Gordon, R. E., & Gordon, K. K. (1960). Social factors in the prevention of postpartum emotional problems. *Obstetrics and Gynecology, 15,* 443–448.

Gordon, R. E., & Gordon, K. K. (1963). *The blight on the ivy.* Englewood Cliffs, NJ, Prentice-Hall.

Gordon, R. E., & Gordon, K. K. (1981). *Systems of treatment for the mentally ill: Filling the gaps.* Grune & Stratton, New York.

Gordon, R. E., & Gordon, K. K. (1983). Predicting length of hospitalization. *Bulletin of Southern Psychiatry, 4,* 4.

Gordon, R. E., Gordon, K. K., & Gunther, M. (1961). *The split level trap.* New York: Bernard Geis Associates. (New York: Dell, 1962, 1964; *Good Housekeeping,* December 1960).

Gordon, R. E., Kapostins, E. E., Gordon,

K. K. (1965). Factors in post partum emotional adjustment. *Obstetrics and Gynecology, 25,* 156–166.

Gordon, R. E., Lindeman, R. H., & Gordon, K. K. (1967). Some psychological and biochemical correlates of college achievement, *Journal of American Colleges Health Association, 15,* 326–331.

Gordon, R. E., Lyons, H. R., & Muniz, C. (1973). The migratory disabled veteran. *Journal of the Florida Medical Association, 60,* 27–30.

Gordon, R. E., Patterson, R., Eberly, D. and Penner, L. (1980). Modular treatment of psychiatric patients. In J. Masserman (ed.). *Current psychiatric therapies* (Vol. 19). New York: Grune & Stratton.

Gordon, R. E., & Webb, S. (1973). The orbiting psychiatric patient. *Journal of the Florida Medical Association, 60,* 27–30.

Guilette, W., Crowley, B., & Savitz, S. (1978). Day hospitalization as a cost effective alternative to inpatient care: A pilot study. *Hospital and Community Psychiatry, 29,* 525–527.

Hogarty, G. E., & Ulrich, R. (1972). The discharge readiness inventory. *Archives of General Psychiatry, 26,* 419–426.

Hollingshead, A. B., & Redlich, F. C. *Social class and mental illness.* New York: Wiley, 1958.

Holmes, T. H., & Rahe, R. H. (1967). The social readjustment rating scale. *Journal of Psychosomatic Research, ll,* 213–218.

Honigfeld, G., Gillis, R. D., & Klett, C. J. (1966). NOSIE-30: A treatment sensitive ward behavior scale. *Psychological Reports, 19,* 180–182.

Kazdin, A. E. (1973). The failure of some patients to respond to token programs. *Journal of Behavior Therapy and Experimental Psychiatry, 4,* 7–14.

Kazdin, A. E. (1975). *Behavior modification in applied settings.* Homewood, IL: Dorsey Press.

Kazdin, A. E. (1977). *The token economy.* New York: Plenum Press.

Kazdin, A. E., & Bootzin, R. R. (1972). The token economy: An evaluative review. *Journal of Applied Behavior Analysis, 5,* 343–372.

Liberman, R. P., King, L. W., DeRisi, W. J.,

& McCann, M. (1975). *Personal effectiveness: Guiding people to assert themselves and improve their social skills.* Champaign, IL: Research Press.

Mahoney, M. J. (1974). *Cognition and behavior modification.* Cambridge, MA: Ballinger Publishing Co.

Manis, M. (1974). *Introduction to cognitive psychology.* Belmont, CA: Wadsworth Publishing Co.

Neumann, G. (1976) *Beyond pregnancy and childbirth: The use of anticipatory guidance in preparing couples for postpartum stress.* Unpublished doctoral dissertation, University of Missouri, St. Louis.

Pankratz, L., & Lipkin, J. (1978). The transient patient in a psychiatric ward: *Summering in Oregon. Journal of Operational Psychiatry, 9,* 42–47.

Patterson, R. L. (1982). *Overcoming the deficits of aging.* New York: Plenum Press.

Paul, G. L., & Lentz, R. J. (1977). *Psychosocial treatment of chronic mental patients: Mileau versus social learning programs.* Cambridge, MA: Harvard University Press.

Rehabilitation Research Foundation Publications. (1977). *Measurements and Evaluations.* Box BV, University of Alabama.

Phillips, E. L., Phillips, E. A., & Fixsen, D. L. (1973). Behavior shaping works for delinquents. *Psychology Today, 7,* 74–79.

Rotter, J. B. (1966). Generalized expectancies for internal versus external control of reinforcement. *Psychological Monographs 80.*

Slater, A., Gordon, K., Patterson, R. and Bowman, L. (1978). *Deinstitutionalizing the elderly in Florida's state mental hospitals: Addressing the problems.* Tampa, FL: University of South Florida, Human Resources Institute, Monograph Series No. 2.

Spielberger, C. D., Gorsuch, R. L., & Lushene, R. E. (1979). *STAI Manual for the State-Trait Anxiety Inventory.* Palo Alto, CA: Consulting Psychologists Press.

Tolsdorf, C. (1976). Social networks, support and coping. *Family Process, 15,* 407–417.

Vagg, P., Archer, R. P., Bedell, J. R., & Leggett, J. A. (1982). *A comparison of cognitive and behavioral treatments of depression.* Tampa, FL: Florida Mental Health Institute (unpublished manuscript available from the Florida Mental Health Institute).

Wallace, C. J., Teigen, J. R., Liberman, R. P. et al. (1973). Destructive behavior treated by contingency contracts and assertive training. *Journal of Behavior Therapy and Experimental Psychiatry, 4,* 273–74.

Weathers, L., Bedell, J., Marlowe, H. Gordon, R., Adams, R., & Reed, V. (1973) Psychotherapeutic games. *Journal of the Florida Medical Association,* 891–896.

CHAPTER 17

Social Skills Training for the Mentally Retarded

FRANK ANDRASIK AND JOHNNY L. MATSON

SOCIAL SKILLS WITH THE MENTALLY RETARDED

Social skills deficits have been recognized as problematic for some time in children (Chittenden, 1942) and the mentally retarded (Doll, 1953). Poor social adjustment has been found to occur at disproportionately high rates among juvenile delinquents (Roff, Sells, & Golden, 1972) and school drop-outs (Ullman, 1957), to result in increased mental health problems (Cowen, Pederson, Babigian, Izzo, & Trost, 1973), and to be a defining characteristic of mental retardation (Grossman, 1977). With this latter group, it is assumed that social skills deficits can lead to a greater incidence of psychopathology (Kolstoe & Shafter, 1961; Zigler & Phillips, 1960). Matson (1980a) has noted that the problems of many hard-core refractory chronic mental health patients and those of the mentally retarded are similar and are social-interpersonal in nature.

A rather large body of research has begun to appear that demonstrates to some degree the nature and extent of the deficiencies in social skills present among the mentally retarded. For example, not only has it been demonstrated that mentally retarded persons are especially deficient in interpersonal skills (McDaniel, 1960; Weiss & Weinstein, 1967) but that the possession of social

skills is related to successful community adjustment (Bell, 1976; Crawford, Aiello, & Thompson, 1979; Schalock & Harper, 1978, 1979). Similarly, it has been reported that when mildly mentally retarded adults are fired from competitive jobs, it is often because of interpersonal difficulties rather than an inability to perform job tasks (Greenspan & Shoultz, 1981). One hypothesis for this problem is that the mentally retarded are at risk because of cognitive limitations leading to a lack of understanding about how to behave in various social settings (Greenspan, 1979).

The relationship of social skills to various forms of psychopathology likewise is well established (Bellack & Hersen, 1978). Thus, socially deficient individuals are much more likely to evince emotional disorders. These data seem to account for the higher prevalence of psychopathology found in mentally retarded persons displaying psychopathology when compared to persons of normal intelligence (Rutter, Tizard, Yule, Graham, & Whitmore, 1976). The assumption that treatment of psychiatric disorders exhibited by these persons is necessary for proper community adaptation is amply supported (Sarason & Gladwin, 1958).

High rates of psychopathology and social skills deficits are likely to be further exacerbated by attitudes of many community members (Rabkin, 1979). These individuals have in many cases resisted the placement of the mentally retarded in hotels and boarding houses to the extent that municipal ordinances to prohibit the existence of various types of group homes and other residential facilities have been enacted.

Based on these data, it seems apparent that social skills deficits are pervasive and problematic in the general population as a whole and in the mentally retarded in particular. Additionally, it would seem that social performance in community settings is highly significant with respect to successful adjustment on a host of variables. The potential for markedly improving such relationships would also seem to be very promising. This is the case because it has been found that enduring, intense, and complex friendships can occur among even the severely mentally retarded (Landesman-Dwyer, Berkson, & Romer, 1979; MacAndrew & Edgerton, 1966), and may be maintained after periods of separation (Gollay, Freedman, Wingaarden, & Kurtz, 1978). In the following section, various definitions and behaviors that seem to constitute this construct will be discussed.

Social Skills Defined

In the field of mental retardation, an exceedingly wide range of behaviors has been defined as social skills. This may be due to the general belief that most severely and profoundly mentally retarded persons have few if any interpersonal skills. Thus, in the American Association on Mental Deficiency Adaptive Behavior Scale, toileting and hygenic behaviors have been called social skills (Nihira, Foster, Shellhaas, & Leland, 1974). This trend is not in line with the field of social skills in general because interpersonal skills have largely been stressed with other groups. Recent studies have begun to emphasize the importance of interpersonal skills within mentally retarded adults, however. This trend has been particularly evident with those in the mild and moderate range of mental retardation (Berkson & Romer, 1980; Matson, DiLorenzo, & Andrasik, 1982; Romer & Berkson, 1980). For the present volume, we wish to adhere to a definition encompassing only interpersonal behavior. This definition is in line with the massive literature with nonretarded populations and is the definition applied historically by Chittenden (1942), Bellack, Hersen, and Turner (1976) and Kelly (1982), to name a few.

Almost all of us have a general concept of interpersonal functioning and the skills required therein. The socially skilled individual is usually seen as one who can easily meet others, converse effectively, convey and elicit information, and leave others with the feeling of enjoyment following the interaction (Kelly, 1982). For those who are mentally retarded, the degree of social impairment is even more evident. This latter point is supported by the fact that interpersonal deficiencies have routinely been associated with this condition (Grossman, 1977).

A number of varying definitions of social skills have been proposed. Kelly (1982), for example, states these behaviors are identifiable, learned behaviors that individuals use in interpersonal situations to obtain or maintain a reinforcing environment. Another definition, and one that has commonly been used has been suggested by Hersen and Bellack (1977). They stated that a social skills definition should emphasize an individual's ability to express both positive and negative feelings in the interpersonal context without loss of reinforcement. Such skills are said to be demonstrated in a large variety of interpersonal contexts and involve the coordinated delivery of appropriate verbal behaviors.

In both of the definitions just mentioned, the reinforcement that can be gained from eliciting specific responses is prominent. These reinforcers can accrue on several levels, including facilitating the establishment of relationships, to preventing others from removing or blocking reinforcement to which an individual is entitled. Typical behaviors trained in mentally retarded adults include conversation skills (Matson, 1979), vocalizations, toy play (Berry & Marshall, 1978), talking loudly, pestering institutional staff (Matson & Earnheart, 1981), appropriate content of statements, appropriate intonations, acceptable number of words in responses to questions, eye contact, appropriate facial expession, and appropriate motor movements (Matson, Kazdin, & Esveldt-Dawson, 1980). Thus, social skills have specific goals and a number of discrete behaviors that may lead toward this goal. The degree to which various behaviors are important depend on a number of factors, including the proficiency of the patient, the social contexts in which the behaviors must be displayed, and the expectations for various social behaviors under differing conditions.

Assessment of Social Skills

Assessment of social skills in mentally retarded adults must involve at least two functions. First, the individual's skills deficits and relative levels of deficiencies on various behaviors must be identified. Second, the effects of treatment for these deficiencies need to be measured. This may be accomplished in a number of ways, One method, devised recently, is referred to as *social validation*.

Social Validation

The two most common methods for establishing criteria for both identifying deficits and evaluating treatment effects are relying on arbitrary significance levels on various mathematical tests (*the most common method*) or applying *social validaton* criteria. The former method has been aptly described elsewhere (Kazdin, 1980; Winer, 1962) and thus will not be reviewed in detail here. Social validation, on the other hand, is quite new and may be of value in clinical settings. The notion of social validation has been introduced to convey the importance of considering the social context in which behavior occurs (Wolf, 1978). One component of social validation is the acceptability of the focus or importance of the behaviors selected for treatment for enhancing everyday functioning of patients. Magnitude of treatment effects, on the other hand, may be evaluated in light of how the client functions in relation to other persons considered to be behaving adequately in everyday life (Kazdin & Matson, 1981). Acceptability of the focus and outcome of treatment using social validation methods is made especially important by the increasing emphasis on normalization in community placement because the "norm" is used as a standard for evaluating performance.

Two methods are used for assessing deficits and evaluating treatment outcome. They are social comparison, which consists of observing the behaviors of persons functioning adequately in everyday life, and subject evaluation, where the opinions of persons who are in a special position by virtue of their expertise or relationship to the patient evaluate particular social behaviors (Kazdin, 1977). The former method consists of obtaining norms on a same-age and same-sex person or persons on the specific behaviors being considered as deficits. Those behaviors that are markedly different across the patient and norm group are deemed inappropriate. With subjective evaluation, specific behaviors are rated by persons not involved in the treatment based on whether or not the behavior appeared appropriate. These methods can add a degree of clinical significance to selection of deficit behaviors and evaluation of treatment outcome. A more detailed description of particular cases in which social validation methods have been used effectively with the mentally retarded has been presented elsewhere (Kazdin & Matson, 1981).

Identifying and Assessing Treatment Effects of Social Skills Deficits

A number of strategies are available for assessing social skills. These methods, which include ranking and sociometric procedures, behavior ratings, checklists, and direct observation, are generally applicable for both identifying deficits and assessing the effects of treatment. Using these assessment methods, the first and basic question to ask is whether or not a problem exists on a gross screening level. Then, more precise measures are taken to determine the nature of the difficulty. Finally, effects of treatment are generally evaluated by using the latter mentioned methods. Two systematic screening methods have been noted as means of evaluating social skills: rankings and sociometrics (Hops & Greenwood, 1980).

Rankings

This method involves the ordering of persons from high to low on a given skill or trait. This can be accomplished, for example, by using frequency of peer verbal interactions or teachers' perceptions and generally takes about 15 minutes. Hops and Greenwood (1980) have suggest that ranking be completed in three steps: (1) the teacher/staff person initially lists all of the mentally retarded in the class, work setting, and so forth; (2) the teacher/staff person divides them into "most" and "least," based on the behavior(s) being rated; and (3) the teacher/staff person rank orders them according to the skill or trait being evalu-

ated. The method requires little training of raters and is frequently used.

Sociometrics

Hops and Greenwood (1980) indicate that sociometrics are more costly than rankings but that they may also be appropriate. This method may be an accurate assessment procedure because it correlates with various measures of social competence (Asher, Oden, & Gottman, 1976; Gottman, Gonso, & Rasmussen, 1975) and is useful in predicting school drop-out (Ullman, 1952), delinquency (Roff et al., 1972), and adult psychiatric referrals (Cowen et al., 1973).

Several sociometric methods are available. One of the most commonly used is described as a partial ranking or peer nomination system. Patients/residents are asked to choose a predetermined number of peers (others at the workshop, group home, classroom) for specific concepts such as "best friend," "persons you would most like to speak to," and the like. Obtained scores from such measures indicate levels of acceptance and rejection.

A second sociometric procedure involves rating of all peers on a Likert scale (e.g., 3–7 points) on the same type of characteristics noted before. This method provides better distribution of scores across the entire group and ensures that all group members are considered (Greenwood, Walker, & Hops, 1977). However, it is a more time-consuming method, and the mentally retarded adult may have no opinion on some peers.

Cohen and Van Tassel (1978) have described a third type of sociometric procedure with preschoolers that also may be appropriate for mentally retarded adults. They have labeled it the *paired comparison technique.* In their case, the child was presented with all possible pairs of pictures of her/his classmates and was asked to make a choice in each case that was dependent upon the referent situation. The system seems to provide data that is most pertinent, but, as with the Likert system just described, this method is very time consuming.

Precise Measures of the Problems

As previously noted, the second major function of assessment is to verify screening data in terms of relationships to more precise behavior. Several methods of accomplishing this are possible. What we believe to be the major methods are noted next.

Checklists

These scales typically consist of from 30 to 150 items, primarily within a Likert format, and are completed by the individual or by reports based on information of significant others. Perhaps the best known of these methods is the American Association on Mental Deficiency Adaptive Behavior Scale (Nihira et al., 1974), which has a subfactor on social behavior. The scale is filled out by a knowledgeable informant based on her/his past experiences with the patient. A second method that falls under this general ruberic is the Social Performance Survey Schedule (SPSS) (Lowe & Cautela, 1978). An empirically based version of this scale has been developed for mild and moderately mentally retarded adults (Matson et al., 1982). The latter scale measures social skills exclusively. It consists of 57 items rated from 1 to 5 based on their prevalence in mild and moderately mentally retarded adults; subfactors of social proficiency are also available.

A number of scales on vocational and general adaptive behavior are available (see Meyers, Nihira, & Zetlin, 1979). However, these methods have generally ignored interpersonal functioning.

Direct Observation

Direct observation in natural or analog settings has been the most frequently employed means of assessment in behavior therapy (Hops & Greenwood, 1980), and the behavioral strategies have been by far the most frequently used means of controlling social behaviors (Matson et al., 1982). Behavioral observation systems vary according to recording techniques such as checklist versus stopwatch, real time versus time sampling and single versus multiple code categories (Sackett, 1978). The method used may vary, based on availability of staff, behaviors assessed, and setting in which observations occur. Direct observation of social behavior using the previously described procedures has been practiced sporadically for over 50 years (Goodenough, 1928) and appears well tested. Most treatment studies conducted on social behaviors of mentally retarded adults have focused primarily on this mode of assessment in recent years. Studies have generally involved the presentation of role-played scenes that typically consist of three parts (Matson et al., 1980). These include the narrator description of the particular circumstances that might occur on the unit, the delivery of a prompt to the subject by the trainer that was to be answered as if they were in the circumstances described by the narrator, and the patient's direct response to the trainer's prompt. Behaviors are typically rated retrospectively from videotape with operationally defined behavior such as physical gestures, facial mannerisms, eye contact, and voice intonation being assessed.

A second means of direct observation employed frequently with children and more recently with mentally retarded adults (Berkson & Romer, 1980; Romer & Berkson, 1980) is based on an interaction model. With these approaches, a wide variety of observable responses of two or more respondents are coded simultaneously. Generally, one person is targeted as the primary individual for observation. However, the object is not only to determine what this target person says and does but what others say and do to him or her. Such a model is generally very time consuming, and the data are quite difficult to collect because highly trained raters are needed. However, the data obtained from such an assessment are much more comprehensive than what are available in most direct observation systems.

Social Skills Training

A number of rationales have been put forward concerning reasons for training social skills. For example, some persons have emphasized that social skills training be viewed within the context of a larger effort to describe and improve general cognitive skills (Simeonsson, 1978). By far the more popular method, however, has involved the direct training of discrete skills within a general behavior modification framework (Matson et al., 1982). Numerous studies have been conducted that support the use of such a method. Following this latter method, several techniques have been proposed. A number of studies will now be reviewed that meet the tenets of methodological rigor necessary for making reliable and valid conclusions.

Contingency Procedures to Enhance Performance of Appropriate Social Behaviors

When faced with a client who is behaving in a socially incompetent manner, it must be decided whether the problem results from a deficient skills repertoire or from a failure of social/environmental contingencies to support more appropriate behaviors (see the assessment section in this chapter). A number of investigators have shown that restructuring of reinforcement contingencies is, on occasion, adequate for improving social functioning. Review of studies utilizing this approach will be brief because our main focus concerns clients with true deficiencies.

Perhaps the first use of reinforcement contingencies was reported by Brodsky (1967). The focus of the study was directed more at correspondence between verbal and nonverbal behaviors rather than social behavior as defined in this chapter, but certain procedures and findings are directly relevant to this chapter and hence are summarized.

Subjects in the investigation were two mentally retarded females, aged 17 and 25, who, although "highly verbal," rarely initiated or responded to social advances. Prior to intervention, base-operant levels were determined for social behaviors and social statements. Social behaviors were assessed in two separate settings: a naturalistic setting (playground located on the ward) and a structured social setting (placed in a "game" setting with a more highly skilled peer in which the stated object was simply to remain together for a set period of time) whereas social statements were determined during structured interviews with the author. Intervention with one subject centered on use of token reinforcement for increasing social statements during the interviews. Reinforcement raised the subject's level of social responses from approximately 10 to 35%, or a near-fourfold increase. No accompanying changes in social behaviors resulted, however. Content analysis of social statements made to the interviewer indicated the statements were often clearly discrepant with actual behaviors. For example, one question asked by the interviewer was, "What do you like to do best on the playground?" Although, during the reinforcement phase, the subject described herself as active during play, no such behaviors actually occurred. The remaining subject was provided reinforcement for social behaviors emitted in the structured social setting. This procedure not only led to significant insession increases in social behaviors, but, in this instance, the effect generalized both to the playground and to the interview situation (although magnitude pf effect was somewhat less pronounced in each setting). In addition to demonstrating effects of contingent reinforcement upon social statements and social behaviors, this study raises questions about the most appropriate mode for intervention.

Whitman, Mercurio, and Caponigri (1970) conducted another early investigation of the utility of operant conditioning for improving the social responses of two severely mentally retarded, withdrawn children. Training occurred in 30 sessions, wherein food and praise were delivered that were contingent upon the children's mutual participation in play. Other children were brought into the training situation at certain points in an attempt to facilitate generalization. Training produced marked increases in social responding that generalized to children not involved in training. Removal of the reinforcement contingency, however, resulted in pronounced deterioration of effects. Other investigators have found similarly positive effects through the use of primary, token, or social reinforcement for improving social interaction skills (Barton, 1973; Deutsch & Parks, 1978; Doljanac, Schrader, & Christian, 1977; Luiselli, Colozzi, Donellon, Helfen, & Pemberton, 1978; Whitman, Burish, & Collins, 1972); cooperative play and related behaviors (McClure, 1968; Paloutzian, Hasazi, Streifel, & Edgar, 1971; Stoudenmire & Salter, 1975; Wehman, Karan, & Rettie, 1976); voice loudness (Jackson & Wallace, 1974); social-greeting responses in the form of handwaving (Stokes, Baer, & Jackson, 1974), and question-asking behavior (Twardosz & Baer, 1973).

The previously mentioned studies relied exclusively upon application of presumably desired consequences. Schutz, Wehman, Renzaglia, and Karan (1978) have described the use of contingent nondesired consequences with similar results. Targets of the study were two severely mentally retarded individuals (ages 16 and 34) who were enrolled in a workshop program, both of whom displayed a number of inappropriate verbal behaviors (talking or grunting outloud to self, outbursts of bizarre laughing, etc.). Following baseline, verbal reprimands (e.g., firmly stating, "R., stop making that noise; you are bothering other workers") were introduced and repeatedly applied until a bout of disruptive behavior terminated. Application of verbal reprimands produced substantial decrements in the inappropriate utterances of both subjects. The authors concluded, that the procedure could be used as an alternative to other behavioral procedures to reduce maladaptive behavior, and further, that it "exemplifies a first approximation of 'normal' control techniques as used in typical social-interpersonal interactions in workshop settings." (Schutz et al., 1978, p. 661). A planned return to baseline (used with only one subject), however, resulted in a complete return to previous levels of performance. Because there is reason to suspect that the procedure may be effective only in the presence of the trainer who provided the reprimand, further documentation is needed before this procedure's overall utility can be determined. One has to wonder, too, about the possibility of adverse modeling effects upon other clients.

INTERVENTION BY SKILLS TRAINING PROCEDURES

The majority of investigations have chosen to remediate social-interpersonal deficits through application of a skills training package found helpful in earlier research with chronic schizophrenics (e.g., Hersen & Bellack, 1976; Hersen, Eisler, & Miller, 1973). Although researchers have made modifications, the basic package contains the following basic elements: (1) instructions conveying knowledge about appropriate ways to respond during interpersonal encounters; (2) modeling of appropriate social behaviors, which may involve live or filmed demonstrations by more skilled peers or nonpeers (i.e., experimenter–trainer, research assistant, college volunteer); (3) role play of training material to practice alternative, preferred ways to respond in social situations; (4) performance feedback from the trainer (and occasionally from other sources as well) that identifies not only areas in need of improvement but behaviors performed in a more socially correct manner; and, lastly, (5) social praise to reinforce progress (which is occasionally accompanied by tangible reinforcers). The basic package can be applied to individuals or groups.

Prior to treatment, it must be decided which behaviors to target for treatment and how to define and quantify their occurrence. Matson and Zeiss (1978) have provided a detailed description of this process that had as its first step a comprehensive review of "nursing notes" recorded on all inpatients around the clock. From this information, tentative lists of problematic social behaviors were developed for each resident, which were then reviewed in small-group discussions with experienced institutional aides (assessment methods described earlier in this chapter might also be used here). Once staff selected residents most in need of intervention, they were asked to help formulate training scenarios and to identify what they believed to be the appropriate responses. Of all institutional personnel, aides have the highest frequency of interaction with residents, and their active inclusion in initial stages of intervention certainly contributes to the success Matson and colleagues have had in their investigations. Matson, Zeiss, Zeiss, and Bowman (1980) took this procedure one step further by limiting the selection of target behaviors to those that staff had expressed a willingness to reinforce on the ward in an attempt to enhance generalization. Al-

though notable, use of this intensive involvement of direct-care staff must be cautioned because it also runs the risk of inadvertently training residents in behaviors that are more of benefit to staff and the institution at large. This does not seem to be in evidence in any of the studies we have reviewed, however. In another study, Matson, Kazdin, and Esveldt-Dawson (1980) used a "norm-referred" approach to socially validate (Kazdin, 1977; Wolf, 1978) intervention-produced change. Use of a similar type of approach during assessment might be useful in the selection of target behaviors.

As Turner, Hersen, and Bellack (1978) have pointed out, the social skills training package seems especially suited for use with developmentally disabled individuals for a variety of reasons. First, the approach emphasizes the training of relatively small, circumscribed components of social responses as opposed to more global responses. This focus limits the number of stimuli to which the individual must attend. Second, deficits evinced by many developmentally disabled individuals are severe, and the technique of modeling has proven to be particularly suited in such instances. Third, throughout treatment, the trainee receives considerable individual attention that stimulates many recalcitrant individuals to respond. Fourth, and related to the preceding, the training environment becomes a highly socially reinforcing milieu, which encourages and supports attempts to acquire more appropriate social responses. Finally, the approach allows (rather demands) ample attempts to "try out" new responses (behavioral rehearsal) in this socially safe environment.

The basic approach just outlined has been applied to developmentally disabled individuals residing in varied settings and, hence, confronted by varied social demands. Our review is arranged by settings in which the study participants reside, beginning with long-term residential care settings and continuing through short-term residential care to community-based programs.

Applications in Long-term Residential Care

Most investigations of skills training with chronic institutional residents have been conducted by Matson and colleagues (Matson, 1978, 1979; Matson & Andrasik, 1982; Matson & Earnhart, 1981; Matson & Stephens, 1978; Matson & Zeiss, 1978, 1979; Matson, Zeiss, Zeiss, & Bowman, 1980; Stephens, Matson, Westmoreland, & Kulpal, 1979); the two remaining institutional studies reviewed were carried out by Wortmann and Paluck (1979) and Lee (1977). These studies are briefly discussed next.

Individuals with Dual Diagnoses

Five of the studies performed in long-term care settings targeted a particularly resilient subgroup—individuals with dual diagnoses of mental retardation and psychosis. However, extreme overt manifestations of psychosis (i.e., delusions, hallucinations) were evident only for subjects treated by Stephens et al. (1979); the remaining subjects' psychotic symptoms were largely controlled by regular administration of psychoactive medication. Subject characteristics and targeted behaviors for the five investigations are summarized in Table 17.1 (arranged by order in which they will be discussed here). The first study will be described in some detail as the remaining investigations are similar in many respects.

Matson and Stephens (1978) treated several individuals with mixed diagnoses who resided on a chronic-care ward of a state hospital. All individuals were known for their aggressive, combative, and uncooperative behavioral repertories. In one case, the patient was so combative that she had to be escorted by hospital security to the initial assessment sessions in leather arm-and-leg restraints. The 11 behaviors listed in Table 17.1 were studied, and each subject's response to training was assessed during role play of conflict situations, for example, other patients attempting "to bum" money or consumables and making insulting or threatening comments. To assess generalization, several measures of social responding were recorded on the subjects' living unit by staff who were unaware of the study's purpose. These measures consisted of frequency counts of arguments and fights (monitored 24 hours per day throughout the study and recorded as occurring only if witnessed by two or more staff members) and ratings of personal appearance, cooperation, requests for attention, and appropriate verbal statements, which were made on a 10-point scale by two independent staff prior to, immediately after, and 12 weeks following completion of training.

The skills training package of instructions, modeling, performance feedback, and social reinforcement paired with role playing was applied in sequential fashion across subjects and behaviors, as is shown in Figure 17.1. Subjects were taken to a small office for individual training sessions. Each session began with the trainer providing feedback and praise for appropriate grooming and dress as well as instructions for improvement. At each training session, six role-play scenes were reviewed over, and training continued until all targeted behaviors were performed in a correct manner or until the patient had attempted three responses for each scene, whichever occurred first. All target behaviors for each subject changed markedly soon after social skills training was begun (generally within the first 3 days of training). Figure 17.1 further reveals that responses to role-play scenes remained

TABLE 17.1. Subject Characteristics and Target Behaviors for Investigations of Individuals with Dual Diagnoses

Authors	Subjects and Characteristics	Target Behaviors	
		Increase Appropriate Use of	Decrease Inappropriate Use of
Matson & Stephens (1978)	4 aggressive adult females, 23 28, 33, & 38 years of age; all diagnosed mental retardation (level unspecified) & psychosis (type unspecified; receiving maintenance dosages of major tranquilizers)	1. Frequency of looking 2. Content 3. Physical appearance 4. Facial mannerisms 5. Posture 6. Affect 7. Overall assertiveness	1. Requests 2. Laughing 3. Comments (irrelevant) 4. Interruptions
Matson & Zeiss (1978)	12 aggressive adult females; mean age = 32; range from 17–61; 8 diagnosed primarily or secondarily as mental retardation; 6 diagnosed primarily or secondarily as schizophrenia, chronic undifferentiated type, & 5 diagnosed primarily or secondarily as epilepsy (all were receiving maintenance dosages of psychoactive medication)	1. Affect 2. Tone of voice 3. Content 4. Personal Appearance 5. Overall assertiveness	1. Physical gestures
Matson & Zeiss (1979)	2 adult females; 32 & 38 years of age; both diagnosed mental retardation (level unspecified) & psychosis (type unspecified; receiving maintenance dosages of psychotropic medication)	None	1. Statements (socially inappropriate) 2. Arguing 3. Tantrum behavior 4. Interruptions
Matson et al. (1980)	12 adult males; mean age = 35, range from 19–62; 4 diagnosed mental retardation (level unspecified); 4 diagnosed mental retardation (level unspecified); & psychosis (type unspecified) combined, & 4 diagnosed schizophrenia	1. Being neat and clean 2. Complying with requests 3. Responding quickly 4. Being cheerful 5. Making positive self-statements 6. Talking clearly 7. Smiling or giggling 8. Mannerisms	None

TABLE 17.1. (*Continued*)

Authors	Subjects and Characteristics	Target Behaviors	
		Increase Appropriate Use of	Decrease Inappropriate Use of
Stephens et al. (1979)			
Experiment 1	1 adult female; 21 years of age; mild mental retardation combined with schizophrenia, chronic undifferentiated type; overt psychotropic symptoms not fully controlled by psychotropic medication	1. Number of words spoken 2. Speech duration 3. Speech volume 4. Physical gestures 5. Overall Assertiveness	None
Experiment 2	1 adult female; 33 years of age; mild mental retardation combined with schizophrenia, chronic undifferentiated type; overt psychotic symptoms not fully controlled by psychotropic medication	None	1. Subject changes 2. Nonsense phrases 3. Talk of past problems 4. Words (inappropriate) 5. Speech duration
Experiment 3	2 adult females; 29 & 61 years of age; 1 severe mental retardation, 1 moderate mental retardation; both additionally diagnosed schizophrenia, chronic undifferentiated type; overt psychotic symptoms	None	1. Response latency 2. Speech volume 3. Subject changes 4. Speech disturbances 5. Physical gestures

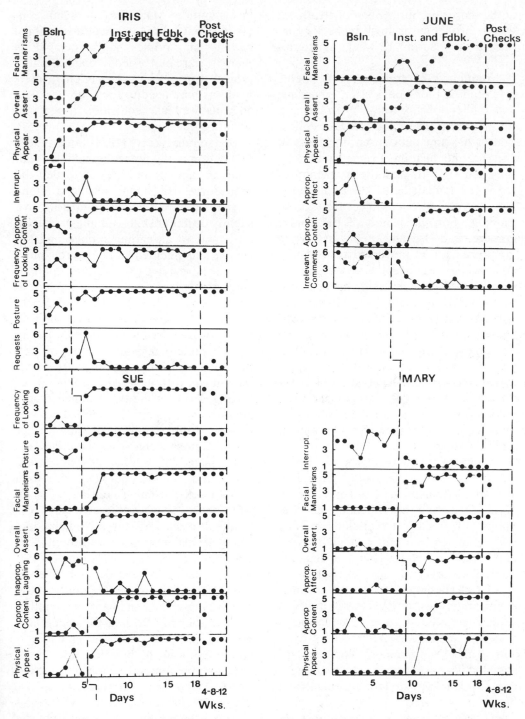

Figure 17.1. Scores on target behaviors during probes for each session across treatment conditions. Reprinted with permission from Matson, J. L. and Stephens, R. M. "Increasing appropriate behavior of explosive chronic psychiatric patients with a social-skills training package." *Behavior Modification,* Vol. 2, No. 1, pp. 61–76. Copyright 1978 Sage Publications, Inc.

at the more appropriate end-of-treatment levels throughout follow-up checks conducted at 4, 8, and 12 weeks posttreatment.

Frequency of arguments and fights was recorded for 4 days prior to baseline data collection for role-play scenes, or for a "prebaseline" period. Once collection of baseline data began, incidents of arguing and fighting dropped markedly for each subject, and the frequency of these problematic behaviors remained at zero for all but one subject throughout training. For the length of the study, arguing and fighting behaviors were monitored for 14 untreated controls for comparison purposes. Control individuals showed no consistent change in onward fights/arguments, suggesting that some aspect of baseline assessment was instrumental for producing the observed decrement. Matson and Stephens (1978) speculated that attentional and expectancy factors may have accounted for the effect. And, finally, the global ratings made by staff revealed most treated subjects to be more skilled at posttreatment and follow-up.

Failure to engage in appropriate social behaviors may stem from skills deficits, performance deficits, or some of both. Findings from Matson and Stephens (1978) suggest that skills training may be unnecessary for remediating certain behavioral excesses of dual diagnostic patients, even though these behaviors may be frequent, intense, and chronic. As an initial test of the contributions of skills versus performance deficiencies in these patients' social repertoires, Matson et al. (1980) compared the standard social skills package to contingent attention, which consisted of feedback and praise for correct performance only. Each procedure was administered sequentially to three separate groups consisting of two subjects each. Improvements were found for both procedures, but those occurring for skills training were more consistent and larger

in magnitude. Matson et al. (1980) concluded that many chronic institutional patients may possess more social skills than they are motivated to display on the typical ward. With such patients, interventions may need to focus on performance as well as acquisition aspects of social competence.

Matson and Zeiss (1978) attempted a replication of the preceding findings with a larger sample, and they extended the procedures by administering training in small groups and by comparing two slightly different skills training packages, the standard as earlier applied and the standard augmented by *in vivo* role play. In the more typical role-play situation, subjects sit passively and respond to prompts by verbal statements alone. In the *in vivo* role-play condition, subjects were now required to act out motorically their complete response, as it was felt this might augment training effects for individuals with lowered cognitive functioning. Each of the two training procedures was sequentially applied to two groups of subjects, with training further lagged across behaviors. Training sessions lasted 40–60 minutes and were conducted 3–5 times per week for a total of 10 weeks; training continued for an additional 5–10 weeks but on a much less frequent basis. All targeted behaviors changed in the appropriate direction as a function of training, with minimal differences being evident for the different procedures. As in the previous study, onward arguments and fights were monitored throughout to test for generalization. In contrast to the earlier findings, participation in the baseline assessment had no apparent effect on arguments/fights. Decrements in these behaviors did not occur until onset of skills training, at which time nearly all subjects showed considerable improvement, regardless of treatment condition. Pre-post ratings by ward staff of six untrained behaviors revealed substantial generalization for two behaviors—lying and personal appearance—but no appreciable change for the four remaining behaviors —cooperation, requests for attention, appropriate content, and cursing.

Results from Matson and Zeiss (1978) provide further support for the standard skills training package and show also that it can be applied successfully within a small-group setting, perhaps resulting in a more cost-effective delivery strategy. Contrary to expectations, having subjects act out role-play responses produced no consistent therapeutic advantage. In a second investigation, Matson and Zeiss (1979) evaluated the utility of yet another procedural modification to the standard skills training approach. Two specific modifications were incorporated in an attempt to improve generalization and maintenance. In this study, training stimuli consisted of problem situations that had actually occurred on the ward, rather than prewritten, preselected vignettes. Material for training was provided by each of the two female participants with each being required to keep a daily record of occurrences on all target behaviors for herself and her "buddy." Additionally, subjects were encouraged to provide feedback about each other's behaviors during problematic situations on the ward, and staff were instructed to reinforce all occurrences of these socially helpful interactions. This self- and other monitoring, paired with peer and staff feedback and reinforcement, constituted the second modification. This modified skills training program resulted in sizable reductions in all targeted behaviors in the actual ward setting. Further, a brief follow-up (6 weeks posttreatment) revealed near-complete elimination of all problematic social behavior for each subject. Because several modifications were made by Matson and Zeiss (1979) to the basic procedure, it is not possible to determine the relative contribution of each. Patient comments, in addition to indicating that a high level of satisfaction and

a sense of responsibility resulted from study participation, suggest that peer feedback was the most critical ingredient. This remains open to empirical evaluation. Further, the study contained no comparison between the modified package and the standard approach. Although it is hazardous to make comparisons across studies, it appears that changes in onward behaviors were more consistent in this study when compared to findings of the former study. Direct comparison seems warranted.

Stephens et al. (1979) have described three separate single-case experiments conducted with individuals dually diagnosed as mentally retarded and psychotic and whose psychotic verbal repertoires were uncontrolled. Each subject was treated by the standard skills training package, tailored slightly to encompass subjects' varied verbal excesses and deficits assumed to be a function of their experiencing hallucinations and delusions. Experiment 1 documented the utility of the skills package for increasing appropriate verbal communication of a withdrawn patient, whereas experiment 2 demonstrated similar effectiveness for reducing "psychotic" talk of another patient. Experiment 3, which sought to replicate the preceding findings and to test for generalization to untrained role-play situations and for maintenance of effects at 2 months, demonstrated that gains from training were durable over time and situations. Periodic administrations of the Nurse's Observation Scale for Inpatient Evaluation (NOSIE-30; Honigfeld, Gillis, & Klett, 1966), a measure of social adaptation to a hospital setting, reflected overall improvement as well. The authors appropriately remind readers that social skills training is neither a panacea for psychotic behavior nor a substitute for psychoactive medication. Rather, the two are seen as complementing one another.

This series of five studies supports the

utility of the social skills training package for remedying a number of social-behavioral excesses and deficits in individuals dually diagnosed as mentally retarded and psychotic, with and without overt symptom expression. Treatment gains in evidence are especially encouraging, given the population at hand. Active participation of a "buddy" (Matson & Zeiss, 1979) during training may enhance treatment effects, but this needs more extensive documentation.

Mental Retardation Alone

Five investigations were found that directly targeted mentally retarded adults receiving chronic care within an institutional setting (Matson, 1978; Matson & Andrasik, 1982; Matson & Earnhart, 1981; Wortmann & Paluck, 1979). A sixth investigation utilized mentally retarded adults as assistants during training and subsequently assessed the indirect effects of training upon them (Matson, 1979).

Wortmann and Paluck (1979) applied a standard skills training program (occasionally augmented by videotape) to five adult females, ranging from severe to moderate mental retardation. Training was designed to promote appropriate expression of assertion in negative interpersonal encounters (e.g., an invader attempts to take food from another resident or to block the view of a resident watching TV). These are important skills for all individuals, but difficult to train even for nondisabled, handicapped, or emotionally disturbed individuals.

All residents met as a group for training that took place in eighteen 1-hour sessions. Role-play responses were assessed to trained and untrained scenes, both within and outside of the group training setting, at pretreatment, post-treatment, and 6-month follow-up. Training produced statistically significant effects for all measures, which maintained over time. Although suggestive of the utility of the standard skills

training package for improving negative assertion abilities, firm conclusions cannot be drawn from the present study for at least two reasons. First, the design would be best termed a "single-group outcome," and, as such, contains no controls for attention, passage of time, and so on. Second, procedures used for scoring and tabulating subjects' responses were not specified, making it impossible to evaluate the clinical significance of the findings.

Matson and Earnhart (1981) designed a single-case experiment to determine whether self-monitoring of behavior and training in the natural environment would further enhance skills acquisition. Two pairs of female inpatients, diagnosed as severe or moderate mental retardation, were exposed alternately to a basic social skills training program combined with instructions to self-monitor target behaviors, termed "no prompting," or to the preceding plus onward training when needed and social reinforcement when earned (for correctly noting and reporting to ward and to their partner the occurrence of an inappropriate targeted response), termed "prompting." All outcome assessments were made on the ward during randomly selected 1-hour intervals, at which time trained observers recorded occurrence of excessively loud talking, fussing (responding to appropriate statements of others by a harsh tone of voice; e.g., cursing or derogating others), or pestering staff, all of which are somewhat typical of chronic psychiatric patients. Prompting quickly eliminated occurrences of all but one target behavior (for one patient only), but all inappropriate behaviors reemerged when a return to baseline was instituted. Introduction of the "no-prompt" condition had no appreciable effect on behaviors; in fact, certain behavioral excesses became more severe. Reintroduction of the "prompt" condition replicated the earlier findings. Follow-up assessments at

1 and 4 months, conducted with onward training and contingent praise still in effect, revealed moderate maintenance of effects.

The prompt condition of Matson and Earnhart (1981) shows particular promise for combating inappropriate social institutional behaviors of chronically hospitalized developmentally disabled individuals. With these four patients, skills training alone was insufficient for behavior change on the ward. Other investigators may need to incorporate similar contingencies to ensure carry-over of training to the natural environment. The prompting condition incorporated several procedures to enhance generalization responsibility for monitoring one's own behavior and for cooperating with peers, training interactions with staff that are designed to be positive in nature, and training around highly relevant situations. Although all would seem to play an important part in the obtained results, research is needed to determine if this is so.

Matson (1978) has described two additional studies examining effects from combining self-monitoring of behavior with standard skills training. The choice of self-monitoring as a method for augmenting behavior change has an extensive base of support for nondevelopmentally disabled populations (cf., Ciminero, Nelson, & Lipinski, 1977). Limited investigation with developmentally disabled individuals preceded applications for enhancing their social behaviors. Nelson, Lipinski, and Black (1976) were perhaps the first to document the feasibility of using self-monitoring with the developmentally disabled. Zegiob, Klukas, and Junginger (1978) conducted a further exploration of the reactivity effects of self-monitoring with two mentally retarded individuals, both of whom displayed inappropriate social/body mannerisms, and they found this procedure effective for decreasing nose and mouth picking as well as head shak-

ing. Other behavioral procedures (praise and feedback) were combined with self-monitoring during later phases of study, and these procedures added to the treatment effect. Although self-monitoring was highly effective for changing subjects' behaviors, each subject's accuracy of recording was poor; this suggested that self-monitored behavioral counts may have limited utility as primary dependent measures. And, finally, Bauman and Iwata (1977) and Wells, Turner, Bellack, and Hersen (1978) showed self-monitoring to be useful for improving meal preparation and housekeeping behaviors and decreasing seizure activity, respectively, of mentally retarded persons.

The first study by Matson (1978) concerned six moderately mentally retarded adults, each of whom displayed extensive undesirable social behaviors ranging from stealing and destroying property of others to poor grooming habits. The basis of intervention was a self-monitoring "report card" subjects carried and marked during certain daily training periods. At the end of each training period a staff member reviewed the subject's report card, noted the occurrence or nonoccurrence of each behavior, provided praise of appropriate behavior, discussed why each behavior was or was not appropriate, and demonstrated more appropriate alternative behaviors. The aggressive nature of each subject's behaviors required that a standard ward time-out procedure remain in effect during the study. Responses to the intervention were varied initially, but by the end of a 4-month training period all subjects showed marked improvements in behaviors, which were maintained at the 7-month follow-up.

In a later study, Matson (1979a) expanded the self-monitoring component so that increased involvement was required of the subject. A 28-year-old moderately mentally retarded female was the focus of investigation, having been selected for regularly making derogatory comments to others (e.g., "You're ugly"; "I hate you"; "Go to hell"; and "This place stinks"). Treatment was implemented each day in two separate settings, following the dictates of the multielement design (Bittle & Hake, 1977). Treatments administered in each setting were highly similar. Treatment 1 was conducted in an offward therapy room where the subject met with a therapist one-on-one. Training centered around interpersonal encounters taken from actual ward incidents. The subject was taught first how to evaluate the appropriateness of the interaction and how to record it correctly. Alternate ways to respond were then discussed, modeled, and practiced with social praise being given as indicated. Unlike previous studies, considerable training was devoted to evaluating one's own behavior rather than simply recording occurrence or nonoccurrence. Treatment 2 was conducted on the ward. Whenever the subject made a negative comment, an observer informed the trainer, who would then approach the subject and examine her self-monitoring record. The subject was required to evaluate what she had done wrong and how she might improve her behavior. Feedback, modeling, rehearsal, and praise were used as needed. Thus, the main difference between the two treatment procedures concerned training stimuli that were live in one instance and reenactments in the other. Both treatments were highly effective for decreasing this subject's negative verbalizations. Unfortunately, effects did not generalize to untrained situations nor did they maintain once training was stopped. Treatment was brief during each experimental phase, and this may account in part for the lack of generalization and maintenance. Of considerable additional interest is the high accuracy level of self-recording. A comparison of the subject's data to that of the observer revealed 84% agreement.

This situation is in marked contrast to the poor results of Zegiob et al. (1977). Whether this improved accuracy is due to recording different response classes or to the more extensive training procedures cannot be determined. These initially promising results, however, suggest that there may be a high payoff for additional research on self-monitoring as an ancillary procedure for remedying social skills deficits of the developmentally disabled. One potential area for research would seem to be using self-monitoring for maintaining gains after treatment is completed.

Matson and Andrasik (1982) have described three separate single-case experiments that were all designed to improve the participation of mentally retarded adults (ranging from mild to moderate in degree) during a conversation hour held several evenings per week. Thus, this study attempted to take social skills technology one step forward by investigating ways to promote appropriate leisure-time social interaction. Skills were more molar in nature and consisted of the following:

Appropriate social interactions. This behavior was scored whenever a subject initiated a positive statement to others. Appropriate social interaction could occur in a variety of ways, such as the following: (a) introducing oneself to or greeting another resident, (b) requesting the use of an item, (c) asking another resident a favor, (d) asking a resident about a question, (e) offering to share an activity with or for another resident, (f) complimenting a resident, and (g) talking politely to staff members or other residents. These interactions have to be reality-based in order to be scored as appropriate. For example, an appropriate social interaction might be, "I like your watch." If this occurred when the person being complimented was not wearing a watch, the response would not be considered appropriate.

Inappropriate social interactions. These interactions were responses considered to be detrimental to the establishment of socially appropriate interactions. Typical responses for this class of behavior included: (a) complaining; (b) making hostile, insulting, and threatening remarks; (c) making responses that did not relate to statements made by others (e.g., person said "How are you today," and the subject responded, "Give me your money"); (d) speaking to oneself, objects, or people not apparent to others; and (e) engaging in verbal or physical aggression. (p. 535)

Frequent reliability checks ensured that observers were able to record the previously mentioned behaviors in an accurate fashion.

Study 1 tested whether reinforcement (consisting of self-applied tokens) alone was sufficient for promoting leisure time verbal interactions. Results indicated minimal effects. Similar to Matson and Earnhart (1981), studies 2 and 3 sought to determine what, if any, procedures were needed above and beyond skills training per se in order for residents to develop and utilize conversational skills in the natural environment. Two self-management procedures—self-reinforcement and self-monitoring—were chosen for study to evaluate whether they, in combination with skills training, could serve as low-cost alternatives to the highly effective but much more effort-intensive prompt procedure of Matson and Earnhart (1981). Study 2 showed that social skills training combined with the two self-management procedures was highly effective for producing clinical change. In study 3, social skills training was alternately introduced with and without the self-management procedures. In all instances, skills training combined with self-management resulted in the greatest frequency of appropriate interactions. Both procedures were similarly effective for eliminating inappropriate conversational remarks, although the combined procedure appears to have been somewhat more effective. The favorable outcomes of these studies support the pursuit of additional interpersonal leisure skills with clients residing in institutional and noninstitutional settings. Although not evaluated, Matson and Andrasik (1982) used other residents as assistant trainers. Anecdotal comments of resident assistants suggested this procedure had considerable utility (save one situation in which a resident trainer continued to offer advice outside of training periods). (The last study to be reviewed in this section was conducted to evaluate more vigorously the inclusion of mentally retarded peers in the training process.)

Results from Matson and Andrasik (1982) and Matson and Earnhart (1981) begin to pinpoint technologies for facilitating generalization. Self-reinforcement and self-monitoring appear to have the most promise, but they may prove to be limited to clients with certain requisite cognitive skills.

In Matson and Andrasik (1982), mentally retarded peers served as role-model prompts during training. Anecdotal evidence suggested that substantial learning resulted while these assistants observed others being trained. Matson (1980b) provided an experimental test of this in the following manner. Two moderately mentally retarded individuals participated as role-model prompts while other mentally retarded individuals were being trained in the standard fashion to increase appropriate and to decrease inappropriate social interactions (defined in a manner similar to Matson & Andrasik, 1982). To evaluate observational learning effects, assistant trainers were observed during informal conversation periods.

Subjects were first taught how to deliver prompts in a therapeutic and accurate manner and received praise when successful. They then served as role-model prompts for three different conditions: baseline assessment; contingent attention, during which trainees received social praise for appropriate responding only (devoid of all instructional techniques); and skills training proper. Contingent attention resulted in few changes from baseline. However, coincident with actual training, both assistant trainers began to show considerable changes in how they interacted with staff and other residents alike during the leisure period. These findings suggest that observational learning may be an effective and low-cost procedure for improving social interaction and, further, that this procedure may promote heightened generalization. Not all behaviors monitored showed significant changes; both assistants showed little change in directing appropriate remarks to staff. Additional intervention seems necessary for change in this response. Matson (1979) identified a number of additional observational research offshoots, including determining effects with lower functioning patients, evaluating the effects more socially skilled patients exert on their peers, and, as is true in other areas of research, developing ways to ensure treatment gains are maintained.

Applications in Short-Term Residential Care

We found five investigations conducted within brief but intensive residential care settings. These studies concern younger adults (below age of 30; Gibson, Lawrence, & Nelson, 1976; Turner, Hersen, & Bellack, 1978); adolescents (Kelly, Wildman, Urey, & Thurman, 1979); and children (Matson, Kazdin, & Esveldt-Dawson, 1980; Nelson, Gibson, & Cutting, 1973).

Young Adults

One of the earliest investigations of a comprehensive skills training package conducted within any setting was reported by Gibson et al. (1976). At the time of this investigation, only limited case and anecdotal reports were available to guide research and application. These authors therefore set out to test

various combinations of three strategies suspected to be beneficial for skill remediation: (1) modeling alone; (2) instructions plus feedback; or (3) all three procedures combined. Three subjects, ranging in age from 20–27 and of moderate to borderline mental retardation, were selected for study. Training was initiated to improve verbalization, recreational behaviors (playing with cards or puzzles, listening to records, etc.), and cooperation with chores. Each subject received nine individual training sessions of 15 minutes duration, and at each session one of three training procedures was applied to one of the three target responses. The order of target responses and training procedures was counterbalanced to control for sequence effect. Undergraduates modeled appropriate interactions that were presented via videotape.

Results indicated a clear additive effect, with the three strategies combined being superior to the two strategies employed together. These methods were in turn superior to modeling alone. Although all three target behaviors changed significantly from baseline, the magnitude of change varied from response to response. The greatest increases occurred for recreational behaviors, the smallest increases occurred for cooperation, with change in verbalization falling in between. Return to baseline probes, conducted repeatedly during training, revealed the effects held only while training was in place. This finding stands in contrast to most other studies reviewed here, which have found training effects to be more durable. The failure to find a lasting treatment effect is most likely attributable to the brevity of training; subjects received only 45 minutes total training for each behavior. This contrasts markedly with the amount of time devoted to training in studies conducted subsequent to this one.

Turner et al. (1978) have reported an interesting single-case experiment with a

19-year-old organically impaired and intellectually deficient male (mild mental retardation), who was undergoing treatment in a day hospitalization program operated within a short-term psychiatric care setting. This young adult had spent approximately three-fourths of his life undergoing assorted treatments at in- and outpatient facilities. Previous diagnoses included mental retardation, depression, obsessive-compulsive personality, and schizophrenia. Social skills training was conducted over two separate occasions. His response to the first training program was considerable, but shortly afterward his overall behavior deteriorated so severely that a series of brief inpatient admissions were necessary over a course of 6 months. Upon return to the partial hospital program, role-play scenes were readministered to test maintenance of earlier learned skills. Substantial levels of maintenance were found for eye contact and response latency and speech loudness; moderate effects were obtained for number of words spoken. Smiles, physical gestures, and intonation revealed near-complete returns to baseline. This level of maintenance appears surprisingly high overall given the patient's intervening turbulent history. A series of booster skills training sessions instituted for those behaviors most in need of treatment quickly resulted in more improved skills. Additional therapy followed after completion of skills training and no more empirical assessments were obtained. Anecdotal information suggested maintenance. Thus, it is difficult to determine fully the lasting outcome of social skills treatment with this difficult patient.

Adolescents

Kelly et al. (1979b) conducted their research with 10 behavior-problem mentally retarded (moderate to mild) males ranging in age from 12–17. All were referred for short-term treatment (6 months) because of commission of juve-

nile offenses or recognized potential for committing offenses. All were referred for training in more advanced conversational skills, consisting of eliciting information from others, making statements that disclose information about oneself, and reinforcing or complimenting others. Training effects were assessed by observing subjects' participation during unstructured conversations with one other peer. Generalization was judged by evaluating subjects when conversing with an unfamiliar nonretarded partner. Skills training (modeling via videotape, group discussion/feedback, and behavior rehearsal) was conducted in a group that met three times per week for 4 weeks, with each session lasting 40 minutes. Durability of training was investigated 1 month following completion of group training.

All three behaviors of focus changed appreciably by the end of training, and all but one (praising others) revealed high levels of maintenance during assessment of conversations with peers. Generalization effects were less pronounced. Eliciting information and complimenting occurred with much higher frequencies by the end of training, but only the former was maintained at follow-up. Minimal change was evident throughout the study for self-disclosing statements. Thus, subjects were able to use all trained skills in an effective manner with their mentally retarded peers and at least one newly acquired behavior with nonretarded individuals, such as those they might encounter when returned to the community.

Children

The investigation by Matson et al. (1980) was conducted within a short-term residential facility and involved two children (aged 11 and 12) who had been hospitalized for conduct disorder paired with moderate mental retardation. Various components of social skills were targeted for treatment, including gestures/mannerisms, eye contact, and speech content/intonation, in an attempt to reduce each child's aggressive and antisocial ways. Treatment effects were assessed by performance during structured role-play situations. For comparison purposes, the entire role-play assessment battery was administered to four additional children of the same age, all of whom seemed to be functioning normally. This permitted the authors to socially validate (Kazdin, 1977; Wolf, 1978) treatment-induced changes.

Skills training, conducted according to standard procedures and applied in lagged fashion across behaviors, was highly effective for improving all targeted skills deficits as supported by responses to trained and untrained scenes alike. Follow-up assessments 4 to 6 weeks posttreatment indicated high levels of maintenance of all newly acquired skills. Further, each subject's skills level now exceeded that of his normal, same-aged peers, which further highlights the significance of these findings. These encouraging findings complement those achieved with adults dually diagnosed as being mental retarded and psychotic by showing that children whose mental retardation is compounded by additional psychiatric difficulties can still profit from this form of treatment. An interesting finding emerged when comparing baseline responding of the two target subjects to the response levels shown by the social validation controls. Certain behaviors for each child were found to be at levels similar to those found for the controls, indicating in hindsight, that these behaviors were in minimal need of remediation. Researchers should find collection of similar types of normative data to be of considerable value for deciding when and at what level of intensity to intervene with patients who appear to evince social skills deficits.

The last investigation conducted within a short-term residential care setting focused on a 7-year-old mildly re-

tarded boy (Nelson et al., 1973). Even though the boy was highly expressive, three significant deficits were present: difficulty asking questions in a grammatically correct form, infrequent smiling in the presence of appropriate stimuli, and a lack of appropriate content when speaking. Three different training procedures—modeling (videotapes of two normal 7-year-olds), instructions plus social reinforcement, and all three procedures combined—were applied consecutively to each target behavior in a modified multiple baseline design. Nine 15-minute sessions were held in all. Statistical analyses revealed a significant training effect. A single, follow-up assessment 3½ months past treatment revealed substantial maintenance for two of the three trained behaviors. Unfortunately, the authors were not able to analyze the relative contributions of each training procedure. (This, however, was done in the study by Gibson et al., 1976, reported earlier).

Applications in Community-Based Programs

As the developmentally disabled move out of institutional settings and into the community, they are faced by new and varied social situations. In the more open community settings, opportunities for social discourse dramatically increase, but along with these opportunities come new interpersonal challenges. Unfortunately, many individuals placed in the community are inadequately prepared for these interpersonal challenges, and their lack of social skills has been identified as a major factor for failure in the community (Eagle, 1967; Windle, Stewart, & Brown, 1961). The absence of adequate social skills often results either "in returning mentally retarded individuals to the institution or in community-based programs becoming 'mini-institutions'" (Stacy, Doleys, & Malcolm, 1979, p. 152). The skills training approach would appear to hold much promise for skills-deficient individuals residing within community settings, and researchers have most recently begun to address this topic. This section reviews the limited research conducted with mentally retarded individuals residing in group homes, sheltered workshops, outpatient clinics, and school programs.

Group Homes

The first community investigation was conducted by Perry and Cerreto (1977) and was designed to compare the relative efficacy of an approach modeled after Goldstein's (1973) Structured Learning Therapy and that of a group discussion training procedure to a no-treatment control. Subjects consisted of 30 adults, the majority of whom fell within the moderate range of mental retardation. The Structured Learning Therapy procedure incorporated all components of the now-standard training package (instructions, modeling via videotape, role play, performance feedback, and social reinforcement) plus the additional components of active group discussion and homework assignments involving outside practice. Modeling and role play were omitted from the second treatment group, termed "discussion," but participants were otherwise treated in a manner identical to that of the first group. Both treatments were administered in a group format; sessions lasted 45 minutes and were held three times per week for 5 weeks. The remaining group received no form of treatment and served as a control. Treatment focused on assorted mealtime and informal social behaviors.

Three dependent measures were collected prior to and at the end of treatment: (1) observations during a regular meal; (2) responses to certain behavioral situation (role play) tests; and (3) counselor ratings on various scales (Walker Problem Behavior Identification Checklist; Walker, 1970, and select scales of the Washington Assessment and Train-

ing Scale, Washington State University, 1973). Nonparametric data analyses revealed a significant improvement in mealtime behavior for participants of Structured Learning Therapy only. However, improvements evinced during the structured situation tests were equivalent for both training procedures. No differences were found for counselor ratings. Although these results appear to lend support to the efficacy of skills training, it is not possible to evaluate their full clinical significance because score values are omitted from the article and the data analysis took into account direction but not magnitude of change.

A second evaluation of a skills training package was conducted by Stacy et al. 1979) and included as subjects 14 mentally retarded adults (mild to moderate), each of whom had been released from an institutional setting within the past 2 years. Three nonverbal (eye–face contact, latency of response, length of response) and four verbal (noncompliance, new request, appreciation, and praise) behaviors were selected for treatment. Readers will note that most verbal behaviors targeted are substantially different from those pinpointed in studies reviewed earlier. Subjects of this study were evaluated primarily for assertion skills, both positive assertion (expressing appreciation) as well as negative assertion (refusing to comply with unreasonable requests and making specific requests for behavior change). All dependent measures were assessed during role play of 12 social encounters.

The 14 subjects were assigned to one of two groups. The first group received a standard assertion skills training package, involving instructions, modeling, behavioral rehearsal, performance feedback, and social reinforcement coupled with token reinforcement for displaying appropriate social skills and assertion in the group home. Each subject received twenty-thirty-minute individual training sessions spaced over 4 weeks. Subjects assigned to the second group received no treatment and served as a control.

Subjects who received assertion training showed significant improvement at posttest for all but one measure (latency of response) during assessment on trained scenes and all but two measures (latency of response and noncompliance) during assessment on unfamiliar scenes (see Figure 17.2a, b). Control group subjects evinced no significant positive changes. In fact, during the brief course of the study, control participants showed a significant *decrease* in noncompliance to unreasonable requests. Stacey et al. (1979) speculated that, without active training, exposure to community living might lead to a deterioration in assertive behavior. This may be worthy of investigation in and of itself.

Stacy et al.'s findings offer more convincing support for the utility of social skills training within group-home settings. Checks for matching of subjects across conditions revealed the experimental group subjects to be younger and less chronic, and it is possible, unfortunately, that this may have biased the findings. Durability and generalization of effects are unknown at present, as is the extent to which such training will impact overall community adjustment. All merit serious research attention. As earlier stated, the work of Stacy et al. (1979) is notable for its pioneering efforts in the area of assertive behaviors. Although laudable, such training may present developmentally disabled individuals with a host of new problems centering on where and when to be assertive. Without well-developed discrimination abilities, assertive behavior can be inappropriately applied to the overall detriment of the individual (Rinn & Wise, 1975). Therefore, sensitivity by the therapist to this issue is necessary, and consideration should be given to incorporating some form of discrimination training to optimize treatment effects. Stacy et al. (1979) suggest that the work of Fiedler

and Beach (1970) and Ross (1969) may prove helpful when designing such training procedures.

Sheltered Workshops

Three interventions have been conducted to improve the social functioning of mentally retarded employees of a sheltered workshop, the first two of which were conducted by Bornstein and colleagues.

The first investigation (Rychtarik & Bornstein, 1979) targeted three mildly mentally retarded employees who were deficient in conversational skills; specifically, maintaining eye contact, initiating questions during conversations, and providing others positive feedback during conversation. Each skills deficit was trained in a 90-minute session, with training implemented in multiple baseline fashion. At the end of training, all subjects showed improvement. Ratings by staff members of overall conversational ability reflected minimal change, however.

In a second investigation (Bornstein, Bach, McFall, Friman, & Lyons, 1980), the authors attempted a direct clinical replication (Hersen & Barlow, 1976) of the earlier study and enhanced certain methodological aspects. These included incorporation of social validation measures (Kazdin, 1977), generalization assessments, and collection of brief follow-up. Six mild to moderately mentally retarded workshop employees participated in the training procedure. Twelve prepared scenes of typical social encounters were administered throughout the study for assessment purposes; subjects were trained on six, whereas the remaining scenes were used to assess generalization. Subjects were trained during eight individual sessions (each approximately of a 50-minute duration) spaced over 4 weeks. Each subject was trained for 4 specific interpersonal skills deficits selected from a list of 12 possible target behaviors. Training was conducted in

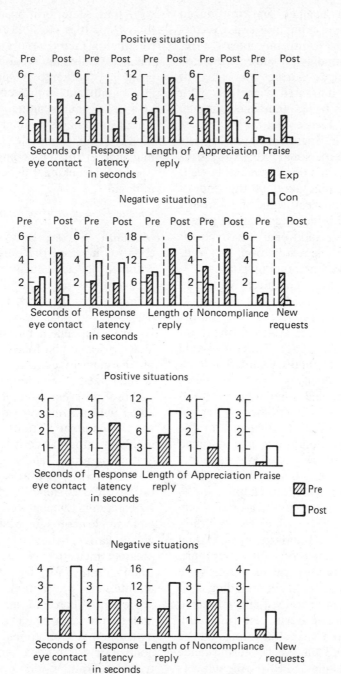

Figure 17.2(*a*)   Mean frequency or duration of response to the Behavioral Assertiveness Test scenes during pre- and posttraining for the experimental (Exp.) and control (Con.) groups. (Maximum score for noncompliance, new requests, praise and appreciation was 6.)(*b*) Mean frequency or duration of response to the Behavioral Assertiveness Test scenes not used during training for the experimental group. (Maximum score for noncompliance was 4.) Reprinted from Stacy, D., Deloyes, D. M. and Malcolm, R. "Effects of social-skills training in a community-based program." *American Journal of Mental Deficiency,* Vol. 84, p. 156. Copyright 1979 the American Association on Mental Deficiency.

the standard manner and introduced sequentially and cumulatively across target behaviors. Uniformly positive results were found as all subjects evinced marked changes during role play of trained and untrained vignettes, with these changes being maintained through 1 month (see Figure 17.3a, b). Pre-post ratings by independent professionals of overall interpersonal effectiveness revealed substantial improvement as well. Social validation taken at the end of treatment had a mean value of 4.4 from a possible 7. This indicates that the judges believed much additional improvement was possible. The results from this well-conducted study are encouraging.

The third study, conducted with individuals selected from five different workshop programs, constitutes one of the few controlled group comparisons (Matson & Senatore, 1981). Thirty-five mild to moderately mentally retarded individuals were randomly assigned to one of three experimental conditions: no treatment, traditional psychotherapy, or social skills training. Participants in the two treatment conditions met in small groups for 10 twice-weekly sessions. Traditional psychotherapy incorporated client-centered techniques applied in the context of an interpersonal growth group (e.g., Yalom, 1975). Social skills training followed the standard approach and targeted production of socially appropriate statements. Several measures were used to evaluate change, including role-play responses to trained and untrained scenes, behavior during informal conversation hours, and staff ratings on the NOSIE-30 and the Social Performance Survey Schedule (SPSS). All subjects returned for a follow-up assessment 3 months after completing treatment.

As expected, untreated controls showed no changes on any of the measures. Highly significant improvements occurred for social skills training on three of the four data sets (the exception being the SPSS) by the end of treatment,

with some deterioration occurring over follow-up. It is possible that "booster" treatments might have enhanced maintenance. Subjects receiving traditional group psychotherapy displayed statistically significant improvement for role-play assessments alone. However, the actual increments in improvement were of very small magnitude. The clinical significance of this procedure for remediation of interpersonal deficits thus seems minimal.

Special Education Programs

Meredith, Saxon, Doleys, and Kyzer (1980) conducted the only investigation within a special education program (at a developmental center). Subjects were all mildly mentally retarded (mean IQ = 65.6); mean age was approximately 20. Five dependent measures were collected prior to and following completion of treatment by exposing subjects to six standardized 2-minute social situations —three different situations, each enacted with a same-sex and an opposite-sex respondent. The three situations involved initiating conversations, cooperating on a task, and expressing anger. Two of the five measures were based on ratings of occurrence/nonoccurrence of 10 behaviors, which were converted to yield single scores for positive behaviors and negative behaviors. The three remaining measures consisted of 7-point Likert ratings for degree of empathy, attention to transaction, and appropriateness of affect. Four males and four females were each assigned to one of two experimental conditions: no-treatment control or group behavioral social skills training. Training incorporated prompts and instructions, response shaping, rehearsal, modeling by peers and group leaders alike, videotape feedback, and delivery of tokens for appropriate behavior. Each session was devoted to one training theme.

Each measure was analyzed by a condition (treatment vs. no treatment) ×

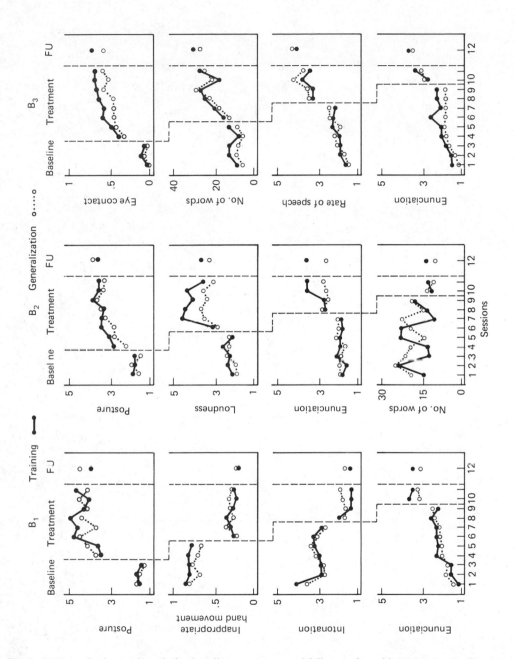

Figure 17.3(*a*). Probe sessions during baseline, treatment, and follow-up for subjects A_1, A_2, A_3. Data are presented in blocks of six scenes. Reprinted from Bornstein, P. H. et al. "Application of a social skills training program in the modification of interpersonal deficits among retarded adults: A clinical replication." *Journal of Applied Behavior Analysis,* Vol. 13, pp. 174–175. Copyright 1980 by the Society for the Experimental Analysis of Behavior, Inc.

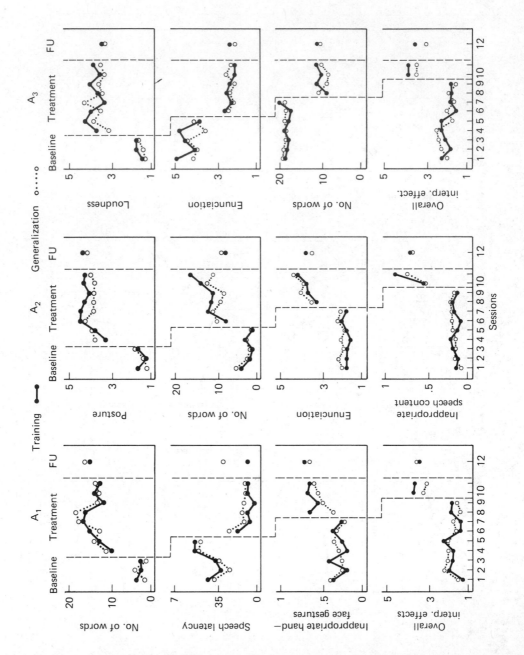

Figure 17.3(b). Probe sessions during baseline, treatment, and follow-up for subjects B_1, B_2, B_3. Data are presented in blocks of six scenes. Reprinted from Bornstein, P. H. et al. "Application of a social skills training program in the modification of interpersonal deficits among retarded adults: A clinical replication." *Journal of Applied Behavior Analysis,* Vol. 13, pp. 174–175. Copyright 1980 by the Society for the Experimental Analysis of Behavior, Inc.

time (pretreatment vs. posttreatment) × sex (male vs. female) × social situation ANOVA. Obtained results were complex because different patterns of significance occurred for the measures. We have summarized the findings in Table 17.2 to simplify discussion. As revealed in Table 17.2, statistically significant effects were found for each variable. For the latter three variables, mean score values were not given; therefore, it is impossible to determine degree of change, which would provide some estimate of clinical significance. Percentage increase in positive behavior shown by treated subjects was only 13% (calculation by present authors), which questions the clinical utility of this finding. Some measure of social validation would be helpful for evaluating this effect. Percentage of education in negative behavior shown by males (47%) and females (42%) was more substantial and clinically meaningful.

Meredith et al. (1980) concluded from their findings that researchers should expand their conceptual models of social skills to take into account situational variables as well as response and consequent variables. A conceptual model for assessment and development of social skills behavior is presented as a guide for future research. Much empirical investi-

gation will be needed to determine the viability of this model.

Outpatient Clinics

Three investigations have been conducted in varied outpatient clinic settings. The most extensive investigation (Senatore, Matson, & Kazdin, 1982) was conducted in a mental retardation outpatient clinic operating within a medical school. Thirty-five subjects with primary diagnoses of mental retardation (2 borderline, 15 mild, 17 moderate, and 1 severe), 11 of whom who had secondary diagnoses of chronic schizophrenia but with symptoms in remission, participated in the study. Subjects were matched for degree of impairment in social skills and then randomly assigned to one of three experimental groups: standad social skills training, standard training augmented by "active rehearsal," or no treatment. Training focused on increasing subjects' frequencies of positive comments and statements acknowledging others and on decreasing complaints. All treatments were conducted in 10 twice-weekly small-group meetings of 1-hour's duration. Performance was assessed pre-post during individual role plays and interviews. At the conclusion of treatment, all subjects attended a

TABLE 17.2.   Summary of Findings from Meredith et al. (1980)

Measure	Highest Order Effect	Source of Significance
Positive behavior	Condition × time	Treatment > No treatment at posttreatment
Negative behavior	Condition × time × sex	Treated males > control males = treated females at pretreatment
		Treated males = treated females < control males at posttreatment
Degree of empathy	Condition × time	Treatment > no treatment at posttreatment
Attention to transaction	Condition × time	Treatment > no treatment at posttreatment
Appropriateness of effect	Social situation	Expressing anger < initiating conversations = cooperating on a task
	Time	Not described

"party," at which a third set of perform- ance measures was collected by under- graduate attendees unaware of condition assignments.

One of the skills training groups re- ceived the standard training package, and this requires no further discussion here. The second treatment procedure was augmented by more "active rehear- sal" in order to enhance effects:

However, this group differed in that clients were required to "act out" the scenes by walking through and overtly rehearsing the situation with the use of prompts by the ther- apist. Props such as tables, chairs, and other paraphernalia were used to enhance the real- ism of the in vivo situations. Also the therapist allowed the clients to "practice" appropriate responding while the therapist was out of the room. (Senatore et al., 1982, p. 319)

This procedure was, in essence, an ex- tension of that employed by Matson and Zeiss (1978). On the role-play and inter- view measures, both training procedures were found to be superior to no treat- ment, but, as shown in Figure 17.4, the gains made by the augmented training procedure far surpassed those made by the standard procedure. Role-play as- sessments alone were conducted at 6- month follow-up, and findings were nearly identical to those immediately fol- lowing treatment. Results from the "party" assessment revealed only the augmented group to be significantly more skilled. Included in the statistical analyses was the determination of Kirk's (1968) W^2, which provides a measure of strength of effect. Depending upon the measure chosen, the treatments ac- counted for 41–77% of the variance in

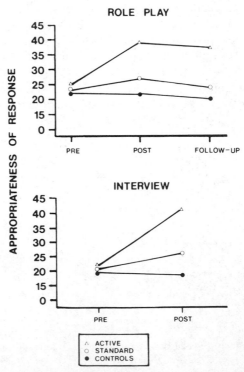

Figure 17.4. Means for all experimental conditions across assessment periods and dependent measures. Reprinted from Senatore, V., Matson, J. L., and Kazdin, A. E. "A comparison of behavioral methods to train social skills to mentally retarded adults." *Behavior Therapy,* Vol. 13, p. 321. Reprinted by permission.

outcome, indicating that the strength of the treatments was substantial.

Active rehearsal appears to have considerable incremental utility in social skills training. A number of procedural variations were made during active rehearsal, so it is not possible to determine what factors were most responsible for the added treatment effect. Matson and Zeiss (1978) found little advantage to motoric rehearsal alone; so it would appear that use of props or fading of therapist instruction and attention contributed most significantly to the findings. This procedure certainly merits replication as well as examination to partial out the necessary and sufficient therapeutic components.

The two remaining investigations targeted individual subjects. Geller, Wildman, Kelly, and Laughlin (1980) successfully trained a 16-year-old mildly retarded female who was having difficulty responding to her peers' derogatory and commendatory comments at school. Training (held weekly for 21 sessions) was highly effective for improving both abilities as assessed by her responses to both males and females during training. Generalization to untrained role-play scenes was variable, with the highest level occurring for refusal assertion. Tofte-Tipps, Mendonca, and Peach (1982) treated two children at an outpatient facility, one of whom was diagnosed as mildly mentally retarded. This 11-year-old female was trained to improve a variety of social skills behaviors during seven weekly sessions, each of 60–90 minutes duration. Evaluation was vigorous; assessments were made to trained and untrained role-play scenes and during extemporaneous conversations with familiar and unfamiliar adults. Training and generalization effects were both substantial. These results, combined with those of Senatore et al. (1982), show that social skills training can be successfully applied in an outpatient setting with infrequent contact (once or twice per week).

SUMMARY

Within the past few years, much research has been conducted on social skills training with the mentally retarded. Data have been collected in both single-case and group studies. Inpatient and outpatient children and adults have been trained, with the heaviest emphasis on adults. Generalization and maintenance were demonstrated in several of the studies reviewed. It seems reasonable to conclude that these effects are achieved best when they are programmed.

ASSESSMENT

Relative to assessment, the bulk of the studies have relied primarily on unidimensional assessment—direct observation of a few targeted behaviors. This approach is viewed as narrow and, given the state of the research now available, should be discarded in lieu of mutimodal assessment. These procedures could include the use of social validation and rating scales along with observation of specific behaviors. These multimethod assessments should give much more detailed and reliable data on the full scope of the treatment's effectiveness. Similarly, social validation procedures should be of value in establishing clinical as well as statistical significance of the treatment effects.

Another problem with assessment that is interrelated with the concern for more broadly based evaluations is that there are few reliable and valid means of assessing social behaviors with the mentally retarded. Researchers interested in behavioral assessment for some time have largely ignored many well-established rules and principles of more traditional assessment methods. The field seems to have matured to the point that the realization of having throw the baby out with the bathwater seems to have emerged. This "discovery" is of considerable importance because it is unlikely that these assessment procedures will be perceived by the larger community of psychologists as legitimate until such modification can be made. Such a trend will, we hope, continue in the future. It has further been argued that researchers in the field of social skills place a moratorium on further treatment studies until more and better ways of assessing social skills excesses and deficits can be established. The recent heavy reliance on role-play tests as a means of evaluating social skills in analog settings and the failure of these effects to generalize to natural settings would seem to further strengthen this argument. We are concerned that assessments of social skills have not been as comprehensive as possible, but it is also felt that the massive amount of treatment data accumulated across the various populations treated would provide sufficient evidence to support further efforts in the field. Thus, the development of more and better ways of assessing social skills should do nothing but further enhance what has already proven to be an important area of investigation. More elaboration assessment methods should, however, further our understanding of social skills treatment procedures.

Most of the studies reviewed employed a social skills training package. This is a positive way to enhance appropriate social behaviors, and in some instances it may also result in the deceleration of aberrant behavior (e.g., Matson & Stephens, 1978). This method has not been employed with the profoundly mentally retarded and is probably not applicable with many severely cognitively impaired persons. This situation is the case because sufficient conceptual skills to understand role playing are necessary. Similarly, speech and some ambulatory skills are highly desirable.

From the data obtained with the mentally retarded to date, several generalizations seem possible. First, make sure that responses to be trained are brief (three or four words) and the terms used can be readily pronounced and understood. Second, do not assume that role-playing or other aspects of training can be understood by explanation of the therapist. Make sure the patient explains and demonstrates the appropriate skills. Third, active role-playing that involves the use of props to recreate settings in as naturalistic a way as possible seems to enhance training efficiency. Fourth, tangible reinforcers may be desirable in many instances to enhance the motivation level of patients. Fifth, patients and staff who are familiar with those to be treated should be questioned to obtain information on problem areas from which scenes can be developed, what reinforcers may be most effective, and so forth.

Other issues in enhancing treatment effectiveness with the mentally retarded also seem worth rating. It has generally been felt that mentally retarded persons, even in the high ranges of mild retardation do not have insight abilities. This rationale has been the primary reason for traditionally trained psychotherapists to avoid this population completely. Skills levels within such a heterogeneous group are not so easily pinpointed. Thus, self-management and the buddy system, where mentally retarded adults were shown capable of monitoring and evaluating their own behaviors and others, were found to be useful and effective. Obviously, however, such skills will only be evident in a segment of this population, and a modification or partial application of these methods may be possible in some situations (e.g., self-evaluation, where alternatives are provided and the mentally retarded person may select from among them).

It should also be emphasized that the early training of social skills with the mentally retarded involved only a few rudimentary behaviors. More recent studies have attempted much more involved behaviors. These strategies do not necessarily mean that the training techniques currently in vogue are more powerful. However, whatever the reason, these data would seem to be encouraging relative to what can potentially be remediated in the way of social behaviors with the mentally retarded. These data, both with respect to assessment and treatment, are encouraging and do suggest much potential for social skills training with the mentally retarded.

REFERENCES

Asher, S., Oden, S., & Gottman, J. (1976). Children's friendship in school settings. In L. Katz (Ed.), *Current topics in early childhood education* (Vol. 1). Hillsdale, NJ: Earlbaum.

Barton, E. S. (1973). Operant conditioning of appropriate and inappropriate social speech in the profoundly retarded. *Journal of Mental Deficiency Research, 17,* 183–191.

Bellack, A. S., Hersen, M., & Turner, S. M. (1976). Generalization effects of social skills training in chronic schizophrenia: An experimental analysis. *Behaviour Research and Therapy, 14,* 391–398.

Bauman, K. E., & Iwata, B. A. (1977). Maintenance of independent housekeeping skills using scheduling plus self-recording procedures. *Behavior Therapy, 8,* 554–560.

Bell, N. J. (1976). IQ as a factor in community lifestyle of previously institutionalized retardates. *Mental Retardation, 14,* 29–33.

Bellack, A. S., & Hersen, M. (1978). Chronic psychiatric patients: Social skills training. In M. Hersen & A. S. Bellack (Eds.), *Behavior therapy in the psychiatric setting.* Baltimore: Williams & Wilkins.

Bellack, A. S., & Hersen, M. (Eds.) (1979). *Research and practice in social skills training.* New York: Plenum.

Berkson, G., & Romer, D. (1980). Social ecology of supervised communal facilities for mentally disabled adults: I. Introduction. *American Journal of Mental Deficiency, 85,* 219–228.

Berry, P., & Marshall, B. (1978). Social interactions and communication patterns in mentally retarded children. *American Journal of Mental Deficiency, 83,* 44–51.

Bittle, R., & Hake, D. F. (1977). A multi-element design model for component analysis in cross-setting assessment of a treatment package. *Behavior Therapy, 8,* 906–914.

Bornstein, M. R., Bellack, A. S., & Hersen, M. (1977). Social-skills training for highly aggressive children in an inpatient psychiatric setting. *Journal of Applied Behavior Analysis, 10,* 183–195.

Bornstein, P. H., Bach, P. J., McFall, M. E., Friman, P. C., & Lyons, P. D. (1980). Application of a social skills training program in the modification of interpersonal deficits among retarded adults: A clinical replication. *Journal of Applied Behavior Analysis, 13,* 171–176.

Brodsky, G. (1967). The relationship between verbal and non-verbal behavior change. *Behaviour Research and Therapy, 5,* 183–191.

Chittenden, G. F. (1942). An experimental study in measuring and modifying assertive behavior in young children. *Monograph in Social Research in Child Development, 7,* 1–87.

Ciminero, A. R., Nelson, R. O., & Lipinski, D. P. (1977). Self-monitoring procedures. In A. R. Cimenero, K. S. Calhoun, & H. E. Adams (Eds.), *Handbook of behavioral assessment.* New York: Wiley.

Cohen, A. S., & Van Tassel, E. (1978). A comparison: Partial and complete paired comparisons in sociometric measurement of preschool groups. *Applied Psychological Measurement, 2,* 31–40.

Cowen, E. L., Pederson, A., Babigian, H., Izzo, L. D., & Trost, M. A. (1973). Long-term follow-up of early detected vulnerable children. *Journal of Consulting and Clinical Psychology, 41,* 438–446.

Crawford, J. L., Aiello, J. R., & Thompson, D. E. (1979). Deinstitutionalization and community placement: Clinical and environmental factors. *Mental Retardation, 17,* 59–63.

Deutsch, M., & Parks, L. A. (1978). The use of contingent music to increase appropriate conversational speech. *Mental Retardation, 16,* 33–36.

Doljanac, R. F., Schrader, S. J., & Christian, J. G. (1977). *Development of verbal interaction skills in the mentally retarded.* Paper presented at the Association for Advancement of Behavior Therapy, Atlanta.

Doll, E. A. (1953). Measurement of social competence: A manual for *Vineland Social Maturity Scale.* Circle Pines, MN: American Guidance Service.

Eagle, E. (1967). Prognosis and outcome of community placement of institutionalized retardates. *American Journal of Mental Deficiency, 72,* 232–243.

Fiedler, D., & Beach, L. R. (1978). On the decision to be assertive. *Journal of Consulting and Clinical Psychology, 46,* 537–546.

Geller, M. I., Wildman, H. E., Kelly, J. A., & Laughlin, C. S. (1980). Teaching assertive and commendatory social skills to an interpersonally-deficient retarded adolescent. *Journal of Clinical Child Psychology, 9,* 17–21.

Gibson, F. W. Jr., Lawrence, P. S., & Nelson, R. O. (1976). Comparison of three training procedures for teaching social responses to developmentally disabled adults. *American Journal of Mental Deficiency, 81,* 379–387.

Goldstein, A. P. (1973). *Structured Learning Therapy: Toward a psychotherapy for the poor.* New York: Academic Press.

Gollay, E., Freedman, R., Wingaarden, M., & Kurtz, W. R. (1978). *Coming back: The community experiences of deinstitutionalized mentally retarded people.* Lambridge: ABT Books.

Goodenough, F. L. (1928). Measuring behavior traits by means of repeated short samples. *Journal of Juvenile Research, 12,* 230–235.

Gottman, J., Gonso, J., & Rasmussen, B. (1975). Social interaction, social competence, and friendship in children. *Child Development, 46,* 709–718.

Greenspan, S. (1979). Social intelligence in the retarded. In N. R. Ellis (Ed.), *Handbook of mental deficiency: Psychological theory and research* (2nd ed.). Hillsdale, NJ: Erlbaum.

Greenspan, S., & Shoultz, B. (1981). Why mentally retarded adults lose their jobs: Social competence as a factor in work adjustment. *Applied Research in Mental Retardation, 2,* 23–38.

Greenwood, C. R., Walker, H. M., & Hops, H. (1977). Some issues in social interaction/withdrawal assessment. *Exceptional Children, 43,* 490–499.

Grossman, H. J. (Ed.). (1977). *Manual on terminology and classification in mental retardation.* Washington: American Association on Mental Deficiency.

Hersen, M., & Barlow, D. H. (1976). *Single-case experimental designs: Strategies for studying behavior change.* New York: Pergamon.

Hersen, M., & Bellack, A. S. (1976). Social skills training for chronic psychiatric patients: Rationale, research findings and future directions. *Comprehensive Psychiatry, 17,* 559–580.

Hersen, M., & Bellack, A. S. (1977). Assessment of social skills. In A. R. Cimenero, S. Calhoun, & H. E. Adams (Eds.), *Handbook for behavioral assessment.* New York: Wiley.

Hersen, M., Eisler, R. M. & Miller, P. M. (1973). Development of assertive responses: Clinical measurement and research considerations. *Behaviour Research and Therapy, 11,* 505–521.

Honigfeld, G., Gillis, R. D., & Klett, C. J. (1966). Noise-30: A treatment-sensitive ward behavior scale. *Psychological Reports, 19,* 180–182.

Hops, H., & Greenwood, C. R. (1980). Social skills deficits. In E. J. Mash & L. G. Terdal (Eds.), *Behavioral assessment of childhood disorders.* New York: Guilford.

Jackson, D. A., & Wallace, R. F. (1974). The modification and generalization of voice loudness in a fifteen-year-old retarded girl. *Journal of Applied Behavior Analysis, 7,* 461–471.

Kazdin, A. E. (1977). Assessing the clinical or applied importance of behavior change through social validation. *Behavior Modification, 1,* 427–452.

Kazdin, A. E. (1980). *Research design in clinical psychology.* New York: Harper & Row.

Kazdin, A. E., & Matson, J. L. (1981). Social validation in mental retardation. *Applied Research in Mental Retardation, 2,* 39–53.

Kazdin, A. E., Matson, J. L., & Esveldt-Dawson, K. (1981). Social skills performance among normal and psychiatric inpatient children as a function of assessment conditions. *Behaviour Research and Therapy, 19,* 145–1152.

Kelly, J. A. (1982). *Social-skills training: A practical guide for interventions.* New York: Springer.

Kelly, J. A., Furman, W., Phillips, J., Hawthorn, S., & Wilson, T. (1979). Teaching conversational skills to retarded adolescents. *Child Behavior Therapy, 1,* 85–97.

Kelly, J. A., Wildman, B. G., Urey, J. R., & Thurman, C. (1979). *Group skills training to increase the conversational repertoire of retarded adolescents.* Paper presented at the Southeastern Psychological Association annual meeting, New Orleans.

Kirk, R. E. (1968). *Experimental design: Procedures for the behavioral sciences.* Belmont, CA: Brooks/Cole.

Kolstoe, O. P., & Shafter, A. J. (1961). Employability prediction for mentally retarded adults: A methodological note. *American Journal of Mental Deficiency, 66,* 287–289.

Landesman-Dwyer, S., Berkson, G., & Romer, D. (1979). Affiliation and friendship of mentally retarded residents in group homes. *American Journal of Mental Deficiency, 83,* 571–580.

Lee, D. Y. (1977). Evaluation of group counseling program designed to enhance social adjustment of mentally retarded adults. *Journal of Counseling Psychology, 24,* 318–323.

Lowe, B. R., & Cautela, J. R. (1978). A self-report measure of social skill. *Behavior Therapy, 9,* 535–544.

Luiselli, J. K., Colozzi, G., Donellon, S., Helfen, C. S., & Pemberton, B. W. (1978). Training and generalization of a greeting exchange with a mentally retarded language-deficient child. *Education and Treatment of Children, 1,* 23–30.

MacAndrew, C., & Edgerton, R. (1966). On the possibility of friendship. *American Journal of Mental Deficiency, 70,* 612–621.

Mahoney, J. J. (1977). Some applied issues in self-monitoring. In J. D. Cone & R. P. Hawkins (Eds.), *Behavior assessment: New directions in clinical psychology.* New York: Brunner/Mazel.

Matson, J. L. (1978). Training socially appropriate behaviours to moderately retarded adults: A social learning approach. *Scandinavian Journal of Behavior Therapy, 7,* 167–175.

Matson, J. L. (1979) Decreasing inappropriate verbalizations of a moderately retarded adult by a staff assisted self-control program. *Australian Journal of Mental Retardation, 5,* 242–245.

Matson, J. L. (1980a). Behavior modification procedures for training chronically institutionalized schizophrenics. In M. Hersen, R. M. Eisler, & P. M. Miller (Eds.), *Progress in behavior modification.* New York: Academic Press.

Matson, J. L. (1980b). *Acquisition of social skills by mentally retarded adult training assistants. Journal of Mental Deficiency Research, 24,* 129–135.

Matson, J. L., & Andrasik, F. (1982). Training leisure-time social-interaction skills to mentally retarded adults. *American Journal of Mental Deficiency, 86,* 533–542.

Matson, J. L., DiLorenzo, T., & Andrasik, F. (1982). A review of behavior modification procedures for treating social skills deficits and psychiatric disorders of the mentally retarded. In J. L. Matson & F. Andrasik (Eds.), *Treatment issues and innovations in mental retardation.* New York: Plenum.

Matson, J. L., & Earnhart, T. (1981). Programming treatment effects to the natural environment: A procedure for training institutionalized retarded adults. *Behavior Modification, 5,* 27–37.

Matson, J. L., Helsel, W., Bellack, A. S., & Senatore, V. (in press). Development of a rating scale to assess social skill deficits in mentally retarded adults. *Applied Research in Mental Retardation.*

Matson, J. L., Kazdin, A. E., & Esveldt-Dawson, K. (1980). Training interpersonal skills among mentally retarded and socially dysfunctional children. *Behaviour Research and Therapy, 18,* 419–427.

Matson, J. L., & Senatore, V. (1981). A comparison of traditional psychotherapy and social skills training for improving interpersonal functioning of mentally retarded adults. *Behavior Therapy, 12,* 369–382.

Matson, J. L., & Stephens, R. M. (1978). Increasing appropriate behavior of explosive chronic psychiatric patients with a social-skills training package. *Behavior Modification, 2,* 61–76.

Matson, J. L., & Zeiss, R. A. (1978). Group training of social skills in chronically explosive, severely disturbed psychiatric patients. *Behavioral Engineering, 5,* 41–50.

Matson, J. L., & Zeiss, R. A. (1979). The buddy system: A method for generalized reduction of inappropriate interpersonal behavior of retarded psychiatric patients. *British Journal of Social and Clinical Psychology, 18,* 401–405.

Matson, J. L., Zeiss, A. M., Zeiss, R. A., & Bowman, W. (1980). A comparison of social skills training and contingent attention to improve behavioral deficits of chronic psychiatric patients. *British Journal of Social and Clinical Psychology, 19,* 57–64.

McClure, R. F. (1968). Reinforcement of verbal social behavior in moderately retarded children. *Psychological Reports, 23,* 371–376.

McDaniel, J. (1960). Group action in the rehabilitation of the mentally retarded. *Group Psychotherapy, 13,* 543.

Meredith, R. L., Saxon, S., Doleys, D. M., & Kyzer, B. (1980). Social skills training with mildly retarded young adults. *Journal of Clinical Psychology, 36,* 1000–1009.

Meyers, C. E., Nihira, K., & Zetlin, A. (1979). The measurement of adaptive behavior. In N. R. Ellis (Ed.), *Handbook of mental deficiency: Psychological theory and research.* Hillsdale, NJ: Erlbaum.

Nelson, R. O. (1977). Methodological issues in assessment via self-monitoring. In J. D. Cone & R. P. Hawkings (Eds.), *Behavior assessment: New directions in clinical psychology.* New York: Brunner/Mazel.

Nelson, R., Gibson, Jr. F., & Cutting, D. S. (1973). Videotaped modeling: The development of three appropriate social responses in a mildly retarded child. *Mental Retardation, 11,* 24–27.

Nelson, R. O., Lipinski, D. P., & Black, J. L. (1976). The reactivity of adult retardates' self-monitoring: A comparison among behaviors of different valences, and a comparison with token reinforcement. *Psychological Record, 26,* 189–201.

Nihira, K., Foster, R., Shellhaas, W., & Leland, H. (1974). *AAMD Adaptive Behavior Scale, Manual.* Washington: American Association on Mental Deficiency.

Perry, M. A., & Cerreto, M. C. (1977). Structured Learning training of social skills for the retarded. *Mental Retardation, 15,* 31–34.

Paloutzian, R. F., Hasazi, J., Streifel, J., & Edgar, C. L. (1971). Promotion of positive social interaction in severely retarded young children. *American Journal of Mental Deficiency, 75,* 519–524.

Rabkin, J. G. (1979). Criminal behavior of discharged mental patients: A critical appraisal of the research. *Psychological Reports, 44,* 1–27.

Rinn, R. C., & Wise, M. J. (1975). Developing assertive responses in retarded adults: An analog study. Unpublished manuscript, Huntsville–Madison County Community Mental Health Center.

Roff, M., Sells, S. B., & Golden, M. M. (1972). *Social adjustment and personality development in children.* Minneapolis: The University of Minnesota.

Romer, D., & Berkson, G. (1980). Social ecology of supervised communal facilities for mentally disabled adults: II. Predictors of affiliation. *American Journal of Mental Deficiency, 85,* 229–242.

Ross, S. A. (1979). Effects of intentional training in social behavior on retarded children. *American Journal of Mental Deficiency, 73,* 912–919.

Rutter, M., Tizard, J., Yule, W., Graham, P., & Whitmore, K. (1976). Isle of Wight studies, 1964–1974. *Psychological medicine, 7,* 313–332.

Rychtarik, R. G., & Bornstein, P. H. (1979). Training conversational skills in mentally retarded adults: A multiple baseline analysis. *Mental Retardation, 17,* 289–293.

Sackett, G. P. (1978). Measurement in observational research. In G. P. Sackett (Ed.), *Observing behavior* (Vol. 2). *Data collection and analysis methods.* Baltimore: University Park Press.

Sarason, S. B., & Gladwin, T. (1958). The severely defective individual. *The Journal of Nervous and Mental Disease, 126,* 64–96.

Schalock, R. L., & Harper, R. S. (1978). Placement from community-based mental retardation programs: How well do clients do? *American Journal of Mental Deficiency, 83,* 240–247.

Schalock, R. L., & Harper, R. S. (1979). Training in independent living can be done. *Journal of Rehabilitation Administration, 3,* 128–132.

Segal, S., & Aviram, V. (1976). Community-based sheltered care. In P. Ahmed & S. Plot (Eds.), *State mental hospitals.* New York: Plenum.

Senatore, V., Matson, J. L., & Kazdin, A. E. (1982). A comparison of behavioral methods to train social skills to mentally retarded adults. *Behavior Therapy, 13,* 313–324.

Schutz, R., Wehman, P., Renzaglia, A., & Karan, O. (1978). Efficacy of contingent social disapproval on inappropriate verbalizations of two severely retarded males. *Behavior Therapy, 9,* 657–662.

Simeonsson, R. J. (1978). Social competence. In J. Wortis (Ed.), *Mental retardation and developmental disabilities* (Vol. 10). New York: Brunner/Mazel.

Stacy, D., Doleys, D. M., & Malcom, R. (1979). Effects of social-skills training in a community-based program. *American Journal of Mental Deficiency, 84,* 152–158.

Stephens, R. M., Matson, J. L., Westmoreland, T., & Kulpal, J. (1979). *Social-skills training with chronic retarded psychotic patients.* Unpublished manuscript.

Stokes, T. F., Baer, D. M., & Jackson, R. L. (1974). Programming the generalization of a greeting response in four retarded children. *Journal of Applied Behavior Analysis, 7,* 599–610.

Stoudenmire, J., & Salter, L. (1975). Conditioning prosocial behavior in a mentally retarded child without using instructions. *Journal of Behavior Therapy and Experimental Psychiatry, 6,* 39–42.

Tofte-Tipps, S., Mendonca, P., & Peach, R. V. (1982). Training and generalization of social skills: A study with two developmentally handicapped, socially isolated children. *Behavior Modification, 6,* 45–71.

Turner, S. M., Hersen, M., & Bellack, A. S. (1978). Use of social skills training to teach prosocial behaviors in an organically impaired and retarded patient. *Journal of Behavior Therapy and Experimental Psychiatry, 9,* 253–358.

Twardosz, S., & Baer, D. M. (1973). Training two severely retarded adolescents to ask questions. *Journal of Applied Behavior Analysis, 6,* 655–661.

Ullman, C. A. (1952). Identification of maladjusted school children. *Public Health Monograph No. 7.* Washington: Federal Security Agency.

Ullman, C. A. (1957). Teachers, peers and tests as predictors of adjustment. *Journal of Educational Psychology, 48,* 257–267.

Walker, H. M. (1970). *Walker Problem Behavior Identification Checklist.* Los Angeles: Western Psychological Services.

Washington Assessment and Training Scale. (1973). Pullman: Washington State.

Wehman, P., Karan, O., & Rettie, C. (1976). Developing independent play in three severely retarded women. *Psychological Reports, 39,* 995–998.

Weiss, D., & Weinstein, E. A. (1967). Interpersonal tactics among mental retardates. *American Journal of Mental Deficiency, 72,* 267–271.

Wells, K. D., Turner, S. M., Bellack, A. S., & Hersen, J. (1978). Effects of cue-controlled relaxation on psychomotor seizures: An experimental analysis. *Behaviour Research and Therapy, 16,* 51–53.

Whitman, T. L., Burish, T., & Collins, C. (1972). Development of interpersonal language responses in two moderately retarded children. *Mental Retardation, 10,* 40–45.

Whitman, T. L., Mercurio, J. R., & Caponigri, V. (1970). Development of social responses in two severely retarded children. *Journal of Applied Behavior Analysis, 3,* 133–138.

Windle, C. D., Stewart, E., & Brown, S. J. (1961). Reasons for community failure of released patients. *American Journal of Mental Deficiency, 66,* 213–217.

Winer, B. J. (1962). *Statistical principles in experimental design.* New York: McGraw-Hill.

Wolf, M. M. (1978). Social validity: The case for subjective measurement or how applied behavior analysis is finding its heart. *Journal of Applied Behavior Analysis, 11,* 203–214.

Wortmann, H., & Paluck, R. J. (1979). Assertion training with institutionalized severely retarded women. *The Behavior Therapist, 2,* 24–25.

Yalom, I. (1975). *The theory and practice of group psychotherapy.* New York: Basic Books.

Zegiob, L., Klukas, N., & Junginger, J. (1978). Reactivity of self-monitoring procedures with retarded adolescents. *American Journal of Mental Deficiency, 83,* 156–163.

Zigler, E., & Phillips, L. (1960). Social effectiveness and symptomatic behaviors. *Abnormal Social Psychology, 61,* 231–238.

PART FIVE

Programs for Couples and Families

CHAPTER 18

The Couple Communication Program

DANIEL B. WACKMAN AND KAREN SMITH WAMPLER

The Couple Communication Program is a social skills training program designed to help couples learn new ways of communicating together. As such, the program is intended to have a system impact in the sense of not only teaching individuals specific communication skills but also helping the couple as a unit to learn new forms of communicating and relating with each other. This joint emphasis on individual and couple learning developed from the bringing together of several different theoretical perspectives emerging in the late 1960s, namely, family development theory, systems theory, and modern communication theory.

HISTORY OF COUPLE COMMUNICATION

In 1968, a small group of family theorists, researchers, and therapists from the University of Minnesota Family Study Center and the Family and Children's Service of Minneapolis began to work on a series of programs aimed at enriching family life. We began by elaborating concepts from the family development framework developed by Reuben Hill and Roy Rodgers (1964). The family development literature suggested that families move through recognizable stages in their careers and that critical role transitions occur as they move from one stage to another. Furthermore, the move from one stage to another appears to be facilitated or hindered by the extent to which the family system deals effectively with various personal and system issues in earlier stages.

The study team was impressed by the necessity for both personal resources and family resources to deal with change —change generated from within the system as family members entered, matured, and departed, and change generated from outside the family in the larger society. Turning to modern systems and communication theory, we learned that families are characterized as "rule-governed systems" (Watzlawick, Beavin, & Jackson, 1967). The rules governing a system delimit how the system interacts, and they have a powerful impact on how effectively it functions. The family system that is believed to function most effectively has two types of rules: (1) rules defining interaction patterns that establish some degree of stability in the family; and (2) rules that provide procedures for changing patterns, thereby maintaining flexibility (Sprey, 1966; Spear, 1970).

In order to provide for both stability and change, we believed couples could benefit by learning more about their communication. Specifically, we thought that learning several frameworks would help increase their understanding of their issues, rules, and interaction patterns. And we believed that learning a number of specific communication skills would help them talk more effectively about their issues, rules, and interaction patterns—and change them if necessary.

We began to translate those theoretical concepts into practice by identifying communication frameworks and skills and developing skills training modalities. We reasoned that the major vehicle for creating change in relationships was communication. And we thought that if couples could learn some principles about communication and skills for modifying relationships, they could more effectively shape their own lives together and with their children.

The first Couple Communication group was conducted in 1968 with participants recruited through the bridal registry of Dayton's Department Store in Minneapolis. (Initially, the program was designed to facilitate the transition from engagement to marriage.) The following year, after a number of groups had been conducted and a model of the program became standardized, it was tested in a field experiment (Miller, 1971; Nunnally, 1972; Miller, Nunnally, & Wackman, 1976). Results of the test were very encouraging, and, as a consequence, we began training others to conduct the program in 1972.

The next four years were spent refining the program, developing materials to support the group experience, and training leaders to conduct the program. In late 1972, *The Minnesota Couple Communication Program Handbook* (Miller, Nunnally, & Wackman) was published to provide couples with material to read about the skills they were learning and with exercises to use at home to practice the skills they were learning during the Couple Communication group. During the next several years, the developers continued to refine the concepts and skills taught in the program and modified

group experiences to keep up with conceptual developments. The conceptual refinements of this period were brought together when *Alive and Aware* (Miller, Nunnally, & Wackman) was published in October 1975, supplemented by a *Couple Workbook* (Miller, Nunnally, & Wackman) published in 1976.

Leadership training began in January 1972. Interpersonal Communication Programs, Inc. (ICP), the organization set up to distribute the program, offered Couple Communication Instructor Workshops to train professionals in teams of two—either professional colleague pairs or married couples. Groups of 6 to 10 instructor teams participated in the 3-day workshops to learn how to conduct Couple Communication groups. For the first year and a half, one workshop was offered each month. After this, workshops began to be held at the rate of 2 or 3 per month. During these first few years, continuing refinement of the instructor workshop design was also occurring.

By the end of 1975, about 500 instructor teams had been trained and over 15,000 couples had participated in a Couple Communication group. During 1976, more than 500 couples were participating in one of the 80–90 Couple Communication groups that were held each month throughout the United States and in Canada. Furthermore, college students began to learn the communication skills taught in Couple Communication in a classroom version of the program developed in 1976. The *Student Workbook* was also published as a supplement to *Alive and Aware*.

During the next 4 years, training of instructors continued at the rate of three to four workshops per month, resulting in increased numbers of CC groups and participating couples. By 1980, over 1000 couples per month were participating in one of the 150 plus CC groups held monthly. By this time, ICP had trained over 2500 instructor teams, although not all of them became active instructors. During this same period, a number of studies of Couple Communication were conducted by Ph.D. candidates in universities throughout the United States. Results of these studies, combined with the developers' continuing refinement of the program, led to further revisions of the basic program, which culminated in the publication of *Talking Together* (Miller, Nunnally, & Wackman) in late 1979. This book replaced *Alive and Aware* as the text for the CC program.

Since 1980, a follow-up program called Couple Communication II has been developed. Additionally, in an attempt to increase opportunities for couples to participate in the Couple Communication program, ICP began to make it possible for qualified persons to become CC instructors without training by directly supplying them with the *Couple Communication Instructor Manual* (Nunnally, Miller, & Wackman, 1978). Feedback from couples indicates that CC continues to be taught effectively by these instructors. Furthermore, ICP has recently developed an audiotape series to help couples learn the skills taught in the Couple Communication program in their own homes. This tape series is entitled *Communication Skills for Couples*.

Despite these broadening efforts, there has been some decrease in participation in the Couple Communication program during the last 2 years, paralleling the experience of most other marriage-enrichment programs. Currently, about 125 CC groups are conducted each month, with over 750 couples participating in them. During the 11 years since its founding in 1972, more than 3500 instructor teams have been trained to offer the program and about 100,000 couples have participated in the program. In addition, over 40,000 college students have learned skills taught in the Couple Communication program through participa-

tion in the classroom version of the program.

MAJOR FEATURES OF THE COUPLE COMMUNICATION PROGRAM

The general educational goal of the Couple Communication program is to encourage personal and relationship growth by increasing competence in interpersonal communication. This goal incorporates two specific educational objectives:

1. Learning cognitive frameworks or "mental" maps for expanding understanding of effective communication.
2. Learning specific communication skills for disclosing self-awareness and listening to partner's disclosures.

The program is designed to achieve both objectives simultaneously and, in the process, help partners integrate their learning and skills to expand the range of choices they are equipped to make. With heightened awareness and skills to express that awareness congruently, partners can become active agents in building their relationship rather than simply being responders to events that happen to them.

Couple Communication groups include five to eight couples who meet with one or two certified CC instructors for 12 hours. Usually, sessions are held over a 4-week period, each session running for 3 hours. Each session includes minilectures, exercises, and skills practice with feedback. Between sessions, participants read and experiment with communication skills. Sessions build upon each other and on the activities between sessions.

Talking Together is provided as a text to increase participants' learning outside the group. *Talking Together* presents descriptions and examples of the communication frameworks and skills taught in CC. Participants are expected to read sections from *Talking Together* between group sessions and to complete some of the exercises in the book that help partners practice skills between sessions, thereby transferring learning to their relationship outside the group. Participants are expected to spend time talking about issues and practicing skills between sessions.

During the first session in the Couple Communication program, partners are introduced to the "awareness wheel." This framework helps participants identify the many different kinds of self-information they have about issues in their daily lives. It creates an overview for understanding complete and incomplete self-awareness. The Awareness Wheel* is basic to the entire program because it is the pivot upon which participants learn to organize and use their self-information. In the first session, participants learn six specific behavioral skills for verbally expressing their self-awareness congruently and self-responsibly.

In the second session, the focus shifts to skills for listening to and helping one's

*The Awareness Wheel has been submitted for registration as a trade mark.

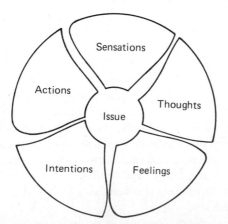

Figure 18.1. The awareness wheel. Reproduced with permission of the authors and publisher, Interpersonal Communication Programs, Inc.

partner express her/his awareness more completely. The major framework taught during this session is "attentive listening" to assure that messages are understood accurately. In session 2, participants learn five specific skills for creating understanding between them.

The third session is built around the "verbal communication style" framework. This framework helps participants identify the kinds of communication alternatives they have and the kinds of impacts different styles have on others. Each style is described in terms of both intentions typically associated with the style and behaviors commonly used in expressing the style. Particular emphasis is given in session 3 to style 4, which is a new communication style for most participants. In the process of becoming more aware of alternative styles, partners become more aware of their choices regarding *how* they can communicate as well as what they communicate.

In the final session, attention centers on heightening each partner's awareness of her/his intention to build, maintain, or diminish both self- and partner's esteem, using the I-count-me/I-count-you framework.

The typical session begins with a presentation of the framework taught in the session. This is followed by an exercise giving participants a chance to use the framework, usually while communicating with their partner. The exercise is usually conducted in a group of three or four people that provides participants with the opportunity to be both observers, using the framework to practice observation of interaction, and actors, practicing the skills taught in the framework. Observers provide feedback to the actors on their use of the skills during the exercise. The group will also usually hold a discussion as a total group about the framework being taught and the related communication principles.

After a break, the session closes with an exercise in which each couple has the chance to talk about one of their own issues in front of the group. The focus of this exercise is on the communication skills taught during the session, not on the topic the couple selects to talk about. The couple's interaction usually lasts from 3 to 5 minutes, and frequently the instructor will stop the discussion before the issue is resolved. Other couples and the instructor then provide feedback on the interaction, restricting their comments to observations about communication skills and patterns. Advice giving to help the couple resolve their issue is not allowed.

Between sessions, participants are expected to read about 15 pages that review the frameworks and skills taught during the session. In addition, they are expected to complete one or two exercises in order to practice the skills taught in the program. Thus, in both group sessions and between-group skills practice, the primary mode of learning is experiential. A major feature of all of the exercises used in the Couple Communication program is that couples have complete choice as to what they will discuss. Further, if they do not want to participate in a particular exercise during the group, they have the right not to do so. Presentations, group discussions, reading, and observation provide alternative modes for learning the material taught in the course, but experiential learning under controlled conditions is central to the program.

In the past few years, a second 4-week program has been developed as a follow-up. Couple Communication II, as it is called, can be taken immediately after the original program or after a time delay. CC II includes sessions on decision making, conflict resolution, intimacy, and marriage as a developmental process. CC II was developed in response to requests by both instructors and couples for more material as well as evidence from research indicating the need for follow-up programming to maintain use of skills (e.g., Brock & Joanning, 1982).

APPLICATIONS AND OUTCOMES

The Couple Communication program has been distributed basically as a marriage-enrichment program. Although the program is relevant for couples at any stage in their relationship, CC appeals most to couples who are in the 25–40 age range. Young couples, in the 21–25 range, and couples in their 40s also attend in fairly large numbers, but these are clearly secondary populations. Very few couples attend after the age of 50.

Demographic data collected in surveys of participants and instructors show that Couple Communication is a middle- and upper-middle-class program. Educational levels of participants are generally quite high; most participants have at least some college education, and most participants have white-collar jobs. Both in terms of the age pattern and demographic patterns, Couple Communication is very similar to other marriage-enrichment programs.

Groups are conducted in a variety of settings, but nearly half are held in churches and a sizable percentage are held at agencies. Lesser numbers are held in school settings and in private settings (homes and counselor offices), and a few are held in such locations as hospitals, drug and alcohol treatment centers, and the like.

Couples learn about the program through a number of different channels. The main three sources of information are churches, friends and relatives, and CC instructors. Less important sources include books, articles about the program, other enrichment programs, advertisements, and brochures.

For more than three-fourths of the couples, CC is their first educational/enrichment experience, and it is likely to be the only such experience for many couples. Marriage Encounter and other church-related weekend events are the programs most often attended by couples who have had other educational/enrichment experiences.

The benefits sought most often by couples are improvement of their relationship and personal growth. Enjoyment of an activity with their partner and a chance to spend time together as a couple are also mentioned frequently as perceived benefits by couples. Thus, participants often appear to have both personal objectives and objectives for their relationship—and the latter often involves multiple objectives.

Finally, to round out the picture, the Couple Communication program appears to be doing an excellent job of fulfilling couples' objectives. More than two-thirds of the participants express very high satisfaction with the program, and less than 5% indicate that CC was "not very" or "not at all" satisfying.

Couple Communication is a heavily researched program. Through July 1982, 22 CC studies were published in some form, as dissertations or journal articles, and at least 7 other studies had been conducted but were not available in published form or had major design flaws. Wampler (1982a, 1982b) has recently completed detailed reviews of this research. Here we will report only the major conclusions of the reviews.

The reviews were based on a critical evaluation of the complete text of the 22 published CC studies. Information on study designs is contained in Table 18.1. With the exception of Campbell (1974), who used a posttest-only design, measures were obtained at both pretest and posttest. The majority included a no-treatment control group. Because of difficulties in recruiting, couples were not assigned randomly in six studies. Some follow-up data, 3 weeks to 6 months after CC, were collected in over half of the studies. In almost all cases, leaders had

received the standard CC instructor's training, and standard measures, with information on reliability and validity, were used. Behavioral measures were used in 12 studies. With few exceptions, appropriate procedures were followed, and adequate levels of interrater reliability were obtained.

The design quality of each study was determined by criteria developed by Gurman and Kniskern (1978) for evaluating studies of marital and family therapies. The quality of CC research can be characterized as good and improving. The quality of the research is significant, considering that all of the CC studies have been field experiments with the host of problems attending such studies. Because of small sample sizes and variations in study design and quality, it is important to examine the evidence concerning the effectiveness of CC over as many studies as possible.

Research participants were obtained from a variety of sources including universities, counseling agencies, churches, and enrichment-group mailing lists. All participants had volunteered for CC as well as for research on CC, except those in one study (Fleming, 1977). With the exception of one study (Davis, 1980), the majority of couples in the CC studies were middle class, well educated, and white (also characteristic of those who volunteer for enrichment programs). Most samples included a mixture of ages, spanning at least three decades. Participants in all studies were male/female couples who were romantically involved with each other.

Evaluation of each study is based on consideration of the complete text of the study, and results are reported only if the conclusions appear warranted. Two approaches will be used in discussing outcomes. First is the statistical significance of results from each original study. In studies where multiple tests of the same data were utilized, we used the finding

TABLE 18.1.   Design Characteristics of CC Studies

Groups	Pre–Post	Pre–Post–Follow-up
CC only	Larsen, 1974 (F)[a] Fleming, 1977 (G)	
CC–no treatment	Miller, 1971 (VG) Nunnally, 1972 (VG) Campbell, 1974 (F)[b] Larson, 1977 (G)[c]	Dillon, 1976 (F)[c] Stafford, 1978 (VG)[d] Thompson, 1978 (G)[c,d] Dode, 1979 (VG) Steller, 1979 (VG)[e] Joanning, 1982 (VG)[c,d]
CC–alternative treatment	Coleman, 1979 (F)[c]	Glisson, 1977 (G)
CC–alternative treatment–no treatment	Brown, 1976 (F)[c] Beaver, 1978 (F)[c] Schaffer, 1981 (VG)	Davis, 1980 (VG)[d] Dillard, 1981 (VG) Schwartz, 1981 (VG)[f] Wampler & Sprenkle, 1980 (VG)[f] Warner, 1982 (VG)

Note. All studies were based on different samples except those by Miller (1971) and Nunnally (1972) and Wampler and Sprenkle (1980) and Schwartz (1981).

[a] Design quality designation based on Gurman and Kniskern (1978) rating system as follows: F = Fair; G = Good; VG = Very Good.

[b] Posttest only.

[c] Groups not assigned randomly.

[d] Only CC group tested at follow-up.

[e] All groups had CC by follow-up.

[f] All but no-treatment group had CC by follow-up.

that includes the most information in the statistical procedure.*

An approach based on statistical significance of results is a very conservative one because it is highly dependent on sample size and the homogeneity of the sample on the measures used. Much information about effect is lost, especially in small-sample field studies like those evaluating CC. For this reason, outcome will also be evaluated in terms of effect size. Effect size is simply a standard score in which the mean for the no-treatment group is subtracted from the mean

of the CC group on a measure and divided by the standard deviation of the no-treatment group. A mean of these standard scores for each category of interest is obtained by summarizing across studies. This approach to the review of research findings is called metaanalysis (Glass, McGaw, & Smith, 1981). An extensive metaanalysis of CC research has been reported elsewhere (Wampler, 1982a).†

We will begin with an examination of studies assessing short-term effects. Very few of the CC studies have been designed to evaluate the program's stated goals of increasing awareness of

*This summary of research results differs somewhat from an earlier review by Wampler (1982b) in that the study, not the measure, is the unit of analysis in this review. Using the study as the unit of analysis eliminates distortions due to variation in the number of measures used, which ranged from one to five measures per study in any one category.

†Effect sizes for the two most recent CC studies (Dillard, 1981; Warner, 1982) are not included in the mean effect sizes. In each case a mean effect size of less than .35 is considered small, .35–.65 moderate, and .66 or more large.

communication processes and teaching communication skills. Rather, most of the studies also evaluated CC as a marriage-enrichment program, using some measure of relationship satisfaction. Perhaps this reflects the fact that the Couple Communication program is promoted as a marriage-enrichment program, not simply as a communication skills programs.

In terms of the primary goal of CC—to change communication behavior in couples—the effects are strongly positive. Of the 12 studies using one or more behavioral measures, 10 found significant positive changes in behavior (Table 18.2). No study reported negative changes. Findings did not appear to vary by type of measure used, which ranged from measures based on skills taught in the program (e.g., use of open style communication) to measures not directly related to program content (e.g., frequency of interruptions). Mean effect size indicates a very large effect of CC on behavior ($ES = 1.07$, $n = 17$ measures from 10 studies).

Findings with respect to couples' subjective ratings of communication quality were more mixed (Table 18.2). Of the 10 studies using such a measure, only 2 found significant positive results. This finding appears to be influenced heavily by study quality, however (Table 18.2). Of the three studies rated as very good, using a measure of communication quality, two (Dode, 1979; Joanning, 1982) found significant positive effects. The one that did not (Schaffer, 1981) has a sample size for the CC group of less than 10 couples. No study found any significant negative results on perceived communication quality.

None of the four studies using measures of self-disclosure (Campbell, 1974; Larson, 1977; Miller, 1971; Steller, 1979) report any significant positive or negative results, indicating that CC has no effect on couple perceptions of self-disclosure. Only a few studies attempted to assess the impact of CC on couples' awareness of partner and awareness of communication patterns, and results

TABLE 18.2.   Immediate Effects of CC from All Studies and Those Rated "Very Good"[a]

Type of Measure	Positive[b] Effect	No Effect	Mixed Effects	Negative Effect
All Studies (N = 22)				
Behavior	10	2	0	0
Self-report				
Communication				
Quality	2	8	0	0
Self-disclosure	0	4	0	0
Perceptual accuracy and congruence	1	2	1	0
Relationship quality	5	8	2	0
"Very Good" Studies (n = 12)				
Behavior	7	2	0	0
Self-report				
Communication				
Quality	2	1	0	0
Self-disclosure	0	2	0	0
Perceptual accuracy and congruence	1	1	1	0
Relationship quality	4	4	1	0

[a] "Very good" refers to quality designation based on Gurman and Kniskern (1978) rating system. See Wampler (1982b) for details.

[b] Positive, negative, and no effects refer to the statistical significance of results. "Mixed" means that the study produced an equal number of positive and neutral results in that category.

were quite mixed. Mean effect size for all of the self-report communication measures indicates a small effect on all three aspects of perceived communication ($ES = .34$, $n = 19$ measures from 15 studies).

Although not a stated goal of CC, many investigators have sought to establish whether or not CC has an effect on relationship satisfaction. Of the 15 studies including a measure of relationship satisfaction, 5 found a positive effect, 8 no effect, and 2, a mixture of positive and no effects (Table 18.2). No study found any negative effect on relationship satisfaction due to CC. The results are almost as varied when only the best studies are considered, with equal numbers reporting positive and no effects and one reporting mixed effects (Table 18.2). Using the effect size measure, however, suggests that CC has a moderately positive effect on relationship satisfaction ($ES = .41$, $n = 24$ measures from 15 studies).

Moving to an examination of longer term effects, we find the following pattern. Four of the studies finding positive effects of CC on communication behavior immediately after the program also included a behavioral measure at follow-up (Table 18.3). Two studies continued to find positive changes in behavior due to CC (Joanning, 1982; Schwartz, 1981). One study (Stafford, 1978) found mixed results, with positive changes maintained on two measures and deterioration on three others. One study found no maintenance of changes in behavior at follow-up (Wampler & Sprenkle, 1980). Mean effect size for behavior remained in the large range, however ($ES = .91$, $n = 10$ measures from four studies). The evidence as to durability of effects is weak because of the small number of studies that included a behavioral measure at follow-up. In two studies, only the CC group was tested at follow-up (Joanning, 1982; Stafford, 1978). That Wampler and Sprenkle (1980) and

Schwartz (1981) produced different findings based on different measures on the same sample further reduces the confidence in any definite conclusion about the maintenance of behavioral effects.

Both studies (Dode, 1979; Joanning, 1982) finding a positive change in perceived communication quality at posttest found these gains maintained at follow-up (Table 18.3). The three studies finding no change at follow-up had not found any change immediately after the program either. Mean effect size indicates a large effect of CC on self-report communication measures at follow-up ($ES = .73$, $n = 9$ measures from seven studies).

Five studies finding positive changes in relationship satisfaction due to CC also obtained information at follow-up (Table 18.3). In three of these (Davis, 1980; Thompson, 1978; Wampler & Sprenkle, 1980), positive changes were maintained. In one study (Joanning, 1982), one measure indicated deterioration whereas the other did not. Finally, one study categorized as mixed at posttest reported no maintenance of effects on relationship satisfaction at follow-up (Stafford, 1978). Mean effect size for relationship satisfaction at follow-up was small ($ES = .26$, $n = 18$ measures from eight studies).

That the effects of CC are due to the impact of the program rather than other factors is indicated by several types of comparisons.

The studies that used an alternative treatment group in addition to a no-treatment group as a means of testing for the effects of nonspecific factors found CC to be superior to the comparison group (Brown, 1976; Schwartz; 1981; Wampler & Sprenkle, 1980). Mean effect size indicates a moderate superiority for CC groups over all types of alternative treatments in effects on attitudes ($ES = .41$, $n = 8$ measures) and a large effect on behavior as compared to alternative treatments ($ES = 1.21$, $n = 2$).

Most studies included more than one

TABLE 18.3.   Longer Term Effects of CC from All Studies and Those Rated "Very Good"[a]

Type of Measure	Positive[b] Effect	No Effect	Mixed Effects	Negative Effect
All Studies (N = 12)				
Behavior	2	3	1	0
Self-report				
Communication				
Quality	2	3	0	0
Self-disclosure	0	1	0	0
Perceptual accuracy and congruence	1	1	0	0
Relationship quality	3	5	1	0
"Very Good" Studies (N = 9)				
Behavior	2	3	1	0
Self-report				
Communication				
Quality	2	0	0	0
Self-disclosure	0	1	0	0
Perceptual accuracy and congruence	1	1	0	0
Relationship quality	2	4	1	0

[a] "Very good" refers to quality designation based on the Gurman and Kniskern (1978) rating system. See Wampler (1982b) for details.

[b] Positive, negative, and no effects refer to the statistical significance of results. "Mixed" means that the study produced an equal number of positive and neutral results in that category.

team of CC leaders. Those that tested for differences found no significant effects by training team (Davis, 1980; Dode, 1970; Joanning, 1982; Larson, 1977; Stafford, 1978; Wampler & Sprenkle, 1980). It can be concluded that the effects of CC are not attributable to qualities of particular instructors.

Even though all 22 studies were designed to evaluate the effectiveness of CC, large variations in design, study quality, sample size, and measures used have produced varied results. Nevertheless, some patterns have emerged. The strongest evidence is with respect to the large positive effect of CC on the communication behavior of couples—a major goal of CC. Although there is some evidence that these positive changes in behavior are maintained over time, more studies, including a behavioral measure at follow-up for both CC and no-treatment groups, are needed. This type of study is among the most difficult to carry out. CC also appears to have a positive effect on communication quality as per-

ceived by the couple. Findings of no effect in this area appear to be related to study quality. Study quality does not explain the variation in results with respect to relationship satisfaction, however, that were mixed both at posttest and follow-up.

CRITICAL EVALUATION AND PROBLEMS

Beside the evaluation of specific outcomes of a program, another set of issues relate to such questions as whether the program attracts participants, how quality is maintained, and how the program handles potential crises.

The Couple Communication program has been highly successful in attracting participants. In fact, CC has enrolled more couples than any other marriage-enrichment program except Marriage Encounter. Whether its success is due to program content, availability, cost, length, or a combination of factors, is not known. What is known is that the program appeals to couples. Further, couples who participate are very positive about the program based on evaluations completed and forwarded to ICP.

Quality control is a second issue. The formal instructor training process was the chief method for assuring quality instruction initially; this was supplemented by a continuing certification review process. More recently, the lengthy and detailed instructor manual has become the major means for assuring quality instruction combined with the certification review process. Additionally, instructors are prohibited from calling their program Couple Communication unless they follow the standard format. Further, the use by couples of *Talking Together* provides another aid to quality control.

The third issue concerns how potential crises are handled by the program. There is growing evidence that enrichment programs, such as CC, attract along with happy couples a number of couples who are troubled but not troubled enough to seek therapy (Powell & Wampler, 1982). Troubled couples can create crises and disrupt an enrichment program. Further, we can ask whether a program like CC gives these couples the help they need or reassures them enough about the benign nature of helpers so that they are less afraid of seeking more help? Or does a program like CC take just enough of the pain away so that the couples do not seek further help if needed?

The possibility that a program like CC might produce a deterioration in the couple's relationship is always a concern. To date, there is no evidence from any of the studies that CC has produced a deterioration on any of the measures used. This is strong support for the contention that CC is a fairly safe (but effective) program.

Several specific steps are taken in the program to lessen the risks of crisis. The preprogram "maxicontract" interview provides information about what the program can and cannot do. It also helps couples who may be in crisis or need another option to make appropriate choices, often by referral to another form of service instead of a CC group. Additionally, instructors are given training on dealing with crises and disruptions that may arise in the group. This is, of course, simply a small supplement to the many years of training and professional counseling experience most CC instructors already have.

Another set of issues arises in the context of the results of research on the Couple Communication program. Couple Communication has been shown to be successful in teaching communication skills, as indicated by the highly consistent results of short-term change in communication behavior. However, the evidence concerning the maintenance of this change over time is mixed, with some studies showing continued change and others showing deterioration of learning. Similarly, findings in relation to measures of relationship quality are also mixed. This pattern of findings leads one to ask such questions as, "Is CC effective enough?" or alternatively, "What can be expected in 12 hours?"

Researchers who have failed to find maintenance of behavioral change or the expected impact of CC on relationship quality typically call for "more": more content, more sessions, more homework, more practice during sessions, and more practice between sessions. As indicated earlier, CC has developed follow-up programming to offer additional content and practice in the form of Couple Communication II. The design of CC II was based on needs and desires expressed by both couples and instructors for (1) more opportunities to practice skills already learned; and (2) sessions dealing with decision making, conflict resolution, and intimacy.

ICP's experience indicates, however, that neither instructors nor couples are very interested in CC II. When the program was initially offered in 1980, a relatively small number of instructors asked for the CC II instructor manual. Among those who did, most reported very few takers when the program was offered to couples. This was true when the program was offered as an immediate 4-week follow-up to the initial CC experience or when it was offered after a delay of 3 to 6 months. Further, when the program was offered as an intact 8-week program, so few couples enrolled that groups were usually canceled by the instructor. For both instructors and participants, the consensus is very clear: More is not better.

STATUS AND FUTURE DIRECTIONS

ICP's experience with Couple Communication II is a microcosm of the dilemma faced by social skills training in general. This is the dilemma of trying to achieve simultaneously the twin goals of high program effectiveness and high program reach. The steps taken to increase program effectiveness almost always create barriers to achieving the goal of reaching large numbers. We will briefly review some of these barriers.

The basic form of communication training—and social skills training generally—is the small group. This is because the small group has been proven to be effective for many forms of skill learning. This form, however, creates a set of constraints to participation:

1.   Many people simply will not join a group.
2.   There are major logistical difficulties in arranging groups. People are so busy, and their schedules are so varied that scheduling a time and place to satisfy everyone who is interested is very difficult. Furthermore, the more sessions included in the program, the more difficult are the logistics for each person and

the harder it is to make a commitment to the program. Programs with more than four sessions usually are harder to fill, and they experience attendance drop-offs after the fourth session.

3.   Powerful experiences usually cost more money. People may be willing to pay large amounts for skills learning with specific payoffs (e.g., management training programs for job improvement), but they do not appear to be willing to pay much for training in everyday social skills, such as parenting skills or marriage enrichment. The result of this is that there is not enough revenue to create or sustain a marriage-enrichment profession and, consequently, program leadership is likely to fall on dedicated volunteers to a considerable extent.

4.   Developing skilled leadership for programs is costly. Conducting leader training events is costly in itself, but this cost is magnified by the one-third–one-third–one-third activity pattern that seems to prevail. In ICP's experience (which has paralleled that of other organizations such as PET*), only about one-third of the instructors who participate in a workshop become active instructors, that is, running two or more groups each year for several years. Another third will run a group or two and then give it up because recruiting is too difficult; they do not enjoy leading the group; and so forth. Another third will run no groups because they did not really intend to run groups but took the training for professional development; they are too busy with other things; or they simply cannot put a group together. To add further to

*Information about activity rates of trained leaders and leader burnout (to be mentioned later) come through a variety of conversations the authors and Sherod Miller have had with leaders of service-providing organizations such as Effectiveness Training, Marriage Encounter, The Association of Couples for Marriage Enrichment (ACME), and other marriage-enrichment organizations participating in The Council of Affiliated Marriage Enrichment Organizations (CAMEO).

the cost of developing skilled leadership is the burnout that most group leaders experience after several years of leading groups: ICP's experience in this regard is paralleled by PET, Marriage Encounter, and a number of other programs. It is the case, in fact, that after a while, all leadership training efforts simply have the effect of replacing those leaders who are no longer conducting groups.

5. Because of these cost considerations, social skills training programs must become imbedded in a social network that can absorb some of the costs of leadership, promotion, and so forth, and supply volunteers to carry out many of these functions. In the marriage-enrichment movement, this has been the church. Other possibilities include the school system, more specifically community education programming, and social service agencies. However, with decreases in government funding of agencies and school districts, these will be less able to absorb costs, leaving the church as a major provider of family-oriented skills training. Because many people do not attend church or participate in church-sponsored activities, a large population segment will be missed.

This set of constraints is imposing, but there probably are a number of others as well. In any case, it is not difficult to understand why almost all of the major marriage-enrichment programs are reporting drop-offs in participation during the last 2 years, some by as much as 50%. It simply takes a lot of energy to carry on a small-group program year after year after year. If communication training—and social skills training in general—continues to rely solely on the small-group experience, it will almost certainly fail to achieve the second goal of reaching many people.

We will now talk about two types of communication training beside skills training and other forms for delivering training beside the small group. The two

other types of communication training might be called perspective giving and situational application.

Even in the most behaviorally oriented programs, some attempt is made to help provide a perspective about how communication works in addition to teaching specific skills. This perspective giving usually occurs in one of two ways.

First, attitudes, motivations, or the "spirit" involved in communication is discussed. Most programs emphasize an attitude of respecting, caring for, and counting the other person, and show how the communication skills that are being taught express this attitude.

A second way involves the presentation of models or frameworks to help participants become aware of broader patterns of communication. Learning perspectives is seen as particularly important in helping participants identify problem spots in communication and in taking steps to change the interaction when trouble occurs.

The third type of communication training—situational application—usually utilizes less active involvement by participants. It most often occurs in large-group settings where a leader lectures about specific communication situations or problems occurring in marriage or family life. Major principles of communication are often presented, followed by specific advice concerning how to apply the principles in everyday situations.

Another approach to advice giving utilizes the mass media, particularly women's magazines, newspapers, and books. Readers are given principles and tips for dealing with specific situations or problems in their lives. This approach reaches many more people than all of the other approaches combined. However, it seldom provides either systematic or comprehensive training, and it almost never provides a context in which the principles or skills that are discussed can be really learned and internalized.

Four major forms are used in delivering the three types of communication training. The *small-group* experience is the best developed form. In this experience, a limited number of participants (usually 20 or less) meet for a number of sessions with a leader or leaders. Participants usually participate in structured experiences and in group discussions. The *large-group* experience includes many people (perhaps as many as several thousand) who listen to a lecture given either in person or via videotape. Sometimes, an opportunity for small-group discussion is provided in the context of the lecture. The *in-home* experience involves only a single couple or family following a self-help program in their own home on their own schedule. Booklets or audiotapes are used to guide and structure the experience. Finally, *individual* experiences involve only a single person participating in the experience alone, usually in her/his home. Again, self-help books, booklets, or audiotapes can be used to guide the experience, but the most common form of individual experience is simply reading a magazine or newspaper article.

The importance of identifying these different delivery forms is that each of the forms has particular strengths and limitations for effectively distributing different kinds of communication training. For example, small-group programs generally focus on the kind of communication training that they are best suited for, namely, skills training with a secondary emphasis on perspective giving. Large groups can best provide perspective and situational application. In-home experiences are best at perspective giving, with some potential for skills training and situational application. Individual experiences are most useful for providing perspective if the experience is created in the form of a booklet, book, or audiotape series, or for situational application if the experience is created in magazine or newspaper articles.

The different strengths and limitations

of these programming forms are a major reason that no single program or program approach is currently designed to provide training in all of the facets of communication discussed here. Yet training in all of them is important for two reasons.

First, the various facets speak to different needs people have in learning how to communicate better in marriage and everyday life. People need to learn more than just skills, which is the primary emphasis of most group communication training programs. They also need to learn some perspectives for understanding communication. And they often need specific advice for dealing with communication situations and problems occurring in their lives.

Second, the different facets of communication training have varying appeal for people, depending on the issues or problems currently being experienced in their own lives. This consideration raises the issue of motivation for learning.

Most current programming involves having the participant come to the program in a church, school, or some other local setting. This creates a barrier for many participants because many people simply do not want to come to small-group experiences. Additionally, when programs involve several members of a social unit, such as a couple or family, it is often the case that one or more members are reluctant participants or, at least, that motivations to participate vary considerably among family members. (This is also true when in-home experiences are provided; family members usually differ considerably in their eagerness to involve themselves.) Further, even when all members of a social unit are reasonably interested in participating in a program, there is a second general motivational issue. Different members vary in the extent to which they take seriously what can be learned in the program.

The fact that participants from the

same unit—as well as participants from different units—are likely to vary in their willingness to participate at all and in their level of participation during the programming experience has important implications for program development, both regarding the content of the program and its form of delivery.

Programming Content

A major motivation for many couples and families to participate in communication training is to be able to spend some time together. Many families simply find it difficult to create time together as a couple or family. A marriage or family program can provide a context for doing so. This suggests that the programs developed for people with this kind of motivation should provide an enjoyable experience that does not require too-hard work. This is especially true when children are involved.

Another significant motivation for participation is that the marriage or family is experiencing a change that is creating some stress. Current research on adult and family development identifies a large number of transitions in normal family development, transitions that provide a motivational basis for programming opportunities. The engagement period, newly wed phase, birth of the first child, the adolescent stage, and so on have all provided opportunities for successful stage-specific programming. But additionally, it is possible to incorporate stage-specific issues with more general communication training (skills and perspective learning) to appeal to people with similar concerns and motivations.

The principle that people's interests influence what they learn carries another specific implication regarding programming: Participants should have some choice regarding what they can work on. Even in relatively structured learning experiences, there should be enough flexibility so that participants have a choice as to what they wish to emphasize in their own learning. As a corollary to this, because people also vary in their willingness to participate in different activities, programming should include several kinds of experiences (e.g., experiential exercises, group discussions, minilectures, reading, etc.) that provide opportunities for various forms of participation. Providing multiple opportunities for learning the same concepts, principles, or skills increases the likelihood that all participants will learn something from a program.

These principles apply for both group and in-home experiences, but in-home experiences have a particular difficulty that group experiences do not have, that is, providing feedback to participants on the experience. This is an especially difficult problem in programs that try to emphasize skills training where feedback on performance can be very important in learning. However, by developing learning aids, such as observer sheets, audiotapes, and the like, it is possible to help participants observe and reflect on their own experience, thereby providing feedback to themselves.

Programming Forms

A truism of modern life is that it is very hard to get any two people together for a series of experiences. When you try to get even more together, such as a whole family, it becomes even more difficult. Thus, the decision that is made regarding the form of the programming experience is even more significant than programming content in determining the ultimate impact of programming efforts.

The hectic pace of modern life suggests that programming efforts should extend over a relatively short period of time. Most successful programs involve only four or five sessions; as noted earlier, those that extend much beyond four sessions either get few people signing up initially or have major drop-offs in attendance for later sessions. This pattern is also true for in-home program involvement.

Many kinds of communication training can effectively utilize alternative delivery systems. Thus, it is possible to develop programming that will use multiple delivery forms. For example, a program might offer the option of a small-group experience or an in-home experience. Or, it might be designed as a one-session program or, as an option, as a multisession program.

Leadership Training

A final important issue in developing communication training programs concerns the role of the leader in the experience and the type of training needed for fulfilling this role. Early communication training programs typically involved highly intensive leadership training. Often, this training was offered only to professionals who had had years of experience in counseling, group work, and the like. Over time, it became clear that this was a self-defeating strategy because professionals could not earn enough by offering communication training for marriage and family living.

Fortunately, the general communication skills levels of many lay people increased substantially during the 1970s making it possible to shift the leadership base to those lay individuals and couples who had participated in the programs. An added benefit from this was these lay people brought an excitement and dedication to the programs that professionals often did not have. Yet, the intensive training process still continued. As noted before, however, most of the leadership training occurring now simply replaces the dedicated volunteers who have moved on to other activities.

As new programming develops, it is important to keep this pattern in mind. Two specific programming considera-

tions are suggested. First, in designing the programming itself, serious considerations should be given to structuring the program so that the leader's role is less demanding than in current programs. This is not meant to suggest that totally leaderless programs are preferable because, in fact, the effectiveness of most small-group programs is highly dependent on a person or couple exerting effective leadership. Rather, what is being suggested is that the leader's functions be shifted away from the kinds of activities requiring intense leadership training (e.g., providing process feedback, providing conceptual input, etc.) to those activities requiring less leadership training (e.g., guiding exercises, managing group process, etc.).

Second, careful attention should be paid to developing teaching aids for use in the group, such as audiotapes to present conceptual materials, worksheets for guiding observers, and so forth. Additionally, well-designed, easy-to-follow instructor manuals should be developed to increase the training that can be done on a self-study basis.

CONCLUDING COMMENTS

In closing, we will suggest some future possibilities for the development of communication and social skill training in the area of marriage and family.

The Idea Life Cycle

It may well be the case that ideas, like products, have a life cycle involving such stages as innovation, growth, maintenance, and finally, decline. If this is the case, the recent downward trend in participation in marriage-enrichment programs may indicate that the ideas presented in these programs are near the end of their idea life cycle. Most of the marriage-enrichment, couple, and family communication programs teach a similar set of skills involving self-expression and more effective listening, and many of the programs utilize a form of dialoguing technique. A number of the programs, like PET, Couple Communication, and Marriage Encounter, experienced substantial growth in the middle and late 1970s, but these same programs are currently experiencing declines. Perhaps this is because the skills and ideas they teach are stale, both to participants and, more importantly, to program leaders.

Attempts have been made by us at Couple Communication and by leaders in other organizations to reverse the decline by repackaging the ideas, using new delivery forms, developing new marketing and advertising approaches, and the like, but none of these efforts has been very successful. It may be that what will be necessary in marriage and family communication is a set of truly new ideas, perhaps an entirely new paradigm. What form that paradigm might take only the future will disclose.

Delivery System Barriers

As noted earlier, the major delivery system for marriage enrichment and communication programming has been the church. However, because of the organization of various denominations in the United States, mixing of programs across denominational lines has been very difficult. Many denominations have created their own programs and expend their primary effort on making these programs work. As a consequence, there is little incentive to cooperate with other programs, even when the programs are complementary rather than competitive. Issues of "doctrinal purity" reinforce the barriers between programs as well. The effect of these tendencies is that a series of small, closed delivery systems have been developed, each serving a single denomination's membership in a limited way. Of the more than 20 denominationally based programs, only two re-

ported reaching more than 1000 couples during the preceding year at a recent meeting of the Council of Affiliated Marriage Enrichment Organizations.

Attempts to shift programming from a small-group context to an in-home form also experienced a formidable barrier, namely the structure of book and tape distribution systems. Bookstores, particularly the chain stores, are dominated by the major publishers and local wholesalers. Organizations with only one or two titles to offer have great difficulty penetrating the bookstore distribution system, and tapes are even more difficult to distribute because only a few bookstores even carry tapes. Using direct mail to reach potential customers is a possibility, but unless the organization has enough titles to offer, with a high-enough purchase price, direct mail is too expensive to be feasible. Organizations with large mailing lists and multiple products, such as the Christian Marriage Enrichment organization, have been successful in reaching potential participants via direct mail. Programs published as books or tapes have penetrated the bookstore market when they are connected with a well-known name, such as James Dobson or Charles Swindol in Christian bookstores, or Thomas Gordon, in regular bookstores. However, there appears to be a life cycle of popularity here too.

Perhaps, the most useful approach to overcoming the delivery system barriers discussed here is to view the church as a provider of a smorgasbord of program possibilities. Programs that might ideally fit into such a smorgasbord would have characteristics like these: short in length —only one or two sessions; little leadership training required; low dependence on published materials for support; programming formats with a segment to enable specific denominations to include their own scriptural basis as part of the experience; and age or topic specific to have direct appeal to at least a segment of the church's membership. Even if an effective program is developed with these characteristics, it is important to recognize that there will still be major barriers to entry, and a substantial "selling" job will be necessary.

Much of what we have said in this concluding section is based on our reading of recent trends in marriage and family programming in the United States. We believe many of the same principles apply to social skills programming generally.

REFERENCES

Beaver, W. A. (1978). Conjoint and pseudo-disjunctive treatment in communication skills for relationship improvement with marital couples (Doctoral dissertation, Marquette University, 1978). *Dissertation Abstracts International, 39,* 3361A-3362A. (University Microfilms No. 78-24, 332)

Brock, G. W., & Joanning, H. (1982). Structured communication training for married couples: A comparison of the Relationship Enhancement Program and the Minnesota Couples Communication Program. *Journal of Marital and Family Therapy, 9,* 413–421.

Brown, R. (1976). *The effects of couple communication training on traditional sex stereotypes of husbands and wives.* Unpublished master's thesis, Appalachian State University, Boone, NC.

Campbell, E. E. (1974). The effects of couple communication training on married couples in the child rearing years (Doctoral dissertation, Arizona State University, 1974). *Dissertation Abstracts International, 35,* 1942A-1943A. (University Microfilms No. 74-23, 420)

Coleman, E. J. (1979). Effects of communication skill training on the outcome of a sex counseling program (Doctoral dissertation, University of Minnesota, 1978). *Dissertation Abstracts International, 39,* 7234A. (University Microfilms No. 79-11, 990)

Davis, G. M. (1980). The differential effect of married couple communication train-ing in groups with the spouse present and spouse not present (Doctoral dissertation, University of North Carolina, 1979). *Dissertation Abstracts International, 40,* 4023B. (University Microfilms No. 80-05, 031)

Dillard, C. K. (1981). Marriage enrichment: A critical assessment of the Couples Communication program model (Doctoral dissertation, Virginia Polytechnic Institute and State University, 1981). *Dissertation Abstracts International, 42,* 2882A. (University Microfilms No. 81262S4)

Dillon, J. D. (1976). Marital communication and its relation to self-esteem (Doctoral dissertation, United States International University, 1975). *Dissertation Abstracts International, 36,* 5862B. (University Microfilms No. 76-10, 585)

Dode, I. L. (1979). An evaluation of the Minnesota Couples Communication Program: A structured educational enrichment experience (Doctoral dissertation, Arizona State University, 1979). *Dissertation Abstracts International, 40,* 1211A. (University Microfilms No. 79-20, 500)

Fleming, M. J. (1977). An evaluation of a structured program designed to teach communication skills and concepts to couples: A field study (Doctoral dissertation, Florida State University, 1976). *Dissertation Abstracts International, 37,* 7633A-7634A. (University Microfilms No. 77-13, 315)

Glass, G. V., McGaw, B., & Smith, M. L. (1981). *Meta-analysis in social research.* New York: Sage.

Glisson, D. H. (1977). A comparison of reciprocity counseling and communication training in a treatment of marital discord (Doctoral dissertation, Washington University, 1976). *Dissertation Abstracts International, 37,* 7973A-7974A. (University Microfilms No. 77-12, 462)

Gurman, A. S., & Kniskern, D. P. (1978). Research on marital and family therapy: Progress, perspective and prospect. In S. Garfield & A. Bergin (Eds.), *Handbook of psychotherapy and behavior change* (2nd ed.). New York: Wiley.

Hill, R., & Rodgers, R. (1964). The developmental approach. In Harold T. Christensen (Ed.), *Handbook on marriage and the family*. Chicago: Rand-McNally.

Joanning, H. (1982). The long-term effects of the Couple Communication program. *Journal of Marital and Family Therapy, 8,* 463–468.

Larsen, G. R. (1974). An evaluation of the Minnesota Couple Communications Training Program's influence on marital communication and self- and mate-perceptions (Doctoral dissertation, Arizona State University, 1974). *Dissertation Abstracts International, 35,* 2627A-2628A. (University Microfilms No. 74-20, 137)

Larson, K. B. (1977). The effects of communication training in small groups upon self-disclosure, marital adjustment, and emotional attachment in marriage (Doctoral dissertation, University of Utah, 1976). *Dissertation Abstracts International, 37,* 5328B. (University Microfilms No. 77-08, 453)

Miller, S. L. (1971). The effects of communication training in small groups upon self-disclosure and openness in engaged couples' systems of interaction: A field experiment (Doctoral dissertation, University of Minnesota, 1971). *Dissertation Abstracts International, 32,* 2819A-2820A. (University Microfilms No. 71-28, 263)

Miller, S., Nunnally, E. W., & Wackman, D. B. (1972). *The Minnesota Couple Communication Program handbook*. Minneapolis: Interpersonal Communication Programs.

Miller, S., Nunnally, E. W., & Wackman, D. B. (1975). *Alive and aware improving communication in relationships*. Minneapolis: Interpersonal Communication Programs.

Miller, S., Nunnally, E. W., & Wackman, D. B. (1976). Minnesota Couples Communication Program (MCCP); Premarital and marital groups. In D. H. L. Olson (Ed.), *Treating relationships*. Lake Mills, IO: Graphic Publishing.

Miller, S., Nunnally, E. W., & Wackman, D. B. (1976). *Couple workbook: Awareness and communication skills*. Minneapolis: Interpersonal Communication Programs.

Miller, S., Nunnally, E. W., & Wackman, D. B. (1979). *Talking together*. Minneapolis: Interpersonal Communication Programs.

Miller, S., Wackman, D. B., & Nunnally, E. W. (1982). *Communication skills for couples*. Minneapolis: Interpersonal Communication Programs.

Nunnally, E. W. (1972). Effects of communication training upon interaction awareness and empathic accuracy of engaged couples: A field experiment (Doctoral dissertation, University of Minnesota, 1971). *Dissertation Abstracts International, 32,* 4736A. (University Microfilms No. 72-05, 561)

Nunnally, E. W., Miller, S., & Wackman, D. B. (1978). *The Couple Communication instructor manual*. Minneapolis: Interpersonal Communication Programs.

Powell, G. S., & Wampler, K. S. (1982). Marriage enrichment participants: Levels of marital satisfaction. *Family Relations, 31,* 389–394.

Schaffer, M. (1981). An evaluation of the Minnesota Couple Communication program upon communication of married couples. (Doctoral dissertation, University of Southern Mississippi, 1980). *Dissertation Abstracts International, 41,* 4643B. (University Microfilms No. 8109897)

Schwartz, R. C. (1981). The relationship among communication style, self-esteem, and the Couple Communication program. (Doctoral dissertation, Purdue University, 1980). *Dissertation Abstracts International, 41,* 3195B. (University Microfilms No. 8102705)

Speer, D. C. (1970). Family systems: Morphostasis and morphogenesis, or "Is homeostasis enough?" *Family Process, 9*(3), 259–278.

Sprey, J. (1966, November). The family as a system in conflict. *Journal of Marriage and the Family, 31,* 699–706.

Stafford, R. R. (1978). Attitude and behavior change in couples as a function of communication training (Doctoral dissertation, Texas Tech University, 1978). *Dissertation Abstracts International, 39,* 2626B. (University Microfilms No. 78-19, 902)

Steller, J. B. (1979). The effects of Couples Communication training upon individualized goals, marriage adjustment, self-disclosure, and the use of communication skills by married couples (Doctoral dissertation, University of Minnesota, 1979). *Dissertation Abstracts International, 40,* 900B-901B. (University Microfilms No. 79-18, 397).

Thompson, K. B. (1978). The effectiveness of couple communication training on interpersonal orientation, couple communication, perceptual congruence, and verbal communication style: A field study. (Doctoral dissertation, University of Iowa, 1978). *Dissertation Abstracts International, 39,* 3009B-3010B. (University Microfilms No. 78-22, 768)

Wackman, D. B., Miller, S., & Nunnally, E. W. (1976). *Student Workbook: Awareness and communication skills.* Minneapolis: Interpersonal Communication Programs.

Wampler, K. S. (1982a). Bringing the review of literature into the age of quantification: Meta-analysis as a strategy for integrating research findings in family studies. *Journal of Marriage and the Family, 44,* 1009–1023.

Wampler, K. S. (1982b). The effectiveness of the Minnesota Couple Communication program: A review of research. *Journal of Marital and Family Therapy, 8,* 345–356

Wampler, K. S., & Sprenkle, D. H. (1980). The Minnesota Couple Communication program: A follow-up study. Journal of Marriage and the Family, 42, 577–584.

Warner, M. D. (1982). Comparison for religious marriage enrichment program with an established communication training enrichment program. (Doctoral dissertation, Purdue University, 1982). *Dissertation Abstracts International, 42,* 3774-3775A. (University Microfilms No. 8200747).

Watzlawick, P., Beavin, J. H., & Jackson, D. D. (1967). *Pragmatics of human communication: A study of interaction patterns, pathologies and paradoxes.* New York: Norton.

CHAPTER 19

Structured Approaches to Couples' Adjustment

NORMAN EPSTEIN

When couples contact a professional for help with relationship problems, it is most often at a point when their level of distress is quite high and their own attempts to maintain a satisfying life together have failed to a significant degree. Distressed partners' daily experiences with one another tend to be characterized by low rates of positive interaction and high rates of reciprocal aversive exchanges (Birchler, Weiss, & Vincent, 1975; Jacobson, Follette, & McDonald, 1982; Jacobson & Margolin, 1979), with associated negative emotions such as anger and depression. At a cognitive level, distressed spouses* are likely to attribute marital conflict to broad, stable causes (Baucom, Bell, & Duhe, 1982) and to negative intent and lack of love on their partner's part (Epstein, Pretzer, & Fleming, 1982). On the one hand, a tendency to attribute problems to a partner can elicit blame that only escalates marital conflict (Doherty, 1981), and, on the other hand, consistent attibutions to global or stable characteristics of the self can constitute a depressive cognitive set (Abramson, Seligman, & Teasdale, 1978).

*Terms associated with marriage, such as *spouses* and *marital* will be used in this chapter in order to be consistent with the marital research and therapy literature, but the author assumes that the procedures described would apply to other intimate relationships.

Whether marital interactions are characterized by outbursts of anger expressed in a destructive manner or by withdrawal, it is likely that members of a distressed couple have diminished hope of improving their relationship by the time they seek treatment. Consequently, therapists working with such couples are faced with the task of designing interventions that will have impact on the behavioral, cognitive, and affective aspects of the marital maladjustment. This chapter describes a variety of structured interventions for modifying dysfunctional marital interaction, emphasizing the effects each can have in the behavioral, cognitive, and affective spheres. The approaches covered in this discussion have been drawn from behavioral marital therapy, communication training, and cognitive therapy—three orientations where structured therapeutic procedures have been outlined clearly and treatment efficacy has been evaluated systematically.

Distressed spouses who do not believe that their relationship has much potential for change tend to be less committed to their marriages, less optimistic about the outcome of marital therapy, and less interested in conjoint marital versus individual treatment (Epstein & Eidelson, 1981). It would appear important, then, for marital therapists to reduce this sense of hopelessness early in the treatment in order to engage the couple in constructive change efforts. This issue is similar to that facing therapists who work with depressed individuals whose sense of hopelessness about their lives contributes to suicidal behavior (Beck, Kovacs, & Weissman, 1975). Just as the major cognitive and behavioral approaches to the treatment of depression use a high level of structure for counteracting hopelessness and modifying ineffective coping skills (e.g., Beach, Abramson, & Levine, 1981; Beck, Rush, Shaw, & Emery, 1979; Lewinsohn & Arconad, 1981; Rehm, 1981), marital interventions that provide structure and order for confused, disappointed, and angry spouses can help overcome distressed couples' pessimism and activate them toward change. This is not to say that the outcome of successful marital therapy consistently will be the continuation of the relationship, but these structured approaches can help couples establish constructive decision making rather than possibly terminating their relationship prematurely or engaging in a spiraling pattern of destructive interaction.

A number of these structured interventions commonly are used in a preventive manner with less-distressed couples seeking marital enrichment and with premarital couples (Markman & Floyd, 1980). When used as such, these behaviorally and cognitively oriented procedures have the goals of expanding the sources of satisfaction spouses have within their relationships and building their skills at changing distressing behaviors that may occur in the future. The sense of hopelessness experienced by clinically distressed couples is much less likely to be a factor in perventive work. The present chapter focuses on the use of structured approaches with couples for whom hopelessness and dysfunctional interaction are immediate threats to their relationships. As described before, the utility of the approaches stems not only from their enhancement of specific skills but also from their impact on couples optimism and motivation regarding their relationships.

A COGNITIVE/BEHAVIORAL MODEL OF MARITAL DYSFUNCTION

The structured approaches described in this chapter include those of behavioral marital therapy, communication training, and cognitive therapy for couples. Marital therapists increasingly have been integrating these three orientations (e.g., Baucom & Lester, 1982; Epstein, 1982; Jacobson, 1984; O'Leary & Turkewitz, 1978) because their theoretical underpinnings tend to be compatible, and together they provide the means for modifying the behavioral, cognitive, and affective components of marital distress.

Behavioral Marital Therapy (BMT) has been based primarily on concepts from social learning theory (Bandura, 1977) and social exchange theory (Thibaut & Kelley, 1959). In social exchange theory, the degree of satisfaction each member of a relationship achieves depends on the ratio of benefits to costs accrued. Although individuals vary considerably in their standards for a benefit/cost ratio, Thibaut and Kelley (1959) note that a person will be dissatisfied with his or her relationship to the extent that he or she perceives more favorable ratios available outside the relationship. In addition, there is considerable evidence of reciprocity between spouses in the exchange of rewards and punishments in a marital relationship over time (Jacobson, 1981).

Jacobson and Margolin (1979) have qualified the behavior exchange model of relationship distress, hypothesizing that not only do distressed couples exchange more negative behaviors than do nondistressed couples, but the day-to-day satisfaction of distressed spouses also is more *reactive* to recent frequencies of positive and negative events. This hypothesis was supported in a study by Jacobson, Follette, and McDonald (1982), and Jacobson (1984) has suggested that distressed spouses' hypersensitivity to each other's negative behaviors is likely to be cognitively mediated. Also, behavioral marital therapists often have noted the idiosyncratic subjective quality of what any individual will experience as rewarding or aversive (Jacobson & Margolin, 1979; O'Leary & Turkewitz, 1978; Weiss, 1978). Thus, efforts in behavioral marital therapy to improve couples' benefit/cost ratios by means of procedures such as contingency contracting must take into account not only observable behaviors but also spouses' appraisals of those acts.

Although social learning theory emphasizes how an individual's behavior is regulated (e.g., elicited, reinforced) by environmental events, it also takes into account internal events, such as cognitions and emotions, that mediate behavioral responses. In a marital relationship, each partner's behavior both controls and is controlled by the other's behavior, and the impact of any behavior will depend on how it is perceived and appraised. For example, if a husband believes that his wife has a global trait of "insensitivity," he is likely to criticize her angrily when she interrupts his reading, even when she has received no message from him that he is not to be interrupted. Each individual's reinforcement history, beliefs about the qualities of a good relationship, and attributions about the meaning and intent of his or her partner's acts are likely to mediate the person's responses to the partner's behavior.

Although early applications of learning principles to marital dysfunction (e.g., Goldiamond, 1965; Goldstein, 1971) were extensions of individual treatment or the use of one spouse to change reinforcement contingencies for the other's behavior, more recent approaches to behavioral marital therapy

tend to involve conjoint treatment designed to modify interaction patterns and sequences (Epstein & Williams, 1981; O'Leary & Turkewitz, 1978). Birchler and Spinks (1980) have developed an integrated behavioral-systems treatment based on a conceptualization of how "family rules" are derived from a gradual mutual shaping of spouses' behaviors by means of reinforcement, punishment, and extinction over the course of their continuing interaction. Initially interacting in a trial-and-error manner, two courting partners shape each other's behavioral repertoires, with many of the interaction "rules" remaining implicit and beyond the awareness of the participants. Birchler and Spinks describe how deviations from established relationship rules are controlled through homeostatic behavioral processes such as negative reinforcement, extinction, and punishment.

Stuart (1980) also describes the behavioral norms that develop at a molar level—an implicit behavioral contract regarding each person's role in ongoing interactions. These relationship contracts include both the guidelines for each person's behavior and the rules regarding the manner in which the agreement can be modified. Stuart notes that a contract must be renegotiated as spouses' needs change over time.

The status quo in a marital interaction also can be maintained by cognitive phenomena that serve as self-fulfilling prophecies (Stuart, 1980). When an individual has developed either negative or positive expectations regarding a partner (e.g., "He ignores me"), that person may act in a manner that elicits the expected behavior (e.g., she nags and he withdraws).

Thus, although the "technology" of behavioral marital therapy has been dominated by procedures designed to modify frequencies of overt behaviors, proponents of these approaches have recognized that the impact of behavioral change depends on intrapsychic (cognitive and affective) phenomena. Jacobson (1984) has argued that behavior change should be conceived of as a means to an end, with the ultimate goal being subjective marital satisfaction.

Some form of communication training is characteristic of most approaches to marital treatment, including psychoanalytic, systems theory, Rogerian, and behavioral orientations (Jacobson, 1981). In a survey of members of the American Association for Marriage and Family Therapy, Geiss and O'Leary (1981) found that therapists ranked communication problems as the most frequently presented complaint of distressed couples and the problem area having the most damaging effects on marital relationships.

The emphasis on modifying communication processes in marital therapy has been derived from two major theoretical bases: family systems theory and behavioral social skills training. Systems theorists (e.g., Satir, 1967; Watzlawick, Beavin, & Jackson, 1967) define *communication* as all system-defining interactions that structure and control the interrelationships of a family's members. All acts, including silence, have message value, and therapists such as Satir stress the importance of metacommunication (explicit descriptions of interaction patterns, especially those involving conflicting messages) to modify dysfunctional relationship patterns. Behaviorally oriented theoreticians emphasize specific skills for the expression and reception of ideas, preferences, and feelings, based on an assumption that a clear, non-aversive exchange of information is necessary to resolve the conflicts and problems of daily married life (Jacobson, 1981). Among the approaches used to improve couples' communication are programs in expressive and empathic listening skills (e.g., Guerney, 1977), problem solving (e.g., Jacobson & Margolin,

1979) and assertion training (e.g., Epstein, 1981).

Some form of communication training has been integrated into most behavioral marital therapy programs (e.g., Jacobson & Margolin, 1979; Liberman, Wheeler, deVisser, Kuehnel, & Kuehnel, 1980; O'Leary & Turkewitz, 1978; Stuart, 1980). Cognitive factors also are considered to be important in the communication process because a mismatch between a communicator's intent and the message received by a listener can be influenced by the listener's appraisal as well as by the sender's expressive skills. For example, one spouse may intend to communicate a compliment, but the other may appraise it as an insult if he or she classifies it as trite. Also, any beliefs the sender has regarding possible negative consequences of open expression may inhibit his or her communication of important information to the partner (Epstein, 1981; Epstein & Eidelson, 1981). Consequently, today a behaviorally oriented approach to marital treatment based on behavior exchange and social learning principles is likely to include structured procedures to maximize exchanges of rewards relative to aversive behaviors, communication training to build skills for clear noncoercive feeling expression and problem solving, and cognitive restructuring to modify spouses' negative idiosyncratic interpretations of each other's behaviors. Epstein et al. (1982) present a model of marital interaction in which each spouse's behavioral response to the other's behavior is mediated by his or her cognitive appraisal of the other's actions. In a continuing cycle, each person's behavior is a joint function of the other's behavior and his or her own evaluation of the behavior.

Any one problem in marital interaction might primarily involve a dysfunctional behavioral skill or dysfunctional cognitive processing, or it may be due to both. Stuart (1980) notes that "microbe-haviors," the high-frequency acts that communicate partners' interest, warmth, and the like toward each other in daily interaction "have the power to shape their broader conceptions of one another, their expectations for the future, and their willingness to act in a reinforcing manner toward each other in the present" (p. 57). Consequently, he argues that changes in such negative behaviors exchanged by distressed couples will improve the subjective quality of their relationships, establishing the trust and collaboration needed for solving broader relationship problems and conflicts.

On the other hand, Jacobson (1984) suggests that dysfunctional cognitive processes can impede the perception of positive behavior changes, interfere with behavior change (e.g., when mistrusting spouses withhold positive behavior with a demand that the partner change first), or become functionally independent of behavior. An example of the last process would be when a person has a narrow, fixed view of the partner and responds reflexively to the latter's mere presence, based on the schema rather than current behavior.

The structured interventions described later can be used to modify problematic behaviors and dysfunctional cognitive processes. The optimal sequence of behavioral and cognitive procedures remains an empirical question, although there has been consensus among clinicians (e.g., Abrahms, 1982; Jacobson & Margolin, 1979; Stuart, 1980) that initial cognitive restructuring to establish a collaborative set is an important prerequisite for engaging distressed couples in behavior change efforts. The unique contributions of behavioral and cognitive treatment components also have not been evaluated as yet, although Baucom and Lester's (1982) preliminary results suggest somewhat broader impact on couples' rela-

tionships when a combined cognitive-behavioral approach was compared with traditional behavioral marital therapy. In the absence of empirical data, the clinician should base treatment strategies on careful ongoing assessment of each couple's responses to particular interventions.

BEHAVIORAL DISCRIMINATION TRAINING

Distressed spouses commonly conceptualize and present their complaints about their marital interactions in terms of global, stable characteristics, particularly attributions of negative traits in their partners. Similarly, their expectations regarding the nature of a "good" marriage and how their partners should behave often are broad and poorly articulated (O'Leary & Turkewitz, 1978). As marital distress intensifies, spouses tend to "track" selectively or attend to negative events, failing to discriminate these from any positive interactions (Jacobson & Margolin, 1979). They also fail to notice which consequences follow which behaviors in which situations (Weiss, 1978). Weiss notes that the lack of clear behavioral referents (rather than trait labels) and a failure to specify the cause–effect sequences in marital interaction impede the identification of changes that could increase spouses' satisfaction. For example,

Thus, a partner is not lazy, in this sense, but the rate of some particular behaviors is too low; the reinforcing contingencies controlling such behaviors are possibly ineffective because of (a) noncontingencies (there are *no* consequences to emitting the responses) or (b) consequences are temporally too distant from the accomplishment itself (recalling two weeks afterwards that someone did a fine job). (p. 201)

Consequently, one of the goals of the treatment program designed by Weiss and his colleagues at the University of Oregon (Weiss & Margolin, 1977) is to increase *objectification*—the ability of spouses to denote and discriminate the behaviors that influence their levels of satisfaction.

As a means of assessing the specific interactional events associated with marital satisfaction and increasing spouses' ability to pinpoint these behaviors, behavioral marital therapists commonly ask couples to keep detailed daily records of pleasant and unpleasant events. Weiss and his colleagues (Weiss, Hops, & Patterson, 1973) developed the Spouse Observation Checklist (SOC) with which spouses report the daily occurrence (or lack thereof) of approximately 400 behaviors categorized a priori as pleasing or displeasing, within 12 content areas (e.g., affection, sex, communication, financial decision making). Higher ratios of "pleases" to "displeases" have been found in nondistressed than in distressed couples in a number of studies, and behavioral marital treatments increase the frequency of "pleases" and decrease the frequency of "displeases" (Christensen & Nies, 1980; Weiss, 1978). As a treatment tool, the SOC can increase a couple's awareness of specific behaviors that influence their level of satisfaction, and this information can be used to plan behavior change agreements between spouses (Jacobson & Margolin, 1979).

A notable result of the Christensen and Nies (1980) study was that agreement between spouses on the events occurring in their daily interactions was low. This underscores the subjectivity of individuals' perceptions of their marriages and suggests that reports on the SOC may be biased by spouses placed in a participant–observer role. From the viewpoint of a cognitive analysis, it would be important to assess and intervene with such distortions and idiosyncratic perceptions. Also, Christensen and Nies note that the SOC includes "displeases" involving only the partner, not dyadic events such as "We got into an argument with one another." Given the importance in marital treatment of fostering spouses' perceptions of marital dysfunction as a dyadic process rather than the fault of one partner, Christensen and Nies recommend the addition of dyadic "displeases" to the SOC.

Christensen, Sullaway, and King (1982) found moderate agreement between spouses who completed questionnaires describing interaction *patterns* in their relationships. The patterns assessed included those in which partners play complementary roles (e.g., one withdraws when the other nags) and those involving symmetry (e.g., the spouses exchange complaints). Many of the patterns had strong correlations with self-reported marital satisfaction, and Christensen et al. argued that their methodology was considerably less costly than most behavioral observation procedures. They suggested that partner agreement might be increased by providing greater behavioral specificity in the questions. It seems that their assessment procedure should help couples achieve one of Weiss's (1978) goals for "objectification," the identification of cause–effect relationships in sequences of interspouse behavior.

Christensen, Sullaway, and King (1983) found modest levels of agreement between members of couples who were asked to report their interactions during the previous 24 hours or the preceding 3 to 4 days, using behavior checklists. Higher agreement was reached with more objective, specific items (good for discrimination), but regardless of item objectivity, there was considerable evidence of an egocentric bias in which participants overrated their own responsibility and underrated their partner's responsibility for both positive and negative events. Egocentric bias with negative events was less as the length of relationship increased; that is, couples who were together longer were more likely to attribute responsibility to the partner or deny their own responsibility for these events. Whether or not this process reflects a diminishing "honeymoon" effect, as Christensen et al. (1983) suggest, the results of the study indicated that systematic biases in spouses' appraisals of their marital interactions occur commonly. Therapists must assess such potential biases carefully in the process of refining a couple's discrimination skills.

Spouses can be asked to share their logs of "pleases" and "displeases" and to discuss their preferences for increases in the pleasing behaviors they have received (Liberman, Wheeler, & Sanders, 1976). This procedure counteracts negative "tracking" by focusing the couple's attention on relationship strengths and specific behaviors they can use to satisfy each other.

Markman, Floyd, Stanley, and Jamieson (1984) stress to couples that negative exchanges often result from global negative complaints regarding a partner's personality or intentions, and they instruct them in the translation of nebulous complaints into positively worded, specific statements with clear implications for relationship change. These "X Y Z" statements identify when an event occurs, what occurs, and its impact on the recipient. For example, the global "You're a slob" becomes "When I come from work and see your coat on the floor, I feel that you are not doing your share around the house and I feel abused." Markman et al. also ask each spouse to describe irritating things about each other in terms of specific requests for behavior change.

During conjoint interviews in the therapist's office, a couple can be instructed in the assessment of their behavioral interactions (Epstein & Williams, 1981). Initially, the therapist can provide feedback about the behaviors of each spouse that precede and follow each of the other's behaviors, thus identifying patterns of mutual influence. Not only does this process help couples discriminate constructive from destructive responses, but it can be a prerequisite for self-control of negative exchanges (see the section on cognitive interventions). When positive behavior patterns are identified, each member of the couple can be coached in increasing his or her behavioral contribution to the beneficial sequence.

Another procedure that serves simultaneously as a means of assessing a couple's interaction and increasing their awareness of discriminations among behaviors with various pleasant or unpleasant consequences is Williams's (1979) Marital Satisfaction Time Lines. Each spouse independently rates 15-minute segments of time spent with the partner each day on a 5-point scale ranging from "very pleasant" to "very unpleasant." They also report the most pleasant and unpleasant specific behaviors occurring during these time periods. Williams found notable discrepancies between partners in thier judgments of the quality of time spent together, particularly among distressed couples. Especially when spouses are unaware of the differences in their subjective experiences, having them compare their time lines can help them discriminate events associated with each person's satisfaction from those that are unpleasant. These data can be used for planning behavior change (Epstein & Williams, 1981).

COMMUNICATION TRAINING

In order to have their needs met in a marriage, spouses must be able to express information about those needs clearly, understand the information about each other's desires accurately, and make requests in a context of negotiation whereby areas of conflict are resolved to their mutual satisfaction (Stuart, 1980). The process of exchange of information in human communication is complex, involving the encoding and decoding of messages in verbal and nonverbal channels. Consequently, there are numerous "communication problems" that can occur (e.g., an individual uses vague, global terminology in describing his or her needs, and the partner has insufficient information to respond appropriately; verbal and nonverbal messages are inconsistent, with one channel communicating a message destructive to goodwill in the relationship; a spouse listening to a partner's message selectively attends to particular aspects, thereby missing important information).

Couples often are unaware of the multiple factors that influence the nature of the pleasing or distressing messages they exchange; therefore, most structured treatments for marital discord include interventions intended to teach couples to communicate in more constructive, effective ways. These approaches emphasize that effective communication depends on both parties—expresser and listener—and a variety of procedures have been developed to train couples in the sending and receiving of messages. Some of these procedures are presented elsewhere in this volume and will be outlined only briefly here; others will be described in greater detail.

Basic Components of Communication Training

Jacobson (1981) notes that behaviorally oriented approaches to communication training have common basic components and methods: instructions, behavior rehearsal, and feedback (corrective and reinforcing). *Instructions* involve didactic presentations regarding the specific characteristics of desirable communication skills. Because a couple's problematic interactions most likely have been at least somewhat effective in influencing each other's behaviors, they must be instructed in what *not* to do as well as what to do (Epstein, 1981). Bibliother-

apy (e.g., Gottman, Notarius, Gonso, & Markman, 1976), brief descriptions of communication skills and processes by the therapist, and modeling of examples of effective communication are major techniques for imparting this knowledge. Modeling may include presentation of standard films, but more commonly it involves demonstrations of specific behaviors by a therapist. For example, the therapist can interrupt a couple's interaction in the office at a point when one spouse has elicited a negative response from the other due to a dysfunctional behavior. The therapist can note that the negative reaction seemed to follow a specific behavior on the part of the first spouse, and (assuming that the therapist believes that the problem involves that behavior rather than a distorted appraisal of it by the other spouse) he or she can suggest and demonstrate an alternative behavior. When a therapist steps in and plays the role of one spouse with the other, it is important to do so with appropriate tact so that the spouse whose role has been taken does not feel criticized and inadequate by comparison.

Jacobson (1981) notes that couples who merely imitate a therapist's behavior without learning the basic underlying principles will be unlikely to apply new skills in future situations, and he suggests that their understanding and learning of communication "rules" will be facilitated by discussions following the modeling demonstration, during which spouses are asked to describe the characteristics of the modeled behavior that produced positive consequences in the dyadic interaction.

In spite of the efficiency of learning through observation of a model, structured approaches to communication training are based on an assumption that mastery of new skills will require repeated *practice*. Given the system of mutual behavioral influence existing in a couple, each spouse is likely to need considerable practice in modifying his or her own responses in the face of continued provocative stimuli from the partner; for example, the partner's mere presence can serve as a discriminative stimulus for fighting (Epstein & Williams, 1981). Only as a couple actively rehearse new skills can they and the therapist assess the degree to which they have modified dysfunctional patterns and identify additional aspects of their behaviors that require change. Rehearsal can include the practice of specific behaviors (e.g., use of "I" statements) with sets of structured exercises, or more natural discussions between spouses utilizing particular communication guidelines.

Frequent behavior rehearsal outside the therapist's office between treatment sessions typically is structured by means of homework assignments. When a couple is given an assignment to practice a particular skill with which they already have demonstrated proficiency in the office, the task should be selected so as to maximize the probability of success. A practice session that ends in an upsetting fight can undermine therapeutic progress. Consequently, it is important to introduce more difficult homework tasks gradually (e.g., moving from discussions of neutral or positive topics to minor conflicts, and then to more central relationship issues). The therapist and couple can devise a hierarchy of behavior-rehearsal tasks based on estimates of probabilities for success (Epstein, 1981).

Feedback to a couple regarding the adequacy of their communication efforts serves two purposes: (1) corrective instruction when changes in specific behaviors are needed; and (2) reinforcement of their constructive efforts. Feedback can focus on either "molecular" behaviors or on larger interaction sequences (Jacobson, 1981), and although it will draw the couple's attention to both the positive and negative aspects of their interaction, even small improvements

should be noted and failures discussed in a spirit of learning from one's mistakes.

Videotape and audiotape playback of a couple's interactions can provide more potent, clear feedback than descriptions provided by a therapist, but the power of such feedback can be quite upsetting to some clients (Alkire & Brunse, 1974), and confrontation should be used judiciously and with support by the therapist (Epstein, 1981; Jacobsen, 1981).

Feedback is used in conjunction with instructions and behavior rehearsal in order to shape clients' responses gradually toward an approximation of more constructive marital interaction.

Nonverbal Communication

Although marital communication training programs tend to focus on restructuring spouses' verbal messages, considerable attention also is paid to nonverbal behavior that can have profound impact on the quality of a relationship. When the verbal and nonverbal components of communication are inconsistent (e.g., when a person paces while saying that he or she is calm), observers tend to give greater weight to the nonverbal message (Mehrabian, 1972). Consequently, marital therapists commonly coach couples toward identifying and clarifying inconsistencies as well as increasing the frequency of positive versus negative nonverbal messages (Stuart, 1980). Because nonverbal behavior, such as facial expressions, eye contact, and posture, often convey messages about a person's definition of the relationship with his or her spouse (e.g., degree of liking, dominance), training couples in constructive communication includes considerable attention to the nonverbal and paralinguistic components (e.g., voice tone, speech rate) as well as the verbal content in marital interaction.

A variety of structured exercises can be used to sensitize couples to their nonverbal behaviors and to substitute pleasing for aversive behaviors. Stuart (1980) suggests asking each spouse to express a message such as desire for closeness to the partner first only nonverbally and then combined with words. By means of feedback (from the therapist or spouse), couples are made aware of how their nonverbal behaviors "comment on" the intent of their verbal messages. They then can discuss how their routine daily behaviors communicate levels of concern or distance between them. These nonverbal behaviors also can be sources of damaging misunderstanding; for example, when one husband arrived home from work very tired, with the idea of taking a brief nap before dinner, he walked in the house and saw his wife in the living room scowling. He said nothing, started to walk upstairs, then returned to the living room and said in a clipped manner, "What's your problem! I'm going upstairs for a nap." His wife responded in a sarcastic tone, "Then why don't you just stay up there!" When this interaction was explored later in the therapist's office, it became clear that the wife had scowled because she had been thinking about her stressful day at work (it had nothing to do with her husband), the husband felt guilty about taking a nap rather than spending time with his wife, and, in general, this couple had never worked out a way of greeting each other after a work day in a manner that communicated mutual caring *as well as* any need either partner may have for some time alone to unwind. The wife was not upset at the idea that her husband might need time by himself and was quite satisfied with an agreement that they would greet each other for a few minutes (communicating mutual interest and caring), exchange information about the general nature of their respective days, and spend some time apart if either needed it. If one spouse had a topic to discuss with the other and the latter wanted time alone, they would make an explicit agreement to talk later in the evening. The therapist also coached the couple in exchanging information about any nonverbal messages they found upsetting; for example, in the future, the husband was to inquire about the meaning of his wife's scowls rather than making assumptions about her feelings and intentions. The interpretations that spouses make of each other's nonverbal and verbal communications can be susceptible to cognitive distortion. Specific interventions for cognitive restructuring are described in a later section of this chapter.

Liberman et al. (1980) present brief exercises that allow couples to experience the impact of variations in the nonverbal delivery of messages. In one exercise, after the therapist and couple select a brief neutral statement such as "Green is a beautiful color," the spouses are instructed to say that sentence in different ways (e.g., make it a demand, say it in a loud voice, imitate the tone of being afraid), with the listener describing the nonverbal message he or she received. The couple can be coached in producing nuances of tone and volume. A second exercise involves expressing a neutral statement with neutral tone but varying eye contact (e.g., look the other straight in the eye; look hard, demanding; make many brief eye contacts). Similar procedures can be used to explore variations in facial expression, gestures, posture, and the pacing and fluency of speech; then couples can practice combinations of these elements, such as looking away and whispering (Liberman et al., 1980).

Videotape feedback can provide valuable information for couples about their nonverbal behavior toward each other. As noted earlier, the therapist should apply this confrontive procedure with care, including preparation of the couple for the "shock" of seeing themselves on tape (Jacobson & Margolin, 1979). A particular advantage of videotape feedback is that it can increase each individual's awareness of his or her own behavior in marital interaction and thereby foster a greater understanding of the *mutual* influence process. Many spouses are surprised to see that their degree of eye contact or their use of particular gestures detracts from a positive exchange with their partners. When providing such feedback, the therapist should take the role of encouraging constructive changes and blocking spouses from criticizing each other for their taped behavior.

The Issue of Skill versus Performance

The use of structured approaches to communication training is based on an assumption that spouses have deficits in certain skills that can be ameliorated by means of procedures such as instruction, behavior rehearsal, and feedback. However, an individual may fail to perform skills in his or her repertoire if he or she doubts that it would make a difference in the relationship. A spouse may be inhibited from expressing feelings due to fear that the partner will use it as "ammunition" in future fights, or he or she may choose not to make direct requests due to a belief that the partner does not care enough to comply. Margolin (1983) argues that skills training based on the therapist's assumption of skills deficits may be misguided, and marital assessment must take into account variables such as spouses' outcome expectations in distinguishing between performance and skill deficits.

Training in Expressive and Listening Skills

Based on a general model of communication in which the accurate exchange of information depends on one person's expressing a message clearly and another person's receiving the information in an undistorted manner, programs of structured marital treatment commonly include specific training in both expressive and listening skills (e.g., Epstein, Pretzer, & Fleming, 1982; Gottman et al., 1976; Halweg, Revenstorf, & Schindler, 1982; Jacobson, 1982; Liberman et al., 1980; Markman & Floyd, 1980; O'Leary & Turkewitz, 1978; Stuart, 1980).

Gottman et al. (1976) emphasize the goal of equating the message one person intends with the actual impact of that message on the receiver. Both parties are held responsible for the successful exchange of information. Gottman et al. describe dysfunctional communication patterns such as the "summarizing self syndrome" in which each spouse repeatedly states his or her position on an issue rather than listening to the other's views and providing feedback to the other about his or her reactions to those views. Because spouses in conflict often fail to listen to one another and often engage in "mind reading" (assuming one knows the other's feelings and intentions without asking for information to validate the assumption), they develop an often well-founded sense that they are misunderstood.

Gottman et al.'s interventions are designed to increase mutual understanding through the exchange of information and to increase goodwill by means of attentive listening and acknowledgment of each other's views. Initially, the couple is given considerable feedback about their dysfunctional communication patterns and coached in interrupting such exchanges as soon as they are noticed. Spouses also are instructed to ask each other for feedback about the impacts of messages they send and to discuss discrepancies between intended and received messages. The therapist stresses that each spouse needs to listen carefully in order to understand the other's thoughts and feelings. Each spouse practices paraphrasing the messages sent by the partner and communicating acknowledgment that the other's point of view has value. This mutual validation is intended to increase spouses' perceptions that they are respected, even when they disagree.

Gottman et al. (1976) require that the sender of a message engage in "constructive leveling" in which verbal attacks are minimized with the use of statements in the form, "When you do X in situation Y, I feel Z." The language to be used should be specific but not derogatory. For clients who lack sophistication in the labeling and expression of emotional states, the therapist can provide reference lists of positive and negative emotions. Also, concerns that either spouse may have about the direct expression of feelings (e.g., potential loss of the other's love) are explored if these appear to be inhibiting communication.

The principles of Guerney's (1977) Relationship Enhancement program approach to communication training have been applied extensively in structured programs of marital treatment (e.g., Epstein, Pretzer, & Fleming, 1982; Halweg, Revenstorf, & Schindler, 1982; O'Leary & Turkewitz, 1978). Guerney emphasizes the educational rather than therapeutic orientation of this approach, in which couples are taught expressive and listening skills, often in a couples' group setting. Practice in nonjudgmental empathic listening as well as exposure to direct didactic presentations stressing the subjectivity of each individual's views is intended to foster each spouse's acceptance of his or her own and the partner's feelings and preferences. The resolution of marital conflicts is expected to follow from such communication of mutual respect and clarification of each person's feelings, needs, and preferences. Guerney also expects Relationship Enhancement training to prevent future marital dysfunction if spouses apply their new communication skills when conflicts arise.

Because Guerney's (1977) program is described elsewhere in this volume, only a basic outline will be presented here.

Spouses are taught to take turns in expressive and empathic listening modes, with additional training in appropriate ways of shifting from one mode to the other. The person using the expresser mode describes his or her thoughts and feelings about a topic, and the partner listens carefully, providing empathic feedback similar to that exhibit by a Rogerian therapist. The expresser then acknowledges the listener's accurate feedback and/or notes any points that the listener missed. The listener then gives any supplemental feedback that may be needed, until the expresser is able to say that the listener has achieved a basic understanding. At this point, the spouses can switch modes.

Based on social learning principles, Guerney (1977) emphasizes highly structured interventions, including modeling of good communication skills by group leaders, verbal instructions and videotaped examples of specific communication skills, repeated practice by clients during sessions and at home, graded expectations for proficiency of clients' performance of the skills, and therapist reinforcement of spouses' successes. Clients begin practice of the communication skills in same-sex pairs before attempting them with their partners, and couples are given an opportunity to practice discussing nonthreatening topics before moving on to areas of minor and major conflict. In the group setting, couples can learn by observing other couples and providing feedback for each other.

The Relationship Enhancement program includes specific communication guidelines for each of the expresser and empathic listener modes. For example, the expresser is to (1) acknowledge the subjectivity of his or her thoughts and feelings; (2) describe feelings, thoughts, and perceptions in specific rather than global terms; (3) state what action he or she would like the partner to take; (4) acknowledge positive aspects of the partner or relationship before stating a complaint or request (to minimize defensive reactions by the listener); and (5) convey empathy for the listener's position. In turn, the empathic listener is to (1) engage in reflective listening; (2) refrain from guiding the expresser with questions or advice; (3) focus on understanding the expresser's perceptions rather than expressing his or her own perceptions; and (4) take a nonjudgmental stance regarding the partner's opinions and preferences.

Research on the Relationship Enhancement program has been encouraging (Guerney, 1977), although most applications have been with highly educated couples who are not experiencing clinical levels of marital distress (Epstein & Williams, 1981; Halweg, Revenstorf, & Schindler, 1982). Halweg et al. used 8 weeks of communication training based on Guerney's program with distressed couples and found considerable improvement when it was applied with individual couples but not with couple groups. Epstein, Pretzer, and Fleming (1982) also found limited improvement with a group communication training program that included and 4 weeks of Relationship Enhancement training 4 weeks of assertion training procedures. These results suggest that more intensive practice of expresser and listener skills may be necessary with clinically distressed couples than may be possible in a group format or that group treatment for such couples must be longer in order to give each couple sufficient time to develop more constructive attitudes and skills. Halweg et al. also found more stable change with a behavioral marital therapy that included training in problem solving than with the communication training, suggesting that distressed couples may need more focused work with conflict resolution skills than is provided in the Relationship Enhancement program. It will be important for future comparative studies to investigate the specific impacts of different interventions, such as training in expressive, empathic listening and problem-solving skills.

My clinical experience with Relationship Enhancement procedures suggests that the structure of the communication modes helps disrupt and control escalation of aversive exchanges between spouses, and in the case of withdrawn individuals, it increases the exchange of information in a manner that reduces the psychological distance in the couple. Certainly, the procedures create a marked departure from the normal flow of conversation and are unlikely to be used routinely in daily exchanges, but couples who have mastered them know they have a means of bringing some order to chaotic and destructive interactions.

The attitudinal shifts that can take place with training in expressive and empathic listening skills may be equally or more important than the behavioral changes. The structure sets the tone for collaboration rather than an adversarial relationship. Both spouses learn that they will be heard, and the common polarization (i.e., the belief that one partner must be right and the other wrong) in marital conflict can be counteracted by this approach that emphasizes the subjectivity of individual experience and the worth of each person's views.

Shifts in spouses' negative attributions about each other's personalities and intentions also can be facilitated with this communication training. For example, one wife believed that her husband was insensitive and uncaring because he did not seem to pay attention to her when she expressed her negative feelings about their relationship. When the couple was coached in the use of expresser and empathic listener modes, the husband demonstrated that he understood his wife well, especially when she expressed her feelings in a nonattacking manner. The wife was pleasantly surprised at her husband's display of empathy, remarking with a grin that she could really tell that he cared.

The preceding example demonstrates a positive attitudinal effect of training in Relationship Enhancement communication skills. However, members of highly distressed couples are likely to have long-standing negative views of one another, and creation of more favorable attitudes and attributions may require much more than a demonstration of empathic listening. Guerney (1977) does not detail how a Relationship Enhancement trainer can deal with highly distressed, hostile spouses, and, in fact, Epstein, Pretzer, and Fleming (1982) found no appreciable changes in negative attitudes and attributions among couples in their communication training group, in contrast to the change found with a cognitively oriented treatment. It may be that negative cognitive sets can be modified in conjunction with communication training, but the means for doing so have not been specified in the literature. Integration of communication training with cognitive interventions such as those described later in this chapter may help rectify this potential limitation of the skill training.

Other Expressive Skills: Assertion, Negative Feeling Expression, and Positive Feeling Expression

The expressive skills fostered in approaches such as the Relationship Enhancement program (Guerney, 1977) facilitate clear, specific messages about a person's preferences, negative feelings, and positive feelings, but a distressed couple also may need communication training focused more intensively on constructive ways of making and refusing requests as well as expressing feelings. Individuals often use threats, demands, and derogatory descriptions of their partners as means of expressing anger, and these forms of "destructive engagement" (Raush, Barry, Hertel, & Swain, 1974) tend to escalate conflict and mutual alienation. On the other hand, suppression of anger or expression of anger through passive, obstructional means may produce a less tumultuous but nevertheless unsatisfying relationship. Consequently, marital therapists commonly intervene to modify destructive forms of feeling expression.

Jacobson (1982) instructs couples to restrict expressions of negative feelings to feeling–cause statements of the form, "I am feeling X because you did Y." Threats, demands, and put-downs that would only elicit defensiveness in the recipient are prohibited. Such statements specify the stimuli associated with negative feelings (of course, these may be accurate perceptions or may involve cognitive distortions on the part of the angered person) and thus can lead to discussions of possible constructive behavior changes.

Stuart (1980) notes that unlimited expression of feelings can be unnecessarily hurtful and destructive to a relationship, and he outlines characteristics of effective statements, including the following:

1. Beginning statements with the pronoun "I" communicates that the expresser takes responsibility for his or her own feelings and acknowledges that others may have different feelings and views.

2. Questions tend to reduce personal responsibility and often elicit defensiveness, so they initially should be avoided.

3. When questions must be asked, they should be prefaced with an I self-statement.

4. Beginning a question with "how" rather than "why" is compatible with a problem-solving rather than an accusatory approach to one's relationship.

5. A question should be followed by a second question asking for more information in order to underscore the

asker's interest and avoid using the answerer's response as material for an attack (e.g., a follow-up question can indicate that one has heard the response and cares to know more about the other person's experience).

6. Self-statements should be present oriented in order to maximize the speaker's responsibility for the message.

7. Statements should be free of qualifiers intended to manipulate the listener's mood and attention (e.g., an anxiety-eliciting preface such as "Don't worry about me, but . . .").

Stuart (1980) argues how this constructive use of self-summarizing statements is important for the establishment of each patient's identity in a relationship, and he describes how a therapist can teach couples how to use them. The preceding rules can be described and even written on note cards for easy reference by couples, and the therapist can use instruction and feedback to shape each spouse's use of the rules as they practice, beginning with neutral topics. Instruction in simple methods of reducing spouses' tendencies to interrupt one another, such as having a speaker hold a pencil vertically when he or she wants to continue talking, can help structure the exchange of self-statements.

Liberman et al. (1980) also stress to couples that constructive expression of negative feelings, such as anger, hurt anxiety, depression, and frustration, is important because these states occur naturally in a close relationship. They recommend that a therapist describe, demonstrate, and discuss with a couple the differences between constructive and indirect, hurtful expression of negative feelings. Examples of inappropriate expression are indirect messages, accusations, "gunnysacking," passive withholding, withdrawal, direct or passive aggression, and interpretation of the other's motives. Liberman et al. note that a therapist must be quite active and directive in order to shift distressed couples from long-standing destructive to constructive modes of expressing negative feelings.

Once again, the distinction between performance and skill is important when one assesses the need for training a couple in constructive expression of negative feelings. Studies by Ryder (1968) and Vincent, Weiss, and Birchler (1975) have indicated that individuals exhibit more constructive communication with strangers than with their spouses. Thus, a person may fail to use constructive responses in his or her repertoire when interacting with the partner, and factors that lead to such a choice should be explored. These may include anxiety about negative consequences of direct expression, punitive withdrawal of positive expression due to a desire for revenge, or a tendency for people to suspend rules of common courtesy when interacting with intimates (Liberman et al., 1980).

Regarding the expression of positive feelings, the initial high rate of compliments and statements of affection characteristic of courtship tends to drop off over time, often because people assume that their partners already are aware of such feelings (Jacobson, 1982). Other reasons for low rates of positive exchange include embarrassment about expressing love, deficits in skills for wording such statements, and concerns among dissatisfied spouses that a partner who hears positives will rest on his or her laurels and assume that no changes are required. Even when spouses do have a sense that the other person appreciates them, positive-feeling expressions can be highly reinforcing (Jacobson, 1982), and partners are likely to maintain positive exchanges if they acknowledge the positives they receive from one another (Liberman et al., 1980). Therapists can coach couples in positive expression; for example, in conjunction with homework in which each spouse is to observe and record "pleases" received from the other. Assessment of factors that may inhibit *performance* when an individual has the skills for expressing positive feeling should be a routine procedure with distressed couples who do not exchange positives.

In order to initiate changes in their relationship, members of a couple must be able to make requests of each other in a manner that conveys specific information about desired behavior and that minimizes the listener's defensiveness. Spouses often are not skilled at discriminating assertive (direct, noncoercive) ways of making requests from aggressive (direct, coercive), passive-aggressive (indirect, coercive), and submissive (indirect, noncoercive) responses (Epstein, 1981). They also can be inhibited from making direct requests due to anxiety about possible negative reactions from the partner, a belief that spouses should be able to read each other's mind, or an expectation that such requests will be ineffective (Eidelson & Epstein, 1982; Liberman et al., 1980; Weiss, 1980).

Spouses who are angry and view their partners as ungiving are likely to continue to use aggression (threats, disparagement, and other aversive stimulation) in order to force compliance with their wishes, in spite of the tendency for this coercion to elicit the partner's defensiveness, anger, and counteraggression or withdrawal. Therapists can help couples substitute assertive forms of requests for direct and passive aggression as well as for submission by training them to discriminate these influence tactics and their differential consequences (e.g., a number of studies have documented that assertion produces more compliance and less hostility than aggression) and coaching them in the practice of constructive request making. As in other forms of communication training, didactic presentations, such as discussions and therapist modeling of the behavior modes, can be followed by extensive behavior rehearsal by clients and feedback by the therapist (Epstein, 1981).

Stuart (1980) suggests that constructive requests should have the characteristics of self-statements described earlier (e.g., begin with "I," be present oriented). He argues that requests phrased as "I want" place the listener under less obligation to comply than those phrased as "I need." Stuart also notes that spouses often must learn better *timing* of their requests—a task that may be more difficult than modifying the form of the requests. At times, the recipient of a request may have more pressing needs than those of the requester, and spouses may need practice identifying cues regarding each other's readiness to respond to requests. Stuart suggests that empathic listening skills can facilitate the reading of such cues, as can direct statements by each spouse about his or her readiness to comply with the other's wishes. Thus, the ability to refuse a partner's request in a direct but nonaggressive manner is another important form of assertion that can be a target for intervention with couples whose methods of influencing one another are ineffective.

Cognitive factors that may inhibit refusal of a request often involve anxiety about the possibility of angering or alienating the requester and a sense of guilt about possibly hurting or depriving the other person. It is important to assess whether an individual needs to become more skilled at refusing requests or needs to develop a less threatening perception of the consequences associated with a refusal. Of course, a person's fears about the partner's negative response may be well founded, and in such a situation, the therapist could work toward modifying the partner's reactions to assertive refusals as well. Also, it is helpful for the therapist to emphasize from the beginning of the assertion training that assertion involves the direct statement of one's preferences without a demand that these be met and that an assertive request may result in an assertive refusal.

Conjoint rather than individual treatment for problems of unassertiveness in marital interaction has an advantage of providing the therapist with an *in vivo* assessment of dysfunctional behavior, and it allows the therapist to inquire about cognitive and affective factors that influence assertive, aggressive, passive-aggressive, and submissive responses at the moment that they occur (Epstein, 1981).

Assertion training traditionally includes practice of other expressive skills, such as constructive expression of negative feelings and giving and receiving compliments (Epstein, DeGiovanni, & Jayne-Lazarus, 1978; Lange & Jakubowski, 1976). Consequently, work with assertive deficits can be integrated with the other communication training procedures described previously.

TRAINING IN PROBLEM SOLVING

Problem solving is a specialized structured approach to communication that can help couples resolve marital conflicts. Its procedures are designed to reduce disruptive and destructive exchanges while a couple generates, evaluates, and selects solutions that are maximally beneficial to both parties. In treatment-outcome studies, problem solving has been demonstrated to be effective in increasing marital satisfaction and decreasing spouses' negative behavioral interactions, both in combination with contingency contracting procedures (Jacobson, 1977) and on its own (Jacobson, 1979).

General goals of problem solving are to substitute clear, specific definitions of problems for global descriptions, maximize effective expression and understanding of each spouse's views, and identify specific behavior changes that would alleviate a problem (Jacobson,

1981). Jacobson stresses that the problem-solving efforts of distressed couples tend to be marked by competitive struggles in which spouses assume there must be a winner and a loser. Consequently, a major therapeutic goal is the establishment of a cooperative, collaborative set in which spouses work together toward solutions involving mutual change. In order to decrease spouses' tendencies to assign blame for problems, it is helpful to coach them in identifying how a problem affects both of them and how there will be maximal progress if both parties make some changes. When a presenting problem clearly involves one spouse more than the other, the partner still can change in ways that would facilitate the former's ability to change.

The communication skills described earlier in this chapter will help establish a positive atmosphere for problem solving. For example, negative descriptions of problems and the use of derogatory trait labels (e.g., "You are lazy") are likely to elicit negative responses rather than constructive behavior change from the recipient. Consequently, skills in behavioral discrimination and positive rather than negative feeling expression should facilitate problem solving. Behaviors that tend to escalate marital conflict (e.g., cross-complaining, overgeneralization, negative nonverbal behaviors) are to be avoided, and constructive expressive and listening skills should be used throughout the problem-solving procedures (Epstein & Williams, 1981; Harrell & Guerney, 1976; Jacobson, 1981; Thomas, 1977). Jacobson (1981) emphasizes the distinction between collaborative problem solving and non-collaborative fighting by instructing a couple to move to a separate part of a room labeled a "fight corner" when engaged in the latter type of interaction.

In addition to following these basic communication procedures, couples are taught two stages of specific problem solving: (1) problem definition and (2) the determination of problem solutions (Jacobson & Margolin, 1979). The two stages are kept distinct, such that solutions are not to be suggested while the couple is in the process of defining the problem, and the generation of solutions is not to be contaminated by additional problem definition. The separation of functions reduces distraction and confusion (Jacobson, 1981). Although the structured, relatively cognitive nature of problem solving may not in itself produce warm exchanges between spouses, it can help highly distressed couples reduce their aversive, often chaotic interactions and gain a sense of greater control over their problems.

Jacobson (1981) and his colleagues have developed sets of guidelines for general problem-solving communication, for problem definition, and for generating solutions. The general guidelines instruct spouses to discuss one problem at a time, paraphrase the partner's remarks before responding to them (to reduce miscommunication and increase empathy), avoid inferences about the partner's motives, attitudes, and feelings (or at least seek information to test the validity of any hypotheses one may have about these), and avoid aversive exchanges.

When defining a problem, a spouse is instructed to begin statements with positives (e.g., prefacing a complaint or request with a reference to something the partner does). This reduces the partner's defensiveness and makes it clear to both parties that the partner is being criticized for one specific behavior and not attacked as a person in general. Also, problems should be defined in terms of specific overt behaviors rather than global characteristics; the impact of a problem on one's thoughts and feelings should be stated (this may increase sympathy); both spouses should acknowledge a role in the maintenance of the problem (which does not at this point imply a commitment to change); and def-

initions should be brief (avoiding discussions of the past, assignment of blame, and other distractions from the task at hand) (Jacobson, 1981).

The solution phase of problem solving initially involves "brainstorming," in which couples generate as many solutions as possible to the problem they have defined. The goal is to be creative and not evaluate or censor any solution at this point. In order to facilitate free expression, the therapist can stress that a solution that at first may seem silly or impractical may develop into a useful alternative when examined in greater detail later. Also, the therapist can model brainstorming, demonstrating a lack of censoring by adding some absurd, humorous solutions to the list (Jacobson, 1981). Brainstorming can reduce tension between spouses and shift them from a rigid approach to their problems to a more creative, flexible approach. Some couples experience a reduction in their sense of hopelessness when they can see that they have alternatives.

During the brainstorming process, the therapist should encourage spouses to try to include solutions that have the potential to be palatable to both of them, and solutions should be stated in specific behavioral terms. It is likely that the therapist will need to intervene in order to prevent couples from evaluating solutions during this phase.

Once a list of solutions has been generated, those that are absurd should be eliminated, and the advantages and disadvantages of each remaining alternative should be listed. Each proposed solution is evaluated in terms of feasibility, costs and benefits to each spouse, and mutual acceptability (Epstein & Williams, 1981).

A final solution may be one or a combination of the proposals. It should reflect collaboration, in that some change should be required of each spouse. The specific behaviors expected of each person should be noted, and the goals for behavior change should be graduated steps rather than major changes that may be difficult to achieve. The criteria for each spouse's performance of his or her role in the solution should be specific in order to facilitate objective evaluation. Vague agreements leave room for idiosyncratic interpretations and later arguments between spouses. Consequently, final agreements should be stated in writing and should include what is to be done, how often, when, and in what situations (Jacobson & Margolin, 1979).

New behaviors also are more likely to replace long-standing habits if cues are built in to remind each spouse of the behavior he or she has agreed to perform. Cues can include the written agreement itself, cards with brief messages posted in locations where they will be highly visible, and brief nonaversive prompts by the partner (Jacobson & Margolin, 1979).

Just as each spouse's performance of his or her behavioral role in the solution can be assessed in an ongoing manner, according to the specific criteria outlined in the formal agreement, the success of the solution in resolving the problem should be evaluated over time. For example, if a couple's problem is that they chronically get to bed so late on weekdays that they are too tired to enjoy sex, and thus their sexual relationship seems restricted to weekends, a solution might involve cooking meals that take little time to prepare and restricting the time spent on household chores during the evening. If ongoing assessment indicates that the spouses are performing as intended but the solution has not led to sufficiently earlier bedtimes, the couple may need to evaluate whether additional components of the problem need to be addressed with a revised solution; for example, routinely turning the television off by a certain hour (Epstein & Williams, 1981).

Although the statements used to define problems are likely to include *descriptions* of emotions, the problem-solving process is designed to be largely cognitive. Expression of feelings is encouraged in other arenas, but this particular task-oriented form of communication is better approached as instrumental rather than affective. As with the other forms of structured communication training described earlier, problem-solving skills can be shaped by means of instructions, repeated behavioral rehearsal, and feedback. Therapists should be active, modeling problem-solving skills, providing corrective feedback to couples as they practice, and reinforcing spouses for their successes.

The behavioral principle of stimulus control, in which the occurrence of certain behaviors is modified by altering the environment in which the behaviors typically occur, can be used to facilitate problem solving. The discriminative stimuli for problem-solving attempts are inappropriate for many couples (e.g., they discuss problems while preparing dinner or while watching television), and it often is important to restrict their problem-solving behavior to a setting that is relatively free of distractions and cues that could elicit competing responses (Weiss, Hops, & Patterson, 1973). Jacobson (1981) also suggests that when a couple follows a rule of deferring problem solving from the moment when they are upset about the occurrence of the problematic behavior to a later scheduled problem-solving time, many conflicts are diffused, and aversive exchanges are avoided.

Problem solving focuses on both process and content in a relationship (Jacobson, 1981). Thus, the outcome of training includes the resolution of particular areas of marital conflict *and* modification of the manner in which a couple interacts in order to resolve conflicts. Also, as a couple is coached toward experimentation with a collaborative effort, the positive consequences can demonstrate to them that teamwork is preferable to competition.

CONTINGENCY CONTRACTING AND MARITAL AGREEMENTS

Based on behavior exchange and social learning principles, early approaches to structured behavior therapy with couples focused on increasing rates of pleasing behaviors emitted by each spouse by means of operant conditioning principles and the establishment of formal contracts specifying the behaviors required of each person (Azrin, Naster, & Jones, 1973; Goldstein, 1971; Knox, 1971; Stuart, 1969).

Although behavioral marital therapists used a variety of procedures with distressed couples, they tended to emphasize formal contracts as the major means of implementing behavior change. These contracts sometimes were based on coercive control, such that the penalties each spouse would accrue for failure to perform were emphasized, and the use of *quid pro quo* contracts tied each partner's behavior to the other's performance; that is, "I will do X if you do Y" (Epstein & Williams, 1981). The use of a "good faith" contract, in which the contingencies for the partners' behaviors are independent and each receives rewards for appropriate performance regardless of what the other person does, has become more popular than the *quid pro quo* contract among clinicians (Epstein & Williams, 1981; Jacobson & Margolin, 1979). Also, there has been a trend toward more informal "marital agreements" in which spouses list behaviors they would like each other to increase, but "intrinsic positive consequences" such as the pleasant aspects of cooperations are used in place of formal contingencies (O'Leary & Turkewitz, 1978) and "holistic agreements" in which each partner has a variety of constructive behaviors he or she can direct toward the partner at any time (Stuart, 1980).

Behavior exchanges are difficult to implement when a couple lacks a collaborative attitude (Jacobson, 1981; Jacobson & Margolin, 1979), and the process of contracting may itself create a negative cognitive set (e.g., an individual may discount his or her partner's behavioral changes by attributing them to the contrived agreement rather than to the partner's positive intentions). However, these procedures do address some important factors in marital conflict. As noted earlier, the development of a relationship is marked by trial-and-error responding in which two partners shape each other's behaviors and establish norms for their interaction (Birchler & Spinks, 1980; Stuart, 1980). These shared expectations about what are acceptable behaviors for each person in the relationship also include sanctions for violations (Stuart, 1980). The norms of a relationship will be some blend of the expectations the two parties bring to the relationship from their past learning experiences (e.g., relationship norms modeled by their parents, standards communicated in the mass media). Although such norms are reflected in explicit rules expressed when partners describe how they want to interact, many of each individual's expectations are likely to be implicit and beyond awareness (Sager, 1976). Sager argues that overt marital conflict often arises when one person's implicit expectations or individual "contracts" are violated in interactions with the partner and the former responds with anger and disappointment as if an explicit pact had been broken. A major goal of marital therapy, then, is to make explicit the nature of each person's individual expectations and needs, identify how the ongoing "interactional contract" between spouses fails to meet individual expectations about costs and benefits to be exchanged and plan changes (in either the individual expectations or the interaction pattern) that will result in a more mutually satisfying relationship.

When spouses (commonly) do not explicitly discuss their expectations regarding their relationship as their interaction pattern is developing, potential areas of significant conflict can be created. Often the characteristics that attract people to one another can be double edged, in that these meet certain individual expectations but simultaneously violate others. For example, a person who wants a sense of security derived from a relationship with a strong, confident partner may be attracted to and enjoy an assertive person, but if that assertiveness also tends to be perceived as domineering behavior, the former individual's desire for supportive, secure caretaking may not be met. When assessing the sources of a couple's conflict with them, the therapist sometimes can reduce hostility between spouses by drawing their attention to how some of the behaviors they find distressing also have positive aspects that, in fact, had been sources of attraction. This approach can facilitate negotiation designed to save the pleasing components of spouses' behaviors while modifying those aspects that are unpleasant.

Thus, couples' relationships naturally are governed by contracts that involve individual and shared expectations and norms as well as repetitive behavioral patterns, and behavior exchange interventions with varying degrees of structure can be used to help a couple understand and modify distressing contracts. Thus, the imposition of a contract or agreement in the course of therapy only makes more explicit a basic characteristic of relationships, and this concept can be explained to couples as a prelude to behavior exchange procedures the therapist may introduce.

Stuart (1980) notes that both implicit and formal (e.g., religious or legal) relationship contracts stabilize marital interactions and specify reciprocal rights and obligations of the parties. These contracts also include sanctions and bonuses for noncompliance and extra effort, respectively. The contracts and agreements used in behavioral marital

therapy tend to have these same characteristics and therefore are not necessarily artificial. The danger lies in applying the "technology" in a superficial manner rather than as a means of making spouses aware of the expectations and desires they have for their relationship, the ways in which their current pattern of exchange fails to meet some of those expectations, and how their interactional pattern could be changed to increase the degree to which each person receives rewards from the other.

As described before, the formality and structure of behavior exchange procedures can vary considerably. In the formal quid pro quo contingency contract, each spouse agrees to behavior changes requested by the partner, with each person's compliance linked to the other's compliance. The standards and contingencies for adequate performance should be specified; the benefits and costs involved in the two partners' behavior changes should be comparable; and a plan for reinstating the exchange after an incidence of noncompliance should be outlined (Jacobson, 1981).

In a good faith contract, the reinforcement each spouse receives for performing behaviors desired by the other is independent of the positive behaviors the partner has agreed to increase. For example, in such a parallel contract a husband's reward for initiating more social activities may be an opportunity to buy some new shirts he has wanted, whereas his wife's reward for working on the family budget may be an opportunity to buy some interesting books. Jacobson (1981) argues that the danger of creating negative attributions with contingency contracts (e.g., that one's partner is behaving positively only because of the contingencies) is great enough that this form of exchange should be used with caution, and unique advantages of contingency contracts that would favor their use have not been demonstrated. Stuart (1980) voices similar concerns, stressing that quid pro quo expectancies of immediate reciprocity are likely to foster marital dissatisfaction.

In contrast, a noncontingent change agreement can help focus spouses' attention on specific behaviors they can increase that will produce greater satisfaction. Weiss (1975) suggests that contracting can serve as a form of stimulus control, providing structure and cues for spouses to behave in ways that are pleasing to each other.

In a "holistic" contract, each spouse lists things he or she would like the other to do, and there is a general expectation that each will do as many of these things as is manageable and at some agreed-upon average frequency. Either spouse can intitiate change, and the fact that each person has a variety of ways of demonstrating commitment to change should make it easier to do *something* positive even when some behaviors on the list seem uncomfortable on any particular day.

Regardless of their structure, *written* agreements are preferable (Jacobson & Margolin, 1979; O'Leary & Turkewitz, 1978). Written agreements can provide stimulus control (concrete reminders of what behaviors each spouse is to perform), increase commitment to the agreement, and avoid later conflicts resulting from differences in spouses' memories of the nature of the agreement (Jacobson, 1981).

In order to establish behavioral contracts or agreements with highly distressed couples who may enter therapy with an orientation more focused on winning than on collaboration, the therapist must establish an atmosphere of cooperation and trust. One means of doing this is for the therapist and spouses to identify clearly the gains each person can expect if the couple establishes a pattern of positive rather than negative exchange. The therapist can demonstrate *in vivo* to the couple how their aversive exchanges in the office cause pain and dissatisfaction, and the value of a "cease fire" can

be stressed. Even if spouses need to be challenged to provide positives for one another during "caring days" (Weiss, Hops, & Patterson, 1973), once the increase in positives creates a more pleasant atmosphere it often will be easier to prompt additional positive behavior. A collaborative set regarding mutual behavior change also can be facilitated with interventions directed at spouses' negative cognitive appraisals of each other and their relationship. Some basic approaches to cognitive restructuring are described next.

COGNITIVE INTERVENTIONS

Throughout this chapter, the role of cognitive processes in marital dysfunction and dissatisfaction has been noted, and ways in which structured behavioral interventions can influence spouses' cognitive appraisals of one another have been described. Although behavioral change indirectly may produce positive cognitive change, procedures focused more directly on cognitive phenomena may be necessary at a number of points when one is working with distressed couples in order to establish an optimistic collaborative set regarding mutual change efforts or to increase the degree to which spouses appraise each other's attempts at constructive behavior in a positive light. Within a cognitive/behavioral model of marital interaction, the value of any behavioral change depends on the meaning it has for the members of a couple. Cognitive variables that can influence the perceived meanings of a partner's behavior as well as approaches to modifying dysfunctional distortions in these phenomena are described next.

Assessment and Modification of Dysfunctional Beliefs

Marital therapists have stressed that unrealistic or exaggerated expectations and beliefs that individuals hold regarding the nature of intimate relationships are likely to elicit negative emotions (e.g., anger) and negative behaviors (e.g., nagging) when they are not met (Epstein & Eidelson, 1981; Jacobson & Margolin, 1979; O'Leary & Turkewitz, 1978; Stuart, 1980). Beliefs and expectations may involve extreme negative views, such as pessimism about the ability of people to change, or unrealistically positive standards, such as an expectation that loving spouses should be able to sense each others' needs without overt communication. The expectations that constitute individual "contracts" in Sager's (1976) model may be unrealistic, and resolution of marital conflicts in such a situation will depend on the establishment of more realistic standards. The perception of a behavior as positive will depend on the standards against which it is judged.

Beliefs and expectations that can affect marital satisfaction can be individually oriented standards (e.g., "Everyone must approve of me or I am worthless") or conceptions of dyadic functioning (e.g., "If my partner and I argue, our relationship will fall apart"), although Epstein and Eidelson (1981) found that the latter were more strongly associated with couples' maladjustment. Assessment of potentially dysfunctional beliefs about the self, partner, and relationship can include standard questionnaires such as Eidelson and Epstein's (1982) Relationship Belief Inventory and systematic inquiries during clinical interviews, such as the idiographic approach developed by Beck and his associates (Beck, Rush, Shaw, & Emery, 1979) in the treatment of depression. The latter procedure involves sequential questioning regarding the meanings of events that a spouse experiences as upsetting. Beginning with "automatic thoughts," or the individual's stream-of-consciousness thinking associated with negative affect, the therapist asks about the significance of the event until a "bottom line" upsetting interpretation or assumption is reached. For example, a man who be-

came anxious when his wife did not become aroused during a sexual encounter initially had the thought "I can't excite her." An inquiry by the therapist with the basic question "If that is so, then what does that mean?" produced the following chain of thoughts: "If I can't excite her, she must be losing interest in me sexually. She'll become interested in other men. She'll leave me for someone else. I have to be a perfect lover to maintain her love and interest." Such a sequence of thoughts (and perhaps visual images) can occur in a rapid reflexive manner, and the content may be distorted at any point. The man's underlying assumption that he must be a perfect lover is likely to leave him susceptible to catastrophic thinking whenever the couple's sexual relationship is other than smooth. The therapist's task is to help the client test the reality of his or her assumptions and beliefs. In the preceding example, the husband could be asked to recount past instances when the couple had an off day sexually, noting whether the wife's reactions had been severe. During conjoint marital sessions, feedback from the wife could be used for additional reality testing (Epstein, 1982).

In addition, the therapist can explore with a couple how their beliefs elicit disappointment and interfere with constructive problem solving (e.g., when the belief that spouses should be able to mind read results in a withholding of information crucial to the identification of a solution that meets a spouse's needs). Repeated reality testing will be more likely than direct challenges by a therapist to reduce spouses' defensiveness and modify long-standing beliefs (Beck et al., 1979).

The challenging of couples' beliefs and expectations is not intended to produce unrealistically positive views but rather to determine the most realistic view of a situation. When a negative expectation is found to be accurate, as when a wife's view that her husband would not tolerate her assertiveness was confirmed, other interventions may be necessary.

Reality testing can be structured with behavioral "experiments" in which spouses try behaving in a manner that they believe will have negative consequences and assess the actual impact on their relationship. Of course, the therapist should help the couple plan an initial experiment whose possible negative consequences would not damage the marriage significantly should they actually occur.

The belief that partners cannot change their relationship has been demonstrated to have a strong association with marital maladjustment (Eidelson & Epstein, 1982), and any cognitive or behavioral interventions that can counteract this hopelessness can be therapeutic. Behavioral experiments that result in changes in even the "microbehaviors" of daily interaction (Stuart, 1980) may decrease the strength of this belief. Also, data from daily records of marital interaction, such as Williams's (1979) Time Lines, can be used to demonstrate situational variation in spouses' behaviors and thereby increase optimism about change.

Modifying Dysfunctional Attributions

Clinical and research data have indicated that distressed spouses tend to attribute negative, global, stable characteristics and malevolent intentions to their partners (Baucom, Bell, & Duhe, 1982; Doherty, 1981; Epstein, 1982). Extreme attributions of malevolent intent may play a role in family violence (Gelles & Straus, 1979), and perceptions of negative traits in one's partner are likely to contribute to a sense of hopelessness about the potential for positive change. Once an individual has attributed a broad characteristic to his or her partner, he or she may be more likely to notice behaviors that are consistent with that conceptualization than those that do not fit. As noted earlier, planned behavior changes

will not have a positive impact on a relationship if an individual discounts a partner's behaviors with negative attributions (e.g., "She is acting positively only because the therapist told her to do so, and down deep she still doesn't care").

It is important to help couples differentiate between attributions that are accurate and those that are distorted. For example, if a wife accurately attributes her husband's silence to a desire on his part to inflict revenge on her for a mistake she made when disciplining the children, the appropriate intervention might include facilitating the husband's direct expression of his displeasure and instituting problem solving to devise more mutually acceptable parenting behavior. On the other hand, if the husband's silence reflects his preoccupation with a work problem, interventions might include communication training to facilitate the accurate exchange of information *and* cognitive restructuring to modify the wife's tendency to jump to conclusions in which she is responsible for her partner's negative states.

Regarding attributions that contribute to hopelessness, Hurvitz (1970) draws spouses' attention to "terminal hypotheses" or causal explanations they pose that suggest no potential for change. Terminal hypotheses a person may have for his or her partner's behavior would include trait attributions and other appraisals that the conditions influencing a problem are unlikely to change over time. Hurvitz emphasizes to a couple how their terminal hypotheses are inconsistent with efforts toward change and coaches them in substituting "instrumental hypotheses" or unstable, specific causal attributions that involve potential for change. Similarly, Baucom and Lester (1982) teach couples to view their problems in terms of specific, unstable causes and to focus on identifying their own roles in the maintenance of problems rather than blaming their partners.

As in the case of dysfunctional beliefs and expectations, problematic attributions can be assessed with standardized questionnaires (e.g., Baucom, Bell, & Duhe, 1982) or by means of systematic clinical inquiry (Beck et al., 1979).

In addition to assessing the content of negative attributions, the therapist should investigate systematic cognitive distortions or styles of thinking that contribute to such attributions. Beck and his associates (Beck et al., 1979) have identified cognitive distortions such as dichotomous thinking, overgeneralization, selective abstraction (attending only to part of the available information), and arbitrary inference, which can produce dysfunctional attributions.

Some dysfunctional attributions can be modified by means of "relabeling," a process by which the therapist substitutes a more benign meaning for the negative attribution attached to a behavior (Epstein, 1982; Jacobson & Margolin, 1979; Stuart, 1980). For example, a spouse's silence can be relabeled as "preoccupation" rather than "passive aggression." It is helpful for the therapist to promote the attitude that attributions are subjective appraisals that may be inaccurate. Training in communication skills can facilitate the exchange of information necessary for couples to test the validity of their attributions about each other.

Self-Instructional Training for the Control of Marital Interaction

The structured behavioral interventions described in this chapter are designed to build couples' skills for controlling the quality and quantity of their marital interaction. When exchanges between spouses tend to be chaotic and fueled by strong emotional responses such as anger and anxiety, self-instructional training such as that used with impulsive children (Meichenbaum, 1977) and angry adults (Novaco, 1975) can be applied to

increase spouses' self-control. Stress-inoculation training (Meichenbaum, 1977) that teaches cognitive and behavioral coping responses (how to prepare for a stressor, how to confront it, how to cope if overwhelmed by it, and how to reinforce oneself for successful coping) can be used to increase spouses' tolerance for upsetting marital interactions. Central to the application of these procedures is the generation of constructive self-statements that guide behavior (e.g., "Do not shout; speak with an even tone") and attenuate emotional responses (e.g., "Stay calm; take a deep breath and relax"). Therapists can use the procedures of modeling, rehearsal (first overt, then covert), and feedback to shape appropriate self-instructions (Epstein, 1982).

Self-instructional procedures intuitively seem quite appropriate for controlling volatile marital interaction, but as yet no research has tested the efficacy of such interventions. Consequently, clinical judgment must guide any current use of this approach with distressed couples.

SUMMARY AND CONCLUSIONS

This chapter has presented a variety of structured approaches to the modification of behavioral and cognitive factors commonly implicated in marital maladjustment. The constructive impacts of behavioral marital therapy and communication training have been demonstrated in numerous research studies, and data from initial studies of cognitive therapy with couples (e.g., Baucom & Lester, 1982; Epstein, Pretzer, & Fleming, 1982) have been encouraging. What remains to be determined is the unique contribution each of these approaches makes toward the alleviation of marital distress. Ongoing studies in several marital study centers are comparing the effects of these procedures, alone and in combination. Until a more extensive data base has been established, questions of comparative treatment efficacy and the optimal sequencing of cognitive and behavioral interventions remain unanswered. However, these structured approaches can provide the marital therapist with a repertoire of treatment strategies that can be used in a flexible manner to modify spouses' hopelessness and destructive exchanges.

REFERENCES

Abrahms, J. L.(1982). *Inducing a collaborative set in distressed couples: Nonspecific therapist–patient issues in cognitive therapy*. Paper presented at the annual meeting of the Association for the Advancement of Behavior Therapy, Los Angeles.

Abramson, L. Y., Seligman, M. E. P., & Teasdale, J. D. (1978). Learned helplessness in humans: Critique and reformulation. *Journal of Abnormal Psychology, 87*, 49–74.

Alkire, A. A., & Brunse, A. J. (1974). Impact and possible casualty from videotape feedback in marital therapy. *Journal of Consulting and Clinical Psychology, 42*, 203–210.

Azrin, N. H., Naster, B. J., & Jones, R. (1973). Reciprocity counseling: A rapid learning-based procedure for marital counseling. *Behavior Research and Therapy, 11*, 365–382.

Bandura, A. (1977). *Social learning theory*. Englewood Cliffs, NJ: Prentice-Hall.

Baucom, D. H., Bell, W. G., & Duhe, A. D. (1982). *The measurement of couples' attributions for positive and negative dyadic interactions*. Paper presented at the annual meeting of the Association for the Advancement of Behavior Therapy, Los Angeles.

Baucom, D. H., & Lester, G. (1982). *The utility of cognitive restructuring as a supplement to behavioral marital therapy*. Paper presented at the annual meeting of the Association for the Advancement of Behavior Therapy, Los Angeles.

Beach, S. R. H., Abramson, L. Y., & Levine, F. M. (1981). Attributional reformulation of learned helplessness and depression: Therapeutic implications. In J. F. Clarkin & H. I. Glazer (Eds.), *Depression: behavioral and directive intervention strategies*. New York: Garland.

Beck, A. T., Kovacs, M., & Weissman, A. (1975). Hopelessness and suicidal behavior. *Journal of the American Medical Association, 234*, 1146–1149.

Beck, A. T., Rush, A. J., Shaw, B. F., & Emery, G. (1979). *Cognitive therapy of depression*. New York: Guilford.

Birchler, G. R., & Spinks, S. H. (1980). Behavioral-systems marital and family therapy: Integration and clinical application. *American Journal of Family Therapy, 8*(2), 6–28.

Birchler, G. R., Weiss, R. L. & Vincent, J. P. (1975). A multi-method analysis of social reinforcement exchange between maritally distressed and nondistressed spouse and stranger dyads. *Journal of Personality and Social Psychology, 31*, 349–360.

Christensen, A., & Nies, D. C. (1980). The Spouse Observation Checklist: Empirical analysis and critique. *American Journal of Family Therapy, 8*(2), 69–79.

Christensen, A., Sullaway, M., & King, C. E. (1982). *Dysfunctional interaction patterns and marital happiness*. Paper presented at the annual meeting of the Association for the Advancement of Behavior Therapy, Los Angeles.

Christensen, A., Sullaway, M., & King, C. E. (1983). Systematic error in behavioral reports of dyadic interaction: Egocentric bias and content effects. *Behavioral Assessment, 5*, 129–140.

Doherty, W. J. (1981). Cognitive processes in intimate conflict: I. Extending attribution theory. *American Journal of Family Therapy, 9*, 3–13.

Eidelson, R. J., & Epstein, N. (1982). Cognition and relationship maladjustment: Development of a measure of dysfunctional relationship beliefs. *Journal of Consulting and Clinical Psychology, 50*, 715–720.

Epstein, N. (1981). Assertiveness training in marital treatment. In G. P. Sholevar

(Ed.), *The handbook of marriage and marital therapy*. New York: Spectrum.

Epstein, N. (1982). Cognitive therapy with couples. *American Journal of Family Therapy, 10*(1), 5–16.

Epstein, N., DeGiovanni, I. S., & Jayne-Lazarus, C. (1978). Assertion training for couples. *Journal of Behavior Therapy and Experimental Psychiatry, 9*, 146–156.

Epstein, N., & Eidelson, R. J. (1981). Unrealistic beliefs of clinical couples: Their relationship to expectations, goals, and satisfaction. *American Journal of Family Therapy, 9*(4), 13–22.

Epstein, N., Pretzer, J. L., & Fleming, B. (1982). *Cognitive therapy and communication training: Comparison of effects with distressed couples.* Paper presented at the annual meeting of the Association for the Advancement of Behavior Therapy, Los Angeles.

Epstein, N. & Williams, A. M. (1981). Behavioral approaches to the treatment of marital discord. In G. P. Sholevar (Ed.), *The handbook of marriage and marital therapy*. New York: Spectrum.

Geiss, S. K., & O'Leary, K. D. (1981). Therapist ratings of frequency and severity of marital problems: Implications for research. *Journal of Marital and Family Therapy, 7*, 515–520.

Gelles, R. J., & Straus, M. A. (1979). Determinants of violence in the family: Toward a theoretical integration. In W. R. Burr, R. Hill., F. I. Nye, & I. L. Reiss (Eds.), *Contemporary theories about the family* (Vol. 1). New York: Free Press.

Goldiamond, I. (1965). Self-control procedures in personal behavior problems. *Psychological Reports, 17*, 851–868.

Goldstein, M. K. (1971). *Behavior rate change in marriages: Training wives to modify husbands' behavior*. Unpublished doctoral dissertation, Cornell University.

Gottman, J., Notarius, C., Gonso, J., & Markman, H. (1976). *A couple's guide to communication*. Champaign, IL: Research Press.

Guerney, B. G., Jr. (1977). *Relationship enhancement*. San Francisco: Jossey-Bass.

Halweg, K., Revenstorf, D., & Schindler, L (1982) Treatment of marital distress: Comparing formats and modalities. *Advances in Behavior Research and Therapy, 4*, 57–74.

Harrell, J., & Guerney, B. G. Jr. (1976). Training married couples in conflict negotiation skills. In D. H. L. Olson (Ed.), *Treating relationships*. Lake Mills, IA: Graphic.

Hurvitz, N. (1970). Interaction hypotheses in marriage counseling. *Family Coordinator, 19*, 64–75.

Jacobson, N. S. (1977). Problem-solving and contingency contracting in the treatment of marital discord. *Journal of Consulting and Clinical Psychology, 45*, 92–100.

Jacobson, N. S. (1979). Increasing positive behavior in severely distressed marital relationships: The effects of problem-solving training. *Behavior Therapy, 10*, 311–326.

Jacobson, N. S. (1981). Behavioral marital therapy. In A. S. Gurman & D. P. Kniskern (Eds.)., *Handbook of family therapy*. New York: Brunner/Mazel.

Jacobson, N. S. (1982). Communication skills training for married couples. In J. P. Curran & P. M. Monti (Eds.)., *Social skills training: A practical handbook for assessment and treatment*. New York: Guilford.

Jacobson, N. S. (1984). The modification of cognitive processes in behavioral marital therapy: Integrating cognitive and behavioral intervention strategies. In K. Halweg & N. S. Jacobson (Eds.), *Marital interaction: Analysis and modification*. New York: Guilford.

Jacobson, N. S., Follette, W. C., & McDonald, D. W. (1982). Reactivity to positive and negative behavior in distressed and nondistressed married couples. *Journal of Consulting and Clinical Psychology, 50*, 706–714.

Jacobson, N. S., & Margolin, G. (1979). *Marital therapy: Strategies based on social learning and behavior exchange principles*. New York: Brunner/Mazel.

Knox, D. (1971). *Marriage happiness: a behavioral approach to counseling*. Champaign, IL: Research Press.

Lange, A. J., & Jakubowski, P. (1976). *Responsible assertive behavior: Cognitive/behavioral procedures for trainers.* Champaign, IL: Research Press.

Lewinsohn, P. M., & Arconad, M. (1981). Behavioral treatment of depression: A social learning approach. In J. F. Clarkin & H. I. Glazer (Eds.), *Depression: Behavioral and directive intervention strategies.* New York: Garland.

Liberman, R. P., Wheeler, E. G., deVisser, L. A. J. M., Kuehnel, J., & Kuehnel, T. (1980). *Handbook of marital therapy.* New York; Plenum.

Liberman, R. P., Wheeler, E., & Sanders, N. (1976). Behavioral therapy for marital disharmony: An educational approach. *Journal of Marriage and Family Counseling, 2,* 383–395.

Margolin, G. (1983). An interactional model for the behavioral assessment of marital relationships. *Behavioral Assessment, 5,* 103–127.

Markman, H. J., & Floyd, F. (1980). Possibilities for the prevention of marital discord: A behavioral perspective. *American Journal of Family Therapy, 8*(2), 29–48.

Markman, H. J., Floyd, F. J., Stanley, S., & Jamieson, K. (1984). A cognitive/behavioral program for the prevention of marital and family distress: Issues in program development and delivery. In N. S. Jacobson & K. Halweg (Eds.), *Marital interaction: Analysis and modification.* New York: Guilford.

Mehrabian, A. (1972). *Nonverbal communication.* Chicago: Aldine Atherton.

Meichenbaum, D. (1977). *Cognitive-behavior modification: An integrative approach.* New York: Plenum.

Novaco, R. (1975). *Anger control: The development and evaluation of an experimental treatment.* Lexington, MA: Heath.

O'Leary, K. D., & Turkewitz, H. (1978). Marital therapy from a behavioral perspective. In T. J. Paolino & B. S. McCrady (Eds.), *Marriage and marital therapy: Psychoanalytic, behavioral and systems theory perspectives.* New York: Brunner/Mazel.

Raush, H. L., Barry, W. A., Hertel, R. K., & Swain, M. A. (1974). *Communication, conflict and marriage.* San Francisco: Jossey-Bass.

Rehm, L. P. (1981). A self-control therapy program for treatment of depression. In J. F. Clarkin & H. I. Glazer (Eds.), *Depression: Behavioral and directive intervention strategies.* New York: Garland.

Ryder, R. G. (1968). Husband–wife dyads versus married strangers. *Family Process, 7,* 233–238.

Sager, C. J. (1976). *Marriage contracts and couple therapy.* New York: Brunner/Mazel.

Satir, V. (1967). *Conjoint family therapy* (rev. ed.) Palo Alto, CA: Science and Behavior Books.

Stuart, R. B. (1969). Operant-interpersonal treatment for marital discord. *Journal of Consulting and Clinical Psychology, 33,* 675–682.

Stuart, R. B. (1980). *Helping couples change: A social learning approach to marital therapy.* New York: Guilford.

Thibaut, J. W., & Kelley, H. H. (1959). *The social psychology of groups.* New York: Wiley.

Thomas, E. J. (1977). *Marital communication and decision making: Analysis, assessment, and change.* New York: Free Press.

Vincent, J. P., Weiss, R. L., & Birchler, G. R. (1975). A behavioral analysis of problem solving in distressed and nondistressed married and stranger dyads. *Behavior Therapy, 6,* 475–487.

Watzlawick, P., Beavin, J. H., & Jackson, D. D., (1967). *Pragmatics of human communication: A study of interactional patterns, pathology, and paradoxes.* New York: Norton.

Weiss, R. L. (1975). Contracts, cognition, and change: A behavioral approach to marriage therapy. *Counseling Psychologist, 5,* 15–26.

Weiss, R. L. (1978). The conceptualization of marriage from a behavioral perspective. In T. J. Paolino & B. S. McCrady (Eds.), *Marriage and marital therapy: Psychoanalytic, behavioral and systems theory perspectives.* New York: Brunner/Mazel.

Weiss, R. L. (1980). Strategic behavioral

marital therapy: Toward a model for assessment and intervention. In J. P. Vincent (Ed.), *Advances in family intervention, assessment and theory: An annual compilation of research* (Vol. 1). Greenwich, CT: JAI Press.

Weiss, R. L., Hops, H., & Patterson, G. R. (1973). A framework for conceptualizing marital conflict, a technology for altering it, some data for evaluating it. In L. A. Hamerlynck, L. C. Handy, & E. J. Mash (Eds.), *Behavior change: Methodology,* *concepts and practice*. Champaign, IL: Research Press.

Weiss, R. L., & Margolin, G. (1977). Marital conflict and accord. In A. R. Ciminero, K. S. Calhoun, & H. E. Adams (Eds.), *Handbook for behavioral assessment*. New York: Wiley.

Williams, A. M. (1979). The quantity and quality of marital interaction related to marital satisfaction: A behavioral analysis. *Journal of Applied Behavior Analysis, 12, 665–678.*

CHAPTER 20

The Relationship Enhancement
Family of Family Therapies

LOUISE GUERNEY AND BERNARD GUERNEY, JR.

HISTORY OF RELATIONSHIP
ENHANCEMENT THERAPIES

In the past, Relationship Enhancement (RE) methods have often been given other names related to the specific programs or populations toward whom the therapy was directed. Child Relationship Enhancement therapy, which was called Filial Therapy (Guerney, 1964), was the first of the Relationship Enhancement programs. It is a form of therapy for children with behavioral and emotional adjustment problems in which the parents are used as the therapeutic agents. The major therapeutic strategy is to teach parents play therapy as practiced by Axline (1969) and other Rogerian child therapists, such as Dorfman (1958), Ginott (1961), and Moustakas (1973). The parents are also taught behavioral techniques helpful in socializing their children. It was a major departure from other therapies in its use of programmatic skill training and the systematic use of parents as psychotherapeutic agents.

Each new development in the RE programs has served to broaden the application of the concepts and principles of RE to additional family constellations. Usually, an RE program of a new type is empirically tested before being introduced to the professional community. Each new program is developed with several objectives in mind:

1. To use the modality for training that is most suitable to the developmental level of the target family members.

2. To contain skills relevant to the relationships addressed.

3. To develop processes that will meet the psychosocial needs of nearly all families or family subunits at their respective ages and stages of family life, thereby reducing the necessity of generating unique prescriptions on a family-by-family basis.

4. To utilize the strengths of the relationships to overcome any deficits present.

5. To promote the acquisition of positive behaviors as the way to eliminate inappropriate behaviors.

6. To build in components that will allow the participants to master the use of skills in daily life as well as inside the training situation.

7. To enhance and enrich the quality of the relationship and to build habits and skills that will help maintain gains, prevent relapse, and avoid the development of new problems.

8. To make the therapeutic strategy and

methods teachable and replicable by other professionals.

9. To test the efficacy of the program through empirical studies.

RE is a blend of psychodynamic, behavioral, and humanistic approaches. Sensitivity and empathy to the feelings of others and awareness and assertion of one's own feelings as well as behavior modification principles and skills are taught using reinforcement and other learning principles. In RE, feelings and interpersonal needs are first clarified; then, in relation to important instrumental issues, task performance and task management are dealt with. The affective components come first and continue to be included in the examination of instrumental solutions.

Although the usual rapport with the therapist and client attribution of expertise to the therapist is essential to RE, over the years since Filial Therapy (FT) was introduced, the method has been developed to place the power to effect changes in the hands of the individuals involved in the relationship. RE therapies tend to promote equality among family members in contributing to decision making and to the process of change. This equality, however, is modified by each participant's capacity (based on experience, intelligence, etc.) to make useful contributions. Hence, the relative power to influence the process and contribute to decisions is correlated with age. The relative inability of young children to be full participants in decision making makes Child RE quite different in some respects from RE with other populations. Thus, in Child RE, more so than in Family RE, the therapist is an active advocate of the child and must teach the parents more skills to allow them to elicit and understand the needs of the child.

The Child, Marital, and Family RE programs regard the relationship as the primary client. So that, even if for some reason beyond the control of all involved, it would be impossible to include all members involved in a family subunit, such as the second marital partner, the relationship with the missing partner may still be a central agenda item.

In the early 1970s, those involved in the development of RE methods paused along the way to look at what they were doing at the metalevel. As the RE programs were being studied and revised, it became apparent that in addition to a new treatment model per se, a new model of intervention services delivery, which was feasible and desirable, was being practiced as well. This has been labeled the *educational model* (Guerney, 1982; Guerney, Guerney, & Stollak, 1971, 1972; Guerney, Stollak, & Guerney, 1970, 1971). The recognition that the systematic use of educational methodology as opposed to medical methodology was a key component to this new model helped us to sharpen our understanding of RE processes. An example of the method is the principle of assigning roles to participants in therapy that allows them to function at their highest and best possible levels. Translated to treatment operations, this means that the therapist does not reserve knowledge and skills for him/herself that clients could learn and apply for therapeutic change in themselves and others. In recent literature in the community psychology field, the concept of *empowerment* has been introduced to mean a similar thing (Jacobs, 1980; Rappaport, 1981)). However, the educational model implies more than the appropriateness of empowerment, or giving participants as much of the knowledge and skill of the professional as is appropriate to age, limits of services, and specific client circumstances. The educational model further suggests that the terminology, technology, institutional and organizational features for implementing the treatment should, whenever feasible, be those of the teacher as opposed to the physician.

In addition, the educational model further implies that the desire for learning skills and the purpose of teaching them need not be rigidly divided into treatment, and primary, secondary, and tertiary prevention. Instead of trying to decide whether clients are "normal" or "pathological," and if the latter, what specifically is "wrong," one asks only the following: What skills could enhance these relationships and increase the family's abilities to succeed in carrying out developmental tasks? When presented with an assignment of program development, the educational model requires the developer to ask: What do family members need to learn and how shall it be taught to them most efficiently? What is the highest/lowest professional level required to provide effective leadership? How can transfer outside of the teaching situation be promoted? How can generalization be furthered? How can we best assure that the skills taught will not fall into disuse and fade?

Such questions greatly simplify the task of program design for new populations or new skills areas. They have enabled us to design special programs for foster parents (L. Guerney, 1976, 1977; L. Guerney & Wolfgang, 1981) and parents of adolescents at risk for maltreatment. Colleagues using the same model have designed programs developed for Child RE for the training of day care workers (Kostelnik, 1978) and child service case workers (Sywulak, 1978). When designing programs for members outside of the family, the educational model requires an analysis of the basic tasks of a role, such as day-care worker. The study of several day-care centers might be required to get such a definition of role tasks if one is designing a generic "day-care worker model." This can then be modified to emphasize the task needs of centers that differ from the generic profile.

The principles of the educational model permit the same flexibility within the Family RE approaches. For instance, in dealing with single parents or parents in reconstituted or "blended" families, if additional skills are seen to be needed, these can be added to the skills of the basic Child or Family RE model.

As the clients in our FT groups tried to use the psychotherapeutic skills taught them, they frequently used them with other family members as well as their young children. Such generalization was encouraged even in the earliest Filial Therapy groups. Their reports of success encouraged us in going on to design the Marital and Family RE programs.

Major Components of Child RE Therapy

Child Relationship Enhancement therapy (CRE) contains both process and content features that classify it as a skills-oriented approach. Skills in play therapy are taught to parents using both modern and age-old methods of behavioral skills training. A group format is preferred for the training for efficiency and the benefits of group support. However, especially in private practice, parents also participate on an individual basis or as couples.

After the first session in which the rationale for the approach and an overview of the program format are presented, sessions follow the following format: (1) play therapy demonstration by the therapist; (2) observed practice by parents; (3) feedback to parents; (4) dynamic processing; and (5) assignment and explanations for the next session. Several phases can be identified in the therapy process: (1) training in play therapy skills; (2) home play sessions; (3) transfer and generalization; and (4) phaseout. During phases 3 and 4 the home assignments are home play sessions or variations on play sessions. Starting with transfer and generalization and on through the phaseout period, training in how to transfer playroom skills outside of the playroom are included. The phases may be briefly summarized as follows.

Each stage is eased into the next stage, overlapping somewhat with the previous and/or next stage rather than being sharply demarcated. As parents evidence not only skilled play session behaviors but also clarity of purpose, ease, and proficiency in the therapist role, it is time to move them onto the next task. A challenge for greater mastery must always be ahead to keep parents motivated. In each stage, references are made to what will be coming in future stages so that parents are primed for them when they are introduced.

Phase 1—Training in Play Therapy Skills

For the first three to five sesssions of a group, depending on group size, the therapist demonstrates how to conduct a child-centered play therapy session, with the parents observing. Following the session, parents are helped to identify how play therapy behaviors differ from ordinary interactions, the effects of the difference, and the qualities of the therapist's verbal and nonverbal responses.

The philosophy, rationale, theoretical basis, and empirical evidence of the approach are presented in relation to the play session behavior of the therapist. Much attention is paid to the child's reactions to the therapist's approach to demonstrate that avoidance of the more typical adult responses of teaching, threatening, and the like can result in desirable child behaviors. The value of both acceptance and reasonable limits are pointed out in events of the demonstration sessions. Parents usually are fascinated to see their children's reactions to the play therapist's approach and become eager to conduct sessions themselves in spite of the fact that at this point most are also apprehensive about their ability to perform in the therapist's role.

Following the demonstrations, subcomponents of the play therapist's role behaviors are taught and practiced by the parents with feedback and much positive reinforcement from the therapist. The principle of shaping and rewarding closest approximations is practiced by the therapist in reinforcing these tentative efforts of the parents. However, there is also much noncontingent encouragement and praise for effort. Observation of performance permits the identification of weakness and strengths. The amount of practice and the pace for the individuals in training can then be determined. In the group format, a group is paced according to the middle-level performers. Accelerated members assist the others. In the rare instances when it is required, group members who are much slower to learn than other group members are offered one or two additional training sessions apart from their group.

At this stage, parents are told not to try to use any of the skills at home. This admonition has two effects. It reassures parents that it is not yet expected that they will really know the finer points of the skills. Mostly, however, it spares them from failure experiences that premature usage might generate.

Observed Parent Practice

After a minimal mastery of the skills and procedures of the play session, parents conduct 15-minute play sessions that are observed by all present. In a couple or group format, other parents observe along with the therapist. Parents play separately with each of their children included in the program (all between the ages of 3–12 are participants as well as the target child). They start with the one that all agree will be the easiest to work with. Following these demonstrations, the therapist and other parents provide *positive* feedback and suggestions for alternate behaviors for future sessions.

Dynamic Processing

Discussions follow or are intermingled with the feedback to provide the parents with an opportunity to process what they have learned and to examine their own feelings and other phenomenological aspects of the new behaviors they are attempting to acquire. It is an important aspect of the dynamic part of our dynamic-didactic approach (Andronico, Fidler, Guerney, & Guerney, 1967). An experiment that omitted the processing or dynamic aspects, dwelling only on teaching and feedback on performance competence, revealed no greater gains in a 13-week period of parent participation than a no-treatment control group of parents, whereas parents engaged in the dynamic-didactic approach showed significantly more improvement in the same length of time (Eardley, 1978). The therapist's behavior in these dynamic exchanges is important to the parent's feelings of being understood and accepted. However, therapist behavior always circles back toward the didactic skills training component.

Phase 2—Home Sessions

After parents have had a minimum of two supervised sessions, they are ready to begin their home sessions. Home sessions are 30–45 minutes long (always starting with only 15 minutes for the first home session). If two parents participate, the child will have one session per week with each parent in most instances. In the event that there are a number of children in the family participating or parents cannot afford that much time, parents will alternate children so that each child will have one session with the father one week and the next week's session with the mother. Other particulars of home sessions—for example, place, toys, and so on—are carefully structured.

Parents report on their home sessions, and positive reinforcement and alternative suggestions are offered. Behavioral replays of difficulties are conducted to help parents handle such situations better in future sessions. By this time in

Group Child RE, other participants, without becoming negative, freely provide feedback and express great empathy for each other's problems in carrying out their roles or in accepting difficult behavior from their children. Husbands and wives typically do not engage in rivalries or carry over negative relationship patterns into the FT sessions. The novelty of the task and the effects of modeling and structuring seem to be so strong that these do not seem to transfer over. This is perhaps assisted by the therapist's strategy of dealing with the parents as individuals instead of as a couple.

Home sessions continue until two criteria for progress are met in relation to the child. First, the parents, teachers, and other relevant observers are able to report significant progress in the outside world of the child. Second, there is evidence in the child's play sessions that she/he is in the final stages of play therapy. This is usually considered to be a point where the child appears to have resolved conflicts and is demonstrating positive feelings and actions toward him/herself and others in his play (Dorfman, 1958; Moustakas, 1973). Demonstrations continue at the treatment site to monitor progress and to keep skills sharpened.

Phase 3—Transfer and Generalization

While conducting play sessions, parents are prepared for trying to use skills outside in daily life by frequent references to future generalizations. In Group CRE, as soon as the *first* parent in the group reaches an appropriate skill level, this parent is guided to think about what happens in "real life" when parent and/or child experience the feelings evidenced in the play sessions. Does the child strike out? Does the parent withdraw? Analyses of differences between processes in the play session and real-life expressions are made. Parents are urged to pick out a specific, easy situation to attempt to introduce the *same elements* into real life that work in the play session. Elements are what is transferred, not the whole structure of the play sessions. From the beginning, with the advice not to try skills until later, every effort is made to be certain that parents do not try to equate parent behavior in play sessions with daily parenting. The different goals and responsibilities in the two roles are spelled out.

At the transference and generalization stage, however, parents are shown through observation and analysis that *certain aspects* of the play therapist role have legitimate application at home. Empathic responses, realistic expectations, structuring for certain behaviors or for eliminating certain behaviors, designation of few but very firm limits, appropriate consequences, allowing maximal self-direction to the child in relation to age and circumstances, and the expectation that the child will behave maturely if he or she is understood and accepted are appropriate in daily life. The parent already understands these concepts and has mastered their application in the play sessions. Now, at this stage, the parent is asked, for example, "How might limit setting work at home?" or "Billy seemed to gather up the courage to try again in the play session when he couldn't get those difficult pieces together. What's different that makes him give up so quickly in the home situation you've just described?" The way the parent handled the situation differently is identified. The way the parent might be able to employ the type of response she or he learned when acting as a therapist is explained. The parent then realizes how the more appropriate response might be applied in daily life situation. Possible complications and resistance by the child are dealt with dynamically and didactically. The reader should remember that the dynamic part is rarely confrontative but nearly always consists of empathic responses and/or open-ended leads.

By the end of the program, parents have carried out many carefully rehearsed applications in a variety of settings. The Rogerian play therapist's skills do not include use of the skills of reinforcement or statement of the adult's personal feelings and desires except in the very narrow area of personal limits on child session behavior. However, it is our belief that in real life, parents must be expert in both these skills as well as those that arise out of play sessionss. Therefore, all of these skills are systematically taught and practiced as presented in a parenting skills manual (Guerney, 1979a) used in parenting skills classes.

Phaseout Stage

The goal at this stage is greater independence for parents. In this phase, the therapist provides the support necessary to achieve independence through further helping parents to generalize the skills and attitudes acquired in the role of play therapist. Parents continue to hold "special times" with their children after play sessions have finished. These are scheduled times for the parent to provide the child with uninterrupted individual attention and caring, as in the play session. Also, as in the play session, the parent permits the child as much self-direction as is possible, starting with the child's selection of what he or she would like to do within the parameters of the parent's ability to accept the activity. Children choose game playing (at home or at video game sites), trips to local stores (spending amounts that are structured in advance) treats at fast-food restaurants, and so forth. The guideline for the child is "something you like to do and don't usually get time to do" with your parent. Discussion of how special times are progressing for both parent and child are conducted in the closeout phase. Meetings are scheduled at this point every 3 to 4 weeks and continue for approximately 3 months after the weekly meetings have finished. The total time for Group Child RE weekly meetings usually lasts about 4 to 5 months and the phaseout time brings the length of the entire treatment to about 6 to 7 months. In a nongroup format, the treatment can require as few as 2 months because the concentration is solely on one parent or one couple.

Overview of Applications and Outcomes

CRE is considered most appropriate for children 3 years through 10 years of age —when play is the major expressive medium. More recently, in order to accommodate child clients older than 10, but still not mature enough to participate fully in Family RE, we have been instructing parents from the beginning of treatment to use special times with these children instead of play sessions.

Although the modal child client has been an 8-year-old boy of white, high-school-eduated parents, neither clinical experience nor empirical evidence suggests that Child RE is inappropriate for children of other backgrounds. Children of both sexes, black and white and Puerto Rican, (Ginsberg, Stutman, & Hummel, 1978) of all (appropriate) ages and socioeconomic backgrounds have responded favorably to CRE. In relation to diagnostic categories of children, there appear to be few restrictions. Although we have not applied it with genuinely autistic children and have not ourselves recommended it for them, a group at the University of Texas at Galveston (Hornsby & Appelbaum, 1978) reports successful use with autistic children.

Early work with the method was confined to children with difficulties of a strictly psychological etiology. Any child whose history indicated even the possibility of brain damage was excluded and given more conventional treatment. However, mainly through inaccurate referral diagnoses, many children have been included who were later revealed to have minimal brain dysfunction (MBD)

and other organically based problems. (L. Guerney, 1979b; Harrell & Dewitt, 1981). As a group, they, too, showed excellent improvement in their social and psychological adjustment. Thus, in the past 10 years, it has been our practice to include for treatment of their psychosocial disturbances children with organically based difficulties including epilepsy and mild cerebral palsy. Maladjusted children with physical handicaps have also participated with successful improvement in their psychosocial adjustment, including some with muscular dystrophy and with hearing and visual impairments. Children who are retarded and whose mental ages are within the appropriate age range have shown similar improvement. The mother of one was herself retarded. She was able to conduct short play sessions at the treatment site (none were assigned for home) in an acceptable manner. Abused and neglected and foster and adopted children are other subgroups who have benefitted from the program.

There are no groups of parents who would, ipso facto, be disqualified for inclusion in Child RE. Child abusers, alcoholics, socially and emotionally immature individuals, and other clinical categories have been seen successfully. Although no single clinical category of parents could now be cited as better or worse than any other, caution should be exercised in recommending CRE to parents who lack the personal and/or instrumental resources to attend sessions on a regular basis for an extended time period. Parents lacking such resources are those most likely to be lost through attrition. There is little point in including such parents if, as a result, one must exclude those who will more likely be able to remain in treatment. For example, the parent who has no car and must depend on a relative's schedule for transportation from a distant community is less likely to find it possible to complete the program than a parent not facing such obstacles to regular attendance. Alternate CRE formats, such as individual marathon and minimarathon sessions have not been attempted with such cases. Such formats might help overcome such problems.

In our programs at Rutgers (Guerney, 1964; Guerney & Stover, 1971) and at Penn State, we have accepted mothers as sole participants either for research reasons or simply because their husbands could not or would not participate. Some Child RE practitioners insist that both parents must attend. Studies conducted at Penn State in Group Child RE have not demonstrated more gains in children with both parents participating than with one parent, when the therapy has been completed (Sensué, 1981; Sywulak, 1977). However, we have noted that parents without partners are more likely to fail to complete the program, primarily because of resource limitations, particularly if they are working mothers.

Our current attrition rate is low, with an acceptance of the treatment recommendation of 85% or better and a completion of the program rate of approximately two-thirds.

Outcomes for children have been consistently favorable, measured in terms of problem reduction (Guerney & Stover, 1971; Horner, 1974; Oxman, 1971; Sensué, 1981; Sywulak, 1977) as reported by parents, therapists, and, in some instances, corroborated by teachers (Eardley, 1978). Child behaviors in play sessions have demonstrated the acquisition of positive behaviors and the reduction of negative behaviors (Guerney & Stover, 1971). Formerly deviant children are not significantly different from normal children following CRE treatment (Oxman, 1971; Sensué, 1981).

Parents have demonstrated their ability to master the play therapist behaviors and to increase the amount of self-direction they permit to children, increase their use of empathic responses, and

increase their active involvement with their children in the play sessions (Guerney & Stover, 1971). They have also increased their acceptance of their children on the Porter Parental Acceptance Scale (Porter, 1954) from pre- to posttreatment, with no changes during an equivalent wait period (Sywulak, 1977). Further, they increase their acceptance scores to exceed those of parents of nonproblematic children in a 3-year follow-up study, during which time they reported continued improvement in their children as well. Prior to and early in treatment, these parents had demonstrated lower scores on the Porter, relative to the norms on the scale (Sensué, 1981).

Current Status of Child Relationship Enhancement Therapy

A number of studies have demonstrated that a great variety of children and parents improve on important dimensions in Child RE and that the changes are not due to time alone or testing and observation alone and that normality is restored to children. However, because of the very formidable practice and methodological problems involved, many questions have not yet been addressed in relation to this treatment approach that should be addressed. Outstanding among these are the following:

1. How does FT compare to other treatment methods used for similar symptoms, for example, behavioral approaches? Or a traditional parent counseling/child play therapy approach that does not give therapeutic responsibilities to the parents?

2. How much generalization of the skills of the playroom to real-life use is made by parents? To date, only anecdotal evidence (and the positive outcomes) indicates that there is.

3. What parts of the Child RE programs are the most critical? We know

that the exclusion of the dynamic elements resulted in less progress (Eardley, 1978). We also know that changes appear to occur in parental acceptance before child problems are reported as significantly decreased (Sywulak, 1977). However, it is not clear whether the training in play sessions or the play sessions at home or which single or combination of components is most essential to promoting the significant changes noted.

MARITAL AND FAMILY RE THERAPIES

Major Components

Marital and Family RE therapies integrate a number of psychotherapeutic theories and practices. The rationale underlying the therapeutic approach includes elements from Freud, Adler, Rogers, Skinner, Bandura, Dollard, and Miller, and, most importantly, Harry Stack Sullivan as his work was further developed by Timothy Leary. Essentially, we regard the task of RE therapy as changing personality and interpersonal relationships by teaching people to consciously control what previously had been unconsciously determined interpersonal behaviors. This brings their behavior into the service of their conscious goals, and, in fact, helps them to understand better what their goals truly are. To implement their own goals, they must learn to coordinate the satisfaction of their needs with the satisfaction of the needs of others. Thus, the objectives sought are greater self-understanding, greater mutual understanding, and a high level of need satisfaction among the family members.

To help them reach these goals, clients are taught nine sets of skills. For each skill, there are clearly specified guidelines to follow (B. Guerney, 1977; Preston & Guerney, 1982). Here, space forbids inclusion of the guidelines. Instead, each skill set will be described in terms of its purpose.

1. *Expressive* skill helps the client (1) to understand his/her own emotional/psychological/interpersonal needs; (2) to express his/her desires and emotions to others in ways that minimize the others' defensiveness, anxiety, conflict, and hostility, and maximize the probability that others will respond sympathetically, with understanding, and with cooperation; and (3) to deal with interpersonal conflicts and problems promptly and positively.

2. *Empathic* skill helps the client (1) to gain an increased understanding of the emotional/psychological/interpersonal needs of others; and (2) elicit from others more prompt, frequent, open, relevant, intimate, honest, and trusting behaviors.

3. *Conversive* ("Mode-Switching") skill helps the client to create and maintain a positive emotional climate when attempting to resolve issues, accomplish goals, solve problems, and negotiate conflicts. It enables the client to avoid unnecessary and damaging sidetracks and to bring discussions to root issues more quickly.

4. *Problem-Solving/Conflict Resolution* skill helps the client to develop and to help others to develop creative solutions to problems and to attain agreement on problems that are mutually satisfactory and are therefore likely to prove sound and durable.

5. *Self-Changing* skill helps the client to implement changes in attitudes/feelings/behaviors in the service of carrying out interpersonal agreements and objectives

6. *Other-Changing* skill helps the client to help others to change their attitudes/feelings/behaviors so as to implement interpersonal agreements and objectives successfully.

7. *Generalization* skill helps the client to train him/herself to use RE skills in daily life.

8. *Teaching* ("Facilitative") skills helps the client to train others to treat the client in ways that are likely to improve the client's self-image, psychological well-being, and interpersonal relations.

9. *Maintenance* skill helps the client to maintain skills over long periods of time.

In teaching these skills, the RE therapist attempts to be honest and compassionate and to convey enthusiasm and competence. When RE is applied in a group format, he or she endeavors also to display impartiality and fairness. The therapist endeavors to motivate and inspire clients to acquire the necessary attitudes and skills by linking them to the clients' important life goals, especially interpersonal goals. The therapist tries to instill and to maintain clients' confidence in their ability to learn and to change. To do this, the therapist elicits and resolves client doubts through evidence, reason, and by pacing skills practice and problem solving in such a way as to promote successful experiences. The therapist uses encouragement and praise very liberally.

Marital and Family RE therapists avoid certain categories of therapeutic responses that are used in most other types of marital and family therapy because they are regarded as generally counterproductive. Among the responses generally avoided are (1) Directive Leads, in which the therapist asks questions designed to direct the client's attention to content areas that the therapist thinks are important to solving the clients' problems; (2) Interpretation (trying to give the clients insight into the nature of specific problems by pointing out causal connections of which the client is unaware; (3) Suggestion, Explanation, or Advice concerning norms or the nature of the clients' problems; (4) Encouragement, Approval, or Reassurance regarding the clients' problems; and (5)

Criticisms or Feedback on Content; for example, comments aimed at improving the clients with respect to their character, motives, attitudes, or behaviors. Instead of using such responses, the therapist teaches the clients skills designed to allow the clients themselves to accomplish the objectives that therapists seek when they use such responses.

The responses the therapist does use to accomplish those objectives are limited to seven. These responses are (1) Administrative (seeing that the session proceeds smoothly); (2) Social Reinforcement; (3) Demonstrating (illustrating skilled behaviors and linking them to the skill guidelines); (4) Modeling, that is, behaving in the same way she or he advocates for clients and also providing specific statements for the client to "copy"; (5) Encouraging and Prompting (eliciting appropriate portions of a skilled response); and (6) Doubling (speaking for clients when they are unable to speak in an appropriately skillful fashion for themselves). Troubleshooting, the seventh response, is infrequently used, but it is very important. It allows the therapist, following certain guidelines, to do things that are generally proscribed in RE therapy. It enables the therapist, *under carefully defined circumstances,* to express her/his own opinion, to offer interpretations, to make suggestions, to discuss her/his own feelings about the client's problems or the therapeutic process, and to provide empathy, nurturance, reassurance, and support *directly* to the client instead of channeling it through other family members as the RE therapist usually does.

In order to maximize chances for success, the clients are guided to choose topics in gradually increasing order of difficulty. First, they discuss their views and feelings on a topic they have strong feelings about, but which in no way involves other family members who may be present. Such topics are used until, and only until, Empathic skill has been learned moderately well. Next, clients discuss their positive attitudes, feelings, and opinions of other family members who are physically present. (With many cases, we have clients begin each homework session, and sometimes each practice session with the therapist, by sharing positive views.) Next, clients discuss enhancement issues. *Enhancement issues* are defined as suggestions that a client has for improving the relationship or improving satisfactions within the family that they believe the others are also likely to find agreeable or at least nonobjectionable. Next, clients are asked to discuss mild problems/conflicts. Then, they discuss moderate problems, next, serious problems. When all significant problems/conflicts are resolved, attention turns to enhancement and enrichment issues once again.

Usually beginning in the very first session, clients are given home assignments to complete. Homework may consist of one or more of the following tasks: reading about the skills; listening to tapes demonstrating the skills; 20 minutes to several hours per week of practicing the skills (sometimes, tape recorded); completion/revision of the Relationship Questionnaire to select topics for discussion; completion of the Home Practice Form that briefly records their reaction to the home practice sessions; and, Generalization Logs that report the how and why of their use or failure to use skills during their daily life.

Intermittently, most frequently in the early stages, clients are asked to listen to audiotapes that illustrate the use of RE skills in discussions of a variety of family problems (Guerney & Vogelsong, 1981). These tapes are from the same series used by the therapist to demonstrate the skills within the sessions. Each of these audiotapes begins with a brief dialogue between the couple showing how the discussion of a given issue or conflict is likely to proceed without the use of skills. That segment is followed by a longer dialogue of about 20 minutes in which the couple discusses the same issue using RE skills. The non-skilled segment is usually not asigned except in the initial introduction to the skills and the first home use of such tapes. (Information about these tapes and about the Relationship Questionnaire and the Home Practice Form is available from B. Guerney at Catherine Beecher House, University Park, PA. 16802.)

Once the basic skills have been learned, the typical sequence in an RE session is as follows. First, the therapist provides supervision and reinforcement of homework. Next, the therapist gives follow-up on previously resolved problems that are due for reevaluation, thus reinforcing the clients for successes and reopening problem solving where difficulties have been encountered. Next, in many cases, the sharing by clients of positive attitudes/feelings/behaviors about one another often takes place. Next, the topics listed on the Relationship Questionnaire by the clients as most important to relationships are reviewed by client and therapist and an appropriate topic is chosen for problem solving. (The therapist does not allow substitutions of less fundamentally important topics however salient they may be unless it arises out of a genuine crisis and urgently requires attention or decision making.) Then, the therapist supervises the clients as they make use of their skills in dealing with the problem issue. Once initiated, each problem is followed directly through to its solution within the session or at home unless it evolves into another deeper problem requiring discussion and problem resolution. In the last 5 minutes or so of each session, the therapist prepares the clients to do their home assignment. (Until the clients have established a record of faithfully executing assignments, the therapist always ascertains the particular time, place, and circumstances when the homework will be carried out.)

RE programs cover virtually the full range of formats. RE enrichment and problem prevention programs typically are "time-limited" therapy, running for a set length of time. RE therapy programs are not time-limited nor are they open-ended. We have coined the term *time-designated* to describe the typical time format of RE. By time-designated, we mean that an initial informal contract about time is worked out by the therapist and the client(s). The amount of time decided upon is not viewed as the upper limit of the number of sessions but rather as a time at which progress will be evaluated to determine whether further sessions are indicated. At that time, it may be decided that the goal has been met. If not, another time is designated for the next evaluation. In our view, this time-designated format is one that best resolves the advantages and disadvantages of the time-limited and open-ended approaches. It provides clients and therapist alike with a goal to strive for and at the same time does not prematurely cut off people who might well profit from further sessions using the therapeutic process.

RE therapy can be used for individual psychotherapy. If interpersonal relations are the primary problem, it could be the primary strategy used in individual therapy. In other cases, where a lack of self-confidence, shyness, or poor self-image is only a part of the problem of the individual, it could be used along with other therapeutic methods. Primarily, however, RE therapy has been used in marital/family therapy. Marital or Family RE therapy can be used with an individual, with a dyad, with a larger family unit, or with a group of individuals, a group of dyads, or group of families. Family RE therapy, for example, can be applied with only one member of a family attending throughout the entire course of therapy if others in the family are unwilling or unable to come (a format we have termed *unilateral* Marital/Fam-

ily RE). Family therapy has been applied with a subgroup from the family—for example, a mother and daughter. It also has been applied with the entire family as a unit, and with groups comprised of two or more whole family units or of subunits of two or more families.

An "intensive" or "extensive" format could be used with any of the preceding groupings. By *intensive*, we mean a marathon session lasting 8 hours or a weekend, or a minimarathon session lasting 3 or 4 hours. *Extensive* refers to sessions lasting an hour or two and spread out over many weeks at the rate of once or twice a week. Combinations of intensive and extensive formats also may be used.

Overview of Applications

Whenever better relationships with others would be of help, RE is appropriate either as the single therapy or in conjunction with other types of therapies. The criterion for screening out clients would be a mental age of less than approximately 10–12 years or the lack of sufficient reality contact to attend to instruction. RE therapy has been found to be helpful with chronic schizophrenics (Malone, 1982; Vogelsong, Guerney, & Guerney, 1983); alcoholic couples (Armenti, 1980; Waldo & Guerney, 1983); spouse abusers (Waldo, Guerney, & Firestone, 1984); in the treatment of depression (Ginsberg, 1981); of severely disturbed delinquents (Welsh, 1982); drug addicts in rehabilitation settings (Cadigan, 1980); and many other severely pathological conditions.

We view RE as the treatment of choice for any type of marital or family difficulty. However, we do not hesitate to refer individuals within the family for other types of treatment along with RE (e.g., Alcoholics Anonymous or individual non-RE therapy) when there are what we view to be problems not treated best by family therapy. (We refer here not to any special characteristics of RE, but rather to family therapy in general. That is, we do not believe that marital or family therapy is the most efficient answer to all types of problems.) Positive outcomes for RE therapy have been experimentally demonstrated with a number of different populations and formats as is summarized next.

Group Marital RE

Group Marital RE therapy (originally called Conjugal Therapy) was first studied by Ely, Guerney, and Stover (1973). The primary objective of this study was to find out whether the couples were able to learn the skills; hence, only the training phase of the therapy was studied. Trained couples were found to gain more in specific skills than a control group. In a later quasi-replication portion of this study, RE clients gained more in the treatment period than they had gained in a comparable time period before treatment began. Significant gains were found in general communication patterns and in the general quality of their relationships.

In a later study, Collins (1977) studied the full course of treatment. Couples in RE therapy showed greater gains than the control couples in marital communication and marital adjustment.

Rappaport (1976) studied an *intensive* Group Marital RE format using an own-control design. Clients showed greater gains during the treatment period than they had during the waiting period on all variables studied. In discussions of emotionally significant topics, the couples expresssed themselves with more sensitivity to their own feelings and in ways deemed less likely to induce argument from their partners and showed more empathic acceptance of their partners. Clients experienced greater improvement in marital harmony and in marital communication. They showed greater gain in trust and intimacy and a greater rate of change in the overall quality of their relationship. They showed more improvement in their marital satisfaction and in their ability to resolve relationship problems satisfactorily.

The preceding studies were followed by a group of studies aimed primarily at assessing the question of whether RE effects were treatment specific rather than being generic (that is, due to placebo, Hawthorne, experimenter-demand, thank-you effects, and the like). These studies compared Group Marital RE to other equally credible and competently administered programs. The first such study was conducted by Wieman (1973). He compared RE with his Reciprocal Reinforcement Program, which drew heavily upon principles and techniques used by Knox (1971), Rappaport and Harrell (1972), and especially Stuart (1969a). The RE program used here was abbreviated and time-limited, lasting only 8 weeks. In comparison to a waiting list control group, the participants in both treatments equally showed greater improvement in measures of marital communication, marital adjustment, and cooperativeness. On 16 semantic differential scales, ratings were generally positive for both treatments, but there were also many significant differences between the treatments on these measures. Clients in the Reciprocal Reinforcement Program evaluated their treatment as being more light, safe, easy, cold, and calm than did the clients in the RE program. Clients in the RE program perceived their treatment experience as being significantly more deep, good, worthwhile, exciting, strong, fair, important, comfortable, and professional than did the clients in the Reciprocal Reinforcement Program.

Another study pertinent to the question of specific versus generic treatment effects was done by Jessee and Guerney (1981). This study compared Group Marital RE to Jessee's Group Gestalt

Relationship Facilitation program. Participants in both groups gained significantly on all variables studied: marital adjustment, communication, trust and harmony, rate of positive change in the relationship, relationship satisfaction, and ability to handle problems. RE participants attained greater gains than Gestalt Relationship Facilitation participants in communication, relationship satisfaction, and ability to handle problems.

Ridley, Jorgensen, Morgan, and Avery (1982) compared RE to a discussion treatment of equal length. Participants in the RE program showed significantly greater improvement in satisfaction, communication, intimacy, sensitivity, openness, and understanding in the marital relationship. Participants in the RE program also showed significantly greater improvement on a measure assessing satisfaction, communication, intimacy, sensitivity, openness, and understanding in the marital relationship.

Maintenance of gains in Group Marital RE was demonstrated in the Wieman study mentioned previously. As did couples in the other treatment, RE participants maintained their gains 10 weeks after the close of treatment.

Dyadic Marital RE

Dyadic Marital RE has been studied by Ross (1982). Five therapists who averaged 6 years in the marital and family therapy experience participated in the study. These therapists, all of whom worked in the same mental health center, were jointly given a 3-day training program in Marital RE. By random assignment, they used their own preferred modes of therapy with half of the clients assigned to them and RE with the other half. At posttesting 10 weeks later, the clients in RE showed greater improvement than the clients treated with the therapist's preferred treatment. This was

true on all variables studied: (1) marital adjustment; (2) the quality of their relationship; and (3) the quality of their communication.

Group Family RE

Group Family RE (mothers and daughters) also has been compared to a traditional group treatment and to a no-treatment control (Guerney, Coufal, & Vogelsong, 1981). The two treatment groups met 2 hours weekly for approximately 13 weeks in a time-limited format. The Traditional and RE methods were very carefully equated in every way: The therapists/leaders were the same for both groups and were perceived as showing virtually identical amounts of empathy, warmth, genuineness, enthusiasm, and competence by the clients. The amount of home assignments was the same and so forth. Three basic hypotheses were confirmed on a wide variety of measures. The RE participants improved more than Traditional treatment and no-treatment subjects with respect to (1) specific empathic and expressive skills as measured both behaviorally and quasi-behaviorally; (2) general patterns of communication; and (3) the quality of the general relationship between the mothers and daughters. This study confirmed similar results found earlier with fathers and sons (Ginsberg, 1977).

Maintenance of gains in the mother–daughter study was followed up 6 months after termination (Guerney, Vogelsong, & Coufal, 1983). In comparison to mothers and daughters who had received no treatment, participants in the traditional treatment showed no greater gains over pretreatment status in specific communication skills, general communication patterns, or the general quality of their relationship in comparison to pretreatment status. Participants in RE, however, showed significantly greater gains in all of these areas relative not only to the control group, but to the traditionally treated group. In addition to demonstrating maintenance of superiority of RE over a traditionally oriented approach, the study demonstrated that long-range as well as immediate gains are treatment specific.

Current Status of RE Marital and Family Therapies

To date, it has been experimentally demonstrated, as briefly summarized before, that Marital Relationship Ennhancement is effective, both with mildly disturbed and seriously distressed couples. (Incidentally, it seems, from cross-study comparisons, that the gains achieved with deeply disturbed relationships are of a much higher magnitude than the also-significant gains achieved with moderately disturbed couples.) Achieving greater gains than alternate equally credible treatment approaches has demonstrated that the gains achieved in RE are treatment specific rather than due to generic effects, such as suggestion, experimenter-demand, and thank-you effects. These treatment specific gains last well beyond termination. The same things have been demonstrated for Family RE. However, the format of the Family RE studies, for practical/research reasons, has been limited to dyadic family subgroups. As practice would indicate, clinical experience suggests that using RE with larger family units is also effective. However, we have not yet done the experimental research necessary to confirm this.

RE therapy research has been complemented by enrichment/prevention research. In this regard, RE methods and skills have been shown to be effective in training elementary students (Vogelsong, 1978) and high school students (Avery, Rider, & Haynes-Clements, 1981; Haynes & Avery, 1979; Rocks, 1980); elementary teachers (Guerney & Merriam, 1972; Hatch, 1973; Merriam & Guerney, 1973), and high school stu-

dents and teachers (Haynes & Avery, 1979; Rocks, 1980). RE methods and skills also have been used successfully to train volunteer paraprofessionals (Avery, 1978; Cadigan, 1980; Guerney, Vogelsong, & Glynn, 1977; Most & Guerney, 1983). Premarital couples also have been successfully trained (Ginsberg & Vogelsong, 1977). We plan to continue this type of complementary research.

In terms of further clinical development of the method itself, we now want to focus primarily on refining our knowledge through additional clinical experience and also by research in two areas: (1) the newer additions to the skills taught; and (2) some of the newer, less frequently used, formats. The new skills are self-change, other change, generalization, and maintenance skills (Guerney, 1983; Preston & Guerney, 1982). All of these features have always been included to some extent in RE. But only in recent years have they been clearly formulated as specific skills to be taught to clients in the same way that the five more basic skills were taught. Refining the training procedures for these newer skills is a present focus in developing RE.

Current focus on improving the state of the art of RE clinically also involves studying some of the less frequently used formats of RE. All except one of the RE formats have been used since the early years of RE. However, we have not researched them either formally or informally as much as we now would like to do. In the area of *composition* format, our keenest current interest is in researching unilateral and group-unilateral formats. In the area of *time* format, the new addition to our formats is of greatest interest to us. We have termed it a *front-loaded* format. By front loading, we mean training participants in all the five basic skills in the first week or so of treatment through a marathon or a couple of minimarathons; this is then followed by briefer weekly sessions. This allows clients the advantage of immediately working on their problems with a full array of the basic skills, and thereafter allows for the advantages afforded by home assignments and spaced learning for the more advanced skills, including generalization and maintenance. We believe that this type of format may prove more appropriate for using skills training with disturbed people than the 50-minute format adopted unthinkingly from traditional therapy. We hypothesize that it will prove to be a superior format in skills training therapies for clients in general, especially for clients who are highly distressed and/or in crisis. By "superior," we mean holding clients better and yielding more gain per therapist-hour spent.

CONCLUSION AND FUTURE DIRECTIONS

Our plans for the future are to continue to assess the efficacy of RE Marital and Family therapy (and prevention and enrichment programs) through evaluation of field projects, through case studies, and through experimental research. We would like to study a broad array of problems, age groups, and composition formats and time formats. The greatest obstacle we must overcome is access to large numbers of subjects suffering from specific types of problems. We do not have access to large numbers of cases of, say, alcoholics, depressives, recovering schizophrenics, and so on in State College, Pennsylvania. We welcome offers of collaborative research from practitioners and from researchers in settings where large numbers of cases suffering such specific problems are available.

In concluding, we would like to make a comment beyond the confines of the RE approach. We have maintained, since our work on the RE approaches began, that in order to meet the mental health needs of the nation, therapy, problem-prevention, and enrichment intervention should be based on the educational model, and especially the skill training model. We believe the work described throughout this volume attests to the fact that this revolution is now very rapidly becoming a reality.

REFERENCES

Andronico, M.P., Fidler, J., Guerney, B. G., Jr., & Guerney, L. (1967). The combination of didactic and dynamic elements in filial therapy. *International Journal of Group Psychotherapy, 17,* 10–17.

Armenti, N. (1980). Personal communication, March 18.

Avery, A. W. (1978). Communication skills training for paraprofessional helpers. *American Journal of Community Psychology, 6,* 583–592.

Avery, A. W., Rider, K., & Haynes-Clements, L. (1981). Communication skills training for adolescents: A five month follow-up. *Adolescence, 16,* 289–298.

Axline, V. (1969). *Play therapy* (rev. ed.). New York: Ballantine Books.

Cadigan, J. D. (1980). *RETEACH program and project: Relationship enhancement in a therapeutic environment as clients head out.* Unpublished doctoral dissertation, The Pennsylvania State University.

Collins, J. D. (1977). Experimental evaluation of a six-month conjugal therapy and relationship enhancement program. In B. G. Guerney, Jr. (Ed.), *Relationship enhancement: Skill-training programs for therapy, problem prevention, and enrichment.* San Francisco: Jossey-Bass.

Dorfman, E. (1958). Personality outcomes of client-centered child therapy. *Psychological Monographs, 72*(3, Whole No. 456).

Eardley, D. (1978). *An initial investigation of a didactic version of filial therapy dealing with self-concept increase and problematic behavior decrease.* Unpublished doctoral dissertation, The Pennsylvania State University.

Ely, A., Guerney, B. G., Jr., & Stover, L. (1973). Efficacy of the training phase of conjugal therapy. *Psychotherapy: Theory, Research and Practice, 10*(3), 201–207.

Ginott, H. (1961). *Group psychotherapy with children.* New York: McGraw-Hill.

Ginsberg, B. G. (1977). Parent–adolescent relationship development program. In B. G. Guerney, Jr. (Ed.), *Relationship enhancement: Skill-training programs for therapy, problem prevention, and enrichment.* San Francisco: Jossey-Bass.

Ginsberg, B. (1981). Personal communication, June 2.

Ginsberg, B., Stutman, J., & Hummel, J. (1978). Notes for practice: Group filial therapy. *Social Work, 23,* 154–156.

Ginsberg, B., & Vogelsong, E. L. (1977). Premarital relationship improvement by maximizing empathy and self-disclosure: The PRIMES program. In B. G. Guerney, Jr. (Ed.), *Relationship enhancement: Skill-training programs for therapy, problem prevention, and enrichment.* San Francisco: Jossey-Bass.

Guerney, B., Jr. (1964). Filial Therapy: Description and rationale. *Journal of Consulting Psychology, 28,* 303–310.

Guerney, B. G., Jr. (1982). The delivery of mental health services: Spiritual versus medical versus educational models. In T. R. Vallance & R. M. Sabre (Eds.), *Mental health services in transition: A policy sourcebook.* New York: Human Sciences Press.

Guerney, B. G., Jr. (1983). Relationship enhancement. In E. K. Marshall & P. D. Kurtz (Eds.), *Interpersonal helping skills.* San Francisco: Jossey-Bass.

Guerney, B. G., Jr., Coufal, J., & Vogelsong, E. (1981). Relationship enhancement versus a traditional approach to therapeutic/preventative/enrichment parent–adolescent programs. *Journal of Consulting and Clinical Psychology, 49,* 927–939.

Guerney, B. G., Jr., Guerney, L., & Stollak, G. (1971/1972). The potential advantages of changing from a medical to an educational model in practicing psychology. *Interpersonal Development, 2,* 283–245.

Guerney, B. G., Jr., & Merriam, M. L. (1972). Toward a democratic elementary school classroom. *Elementary School Journal, 72,* 372–383.

Guerney, B. G., Jr., Stollak, G. E., & Guerney, L. (1970). A format for a new mode of psychological practice: Or, how to escape a zombie. *The Counseling Psychologist, 2,* 97–104.

Guerney, B. G., Jr., Stollak, G. E., & Guerney, L. (1971). The practicing psychologist as educator—An alternative to the medical practitioner model. *Professional Psychology, 2,* 276–282.

Guerney, B. G., Jr., & Stover, L. (1971). *Filial Therapy: Final report on MH 1826401.* State College, PA., mimeograph, 156 pp.

Guerney, B. G., Jr., & Vogelsong, E. (1981). *Relationship Enhancement Demonstration Tapes.* Individual and Family Consultation Center, The Pennsylvania State University, Catharine Beecher House, University Park, PA., 16802.

Guerney, B. G., Jr., Vogelsong, E., & Coufal, J. (1983). *Relationship enhancement versus a traditional treatment: Follow up and booster effects.* In D. H. Olson & B. Miller (Eds.), *Family studies review yearbook* (Vol. I). Beverly Hills, CA: Sage.

Guerney, B. G., Jr., Vogelsong, E. L., & Glynn, S. (1977). *Evaluation of the family counseling unit of the Cambria county probation bureau.* State College, PA: Ideals, mimeographed, 45 pages.

Guerney, L. F. (1976). A program for training agency personnel as foster parent trainers. *Child Welfare, 55,* 652–660.

Guerney, L. F. (1977). A description and evaluation of a skills training program for foster parents. *American Journal of Community Psychology, 5,* 361–371.

Guerney, L. F. (1979a). *Parenting: A skill training manual.* State College, PA: The Institute for the Development of Emotional and Life Skills (Ideals).

Guerney, L. F. (1979b). Play therapy with learning disabled children. *Journal of Clinical Child Psychology, 9,* 242–244.

Guerney, L. F., & Wolfgang, G. (1981). Long-range evaluation of effects on foster parents of a foster parent skill training program. *Jounal of Clinical Child Psychology, 10,* 33–37.

Harrell, J., & Dewitt, M. (1981, April). *An intervention program to increase parental competence of mothers with learning disabled children*. Paper presented at the American Educational Research Association meeting, Los Angeles.

Hatch, E. (1973). *An empirical study of a teacher training program in empathic responsiveness and democratic decision making*. Unpublished doctoral dissertation, The Pennsylvania State University.

Haynes, L. A., & Avery, A. W. (1979). Training adolescents in self-disclosure and empathy skills. *Journal of Counseling Psychology, 26,* 526–530.

Horner, P. (1974). *Dimensions of child behavior as described by parents: A monotonicity analysis*. Unpublished master's thesis, The Pennsylvania State University.

Hornsby, L., & Appelbaum, A. (1978). Parents as primary therapists: Filial therapy. In L. Arnold (Ed.), *Helping parents help their children*. New York: Brunner/Mazel.

Jacobs, M. (1980). Foster parent training: An opportunity for skills enrichment empowerment. *Child Welfare, 59,* 615–624.

Jessee, R., & Guerney, B. G., Jr. (1981). A comparison of gestalt and Relationship Enhancement treatments with married couples. *American Journal of Family Therapy, 9,* 31–41.

Knox, D. (1971). *Marriage happiness: A behavioral approach to counseling*. Champaign, IL.

Kostelnik, M. (1978). *Evaluation of a community and group management skills training program for child development personnel*. Unpublished doctoral dissertation, The Pennsylvania State University.

Malone, H. (1982). Personal communication, November 8.

Merriam, M. L., & Guerney, B. G., Jr. (1973). Creating a democratic elementary school classroom: A pilot training program involving teachers, administrators, and parents. *Contemporary Education, 45,* 34–42.

Most, R. K., & Guerney, B. G., Jr. (1983). An empirical evaluation of the training of lay volunteer leaders for premarital Relationship Enhancement. *Family Relations, 32*(2).

Moustakas, C. (1973). *Children in play therapy*. New York: Jacob Aronson.

Oxman, L. (1971). The effectiveness of filial therapy: A controlled study. Unpublished doctoral dissertation, Rutgers University.

Porter, B. (1954). Measurement of parental acceptance of children. *Journal of Home Economics, 46,* 176–182.

Preston, J., & Guerney, B. G., Jr. (1982). *Relationship enhancement skill training*. Xeroxed Manual available from B. Guerney, Catharine Beecher House, University Park, PA, 16803.

Rappaport, A. F. (1976). Conjugal relationship enhancement program. In D. H. Olson (Ed.), *Treating relationships*. Lake Mills, IO: Graphic Publishing Co.

Rappaport, A. F., & Harrell, J. (1972). A behavioral exchange model for marital counseling. *Family Coordinator, 21,* 203–212.

Rappaport, J. (1981). In praise of paradox: A social policy of empowerment over prevention. *American Journal of Community Psychology, 9*(1), 1–22.

Ridley, C. A., Jorgensen, S. R., Morgan, A. C., & Avery, A. W. (1982). Relationship Enhancement with premarital couples: An assessment of effects on relationship quality. *The American Journal of Family Therapy, 10,* 41–48.

Rocks, T. (1980). *The effectiveness of communication skills training with underachieving, low communicating secondary school students and their teachers*. Unpublished doctoral dissertation, The Pennsylvania State University.

Ross, E. (1982). Comparative effectiveness of relationship enhancement versus therapist's preferred therapy on marital adjustment. (Doctoral dissertation, The Pennsylvania State University). *Dissertation Abstracts International,* 1982, *42,* 4610A.

Sensué, M. E. (1981). *Filial Therapy follow-up study: Effects on parental acceptance and child adjustment*. Unpublished doctoral dissertation, The Pennsylvania State University.

Stuart, R. B. (1969a). Operant-interpersonal treatment for marital discord. *Journal of Consulting and Clinical Psychology, 33*, 675–682.

Sywulak, A. E. (1977). *The effect of Filial Therapy on parental acceptance and child adjustment*. Unpublished doctoral dissertation, The Pennsylvania State University.

Sywulak, A. (1978). *Case work skills training manual*. State College, PA: Child Care Systems, Inc.

Vogelsong, E. L. (1978). Relationship Enhancement training for children. *Elementary School Guidance and counseling, 12*(4), 272–279.

Vogelsong, E., Guerney, B. G., Jr., & Guerney, L. F. (1983). Relationship Enhancement therapy with inpatients and their families. In R. Luber & C. Anderson (Eds)., *Family intervention with psychiatric patients*. New York: Human Sciences Press.

Waldo, M., & Guerney, B. G., Jr. (1983). Marital Relationship Enhancement therapy in the treatment of alcoholism. Journal of Marital and Family Therapy, 9, 321–323.

Waldo, M., Guerney, B. G., Jr., & Firestone, L. (1984). *Brief report: A case study of a Relationship Enhancement group for battering couples*. Manuscript submitted for publication.

Welsh, (1982). Personal communication, November 22.

Wieman, R. J. (1973). *Conjugal relationship modification and reciprocal reinforcement: A comparison of treatments for marital discord*. (Doctoral dissertation, The Pennsylvania State University, 1973). *Dissertation Abstracts International, 35*, 493B.

PART SIX

Current Status and Future Directions

CHAPTER 21

Skills Training for Professional Helpers

MARYANNE GALVIN

"I feel depressed all the time. Sometimes I even think about killing myself."

What would you, a professional helper, say next? This is the central dilemma for every beginning counselor. You may understand and empathize with your client's emotional conflict, and you may even have a sense of its origins and of the insights you would wish your client eventually to attain. But what do you say next? Microtraining can help you to learn specifically how to respond to a client with respect for his or her individuality, for his or her particular needs, temperament, and cultural background.

Microtraining, a form of skills training, is the teaching of individual helping skills and concepts in a systematic program that increases counselor and human effectiveness and clarifies the helping process (Ivey, 1971). At its inception in 1968, microcounseling—a systematic design for interviewing training—was directed at the education of professional helpers but has evolved into numerous other areas ranging from medical education to management training and even to direct instruction of parents in relationship building. Its chief advantage is that it applies mutually to therapist and client: Once learned by the professional helper, it becomes a learning tool for the client seeking help.

In a review of psychotherapy research, Cartwright (1968) asserted that the educational process for training novice clinicians needed systematic evaluation. Microtraining and microcounseling techniques have done much to fill that vacuum, and they have supplemented traditional and experiential-didactic training. The microcounseling model is unique in that it combines theoretical and practical training in a systematic way, teaching necessary skills not by chance but through practice of clearly delineated interviewer behaviors.

Various psychotherapeutic training programs have been designed to help train a diverse group of professionals and paraprofessionals in the art of interviewing or in basic clinical skills. Common to all, however, is a basic pragmatism (Galvin & Ivey, 1981). Carkhuff's Human Relations Development (1969) and Guerney's Filial Therapy (1964) are based on a client-centered approach. Goldstein's Structural Learning Therapy (1973) and Ivey's microcounseling (1971) most closely relate to a social learning model, whereas Kagan's interpersonal process recall (1972) is influenced by psychodynamic thinking. Skills training has been consistently effective for more than 15 years, combining theory and practice in a unique working combination in which individual trainers and trainees can immediately test whether the concepts have validity.

In the more traditional approaches,

such as psychodynamic training, the conceptual strategic skills of interviewing are emphasized at the expense of facilitative and interpersonal behavior. The traditional approaches seemed to lack a discernible transition from classroom to actual practice.

When investigation of the skills training movement for professional helpers began, there was basically no preconceived theory. Thus, the question was generated: What steps would one take in order to cultivate in a helping professional the knowledge that she or he will need if she or he is to teach others to live the happy and contented life that comes from a sense of efficiency in all essentials?

To have knowledge without practical power, to have insight and yet be incapable of applying it in everyday life—what more dreadful fate could even an unfriendly spirit devise for us? Human needs and cravings are many. People must know and think in order to satisfy those needs, it is true, but they must also act. Indeed, knowledge and action are so closely connected that if one ceases the other ceases also. But that can never happen if practical skills keeps pace within growing needs.

Training in practical skills is based upon the same laws as the training of the intellect. Nature affects plants, unreasoning beasts, and humans in much the same way, though humans are not only sensitive to external impressions, but are also capable of voluntary action. Nature's consistency is also seen in the threefold results she may produce in me, the author. Nature may produce a purely mechanical result, such as she produces upon animals, or she may act through sensory impressions that partially determine my judgment, my inclinations, and my will, or she may lead me to acquire skill, inasmuch as my will accepts the recognized needs of my situation. But this acquisition of skill must not be left entirely to nature, because nature is too

capricious in her action on the individual. We must transfer responsibility for learning skills to those intelligent powers that human beings acquired long ago to their common advantage. Thus, the microskills model of skills training can answer the basic question: What treatment, by *whom,* is most effective for *this* individual with *that* specific problem, and under *which* set of circumstances? (Paul, 1967, p. 111).

Microtraining, human relations development, assertiveness training, values clarification, or any others from a wide array of skills training and psychoeducational programs all focus on the development of *intentionality*. Intentionality is the ability to choose among a number of different actions.

The person who acts with intentionality has a sense of capability. He or she can generate alternative behaviors in a given situation and "approach" a problem from different vantage points. The intentional, fully functioning individual is not bound to one course of action but can respond in the moment to changing life situations and look forward to longer term goals. (Ivey & Simek-Downing, 1980, p. 8)

Generating increased response capability is a goal of microtraining as well as, it may be suggested, of skills training in general. The main premise and commonality of skills training is that all skills training programs are ultimately concerned with developing intentionality and freeing helpers as well as clients to *generate* an ever-increasing ray of sentences, metaphors, and behaviors that will enable them to commit themselves in the world from a position of many options, rather than of limitations. The word *generate* is analogous to Chomsky's (1965) transformational or generational grammar.

Clients come to skills training programs (or psychotherapy) unable to generate the full array of sentences and behaviors that they are capable of generating. They, too, can be helped by skills training. Fritz Perl's inelegant term *stuckness* is perhaps most descriptive of the immobility of clients unable to cope with difficult situations. Various schools of psychotherapy help clients deal with certain types of "stuckness," such as logical inconsistencies (rational emotive therapy), behavior deficits (behavior therapy), polarities (psychodynamic therapy), and rigid scripts (transactional analysis). Skills training can be highly therapeutic, but because of its broader base, it is perhaps more able than traditional therapy to increase client alternatives.

The microtraining approach to teaching basic therapy skills to professional helpers begins with a simple exercise. A brief "videovignette," in which a client speaks directly from the TV and presents an immediate concern or problem is viewed by all. The tape is stopped, and students are asked to respond to the following question: What would you say next to this particular client? There are, of course, a variety of different student responses; the instruction begins with the basic and critical insight that *different people* respond to the *same stimulus differently, and that depending on context, any response by the therapist-in-training may be appropriate.*

The students then move on to an in-depth examination of specific *skills* used by therapists and counselors in many different domains, including the very familiar ones of open and closed questions, paraphrasing, reflecting feelings, and giving directives and interpretations. The microcounseling format for learning each of these one at a time is as follows:

1. Brief introduction of the skill.
2. Viewing of video modeling tape of the skill being demonstrated by an experienced therapist.
3. Presentation of reading material elaborating on the concepts just viewed.

4. Immediate practice in small groups, with video- or audiotape equipment, on the single skill previously experienced.

Thus, both the theory and the practice of each skill are demonstrated, followed by immediate application by the student. Student groups ranging from 12 to 60 or more have participated in single-skills training.

Figure 21.1 presents several ways in which skills differ in various forms of therapy. In approximately 2 to 4 hours, students learn each of these skills in class workshops. Not surprisingly, there is a direct positive correlation between the amount of time that students engage in actual practice with the skill and the level of competency they achieve.

Students also learn to focus their response on the client in a variety of ways. For example, a client may say, "I just had an abortion," to which the therapist may respond, "You seem to be really worried." What the client says next is heavily determined by the subject or theme of the counselor's lead. The beginning student attains full mastery when she or he is able to focus the client at will and to complete focusing with other microskills.

The microskills model even goes so far as to express empathy dimensions (confrontation, concreteness, respect, warmth) in operational terms. For example, students are taught to notice what verb tense the client or therapist is using and to move toward immediacy (present tense) in their work. Interventions posed in the present tense tend to be most powerful, although not, of course, appropriate at all times.

For approximately one-half of the 45-hour training period, the students are engaged in learning the basic attending skills as well as the concepts of focus and empathy in the interview. Systematic observation of interviews on videotape stress the nonverbal dimensions of com-

Theory	Microskills: Quantitative Dimensions											Focus						Empathy: Qualitative Dimensions								
	Closed Question	Open Question	Min. Encourage	Paraphrase	Reflect. Feeling	Summarization	Directive	Express. Content	Express Feeling	Inf. Summarization	Interpretation	Helpee	Others	Topic	Helper	Mutual	Cultural-Envir.	Primary Empathy	Additive Empathy	Positive Regard	Respect	Warmth	Concreteness	Immediacy	Confrontation	Genuineness
Psychodynamic		X	X			X					XX	XX	X					X	XX	X	X		X	P	X	
Behavioral	XX	XX	X	X	X	X	XX	XX			X	XX	X	XX				X	XX	X	X		XX	F	X	
Non-Directive			X	XX	XX	X						XX						XX		XX	XX	XX		H	X	X
Modern Rogerian			X	XX	XX	X			X			XX			X	XX		XX	X	XX	XX	XX		H	X	XX
Exist.-Humanist.		X		X	X	X			X		XX	XX			X	X	X	X	X		X	XX	X	H	X	X
Gestalt	X	X					XX	X			XX	XX						XX	X				X	H	XX	X
Transpersonal	X	X	X	X	X	X	XX	XX	X		X	XX	XX	X	X	X	X	X	XX	XX	XX	X	X	F	X	XX
Trait & Factor	X	XX	X	X	X	X	X	X	XX	X	X	X	XX				X	X	X	X	X	X	XX	F	X	X
Rational-Emot.	X	X					X	XX			X	XX	XX	XX			X	X	XX	X	X		X	P/H	X	
Trans. Analysis		X	X	X	X	X	X	X	XX		X	XX	XX	XX				X	XX	X			X	P/H	XX	X
Reality Therapy	X	X	X	X	X	X	X	XX	X	X	X	XX	X	XX	X	X	XX	X		X	XX	X	X	P/F	X	XX
Strategic	X	X					XX				X	XX		X				X	XX	X			XX	P/H	XX	

Legend

XX	Most frequently used dimension.
X	Frequently used dimension.
	Dimension may be used, but is not a central aspect of theory.

P   Primary emphasis on past tense immediacy.
H   Primary emphasis on present tense immediacy.
F   Primary emphasis on future tense immediacy.

Figure 21.1. Skills used in different therapies.

munication. In small groups, students practice giving and receiving direct feedback from the taped sessions. They learn to rate and classify specific interviewer behaviors. The clearly defined single-skills approach and the mechanics of video feedback training combined with a high level of observational skills provide impressive information about their own and the clients' nonverbal behavior in the session. In the remainder of the course, the students apply skills in different theoretical orientations.

THE ABC'S OF MICROCOUNSELING: APPLYING SKILLS METHODS TO ALTERNATE THEORIES OF THERAPY

Imagine that you are the therapist who is responding to our introductory client statement: "I feel depressed all the time. Sometimes I even think about killing myself." Examine your original response to this statement. Did you preface your response with the words "It sounds like . . ."; with focus on the topic at hand and then direct the client to "please go on"? Then, perhaps, you are inclined to move in the psychodynamic direction in this session. If you compare your response with those of fellow counselors, you will find that they probably respond differently from you. A key question is, "Who had the correct response in this case?"

The solution to "correctness" is that there are many possible useful responses in an interviewing situation. At one time, an open question ("Could you tell me more?" may be most facilitative. Another time, it may be more useful to reflect immediate feelings here and now ("Looks like you feel terribly anxious and upset over a recent incident?"). Again, there are times when self-disclosure and direct advice may be what is needed (My experience with my low periods is . . . and I suggest you try . . .").

Beginning therapists are often eager to find the "right" answer for the client. Trainers and books sometimes reinforce this desire to find the "perfect empathic response" that will unlock the door to the client's world. However, the very tendency to search for the single "right" response can be damaging.

Intentional interviewing is concerned not with which one single response is correct but how many responses may be helpful. Intentionality is a core goal of microtraining. Figure 21.1 demonstrates the building blocks for constructing an intentional therapist.

Different orientations in therapy tend to use different skills and manifest empathy in various forms. For instance, Figure 21.1 reveals that classical, nondirective therapists tend to use paraphrase and reflection of feeling whereas psychoanalytically oriented therapists tend to use the interpretation skills. In teaching the theoretical approach to students, key concepts are presented that are followed by observation of a therapist's demonstrating that point. Reference to Figure 21.1 assists trainees in clarifying which specific skills are used with which theories. Then, the concepts of self-actualization, positive regard, and so forth are presented in lecture form and students then observe a film of Carl Rogers demonstrating these concepts. Students are then able to analyze the behavior of the therapist and note the sequence of skills usage and any special techniques before breaking into small groups to practice.

Skills training may be a form of therapy, though its relationship to traditional treatment is at present still tentative. Skills training has largely served as an adjunct to traditional therapies but has been demonstrated to be a viable treatment approach in itself (Goldstein, 1973; Ivey, 1973). Whereas research on the effectiveness of therapy (Garfield & Bergin, 1978; Gurman & Razin, 1977) has had mixed results, research on the effectiveness of skills training seems more positive and hopeful. Skills training may indeed be the treatment of choice.

The identification and acquisition of new behaviors through skills training is similar to the fixed-role therapy of Kelly (1955). A special role is identified, and the key constructs associated with that role are made explicit. In skills training, a client can test a role or behavior in a simulated situation with little danger to him/herself or others. The power and elegance of this simple social learning model is evidenced by the surprising levels of competence attained.

Students who are given an elementary introduction to experiential Freudian techniques learn to generate on their own concepts and ideas, like unconscious material, heretofore usually "learned" in lecture. Students view a videotape about a client's dream in which the therapist uses the microskills of closed and open questions, paraphrasing, reflection of feeling, and summarization to draw out details of the dream. The client is then directed to free associate to an earlier childhood memory; again, the basic listening skills are used to obtain specifics of the early experience. Role-played clients and trainees then transfer this set of theoretical constructs and skills sequence to practice sessions.

TOWARD A THEORY OF SKILLS TRAINING

Skills training is rooted in theory as well as in practice. Based on the major premise of skills training stated earlier—that intentionality is the primary goal of therapy for both helper and client—the following assumptions may be useful in leading to a general theory applicable to the many alternative skills training programs.

Assumption 1. The major alternative approaches to skills training may be thought of as systematic constructs for construing the world and acting out more intentionally. These systematic constructs permit the alternation of actions and the generation of new sentences and behaviors by the client.

Assumption 2. Skills training programs have in common rigorous specification of the alternative sentences, metaphors, and behaviors they wish to teach. These specifics are taught in such a way that learned constructs may be tested first in the laboratory environment of the training program and then generalized systematically to the home environment. One of the reasons that skills training works is that specific and limited objectives are established prior to training.

Assumption 3. Different modes of skills training will be useful in varying degrees to people who present different types of issues, come from different backgrounds, and have special histories of personal and environmental transaction.

To compare the relative merits of the several training programs, we need to define specific goals and objectives. If a basic assumpttion of a skills training theory is that different people may require different training, then perhaps we can avoid the age-old question of which training modality is most effective and ask instead, Which training modality is most effective for what? A corollary is that we can expect some clients to benefit more from traditional psychotherapy or counseling than from skills training. Such a client might be one raised in a culture that believes in the medical model of healing.

All skills training programs have experienced resistance and difficulty with some client populations. This has led to a flexibility of training and an effort on the part of trainers to offer something to every person in a training group. This ability to adapt programs to meet special needs is a unique strength of skills training. Some competition between programs has arisen from time to time, but trainers have generally respected differences and learned from one another, recognizing that no one skills training program has all the solutions.

With research and theory (Berzins, 1977; Goldstein & Stein, 1976) suggesting that systematic planning of appropriate treatment modes may be possible, a major challenge for skills training over the next few years is to determine the specific methods and techniques that are most suitable for clients pressenting different concerns.

If skills training can be compared to developing an artistic capacity, we need to examine the intellectual foundation of practical skill. Skills training suggests that a trainee who has learned to measure, to count, or to draw on "elementary" lines has within her/him the intellectual foundations for the practical skills. It only remains to train the external dexterities necessary to the particular art that she or he desires to master. The course of training for all mechanical dexterities goes through four stages: The first concerns the correct apprehension of forms; the second, power to reproduce them; the third, delicacy in their representation; and the fourth, freedom and independence in applying them. Experience has shown us that this is true of writing, drawing, singing, piano playing—so why not of psychotherapy?

Despite their differences, all skills training programs tend to follow some variant of the psychoeducational model. Authier and his colleagues (1975) have perhaps said it best:

Most of the advocates of such an approach [psychoeducation skills training] agree that the educational model means psychological practitioners seeing their function not in terms of abnormality (or illness)—diagnosis —prescription—therapy—cure; but rather in terms of client dissatisfaction (or ambition)— goal setting—skill teaching—satisfaction of goal achievement. The person being served is seen as analogous to a pupil, rather than a patient. (p. 31)

This distinction leads to another basic assumption of the skills training model.

Assumption 4. Skills training is concerned with teaching rather than remediation, with prevention rather than cure. This, however, does not mean that skills training is not therapeutic. It is a distinct alternative or supplement to traditional therapy.

Microtraining and human relations development evolved from attempts by counseling psychologists to understand therapy. The majority of skills trainers came from traditional therapeutic backgrounds. Through their investigations, the generic aspects of the process were uncovered, and the psychoeducational skills training approach was developed.

Assumption 5. Skills training programs generally rest on systematic technology. Through experience and research, the technology has been shaped and adapted to many types of individuals and groups. Most skills training technologies contain cognitive information about a construct, sample experiential exercises to illustrate the construct, practice experiential exercises to try out the construct, and systematic practice leading toward generalization beyond the skills training program.

Although the influence is not universal, some form of the social learning models seems to pervade skills training. In Kelly's work, theoretical concepts are seldom explicit, but in skills training programs, a scientific view of human relations is emphasized, the knowability of one's own constructs is taught, and the need to test out constructs through some form of role play or practice is considered essential. Further, skills trainers seldom believe they have the final answer to all questions but emphasize that the skills learned are just a part of the solution to the client's problems.

>   *Assumption 6.*   Skills training is generic in nature, teaching a basic set of human interactions that may be used by many people in differing settings.

Microtraining has been used with patients and parents and physicians and paraprofessionals in settings ranging from the Canadian Arctic to aboriginal Australia. The universal application of skills training inevitably ressults in resistance from specialists who deny that psychologists and counselors can generalize behavior to multiple settings and who emphasize the "professionalization" of psychology and the importance of unique contributions that can be "owned." Skills trainers, on the other hand, are often interested in sharing basic generic concepts with the lay population and making psychology public and available to all. An important intent of skills training is the demystification of the helping process.

>   *Assumption 7.*   Skills training, like psychotherapy, is a cultural phenomenon primarily representative of Western culture, so that cultural uniqueness and cultural differences must be taken into account as skills training becomes more broadly available.

Marsella and Pedersen (1980) have described the issue of cross-cultural communication and skills training. Experience has revealed that microtraining works, but it works differently in different cultures. Different cultural groups have differing patterns of communication and microskills usage. Intentional

interviewing demands awareness of this key point.

Eye-contact patterns differ, for example. Middle-class patterns call for rather direct eye contact in our culture, but in some groups, direct eye contact is considered rude and intrusive. Some groups find the rapid-fire questioning techniques of many North Americans offensive. Many Hispanic groups have more varying vocal tones and sometimes a more rapid speech rate than English-speaking people.

Skills of questioning, popular in the white middle-class population, turn out to be inappropriate in other cultures where a more subtle approach is better suited. Because of its vagueness, psychotherapy often flounders when dealing with cultural differences. In contrast, the precision of skills training allows specific differences in behaviors and attitudes to be identified, specified, and eventually taught. A true frontier for skills training is to outline effective modes of cross-cultural communication accurately.

The major premise and the seven basic assumptions given here should be considered only the beginning of a comprehensive theory of skills training. We are still left with the question cited earlier in this chapter (Paul, 1967, p. 111). "Which treatment, by whom, under what condition . . ." At this time, we do not know which skills training programs can substitute for therapy, which will be most effective for different types of individuals, or even which are most cost-effective, given a certain goal. These and other questions will serve as a basis for further research and investigations.

It is therefore incorrect to assume that the communication patterns emphasized in this chapter will work for everyone, regardless of cultural backgrounds. However, the microskills model can provide clues as to why *your* interviewing technique may not be working. For instance, recent research has revealed that men and women may differ at times in their interviewing styles. Women often tend to use reflective listening techniques (e.g., paraphrase and reflection of feelings), whereas men may use more questioning and interpretive statements. Again, less advantaged socioeconomic groups often expect advice and suggestion rather than drawn-out talk and analysis of the problem.

RESEARCH AND APPLICATIONS

The theoretical framework for the psychoeducational model of teaching basic helping and communication skills emerged in response to a need to help people cope more efficiently and effectively with their environments and themselves (Ivey & Alschuler, 1973). There has been considerable psychoeducational research in teaching communication skills to paraprofessionals, counseling students, professional psychologists, and incarcerated persons, among many others. Ivey et al. (cited in Kasdord & Gustafson, 1978) have generated more than 150 data base studies, a few of which are presented here. To these studies should be added more than 15 years of clinical testing of the model with trainees in counseling, business, and other settings. The basic finding of the research data is the classical conclusion that "more research is needed." However, the following studies will provide an overview.

Chilsom (1977) trained graduate students in counseling as well as public offenders in jails in a systematized program of human relations. The results showed that both graduate students and public offenders could acquire and demonstrate helping skills after only 50 hours of training.

Terrell (1977) used microcounseling training with applicants for the position of orientation leader at a major university and discovered that the number of eye contact breaks and arm, hand, leg, and foot movements were significantly reduced after training; he also noted an increase in general attending behavior.

Higgins, Ivey, and Uhlemann (1970) instructed students in the interpersonal skills of direct mutual communication, that mystical communication between people who are committed and able to be truly themselves in relationship to another person (Ivey & Gluckstern, 1974). They obtained significant results, showing that microcounseling can be used to train counseling students in extremely complex interpersonal skills, which can be transferred to the therapeutic process as well as to daily human interaction.

In the area of field practicum and supervision, the microcounseling literature reveals some particularly worthwhile research findings. Shea (1975) studied 30 graduate students in two groups who received distinctly separate field practicums. The experimental group (n = 15) received 5 weeks of microcounseling training with supervised fieldwork. The control group received only live, on-site supervision. As compared to controls, the microtrained group achieved higher scores in their taped interviews in confrontative and directive behavior as well as in encouraging clients to make decisions and to take action.

Though this review of research is cursory, it does indicate some of the positive outcomes that result from training students, professionals, and paraprofessionals, and, by extension, clients in the microcounseling model of helping. Current research is revealing some of the model's deficits and is turning up concrete suggestions for future development. For instance, discrepancies have been detected in some studies of the impact of supervision on the learning of interviewing skills. Frankel (1971) gave early indications that supervision is unnecessary in imparting interviewing skills to trainees. In contradiction to this hypothesis, Authier et al. (1975) moved to support acquisition of established skill paradigms. And Berg and Stone (1980) have laid the groundwork for extensive elaboration of some important questions. Their findings suggest three possible directions for future investigation of microtraining effectiveness: (1) studying the impact of individual learning styles in the microtraining process; (2) examining with equal emphasis the quantitative as well as the qualitative dimensions of interviewing behavior; and (3) conducting more concise and precisely controlled studies of the multidimensional nature of the supervisory process, in which such variables as supervisory style, relationship factors, and types and amount of reinforcing feedback are accounted for.

The following practical points may be made with some assurance after reviewing the research literature:

1. The skills of the microskills hierarchy have been repeatedly borne out and show consistent construct validity.

2. Students who are trained by means of the model used in this chapter are able to recognize and classify interviewing skills with accuracy.

3. Students are able to demonstrate their mastery of these skills on audiotape or videotape following completion of training.

4. Students do improve and change their pattern of microskills usage as a result of this training. If a trainee goes on to practice the skills learned, she or he will maintain them as part of a skills repertoire.

5. Clients of students who have gone through microskill training appear to change their verbal patterns and to have more complex conceptual patterns of thinking.

6. The complete training package of introductory exercises, video or audio model, reading, and experiential practice seems to be most effective. Practice with the single skills to mastery levels appears to be particularly important to the development of competence.

7. Different counseling theories do indeed appear to have differing patterns of microskills usage, and the microtraining framework may be used to teach complex interviewing behavior according to alternative theoretical perspectives on the interview.

FUTURE DIRECTIONS

Skills training holds much promise for the future. The research data, the explicitness of the various programs, the promising patterns of cost-effectiveness, and the ease and simplicity of training all point to its potential. This chapter has suggested some beginning theoretical formulations for an integrated view of skills training, but much remains to be done. For instance, we need comparative analyses of the skills and the traditional approaches to therapy. This issue is difficult to address because psychotherapy is generally individual in nature and skills training is most often a group process; nevertheless, individual work in structural learning therapy and microtraining, for example, are clearly possible. Could it be demonstrated that such approaches are viable alternatives to individual therapy? Such data will be required in order to obtain funds and insurance payments to support the development of skills training as a viable method.

Given the back-to-basics movement of the late 1970s and early 1980s, skills training must prove its validity and win a more secure place in the educational curriculum of universities and colleges. Simply because it is new on the scene, skills training may have difficulty maintaining momentum in a time of budgetary cutbacks.

Again, although skills training has

been conducted among many professional groups, including social workers and the various divisions of the American Psychological Association, trainers have had little contact among themselves. It may be either time to form a national association of skills trainers, or to work within the existing organization to help further the movement.

At present, skills training remains an appendage to other theoretical frameworks. Can skills training develop its own independant theory? On the other hand, a separate, theoretically based movement might pose problems for the counseling, social work, and psychological establishments.

Finally, proponents and critics of the microtraining paradigm agree that a delicate balance is needed in the dissemination of these skills—that is, a delicate balance between overly strict adherence to training methodologies and behavioral technology on the one hand, and careful attention on the other to critical human dimensions such as individual learning style and cultural environmental indicators. Follow-up information for trainers to insure maintenance of acquired skills will also be necessary.

SUMMARY

New theoretical assumptions in combination with microcounseling technology should provide a system for relating many types of counseling and therapy and for passing microskills onto trainees more quickly and efficiently at higher levels of quality. The last 15 years have yielded a useful beginning in microskills development. However, the real value of the framework lies in the questions that have been unearthed over time. The metatheoretical assumptions that now underlie the framework appear to be the points for examination in microskills research and training. Most critical will be investigation of *how* clients are affected by counselors' use of skills. As stated throughout this chapter, the pinnacle issue of maintenance of behavior as determined by the impact a person can have on someone else needs closer examination. Continuous monitoring of training-process features such as client/counselor match will represent a step in the direction of providing a "map" for generating effective outcome through intentional interactions in therapy.

REFERENCES

Authier, J., et al. (1975). The psychological practitioner as a "teacher." *The Counseling Psychologist, 5,* 31–50.

Berg, K., & Stone G. (1980). Effects of conceptual level and supervision structure on counselor skill development. *Personnel and Guidance Journal, 27,*(5), 500–509.

Berzins, J. (1977). Therapist–patient matching. In A. Gurman & A. Razin (Eds.), *Effective psychotherapy*. Elmsford, NY: Pergamon.

Carkhuff, R. (1969). *Helping and human relations* (2 vols.). New York: Holt, Rinehart & Winston.

Cartwight, R. (1968). Psychotherapeutic process. *Annual Review of Psychology, 19,* 387–416.

Chilsom, A. (1971). *Some effects of systematic human relations training on offenders' ability to demonstrate helping skills*. Unpublished Doctoral Dissertation. University of Georgia *37,* 4857A.

Chomsky, N. (1965). *Aspects of the theory of syntax*. Cambridge: M.I.T. Press.

Frankel, M. (1971). Effects of videotape modeling and self-confrontation techniques on microcounseling behaviors. *Journal of Counseling Psychology, 18,* 465–471.

Galvin, M., & Ivey, A. (1981). Researching one's own interviewing style: Does your theory of choice match your actual practice? *Personnel and Guidance Journal, 59* (8) 536–541.

Geurney, B. (1964). Filial Therapy. *Journal of Consulting Psychology, 28,* 303–310.

Goldstein, A. (1973). *Structural learning therapy.* New York: Academic Press.

Goldstein, A. P., & Stein, N. (1976). *Prescriptive psychotherapies.* Elmsford, NY: Pergamon.

Gurman, A., & Razin, A. (1977). *Effective psychotherapy.* Elmsford, NY: Pergamon.

Higgins, W., Ivey, A., & Uhlemann, M. (1970). Media therapy: A programmed approach to teaching behavioral skills. *Journal of Counseling Psychology, 20,* 101–104

Ivey, A., et al. (1968). Microcounseling and attending Behaviors: An approach to pre-practicum counselor training. *Journal of Counseling Psychology, 15,* 1–12

Ivey, A. (1971). *Microcounseling.* Springfield, IL: Charles C Thomas.

Ivey, A. (1973). Media therapy: Educational change planning for psychiatric patients. *Journal of Counseling Psychology, 20,* 338–343

Ivey, A., & Alschuler, A. (1973). Psychological education: A prime function of the counselor. *Personnel and Guidance Journal, 5,* 591–597.

Ivey, A., & Gluckstern, N. (1974). *Basic attending skills: Leader and participant manuals and basic influencing skills.* North Amherst, MA: Microtraining Association.

Ivey, A., & Simek-Downing, L. (1980). *Counseling and psychotherapy: Skills, theories and practice.* Englewood Cliffs, NJ: Prentice-Hall.

Kagan, N. (1972). *Influencing human interaction.* East Lansing: Michigan State University Press.

Kasdord, J., & Gustafson, K. (1978). Research Related to microtraining. In A. Ivey & J. Authier (Eds.), *Microtraining.* Springfield, IL: Charles C Thomas.

Kelly, G. (1955). Psychology of personal Constructs. New York: Norton.

Marsella, A., & Pedersen, P. (1980). *Cross-cultural counseling and psychotherapy.* Elmsford, NY: Pergamon.

Paul, G. (1967). Strategy of outcome research in psychotherapy. *Journal of Consulting Psychology, 31,* 109–119.

Shea, J. (1975). An evaluation of the effectiveness of microcounseling in training counselors to use selected behaviors in an urban field practice. *Dissertation Abstracts International. 3*(6-A):3419–20

Terrell, T. (1977). The effects of microtraining in attending behavior in response behavior of paraprofessional orientation leaders. *Dissertation Abstracts International, 37* (7-A), 4149.

CHAPTER 22

Toward Effective Supervision in Business and Industry

JUDITH L. KOMAKI AND STACEY ZLOTNICK

Corporations spend an estimated $100 billion annually on the training of their personnel (Gilbert, 1976). Although it is difficult to estimate what proportion of this expense is used specifically for the training of management-level employees, it is generally considered to be quite substantial. Besides funding internal training departments and corporate "universities," most large companies spend millions of additional dollars on management programs given by external training consultants (Smith, 1980).

To the corporate consumer's eye, the promises made by training specialists are impressive. A sample of the promotional literature gives a clue to their appeal. These programs typically promise to teach managers how to do the following:

Tune into employee attitues.

Spot motivation killers.

Increase employee commitment.

Diagnose potential conflict producers.

Turn problems into opportunities.

Get the most out of your people.

Develop an effective management style.

Unfortunately, even the most well-regarded programs fall short of their promises. Why this is so and what can be done are among the topics of our chapter.

To put the current emphasis on the so-cial skills of managerial personnel into perspective, we will first trace the origin and growth of management training in industry. We will then describe the current crop of management development programs: their models of an ideal manager, components, methods of instruction, and evidence. Lastly, we will show why these programs usually fall short, and what can be done to upgrade the social skills of one group of the most vital people in work organizations—managers.

HISTORY OF MANAGEMENT TRAINING

To begin our discussion of management training and development, we will first take a brief look at the origin and growth of these programs.

Prior to World War II, programs in management training were virtually non-existent. The growth of management training occurred after World War II when there appeared a marked increase in the number of both in-company and out-of-company training programs. In 1935, for example, only 3% of 2500 companies surveyed by the National Industrial Conference Board reported that they had executive training programs. By 1946, this figure had risen to only 5% of some 3000 companies (Habbe, 1950, cited in Bridgman, 1959). However, a survey by the American Management Association in 1952 found that 38% of 2000 companies and in 1954, 54% of 500 companies were using management development programs (Trichett, 1954, cited in Bridgman, 1959). By 1957, Clark and Sloan (cited in Bridgman, 1959) reported that of 350 companies surveyed, 77% provided management training and development programs. Although it is difficult to make comparisons between these data, the findings nevertheless indicate that "a dramatic increase in management training has taken place" (Campbell, Dunnette, Lawler, & Weick, 1970, p. 41).

Although there are probably many factors that contributed to this sudden upsurge, two events were most significant. First, America's entrance into World War II brought a need to train a huge influx of new soldiers as well as the many workers who had replaced them in the factories back home. To meet this challenge, psychologists, for the first time and on a massive scale, designed training programs for both military and industrial personnel (Bridgman, 1959; Smith, 1980). As the benefits of these programs became apparent, the training movement continued to thrive even after the war.

A second impetus behind the growth of management training was the influence of organized labor. The passage of prolabor legislation in the 1930s had given rise to a growing number of unionized workers. Threats of labor disturbances and union interference created a need for foremen, supervisors, and first-line managers who could handle grievances and avoid walkouts. By the 1940s, with new training methodologies now in hand, industries began human relations programs to teach managers how to develop rapport with workers, encourage cooperation, and generally to minimize conflict on the bottom line (Barkin, 1950; Kestnbaum, 1940; Smith, 1980).

The increase in white-collar workers, by the 1960s, continued to fuel the growth of training programs. The greater costs of selection and training of these personnel and thus the greater loss from turnover created a concern for developing managers who could promote satisfaction, commitment, and motivation of these workers (Bowden, 1952; Phelps, 1962). By the 1970s and 1980s, rapid technological growth and changing economic conditions amplified the problems of management by removing the stability of established products and markets. To keep pace with competition, organizations needed to develop managers who could adjust to and plan for technological change and also limit time and costs by motivating the effectiveness and productivity of workers.

Given this range of demands, it is no wonder that leadership and supervisory skills training is considered to be the most important area of management training today (Neider, 1981).

REPRESENTATIVE TRAINING PROGRAMS

A glance at the training literature reveals that management training programs cover a wide variety of topics. Using Campbell et al.'s (1970) classification system, we find that these programs can be grouped into five categories:

1. Factual content.
2. Approaches and techniques for problem solving and decision making.
3. Attitudes.
4. Self-knowledge.
5. Interpersonal skills.

The focus of this chapter is on this last category—interpersonal skills programs. Included in this category are programs that emphasize improving a manager's ability to communicate, listen, and influence/motivate others. Even within this group, however, the rationale and approaches to training vary widely. For purposes of illustration, we have selected four programs. The first pair of these programs—Managerial Grid Seminars and Double-Loop Learning—employ sensitivity-training experiences to encourage managers to experiment and adapt new styles that are consistent with a specific model of management. The second pair of programs—Behavior Modeling and Positive Reinforcement—employ principles of learning to broaden managers' overall repertoires of effective supervisory behaviors.

Grid Seminars

Model of Ideal Manager

Blake and Mouton's (1964, 1978) Grid Seminars are based on a model known as the "managerial grid" that characterizes leadership behavior along two dimensions—concern for production and concern for people. Concern for production, for example, includes problems of work load and efficiency, whereas concern for people includes problems such as worker satisfaction and morale. These two concerns form the axes of a 9 × 9 point grid, with 1 representing minimum and 9 representing maximum effort or emphasis. Thus, a manager's style can be located on the grid by a pair of coordinates, the first number representing the degree of concern for production, and the second, for people.

Instead of balancing concerns for people and production, Blake and Mouton claim that most managers emphasize one concern at the expense of the other. For example, a 1,9 manager pays little attention to the task and instead works toward the maintenance of friendly and satisfying staff relationships. A 9,1 manager, by contrast, demands authority and obedience: He or she strives to get the work done with minimal interference of human factors. The 9,9 position represents the ideal style on the managerial grid because it optimizes both people and production concerns.

Training Program

The focus of the Grid Seminars is to move managers from a polarized concern for either people or production toward a 9,9 management style that maximizes both concerns. The complete program entails a six-phase organizational development strategy spanning 3 to 5 years. Because only Phase 1 of the seminar focuses on management development, this will be the only part of the training that we will discuss here.

Phase 1 begins with 30 hours of pre-seminar instruction to introduce managers to grid analysis. This is followed by 5 days of laboratory training conducted by outside consultants or in-house management familiar with the seminar materials and methods. Trainees are divided into study teams of between five and nine managers, representing a "diagonal slice" of different departments, divisions, and levels within the organization.

Each team is given a series of problems to solve that are designed to illustrate the influence of interpersonal behavior on task performance. The teams work on these problems, measure their performance, and evaluate their effectiveness in relation to the performance of other teams. Team members are encouraged to critique their own and other's leadership behaviors, and to practice team management skills in solving conflict, earning cooperation, and facilitating group planning and problem solving. Again, the objective of the seminar is to encourage managers to disregard their old, ineffective styles of managing and adopt a 9,9 or team management style.

Evaluation

Despite an intuitive appeal, there exists no substantial body of evidence to support the position that a balanced concern for people and production is the most effective leadership type (Fiedler & Chemers, 1974). Even if the 9,9 style of management was highly effective, it is not clear from the grid model just what a manager would do to optimize people and production concerns.

To date, there have been no studies that document the effectiveness of phase 1 of the Grid Seminars. In an evaluation study of the entire six-phase program, Blake, Mouton, Barnes and Greiner (1964) reported a rise in plant productivity and profitability as a result of grid training. However, because a control group was not used in the study, we cannot be sure that these increases were not caused by environmental factors. In fact, the figures used as a pretest comparison were collected only 2 years prior to the intervention when the plant was in the midst of a corporate merger. Furthermore, Bass (1981) points out that the program was introduced during a period of economic growth when businesses in general were gaining in profits.

Even if we could accept these results, the investigators offer no observational or other objective data to support their claim that these increases were due to behavioral changes in the direction of the 9,9 management style. All that is reported is the questionnaire responses of staff that show slight improvements in their perception of their supervisors' behaviors. The staff had also participated in the seminars and were asked in the questionnaire to recall their supervisors' behaviors from over a year ago. Given these circumstances, it is likely that the staff responses were distorted by both time and sensitivity to training. Thus, until more sound evidence is presented, we cannot as yet draw any conclusions as to the effectiveness of the Grid Seminars.

Double-Loop Learning

Model of Ideal Manager

The ideal manager, according to Argyris (1976b; Argyris & Schon, 1974), is a master of double-loop learning; he or she will advocate a position, yet also encourage inquiry, challenge, and modification of this position in order to produce a decision that is based on the most complete and current information. Although most managers may believe and espouse "model 2" theories of behavior that are consistent with double-loop learning, they actually use "model 1" theories that promote only one-way or single-loop learning.

Single-loop learning is initiated by managers who operate according to model 1 theories-in-use. These managers strive to (1) unilaterally define and achieve their goals; (2) win, not lose; (3) minimize negative feelings; and (4) always be rational. In order to satisfy these four values, model 1 managers maximize control over their environment, the task, and people. Co-workers, in turn, feel controlled and manipulated, and they respond by withholding information and ideas, refusing to give valid feedback, and behaving in a generally defensive and conforming manner. What results is rigid channels of communication in which there is little public testing of ideas and where learning is single loop or self-sealing, in that managers only learn what they already know.

Managers who operate according to model 2 theories-in-use strive to attain valid information, free and informed choice, and internal commitment. These managers build channels for double-loop learning by inviting public scrutiny, criticism, and modification of their ideas. This creates channels for the two-way flow of information and feedback from which sound and effective decisions can be made.

Training Program

The focus of the training program is to make managers aware of the discrepancy between their espoused theories and their theories-in-use, so as to move them from model 1 to model 2 behavior. Trainees first study material covering model 1 and model 2 theories and then review these concepts in a group discussion. The trainees are then presented with a case study and asked to formulate a solution to the problem. These solutions are analyzed by the trainer to determine the extent to which they fit model 1 or model 2 theories of action. The trainees are then divided into small groups, and each group is given one of the solutions developed in the previous activity and then instructed to propose an alternative solution to the problem that approaches model 2 behavior. The groups then rejoin to discuss their model 2 strategies. One member from each subgroup then role plays the solution with the trainer, and the group provides feedback on the congruence of the strategy with model 2 behavior and its effectiveness in solving the original problem.

Evaluation

Reports on the overall effectiveness of double-loop training have shown that although trainees can be taught to develop model 2 solutions, they still cannot change their behavior in accordance with model 2 actions (Argyris, 1976a). Apparently, the training provides ample opportunity to learn model 2 thinking but not to practice model 2 behaving (Wexley & Latham, 1981). Like the managerial grid, model 2 theories define a general objective or leadership strategy but fail to provide sufficient behavioral specificity. There is generally also no consistent evidence to suggest that managers who encourage two-way communication are more effective than managers who do not (Vroom, 1976).

Positive Reinforcement Seminars

Model of Ideal Manager

Unlike Grid Seminars and Double-loop Learning, the positive reinforcement or applied behavior analysis approach (Keller, 1969; Skinner, 1974) does not put forth an explicit model of an ideal manager. Rather, the model is more subtle or implied.

The behavior analysis approach emphasizes the lawful relationships that exist between behavior and its consequences. Workers are thought to improve or decrease their levels of performance, depending on the consequences that follow their behavior. If the consequence is positively reinforcing, performance improves. If the event is punishing, or if no event occurs, performance eventually drops to a baseline level. Poor performance, then, is viewed as stemming from management's misuse of the consequences it provides for worker behavior.

Thus, the implicit model of an effective manager is one who judiciously and systematically delivers consequences based on worker performance. An effective manager, for example, would make it clear what is expected, accurately and fairly appraise performance, and then regularly provide consequences contingent on desired or undesired behavior. An ineffective manager, on the other hand, would probably leave tasks ambiguously defined, appraise performance infrequently, if at all, and then arbitrarily notice only poor performance.

Training Program

The focus of the Positive Reinforcement Seminars is to teach managers how to influence workers' performance through specifically clarifying desired behaviors, frequently monitoring those behaviors, and systematically providing consequences contingent on satisfactory performances. Although the specific content and format of these seminars varies with the individual and firm providing training, all seminars include:

1. A didactic presentation of the behavioral principles.
2. Examples that illustrate how to apply these principles to actual work settings.

During the seminar sessions, trainees are taught the principles of positive and negative reinforcement, punishment, and extinction; what effect each principle has on performance; and how and when to apply each principle to change or maintain worker behavior. In particular, trainees learn the various types of reinforcers, which include (1) social reinforcers, such as recognition; (2) informational reinforcers, such as feedback; (3) generalized reinforcers, such as money; and (4) organizational reinforcers, such as promotions. Social reinforcers are often recommended as the most feasible and powerful form of reinforcement supervisors can provide on a daily basis (Rosen & Daniels, in press). Informational reinforcers are also suggested as a particularly potent and practical means of enhancing employee motivation (Komaki, Collins, & Penn, 1982).

Trainees are then taught to apply these principles to problems in actual work settings. Examples are provided that illustrate how to (1) identify or pinpoint desirable behaviors; (2) objectively monitor behaviors; and (3) provide consequences contingent on performances. In the area of occupational safety, for instance, (1) safe behaviors would be specified; (2) frequent observations of safety behaviors would be conducted at the work site; and (3) feedback regarding the level of safety performances would be discussed with workers.

Participants are then encouraged to implement this three-step procedure in their own organizations. Trainees practice identifying or pinpointing desired behaviors and brainstorm how best to recognize subordinates for performing well. For training sessions held on a regular basis, participants often select a problem area in their organizations. They then learn how to define desirable behaviors specifically, to monitor those behaviors, and to chart performance levels on graphs. Some firms provide extensive follow-up services in which their personnel remain at the organization to provide assistance as needed.

Evaluation

Only indirect evidence exists for the effectiveness of Positive Reinforcement Seminars. Recent reviews (Andrasik, Heimberg, & McNamara, 1981; Frederiksen, 1982; O'Brien, Dickinson, & Rosow, 1982) of behavior analysis applications to work settings, for example, reference numerous studies demonstrating the efficacy of this three-step process of clarifying, monitoring, and providing performance consequences. However, virtually no studies have focused on the behaviors of managers following participation in these seminars. Thus, no direct evidence exists showing that the trainees actually learn the behavioral principles and, more importantly, that they actually modify their own behaviors when interacting with subordinates.

Behavior Modeling

In contrast to the previous approaches, behavior modeling focuses on the process by which persons learn new behaviors rather than teaching trainees specific leadership styles. This training approach is based on social learning theory (Bandura, 1977), which holds that most human behavior is learned observationally through modeling. Thus, although people can learn from the consequences of their own behaviors, they can also learn from observing the actions of others.

As originally presented by Goldstein and Sorcher (1974), the three major components that constitute the behavior modeling approach are:

1. Modeling, in which trainees watch filmed interactions between supervisors and subordinates in order to observe effective ways of handling problem situations.
2. Role playing, in which trainees practice and rehearse the specific behaviors demonstrated by the filmed models.

3. Social reinforcement, in which trainees receive praise, reward, and constructive feedback for demonstrating appropriate supervisory behaviors.

Training Program

Latham and Saari (1979) introduced a behavior modeling program designed to increase the effectiveness of first-line supervisors. The 18-hour program consisted of nine training sessions focused on the following supervisory situations: (1) orienting a new employee; (2) giving recognition; (3) motivating poor performance; (4) correcting poor work habits; (5) discussing potential disciplinary action; (6) reducing absenteeism; (7) handling a complaining employee; (8) reducing turnover; and (9) overcoming resistance to change. Each session was conducted according to the following format:

a) Introduction of the topic by two trainers (attentional processes).

b) Presentation of a film that depicts a supervisor model effectively handling a situation by following a set of 3 to 6 learning points that were shown in the film immediately before and after the model was presented (retention processes).

c) Group discussion of the effectiveness of the model in demonstrating the desired behaviors (retention processes).

d) Practice in role playing the desired behaviors in front of the entire class (retention processes, motor reproduction processes).

e) Feedback from the class on the effectiveness of each trainee in demonstrating the desired behaviors (motivational processes). (Latham & Saari, 1979, p. 241)

In the role-playing activity, trainees reenacted a personal experience relevant to the topic covered in the film and were given the opportunity to play both the role of themselves and the subordinate. To facilitate transfer of training, trainees were given a list of learning points, or behavioral goals, and asked to practice their new supervisory skills with one or more employees during the upcoming week. Moreover, to increase the likelihood that supervisors would perform these new behaviors, their superintendents attended an accelerated behavior modeling program that stressed the importance of praising supervisors for demonstrating the desired behaviors on the job.

Results of the preceding study revealed that trained supervisors performed significantly better than untrained supervisors on both learning and behavioral criteria. Six months after the program, trained supervisors scored higher than untrained supervisors on solutions given on a paper-and-pencil test of problem situations. They also received higher ratings from their superintendents on (1) role plays of supervisor–employee problems; (2) behavioral observation scales; and (3) company performance appraisal measures. However, these results did not demonstrate that the behaviors of the trained supervisors were related to improvements in employee performance. Without such evidence, we do not know if their behaviors were in fact more effective, only that they were perceived as more effective by their superintendents.

Despite an emphasis on behavioral observation and rehearsal, the behavior modeling approach does not specify how to supervise effectively, beyond providing general objectives or goals for behaviors. For example, the learning points for the session on handling a complaining employee are (1) avoid responding with hostility or defensiveness; (2) ask for and listen openly to the employee's complaints; (3) restate the complaint for thorough understanding; (4) recognize and acknowledge his or her viewpoint; (5) if necessary, state one's position nondefensively; and (6) set a specific date for a follow-up meeting. Just how a supervisor would "listen openly," "recognize and acknowledge" an employee's viewpoint, or state a position "nondefensively" is left undefined. It is even questionable as to whether achieving these objectives would lead to better supervision.

Evaluation

Of all the management training programs discussed thus far, the behavior modeling approach has been evaluated most frequently. Several investigators (Burnaska, 1976; Byham, Adams, & Kiggins, 1976; Moses, 1978; Moses & Ritchie, 1976) have reported that managers trained with behavior modeling scored higher than untrained managers on performance ratings and employee evaluations. In addition, Smith (1976) reported that training using modeling and modeling plus team building was more effective in improving communication skills than traditional management training approaches. However, as McGhee and Tullar (1978) have pointed out, because all these studies used nonmatched or nonrandomized control groups, the initial differences between subjects in the trained and untrained groups may have biased these results. Thus, the verdict is still out on the behavior modeling approach as well as interpersonal skills training programs in general.

CRITICAL EVALUATION

No One Really Knows What Managers Should Do to Enhance Their Effectiveness

Management training is in serious trouble. Its major problem is definitional: Training programs are based on either vague or unempirical models of an ideal manager or on no models at all. Without a clear understanding of what behaviors define an effective manager, we cannot adequately prescribe the goals of management training, design appropriate training packages, or expect to evaluate

realistically whether these programs improve supervisory skillfulness. At present, we have no solid evidence that shows what effective managers actually do that distinguishes them from ineffective managers. We have not even defined or investigated what managers, effective or otherwise, do when interacting with their subordinates.

Four reasons have been suggested for this lack of precise information on managerial behavior and effectiveness (Campbell et al., 1970). First, the fact that managers contribute to their organizations through their subordinates makes it difficult to measure the tangible outcomes of their work. Second, it is difficult to compare the effectiveness of managers across different levels and functions in an organization. Outcome measures, such as the volume of new accounts, may be appropriate for the marketing director but not for the director of research and development. Global measures, such as rankings of total managerial effectiveness, lack specificity and raise many questions of rater bias. Other measures, such as salary and seniority, reflect function and organizational level in addition to supervisory effectiveness.

The imprecise methods used to study managerial performance are another reason for the lack of a documented model. These are (1) *questionnaire/interview* (Dowell & Wexley, 1978; Hemphill, 1959; Morse & Wagner, 1978; Orpen, 1973; Tornow & Pinto, 1976; Tscheulin, 1973); and (2) *diary* (Brewer & Tomlinson, 1964; Burns, 1954, 1957; Carlson, 1951; Copeman, 1963; Dubin & Spray, 1964; Ellis & Child, 1973; Hinrichs, 1976; Horne & Lupton, 1965; Marples, 1967; Stewart, 1964; Thomason, 1966a, 1966b). Growing evidence suggests that managers' self-reports of their activities on questionnaires and interviews are often quite inaccurate (Lewis & Dahl, 1976). Although the diary technique provides more direct, and therefore, presumably more accurate information than do questionnaire/interview methods, several investigators have questionned whether managers can reliably record their own activities, given the hectic shift and pace of their day (Burns, 1957; Carlson, 1951; Marples, 1967).

A fourth reason concerns the way in which these data have typically been collected and analyzed. In the questionnaire and interview studies, categories are so vague that one can hardly reach sound conclusions about the specifics of managerial actions. In diary studies, the information is more concrete but behaviorally sterile. Although it surely expands our knowledge base to learn that the manager's work is primarily oral and that his or her interactions are brief (McCall, Morrison, & Hannan, 1978), this knowledge does not reveal exactly how managers should interact with their subordinates.

Even observational studies, which overcome many of the methodological problems of questionnaire/interview and diary studies, analyze behaviors in terms of time spent engaged in each category of the classification scheme (Guest, 1956; Jasinski, 1956; Landsberger, 1961; Ponder, 1957). In a now-classic observational study of managers, Mintzberg (1973) attempted to obtain more meaningful information by developing categories as the observations took place rather than beginning the study with a set of categories developed prior to observing. After five managers had been observed for 1 week each, the data were examined, the rough categories used in collecting the data were refined, and all the observations were recoded to reflect what had been learned about managerial behavior during the observations. Though the Mintzberg data were painstakingly collected, analyzed, and reanalyzed, the study produced information only on what managers do—not what they should do.

In short, despite the considerable body of descriptive research on managers, we still lack sufficient information to define "managerial effectiveness" adequately.

This definitional problem means that:

1. The goals of most training programs are necessarily vague or nonexistent.
2. Trainees' strengths and weaknesses are rarely diagnosed before training.
3. Training is not tailored to meet the needs of individuals with different skills levels or situational problems.
4. Lastly, program effectiveness is uncertain.

Claims About Management Training Need to Be Substantiated

Despite these problems, there are literally hundreds of programs that offer interpersonal skills training for managers. For each program, there is a stated or implied claim that the particular training program will enhance performance on the job, make subordinates more receptive, or create improvements on the bottom line. Unfortunately, few of the programs advertised can live up to their press. The evidence simply does not exist to back up their claims.

More often than not, training programs are not carefully and specifically evaluated to determine their effectiveness (Staw, 1977). Instead, they are assumed to be naturally beneficial, or their effects are only cursorily examined, with management accepting testimonials from nonneutral parties as primary evidence. Goldstein (1980) in a comprehensive review of training in work organizations acknowledges this unfortunate situation, noting that most "decisions are based upon anecdotal trainee and trainer reactions" (p. 238). Given such uncertainty, it is no wonder that decisions in this area are little better than shots in the dark.

How, then, does one separate fact from fantasy in claims made by training programs?

The established method is to use what is referred to as between-group or control-group designs. In the simplest case, persons are assigned by lot to one of two groups. One is labeled the *treatment group*; the other, the *control group*. Persons in the treatment group are exposed to the program, whereas persons in the control group are not. Potential factors are effectively ruled out because random assignment essentially equalizes both groups on all dimensions except the treatment. It is just as likely that one group of managers will experience a significant event—an innovative marketing technique, a new influx of personnel—or will get more practiced at a task than the other group will. If improvements occur in the treatment group and not in the control, one can confidently say that the program was responsible for the improvements. For a further description of these designs and potentially confounding effects, we refer the reader to the classic text by Campbell and Stanley (1963/1966).

Although control-group designs are widely acknowledged as an ideal way to rule out alternative hypotheses, suitable control groups are difficult to arrange in most work settings. Rarely, outside of laboratories, can one randomly assign persons to different groups with the purpose of exposing only one of the groups to an intervention. Managers in the West typically stay in the West; managers in the Southeast stay in the Southeast. Seldom can individuals from two such areas be reassigned by lot so that some in the West are now in the Southeast and vice versa, and persons in newly formed group 1 are exposed to in-house training, whereas persons in newly formed group 2 are not. Despite the importance of precise evaluation, it is a simple fact of organizational life that presently constituted groups tend, and rightfully, to be left intact.

FUTURE DIRECTIONS

Given our lack of certainty regarding the skills that determine the quality of super-

vision, we recommend that future research attempt to resolve the definitional problem by examining basic differences in behavior between effective and less effective managers.

Proposal: Toward Effective Supervision

As a first step in enhancing managers' supervisory skills, we suggest that research be conducted to:

1. Determine exactly what managers do when interacting with subordinates by observing the frequency and variety of performance antecedents, monitors, and consequences that managers provide.
2. Identify what constitutes effective supervision by contrasting the actions of effective and less effective managers on these three dimensions.

Observational Measurement System

This research, like Mintzberg's, should collect data primarily through observations. A trained observer could track and record the interactions between a manager and his or her subordinates across a variety of occasions. One could thus collect relatively nonfiltered information about managerial behaviors, as several researchers have suggested (Campbell, 1977; Luthans, 1979; McCall, Morrison, & Hannan, 1978; Sims, 1979).

Focus on Performance Antecedents, Monitors, and Consequences

This measurement system would classify behavior according to what operant psychologists regard as the heart of supervision—those activities in which managers clarify, appraise, and provide consequences for worker performance.

Information would then be available on the percentage of time each manager spent providing the following:

1. Performance consequences (which include those occasions in which a

manager indicates knowledge of a subordinate's performance).

2. Performance monitors (which include those occasions in which a manager collects information about a subordinate's performance).

3. Performance antecedents (which include those occasions in which a manager instructs, reminds, or conveys an expectation of performance for a subordinate).

Within the category of performance consequences, one could see whether a manager delivers appraisals directly to the subordinate or indirectly to someone else and whether the evaluation given for performance is positive, negative, or neutral. Within the category of performance monitors, one could see whether a manager typically collects information about performance through actual work samples or self-reports. Within the category of performance antecedents, one could examine the degree of specificity a manager uses to convey expectations of performance. One could also see whether a manager typically invites subordinate participation.

Contrast Effective and Less Effective Managers

Those managers rated high in supervision by both their superiors and subordinates would be placed in an effective group, whereas those rated low in supervision would be placed in an ineffective group. Only managers rated particularly effective or ineffective would be included in the sample, so as to accentuate any differences that might exist.

The value of obtaining information on these two contrasted groups is that it allows for a comparison. One could then determine whether one group performs a certain set of activities and the other group does not, or whether one group engages in certain activities more frequently than the other.

Benefits

This research program would begin to address questions of what managers *should* do to enhance their effectiveness. For example,

1. Do effective managers monitor and provide performance consequences more or less often than ineffective managers?

2. Do effective managers instruct and remind subordinates as frequently as ineffective managers?

3. Do ineffective managers deliver primarily positive or negative performance consequences?

4. What happens when managers deliver consequences without monitoring performance?

5. Should managers invite worker participation?

The proposed research would also provide a rich source of information about how managers actually instruct, monitor, and provide performance consequences. One might find, for example, that managers do not communicate evaluations in blatant or overt statements, such as "I'm pleased with you for completing that sales report." Instead, we might find that managers express consequences in language like, "I passed your report on up the line," in which the evaluation is more subtle or implied.

The results of the proposed research would help to clarify training goals: One could specify exactly how managers should perform following participation in a training program.

Another advantage is that training evaluators could use the proposed observational instrument to assess managers' performance before and after training. Brief simulated social situations could be arranged similar to those used by Curran (1982) for judging entry- and exit-level social skills of psychiatric patients. In Curran's Simulated Social Interaction

Test, for example, a narrator describes a social situation and a confederate delivers a prompt:

NARRATOR: You are at work, and one of your bosses has just finished inspecting one of the jobs that you have completed. He says to you . . .

CONFEDERATE: That's a pretty sloppy job. I think you could have done better.

Videotaped simulations like these, rewritten to reflect those that managers typically encounter, could then be rated by trained observers.

The pretraining assessments could be used by training developers to tailor instruction based on participant needs and wishes. Posttraining assessments could be used to see how closely persons come to meeting course objectives and to revamp the course content and procedures. The observational instrument could also be used to evaluate transfer of training to on-the-job behavior. Observers could record managers' interactions with their subordinates prior to, during, and following participation in a training program.

In short, the proposed research would provide an empirical basis of effective supervisory behavior on which to evaluate the claims made about management training programs.

Alternative Evaluation Strategies: Within-Group Designs

Our second recommendation concerns an alternative strategy for evaluating training programs. Instead of comparing a treatment group with a control group, we suggest using within-group designs (Komaki, 1982). The advantage of within-group designs is that one can determine the effectiveness of an intervention, while avoiding the problems and complexities of setting up a control group.

Among within-group designs, the multiple baseline design is particularly appropriate for assessing the effects of training programs. As its name indicates, it involves the collection of data on two or more baselines. The second characteristic of this design is that the training is introduced in a staggered fashion across baselines.

In a multiple baseline design across behaviors, for example, the treatment is first introduced with one behavior. When the desired change has occurred (or a certain amount of time has passed, or a number of data points have accumulated), the training is begun with the second behavior. Again, following an observed change, the treatment is introduced with the next behavior, and so on until training has been introduced with all the behaviors.

Suppose you are conducting a 12-week training course on interpersonal skills for first-line supervisors and you wish to evaluate whether the training is having the desired effect. You could use a multiple baseline design across behavior as demonstrated by Miller and Weaver (1972). You would first divide the content area into components, such as clarifying, monitoring, and providing performance consequences. You would repeatedly assess how well the new supervisors performed each category and then introduce the training, one category at a time. After assessing knowledge and skills in these areas, you would present the instructional package for the first category—antecedents. Once the trainees demonstrated a mastery of the first component, you would introduce the second one. If the supervisors demonstrated mastery of the second component and were still able to score well on the first, then you would introduce the third and last component.

Another alternative is to use a multiple baseline design across groups. In a recent study by Komaki, Heinzmann, and Lawson (1980), for example, a safety training program was introduced to the sweeper section of a vehicle maintenance division after 4 weeks of baseline. One week later the preventive maintenance section received the training. Again, following one week, training was introduced in the third and fourth departments.

The rationale underlying the multiple baseline design is that comparisons can be made between phases and the results can be checked to see whether effects are replicated at different times. To determine whether a particular program is responsible for improvements, one must examine whether performance changes after the program are introduced and whether other groups, yet to receive the program, continue at their baseline rates.

Because performance in the preceding study did not improve significantly following training in the first department and this result occurred again when the training was introduced in the second, third, and fourth departments, it was concluded that the training program was not effective in obtaining the desired on-the-job improvements. If performance improved following training and this effect was replicated in all the departments, then one could conclude that the training program caused on-the-job improvement.

Because within-group designs can verify cause—effect relationships without using control groups, we highly recommended them as a method for sustantiating claims about management training programs.

SUMMARY

In summary, this chapter has described how interpersonal skills are typically viewed and taught in business and industry. Four programs—Managerial Grid Seminars, Double-Loop Learning, Positive Reinforcement Seminars, and behavioral modeling—illustrate the gamut of courses offered to supervisors and managers.

Management training lags considerably behind the ideal, however. Its primary problem, which also plagues the entire social skills training area (Bellack, 1979; Conger & Kane, 1981; Curran, 1979), is definitional: No one really knows what managers should do to enhance their effectiveness. As a result, it is not clear what the goals of training should be. The lack of training goals, in turn, adversely effects how well we can evaluate training programs.

At the same time, the established method of evaluating programs, using between-group designs, is often unsuitable for work settings. The net result is that training programs are rarely, if ever, adequately evaluated. And thus, many of the glowing testimonials about management training are probably grossly exaggerated.

To correct this problem, we suggest that future researchers determine exactly what actions distinguish effective from ineffective managers. Assuming that differences are found, then a model of effective supervision could be put forward that was empirically based and specific. Second, we recommend that researchers employ within-group designs when evaluating training programs. These designs are particularly useful in work settings and permit one to draw sound conclusions regarding program effectiveness. By implementing these suggestions, we will enhance the utility of supervisory skills training considerably and be well on our way toward improving the quality of supervision.

REFERENCES

Andrasik, F., Heimberg, J. S., & McNamara, J. R. (1981). Behavior modification of work and work-related problems. In M. Hersen, R. M. Eisler, & P. M. Miller (Eds.) *Progress In behavior modification*. New York: Academic Press.

Argyris, C. (1976a). Theories of action that inhibit individual learning. *American Psychologist, 31,* 638–654.

Argyris, C. (1976b). *Increasing leadership effectiveness.* New York: Wiley.

Argyris, C., & Schon, D. (1974). *Theory in practice.* San Francisco: Jossey-Bass.

Bandura, A. (1977). *Social learning theory.* Englewood Cliffs, NJ: Prentice-Hall.

Barkin, S. (1950). A trade unionist appraises management personnel philosophy. *Harvard Busines Review, 18,* 59–64.

Bass, B. M. (1981). *Stogdill's handbook of leadership.* New York: Free Press.

Bellack, A. S. (1979). Behavioral assessment of social skills. In A. S. Bellack & M. Hersen (Eds.), *Research and practice in social skills training.* New York: Plenum.

Blake, R. R., & Mouton, J. S. (1964). *The managerial grid.* Houston: Gulf.

Blake, R. R., & Mouton, J. S. (1978). *The new managerial grid.* Houston: Gulf.

Blake, R. R., Mouton, J. S., Barnes, J. S., & Greiner, L. E. (1964). Breakthrough in organizational development. *Harvard Business Review, 42,* 133–155.

Brewer, E., & Tomlinson, J. W. C. (1964). The manager's working day. *The Journal of Industrial Economics, 12,* 191–197.

Bridgman, D. S. (1959). Company management development programs. In F. C. Pierson (Ed.), *The education of American businessmen.* New York: McGraw-Hill.

Bowden, G. T. (1952). The problem of employee turnover. *Harvard Business Review, 30*(5), 72–82.

Burnaska, R. F. (1976). The effects of behavior modeling training upon managers' behaviors and employees' perceptions. *Personnel Psychology, 29,* 329–335.

Burns, T. (1954). The directions of activity and communication in a departmental executive group. *Human Relations, 7,* 73–97.

Burns, T. (1957). Management in action. *Operational Research Quarterly, 8,* 45–60.

Byham, W. C., Adams, D., & Kiggins, A. (1976). Transfer of modeling training to the job. *Personnel Psychology, 29,* 345–349.

Campbell, J. P. (1977). The cutting edge of leadership: An overview. In J. G. Hunt & L. L. Larson (Eds.), *Leadership: The cutting edge.* Carbondale: Southern Illinois University Press.

Campbell, J. P., Dunnette, D., Lawler, E., III, & Weick, K. E., Jr. (1970). *Managerial behavior, performance, and effectiveness.* New York: McGraw-Hill.

Campbell, D. T., & Stanley, J. C. (1966). Experimental and quasi-experimental designs for research on teaching. In N. L. Gage (Ed.), *Handbook of research on teaching.* Chicago: Rand McNally, 1963. Reprinted separately as *Experimental and quasi-experimental designs for research.* Chicago: Rand McNally.

Carlson, S. (1951). *Executive behavior: A study of the work load and the working methods of managing directors.* Stockholm: Strombergs.

Conger, J. C., & Kane, S. P. (1981). Social skills intervention in the treatment of isolated or withdrawn children. *Psychological Bulletin, 90,* 478–495.

Copeman, G. (1963). How British executives spend their day. In G. Copeman, H. Luijk, & F. de P. Hanika, *How the executive spends his time.* London: Business Publications.

Curran, J. P. (1979). Social skills: Methodological issues and future directions. In A. S. Bellack & M. Hersen (Eds.), *Research and practice in social skills training.* New York: Plenum.

Curran, J. P. (1982). A procedure for the assessment of social skills: The simulated social interaction test. In J. P. Curran & P. M. Monti (Eds.), *Social skills training.* New York: Guilford.

Dowell, B. E., & Wexley, K. N. (1978). Development of a work behavior taxonomy for first line supervisors. *Journal of Applied Psychology, 63,* 563–572.

Dubin, R., & Spray, S. L. (1964). Executive behavior and interaction. *Industrial Relations, 3,* 99–108.

Ellis, T. T., & Child, J. (1973). Placing stereotypes of the manager into perspective. *Journal of Management Studies, 10,* 233–255.

Fiedler, F. A., & Chemers, M. M. (1974). Leadership and management. In J. W.

McGuire (Ed.), *Contemporary management: Issues and viewpoints*. Englewood Cliffs, NJ: Prentice-Hall.

Frederiksen, L. W. (Ed.). (1982). *Handbook of organizational behavior management*. New York: Wiley.

Gilbert, T. F. (1976). The high cost of knowledge. *Personnel*, March–April, 11–23.

Goldstein, A. P., & Sorcher, M. (1974). *Changing supervisor behavior*. New York: Pergamon.

Goldstein, I. L. (1980). Training in work organizations. *Annual Review of Psychology, 31*, 229–272.

Guest, R. H. (1956). Of time and the foreman. *Personnel, 32*, 478–486.

Hemphill, J. K. (1959). Job descriptions for executives. *Harvard Business Review, 37*, 55–67.

Hinrichs, J. R. (1976). Where has all the time gone? *Personnel, 53*(4), 44–49.

Horne, J. H., & Lupton, T. (1965). The work activities of "middle" managers—An exploratory study. *The Journal of Management Studies, 2*, 14–33.

Jasinski, F. J. (1956). Foreman relationships outside the work group. *Personnel, 33*, 130–136.

Keller, F. S. (1969). *Learning: Reinforcement theory*. New York: Random House.

Kestnbaum, M. A. (1940). Study of management prerogatives. *Harvard Business Review, 19*(1), 88–98.

Komaki, J. (1982). A case for the single case: Making judicious decisions about alternatives. In L. W. Frederiksen (Ed.), *Handbook of organizational behavior management*. New York: Wiley.

Komaki, J., Collins, R. L., & Penn, P. (1982). Role of performance antecedents and consequences in work motivation. *Journal of Applied Psychology, 67*, 334–340.

Komaki, J., Heinzmann, A. T., & Lawson, L. (1980). Effect of training and feedback: Component analysis of a behavioral safety program. *Journal of Applied Psychology, 65*, 261–270.

Landsberger, H. A. (1961). The horizontal dimension in bureaucracy. *Administrative Science Quarterly, 6*, 229–332.

Latham, G. P., & Saari, L. M. (1979). The application of social learning theory to training supervisors through behavior modeling. *Journal of Applied Psychology, 64*, 239–246.

Lewis, D. R., & Dahl, T. (1976). Time management in higher education administration: A case study. *Higher Education, 5*, 49–66.

Luthans, F. (1979). Leadership: A proposal for a social learning theory base and observational and functional analysis techniques to measure leader behavior. In J. G. Hunt & L. L. Larson (Eds.), *Crosscurrents in leadership*. Carbondale: Southern Illinois University Press.

Marples, D. L. (1967). Studies of managers: A fresh start? *Journal of Management Studies, 4*, 282–299.

McCall, M. W., Jr., Morrison, A. M., & Hannan, R. L. (1978). *Studies of managerial work: Results and methods* (Tech. Rep. No. 9). Greensboro, NC: Center for Creative Leadership.

McGhee, W., & Tuller, W. L. (1978). A note on evaluating behavior modification and behavior modeling as industrial training techniques. *Personnel Psychology, 31*, 477–484.

Miller, L. K., & Weaver, F. H. (1972). A multiple baseline achievement test. In G. Semb (Ed.), *Behavior analysis and education*. Lawrence: Support and Development Center for Follow Through, Department of Human Development, University of Kansas.

Mintzberg, H. (1973). *The nature of managerial work*. New York: Harper & Row.

Morse, J. J., & Wagner, F. R. (1978). Measuring the process of managerial effectiveness. *Academy of Management Journal, 21*, 23–25.

Moses, J. L. (1978). Behavior modeling for managers. *Human Factors, 20* (2), 225–232.

Moses, J. L., & Ritchie, R. J. (1976). Supervisory relationships training: A behavioral evaluation of a behavior modeling Program. *Personnel Psychology, 29*, 337–343.

Neider, L. L. (1981). Training effectiveness: Changing attitudes. *Training and Development Journal, 35* (12), 24–28.

O'Brien, R. M., Dickinson, A. M., & Rosow,

M. (Eds.). (1982). *Industrial behavior modification*. New York: Pergamon.

Orpen, C. (1973). An empirical assessment of the job performance of high-level executives by means of multitrait-multimethod matrix. *Psychologia Africana, 15*, 7–14.

Phelps, E. D. (1962). Help your engineers to get ahead. *Harvard Business Review, 40*(1), 125–132.

Ponder, Q. D. (1957). The effective manufacturing foreman. In E. Young (Ed.), *Proceedings of the Tenth Annual Meeting of the Industrial Relations Research Association (pp. 41–54)*.

Rosen, T. A., & Daniels, A. C. (in press). *Performance management*. Atlanta: Performance Management.

Sims, H. P., Jr. (1979). Limitations and extensions to questionnaires in leadership research. In J. G. Hunt & L. L. Larson (Eds.), *Crosscurrents in leadership*. Carbondale: Southern Illinois University Press.

Skinner, B. F. (1974). *About behaviorism*. New York: Vintage.

Smith, A. P. (1980). Wither T + D—And you? *Training and Development Journal, 34*(5), 88–94.

Smith, P. E. (1976). Management modeling training to improve morale and customer satisfaction. *Personnel Psychology, 29*, 351–359.

Staw, B. M. (1977). The experimenting organization: Problems and prospectss. In B. M. Staw (Ed.), *Psychological foundations of organizational behavior*. Santa Monica: Goodyear.

Stewart, R. (1964). The use of diaries to study managers' jobs. *The Journal of Management Studies, 2*, 228–235.

Thomason, G. F. (1966a). Managerial work roles and relationships (Part I). *The Journal of Management Studies, 2*, 228–235.

Thomason, G. F. (1966b). Managerial work roles and relationships (Part II). *The Journal of Management Studies, 3*, 270–284.

Tornow, W. W., & Pinto, P. R. (1976). The development of a managerial job taxonomy: A system for describing, classifying, and evaluating executive positions. *Journal of Applied Psychology, 61*, 410–418.

Tscheulin, D. (1973). Leader behavior measurement in German industry. *Journal of Applied Psychology, 57*, 28–31.

Vroom, V. H. (1976). Leadership. In M. D. Dunnette (Ed.), *Handbook of industrial/organizational psychology*, Chicago: Rand McNally.

Wexley, K. N., & Latham, G. P. (1981). *Developing and training human resources in organizations*. Glenview, IL: Scott, Foresman.

CHAPTER 23

Social Skills Training

A European Perspective

ADRIAN FURNHAM

In England it is bad manners to be clever, to assert something confidently. It may be your own personal view that two and two make four, but you must not state it in a self-assured way, because this is a democratic country and others may be of a different opinion.

G. Mikes's "How to be an alien," 1938

The English are a shy and different race, and can sometimes be seen looking lost and lonely at parties because they do not know the other people in the room and are too timorous to introduce themselves.

Debrett's "Etiquette and Modern Manners," 1981.

The difference in perspective between North American and European theory and research in social skills training can best be seen in the different histories of the development of the concept. Although it may be argued that American research on social skills grew out of the work of the behavior therapists of the 1950s such as Wolpe (1958) and studies on social competence (Philips & Zigler, 1961; Zigler & Philips, 1960) in the 1960s, the European research had a quite different origin in social psychology and ergonomics (Furnham, 1979; Furnham & Argyle, 1981).

Welford (1981) has noted:

The modern concept of social skill came into focus with a study by Crossman (1960) of the operators of automated process plants. . . . Many of the concepts formulated in the course of earlier research on sensory-motor performance and information processing appeared to have close analogies in social situations. . . . Credit for the expansion of social skill from an idea into a considerable area of research and interest is due to Argyle (1967), who collaborated with Crossman in starting a major research project while they were both at Oxford and who has with his co-workers played a leading part in developing the area since. (pp. 847–848)

American researchers on the other hand, like Eisler (1978), trace the ideas of social skills back to the neopsychoanalyst Sullivan and to Wolpe and Lazarus. Thus, whereas for North America, social skills training is firmly rooted in clinical and counseling psychology, in Britain and Europe the research in social skills owes more to occupational and social psychology. The difference in these origins still reflects itself in the work done by social skills researchers on both sides of the Atlantic.

There are, however, other differences between European and North American social skills training that are probably a function of the general difference be-

555

tween the two continents' approach to psychological research. This general difference has been well illustrated in the person–situation debate that has overflowed into the social skills area (Curran, 1979; Furnham, 1983b). Whereas European schools of psychology have followed a Leibnitzian tradition, American schools have tended to follow a Lockean tradition. That is, in the European approach it is the organism (individual) that is important, and causes of social behavior are seen as internal; whereas in the latter tradition, the organism is seen as reactive to social events external to it that are the primary causes of social behavior (Pervin, 1978). Britain, however, has often leaned more toward the American than the European tradition both theoretically and empirically.

Apart from the historical and philosophic differences in the two approaches, it seems that British and American researchers have adopted different paradigms. Ellis and Whittington (1981) have suggested that there are four "paradigms" or approaches to the acquisition of social skills and the way in which programs are conceived, planned, operated, and evaluated. These they have labeled "conditioning," "cybernetic," "experiental," and "teleological." It is quite clear that whereas American social skills training owes much to the conditioning behavioristic paradigm, the British, and to a lesser extent European, social skills researchers lean toward a more cybernetic, cognitive approach. With the coming of the "cognitive revolution" in American social psychology, this difference may, however, be lessening.

Whatever the origins of the different perspectives, there are a number of different emphases between European and American psychologists interested in social skills and social competence. It should be pointed out at the onset of this chapter that the observations that follow are of necessity generalizations. It would

not be difficult to find contrary examples for each of the distinctions made. Nevertheless, the purpose of this chapter is to attempt to outline some of the major differences between North American and European perspectives on social skills training.

DIFFERENT EMPHASES

Assertiveness Versus Friendship Formation

Perhaps the most obvious difference between the two approaches has been the important stress American researchers place on assertiveness, whereas the British, on the other hand, have almost neglected the topic altogether. For some American researchers, assertiveness is synonymous with social skills (Gambrill, 1977), and much effort has gone into devising valid and reliable instruments to measure assertiveness (Hersen & Bellack, 1976). The interest in assertiveness in America can also be measured by the many popular books available to the layman (Bower & Bower, 1976).

Craighead, Kazdin, and Mahoney (1976) have argued:

The concept of assertiveness (or its lack) may be as broad as the notion of social skills; they are often used interchangeably. Assertiveness training may cover such varied skills as learning to say "Yes" and "No" appropriately, ability to express anger, noting and expressing disappointment, speaking up for one's rights, realizing that depressive aftermaths may represent a failure in interpersonal relations to act on what one covertly feels or intends to go on. One of the most succinct ways to increase social skills generally is to proceed through assertiveness training." (p. 363)

Despite the enthusiasm for the concept of assertivessness and much research in the definition, measurement, and training of assertiveness (Heiberg, Montgomery, Madsen, & Heimberg, 1977), some researchers are becoming more cautious about the usefulness of this research. Galassi, Galassi, and Vedder (1981) have concluded that:

first and foremost, the assertion construct is outmoded and should be relinquished. The construct has proven to be vague, difficult to define, and to be laden with assumptions reflecting traditional rather than more contemporary views of personality and behavior change. In the future, we need to concentrate more on response- and situation-specific behaviors falling under the rubric of social skills-social competence and retire the assertiveness (assertion) construct. (p. 330)

However, it should not be presumed that no interest has been taken in assertiveness in Britain. Furnham and Henderson (1981) administered five widely used self-report assertiveness inventories to 200 adult British males and females, none of whom were undergraduates. By and large, the British populations' scores were comparable with other studies done in America and Australia. However, of the six scores derived from the five scales, all showed significant male–female differences, with men reporting more assertiveness than females on five of the six, and females greater assertion on the sixth. These results also reflect studies and reviews on sex differences in assertiveness in Australia (Crassini, Law, & Wilson, 1979; Hollandsworth & Wall, 1977). Furnham and Henderson (1984) also undertook a content and correlational analysis of assertiveness inventories, noting their various biases.

The relative neglect of assertiveness as a topic for investigation among social skills researchers in Britain has been compensated by a great interest in friendship formation and interpersonal attraction. Indeed, for Trower, Bryant, and Argyle (1978), social rejection and isolation and the inability to make friends is a fundamental component of social skill. Cook (1978) has applied the social skill model to interpersonal perception. He notes:

. . . There is more to attraction than the variables traditionally thought important by psychologists, such as similarity (or complementarity) of personality, intelligence, attitudes, social background, proximity, or for that matter the variables thought important by the layman, such as appearance or money. These may well be necessary conditions, but are not sufficient—being similar, available, nice-looking, and rich doesn't guarantee a person friends or lovers; attractive people may not enjoy the rich social and sexual lives they are in a sense entitled to because they lack *social skill* that is, the ability to get on with other people. Making friends with someone is not an instantaneous process and does not occur magically or automatically, given similarity, proximity, etc; it depends on a complicated, drawn out sequence of moves, directed, by a general plan, and triggered by what each person's previous actions were. . . . Making friends with someone is a skilled performance, in the same sense that driving a car, or playing tennis, or turning a chair leg are skilled process. (p. 320)

Argyle (1978) has pointed out that clients presenting themselves for social skills training often have very few friends. They tend on the whole to be very emotionally inexpressive in face and voice, very socially unrewarding, and not really interested in other people.

Thus, whereas for American researchers lack of assertiveness is often seen as an index of social inadequacy, in Britain lack of friends is considered a more useful index of friendships formation (Furnham & Bochner, 1982; Trower et al., 1978). Despite this emphasis on friendship formation, those British psychologists who are most actively researching in the area do not exclusively take a social skills approach (Duck, 1973, 1977; Foot, Chapman, & Smith, 1980). The American studies on heterosexual social anxiety (Curran, 1977; Twentyman, Boland, & McFall, 1981), although concerned with opposite-sex friendship, are, however, very different from the British studies.

Clinical Versus Social Psychological Approaches

It has already been pointed out that, whereas social skills training in America is deeply rooted in clinical psychology, in Britain there are close ties between social psychology and social skills training. These different approaches can perhaps be most clearly seen in the pure and applied work in social skills training.

Though it is probably an exaggeration, particularly if one consults the work of Hersen, Bellack, and others at Pittsburgh, it does seem as if British research has concentrated particularly on nonverbal behavior and the minutae of social interaction, rather than on more gross forms of behavior, or subjective reports of feelings, perceptions, and the like (Argyle, Alkema, & Gilmour, 1972; Trower, 1980). Similarly, British researchers have used nonpsychiatric samples more than American researchers (Bryant & Trower, 1974; Furnham & Henderson, 1981), although some careful and detailed studies have been done on psychiatric patients (Bryant, Trower, Yardley, Urbieta, & Letemendia, 1976). On the whole, British researchers appear to use questionnaires and other self-report measures very little, preferring to measure skills by using peer ratings or behavioral measures. Some attempts have been made to developed self-report measures such as the "social situations questionnaire" (Trower et al., 1978), but it has received little psychometric assessment. Similarly, Spence (1980) has provided some useful but as yet quite unvalidated self-report measures of social competence in adolescence. However, Lindsay and Lindsay (1982) have attempted to develop, standardize, and validate a questionnaire about social difficulty for adolescence. Thus, although many British social skills researchers

have done careful and exhaustive work measuring the minutae of social behaviors from videotapes, they have been somewhat cavalier in the development and use of self-report measures. American researchers, on the other hand, seem generally to expend less energy measuring such a wide range of minor social behaviors, perferring to develop valid, reliable, multidimensional self-report measures of social skills.

The clinical versus social psychological differences can also been seen in the application of social skills research. Whereas the application of social skills training in America always appears to have a clinical flavor, in Britain it is just as often occupational.

Social skills training has been used in America for schizophrenics (Wallace et al., 1980), delinquents (Freedman, Rosenthal, Danahoe, & McFall, 1979), alcoholics (Foy, Massey, Duer, Ross, & Wooten, 1979), and many other groups. Furthermore, there exist a whole range of self-help or popular instruction books about aspects of social skills training that simply do not exist in Britain in the same profusion. Indeed, they are few and far between, showing perhaps the Europeans dislike of such programs.

On the other hand, social skills training in Britain has been extensively and successfully applied to occupation, industrial, and administrative settings. In the book *Skills with People: A Guide for Managers,* Sidney, Brown, and Argyle (1973) have attempted to describe the basis of social skills theory, but they spent the vast portion of the book looking at such skills as speaking and writing, interviewing, chairing committees, maintaining long-term relationships, and building and leading work groups. Similarly, Argyle (1974) in *The Social Psychology of Work* has a chapter on social skills and work. In this chapter, he acknowledges the work by Mayo and Likert on the importance of social skills in the work place, but references to these writers are rarely found in the mainstream American social skills literature. Indeed, for Argyle, the very first social skills to be trained were with those professionals like supervisors and teachers, and the first research in this area was that of industrial and organizational psychologists comparing the behavior of effective and ineffective supervisors. More recently, Argyle (1981a) has edited a book exclusively concerned with social skills and work, which contains chapters concerned with negotiating and bargaining, public speaking, and intercultural communication.

Hence, the difference between the social and clinical approaches to social skills training can to some extent be seen in the pure and applied research of people on both sides of the Atlantic.

Theory versus Practice in Social Skills Training

Despite the rapid expansion of social skills training on both sides of the Atlantic and euphoric expectations for a new treatment method, a more reflective period of critical evaluation and empirical assessment has set in. Some reviewers have been particularly scathing (Stravinsky, 1978), whereas others have been both more complimentary and more optimistic for the future (Curran, 1980). The criticisms of social skills training have been theoretical, methodological, and therapeutic (Furnham, 1983b).

By and large, the British researchers have been more concerned with theoretical critiques of the social skills model and the definition of skill, whereas American researchers have been more concerned with the methodological and practical critiques, though, of course, there are exceptions.

Theoretical Critiques

One of the major problems with social skills training is that it is somewhat atheoretical. The social skills model of

Argyle and Kendon (1967) was very roughly adapted from a perceptual and motor skills model and has seen very little modification or development. The model has been reproduced again and again and has been described as a useful heuristic (Robinson, 1974). For Argyle (1979), the developer of the model, it has been "heuristically very useful in drawing attention to the importance of feedback and hence to gaze: It also suggests a number of different ways in which social performance can fail, and suggests the training procedures that may be effective through analogy with motor skills training" (p. 139).

However, it has a number of problems, predominantly in what it omits. Pendleton and Furnham (1980) have noted that the model does not include any explicit cognitive component such as higher order cognitions in the form of knowledge of social conventions and appropriate behavioral patterns. Affect, too, is neglected in the model despite its being a central component in skills deficits and the fact that the recognition and display of emotions is considered an extremely important aspect of social skills. The social skills model does not distinguish between interpersonal perception (the perception of others), self-perception (the perception of oneself in relation to others and situational constraints), and metaperception (the perception of other people's perception of oneself in interaction). Thus, unless the various types of perceptions are distinguished in the social skills model, it is not clear whether social skills perceptual deficits are due to inaccurate perception of others, faulty self-monitoring, or inaccurate metaperceptions. Finally, and paradoxically, although the social skills model is a model of social interaction, it is not itself interactive, as there have been problems in specifying a two-person model, though some exist.

But, as Furnham (1983b) has pointed out, Argyle and his co-workers (Argyle,

1979; Furnham & Argyle, 1981) have always been aware of the limitations of applying a model from the human–machine interaction area and applying it to social interaction. Hence, certain special features of social skills, such as the role of reinforcement, empathy, and self-presentation, have been pointed out that are not obviously present in manual skills.

Yardley (1979) complains about the model's lack of explanatory power and definitions of skills that are scarce, inadequate, or tautological. She writes:

The social skills model of social interaction was found wanting in explanatory power particularly in the area of the understanding and establishment of meaningful behavior. Notions of criteria achievement, superordinate goals, and restricted course limited the possibilities of social behavior. The very ideas of social skill and social effectiveness, as their antithesis, represented in the person of the social inadequate do not lead to self-evident goals of therapy but raise contentious problems. A particular problem that arises is the question of defining therapeutic targets and who shall define such targets. (p. 61)

Potter (1982) has argued that, with regard to social skills theory and therapy, the interchange between theory and application is less common than might be expected from traditional models of application. From a review of the social skills literature and an interview with an anonymous researcher, Potter (1982) has concluded that the utilization of theory tends to be grounded more in previous practice than theory and that changes in applied social psychology tend to originate in practice rather than any change in theory. This fact is no doubt due to the fact that, whereas practitioners work in a more or less behavioristic framework, many theoretically oriented researchers are less sympathetic to behaviorist ideas and methods.

It has perhaps unfairly been suggested in other areas of psychology, such as psychological differentiation (Witkin, Goodenough, & Oltman, 1978), that

we have techniques in search of theories. It may equally be suggested (perhaps equally unfairly) that social skills training is a therapy in search of a theory. As Ellis and Whittington (1981) have pointed out:

All social skills trainers accept, by definition, that social behavior can be properly described as skilled, that skills can be identified and that these skills can be systematically taught. Obvious though it may seem, and tedious to repeat, a social skill trainer must know what social skills are and how he can arrange for his trainees to acquire or develop them. The routes by which trainers arrive at this knowledge, however, vary considerably and are related at least in part to broader issues of truth, evidence and enquiry. There tends to be a consonance between approaches to the identification of skills, the kinds of skills described and the training programmes associated with them. Thus the trainer who accepts a generally behaviorist view might be expected to account for SST in terms of conditioning and to apply a rigorous empiricism to the identification of units of social behavior. A more cognitively-oriented trainer might account for acquisition in terms of information theory and might be more prepared to discuss internal events such as plays and strategies in relation to skilled behavior. . . . Approaches to the acquisition of social skills and the way in which training programmes are conceived, planned, operated and evaluated relate clearly to views of how learning occurs. Thus basic positions regarding human learning are reflected in the various social skill training programmes which exist. We have used four categories to describe these approaches and have called them conditioning, cybernetic, experiential and teleological. (p. 20)

It is because of this theoretical malaise that critics have pointed to the "uniformity myths" in the social skills training literature, suggesting that the apparent homogeneity in theory and practice between practitioners was a poor attempt to paper over wide cracks in a very heterogeneous research population (Stravinski, 1978). This lack of theoretical base may also account for the lack of agreement as to the definitive list or compendium of skills that needs to be measured or trained. Romano and Bellack (1981) have noted:

There is little empirical support for the particular components typically assessed as indices of social skill. These diverse response elements have been selected for study on the basis of face validity and general examination of the literature on interpersonal communication rather than an objective analysis of the various molar skill categories. . . . The need for a clearly defined and operationalized set of behavioral referents of social skill has been by a number of researchers. (p. 479)

It is, therefore, not surprising that a myriad of definitions of social skills exist. Phillips (1978) listed 18 very different definitions, whereas Van Hasselt, Hensen, Whitehill, & Bellack (1979) and Curran (1979) have recently attempted to clarify the definitional problems. Certainly, that task will be made much easier once an explicit and uniform theory for social skills training has been developed.

Practical Critiques

Whereas many British (and some American) researchers have agonized over the theoretical problems in social skills training, many American (and some British) researchers have been more concerned with the more pragmatic question of, Does it work? Researchers have been particularly interested in methodological critiques of the studies done, whereas therapists have been particularly interested in a careful evaluation of the outcomes of treatment.

Methodological and research criticisms have revolved around a number of issues. Many researchers have lamented the poor psychometric quality of assessment techniques, particularly self-report inventories (Hersen & Bellack, 1976). Few have good reliability or validity figures; they are often multidimensional, culture and situation specific, and poor predictors of performance. A second re-

lated problem is the ecological validity of the training situation—that is, how representative the training situation is of real life. Often, experiments are run and training is done in environments that bear only a slim resemblance to those in the real world, and hence generalizability becomes a problem (Bellack, Hersen, & Lamparski, 1979). Another problem in both research and therapy is the selection of subjects. They are often self-selecting, highly heterogeneous, and of higher intelligence than average patients. Curran (1980) suggested that multiple screening procedures be used to attempt to delineate specific skills deficits in subjects before the onset of training so that the full and specific effects of training may be measured. Few studies have attempted a careful, extended follow-up assessment to test the generalizability of findings across time, situations, and skills (Furnham, 1983b). The problem of generalization has been extensively discussed; yet it still appears to be the Achilles' heel of social skills training. Finally, from a methodological point of view, the analysis of multivariate data has, for the most part, been crude and often inappropriate. The fact that many dependent measures are highly correlated suggests descriptive analysis as well as such techniques as MANOVA and discriminant analysis rather than simple nonparametric analyses on each dependent variable.

It is not only the methodology of research that has received criticism in America (Curran, 1980; Hersen & Bellack, 1976), but criticisms concerning the therapy also exist.

Therapeutic Critiques

Marzillier (1978) has offered a critique of various aspects of social skills therapy. These criticisms refer essentially to four aspects of therapy: (1) the type of social skills therapy offered; (2) therapist effects; (3) the neglect of individual differences; and (4) measures of the significance of change.

As regards the exact type of social skills training programs offered there are a number of problems. First, courses differ radically according to their content, length, and emphasis on various training methods, and therefore to compare different methods or do a metaanalysis of different studies is fraught with problems. Thus, in order to assess the effectiveness of different training programs, it is important that all groups should have the equivalent amounts and types of treatments. Another problem concerns the fact that with nearly all inpatients and also with a number of outpatients additional therapies (drug, relaxation, psychoanalytic, etc.) are being conducted alongside social skills training. It, therefore, becomes very difficult to establish the cause of change (or lack of change) over time because it could be the social skills training, the other therapy, or the particular combination of the two. A related problem is the amount of spillover or leakage between patients of the different therapies they are receiving. Therefore, for any evaluation of therapy to be done, it is important to ensure that patient groups are undergoing equivalent treatments that are uncontaminated by other therapies or information.

Second, it has been shown in all forms of therapies that certain characteristics or attributes of the therapist (age, sex, personality, enthusiasm) can greatly effect the behavior of the patients. This can mean that if one treatment shows poorer effects than another, the cause lies in the personality of the therapist rather than in the treatment received. Similarly therapist's effects may also occur in the rating of patients before and after therapy. Only carefully balanced therapy programs and carefully trained rates can overcome this problem.

Third, many effectiveness and assessment studies have neglected individual differences. However, because there is such variation and heterogeneity between patients, it is important to look more closely at individual differences both in the planning of individual treatment and conducting evaluative research. Furthermore, a thorough analysis of individual differences before treatment would allow for an analysis of patients who drop out of treatment in order to establish potential reasons.

Finally, there is the criticism associated with the measurement of change (Curran, 1979). It becomes problematic deciding who evaluates change—the patient, her/his peers, the therapist—and according to what criteria—namely global rating scales of warmth, assertiveness, happiness or detailed fine-grained measures of eye contact and the like. Furthermore, as skills are not culture free, inflexible, or stable over time, it becomes difficult to determine absolutely the nature of the change. Statistical significance in the form of changes in social behavior before and after treatment may not in itself be a very good measure of change. These criticisms of social skills training on both sides of the Atlantic are important but not damning. Indeed, recent reviewers, both in America (Curran, 1979; Smye & Wine, 1981) and in Britain (Shepherd, 1980; Trower, 1980), seem optimistic for the future of social skills training. Furnham (1983b) offers three reasons for guarded optimism: (1) the awareness on the part of social skills theorists and researchers of the deficiencies in social skills research; (2) the advantages of social skills training over other types of psychotherapy; and (3) finally, the encouraging evidence regarding the effectiveness of social skills training with a wide range of population groups.

Social Norms: Situational and Cultural Specificity

Situational Specificity

Partly as a consequence of the person–situation debate (Argyle, Furnham, &

Graham, 1981) and partly because of the problems associated with skills assessments (Kazdin, 1979), social skills researchers have become much more aware of the situational specificity of social performance. As Curran (1979) has noted:

Social Skills should not be viewed as an invariant trait. An individual's social skills performance in one particular situation may not be predictive of his performance in other criterion situations. Social skills are not a disposition but a response capability. Questions of stability and cross-situational generality need to be determined on empirical bases. (pp. 68–69)

Indeed, the situational, specific nature of many social skills has been emphasized for some time (Eisler, Hersen, Miller, & Blanchard, 1975). Most techniques developed to assess social skills involve some form of assessment of behavior in difficult social situations, either role play or self-report. Rehm and Marston (1968) developed the Situation Test, which consists of 10 situations requiring some form of heterosexual interaction. Male subjects are informed of the nature of the situation and have to reply to a line of dialogue spoken by a female confederate that is later rated. Twentyman and McFall (1975) devised a similar Social Behavior Situations task that requires lengthy role playing in six "difficult situations." Freedman et al. (1978) conceptualized delinquent behavior as a manifestation of situation-specific social-behavioral skills deficits. They identified a number of adolescent problem situations that were validated by role-playing analysis, and they were able to demonstrate that nondelinquents were rated as more competent in these situations than delinquents.

There is a host of self-report inventories used on student or psychiatric populations to assess difficulty in specific situations: Friedman (1968), Action Situation Inventory; Goldsmith and McFall (1975), Interpersonal Situation Inventory; and Wolpe and Lazarus Assertiveness Inventory (1966). Popular guides to learning social skills and assertiveness in particular also use situation training. Bower and Bower (1976) considered a set of standard "problem" situations requiring assertive behavior, and they offered a sample solution script for each as an example of how to behave.

As Hersen and Bellack (1976) in their review of social skills assessment concluded:

Rather than providing a single, global definition of social skill, we prefer a situation-specific conception of social skills. The overriding factor is effectiveness of behavior in social interactions. However, determination of effectiveness depends on the context of the interaction, and, given any context, the parameters of the specific situation. (p. 512)

Despite the recognition of the situational specificity of social skills, few researchers have attempted to provide ways by which social situations may be analyzed and the appropriate skills taught. An exception are the Oxford-based researchers, Argyle and colleagues, (1981) who, in a functional analysis, attempted to outline the fundamental features of social situations. They argued that most social behavior is goal directed and that various social situations afford the opportunity to attain various goals, such as to make friends, obtain information, and so forth. Graham, Argyle, and Furnham (1980) have argued that these goals are hierarchically structured in everyday social situations. Hence, in skills training, clients need to understand the implicit and explicit nature of the goal structure of the situation and to select or avoid situations that achieve or hamper the goal development. Argyle et al. (1981) also place great stress on social rules and conventions that dictate which behaviors are permitted, are required, or are not allowed. Rules are generated in social situations in order to regulate and coordinate behavior so that various goals may be attained. Clients in social skills training must be made familiar with the etiquette and conventions of specific situations in a subculture as well as the function of that rule and when it is applied. A third important feature of all social situations is the specified social roles that people are required to play, such as hostess, interviewer, and so forth. Roles change with situations, though it is possible to hold more than one role in a social situation. These roles emcompass various duties, obligations, and rights, are often interdependent, and involve many expectations about the actions, beliefs, feelings, attitudes, and values of the person holding the roles.

Argyle et al. (1981), in their functional analysis of situations, also specified other situational features, such as the repertoire of acceptable behaviors in a social situation, the sequences of those behaviors, and the shared social concepts that are necessary for understanding various social situations.

This structural approach to situations allows a new approach to skills training. The first stage of situational analysis involved discovering the range of situations that the patient or client found most difficult and those they could cope with. Social skills training is then directed primarily to the problem situations. The second stage of the training may then involve a lengthy discussion about the nature of these situations and an attempt to make their goal structure, social rules, norms, repertoires of behaviors, and so on explicit. Difficulties and ambiguities may be analyzed, and a number of possible skilled solutions discussed. The third stage of training actually involves modeling and role play with feedback in similated social situations as closely akin to the "real-life" situations as possible. The fourth stage involves a client doing "homework," which is the exercise and self-monitoring of his or her newly ac-

quired skills. Cognitive aspects of skills are continually emphasized in order to make the clients *perceptive* to the skills requirements of various situations and *flexible* in their range of responses.

Another British psychologist has offered a situational analysis of the components and processes of the behavior of socially inadequate patients. Trower (1980) has stressed the need for information on "normal" social behavior norms:

The second requirement is a body of scientifically validated knowledge of normal social behaviour to provide training targets and assessment criteria. One problem here is that clinicians usually rely on experience and intuition in deciding what skills should be taught, with the danger that the wrong or irrelevant skills may be selected. (p. 327)

Thus, there is a strong tradition among British social skills researchers for a situational analysis of social skills and an understanding of the social norms. It is suggested that only by knowing the situational features that shape and guide normal social behaviors one can hope to train socially inadequate patients.

Cultural Specificity

This emphasis on social norms extends beyond situational determinants to cultural determinants of social behaviors. Social skills researchers, particularly in Europe, have been slow in recognizing the culture-specific nature of their work and the inapplicability of certain concepts and techniques in other cultures. For instance, Furnham (1979) has pointed out that although assertiveness may be seen as an index of mental health and lack of assertiveness a major source of unease, anxiety, and inadequacy, in many other cultures asserting oneself in the way that is normative in North America and parts of Europe is neither encouraged nor tolerated. "Humility, subservience and tolerance are valued above assertiveness in many other cultures especially for women. Furthermore, lack of assertiveness is not necessarily a sign of inadequacy or anxiety, though in instances it may be" (p. 522). Furnham (1979) demonstrated that matched groups of European, Indian, and African nurses differed in their self-reported assertiveness, which was interpreted in terms of the cultural norms for desirable female behaviors of the three cultures and the sociopolitical structures of the country in which they lived (South Africa). In a later study, Furnham (1983a) found significant differences between the same three groups' self-reported social difficulty with the Europeans' least social difficulty and the Africans' most. He concluded:

Tests of social difficulty may actually be measuring aspects of a given structure and/or subjects' experience within a subculture, rather than social skills within it. The three groups had had different experiences of these social situations, some of which they were unfamiliar with and hence were revealing their lack of experience rather than their lack of social skill. . . . The different role of women in the three cultures may also account for some of the differences, as certain behaviour in social situations may be prohibited, anti-conformist or considered the domain of the male role. Traditionally African and Indian women are socialized into being more subservient and obedient than their white counter-parts and hence may experience more difficulty in social situations where they are called upon to be assertive, initiating or confident. (pp. 223–224)

However, few other cross-cultural studies of social difficulty appear to have been done, comparing social difficulty in similar types of social situations between different cultural groups. Rim (1976) administered the Bryant and Trower (1974) Social Situations Questionnaire to a group of British and Israeli students in their respective countries and found a number of differences, both between the cultures and between the sexes within

each culture. The samples, however, were not carefully matched nor was the analysis systematic. British students reported more difficulty with heterosexual interaction and initiating friendships than did Israelis, whereas Israeli women found it more difficult to go to dances, make decisions affecting others, have people look at them, and go into pubs than did men in their culture. Spinks and Moerdyk (1980) found differences in manifest anxiety between groups of South African Europeans and Indians, the former reporting more anxiety than the latter, though this difference decreased with increases in educational level. They warned against the use of interpreting data from anxiety measures when used in non-Western societies. In America, Hall and Beil-Warner (1978) found that Mexican-American male college students had lower scores than Anglo-American students on measures of assertiveness with parents, same-sexed peers, and business relations. Thus, situation-specific assertiveness behavior appears to be a function of the needs and cultural experiences of different cultural groups. In Europe, Magnusson and Stattin (1978), on the other hand, found considerable similarity between the reaction patterns of Swedish, Japanese, and Hungarian schoolchildren to 17 hypothetical anxiety-provoking situations categorized in terms of ego threat, anticipation threat, and inanimate threat. However, the findings are not surprising given the fact first, that many of the situations were not social, in the sense that they involved social interaction, and second, they were all fairly unusual and anxiety provoking.

Furnham and Bochner (1982) extended social skills specifically to an analysis of cross-cultural interaction. They suggested that for visitors to an unfamiliar culture (tourists, students, immigrants, refugees) the mundane, everyday interpersonal encounters with members of the host society are a source of stress, anxiety, and misunderstanding as they are unaware of the risks, conventions, and implicit messages being given. They argued:

Socially unadequate individuals are people who have failed to learn a wide range of interpersonal skills due to poor parent and peer group relationships, and because of other forms of social and physical deprivation. Thus it could be said that socially inadequate individuals are often like strangers in their own land and culture. . . . Turning this argument around, it follows that people who are new to a culture or subculture will not have been socialized in the rules and routines of behaviour pertaining to that society and will, therefore, at least initially be socially unskilled in their new environment." (pp. 165–166).

Previously, the sojourn experience had been conceptualized in clinical terms in such ideas as culture or role shock and culture fatigue. Sojourners who experience difficulties are considered to have suffered a breakdown in their normal, healthy, psychological functioning, and this requires counseling or individual therapy. However, the social skills approach asserts that cross-cultural incompetence is due to inadequate or absent learning rather than being inherited or the manifestation of neurosis. This approach, furthermore, takes away some of the stigma of being socially incompetent in a new culture as it implies the opportunity of making up for lost ground rather than inferiority and hence increasing the likelihood that persons will seek or accept remedial treatment.

In a extensive study of 150 foreign students, Furnham and Bochner (1982) found that the stress experienced by sojourners was largely due to their lacking the requisite social skills with which to negotiate specific social situations; often sojourners were not in a very good position to acquire the social skills appropriate to their new culture because they were being denied the services of infor-

mal culture guides and trainers due to the paucity of their links with host members.

Cross-cultural studies of social skills deficits, therefore, have two major implications. The first is that social norms and hence social skills are culture specific. For instance, Argyle (1975) has noted that the Japanese are taught not to express negative emotions and to avoid mutual eye gaze, whereas Arab males touch each other much in social conversation and have very high rates of mutual eye gaze. Thus, definition and measurements of social adequacy or inadequacy in one culture may be totally inapplicable in another because the norms of "healthy, normal, skilled" socially accepted behaviors differ considerably. The second implication is that social difficulty in a foreign culture (or culture shock) may be seen as a deficiency in social learning rather than as a manifestation of psychopathology, and hence social skills training rather than psychotherapy is the most appropriate form of treatment.

CENTERS OF EXCELLENCE

There are at least four reasons to be cautious in listing "centers of excellence" in any research area. First, the bestowing of the honor of excellence on an institution is itself difficult as research groups change quite noticeably over time and, although they may be excellent (or at least strong) for a certain period, they may decline rapidly, whereas others that are characterized by only intermittent or average research, may suddenly begin producing excellent publications. Second, the concept of excellence is itself difficult to define—some departments may do extensive, careful, and exhaustive, if pedestrian, research, whereas others may be more interested in theoretical problems and prefer a conceptual approach. Depending on the biases of the bestower of excellence, then, one institution or department could be perhaps unfairly ranked above all others. A third problem lies in getting information about institutions or departments doing research in an area. Whereas some departments are unashamedly proselytizing in their annual reports or glossy booklets on current research, others do little to advertise their activities. This problem is made all the worse by the fact that the range of journals in which one might publish research (in social skills training) is quite enormous, and unless one obsessively checks all the relevant journals, important papers may not come to the notice of many researchers. Finally, it is inevitable that some departments or research groups get overlooked (much to their consternation), whereas others get included (much to their delight) as centers of excellence, and hence the judgment of the bestower of this honor is questioned.

Despite these dangers, four centers of excellence for social skills research in Britain have been selected and will be briefly described.

Oxford

There is no doubt that the social skills research at Oxford has been the longest established and has produced the widest range of research in Europe. The interest in social skills research at Oxford can be traced back to the early 1960s when Argyle began working with Crossman on social skills (Welford, 1981). Argyle's first references to social skills were a chapter in the first edition of his paperback *The Psychology of Interpersonal Behaviour,* which appeared in 1967 as well as a paper with Adam Kendon in Volume 3 of *Advances in Experimental Social Psychology* (1967.

In the chapter in his first edition, Argyle (1967) wrote:

In this chapter we shall try to break through the conceptual barriers which are holding up the study of social interaction by introducing a theoretical model, and its associated language for describing these events. This chapter contains our main theoretical contribution, and in the rest of the book we shall make use of this analysis offered. The suggestion is simply this: that the sequence of individual behaviour which occurs during social interaction can usefully be looked at as a kind of motor skill. By motor skill are meant such things as cycling, skating, driving a car, playing the piano, typing, sending and receiving morse, performing industrial tasks, playing tennis and other games. These have been extensively studied in the field and in laboratory experiments, and their psychological components are now well understood. Social interaction has many resemblances to other motor skills: the point of our suggestion is to pursue the basic psychological similarities in more detail, to see if the same processes operate. (p. 85)

In the chapter, Argyle goes on to look at the similarities between social interaction and serial motor skills, special features of social skills, and the concept of social competence.

However, the book also contains two further chapters on social skills. One is entitled "Some Professional Social Skills" and concerns such topics as the social survey interview, the assessment interview, selling, public speaking, the supervision of work groups, the personnel interview, teaching, psychotherapy and counseling, and child rearing. Finally, the penultimate chapter is entitled "Training in Social Skills" and contains a short section on training by sheer repetition, role playing, imitation of models, T-group training, alternative kinds of sensitivity training, and finally lectures, discussion, case studies, and readings.

In the chapter with Kendon, Argyle deals much more systematically with aspects of nonverbal communication, a research area that he was to pursue for the next 10 years. Argyle and Kendon (1967) paid much attention to the structure of social performance, looking at what they called standing features, such as in-

terpersonal distance orientation and posture and physical contact as well as
dynamic features such as the sequential
structure of actions in time, language and
speech, usual orientation, body movement, facial expression, and looking patterns. A section of this chapter was also
dedicated to self-presentation and social
competence; it drew heavily on the work
of Goffman and other symbolic interac-
tionists. Argyle and Kendon (1967) concluded:

As we have tried to make clear in the discussion of self-presentation and competence in
social skill, the more we know about how the
social performance is organized, what its
components are, the better we shall be able to
understand the nature of interpersonal process. We have stressed the idea that there are
a number of different social skills, each specific in function, and a detailed understanding
of their organization opens up the possibility
of social skills training, analogous to training
in industrial skills which has followed so
fruitfully upon the analysis of sensorimotor
performance. This may have an important application in dealing with mental illness insofar
as these may be seen as breakdowns in social
skill. (p. 91)

These early writings of Argyle show
quite clearly the direction in which the
Oxford group was to move. Essentially
four areas of research were pursued that
produced ideas that were skilfully cross-
fertilized over the different research
areas: nonverbal communication, social
skills training with abnormal populations, professional social skills training,
and a situational and sequential analysis
of social behaviors. Among the books
produced from this research are the following: Argyle, *Bodily Communication*
(1975); Argyle and Cook, *Gaze and Mutual Gaze* (1976); Trower, Bryant, and
Argyle, *Social Skills and Mental Health*
(1978); Argyle, *Social Skills and Health*
(1981b); Argyle, *Social Skills and Work*
(1981a); and Argyle, Furnham, and Graham, *Social Situations* (1981).

Apart from the work inspired by Argyle, there has been an active research
group over the years that has sought to
expand the concept of skill and the application of social skills training. Hence,
the work of Pendleton (in press) on skills
training for general practitioners, Henderson (1982) on skills deficits in violent
prisoners, and Young and Martin (1981)
on self-perception in neurotics.

The Oxford group continues to be the
foremost researching and publishing
group in this area, probably in the whole
of Europe. Although the projects have
changed since the late 1960s, the theme
of social skills remains a topic of interest
and research. This can be seen by Argyle's latest interest in long-term relationships (Argyle & Furnham, 1982,
1983).

Birmingham

The University of Birmingham has also
been active in the area of social skills
training and research. Whereas in Oxford, social skills research has been pre-
dominated by social psychologists, the
Birmingham team are mainly clinical
psychologists. The research of two people at Birmingham perhaps best reflects
the research at that department.

Marzillier has done a number of evaluative studies on social skills training.
He has written a chapter in Trower, Bryant, and Argyle (1978) on the outcome of
skills training. It is a careful, thoughtful
critique of outcome research on both in-
and outpatients and volunteer subjects.
From this review, he has suggested three
future research needs:

A priority in future research is to establish
methods of maintaining new behaviour and
generalizing it to real life. . . . A second important area for future research is further investigations into the various components
of training. . . . The focus of such investigations should be on the importance of different types of modelling, role-playing and
feedback. . . . More attention should also be

paid to cognitive processes and the extent to which training can improve the individual's ability to induce rules of social behaviour. Finally, more research is needed on the characteristics of patients who would be suitable for various training approaches. (pp. 126–127)

Marzillier's own work has been careful and well planned. Marzillier, Lambert, and Kellett (1976) compared social skills training with systematic desensitization and with a no-treatment control on 21 psychiatric outpatients who complained of major social difficulties and found support for social skills training. However, the authors note the problems of the research design. Later, Marzillier and Winter (1978) did an intensive study on four psychiatric outpatients to investigate individual differences that are clearly important in both the planning of individual treatment and the carrying out of evaluative research. Kellett, Marzillier, and Lambert (1981) investigated the relationship between social skills and somatotypes. They found a number of differences between ectomorphs, endomorphs, and mesomorphs, and they found that social skills training benefited the shorter, plumper physique more than the linear ectomorph.

Feldman (1980), at Birmingham, has been particularly interested in skills training with offenders and homosexuals and the etiology of these conditions. Although not directly in the British social skills tradition, Feldman's work tends to stress the social context of psychological problems.

Overall, there is an active research group in Birmingham whose research is characterized by careful, detailed studies, usually on clinical populations.

London

London University is more like a collection of universities (like New York University, the University of California), and hence the interest in social skills is more predominant at some colleges than others. The most impressive research has come out of the Psychology Department at the Institute of Psychiatry. Two researchers and their colleagues appear to have done the most outstanding research in London.

Spence has done considerable research in the area of social skills. She has written a number of papers on social skills with adolescent delinquents and offenders (Spence & Marzillier, 1979, 1981; Spence, 1981). In all these studies, she has demonstrated that on a variety of self-report and behavioral measures, delinquents appear to be less socially skilled than a comparable group of controls and hence recommends social skills training for offenders. She is particularly interested in the measurement of social skills (Spence, 1981) and has in fact produced a very useful counselor's manual entitled *Social Skills Training with Children and Adolescents*. Yet, her interest in behavioral assessment has not meant that she has neglected cognitive changes associated with social skills training (Spence & Spence, 1980).

A careful and concerned critique of social skills training has been offered by Shepherd (1977, 1978). Shepherd has been particularly concerned with the generalization problem in social skills training. Accrding to Shepherd (1980), one reason why so little generalization has been found is that so little good research has been spent looking for it. However, he argues that the problems of generalization and durability of treatment in social skills training are also encountered in other treatments. He suggests that poor generalizability is due primarily to two things: reactivity of measurements and not programming for generalization. Where measures of generalizability are attempted in the "real world," they are often plagued by methodological problems such as their reliability, reactivity, and validity. Second, not all social skills programs attempt programming for generalization by, for instance, designing treatment programs that contain conditions as similar as possible to those in real life. Shepherd concludes:

Firstly, we could discard our rather strict learning theory model and aim at producing changes in underlying cognitions in the hope that they would exert a determining influence on behaviour which would then generalize. . . . Alternatively, both in the same vein, we might argue that an approach which aims at teaching the rules of appropriate interaction rather than specific responses might be more effective in promoting generalization. . . . Thirdly, we might hope that a better understanding of individual differences would contribute to a better match between problems and techniques and hence to more strongly established responses during the training phase (and so, presumably, to more generalization). (p. 264)

As well as the Institute of Psychiatry, there are researchers at other London University colleges who are interested in social skills training and research. Among these are Summerfield at Birkbeck College (Summerfield & Lake, 1977), Furnham at University College (Furnham, 1983a,b), and Gaskell at the London School of Economics.

Ulster Polytechnic

One of the most active centers in social skills training in Great Britain is at Ulster Polytechnic outside Belfast. The history and development of social skills training there has been clearly described in Ellis and Whittington (1981). Their approach is based heavily on educational microteaching, which has dominated all their research. This is particularly apparent in the work of Hargie, Saunders, and Dickson (1981), whose chapter headings, for example, Reinforcement, Questioning, and Set Induction and Closure, reflect the stress on microteaching.

In 1979–1980, the staff of the social skills program taught over 600 students within their sophisticated social skills laboratories. The students were not only psychology undergraduates or trainee teachers but also social workers, community workers, youth leaders, health visitors, counselors, careers officers, employment advisory officers, speech therapists, physiotherapists, occupational therapists, and junior executives! Each appears to have had a 25–30-week course of 5 hours per week (often with one-to-one training), which is perhaps the best organized and most extensive and intensive training program in Britain. In their conclusion, Ellis and Whittington (1981) write that "central to the work of the unit are the views that

(1) professional education and training should focus on informed practice

(2) social skill constitutes a key element in this practice

(3) the understanding of social skill, and its development for training purposes is best approached scientifically and empirically. (p. 146).

Later, they again stress their belief in applied social skills training:

Developmental social skills training is in our view the weakest area in its atheoretical eclecticism and polarization into, on the one hand, ill-defined social education and, on the other, overly-rigid behaviour modification. The area is an important one bringing a new dimension to formal schooling and in many cases bridging school and work, immaturity and adulthood. It deserves better. (p. 200)

Three books have come out of the Ulster unit: Hargie, Saunders and Dickson, *Social Skills in Interpersonal Communication* (1981); Ellis and Whittington, *A Guide to Social Skill Training (1981); and Ellis and Whittington, New Directions in Social Skill Training* (1982). However, a number of papers have also been published in professional journals explaining the role and usefulness of social skills training. Yet, they have not done many empirical or assessment studies. Their strengths lie clearly in the application of social skills methods to various professional groups and the setting up of clearly thought out syllabuses for training rather than in the development of assessment tools or controlled empirical studies. They have also attempted some empirical work—for instance, a study by Tittmar, Dickson, and Hargie (1979) on the relationship between social anxiety and attitudes to social skills training.

It would be quite wrong to suggest that no other universities or polytechnics are conducting research into social skills and related areas. Students and staff at many other departments are involved in research in this area (the University of Kent and North East London Polytechnic both have members of staff researching various aspects of social skills). Furthermore, much research is being conducted by clinical psychologists at various hospitals in the country, for example, Capon has been an active researcher in this area (Capon, 1979; Furnham & Capon, in press) as have been Lindsay and colleagues (Lindsay, Symons, & Sweet, 1979; Lindsay & Lindsay, 1982).

RESEARCH IN THE REST OF EUROPE AND THE COMMONWEALTH

British academics from many areas of psychology often complain about American ethnocentrism as they perceive Americans as only reading and publishing in American journals. Though this may be quite true, it is perhaps not nearly as ethnocentric as that displayed by the English-speaking world in general to psychological research emanating from other countries. Because the author is guilty of the latter ethnocentrism (be-

ing practically monolingual), the review that follows is somewhat limited.

Research in Europe

In 1979 a conference was held in Europe that was later published as Singleton, Spurgeon, and Stammers (1980), *The Analysis of Social Skill,* in which a number of Europeans presented their work. Among them was de Jong from Holland who looked at the social skills aspects of industrial organizations and Scherer and Scherer who were interested in the skills necessary in interactions between government officials and clients. Indeed, the latter group has been very active in many areas related to social skills training.

Other work has been and is being done in Europe on social skills training: Holland (Pendleton, in press); Norway (Braaten, 1979); as well as Italy, Spain, and Greece (Argyle, personal communication, 1983). However, most of their published work is in house journals rarely read by people outside their own countries.

Research in the Commonwealth

By far the most prolific Commonwealth country producing research in this area is Australia. (Canada, for the purposes of this review, will not be considered part of the Commonwealth because the research interests and traditions are too similar to those of researchers in the United States.)

Many studies have been done on assertiveness in Australia (Crassini et al., 1979; Leah, Law, & Snyder, 1979; Law, Wilson, & Crassini, 1979). Furthermore, other studies have concerned social skills in delinquent adolescent groups (Gaffney & McFall, 1981) as well as social skills training with alcoholics (Oei & Jackson, 1980). Many Australian psychologists have done work related to social skills research. Furthermore, psychologists in New Zealand also appear to be taking more and more interest in social skills training (Argyle, personal communication, 1983).

One of the major problems of this area for any reviewer of the literature is not only that it is in different languages but that it appears in a number of different journals. Social skills research is published in clinical, social, occupational, industrial, educational, medical, and applied psychology journals as well as in professional magazines. This makes it extremely difficult for any reviewer to be thorough. There certainly appears to be a need for a journal specifically for research on social skills training.

APPLIED SOCIAL SKILLS RESEARCH IN EUROPE

Furnham and Argyle (1981) have noted that because of its efficacy, cost-effectiveness, viability, and adaptability, social skills training has been applied as a form of teaching and therapy with a wide number of groups. Earlier, Furnham, King, & Pendleton (1980) had listed four reasons why they believed social skills training had advantages over other sorts of educational training or psychotherapy:

1. The social skills trainer does not require years of psychological or analytic training before he or she can lead a group. However, a certain amount of theory must be learned, coupled with experience and training in group therapy and psychotherapy in general. Manuals may easily be obtained (Capon, 1979); Priestley McGuire, Flegg, Hemsley, & Welham, 1978), and the equipment required, apart from video equipment, is minimal and relatively cheap.

2. Social skills training may be easily adapted for the precise needs of specific groups. Much standard social skills training is appropriate for all client groups; however, additional training in certain skills may be required to cope with special problems resulting from psychological or physical handicaps.

3. Social skills training can be done most beneficially in small groups, and results are obtained relatively quickly compared to other types of therapy, which may extend over several years.

4. Social skills training is a positive approach to personal problems and adjustment because it asserts that social competence is learned rather than inherited, and therefore it can be learned for the first time if absent previously or relearned where the initial learning experience has been inadequate.

As a result, applied social skills researchers have turned their attention to various groups of patients or clients thought to benefit from social skills training. Essentially, six groups have attracted most attention from social skills trainers and researchers: mental patients, criminals and delinquents, alcoholics and drug addicts, children and adolescents, handicapped people, and professionals. It is only social skills training with the handicapped (Gresham, 1981) that appears not to have attracted much attention in Europe; otherwise, all the other groups have been used for research and training.

Social Inadequates and Mental Patients

Trower, Bryant, and Argyle (1978) have suggested that some forms of mental disorders are caused or exacerbated by lack of social skills. They include among the mental patients likely to be socially unskilled, chronic schizophrenics, depressives, anxious patients, and social phobics.

In a survey of psychiatric outpatients

aged between 18 and 49, Bryant et al. (1976) found that 28% were rated by psychiatrists as socially inadequate. On most of the 24 behavioral criteria, divided into nonverbal (voice and body), verbal (form and content), and 7 overall judgments on such things as warmth, assertiveness, and control, socially inadequate patients were markedly inferior to others. There appear to be both clinical factors and social factors associated with deficiency in social skills among mental patients.

A number of studies have been done on mental patients in Britain, including studies comparing social skills training and psychotherapy (Argyle, Bryant, & Trower, 1974) and social skills training and systematic desentization (Marzillier, Lambert, & Kellett, 1976). Earlier Argyle, Trower, and Bryant (1974) looked at the feasibility of social skills training with personality-disordered and neurotic patients. Also Trower (1980) performed a situational analysis of the components and processes of social behavior of socially skilled and unskilled patients. Pillay and Crisp (1981), however, have reported that social skills training was not found to be a very powerful form of intervention with anorexic-nervosa inpatients.

Certainly, with the popularity of social skills training in psychiatric and general hospitals all over Britain, more and more research is being done with social inadequates and mental patients.

Criminals and Delinquents

One of the most interesting applied areas of social skills training has been with recidivists, delinquents, offenders, and prisoners. The extensive and careful work of Spence in this area has already been mentioned. However, there are many other British researchers working in this field. Fawcett, Ingham, McKeever, and Williams (1979) instituted a program of social skills training for young prisoners who were demonstrably lacking in various interpersonal skills. In their training, they paid particular attention to aggression, embarrassment, assertiveness, appeasement, and relationships with authority. Though they did not take careful behavioral measures, they did conclude that the program was a success.

Similarly, Burgess, Jewitt, Sandham, and Hudson (1980) found that sex offenders had both deficiencies in interpersonal skills and high levels of anxiety in everyday social interactions. Using role play, modeling, reinforcement, and homework (practice), they focused on three specific behaviors, namely eye contact, voice control, and bodily movements. Self-reported questionnaires and videotaped ratings indicated that the intervention program was successful in a population of socially unskilled prisoners.

Hollin and Henderson (1981) carried out a social skills training program with incarcerated delinquent adolescents. They found that although social skills training did not significantly affect either locus of control or undercontrolled personality measures, trainees did report significantly fewer personal problems upon completion of the social skills training. The number of institution disciplinary reports was also reduced compared to a comparison group of delinquents not receiving social skills training.

The rise in social skills training in prisons and correction institutions is encouraging. By emphasizing the acquisition of skills, the approach asserts that antisocial or criminal behavior is primarily due to inadequate or absent social learning rather than being inherited or the manifestation of unresolved childhood conflicts. This interpretation takes away some of the stigma that offenders might feel, implying as it does opportunities for making up lost ground rather than genetic inferiority or psychopathology, which in turn might increase the likelihood that persons will seek help or accept training.

Alcoholics and Drug Addicts

Although much social skills training and research has been done on the previously mentioned groups in America, very little has been done in Britain or Europe. There are, however, two exceptions.

Oie and Jackson in Australia (Jackson & Oei, 1978; Oei & Jackson, 1980) have done some very interesting work on social skills training with alcoholics. They (1980) compared the long- and short-term effects of group and individual social skills training with traditional supportive therapy on 32 alcoholics over ½ months. They found that group social skills training produced faster improvement in necessary social skills and an equivalent reduction in alcohol consumption than individually trained subjects and that social skills training produced a significantly larger reduction of alcohol consumption than traditional supportive therapy, whether the subjects were treated in a group or individually.

Although not strictly within a social skills tradition, O'Connor (1980) demonstrated that smokers can be reliably typed on the situational contexts of their habit and situations that are the best predictors of difference in habit tend to emphasize different information-processing styles. Argyle, Furnham, and Graham (1981) found that these sorts of situational analyses can be very useful in social skills training for alcoholism, obesity, and smoking. Patients are required first to monitor closely the situations in which they eat, drink, or smoke to make them attempt to find alternative behavioral repertoires to cope with the stimuli that these situations evoke.

Certainly, many self-help groups such as Alcoholics Anonymous and Weight Watchers might benefit from the use of such techniques as social skills training.

Children and Adolescents

Many social skills researchers in Britain have been interested in training children and adolescents. Trower (1978) has argued:

Adolescence is a crucial period in the acquisition of social skills, since it is the time when the individual must learn the fundamentals of a repertoire of adult social behaviour. It is well recognised that adolescence is a period of stressful transition from childhood to adulthood, and it has been argued that adolescents need to develop a special set of social skills for a special set of problems. (p. 327)

Lindsay et al. (1979) have, in fact, described in some detail a social skills program for socially inept adolescents, including initiating conversations, assertion and interviewing skills, dealing with authority figures, and heterosexual interaction. Porteous (1979), in a survey of problems of normal 15-year-olds found that many were concerned with skills deficits such as self-confidence, adequacy, and peer acceptance. Lindsay and Lindsay (1982) have developed a self-report questionnaire dealing with peer relationships, adult relationships, and general social difficulties for British adolescents. Spence (1980) has, in fact, produced a very useful and comprehensive counselor's manual for social skills training with children and adolescents.

Professional Groups

Social skills training has also been directed toward professionals of various kinds—doctors, nurses, occupational therapists, social workers, managers, salesmen, and so on (Argyle, 1978; Ellis & Whittington, 1981). Professionals are assumed to be socially adequate but need to acquire specific skills related to their jobs. Some also are required to learn how to teach social skills to others.

Argyle (1978) has mentioned a number of professional social skills that are regularly taught: selling, interviewing, counseling, supervision, committee chairpersonship, teaching, and public speaking. He suggests that professional skills involve rather special techniques that are not necessarily acquired as a result of everyday experience and they also require a certain amount of specialist knowledge.

Most of the social skills work with professionals has been done with those working within a medical setting. Pendleton and Furnham (1980) have outlined some of the skills that general practitioners need to learn for their job, whereas Furnham, King, and Pendleton (1980) have pointed out the necessity of occupational therapists learning certain interpersonal skills to improve their interaction with patients and peers.

Similarly, Haines (1978) has listed three areas of social skills that need to be acquired by social workers: relationship skills, transactional skills, and organizational skills.

CONCLUSION

This chapter has attempted to take a European, and a particularly British, perspective on social skills training. Some of the differences in research and training between Europe and America were attributed to different historical origins of the concept of social skills and others to different philosophical and empirical traditions. Specifically, it was suggested that, whereas British research stresses problems in friendship formation, American research has been more interested in problems of interpersonal assertiveness; that British research is more closely linked to social psychology and American research to clinical psychology; that, of the critiques made of social skills training and research, British and European researchers have made more theoretical and practical criticisms,

whereas American researchers have been more concerned with methodological critiques; and finally, that although American social skills researchers are aware of the situational specificity of social skills, British and European researchers are equally aware of the cultural specificity of social skills.

Various centers of excellence with social skills research were mentioned, though the dangers of this idiosyncratic nomination were outlined. Furthermore, research in the rest of Europe and the Commonwealth were noted, though this overview was probably inadequate, given the extensive amount of research and training going on in these countries.

Finally, applied social skills training in Europe was reviewed. British and European researchers have been particularly interested in the application of social skills training to three groups: delinquents, offenders, and recidivists; children and adolescents; and professionals, whereas American researchers have concentrated on two other groups (as well as those previously mentioned): addicts and the handicapped. Both groups have predictably been very interested in mental patients.

This diversity in emphases in social skills training may be seen more as an asset than a disadvantage. Unlike other forms of therapy and training, social skills training is rarely narrowly doctrinal or restrictive. However, there is a danger that it becomes all encompassing and looses its distinctive theoretical and therapeutic characteristics. Yet, a period of rapid expansion and application has been replaced by a period of critical evaluation and empirical assessment. Certainly, British reviewers of the current state of the art (Argyle, 1981a, b; Ellis & Whittington, 1981, 1982; Furnham, 1983b; Trower, 1980) are cautiously optimistic about the future.

There are, I believe, three reasons to be optimistic about the future of social skills therapy and theory. Firstly most researchers and therapists are aware of the many deficiencies in social skills research. This awareness, rather than leading to dispair, has led to a renewed effort to improve methodology and assessment, and attempted to clarify some of the major theoretical issues. . . . Secondly social skills training has a number of advantages over other types of psychotherapy. . . . These advantages can only mean that social skills training will be adopted by more and more trainers for use with wider and wider groups of people. . . . Finally social skills training works; by-and-large there is good evidence for the effectiveness of training. (Furnham, 1983b, pp. 291–293

REFERENCES

Argyle, M. (1967). *The psychology of interpersonal behaviour (1st ed.). Harmondsworth: Penguin.*

Argyle, M. (1974). *The social psychology of work.* Harmondsworth: Penguin.

Argyle, M. (1975). *Bodily communication.* London: Methuen.

Argyle, M. (1978). *The psychology of interpersonal behaviour* (3rd ed.). Harmondsworth: Penguin.

Argyle, M. (1979). *New developments in the analysis of social skill. In A. Wolfgang (Ed.), Nonverbal behavior: Applications and cross-cultural implication.* New York: Academic Press.

Argyle, M. (1981a). *Social skills and work.* London: Methuen.

Argyle, M. (1981b). *Social skills and health.* London: Methuen.

Argyle, M., & Cook, M. (1976). *Gaze and mutual gaze.* Cambridge: Cambridge University Press.

Argyle, M., Alkema, F., & Gilmour, R. (1972). The communication of friendly and hostile attitudes by verbal and nonverbal signals. *European Journal of Social Psychology, 1,* 385–402.

Argyle, M., Bryant, B., & Trower, P. (1974). Social skills training and psychotherapy: A comparative study. *Psychological Medicine, 4,* 435–444.

Argyle, M., & Kendon, A. (1967). The experimental analysis of social performance. *Advances in Experimental Social Psychology, 3,* 55–98.

Argyle, M., Furnham, A., & Graham, J. (1981). *Social situations.* Cambridge: Cambridge University Press.

Argyle, M., Trower, P., & Bryant, B. (1974). Exploration in the treatment of personality disorders and neuroses by social skills training. *British Journal of Medical Psychology, 47,* 63–72.

Argyle, M., & Furnham, A. (1983). Sources of conflict and satisfaction in long-term relationships. *Journal of Marriage and the Family, 45,* 481–493.

Argyle, M., & Furnham, A. (1982). The ecology of relationships: Choice of situation as a function of relationship. *British Journal of Social Psychology, 21,* 259–261.

Bellack, A., Hersen, M., & Lamparski, D. (1979). Role play tests for assessing social skills: Are they valid? *Journal of Consulting and Clinical Psychology, 47,* 335–345.

Bower, S., & Bower, G. (1976). *Asserting yourself.* Reading, MA: Addison-Wesley.

Braaten, L. (1979). Some ethical dilemmas in sensitivity training, encounter groups and related activities. *Scandanavian Journal of Psychology, 20,* 81–91.

Bryant, B., & Trower, P. (1974). Social difficulty in a student sample. *British Journal of Educational Psychology, 44,* 13–21.

Bryant, B., Trower, P., Yardley, K., Urbieta, H., & Letemendia, F. (1976). A survey of social inadequacy among psychiatric outpatients. *Psychological Medicine, 6,* 101–112.

Burgess, R., Jewitt, R., Sandham, J., & Hudson, B. (1980). Working with sex offenders: A social skills training group. *British Journal of Social Work, 10,* 133–142.

Capon, M. (1979). *Basic course in social skills training.* Unpublished manual.

Cook, M. (1978). The social skill model and interpersonal attraction. In S. Duck, (Ed.), *Theory and practice in interpersonal attraction.* London: Academic Press.

Craighead, W., Kazdin, A., & Mahoney, M.

(1976). *Behavior modification: Principles, issues and applications*. Boston: Houghton-Mifflin.

Crassini, B., Law, H., & Wilson, E. (1979). Sex differences in assertive behavior? *Australian Journal of Psychology, 31,* 15–19.

Crossman, E. (1960). *Automation and skill.* London: HMSO.

Curran, J. (1977). Skills training as an approach to the treatment of heterosexual social anxiety: A review. *Psychological Bulletin, 84,* 140–154.

Curran, J. (1979). Pandora's box reopened? The assessment of social skills. *Journal of Behavioural Assessment, 1,* 55–71.

Curran, J. (1980). Social skills: Methodological issues and future directions. In A. Bellack & M. Hersen (Eds.), *Research and practice in social skills training.* New York: Plenum.

Duck, S. (1973). *Personal relationships and personal constructs.* London: Wiley.

Duck, S. (1977). *The study of acquaintance.* London: Saxon House.

Eiser, R. (1978). The behavioral assessment of social skills. In M. Hersen & A. Bellack (Eds.), *Behavioral assessment.* New York: Pergamon.

Eisler, R., Hersen, M., Miller, P., & Blanchard, E. (1975). Situational determinants of assertive behaviours. *Journal of Consulting and Clinical Psychology, 43,* 330–340.

Ellis, R., & Whittington, D. (1981). *A guide to social skills training.* London: Croom Helm.

Ellis, R., & Whittington, D. (1982). *New Directions in social skill training.* London: Croom Helm.

Fawcett, B., Ingham, E., McKeever, M., & Williams, S. (1979). Social skills group for young prisoners. *Social Work Today, 10,* 16–18.

Feldman, P. (1980). The making and control of offenders. In P. Feldman & J. Orford (Eds.), *Psychological problems: The social context.* London: Wiley.

Foot, H., Chapman, A., & Smith, J. (1980). *Friendship and social relations in children.* London: Wiley.

Foy, D., Massey, F., Duer, J., Ross, J.,

& Wooten, S. (1979). Social skills training to improve vocational interpersonal competency. *Journal of Counseling Psychology, 26,* 128–142.

Freedman, B., Rosenthal, L., Danahoe, C., & McFall, R. (1978). A social behavioural analysis of skills deficits in delinquent and non-delinquent adolescent boys. *Journal of Consulting and Clinical Psychology, 46,* 1148–1163.

Friedman, P. (1968). The effects of modeling and role playing on assertive behavior. Unpublished thesis, University of Washington.

Furnham, A. (1979). Assertiveness in three cultures: Multidimensionality and cultural differences. *Journal of Clinical Psychology, 35,* 522–527.

Furnham, A. (1983a). Social difficulty in three cultures. *International Journal of Psychology, 18,* 215–228.

Furnham, A. (1983b). Research in social skills training: A critique. In R. Ellis & D. Whittington (Eds.) *New directions in social skills training.* London: Croom Helm.

Furnham, A., & Argyle, M. (1981). The theory, practice and application of social skills training. *International Journal of Behavioural Social Work, 1,* 125–143.

Furnham, A., & Bochner, S. (1982). Difficulty in a foreign culture: An empirical analysis of culture shock. In S. Bochner (Ed.) *Culture in contact: Studies in cross-cultural interaction.* Oxford: Pergamon.

Furnham, A., & Capon, M. (1983). Social skills and self-monitoring processes. *Personality and Individual Differences, 4,* 171–178.

Furnham, A., & Henderson, M. (1981). Sex differences in self-reported assertiveness in Britain. *British Journal of Clinical Psychology, 20,* 50–62.

Furnham, A., & Henderson, M. (1984). Assessing assertiveness: A content and correlational analysis of five assertiveness inventories. *Behavioural Assessment, 6,* 79–88.

Furnham, A., King, J., & Pendleton, D. (1980). Establishing rapport: Interactional skills and occupational therapy.

British Journal of Occupational Therapy, 43, 322–325.

Furnham, A., & Pendleton, D. (1983). The assessment of skills deficits in the elderly. *International Journal of Aging and Human Development, 17,* 29–38.

Gambrill, E. (1977). *Behavior Modification.* San Francisco: Jossey-Bass.

Gaffney, L, & McFall, R. (1981). A comparison of social skills in delinquent and non delinquent adolescent girls using a behavioural role-playing inventory. *Journal of Consulting and Clinical Psychology, 6,* 959–967.

Gallassi, J., Gallassi, J., & Vedder, M. (1981). Perspectives on assertion as a social skills model. In J. Wine & M. Smye (Eds.), *Social competence.* New York: Guilford.

Goldsmith, J., & McFall, R. (1975). Development and evaluation of an interpersonal skill-training program for psychiatric patients. Journal of Abnormal Psychology, 84, 51–58.

Graham, J., Arygle, M., & Furnham, A. (1980). The goal structure of situations. *European Journal of Social Psychology, 10,* 345–366.

Gresham, F. (1981). Validity of social skills measures for assessing social skills in low status children. *Developmental Psychology, 17,* 390–398.

Haines, J. (1978). *Skills and methods in social work.* London: Constable.

Hall, J., & Beil-Warner, D. (1978). Assertiveness of male Anglo- and Mexican-American college students. Journal of Social Psychology, 105, 170–178.

Hargie, O., Saunders, C., & Dickson, D. (1981). *Social skills in interpersonal communication.* London: Croom Helm.

Heimberg, R., Montgomery, D., Madsen, C., & Heimberg, J. (1977). Assertiveness training: A review of the literature. *Behaviour Therapy, 8,* 953–971.

Henderson, M. (1982). An empirical classification of male prisoners with convictions for violent offenders. *British Journal of Criminology, 22,* 128–139.

Hersen, M., & Bellack, A. (1976). Assessment of social skills. In A. Ciminero, K. Calhoun, & H. Adams (Eds.), *Hand-book of behavioral assessment.* New York: Wiley.

Hollandsworth, J., & Wall, K. (1977). Sex differences in assertive behaviour: An empirical investigation. *Journal of Counseling Psychology, 23,* 108–111.

Hollin, C., & Henderson, M. (1981). The effects of social skills training on incarcerated delinquent adolescents. *International Journal of Behavioural Social Work, 1,* 145–156.

Jackson, P., & Oei, T. (1978). Social skills training and cognitive restructuring with alcoholics. *Drug and Alcohol Dependence, 3,* 369–374.

Kazdin, A. (1979). Situational specificity: The two edged sword of behavioural assessment. *Behavioural Assessment, 1,* 57–76.

Kellett, J., Marzillier, J., & Lambert, C. (1981). Social skills and somatotype. *British Journal of Medical Psychology, 54,* 149–154.

Law, H., Wilson, E., & Crassini, B. (1979). A principal components analysis of the Rathus Assertiveness Schedule. *Journal of Consulting and Clinical Psychology, 47,* 631–633.

Leah, J., Law, H., & Snyder, C. (1979). The structure of self-reported difficulty in assertiveness. *Multivariate Behavioural Research, 14,* 443–462.

Lindsay, W., & Lindsay, I. (1982). A self-report questionnaire about social difficulty for adolescents. *Journal of Adolescence, 5,* 63–69.

Lindsay, W., Symons, R., & Sweet, T. (1979). A programme for teaching social skills to socially inept adolescents. *Journal of Adolescence, 2,* 215–218.

Magnusson, D., & Stattin, H. (1978). A cross-cultural comparison of anxiety responses in an interaction frame of reference. *International Journal of Psychology, 13,* 317–322.

Marzillier, J. (1978). Outcome studies of skills training: A review. In P. Trower, B. Bryant, & M. Argyle (Eds.), *Social skills and mental health.* London: Methuen.

Marzillier, J., Lambert, C., & Kellett, J. (1976). A controlled evaluation of systematic desensitization and social skills training for social inadequate psychiatric patients. *Behaviour Research and Therapy, 14,* 225–228.

Marzillier, J., & Winter, K. (1978). Success and failure in social skills training: Individual differences. *Behaviour Research and Therapy, 16,* 67–84.

O'Connor, K. (1980). Individual differences in situational preferences amongst smokers. *Personality and Individual Differences, 1,* 57–72.

Oei, T., & Jackson, P. (1980). Long-term effects of group and individual social skills training with alcoholics. *Addictive Behaviours, 5,* 129–136.

Pendleton, D. (in press). *The consultation.* Oxford: Blackwells.

Pendleton, D., & Furnham, A. (1980). Skills: A paradigm for applied social psychological research. In W. Singleton, R. Spurgeon, & R. Stammers (Eds.), *The analysis of social skill.* New York: Plenum.

Pervin, L. (1978). *Current controversies and issues in personality.* New York: Wiley.

Phillips, E. (1978). *The social skills bases of psychopathology.* London: Grune & Stratton.

Philips, L., & Zigler, E. (1961). Social competence: The action–thought parameter and vicariousness in normal and pathological behaviour. *Journal of Abnormal and Social Psychology, 63,* 137–146.

Pillay, M., & Crisp, A. (1981). The impact of social skills training with an established in-patient treatment programme for anorexia nervosa. *British Journal of Psychiatry, 139,* 533–539.

Potter, J. (1982) "Nothing as practical as good theory. . . ." The problematic application of social psychology. In P. Stringer (Ed.), *Confronting social issues: Applications of social psychology.* London: Academic Press.

Porteous, M. (1979). A survey of the problems of normal 15-year-olds. *Journal of Adolescence, 2,* 307–323.

Priestley, P., McGuire, J., Flegg, D., Hemsley, V., & Welham, D. (1978). *Social skills in personal problem solving.* London: Tavistock.

Rehm, L., & Marston, A. (1968). Reduction of social anxiety through modification of self-reinforcement. *Journal of Consulting and Clinical Psychology, 32,* 565–574.

Rim, Y. (1976). A note on personality, psychosocial disturbance and difficulty in social groups in two cultures. *Interpersonal Development. 2,* 91–95.

Robinson, W. (1974). *Language and social behaviour.* Harmondsworth: Penguin.

Romano, J. & Bellack, A. (1981). Social validation of a component model of assertive behaviour. *Journal of Consulting and Clinical Psychology, 48,* 478–490.

Shepherd, G. (1977). Social skills training: The generalization problem. *Behaviour Therapy, 8,* 1008–1009.

Shepherd, G. (1978). Social skills training: The generalization problem, some further data. *Behaviour Research and Therapy, 16,* 287–288.

Shepherd, G. (1980). The treatment of social difficulty in special environments. In P. Feldman & J. Orford (Eds.), *Psychological problems: The social context.* London: Wiley.

Sidney, E., Brown, M., & Argyle, M. (1973). *Skills with people: A guide for managers.* London: Hutchinson.

Singleton, W., Spurgeon, P., & Stammers, R. (Eds.). (1980). *The analysis of social skill.* New York: Plenum.

Smye, M., & Wine, J. (Eds.). (1981). *Social competence.* New York. Guilford Press.

Spence, S. (1980). *Social skills training with children and adolescents: A counsellor's manual.* Windsor: NFER.

Spence, S. (1981). Differences in social skills performance between institutionalized juvenile male offenders and a comparable group of boys without offence records. *British Journal of Clinical Psychology, 20,* 163–172.

Spence, S., & Marzillier, J. (1979). Social skills training with adolescent male offenders I. Short-term effects. *Behaviour Research and Therapy, 17,* 7–16.

Spence, S., & Marzillier, J. (1981). Social skills training with adolescent male offenders II. Short-term, long-term and generalized effects. *Behaviour Research and Therapy, 19,* 349–368.

Spence, A., & Spence, S. (1980). Cognitive changes associated with social skills training. *Behaviour Research and Therapy, 18,* 265–272.

Spinks, P., & Moerdyk, A. (1980). A comparison of responses between Indian and European South Africans to the Taylor MAS. *International Journal of Psychology, 15,* 43–52.

Stravinski, A. (1978). The "Emperor's Clothes" revealed or social skills vs. research skills. *Behavioural Psychotherapy, 6,* 91–96.

Summerfield, A., & Lake, J. (1977). Non-verbal and verbal behaviours associated with parting. *British Journal of Psychology, 68,* 133–136.

Tittmar, H. G., Dickson, D., & Hargie, O. (1979). *The relationship between anxiety and student attitudes to microteaching.* Unpublished paper, Ulster Polytechnic.

Trower, P. (1978). Skills training for adolescents' social problems: A viable alternative. *Journal of Adolescence, 1,* 319–329.

Trower, P. (1980). Situational analysis of the components and processes of behaviour of socially skilled and unskilled patients. *Journal of Consulting and Clinical Psychology, 48,* 327–339.

Trower, P., Bryant, B., & Argyle, M. (1978). *Social Skills and mental health.* London: Methuen.

Twentyman, C., & McFall, R. (1975). Behavioural training of social skills in shy males. *Journal of Consulting and Clinical Psychology, 4,* 364–375.

Twentyman, C., Boland, T., & McFall, R. (1981) Heterosexual avoidance in college males. *Behaviour Modification, 5,* 523–552.

Van Hasselt, V., Hersen, M., Whitehill, M., & Bellack, A. (1979). Social skills assessment and training for children. *Behaviour Research and Therapy, 17,* 413–437.

Wallace, C., Nelson, C., Liberman, R., Aitchinson, R., Lukoff, D., Elder, J., & Ferris, C. (1980). A review and critique of social skills training with schizophrenic patients. *Schizophrenia Bulletin, 6,* 42–65.

Welford, A. (1981). Social skills and social class. *Psychological Reports, 48,* 847–852.

Witkin, H., Goodenough, D., & Oltman, P. (1978). Psychological differentiation: Current status. *Journal of Personality and Social Psychology, 37,* 1127–1145.

Wolpe, J. (1958). *Psychotherapy by reciprocal inhibition.* Stanford: Stanford University Press.

Wolpe, J., & Lazarus, A. (1966). *Behavior therapy techniques: A guide to the treatment of neurosis.* New York: Pergamon.

Yardley, K. (1979). Social skills training: A critique. *British Journal of Medical Psychology, 52,* 55–62.

Young, G., & Martin, M. (1981). Processing of information about self by neurotics. *British Journal of Clinical Psychology, 20,* 205–212.

Zigler, E., & Philips, L. (1960). Social effectiveness and symtomatic behaviours. *Journal of Abnormal and Social Psychology, 61,* 231–238.

CHAPTER 24

Enrichment, Structured Enrichment,
Social Skills Training,
and Psychotherapy

Comparisons and Contrasts

LUCIANO L'ABATE, DAVID KEARNS, WILLIAM RICHARDSON, AND WAYNE DOW

The past 25 years in the history of the behavioral sciences have been characterized by flux and change. Many established ideas concerning both the etiology and treatment of psychological disorders have come under careful scrutiny (Torrey, 1974), as has the effectiveness of treatment procedures in bringing about change.

With this scrutiny has come a dramatic shift in what some practitioners conceptualize as the most appropriate locus of intervention. A movement has occurred away from the once-common practice of treating persons in isolation from significant others, often with (at best) a limited analysis of how these significant others influence and in turn are influenced by the "identified patient." Such an appreciation for the contextual base of behavior and for the reciprocal influence that people have on each other is one of the hallmarks of the more systemic notions of marital and family treatment that have blossomed since the mid-1950s (Haley, 1981).

This broad conceptual shift, however, represents only part of the change in the development of ideas that has characterized the past 25 years. With an appreciation of the notion of context and how the behavior of those in marriages and families cannot be considered apart from it, researchers and practitioners have busied themselves by probing, analyzing, and theorizing about methods that are commensurate with a contextual/systemic position: methods that can most efficiently and effectively be used to influence and change marital and family behavior (Hansen & L'Abate, 1981).

A CONTINUUM OF INTERVENTIONS

In a global sense, a continuum of interventions has been created. Many of the methods on this continuum stand in bold contrast to traditional, individually focused notions of treatment and intervention. In the marriage and family area, L'Abate (1974) suggested that the end points of such a continuum include, on one side, the structured methods of family life education, and on the other, those of unstructured family therapy. Between these two extremes, L'Abate included the work of those interested in family problem solving (Aldous, Condon, Hill, Straus, & Tallman, 1971) as well as that of the more behaviorally oriented practitioners in the area of marital and family work (Patterson & Hops, 1972).*

L'Abate and Rupp (1981) noted that, whereas each of these methods has been successful, their success cannot be viewed apart from what they see as some obvious limitations. With reference to family life education, these authors see these procedures as seriously lacking an overriding theoretical framework within which the methods used can be viewed. On the opposite side of the proposed continuum, family therapy, by way of limitations, is seen as being available to only a limited (oftentimes affluent) clientele, and can only be performed by practitioners who have been the recipients of a highly specialized, generally expensive training. Similarly, L'Abate and Rupp conceptualize behavior therapy as being inappropriate for the training of certain complex, relationally based skills, such as negotiation, conflict resolution, and alternatives to usually repetitive, self-defeating behaviors within marital and family systems.†

L'Abate and Rupp suggested that an alternative methodology also exists along the continuum of interventions noted before, which they see not only as not having the limitations of the methods

and procedures just described but also a particular advantage as well. It is focused toward prevention rather than therapy (i.e., a method of primary prevention for normal couples and families and one of secondary or tertiary prevention for clinical couples and families.) This alternative is described under the general rubric of "family enrichment" (L'Abate, 1974, 1981; L'Abate & Rupp, 1981). Not surprisingly, like each of the methods listed before, the various models of family enrichment have their own characteristic sets of methods and procedures. The next section surveys the area of marriage and family enrichment (MFE) and has devised a listing of the features that are common to the various existing models. Based on these commonalities, a definition of marriage and family enrichment includes the salient features of the major models and programs that are available.

MARRIAGE AND FAMILY ENRICHMENT (MFE)

Marriage and Family Enrichment (MFE) is a movement that is touching the lives of hundreds of thousands of couples and families in the United States and other countries (Otto, 1976). However, when one begins to seriously ask the question "What is MFE?" satisfactory answers become illusive. Smith, Shoffner, and Scott (1979) wrote that MFE had "yet to be defined adequately." Today the criticism still holds true. In fact, a search for answers in the literature only leads to more confusion. A few illustrations sufficiently demonstrate this point.

Hof and Miller (1981), whose definitional treatment of MFE is markedly superior, begin their book with these words: "Marital Enrichment is an educational and preventive approach to relationship enhancement" (p. 3). They define *preventive* as "dealing with peo-

---

*It is not the intent of this section to provide a history of any particular part of this continuum. Such histories are available in the existing literature, and the interested reader is asked to consult the following sources: Somerville (1971) for a discussion of family life education; Aldous, Condon, Hill, Straus & Tallman (1971) on family problem solving; L'Abate (1974, 1981) for a discussion of the historical antecedents of marital and family enrichment programs; and Gurman and Kniskern's (1981) overview of the family therapy field.

†A behavioral rejoinder to these proposed limitations would undoubtedly include references to Harrell and Guerney's (1976) and Rappaport and Harrell's (1972) work on the training of couples in the use of conflict negotiation skills as well as a body of literature describing skills training via negotiation or training and behavioral exchange (Liberman, 1970; Patterson & Hops, 1972; Stuart, 1969, 1980). (See Birchler, 1979, for more specific details.)

ple in marriages which are basically functional'' (p. 11). Yet, they also write that an increasing number of enrichment programs are aimed at "troubled, dysfunctional or clinical couples" (p. 1). What is MFE—a preventive strategy for functional families or an intervention strategy for clinical populations? Is it either of these or some combination of both? We are left confused.

At various times in the literature, MFE has been made synonymous with social skills training (SST)—a behavioristically oriented model of psychoeducation. At other times, MFE has been seen as a subcategory of SST (L'Abate, 1981). Is MFE synonymous with SST or a separate entity? Or, is MFE a subcategory of SST, or is this situation reversed? Again, we are left confused.

In general, it appears that two problems prevail when attempting to define this field as a whole. First, various authors have their own conceptions of enrichment, that is, their own beliefs regarding what should be the process and the content of MFE. Second, the field itself, though relatively new (early 1960s) is evolving. It is changing over time, and some earlier definitions of MFE may no longer seem adequate.

Though these problems exist, it is also true that the definition of this field is of paramount importance. If the contemporary family may be "sinking deeper and deeper in a sea of trouble" (Mace, 1975) (as virtually all authors in this field point out), then it seems apparent that MFE needs to be as effective as it possibly can. MFE can only begin to reach its maximum effectiveness if it is carefully researched. Yet, until some consensus is reached regarding what MFE is and what MFE is not, systematic research that will facilitate the maturity of this young field may not occur. The goal of this section is to offer a more precise, comprehensive, and current definition of MFE than has been previously available. We hope that a clearer definition will facilitate re-

search that will, in turn, heighten the effectiveness of the MFE field.

EARLY DEFINITIONS

MFE began primarily as a religious phenomenon (L'Abate, 1977; 1981, Hof & Miller, 1981). The first definition to come into fairly widespread use was from a religious organization. In 1973, a conference coordinated by the Committee on Marriage and the Family of the National Council of Churches developed the following definitions of MFE programs:

Marriage Enrichment Programs are for couples who have what they perceive to be fairly well-functioning marriages and who wish to make their marriages even more mutually satisfying. (The programs are not designed for people whose marriages are at a point of crisis or who are seeking counseling help for marital problems.) Marriage Enrichment programs are generally concerned with enhancing the couple's communication, emotional life, or sexual relationship; with fostering marriage strengths, personal growth and the development of marriage and individual potential, maintaining a consistent and primary focus on the relationship of the couple. (Otto, 1976, pp. 13–14)

The definition of family enrichment programs is identical to the preceding except for obvious replacements of "family" for "marriage" or "couple" and inclusions of concepts such as parenting skills, parent–child relationships, and emphasis on involvement of children in the enrichment program. This definition is often cited in the enrichment literature (Otto, 1976). Its salient features are: (1) nonclinical population; (2) growth oriented; (3) primary focus on relationship; and (4) common content of communication, sexual relationships, and so forth.

Other authors have given their lists of common enrichment components. Smith et al. (1979), for instance, gave (1) normal populations; (2) informal settings; and (3) experiential learning. Mace (1975) used (1) nonclinical couples; (2) experiential learning; and (3) preventive education. L'Abate (1981) used (1) time-limited contracts; (2) specific topics agreed upon by clients; (3) nonclinical clients; (4) skills education; and (5) preventive.

Some overlap in these lists is obvious. The question remains as to what elements are characteristic of all MFE programs. Also, what accounts for variance among programs. From a review of the literature, it appears that there are five common characteristics and also five dimensions or continua along which enrichment programs vary. The remainder of this section will elaborate on these characteristics and dimensions. The common characteristics of most MFE approaches follow.

1. Relationship orientation. Whereas personal growth is a subgoal of enrichment programs, relationship enhancement is the primary focus of all MFE programs. Regardless of theoretical orientations and varying processes and contents, all MFE programs seek to treat relationships among intimate individuals (L'Abate, 1981).

2. Theoretical underpinnings. In a review of MFE programs (L'Abate, 1981), there are two common theoretical bases: (1) the humanistic-existential movement and (2) the learning theory movements. The common thread designated *humanistic-existential* is characterized in Otto's (1976) human potential hypothesis. This thesis states that all persons function at a fraction of their potential and in every person or family there is potential for growth. This is not the same as focusing on nonclinical populations. Instead, this is a philosophical mind set toward all persons, across client populations. All persons have inherent tendencies toward growth and realization of potential under the proper conditions.

The other common theoretical thread is learning theory, especially in the form of operant reinforcement theory (Hof & Miller, 1981). This thread emerges in the form of specific skills training, behavioral rehearsal, social reinforcement, modeling, and so forth. Together, these two theoretical commonalities account for the experiential learning and educative characteristics of MFE programs.

Whereas some programs have additional conceptual footings (e.g., systems theory, group process theory), the two theories mentioned before contribute to MFE programs in general.

Contractual Nature

MFE programs are contractual in nature, that is, there is a mutual agreement between client and enricher with regard to duration and the content of the programs. Programs vary according to content offered as well as time involved; yet the mutual agreement is common. For example, when a couple signs up for a Couple Communication Program (Miller, Nunnally, & Wackman, 1975) or a weekend with the Maces (Mace & Mace 1974), the experiences vary greatly, but the nature of the experience and its duration is clearly understood.

The three previously mentioned characteristics are common to MFE, but they do not necessarily differentiate MFE from other modes of intervention, for example, SST is contractual and Strategic Family Therapy is relationship oriented. The remaining two characteristics are unique to MFE. (Yet all five characteristics compose a defining set of commonalities.)

Prescribed Mode of Intervention

Regardless of the particular mode of intervention, that is, the actual behaviors of leader and clients, those behaviors are ultimately prescribed beforehand by an outside authority—the MFE program developer. Behavior of enricher and enrichee is prescribed by a written program in contrast to the behavior of the therapist in the typical psychotherapy session, who is free to direct the session at will. In MFE, the program dictates beforehand the behavior of the enricher. This characteristic is obvious in some MFE programs (L'Abate & Rupp, 1981; Miller et al., 1975), but even in others, where the programs are less structured and the prescription is less obvious (Mace, 1975; Calvo, 1975), the overall mode of enricher behavior (and therefore enrichee behavior) is prescribed by the program. An interesting contrast is seen here between SST and MFE. The intervention of the SST leader is guided by behavioral assessment, not programs.

Education for Many

MFE is intended for large numbers of people, that is, society in general. A goal of MFE is to revitalize a corrupting family structure seen throughout society. The application in intention and implication is uniquely global.

VARIABLE DIMENSIONS

The preceding five characteristics are common to all MFE programs. The following dimensions are common to all as well but only in the sense that MFE programs vary along these dimensions. The dimensions can be conceptualized as continua with each enrichment program falling somewhere on each of those spectrums.

Prevention–Remediation

It is difficult (i.e., if it is possible) to distinguish qualitatively between prevention and remediation. The Maces (1976) notes that all therapy is preventive. This certainly muddles a distinction. L'Abate (1973) calls prevention "improving incipiently dysfunctional patterns." It could be argued that "incipiently dysfunctional" is not different from dysfunctional. If this is the case, changing dysfunctional patterns can be called remedial as well as preventive. Again, the distinction is muddled. Finally, Eisenberg's (1962) categorization of prevention also classifies remedial interventions as types of preventions (secondary and tertiary). It is hard (at best) to distinguish between preventive and remedial.

MFE has traditionally called itself preventive. This assertion is misleading. MFE programs vary along a dimension of preventions, some educating families, some correcting families. At one end of the continuum, MFE is preventive; at the other end remedial. This issue is closely tied to target populations.

Population

Again, traditionally, MFE has claimed to work with mostly nonclinical populations. Today, this is clearly not the case for all MFE programs (Hof & Miller, 1981, p. 2). Although some programs are clearly preventive for nonclinical populations, others are remedial for clinical populations.

Process

MFE programs vary in terms of their process, that is, method of intervention. As we shall see, there is a range of processes from the very structured skills training approach to the much less structured style of groups of couples interacting a la ACME enrichment weekends (L'Abate, 1981).

Content

This has been alluded to earlier. Some commalities may exist, but it is apparent from a review of various programs that there is much uniqueness within various MFE programs. Content ranges from intimacy to problem solving, effectiveness, and so forth.

Time

It has already been pointed out that MFE program writers prescribe various lengths of time for sessions and for overall duration of programs. It would be possible to define any MFE program *graphically* by plotting the particular program as it would fall on each dimension. Also, using the scheme of the five variable dimensions, it would be possible to carry out interactional design research on MFE programs (e.g., a 2×2 design to investigate which types of clientele (clinical vs. nonclinical) benefit more from which types of program process (didactic vs. experiential) or very structured vs. less structured, etc.).

Summary

After considering five common characteristics of MFE programs as well as five variable dimensions, we can define MFE programs as *prescribed and contractual programs of marriage and family intervention that are theoretically based in growth potential and learning theory concepts. Programs consist of experiential learning and skills training and vary along dimensions of prevention–remediation, target populations, processes, contents, and time.* This movement intends its programs for the masses in the hopes of obtaining societal reform for marriages and families.

STRUCTURED ENRICHMENT (SE)

Within the past decade, L'Abate, with the assistance of his students, has developed and started to refine a particular set of structured family enrichment programs and procedures. SE programs (L'Abate, 1985a) for marriages and families can be compared and contrasted in terms of content and structural and procedural similarities and differences with other enrichment and relational skills training programs (L'Abate, 1981).

Although the purpose of this section is *not* to provide a complete overview of the SE process (a task that has been performed in a number of articles and chapters), a brief summarization of the theoretical, procedural, and functional bases of SE is seen as necessary. (The reader is referred to L'Abate, 1981, and L'Abate & Rupp, 1981, for a more complete elaboration of the points that follow.)

Background

Initial intentions for devising SE procedures (not SE until more recent writings) were (1) to create standard procedures of use with families who, although not dysfunctional in the usual therapeutic sense of the word, were in need of "some basic groundwork that would allow their members to communicate with each other more effectively" (L'Abate, 1968, p. 32) (b) as an application of the laboratory method to devise programs that through a standard format could be used by less trained intermediaries (under the supervision of an experienced clinician) as a way of efficiently serving a larger number of families than was possible with traditional methods of family therapy; and (3) to use these structured programs as a starting point of a stepwise training process for those learning to work with families.

The functions of SE are (1) the evaluation of couples and families through actual interaction rather than paper-and-pencil tests; (2) the dydactic, stepwise training of students in family work (from structured to eventually less structured experiences); (3) for the couples and families seen, the prevention of relational difficulties in the future; and (4) research. Each of these functions has been clearly and completely elaborated upon in other sources (L'Abate, 1981; L'Abate & Rupp, 1981).*

Theoretical base

The theoretical base of SE is eclectically varied. Its influences reportedly include general information-processing theory, communication theory, transactional psychology, and (more recently) a view of systemic dysfunction as being the result of some type of skills deficit within the marital or family system (L'Abate, 1981; L'Abate & Rupp, 1981), especially deficits in negotiation and problem solving.

Procedures

The procedures followed in SE are (true to its name) structured and standard. The process typically starts with an interview of the couple or family to determine their suitability for SE. A series of preenrichment evaluations are then performed (using rating sheets and paper-and-pencil tests), and, based on the results of the interviews, observations by the enrichers and the preenrichment evaluations, several possible SE programs are selected with the assistance of

---

*With this focus on prevention, SE ties together a number of points that are prevalent in the fields of MFE. This is expecially evident in the discussion of the need for structured (primary preventive) interventions for normal couples and families and for carefully selected clinical samples (thus being preventive in the secondary or tertiary sense). Such procedures reportedly would make it possible to reach larger numbers of clients than is possible with traditional clinical procedures. L'Abate's discussion of the importance of the laboratory method is also representative here, given that it is proposed that these services be carried out by supervised, but often clinically unskilled personnel, thus making the services available at a fraction of the cost that is typical with more unstructured marital or family interventions (L'Abate, 1968, 1969, 1974; L'Abate & Rupp, 1981).

the supervisor. Exercises in selected program(s) are then carried out on a weekly basis of the course of six sessions. A reevaluation follows to assess change relative to the preenrichment rating sheet and test results. A final feedback meeting with the couple or family provides the enrichers an opportunity to provide information to the participants about particular patterns noted about them during the course of the SE and to make recommendations for the future (e.g., no further intervention, further enrichment, therapy, etc.) (L'Abate & Rupp, 1981).

Just as the procedure utilized as part of L'Abate's SE is standardized, so too are the programs and exercises that provide the focus of the six SE sessions. A wide variety of programs are available that cover a number of areas and issues that are specific to marital and family life. To date, these include (in part) affective and cognitively based programs, those covering financial management, democratic living, the use of behavioral principles as a means of family life as well as a variety of special purpose programs (e.g., single parents, adopted children, drug-oriented youngsters, physically handicapped and mentally retarded children, and families of alcoholics) (L'Abate, 1975a). Programs are also available that address issues that are common to particular stages of the family life cycle (L'Abate, 1975b, 1977; L'Abate & Rupp, 1981).

Usually, a couple, drawn from the undergraduate population, signs up for experimental credit in a lower level class. The student partner agrees to bring the other partner and to receive 4 hours of credit for what amounts to an 8-hour experience. They are first interviewed by the enricher(s) to learn whether they are (1) suitable for SE; (2) to establish rapport; (3) to learn what areas of their relationship they want or need to work on; and (4) to sign a consent and contract form. After the interview, they are given a paper-and-pencil battery. Once this battery is scored and evaluated, a decision on what SE programs to be presented to them is made on the basis of their expressed wants and the enricher's evaluation of what is seen to be needed. Thus, during the first session, at least three SE programs that approximate the couple's desires or needs and the enricher's evaluation are briefly presented and described. The couple is to negotiate a choice. They are also reassured that if their choice does not seem to work well for them, they can switch to another program. A program consists of six lessons, and each lesson consists of approximately six exercises. The exercise is the smallest unit of SE and may consist of a question, a task, or presentation of problem-solving issues ("What does love mean to you?" "How do you define care in your marriage?"). Once the program is selected and agreed upon, it is usually followed by most couples. However, exceptions do occur, and if it appears that the program is not going well, changes to other programs or to specific lessons of other programs are easily made. The library of programs (over 70) and of exercises (over 2500) available is so large that there is no problem tailoring lessons and exercises to fit the specific needs of each couple or family.

After finishing six lessons of SE, the couple or family is reevaluated (with the same battery used pre-SE), and a feedback session is arranged within a week or so from completion of the program to allow the couple to express how they feel about the process of SE, to allow the enrichers to feedback to the couple what they learned about them from this paper, and what they may still need to work on. Finally, each couple is given all the choices available at the Georgia State University Family Study Center: (1) complete termination; (2) covenant contracting; (3) intimacy workshops for couples; or, if needed, (4) therapy.

SE and Social Skills Training

As noted before, SE procedures represent a subset of a broader group of programs and procedures known simply as family enrichment.

In more recent writings, however, L'Abate (1981) has referred to SE as what may be viewed as a subset of yet another more global set of procedures—those of the social skills training movement. This is most obvious with reference to L'Abate's (1981) chapter review of marriage and family interventions (including SE that are seen neither as *therapy* or *"therapeutic"* in the traditional meaning of these terms. A second indication of L'Abate's view of this skills training connection is provided in his elaboration of the theoretical underpinnings of SE (L'Abate & Rupp, 1981). Here (as briefly noted before), SE is seen as having its theoretical roots (in part) in a set of ideas that suggests that marital or family difficulties may be the result of skills deficiencies existing in the marital or family system. Through the training of new skills, these deficiencies may be remediated, and it is proposed that future difficulties may be prevented.

Because L'Abate has conceptualized the SE process as a subset of social skills training procedures, much of the remainder of this section is devoted to a check as to the goodness-of-fit of the former with the latter. Before this occurs, however, a brief overview of the social skills training area (specifically, that with a relational focus) is necessary.

Social Skills Training with Couples and Families

An examination of the existing social skills training literature, particularly that that involves work with marital systems, quickly reveals that the literature is largely a behavioral one (Hersen & Bellack, 1976; Jacob, 1976; Jacobson, 1982) and is closely aligned with basic tenets of social learning theory (Bandura, 1969, 1978; Stuart, 1980). Although this description is admittedly abbreviated, the behavioral social skills training position has largely been one in which behavioral principles have been applied as a way of assisting couples in the development of communication skills (Lieberman, Wheeler, & Sanders, 1976).

The behavioral focus of the social skills training area is made even more evident when the behavioral influence on primarily nonbehavioral programs is considered. Birchler (1979) commented that a behavioral methodology has become part of many originally nonbehavioral communication skills training programs in the relationship enhancement area. For example, programs such as the Minnesota Couples Communication program (Chapter 18) now routinely employ behavioral techniques as part of their methodology. Indeed, some of the ideas and procedures that once served to demarcate the behavioral and enrichment/relationship enhancement camps from each other are, over time, becoming points of commonality.

Birchler (1979) has commented on the convergence of methodologies across some of the behavioral social skills training procedures and those with a more humanistic, relationship enhancement focus. Specifically, the proponents of some of the Rogerian-based relationship enchancement programs that call for the development of skills in expressing feelings and empathic listening have extended their focus to include the development of more behaviorally oriented conflict–negotiation skills. The concern of some behaviorists with aspects that historically have been considered the province of a more humanistic tradition —like feelings—is also evident.

Some behavior therapists who have focused on training marital skills related to negotiation and behavior exchange (cf. Lieberman, 1970; Patterson & Hops, 1972; Stuart, 1969) have increasingly emphasized the importance of employing communication modules that facilitate the marital partners' expression of support and understanding, that is, relationship skills (Lieberman et al., 1976; Margolin & Weiss, 1978).

The preceding certainly has been intended as no more than a brief statement concerning the behavioral social skills training area. However, the intent was to suggest that (1) whereas some behavioral practitioners in the social skills training area have slowly adopted more traditionally humanistic concerns (e.g., concerns for the expression of feelings, active listening, etc.) as component parts of their training packages, their training procedures have remained behavioral; and (2) the behavioral methodology is increasingly being used as part of the training that occurs in many generically nonbehavioral relationship enhancement programs. Quite simply, the behavioral position is a dominant one in the social skills training area and appears to be gaining strength in the relationship enhancement areas as well (e.g., as the growing behavioral focus of the couple communication program (Chapter 18).

Despite the implied connection between SE and the more global set of behavioral programs and procedures in the social skills training area, L'Abate has unfortunately provided little information that highlights the specific nature of this connection. Information concerning the nature of the connection between the two areas seems invaluable because, given the behavioral flavor of much of the marital skills training (communication training generally) literature, it is not unlikely that L'Abate's proposed SE procedures will be compared, contrasted, and potentially criticized with reference to the overeaching behavioral frame of reference. Points of similarity and difference between the two sets of procedures need to be carefully elaborated. The similarities and differences between the processes of SE and behavioral social skills training (BSST) are to be discussed in the following sections. This discussion is preceded by overviews of the processes of SE and BSST. Figures 24.1 and 24.2 are provided as guides to structure the discussion that follows.

PROCESS CONSIDERATIONS

The Process of SE

The SE process, as noted in Figure 24.1, begins with an initial interview. Besides the rapport-building function of the interview, it is the task of the enrichers to provide an overview for the couple or family of the SE process and to elicit information from them (via both interview and behavioral observations) as to particular issues or problems that may serve as a central focus of the process to follow (L'Abate, 1981; L'Abate & Rupp, 1981). Besides its use in the planning of the subsequent programs, this information also serves a valuable function in that it is used in part to determine the suitability of the couple family for SE. L'Abate and Rupp (1981) have commented at length about how the SE process was intended for use with normal couples or families, or with certain carefully selected clinical

couples or families. Procedurally, it is not intended for use with couples or families that (1) are chaotic or severely disorganized; (2) are in extreme crisis (e.g., dealing with a death, divorce, separation, etc.); (3) are uncooperative; or (4) evidence entrenched patterns of symptomatology (e.g., behaviors labeled as "psychosomatic," "paranoid," "psychotic," etc.). L'Abate and Rupp caution that even keen observational and interviewing skills on the part of the enrichers during the first meeting may not provide enough information to categorize successfully all of the couples or families that fall within the typology noted before. Their inappropriateness for SE may become clear only after information is gained, for example, after an analysis of their inability or failure to complete particular SE exercises, and the like. Nonetheless, the information and observational information gained as part of this initial meeting with the family is invaluable in the planning of how the subsequent enrichment programs will be structured (L'Abate & Rupp, 1981).

A pre-enrichment evaluation is also part of this initial meeting. Each member of the couple is asked to complete a series of pencil-and-paper rating sheets (i.e., Holmes and Rahe Schedule of Events; the Dyadic Adjustment Scale; Family Adjustment Inventory; and a Feelings Questionnaire). The GSU Fam-

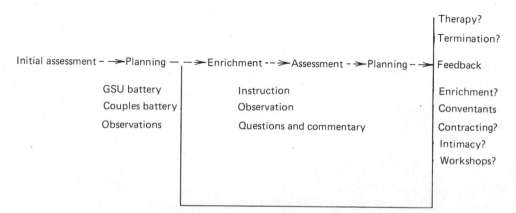

Figure 24.1 The process of structured enrichment.

ily Battery is composed of four separate tests (i.e., the Bell-Fagan Symbol Test; Feelings in the Family; Family Situations Test; and Animal Concepts Picture Series) (see L'Abate & Wagner, 1985b, for a discussion of the use of laboratory psychodiagnostic batteries). These tests call for each family member to evaluate either the family as a whole, or each family member (including themselves) with reference to the symbolic or visual information that is specific to each test. Based on the information provided, these data are used to represent the family graphically (as well as particular members in it) along a variety of cognitive and affective dimensions.

These interviws, observations, and test data about the couple or family are then taken to a planning and supervision meeting with the Enrichment supervisor (see Figure 24.1). It is during this meeting that the data obtained are discussed, along with the enricher's impressions of the couple or family. Based on the data provided, several possible SE programs are selected that are appropriate to the structural, developmental, and systemic characteristics of the couple or family (L'Abate & Rupp, 1981).

The actual SE begins with the presentation of the program alternatives to the couple or family. When there is agreement between all concerned about the program(s) to be used, the actual enrichment process begins. (Because this process was briefly discussed in the preceding section, it will only be briefly reviewed here.)

Procedurally, the enrichers read for the couple or family the instructions for the various lessons and exercises of the selected Enrichment programs. As noted in Figure 24.1, they then observe the couple or family's performance of the requested tasks and activities, most of which have an experiential, relational focus. According to the instructions in the Enrichment program, the enrichers may ask particular questions for the cou-

ple or family that are specific to the exercises performed.

Usually, one lesson is completed at each Enrichment session, with each lesson consisting of five or six particular exercises. The results of each Enrichment session are brought before the Enrichment supervisor before the next session is held (see Planning–Enrichment loop, Figure 24.1). This supervisory experience provides an opportunity for an ongoing analysis (based on the observations made during the previous session) of the appropriateness of the program(s) initially selected and a possible fine tuning of the procedures to be followed in subsequent sessions (i.e., the selection of alternative lessons and exercises, etc.). This alternation between Enrichment and supervision continues until the six lessons of the SE process have been completed. At this time a reevaluation meeting is held in which the couple again completes the GSU Couples Battery, whereas families complete the GSU Family Battery. These results are taken to yet-another planning and supervision meeting (Figure 24.1), and the feedback information to be provided to the couple or family at the final meeting is discussed. This feedback is based on the overall impressions of both the Enrichers and the supervisor about the couple or family, according to their performance on the various Enrichment program tasks, observational data from the sessions, and the evaluation data noted before.

The feedback session is usually divided into four parts. During the first part, the Enrichers ask the couple or family to discuss their reactions (both positive and negative) to the SE process. Second, the Enrichers provide positive comments about particular aspects of the couple or family's behavior that they see as functional and adaptive. Section 3 includes an elaboration by the Enrichers of particular issues or behaviors that were noted during the course of the Enrichment program that were seen as being particularly troublesome. This elaboration may include descriptions of both positive and negative features as well as strengths and weaknesses. Finally, recommendations are made by the couple or family (based on the observations noted above). For some couples or families, the SE just completed is viewed as an end in itself. For others, further Enrichment program activities are recommended, whereas for still others (who had more severe problems and difficulties become evident during the course of the Enrichment program, e.g., more entrenched patterns of behavior), more traditional clinical interventions may be recommended (i.e., therapy, marital contracting, etc.). In these cases, particular referral sources are recommended, should the couple or family request them. For those couples or families in which further Enrichment program activities are recommended (usually with a new program, lesson and exercise format), the Enrichment process begins again with the first planning and supervision session noted in Figure 24.1 but not pretesting.

The Process of Behavioral Social Skills Training (BSST)

Figure 24.2 provides an overview of a behaviorally oriented social skills training procedure. Although the component parts of this figure are not specific to a particular author or set of researchers, it nonetheless describes the basic training process utilized by a number of behavioral practitioners (Jacobson, 1982; Liberman et al., 1976; Stuart, 1980).

It is commonly noted in the behavioral literature on marital skills training (which is largely communication training based) that the most critical task for those working in this area is to identify correctly the interactional behaviors (or lack thereof) that will serve as the targets for skill training (Hersen & Bellack, 1978). Along this line, Jacob (1976) has succinctly summarized the task of behavioral assessment as involving "the identification, description and systemic evaluation of: (a) problem behaviors and desired alternatives, (b) events and behaviors which are functionally related to problems and desired interactions, and (c) strategies for rearranging behavioral sequences so as to increase the frequency and magnitude with which desired behaviors occur" (p. 397).

In an effort to facilitate this assessment task, a variety of strategies have been developed in recent years. Some of the common strategies developed are briefly discussed next.

The initial skills training assessment often begins with a structured interview (see Figure 24.2). An interpersonal history is often taken. The interview is important because it allows the members

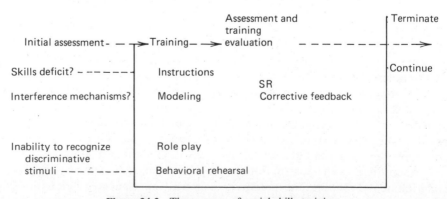

Figure 24.2   The process of social skills training.

of the couple to provide their own subjective evaluation of interpersonal difficulties that they may be experiencing. Although the interview may provide data that are only situationally specific to the interview setting and not representative of the interpersonal behaviors that actually occur in the natural environment, these data are nonetheless invaluable for generating hypotheses as to the nature of the difficulty and for planning possible future assessments and interventions (Hersen & Bellack, 1976).

Besides the use of data gained through structured interviews, a variety of pencil-and-paper inventories have been developed for use as part of the preskills training assessment (as well as for use in monitoring changes throughout skills training). Typically used are a variety of measures that tap spouses' *reports* both of themselves and their partners (Jacob, 1976). Such reports include, for example, Stuart's Marital Precounseling Inventory (MPI) (Stuart & Stuart, 1972), Knox's (1971) Marital Inventory (MI), the Locke-Wallace Marital Adjustment Scale (MAS) (Locke & Wallace, 1959), the Areas of Change Questionnaire (A-C) (Weiss, Hops, & Patterson, 1973), and the Marital Conflict Form (MCF) (Weiss & Margolin, 1975). Collectively, these procedures provide a myriad of self-reported data, including information concerning spouse desires, suggestions for skills training interventions, and baseline data on specific target behaviors (Jacob, 1976).

Other procedures of use in the initial assessment have been devised to tap information concerning spouses' *observations* of themselves and their partners (Jacob, 1976). Briefly, these include measures such as Patterson and Hops (1972) Pleasant Thoughts (PT) procedure, which was designed to assess cognitive correlates of marital relationship behaviors. Also representative is Weiss et al.'s, (1973) Marital Activities Inventory—Together, Other, Alone (MAITOA) as well as their Spouse Observation Checklist (SOC), which depicts discreet behaviors performed by spouses either alone or together.

With increased sophistication, some practitioners (e.g., Weiss & Margolin, 1975) have videotaped interactional sequences between husbands and wives and had them monitor and label themselves on spouse behaviors that each sees as relevant to their communication difficulties. Their responses are then used in the planning of their subsequent skills training.

Though both expensive and impractical for the general practitioner, assessments (both initial and ongoing) have been performed with the use of home-based automatic recording devices. These assessments presumably provide a more naturalistic (though probably not unreactive) view of the actual interactional behaviors of the husband and wife (Johnson & Bolstad, 1975).

As noted by Jacob (1976), potentially the most reliable means of behavioral assessment comes from the use of trained observers (including those doing structured interviews) who monitor actual or recorded sequences of interactional behaviors between spouses. These interactions may be in response either to interview questions (Jacob, 1976), or to structured, staged marital interactions (e.g., discussions of particular topics, role plays, etc.) (Hersen & Bellack, 1976). Although each of the measures and procedures noted before is discussed with reference to the initial assessment phase of the behavioral skills training process (see Figure 24.2), all can potentially be used to monitor behavioral changes over time following the implementation of the selected skills training procedures.

Another important task completed during the initial assessment phase of the skills training process (besides attempting to determine the nature of possible skills deficits as noted before) concerns an analysis of the possible influence of interference mechanisms on interpersonal behavior.

Eisler (1976) discussed the importance of determining whether the interpersonal difficulty was the result of an actual skills deficit or whether factors such as anxiety (or potentially, an inability to recognize discriminative stimuli important for interpersonal behavior) may be short-circuiting the performance of behaviors that are already in the behavioral repertoire of one or both members of the couple. This is an essential part of the assessment in that different courses of action in terms of skills training will follow, depending on the identified locus of the interpersonal difficulty.

The training phase of the process (noted in Figure 24.2) highlights, at least initially, the active role of the trainer or clinician as part of the skills training process. With an agreed-upon course of action, that is, an understanding of the interpersonal behaviors to be trained), the behavioral skills trainer commonly instructs, models, and/or sets the stage for role plays in which the desired behaviors are the focus as well as the subsequent rehearsal of these behaviors (Curran, 1979). What is important is that there is an ongoing feedback component built into the skills training process. Here, after instructing, modeling, and so forth, the trainer observes and assesses the resulting interpersonal behaviors of the couple. Correct performance is reinforced, whereas corrective feedback is offered as to ways of fine tuning or modifying less successful behaviors. This training–assessment–reinforcement or corrective feedback progression (see Figure 24.2) is often continued until the desired behavior initially agreed upon by both the trainer and couple is performed to satisfaction. When this occurs, training is either terminated, or a determination is made as to other skills that might be trained according to the process noted before in Figure 24.2.

With this very complex interpersonal

skills sequence (as in the communication skills area) the training is often initially directed toward simple unitary behaviors. When this bit of behavior has been shown to be performed successfully, however (and at least in the session, reliably performed), progressive, stepwise additions are made in terms of the complexity of the terminal behaviors expected.

During the assessment or training phase of the process (see Figure 24.2), besides a concern for actual observed behavior, many practitioners often re-evaluate the couple according to some of the paper-and-pencil inventories noted in the comments on the initial assessment presented previously. It is not uncommon for termination from many skills training programs to be based not exclusively on actual behavior observed as part of the training process but rather on self-report data obtained from more indirect assessment tools (i.e., statements of relational satisfaction following skills training, etc.).

SIMILARITIES AND DIFFERENCES BETWEEN SE AND BSST

The information presented in the preceeding sections highlights the overall nature of the basic processes involved in both SE and BSST, that is, the activities and procedures that constitute each. In this section, an elaboration is made about some of the similarities and differences that exist between the two procedures.* The listing is certainly not exhaustive, but rather it highlights some of the more salient points of convergence and divergence of the two.† The process

---

*This elaboration is largely the creation of the senior author because the nature of the connection between the SE program and SST has not been discussed in the existing literature. For this reason, new reference citations are included throughout the remainder of the chapter.

†A major similarity that is not addressed in the chapter concerns the fact that both procedures rep-

components of Figures 24.1 and 24.2 will serve as guides for the presentation of information.

It is stressed at the onset that the similarities and differences noted should not be viewed as information suggesting that one procedure is better or more sound in some way than the other. Rather, this section is concerned only with indications of similarity and difference, not with statements as to the relative value or effectiveness of either procedure.

Assessment

Both similarities and differences emerge when the area of assessment is examined. One similarity is that there is a general compatibility across the two procedures in terms of the manners in which assessments are gathered. Both procedures place an emphasis on interview and observation-derived information. Also, both utilize data from paper-and-pencil instruments to provide a multidimensional view of the interpersonal behavior being seen (Stuart, 1980). This similarity in terms of paper-and-pencil data is most evident when skills training and SE with couples are compared. In both instances, the couples are routinely asked to complete inventories (see process sections that call for members of the couple to report the occurrence of particular interpersonal behaviors, and often, their subjective reactions to them. Although these reports are admittedly removed from the actual behavior from which the reports are derived, the information requested is nonetheless behaviorally related.‡

A behaviorally related focus in terms of paper-and-pencil assessment of couples does not seem to extend to work done with families, however. Except for Patterson, this is a relational configuration on which the behaviorists have concentrated very little, if at all (Bellack & Hersen, 1979). Even if this were not the case, measures and rating sheets typically used for dyadic relationships could not be used to evaluate families.

Although SE can be performed with both couples and families, the paper-and-pencil assessment data solicited from family members are qualitatively different from those requested when working with couples. Here, via the GSU Family Battery, the information tapped is more projective and symbolic rather than behaviorally derived (as is more characteristic of the GSU Couples Battery). Therefore, in work with couples, both SE and BSST concentrate heavily on behaviorally focused information (e.g., interviews, direct observation, test data) as part of the assessment process. This pattern does not extend, however (at least in terms of behaviorally related test data) to work with families.

Despite the overall similarity that exists between SE and BSST in terms of the manners in which data about couples are obtained, a difference does exist between them as to a type of information that is commonly collected. As noted earlier (Eisler, 1976), many behaviorists assess whether a deficit in interpersonal performance is related to an actual skills deficiency (e.g., a lack of information about how or what to perform) or whether the skills deficiency is related more to an inability to perform an already existing pattern of behavior. Here, factors such as anxiety may be preventing a person's performance of behaviors that have already been learned. The information gained as part of this assess-

resent alternatives or traditional methods of diagnosis and treatment (L'Abate & Rupp, 1981; Phillips, 1978). A difference that will require further elaboration is how SST potentially stands up against the SE program in terms of the application of L'Abate's laboratory method (1968, 1974).

‡It is recognized, however, that this focus on assessment in the SE program has more relevance in situations where couples or families specifically identify areas of concern or difficulty. Assessment is probably less critical, however, in those in-

stances where a couple or family is interested simply in participating in an experiential process—one that is not necessarily issue-or problem-specific.

ment has implications for the skills training procedure that will be planned. With an assessed skills deficiency, skills training is likely to be the plan of choice. If anxiety is interfering with performance, anxiety-reduction procedures may indeed be called for. In situations in which both factors are operative, skills training and anxiety reduction may occur in tandem (Eisler, 1976; Stuart, 1980). This type of determination does not, however, seem to be a central component of the initial assessment in SE because anxiety is not a transactional concept.

Enrichment and Training

More obvious differences emerge between SE and BSST when the actual enrichment and training phases represented in Figures 24.1 and 24.2 are considered. Here SE differs from BSST largely with reference to the relative inactivity of the enrichers in comparison to those expected of the Skills Trainer(s). The enricher is basically responsible for reading the instructions of the lessons and exercises and then observing the interpersonal behavior that follows. His/her/their role(s) may involve asking questions at the end of an exercise, but the questions asked are generally preplanned as part of the standardized features of the written exercises. In essence, once the stage is set for the performance of the exercises, the couple or family generates virtually all of the behavior that follows. The enricher's task is one of observation. This pattern of inactivity is intentional because, in devising the SE process, it was important to create procedures in which the program and related exercises, rather than the persons presenting them, were the primary focus. This focus is very important in relationship to delivery costs and personnel–power considerations.

The activity of the behavioral trainer stands in bold contrast to the relative inactivity of the enricher. Although the trainer may "fade out" as the performance of the couple in training improves, initially, he/she/they/is/are the focus of the training procedure. Not only do the trainers offer instructions to the couple about the behavior expected, they also are often involved in the role play or modeling of the expected performance as well as in setting the stage for behavioral rehearsals. Likewise, as part of an ongoing assessment procedure, the trainers are responsible for monitoring the interpersonal performance being trained and for providing either positive reinforcement or corrective feedback to the couple as a result.

The Timing of Feedback to Clients

An important aspect of both SE and BSST is the provision of feedback to those receiving the respective services. In terms of the overall process, the procedures differ in the timing of the delivery of feedback. With SE, feedback from the enricher as to the behaviors noted during the various sessions is not given until all sessions, including the reevaluation meeting, have been completed. A different picture emerges, however, with reference to BSST. Here, feedback as to performance is an integral part of each session. The delivery of feedback is integrally connected with the positive feedback and possible suggestions as to improved performance.

Parallel Between SE Supervision and BSST

There is a procedural similarity in the manner in which those doing SE are supervised and the way in which BSST trains clients. This is especially evident with reference to the recurrent supervision–enrichment–supervision loop of the SE process (see Figure 24.1) and the training–feedback–training alternation of BSST (see Figure 24.2). The obvious difference here concerns who is being trained (in the traditional skills training meaning of the term). In SE, it is the behavior of the enricher(s) (in relation to that of the couple or family) that is of central importance. In the case of BSST, it is the behavior of the client in relation to the tasks performed by the trainer (e.g., modeling, instruction, etc.) that is the focus of the recurrent feedback. In both cases, correct, acceptable performances are reinforced, and corrective feedback is provided to help set the stage for the improved future performance. Thus, there appears to be a global similarity between the manner in which those doing SE are supervised and the way in which BSST trains clients. It is when these aspects of the two processess are examined that SE can be seen as most like traditional BSST.

Ideas Concerning Change

It is proposed here that SE and BSST differ in terms of the manners in which the changes observed in couples and families are explained. On a global level, the changes that result from SE must be explained differently than those potentially resulting from BSST. Considering BSST first, the methods that are employed as part of the training process (e.g., instruction, modeling, positive reinforcement, etc.) and the connection of these procedures with empirical data as to their effectiveness provide a specific means of explanation for the behavioral changes that may be noted.

A different type of explanation must be posited to explain results obtained with SE. Here, an educational explanation does not seem relevant because tasks are generally performed with only a limited set of instructions as to the performance expected. Also, given the relative passivity of the enricher(s) (except for observation and occasional commentaries at the end of exercises), their task is not that of "training" new behaviors in the BSST sense of the word. There-

fore, explanations of change seemingly must come from within the SE experiential frame of reference.

One explanation from within this perspective might be that SE provides a contextual setting and a time during which marital partners or family members come together to converse and interact in ways that are uncharacteristic of their current interactions in everyday life. From these experiences, potentially new (or at least different) patterns of behavior, both verbal and interactive, might be said to result. For couples, potentially it could be said that SE serves as a metaphor for their courtship period. The experiential focus of the meetings and the feeling content of many of the lessons may be suggestive of earlier experiences together. Though admittedly contrived, this metaphor suggests an experientially focused explanation of SE-induced change.

Those utilizing BSST could use the same experiential explanation of change for their procedures as well. The difference that emerges is that although educational, training, and experiential explanations of change are potentially available to those utilizing a BSST procedure (in the behavioral sense), of these choices, only the experiential explanation of change seems to apply with reference to SE. If indeed this is the case, this represents a major difference between the procedures—contextual versus acontextual procedures.

Outcome Assessment

A final process similarity between SE and BSST concerns a limitation that exists for both. Those who work in these areas have an obvious interest in facilitating positive outcomes. Like those in most areas of intervention, however, enrichers and trainers are in a position where they must ask themselves similar questions in assessing the effectiveness of their procedures: (1) In terms of validity, do the methods used to assess in-session changes in behavior (e.g., interviews, test data, etc.) actually provide an indication of behavior change? (2) Should positive changes be reflected through the methods of assessment used, are the changes indeed incorporated into the real-world lives of the couples or families seen?

Not surprisingly, these questions are probably more often asked than answered. Their very existence, however, suggests that those in the areas of SE and BSST must work to create clearer, more accurate means of assessing the utility of the methods employed. To focus on these concerns is to address an area of importance with reference to all types of marital and family interventions (Gurman & Kniskern, 1977; Zuk, 1976).

Summary

The information provided suggests that there, indeed, are some salient similarities and differences in terms of the processes of SE and BSST. In the area of assessment, it is suggested that there is a similarity between the two procedures in terms of the manner in which initial and outcome assessment data are collected. They presumably differ, however, with reference to the amount of attention that is devoted to the assessment of the role of anxiety in instances of skills deficiencies; this is more characteristic of the behavioral position. SE and BSST have also been shown to differ in terms of the extent to which the enrichers and skills trainers are involved in the activities of the various SE sessions, whereas much more involvement is characteristic in traditional BSST. The procedures also differ with reference to the timing of the feedback provided to the clients seen. With SE, there is often a single feedback session after all aspects of the process have been completed, whereas with BSST, a feedback component is a central component of all training sessions. It is

proposed that the two procedures also differ as to the manner in which changes resulting from the application of each can be explained. Differences resulting from BSST can potentially be accounted for with reference to educational, training-related, or experiential frames of reference. An experiential explanation seems most viable in explaining changes induced by SE. Finally, a suggestion has been made that the two procedures share two final similarities. First, there is a similarity in the manner in which enrichers are supervised, and the way in which BSST trains clients. Second, both methods of intervention are limited in terms of the methods of assessment now used.

It is suggested that this list of similarities and differences is not an exhaustive one, but rather an initial attempt to elaborate more clearly some salient points of convergence between SE and BSST.

FAMILY THERAPY (FT) AND STRUCTURED ENRICHMENT (SE): IMPLICATIONS FOR COST-EFFECTIVENESS

This section addresses some of the differences between traditional family psychotherapy (FT) and SE for working with couples and families (L'Abate and Rupp, 1981). This topic is relevant because for certain target populations SE may constitute a cost-effective adjunct or alternative to FT.

SE and FT are different from each other. In some respects, their differences are conceptual. Otherwise, differences may be represented along linear dimensions. For example, as practiced, an enrichment program is of shorter duration and costs less than most forms of therapy. Usually, it occurs in six 1-hour lessons with an intake interview and a follow-up session. The conceptual difference along this dimension is that the duration, and therefore the cost, of an enrichment program is predetermined, whereas the duration of therapy is usually determined by how close therapists and clients have come to achieving their respective goals.

Due to changing social and economic factors, both therapy and enrichment programs are under pressure to change; therefore, the differences between the two are not static. Furthermore, because SE and FT share the general goal of improving the human condition, the direction of change for both modes of intervention is toward the other.

Although the task of identifying some of the dimensions along which FT and SE differ is central to this section, it should be noted that the two modes of intervention have developed from distinct historical roots and therefore will always be different from each other. Most nonbehavioral theories of FT have direct or indirect links to traditional Freudian psychoanalytic psychotherapy. Each of the various therapeutic approaches share some core concepts with tradition and have advanced others in reaction to it. For example, Freud popularized the notion that psychological problems resulted from functional illnesses of the mind (Bowen, 1976). Most theories of therapy have accepted this notion and have assumed that the treatment of emotional disorder is the primary goal of therapy.

The roots of SE have been described in detail (L'Abate and Rupp, 1981). At present, an enrichment program is most closely aligned with the BSST tradition. A key conceptual difference between BSST programs and the various therapeutic approaches is that social skills trainers think of psychological problems in terms of skills deficits rather than as symptoms of illnesses. Social skills interventions, therefore, are more like education than therapy. One implication for SE is that it is available as a preventive tool more than is therapy.

A second of Freud's core concepts is that the transference phenomenon, as it develops in the context of the therapist–patient relationship, is the primary mode of psychological change. The centrality of this concept is widely acknowledged in terms of the therapist–patient relationship, with its interpersonal experiences, that is, "resistance." In some nontraditional therapy approaches, such as strategic and Bowenian family therapies, transference is avoided, and the importance of the therapeutic relationship is deemphasized.

Likewise, behavior therapy is not concerned with therapist–client relationships, and most behaviorists, because of the subconscious aspects, would deny that the transference phenomenon occurs. Yet, as behavior therapists manipulate their clients' behavioral environments, including providing for the distribution of reinforcements, they are the primary agents of change. In this sense, the behavior therapist–client relationship can be described in traditional terms.

On the other hand, psychological change resulting from SE could not easily be described in traditional terms. Instead of the enrichers, the programs themselves are seen as the primary agents of change (L'Abate, 1977). Traditionalists might respond that psychological change does not occur as a result of enrichment. In fact, SE does not directly promote personality or character change in the traditional sense. Instead, an enrichment program is concerned with enhancing relationships through the addition of structured interpersonal experiences. If psychological change does occur as a result of intervention, then it occurs in the context of changing intrafamilial rather than therapeutic relationships.

Consistent with the foregoing notions, the enricher–client relationship is moving in the direction of traditional therapeutic relations. While training graduate students in SE, the use of prescribed responses as contained in the published manual are encouraged. However, we all recognize that each family is a unique system with needs that are best met when we deviate occasionally from the prescription. What often happens in supervision is that students present a rationale for making changes in a given program. Rationales for changes are generally supported by subjective as well as objective data, and in this sense, the person of the enricher becomes important to the process of psychological change. Students have sometimes referred to this as "creative enrichment."

Thus far, several differences between FT and SE have been identified. The core conceptual differences are (1) that FT focuses on the treatment of disorder whereas SE is concerned with social skills development in the family; and (2) in traditional and other forms of FT, the therapist–client relationship is seen as the mode of psychological change whereas in SE, the programs are the agents of change. As a result of these two conceptual differences, FT and SE differ radically along the linear dimension of duration that causes a radical difference in costs. The two conceptual differences also combine directly to influence the relative costs of SE and FT. Specifically, as a result of the differences, the cost of training and supervising people to do an enrichment program is next to nothing compared to the cost of training therapists. Enrichers, for instance, do not have to diagnose and treat as do therapists, nor do they have to learn to be in therapeutic relationships as do therapists. They only have to be literate, interested, caring, and able to spend time with others.

Another major difference between the two modes of intervention, and the last one to be discussed here, relates to their respective consumer populations. Presumably, this factor and the cost of the intervention affect each other. For instance, one practical effort is that some people who are discouraged from entering FT because of its high cost may be available for an alternative such as an enrichment program. Theoretically, because of the low cost of SE and because of the way psychological problems are defined in the social skills training tradition, SE can be used in prevention. This means that SE is available for functional nonclinical families and couples. In different words, families do not have to have problems in order to profit from and enjoy an enrichment program. In practice, follow-up study after 3 to 6 months to research consumer satisfaction (L'Abate & Rupp, 1981) indicates that approximately 80% of the respondents are satisfied or very satisfied about their participation in SE.

None of this is to say that functional family groups could not also profit from FT. To the contrary, some functional families could profit from some form of FT. However, most families would not have chosen to enter FT because of its high cost and because of its identification with the treatment of emotional illnesses.

Nor is any of this to say that SE is not available to clinical populations. Although L'Abate and Weeks (1976) have identified four types of families for which they believe that an enrichment program is useful (as noted previously in this chapter), SE can be made available to all types, including the most difficult of clinical families. For instance, where most clients are clinical families in crisis, one could use enrichment-like lessons within the framework of a larger therapeutic environment. SE is especially appropriate when its activities have a minimum of overlap with FT, like in play. The use of playful activity in SE has implications for all clinical families. For instance, chaotic or uncooperative families may be unavailable for improving their ability to solve problems verbally; however, they may be available to learn to play games together and thereby create a whole new level on which to attack their problems.

In general, the use of SE as a sole mode of intervention with clinical families would be ineffective, but in conjunction with other interventions including FT, SE may be very valuable indeed.

In summary, SE is different from FT along a number of conceptual and linear dimensions. As these differences translate directly into a lower cost, SE should be recognized as a viable cost-effective mode of systemic intervention. Although SE was initially intended for a consumer population different from that of FT, it is not theoretically so limited; in fact, SE can be integrated into a comprehensive treatment program for clinical families.

CONCLUSION

The purpose of this chapter was to compare and contrast the field of marriage and family enrichment, as exemplified by the Structured Enrichment program with behavioral, marital, and family-oriented (parent-oriented, really) social skills training and family therapy programs. The similarities and differences do highlight how the field of enrichment—structured and unstructured—stands as an additional preventive and quasi-therapeutic procedure in the field of mental health delivery.

REFERENCES

Aldous, J., Condon, T., Hill, R., Straus, M., & Tallman, I. (1971). *Family problem solving: A symposium on theoretical, methodological and substantive concerns*. Hindsdale, IL: The Dryden Press.

Bandura, A. (1969). *Principles of behavior modification*. New York: Holt, Rinehart & Winston.

Bandura, A. (1977). *Social learning theory*. Englewood Cliffs, NJ: Prentice-Hall.

Bellack, A. S., & Hersen, M. (1979). *Research and practice in social skills training*. New York: Plenum.

Birchler, G. R. (1979). Communications skills in married couples. In A. S. Bellack & M. Hersen (Eds.), *Research and practice in social skills training*. New York: Plenum.

Bowen, M. (1976). Theory in the practice of psychotherapy. In P. Guerin (Ed.), *Family therapy: Theory and Practice*. New York: Gardner Press.

Curran, J. P. (1979). Social skills. Methodological issues and future directions. In A. S. Bellack & M. Hersen (Eds.), *Research and practice in social skills training*. New York: Plenum.

Eisenberg, L. (1962). Possibilities for a preventive psychiatry. *Pediatrics, 30,* 815–828.

Eisler, R. M. (1976). Assessment of social skills. In M. Hersen & A. S. Bellack (Eds.), *Behavior assessment: A practical handbook*. Englewood Cliffs, NJ: Prentice-Hall.

Guerney, B. G. (1964). Familial therapy: Description and rationale. *Journal of Consulting Psychology, 28,* 304–310.

Gurman, A. S., & Kniskern, D. P. (1977). Enriching research on marital enrichment programs. *Journal of Marriage and Family, 5,* 3–11.

Gurman, A. S., & Kniskern, D. P. (1981). *Handbook of family therapy*. New York: Brunner/Mazel.

Haley, J. (1981). *Reflections on therapy*. Chevy Chase, MD: Family Therapy Institute of Washington, DC.

Hansen, J. C., & L'Abate, L. (1982). *Approaches to family therapy*. New York: Macmillan.

Harrell, J., & Guerney, B. (1976). Training married couples in conflict negotiation skills. In D. H. Olson (Ed.), *Treating relationships*. Lake Mills, IO: Graphic.

Hersen, M., & Bellack, A. S. (1976). Social skills training for chronic psychiatric patients: Rationale, research and future directions. *Comprehensive Psychiatry, 17,* 559–580.

Hof, L., & Miller, W. (1981). *Marriage enrichment: Philosophy, process, and program*. Bowie Maryland: Robt. J. Brady.

Jacob, T. (1976). Assessment of marital dysfunction. In M. Hersen & A. S. Bellack (Eds.), *Behavioral assessment: A practical handbook.* Englewood Cliffs, NJ: Prentice-Hall.

Jacobson, N. S. (1982). Communication skills training for married couples. In J. P. Curran & P. M. Monti (Eds.), *Social skills training.* New York: Guilford.

Johnson, S. M., & Bolstad, O. D. (1975). Reactivity to home observation: A comparison of audio recorded behavior with observers present or absent. *Journal of Applied Behavior Analysis, 8,* 181–189.

Knox, D. (1971). Marriage happiness: A behavioral approach to counseling. Champaign, IL: Research Press.

L'Abate, L. (1964). *Principles of clinical psychology.* New York: Grune & Stratton.

L'Abate, L. (1968). The laboratory method in clinical psychology: An attempt at innovation. *The Clinical Psychologist, 21,* 183–184.

L'Abate, L. (1969). The continuum of rehabilitation and laboratory evaluation: Behavior modification and psychotherapy. In C. M. Franks (Ed.), *Behavior therapy: Appraisal and status.* New York: McGraw-Hill.

L'Abate, L. (1974). Family Enrichment programs. *Journal of Family Counseling, 2,* 32–38.

L'Abate, L. (1975a). *Manual: Enrichment programs for family life cycles.* Atlanta: Georgia State University.

L'Abate, L. (1975b). *Manual: Family Enrichment programs.* Atlanta: Georgia State University.

L'Abate, L. (1977). *Enrichment: Structured interventions for couples, families and groups.* Washington, D.C.: University Press of America.

L'Abate, L. (1981). Skills training for couples and families. In A. S. Gurman & D. P. Kniskern (Eds.), *Handbook of family therapy.* New York: Brunner/Mazel.

L'Abate, L. (1983). Prevention as a profession: Toward a new conceptual frame of reference. In D. Mace & V. Mace (Eds.), *Toward family wellness: The need for preventive services.* Beverly Hills, CA: Sage.

L'Abate, L. (1985). Structured enrichment (SE) with couples and families. *Family Relations* (in press).

L'Abate, L., & Wagner, V. (1985). Theory-derived, family-oriented test batteries. In L. L'Abate (Ed.), *Handbook of Family Psychology.* Homewood, IL: Dow-Jones-Irwin.

L'Abate, L., & Rupp, G. (1981). *Enrichment skills training for family life.* Washington: University Press of America.

L'Abate, L., & Weeks, G. (1976). Testing the limits of enrichment: When enrichment is not enough. *Journal of Family Counseling, 4,* 70–74.

Liberman, R. (1970). Behavioral approaches to family and couple therapy. *American Journal of Orthopsychiatry, 40,* 106–118.

Liberman, R. P., Wheeler, E., & Sanders, N. (1976). Behavioral therapy for marital disharmony: An educational approach. *Journal of Marriage and Family Counseling, 21,* 251–255.

Locke, H. J., & Wallace, K. M. (1959). Short marital adjustment and prediction tests: Their reliability and validity. *Marriage and Family Living, 21,* 250–255.

Mace, D. (1975). We call it ACME. *Small Group Behavior, 6,* 31–44.

Mace, D., & Mace, V. (1976). Marriage enrichment. In D. Olson (Ed.), *Treating relationships.* Lake Mills, IO: Graphic.

Mace, E., & Mace, V. (1974). *We can have better marriages—If we really want them.* Nashville: Abingdon Press.

Miller, S., Nunnally, E., & Wackman, D. (1975). *Alive and aware.* Minneapolis, MN: Interpersonal Communications Program.

Margolin, G., & Weiss, R. L. (1978). Communication training and assessment: A case of behavioral marital enrichment. *Behavior Therapy, 9,* 508–520.

Otto, H. (Ed.). (1976). *Marriage and family enrichment: New perspectives and programs.* Nashville: Abingdon Press.

Patterson, G. R., & Hops, H. (1972). Coercion: A game for two: Intervention techniques for marital conflict. I. R. Ulrich & P. Mountjoy (Eds.), *Experimental analysis of social behavior.* New York: Appleton-Century-Crofts.

Phillips, E. L. (1978). *The social skills basis*

of psychopathology. New York: Grune & Stratton.

Rappaport, A. F. (1976). Conjugal relationship enhancement program. In D. H. Olson (Ed.), *Treating relationships.* Lake Mills, IO: Graphic.

Rappaport, A. F., & Harrell, J. E. (1972). A behavioral-exchange model for marital counseling. *The Family Coordinator, 21,* 203–212

Smith, R., Shoffner, S., & Scott, J. (1979). Marriage and family enrichment: A new professional area. *The Family Coordinator, 28,* 87–93.

Somerville, R. M. (1971). Family life and sex education in the turbulent sixties. In C. B. Broderick (Ed.), *A decade of family research and action.* Minneapolis: National Council on Family Relations.

Stuart, R. B. (1969). Operant interpersonal treatment of marital discord. *Journal of Consulting and Clinical Psychology, 33,* 675–682.

Stuart, R. B. (1980). *Helping couples change.* New York: Guilford.

Stuart, R. B., & Stuart, F. (1972). *Marital pre-counseling inventory.* Champaign, IL: Research Press.

Torrey, E. F. (1974). *The death of psychiatry.* Radnor, PA: Chilton.

Wampler, K. S. (1982). The effectivenss of the Minnesota Couples Communication Programs; A review of research. *Journal of Marital and Family Therapy, 8,* 345–355.

Weiss, R. L., Hops, H., & Patterson, G. R. (1973). A framework for conceptualizing marital conflict, a technology for altering it, some data for evaluating it. In L. A. Hammerlynck, L. C. Handy, & E. J. Mash (Eds.), *Behavior change: Methodology, concepts and practice.* Champaign, IL: Research Press.

Weiss, R. L., & Margolin, G. Marital conflict and accord. (1975). In A. R. Cinimero, K. S. Calhoun, & H. E. Adams (Eds.), *Handbook for behavioral assessment.* New York: Wiley.

Whitaker, Carl. (1976). The hindrance of theory in clinical work. In P. Guerin (Ed.), *Family therapy: Theory and practice.* New York: Gardner.

Zuk, G. H. (1976). Family therapy: Clinical hodgepodge or clinical science? *Journal of Marriage and Family Counseling, 2,* 299–303.

CHAPTER 25

Implications of Social Skills Training for Social and Interpersonal Competence

DENNIS BAGAROZZI

THE LIMITS OF SOCIAL SKILLS TRAINING

With the advent of each new therapeutic approach, a prophet has appeared on the scene. Psychoanalysists have had their Dr. Freuds as behaviorists have had their Dr. Skinners. As yet, the Social Skills Training movement has not produced a prophet. However, this volume might well become a prophetic Social Skills Training Encyclopedia. As a precautionary measure, therefore, I would like to outline some of the limitations of social skills training. By doing this, I hope to calm some of the overzealous readers—to take some of the wind out of the sails of those Social Skills Training enthusiasts who are ready to proclaim the benefits of Social Skills Training as a panacea for all ills.

Probably, the most obvious limitation to identify is that imposed by the degree of dysfunctionality of a given population of clients (e.g., psychotic individuals, autistic children and adults, brain damaged and retarded citizens, etc.). When working with such populations, the social skills trainer must be able to make realistic appraisals of what these clients can achieve. Setting goals that are too high and unattainable will lead only to frustration. Setting goals that are be-

neath the trainee's potential will have a negative effect upon the trainee's self-esteem and self-respect.

The second limitation is that which stems from the degree of distress or upset in the individual client, married couple, or family system. Thorough screening procedures are necessary to assure that only clients who can benefit from a particular structured learning program are allowed to participate. Social skills trainers must be able to assess the degree of individual psychological distress as well as the severity of interpersonal disturbances by using appropriate diagnostic measures, instruments, questionnaires, observational techniques, standardized tasks, and interviewing procedures specifically designed for such purposes. It would be naive to assume that all individuals who seek social skills training experiences are, in fact, appropriate candidates for such programs. Such a self-selection process cannot be considered a substitute for a thorough screening of applicants. This is true especially when social skills training programs are conducted by inexperienced clinicians and students in training. For example, persons in the throes of crises; individuals seeking magical solutions to long-standing problems; people evidencing severe psychological and psycho-somatic symptoms; uncooperative, disruptive, and hostile clients; extremely defensive, suspicious, and potentially assaultive persons, and so on all may be considered inappropriate for social skills training. Many of these individuals may benefit from a structured learning program, however, once these problematic behaviors have been brought under control through more traditional forms of psychotherapy.

A final consideration facing social skills trainers has to do with client motivation. Clients who enroll in social skills training seminars, workshops, and institutes rarely are "hurting." Indeed, the selection and screening procedures suggested above virtually prohibit such participants from entering social skills training programs. Distressed clients are motivated, at least initially, to enter more intensive psychotherapeutic experiences, because they expect that therapy will remove, or at least help alleviate, the sources of their discomfort. This motivation does not exist for most social skills trainees. The social skills trainer is confronted with a marketing problem. He/she is faced with the task of creating a need or a desire (in the minds of potential consumers) to possess or acquire a particular social skill. His/her problem is not dissimilar from that faced by physicians and dentists who try to get their patients to undergo periodic check ups even when they are not feeling ill.

It seems to me that the social skills trainer may have to develop charisma to entice potential participants into giving social skills training a try. However, this zeal should be tempered with some sound understanding of the limits of social skills training.

GOALS OF SOCIAL SKILLS TRAINING

I would now like to offer some observations about social skills training and re-

search as conceptualized by the majority of contributors to this volume. For these writers, social skills training is much more than a "new" or "different" approach to working with individuals, groups and family systems; it is a sociopolitical movement whose time has come! Proponents of social skills training view dysfunctional behavior, for the most part, as a skills deficit and as a product of faulty learning rather than as symptomatic manifestations of perverted instinctual drives and unresolved unconscious conflicts. Each empirical study cited in this volume and each program that has been reviewed herein stands as a political statement that reaches far beyond the substantive findings presented to the readers. The political nature of this volume is reflected in the terms used to describe social skills training, for example, "educational," "psychoeducational," and the like. The choice of such terms sets social skills approaches apart from more traditional trait conceptions of personality, deviance, and medical notions of psychopathology.

Researchers and clinicians from a variety of disciplines who have been dissatisfied for a long time with medical models of human behavior and behavior change have finally found a common banner around which to rally. Although it may be accurate to say that proponents of social skills have broken away from more traditional psychotherapeutic approaches to alleviating human suffering, it would be erroneous to assume that there is unanimous agreement about the goals of social skills training. For example, Phillips (Chapter 1) presents what can be considered the philosophical premise or value base of the social skills movement as he sees it. He makes a number of assumptions about the goals of social skills training that deserve consideration because of the far-reaching implications they hold for the refinement of social skills training and the future of the social skills movement. For Phillips, the major purpose of social skills training is to teach participants how to communicate and interact with each other in ways that respectfully uphold the rights of all parties involved in any type of social exchange or interpersonal transaction. The outcome of such training, if successful, is a person who is prosocial and proactive and who engages in mutually reinforcing social interactions that are not exploitive or coercive. It is probably not correct to assume that all proponents of social skills training agree with these objectives. However, this prosocial orientation is implicit in many of the social skills programs presented in this volume. If one accepts the premise that the goal of social skills training is to foster prosocial behavior, spokespersons for the social skills movement may find that they have left themselves open to criticism from a number of quarters. For example, it is conceivable that some critics might argue that such a goal is actually a veiled attempt to impose white middle-class values and standards of behavior on ethnic and racial minorities. In this instance, social skills training may be perceived as a means of social control—a subtle attempt to maintain economic repression of the poor and disadvantaged.

Conversely, when social skills training is used to teach morality, altruism, and reciprocal sharing to children in a "social curriculum" in public schools, a number of concerns arise, for example, the separation of church and state, the selection of the "correct" morality, the subtle indoctrination of schoolchildren in anticapitalist ideologies, and so forth. Another criticism one might encounter is that training in prosocial, noncompetitive, and altruistic behavior may actually do a disservice to children because it does not equip them with the survival skills necessary to exist in an extremely competitive world of dwindling resources where aggression is frequently rewarded. Although these

criticisms might seem trivial to some, advocates of social skills training should be aware of the possible negative consequences that might result if social skills training is so narrowly defined and/or perceived. It would be unwise for patrons of the social skills movement to endorse a particular ideological goal. A more fruitful course would be to devote time and energies to answering important empirical questions such as: How does the sequencing and the timing of social skills acquisition affect social skills maintenance and transfer? How does one go about integrating newly learned skills systems with those skills systems that already exist in the learner's repertoire?

BEHAVIORAL ACQUISITION AND THE ACQUISITION OF A SOCIAL SKILL

Anyone who has tried to teach a social skill to another knows what a difficult and complex task this is. After teaching social skills for only a short period of time, one quickly realizes that the acquisition of specific behaviors or behavioral systems is quite different from becoming proficient in the use of a given skill or set of skills. Skill, or competence, in the use of any interpersonal behavior can be said to have been achieved only when the trainee or learner has been able to:

1. Master all the behavioral components (gross and subtle) in their correct sequence without the aid of supervision.

2. Achieve nonmechanical, spontaneous, and reliable reproduction of the desired skills in environments other than those where they were actively learned and practiced.

3. Exhibit the desired behavior or behavioral sequences only after carefully considering their appropriate-

ness for the time, place, setting, and interpersonal context in which the learner finds himself/herself. The prudent and judicious use of feedback from various sources in the person's environment is a critical factor in determining whether newly acquired responses are being used skillfully.

Obviously, a distinction is being made between the acquisition and reproduction of novel responses and the cultivation of a true skill. It would be naive to believe that a trainee actually had acquired a skill when all that had been mastered was the rote performance of a carefully choreographed and ordered set of behavioral sequences. The development of a skill requires some degree of talent or artistry on the part of the learner that cannot be taught by the social skills trainer. In the future, therefore, social skills trainers and researchers should begin to experiment with new methods of teaching social skills that require the learner to be creative, to improvise, to modify, and to mold the skills into a pattern that "fits" well with his/her own personal style.

The most difficult part of social skills development occurs after the trainee has learned to perform all the steps and various components of a particular program and begins to struggle with the difficult tasks of incorporating these newly learned behaviors into his/her existing behavioral repertoires and exhibiting the desired responses spontaneously at the appropriate times. For example, in follow-up evaluations of two social skills training programs, the Premarital Education and Training Sequence—PETS (Bagarozzi & Bagarozzi, 1982; Bagarozzi, Bagarozzi, Anderson, & Pollane, in press) and Structured Behavior Exchange (Russell, Bagarozzi, Atilano, & Morris, in press), participating couples indicated that they did not routinely use the communication, conflict negotiation, and joint problem-solving skills that they had learned in these programs to resolve interpersonal disputes and disagreements. However, the majority of couples who had completed these training programs reported that they resorted to using these "skills" in times of crisis or when all other means to resolve their difficulties had "failed." Although one of the goals of both these programs was to help participants incorporate constructive communication, joint problem solving, and contingency contracting into their everyday exchanges and life-styles as couples, this goal was not realized even though all couples who participated in these two programs were able to reproduce these behaviors in observations made during post-testing and follow-up evaluations conducted 60 and 120 days after training had been completed (Russell, Bagarozzi, Atilano, & Morris, in press). These findings led me to postulate that if new behavior is to become part of a person's or couple's characteristic way of functioning, the social skills trainer must take into consideration how to facilitate the integration of new behavioral systems with those skills systems already possessed by the learner. Schlundt and McFall (Chapter 2) briefly review some issues that social skills trainers should consider when adopting a systems approach to skills training, for example, subdividing the skills systems into separate but related task domains; outlining various subtasks of which each domain is comprised; specifying the relationship between and among various domains, tasks, and subtasks; and considering the hierarchical ordering and relationships among major tasks, domains, and social skills systems. These suggestions become especially difficult to implement when one attempts to provide training on a large scale, for example, Life Skills Training as proposed by Gazda and Brooks (Chapter 4), when one tackles the complexities of family life (Relationship Enhancement Therapies, Chapter 20) or when one struggles with the delicacies of intimate associations (sexual fulfillment, Chapter 7).

Conceptualizing social skills training according to a systems approach and taking into account the issues outlined before may change a central aspect of social skills training as currently practiced; that is, the training process may be lengthened considerably. This prospect may be an unpleasant one for social skills enthusiasts who were attracted to the social skills movement because of the relatively short-term nature of many skills training programs. However, if social skills training is to become recognized as a legitimate alternative to traditional psychotherapeutic approaches, social skills trainers and researchers must develop training methods that will help clients incorporate newly acquired skills into already existing behavioral systems in order to insure skills maintenance after training has been completed.

ASSESSMENT

Throughout this volume much consideration has been given to assessing skills deficits, but relatively little has been said about how one goes about assessing which persons, groups, families, and so forth are appropriate candidates for which types of social skills training programs. Similarly, little has been said about what realistic gains one can expect to achieve with certain populations, for example, chronic psychiatric patients and criminal offenders who have long histories of institutionalization. It would be unrealistic to assume that a brief training program would be sufficient to prepare such individuals for productive and fulfilling lives outside the institution. A fertile area for future research and training lies with these societal outcasts who desperately need to acquire social

skills. What is particularly exciting about the social skills movement is the promise it holds for reaching larger groups of consumers and persons not usually seen by psychotherapists (e.g., the poor, elderly, economically disadvantaged as well as some ethnic and racial minorities).

MAJOR CONSIDERATIONS

Throughout this volume, contributors have grappled with the issue of transfer and generalization of newly acquired skills to environments and interpersonal contexts other than those where skills were learned and training originally had taken place. From my experiences teaching social skills to individuals, couples, families, and professional helpers, several factors have been found that seem to influence the degree to which skills systems will generalize once they have become an integral part of the trainee's social skills repertoire.

Environmental Supports for Newly Acquired Behavioral Systems

An important factor in determining whether a trainee will successfully transfer a new skills system to localities outside the training setting is whether the environment is supportive of the behavior and reinforces the client or whether the environment is antagonistic and punishing of the trainee's attempt to put these new behavioral skills into operation.

For example, a ghetto youth who has learned prosocial ways to resolve interpersonal conflicts may find that prosocial problem-solving attempts are dysfunctional in the street culture in which he or she must live on a day-to-day basis. Under such circumstances, social skills training programs should include components that help such clients learn how to seek out environments that encourage and reward the continued use of prosocial behaviors. Training of this sort is not the same as teaching someone how to assess whether the times, settings, interpersonal contexts, and the like are right for the enactment of a given skill. This type of training requires the trainee to actively seek out supportive environments. A more radical, yet creative, approach would be to teach clients how to design environments that would be supportive and thus insure transfer.

Those of us who have spent many hours training graduate students in the development of clinical interviewing skills often find it frustrating when students who perform well in the training laboratory show marked decreases in their social skills levels (e.g., core conditions) once they have become immersed in their clinical internship or practica. A number of factors may account for this drastic change:

1. The student's immediate supervisor may be of a different or antagonistic theoretical and clinical persuasion. She or he may actively discourage or punish the student for utilizing client-centered interviewing techniques.

2. The student's immediate supervisor may be of a different theoretical and clinical persuasion, but does not prevent the student from using, for example, a client-centered approach. However, she or he may not possess these skills. Therefore, she or he is unable to offer corrective feedback or to serve as a model.

3. The clinical setting in which the student is placed may not be equipped with observation rooms, or audio and video devices that permit the supervisor to monitor the student's intherapy behavior. As a result, the student may rarely receive any feedback concerning her/his level of skill performance. Correcting factors 1 and 2 can be accomplished easily by making sure that students are supervised by persons pos-

sessing the skills in question. However, when students are placed in agencies that do not have adequate facilities for live observation or electronic reproduction, it is the training institution's responsibility to see to it that the agency has access to equipment that makes it possible for the student to record her/his work with clients so that she or he can receive the feedback necessary for skills maintenance.

Contextual Issues in Skills Maintenance

Family systems clinicians (e.g., Bateson, Jackson, Haley, & Weakland, 1956; Haley, 1959, 1963, 1976, 1980; Hoffman, 1981; Watzlawick, Beavin, & Jackson, 1967) have stressed the importance of examining the interpersonal contexts in which a person finds herself/himself in order to understand that person's behavior. For family systems thinkers and clinicians, it would be absurd to attempt to effect long-lasting changes in a person's behavior without changing the interpersonal context in which that person is expected to function. In this volume, little consideration has been given to the central role of interpersonal context in the development, maintenance, and transfer of behavioral systems. This issue is particularly relevant for social skills training with institutionalized individuals and young children who must return home to live in interpersonal contexts that, if family systems thinkers are correct, require the "identified patient" to exhibit dysfunctional behaviors in order to maintain the system's homeostatic equilibrium.

This issue is conceptually and epistemologically distinct from the one raised earlier concerning the ghetto youth who returns to an environment that does not support his or her newly acquired skills. In that example, the youth is able to leave the field. He or she is not compelled to remain in a rigid interpersonal system that will move to counteract any new behavior that deviates too drastically from the norm. However, in the case of most institutionalized individuals and children and in the case of many marriages, people must remain in families and relationship contexts that can only be described as "nonvoluntary" (Bagarozzi, 1983; Bagarozzi & Wodarski, 1977, 1978). Under such circumstances, it may be incorrect to assume that a person behaves as one does or fails to behave appropriately because (1) the person has a skills deficit; (2) does not know the proper behavior; (3) knows the proper behaviors but is unable or unwilling to exhibit them; and (4) was not taught general rules, concepts, and strategies for using social skills, and the like. It may be more accurate to say that the person does not exhibit certain behaviors and social skills because doing so is perceived to have dire consequences for herself/himself as well as for the integrity of the social group in which the person is an essential component.

More consideration must be given to understanding the roles played by interpersonal contexts in the acquisition, maintenance, and generalization of social skills. In the future, social skills researchers and practitioners who ordinarily do not treat relationship systems must give serious thought to how they might begin to effect changes in the trainee's interpersonal contexts, especially those interpersonal systems that are resistant to any planned attempts at intervention.

In keeping with this perspective, an essential component of the assessment process becomes the careful analysis of how the client's dysfunctional behavior "fits" and has meaning in specific relationship contexts. Serious consideration must be given to how newly acquired skills systems will impact significant interpersonal systems in which the trainee is expected to function. Therefore, social skills trainers are faced with three con-

siderations when devising social skills training programs.

1. To design skills training programs so that they take into account how the skills systems to be acquired by the learner can be integrated with social skills systems that are already part of the learner's repertoire.

2. To assess the possible impact of a newly acquired skills system on the interpersonal systems in which the learner is expected to live and function.

3. To decide whether social skills training should focus on (1) the individual learner or (2) the important social systems and interpersonal contexts in which the client is an integral part and from which she/he cannot be separated.

Perception of Social Skills Training

The extent to which the social skills training movement becomes an accepted and legitimate intervention strategy will depend, to a large degree, upon whether social skills training advocates can change some basic perceptions and prejudices of the general public as well as those of other mental health professionals. Consumers will be more likely to participate in social skills training programs if they perceive that what they stand to gain from their involvement will enable them to achieve goals that are thought to be personally meaningful and pragmatically useful. Frequently, social skills training programs are advertised as "enrichment" experiences. This label may be producing negative consequences that hinder the development of the social skills movement. For example, the experience recounted by Wackman and Wampler (Chapter 18) illustrates this point. Little enthusiasm was shown by trainers and potential workshop participants alike for Couple Communication II. One would venture to speculate that a contributing factor for this lack of interest was that Couple Communication II was perceived as "more of the same." Although one is unable to produce or cite any empirical studies that would substantiate this contention, one suspects that "enrichment" programs, in general, are perceived as luxuries that people engage in only if they have the time, money, interest, and inclination to do so. However, "enrichment" probably is not seen by most people as offering something "essential," "needed," or "important."

Similarly, most social skills training programs are of short duration. Although the relative brevity of social skills programs is considered a source of pride for social skills proponents, it may be having detrimental effects. For instance, brief psychotherapy, for many people, is thought to represent a superficial approach that does not address the "true roots" of the problem.

Finally, enrichment programs are not seen as experiences that one engages in continually. Repeated involvement in such training programs may be seen, by some, as self-indulgent. For others, frequent participation may be thought to represent a disguised quest for help with more serious personal problems and relationship difficulties. An important task for social skills practitioners, in the future, is the education of the lay public and the mental health community concerning the nature, goals, scope, and so forth of social skills training.

In this age of professional accountability, mental health practitioners will be more likely to accept the social skills movement as legitimate and refer clients for social skills training if a solid empirical foundation exists to attest to the efficacy of specific programs with various populations, presenting problems, and so forth. It would be foolish and self-defeating to portray social skills training as the treatment of choice for all clients and as a panacea for all human difficulties.

Social Skills Training and Sociocultural Contexts

In Chapter 13, Solomon and Rothblum demonstrate how sex differences have been neglected in the design, development, standardization, and packaging of assertion training programs. They show how such programs routinely prepare trainees to deal only with specific problems in a limited number of settings, situations, and interpersonal contexts. However, the learner is not taught how to identify similarities that exist across situations that reflect a broader societal expectation about what is considered to be appropriate behavior for women, for instance, that they be passive, compliant, submissive, and emotionally supportive. Therefore, transfer becomes less likely. Solomon and Rothblum question one of the central assumptions underlying all assertion training programs, that is, that assertive behavior will be well received, rewarded, and approved of by others in the trainee's environment. As a result of this assumption, little research has been undertaken to investigate the consequences that might befall women who have not been taught to discriminate those situations where assertive behavior is appropriate from those where being assertive may result in negative or even physically harmful consequences. Solomon and Rothblum conclude that because the impact of assertive responding in certain interpersonal situations is not known (e.g., with an abusing spouse or a rapist), the wholesale promotion of assertiveness training for women should be discontinued until some solid empirical data become available.

In their discussions of assertion training, Solomon and Rothblum have brought into focus a broader issue that social skills trainers must address. In addition to paying attention to the sex of the trainees, program developers must begin to consider other salient factors that have been ignored. For example, age, race, ethnic identification, subcultural norms and mores, religious beliefs, geographical location, and regional affiliation all must be taken into account. These factors play an important role in determining the degree to which social skills will be learned, utilized, maintained, and transferred. In order to illustrate this point, the following example is offered.

Over the years, I have had the opportunity to work with individuals, families, and primary groups from a variety of socioeconomic, ethnic, and racial backgrounds. Some of these clients came from large urban centers; others lived in small and isolated rural communities. The more I worked with diverse client populations, the more it became apparent that prepackaged, standardized programs had to be modified, sometimes drastically, to meet the needs of specific client groups and populations.

In many isolated rural areas, inner cities, and among certain ethnic and religious groups, for example, sexism and male supremacy are subcultural norms that are upheld by men and women alike. Typically, in such subcultures, women have little status, possess few rights, and are considered second-class citizens. Acceptable roles for women are limited to those of housewife, mother, nurse, secretary, and the like. For the most part, women are expected to be passive, submissive, and dependent.

In some rural areas, wives are not supposed to enjoy sex. Sex is considered a duty that is performed to satisfy one's husband and to procreate children. Contraception is believed to be unnatural and conflicts with fundamentalist religious values. In many cases, contraception is forbidden by husbands who see

their wives' pregnancies as affirmations of their virility. If contraception is used, it is usually the woman who must take the responsibility for preventing pregnancies. Extramarital relationships are acceptable for men but are not permitted for women. Physical punishment is frequently used by men and women to resolve domestic conflicts, discipline children, and settle interpersonal differences. Complex kinship networks form the fabric of community life, multigenerational households are common, and mistrust of all outsiders is the unspoken rule (Bagarozzi, 1982).

Obviously, assertion training for women who live in such communities should differ substantially from assertion training that a career woman living in a large urban center would receive. It would be disastrous for women living in these communities to receive the same training that one would make available to females who live in large metropolitan centers, who may be living alone, who are struggling to build successful careers in business, and who must learn how to compete, on an equal footing, with highly competitive men. Similarly, it would be foolish to use marital enrichment programs or marital therapy, as suggested by Solomon and Rothblum, to encourage wives living in such subcultures to act independently of their husbands, to ask their husbands to rotate or share household responsibilities and tasks, and to have separate checking accounts. The ideal of achieving an egalitarian power structure and marital relationship may be totally inappropriate for members of some ethnic groups, religious denominations, subcultures, and so forth. However, this ideal may be pursuable for other couples (e.g., middle-class, college-educated couples, and dual-career marriages). The issue of relevance of program goals is underscored by Gambrill (Chapter 14) in her discussions of social skills training for the elderly. Although her recommendations for an effective social skills training program are offered to improve social skills programs developed for the elderly, her suggestions are relevant for social skills training programs in general. She points out that effective programs should include (1) a typology of social situations that are relevant and meaningful for each client; (2) an appraisal of how frequently the target group of clients is likely to encounter a particular situation; (3) the goals that could be effectively pursued within each situation; and (4) the skills required to attain these goals for different subpopulations of the elderly. Gambrill stresses that more attention needs to be given to what she terms the "social validity" of program goals. To achieve social validity, Gambrill urges a return to individualized assessment, which is considered to be the hallmark of behavioral approaches to social skills training. Individualized assessment is crucial for determining which situations are the most problematic for specific clients, for identifying the most effective response options available to clients in given situations, for isolating those factors that interfere with competent performance, and for determining which factors contribute to effective responding. What Gambrill is suggesting is a pragmatic approach to social skills training that takes into account the uniqueness of the client and the goals that she or he would like to achieve in specific situations and interpersonal contexts. In order to develop a highly individualized social skills training program, assessment procedures should be developed that make it possible for trainers to consider the uniqueness of each client, the specific interpersonal situations and contexts that the client identifies as troublesome, and the goals that the client wishes to pursue in each of these situations and contexts. In addition to these three factors, however, program developers also must consider what Goldstein, Gershaw, and Sprafkin (Chapter 12) refer to as the

"trainee × trainer × training method match." In sum, the interaction among five factors must be taken into account:

1. Relevant client characteristics.
2. Situational and contextual considerations.
3. Factors related to goal attainment.
4. Relevant trainer characteristics.
5. Appropriateness of training method.

In light of the previous comments, one may suggest that the following characteristics be included in developing profiles for both clients and trainees: age, sex, race, ethnic background, religious affiliation, socioeconomic status, educational attainment, intelligence, regional identification, characteristic environmental setting (urban, inner city, suburban, small community, isolated rural, etc.), and subcultural considerations (e.g., relevant norms, mores, expectations, etc.) In addition, certain personality factors may be included (e.g., internal-external locus of control, introversion–extroversion, anxiety, achievement motivation, cognitive moral reasoning, learning style, and cognitive complexity).

The prospect of conducting detailed assessments, developing highly individualized training programs, and matching clients with appropriate trainers and methods may be disconcerting to some social skills enthusiasts for a number of reasons. For example:

1. Training procedures for clients may have to be lengthened considerably.
2. It may become more difficult to train large numbers of clients in heterogeneous groups.
3. The training and skills required for the successful implementation of such highly individualized programs may limit the extent to which paraprofessionals can be used.
4. The time needed to prepare trainers

(professional and paraprofessional) may be lengthened.

5. The assistance of a computer might be required to determine the appropriate client × situation and context × goal × trainer × training method match.

Developing highly individualized training programs does not necessarily mean that standardized treatment packages will have to be discontinued altogether. What this does mean is that prepackaged programs will be used in the initial stages of social skills training to teach heterogeneous groups of clients basic or generic skills. However, once clients have mastered these skills and deficits have been removed, training becomes more individualized, and clients can be assigned to programs specifically tailored to meet their ideosyncratic needs.

The Importance of a Developmental Perspective in the Design of Social Skills Training Programs

Social skills trainers have given much thought and consideration to problems associated with transfer, maintenance, and generalization of skills. They also are beginning to recognize the importance of taking into account the roles played by cognitive processes and interpersonal contexts in the generalization, transfer, and maintenance of newly acquired behaviors. However, little attention has been given to certain developmental issues that I believe to be important.

First, social skills usually are taught to clients with the implicit assumption that once a particular skill has been mastered, she or he will be able to use that skill (*unchanged*) throughout the course of her/his lifetime. Program developers do not seem to take into consideration the possbility that skills learned and developed to achieve specific goals at one time during a person's lifetime may be of limited value at another point in her/his

life cycle. For example, the skills needed to make isolated, withdrawn, rejected, and lonely children socially competent with their peers (Chapter 9) may not be useful or appropriate at later stages of the life cycle. In the future, social skills researchers will have to undertake longitudinal studies to answer a number of important questions. Some of these might include:

1. Is it possible to identify a predictable sequence and/or hierarchical ordering in the development of certain social skills?
2. What, if any, is the relationship between and among the developmental courses of various social skills?
3. Is it possible to identify critical periods in the course of human development when certain skills must be learned? If so, what are they?

Second, when teaching complex interpersonal relationship skills to individuals, social skills trainers must begin to pay closer attention to recognized theories of relationship formation and relationship development than they have in the past. For example, in Chapter 6, Curran, Wallander, and Farrell reviewed the research on heterosocial skills training. As I read this chapter, it was amazing to discover that none of the programs reviewed identified a theoretical framework of relationship formation or relationship development that served as a guide for selecting program contents and skills to be mastered by trainees. As far as I can determine, heterosocial skills training is not an accurate description of what actually takes place in such programs. Upon close examination, one finds that heterosocial skills training programs actually are designed to teach *relationship initiation and dating skills to men*. They are not programs designed to offer both men and women the opportunity to acquire the varied and complex skills they need to progress successfully through the various stages of heterosexual relationship development. For example, Lewis (1972) has presented a developmental model of dating and courtship. This developmental process begins with the couple's perceiving similarities along a number of dimensions (e.g., socioeconomic status, cultural background, values, interests, and personality characteristics) and ends with the process of dyadic crystallization. This final stage of dyadic crystallization is marked by the couple's functioning as an autonomous dyadic system, establishing barriers, becoming committed as a pair, and forming a solid identity as a couple. The major stages of this developmental process are as follows:

1. The process of perceiving similarities.
2. The process of achieving pair rapport.
3. The process of inducing self-disclosure.
4. The process of role taking.
5. The process of achieving interpersonal role fit.
6. The process of achieving dyadic crystallization.

In order to complete each stage successfully in this developmental sequence, both partners must acquire individual social skills. In addition, both participants must learn to function successfully as a dyad at each stage of the process. To be successful, therefore, individual social skills and couple social skills are necessary.

We do clients a disservice if we simply teach them relationship initiation skills but do not offer them a comprehensive training program that will enable them to function successfully throughout the course of an intimate relationship. Many relationship problems seen in distressed marriages can be traced to skills deficits in one or both partners. The following example is offered to illustrate this point.

Over the years I have treated numerous couples who have come for marital therapy with the same presenting problems. Usually the wife laments that her husband no longer loves her, that the romance has gone out of their marriage, that her husband rarely shows any sexual interest in her, and so forth. The husband, on the other hand, complains that his wife does not understand him, that she nags him constantly, and that she does not appreciate him. If one traces the history of the problem, one often finds that these feelings and perceptions began shortly after the couple married. Upon closer examination, it becomes apparent that both spouses are victims of a dating and courtship system in Western culture that requires each participant to play specific roles for the duration of the courtship process. However, after the couple is formally wedded, each spouse adopts a different set of roles. In many traditional relationships, for example, the husband becomes absorbed in his work, career, profession, and so forth. For him, this behavior is not unusual. He sees it as fulfilling his role as husband and provider. However, he is not the attentive, solicitous, and affectionate man he was during the courtship process. His wife, on the other hand, perceives this same behavior as an indication that her husband is losing interest, that he no longer cares for her, and that he is unromantic. As a result, she may begin to press him to become more involved with her. In many instances, the husband experiences these requests for more closeness as nagging. From his point of view, his wife does not appreciate all the work he is doing so that he and his wife can live a comfortable life. He begins to perceive her requests for more involvement as demands. The more she demands, the more he resists. The more he resists, the more she demands, and so on. Eventually, he does begin to lose interest in her.

The change in spouses' behaviors after marriage may come about for other reasons, for instance, one or both spouses reverts to previous, more characteristic behavior patterns that were temporarily replaced by courtship behaviors, or spouses adopt the marital roles they learned through observing parental models. Regardless of the explanation used to account for such drastic shifts in behavior after marriage, these and many other marital difficulties can be said to stem from social skills deficits, that is, one or both spouses may not possess the social skills necessary to carry them successfully past the dating and courtship stage of family development. In the Premarital Education and Training Sequence (PETS) mentioned earlier (Bagarozzi & Bagarozzi, 1982; Bagarozzi, Bagarozzi, Anderson & Pollane, in press), couples are taught skills that will help them resolve the major developmental tasks associated with that stage of the family life cycle before the birth of the first child (if the couple elects to have children). This program's contents are derived from recognized theories of marital and family development (e.g., Duvall, 1977; Hill, Foote, Aldous, Carlson, & Macdonald, 1970; Rogers, 1973).

The importance of designing social skills training programs that are solidly grounded in recognized theories of interpersonal behavior and relationship development cannot be overestimated. The key to finding solutions to some of the central problems that plague social skills researchers (e.g., skills maintenance) may be a better understanding of the dynamics of social skills development over time. Similarly, problems of transfer and generalization may be resolved once we begin to understand how various social skills are influenced by the process of relationship development.

SUMMARY AND CONCLUSION

At this time in the development of the social skills training movement, it seems accurate to say that social skills trainers have come a long way in refining techniques for teaching selected social skills to various groups of clients and trainees. However, problems of skills maintenance, transfer, and generalization still remain unsolved. For the most part, social skills proponents have relied upon behavioral technology to help their clients and trainees acquire new skills. Even program developers who cannot be considered "behaviorists" by any stretch of the imagination use a variety of learning principles and procedures in their work (e.g., reinforcement, shaping, modeling, feedback, practice, homework, etc.). However, this emphasis on behavioral technology has had some negative consequences. In some instances, for example, social skills training programs have been developed by persons who have little or no theoretical understanding of the problems with which they are dealing. Rather than turning to theories of human behavior, individual and interpersonal development across the life cycle, the nature of living systems, and so forth to find solutions to problems of skills maintenance and generalization, these program developers seem to believe that if only they can discover the "right" technology, these difficulties can be overcome. In essence, the reliance upon technology has replaced sound reasoning.

It can be said that many social skills training programs are based upon a linear view of human behavior and skills acquisition, that is, specific skills are taught to trainees—trainees acquire these skills—trainees enact these newly acquired behaviors in static environments and rigid interpersonal contexts. Although this view of social skills training may be appealing, it fails to take into consideration the fact that the learning process is not linear; it is interactive and dynamic. In the future, social skills trainers and researchers will have to give serious thought to planning programs that adequately deal with the client × situations and context × goal × trainer × training method match problems outlined previously. I sincerely hope that the comments offered in this chapter stimulate research in these areas.

REFERENCES

Bagarozzi, D. A. (1982). The family therapist's role in treating families in rural communities: A general systems approach. *Journal of Marital and Family Therapy, 8,* 51–58.

Bagarozzi, D. A. (1983). Methodological developments in measuring social exchange perceptions in marital dyads (SIDCARB): A new tool for clinical assessment. In D. A. Bagarozzi, A. P. Jurich, & R. W. Jackson (Eds.), *Marital and family therapy: New perspectives in theory, research and practice.* New York: Human Sciences Press.

Bagarozzi, D. A., & Bagarozzi, J. I. (1982). A theoretically derived model of premarital intervention: The making of a family system. *Clinical Social Work Journal, 10,* 52–62.

Bagarozzi, D. A., Bagarozzi, J. I., Anderson, S. A., & Pollane, L. (in press). Premarital education and training sequence (PETS): A three year follow up of an experimental study. *Personnel and Guidance Journal.*

Bagarozzi, D. A., & Wodarski, J. S. (1977). A social exchange typology of conjugal relationships and conflict development. *Journal of Marriage and Family Counseling, 3,* 53–60.

Bagarozzi, D. A., & Wodarski, J. S. (1978). Behavioral treatment of marital discord. *Clinical Social Work Journal, 6,* 135–154.

Bateson, G., Jackson, D. S., Haley, J., & Weakland, J. H. (1956). Toward a theory of schizophrenia. *Behavioral Science, 1,* 251–264.

Duvall, E. M. (1977). *Marriage and family development.* Philadelphia: Lippincott.

Haley, J. (1959). The family of the schizophrenic: A model system. *Journal of Nervous and Mental Disease, 129,* 357–374.

Haley, J. (1963). *Strategies of psychotherapy.* New York: Grune & Stratton.

Haley, J. (1976). *Problem solving therapy.* San Francisco: Jossey-Bass.

Haley, J. (1980) *Leaving home.* New York: McGraw-Hill.

Hill, R., Foote, N., Aldous, J., Carlson, R., & Macdonald, R. (1970). *Family development in three generations.* Cambridge, MA: Schenkman.

Hoffman, L. (1981). *Foundations of family therapy: A conceptual framework for systems change.* New York: Basic Books.

Lewis, R. (1972). A developmental framework for the analysis of premarital dyadic formation. *Family Process, 11,* 17–49.

Rogers, R. (1973). *Family interaction and transaction: The developmental approach.* Englewood Cliffs, NJ: Prentice-Hall.

Russell, C. S., Bagarozzi, D. A., Atilano, R. B., & Morris, J. E. (in press). A comparison of two approaches to marital enrichment and conjugal skills training: Minnesota Couples Communication Program and Structured Behavioral Exchange Contracting. *American Journal of Family Therapy.*

Watzlawick, P., Beavin, J. H., & Jackson, D. D. (1967). *Pragmatics of human communication.* New York: Norton.

Author Index

Numbers in *italics* indicate pages on which full references appear.

Abel, G. C., 28, *45*
Abel, G. G., 50, 53, 58, *66*, 142, *165*
Abidin, R., 264, 268, 269, *280*
Abraham, D., 56, 72
Abrahams, J. P., 350, *352*
Abrahms, J. L., 481, *502*
Abrahs, L., 349, *352*
Abramson, L. Y., 477, 478, *502*
Adams, D., 546, *552*
Adams, H. E., 173, 175, 176, *190*, *505*, *603*
Adinolphi, A., 55, *70*
Adkins, W. R., 79, *97*
Adler, A., 136, *165*
Agras, W. R., 294, *299*
Aiello, J. R., 418, *419*
Aitchinson, R. A., 372, *378*, 558, *580*
Alberti, R. E., 101, *129*, 373, *383*
Aldous, J., 581, 582, *601*, 616, *617*
Alexander, J. F., 250, 251, 256, 258, *259*
Alford, H., 139, *166*
Alkema, F., 558, *576*
Alkire, A. A., 485, *502*
Allen, G. J., 53, 54, *66*, 150, 151, 156, 158, *165*, 378, *383*
Allen, K. E., 119, *129*, 224, 233, 237, *240*
Allen, P., 122, 123, *131*
Allen, V. L., 246, *259*
Allin, J., 39, *47*, 62, 63, *69*
Allison, P. D., 39, *44*
Allison, S., 122, *129*
Allison, T., 122, *129*
Alschuler, A., 535, *538*
Altman, K., 252, *259*
Altmann, S. A., *44*
Ames, L. B., 78, *98*, *99*
Anchor, K., 264, *280*
Anderson, C., 175, *189*, *524*
Anderson, G. L., 10, *18*
Anderson, H. H., 10, *18*
Anderson, J., 143, 145, *165*, 367, 368, *384*
Anderson, L., 297, *299*
Anderson, N. H., 34, *44*
Anderson, S. A., 607, 616, *617*
Andrasik, F., 109, 116, *132*, 419, 422, 423, 426, 427, 430, 432, 434, 435, 437

Andronico, M. P., 510, *521*
Annon, J. S., 182, 186, *188*
Anthony, W. A., 344, *352*
Appelbaum, A., 512, *523*
Aranson, V., 56, *72*
Arbuthmet, J. B., 7, 14, *18*
Archer, D., 42, *48*
Arconard, M., 478, *504*
Areyzo, D., 236, *244*, 257, *261*
Argyle, M., 5–7, 13–15, *18*, *19*, *21*, 26, 29, *47*, 63, *72*, 137, 139, *165*, 176, *188*, 326, 327, 346, 347, 351, *353*, 376, *387*, 555, 557–560, 562–564, 567, 568, 571–575, *576*, *577*, *578*, *579*, *580*
Argyris, C., 542, 543, *552*
Arkowitz, H., 28, 33, 37, *44*, *45*, 48, 50–57, 61, 63, 64, *66*, 67, 69, *72*, 143–145, 149, 151, 152, 157, 158, *165*, *166*, *168*, 367, 368, 377, 378, *383*, *384*
Arland, S., 53, 57, 62, *71*
Armenti, N., 517, *521*
Arnkoff, D., 95, 96, *99*, 128, *132*
Arnold, S., 249, 250, 256, *259*
Arthur, G. L., 78, *100*
Asbury, F. R., 78, 86, *98*
Asher, S. R., 219, 221–226, 228–233, 235, 236, 238, 240, *243*, *244*, 245, 248, *259*, *261*, 421, *449*
Atilano, R. B., 607, *617*
Atlas, L., 349, *356*
Authier, J., 78, 93, *97*, 275, *280*, 533, 535, *537*, *538*
Avery, A. W., 14, *19*, 202, 204–212, *214*, *215*, 519, 520, *521*, *523*
Aviram, V., *453*
Ax, A., 103, *129*
Axline, V., 506, *521*
Ayllon, T., 119, 121, *129*, 362, *383*
Azrin, N. H., 121, 123, *129*, 130, 146, *165*, 362, 379, *383*, *385*

Babigian, H., 221, *241*, 245, *260*, 418, 421, *449*
Bach, D. J., 440, 443, 444, *449*
Baer, A., 124, *130*
Baer, D., 124, 126, *129*, *130*, 251, 253, *260*, *261*, 349, 350, *353*, *354*
Baffra, G. A., 326, *353*
Bagarozzi, D. A., 607, 610, 612, 616, *617*
Bagarozzi, J. I., 607, 616, *617*

619

Bailey, J., 122, 127, *129*, *131*
Bakeman, R., 34, 39, *44*
Baker, V., 107, 120, *135*
Baltes, M. M., 348, *353*
Baltes, P. B., 174, *188*, 350, *353*
Balzer, F. J., 78, 86, *98*
Bander, K. W., 53, 54, *66*, 150, 151, 156, 158, *165*, 378, *383*
Bandura, A., 3, *19*, 54, *66*, 84, *97*, 101, 102, *129*, 137, 144, *165*, *168*, 223, *240*, 285, 289, *299*, 544, *552*, 589, *601*
Barbee, J. R., 379, *383*
Barber, R. G., 26, 34, *44*
Barclay, J. R., 95, *97*
Bardill, D., 120, *129*
Barkin, S., 540, *552*
Barlow, D. H., 28, *45*, 50, 53, 58, 62, *66*, 109, *131*, 139, 142, *165*, *450*
Barnes, J. S., 542, *552*
Barocas, R., 56, *66*
Baron, R., 101, *129*
Barrera, F., 122, 124, 125, *130*
Barry, W. A., 490, *504*
Barth, R., 334, 336, 347, *354*
Bartol, K. M., 311, *322*
Barton, E. M., 348, *353*
Barton, E. S., 424, *449*
Barton, W. M., 348, *353*
Bass, B. M., 542, *552*
Bateson, G., 609, *617*
Baucom, D. H., 477, 478, 481, 500, 501, *502*
Bauman, E. E., 361, *383*
Bauman, K. E., 433, *449*
Baumgarten, L., 368, *384*
Baumrind, D., 245, *260*
Bayer, R., 179, *188*
Beach, L. R., 55, *68*, 440, *450*
Beach, S. R. H., 478, *502*
Bean, L. L., 287, *301*
Beaver, W. A., 463, *474*
Beavin, J. H., 457, *475*, 480, *504*, 607, *617*
Beck, A. T., 478, 499, 501, *502*
Beck, P., 346, 347, *355*
Becker, M. D., 375, *386*
Becker, W., 118, 119, *132*, 248, *261*, 270, *281*
Beil-Warner, D., 565, *578*
Bell, A. P., 170, *188*
Bell, D. A., 27, *45*
Bell, N. J., 418, *449*
Bell, W. G., 477, 500, 501, *502*
Bellack, A. S., 3, 4, *19*, 22, 28, 33, 36, 40, 44, *45*, *47*, *49*, 50–52, 55, 57, 58, 61, 63, 64, *66*, 69, 70, *72*, 109, 126, *129*, 155, *165*, 246–248, 253, *259*, *262*, 298, *299*, 361–364, 366, 368, 371, 372, 374–376, 382, *383*, *385*, *386*, 418, 419, 422–425, 427, 430, 433, 436, 437, 440, *449*, 450, *451*, *453*, 551, *552*, 556, 558, 561, 563, *578*, *579*, *580*, 588, 592, 593, 595, *601*
Bengston, V. L., 326, *355*
Benner, P., 346, *357*
Bergain, A., *474*

Berg, K., 536, *537*
Berger, R. M., 335, 340, 351, *353*
Bergin, A. E., 95, *98*, 531
Berkman, L., 326, *353*
Berkowitz, L., 102, *129*
Berkson, G., 419, 422, *449*, *451*, *452*
Berler, E. S., 252, *259*, 364, 365, 368, 372, 375, 376, 378, 379, 380, 382, *385*, 386
Berlin, R. J., 297, 298, *299*
Bernal, M., 119, *129*, 280, *281*
Bernstein, D. A., 141, *168*
Berry, P., 420, *449*
Berry, W. A., 28, 34, *48*
Berscheid, E., 55, 56, *67*, *68*
Berzins, J., 533, *537*
Bettleheim, B., 16, *19*
Bhargava, D., 116, 128, *131*
Biddle, B. J., 226, *241*
Bierman, K. L., 232, *240*
Biglam, A., 41, *45*, 53, 59, *68*
Bijon, S., 122, *134*
Bikson, J. K., 327, 328, 346, 348, *356*
Binder, A., 39, *45*
Birchler, G. R., 477, 479, 491, 496, *502*, *504*, 582, 589, *601*
Bird, E., 370, *386*
Bittle, R., 434, *449*
Bixler, J., 95, *97*
Black, E., 350, *355*
Black, J. L., 433, 438, *452*
Blackham, G., 120, *129*
Blackman, D. K., 348, 349, *353*
Blackwood, R., 114, *129*
Blake, R. R., 85, *100*, 541, 542, *554*
Blakeney, P. E., 184, *189*
Blanchard, E. B., 28, 36, *45*, 50, 53, 58, 61, 62, *66*, *68*, 142, *165*, 305, 323, 363, 364, 366, 367–369, 371, 375, 376, 382, *384*, 563, *577*
Blashfield, R. K., 29, *48*
Blechman, E. A., 250, 251, 256, *259*
Blenker, M., 351, *353*
Bloom, B. L., 315–317, *322*
Bloom, B. S., 82, 84, 92, *97*
Bloom, M., 351, *353*
Bochner, S., 557, 565, 566, *577*
Bohart, A. C., 85, *97*
Boland, T., 52, 55, 57, 61, 64, *72*, 557, *580*
Bolstad, O. D., 122, *129*, 593, *602*
Bowden, G. T., 540, *552*
Bowen, M., 599, *601*
Bower, G., 556, 563, *576*
Bower, S., 556, 563, *576*
Bowerman, E. C., 12, *19*
Bowers, K., 121, *133*
Bowles, E., 348, 350, *353*
Bowman, W., 422, 423, 425–427, 430, 437, *452*
Boyd, S. B., 379, *384*
Braatere, L., 571, *576*
Bradford, L., 85, *97*
Bradlyn, A. S., 371, *383*
Brady, J. E., 223, *243*

Brahoe, C. I., 346, *353*
Brakke, N. P., 226, *241*
Brandwein, R. A., 316, *322*
Brankmann, C. J., 37, 48, 58, 71, 371, 382, *386*
Brehony, K. A., 318, *324*, 383, *386*
Brewer, E., 546, *552*
Bricker, W., 101, 120, 124, *133*, 223, *243*
Bridger, W. H., 140, *166*
Bridgewater, C. A., 309, *323*
Bridgman, D. S., 539, 540, *552*
Briggs, D., 269, *281*
Bristow, A. R., 28, 45, 50, 53, 62, *66*, 142, *165*
Brock, G. W., 14, *19*, 263, 265, 278, *281*, 461, *474*
Broderick, C. B., *603*
Broderick, J., 102, *113*
Brodsky, G., 423, *449*
Brody, G. H., 223, *240*
Brooking, J. Y., 347, *355*
Brooks, D. K., Jr., 79–81, *97*, *98*
Broverman, D. M., 303, 305, 308, *322*
Broverman, I. H., 303, 305, 308, *322*
Brown, C. A., 192, *214*, 316, 322
Brown, G. W., 13, *19*
Brown, J. L., 78, *98*
Brown, L., 186, *189*
Brown, M., 558, *579*
Brown, N., 104, 107, 128, *134*
Brown, P., 119, *130*
Brown, R., 463, 465, *474*
Brown, R. C., 102, *134*
Brown, R. S., 93, *97*
Brown, S. D., 94, *97*
Brown, S. J., 438, *454*
Browning, R., 125, *130*
Brumage, M. E., 305, *322*
Brunse, A. J., 485, *502*
Brunswik, E., 30, 40, *45*
Bryant, B. M., 6, 13, 15, *19*, *21*, 51, 63, *67*, *72*, 141, 162, *165*, *169*, 327, 344, 346, *357*, 362, 376, *387*, 557, 558, 565, 568, 572, 573, *576*
Bucher, B., 126, *130*
Budd, K. S., 251, 255, *259*
Buell, Bradley & Associates, 11, 13, *19*
Buell, J. S., 224, 233, 237, *240*
Bullis, G. E., 78, *98*, *99*
Burchard, J., 122, 124, 125, *130*
Burgess, R., 573, *576*
Burish, T., 424, *454*
Burnaska, R. F., 546, *552*
Burns, T., 546, 547, *552*
Burr, W. R., *503*
Burruss, G., 221, 225, *243*
Buswell, N. M., 221, *240*
Butler, L., 54, *71*
Butler, R., 348, *353*
Butterfield, D. A., 310, 311, *322*, *324*
Byham, W. C., 546, *552*
Byrne, D., 55, *67*

Cadigan, J. D., 517, 520, *521*
Cairns, R. B., 245, *260*

Calhoun, K. S., 55, 59, 70, 152, 153, 161, *167*, *505*, *603*
Callahan, S., 276, *281*
Callantine, M. F., 293, *299*
Callner, D. A., 139, *165*
Calvo, 585
Camp, B., 113, 114, 116, 127, *130*
Campbell, D. T., 548, *552*
Campbell, E. E., 462– 464, *474*
Campbell, J. D., 227, *240*
Campbell, J. P., 540, 546, 548, *552*
Campbell, R. Z., 340, *356*
Campbell, W. H., 349, *353*
Cannon, J. R., 344, *352*
Cantela, J. R., 422, *451*
Cantor, D., 268, *281*
Cantor, M., 328, *353*
Capanigri, V., 424, *454*
Capon, M., 571, 572, *576*, 577
Carbanell, J., 295, *300*
Carkhuff, R. R., 78, 84, 88, *97*, 340, *353*, 527, *537*
Carlson, C. G., 362, *383*
Carlson, N. R., 186, *188*
Carlson, P. M., 224, 233, *242*
Carlson, R., 616, *617*
Carlson, S., 546, 547, *552*
Carmichael, L., 10, *19*
Carpenter, W. T., 138, *169*
Carrera, M. A., 175, *188*
Carter, D. K., 316, *324*
Cartledge, G., 16, *19*, 237, *240*, 257, *260*
Cartwright, R., 527, *537*
Castlellan, N. J., Jr., 31, *45*
Cayner, J., 122, *130*
Ceininero, A. R., 33, 54, 61, 64, *73*, 433, *449*, 603
Cerreto, M. C., 439, *452*
Chamberlin, P., 267, *282*
Chan, F. A., 184, *189*
Chapman, A., 557, *577*
Charlesworth, R., 227, 228, *242*
Chatfield, C., 38, *45*
Chemers, M. M., 541, *552*
Cheney, T. H., 41, *47*, 53, 59, 62, *70*, 142, 152, 153, 161, *167*, 378, *386*
Chesney, A. P., 184, *189*
Chiff, P. J., 349, *353*
Child, J., 546, *552*
Childers, W. C., 78, 86, 94, 95, *97*, *98*
Chilsom, M., 535, *537*
Chiriboga, D., 330, *356*
Chittenden, G., 112, *130*
Chittenden, G. F., 418, 419, *449*
Chomsky, N., 528, *537*
Christensen, A., 54, 67, 143, 145, *165*, 367, 368, *384*, 482, 483, *502*
Christian, J. G., 424, *450*
Christoff, K. A., 369, 383, *384*
Claiborne, M., 364–366, 368, 372, 375, 376, 378– 380, 382, *385*
Clark, E. R., Jr., 12, *19*, 124, *130*
Clark, H. B., 379, *384*

Clark, J., 28, 33, *45*
Clark, J. V., 55, *67*
Clark, K. W., 144, *165*
Clarke-Stewart, K., 263, *281*
Clarkin, J. F., *502*, *504*
Clarkson, F. E., 303, 305, 308, *322*
Clausen, J., 221, *242*
Clayton, M. S., 78, 95, *100*
Cobb, J., 101, 102, 120, 124, *133*
Coe, W., 124, 126, *130*
Cohen, A. S., 421, *449*
Cohen, B. M., 379, *384*
Cohen, C. I., 328, 350, *353*
Cohen, J., 85, *98*, 149, 158, 162, *167*
Cohen, M. R., 344, *352*
Coie, J. D., 221, 225–228, *241*
Cole, C. M., 184, *189*
Coleman, E., 186, *189*
Coleman, E. J., 463, *474*
Colgan, P. W., 34, 38, *45*
Collett, P., 32, 42, *45*
Collingwood, T. R., 93, *98*
Collins, C., 424, *454*
Collins, J. D., 518, *521*
Collins, R. L., 544, *553*
Colozzi, G., 424, *451*
Combs, M. L., 127, *130*, 245, 247, *260*
Condon, T., 581, 582, *601*
Conger, A. J., 53, 54, 57, 58, 62, 63, *67*, *72*, *73*, 142,
    153, 154, 162, *165*, *169*, 378, *384*
Conger, A. M., 58, *68*
Conger, J. C., 28, 34, *45*, 53, 57–59, 62, 63, *67*, *68*,
    71, *73*, 142, 152–154, 162, *165*, *169*, 219, 225, 233,
    241, 246–248, *260*, 378, *387*, 551, *552*
Constantine, L., 265, *281*
Cook, A. R., 39, *49*
Cook, M., 557, 568, *576*
Cooper, A., 140, *166*
Copeman, G., 546, *552*
Coppotelli, H., 226, 228, *241*, 326, *357*
Corby, N., 343, *353*
Corrigan, B., 31, *45*
Corriveau, D. P., 33, *45*
Corsini, D. A., 227, *241*
Corsini, R. J., 79, 85, *98*, *100*
Corwin, B. J., 308, *323*
Cotler, S. B., 371, *384*
Coufal, J., 14, *19*, 263, 265, 266, *281*, *282*, 519, *522*
Cowan, G., 308, *322*
Cowen, E. L., 221, *241*, 245, *260*, 418, 421, *449*
Cox, M., 315, 316, *323*
Cox, R., 315, 316, *323*
Coyne, J. C., 13, *19*
Craig, R., 55, *68*
Crane, V. R., 38, *45*
Crassini, B., 557, 571, *577*, *578*
Crawford, J. L. 418, *449*
Crayhead, W., 556, *576*
Crimins, D. B., 371, *383*
Crisp, A., 573, *579*
Cristoff, K. A., 371, *383*

Crites, J. O., 77, *100*
Croake, J. W., 347, *355*
Crosby, F., 314, *322*
Crossman, E., 555, *577*
Crossman, E. R. F. W., 6, *19*
Crumbaugh, J. C., 95, *98*
Curran, J., 109, 126, *130*, 556, 557, 559, 561–563,
    577
Curran, J. P., 28, 33, *45*, 50, 52–58, 60, 64, 65, *67*,
    68, *71*, *72*, 138, 139, 141, 143–146, 148, 149, 151,
    154–156, 158, 160, 162, *166*, 377, 378, *384*, 503,
    549, 551, *552*, 594, *601*, *602*
Cutting, D. S., 438, *452*
Cuvo, A. J., 361, *385*

Dabbs, J. M., 34, *44*, 59, 62, *68*, *72*
Dahl, T., 546, *553*
Danahoe, C., 558, 563, *577*
Daner, S., 39, *47*, 62, 63, *69*
Daniels, A. C., 544, *554*
Daniels-Beirness, T., 227,, *244*
Danish, S. J., 179, 181, *189*, 278, *281*
Dann, S., 223, *241*
Darbyshire, M., 370, *386*
D'Augelli, A. R., 179, 181, *189*
D'Augelli, J., 268, 270, *281*
Davidson, N., 246, *260*, 280, *281*
Davis, G. M., 462, 463, 465, 466, *474*
Davis, J., 107, 125, *132*
Davis, M., 56, *68*
Dawes, R. M., 31, *45*
Dean, S., 298, *299*
deAngelis, M., 16, *19*
Deaux, K., 303, *323*
DeGiovanni, I. S., 493, *503*
DeGroot, J., 103, 104, 128, *133*
deJong, J. R., 14, *19*
deLissovoy, V., 277, *281*
Deluquch, J., 39, *45*
Denmark, F. L., 309, *323*
Depaulo, B. M., 42, *48*
DeRisi, W. J., 345, *355*, 365, *386*
Deselle, E., 78, *98*
Deutsch, M., 424, *449*
Dever, S., 309, 310, *325*
deVisser, L. A. J. M., 480, 486, 487, 491, 492, *504*
deVrioste, R., 227, *241*
Dewitt, M., 512, *523*
Diament, C., 35, *48*
Dickinson, A. M., 544, *553*
Dickson, D., 14–16, *19*, 570, 571, *578*, *580*
Dignum-Scott, J. E., 340, *353*
Dilbonis, P. A., 51–54, 62, *71*
Dillard, C. K., 463, *474*
Dillon, J. D., 463, *474*
Dillow, P., 103, 104, 128, *133*
DiLorenzo, T., 419, 422, 423, 427, 430, 437, *451*
DiMarco, N., 310, *324*
Dimateo, M. R., 42, *48*
Dinkmeyer, D., 258, *260*, 263, 265, *281*
Dion, G., 186, *190*

Dion, K., 55, *68*
Divens, S., 350, *352*
Dobson, J., 270, *281*
Dode, I. L., 463–465, *474*
Dode, J. D., 466
Dodge, K. A., 24, 35, 36, 39, *45*, *47*, 221, 225–229, *241*
Dodson, F., 269, *281*
Doherty, W. J., 477, 500, *502*
Dohrenwend, B. R., 12, *19*
Doleys, D. M., 438–442, 445, *452*, *453*
Doljanac, R. F., 424, *450*
Doll, E. A., 418, *450*
Dollinger, S., 112, *134*
Donahoe, C. P., Jr., 26, 32, *45*, *46*, 60, 61, *68*, 142, *166*
Donellon, S., 424, 451
Donelson, E., 314, 315, 323
Doornick, W., 114, 116, 127, *130*
Dorfman, E., 506, 510, *521*
Dornbush, R. L., 184, *190*
Dorsett, P. G., 48, 59, 68, *70*, 102, 105, 106, 109, *132*
Doughty, R., 125, *131*
Douvan, E., 181, *191*
Dow, M. G., 41, *45*, 53, 59, *68*
Dowell, B. E., 546, *552*
Drake, L. R., 379, *384*
Drasgow, J., 78, 93, *100*
Dreikurs, R., 264, 270, *281*
Dreikurs, R. S., 258, *260*
Dressel, M. E., 368, 379, *385*
Drolette, M., 103, *131*, 252, *259*
Drum, D. J., 81, *98*
Dubin, R., 546, *552*
Duck, S., 55, 64, *68*, 557, *577*
Duer, J., 376, *384*, 558, *577*
Duke, A. D., 477, 500, 501, *502*
Duncan, C. P., 293, *299*
Duncan, J. A., 78, *98*
Duner, A., 246, 253, *260*
Dunkin, M. J., 226, *241*
Dunnette, D., 540, 546, *552*
Dunnington, M. J., 228, *241*
Dupont, H., 78, *98*
Dupree, L. W., 337, 343, 344, *356*
Duvall, E. M., 616, *617*
Dweck, C. S., 229, *241*
D'Zurilla, T. J., 26, *46*, 60, *69*, 93, *98*, 112, *130*, 148, 151, 155, *166*, 332, 347, *354*, *356*

Eagle, E., 438, *450*
Eardley, D., 510, 513, 514, *521*
Earnhart, T., 420, 422, 423, 426, 427, 430, 432, 433, 435, 437, *451*
Eberly, D. A., 337, 343, 344, *354*, *356*
Eckman, T. H., 365, *386*
Edelman, E., 51, 53, 55, *68*, *71*, 109, *130*, 150, 151, *166*, 363, 364, 376, *384*
Edelstein, B. A., 383, *384*
Ederton, R., *451*
Edgar, C. L., 424, *452*

Edinberg, M. A., 332, 338, *354*
Edwards, A., 349, *350*
Edwards, J. N., 175, *189*
Edwards, K., 349, *350*
Edwin, D., 55, *69*
Eggers, J., 63, *70*
Eidelson, R. J., 477, 480, 492, 499, 500, *502*, *503*
Einhaun, H. J., 31, *45*
Eisenberg, L., 585, *601*
Eiser, R., *577*
Eisler, E., 108, 109, 128, *131*
Eisler, R., 555, 563, *577*
Eisler, R. M., 4, *19*, 22, 36, *45*, *46*, 50, 53, 55, 61, *68*, 102, 108, 128, *130*, *131*, 139, *166*, *168*, 305, 318, *323*, 334, 344, *354*, 362–364, 366–369, 371, 373, 375, 376, 382, *383*, *384*, 424, *450*, 594–596, *601*
Ekchannrar, B., 29, *46*
Ekman, P., 35, *46*
Elder, J., 55, *68*, 109, *130*, 150, 151, *166*, 372, *387*, 558, *580*
Elliot, R., 119, *130*
Ellis, A., 111, *130*, 178, 182, 183, *189*, 319, *323*
Ellis, H., 293, *299*
Ellis, R., 14, *19*, 556, 560, 570, 574, 575, *577*
Ellis, T. T., 546, *552*
Ellison, C. R., 177, 182, 186, *191*
Ely, A., 518, *512*
Embry, L. H., 251, *260*
Emcry, G., 478, 499, 501, *502*
Emmons, M. L., 101, *129*, 373, *383*
Endler, N. S., 27, *46*, *47*
Epstein, N., 477–480, 483–485, 487–490, 492–496, 499–501, *502*, *503*
Epstein, R. C., 307, *323*
Erikson, E. H., 77, *98*, 136, *166*
Eron, L., 102, *132*
Ersner-Hershfield, R., 186, *189*
Eskilson, A., 312, *324*
Estes, C. L., 328, *354*
Esveldt-Dawson, K., 41, *47*, 109, 110, *132*, 370, *385*, *386*, 420, 422, 423, 425, 427, 430, 436, 437, *451*
Etheridge, J. M., 379, *384*
Evans, D., 103, 104, *130*, *131*
Evans, M., 9, 184, *191*
Everett, D., 119, *129*
Evers, W., 233, 237, *241*
Evers-Pasquale, W., 225, *241*

Fabry, D. L., 350, *354*
Fagen, R. M., 34, *46*
Falloon, I. R. H., 372, *384*
Fanshel, D., 328, *355*
Farrell, A. D., 28, 33, 34, *45*, 53, 54, 57–59, 62, 63, *67*, *68*, *73*, 142, 152, 154, *165*, *166*, 378, *384*
Faust, D., 7, 14, *18*
Fawcett, B., 573, *577*
Feinberg, S. E., 38, *46*
Feldberg, R., 192, *214*
Feldman, P., 569, *577*
Feldman-Summers, S., 313, *324*
Ferris, C., 372, *387*, 558, *580*

Fidler, J., 510, *521*
Fiedler, D., 55, 68, 440, *450*
Fiedler, F. A., 541, *552*
Field, G. D., 376, *384*
Fine, M., 279, *281*
Fineman, K., 121, *130*
Fink, S., 340, *357*
Firestone, L., 517, *524*
Firestone, P., 128, *130*
Firth, E. A., 63, *68*
Fischetti, M., 53, 57, 62, 68, *71*, 146, 148, *166*
Fischoff, B., 43, *49*
Fisher, B., 195–197, 203, 204, 206–211, *214*
Fisher, J. D., 27, *45*
Fisher-Beckfield, D., 60, 61, *68*
Fishman, P., 314, *323*
Fishman, S., 140, *166*
Fitts, H., 363–369, 371, 372, 375–380, 382, *384*, *385*
Fixsen, D. L., 37, *48*, 58, *71*, 256, *261*, 371, 382, *386*
Flavell, J. H., 78, *98*
Flegg, D., 572, *579*
Fleming, B., 477, 480, 487–490, 501, *503*
Fleming, L., 294, *299*
Fleming, M. J., 462, 463, *474*
Flores, T., 146, *165*, 379, 383
Floyd, F. J., 478, 484, 487, *504*
Fodor, I. G., 304, 306, 307, *323*
Follette, W. C., 477, 479, *503*
Follingstad, D. R., 186, *190*
Foot, H., 557, *577*
Foote, N., 616, *617*
Fordyce, W., 122, *134*
Forehand, R., 122, *130*, 249, 250, 256, 257, *259*, *261*
Forgas, J. P., 28, 29, *46*
Forman, S., 114, 116, 127, *130*
Forrest, D. V., 368, *384*
Foster, R., 419, 422, *452*
Foster, S. L., 22, *46*, 247, 250, 251, 253, 256, *260*, *261*
Fowler, R., 122, *134*
Fox, E. M., 192, *214*, 316, *322*
Fox, J. J., 252, 253, *261*
Foxx, R., 123, *130*
Foy, D. W., 108, 109, 128, *131*, 344, *354*, 363, 364, 376, *384*
Frame, C. L., 229, *241*
Framer, J. A., 148, 151, *167*
Francoeur, R. T., 188, *189*
Frank, E., 175, *189*
Frank, J. D., 4, *19*
Frankel, M., 535, *537*
Franks, C. M., 365, 381, *384*
Frederiksen, L. W., 50, 55, *68*, 102, 109, 128, *130*, *131*, *134*, 318, *323*, 363–365, 368, 372, 375, 376, 378–380, 382, *384*, *385*, *386*, 544, *553*
Fredicksen, N., 29, *46*
Freedman, B. J., 26, 28, *45*, 142, *166*
Freedman, P., 563, *577*
Freedman, R., 419, *450*
Freeman, B., 122, 123, *131*, 558, 563, *577*
Freeman, S., 265, *281*

French, A., 223, *241*
French, J. R. P., 85, *98*
Freumann, W. J., 55, *68*, 150, 151, *166*
Friman, P. C., 440, 443, 444, *449*
Fry, R., 112, *134*
Funkstein, D., 103, *131*
Furman, W., 222, 232, *240*, *241*, 364–366, 368, 371, 372, 375–379, 380, 382, *385*, 437, *451*
Furnham, A., 26, 29, *47*, 326, 327, 346, 347, *353*, 555–566, 568, 570–572, 574–576, *576*, *577*, *578*, *579*
Furst, J. B., 140, *166*

Gaffney, L., 571, *578*
Galassi, J. P., 15, *19*, 52, 54, 58, 61, 63, 64, *69*, *71*, 141, 151, 152, *166*, 557, *578*
Galassi, M. D., 15, *19*, 52, 54, 58, 61, 64, *69*, 141, 151, 152, *166*
Galbraith, J. R., 146, *167*
Gale, M. E., 232, *244*
Galvin, M., 527, *537*
Gambrill, E. D., 4, *19*, 28, *46*, 334, 336, 339, 345, 347, *354*, 556, *578*
Ganzer, V. J., 146, *168*
Gardner, W., 38, *47*
Garfield, S. L., 95, *98*, *474*, 531
Garret-Fulks, N., 315, 316, *325*
Gatson, E., 114, 116, 127, *130*
Gaupp, L. A., 141, *167*
Gazda, G. M., 77–80, 86, 94, *98*, *100*
Geary, J. M., 54, *69*
Geiss, S. K., 480, *503*
Geleerd, E., 126, *131*
Geller, M., 366, 379, *385*
Geller, M. T., 447, *450*
Gelles, R. J., 500, *503*
George, C. H., 255, *259*
Gershaw, N. J., 94, *99*, 108, *131*, 297, *300*, 337, 341, 344, *354*, *355*
Gerson, A. C., 328, *356*
Gesell, A., 78, *98*, *99*, 269, *281*
Gettleman, S., 192, *214*
Gibat, C. C., 307, *324*
Gibson, F. W., Jr., 436, *450*, *452*
Gilbert, F. S., 53, 54, 56, *67*, 144, 145, 146, 149, 151, 156, 158, 160, *166*
Gilbert, T. F., 539, *533*
Gilchrist, L. D., 375, 382, *386*
Gillis, R., 95, *99*, 431, *450*
Gilmore, R., 558, *570*
Gilmore, S. K., 53, 61, *71*, 144, 145, 149, 151, 157, *168*, 267, *283*
Gilner, F. H., 28, *49*, 184, *190*, 376, *386*
Ginott, H. G., 258, *260*, 269, *281*, 506, *522*
Ginsberg, B. G., 266, *281*, 512, 517, 519, 520, *522*
Gittelman, M., 113, 116, *131*
Gladwin, T., 139, *166*, 418, *453*
Glaser, S. R., 41, 45, 53, 59, *68*
Glasgow, R. E., 53–55, 61, 63, 64, *69*, 152, *166*
Glass, C. R., 55, *68*, *69*, 140, 149, 159–161, *166*, 326, *354*

Glass, G. V., 38, *46*, 463, *474*
Glazer, H. I., *503*, *504*
Glazer, J. A., 227, 228, *242*
Glazeski, R. C., 379, *385*
Gleser, G. C., 332, *354*
Glick, B., 108, *131*
Glisson, D. H., 463, *474*
Gluckstern, N., 535, *538*
Glynn, S., 520, *522*
Godole, M., 337, 343, 344, *356*
Goedhart, A., 294, 297, *300*
Goethals, K., 206, *214*
Goethe, K. E., 150, 161, *169*
Goetz, T. E., 229, *241*
Goldberg, L. R., 31, *46*
Golden, M. M., 221, *244*, 246, 253, *261*, 418, 421, *452*
Goldfarb, A. L., 251, *259*
Goldfoot, D. A., 220, *242*
Goldfried, A., 319, *324*
Goldfried, A. P., 58, *70*
Goldfried, M. R., 24, 26, *46*, 58, 60, *69*, *70*, 93, *98*, 112, *130*, 148, 151, 155, *166*, 319, *324*, 332, *354*
Goldiamond, I., 479, *503*
Goldman, J. A., 227, *241*
Goldman, M. S., 54, *69*
Goldman, W., 56, *69*
Goldsmith, J. B., 60, *69*, 149, *167*, 371, 372, 375, 376, *385*, 563, *578*
Goldstein, A. P., 94, *99*, 108, *131*, 284, 288, 289, 294, 295, 297, 298, *299*, *300*, *301*, 337, 341, 344, *354*, *355*, 439, *450*, 527, 531, 533, *538*, 544, 547, *553*
Goldstein, I. L., *553*
Goldstein, M. K., 479, 496, *503*
Goldstein, R. S., 350, *354*
Gollay, E., 419, *450*
Gonso, J., 227–230, *241*, 248, *260*, 421, *450*, 484, 487, 488, *503*
Goodchilds, J. D., 327, 328, 348, *356*
Goodenough, D., 560, *580*
Goodenough, F. L., 422, *450*
Goodman, L. A., 38, *46*
Goodwin, S., 112, *131*
Goodwin, W., 234, *242*
Gordon, R. D., 343, *354*
Gordon, S., 280, *281*
Gordon, S. B., 246, 258, *260*
Gordon, T., *260*, 263, 264, 269, 270, 277, *281*
Gormally, J., 56, *69*, 146, *167*
Götestam, K. G., 349, *355*
Gottlieb, B. H., 350, *354*
Gottman, J. M., 28, 36, 38, 39, *46*, 55, *69*, 140, 142, 149, 159, 160, 161, *166*, *169*, 223, 225–229, 232, 236, *240*, *241*, *243*, 248, *260*, 368, *385*, 421, *449*, *450*, 484, 487, 488, 503
Gottula, P., 349, *350*
Goula, J. W., 265, *281*, 347, *355*
Gove, W. R., 317, *323*
Goy, R. W., 220, *242*
Graham, J., 562–564, 568, 574, *576*

Graham, J. A., 26, 29, *47*, 326, 327, 346, *353*
Graham, P., 418, *452*
Granvold, D., 200–202, 209–211, *214*, *215*
Graves, K. G., 371, *383*
Graziano, A., 118, *131*
Graziano, A. M., 247, 248, *260*
Green, D. R., 250, 251, 256, *260*
Greenleaf, D., 294, 297, *300*
Greenspan, S., 418, *450*
Greenwald, D. P., 28, 40, *47*, 53–55, 62, *69*
Greenwood, C. R., 248, 251, 253–255, *262*, 421, 422, *450*
Greiner, L. E., 542, *552*
Gresham, F., 572, *578*
Gresham, F. M., 231–233, *242*
Grey, L., 258, *260*
Grober, B., 173, 181, 183, *189*
Gronlund, N. E., 221, 226, *242*
Gross, A. M., 252, *259*
Grossman, H. J., 418, 419, *450*
Grossnickle, W. F., 308, *323*
Gruber, R. P., 294, *300*
Gruson, L., 54, *71*
Gubrium, J. F., 347, *354*
Guerin, P., *603*
Guerney, B. G., 78, 93, *97*, 265, 266, 269, 275, 527, 528, 582, *601*
Guerney, B. G., Jr., 203, *214*, 275, *280*, 480, 488, 490, 493, *503*, 506, 507, 510, 513, 514, 516, 517, 519, 520, *521*, *522*, *523*, *524*
Guerney, L. F., 93, *99*, 263–265, 268–270, *282*, 507, 508, 510, 511, 512, 517, *521*, *522*, *524*
Guerra, J. J., 371, *384*
Guest, R. H., 547, *553*
Gullian, M. E., 294, *301*
Gullion, M., 101, 120, 124, *133*, 270, *282*
Gurman, A. S., 462–464, 466, *474*, 503, 531, *538*, 582, 598, *601*
Gustafson, K., 78, 93, *97*, 275, *280*, 535, *538*
Gutride, M. E., 294, *300*
Guzzetta, R. A., 294, *300*

Haas, A., 305, *323*
Haas, S., 346, *353*
Hager, R., 186, *191*
Hagerman, S., 33, *45*
Hahlweg, K., 38, *48*
Haines, J., 575, *578*
Hake, D., 123, *135*
Hake, D. F., 434, *449*
Haley, J., 581, *601*, 609, *617*
Haley, W. E., 350, *354*
Hall, J., 565, *578*
Hall, J. A., 42, *48*
Hall, M., 263, 267, *282*
Halsdorf, M., 250, 256, *259*
Halverson, C. F., 221, *244*
Halweg, K., 487–489, *503*
Hamerlynck, L. A., *505*
Hamilton, J., 122, 123, *131*
Hammen, C. L., 340, *357*

Hammersmith, S. K., 170, *188*
Hammond, K., 30, 31, *47*
Hammond, K. R., 31, *49*
Hampson, R., 279, *282*
Handy, L. C., *505*
Hanley, D., 264, *282*
Hannan, R. L., 547, 548, *553*
Hansen, J. C., 581, *601*
Hargie, O., 14–16, *19*, 570, 571, *578*, *580*
Harlow, H. F., 220, *242*, *244*
Harper, R. A., 319, *323*
Harper, R. S., 418, *453*
Harré, R., 14, *19*, 137, *167*
Harrell, J., 493, *503*, 512, 518, *523*, 582, *601*, *603*
Harris, F. R., 224, 233, 237, *240*
Harris, T., 13, *19*
Harrison, D. F., 58, 62, *69*
Hart, B., 224, 233, 237, *240*
Hart, N., 192, *214*
Hartmann, D. P., 38, *47*
Hartrup, W., 223, 236, 242, *243*
Hartup, W. W., 222, 223, 227, 228, *241*, 245, *260*
Harvey, J., 116, 128, *131*
Hasazi, J., 121, *133*, 424, *452*
Hasazi, S., 121, *133*
Hatch, E., 520, *523*
Hattwick, L. A., 221, *244*
Havighurst, R. J., 77, 80, *99*
Havighurst, R. M., 50, *69*
Hawkins, J., D., 350, *355*
Hawkins, N. G., 12, *19*
Hawthorne, S., 364, 365, 368, 371, 372, 375, 376, 378–380, 382, *385*, 437, *451*
Hay, L. R., 33, *45*
Hay, R. A., Jr., 38, *47*
Haynes, L. A., 520, *523*
Haynes, S. N., 187, *190*
Haynes-Clements, L., 520, *521*
Hays, W. L., 37, *47*
Hayvren, M., 227, *244*
Healy, J. A., 298, *300*
Hearn, M., 103, 104, *130*, *131*
Heatherington, E., 102, 120, *131*
Hebert, F., 114, 116, 127, *130*
Heim, M., 328, 346, *356*
Heiman, J. R., 176, 177, *191*
Heimberg, G., 28, *47*
Heimberg, J., 557, *578*
Heimberg, J. S., 544, *551*
Heimberg, R., 556, *578*
Heimberg, R. A., 144, 151, 159, 160, *167*
Heimberg, R. G., 54, 58, 62, *69*, 378, *385*
Heinzman, A. T., 550, *553*
Helfen, C. S., 424, *451*
Helmreich, R., 311, 312, *324*
Helsel, W., 422, 423, 427, 430, 434, *451*
Hemphill, J. K., 546, *553*
Hemsley, V., 572, *579*
Henderson, M., 557, 558, 568, *572*, 573, *578*
Henley, N., 314, *323*
Hereford, C., 264, *282*

Herell, J., 103, 104, *131*
Heriksen, K., 125, *131*
Herman, J., 103, 104, 128, *133*
Hersen, J., 433, *453*
Hersen, J., 3, 4, *19*, 22, 28, 36, 40, 44, *45*, *46*, 47, *49*, 50–52, 55, 57, 58, 61, 63, 64, 67, *68*, *69*, *70*, 102, 109, 129, *131*, *132*, *133*, 138, 139, *166*, *167*, *168*, 247, 248, 253, *259*, *262*, 298, *299*, 305, *323*, 326, 334, *354*, 361–364, 366, 368, 371, 372, 374–382, *383*, *384*, *385*, *386*, 418, 419, 424, 425, 436, 440, *449*, *450*, *453*, 556, 558, 561, 563, *576*, *577*, *578*, 580, 588, 592, 593, 595, *601*
Hertel, R. K., 28, 34, *48*, 490, *504*
Hess, B. B., 348, *354*
Hess, E. P., 309, *323*
Hesselbrock, V. M., 222, *242*
Hesselhund, H., 175, *189*
Hetherington, E. M., 315, 316, *323*
Hetrick, E., 264, *282*
Heyl, B. S., 184, *189*
Higbee, G. H., 63, *68*
Higgins, W., 535, *538*
Hill, C. E., 146, *167*
Hill, G., 104, 107, 128, *134*
Hill, R., 457, *474*, *503*, 581, 582, *601*, 616, *617*
Hilsman, G., 139, *168*
Himadi, W., 51, 54, 55, *66*, *71*
Himadi, W. G., 51, 61, 64, *69*, 371, *383*
Hines, D., 349, *352*
Hines, P., 28, 33, 37, *44*, 53–55, *66*, 152, *165*
Hinrichs, J. R., 546, *553*
Hinton, R., 51, 54, 55, 61, 64, *66*, *69*, *71*
Hirsch, C., 30, 31, *47*
Hite, S., 178, *189*
Hobbs, S. A., 41, *47*, 53, 55, 59, 62, *70*, 142, 152, 153, 161, *167*, 378, *386*
Hof, L., 582–585, *601*
Hoffman, L., 607, *617*
Hoffman, P., 31, *47*
Hogan, D. R., 184, *189*
Holland, C. J., 84, *99*
Hollandsworth, J. G., 63, *69*, 304, 305, *323*, 557, 578
Hollandsworth, J. G., Jr., 368, 379, *385*
Hollin, C., 573, *578*
Hollingshead, A. B., 13, *19*, 287, *300*
Holmes, T. H., 12, *19*
Honigfeld, G., 95, *99*, 431, *450*
Hopper, C. H., 59, 62, *68*, 72
Hops, H., 224, *242*, 246–248, 251, 253–255, *260*, *262*, 421, 422, *450*, 482, 495, 498, 505, 581, 582, 589, 593, *602*
Horne, J. H., 546, *553*
Horner, P., 513, *523*
Horney, K., 136, *167*
Hornsby, L., 512, *523*
Horton, L., 121, *131*
Hovell, M. F., 251, *261*
Howe, M., 348, *353*
Howe, M. W., 349, *355*
Hoyer, W. J., 297, *300*, *301*

Hoyer, W. T., 337, *355*
Hudson, B., 573, *576*
Hudson, B. L., 348, *354*
Huesman, R., 102, *132*
Hull, D. B., 309, *323*
Hummel, J., 512, *522*
Hummel, J. W., 294, 297, *300*
Hummel, R. C., 77, *100*
Hunter, G. F., 294, *300*
Huntsinger, G., 116, 128, *132*
Hurvitz, N., 500, *503*
Hussian, R. A., 347, *354*
Huston, T., 177, *189*
Huyck, E. T., 85, *99*
Hymel, S., 221, 222, 224, 225, 231-233, 236, *240*

Ilg, F. L., 78, *98, 99*, 269, *281*
Ingham, E., 573, *577*
Ingram, D., 14, *20*
Ispa, J., 223, *242*
Ittelson, W. H., 27, *48*
Itzbowitz, J. S., 149, 250, 255, 257, *259, 261*
Ivey, A., 527, 528, 531, 535, *537, 538*
Ivy, A. E., 340, *354*
Iwata, B. A., 361, *383*, 433, *449*
Izzo, L. D., 221, *241*, 245, *260*, 418, 421, *449*

Jack, L. M., 8, 9, 11, *19*
Jackson, D. S., 609, *617*
Jackson, D. A., 424, *450*
Jackson, D. D., 457, *475*, 480, *504*, 607, *617*
Jackson, G. M., 326, 337, 343, 344, *356*
Jackson, P., 571, *574, 578, 579*
Jackson, R. L., 424, *453*
Jackson, R. W., *617*
Jacob, T., 588, 592, *602*
Jacobi, L., 361, *384*
Jacobs, L. I., 178, *189*
Jacobs, M., 507, *523*
Jacobsen, E., 115, *131*
Jacobson, N. S., 477-482, 484-487, 490, 491, 493-
    499, 501, 588, 592, *602*
Jakibchuk, Z., 233, *242*
Jakubowski, S. P., 304, 305, 319, *323*, 373, *386*, 493,
    504
James, R. R., 38, *47*
Jamieson, K., 484, *504*
Janes, C. L., 222, *242*
Janoff-Bulmann, R., 346, *354*
Jaremko, M. E., 39, *47*, 62, 63, *69*
Jasinski, F. J., 547, *553*
Jason, L. A., 348, *356*
Jayne-Lazarus, C., 493, *503*
Jeffers, J., 122, *132*
Jenkins, J., 108, 109, 128, *131*
Jenkins, J. O., 363, 364, *384*
Jenkins, R., 102, *131*
Jensen, V., 370, *380*
Jerdee, T. H., 311, 312, *324*
Jessee, R., 518, *523*
Jewett, R., 573, *576*

Joanning, H., 14, *19*, 202, 204-206, 208-212, 215,
    461, 463-466, *474, 475*
Joffee, J. R., 12, *19*
Johnson, B. F., 361, *385*
Johnson, D. A., 186, *188*
Johnson, M., 122, 127, *131, 134*
Johnson, S., 102, 123, *129, 131, 135*
Johnson, S. M., 593, *602*
Johnson, V. E., 174, 175, 178, 182-184, *189*
Johnson, W. G., 382, *387*
Johnston, J., 125, *131*
Jones, M. C., 3, *20*
Jones, R., 496, *502*
Jones, R. J., 379, *385*
Jorgensen, S. R., 519, *523*
Jose, P., 314, *322*
Judd, B. B., 35, *47*
Juhasz, A. M., 175, *189*
Junginger, J., 433, 434, *454*
Jurich, A. P., *617*
Justman, A., 108, *129*

Kagan, N., 527, *538*
Kahana, B., 331, *354*
Kahana, E., 331, *354*
Kahn, A., 56, *71*
Kahneman, D., 42, *49*
Kalish, H. I., 13, *20*
Kallman, W. M., 150, 161, *169*
Kaloupek, D., 33, *45*, 51, 53, *67*, 140, *165*
Kane, R. A., 326, 331, 346, *355*
Kane, R. L., 326, 331, *355*
Kane, S. P., 551, *552*
Kanfer, F., 139, 143, *167*, 295, 297, *300*
Kaplan, H. R., 379, *384*
Kaplan, H. S., 182-184, *189*
Kaplan, S. J., 146, *165*, 379, *383*
Karan, D., 116, 128, *131*, 424, *453*
Karoly, P., 56, *66*, 295, 297, *300*, 332, *354*
Kasdorf, J., 78, 93, *97*, 275, 281, 535, *538*
Kaslow, F., 193, 210, *214*
Katz, L. G., 239, *242*
Kauffman, L., 107, *131*
Kazdin, A., 556, 563, *576, 578*
Kazdin, A. E., 38, 41, *47*, 58, *69*, 144-146, 151, *167*,
    295, *300*, 362, 370, *385*, 420-423, 425, 427, 430,
    436, 437, 440, 445-447, *450, 451, 453*
Keane, A. P., 219, 225, 233, *241*
Keane, S. P., 246, 247, 248, *260*
Keane, T. M., 308, *323*, 364, 365, 368, 372, 375, 376,
    378-380, 382, 383, *385*
Kear, K., 174, *189*
Kedward, H. B., 139, *169*
Keeley, S. M., 295, *300*
Kehoe, B., 370, *386*
Keil, E. C., 379, *383*
Keller, F. S., 543, *553*
Keller, J. F., 347, *355*
Keller, M. F., 224, 233, *242*
Kellett, J., 372, *386*, 569, 573, *578*
Kelley, H. H., 478, *504*

Kelley, J. A., 53, *72*
Kelley, J. D., 305, *325*
Kelley, M. L., 251, *260*
Kelly, C. D., 337, 343, 344, *356*
Kelly, G., 532, 533, *538*
Kelly, J. A., 50, 53, *69*, 308, 318, *323*, *324*, 363–376, 378–383, *384*, *385*, *386*, 419, 436, 437, 447, *450*, *451*
Kendal, P., 122, *132*
Kendall, P. C., 246, 248, 250, 253, *261*
Kendon, A., 6, *19*, 137, 139, *165*
Kent, R., 250, 251, 256, *261*
Kent, R. N., 24, 35, *46*, *48*
Kern, J. M., 63, *70*, 308, *323*, 364, 365, 368, 372, 375, 376, 378–380, 382, 383, *385*
Kerndon, A., 559, 567, 568, *576*
Kessler, S., 197–200, 202, 205, 207–212, *214*
Kestnbaum, M. A., 540, *553*
Kiesler, D. J., 298, *300*
Kifer, R. E., 250, 251, 256, *260*
Kiggins, A., 546, *552*
Kiland, J., 122, *130*
Kilmann, P., 186, *190*
Kilmann, P. R., 172, *189*
King, C. E., 482, 483, *502*
King, J., 572, 575, *577*
King, L. W., 345, *355*, 365, *385*
King, S., 103, *131*
Kirk, R. E., 446, *451*
Kirkley, B. G., 308, *323*, 364, 365, 368, 372, 375, 376, 378–380, 382, 383, *385*
Kirsh, B., 314, *323*
Klaus, D., 51, 52, 63, 64, *70*
Klausmeier, H. J., 234, *242*
Klein, P., 297, *300*
Klett, C., 95, *99*
Klett, C. J., *450*
Klorman, R., 139, *169*
Klubas, N., 433, 434, *454*
Kniskern, D. P., 462–464, 466, *474*, *503*, 582, 598, *601*, *602*
Knott, J. E., 81, *98*
Knox, D., 496, *503*, 518, *523*, 593, *602*
Kobasigawa, A., 84, *99*, 223, *242*
Koch, H. L., 221, 226, 227, *242*
Kohen, J., 192, *214*
Kohen, J. A., 328, *355*
Kohlberg, L., 78, *99*
Kohn, M., 220, 221, *242*
Kokes, R. F., 139, *169*
Kolko, D. J., 53, 58–62, 64, *68*, *70*, 102, 105, 106, 109, 111, *132*
Kolodny, R. C., 184, *190*
Kolotkin, R. A., 35, *47*, 61, *70*
Kolstoe, O. P., 418, *451*
Konopka, G., 192, *214*, 320, *323*
Kosinski, J., 188, *189*
Kostelnik, M., 508, *523*
Kovacs, M., 478, *502*
Koziej, J., 308, *322*
Kraft, T., 139, *167*

Kramer, J. A., 53, *70*, 146, 149, 158, 167
Kramer, S. R., 54, *70*, 144, *167*
Krantzler, M., 192, *214*
Krasner, L., 101, 121, *132*
Krebs, D., 55, *70*
Krebs, L. L., 95, *99*
Krumboltz, H., 270, *282*
Krumboltz, J., 270, *282*
Kuehnel, J., 480, 486, 487, 491, 492, *504*
Kuehnel, T., 480, 486, 487, 491, 492, *504*
Kulka, R. A., 181, *191*
Kulpal, J., 426, 428, 431, *453*
Kupers, C. J., 84, *97*
Kupersmidt, J., 225, 227, 288, *241*
Kupke, T. E., 41, *47*, 53, 55, 58, 59, 62, *70*, 142, 152, 153, 161, *167*, 378, *386*
Kurtz, P. D., *522*
Kurtz, W. R., 419, *450*
Kutner, B., 328, *355*
Kuypers, J. A., 326, *355*
Kyzer, B., 442, 445, *452*

L'Abate, L., 12, 13, 18, *20*, 581–591, 595, 598–600, *601*, *602*
Labouvie-Vief, G., 347, *355*
Lack, D. Z., 294, 297, *300*
Ladd, G., 219, 222, 224, 228, 229, 231–237, *242*, *243*
Ladd, G. W., 228, 230, *242*, *244*
LaGreca, A. M., 231, 232, *243*
Lake, J., 570, *580*
Lakoff, R., 313, *323*
Lally, M., 350, *355*
Lamb, M. E., 245, *260*
Lambert, C., 372, *386*, 569, 573, *578*
Lamparski, D., 44, *45*, 58, 61, 63, *67*, 561, *576*
Landesman-Dwyer, S., 419, *451*
Landsberger, H. A., 547, *553*
Landy, D., 56, *72*
Landy, F. J., 141, *167*
Lange, A. J., 319, *323*, 373, *386*, 493, *504*
Langer, E., 329, 346, 347, 350, *355*, *356*
Langer, T., 328, *355*
Lao, R. C., 308, *323*
Larsen, G. R., 463, *475*
Larson, K. B., 463, 464, 466, *475*
Larson, R., 264, *282*, 328, *355*
Latham, G. P., 543, 545, *553*, *554*
LaTorre, R. A., 174, *189*
Laughlin, C., 53, *72*, 364–366, 368, 372, 375, 376, 378–380, 382, *385*
Laughlin, C. S., 366, 368, 371, 372, 378, 382, *387*, 447, *450*
Lavigueur, H., 248, *260*
Lavin, P. F., 58, *70*
Law, H., 557, 571, *577*, *578*
Lawler, E., III, 540, 546, *552*
Lawrence, P. S., 347, *354*, 436, 438, *450*
Lawson, L., 550, *553*
Lazarus, A., 373, *386*
Lazarus, A. A., 3, *20*, 54, *73*, 94, *99*, 139, 143, *167*, *169*, 289, *300*, 305, *324*, 555, 563, *580*

Lazarus, P. S., 346, *357*
Leah, J., 571, *578*
Leavitt, S., 236, *244*, 257, *261*
Leavitt, S. E., 256, 257, *260*
Leborgne, B., 59, *72*
Ledingham, J., *242*
Lee, D. Y., 426, *451*
Lee, L. C., 228, *243*
Leech, S., 347, *355*
Lefkowitz, M., 102, *132*
Leiberman, M. A., 329, *357*
Leiblum, S. R., 186, *189*
Leibowitz, J. M., 251, *259*
Leitenberg, H., 122, *132*
Leland, H., 419, 422, *452*
Lemon, R. E., 38, *45*
Lentz, R. J., 139, *168*
Leon, J., 346, *353*
Lesinsohn, P. M., 362, *386*
Lesser, G. S., 228, *243*
Lester, G., 478, 481, 500, 501, *502*
Letemendia, F., 57, *67*, 141, *165*, 558, 573, *576*
Levenson, R. W., 28, *47*
Levine, F. M., 478, *502*
Levine, J., 138, *169*
Levinger, G., 177, *189*
Levy, S., 249, 250, 257, *261*
Lewin, K., 25, *47*
Lewinsohn, P. M., 4, 15, *20*, 63, *70*, 139, *167*, 478, *504*
Lewis, D. R., 546, *553*
Lewis, M., *244*, 348, *353*
Lewis, M. A., 250, 251, 256, *260*
Lewis, P., 56, , *69*
Lewis, R., 615, *617*
Liberman, A. F., 236, *243*
Liberman, B., 297, *300*
Liberman, R., 107, 120, 125, *132*, *135*, 558, *580*
Liberman, R. P., 345, *355*, 365, 372, *386*, *387*, 480, 483, 486, 487, 491, 492, *504*, 582, 589, 592, *602*
Libet, J. M., 4, *20*, 63, *70*, 139, *167*, 362, *386*
Lichtenstein, E., 28, 33, 37, 43, *44*, *49*, 53–55, *66*, 151, *165*
Lieberman, M. A., 77, *99*
Lifton, W. M., 77, *99*
Liken, J. K., 39, *44*
Lillesand, D. B., 22, *48*, 363, *386*
Lillibridge, E., 264, *282*
Lindley, P., 372, *384*
Lindquist, C. W., 148, 151, *167*
Lindsay, J., 558, 571, 574, *578*
Lindsley, O. R., 330, 347, 348, *355*
Lineham, M. M., 54, 58, 60, *70*
Linehan, M., 319, *324*
Linehan, M. H., 24, *46*
Linquist, C. U., 53, *70*, 146, 149, 158, *167*
Linsk, N., 349, *355*
Lipinski, D. P., 433, 438, *449*, *452*
Lippitt, R., 227, *243*
Lipsett, L. P., 174, *188*
Lipton, D. N., 53, 61, 64, *70*

Liss-Levinson, N., 186, *189*
Little, L. M., 28, *45*, 53, 54, *67*, 145, 146, 149, *166*
Littman, R., 101, 120, 124, *133*
Littman, R. A., 223, *243*
Litwack, S. E., 294, 297, *301*
Lively, L., 150, 151, *166*
Lobitz, G., 102, *131*
Locke, H. J., 593, *602*
Loevinger, J., 78, *99*
Lomont, J. F., 376, *386*
London, O., 55, *67*
Long, J., 115, 117, *134*
Loomis, R. L., 27, *45*
Lopata, H. Z., 347, 350, *355*
Lopez, M., 294, 297, *301*
Lopez, M. A., 297, 298, *300*, 337, 341, 342, *355*
LoPiccolo, J., 172, 183, 184, *190*
LoPiccolo, L., 172, 184, *190*
Lovaas, O., 126, *130*
Lowe, B. R., 422, *451*
Lowenstein, R., 329, *356*
Luber, R., *524*
Luiselli, J. K., 424, *451*
Lukoff, D., 273, *387*, 558, *580*
Lupton, T., 546, *553*
Luthans, F., 548, *553*
Lynch, J. J., 326, *355*
Lyons, P. D., 440, 443, 444, *449*

MacAndrew, C., *451*
McArthur, G. N., 15, *20*
McCall, M. W., Jr., 547, 548, *553*
McCandless, B. R., 227, *243*
McCann, M., 345, *355*
McClannahan, L. E., 349, *355*
McCleary, R., 38, *47*
McClelland, D. C., 303, *324*
McClure, R. F., 424, *452*
McConohey, D., 121, *132*
McCrady, B. S., *504*
McCullough, J., 116, 128, *132*
McDaniel, J., 418, *452*
McDonald, D. W., 477, 479, *503*
MacDonald, M. L., 26, *47*, 53, *70*, 142, 146, 148, 149, 151, 158, 162, *167*, 349, *355*
Macdonald, R., 372, *384*, 616, *617*
McDonel, E. C., 24, *48*
MacDonough, S., 122, *130*
Mace, D., 583–585, *602*
Mace, E., 584, *602*
Mace, V., 584, 585, *602*
McEwan, S., 51, 52, *70*
McFall, M. E., 440, 443, 444, *449*
McFall, R., 557, 558, 563, 571, *577*, *578*, *580*
McFall, R. M., 22, 24, 25–29, 33, 40–42, *46*, *47*, *48*, *49*, 52–55, 57–61, 64, *69*, *70*, *71*, *72*, 139, 142, 143, 146–148, 150–152, 161, 162, *166*, *167*, *168*, *169*
McGhee, W., 546, *553*
McGovern, K., 28, 33, 37, *44*, 53–55, *66*, 154, *165*
McGovern, K. B., 53, 61, *71*, 144, 145, 149, 151, 157, *168*

McGrath, R. A., 53, *70*, 146, 148, 149, 151, 158, *167*
McGraw, B., 463, *474*
McGuire, J., 572, *579*
McGuire, J. M., 228, *243*
McKay, G., 263, 265, *281, 282*
McKay, G. D., 258, *260*
McKeever, M., 573, *577*
MacKinnon, C. E., 223, *240*
McMahon, R. J., 257, *261*
McNabb, C. E., 28, *47*, 54, 62, *69*, 144, 151, 159, 160, *167*
McNamara, J., 113, 116, *132*
McNamara, J. R., 544, *551*
McPhail, P., 14, *20*
Macrae, J. W., 379, *384*
McWhiter, D. P., 187, *190*
Maddock, J. W., 172, 184, 185, 187, *190*
Madison, L. S., 255, *259*
Madsen, C., 118, 119, *132*, 557, *578*
Madsen, C. H., 18, *47*, 54, 58, 62, *69*, 144, 151, 159, 160, *167*, 378, *385*
Magnusson, D., 27, 29, *46, 47*, 246, 253, *260*, 565, *578*
Maholick, L. T., 95, *98*
Mahoney, J. J., *451*
Mahoney, M., 112, *131*, 556, *576*
Mahoney, M. J., 95, 96, *99*, 111, 128, *132*
Mai-Dalton, R. R., 313, *324*
Malamuth, N. M., 307, *324*
Malcom, R., 438-441, *453*
Malone, H., 517, *523*
Maples, M. F., 78, *98*
Margolin, G., 239, *243*, 477-482, 486, 487, 494-496, 498, 499, 501, *503, 504, 505*, 589, 593, *602, 603*
Marholin, D., 295, *301*
Markell, R. A., 222, 224, *240*
Markle, A., 221, 244, 247, 248, 252, *261*, 264, *282*
Markman, H. J., 236, *241*, 484, 487, 488, *503*
Markowitz, J., 192, *214*
Marks, I. M., 372, *384*
Marlot, G. A., 307, *324*
Marples, D. L., 546, 547, *553*
Marques, J. K., 307, *324*
Marquis, 327, 328, *355*
Marriotto, M. J., 54, 57, 58, 60, 63, *67, 68, 72, 73*, 146, 153-155, *166*, 378, *384, 387*
Marsella, A., 534, *538*
Marshall, B., 420, *449*
Marshall, E. K., *522*
Marshall, H. R., 227, *243*
Marston, A., 563, *579*
Marston, A. R., 22, *48*, 55, *72*, 143, 146, 156, 158, 159, *168*, 363, *386*
Martin, B., 102, 120, *131*, 245, *260*
Martin, C. E., 175, *190*
Martin, G., 370, *387*
Martin, G. L., 370, *386*
Martin, M., 568, *580*
Martin, R., 118, *132*
Martinez-Diaz, J. A., 51, 53, *71*
Martinson, W. D., 54, *71*, 140, 141, 143, 150, 158, *167*

Martorano, R. D., 145, *168*
Marzillier, J., 15, *20*, 109, *134*, 372, *386*, 561, 568, 569, 573, *578, 579*
Mash, E. J., *505*
Massaro, D. W., 41, *47*
Massengill, D., 310, *324*
Massey, F., 376, *384*, 558, *577*
Masters, D., 103, 104, 119, 120, 128, *134*
Masters, W. H., 174, 175, 178, 182, 183, 184, *189*
Mastroianni, M., 94, *100*
Mathes, W. D., 56, *71*
Mathews, S. H., 347, *355*
Mathiew, M., 184, *191*
Matson, J. L., 41, *47*, 108-110, 123, 126, *132*, 249, 250, 256, *260*, 370, *385, 386*, 418-423, 425, 426-428, 430-437, 442, 445-448, *451, 452, 453*
Mattison, A. M., 187, *190*
Maxwell, G. M., 15, *20*
May, H. J., 79, 94, *99*
Mead, D., 276, *282*
Mead, M., 193, *214*
Megarqu, E., 101, *132*
Mehrobin, A., 485, *504*
Meichenbaum, D., 54, 71, 110, 113, 117, 121, *132, 133*, 159, *168*, 347, *355*, 501, *504*
Melin, L., 349, *355*
Melnick, J., 53, *71*, 145, *168*
Melnick, J. A., 146, 149, 151, 156, 158, *168*
Mendonca, P., 447, *453*
Menlove, F. L., 223, *240*
Mercer, S., 345, *356*
Mercurio, J. R., 424, *454*
Meredith, R. L., 442, 445, *452*
Merluzzi, T. V., 326, *354*
Merriam, M. L., 520, *522*
Meston, J. T., 187, *190*
Mewcomb, A. F., 223, *243*
Meyer, R., 298, *301*
Meyers, J. A., 287, *301*
Michael, C. M., 221, 225, *243*
Michael, J., 119, *129*
Middleton, D., 14, *20*
Milan, M. A., 18, *20*, 53, 58-62, 64, *68, 70*, 102, 105, 106, 109, 111, 121, *129, 132, 133*
Milburn, D., 16, *20*
Milburn, J. F., 16, *19*, 237, *240*, 257, *260*
Miles, J., 264, *282*
Miles, M. B., 77, *99*
Miller, C., 63, *70*, 337, 343, 344, *356*
Miller, D. B., 329, *356*
Miller, G. D., 79, *99*
Miller, I. W., 138, 146, *166*
Miller, L. K., 550, *553*
Miller, P., 563, *577*
Miller, P. M., 4, *19*, 22, 36, *45, 46*, 61, 68, 139, *166, 168*, 305, *323*, 334, *354*, 363, 365, *384*, 424, *450*
Miller, S., 458, 459, 468, *475*, 584, 585, *602*
Miller, S. L., 458, 463, 464, *475*
Miller, V. H., 184, *190*
Miller, W., 119, 129, 582-585, *601*
Milsum, J. H., 86, *99*

Mindell, C., 251, *259*
Minkin, B., 58, *71*
Minkin, B. L., 37, *48*, 371, 382, *386*
Minkin, N., 37, 38, *48*, 71, 371, 382, *386*
Mintzberg, H., 547, 548, *553*
Mira, M., 252, *259*
Mischel, W., 27, *48*, 137, *168*, 331, *356*
Mitchell, T. R., 313, *324*
Mize, J., 219, 233–237, *243*
Moeller, T. P., 340, *350*
Moerdyk, A., 565, *580*
Moisan-Thomas, P. C., 62, *71*
Molloy, J. T., 369, *386*
Montgomery, D., 28, *47*, 54, 58, 62, *69*, 144, 151, 159, 160, *167*, 378, *385*, 556, *578*
Monti, P. M., 33, *45*, 50, 54, *68*, 138, 146, *166*, *503*, *602*
Moody, K. A., 85, *99*
Moore, S., 39, *47*, 62, 63, *69*
Moore, S. G., 227, *243*
Moos, R. H., 27, *48*
Morehouse, N., 116, 128, *131*
Moreno, J. L., 226, *243*
Morgan, A. C., 519, *523*
Morgan, J. J. B., 10, *20*
Morgan, J. M., 144, *168*
Morris, D. P., 221, 225, *243*
Morris, H., 102, *133*
Morris, J. D., 193 196, 207 211, *214*
Morris, J. E., 607, *617*
Morrison, A. M., 547, 548, *553*
Morrison, D. C., 248, *262*
Morse, J. J., 546, *553*
Morton, T. L., 186, *190*
Moser, H. P., 77, *100*
Moses, J. L., 546, *553*
Mosher, P. M., 348, *357*
Mosher, R. L., 79, *99*, *100*
Mosner, D. L., 53, 54, *66*, 150, 151, 156, 158, *165*, 176, 178, 181, *190*, 378, *383*
Most, R. K., 520, *523*
Mountjoy, P., *602*
Moustakas, C., 506, 510, *523*
Mouton, J. S., 85, *100*, 541, 542, *552*
Muehlenhard, C. L., 52, 59, *71*, 305, *324*
Mueller, D. J., 349, *356*
Muller, A., 121, *133*
Mullinix, S. B., 63, *71*
Murphy, G., 8, 9, 14, *20*
Murphy, L. B., 8, 9, 14, *20*
Murstein, B., 56, *71*
Myers, C. E., 422, *452*
Myers, E. J., 39, *47*, 62, 63, *69*

Nagle, R. J., 231–233, *242*
Narfeh, S., 108, *129*
Narick, M., 109, *130*
Naster, B. J., 496, *502*
National Assessment of Educational Progress, 79, *99*
Navaco, R., 102, 103, 114–116, 127, 128, *133*

Nawas, M., 140, *166*
Nay, W., 116, 122, 128, 132
Neider, L. L., 540, *553*
Nelson, C., 558, *580*
Nelson, C. J., 372, *387*
Nelson, R. O., 53, 61, 64, *70*, 433, 436, 438, *449*, *450*, *452*
Newcomb, T. M., 8, 9, 14, *20*
Newman, J. P., 229, *241*
Nezu, A., 347, *356*
Nielsen, G., 123, *135*
Nielson, M., 351, *353*
Nies, D. C., 482, *502*
Nietzel, M. T., 145, *168*
Nihira, K., 422, *452*
Northway, M. L., 226, *243*
Norwood, R. M., 52, *73*
Notarius, C., 38, 39, *47*, 484, 487, 488, *503*
Novaco, R., 502, *504*
Nunnally, E. W., 458, 459, 463, *475*
Nye, F. I., *503*
Nyquist, L., 314, *322*

O'Banian, K., 55, *71*
O'Barr, W., 314, *324*
O'Brien, D., 298, *301*
O'Brien, G. T., 33, *45*, 51, 53, *68*, 140, *165*
O'Brien, R. M., 544, *553*
O'Connell, W. G., 85, *99*
O'Connor, K., 574, *579*
O'Connor, R. D., 224, 233, *243*
O'Dell, S. L., 247, *261*
Oden, S., 222, 228, 229, *243*, 248, *261*, 421, *449*
Oden, S. L., 224, 230–233, 236, 238, *240*, *243*
Oei, T., 571, 574, *578*, *579*
O'Leary, K., 102, *133*
O'Leary, K. D., 35, *48*, 248, 250, 251, 256, *261*, 478–481, 487, 488, 496, 499, *503*
O'Leary, S., 248, *261*
O'Leary, V. E., 310, *324*
Ollendick, T., 109, *132*, *133*
Olson, D. H., *523*, *601*, *603*
Olson, D. H. L., 250, 256, *259*, *475*
Oltman, P., 560, *580*
Oltmanns, T., 102, *133*
Orenstein, R., 297, *301*
Orpen, C., 546, *554*
Orzech, M. J., 348, *353*
Osgood, C. E., 293, *301*
O'Sullivan, M., 42, *48*
O'Sullivan, M. J., 337, 343, 344, *356*
Otis, M., 146, *167*
Otto, H., 582–584, *602*
Overstreet, P. L., 77, *100*
Oxman, L., 513, *523*

Page, L. M., 9, 11, *20*
Palmore, E., 350, *356*
Paloutzian, R. F., 424, *452*
Paluck, R. J., 426, 432, *454*
Paolino, T. J., *504*

Parkham, I. A., 328, *357*
Parkhurst, J. T., 223, *241*
Parks, L. A., 424, *449*
Parsons, B. V., 250, 251, 256, 258, *259*
Patterson, G., 101, 102, 120, 121, 124, 125, 128, *133*, 267, *283*
Patterson, G. R., 223, *243*, 263, 267, 270, *282*, 294, *301*, 482, 495, 498, *505*, 581, 582, 589, 593, *602*
Patterson, J., 364–366, 368, 371, 372, 375–380, 382, 383, *385*
Patterson, J. N., 308, *323*
Patterson, J. T., 53, *69*
Patterson, R. L., 248, *261*, 326, 337, 343, 344, *354*, *356*
Paul, G., 528, 534, *538*
Paul, G. L., 139, 141, 156, *168*
Paul, S., 112, *134*
Paul, W., 108, *129*
Paulson, T. L., 146, *169*
Peach, R. V., 447, *453*
Pedersen, P., 534, *538*
Pederson, A., 221, *241*, 245, *260*, 418, 421, *449*
Peery, J. C., 226, *243*
Pemberton, B. W., 424, *451*
Pendergrass, V., 123, *133*
Pendleton, D., 559, 568, 571, 572, 575, *577*, *578*, *579*
Penn, P., 544, *553*
Penner, L., 343, *354*
Penner, L. A., 337, 343, 344, *356*
Peplau, L. A., 327, 328, 346, 348, *356*
Pepper, M. P., 287, *301*
Perl, J., 51, 54, 55, 61, 64, *66*, *69*, *71*
Perlman, D., 328, *356*
Perri, M., 26, *48*
Perri, M. G., 53, 55, 60, *71*
Perrin, T. O., 379, *386*
Perry, M. A., 439, *452*
Pervin, L., 556, *579*
Peterson, D., 27, *48*
Peterson, G. L., 55, *68*, 318, *323*
Peterson, J., 53, 57, 62, *71*
Peterson, R. G., 248, *262*
Petti, T., 109, 110, *132*
Petty, B. J., 340, *356*
Phelps, E. D., 540, *554*
Phibbs, J., 61, *71*
Phillips, E., 58, *71*, 124, *133*, 561, *579*
Phillips, E. A., 256, *261*
Phillips, E. L., 12–15, *20*, 37, *48*, 52, *71*, 138, *168*, 250, 251, 256, *260*, *261*, 371, 382, *386*, 595, *602*
Phillips, J., 139, 143, *167*, 363–365, 368, 371, 372, 375, 376, 378–380, 382, *385*, 437, *451*
Phillips, L., 3, 6, 7, 11–14, *20*, *21*, 138, *168*, *169*, 362, *387*, 418, *454*, 555, *579*, *580*
Pierce, M., 121, *133*
Pierce, R., 78, 93, *100*
Pierce, R. M., 344, *352*
Pilkonis, P. A., 28, *48*, 51, *73*, 140, *168*
Pillay, M., 573, *579*
Pinkston, E. M., 348, 349, 353, *355*
Pinkston, S., 108, 128, *131*, 344, *354*

Pinto, P. R., 546, *554*
Pinto, R. P., 379, *386*
Plthers, W. D., 307, *324*
Planty, E. G., 85, *100*
Platt, J. J., 250, *261*
Pollane, L., 607, 616, *617*
Pollock, D., 349, *352*
Polyot, C. J., 349, *352*
Ponder, Q. D., 547, *554*
Porteous, M., 574, *579*
Porter, B., 513, *523*
Potter, J., 560, *579*
Powell, G. N., 310, *324*
Powell, G. S., 467, *475*
Powell, M. F., 78, 95, *100*
Powell, T. H., 249, 250, 253, 256, 257, *261*
Pratt, A. B., 95, *100*
Prescott, M. R., 193–196, 207–211, *214*
Preston, J., 514, 520, *523*
Pretzer, J. L., 477, 480, 487–490, 501, *503*
Price, H. A., 255, *259*
Price, J., 237, *243*
Price, R. H., 29, *48*
Priestley, P., 572, *579*
Prinz, R., 250, 251, 256, *261*
Prinz, R. J., 219, 224, 225, 233, *244*
Proshansky, H. H., 27, *48*
Prusoff, B. A., 317, *324*
Purvis, J. A., 59, 62, *68*, *72*
Putallaz, M., 225, 227, *243*

Quatbrochi-Tubin, S., 348, *356*
Quayhagen, M. P., 330, *356*

Rabinowitz, J. A., 154, *166*
Rabkin, J. G., 419, *452*
Rachlin, H., 117, *133*
Radl, S. L., 257, *262*
Radloff, L., 317, *324*
Rake, D. F., 222, *241*
Ramsay, R. W., 146, *167*, 350, *356*
Raphael, R., 55, *69*
Rappaport, A. F., 518, *523*, 582, *603*
Rappaport, J., 507, *523*
Raschke, H. J., 192, *214*
Rasmussen, B., 227–229, *241*, 248, *260*, 421, *450*
Rausch, H. L., 28, 34, 38, *48*, 490, *504*
Rawlings, E. I., 316, *324*
Ray, R., 101, 102, 120, 124, *133*, 267, *282*
Razin, A., 531, *538*
Read, J., 207–211, *214*
Reagor, P., 119, *129*
Reckman, R. F., 55, *72*
Redlich, F. C., 13, *19*, 287, *300*
Reese, H. W., 174, *188*
Reeves, K., 55, *67*
Rehm, L., 563, *579*
Rehm, L. P., 22, *48*, 55, *72*, 143, 146, 156, 158, 159, *168*, 478, *504*
Reid, D. H., 350, *354*
Reid, J., 101, 120, 124, *133*, 267, *282*

Reiss, I. L., 173, 178, 180, 188, *190*, *503*
Renshaw, P. D., 219, 228–230, 235, 236, *244*
Renzaglia, A., 424, *453*
Resch, J., 346, *353*
Rettie, C., 424, *453*
Revenstorf, D., 38, *48*, 487–489, *503*
Rhyne, L. D., 53, *70*, 146, 148, 149, 151, 158, *167*
Richards, C. A., 55, *71*
Richards, C. S., 26, 48, 53, 60, *71*
Richardson, F. C., 28, *48*
Richey, C. A., 28, *46*, 53, *72*, 339, *354*
Ricks, C., 279, *282*
Rider, K., 520, *521*
Ridley, C. A., 519, *523*
Riley, M. W., 327, *350*
Rim, Y., 565, *579*
Rime, B., 54, *72*
Rimm, D., 101–104, 107, 119, 120, 128, *133*
Riner, L. S., 251, *259*
Rinn, R., 264, *282*
Rinn, R. C., 221, *244*, 247, 248, 252, 255, *261*, 440, *452*
Risley, T., 125, *134*, 349, *356*
Risley, T. R., 349, *355*
Ritchey, W. L., 247, 253, *260*
Ritchie, R. J., 546, *553*
Ritvo, E., 122, 123, *131*
Rivlin, L. G., 27, *48*
Roberts, E. J., 172, 174, 175, *190*
Roberts, M. D., 121
Robertson, B., 298, *301*
Robin, A., 115, *134*, 250, 251, 256, 258, *261*
Robins, L., 102, *134*
Robins, L. N., 221, *244*, 245, *261*
Robinson, E. H., III, 95, *100*
Robinson, R., 297, *301*
Robinson, W., 559, *579*
Rocks, T., 520, *523*
Rodgers, R., 457, *474*
Rodin, J., 329, 346, 347, 350, *355*, *356*
Roff, M., 221, 222, *244*, 246, 253, *261*, 418, 421, *452*
Rogers, P. L., 42, *48*
Rogers, R., 616, *617*
Romano, J. M., 58, 63, *72*, 383, *386*, 561, *579*
Romanzyk, R. G., 34, *48*
Romer, D., 419, 422, *449*, *451*, *452*
Rook, K. S., 327, 328, 346, 348, *356*
Rooke, M. L., 328, 329, *357*
Rose, S. D., 146, *168*, 333, 335, 339, 340, *353*, *357*
Rose, Y. J., 161, *168*
Roseblum, L. A., 35, *48*, *244*
Rosen, B., 311, 312, *324*
Rosen, M., 374, 375, *387*
Rosen, R. C., 186, *189*
Rosen, T. A., 544, *554*
Rosenkrantz, P. S., 303, 305, 308, *322*
Rosenthal, L., 26, *46*, 60, 61, *68*, 558, 563, *577*
Rosenthal, R., 42, *48*
Rosenthal, T., 144, *168*
Rosow, M., 544, *554*
Ross, D., 144, *165*

Ross, E., 519, *523*
Ross, H. E., 139, *169*
Ross, J., 376, *384*, 558, *577*
Ross, M., 349, *352*
Ross, R., 121, *133*
Ross, S. A., 144, *165*, 440, *452*
Ross, S. M., 139, *165*
Rothblum, E. D., 318, *324*, 383, *386*
Rothenberg, A., 101, *134*
Rotheram, M. J., 326, *357*
Rothman, L., 56, *72*
Rouillan, F., 59, *72*
Rounsaville, B. J., 317, *324*
Rowberry, T., 124, *130*
Rowland, K. F., 187, *190*
Royce, W. S., 28, 41, *48*, *49*, 54, 59, *72*, 144, *168*
Rubenstein, D., 175, *189*
Rubin, K., *242*
Rubin, K. H., 224, 227, *244*
Rubin, L. J., 79, *100*
Rubin, T., 101, *134*
Rubin, Z., 245, 254, 257, *261*
Rueveni, V., 127, *134*
Rule, S., 249, 250, 257, *261*
Rupp, G., 582, 585–588, 590, 591, 595, 598–600, *602*
Rush, A. J., 478, 499, 501, *502*
Rushton, J. P., 223, *244*
Russell, C. S., 607, *617*
Russo, S., 119, *134*
Rutledge, P., 310, *324*
Rutter, M., *452*
Rychtarck, R., 108, *129*
Rychtarik, R. G., 440, *453*
Ryder, R., 279, *281*
Ryder, R. G., 491, *504*

Saari, L. M., 545, *553*
Sabalis, R. F., 172, *189*
Sabre, R. M., *522*
Sachs, D., 122, *134*
Sackett, G. P., 34, 35, *49*, 422, *453*
Sager, C. J., 496, 499, *504*
Salter, A., 3, *20*
Salter, L., 424, *453*
Salzberg, C. L., 249, 250, 257, *261*
Samel, J., 370, *387*
Sampen, S. E., 248, *262*
Sampson, E. E., 15, *20*
Sand, P., 122, *134*
Sanders, N., 483, *504*, 589, 592, *602*
Sandhane, J., 573, *576*
Santogrossi, D. A., 231, 232, *243*
Sapon-Shevin, M., 257, *261*
Sarason, T. G., 55, *72*, 146, *168*, 418, *453*
Sarrel, L. J., 174, *190*
Sarrel, P. M., 174, *190*
Satir, V., 480, *504*
Saunders, C., 14–16, *19*, 570, *578*
Sawyer, J., 31, *49*
Saxe, L., 56, *72*
Saxon, S., 442, 445, *452*

Scanzoni, J., 177, *190*
Schaffer, M., 463, 464, *475*
Schaie, K. W., 328, *357*
Schalock, R. L., 418, *453*
Schauble, P. B., 93, *100*
Scheidt, R. J., 330, *357*
Scheim, V. E., 310, *324*
Scherer, K. R., 14, *20*
Scherer, U., 14, *20*
Schindler, L., 38, *48*, 487–489, *503*
Schinke, S. P., 375, 382, *386*
Schlundt, D. G., 26, 29, 32, 34, 38, 39, 41, 42, *46*, *49*, 60, 61, *68*, 142, *166*
Schmitz, K., 264, *283*
Schneider, B., *242*
Schneider, M., 115, *134*
Schneider, P. A., 63, *68*
Schneiman, R., 297, *301*
Schocken, I., 39, *45*
Schofield, R., 264, *283*
Schon, D., 542, *552*
Schornagel, C. Y., 250, 256, *259*
Schrader, C., 115, 117, *134*
Schrader, S. J., 424, *450*
Schroeder, H. E., 309, *323*
Schuler, P., 230, *241*
Schulte, M., 279, *282*
Schutz, R., 424, *453*
Schwartz, R. C., 463, 465, *475*
Schwarz, J. C., 223, *244*
Schwarz, P. M., 142, *169*
Schwarz, S. A., 233, 237, *241*
Schwitzgebel, R., 126, *134*
Scott, J., 582, *603*
Searle, J. A., 35, *49*
Sechrest, L., 293, *301*
Secord, P. F., 137, *167*
Segal, S., *453*
Seligman, M. E. P., 477, *502*
Sells, S. B., 29, *49*, 221, *244*
Senatore, V., 246, 253, *261*, 418, 421–423, 427, 430, 437, 442, 445–447, *451*, *452*, *453*
Sensué, M. E., 513, *523*
Shafter, A. J., 418, *451*
Shaie, K. W., 330, *357*
Shapiro, E., 123, *134*
Shaultz, B., 418, *450*
Shaw, B. F., 478, 499, 501, *502*
Shaw, D., 267, *282*
Shaw, M. E., 85, *100*, 310, *324*
Shaw, P., 162, *169*
Shea, J., 535, *538*
Shellhaas, W., 419, 422, *452*
Shemberg, K. M., 295, *300*
Shepherd, G., 562, 569, 570, *579*
Sherfey, J. A., 58, 62, *69*
Sherif, C., 271, *283*
Sherman, J. A., 251, *261*
Sherman, M., 108, *131*, 225, *241*
Shmurak, S. H., 50, 55, 69, *72*, 140, 149, 159, 160, 161, *166*, 368, *385*

Shoemaker, M. E., 146, *169*
Shoffner, S., 582, *603*
Shofield, W., 287, *301*
Shore, E., 293, *301*
Shumaker, J. B., 251, 257, *261*
Shure, M. B., 42, *49*, 248, 250, 251, *261*
Sidney, E., 558, *579*
Siegel, J. S., 329, *357*
Sigall, H., 56, *72*
Silberman, A., 120, *129*
Silverman, A. G., 346, *357*
Silverstane, B., 349, *357*
Simek-Downing, L., 528, *538*
Simeonsson, R. J., 423, *453*
Simon, S. J., 108, 134, 366, 379, *385*
Sims, H. P., Jr., 548, *554*
Singer, J., 56, *72*
Singleton, W. T., 12, 13, 18, *20*, 571, *579*
Siperstein, G. N., 232, *244*
Sipps, G., 55, *69*
Sisson, P. J., 78, *100*
Skillings, R. E., 375, *386*
Skinner, B. F., 110, *134*, 543, *554*
Skinner, K. K., 376, *386*
Slaby, D. A., 127, *130*, 245, 247, *260*
Slavson, S. R., 77, *100*
Sloane, H. N., 248, *262*
Slovic, P., 43, *49*
Smeriglio, V. L., 233, *242*
Smith, A. P., 539, 540, *554*
Smith, G., 337, 343, 344, *356*
Smith, J., 38, *45*, 557, *577*
Smith, M. L., 463, *474*
Smith, P. E., 546, *554*
Smith, R., 103, *134*, 582, *603*
Smith, R. B., 102, *134*
Smith, R. E., 55, *72*
Smith, T. E., 375, 382, *386*
Smye, M., 562, *579*
Sneath, P. H. A., 29, *49*
Snoek, J. D., 177, *189*
Snowdon, E. E., 364, 365, 368, 372, 375, 376, 378–380, 382, *385*
Snyder, C., 571, *578*
Snyder, J., 114, 116, 117, 127, *134*
Sokal, R. R., 29, *49*
Sololovsky, 328, 350, *353*
Solomon, E., 294, 297, *301*
Solomon, L. J., 318, *324*, 383, *386*
Soltz, V., 264, 270, *281*
Somerset, T., 122, 123, *131*
Somerville, R. M., 582, *603*
Sonnenshein-Schneider, M., 175, *189*
Sorcher, M., 297, *300*, *301*, 544, *553*
Soroker, E., 221, 225, *243*
Sotile, W. M., 186, *190*
Spanier, G. B., 174, *190*
Spector, N. J., 376, *386*
Speer, D. C., 457, *475*
Spence, A., 569, *580*
Spence, J. T., 311, 312, *324*

Spence, S., 57, 59, *72*, 109, *134*, 558, *579*, *580*
Spender, D., 314, *324*
Spenks, P., 565, 569, *580*
Speroff, B. J., 85, *100*
Spinks, S. H., 479, 496, *502*
Spinner, B., 328, *356*
Spitzer, L., 347, *355*
Spivak, G., 42, *49*, 248, 250, 251, *261*
Sprafkin, R. P., 94, *99*, 108, *131*, 297, *301*, 337, 341, 344, *354*, *355*
Spray, S. L., 546, *552*
Sprenkle, D. H., 463, 465, 466, *475*
Sprey, J., 257, *475*
Springbett, B. M., 379, *386*
Sprinthall, N. A., 79, *99*, *100*
Spurgeon, P., 13, 18, *20*, 571, *579*
Stacey, D., 438–441, *453*
Stafford, R. R., 463, 465, 466, *475*
Stahl, G. R., 85, *100*
Stalonas, P. M., 382, *387*
Stammers, R. B., 13, 18, *20*, 571, *579*
Stanley, J. C., 548, *552*
Stanley, S., 264, *283*, 484, *504*
Statein, H., 565, *578*
Staub, E., 4, 7, 14, 16, *21*, 101, *134*
Staw, B. M., 547, *554*
Stearn, M., 264, *283*
Steffens, J. J., 52, 72, 295, 297, *300*
Stein, N., 295, *300*, 533, *538*
Steinke, G. V., 53, 54, *66*, 150, 151, 156, 158, *165*, 378, *383*
Steller, J. B., 463, 464, *475*
Stengel, E., 221, *244*
Stephans, T. M., 236, *244*
Stephens, L., 122, 123, *131*
Stephens, R. M., 108–110, 123, *132*, 422, 423, 426–428, 430, 431, 437, 448, *452*, *453*
Stevens, J., 368, 379, *385*
Stever, J. L., 340, *357*
Stewart, E., 438, *454*
Stewart, R., 546, *554*
Stocker, R. B., 146, *168*
Stocking, H. S., 236, *244*, 257, *261*
Stokes, T. F., 252, *261*, 424, *453*
Stollak, G., 93, *99*, 507, *522*
Stone, B. A., 379, *384*
Stone, G., 536, *537*
Stone, N. M., 33, *45*, 51, 53, *67*, 140, *165*
Stoneman, Z., 223, *240*
Stoudenmire, J., 424, *453*
Stout, R. L., 138, 146, *166*
Stover, D., 125, *130*
Stover, L., 513, 518, *521*
Strain, P. S., 252, 253, *261*
Straus, M. A., 500, *503*, 581, 582, *601*
Strauss, J. S., 138, 139, *169*
Streifel, J., 424, *452*
Strewinski, A., 559, 560, *580*
Stuart, F., 593, *603*
Stuart, J., 104, 107, 128, *134*
Stuart, R. B., 120, 128, *134*, 479–481, 483, 485–487,

490–492, 496, 497, 499–501, *504*, 518, *524*, 582, 589, 592, 593, 595, 596, *603*
Stubbs, D. A., 349, *352*
Sturgis, E., 249, 250, 256, *259*
Sturn, D., 297, 298, *301*
Stutman, J., 512, *522*
Sullaway, M., 482, 483, *502*
Sullivan, B., 172, *189*
Sullivan, H. S., 136, *169*
Summerfield, A., 570, *580*
Suomi, S. J., 220, *244*
Super, D. E., 77, *100*
Supko, R., 361, *384*
Sutton-Simon, L., 297, *301*
Swain, M. A., 28, 34, *48*, 490, *504*
Swanstron, C., 297, *301*
Sweeney, T., 108, *129*
Sweeney, T. M., 309, *323*
Sweet, T., 571, 574, *578*
Sylph, J. A., 139, *169*
Syme, M. D., 16, *21*
Syme, S. L., 326, *353*
Symons, R., 471, 574, *578*
Sywulak, A. E., 508, 513, 514, *524*
Szasz, T., 173, 178, 180–182, *190*

Tallman, I., 581, 582, *601*
Tasto, D. L., 28, *48*
Tavormino, J., 271, 279, *283*
Taylor, A. R., 229, 235, 236, *240*, *244*
Teasdale, J. D., 477, *502*
Tedeschi, J. T., 102, *134*
Teigen, J., 107, 120, 125, *132*, *137*
Telleen, S., 330, *357*
Terrell, T., 535, *538*
Test, M. A., 376, *384*
Tharp, R., 120, *134*, 270, *283*
Tharp, R. G., 294, *301*
Thelen, M., 112, *134*
Therrien, M., 264, *283*
Thibaut, J. W., 478, *504*
Thiessen, J., 202–212, *214*, *215*
Thomander, L. D., 52, *72*
Thomas, D., 118, 119, *132*
Thomas, E. J., 493, *504*
Thomason, G. F., 546, *554*
Thomason, T., 246, *280*
Thompson, D. E., 418, *449*
Thompson, G. G., 8, 10, *21*
Thompson, K. B., 463, 465, *475*
Thompson, T., 121, *132*
Thoresen, C., 120, *135*
Thorndike, E. L., 293, *302*
Thorne, B., 314, *323*
Thorne, G., 120, *134*
Thornock, M., 350, *355*
Thorpe, G. L., 145, *169*
Thurman, C., 436, 437, *451*
Thurman, C., 371, 372, 375–380, 382, *386*
Timbers, B., 58, *71*
Timbers, B. J., 37, *48*, 371, 382, *386*

Timbers, G., 58, *71*
Timbers, G. D., 37, *48*, 371, 382, *386*
Tittmer, H. G., 571, *580*
Tizard, J., 418, *452*
Tobey, T., 120, *135*
Tobin, S. S., 329, *357*
Todd, F., 30, 31, *47*
Todd, F. J., 31, *49*
Todd, N. M., 248, 254, *262*
Tofte-Tipps, S., 447, *453*
Togo, A., 328, *355*
Tollison, C. D., 173, 175, 176, *190*
Tomlinson, J. W. C., 546, *552*
Tornow, W. W., 546, *554*
Torrey, E. F., 581, *603*
Toseland, R., 333, 334, 339, *357*
Touchette, *301*
Treffrey, D., 370, *387*
Trief, P., 297, *302*
Trieschman, R., 122, *134*
Trost, M. A., 221, *241*, 245, *260*, 418, 421, *449*
Trower, P., 6, 11, 13, 15, *19, 21*, 44, *49*, 57, 63, *72*,
    138, 142, 161–163, 169, 176, *190*, 326, 327, 344,
    346, *357*, 362, 370, 375, 376, *387*, 557, 558, 562,
    564, 565, 568, 572–575, *576, 580*
Trower, P. E., 51, *67*
Trower, R., 141, *165*
Tryon, W. W., 161, *168*
Tscheulin, D., 546, *554*
Tschirgi, H. D., 379, *387*
Tuller, W. L., 546, *553*
Tullman, G. D., 184, *190*
Tullman, G. M., 184, *190*
Tunstall, J., 328, *357*
Turiel, E., 78, *99*
Turkewitz, H., 478–481, 487–489, 496, 499, *504*
Turner, A. J., 250, 256, *259*
Turner, B. F., 329, *357*
Turner, K., 119, *129*
Turner, S. M., 28, 36, 40, *47*, 55, 57, 58, 61, 63, *67*,
    363, 364, 366, 374, 376, 382, *383*, 419, 425, 433,
    436, *449, 453*
Tversky, A., 42, *49*
Twardosz, S., 424, *453*
Twentyman, C., 110, 126, *135*, 557, 563, 580
Twentyman, C. T., 15, *21*, 27, 28, 38, *49*, 52–55, 57,
    61, 64, *71, 72*, 139, 143, 144–146, 150–152, *168,
    169*, 557, 563, 580

Uhlemann, M., 535, *538*
Ulbreta, H., 558, 573, *576*
Ulinegardner, J., 108, *129*
Ullman, L. P., 101, 121, *132*
Ullmann, C. A., 221, *244*
Ulman, C. A., 421, *453*
Ulrich, I. R., *602*
Upchurch, W. H., 308, *323*
Updegraff, R., 227, *243*
Urbain, E. S., 246, 248, 250, 253, *261*
Urbieta, H., 51, *67*, 558, 573, *576*

Urbieta, K., 141, *165*
Urey, J. R., 53, *69, 72*, 364–366, 368, 371, 372, 375–
    380, 382, *385, 386, 387*, 436, 437, *451*

Vallance, T. R., *522*
Van Alstyne, D., 221, *244*
VandenBencken, J. H. L., 39, *49*
VanHasselt, V., 561, *580*
VanHasselt, V. B., 22, *49*, 247, 248, 253, *262*
VanTassel, E., 421, *449*
Varvil-Weld, D., 55, *69*
Vaught, R. S., 38, *47*
Vedder, M., 15, *19*
Vedder, M. J., 61, *69*
Vedeler, M., 557, *578*
Verhulst, J., 176, 177, *191*
Veroff, J., 181, *191*
Vincent, J. P., 477, 491, *502, 504*
Vitalo, R., 93, *100*
Vogel, S. R., 303, 305, 308, *322*
Vogelsong, E., 266, *282*, 516, 517, 519, 520, *522, 524*
Vroom, V. H., 543, *554*
Vukelich, R., 123, *135*

Wackman, D., 584, *602*
Wackman, D. B., 458, 459, *475*
Wadsworth, B. J., 78, *100*
Wagner, B., 107, *131*
Wagner, C. A., 175, *191*
Wagner, F. R., 546, *553*
Wagner, M., 105, *135*
Wagner, V., 591, *602*
Wahler, R. G., 248, *262*
Walder, L., 102, *132*
Waldo, M., 517, *524*
Waldrop, M. F., 221, *244*
Walen, S. R., 173, *191*
Walker, H. M., 248, 251, 253–255, *262*, 421, 439,
    450, 453
Walker, J., 150, 151, *166*
Wall, K., 557, *578*
Wall, K. E., 63, *69*, 304, 305, *323*
Wallace, C., 107, 125, *132, 135*, 558, *580*
Wallace, C. J., 344, *357*, 372, *387*
Wallace, K. M., 593, *602*
Wallace, R. F., 424, *450*
Wallach, H. F., 350, *352*
Wallander, J. L., 57–59, *67, 68, 72*, 146, 148, 153,
    154, *165, 166, 169*, 378, *384*
Walster, E., 55, 56, *67, 68, 72*
Walter, H., 267, *283*
Walters, E., 340, *357*
Walters, R. P., 78, 86, 94, *98*
Wampler, K. S., 462–467, *475, 603*
Wanlass, R. L., 172, *189*, 219, 224, 225, 233, *244*
Ward, D., 57, 58, *67*, 153, 154, *166*
Warnatl, C. F., 77, *100*
Warner, M. D., 463, *475*
Warren, J. M., 293, *299*
Warren, W. J., 28, *49*

Watson, C., 370, *387*
Watson, D., 270, *283*
Watzlawick, P., 457, *475*, 480, *504*, 607, *617*
Waxer, P. H., 59, *73*
Weaver, F. H., 550, *553*
Weekland, J. H., 609, *617*
Weeks, G., *602*
Weener, J., 268, 270, *281*
Wehman, P., 424, *453*
Weike, K. E., Jr., 540, 546, *552*
Weinberg, M. S., 170, *188*
Weinman, C., 346, 347, *355*
Weinstein, E. A., 418, *453*
Weiser, S. A., 35, *47*
Weiss, D., 418, *453*
Weiss, D. M., 298, *302*
Weiss, R. L., 28, 41, *49*, 59, *72*, 477, 479, 481, 482, 491, 492, 495, 498, *502*, *504*, *505*
Weiss, R. S., 193, *215*
Weissman, A., 478, *502*
Weissman, M. M., 317, *324*
Welch, G., 200–202, 209–211, *214*, *215*
Welford, A., 555, 567, *580*
Welford, A. T., 5, 7, *21*
Welham, D., 572, *579*
Wells, K. D., 433, *453*
Welsh, 517, *524*
Wessberg, H. W., 53, 57, 58, 62, *68*, *73*, 146, 155, *166*, 378, *387*
West, B. L., 150, 151, *169*
Westmoreland, T., 426, 428, 431, *453*
Wetzel, R., 120, *134*, 294, *301*
Wexby, K. W., 543, 546, *552*, *554*
Wheller, E., 589, 592, *602*
Wheller, E. G., 480, 483, 486, 487, 491, 492, *504*
Wheller, V. A., 226, 230, *240*, *246*
Whitaker, C., *603*
White, B., 340, *357*
White, G., 123, *135*
White, M., 114, 116, 117, 127, *134*
White, R., 136, 137, *169*
White, S. W., 315–317, *322*
Whitehill, M., 561, *580*
Whitehill, M. B., 22, *49*, 247, 248, 253, *262*
Whitelye, J., 199, *214*
Whitemore, K., 418, *452*
Whiting, H., 271, *283*
Whitman, T. L., 424, *454*
Whittington, D., 14, *19*, 556, 560, 570, 574, 575, *577*
Wieman, R. J., 518, *524*
Wilcox, D., 186, *191*
Wildman, B. G., 364, 365, 368, 371, 372, 375, 376, 378–380, 382, *385*, *386*, 436, 437, *451*
Wildman, H. E., 447, *450*
Wiley, M. G., 312, *324*
Willems, E. P., 27, *49*
Williams, A. M., 479, 483, 485, 489, 493–496, 500, *503*, *505*
Williams, C. A., 311, *324*
Williams, C. L., 53, 54, 61, 64, *78*

Williams, D., 119, *129*
Williams, H. M., 8, *21*
Williams, J. G., 363, 364, 376, *384*
Williams, J. H., 315, *324*
Williams, S., 573, *577*
Willis, S. L., 350, *353*
Wilson, E., 557, 571, *577*, *578*
Wilson, G., 111, *135*
Wilson, R. R., 93, *100*
Wilson, T., 364, 365, 368, 371, 372, 375, 376, 378–380, 382, *385*, 437, *451*
Wilson, V. L., 38, *46*
Wilty, N., 267, 280, *283*
Windle, C. D., 438, *454*
Wine, J., 562, *579*
Wine, J. D., 15, *21*
Winer, B. J., 420, *454*
Wingaarden, M., 419, *450*
Wingrove, C. R., 328, 329, *351*
Winkel, G. H., 248, *262*
Winship, B. J., 305, *325*
Winston, R., 329, *356*
Winter, K., 569, *579*
Wise, M. J., 440, *452*
Wiseman, J. P., 176, *191*
Wisocki, P. A., 348–350, *357*
Witkin, H., 560, *580*
Witte, K. L., 347, *355*
Wodarski, J. S., 610, *617*
Wolf, M., 58, *71*, 349, *353*
Wolf, M. M., 37, *48*, 58, *73*, 256, *261*, 371, 382, *386*, 420, 425, 438, *454*
Wolfe, M. A., 224, 233, 237, *249*
Wolfgang, G., 508, *522*
Wolin, B. R., 39, *45*
Wolk, S., 330, *357*
Wolpe, J., 3, 4, *21*, 54, *73*, 103, 111, *135*, 139, *169*, 362, 373, *387*, 555, 563, *580*
Wolpe, J. L., 182, *191*
Womeldorf, J. A., 150, 151, *166*
Wong, S. E., 375, 382, *386*
Wong-McCarthy, W., 314, *322*
Wood, D., 365, *386*
Wood, M., 294, 297, *302*
Woodworth, R. S., 293, *302*
Woolfolk, R. L., 309, 318, *320*
Wooten, L., 376, *384*
Wooten, S., 558, *577*
Worell, J., 315, 316, *325*
World Health Organization, 171, *191*
Wortmann, H., 426, 432, *454*
Wright, J. R., 184, *191*
Wrubel, J., 346, *357*
Wylie, R. C., 203, *215*
Wynter, L., 349, *357*

Yalom, I., 442, *454*
Yalom, I. D., 77, *99*
Yardley, K., 51, *67*, 141, 162, *165*, *169*, 558, 560, 573, *576*, *580*

Yarrow, M. R., 227, *240*
Young, D. Y., 34, *46*
Young, G., 568, *580*
Young, L. D., 28, *45*, 50, 53, 58, 62, *66*, 142, *165*
Yule, W., 418, *452*

Zarit, S. H., 326, 347, *353*, *357*
Zegiob, L., 433, 436, *454*
Zeilberger, J., 248, *262*
Zeiss, A. M., 422, 423, 425–427, 430–432, 437, *452*
Zeiss, R., 108, 110, 126, *132*
Zeiss, R. A., 422, 423, 425–427, 430, 431, 437, 446,
    447, *452*
Zerface, J. P., 54, *71*, 140, 141, 143, 156, 158, *167*

Zetlin, A., 422, *452*
Zetterblom, G., 246, 253, *260*
Zielinski, C., 346, *353*
Zigler, E., 3, 7, 11, *21*, 138, *168*, *169*, 362, *387*, 418,
    454, 555, *579*, *580*
Zilfergeld, B., 177, 182, 184, 186, *191*
Zimbardo, P., 51, *73*
Zimbardo, P. G., 15, *21*, 257, *262*
Zimering, R., 110, 126, *135*
Zimering, R. T., 15, *21*, 144–146, *169*
Zimmerman, R., 121, *132*
Zisfein, L., 374, 375, *387*
Zuk, G. H., 598, *603*
Zwick, W. R., 33, *45*, 138, 146, *166*

Subject Index

Acquisition, skill, 286, 297
Adjustment, community, 418
Admonitions, concrete, 287
Aggression, 101, 103, 108–110, 112–127, 128, 329
Aggressive persons:
  adolescents, 108
  overcontrolled, 101
  undercontrolled, 101
Analysis:
  lag sequential, 39
  Markov chain, 39
  task, 24
Anger, 101, 104, 107, 109, 110, 114–115, 117, 122, 128
Appearance:
  persona, 426, 430, 431
  role in social skills, 369, 370
Arguments:
  explosive, 344
  and fights, 426, 430
Assertion Inventory, 339–340
Assertiveness skills:
  benefits of, 373–377
  commendatory, 374
  conversational aspects of, 374
  definition of, 373
  praise statements in, 374
  of psychiatric patients, 363–364, 373
  refusal, 373–374, 382
  request, 375–376
  situational specificity of, 374
Assertiveness skills training:
  client evaluation preceding, 374
  component behaviors for, 374
  generalization issues in, 377
  goals of, 376
  with groups, 376
  with individuals, 376
  interventions for, 363, 375–376
  for psychiatric patients, 363–364, 373
  response discrimination issues in, 374
  stylistic aspects of, 374
  suitable clients for, 374
Assessment:
  assertiveness skills, 374
  behavior analytic techniques in, 365

of consequences, 89
conversational skills, 370
heterosocial skills, 377–378
important ingredients of, 331
individual, 345, 348, 352
intervention, 368
job finding skills, 378–380
job interviewing skills, 378–380
in natural environment, 366
objective, 104
role playing techniques, 366, 377
self-care skills, 370
of social skills, 420
using practice interactions, 366
Attitude, negative, 329
Attractiveness, physical, 55–56
Atrributions, 329, 347, 352

Baseline, 352
Beck Depression Inventory, 347
Behavior:
  analytic approach, 332
  analytic identification, 105
  analytic validation, 105
  antisocial patterns, 102
  grooming, 330
  heterosocial approach, 61
  imitative, 104
  modeling, 544
  modification, 285
  nonverbal, 337, 343
  psychotic patterns, 102
  rehearsal, 104, 107, 285, 366, 368
  requesting changes, 330
  self-monitoring of, 432
  steps, 290
  verbal, 337
Behavioral analytic method, 28
Behavioral parent training, 248, 258
Behavioral role play test, 340
Behavior analysis:
  nonsequential, 36
  sequential, 38
Brat syndrome, 119
Business, 539–551

Capabilities, sensory, 345, 347
Cards, task, 346
Cassettes:
    audio taped, 346, 348
    videotape, 346
CB radios, 348
Centers, senior, 333, 334, 339
Character Education Movement, 285
Checklists, 349, 422
Children:
    intervention strategies, methods, 228–233. *See
            also* Social skills
        empirical studies of, 228–233
        implementation, 230–232
        theories of skill learning, 88
        training models, 88–91
            modeling, 88
            shaping, 88
                coaching, 89, 230
            training manipulations, 88–91
                cognitive-social learning methods, 88–91
                ethics, 92
                evaluation of, 92
    modification of aggression, 229–233
    peer relations:
        activities, 73, 223
        disorders of, 69–72, 220–222
        models, 223
        reinforcement, 73, 223
        socialization, 74, 223
        teachers, 73, 223
    peer status, 74
        acceptance, 74, 75, 224
        friendlessness, 75, 76, 225, 226
        neglect, 74, 75, 77, 80, 224, 225, 226, 228, 230
        popularity, 74, 75, 76, 83, 224, 226, 227
        rejection, 74, 75, 76, 80
    rate of interaction, 75
        low rates, 74, 75, 224
        peer neglect, 74, 80, 224, 225, 228
        peer withdrawal, 74, 75, 224, 226
        social isolation, 74, 224, 226
    social adjustment, 68–72, 75
        behavior problems, 71, 221
        delinquency, 71, 221–222
        predictors of, 67–72, 219
        psychiatric disorders, 7, 221
        research with humans, 69, 220
        research with primates, 69, 220
        social failure, 70, 221
    social competence:
        behavioral relevance, 79, 227
        contributions of peers, 72, 223
        popularity, 75
        prosocial behavior, 79, 227
        responsiveness to peers, 80, 227, 228
        social goals, 82, 92, 229
        social knowledge, 81, 82, 89, 92, 228, 229
    social isolation, 74
        peer neglect, 74, 80, 224
        peer withdrawal, 74, 75, 224, 226

    unpopular children, 75, 224
        isolates, 77, 226
    social skills training with children, 67–105
        candidates for, 74, 224–225
        cognitive-social learning model, 89
        concept instruction, 90
            evaluation, 92
        empirical studies, 83–88, 228–233
        ethics, 92
        implementaion, 93–95
        purposes of, 68, 92, 219
        rationales, 72, 92, 222
        teachers, 93
        training methodology, review of, 88–91
    sociometric status, 77. *See also* Peer relations;
            Social competence
        behavioral correlates, 78, 227
        classification schemes, 75, 77, 224, 226
        controversial children, 78
        definition of, 77, 226
        neglected children, 78, 80, 228
        popular children, 78, 228
        rejected children, 78, 80, 228
        social cognitive correlates, 81–83
        unpopular children, 78, 83, 228
    unassertive, 109
Children's skills training and peer relations:
    candidates, 224–226
    contribution of peer relations, 222–224
    definitions of, 4–5
        general, 4, 5
        sharing, in social skills, 4, 7
        specific, 5, 6
    ergonomics, 5
    ethical issues:
        in training with children, 238–239
        parents, teachers or educators, 236–238
        research on poor peer relations:
            with humans, 220–222
            methodology, 223–235
            with primates, 220
    process and outcomes, 235–236
    skill deficits, 224, 225
    sociometric status and social skills:
        behavior anticedents, 226–228
        identification of types, 226
        research, 228–230
        unpopular children, 230–233
Chronic patients:
    assessing patients, 405–407
    Community Network Development Program
            discharge, 401–403
    disincentives, overcoming obstacles, 412–414
    dynamic therapy, 404, 405
    improving functional level:
        aggravative stress, 389–390
        biomedical impairments, 390–391
        coping skills, 391
        directive power, 391–392
        environmental support, 392
        functional level, 389

managing problem behavior, 403–404
  skills deficits, 388–389
  skills training:
    categories, 393–395
    patients' special needs, 397–401
  treatment planning, 407–410
Coaching, 104, 108, 126
Cognitive restructuring, 480, 481, 498–501
Communication:
  cognitive factors in, 480
  marital, 484–493
  nonverbal, 485, 487
  skills vs. performance deficits in, 487, 491
  training, 480, 484–493
Communicative skills:
  self-awareness, 459–460
  self-disclosure, 459, 464
Communication training:
  barriers to participation, 467–468, 469, 470
  forms of delivery, 470
  leadership, 468, 472
  types of training, 467
  ways to overcome barriers, 471, 473
Community-based programs, applications in, 438–447
Competence, heterosocial, 50
Competence, interpersonal:
  assessment, 608
  behavioral acquisition, 606–608
  goals, 605, 606
  limits, 604–605
  major considerations:
    contextual issues, 609–610
    developmental perspective, 614–616
    environmental supports, 608–609
    perception of social skills, 609
      training, 610–611
    sociocultural contexts, 611–614
Compliance, 334
Component analyses, 116
Component behaviors:
  change in to evaluate intervention, 382
  commendatory assertiveness, 374
  conversational skills, 362, 371, 382
  dating, 377
  defining social skill by, 369, 382
  heterosocial skills, 377
  job finding skills, 378–379
  job interview skills, 378–379
  refusal assertiveness, 373, 382
  in relation to overall skill, 368, 382
  request assertiveness, 374
Confederate responsivity, 62
Content:
  appropriate, 438
  inappropriate, 438
Contingencies, group, 121
Contingency contracting, 107, 117, 119–121, 124, 128
Contingency management, 103, 109, 117, 118, 127–128, 362

Contingency procedures, to enhance performance of appropriate social behaviors, 423–424, 432, 434
Contrasting groups, methodology, 40
Control, personal, 328
Conversational skills:
  as components of assertion, 372
  as components of heterosocial skills, 377
  as components of job interview skills, 378
  definition of, 370
  as determinants of social competence, 370
  of psychiatric patients, 370–374
Conversational skills training:
  client evaluation preceding, 371
  component behavior for, 362, 371–373, 382
  generalization issues in, 371, 373
  goals of, 370–373
  with groups, 372–373
  interventions for, 372
  for psychiatric patients, 370–371
  suitable clients for, 370–371
Cooperation, 426, 431, 436, 442
Cost:
  effectiveness, 431, 435
  response, 124–125
Counseling:
  bereavement, 350
  peer-group, 340
Counseling programs, paraprofessional, 340
Couples' adjustment:
  behavioral discrimination training, 481–483
  cognitive/behavioral model, of marital dysfunction, 478–481
  cognitive intervention:
    assessment dysfunctional beliefs, 489–500
    modifying dysfunctional attribution, 500–501
    self-instructional training, 501
  communication training:
    applications, 461–466
    comments:
      delivery system, 473, 474
      idea for life cycle, 472–473
    critical evaluation, 466–468
    history, 457–459
    major features, 459–461
    status and future:
      content, 471
      forms, 471–472
      leadership training, 472
        basic components, 484–485
        nonverbal, 485–487
        other expressive skills, 490–493
        skill vs. performance, 487
        training in expressive and listening skills, 487–490
  contingency contracting, 496–498
  problem-solving, 493–495
Couples Communication Program, Minnesota:
  awareness wheel, 460
  effects on communication, 464–466
  effects on relationship satisfaction, 465–466

Couples Communication Program, Minnesota
  (*Continued*)
    format, 68, 460–461
    history, 457–459
    instructor training, 458, 465–466, 468, 469
    maxi-contract, 467
    participation patterns, 459, 461–462, 473
    research design, 462–463
    supporting material, 458–459
    talking together, 459–460
    theoretical background, 457–458
Covert instructions, 113
Criteria, 333, 335
Cross-validation, 332
Cue fading, 108
Cueing, 108
Cursing, 431

Data, group, 345
Dating:
  component behaviors of, 377
  practice, 54, 145, 156
Dating anxiety:
  cognitive, 158
  frequency of, 140
  research target behavior, 140
Dating problems:
  sex differences, 52
  types, 52
Deficits, sensory and cognitive, 345
Definitions, cohort, 327
Deinstitutionalization, 286, 290
Dependence, 348
Desensitization, 54
Design:
  architectural, 349
  experimental, 297
  group, 109
  multiple baseline, 108, 109, 344
  representative, 40
  single case, 109
Developing skills program:
  actuarial approach to, 148
  ideographic approach to, 147
Differences:
  cultural, 351
  gender, 332
Direct observation, 422
Disclosure, 343
Displeasure, expression of, 337
Distortions, cognitive, 55
Divorce:
  adjustment groups, 197–200
  after, 207–287
  communication skills training, 202–208
  consequence of, 33, 192
  effects of, 34, 192
Divorce adjustment programs:
  criteria for, 194
  Fisher Divorce Adjustment Scale, 195–197, 203,
    204
  Fisher Divorce and Growth Seminar, 195–197
  future directions, 211–213
  idealized program, 213–214
  primary features, 208–211
  Read, 207, 211
  research on, 196, 197, 199, 201
  termination groups, 193–195
  treatment seminar, 200–202
Dual diagnoses, individuals with, 426–432

Effective motive, 137
Elements, identical, 43
Empathy, 109, 110
Enrichment, structured:
  continuum of intervention, 581–582
  early definitions:
    contractual nature, 584
    education for many, 585
    prescribed mode intervention, 584, 585
  family therapy and structural enrichment cost
    effectiveness, 598–601
  marriage and family enrichment, 582–583
  process considerations:
    behavioral social skills, 592–594
    structured enrichment training, 590–592
  similarities and differences between SE and
    BSST:
    assessment, 595–596
    enrichment and training, 596
    ideas for change, 597
    outcome assessment, 597–598
    parallel between SE & BSST supervision, 596–
      597
    timing of feedback, 596
  variable dimensions:
    content, 585–586
    population, 585
    prevention-remediation, 586
    process, 585
    time, 586
Environment:
  natural, 104, 109
  physical, 349
Environmental fit, 331
Evaluation, subjective, 420
Event sampling, 34
Expectations:
  appropriate, 327
  inappropriate, 340
  role, 331
Expression, facial, 106
Eye contact, 106, 437, 440

Factors:
  cognitive, 344
  emotional, 344
  physiological, 348
Fallacy:
  of age verification, 327
  of cohort centrism, 327
  life course, 327

Family management skills, 270
    problem solving, 270–271
Feedback, 26, 289–290, 327, 345, 442
Foster home, 349

Galvanic skin responses, 103
Gender, 328
Generalization, 107, 110, 112, 116, 126, 340, 342,
        345, 352, 363, 368, 381
    programming for, 253
    techniques that promote, 368, 381, 436
General principles, provisions of, 293
Goals, 327, 330, 333, 337, 340, 342, 344–345, 346
Gray Panthers, 348
Grooming habits, poor, 433
Group:
    cognitive restructuring, 114
    relearning, 113
    response cost, 114
    support, 340
    therapy, contractual arrangements in, 120

Health:
    benefits, 346
    problems, 328
Heterosocial difficulties:
    conceptual models for, 52
    prevalence of, 50
    severity of, 51
Heterosocial interactions, naturalistic, 63
Heterosocial skills:
    assessment implications, 377–378
    conversational aspects of, 377
    dating, 377–378
    deficits, 53
    definition of, 377
    identification, 58
    methodological limitations, 57
    psychiatric patients of, 377–378
    training, 53
Heterosocial skills training:
    client evaluation preceding, 377–378
    component behaviors for, 377–378
    dating behavior, 377–378
    generalization issues in, 378
    goals of, 377–378
    interventions for, 378
    psychiatric patients for, 377–378
    rationale for, 378
    stylistic aspects in, 378
    suitable clients for, 377–378
Hierarchies, 27
History, social skills:
    aggressiveness, 8
    anxiety, 4
    ascendence, 8, 9
    assertiveness, 3, 4
    early, 7, 8
        development trends, shyness, 8
        trends, 17–18
    individualistic culture, 15

Minnesota Multiphasic Personality Inventory, 15
Mooney Problem Checklist, 15
    person-environment context, 12
    psychopathology, 11
    psychotherapy:
        catharsis, 15
        prosocial, 4, 24
    social curriculum, 7
    training, 17
        general, 15–16
        specific, 14
        traits, 14
Hospitalized patients, aggressive, 107
Humor, 104

Impairment, cognitive, 328
Incentive, monetary, 342
Incomes, 329
Index, heterosocial anxiety, 54
Indicators, progress, 327
Industry, 539–551
Inoculation, 115
Inpatients, low income, 287
Instruction, behavioral, 368
Instrument, heterosocial assessment, 60
Instrumental aggression, 101
Interactions, practice in assessment method, 366
Interpersonal alternatives to aggression, 102
Interpersonal Situation Inventory, 341
Intonation, 437
Issues, ethical, 350

Job finding skills:
    definition of, 378
    of psychiatric patients, 378–379
Job finding skills training:
    client evaluation preceding, 379
    component behaviors for, 379
    goals of, 379
    interventions for, 379
    for psychiatric patients, 379
    suitable clients for, 379
Job interview skills:
    conversational aspects of, 379
    definition of, 379
    of psychiatric patients, 379
Job interview skills training:
    client evaluation preceding, 379
    component behaviors for, 379
    conversational aspects of, 379
    generalization issues in, 379
    goals of, 378–379
    with groups, 380
    interventions for, 379
    for psychiatric patients, 379
    stylistic aspects of, 379
    suitable clients for, 379
Judgement:
    clinical, 106
    competence, 22
Juvenile delinquents, 418

Learning, double-loop, 542
Lens model:
    Brunswik, 30
    competence assessment, 31, 41
Life skills training:
    background, group counseling, 77–80
    clinical considerations:
        assessment of progress, 90–91
        diagnosis, 90
        release, 91
    prediction, 95–97
    preventive applications
        LST unit for elementary, 91–92
        LST unit for high school, 92–93
    rationale, 80–81
    research, 94–95
    training:
        essential elements, 82–83
        example LST unit, case example, 88–89
            history, 88
            progress, 89
        organizational support, 86–87
        pyramid of training, 83
        trainer:
            facilitator, 84
            leader as model, 84–85
            role-playing, 85
            teacher, 83–84
            transfer of training, 85–86
        training materials, 86
Life space, 25
Loneliness, 328, 348
Longitudinal studies, 331
Lying, 430

Maintenance:
    programming for, 253
    of skills, 340, 343, 345, 352
Management training:
    evolution of, 546–548
    history, 539–540
    programs, 540–546
    recommendations, 548–551
Managerial grid seminars, 541–542
Manner, prescriptive, 286
Marital distress:
    behavioral marital therapy for, 478–479
    communication training for, 480, 484–493
    contingency contracting for, 496–498
    discrimination training for, 481–483
    dysfunctional attributions in, 477, 490, 497, 500–
        501
    dysfunctional beliefs and expectations in, 489,
        490, 498–500
    group treatment for, 489
    and hopelessness, 477–478, 500–501
    problem solving training for, 493–495
    self-instructional training for, 501
    and social exchange theory, 478
Markov chain, 38
Marriage encounter, 468–469, 473

Marriage enrichment programs, 464, 472–473
Measurement, scale of, 37
Measurement problems, 331
Mentally retarded, 418
Microcounseling procedures, 340
Minnesota Multiphasic Personality Inventory, 104
Minorities, ethnic, 352
Model:
    behavior-analytic, 60
    coping, 111
    criterion validity, 59
    functional, 60
    mastery, 111
    skills training, 105
    two-tiered, 24
Modeling, 108, 113, 126, 127, 144, 289, 295, 338,
        368, 373, 380, 544–545
Modification:
    behavior, 285
    cognitive, 111
Modular psychoeducational skills training, see
        Chronic patients
Motivation, 347

Norms:
    absence of general, 348
    age, 331
Nurses' Observation Scale for Inpatient Evaluation,
        431
Nursing home, 340, 346, 350

Opportunities, preventative, 350
Option:
    aggressive, 332
    assertive, 332
    coping, 331
    passive, 332
    response, 333
Outcomes:
    long-term, 40
    personal, 333, 346
    short-term, 39
    social, 346
Outpatient clinics, 439, 445
Overcorrection, 123
Overlearning, 293

Paired comparison technique, 421
Parent education:
    existing group programs:
        behavioral, 266–268
        eclectic, 268
        parent–adolescent relationship development,
            266
        parent–child relationship enhancement, 265–
            266
        parent effectiveness training, 264, 468–469,
            473
        systematic training for effective parenting,
            264–265
    future, 279–280

generic program contents:
changing child, 270
changing family, 270–271
communication skills, 269–270
parent self-change, 269
planning environment, 269
parent-educator competencies:
evaluation, 278
implementation, 278
marketing, 276–278
planning, 275–276
training process:
describe skill, 272
evaluate level, 273
practice skill, 272–273
Parent effectiveness training, 264, 468–469, 473
Parents, 245–259
Patients:
chronic, 286
geriatric, 337
institutionalized elderly, 337
low income, 286
psychiatric, 361–383
Yavis, 287
Peer relations, 245
Perceived Environmental Control Scale, 330
Performance:
criterion-meeting, 104
deficit in, 102
Play, cooperative, 424
Pleasure, expression of, 337
Positive reinforcement seminars, 543–544
Post training assessment, for individuals, 368
Power, 350, 352
Praise statements, in commendatory assertiveness, 375
Precounseling session, 342
Prediction, cross-situational, 23–24
Prescriptions:
conformity, 288
reformity, 289
Prescriptiveness, 286, 297
Problem Inventory for College Students, 26
Problems:
definitional, 546
evaluative, 247–248, 550–551
Problem solving:
description, 112
dimensions, 124
of elderly people, 345, 347
group, 339
interpersonal, 329
interventions designed to enhance skills of family members, 250
involving parents in intervention, 251
Processes:
covert, 103
formal review, 118
Process model:
of social competence, 352
of social skill, 326, 346

Professional helpers:
applying methods to alternate therapies, 531–532
future directions, 536–537
research and application, 535–536
theory of skills training, 532–535
Program development, 337
Programs:
aggression treatment, 107
cognitive based treatment, 55
companion, 348, 349
foster grandparents, 349
moral education, 285
outreach, 351
reattribution, 346
special education, 442
values clarification, 285
Prompting, 108
Prompts, 334
Prosthetic aids, 348, 351
Provocations, in vivo, 108
Psychiatric patients:
assertiveness training for, 363, 373
contingency management programs for, 362
conversational skills training for, 371
heterosocial skills training for, 377
job finding skills training for, 378
rationale of skills training for, 361
response discrimination of, 369
self-care skills training for, 369
social skills deficits of, 361–383
social skills training for, 361–383
Psychopathology, 418
for training social skills, 442

Rage, explosive, 108
Rankings, 421
Ratings:
competence, 32
intermediate, 154
Rating scales, binary, 35
Reactions:
emotional, 340
physiological, 341
Recidivism, 343
Records, self-monitoring, 26
Rehearsal:
behavior, 105, 107, 285
covert, 99, 338
verbal, 338
in vivo, 108
Reinforcement:
contingencies, 423
differential, 117–119
naturally occurring, 350
in normal skills development, 363
optimal, 347
real life, 294
sampling, 350
self, 100, 294
social, 108, 113, 126, 285

Reinforcement (*Continued*)
token, 117, 121–122, 124, 127
in training sessions, 368
Relationship enhancement:
current status child relationship enhancement, 513
history, 5, 13
major components CRE, 514
dynamic processing, 509–510
home sessions, 570
observed parent practice, 509
phaseout stage, 511–512
play therapy skills, 509
transfer and generalization, 510–511
marital and family RE therapies:
current status, 520–521
major components, 514–521
overview, 518–520
Relationships, heterosocial, 64
Relatives, 335
Relaxation, 103–104
Reprimands, verbal, 424
Requests:
for attention, 426, 431
for new behavior in assertiveness responses, 414
Residential care, long-term, 426
Residents:
as assistant trainers, 435
depressed institutionalized, 347
expectations of, 347
nursing home, 347
Respondent aggression, 101
Response:
controlled, 110
discrimination, 369
latency, 105, 437
prosocial repertoires, 110
social greeting, 424
verbal, 106
Response acquisition treatment, 139
Rewardingness, 330
Risk taking, 338
Role play:
assertiveness skills, 374
as assessment method, 366
conversational skills, 371–372
ecological validity of, 63
heterosocial skills, 61, 317
job interview skills, 379
validity of, 367
Role playing, 105, 108, 289, 290
Rules, 118, 327

Schedules, reinforcement, 330, 347, 352
Scripts, 326, 333
Self-blame, 346
Self-care skills:
dressing, 369–370
grooming, 369–370
of psychiatric patients, 369–370
social responses to, 369–370

Self-care skills training:
client evaluation preceding, 370
component behaviors for, 369–370
interventions for, 370
for psychiatric patients, 370
rationale for, 369–370
stylistic aspects of, 370
suitable clients for, 370
Self-confidence, 326
Self-control:
cognitive forms of, 111, 116, 128
definition of, 110
training, 110
Self-efficacy, 137, 346, 351
Self-esteem, 329, 346, 351–352
Self-monitoring, 432–433, 435
Self-presentation, 327
Setting:
group, 345
residential, 344
Sexual functioning:
contextual, 178–179
individual, 173–175
interpersonal, 175–178
Sexual skills and competence:
enhancement programs, 184–187
gay population, 187–188
life development, 179–182
sex therapy, 182–184
Sheltered workshops, 440–442
Short-term residential care, applications in, 436–438
Significant others, 337, 345–346, 350, 352
Situations:
definition of, 28–29
methods for operationalizing, 27
real-life, 117
simulating, 28–29
social conversational, 28–29
Skill cards, 342
Skills:
aggression control, 105
cognitive, 111, 339
coping, 350
decision-making, 42–43, 330
deficit, 102
emotion-coping, 329
idiosyncratic, 107
interpersonal, 418
leisure, 343
negotiation, 330
process, 62
social, 102, 424
verbal and cognitive, 102
verbal self-control, 114
Social class, 285–286
Social comparison, 328, 420
Social competence, 23, 327
Social episode, 28
Social functioning, measures of, 331

Social gerontology, 330, 331, 352
Social goals, 330, 347, 350, 351
Social group work, 204, 339
Social incompetence, as major psychological deficit, 138
Social interactions, inappropriate, 434
Social isolation, 326, 328
Social learning theory, 101, 102, 285
Social networks, 350, 351, 352
Social performance, 327
Social Performance Survey Schedule, 442
Social prompts, 349
Social satisfaction, 328
Social signals, 327
Social skills:
    appearance aspects, 369–370
    behavior-analytic identification of, 105
    behavior-analytic validation of, 105
    deficits:
        due to attainable goals lacking reinforcement values, 367
        due to insufficient natural reinforcement, 367
        due to no opportunity to practice, 367
    definition of, 23, 247, 369, 419
    information processing model, 41
    of psychiatric patients, 361–383
    situational specificity of, 367
    stylistic aspects of, 382
    types of, 361
Social support system, 350, 352
Social task, 27
Social validation, 58, 109, 352, 420, 438, 440
Sociology, of aging, 327
Sociometrics, with mentally retarded, 421–422
Sources, valid, 331
Staff, residential, 349
Statistical testing, 38
Stealing, 433
Stereotypes, 326, 327, 329, 352
Stimulation, aversive, 125–126
Strategies:
    cognitive behavioral, 127
    intervention, 102
Stress inoculation model:
    application practice, 114
    cognitive preparation, 114
    skill acquisition, 114–115
Structured learning therapy, 108, 289, 290, 341
Survey of Heterosexual Interactions, 27
System:
    buddy, 146, 345
    coercive family, 102
    support, 351
Systematic desensitization, 103, 104

Task:
    analysis, 24
    domains, 27
    respite from care giving, 350

    social, 27
Taxonomics:
    numerical, 29
    situational, 29
Therapists, paraprofessional, 288
Therapy:
    cognitive behavior, 111
    family oriented problem solving, 250
    group, 120
Time frame, 331
Time-out, 108, 116, 122–124, 128, 329
Time sampling, 34
Time series analysis, 38
Token economy, 121–122
Tokens, 343, 345, 349
Training:
    assertiveness, 107, 343, 344, 363–364, 373–377
    business, 539–554
    coping skills, 111
    group assertion, 107
    industry, 539–554
    interpersonal skills program, 108
    management, 539–554
    modules, 343
    rational-emotive, 347
    self-control, 115
    self-instruction, 111, 112, 113–114
    social skills, 108, 126
    social validity, 105
    stress inoculation, 111, 112, 114–115
    supervisory, 539–554
    transfer of, 290, 292, 341
Transfer:
    skill, 286, 297
    of training, 290, 292, 341
Transitions, 329
Treatment, maintenance of, 110
Turtle Technique, The, 115
Typology, 330

Validation, social, 383
Validity:
    content, 60
    face, 107
Values, subjective, 327
Variables:
    conversational, 62
    motivational, 352
Verbalization, 436
Videotapes, 112, 346
Vignettes, 342
Voice loudness, 106

Walker Problem Behavior Identification Checklist, 439
Washington Assessment and Training Scale, 439
Well-being, subjective, 328, 331
Widowers, 334
Widows, 334

Women:
    assertion, 303–304, 306–308, 317, 321–322
    intervention, 304, 314, 317, 319–321, 322
    linguistic style, 304, 313–314, 313
    marital disruption, 314, 316–317
    perceptions of assertion, 304, 305–306, 308, 310,
        317–319
    prevention, 304, 317, 320, 322
    work-setting, 304, 306–307, 310, 312–313, 317–
        318, 321

Yavis, 287

Handbook of Adolescent Psychology
edited by Joseph Adelson

Psychotherapy Supervision: Theory, Research and Practice
edited by Allen K. Hess

Psychology and Psychiatry in Courts and Corrections: Controversy and Change
by Ellsworth A. Fersch, Jr.

Restricted Environmental Stimulation: Research and Clinical Applications
by Peter Suedfeld

Personal Construct Psychology: Psychotherapy and Personality
edited by Alvin W. Landfield and Larry M. Leitner

Mothers, Grandmothers, and Daughters: Personality and Child Care in Three-Generation Families
by Bertram J. Cohler and Henry U. Grunebaum

Further Explorations in Personality
edited by A. I. Rabin, Joel Aronoff, Andrew M. Barclay, and Robert A. Zucker

Hypnosis and Relaxation: Modern Verification of an Old Equation
by William E. Edmonston, Jr.

Handbook of Clinical Behavior Therapy
edited by Samuel M. Turner, Karen S. Calhoun, and Henry E. Adams

Handbook of Clinical Neuropsychology
edited by Susan B. Filskov and Thomas J. Boll

The Course of Alcoholism: Four Years After Treatment
by J. Michael Polich, David J. Armor, and Harriet B. Braiker

Handbook of Innovative Psychotherapies
edited by Raymond J. Corsini

The Role of the Father in Child Development (Second Edition)
edited by Michael E. Lamb

Behavioral Medicine: Clinical Applications
by Susan S. Pinkerton, Howard Hughes, and W. W. Wenrich

Handbook for the Practice of Pediatric Psychology
edited by June M. Tuma

Change Through Interaction: Social Psychological Processes of Counseling and Psychotherapy
by Stanley R. Strong and Charles D. Claiborn

Drugs and Behavior (Second Edition)
by Fred Leavitt

Handbook of Research Methods in Clinical Psychology
edited by Philip C. Kendall and James N. Butcher

A Social Psychology of Developing Adults
by Thomas O. Blank

Women in the Middle Years: Current Knowledge and Directions for Research and Policy
edited by Janet Zollinger Giele

Loneliness: A Sourcebook of Current Theory, Research and Therapy
edited by Letitia Anne Peplau and Daniel Perlman

Hyperactivity: Current Issues, Research, and Theory (Second Edition)
by Dorothea M. Ross and Sheila A. Ross

Review of Human Development
edited by Tiffany M. Field, Aletha Huston, Herbert C. Quay, Lillian Troll, and Gordon E. Finley

Agoraphobia: Multiple Perspectives on Theory and Treatment
edited by Dianne L. Chambless and Alan J. Goldstein

The Rorschach: A Comprehensive System. Volume III: Assessment of Children and Adolescents
by John E. Exner, Jr. and Irving B. Weiner

Handbook of Play Therapy
edited by Charles E. Schaefer and Kevin J. O'Connor

Adolescent Sexuality in a Changing American Society: Social and Psychological Perspectives for the Human Service Professions (Second Edition)
by Catherine S. Chilman